ENCYCLOPEDIA OF
SCIENCE AND RELIGION

ENCYCLOPEDIA OF
SCIENCE AND RELIGION

VOLUME 1
A-I

J. Wentzel Vrede van Huyssteen,
Editor in Chief

**MACMILLAN
REFERENCE
USA™**

THOMSON

™

GALE

New York • Detroit • San Diego • San Francisco • Cleveland • New Haven, Conn. • Waterville, Maine • London • Munich

THOMSON
★
GALE

Encyclopedia of Science and Religion

J. Wentzel Vrede van Huyssteen

© 2003 by Macmillan Reference USA.
Macmillan Reference USA is an imprint of
The Gale Group, Inc., a division of
Thomson Learning, Inc.

Macmillan Reference USA™ and
Thomson Learning™ are trademarks used
herein under license.

For more information contact
Macmillan Reference USA
300 Park Avenue South, 9th Floor
New York, NY 10010
Or you can visit our Internet site at
http://www.gale.com

Cover image reproduced by permission of
Corbis (Shooting Stars Over the Meteor
Crater).

While every effort has been made to ensure
the reliability of the information presented in
this publication, The Gale Group, Inc. does not
guarantee the accuracy of the data contained
herein. The Gale Group, Inc. accepts no pay-
ment for listing; and inclusion in the publication of any organization, agency, institution,
publication, service, or individual does not
imply endorsement of the editors or publisher.
Errors brought to the attention of the publisher and verified to the satisfaction of the publisher will be corrected in future editions.

Macmillan Reference USA
300 Park Avenue South, 9th Floor
New York, NY 10010

Macmillan Reference USA
27500 Drake Road
Farmington Hills, MI 48331-3535

LIBRARY OF CONGRESS CATALOGING-IN-PUBLICATION DATA

Encyclopedia of science and religion / J. Wentzel Vrede van Huyssteen,
editor in chief. — 2nd ed.
    p. cm.
  Includes bibliographical references and index.
    ISBN 0-02-865704-7 (alk. paper) — ISBN 0-02-865705-5 (v. 1 : alk. paper)
    — ISBN 0-02-865706-3 (v. 2 : alk. paper)
    1. Religion and science—Encyclopedias. I. Van Huyssteen, Wentzel.

  BL240.3 .E43 2003
  291.1'75—dc21
                                                    2002152471

Printed in the United States of America
10 9 8 7 6 5 4 3 2

CONTENTS

ENCYCLOPEDIA OF SCIENCE AND RELIGION
1

Editorial and Production Staff

Ray Abruzzi and Michael J. McGandy
Project Editors

Deirdre Graves and Christine Slovey
Contributing Editors

Judith Culligan
Copy Editor

Elizabeth Merrick
Proofreader

Cynthia Crippen
AEIOU, Inc.
Indexer

Jennifer Wahi
Art Director

Argosy
Compositor

GGS Information Services
Line Art

Mary Beth Trimper
Composition Management

Evi Seoud
Assistant Production Manager

Rhonda Williams
Buyer

MACMILLAN REFERENCE USA

Frank Menchacca
Vice President

Hélène Potter
Director, New Product Development

PREFACE

The dialogue between science and religion is one of the most prominent and visible discourses of our time. The complex but enduring relationship between the sciences and diverse world religions has now transformed itself into what some are calling a new scholarly field of *science and religion*. This multifaceted conversation has developed into a sustained and dynamic discourse with direct implications for contemporary culture. This discourse affects all religions, in both their intellectual and social dimensions. It also analyzes, supports, and constrains the global impact of the sciences of our times.

The *Encyclopedia of Science and Religion* reflects the breathtaking scope and pluralistic character of this ongoing dialogue. It is the most comprehensive work of its kind, and it is designed to be accessible to a wide readership from high school students to independent researchers and academics. Anyone fascinated by the ever-evolving impact of the sciences on religious belief in a global context will find the *Encyclopedia* a rich resource, for the historical relationship between science and religion certainly ranges from harmony and mutual support to stormy periods of intense conflict.

In the last two decades public awareness of and interest in this complex and often contentious relationship between science and religion has reached an unprecedented level. Courses in science and religion are now taught worldwide at a great number of educational institutions. Centers for the study of science and religion are actively pursuing the challenges and complexities of this dialogue; local and international societies for science and religion have been, and are being, established. There is also an exploding number of publications, journals, newsletters, and papers. Most recently, the science and religion dialogue has established an impressive new presence on the Internet.

All of these issues, interests, and constituencies are reflected in the *Encyclopedia of Science and Religion*. The challenging conversation between the sciences and religions is highlighted with entries focusing on issues that bear on topics such as behavioral studies and the human sciences; cognitive science and the neurosciences; computer science and information technology; physical sciences and cosmology; ecology; ethics and value theory; evolution; genetics; feminist and womanist issues; mathematics; methodology; medicine; philosophy; biology; paleontology and the anthropological sciences; and technology. World religions as varied as Bahá'í, Buddhism, Chinese religions, Christianity, Hinduism, Islam, Judaism, and Shinto are represented with individual entries or clusters of entries.

There are more than four hundred entries in the *Encyclopedia of Science and Religion,* all arranged in alphabetical order for easy reference. The entries range in length from several thousand words on broad topics, to a hundred words or so for key terms in the various sciences and religions. The editors see this work primarily as a reflection on the most important issues in the contemporary dialogue between the sciences and religions. A glance over the list of entries, however, indicates that the *Encyclopedia* also covers the critical history of the relationship between science and religion and offers historical biographies of a select number of important figures. All entries guide readers to further sources of information and exhaustive cross-references quickly and easily lead to related topics. The authority of the *Encyclopedia* is assured by the experts who have written the entries. The authors have written so as to make this *Encyclopedia* accessible for students in general, for the public at large, and for scholars in a variety of disciplines. In this way we have created a rich reference resource that is well suited to diverse library environments.

The frontmatter features a Synoptic Outline, covering the complete scope and every entry of the *Encyclopedia of Science and Religion.* The purpose of this Outline is to make the *Encyclopedia* even more accessible by grouping all entries into broad, topical categories. Teachers and readers are offered an organized map of the whole field of science and religion. In addition, a comprehensive Index provides readers with yet another means of access to the wealth of information contained in these two volumes, while an Annotated Bibliography of selected works introduces readers to those published works currently regarded as indispensable in the field of science and religion.

The editors would like to thank Ian Barbour, one of the most prominent scholars in the field, for graciously agreeing to act as a consultant at the initial planning phase of the *Encyclopedia of Science and Religion.* His advice was invaluable to us. We also thank the expert staff at Macmillan Reference USA for their outstanding support throughout this project. We extend our appreciation to the following persons at Macmillan: Elly Dickason, former publisher of Macmillan, for her initiative and encouragement at the beginning of this project; Michael McGandy, who was a pleasure to work with, and who guided us with unfailing professionalism and expertise; Hélène Potter, who oversaw the project with great vision, and was responsible in the end for pulling everything together; and Judy Culligan for all her hard work and a very professional level of copy editing. Here at the Princeton Theological Seminary my assistant Ryan Valentine did an outstanding job. He devoted a great deal of time developing the database that was critical to the beginning phase of this project and later assisted in the editing process. He was also responsible for preparing the Synoptic Outline and checking all cross-references. Taede Smedes did a first rate job of helping us put together the Annotated Bibliography.

The editors, finally, would like to express our deep gratitude to family members and loved ones who so consistently acknowledged and supported our work on this project.

J. WENTZEL VREDE VAN HUYSSTEEN

INTRODUCTION

The publication of the *Encyclopedia of Science and Religion* is a significant milestone marking the maturation of the contemporary dialogue between the sciences and religions. Not only does this *Encyclopedia* offer a massive amount of interdisciplinary and interreligious information, but it mirrors one of the most fascinating stories of our time: the emergence of an extensive international discussion among scientists of various specializations, philosophers of nearly all persuasions, and religious thinkers from all the major world religions. Spectacular advances in the sciences no longer easily threaten religions around the world because the risks and devastating consequences of new technologies have problematized the formerly unquestioned ideal of scientific progress. Scientific advances still challenge basic religious convictions, however, and the intellectual representatives of the world's religious traditions grapple with scientific knowledge more effectively and pervasively than ever before, thanks to the science-religion dialogue. Today sciences as varied as the neurosciences, ecology, and biotechnology raise questions about human beings and the future of our planetary home, perhaps especially for those who possess a sense of the divine. Similarly, chaos theory, quantum mechanics, and the ever-deepening understanding of the role of chance in biological systems conspire to challenge the notions of ultimate reality and divine action espoused by religious traditions and sacred texts.

At the same time, partly because of the unwanted side effects of science-driven technologies, there is a growing conviction that science in itself may never yield an ultimately satisfying explanation of human life and the world we inhabit. And yet the information about reality produced by the sciences is invaluable. Perhaps we have two domains of meaning here, with science and religion each ruler of its own domain. Or perhaps the structures and patterns of nature disclosed by the sciences connect with the more elusive yet existentially more immediate meaning typical of religious faith. Even as the religions of the world grow more accepting of the sciences, at least some intellectuals are noting how scientific methods and aims can enhance and perhaps support religious faith. Therefore, contrary to popular misconceptions, the relationship between the sciences and the various religions at the beginning of the twenty-first century is not about conflict or confrontation only. Those who participate actively in this dialogue are often deeply committed, not only to a specific science, but also to specific religious beliefs. Even scholars who are agnostic or atheistic are taking the interaction among sciences and the religions seriously because this relationship involves two of the dominant cultural forces of our time. Complicated and multilayered, the relationships among the various sciences and diverse world religions are not merely adversarial, nor simply a matter of neatly separable domains of discourse.

In the West the success and prestige of science has had a fundamental influence on the way that the voices of popular culture describe our world. As a result, relationships among the religions and the sciences have often suffered from what some intellectuals have called the modernist dilemma, where the objective and universally true claims of science are often unfairly contrasted with subjective and irrational religious beliefs. This has led to sharp distinctions between objective descriptions and subjective experiences, between scientific and symbolic uses of language, and between empirically justified scientific truths and privately held religious opinions. The appeal of such stark oppositions, however, has waned. *Scientism* is the term of approbation used for the attitude that takes for granted the alleged rational superiority of science and exclusive value of the scientific method for gaining knowledge. The reductionist views that define scientism are now being attacked relentlessly by scholars who point out that both scientific and religious beliefs, in spite of important differences, are historically and culturally embedded and shaped by comprehensive worldviews. The polarization between inappropriately reified and ahistorical notions of science and religion is collapsing and in its place is arising an appreciation for the integrity of diverse discourses and social activities, including those usually called the religions and the sciences. At least as importantly, scholars are attempting to uncover the profound rational and historical linkages that connect, as well as individuate, the religions and the sciences. These historical and philosophical exertions have shown not only that the great discoveries about the nature and history of the physical world have affected religious discourses in nearly all their manifestations, but also that the claims of the various world religions about our capacity to know, the ultimate meaning of the cosmos, and the place of human beings in an evolving universe often impact the way scientific inquiry is conducted.

In the contemporary discussion among the religions and the sciences, particularly as it has transpired in the West, the most influential attempt at representing the complex relationship between these two cultural forces has been Ian Barbour's fourfold typology. Barbour describes the different ways that the sciences have actually related and might possibly relate to the religions as *conflict, dialogue, independence,* and *integration.* Many subsequent models for relating religion and science have built on the legacy of this pioneering analysis. Even as contemporary factors from cultural pluralism to postmodern philosophy suggest other ways of relating the sciences to religion, Barbour's typology remains applicable and instructive. The literature today expresses an increasing awareness that the relations between science and religion can only be properly understood if the specific cultural, historical, and intellectual contexts have been taken into account. The vast amount of information collected in this *Encyclopedia of Science and Religion* illustrates the richness and complexity of this interpretative task.

The growing conversation between science and religion that emerged with new vigor in the late twentieth century has a number of striking features. First, though once considered an esoteric field, the study of the relationship between science and religion is no longer a highly specialized discourse, open only to the few intellectuals who are privy to the complexity of the issues involved. The science and religion debate has become a public affair. The active presence of the debate on the Internet, as well as an explosion of published newsletters, papers, books, and conferences, further enhances this high public profile. Second, whereas there are new debates and ideas within science and religion, in many ways the dialogue extends familiar and longstanding debates known by different names: "faith and reason" or "faith and culture" (in the West) and *"pramana the-ory"* (in South Asian debates on valid sources of knowledge). Third, not only is the science and religion conversation alive and well in many cultures all over the world but, as this *Encyclopedia* clearly shows, a number of academic centers and scholarly associations now concentrate their considerable intellectual and financial resources on issues at the interface of science and religion. The discussion among the sciences and the religions has also found a permanent place in schools, colleges, seminaries, and universities. Courses in religion and science are now taught on all academic levels throughout the world, complemented by a number of high-profile endowed chairs in the field. Finally, one of the most important milestones in this ever-growing field was the founding of the *International Society of Science and Religion* in August 2002 in Granada, Spain.

The *Encyclopedia of Science and Religion* is directed mainly at students and their teachers. They will find all of the most important issues in this field addressed in an accessible and inclusive manner. Outstanding experts from around the world have contributed to the *Encyclopedia*. The comprehensive list of entries focuses on the principal sciences and the major scientific discoveries of our time and on all the challenging and controversial topics that have emerged from this context and have affected the world religions in different ways. Both historical and contemporary issues in science and religion are treated under the headings of the major world religions. The religions represented here include Buddhism, Bahá'í, Chinese religions (Confucianism and Daoism), Christianity (Anglican, Evangelical, Lutheran, Orthodox, Pentecostalism, Radical Reformed, Reformed, Roman Catholic), Hinduism, Islam, Judaism, and Shinto. The various sciences represented in the entries of this *Encyclopedia* cover a wide spectrum of disciplines, such as behavioral studies and the human sciences; cognitive science and neuroscience; computer science and information technology; cosmology; ecology; evolutionary sciences; genetics; primatology; mathematics; medicine; the physical sciences (including chemistry and physics); and the life sciences (including biology, paleontology, and the anthropological sciences). There is also a series of entries on relevant disciplines within the humanities, including ethics and value theory; feminism; philosophy (including methodology, epistemology, philosophy of science, philosophy of religion); theology and religious thought; and technology.

There are interesting, if controversial, reasons why Christian theologians have often taken the lead in discussing the relationship of the sciences to the religions. An unfortunate side effect of this leadership is that, at certain times and places in recent decades, the dialogue has seemed limited by the caricature that only Christianity fostered modern science. But this version of events is historically inaccurate and deeply misleading. The evidence is that all religious traditions and all forms of scientific work have something to gain as well as lose in the process of mutual interaction, and the historical record demonstrates profound and longstanding engagement between science and religion in all literate cultures. Selecting entries and authors to express this guiding conviction and to represent the truly global character of the dialogue has been one of the main goals of this *Encyclopedia*.

The *Encyclopedia of Science and Religion* highlights for our readers the dynamic and ongoing discussion among the religions and the sciences, and demonstrates that it is both possible and fruitful to bring together the spectacular success of science and the wisdom of religion in a constructive interchange. In doing this, the difficult but exciting interdisciplinary conversation between science and religion moves forward to a more challenging phase of interreligious dialogue where religions could be in conversation with each other through their relationship to the sciences. This may go beyond regular interfaith dialogue. If this can be achieved successfully, the multileveled and comprehensive scope of this work will serve well the future of the science and religion interchange.

J. WENTZEL VREDE VAN HUYSSTEEN
NIELS HENRIK GREGERSEN
NANCY R. HOWELL
WESLEY J. WILDMAN

LIST OF ARTICLES

LIST OF ARTICLES

LIST OF CONTRIBUTORS

WOLFGANG ACHTNER
Universität Giessen
Attractor
Butterfly Effect
Chaos, Quantum
Chaos Theory

STACEY A. AKE
Metanexus Institute on Religion and Science,
Philadelphia
Science and Religion in Public
Communication

GEORGE ALLAN
Dickinson College
Aesthetics
Axiology
Beauty
Value
Value, Value Theory

PAUL ALLEN
Concordia University, Montréal
Apologetics

BRAD ALLENBY
AT&T
Humanism

V. ELVING ANDERSON
University of Minnesota
Behavioral Genetics

JENSINE ANDRESEN
Boston University
Buddhism
Mystical Experience
Mysticism
Mystics
Spirituality and Faith Healing
Spirituality and Health

MARIANO ARTIGAS
University of Navarra, Pamplona, Spain
Causality, Primary and Secondary

FRANCISCO J. AYALA
University of California, Irivine
Evolution, Biological

MATTHEW C. BAGGER
Columbia University
Experience, Religious: Philosophical Aspects
Religion, Theories of

OSMAN BAKAR
Center for Muslim-Christian Understanding, Georgetown
University
Islam

YURI V. BALASHOV
University of Georgia, Athens
Laws of Nature
Symmetry

IAN BARBOUR
Carleton College
Science and Religion, Models and Relations

JOHN D. BARROW
Cambridge University
Copenhagen Interpretation
EPR Paradox
Heisenberg's Uncertainty Principle
Indeterminism
Locality
Planck Time
Quantum Cosmologies
Quantum Field Theory
Schrödinger's Cat
Wave-particle Duality

SIGURD BERGMANN
Norwegian Institute of Science and Technology
Pneumatology

LIST OF CONTRIBUTORS

DENNIS BIELFELDT
South Dakota State University
Monism
Ontology
Physicalism, Reductive and Nonreductive
Pluralism
Reductionism

ALISA BOKULICH
Boston University
Philosophy of Science
Philosophy of Science, History of

SUSAN POWERS BRATTON
Baylor University
Human Ecology

JAN BREMMER
University of Groningen
Life after Death

HOWARD BRODY
Michigan State University
Placebo Effect

JOHN HEDLEY BROOKE
Harris Manchester College, Oxford University
Science and Religion, History of Field

WARREN S. BROWN
Graduate School of Psychology, Fuller Theological Seminary
Neurophysiology
Neuropsychology
Neurosciences

DAVID B. BURRELL
University of Notre Dame
Maimonides

ANNA CASE-WINTERS
McCormick Theological Seminary
Design
Design Argument

AUDREY R. CHAPMAN
American Association for the Advancement of Sciences
Behavioral Genetics

PHILIP CLAYTON
Claremont School of Theology and Claremont Graduate University
Deism
Emergence
God
Monotheism
Theism

JOHN COBB
Claremont, California
Gaia Hypothesis

R. DAVID COLE
University of California, Berkeley
DNA
Mutation

RONALD COLE-TURNER
Pittsburgh Theological Seminary
Biotechnology
Cloning
Genetic Engineering

MICHAEL A. COREY
Charleston, West Virginia
Anthropic Principle

HAROLD COWARD
University of Victoria, British Columbia
Dharma
Hinduism
Hinduism, Contemporary Issues in Science and Religion
Karma
Reincarnation

GEORGE COYNE
Vatican Observatory
Christianity, Roman Catholic, Issues in Science and Religion

WILLIAM LANE CRAIG
Talbot School of Theology
Miracle

ANNE A. DAVENPORT
Boston College
Cartesianism
Descartes, René
Infinity

EDWARD B. DAVIS
Messiah College
Christianity, History of Science and Religion

TERRENCE W. DEACON
University of California, Berkeley
Language

CELIA DEANE-DRUMMOND
Chester College of Higher Education, UK
Biology
Life Sciences

JOHN W. DE GRUCHY
University of Cape Town
Liberation Theology

WILLIAM A. DEMBSKI
Baylor University
Algorithm
Algorithmic Complexity
Boundary Conditions
Dissipative Structure
Teleological Argument

ALNOOR R. DHANANI
Harvard University
Islam, History of Science and Religion

STEVEN J. DICK
United States Naval Observatory
Exobiology
Extraterrestrial Life

W. MICHAEL DICKSON
Indiana University
Many-worlds Hypothesis
Phase Space
Physics, Quantum

WILLEM B. DREES
Leiden University
Naturalism

CHRISTIAN EARLY
Eastern Mennonite University
*Christianity, Radical Reformed, Issues in Science and
  Religion*

PAUL ELBERT
Church of God Theological Seminary
*Christianity, Pentecostalism, Issues in Science and
  Religion*

DENIS EDWARDS
School of Theology, Flinders University
Chaos, Religious and Philosophical Aspects
Geocentrism

GEORGE F. R. ELLIS
University of Cape Town
Astronomy
Astrophysics
Gravitation
Inflationary Universe Theory
Relativity, General Theory of
Singularity

CLAUS EMMECHE
University of Copenhagen
Artificial Life
Biosemiotics

ABIGAIL RIAN EVANS
Princeton Theological Seminary
Eugenics

DIRK EVERS
Institute of Hermeneutics, University of Tübigen, Germany
Atomism
Disorder
Time: Physical and Biological Aspects
Unpredictability

LAWRENCE W. FAGG
Catholic University of America
Entropy

FREDERICK FERRÉ
University of Georgia
Technology
Technology and Ethics
Technology and Religion
Value, Scientific

KAI FINSTER
University of Aarhus, Institute of Biological Sciences
Life, Origins of

ANNE FOERST
St. Bonaventure University
Cyborg
Robotics
Virtual Reality

HENRY J. FOLSE, JR.
Loyola University, New Orleans
Bohr, Niels

MATTHEW FOX
University of Creation Spirituality
Sacramental Universe

NANCY FRANKENBERRY
Dartmouth College
Pantheism

GAD FREUDENTHAL
CNRS, France
Judaism, History of Science and Religion, Medieval Period

STEPHEN R. FRIBERG
Lambda Control, Inc.
Bahá'í

LUDOVICO GALLENI
University of Pisa
Teilhard de Chardin, Pierre

MARY GERHART
Hobart and William Smith Colleges
Metaphor

KARL GIBERSON
Eastern Nazarene College
Science and Religion, Periodical Literature

MARCELO GLEISER
Dartmouth College
Myth

JOSEPH A. GOGUEN
University of California at San Diego
Consciousness Studies

ULF GÖRMAN
Lund University, Sweden
Theodicy

COLIN GRANT
Mount Allison University
Altruism

EDWARD GRANT
Indiana University, Bloomington
Aristotle
Thomas Aquinas

LIST OF CONTRIBUTORS

WILLIAM J. GRASSIE
Metanexus Institute, PA
Hermeneutics in Science and Religion

MARION GRAU
Graduate Theological Union
Cybernetics

NIELS HENRIK GREGERSEN
University of Aarhus, Denmark
Christianity, Lutheran, Issues in Science and Religion
Complexity

FREDERICK GREGORY
University of Florida
Kant, Immanuel

ARNE GRØN
University of Copenhagen
Idealism
Truth, Theories of

BRUNO GUIDERDONI
Centres Nationals de Recherche Scientifique
Islam, Contemporary Issues in Science and Religion

ARN O. GYLDENHOLM
University of Aarhus, Denmark
Catastrophism
Competition
Punctuated Equilibrium

TOMAS HANCIL
Protestant Theological Faculty, Charles University, Prague
Evolutionary Epistemology
Hypothetical Realism

NIELS VIGGO HANSEN
Agri, Denmark
Science Wars

MASAKAZU HARA
Seiwa College, Japan
Shinto

PETER HARRISON
Bond University, Australia
Science, Origins of

JOHN HAUGHT
Georgetown University
Atheism
Evolution, Theology of
Incarnation
Kenosis

MICHAEL HELLER
Vatican Observatory
Geometry, Modern: Theological Aspects

JAN-OLAV HENRIKSEN
Norweigan Lutheran School of Theology, Oslo
Human Nature, Religious and Philosophical Aspects
Theological Anthropology

MATTHEW HENRY
Eastern Nazarene College
Free Will Defense

EBERHARD HERRMANN
Uppsala University, Sweden
Explanation
Pragmatism

NOREEN L. HERZFELD
St. John's University, Minnesota
Artificial Intelligence
Science Fiction

PETER M. J. HESS
Center for Theology and the Natural Sciences, Berkeley
Lamarckism
Two Books

NORRISS HETHERINGTON
University of California, Berkeley
Biblical Cosmology
Cosmology
Cosmology, Religious and Philosophical Aspects

SUZANNE HOLLAND
University of Puget Sound
Reproductive Technology
Stem Cell Research

BARBARA A. HOLMES
Memphis Theological Seminary
Ethnicity
Womanist Theology

MUZAFFAR IQBAL
Center for Islam and Science
Averröes
Avicenna

ANTJE JACKELÉN
Lutheran School of Theology at Chicago
Paradigms

MAX JAMMER
Bar-Ilan University
Einstein, Albert
Materialism

ANDERS JEFFNER
Uppsala University, Sweden
Philosophy of Religion

HANS J. L. JENSEN
University of Aarhus, Denmark
Ritual

CHRISTOPHER B. KAISER
Western Theological Seminary
Genesis

BOJE KATZENELSON
Risskov, Denmark
Aggression

STEPHANIE KAZA
University of Vermont, Burlington
Ecology, Science of

CATHERINE KELLER
Drew University
Embodiment

KLAUS K. KLOSTERMAIER
University of Manitoba
Hinduism, History of Science and Religion

CHRISTOPHER C. KNIGHT
Von Hügel Institute, St. Edmunds College, Cambridge
Revelation

DAVID M. KNIGHT
University of Durham, England
Chemistry

HAROLD G. KOENIG
Duke University Medical Center
Medicine

THIEMO KRINK
EVALife Group, University of Aarhus, Denmark
Automata, Cellular
Thinking Machines
Turing Test

ROALD E. KRISTIANSEN
University of Tromsø, Norway
Anthropocentrism
Deep Ecology

MATHIJS LAMBERIGTS
Katholieke Universiteit Leuven
Augustine

BRIAN L. LANCASTER
Liverpool John Moores University
Self-transcendence

RICHARD LANDES
Center for Millennial Studies, Boston University
End of the World, Religious & Philosophical Aspects of
Millenialism

DUANE H. LARSON
Wartburg Theological Seminary
Death
Sacraments

KATHIA CASTRO LASZLO
Instituto Tecnológico y de Estudios Superiores de Monterey, Mexico
Systems Theory

KAREN LEBACQZ
Graduate Theological Union
Gene Patenting

ANDREW LINZEY
University of Oxford; University of Birmingham
Animal Rights

JAMES E. LODER
Princeton Theological Seminary
Paradox
Self-reference

VOLKER LOESCHKE
University of Aarhus, Denmark
Adaptation
Fitness
Gradualism
Neo-Darwinism

DAVID MANLEY
Rutgers University
Cosmological Argument
Ontological Argument

MARTIN E. MARTY
University of Chicago
Fundamentalism

JAY MCDANIEL
Hendrix College
Ecology, Religious and Philosophical Aspects

DONNA M. MCKENZIE
Fordham University
Genetically Modified Organisms
Xenotransplantation

HUBERT MEISINGER
Protestant Church of Hessen and Nassau, Darmstadt, Germany
Created Co-Creator
Functionalism

WILLIAM W. MEISSNER, S.J.
Boston Psychoanalytic Institute and Boston College
Freud, Sigmund

THEO C. MEYERING
Leiden University, The Netherlands
Causation
Downward Causation
Supervenience
Upward Causation

MARY MIDGLEY
Newcastle upon Tyne, UK
Memes
Selfish Gene

JAMES MILLER
Queen's University
Dao

STEVEN MITHEN
University of Reading
Cognitive Fluidity

SIMON CONWAY MORRIS
University of Cambridge
Convergence

KENNETH MOWBRAY
American Museum of Natural History
Evolution, Human
Paleontology

NANCEY MURPHY
Fuller Theological Seminary
Christianity, Radical Reformed, Issues in Science and
Religion

PAUL D. MURRAY
Ushaw College, Durham
Epistemology

NAOKI NABESHIMA
Ryukoku University, Kyoto
Buddhism, History of Science and Religion

RONALD Y. NAKASONE
Graduate Theological Union, Berkeley
Buddhism, Contemporary Issues in Science and Religion

JAMES A. NASH
Boston University School of Theology
Ecology, Ethics of

ALEXEI NESTERUK
University of Portsmouth, UK
Christianity, Orthodox, Issues in Science and Religion

ROBERT CUMMINGS NEVILLE
Boston University
Imagination
Theology
Theology, Theories of
Value, Religious

ANDREW B. NEWBERG
University of Pennsylvania
Experience, Religious: Cognitive and Neurophysiological
Aspects

GEORGE NEWLANDS
University of Glasgow, Scotland
Hope

KEES VAN KOOTEN NIEKERK
University of Aarhus, Denmark
Critical Realism

DAVID H. NIKKEL
University of North Carolina, Pembroke
Panentheism

ULRIK B. NISSEN
University of Aarhus, Denmark
Natural Law Theory
Naturalistic Fallacy
Nature

JENS NOECKEL
Yale University
Chaos, Quantum

PETER ØHRSTRØM
Aalborg University, Denmark
Time: Religious and Philosophical Aspects

PALMYRE M. F. OOMEN
Heyendaal Institute, University of Nijmegen, The Netherlands
Neurotheology
Self-organization

THOMAS JAY OORD
Northwest Nazarene College
Free Process Defense
Free Will Defense
Process Thought
Whitehead, Alfred North

ALAN G. PADGETT
Luther Seminary
Christianity, Evangelical, Issues in Science and Religion

ANN PEDERSON
Augustana College
Abortion
Feminist Cosmology
Feminist Theology

TED PETERS
Graduate Theological Union; Pacific Lutheran Theological
Seminary
Freedom
Genetic Determinism
Genetics
Human Genome Project
Playing God
Sin
UFO

RODNEY L. PETERSEN
Boston Theological Institute
Morality

GREGORY R. PETERSON
South Dakota State University
Evolutionary Algorithms
Hierarchy
Imago Dei
Immanence
Level Theory
Primatology
Science and Religion, Methodologies

JOHN POLKINGHORNE
Queens' College, Cambridge, UK
Physics, Particle

STEPHEN PRIEST
Wolfson College, Oxford
Mind-body Theories
Mind-brain Interaction

W. M. PRIESTLEY
University of the South
Gödel's Incompleteness Theorem
Mathematics

ANNE PRIMAVESI
Birkbeck College, University of London
Ecofeminism

JOHN C. PUDDEFOOT
Eton College, UK
Geometry: Philosophical Aspects
Information
Information Technology
Information Theory

PHILIP L. QUINN
University of Notre Dame
God, Existence of

RICHARD O. RANDOLPH
Saint Paul School of Theology
Global Warming
Greenhouse Effect
Nuclear Energy

MICHAEL L. RAPOSA
Lehigh University
Semiotics

DAVID RAYNOR
Univesity of Ottawa
Hume, David

K. HELMUT REICH
Senior University, Richmond, British Columbia
Complementarity
Psychology of Religion

KURT ANDERS RICHARDSON
McMaster Divinity College, Hamilton, Ontario
Scriptural Interpretation

HOLMES ROLSTON, III
Colorado State University
Biological Diversity
Ecology
Life, Biological Aspects
Life, Religious and Philosophical Aspects
Nature versus Nurture
Religion and Values, Origins of
Skyhooks

GEORGE H. RUDEBUSCH
Northern Arizona University
Plato

MICHAEL RUSE
Florida State University
Evolution
Evolution, Biocultural
Gould, Stephen Jay
Mitochondrial Eve
Progress
Selection, Levels of
Sociobiology

ALLAN M. RUSSELL
Hobart & William Smith Colleges
Metaphor

ROBERT JOHN RUSSELL
Center for Theological and Natural Studies, Berkeley
Cosmology, Physical Aspects
Science and Religion

NORBERT M. SAMUELSON
Arizona State University
Judaism, History of Science and Religion, Modern Period

ANDY F. SANDERS
University of Groningen, The Netherlands
Naturalized Epistemology
Tacit Knowledge

H. PAUL SANTMIRE
Watertown, Massachusetts
Ecotheology

JEFFREY P. SCHLOSS
Westmont College, Santa Barbara
Evolutionary Ethics
Symbiosis

RAYMUND SCHWAGER
Faculty of Theology, University of Innsbruck
Fall

HANS SCHWARZ
University of Regensburg, Germany
Behaviorism
Christology
Holy Spirit

WILLIAM R. SHEA
Université de Strasbourg
Galileo Galilei

JIANG SHENG
Shandong University, China
Chinese Religions, Daoism and Science in China

NIU SHI-WEI
Academia Sinica, Beijing
Quantum Vacuum State

F. LeRon SHULTS
Bethel Theological Seminary
Coherentism
Foundationalism
Nonfoundationalism
Postfoundationalism
Postmodern Science

ERNEST SIMMONS
Concordia College
God of the Gaps
Meditation
Transcendence
Transmigration

LIST OF CONTRIBUTORS

TAEDE A. SMEDES
University of Gronigen
Chaos Theory
Determinism

STEPHEN D. SNOBELEN
University of King's College, Halifax
Newton, Isaac

CHRISTOPHER SOUTHGATE
University of Exeter, UK
Holism
Science and Religion, Research in

MICHAEL L. SPEZIO
University of California, Davis
Human Nature, Physical Aspects

ERIC O. SPRINGSTED
General Theological Seminary
Faith

MAX L. STACKHOUSE
Princeton Theological Seminary
Economics

LISA L. STENMARK
San José State College
Feminisms and Science

MIKAEL STENMARK
Uppsala University, Sweden
Contextualism
Fallibilism
Falsifiability
Scientism
Worldview

WILLIAM R. STOEGER
Vatican Observatory Research Group, University of Arizona
Age of the Universe
Eschatology
Field
Field Theories
Grand Unified Theory
New Physics
String Theory
Superstrings
Thermodynamics, Second Law of

JEROME A. STONE
Meadville-Lombard Theological School
Empiricism

WILLIAM H. SWATOS, JR.
Association for the Sociology of Religion
Sociology

STEPHEN SYKES
University of Durham, St. John's College
Christianity, Anglican, Issues in Science and Religion

CHARLES TALIAFERRO
St. Olaf College
Dualism
Soul
Special Providence

IAN TATTERSALL
American Museum of Natural History
Evolution, Human
Missing Link
Paleoanthropology
Paleontology

ALFRED I. TAUBER
Boston University
Medical Ethics

JOHN A. TESKE
Elizabethtown College
Evolutionary Psychology
Neural Darwinism
Spirit

JOHN J. THATAMANIL
Millsaps College
Liberation

GÜNTER THOMAS
University of Heidelberg, Theology Faculty
Autopoiesis
Constructivism

HAVA TIROSH-SAMUELSON
Arizona State University
Judaism

THOMAS F. TRACY
Bates College
Divine Action
Double Agency
Providence
Special Divine Action

ROGER TRIGG
University of Warwick, England
Positivism, Logical
Realism

LOU ANN G. TROST
Center for Theology and the Natural Sciences, Berkeley
Models

JENNIFER L. TRUSTED
Emerita, Open University and the University of Exeter
Space and Time

LÉON TURNER
Faculty of Divinity, University of Cambridge
Self

LUCO J. VAN DEN BROM
University of Groningen
Eternity
Omnipotence
Omnipresence
Omniscience

JITSE M. VAN DER MEER
Redeemer University
Metaphysics
Order

PETER VAN NESS
Yale University School of Medicine
Spirituality and the Practice of Science

HOWARD J. VAN TILL
Calvin College
Clockwork Universe
Creation Science
Creationism
Forces of Nature
Intelligent Design
Physics
Physics, Classical
Relativity, Special Theory of

GRAHAM WARD
University of Manchester
Postmodernism
Supernaturalism

KEITH WARD
Oxford University
Chance
Christianity
Contingency
Creatio Continua
Creatio Ex Nihilo
Creation
Evil and Suffering
Natural Theology
Teleology

PAUL K. WASON
John Templeton Foundation
Anthropology
Anthropology of Religion
Art, Origins of
Culture, Origins of

BRENT WATERS
Garrett-Evangical Theological Seminary
Gene Therapy
Genetic Defect
Genetic Testing

WILLIAM J. WATSON
University of South Dakota School of Medicine
Abortion

FRASER WATTS
Faculty of Divinity, University of Cambridge
Prayer and Meditation
Psychology
Self

GEORGE E. WEBB
Tennessee Technological University
Scopes Trial

KIRK WEGTER-McNELLY
Graduate Theological Union, Berkeley
Science and Religion

RICHARD C. WEIKART
California State University, Stanislaus
Mendel, Gregor

CLAUDE WELCH
Graduate Theological Union
Historical Criticism

MICHAEL WELKER
University of Heidelberg, Germany
Modernity

E. DAVID WILLIS
Princeton Theological Seminary
Calvinism
Christianity, Reformed, Issues in Science and Religion

CLAIRE E. WOLFTEICH
Boston University
Spirituality

MARK WORTHING
Tabor College, Adelaide, Australia
Big Bang Theory
Big Crunch Theory
Black Hole
Closed Universe
Cyclical Universe
Omega Point Theory
Open Universe
Steady State Theory
T = 0

ADRIAN M. WYARD
Counterbalance Foundation
Science and Religion in Public Communication

HING KAU YEUNG
China Graduate School of Theology
Chinese Religions and Science
Chinese Religions, Confucianism and Science in China
Chinese Religions, History of Science and Religion in China

AMOS YONG
Bethel College
Christianity, Pentacostalism, Issues in Science and Religion

LAURIE ZOLOTH
San Francisco State University
Judaism, Contemporary Issues in Science and Religion

SYNOPTIC OUTLINE

BEHAVIORAL STUDIES AND HUMAN SCIENCES

Altruism

Anthropocentrism

Anthropology

Anthropology of Religion

Behaviorism

Economics

Evolution, Biocultural

Evolutionary Psychology

Freud, Sigmund

Human Nature, Physical Aspects

Human Nature, Religious and
  Philosophical Aspects

Linguistics

Psychology

Psychology of Religions

Ritual

Self

Self-transcendence

Semiotics

Sociobiology

Sociology

Systems Theory

BIOGRAPHIES

Aristotle

Augustine

Averröes (Ibn Rushd)

Avicenna (Ibn Sina)

Bohr, Niels

Charles, Darwin

Descartes, René

Einstein, Albert

Freud, Sigmund

Galileo Galilei

Gould, Stephen Jay

Hume, David

Kant, Immanuel

Maimonides

Mendel, Gregor

Newton, Isaac

Plato

Teilhard de Chardin, Pierre

Thomas Aquinas

Whitehead, Alfred North

COGNITIVE SCIENCE AND NEUROSCIENCES

Art, Origins of

Cognitive Fluidity

Cognitive Science

Consciousness Studies

Experience, Religious: Cognitive
  and Neuropysiological Aspects

Human Nature, Physical Aspects

Human Nature, Religious and
  Philosophical Aspects

Language

Linguistics

Meditation

Mind-body Theories

Mind-brain Interaction

Mystical Experience

Neural Darwinism

Neurophysiology

Neuropsychology

Neurosciences

Neurotheology

Prayer and Meditation

Science, Origins of

Semiotics

Supervenience

COMPUTER SCIENCE AND INFORMATION TECHNOLOGY

Algorithm

Artificial Intelligence

Artificial Life

Automata, Cellular

Chaos Theory

Complexity

Cybernetics

Cyborg

Evolutionary Algorithms

Information

Information Technology

Information Theory

Thinking Machines

Turing Test

Virtual Reality

COSMOLOGY

Age of the Universe

Anthropic Principle

Astronomy

Astrophysics

Big Bang Theory

Big Crunch Theory

Black Hole

Boundary Conditions

Closed Universe

SYNOPTIC OUTLINE

PHYSICAL SCIENCES

Technology

Technology and Ethics

Technology and Religion

Thinking Machines

Virtual Reality

THEOLOGY AND RELIGIOUS THOUGHT

Abortion

Altruism

Animal Rights

Anthropocentrism

Anthropology of Religion

Apologetics

Biblical Cosmology

Causality, Primary and Secondary

Clockwork Universe

Cosmology, Religious and
Philosophical Aspects

Created Co-Creator

Creation

Creatio Continua

Creatio Ex Nihilo

Creationism

Death

Dharma

Divine Action

Double Agency

Miracle

Providence

Skyhooks

Special Divine Action

Special Providence

Embodiment

End of the World, Religious and
Philosophical Aspects of

Eschatology

Eternity

Evil and Suffering

Evolution, Theology of

Experience, Religious:
Philosophical Aspects

Faith

Fall

Free Process Defense

Freedom

Fundamentalism

Genesis

God

Atheism

Deism

Monotheism

Panentheism

Pantheism

Theism

God of the Gaps

Historical Criticism

Holy Spirit

Hope

Human Nature, Religious and
Philosophical Aspects

Imagination

Imago Dei

Immanence

Karma

Kenosis

Liberation

Life, Religious and Philosophical
Aspects

Life after Death

Eternity

Reincarnation

Transmigration

Meditation

Metaphor

Millennialism

Moral Cosmologies

Morality

Mystical Experience

Mysticism

Mystics

Myth

Natural Law Theory

Omnipotence

Omnipresence

Ontological Argument

Paradox

Philosophy of Religion

Pluralism

Pneumatology

Prayer and Meditation

Process Thought

Religion and Values, Origins of

Religion, Theories of

Revelation

Ritual

Sacramental Universe

Science Fiction

Scriptural Interpretation

Self-transcendence

Sin

Soul

Spirit

Spirituality

Spirituality and Faith Healing

Spirituality and Health

Spirituality and the Practice of
Science

Supernaturalism

Teilhard de Chardin, Pierre

Teleology

Theodicy

Theological Anthropology

Theology

Ecotheology

Feminist Theology

Liberation Theology

Natural Theology

Neurotheology

Theology, Theories of

Thomas Aquinas

Transcendence

Two Books

Value, Religious

ABORTION

Abortion is the termination of a pregnancy before the time of extrauterine viability. An abortion terminates the life of the embryo (the fertilized egg before three months of growth) or the fetus (after three months). *Spontaneous abortions,* also called *miscarriages,* occur when the fetus or embryo is spontaneously expelled by the body. An *induced abortion* occurs when there is deliberate human intervention to end the pregnancy. Induced abortions can be accomplished medically or surgically.

Medically induced abortions are accomplished by giving drugs like mifepristone (RU-486), which block the work of the hormone progesterone and soften the lining of the uterus, thus ending the pregnancy. Medically induced abortions can generally only be used if the woman is less than seven weeks from her last menstrual period. Mifepristone is administered in conjunction with another medicine called misoprostol, which causes the uterus to cramp and expel the embryo.

Within the first trimester of pregnancy, the most common form of surgical abortion is *vacuum aspiration*. During the second trimester, *dilation* and *evacuation* procedures (D & E) are performed. Finally, stimulating contractions that expel the fetus from the uterus can also induce abortion.

Ethical issues

Abortion raises significant scientific, legal, religious, and ethical issues: the understanding of life and death, the definition of a human person, the rights of the mother and the fetus, and the impact of new scientific discoveries on reproduction. Certain scientific and technological discoveries, including stem cell research, cloning, and artificial reproduction, have complicated the abortion issue. The status of the fetus is probably the most controversial issue: Is the fetus a person with the same rights as those who are born? Some argue that the embryo from the moment of conception has the same rights as a person *extra utero*. Others argue that the early embryo is human life but not a human person. The political state also has an interest both in the autonomy of the mother and the health of the baby. Sometimes, the autonomy of the mother can be in tension with her maternal responsibility to the fetus.

With the increased use of fertility drugs and assisted reproductive technologies, many patients can conceive who were unable to conceive in the past. Some of these technologies may result in high order multiple pregnancies (with four or more fetuses), which have a substantial risk of the loss of all fetuses before the period of extra-uterine viability (twenty-two to twenty-four weeks gestation). The parents' options include carrying all of the fetuses until birth, eliminating all of them, or selectively terminating some fetuses. Selective reduction may enhance the chance of survival of some fetuses in a high order multiple pregnancy.

Discovery, diagnosis, prevention, and therapy of certain genetic or medical diseases complicate decisions surrounding abortion. Parents can now determine when the fetus is in-utero whether it carries possible genetic predispositions to diseases like cystic fibrosis, Huntington's chorea, early Alzheimer's, and sickle cell anemia. Prenatal testing also allows detection of chromosomal abnormalities, such as Down syndrome. Ultrasound, now widely used during pregnancy, can document a wide variety of birth defects. Although some of these problems may be treatable in-utero, in most cases no therapy is available, and the parents must decide whether to continue the pregnancy. In addition, some maternal medical conditions, such as pulmonary hypertension, may pose a significant threat to the mother's life if pregnancy continues.

Physicians, parents, and insurance companies face difficult decisions about abortion. The human and economic costs of caring for children with medical or genetic disorders can be great. Opponents of abortions that are performed to address these problems raise the concern that the weak and vulnerable in society will have no rights. There is potential for discrimination based on genetic information.

Religious views

Religious views on abortion are pluriform, ranging from those who consider abortion as murder to those who justify it as a necessary means to an end. The spectrum of diversity can be found not only among world religious traditions, but also within religious traditions. The discussion focuses primarily on the status and rights of the fetus, the status and rights of the mother, the role of medical technology, the value of life (quantity and quality), the political and socioeconomic concerns surrounding fertility and infertility, and the nature of what it means to make difficult ethical decisions in a community of faith.

Judaism, Islam, and Christianity are related monotheistic religions that use religious texts, human reason, and teaching authorities for making ethical decisions. Within and among these three traditions, there are deep and potentially divisive views on abortion. For example, some religious scholars believe that God creates all life. According to this view, the embryo is a human person endowed with rights from the moment of conception. To reject this life is to reject the creation of God. Abortion is considered a sin against life along with murder, genocide, and self-destruction, and any destruction of an embryo would be considered sin, even when done in response to prenatal diagnosis of genetic disease.

In contrast, some scholars of religion, including Daniel Maguire, explain that abortion may be permissible for many reasons. Maguire points out in *Sacred Choices* (2001) that there is only one direct reference in scripture to accidental abortion—Exodus 21:22, which states that someone who injures a woman and causes her to miscarry must pay a fine paid to her husband. If the woman dies from her injuries, however, the punishment for the person who injured her is death. Clearly, in this text, the fetus is not considered a person with the same status as the woman, and abortion would be permitted for some reasons, such as preventing extreme fetal abnormalities and saving the life of the mother.

Judaism. Some Jewish scholars, such as Laurie Zoloth, connect reproduction to justice. Judaism takes into account the good of the entire community in making decisions about abortion. This approach derives from Judaism's root commitment that every human being is a child of God, born in the image of God. Reproduction is undertaken not merely for its own sake, but for the sake of the community. Abortion is thus permitted for the woman to avoid disgrace or for health reasons of both mother and fetus. In some Jewish traditions, the first forty days of conception are considered like "water" and the fetus does not have an ontological status of a person.

Islam. The approach from Islam concerning abortion and contraception has generally been one that considers the common good of the community. Muslims see themselves as vice regents of God, called to do God's work in this world. Islam's ethical practices are flexible and are often adapted to political and social climates. As Gamal Serour points out in *The Future of Human Reproduction* (1998), for Muslims abortion can be "carried out to protect the mother's health or life or to prevent the birth of a seriously handicapped child" (p. 196).

Christianity. Within the Christian tradition, perspectives on abortion vary dramatically. For example, within Roman Catholicism different scholars draw different conclusions about permitting abortion. Many consider the official Catholic position on abortion to derive from the 1930 encyclical *Casti Connubii* (On Christian Marriage) of Pope Pius XI and the 1987 *Donum Vitae* (Gift of Life) of Pope John Paul II. On the issue of genetic screening for selective abortion, *Donum Vitae* states that "a woman would be committing a gravely illicit act if she were to request such a diagnosis with the deliberate intention of having an abortion should the results confirm the existence of a malformation or abnormality." Furthermore, humans cannot assume the role of God when using embryos in research from IVF (in vitro fertilization). *Donum Vitae* states that the researcher "sets himself up as the master of the destiny of others inasmuch as he arbitrarily chooses whom he will allow to live and whom he will send to death and kills defenseless human beings." However, Maguire and others have pointed out that papal statements on abortion are not considered infallible and explain that abortion would be permitted for some reasons.

Protestant denominations vary on their stance on abortion. Within Protestantism, decisions about abortion are not made by a central teaching magisterium but within a community of shared discernment. Denominations such as the Evangelical Lutheran Church in American and the United Church of Christ do not take an official stand on the status of the fetus. Both the fetus and the mother are taken into account when confronting decisions concerning abortion. Other Protestant teachings are more consistent with Roman Catholicism and consider abortion a sin. In some cases, exceptions are made for the life of the mother.

Asian religions. According to Maguire, Asian religions like Daoism and Confucianism have understood abortion as a necessity in some cases and have extended compassion to those involved. These nontheistic religions emphasize the family and community as the primary social unit, and decisions about abortion are made within this social context. Buddhism considers all life as linked and interdependent, and most Buddhists believe in reincarnation and understand that life begins at conception. These beliefs could preclude abortion at any stage, but many Buddhists permit abortion, particularly for the sake of the mother. Intention is central to Buddhist morality and so the action of abortion must also include the intentions of the moral actors.

See also BUDDHISM; CHINESE RELIGIONS,
    CONFUCIANISM AND SCIENCE IN CHINA; CHINESE
    RELIGIONS, DAOISM AND SCIENCE IN CHINA;
    CHRISTIANITY, LUTHERAN, ISSUES IN SCIENCE AND
    RELIGION; CHRISTIANITY, ROMAN CATHOLIC, ISSUES
    IN SCIENCE AND RELIGION; CLONING; DAO;
    GENETIC TESTING; HUMAN GENOME PROJECT;
    ISLAM, CONTEMPORARY ISSUES IN SCIENCE AND
    RELIGION; JUDAISM, CONTEMPORARY ISSUES IN
    SCIENCE AND RELIGION; REPRODUCTIVE
    TECHNOLOGY; STEM CELL RESEARCH

Bibliography

ACOG-American College of Obstetricians and Gynecologists. "Medical Management of Abortion." *ACOG Practice Bulletin* 26 (2001):1-13.

Congregation for the Doctrine of the Faith. *Donum Vitae*: *Instruction on Respect for Human Life in Its Origin and on the Dignity of Procreation: Replies to Certain Questions of the Day*. Washington, D.C.: United States Catholic Conference, 1987. In *Intervention and Reflection: Basic Issues in Medical Ethics,* 6th edition, ed. Ronald Munson. Belmont, Calif.: Wadsworth, 2000. Also available from: http://www.nccbuscc.org/prolife/tdocs/donumvitae.htm.

Evangelical Lutheran Church in America. "A Social Statement on Abortion." Adopted at the second biennial Churchwide Assembly of the Evangelical Lutheran Church in America, Orlando, Fla., Aug 28–Sept 4, 1991. Available from: http://www.elca.org/dcs/abortion.pf.html.

Maguire, Daniel. *Sacred Choices: The Right to Contraception and Abortion in Ten World Religions*. Minneapolis, Minn.: Fortress Press, 2001.

Paul, Maureen, ed. *A Clinician's Guide to Medical and Surgical Abortion*. New York: Churchill Livingstone, 1999.

Peters, Ted. "In Search of the Perfect Child: Genetic Testing and Selective Abortion." *Christian Century* 113, no. 31 (1996): 1034–1037.

Pope Pius XI. "*Casti Connubii*: Encyclical On Christian Marriage," December 31, 1930. Available from: http://www.vatican.va/holy_father/pius_xi/encyclicals.

Rispler-Chaim, Vardit. "The Right Not To Be Born: Abortion of the Disadvantaged Fetus in Contemporary Fatwas." *The Muslim World* 89, no. 2 (1999): 130–143.

Rogers, Therisa. "The Islamic Ethics of Abortion in the Traditional Islamic Sources." *The Muslim World* 89, no. 2 (1999): 122–129.

Serour, Gamal I. "Reproductive Choice: A Muslim Perspective." In *The Future of Human Reproduction,* eds. John Harris and Soren Holm. Oxford: Clarendon Press, 1998.

Zoloth, Laurie. "The Ethics of the Eight Day: Jewish Bioethics and Research on Human Embryonic Stem

Cells." In *The Human Embryonic Stem Cell Debate: Science, Ethics and Public Policy,* eds. Suzanne Holland, Karen Lebacqz, and Laurie Zoloth. Cambridge, Mass. and London: The MIT Press, 2001.

ANN PEDERSON
WILLIAM J. WATSON

eye to light and dark, or they may be long-lasting, such as the increased number of red blood cells in humans who live at high altitudes.

See also EVOLUTION; FITNESS; LIFE SCIENCES; SELECTION, LEVELS OF

VOLKER LOESCHCKE

ADAPTATION

The term *adaptation* refers to changes in an organism's structure, function, or behavior that increase its ability to live in a particular environment. As such, adaptation is a central term in the life sciences. The many known examples of animals and plants adapting to their environment were the basis for the theories of evolution formulated by Charles Darwin (1809–1882) and Jean–Baptiste de Lamarck (1744–1829). Adaptation in the Darwinian sense describes a process of evolutionary change by natural selection. In this process the average performance of the individuals in a population with respect to survival and reproduction is improved.

The term adaptation is also used to describe the result of the process of evolutionary change (the state of being adapted) or to describe the "solution" to a problem that is set by the environment. The word is used this way in the *adaptationist program,* which has been criticized for explaining traits post hoc as having evolved to serve certain functions. Because the environment of any organism is continuously changing, the degree of adaptation is never optimal, and adaptation is, therefore, a never-ending process.

Not all traits in an organism or features of an organism's appearance are necessarily the result of adaptation; they may be by-products of selection acting on other traits. For example, the increased brain size in humans is considered to be a side effect of selection favoring increased body size. Specific traits can also be the result of adaptations for other functions that have since changed. For example, feathers in birds originally evolved to provide insulation, and only later were they used for flying. Physiological adaptations are plastic responses to the physical environment that occur within a lifetime and are not inherited by the next generation. Such adaptations can be of short duration and reversible, such as the adaptation of the

AESTHETICS

Aesthetics is the aspect of axiology that deals with the intrinsic value found in people's immediate sense experiences or their responses to sense experiences: judging them ugly, beautiful, or sublime. Aesthetics, which focuses on the uniquely particular, contrasts with science, which focuses on the general laws those particulars illustrate. Aesthetic theories can be about experiences of natural objects and events, but are usually concerned with art works and artistic creations. Aesthetic judgments are usually said to be disinterested, an enjoyment of the unique content of an immediate experience for its own sake. Marxists, postmodernists, and feminist theorists disagree, however, claiming that all such judgments are expressions of an interest.

See also AXIOLOGY; BEAUTY; VALUE; VALUE, SCIENTIFIC

GEORGE ALLAN

AFTERLIFE

See LIFE AFTER DEATH

AGE OF THE UNIVERSE

In contemporary scientific cosmology, the age of the universe is the time that has elapsed since the Big Bang, which in standard cosmological models is the past limit to the hotter, denser phases that are encountered as one goes farther and farther back into the past. In these models the Big Bang is a singularity, a region characterized by infinite density, temperature, and curvature. Quantum gravitational and quantum cosmological treatments of the

Big Bang, using concepts like superstrings, are beginning to provide a more adequate description of this primordial cosmological epoch, which is often referred to as the Planck era, during which the temperature of the universe was above 10^{32} K (kelvin). Here, classical relativistic gravitational theory (Albert Einstein's General Relativity) breaks down. It is from this extremely hot Planck era that the universe emerges with its three spatial dimensions, its one time dimension, its four basic physical interactions, and its matter and radiation. Before that emergence they were all unified in ways that are not yet completely understood.

A rough upper limit on the age of the universe, t_H is given by the reciprocal of the Hubble parameter now, H_0, which gives the rate of expansion of the universe per unit distance. Thus, $t_H = 1/H_0$. Using the currently measured range of values of H_0, t_H is between twelve to sixteen billion years. Compare this to the very reliable age of the Earth and the sun, which is about 4.8 billion years. These ages have been confirmed by a variety of astronomical and isotopic techniques, including the measurement of the ages of stars in globular clusters (which are very old), and the estimation of how much uranium has decayed to lead and how much rubidium has decayed to strontium.

From the point of view of prescientific cultural and religious traditions, the age of the universe is the time that has elapsed since the world or the universe was created. In many traditions the creation is also taken to be the "event" in which time itself began. Some of those who interpret the Genesis creation and pre-Abraham historical accounts literally—as scientifically and historically reliable documents describing the formation of the universe and of the world, and earliest human history—have calculated the age of the world and of created reality (the universe) to be about 6,000 years, having begun in 4004 B.C.E. This has been done by counting the generations listed in Genesis from Adam and Eve to Abraham, and then estimating the number of years from Abraham to Moses, both of which are fairly well known, to the present. Experts have disputed this literal approach, of course, particularly because it is strongly contradicted by independent bodies of evidence from both the natural and the human sciences. It also fails to recognize the mythological and legendary character of the relevant Genesis sources. This does not mean that the Genesis sources are not revealing and expressive of important truths, but it does mean that those truths are neither scientific nor directly historical, but rather religious and theological truths.

The cosmological age of the universe since the Big Bang, although it certainly has important theological significance, cannot be interpreted as the time since the creation of the universe, if *universe* is understood to mean all that exists and not God. There could have been and there could be many other regions of reality, either completely separate from or linked with ours only at the Big Bang itself, which preceded or are older than our observable universe. Furthermore, it is unclear whether "creation" or "the first moment of creation" took place at any definite time. However, it does make some sense to date the beginning of the observable universe at the Big Bang, even though the coordinated manifold of primordial quantum events is not adequately understood.

See also BIG BANG THEORY; COSMOLOGY, PHYSICAL ASPECTS; SINGULARITY; STRING THEORY

Bibliography

Börner, Gerhard. *The Early Universe: Facts and Fiction,* 3rd edition. Berlin, Heidelberg, and New York: Springer-Verlag, 1993.

Coles, Peter, and Lucchin, Francesco. *Cosmology: The Origin and Evolution of Cosmic Structure.* New York: Wiley, 1995.

Kolb, Edward W., and Turner, Michael S. *The Early Universe.* Reading, Mass.: Addison-Wesley, 1990.

WILLIAM R. STOEGER

AGGRESSION

Aggression is behavior or a behavioral urge with the object of threatening or harming primarily members of one's own species. Several theories attempt to explain aggression.

Theories of aggression

The theory of instinct in ethology, as proposed by Konrad Lorenz (1903–1989), supposes that humans, like other biological creatures, are so constituted that they either continuously or periodically produce physiological energies that must seek outlet in certain kinds of species-specific aggressive behavior. Other ethologists argue that although innate genetic codes, as well as neural and hormonal processes, account for an aggressive disposition, there is no reason to assume the existence of aggressive energies. All ethologists agree, however, that aggression has arisen in the course of evolution and serves the same basic functions in animals and humans in regulating the intercourse between members of a species, although the regulation involves more psychological and cultural aspects with humans than with other animals.

This assumption is endorsed by sociobiology, first systematized by Edward O. Wilson (1929–), which studies the social behavior of humans using evolutionary methods. Like ethologists, sociobiologists presume an innate aggressive disposition in humans, but sociobiologists define innateness as the measurable *probability* that aggressiveness will develop in a species within a specified set of environments, not the *certainty* that it will develop in all kinds of environments.

The psychoanalytic drive theory of Sigmund Freud (1856–1939) resembles the instinct theory of Lorenz in the assumption that innate drives represent physiological energies. Freud departs from Lorenz, however, by assuming that the activity of the drives does not result in species-specific behavior patterns. Freud concluded that two drive complexes embodied in human beings constitute the basic sources of all human behavior; these were the life-building *Eros* and the life-demolishing *Thanatos,* with aggression, directed both outwards against others and inwards against oneself, as its central feature.

The theory of needs by Henry Murray (1893–1988) put forward a list of about twenty presumably universal human needs, among them aggression. In need theory there is no place for physiological energies. If a certain need, such as aggression, is dominant within a person in many different situations, it also appears as a personality trait.

The frustration theory, first presented by John Dollard (1900–1980) and his colleagues, explains aggression in a different way. Although aggression probably is a universal human disposition, aggressive behavior arises only as a reaction to incidents where purposeful behavior is blocked. Because this theory can only explain some kinds of aggression, it was modified by Leonard Berkowitz (1926–), who argued that aggression might still be a basic reaction to frustration.

The theory of learning proposed by Albert Bandura (1925–) and others places the origin of aggression solely in the social environment in assuming that aggressive behavior is learned during life history. Aggression is learned either because it is rewarded, or at least not sanctioned, and thereby reinforced. It may also be learned by observing aggressive behavior at home, on the streets, or from the media and entertainment industries, which show that aggression is worthwhile because it gets results, with aggressive people becoming models for imitation.

There might be elements of truth in all the theories, depending on which kind of aggression is in question in which kind of context: physical or mental, intended or reactive, instrumental or spontaneous, hostile or teasing, assaulting or defending, directed toward others or toward oneself, status demonstration, group conflict, sex, age, personality, and so on. Innumerable circumstances may influence the causes of aggression and aggressive behavior may involve a wide spectrum of explanations.

Aggression as evil

Anger is a faithful partner to aggression. For medieval Christians wrath was one of the seven deadly sins. Only God could pass judgment on righteous and unrighteous deeds, and in many cases anger arises when an offense is experienced as unjust. This tenet might have left deeper marks on culture than people are aware of, showing up in the widespread condemnation of anger and aggression. While moderate anger can instigate constructive action, blind anger often leads to destructive aggression. Yet to psychology and biology even furious anger and aggression cannot in itself be sinful, let alone evil. Because aggression is probably an unavoidable human trait, be it conceived of as innate or acquired, from a scientific point of view the very occurrence of aggression cannot be malice, and the absence of aggression cannot be kindness. For conceptions of good and evil to make scientific sense, evil must be viewed as the absence of an attempt to control aggression, thus preventing love to prevail.

In the animal kingdom human beings alone are able to curb their natural impulses and their learned habits, at least to some extent, and to listen to the voice of conscience, moral qualities that can be learned and even taught using psychological techniques. The attempt to curb aggressive behavior might not succeed, which in itself is not evil because it is bound to happen now and then. Evil is only the absence of the attempt to curb aggression, and the absence of remorse at not doing so. In psychological terms, such remorse could be called guilt in a more general sense than the concrete failure of the attempt, due to the conscience, which in its innermost voice tells a person that every concrete failure is a sin against the general good or a sin against love understood as the basic source of bonding and attachment in personal and social life. In this way, the concrete failure to curb aggression makes a person guilty against humankind, not only against the victim of the concrete failure. If a person grasps this idea of aggressive behavior, and yet in defiance and pride does not attempt to control aggression or seek atonement for the sin of failing to control it, then this person might be called evil. If so, probably all people are evil now and then, and many are evil fairly often. However, control can take the shape of inhibition and aggression can be turned inwards, which is not always mentally healthy either.

See also ALTRUISM; EVIL AND SUFFERING; PSYCHOLOGY; SOCIOBIOLOGY

Bibliography

Bandura, Albert. *Aggression: A Social Learning Analysis.* Englewood Cliffs, N.J.: Prentice-Hall, 1973.

Berkowitz, Leonard. *Aggression: Its Causes, Consequences, and Control.* New York: McGraw-Hill, 1993.

Dollard, John; Doob, Leonard W.; Miller, Neal E.; Mowrer, Orval Hobart; and Sears, Robert R. *Frustration and Aggression.* New Haven, Conn.: Yale University Press, 1939.

Freud, Sigmund. *Beyond the Pleasure Principle* (1920), trans. C. J. M. Hubback. London: Hogarth Press, 1953.

Lorenz, Konrad. *On Aggression* (1963), trans. Margaret Kerr Wilson. New York: Harcourt, 1966.

Murray, Henry A., et al. *Explorations in Personality: A Clinical and Experimental Study of Fifty Men of College Age.* New York: Oxford University Press, 1938.

Wilson, Edward O. *Sociobiology.* Cambridge, Mass.: Harvard University Press, 1975.

BOJE KATZENELSON

ALGORITHM

An algorithm is any well-defined procedure for solving a given class of problems. Ideally, when applied to a particular problem in that class, the algorithm would yield a full solution. Nonetheless, it makes sense to speak of algorithms that yield only partial solutions or yield solutions only some of the time. Such algorithms are sometimes called "rules of thumb" or "heuristics."

Algorithms have been around throughout recorded history. The ancient Hindus, Greeks, Babylonians, and Chinese all had algorithms for doing arithmetic computations. The actual term *algorithm* derives from ninth-century Arabic and incorporates the Greek word for number (*arithmos*).

Algorithms are typically constructed on a case-by-case basis, being adapted to the problem at hand. Nonetheless, the possibility of a universal algorithm that could in principle resolve all problems has been a recurrent theme over the last millennium. Spanish theologian Raymond Lully (c. 1232–1315), in his *Ars Magna,* proposed to reduce all rational discussion to mechanical manipulations of symbolic notation and combinatorial diagrams. German philosopher Gottfried Wilhelm Leibniz (1646–1716) argued that Lully's project was overreaching but had merit when conceived more narrowly.

The idea of a universal algorithm did not take hold, however, until technology had advanced sufficiently to mechanize it. The Cambridge mathematician Charles Babbage (1791–1871) conceived and designed the first machine that could in principle resolve all well-defined arithmetic problems. Nevertheless, he was unable to build a working prototype. Over a century later another Cambridge mathematician, Alan Turing (1912–1954), laid the theoretical foundations for effectively implementing a universal algorithm.

Turing proposed a very simple conceptual device involving a tape with a movable reader that could mark and erase letters on the tape. Turing showed that all algorithms could be mapped onto the tape (as data) and then run by a universal algorithm already inscribed on the tape. This machine, known as a universal Turing machine, became the basis for the modern theory of computation (known as recursion theory) and inspired the modern digital computer.

Turing's universal algorithm fell short of Lully's vision of an algorithm that could resolve all problems. Turing's universal algorithm is not so much a universal problem solver as an empty box capable of housing and implementing the algorithms placed into it. Thus Turing invited into the theory of computing the very Cartesian distinction between hardware and software. Hardware is the mechanical device (i.e., the empty box) that houses and implements software (i.e., the algorithms) running on it.

Turing himself was fascinated with how the distinction between software and hardware illuminated immortality and the soul. Identifying personal identity with computer software ensured that humans were immortal, since even though hardware could be destroyed, software resided in a realm of mathematical abstraction and was thus immune to destruction.

It is a deep and much disputed question whether the essence of what constitutes the human person is at base computational and therefore an emergent property of algorithms, or whether it fundamentally transcends the capacity of algorithms.

See also COMPLEXITY

Bibliography

Berlinski, David. *The Advent of the Algorithm: The Idea That Rules the World.* New York: Harcourt Brace, 2000.

Hodges, Andrew. *Alan Turing: The Enigma.* New York: Simon & Schuster, 1983.

Leibniz, Gottfried Wilhelm. *Theodicy,* ed. Austin Marsden Farrer. LaSalle, Ill.: Open Court, 1985.

Rogers, Hartley. *Theory of Recursive Functions and Effective Computability.* Cambridge, Mass.: MIT Press, 1987.

Turing, Alan M. *Collected Works of A. M. Turing: Mechanical Intelligence,* ed. Darrel. C. Ince. Amsterdam and London: North Holland, 1992.

WILLIAM A. DEMBSKI

ALGORITHMIC COMPLEXITY

Algorithmic complexity measures the computational resources needed to solve computational problems. Computational resources are measured in terms of either time (i.e., number of elementary computational steps per second) or space (i.e., size of memory, usually measured in bits or bytes) or some combination of the two. If computational devices had unlimited memory and could perform calculations instantaneously, algorithmic complexity would not be an issue. All real-world computers, however, have limited memory and perform calculations at fixed rates. The more time and space required to run an algorithm, the greater its algorithmic complexity.

See also COMPLEXITY

WILLIAM A. DEMBSKI

ALTRUISM

Altruism is a modern concept attributed to Auguste Comte, a French philosopher who founded the field of sociology in the mid-nineteenth century. The idea of altruism has antecedents in the early modern discussion of benevolence and in such ancient religious notions as Buddhist compassion and Christian *agape.* An important difference is the explicit focus in altruism on the other as the object of concern, which, in turn, reflects the sharper focus on the self that is characteristic of modern self-consciousness. For Comte, altruism identified the concern for others that he expected would characterize the positive religion of humanity that was destined to replace the false religion of the prescientific, theological, and metaphysical eras. Although Comte would have been disappointed with the extent to which altruism has actually flourished, his concept has become an enduring, if ambiguous, staple of modern Western understanding.

Altruism in biology and sociobiology

The notion of altruism has been accorded a significant role in biology, and especially in the refinements of sociobiology, where the term has a technical meaning that narrows the conventional sense of concern for others in terms of the biological concentration on reproduction. As, from a biological perspective, the point of life is reproduction, altruism acquires the meaning of actions that diminish the reproductive prospects of the altruist, while enhancing those of the recipient of the action. For biology and sociobiology, altruism represents something of an anomaly. Because evolution favors the development of inclusive fitness, altruism should have been selected out of existence. But it is firmly present, in the strictest biological sense, in whole classes of nonreproductive workers like ants and bees. Sociobiology has resolved this anomaly by defining altruism out of existence. What may look like altruism on the behavioral level may turn out to be decidedly selfish on the gene level if the recipient of the altruistic behavior is a relative of the putative altruist and so shares the same genes. The concept of *kin altruism* thus explains the sacrifice of reproductive prospects for those who share the same genes. Cases where the beneficiary has no identifiable relation are covered by the notion of *reciprocal altruism*. Here again, what appears to be altruistic behavior is really selfish because it is done with the expectation, genetically speaking, of reciprocal aid that may be required by the altruist in the future. The imperialism of selfish genes thus destroys any semblance of altruistic behavior at the biological level.

Altruism in social science and ethics

The assumption of the primacy of self-interest that dominates sociobiology has been questioned in the social sciences with research into altruism and helping behavior, and yet here too the self-interest assumption remains strong. The favored alternative to a self-interest reading involves a calculative or caring mutuality, for which expectations of altruism may be more detrimental than self-interest. Altruism represents a morality of service and self-sacrifice. Critics point out that such a noble and self-deprecating approach has often been expected of other people; even when its advocates have taken it seriously themselves, it can constitute an individualistic heroism that deflects attention and action from the real possibilities of mutuality inherent in the actual social relations in which people find themselves. Approaches as diverse as the justice procedures of John Rawls (which challenge one to imagine one is designing a society in which one does not know where one will be placed so that one will have to take into account the state of

those on the lowest rungs of the social and economic ladders because one might be one of those people) and the alternative stance of feminist care morality (which sees a focus on individual moral action, even, and perhaps especially, the most heroic, as misguided neglect of the social relations of give and take that daily lives actually involve) agree on the superiority of social mutuality over allowance for, much less expectations of, altruism.

Limitations of the concept

Altruism does carry the liabilities of its origins. As a social concept, meant to counterbalance the excesses of self-interest, altruism is finally only intelligible in relation to the self-interest with which it is contrasted; it is concern for others, rather than what is taken to be the natural and virtually inevitable concern for self. Because it carries this legacy, altruism bears the liability of undermining itself through its own deliberateness. Deliberate focus on the other as the object of one's concern may represent an implicit interest in the self as the source of this concern—a consideration that prompted the nineteenth-century American writer Henry David Thoreau to allow that he would run for his life if he knew that someone was coming to see him with the deliberate intention of doing him good. It is this lack of attention and openness to the other that bothers many contemporary critics of the loss of mutuality in the focus on altruism. That such dangers warrant a dismissal of the whole notion, however, is another matter. Without the moral heroism that altruism entails, reliance on the mutuality of social relations may amount to a frightening leveling down of moral expectations and results. The saints, the philosopher William James contended, are the impregnators of culture, raising it to higher levels through their risking ways of living that hold no obvious benefit for themselves. The philosopher and ethicist Edith Wyschogrod has nominated altruists as the saints of secular culture.

Religious altruism

Suspicion of altruism may be a reflection of the secularization of contemporary culture, and the concept itself may be indicative of a lingering religious sensibility in Comte, who still expected a religion of humanity to develop. As such, it suggests that concern for others is finally only feasible through the deliverance from self that is offered by and celebrated in religion. This allows for the indirection that makes the aims of altruism possible, without the short-circuiting of a focus on altruism itself, and hence on the altruist. Of course, this in no way entails that devotees of religion exemplify the reality to which altruism points. Fortunately, religion also offers forgiveness along with the altruistic vision. This could represent the counsel of complacency that advocates of mutuality fear, but it could also represent the heroic initiative and extravagant saintliness that the realism of social mutuality threatens to undermine.

See also ANTHROPOLOGY; BEHAVIORISM; CHRISTIANITY; EVOLUTION; SELF; SELFISH GENE; SOCIOBIOLOGY.

Bibliography

Dawkins, Richard. *The Selfish Gene.* London: Granada, 1978.

Grant, Colin. *Altruism and Christian Ethics.* Cambridge, UK: Cambridge University Press, 2001.

Kittay, Eva Feder, and Myers, Diana T., eds. *Women and Moral Theory.* Totawa, N.J.: Rowman and Littlefield, 1987.

Mansbridge, Jane J., ed. *Beyond Self-Interest.* Chicago: University of Chicago Press, 1990.

Paul, Ellen Frankel; Miller, Fred D., Jr.; and Paul, Jeffrey, eds. *Altruism.* Cambridge, UK: Cambridge University Press, 1993.

Rawls, John. *A Theory of Justice.* Cambridge, Mass.: Harvard University Press, 1971.

Wyschogrod, Edith. *Saints and Postmodernism: Revisioning Moral Philosophy.* Chicago: University of Chicago Press, 1990.

COLIN GRANT

ANABAPTIST

See CHRISTIANITY, RADICAL REFORMED, ISSUES IN SCIENCE AND RELIGION

ANGLICANISM

See CHRISTIANITY, ANGLICANISM, ISSUES IN SCIENCE AND RELIGION

ANIMAL RIGHTS

The modern animal rights movement, which originated in the 1970s, may be understood as a reaction to dominant emphases within science and religion (principally, though not exclusively, Christianity). When the Jesuit Joseph Rickaby wrote in 1888 that "Brute beasts, not having understanding and therefore not being persons, cannot have any rights" and that we have "no duties of charity or duties of any kind to the lower animals as neither to stocks and stones" (*Moral Philosophy,* vol. II, pp. 248–9), he was only articulating, albeit in an extreme form, the moral insensitivity that has characterized the Western view of animals.

That insensitivity is the result of an amalgam of influences. The first, and for many years the most dominant, was the "other worldly" or "world denying" tendency in Christianity, which has, at its worst, denigrated the value of earthly things in comparison with things spiritual. Traditional Catholicism has divided the world into those beings that possess reason and therefore immortal souls, and those that do not. The result of this schema has inevitably been disadvantageous to animals who have been regarded as bereft of an interior spiritual life, as well as the benefits of immortality. Christian spirituality has not consciously been at home with the world of non-human creatures—either animal or vegetable. Classic accounts of eternal life as found in Augustine of Hippo (354–430), Thomas Aquinas (c. 1225–1274), or John Calvin (1509–1564) make little or no reference to the world of animals. Animals, it seems, are merely transient or peripheral beings in an otherwise wholly human-centric economy of salvation.

The second idea—common to Christianity, Judaism, and Islam—is that animals, along with vegetables and minerals, exist instrumentally in relation to human beings; they are made for human beings, even belong to human beings, as resources in creation. This idea predates Christianity and is found notably in Aristotle (384–322 B.C.E.), who argues that "since nature makes nothing to no purpose, it must be that nature has made them [animals and plants] for the sake of man" (*The Politics,* 1, viii). This idea, largely unsupported by scripture, was nevertheless taken over by Aquinas, who conceived of creation as a rational hierarchy in which the intellectually inferior existed for the sake of the intellectually superior. Hence Aquinas posits that "It is not wrong for man to make use of them [animals] either by killing or in any other way whatever" (*Summa contra Gentiles,* Third Book, Part II, cvii).

Such instrumentalism, which features rationality as the key factor dividing human beings from "brute beasts," has in turn buttressed the third influence, namely the notion of human superiority in creation. Human superiority need not, by itself, have led to the neglect of animal life, but when combined with the biblical ideas of being made "in the image of God" (Gen. 1: 26–27) and God's preferential choice to become incarnate in human form, some sense of moral as well as theological ascendancy was indicated. As a result, Christianity, and to a lesser extent Judaism, have been characterized historically by an overwhelming concern for humanity in creation rather than an egalitarian concern for all forms of God-given life. That humans are more important than animals, and that they self-evidently merit moral solicitude in a way that animals cannot, has become religious doctrine. Thus the *Catechism of the Catholic Church* (1994) maintains that "it is . . . unworthy to spend money on them [animals] that should as a priority go to the relief of human misery" (para. 2418).

These influences have in turn enabled and justified the scientific exploration of the natural world and specifically the subjection of animals to experimentation. Francis Bacon (1561–1626) pursued his scientific investigations in the belief that humanity should "recover that right over nature which belongs to it by divine bequest" (*Thoughts and Conclusions on the Interpretation of Nature,* IV, p. 294). Since animals were made for human use and are incapable of rationality or the possession of an immortal soul, it was only a short philosophical step to conceive of them as automata devoid of self-consciousness, even incapable of pain. René Descartes (1596–1650) famously likened the movements of a swallow to the workings of a clock, and maintained that "There is no prejudice to which we are more accustomed from our earliest years than the belief that dumb animals think" (*Philosophical Letters,* 1649.). Physiologist Claude Bernard (1813–1878) completed the scientific objectification of animals by pursuing ruthless vivisections of living animals, and inaugurating an era in which experimental science, following theology, became largely blind to the sufferings of non-human creatures.

Yet, if science and religion have provided the dominant influences against which animal rights advocates react, they have also variously provided some key justifications for a contemporary animal rights position. Although Charles Darwin (1809–1882) cannot be counted an animal rights advocate (since he shot birds for sport and was not wholly opposed to vivisection), his theory of evolution challenged prevailing religious notions of a difference in kind between humans and animals. In so doing, he laid the foundation for a less hierarchical view of creation and encouraged subsequent discoveries of similarities between species. The irony is that a century of (often abusive) experimental work on animals has demonstrated the range and complexity of their behavior.

It is increasingly difficult to deny self-consciousness, mental states, and emotional complexity to other mammals. Indeed, there is a consensus now among scientists that animals suffer fear, anxiety, trauma, shock, terror, stress, and suffer only to a greater or lesser degree than humans do. Although the case for animal rights does not depend upon any exact similarity between "them" and "us" (except the need for sentiency, defined as the capacity to experience suffering), the question has to be asked: Given what we know now of the similar biological capacities of humans and animals, how can we justify a total difference in our moral treatment of them?

Similarly, religious traditions, especially Christianity, have rekindled more generous insights about animals. Chief among these are the notions that animals too are created by God and have intrinsic value and that human "dominion" over animals means exercising a God-given responsibility of care, and, not least of all, an appreciation that there are moral limits to what humans may do to other creatures. Such a notion of moral limits is explicit in the Hebrew Bible and has formed the basis of the traditional rabbinic injunction not to cause animals unnecessary suffering. Although it came rather late in the day, the humanitarian movement of the nineteenth century in England and the United States focussed religious sensibilities on the suffering of innocents (children as well as animals). Both Christians and Jews, including

Arthur Broome and Lewis Gompertz, were involved in the foundation in London in 1824 of the Society for the Prevention of Cruelty to Animals (SPCA), the world's first national animal welfare organization. Some modern theologians have argued that there is a specifically theological basis for animal rights based on God's prior right as creator to have what is created treated with respect.

Although people in Eastern countries, dominated by the religions of Hinduism, Buddhism, and Jainism, have in practice treated animals with as little respect as people in Western countries, their religions have nevertheless retained notions of respect and nonviolence (*ahimsa*) toward animal, as well as human, life. In the doctrine of *samsara* (reincarnation) a continuity of soulfulness is presupposed (however much it may presuppose a moral hierarchy of life itself), and in Buddhism the first precept against killing is still normative. Specifically, the *bodhisattva's* example of compassionate postponement of buddhahood in order to liberate other suffering beings is a powerful religious ideal expressing the regard that the strong ought to have for the weak.

This ideal also expresses the best in traditional Jewish and Christian theology as summed up in the line that the "good shepherd lays down his life for the sheep" (John 10: 11). Our very God-given power over animals should inspire a view of ourselves not as the "master species but rather as the servant species" (Linzey 1994, p. 45). The irony for animal rights advocates is that traditions that have supported and justified animal abuse also contain within themselves the seeds of an enlightened, even generous, attitude toward the non-human.

See also ARISTOTLE; AUGUSTINE; BUDDHISM; CHRISTIANITY, ROMAN CATHOLIC, ISSUES IN SCIENCE AND RELIGION; DARWIN, CHARLES; DESCARTES, RENÉ; HINDUISM; IMAGO DEI; JUDAISM; PRIMATOLOGY; SOUL; THOMAS AQUINAS

Bibliography

Bacon, Francis. *Thoughts and Conclusions on the Interpretation of Nature,* IV. In *The Works of Francis Bacon,* eds. J. Spedding, R.L. Ellis and D.D. Heath. London: 1857.

Bekoff, Marc. *Minding Animals: Awareness, Emotions, and Heart.* Oxford: Oxford University Press, 2002.

Catechism of the Catholic Church (English translation). Vatican City: Libreria Editrice Vaticana, 1994. Available from: http://www.vatican.va/archive/ccc.

Chapple, Christopher K. *Non-Violence to Animals, Earth, and Self in Asian Traditions.* Albany: State University of New York Press, 1993.

DeGrazia, David. *Taking Animals Seriously: Mental Life and Moral Status.* Cambridge, UK: Cambridge University Press, 1996.

Descartes, René. Letter to Henry Moore. February 5, 1649. In *Descartes: Philosophical Letters,* trans. and ed. Anthony Kenny. Oxford: The Clarendon Press, 1970; extract in *Animal Rights and Human Obligations,* second edition, eds. Tom Regan and Peter Singer. New York: Prentice-Hall, 1989.

Griffin, Donald R. *Animal Thinking.* Cambridge, Mass.: Harvard University Press, 1984.

Klug, Brian, "Lab Animals, Francis Bacon, and the Culture of Science." In *Judaism and Animal Rights: Classical and Contemporary Readings,* ed. Roberta Kalechofsky. Marblehead, Mass.: Micah, 1992.

Linzey, Andrew. *Christianity and the Rights of Animals.* London: SPCK, 1987; New York: Crossroad, 1991.

Linzey, Andrew. *Animal Theology.* London: SCM Press, 1994; Chicago: University of Illinois Press, 1995.

Linzey, Andrew, and Cohn-Sherbok, Dan. *After Noah: Animals and the Liberation of Theology.* London: Mowbray, 1997.

Linzey, Andrew, and Yamamoto, Dorothy, eds. *Animals on the Agenda: Questions about Animals for Theology and Ethics.* London: SCM Press; Chicago: University of Illinois Press, 1998.

Parker, Taylor; Mitchell, Robert W.; and Boccia, Maria, eds. *Self-Awareness in Animals and Humans: Developmental Perspectives.* Cambridge, UK: Cambridge University Press, 1994.

Rachels, James. *Created from the Animals: The Moral Implications of Darwinism.* Oxford: Oxford University Press, 1991.

Rickaby, Joseph. *Moral Philosophy.* Vol. II. London: Longmans, 1888.

Rollin, Bernard E. *The Unheeded Cry: Animal Consciousness, Animal Pain, and Science.* Oxford: Oxford University Press, 1989.

Salisbury, Joyce E. *The Beast Within: Animals in the Middle Ages.* London and New York: Routledge, 1994.

Schochet, Elijah Judah. *Animal Life in the Jewish Tradition: Attitudes and Relationships.* New York: KTAV, 1984.

Thomas, Keith. *Man and the Natural World: Changing Attitudes in England, 1500–1800*. London: Allen Lane, 1983.

Webb, Stephen H. *On God and Dogs: A Christian Theology of Compassion for Animals*. Oxford: Oxford University Press, 1998.

ANDREW LINZEY

ANTHROPIC PRINCIPLE

The Anthropic Principle asserts that the existence of human life places certain necessary constraints on cosmological and metaphysical theories. It is an *ex post facto* methodological tool that attempts to relate the structure of the universe to the underlying conditions that are necessary for the existence of observers.

The Anthropic Principle attempts to explain the universe's many life-supporting "coincidences" in two distinct ways: 1) by appealing to an all-encompassing selection effect amongst a variety of universes (e.g., the Weak Anthropic Principle); 2) by asserting that the evolution of life is the necessary outcome of the laws of nature (e.g., the Strong Anthropic Principle). It is this latter form that suggests the possible creative activity of an Intelligent Designer.

Formulated in 1974 by the British astrophysicist Brandon Carter, the Anthropic Principle is an attempt to limit the Copernican dogma, which asserts that the Earth does not occupy a privileged central position in the universe. However, while the Earth may not be special or privileged in *every* way, this does not mean that it cannot be privileged in *any* way. Indeed, Carter pointed out that the location of the Earth in space is "necessarily privileged to the extent of being compatible with our existence as observers" (p. 291).

The Anthropic Principle is controversial because it implies a teleological link between the structure of the universe and the existence of human beings. Several theorists have taken this idea one step further by incorporating the Anthropic Principle into a larger design argument for the existence of God.

Teleology and fine-tuning

The Anthropic Principle makes this type of goal-directed argument possible by highlighting the various prerequisites for the existence of life. When these prerequisites are duly examined, a striking number of "cosmic coincidences" are discovered to exist between distant branches of physics. These anthropic coincidences are noteworthy because they are essential for the existence of life and because they require tremendous "fine-tuning" before they can be operational. The gravitational constant (G), for instance, appears to be exceedingly fine-tuned for the existence of life. If it were slightly larger, stars would have burned too hot and much too quickly to support the fragile needs of life; if it were slightly smaller, the intrastellar process of nuclear fusion would have never initiated, and life would have been incapable of arising on the Earth.

This same rationale can also be applied to the expansion rate of the nascent universe. This crucial factor is determined by the cooperative interplay between several distinct cosmic parameters, including the mass density of the universe, the explosive vigor of the Big Bang, and the strength of the gravitational constant. If the resulting cosmic expansion rate happened to be slightly greater than the presently observed value, life-supporting galaxies would have been unable to form; if it were slightly smaller, the early universe would have collapsed back in on itself shortly after the Big Bang. Either way, no life forms would have been possible.

This is significant, because the various parameters that comprise the cosmic expansion rate also had to be fine-tuned to better than one part in 1060 in order to generate a "flat" universe, so that normal Euclidian geometry (in which the sum of a triangle's three angles adds up to 180 degrees) could then become applicable. A similar degree of fine-tuning can be found throughout the remainder of nature's fundamental parameters.

The challenge is to find a plausible explanation for this fine-tuning. According to the British mathematical physicist Roger Penrose, the odds that a fine-tuned biocentric universe could have accidentally evolved are an astounding one in ten to the 10^{123}, a number so vast that it could not be written on a piece of paper the size of the entire visible universe. This is why many theorists have posited the existence of a "supercalculating intellect" to account for this fine-tuning.

Others, however, have scoffed at this teleological interpretation of cosmological history. They point out that this fine-tuning could have been generated randomly over billions of years if the universe turns out to be merely one of many. In this case, life would have evolved only in those regions that happened to possess the "correct" configuration of fundamental parameters, and human beings would then find themselves living in this special region as a straightforward selection effect. Critics, however, charge that this position is question-begging by its very nature, since it assumes the prior existence of these unexplained worlds.

Definitions

The Anthropic Principle comes in a variety of permutations, each with its own set of implications.

Weak Anthropic Principle. The broadest and least controversial permutation is known as the Weak Anthropic Principle (WAP). Given the reality of human life, the physical universe must contain areas that are compatible with the existence of human beings as observers. The WAP states that humans never could expect to observe a universe that is significantly different from their own, because human existence *depends* on the prior existence of just such a universe. The WAP thus doesn't try to explain how or why the universe came to be life-supporting. It merely notes that, while the universe is biocentric for unknown reasons, given the current existence of humans it couldn't possibly have been otherwise.

One of the advantages of the WAP is that it highlights the many diverse structural parameters that are necessary for the existence of life. Nevertheless, many people find the WAP deeply unsatisfying because it merely states what is already known to be true; namely, that the universe *has* to be structured in its present form before it can be capable of supporting carbon-based life. The WAP is thus incapable of explaining *why* the universe is structured in this biocentric manner.

Strong Anthropic Principle. The more potent Strong Anthropic Principle (SAP) attempts to explain why the universe has a biocentric structure. According to the SAP, the universe must have properties that will allow life to develop within it at some stage of its history. The key element is the word *must;* it means that the universe *had* to be life-supporting at some stage of its history. This possibility is suggested by the many astonishing coincidences between distant branches of physics that all work together, against all the odds, to make life possible. The conventional SAP, however, does not attempt to explain why the universe must be biocentric. It simply states that this must be so.

Design-Centered Anthropic Principle. The SAP thus comes close to positing the existence of a cosmic designer because there doesn't seem to be any other plausible way of explaining why the universe had to be life-supporting. For this reason the physicist Heinz R. Pagels (1939–1988) once quipped that the SAP is "the closest that some atheists can get to God." One interpretation of the SAP explicitly credits a designer for the Earth's many biocentric features. This interpretation, which can be called the Design-Centered Anthropic Principle (DCAP), holds that the universe is biocentric because it was deliberately designed to be this way by a higher power.

Participatory Anthropic Principle. A second version of the SAP, derived from the findings of modern theoretical physics, has been dubbed the Participatory Anthropic Principle (PAP) by physicist John Wheeler (b. 1911). This version holds that observers are necessary to bring the universe into being. The PAP follows from the standard Copenhagen interpretation of quantum mechanics, in which some type of living consciousness is required to make events "real." According to this interpretation, developed by physicist Neils Bohr (1885–1962), there is no such thing as a concrete quantum reality until a living observer exists to "collapse" the appropriate quantum wave function. Without this act of observation, reality seems to be held in a paralyzing state of indecision.

Some theorists have gone so far as to argue that life is necessary to make the universe itself real. The physicist George Greenstein (b. 1940) has conceived of a "symbiotic universe" in which both life and the universe exist in a classic state of symbiosis; the universe provides the physical foundation for the existence of life, and life symbiotically responds by imparting a concrete state of reality to the cosmos.

The problem with this conceptualization is that life did not evolve until billions of years after the

Big Bang. In order for Greenstein's theory to be plausible, a noncorporeal form of life had to have been responsible for observing the universe into being long ago. The only candidate for this role would be the "Ultimate Observer" spoken of by John Barrow and Frank Tipler. This observer alone would have been in a position to observe the entire universe into being.

Final Anthropic Principle. A third version of the SAP has been dubbed the Final Anthropic Principle (FAP). According to FAP, intelligent life must come into existence in the universe, and, once it comes into existence, it will survive forever and become infinitely knowledgeable as it strives to mold the universe to its will. The FAP thus possesses an obvious religious quality because it states that there is a positive universal purpose to human life that cannot be thwarted by any possible power. In this sense, the FAP is analogous to the tenets of generic theism, particularly in its affirmation of an afterlife. However, the FAP does not explain why intelligent life will endure forever. It merely states that it will do so.

Anthropic coincidences

It is important to distinguish between the Anthropic Principle and a curious set of physical facts known as *anthropic coincidences*. The Anthropic Principle proper is a speculative hypothesis regarding the possible role of humanity in the cosmos, whereas the various anthropic coincidences are empirical observations that relate the apparent fine-tuning of the universe to the needs of life. This, in turn, seems to provide some degree of empirical support for certain forms of the Anthropic Principle.

The value of the gravitational constant *G*, the mass density of the universe, and the explosive vigor of the Big Bang have all seemingly been fine-tuned to cooperate with one another to generate a smoothly expanding universe of coherent galaxies, each containing an abundance of medium-sized biocentric stars like the sun. Numerous other fine-tuned anthropic coincidences are also at work in the universe to make life possible. A partial list includes the following:

(1) the values of nature's fundamental constants;

(2) the existence of three spatial dimensions;

(3) the ratio of the electromagnetic force constant to the gravitational constant;

(4) the mass ratio of the electron and proton;

(5) the ratio of protons to electrons;

(6) the cosmic entropy level;

(7) the speed of light;

(8) the age of the universe;

(9) the mass excess of the neutron over the proton;

(10) the initial excess of matter over antimatter; and

(11) the sun's historical change in luminosity, which happened to coincide with the specific needs of Earth-based life forms.

One of the most notable anthropic coincidences was discovered in 1953 by the British astronomer Fred Hoyle (1915–2001), a former atheist. Hoyle had been researching the intrastellar process of carbon synthesis when he stumbled upon a remarkable series of coincidences pertaining to the stepwise assembly of the carbon atom. To his great surprise, Hoyle discovered that the nuclear resonance levels of both carbon and its immediate precursors (helium and beryllium) were fine-tuned to work together to encourage carbon synthesis. He also found that oxygen's nuclear resonance level is half a percent too low to encourage the nuclear conversion of carbon into oxygen. The result of this remarkable series of coincidences is that carbon can be manufactured inside dying stars in sufficient quantities to make organic life possible. Hoyle concluded that the universe is a "put up job," and that a "supercalculating intellect" had to have "monkeyed" with the basic parameters of physics and cosmology. Otherwise, one would never expect so many unrelated and improbable coincidences to work seamlessly together to generate a biocentric universe.

The Anthropic Design argument

Given the many intercoordinated steps that are required to generate a fine-tuned biocentric universe, many theorists find it astonishing that any form of life could have evolved on this planet. There are simply too many ways in which cosmic evolution could have gone wrong with respect to life, particularly given the universality of the Second Law of Thermodynamics, which states that the total amount of disorder in the universe is always increasing. It is the Second Law that leads one to expect a non-biocentric outcome at each stage of the universe-building process, yet the correct biocentric result nevertheless happened at each bifurcation point.

It is the fine-tuning of nature's fundamental constants at the Big Bang that probably enabled this to happen. Indeed, given the brute fact of human existence, it is *necessarily* the case that the universe be fine-tuned enough for it to overcome the many thermodynamic hurdles that naturally exist on the way to life. This, in turn, seems to suggest a strong element of necessity in the universe's underlying ability to generate life. Insofar as this is so, it constitutes evidence in favor of the Strong Anthropic Principle.

Moreover, since the general cosmic tendency is always towards an increased amount of disorder, some thinkers conclude that there must have been some type of constraining force at work in the past. Otherwise, this predisposition towards disorder would likely have put the universe on a non-biocentric path long ago, despite the fact that order can sometimes be generated within an open thermodynamic system by adding energy to it.

Traditional cosmology has been unable to account for this mystery, except insofar as it has used the principle of cumulative selection to explain the successive preservation of small instances of order, each of which possibly could have been random in origin. The problem with this hypothesis is that the universe had to have evolved to a relatively advanced stage before any type of cumulative selection could have taken place. For this reason many find the Strong Anthropic Principle to be compelling. How else can one explain the trillions of correct choices on the way to life, despite the Second Law, if it weren't structurally necessary for the universe to evolve life at some point in its history?

The Weak Anthropic Principle is typically invoked to refute this conclusion. According to this view, humans shouldn't be surprised at their own existence because they are merely experiencing a selection effect, since it is not possible for them to have observed a non-biocentric universe. While this may be so, it does not necessarily follow that human existence is not surprising. In the same way that a condemned criminal facing a one hundred-man firing squad would naturally be surprised if all one hundred rifles misfired simultaneously, it is

also appropriate for human beings to be astonished at their own existence.

Many Worlds Interpretation. A potent counterargument to this anthropic viewpoint has been provided by Hugh Everett's (1930–1982) Many Worlds Interpretation of quantum mechanics. According to this hypothesis, there are an infinite number of "compartments" or worlds in existence within a much larger "multiverse," each possessing its own randomly varying set of fundamental constants. Humans therefore shouldn't be surprised at their own existence, because it is only natural for life to evolve in the one region of the multiverse that is capable of supporting its existence. This is a prime example of how the Weak Anthropic Principle can be used within a nontheistic worldview to account for the existence of life.

There are three problems with the Many Worlds approach, however. First, there is no evidence for *any* of these other possible worlds, nor can there be any such evidence in the future because these alternative domains are believed to be utterly beyond human observational powers, even in principle. Secondly, this approach begs the question, since it assumes the prior, unexplained existence of the multiverse itself. Finally, the use of an infinite number of unobservable worlds to explain the existence of our own world is an unprecedented violation of Ockham's Razor, which states that the simplest explanation in any set of natural circumstances is probably the correct one.

Anthropic explanations

Critics of the Anthropic Principle believe it to be scientifically sterile, since it doesn't initially seem to explain much about the cosmos in which humans live. Supporters of the Anthropic Principle, by contrast, believe that it holds the key to an intriguing relationship between the structure of the universe and the existence of human observers. The size and age of the universe provide an excellent case in point. Prior to the advance of modern cosmological science, it was believed that both the physical and temporal dimensions of the universe were unrelated to the existence of living observers. The mathematician and philosopher Bertrand Russell, for instance, believed that the universe's enormous size and age naturally rendered the concept of intelligent design implausible, since one would naturally expect a deity to have created the best things in the world (e.g., human beings) first rather than last.

This viewpoint has been supplanted by modern cosmological findings that indicate that a certain minimum time frame is inherently required for the intrastellar synthesis of carbon by natural evolutionary pathways. The amount of time that is necessary for this outcome amounts to several billion years, which is roughly equivalent to the time required to synthesize carbon and other heavy elements inside dying red giant stars. During this entire carbon-making epoch, though, the universe itself has been relentlessly expanding. Therefore, it is only in a universe that is sufficiently old, and hence sufficiently large, that carbon-based observers can evolve. The enormous size of the visible universe (approximately fifteen billion light years in spatial extent) is thus directly related to the time required for intrastellar carbon synthesis, due to the ongoing cosmic expansion. This is a genuine anthropic explanation because it links several aspects of the universe to the conditions necessary to generate living observers.

Anthropic versus biocentric

The Anthropic Principle is actually a philosophical misnomer, since it is primarily an argument about the centrality of biological life in general. As such, it could legitimately be called the "Biocentric Principle." A separate argument is thus required to generate an Anthropic Principle from the biocentric evidence. The Greek word *anthropos,* however, refers to uniquely human life, so the possible existence of intelligent beings elsewhere would technically invalidate the Anthropic Principle. In order to allow for this possibility, it has been suggested that the Anthropic Principle be renamed the *Humanoid Principle.*

Three distinct arguments are thus conflated within the Anthropic Principle: (1) a biocentric argument, which refers to the centrality of biological life forms in general; (2) a humanoid argument, which refers to the centrality of intelligent humanoid life; and (3) a specific anthropic argument, which argues for the exclusivity of Earth-based intelligent life. These conflations, however, are widely deemed to be irrelevant to the central thrust of the Anthropic Principle, since it is generally assumed that human life would be the ultimate goal of any cosmic intention to evolve Earth-based life. It is also assumed that the possible existence of other humanoid life forms would not invalidate the Anthropic Principle itself. Instead, it would simply provide other cosmic loci by which the biocentric nature of the universe could be explained.

Conclusion

The basic purpose of the Anthropic Principle is to relate the underlying structure of the universe to the fact of human existence. Although many thinkers find this goal unrealistic, others believe that the uniqueness of human consciousness is a fact of fundamental significance in the cosmos. For it is primarily through the vehicle of human awareness that the universe has somehow become aware of itself, and no other known entity appears to possess this marvelous capacity.

See also ANTHROPOCENTRICISM; COPENHAGEN INTERPRETATION; COSMOLOGY, PHYSICAL ASPECTS; DESIGN; ENTROPY; GEOCENTRICISM; MANY-WORLDS HYPOTHESIS; PHYSICS, QUANTUM; THERMODYNAMICS, SECOND LAW OF

Bibliography

Barrow, John D., and Tipler, Frank J. *The Anthropic Cosmological Principle.* Oxford: Oxford University Press, 1986.

Barrow, John D. *The World Within the World.* Oxford: Oxford University Press, 1990.

Barrow, John D. *Theories of Everything: The Quest for Ultimate Explanation.* Oxford: Oxford University Press, 1991.

Carter, Brandon. "Large Number Coincidences and the Anthropic Principle in Cosmology." In *Confrontation of Cosmological Theories with Observation,* ed. Malcolm S. Longair. Dordrecht, Netherlands: Reidel, 1974.

Corey, Michael A. *God and the New Cosmology: The Anthropic Design Argument.* Lanham, Md.: Rowman & Littlefield, 1993.

Corey, Michael A. *The God Hypothesis: Discovering Design in our Just Right Goldilocks Universe.* Lanham, Md.: Rowman & Littlefield, 2001.

Danielson, Dennis R. "The Great Copernican Cliché." *American Journal of Physics* 69, no. 10 (2001): 1029–1035.

Davies, Paul. *Are We Alone? Philosophical Implications of the Discovery of Extraterrestrial Life*. New York: Basic Books, 1995.

Davies, Paul. *God and the New Physics*. New York: Simon & Schuster, 1983.

Davies, Paul. *The Accidental Universe*. New York: Cambridge University Press, 1982.

Davies, Paul. *The Cosmic Blueprint: New Discoveries in Nature's Creative Ability to Order the Universe*. New York: Simon & Schuster, 1989.

Davies, Paul. *The Fifth Miracle: The Search for the Origin and Meaning of Life*. New York: Simon & Schuster, 1999.

Davies, Paul. *The Mind of God: The Scientific Basis for a Rational World*. New York: Simon & Schuster, 1992.

Dawkins, Richard. *The Blind Watchmaker: Why the Evidence of Evolution Reveals a Universe Without Design*. New York: Norton, 1987.

Gillespie, Neal C. *Charles Darwin and the Problem of Creation*. Chicago: University of Chicago Press, 1979.

Gribbin, John. *In the Beginning*. Boston: Little, Brown, 1993.

Griffin, David Ray. *Reenchantment Without Supernaturalism: A Process Philosophy of Religion*. Ithaca, N.Y.: Cornell University Press, 2001.

Henderson, Lawrence J. *The Fitness of the Environment: An Inquiry into the Biological Significance of the Properties of Matter* (1913). Gloucester, Mass.: Peter Smith, 1970.

Hoyle, Fred. "The Universe: Past and Present Reflections." *Annual Review of Astronomy and Physics* 20 (1982): 1-35.

Hume, David. *Dialogues Concerning Natural Religion* (1779). London: Penguin, 1990.

Kauffman, Stuart A. *At Home in the Universe: The Search for Laws of Self-Organization and Complexity*. New York: Oxford University Press, 1995.

Schrödinger, Erwin. *What is Life?* Cambridge, UK: Cambridge University Press, 1967.

Schroeder, Gerald L. *The Science of God: The Convergence of Scientific and Biblical Wisdom*. New York: Free Press, 1997.

Scriven, Michael. "The Presumption of Atheism." In *Philosophy of Religion: An Anthology,* ed. Louis P. Pojman. Belmont, Calif.: Wadsworth, 1987.

Ward, Keith. *God, Chance, and Necessity*. Oxford: Oxford University Press, 1996.

Weinberg, Steven. *The First Three Minutes: A Modern View of the Origin of the Universe*. London: André Deutsch, 1977.

MICHAEL A. COREY

ANTHROPOCENTRISM

Anthropocentrism (human-centered) is a term used to describe certain philosophical perspectives that claim that ethical principles apply to humans only, and that human needs and interests are of the highest value and importance. Anthropocentrism is found in both religious and secular philosophies. In science, anthropocentrism has played an important role in liberating human knowledge from external authorities, and in promoting the interests of humanity as a whole against particular interests. Both scientists and theologians have drawn on anthropocentrism to defend specific views about nature, scientists often on the basis of a perspective on evolution in which humans are considered the highest form of life on Earth, and theologians on the basis of a divinely mandated right for humans to exercise dominion over nature.

Beginning in about 1970, anthropocentrism became common in environmental discourse. Anthropocentric ethics evaluates environmental issues on the basis of how they affect human needs and attaches primary importance to human interests. The term contrasts with various *biocentric* (life-centered) perspectives, which assume that nonhumans are also carriers of moral value.

Anthropocentrism in ethics is found in two main forms: *consequential* ethics and *deontological* ethics. Basic to both is the perception of a discontinuity between humans and the rest of nature. Humans are considered superior to animals for various reasons, including their ability to think and speak, plan, organize projects, and so on. According to the German philosopher Immanuel Kant (1724–1804), humans alone have self-consciousness. Humans are therefore fundamentally different in rank and dignity from all other beings, while animals can be treated as means to human ends. The moral status of humans is thus awarded on the basis of "excellence." Values are grounded in the fact that something is valuable for humans, and so human actions should be valued on the basis of their usefulness for humans.

The basic idea of consequentialist anthropocentrism is that human actions are valued according to their consequences for other humans. In a market-oriented society, consequentialist anthropocentrism is often linked to the idea that problems in relation to society and nature are technical. Both human and natural resources are considered unlimited and available for human consumption. If there is a shortage, then replacement products will always be made available on the basis of the law of supply and demand. High status is awarded to technical products such as buildings, bridges, dams, and highways. The basic premise is the idea that human interests rule the world, and that nature is considered relevant only as a resource to be exploited by humans. If a crisis arises with regard to available resources, it is primarily a technical problem, which can be solved by adjustments. In its simplest form this could mean that humans need to move to a new place. When no new place is available, other measures can be taken, such as moving pollutants to a different place or using technology to get rid of toxic elements. The ideal is "business as usual" for the benefit of humans, modified by ad hoc measures to prevent discomfort for human society. Consequentialist anthropocentrism is also the central approach in policies of resource management that respond to the problem of limited resources by adjusting production and consumption, and by avoiding extreme pollution. The anthropocentric attitude is expressed through the ideals of wise use and sustainable development. The central concern is to secure the demands of the present without endangering future needs.

Deontological anthropocentrism in ethics deals primarily with rights and duties that are carried by ethical subjects or by those affected by intended actions. An important issue is who or what may count as a moral subject. In deontological anthropocentrism, only humans have ethical duties and rights. A major concern is therefore to find reasons why humans alone have qualities that set them apart from all other creatures. This is a difficult task because it is hard to define qualities that include all humans while at the same time excluding other living beings. In the Kantian tradition, the hallmark of humans has been connected to the ability of human beings to take moral demands upon themselves. To be an authentic human being is to exercise the freedom to accept morally binding restrictions on "free" choices of actions, thus rejecting selfishness for the sake of a higher moral rationality. Humans are by virtue of their possibility of free choice a "moral community," distinct from other communities on Earth. From a Kantian perspective, one may have indirect duties towards nonhumans, but such duties are only relevant in so far as they have instrumental importance and ultimately lead toward the promotion of human freedom.

Anthropocentrism is common in the Judeo-Christian tradition and in Islam, in part because God is perceived in anthropomorphic categories, but also because the primary concern of theology is humanity's relation with God (*theological anthropocentrism*). With regard to environmental concerns, theistic traditions affirm that humans have an obligation to treat the natural world with respect and care in much the same way as a farmer cultivates the land (*stewardship ethics*). In some Eastern religions (e.g., Mahayana Buddhism), the salvific interest is more universal. All sentient beings, however, have to reach the level of human existence before they can attain *nirvana*.

Since the 1960s awakening of ecological consciousness, the anthropocentric attitude has been strongly criticized, especially regarding its role in theology and ethics, and in secular science and public policy making. Some have attempted to "soften" anthropocentrism by correcting the perceived misconception of humanity as distinct and separate from the natural world. They have argued that anthropocentric concerns for human well-being should be based on enlightened self-interest in which humans regard themselves as partly constituted by the natural world and pay sufficient attention to sound metaphysics, scientific theories, aesthetic values, and moral ideals. This self-interest will naturally lead to respect for the nonhuman world, thus preventing it from degradation and destruction. Others claim this view to be shallow and assert the need for a total reversal of the anthropocentric perspective, as in *biocentrism,* in which the biotic community is seen as the central concern.

See also DEEP ECOLOGY; ECOLOGY, ETHICS OF; FREEDOM; KANT, IMMANUEL; VALUE, RELIGIOUS; VALUE, SCIENTIFIC

Bibliography

Næss, Arne. "The Shallow and the Deep, Long-Range Ecology Movements." *Inquiry* 17 (1973): 95-100.

Næss, Arne. *Ecology, Community and Lifestyle. Outline of an Ecosophy*. Trans. and rev. David Rothenberg. Cambridge, UK: Cambridge University Press, 1989.

Sessions, George, ed. *Deep Ecology for the Twenty-first Century*. Boston: Shambhala, 1995.

Warren, Karen J., ed. *Ecological Feminist Philosophies*. Bloomington: Indiana University Press, 1996.

Zimmerman, Michael E., ed. *Environmental Philosophy. From Animal Rights to Radical Ecology*. Upper Saddle River, N.J.: Prentice-Hall, 1998.

ROALD E. KRISTIANSEN

ANTHROPOLOGY

Anthropology is the study of humanity, in all its aspects, in all times and all places. In this sense, everyone is an anthropologist, for everyone is curious about themselves and their fellow humans, and people often ask anthropological questions. Anthropology is distinctive not so much in subject as in approach. Much of the character of the field, and the heart of its contribution, have come through ethnographic fieldwork, which comprises a large suite of techniques for studying people in qualitative and quantitative depth, typically while living among them for extended periods. The anthropologist's ideal is to learn a people's language, live with them, observe them in their day to day lives and in special events, all the while taking measurements, listing names, and holding extended discussions about their gods, cosmologies, and opinions of each other. Participant observation in which anthropologists do things with the people they are studying to the extent they allow brings such a wealth of knowledge that many anthropologists spend the rest of their lives discovering new insights from even their first trip to the field.

Themes and approaches

This wealth of information is studied in distinctive ways. Anthropologists are divided on whether the discipline can or even should be considered a science, but even the most scientific anthropologists recognize that a qualitative, interpretive study of ethnographic findings must play a major role. Understanding another group of people involves the search for meaning in what they do and say. The difference between the simple empirical observation that someone's eyelid twitched and understanding what someone was really up to when he winked at another person, entering the web of social relations and subtle meanings behind this little conspiracy, is what Clifford Geertz, following philosopher Gilbert Ryle, calls "thin description versus thick description." Ethnography, he concludes, is thick description. This is also what is needed for any broader, more abstract comparative study in anthropology.

Anthropological questioning is also guided by certain basic concepts or themes, such as *cultural relativism*. Often contrasted with *ethnocentrism*, cultural relativism is the insistence on evaluating customs and ideas in terms of that culture's own values rather than those of another culture. Such an approach is sometimes confused with the different and not particularly viable idea that all customs are of equal practical and moral value. Anthropology seeks to understand, for example, why female circumcision or ritual cannibalism have been so important to certain peoples, and how such practices function within those cultures. Everyone benefits from this greater understanding, but it does not follow that everyone must find these practices acceptable.

A second theme is *holism*, the attempt to comprehend the breadth and depth of what is human and how it fits together. Thus, anthropology's concern is not just with, for example, the economy itself, but with questions such as "How does the economy relate to kinship, status, and political considerations?" and "How do all these together affect what it is like being a woman in such a situation rather than a man?" Anthropology also strives to comprehend the breadth of human cultural, social, and physical variation. For example, compared to the specialized field of economics, anthropology explores the full range of what human economies can be like. Similarly, anthropology seeks to understand the nature of political leadership in the broadest terms, not just by comparing, for example, various types of centralized states (democracy with theocracy with monarchy), but by adding Polynesian and African chiefdoms, Micronesian big-man leadership, and the rise of leaders among less centralized or hierarchical hunter-gatherer societies. Without denying that democracies and monarchies differ, these differences are like shades of red compared to the full spectrum of human possibilities. And knowing as much as possible about the full range of human customs can be helpful in answering questions such as "What is economy?" "What is religion?" and "What is art?" as well as corollary questions such as "In what sense is religion a part of what it means to be human?"

Interestingly, an opposing perspective, usually labeled *particularist,* has occasionally swept the field. During such times the common wisdom is that culture is not an integrated system, and comparison among cultures is inevitably more misleading than helpful. Typologies of culture such as savagery, barbarism, and civilization, or the more recent band, tribe, chiefdom, and state model of neo-evolutionists such as Steward, Service, Fried, and Earle, are scorned as constraining, simplistic, wooden, or even propaganda promoting Western hegemony.

There is also value in balancing holism and high-level comparisons with an emphasis on that which is unique about each known people. Recent anticomparativist trends have been enmeshed in postmodern philosophical concerns, eliciting the same sometimes rancorous arguments found in other fields. But anthropology's expansive ambitions have always been shadowed by occasional epistemological failure of nerve. One does not have to claim that "all human knowledge is impossible" to appreciate the difficulty of demonstrating how deeply human thought is influenced by cultural upbringing, and the difficulty of correctly describing the important depths of another people's culture.

Perspectives toward culture

Probably the field's greatest conceptual contribution to human understanding comes through developing and elaborating the concept of culture. In his *Primitive Culture* (1871), Edward Burnett Tylor introduced the term *culture* into his new science of humanity, which he called *anthropology.* Despite many suggestions for alternative definitions, Tylor's is still popular: "that complex whole which includes knowledge, belief, art, morals, custom and any other capabilities and habits acquired by man as a member of society" (Tylor, p.1). An increasing number of anthropologists prefer not to include behavior within the category, seeing culture as socially transmitted information, or as Geertz puts it,

patterns for behavior, not patterns of behavior. This approach avoids the difficulty of explaining culture in terms of itself and highlights the common disparity between what people say and what they do. This approach also reminds us that not all behavior is cultural (for example, blinks vs. winks).

Anthropologists have traditionally understood culture as radically separate from biology. Alfred Kroeber's influential "superorganic" notion views culture as having almost a life of its own, molding each individual far more than the individual molds culture. Franz Boas and his students, including Margaret Mead and Ruth Benedict, set out early in the twentieth century to demonstrate a radical cultural relativism. Mead's *Coming of Age in Samoa* (1928) convinced generations of Americans that even something assumed to be biological and inevitable, such as the rocky period of adolescence, was not experienced in Samoa. Thus, if not all people behave the same way, the reasons must be cultural rather than biological. Derek Freeman has argued convincingly that Mead's conclusion was largely in error, partly as a result of mistaken interpretation, but also because Mead's teenage informants enjoyed playing games with the naïve outsider.

The emphasis on culture, particularly as a variable that is both influential and somewhat independent of biology, is nevertheless an important theme in anthropology. This perspective has also ensured that anthropologists became among the most ardent critics of sociobiology. Along with many reductionistic ideas popular in Western academia, sociobiology puts itself in the strange position of imaginatively crafting reasons we should choose to believe even our cultures are controlled by genes and both imagination and human choice are illusory. Anthropologists do not necessarily defend freedom of the will; a more typical argument is that while humans may be deeply constrained, culture, which is highly symbolic and essentially arbitrary, is as strong a determining influence on the individual as biology.

Nevertheless, interest in biological influences has grown among anthropologists who are exploring a range of approaches from gene-culture coevolution and dual inheritance to memetics. While memetics has its reductionistic aspects (Susan Blackmore has said that culture is a meme's way of replicating itself), in very important ways, memetics recognizes culture as relatively autonomous, beyond either the thought or the biology of the individual.

The search for human universals, an intense preoccupation of anthropology in its early days, but periodically out of favor, has also become more acceptable since the publication of Donald Brown's *Human Universals* in 1991. Brown offers many examples of human traits that are universal, including difficulties during adolescence and the practice of joking. Even examples illustrating how different cultures can be from each other contain elements of universality; for example, people express social respect in an extraordinary variety of ways, but the fundamental idea behind such behaviors is more or less the same. It is, of course, no easy matter to demonstrate that something is truly universal, and attempts to do so have provoked many arguments about whether a certain group of people genuinely constitutes an exception. But the issue itself is of immense importance, for once it is acknowledged that all people have many things in common, the radical individualism and subjectivism of certain philosophies, as well as categorical assertions that, for example, males could never understand females, rich the poor, or one "race" the thinking of someone from another, lose some of their force.

Subdisciplines of anthropology

Despite an emphasis on certain perspectives, methods, and themes, anthropology remains exceptionally broad and has traditionally been divided into subdisciplines. The standard approach in the United States is the "four-field" model:

(1) Physical or biological anthropology involves any study of human physical nature, especially as related to human evolution. Retrospective objections to anthropology's long fascination with race fail to appreciate the contribution of this work to demonstrating the central role of cultural bias in common racial classifications and stereotypes.

(2) Cultural anthropology studies the customs, beliefs, values, social interactions, and physical products (the culture and society) of people known historically or ethnographically. Longstanding goals include studying traditional ways of life before they succumb to modernization, and discovering the fullest possible range of human practice. But it is not simply a matter of collecting exotic customs, nor is cultural anthropology limited to the study of "primitive" peoples. Cultural anthropology attempts to study the full variety of humanity. Also, because the cultural viewpoint of the anthropologist, not just that of the people being studied, is important, the richness of the field grows in part from the fact that there are trained anthropologists from many parts of the world. In the United Kingdom social anthropology, which gives particular emphasis to social relations and social structures, has been very influential from the early work of Malinowski, Firth, Radcliffe-Brown, Evans-Pritchard and Kuper through Rodney Needham, Mary Douglass and many others.

(3) Archaeology has origins in ancient history and the classics, biblical studies, and art history, as well as in the practice of collecting and its institutional cousin, the museum. Most broadly, archaeology is the study of the material remains of humans who lived in the past, and as such it is not always considered a branch of anthropology. Yet archaeologists will often ask anthropological questions, and many view their quest as a cultural anthropology of extinct peoples.

(4) Anthropological linguistics is the anthropological study of human languages, ancient and modern, oral and written. To the extent that an anthropological perspective on linguistics differs from the separate field of linguistics, it will emphasize communication as an element of culture and as a crucial development in human evolution. Archaeologist Colin Renfrew is using linguistics to aid in reconstructing human movements in the past. Language study is also central to work in cognitive evolution.

Anthropology and the science-religion dialogue

Anthropology is not clearly a science, as indicated by the importance of divergent perspectives or schools of thought (social evolutionism, functionalism, historical particularism, cultural materialism, structuralism). It is thus difficult for a scholar of religion to discover the anthropological understanding of a topic. For example, a biblical scholar who painstakingly applies the structuralist insights of Claude Levi-Strauss to a particular text may be surprised and disheartened when her work is ignored by anthropologists sympathetic to Christianity, simply because they are not sympathetic to structuralism.

Anthropology may have more to contribute through its rich body of ethnographic, linguistic, archaeological, and paleoanthropological literature, and through more widely accepted conceptual categories such as culture, holism, and cultural relativism. In some cases the anthropology-religion connection can be put to practical use. Kenneth Pike, Thomas Headland, and others with SIL International (formerly the Summer Institute of Linguistics), for example, are using anthropology to help ensure that translations of the Bible make sense in the local cultural context.

Perhaps most promising is the use of anthropological insights to address issues that grow from theology itself or from the science-religion dialogue. Such issues include sin, human destiny, consciousness, the environment, technology and religion, cognitive evolution, mind-body questions, and the fundamental nature of humanity. The opportunity for the science-religion dialogue to be conducted using questions drawn from theology rather than for theology to follow along and comment on science is potentially of great value.

A striving to understand what it is to be human is a central theme of both anthropology and theology, and systematic theologies often include a major section on the subject. The nineteenth-century Princeton theologian Charles Hodge gave the title *Anthropology* to the second volume of his three-volume *Systematic Theology* (1872), and he devoted some 730 pages to this subject and to salvation. Primary topics included the origins and nature of human beings, the soul, unity of the human race, original state, covenant of works, the fall, sin, and free agency. More than a century later the second volume of Wolfhart Pannenberg's *Systematic Theology* (1991) covers some of the same topics, though in different ways, in no small part because Pannenberg has given serious attention to the findings of academic anthropology, a field that did not exist when Hodge wrote *Systematic Theology*.

Pannenberg is a good model of serious theological engagement with anthropology without allowing the theological agenda to be overwhelmed. This is not an easy balance, for as F. LeRon Shults

points out, theology has not come to grips with the changing view of humanity and human origins carefully constructed by anthropology (and evolutionary biology). It is possible for these topics to be explored philosophically, biblically, and in light of the history of theology, but without much contact with the growing anthropological understanding of what it is to be human. Shults, who is a leading expert on Pannenberg's thought, has himself made a major contribution to rethinking the fundamental theological doctrines of human nature, sin, and the image of God in light of anthropology.

Theologian J. Wentzel van Huyssteen is researching Paleolithic cognition to help understand the origins and nature of the human capacity for religion, a topic also being addressed by an interdisciplinary group of scholars organized by biologist William Hurlbut and anthropologist William Durhamat Stanford University in California. Taking a somewhat different approach, theologian Philip Hefner is engaged in extensive exploration of the theological relevance of sociobiology and biocultural evolution. Hefner suggests that humans should be viewed as "created co-creators." And from a yet different perspective, population geneticist David Wilcox has written a series of articles exploring paleoanthropological findings from a traditionally evangelical, but not creationist, perspective.

Anthropologist Ward Goodenough, perhaps best known for his research on the people of Truk, has written a series of articles for *Zygon* on such subjects as the human capacity for belief. And the biological anthropologist and polymath Solomon Katz has contributed to the understanding of a great range of issues including religion and food, human purpose, and what it means to have a science of humanity. He has also developed and is now working out a model connecting religious change to subsistence change, arguing in particular that a change in religion was an enabler for the Neolithic adoption of agriculture.

See also ANTHROPOLOGY OF RELIGION; CONSCIOUSNESS STUDIES; CREATIONISM; CULTURE, ORIGINS OF; EVOLUTION; EVOLUTION, BIOCULTURAL; FREEDOM; IMAGO DEI; MEMES; MIND-BODY THEORIES; SIN; SOCIOBIOLOGY; TECHNOLOGY

Bibliography

Blackmore, Susan. "The Meme's Eye View." In *Darwinian Culture: The Status of Memetics as a Science,* ed.

Robert Aunger. Oxford, UK: Oxford University Press, 2000.

Brown, Donald E. *Human Universals*. New York: McGraw-Hill, 1991.

Cronk, Lee. *That Complex Whole: Culture and the Evolution of Human Behavior*. Boulder, Colo.: Westview Press, 1999.

Evans-Pritchard, Edward E. *The Nuer: A Description of the Modes of Livelihood and Political Institutions of a Nilotic People*. Oxford: Oxford University Press, 1940.

Freeman, Derek. *Margaret Mead in Samoa: The Making and Unmaking of an Anthropological Myth*. Cambridge, Mass.: Harvard University Press, 1983.

Geertz, Clifford. *The Interpretation of Cultures*. New York: Basic Books, 1973.

Goodenough, Ward H. "Evolution of the Human Capacity for Beliefs." *Zygon* 28, no. 1 (1993): 5–27.

Harris, Marvin. *The Rise of Anthropological Theory: A History of Theories of Culture*, updated edition. Walnut Creek, Calif.: Altamira Press, 2001

Hefner, Philip. *The Human Factor: Evolution, Culture, and Religion*. Minneapolis, Minn.: Fortress Press, 1993.

Hicks, David, and Gwynne, Margaret A. *Cultural Anthropology*, 2nd edition. New York: Harper, 1996.

Hodge, Charles. *Systematic Theology*, vol. 2: *Anthropology*. New York: Scriber, 1872.

Kroeber, Alfred L. "The Superorganic." *American Anthropologist* 37 (1917): 539–569.

Kuper, Adam. *The Invention of Primitive Society: Transformations of an Illusion*. London: Routledge, 1988.

Mead, Margaret. *Coming of Age in Samoa*. New York: Morrow, 1928.

Pannenberg, Wolfhart. *Anthropology in Theological Perspective*, trans. Matthew J. O'Connell. Philadelphia: Westminster Press, 1985.

Pannenberg, Wolfhart. *Systematic Theology*, vol. 2, trans. Geoffrey W. Bromiley. Grand Rapids, Mich.: Eerdmans, 1991.

Shults, F. LeRon. *Reforming Theological Anthropology after the turn to Relationality*. Grand Rapids, Mich.: Eerdman, 2002.

Tylor, Edward Burnett. *Primitive Culture: Researches into the Development of Mythology, Philosophy, Religion, Language, Art, and Custom*. London: Murray, 1871.

Ward, Keith. *Defending the Soul*. Oxford: One World, 1992.

Wilcox, David L. "Adam, Where are You? Changing Paradigms in Paleoanthropology." *Perspectives on Science and the Christian Faith* 48, no. 2 (1996): 88–96.

PAUL K. WASON

ANTHROPOLOGY OF RELIGION

No known society is without religion. Anthropologists study this species-wide phenomenon as a human trait or institution, an element of culture, seeking a deep understanding of all, not just the "world," religions and their local significance. From this breadth, anthropologists of religion ask: What is religion? Are there any common elements? How did it originate? Intentionally nontheological, the anthropology of religion is less concerned with, for example, whether ancestor spirits of the New Guinea Maring people really interact with the living people than with how that perception influences culture. Despite the intention of objectivity, a strong thread of philosophical naturalism permeates the field from E. B. Tylor, James Fraser, and Emile Durkheim to Raymond Firth and Stewart Guthrie. Important exceptions include Edward Evans-Pritchard, Victor Turner, and Roy Rappaport.

See also ANTHROPOLOGY; NATURALISM

Bibliography

Guthrie, Stewart Elliott. *Faces in the Clouds: A New Theory of Religion*. Oxford: Oxford University Press, 1993.

Rappaport, Roy A. *Ritual and Religion in the Making of Humanity*. Cambridge, UK: Cambridge University Press, 1999.

PAUL K. WASON

ANTI-REALISM

See REALISM

APOLOGETICS

From the Greek roots *apo* and *leg* (*apologia*), the term *apologetics* can be translated as "speech with cause." In the Christian context, apologetics is important in science and religion discourse because it aims to provide religious faith with credibility. Particularly since the seventeenth century, a shared understanding of divine action in the world has progressively diminished due to new, scientific explanations for natural events that were previously accounted for in terms of supernatural agency. Apologetics increasingly incorporates scientific material in recognition of the universal scope of scientific knowledge in contrast to theology's alleged lack of empirical basis. It is a hybrid form of theology that aims to provide credibility for divine revelation under the light of human reason. In theological terms, apologetical literature aims to account for foundational elements in doctrine under the perspective of a religious conversion, while providing a systematic way for that doctrine to be understood. It "is the theoretical and methodical exposition of the reasons for believing in Christianity." (Bouillard, p. 11)

Early Christian apologetics

In historic Christian theology, apologetics has been characterized by skilled, often impassioned rhetoric. In the New Testament, the word *apologia* is translated as a defense of the hope that inspires the believer to remain upright (1 Peter 3:15), and for Paul and Luke, *apologia* is employed in situations of mission or conflict. This usage expands on the Old Testament usage, where it possesses sapiential qualities (Wis. 6:10). In neither case does it connote a legal or even a rigorous philosophical justification of religious faith.

In early Christianity, apologetics arose as a theological response to political crisis and as the theoretical expression for ecclesial community. Early Christian apologetics focused primarily on the significance of the person and work of Jesus Christ in arguments with Jews (as in Justin Martyr's *Dialogue with Trypho*) and later with pagan culture through varying critical incorporations of Platonist and gnostic ideas (as in Origen's *Contra Celsum* or Tertullian's *On Prescription Against Heretics*). Theological arguments turned toward civil authorities regarding the toleration of Christianity until the time of fourth century Roman Emperor Constantine. Early Christian apologetics reached a high point with Augustine of Hippo's *City of God,* and especially *The Literal Meaning of Genesis,* which is often cited in modern attempts to cohere a reading of the biblical text with science.

In the medieval period, apologetics was diverted by the encounter with early Islam, evident through Thomas Aquinas's *Summa Contra Gentiles*. As a result, a theological distinction in religious knowledge between revelation and reason was forged and intensified in a full development of theology as a scientific discipline. Through tensions resonant in early Protestant appeals to natural theology, Calvinist apologetics emerged as a formidable stream of thought that is still manifest in several modern theological schools. Against traditional Aristotelian metaphysics and natural theology, John Calvin's *Institutes of the Christian Religion* (1536) stressed the complete sovereignty of God's Word over the instrumental causes of natural powers.

Science and technology

The rise of science and technology in Europe during the sixteenth and seventeenth centuries brought about a stricter, empirical notion of objectivity, which had a pivotal impact on theological apologetics. Combined with a new reluctance on the part of theologians to refer to Christian revelation, the rise of the natural sciences led to diminished religious grounds for natural philosophy. In this new situation, the religious engagement with Enlightenment reason led to a diversity of theological responses to the new sciences. Since the seventeenth century, apologetic writing has stressed a harmony between science and religion, by selecting or neglecting different aspects of scientific and religious knowledge. Only in the late twentieth century has attention turned to uncovering a method of selection that might fruitfully anticipate ongoing discoveries, updates, and new evaluations for expressing theological knowledge.

Five historical questions are particularly important in illustrating this pattern: Copernicanism, the rise of physico-theology, Darwinism, biblical criticism, and scientism. In each case, the initial theological reaction to new scientific learning was confusion and disagreement, followed by concord and agreement.

First, echoing Augustine's hermeneutic that the biblical text is revealed in a way accessible to the uneducated, Galileo Galilei's *Letter to the Grand Duchess Christina* (1615) was a classic attempt to render Copernican astronomy and Catholicism compatible. No recourse to a natural proof for the existence of God was offered in the Galilean controversy.

Second, adopting contrary positions, in the spirit of William Derham's 1713 work *Physico-theology,* thinkers like Samuel Clarke, John Ray, Nicolas Malebranche, and René Descartes speculated on which fundamental natural principles (mechanics or mathematics) ground a proof for God's existence. Isaac Newton's position was the pivotal argument from design and is found in writings such as the *Opticks* (1704), rather than the crucial *Principia* (1687).

Third, after the mid-nineteenth century, Darwinism took this range of opinion and expanded it further into two discernible currents in the English-language world. Initially, there were those who incorporated the Darwinian mechanism of natural selection and adaptation into theological reflection (Asa Gray, Charles Kingsley, Aubrey Moore). Then, there were those who sought to confront and to critique evolution altogether (Charles Hodge, Samuel Wilberforce).

Fourth, advancing beyond the various attempts by philosophers Immanuel Kant, Friedrich Ernst Schleiermacher, Georg Wilhelm Hegel, and theologian John Henry Newman to reestablish a synthesis in knowledge, was scientific historical biblical criticism (David Strauss, Hermann Reimarus, Albert Schweitzer) and its impact upon biblical hermeneutics. This research and that which followed it quickly eclipsed nineteenth and early twentieth century defense of a historically precise text (Pope Pius IX, Karl Barth).

Fifth, from the middle of the twentieth century, a growing chorus of critique against scientific reductionism or *scientism* has developed within the natural sciences, as positivist assumptions of earlier scientific investigation have been shown to be limited.

Twentieth-century apologetics

Still common in the thought of evangelical Protestants, conservative Catholics, and orthodox Judaism, theological apologetics resembles much historical literature in its continuing reference to Christian doctrines such as incarnation, resurrection, creation, and immortality of the soul. However, in other quarters, apologetics has evolved beyond the focus on doctrine and has transformed itself to accommodate the specialization of knowledge and the secularization of university life. This is reflected in the natural theology offered in the prestigious Gifford Lectures offered at Scottish universities since 1889. In Roman Catholicism since 1950, apologetics has been designated as "fundamental theology." Ecumenism and interfaith dialogue have also shaped the importance and impact of theological apologetics.

Late twentieth-century apologetic literature with a scientific accent and doctrinal focus is represented in the writings of the scientist-theologians Stanley Jaki, Alister McGrath, Arthur Peacocke, John Polkinghorne, Robert John Russell, and Thomas Torrance. A less precise theological reconstruction of apologetics exists. It transposes Christian doctrine philosophically through a capacious theoretical commitment. This method is present in the writings of scientists such as Pierre Teilhard de Chardin and Alfred North Whitehead, contemporary philosophers Nancey Murphy, Joseph Bracken, and Holmes Rolston III, as well as the theologians Wolfhart Pannenberg and John Haught.

See also NATURAL THEOLOGY

Bibliography

Bouillard, Henri. *The Logic of Faith.* New York: Sheed and Ward, 1967.

Buckley, Michael. *At the Origins of Modern Atheism.* London and New Haven, CT: Yale University Press, 1987.

Dulles, Avery. *A History of Apologetics.* New York: Corpus, 1971.

Lindberg, David C., and Numbers, Ronald L., eds. *God and Nature: Historical Essays on the Encounter Between Christianity and Science.* Berkeley and Los Angeles: University of California Press, 1986.

Lonergan, Bernard. *Method in Theology.* Minneapolis, MN: Seabury Press, 1979.

PAUL ALLEN

AQUINAS, THOMAS

See THOMAS AQUINAS

ARISTOTLE

The great monotheistic religions have regarded Aristotle's philosophy with both appreciation and hostility. Christian, Islamic, and Jewish theologians generally approved of his well-ordered, teleological world in which final causes ordained that natural processes were directed toward the fulfillment of particular ends. Yet Aristotle rejected various important monotheistic tenants, including the belief that God is the ultimate cause of the existence of the world, the resurrection of the body, and the full immortality of the soul. As unqualified believers in these latter doctrines, Christians were particularly compelled to repudiate Aristotle. Theologians thus tended to reject or reinterpret what they took to be Aristotle's offensive opinions while generally accepting his larger natural philosophy.

Life and work

Aristotle was born in the town of Chalcidice in northern Greece in 384 B.C.E. His father was a physician to the King of Macedon. In 367, at the age of seventeen, Aristotle was sent to Athens to study at Plato's Academy, where he remained for twenty years, until Plato's death in 347. Since he was not chosen to replace Plato as the head of the Academy, Aristotle began a period of travel in Asia Minor, living for awhile in Assos (where he married a woman named Pythias) and then Lesbos until 342, when he accepted King Philip of Macedon's invitation to tutor his son, the future Alexander the Great, then fourteen years old. When Alexander succeeded his father as ruler in 335, Aristotle returned to Athens where he founded his famous school, the Lyceum. Thus began Aristotle's most productive period, which endured until 323, when news of the death of Alexander the Great provoked anti-Macedonian feelings in Athens. A false charge of impiety was made against Aristotle, who then fled Athens to Chalcis in Euboea, where he died in the following year, at the age of sixty-two.

It would be difficult to exaggerate the importance of Aristotle in the history of Western civilization. Not only were his numerous works a dominant factor in at least three civilizations (the Byzantine Empire, Islam, and the Latin West) using three different languages (Greek, Arabic, and Latin, respectively), but his works and ideas remained influential for approximately two thousand years. Aristotle's enormous influence derives not only from his overall brilliance, but also from the fact that he wrote treatises on a remarkable range of topics, which included metaphysics, logic, natural philosophy, biology, ethics, psychology, rhetoric,

poetics, politics, and economics (or household management). He is regarded as the founder of two disciplines, logic and biology. The first book of Aristotle's *Metaphysics* is the first history of philosophy as well as the first history of science, while his *Posterior Analytics* is regarded as the first treatise on the philosophy, or methodology, of science. Finally, in six or seven treatises, Aristotle described the structure and operation of the world, thereby formulating a natural philosophy that served as the primary guide for natural philosophers from late antiquity to the seventeenth century in Western Europe, when it was displaced by a new world view associated with Nicolaus Copernicus, Galileo Galilei, Isaac Newton, and many others.

Aristotle reveals a scientific temperament in all his treatises, always emphasizing reason and reasoned argument. He was highly analytic, dividing and categorizing before arriving at important principles and generalizations. He always gives the impression of objectivity and detachment. In coping with any particular problem, Aristotle considered alternative solutions as carefully as possible before resolving the problem.

Aristotle and the divine

Aristotle's views about religion and divinity play a role in his overall conception of the cosmos and its workings. In Book Eight of his *Physics,* he describes what he calls the "Unmoved Mover" or "Prime Mover," which is the ultimate source, or cause, of motion in the universe, but is itself unmoved. For Aristotle this is God, who dwells at the circumference of the universe and causes motion by being loved. The closer to the Unmoved Mover a body is, the more quickly it moves. Although the Unmoved Mover is God, it did not create the world, which Aristotle regarded as uncreated and eternal. As the prime mover, God enjoys the best kind of life, being completely unaware of anything external to itself and, being the most worthy object of thought, thinks only of itself.

Aristotle's God was clearly not a divinity to be worshipped. Apart from serving as the ultimate source of motion, God, ignorant of the world's existence, could play no meaningful role in Aristotle's natural philosophy. Nevertheless, Aristotle seems to have had a strong sense of the divine, which manifested itself in a sense of wonderment and reverence for the universe.

Aristotle's sense of God was unacceptable to Christians, Muslims, and Jews. Although Plato's concept of a God who created from pre-existent matter was also unacceptable, it was far more palatable to monotheists than was Aristotle's Unmoved Mover, who did not create the world. Indeed, it could not have created the world because, argued Aristotle, the world is eternal, without beginning or end. Aristotle insisted that the material world could not have come into being from another material entity, say *B*. For if it did, one would have to ask from whence did *B* come? Such an argument would lead to the absurdity of an infinite regression, prompting Aristotle to argue that the world has always existed, an interpretation that posed further problems for Muslims and Christians. Consistent with his assumption of an eternal world, Aristotle regarded creation from nothing as impossible.

Aristotle's concept of nature was fully compatible with those of the major religions. Indeed he provided basic interpretations that were widely adopted. Aristotle distinguished four operative causes in nature:

(1) the material cause, or that from which something is composed;

(2) the efficient cause, or the agent that made something come into being;

(3) the formal cause, or the characteristics that make it what it is; and

(4) the final cause, or the purpose for which something exists.

It is the last cause that makes Aristotle's system teleological. Although he did not believe that conscious purposes existed in nature, he was convinced that processes in nature aim toward an end or goal and that "nature does nothing in vain." It is therefore appropriate to characterize Aristotle's natural philosophy and science as teleological, a view of nature's operations that fits nicely into the Christian conception of God's creation.

The manner in which Aristotle argued and rendered judgments provoked Christian theologians in the Middle Ages. On a number of issues, Aristotle produced arguments about the physical world that led him to conclude the impossibility of certain phenomena. For example, in the fourth book of *Physics,* Aristotle argued that the existence of a vacuum is impossible inside or outside of our world. Space is always full of matter, which resists the motion of bodies. In the absence of matter in a vacuum, resistance to motion of any kind would be impossible. Without resistance to its motion, a body would move instantaneously, which is impossible.

In the first book of his treatise *On the Heavens,* Aristotle showed the impossibility of the existence of other worlds. Our world, Aristotle argued, contains all the matter there is, with no surplus left to form one or more other worlds, from which he concludes that "there is not now a plurality of worlds, nor has there been, nor could there be."

Aristotle also argued that without exception all accidental properties—that is, properties that are not essential for the existence of a thing—such as colors, the height of an individual, the size of one's foot, and so on, had of necessity to inhere in the substances of which they were the property. It was impossible that an accidental property exist independently of its subject.

In these, and similar instances, Christians were alarmed at the implications of Aristotle's arguments, for it seemed to place limits on God's absolute power to do whatever God pleased, short of a logical contradiction. Did those who accepted Aristotle's natural philosophy and metaphysics believe that God could not supernaturally create a vacuum just because Aristotle had argued that it was naturally impossible? Did they believe that God could not create other worlds if God wished, simply because Aristotle had argued that other worlds were impossible? And did they regard Aristotle's argument as unqualifiedly true when he declared it impossible that accidents of a substance could exist independently of that substance? The latter claim violated the doctrine of the Eucharist, namely that when God transforms the bread and wine of the Mass into the body and blood of Christ, the accidents of the bread and wine continue to exist without inhering in any substances. The uneasiness with limitations on God's absolute power led theologians in the thirteenth century to place restrictions on Aristotle's natural philosophy. Despite the attempt to circumscribe Aristotle's ideas, the effort did not in any way dampen the enthusiasm with which his works were received in the Latin West, where, during the fourteenth to early seventeenth centuries, they functioned as the curriculum in the arts faculties of virtually all of the sixty to seventy universities that had come into existence by that time.

Conclusion

Why did the works of Aristotle become so popular in the West despite the many ideas he had proposed that were offensive to Christians and Christianity? The answer is quite simple: His collected works ranged over many themes and subjects and were therefore too valuable to ignore. Moreover, no rival body of literature existed that could pose even a remote challenge to it. By the early seventeenth century, however, numerous new currents of thought came together to subvert Aristotle's natural philosophy, which was largely overwhelmed and by-passed by the end of the seventeenth century.

See also GALILEO GALILEI; GOD; ISLAM; METAPHYSICS; NEWTON, ISAAC; PLATO; TELEOLOGY

Bibliography

Barnes, Jonathan. *Aristotle*. Oxford: Oxford University Press, 1982.

Grant, Edward. *The Foundations of Modern Science in the Middle Ages: Their Religious, Institutional, and Intellectual Contexts*. Cambridge, UK: Cambridge University Press, 1996.

Lloyd, G. E. R. *Aristotle: The Growth and Structure of His Thought*. Cambridge, UK: Cambridge University Press, 1968.

Van Steenberghen, Fernand. *Aristotle in the West: The Origins of Latin Aristotelianism*, trans. Leonard Johnston. Louvain, Belgium: Nauwelaerts, 1955.

EDWARD GRANT

ART, ORIGINS OF

Some thirty-three thousand years ago a human being living in what is now Germany carved a figure like a man with a lion's head from a piece of mammoth tusk. Other ivory figurines were made nearby—felines, horses, bison, and mammoth—some with incised markings. Personal decorations appear even earlier. Some beads made from shells from distant shores indicate something special about the materials themselves. Some of the paintings in Chauvet Cave in France have been dated to thirty thousand years before the present, and other cave art may be just as old. Painted slabs from South Africa's Apollo Cave are more than twenty-seven thousand years old, and Australian wall engravings, though less securely dated, may be forty thousand years old. Early Aurignacian sites from thirty-two thousand years ago have produced multiholed bone flutes. Percussion instruments are nearly as old. Footprints beaten into the floors of some Paleolithic caves may suggest dancing.

Over twelve thousand items of Paleolithic portable art have been found in Western Europe alone. There are now three hundred decorated cave sites known, some with only a handful of figures, others with thousands. Humans have been producing art for at least three hundred centuries, portable and parietal, in varied materials, and in widely separate parts of the world. Unfortunately, it is not clear how much this knowledge reveals about the origins of art.

Temporal beginnings and the nature of art

Even asking where and when art began is more complicated than it seems. Because researchers depend on the vagaries of preservation and sometimes chance discovery, it is likely that many other works were created but not (yet) found. Even Chauvet Cave was unknown before 1994. A further complication concerns what qualifies as art or can be conceived as a "precursor" to art. The zoologist Jane Goodall observed wild chimpanzees engaged in a kind of rain dance. Desmond Morris found that apes like to paint—they do so without rewards—and their paintings show balance, control, and varied themes. John Pfeiffer detected among *Homo habilis* (an extinct member of the human genus that lived in Africa approximately 2.5 million years ago) a possible a preference for green lava and smooth pink pebbles, and the geologist and anthropologist Kenneth Oakley notes that fossils that may have been used as charms are common in Paleolithic sites. A rough female form on a pebble from Berekhat Ram, Israel, dated to 230,000 years ago. Is this art or our own imagination? The amazingly early date makes it both more interesting and more difficult to accept.

Art is not easily defined. Robert Layton notes an imprecise, shifting boundary, and different approaches that are hard to correlate, especially with regard to the aesthetic perspective and to art as communication. Anthropologists now commonly shy away from using the term *art*. Margaret Conkey and Olga Soffer advocate not thinking of these images as art but studying them as examples of human symbolic behavior. Some forms of art, such as song, dance, and storytelling, are transient, but other art is more enduring, separating communication from the constraints of time and location. External symbolic storage is of inestimable value in human history, and the arts were among the first media so used.

Sources of art: cogitations, motivations, adaptations, and inspirations

Just as fundamental as the timing and context of its first appearance are the sources from which art arose. Steven Mithin believes the dramatic development of culture, seen in some places as early as fifty thousand years ago and established wherever humans lived by thirty thousand years ago, represents a major redesign of the human mind. The premodern mind had consisted of a suite of relatively separate, specialized intelligences (social, linguistic, natural historical, technical) and the rapid appearance of art and religion is evidence that a generalized intelligence, similar to that of modern humans, allowed people to combine thoughts from the formerly separate intelligences.

Psychological explanations had proliferated even by 1900 when Yrjö Hirn's *The Origins of Art* reviewed many suggestions, from James Mark Baldwin's "self-exhibiting impulse" to Hirn's own preference for locating the art impulse in the human tendency to externalize feeling states, heightening the pleasure and relieving the pain of these feelings and awakening similar feelings in others. The nineteenth-century Russian novelist Leo Tolstoy similarly saw art as a communication of feelings, dependent upon and nurturing empathy. Jumping ahead many years and theories, Nancy Aiken also attributes the origins of art to its emotional effects. This need not involve beauty but could engage any emotion. Some of the same stimuli (lines, shapes) that naturally trigger reactions

are used in art to trigger emotional responses that are evaluated as aesthetic. This connection with biologically built-in responses accounts for the universality of the human aesthetic response.

Many models are *selectionist,* proposing more or less plausible scenarios for how art aids adaptation and so is increasingly favored in early populations. Charles Darwin suggested that the ability to create feelings with music gave certain individuals an edge in attracting mates. Interestingly, his fellow discoverer of natural selection, Alfred Russel Wallace, believed natural selection could not account for artistic faculties and proposed a "spiritual essence," a kind of God-of-the-gaps view of human development. Some arguments involve ecological adaptation rather than the psychology of emotion or sexual selection. Pfeiffer proposed that art arose out of necessity to hold the group together, reduce conflict, and pass on a growing body of wisdom. Looking back, art is an advance, but Terrence Deacon believes it was really a desperate response to change, perhaps to a degrading environment. Such models seem to take a pessimistic view of human freedom and creativity, yet wracking one's brains for a solution takes as much creativity as dreaming on a sunny afternoon.

Ellen Dissanayake's ethological approach involves finding core behaviors that natural selection could work on. Most important is "making special," through which reality is elaborated, reformed, and placed in a different realm, usually a magical or supernatural world, though often today a purely aesthetic realm. In contrast Helena Cronin suggests a pre-adaptation route in which art arose as an unselected by-product of some other adaptation. This may be true of many potentials of the human mind, some of which, perhaps, have yet to be discovered.

John Barrow pushes the causal nexus with the fascinating notion that the structure of the universe itself helped shape human creativity and aesthetic sense. Scale is important—if people were the size of ants, they would lack the strength to break chemical bonds as they do when chipping stones or carving ivory. Human associations of colors with emotions may relate to properties of light. Barrow also attempts to trace some aesthetic preferences to human adaptation to an ancestral savanna homeland. While intriguing, however, there really was no single "ancestral environment" upon which to base such an argument. Indeed, Rick Potts convincingly argues that the time of human evolution was marked by intense environmental variability and that the flexible cognition of human beings was an adaptation to instability. Perhaps human creativity and the aesthetic sense also developed in response to environmental instability.

Or did the arts grow from the human need to impose order on human intelligence and its capacity for self-revelation? Once human beings "left the garden," they needed art to cope with their new knowledge, for natural selection could not keep up. In thus recognizing art's connection with the deepest questioning of humans, sociobiologist Edward O. Wilson offers an almost theological argument, though his aim is *consilience,* the interlocking of causal explanations across disciplines.

Because of the human predicament Wilson captures so well, the arts have been deeply connected with religion. Much of the world's art is religious and so are many interpretations. Returning to the caves, the most influential is the idea, championed by the Abbé Breuil, that the art was involved in hunting magic. Structuralism, via Annette Laming-Emperaire and André Leroi-Gourhan, has also been important. Whatever one thinks of structuralism, art is deeply symbolic, and its meaning not easily perceived from another culture. David Lewis-Williams notes that Leonardo da Vinci's *Last Supper* has little to do with men eating. And for Clifford Geertz, the cultural significance of art is a "local matter." Jean Clottes and Lewis-Williams argue for a connection with shamanism in which the caves are spaces for ritual such as making images expressing the trance and hallucinatory experiences of shamanic activity.

Noting Jeremy Begbie's defense of art as knowledge, John Polkinghorne sees art as a vehicle for access to truth, a view not uncommon among artists and writers such as Madeleine L'Engle, C. S. Lewis, Larry Woiwode, and John Keats, who famously wrote in *Ode on a Grecian Urn* that "Beauty is truth, truth beauty." Ursula Goodenough also sees in art a source of nobility, grace, and pleasure, and Thomas Dubay notes that even in mathematics and science, beauty is evidence for truth. Beauty and art are not coextensive but surely related. Polkinghorne points out "That a temporal succession of vibrations in the air can speak to us of eternity is a fact that must be accommodated in

any adequate account of reality" (p. 45). Intimations of truth and contact with eternity are powerful motivations. In art and music, like religion, there is a dimension of reality that transcends the material world. Indeed, Alejandro García-Riviera suggests that if God is truth, goodness, and beauty, experience of these is an experience of God.

Interlocking causal explanations

An interlocking of explanations may be crucial for understanding the origins of art. Theological perspectives are not necessarily at odds with other ideas, and they may add an important dimension to theories of art's causation and motivation. Art as a window onto truth not otherwise apprehended makes sense of the deepest experience of art. It is a motivation for "making special" and may also be why the shaman creates art after one spiritual journey as an aid to the next. In some models, this "truth" consists in the capture and communication of an experience or feeling. This also makes sense, for whatever their *ultimate* sources, revelations and intimations come to an artist through experiences or feelings dependent on the human nervous and cognitive systems. And by whatever route, people have natural selection to thank for this wonderful facility for exploring truth. It is the universality of certain human experiences and certain truths so conveyed that allows (some) art to communicate across generations. Lascaux, arguably the most famous of the painted prehistoric caves in France, still conveys real truth, very possibly some of what the artists had in mind, if only in the back of their minds, so many centuries ago.

See also ANTHROPOLOGY; CULTURE, ORIGINS OF; PALEOANTHROPOLOGY

Bibliography

Aiken, Nancy E. *The Biological Origins of Art.* Westport, Conn.: Praeger, 1998.

Bahn, Paul, and Vertut, Jean. *Images of the Ice Age.* Leicester, UK: Winward, 1988.

Barrow, John. *The Artful Universe: The Cosmic Source of Human Creativity.* Boston: Little, Brown, 1996.

Clottes, Jean, and Lewis-Williams, David. *The Shamans of Prehistory: Trance and Magic in the Painted Caves.* New York: Abrams, 1998.

Conkey, Margaret W.; Soffer, Olga; Stratmann, Deborah, eds. *Beyond Art: Pleistocene Image and Symbol*. San Francisco: California Academy of Sciences, 1997

Dissanayake, Ellen. *What is Art For?* Seattle: University of Washington Press, 1988.

Geertz, Clifford. "Art as a Cultural System." In *Local Knowledge: Further Essays in Interpretive Anthropology,* 2nd edition, ed. Clifford Geertz. New York: Basic Books, 2000.

Hirn, Yrjö. *The Origins of Art: A Psychological and Sociological Inquiry*. London: Macmillan, 1900.

Layton, Robert. *The Anthropology of Art,* 3rd edition. Cambridge, UK: Cambridge University Press, 1991.

Lewis-Williams, J. D. *Discovering South African Rock Art*. Cape Town, South Africa: David Philip, 1990.

Mithin, Steven. *The Prehistory of the Mind: The Cognitive Origins of Art, Religion, and Science*. New York: Thames and Hudson, 1996.

Pfieffer, John E. *The Creative Explosion: An Inquiry into the Origins of Art and Religion*. Ithaca, N.Y.: Cornell University Press, 1982.

Polkinghorne, John. *The Faith of a Physicist: Reflections of a Bottom-up Thinker*. Princeton, N.J.: Princeton University Press, 1994.

Renfrew, Colin, and Scarre, Chris, eds. *Cognition and Material Culture: The Archaeology of Symbolic Storage*. Cambridge, UK: McDonald Institute for Archaeological Research, 1998.

Tattersall, Ian. *Becoming Human: Evolution and Human Uniqueness*. New York: Harcourt, 1998.

PAUL K. WASON

ARTIFICIAL INTELLIGENCE

Artificial intelligence (AI) is the field within computer science that seeks to explain and to emulate, through mechanical or computational processes, some or all aspects of human intelligence. Included among these aspects of intelligence are the ability to interact with the environment through sensory means and the ability to make decisions in unforeseen circumstances without human intervention. Typical areas of research in AI include game playing, natural language understanding and synthesis, computer vision, problem solving, learning, and robotics.

The above is a general description of the field; there is no agreed upon definition of artificial intelligence, primarily because there is little agreement as to what constitutes intelligence. Interpretations of what it means to be intelligent vary, yet most can be categorized in one of three ways. Intelligence can be thought of as a quality, an individually held property that is separable from all other properties of the human person. Intelligence is also seen in the functions one performs, in actions or the ability to carry out certain tasks. Finally, some researchers see intelligence as a quality that can only be acquired and demonstrated through relationship with other intelligent beings. Each of these understandings of intelligence has been used as the basis of an approach to developing computer programs with intelligent characteristics.

First attempts: symbolic AI

The field of AI is considered to have its origin in the publication of British mathematician Alan Turing's (1912–1954) paper "Computing Machinery and Intelligence" (1950). The term itself was coined six years later by mathematician and computer scientist John McCarthy (b. 1927) at a summer conference at Dartmouth College in New Hampshire. The earliest approach to AI is called *symbolic* or *classical* AI and is predicated on the hypothesis that every process in which either a human being or a machine engages can be expressed by a string of symbols that is modifiable according to a limited set of rules that can be logically defined. Just as geometry can be built from a finite set of axioms and primitive objects such as points and lines, so symbolicists, following rationalist philosophers such as Ludwig Wittgenstein (1889–1951) and Alfred North Whitehead (1861–1947), predicated that human thought is represented in the mind by concepts that can be broken down into basic rules and primitive objects. Simple concepts or objects are directly expressed by a single symbol while more complex ideas are the product of many symbols, combined by certain rules. For a symbolicist, any patternable kind of matter can thus represent intelligent thought.

Symbolic AI met with immediate success in areas in which problems could be easily described using a limited domain of objects that operate in a highly rule-based manner, such as games. The game of chess takes place in a world where the only objects are thirty-two pieces moving on a sixty-four square board according to a limited number of rules. The limited options this world provides give the computer the potential to look far ahead, examining all possible moves and countermoves, looking for a sequence that will leave its pieces in the most advantageous position. Other successes for symbolic AI occurred rapidly in similarly restricted domains such as medical diagnosis, mineral prospecting, chemical analysis, and mathematical theorem proving.

Symbolic AI faltered, however, not on difficult problems like passing a calculus exam, but on the easy things a two year old child can do, such as recognizing a face in various settings or understanding a simple story. McCarthy labels symbolic programs as brittle because they crack or break down at the edges; they cannot function outside or near the edges of their domain of expertise since they lack knowledge outside of that domain, knowledge that most human "experts" possess in the form of what is known as common sense. Humans make use of general knowledge—the millions of things that are known and applied to a situation—both consciously and subconsciously. Should it exist, it is now clear to AI researchers that the set of primitive facts necessary for representing human knowledge is exceedingly large.

Another critique of symbolic AI, advanced by Terry Winograd and Fernando Flores in their 1986 book *Understanding Computers and Cognition* is that human intelligence may not be a process of symbol manipulation; humans do not carry mental models around in their heads. Hubert Dreyfus makes a similar argument in *Mind over Machine* (1986); he suggests that human experts do not arrive at their solutions to problems through the application of rules or the manipulation of symbols, but rather use intuition, acquired through multiple experiences in the real world. He describes symbolic AI as a "degenerating research project," by which he means that, while promising at first, it has produced fewer results as time has progressed and is likely to be abandoned should other alternatives become available. This prediction has proven fairly accurate. By 2000 the once dominant symbolic approach had been all but abandoned in AI, with only one major ongoing project, Douglas Lenat's Cyc (pronounced "psych"). Lenat hopes to overcome the general knowledge problem by providing an extremely large base of primitive facts. Lenat plans to combine this large database with the ability to communicate in a natural language,

hoping that once enough information is entered into Cyc, the computer will be able to continue the learning process on its own, through conversation, reading, and applying logical rules to detect patterns or inconsistencies in the data Cyc is given. Initially conceived in 1984 as a ten-year initiative, Cyc has not yet shown convincing evidence of extended independent learning.

Functional or weak AI

In 1980, John Searle, in the paper "Minds, Brains, and Programs," introduced a division of the field of AI into "strong" and "weak" AI. Strong AI denoted the attempt to develop a full human-like intelligence, while weak AI denoted the use of AI techniques to either better understand human reasoning or to solve more limited problems. Although there was little progress in developing a strong AI through symbolic programming methods, the attempt to program computers to carry out limited human functions has been quite successful. Much of what is currently labeled AI research follows a functional model, applying particular programming techniques, such as knowledge engineering, fuzzy logic, genetic algorithms, neural networking, heuristic searching, and machine learning via statistical methods, to practical problems. This view sees AI as advanced computing. It produces working programs that can take over certain human tasks. Such programs are used in manufacturing operations, transportation, education, financial markets, "smart" buildings, and even household appliances.

For a functional AI, there need be no quality labeled "intelligence" that is shared by humans and computers. All computers need do is perform a task that requires intelligence for a human to perform. It is also unnecessary, in functional AI, to model a program after the thought processes that humans use. If results are what matters, then it is possible to exploit the speed and storage capabilities of the digital computer while ignoring parts of human thought that are not understood or easily modeled, such as intuition. This is, in fact, what was done in designing the chess-playing program Deep Blue, which in 1997 beat the reigning world chess champion, Gary Kasparov. Deep Blue does not attempt to mimic the thought of a human chess player. Instead, it capitalizes on the strengths of the computer by examining an extremely large number of moves, more moves than any human player could possibly examine.

There are two problems with functional AI. The first is the difficulty of determining what falls into the category of AI and what is simply a normal computer application. A definition of AI that includes any program that accomplishes some function normally done by a human being would encompass virtually all computer programs. Nor is there agreement among computer scientists as to what sorts of programs should fall under the rubric of AI. Once an application is mastered, there is a tendency to no longer define that application as AI. For example, while game playing is one of the classical fields of AI, Deep Blue's design team emphatically states that Deep Blue is not artificial intelligence, since it uses standard programming and parallel processing techniques that are in no way designed to mimic human thought. The implication here is that merely programming a computer to complete a human task is not AI if the computer does not complete the task in the same way a human would.

For a functional approach to result in a full human-like intelligence it would be necessary not only to specify which functions make up intelligence, but also to make sure those functions are suitably congruent with one another. Functional AI programs are rarely designed to be compatible with other programs; each uses different techniques and methods, the sum of which is unlikely to capture the whole of human intelligence. Many in the AI community are also dissatisfied with a collection of task-oriented programs. The building of a general human-like intelligence, as difficult a goal as it may seem, remains the vision.

A relational approach

A third approach is to consider intelligence as acquired, held, and demonstrated only through relationships with other intelligent agents. In "Computing Machinery and Intelligence" (1997), Turing addresses the question of which functions are essential for intelligence with a proposal for what has come to be the generally accepted test for machine intelligence. An human interrogator is connected by terminal to two subjects, one a human and the other a machine. If the interrogator fails as often as he or she succeeds in determining which is the human and which the machine, the machine could be considered as having intelligence. The Turing Test is not based on the completion of tasks or the solution of problems by the machine, but on the machine's ability to relate to a human being in conversation. Discourse is unique among human activities in that it subsumes all other activities within itself. Turing predicted that by the year 2000, there would be computers that could fool an interrogator at least thirty percent of the time. This, like most predictions in AI, was overly optimistic. No computer has yet come close to passing the Turing Test.

The Turing Test uses relational discourse to demonstrate intelligence. However, Turing also notes the importance of being in relationship for the acquisition of knowledge or intelligence. He estimates that the programming of the background knowledge needed for a restricted form of the game would take at a minimum three hundred person-years to complete. This is assuming that the appropriate knowledge set could be identified at the outset. Turing suggests that rather than trying to imitate an adult mind, computer scientists should attempt to construct a mind that simulates that of a child. Such a mind, when given an appropriate education, would learn and develop into an adult mind. One AI researcher taking this approach is Rodney Brooks of the Massachusetts Institute of Technology, whose lab has constructed several robots, including Cog and Kismet, that represent a new direction in AI in which embodiedness is crucial to the robot's design. Their programming is distributed among the various physical parts; each joint has a small processor that controls movement of that joint. These processors are linked with faster processors that allow for interaction between joints and for movement of the robot as a whole. These robots are designed to learn tasks associated with human infants, such as eye-hand coordination, grasping an object, and face recognition through social interaction with a team of researchers. Although the robots have developed abilities such as tracking moving objects with the eyes or withdrawing an arm when touched, Brooks's project is too new to be assessed. It may be no more successful than Lenat's Cyc in producing a machine that could interact with humans on the level of the Turing Test. However Brooks's work represents a movement toward Turing's opinion that intelligence is socially acquired and demonstrated.

The Turing Test makes no assumptions as to how the computer arrives at its answers; there need be no similarity in internal functioning between the computer and the human brain. However, an area of AI that shows some promise is that of neural networks, systems of circuitry that reproduce the patterns of neurons found in the brain. Current neural nets are limited, however. The human brain has billions of neurons and researchers have yet to understand both how these neurons are connected and how the various neurotransmitting chemicals in the brain function. Despite these limitations, neural nets have reproduced interesting behaviors in areas such as speech or image recognition, natural-language processing, and learning. Some researchers, including Hans Moravec and Raymond Kurzweil, see neural net research as a way to reverse engineer the brain. They hope that once scientists can design nets with a complexity equal to the human brain, the nets will have the same power as the brain and develop consciousness as an emergent property. Kurzweil posits that such mechanical brains, when programmed with a given person's memories and talents, could form a new path to immortality, while Moravec holds out hope that such machines might some day become our evolutionary children, capable of greater abilities than humans currently demonstrate.

AI in science fiction

A truly intelligent computer remains in the realm of speculation. Though researchers have continually projected that intelligent computers are immanent, progress in AI has been limited. Computers with intentionality and self consciousness, with fully human reasoning skills, or the ability to be in relationship, exist only in the realm of dreams and desires, a realm explored in fiction and fantasy.

The artificially intelligent computer in science fiction story and film is not a prop, but a character, one that has become a staple since the mid-1950s. These characters are embodied in a variety of physical forms, ranging from the wholly mechanical (computers and robots) to the partially mechanical (cyborgs) and the completely biological (androids). A general trend from the 1950s to the 1990s has been to depict intelligent computers in an increasingly anthropomorphic way. The robots and computers of early films, such as Maria in Fritz Lang's *Metropolis* (1926), Robby in Fred Wilcox's *Forbidden Planet* (1956), Hal in Stanley Kubrick's *2001: A Space Odyssey* (1968), or R2D2 and C3PO

in George Lucas's *Star Wars* (1977), were clearly constructs of metal. On the other hand, early science fiction stories, such as Isaac Asimov's *I, Robot* (1950), explored the question of how one might distinguish between robots that looked human and actual human beings. Films and stories from the 1980s through the early 2000s, including Ridley Scott's *Blade Runner* (1982) and Stephen Spielberg's *A.I.* (2001), pick up this question, depicting machines with both mechanical and biological parts that are far less easily distinguished from human beings.

Fiction that features AI can be classified in two general categories: cautionary tales (*A.I., 2001*) or tales of wish fulfillment (*Star Wars*; *I, Robot*). These present two differing visions of the artificially intelligent being, as a rival to be feared or as a friendly and helpful companion.

Philosophical and theological questions

What rights would an intelligent robot have? Will artificially intelligent computers eventually replace human beings? Should scientists discontinue research in fields such as artificial intelligence or nanotechnology in order to safeguard future lives? When a computer malfunctions, who is responsible? These are only some of the ethical and theological questions that arise when one considers the possibility of success in the development of an artificial intelligence. The prospect of an artificially intelligent computer also raises questions about the nature of human beings. Are humans simply machines themselves? At what point would replacing some or all human biological parts with mechanical components violate one's integrity as a human being? Is a human being's relationship to God at all contingent on human biological nature? If humans are not the end point of evolution, what does this say about human nature? What is the relationship of the soul to consciousness or intelligence? While most of these questions are speculative in nature, regarding a future that may or may not come to be, they remain relevant, for the way people live and the ways in which they view their lives stand to be critically altered by technology. The quest for artificial intelligence reveals much about how people view themselves as human beings and the spiritual values they hold.

See also ALGORITHM; ARTIFICIAL LIFE; CYBERNETICS; CYBORG; IMAGO DEI; THINKING MACHINES; TURING TEST

Bibliography

Asimov, Isaac. *I, Robot*. New York: Doubleday, 1950.

Brooks, Rodney. "Intelligence without Representation." In *Mind Design II: Philosophy, Psychology, Artificial Intelligence,* rev. edition, ed. John Haugeland. Cambridge, Mass.: MIT Press, 1997.

Crevier, Daniel. *AI: The Tumultuous History of the Search for Artificial Intelligence*. New York: Basic Books, 1993.

Dreyfus, Hubert. *Mind over Machine: The Power of Human Intuition and Expertise in the Era of the Computer*. New York: Free Press, 1986.

Kurzweil, Raymond. *The Age of Spiritual Machines*. New York: Viking, 1999.

Lenat, Douglas. "CYC: A Large-Scale Investment in Knowledge Infrastructure." *Communications of the ACM* 38 (1995): 33–38.

Minsky, Marvin. *The Society of Mind*. New York: Simon and Schuster, 1986.

Moravec, Hans. *Mind Children: The Future of Robot and Human Intelligence*. Cambridge, Mass.: Harvard University Press, 1988.

Searle, John. "Minds, Brains, and Programs." *The Behavioral and Brain Sciences* 3 (1980): 417–424.

Stork, David, ed. *HAL's Legacy: 2001's Computer as Dream and Reality*. Cambridge, Mass.: MIT Press, 1997.

Turing, Alan. "Computing Machinery and Intelligence." In *Mind Design II: Philosophy, Psychology, Artificial Intelligence,* rev. edition, ed. John Haugeland.Cambridge, Mass.: MIT Press, 1997.

Telotte, J. P. *Replications: A Robotic History of the Science Fiction Film*. Urbana: University of Illinois Press, 1995.

Turkel, Sherry. *The Second Self: Computers and the Human Spirit*. New York: Simon and Schuster, 1984.

Warrick, Patricia. *The Cybernetic Imagination in Science Fiction*. Cambridge, Mass.: MIT Press, 1980.

Winograd, Terry, and Flores, Fernando. *Understanding Computers and Cognition: A New Foundation for Design*. Norwood, N.J.: Ablex, 1986. Reprint, Reading, Mass.: Addison-Wesley, 1991.

Other Resources

2001: A Space Odyssey. Directed by Stanley Kubrick. Metro-Goldwyn-Mayer; Polaris, 1968.

AI. Directed by Steven Spielberg. Amblin Entertainment; Dreamworks SKG; Stanley Kubrick Productions; Warner Bros., 2001.

Blade Runner. Directed by Ridley Scott. Blade Runner Partnership; The Ladd Comany, 1982.

Forbidden Planet. Directed by Fred Wilcox. Metro-Goldwyn-Mayer, 1956.

Metropolis. Directed by Fritz Lang. Universum Film, A.G., 1926.

Star Wars. Directed by George Lucas. Lucasfilm Ltd., 1977.

NOREEN L. HERZFELD

ARTIFICIAL LIFE

Artificial life is a cross-disciplinary field of research devoted to the study and creation of lifelike structures in various media (computational, biochemical, mechanical, or combinations of these). A central aim is to model and even realize emergent properties of life, such as self-reproduction, growth, development, evolution, learning, and adaptive behavior. Researchers of artificial life also hope to gain general insights about self-organizing systems, and to use the approaches and principles in technology development.

Evolution of research

The historical and theoretical roots of the field are manifold. These roots include:

- early attempts to imitate the behavior of humans and animals by the invention of mechanical automata in the sixteenth century;

- cybernetics as the study of general principles of informational control in machines and animals;

- computer science as theory and the idea of abstract equivalence between various ways to express the notion of computation, including physical instantiations of systems performing computations;

- John von Neumann's so-called self-reproducing Cellular Automata;

- computer science as a set of technical practices and computational architectures;

- artificial intelligence (AI)

- robotics;

- philosophy and system science notions of levels of organization, hierarchies, and emergence of new properties;

- non-linear science, such as the physics of complex systems and chaos theory; theoretical biology, including abstract theories of life processes; and

- evolutionary biology.

Despite the field's long history, the first international conference for artificial life was not held until 1987. The conference was organized by the computer scientist C. G. Langton, who sketched a future synthesis of the field's various roots and formulated important elements of a research program.

In the first five years after 1987, the research went through an exploratory phase in which it was not always clear by what criteria one could evaluate individual contributions, and some biologists were puzzled about what could falsify a specific piece of research. Later the field stabilized into clusters of research areas, each with it own models, questions, and works in progress. As in artificial intelligence research, some areas of artificial life research are mainly motivated by the attempt to develop more efficient technological applications by using biologic inspired principles. Examples of such applications include modeling architectures to simulate complex adaptive systems, as in traffic planning, and biologically inspired immune systems for computers. Other areas of research are driven by theoretical questions about the nature of emergence, the origin of life, and forms of self-organization, growth, and complexity.

The media of artificial life

Artificial life may be labeled *software, hardware,* or *wetware,* depending on the type of media researchers work with.

Software. Software artificial life is rooted in computer science and represents the idea that life is characterized by form, or forms of organization, rather than by its constituent material. Thus, "life" may be realized in some form (or media) other than carbon chemistry, such as in a computer's central processing unit, or in a network of computers, or as computer viruses spreading through the Internet. One can build a virtual ecosystem and let small component programs represent species

of prey and predator organisms competing or cooperating for resources like food.

The difference between this type of artificial life and ordinary scientific use of computer simulations is that, with the latter, the researcher attempts to create a model of a real biological system (e.g., fish populations of the Atlantic Ocean) and to base the description upon real data and established biologic principles. The researcher tries to validate the model to make sure that it represents aspects of the real world. Conversely, an artificial life model represents biology in a more abstract sense; it is not a real system, but a virtual one, constructed for a specific purpose, such as investigating the efficiency of an evolutionary process of a Lamarckian type (based upon the inheritance of acquired characters) as opposed to Darwinian evolution (based upon natural selection among randomly produced variants). Such a biologic system may not exist anywhere in the real universe. As Langton emphasized, artificial life investigates "the biology of the possible" to remedy one of the inadequacies of traditional biology, which is bound to investigate how life actually evolved on Earth, but cannot describe the borders between possible and impossible forms of biologic processes. For example, an artificial life system might be used to determine whether it is only by historical accident that organisms on Earth have the universal genetic code that they have, or whether the code could have been different.

It has been much debated whether *virtual life* in computers is nothing but a model on a higher level of abstraction, or whether it is a form of genuine life, as some artificial life researchers maintain. In its computational version, this claim implies a form of Platonism whereby life is regarded as a radically medium-independent form of existence similar to futuristic scenarios of disembodied forms of cognition and AI that may be downloaded to robots. In this debate, classical philosophical issues about dualism, monism, materialism, and the nature of information are at stake, and there is no clear-cut demarcation between science, metaphysics, and issues of religion and ethics. If it really is possible to create genuine life "from scratch" in other media, the ethical concerns related to this research are intensified: In what sense can the human community be said to be in charge of creating life de novo by non-natural means?

Hardware. Hardware artificial life refers to small animal-like robots, usually called *animats,* that researchers build and use to study the design principles of autonomous systems or *agents.* The functionality of an agent (a collection of modules, each with its own domain of interaction or competence) is an emergent property of the intensive interaction of the system with its dynamic environment. The modules operate quasi-autonomously and are solely responsible for the sensing, modeling, computing or reasoning, and motor control that is necessary to achieve their specific competence. Direct coupling of perception to action is facilitated by the use of reasoning methods, which operate on representations that are close to the information of the sensors.

This approach states that to build a system that is intelligent it is necessary to have its representations grounded in the physical world. Representations do not need to be explicit and stable, but must be situated and "embodied." The robots are thus situated in a world; they do not deal with abstract descriptions, but with the environment that directly influences the behavior of the system. In addition, the robots have "bodies" and experience the world directly, so that their actions have an immediate feedback upon the robot's own sensations. Computer-simulated robots, on the other hand, may be "situated" in a virtual environment, but they are not embodied. Hardware artificial life has many industrial and military technological applications.

Wetware. Wetware artificial life comes closest to real biology. The scientific approach involves conducting experiments with populations of real organic macromolecules (combined in a liquid medium) in order to study their emergent self-organizing properties. An example is the artificial evolution of ribonucleic acid molecules (RNA) with specific catalytic properties. (This research may be useful in a medical context or may help shed light on the origin of life on Earth.) Research into RNA and similar scientific programs, however, often take place in the areas of molecular biology, biochemistry and combinatorial chemistry, and other carbon-based chemistries. Such wetware research does not necessarily have a commitment to the idea, often assumed by researchers in software artificial life, that life is a composed of medium-independent forms of existence.

Thus wetware artificial life is concerned with the study of self-organizing principles in "real chemistries." In theoretical biology, *autopoiesis* is a term for the specific kind of self-maintenance produced by networks of components producing their own components and the boundaries of the network in processes that resemble organizationally closed loops. Such systems have been created artificially by chemical components not known in living organisms.

Conclusion

Questions of theology are rarely discussed in artificial life research, but the very idea of a human researcher "playing God" by creating a virtual universe for doing experiments (in the computer or the test tube) with the laws of growth, development, and evolution shows that some motivation for scientific research may still be implicitly connected to religious metaphors and modes of thought.

See also ARTIFICIAL INTELLIGENCE; CYBERNETICS; CYBORG; INFORMATION TECHNOLOGY; PLAYING GOD; ROBOTICS; TECHNOLOGY

Bibliography

Adami, Christoph; Belew, Richard K.; Kitano, Hiroaki; and Taylor, Charles E., eds. *Artificial Life VI: Proceedings of the Sixth International Conference on Artificial Life.* Cambridge, Mass.: MIT Press, 1998.

Boden, Margaret A., ed. *The Philosophy of Artificial Life.* Oxford: Oxford University Press, 1996.

Emmeche, Claus. *The Garden in the Machine: The Emerging Science of Artificial Life.* Princeton, N.J.: Princeton University Press, 1994.

Helmreich, Stefan. *Silicon Second Nature: Culturing Artificial Life in a Digital World.* Berkeley and Los Angeles: University of California Press, 1998. Updated edition, 2000.

Langton, Christopher G, and Shimohara, Katsunori, eds. *Artificial Life V: Proceedings of the Fifth International Workshop on the Synthesis and Simulation of Living Systems.* Cambridge, Mass.: MIT Press, 1997.

Langton, Christopher G. *Artificial Life,* Vol. 6: Santa Fe Institute Studies in the Sciences of Complexity. Redwood City, Calif.: Addison-Wesley, 1989.

Morán, Federico; Moreno, Alvaro; Merelo, Juan Julián; and Chacón, Pablo, eds. *Advances in Artificial Life.* Lecture Notes in Artificial Intelligence 929. Berlin and New York: Springer, 1995.

Varela, Francisco J. and Bourgine, Paul, eds. *Toward a Practice of Autonomous Systems.* Cambridge, Mass.: MIT Press, 1992.

CLAUS EMMECHE

ASTRONOMY

Astronomy is the scientific study of the objects visible in the night sky by means of telescopes and associated instruments that analyze the radiation received from these objects. Using such instruments, astronomers determine their positions, apparent motions, distances, sizes, and total radiation emitted. From their spectra (the decomposition of light received from them into wavelengths) astronomers determine their chemical composition and radial motion. Astronomy distinguishes planets from stars, and identifies the way stars are spatially associated in star clusters, galaxies, and clusters of galaxies. Astronomy has ancient roots arising from peoples' attempts to relate the annual change of seasons to positions of stars in the sky. Astronomy is to be distinguished from astrology, which purports to relate the events in human lives to positions of the planets at the time of one's birth.

See also COSMOLOGY, PHYSICAL ASPECTS

GEORGE F. R. ELLIS

ASTROPHYSICS

Astrophysics is the analysis of the physical structure and evolution of objects studied by means of astronomical observations (e.g., stars, galaxies, radio sources, X-ray sources, quasi-stellar objects). The physical structure of such objects depends on a balance of gravitation, radiation pressure, and centrifugal forces, while their evolution depends on their initial composition and the reactions that take place between matter and radiation. In particular, nuclear reactions create new elements in the interior of stars and provide their major energy source. Detailed analysis discloses important relations between the color of light emitted by a star and its total radiation output; this relation changes with the age of the star. At its life's end, a star may die in a supernova explosion, or it may end up as

a white dwarf star, neutron star, or black hole, depending on its mass.

See also ASTRONOMY; BLACK HOLE; COSMOLOGY, PHYSICAL ASPECTS; GRAVITATION

GEORGE F. R. ELLIS

ATHEISM

Atheism, a term that began to appear with frequency only in modern times, literally means the denial of *theism,* that is, belief in the existence of a personal God who creates the world and exists independently of it. This denial may be formal and explicit, as in the writings of Karl Marx (1818–1883), Friedrich Nietzsche (1844–1900), Sigmund Freud (1856–1939), and Jean-Paul Sartre (1905–1980); or it may be an implicit "practical" atheism in which a person or community tacitly assumes that nothing transcends, or exists beyond, the physical universe. In both cases the justification for atheism is usually rooted in the alleged absence of positive evidence for God's existence. Often vaguely referred to as "unbelief," atheism comes in many varieties, but it is those forms that emphasize the lack of "evidence" for God that are of special interest in discussions of science and religion.

Atheism also arises, of course, among those who consider it impossible logically to reconcile the idea of an all-powerful and omnibenevolent God with the fact of evil and suffering in the world. The physicist and Nobel laureate Steven Weinberg (1933–), for example, has stated that it is not only the absence of evidence but, even more, the fact of evil and suffering that grounds his own atheism. Along with many others today, he finds in the suffering of living beings, especially as this has been exposed by evolutionary biology, a stronger reason for rejecting theism than the mere absence of physical evidence warrants. Since the days of Charles Darwin (1809–1882) the indifference of natural selection to the pain and the extinction of sentient organisms has often been cited as a clinching scientific reason for atheism. Darwin himself was unable to reconcile the idea of an intelligent divine designer with the disturbing life-struggle that his own evolutionary science uncovered. And among scientists today it is more often biologists than physical scientists who reject the notion of a personal God.

It should be noted, however, that the renunciation of theism because of innocent suffering has been a strong temptation quite apart from any specifically scientific information given by evolutionary biology. Darwinian depictions of life may add support to an atheism already based on a compassionate protest against suffering, but the question of how to hold together the idea of God and the fact of suffering is as old as theism itself. Indeed, belief in God arose in the first place, in part at least, as a response to the fact of suffering; and biblical as well as other religious portraits of ultimate reality find in God a compassionate will to conquer suffering and death.

Consequently, as far as the question of science and religion is concerned, atheism is of interest primarily when its proponents accuse theism of failing to provide adequate evidence for its claims. Here *evidence* means empirically available and publicly accessible data that might reasonably confirm theistic claims. To many scientific thinkers such evidence is ambiguous at best and completely lacking at worst. Although the sixteenth- and seventeenth-century founders of modern science (Nicolaus Copernicus, Francis Bacon, René Descartes, Galileo Galilei, Isaac Newton, Robert Boyle, and others) were convinced theists, there is little question that they ironically bequeathed to Western intellectual culture, and especially to modern philosophy, an understanding of truth-seeking (or an epistemic method) that has led many educated people to be skeptical of all propositions unsupported by experimental evidence. And since it is the very nature of theism to refer to a deity that is sensually unavailable, or to propose that believers wait patiently in unconditional trust for a future revelation of indisputable evidence of the divine, the idea of God seems especially uncongenial to confirmation by scientific method.

To those who elevate scientific method to the status of sole or primary arbiter of truth, therefore, all references to a hidden personal deity will be suspect. In the absence of empirical evidence, they ask, how can scientifically educated people be expected to take seriously theistic beliefs about the creation of the world, the eternal love of God, or the ultimate purpose of the universe? The renowned British philosopher Antony Flew (1923–),

applying Karl Popper's (1902–1994) criterion of falsifiability to the question of God's existence, has argued that since no counter-evidence would ever be enough to uproot the beliefs of a confirmed theist, theism violates the (scientifically shaped) rules of rational inquiry. If God lies beyond the domain of possible empirical verification or falsification, the claim goes, then theism cannot pass the most elementary test for truth.

At times the demand for theists to provide empirical evidence of God's existence is framed as a moral requirement, any violation of which is held to be indicative not only of cowardice but also of unethical insensitivity to the value of truth. The famous French biochemist and professed atheist Jacques Monod (1910–1976), for example, sought to base all of culture on what he called the postulate of (scientific) objectivity, which for him constituted the core of a new ethic of knowledge being ushered in by the modern age of science. Accordingly he dismissed theistic affirmations and all religious hope for final redemption as instances not only of cognitive but also moral delinquency. An earlier example of such passionate commitment to an "ethic of knowledge" is that of the American philosopher W. K. Clifford (1845–1879), whose essay "The Ethics of Belief" (1879) became famous in William James's (1842–1910) criticism of it in the "The Will to Believe." Clifford had stated that "it is wrong always, everywhere, and for anyone to believe anything upon insufficient evidence" (p. 183), an assertion that James along with others chastised for its puritanical extremism. In any case, among the beliefs for which sufficient evidence is especially lacking, at least according to Clifford's standards, are those of theists.

Does science support atheism?

The important question, then, is whether science, or the "scientific spirit," provides an incontestable basis for atheism. Although many atheists claim that it does, strictly speaking science as such can in principle justify neither atheism nor theism. By definition scientific method places theological interests beyond the compass of its concerns. Science does not as such ask about values, meaning, or God. Consequently the assertion that science sanctions atheism is logically spurious. Such a claim emanates not from science but from *scientism,* the belief that science is the only road to reliable knowledge. But one may legitimately ask whether this particular belief (scientism) orients the human mind reliably to the fullness of being or truth. Since it is impossible to conceive of an experimental situation that could in principle confirm or falsify the belief that science is the sole avenue to truth, it may be argued that scientism is a self-refuting proposition.

Nevertheless, it is undeniable that the progress of modern science has been accompanied historically by a rising skepticism, especially in the intellectual world, about the existence of a personal God. To many scientific thinkers the decline of theistic religion in modern times, especially among educated people, is a logical and not simply historical correlate of the advance of science. Albert Einstein (1879–1955), for example, famously asserted that the existence of a personal God, one capable of miraculously intervening in nature or history, would be incompatible with a basic assumption of all modern science, namely, that the laws of nature are utterly inviolable and invariant. For a scientist to believe in a responsive, personal God, a God who answers prayers, would be inconsistent with the very essence of scientific inquiry, which can tolerate no exceptions to natural laws.

Einstein, however, did not accept the label of "atheist" since it seemed a term of opprobrium and one that during his lifetime often implied moral relativism, which he vehemently opposed. Moreover, as a disciple of the famous Dutch pantheist Baruch Spinoza (1632–1677), he was not opposed to using the term *God* to refer to the mystery of "intelligence" that pervades the universe and makes possible the whole enterprise of scientific exploration. Einstein considered himself a deeply religious man, provided that "religion" is taken to mean a firm commitment to universal values (goodness, beauty, truth) and a cultivation of the insurmountable "mystery" encompassing the universe. But he considered the idea of a personal God dispensable to living religion.

Responding to Einstein, theologian Paul Tillich (1886–1965) insisted that living religion cannot dispense with the idea of a personal God since an impersonal deity would be lower in being than persons are. God must be "at least personal" in order to evoke the attitude of religious worship. God is much more than personal, of course, and so theology must acknowledge that personality is one among many symbols that religion employs in its attempts to understand ultimate reality; but it is not optional to theism. Addressing the objection by scientific atheists that God does not fall among the objects of empirical investigation, Tillich replied that God by definition cannot be one "object" among others—even if the most exalted of these—without ceasing thereby to be God. If God is to be taken as the deepest reality it would be as the "ground of being" rather than as one being among others. Religious awareness of such a reality, however, comes not by grasping it empirically or scientifically, but only by allowing oneself to be grasped by it.

See also EVIL AND SUFFERING; FALSIFIABILITY; THEISM

Bibliography

Buckley, Michael. *At the Origins of Modern Atheism.* New Haven, Conn.: Yale University Press, 1987.

Clifford, W. K. "The Ethics of Belief." In *Lectures and Essays.* London: Macmillan, 1879.

Dawkins, Richard. *The Blind Watchmaker.* New York: Norton, 1986.

Einstein, Albert. *Ideas and Opinions.* New York: Crown, 1954.

Flew, Antony. *God: A Critical Enquiry.* LaSalle, Il.: Open Court, 1984.

Freud, Sigmund. *The Future of an Illusion* (1927). New York: Norton, 1961.

Larson, Edward J., and Witham, Larry. "Scientists and Religion in America." *Scientific American* 281, no. 88 (1999).

Marty, Martin. *Varieties of Unbelief.* New York: Holt, Rinehart, and Winston, 1964.

Monod, Jacques. *Chance and Necessity: An Essay on the Natural Philosophy of Modern Biology,* trans. Austryn Wainhouse. New York: Knopf, 1971.

Stenmark, Mikael. *Scientism: Science, Ethics and Religion.* Aldershot, UK: Ashgate, 2001.

Tillich, Paul. *Theology of Culture,* ed. Robert C. Kimball. New York: Oxford University Press, 1959.

Weinberg, Steven. *Dreams of a Final Theory.* New York: Pantheon, 1992.

JOHN HAUGHT

ATOMISM

Atomism (from Greek *átomos:* indivisible) considers every substance (including living beings) to be made up of indivisible and extremely small material particles, the *atoms.* Every sensual quality of perceptible bodies has to be explained by the qualities, configurations, and changes of the atoms composing it, so that the (secondary) qualities of a compound are completely determined by and reducible to the (primary) qualities of its component atoms.

Historically, atomism can be traced back to antiquity, namely to the pre-Socratic philosophers of nature, Leucippus (born c. 480/470 B.C.E.) and Democritus (c. 460–370 B.C.E.). Due to Aristotle's convincing arguments against atomism, and because of its materialistic and atheistic worldview, it was unimportant during the Middle Ages. It was only with the seventeenth century that atomism was transformed into a scientific theory. Pierre Gassendi (1592–1655) revived classical atomism and explained the physical world as being constituted by finitely many atoms, which move in a void and have been endowed by God with a conserving momentum, thus freeing atomism from the stigma of being atheistic. Gassendi already allowed atoms to form compounds, which he called *moleculae* or *corpuscula.* The eighteenth and nineteenth centuries then gave rise to chemical atomism, which distinguished element from compound. Although Isaac Newton (1642–1727) had already speculated in detail on the atomic nature of matter and light in his *Opticks* (1704), physical atomism became widely accepted only after the development of the kinetic theory of gases in the nineteenth century. Atomism strongly supported the deterministic worldview of classical mechanics.

With the discovery of the electron and of radioactive decay, atoms themselves were recognized as composites and not indivisible units. The first atomic models were constructed in analogy to a macroscopic planetary system obeying classical laws of motion (negative electrons circling around a nucleus of neutrons and positively charged protons), but these models proved to be inconsistent. Erwin Schrödinger (1887–1961) and others then applied quantum mechanics to the atom. They substituted the electron orbits with probability distributions (*orbitals*), which indicate in which regions of space the electron is most likely to be found. The transition from one state of the atom to another also follows quantum principles, which imply fundamental uncertainties. It has also been shown that two quantum objects that interacted once stay correlated in some of their properties, even if they move away from each other (*EPR effect*). Thus, modern atomism with its dynamic view of matter has overcome the mechanistic tendencies of classical atomism and presents material reality as a holistic, fluctuating, and not fully determined net of coherence, which cannot be reconstructed as a set of completely separable massive objects that follow determined trajectories. Consequently, Alfred North Whitehead (1861–1947) suggested that processes ("actual entities") rather than substances are "the final real things of which the world is made up" (Whitehead, p. 18).

Thus, contemporary atomism opens new perspectives for the dialogue between science and religion, insofar as nature can be envisioned as being open for divine and human creative action. Living beings, human values, the act of striving for meaning and fulfillment in life, religious beliefs, and science itself are not mere agglomerations and idle enterprises in a mechanical world of swirling atoms, but can be understood as emergent and meaningful phenomena in an evolving process of creation.

See also EPR PARADOX; MATERIALISM

Bibliography

Gregory, Joshua C. *A Short History of Atomism: From Democritus to Bohr.* London: A&C Black, 1931.

Pais, Abraham. *Inward Bound: Of Matter and Forces in the Physical World.* Oxford: Clarendon, 1986.

Whitehead, Alfred North. *Process and Reality: An Essay in Cosmology,* (1929) corrected edition, ed. David Ray Griffin and Donald W. Sherburne. New York: Free Press, 1978.

DIRK EVERS

ATTRACTOR

Attractor is a technical term in the theory of dynamic systems. An attractor can be defined as a part of the phase space of a dynamic system to which the system confines itself in the course of time, until it is trapped in it. The simplest example of an attractor is the point of rest of a pendulum, which is geometrically represented by a simple point. More complicated dynamic systems have attractors that require complicated geometric representations. *Strange attractors,* the attractors of chaotic dynamic systems, have fractal geometric representations.

See also CHAOS THEORY

WOLFGANG ACHTNER

AUGUSTINE

Augustine (354–430 C.E.) was born on November 13 in Thagaste in present-day Algeria. His father Patricius, a town councilor with a modest income, was a pagan who was only baptized on his deathbed. Patricius was married to a Christian woman named Monnica, with whom he had three children.

As a young man, Augustine studied grammar and rhetoric in Madaura. Owing to the limited financial means of his family, he was obliged to return home when he was sixteen. Thanks to help from friends, however, he was able to travel to Carthage, where he completed his studies. At the age of eighteen he read Cicero's *Hortensius,* which impressed him and awakened in him a desire for wisdom. He was disappointed with his first reading of the Scriptures, however, largely because of what he deemed to be their inferior literary quality. He turned to the Manichaeans for the next nine or ten years, attracted by their promise of knowledge without faith. Around 372 he met a woman, with whom he would live for thirteen years and with whom he would have a son, Adeodatus. To earn a living, he taught rhetoric in Carthage, but he was disappointed in his students, who apparently were far from attentive and did everything to disrupt the classes. In 383, he left Carthage and traveled to Rome but was similarly dismayed when his students there failed to pay for their lessons. He then traveled to Milan, at that time the capital of the Roman Empire in the West, where his Manichaean friends and the prefect of Milan, Symmachus, secured for him a post as a teacher of rhetoric.

While in Milan, Augustine heard sermons by Ambrose, the bishop of Milan, whose stylish appearance and impressive performance profoundly impressed Augustine. Disappointed by the Manichaeans' failure to deliver the promised insight, Augustine decided to leave the movement, and for a short time he leaned toward skepticism because he thought he would never gain the truth he desired.

In Milan he was joined by his mother, who sent away Augustine's mistress and sought a fitting wife for him. Adeodatus remained with his father. The matchmaking efforts failed, however, when Augustine came under the influence of Platonism, in part due to the strong Platonic bias of Ambrose's sermons. In Platonic thought, Augustine found an answer to the then existential question: *unde malum* (Where does evil come from?). His inability to renounce physical desire delayed his conversion until the autumn of 386. But after reading Romans 13:13–14 he became convinced of the need to renounce "worldly depravity," and on Easter night 387 he received baptism. He thereafter decided to return to Africa but was forced to wait until 388 because of the political turmoil. A revolt of the Roman troops in Africa postponed his return.

Augustine founded a religious community in Thagaste, where he spent his time in study and writing, and soon became a respected scholar. He traveled to nearby Hippo in 391, where he was persuaded to become a priest and to assist Valerius, the bishop of Hippo. Augustine succeeded Valerius as bishop in 395 or 396, a role he fulfilled with great dedication for the rest of his life. He also served as pastor in the liturgy and as a judge, and he took great care in attending to people's material needs. Letters discovered in 1975 (first critical edition: 1981) reveal his profound concern for the condition and well-being of the poor and the slaves. Augustine also worked to refute the Manichaeans, and he was involved in discussions with the Donatists, a local Christian movement, which actively opposed Roman oppression.

Around 411, Augustine decided to address Pelagianism, a strong ascetically oriented movement, which Augustine felt put too little emphasis on God's saving grace in Jesus Christ and depended too heavily on the moral potential of human beings themselves. Augustine's dispute with the Pelagians lasted until the end of his life. Especially in his last works, which were destined to be read by monks in Hadrumetum and Marseille, Augustine emphasized predestination, creating the impression that he had given up on the capacity of the human will. Because of this, and also because of his negative opinion of *concupiscentia carnis* (sinful desire, mainly in its sexual manifestation), scholars assess this period of his life to have been pessimistic.

Works

Augustine was the most productive author in Latin antiquity. His autobiographical *Confessions* describes his life up to his conversion. This work and Augustine's *De civitate Dei* (*City of God*), written after the fall of Rome in 410, have become classics of world literature. Because of his intellectual prestige, he was asked to offer his views on a wide range of matters. In addition to *Confessions* and *De civitate Dei,* his most important works are *Enarrationes in Psalmos* (Explanations of the Psalms c. 418), *De Trinitate* (The Trinity c. 420), and *Enchiridion* (A Handbook on Faith, Hope, and Love 422). His late works form part of the basis for the theological developments of the Reformation and the Jansenism movement during the sixteenth and seventeenth centuries.

Views on science and religion

The correlation between faith and reason arose during Augustine's time, and his thinking was influenced by such trends as Stoicism, neo-Platonism, and Manichaeism. He was, of course, greatly influenced by the Scriptures and the writings of his Christian predecessors. The Scriptures represented ultimate authority and the source of all truth for Augustine. His reflections on the relation between faith, knowledge, and "science" developed within his theocratic image of the world and humankind. For Augustine, the one and only (Jewish-Christian) God is the creator of the universe and humankind (body and soul). Humans, like all parts of nature, are dependent on the creator. Such a view involves an inherent teleology, toward which the universe as process is ultimately ordered (*Confessions* 9, 23, 24). It also means that true knowledge is dependent on having a correct relationship with a personal and provident God, a view that deviates from the classical philosophy of, for example, the Stoa, where the cosmos as a whole represents a living and rational reality. According to

Augustine, humans look for knowledge of self and God through reason because this will provide them with true happiness; religion cannot be disconnected from an active pursuit of truth. Religion and truth are closely bound, and knowledge occurs by means of an inward upward movement in the course of which truth reveals itself. For Augustine, one must search for truth in one's heart, and this inward movement must lead to a transcendent movement toward God, the truth. In this process God, who is love, plays an essential role because knowledge and love are bound together: As Augustine states in *De Trinitate* (9, 2, 2), "There is no knowing without loving, and no loving without knowing." For Augustine, body and soul are also closely linked, and Augustine's reflections on body and soul helped form the basis of the Western concept of "self." Furthermore, human freedom and autonomy for Augustine do not have the same importance as they enjoy in modern thought. Philosophy, psychology, anthropology, and theology are always intrinsically linked and cannot be separated. Augustine's view of human history is essentially determined by his belief in the God of Jesus Christ and in the crucial part that Christ, as sole intermediary, plays in history. Augustine was convinced that there can be no true knowledge, salvation, or welfare outside of faith in Christ. The only criterion of judgment is the Christian faith.

The soul must guide the body and serve as reference to God; it is the image and likeness of God, which is why human beings, of all creatures, are closest to God. The soul hosts the memory and makes humans rational beings. Augustine distinguishes between superior reason (also called *intellectus* and *sapientia*), which is concerned with knowledge of unchanging principles, and inferior reason, which is focused on temporary things and is related to science. It is via superior reason that humans can see the truth "in" God.

Augustine is less univocal in his discussion of the body, which he judges in both positive and negative terms. He often spoke of love for the body and the duty to take care of it. When reacting to Manichaean dualism, he emphasized that the body is an essential part of the human person, and he strongly defended the resurrection of the body. At the same time, he regarded the body as a hindrance to the soul in the search for true happiness and as a source of sinfulness and mortality. In this connection he often spoke in a Pauline sense about life according to the flesh, in which the soul itself is always actively involved. Especially during the Pelagian controversy, Augustine emphasized that there is a sinful longing in all people (*concupiscentia carnis*), which prevents them from doing the good they want to do.

Augustine's life can be described as a continuous search for the truth, although he was not a scientific theologian in the medieval or modern meaning of the word. Especially in his early period, he looked for mathematical (positive-scientific) certainty in his search for truth, which helps explain his interest in astrology. Augustine quickly discovered, however, that astrology did not lead him to the truth he sought, and his initial sympathy would, after a period of skeptical doubt, disappear. Around 400, he rejected the power of astronomy to predict people's fate on the basis of heavenly signs. He thereafter fiercely and repeatedly criticized astrology, although Bernard Bruning has suggested that Augustine may have traded his initial astrological fatalism for a divine fatalism (predestination). Nonetheless, after his conversion Augustine became convinced that true knowledge could only be gained through Christian revelation, even though this knowledge would always remain fragmentary and incomplete in this world.

See also EMBODIMENT; FAITH; FREEDOM; GOD; IMAGO DEI; REVELATION; SOUL; TELEOLOGY

Bibliography

Augustine. *Oeuvres de Saint Augustin,* bibliothèque augustinienne. Paris: Desclée de Brouwer, 1941.

Augustine. *The Works of Saint Augustine: A Translation for the 21st Century,* ed. Edmund Hill and John E. Rotelle. New York: New City Press, 1990.

Brown, Peter R. L. *Augustine of Hippo: A Biography* (1967). Berkeley: University of California Press, 2000.

Bruning, Bernard. "De l'astrologie à la grace." *Augustiniana* 50 (1990): 575–643.

Duffy, Stephen J. "Anthropology." In *Augustine through the Ages: An Encyclopedia,* ed. Allan D. Fitzgerald. Grand Rapids, Mich.: Eerdmans, 1999.

Fitzgerald, Allan D., ed. *Augustine through the Ages: An Encyclopedia.* Grand Rapids, Mich.: Eerdmans, 1999.

Lamberigts, Mathijs. "Julien d'Eclane et Augustin d'Hippone: Deux conceptions d'Adam." *Augustiniana* 40 (1990): 373–410.

Lancel, Serge. *Saint Augustine,* trans. Antonia Neville. London: SCM Press, 2002.

Mayer, Cornelius P., ed. *Augustinus-Lexikon.* Basel, Switzerland: Schwabe, 1986.

O'Daly, Gerard. *Augustine's Philosophy of Mind.* Berkeley: University of California Press, 1987.

Pacioni, Vingilie. *L'unità teoretica del "De ordine" di S. Agostino.* Rome: Millenium, 1996.

Rist, John M. *Augustine: Ancient Thought Baptized.* Cambridge, UK: Cambridge University Press, 1994.

van Bavel, Tarsicius J. "No One Ever Hated His Own Flesh: Eph. 5:29." *Augustiniana* 45 (1995): 45–93.

MATHIJS LAMBERIGTS

AUTOMATA, CELLULAR

A cellular automata (CA) is a network of connected, identical, finite state automata, which are typically arranged in a one-, two-, or three-dimensional grid, where each grid cell corresponds to one automaton. A *finite state automaton* is a simple mathematical model for processes that can be described by a table of state transitions and limited memory, which only allows immediate calculations without delays. Each automaton has a state and a set of program rules defined in the state transition table. The state transitions are defined as a function of the current state and the state of its neighbors according to the program rules. Time and space in CAs are discrete—that is, they are represented as discrete time steps and a finite number of cells respectively. During runtime, the state of all automata is updated between time step t and $t + 1$ based on the states of all automata at time t, resulting in synchronized state transitions.

The neighbors of each automaton are defined by a neighborhood topology, typically (but not necessarily) specified as the immediate neighboring cells. In the case of the most common two-dimensional grids with square cells, these are often five (center, right, left, above, below) and nine (the five neighborhood and all diagonals) cell neighborhoods. Often CAs are also defined as discrete dynamic systems in contrast to differential equations that describe continuous dynamic systems.

CAs were introduced by computer pioneers John von Neumann (1903–1957) and Stanislaw Ulam (1909–1984) in the 1940s. The original work was published in the 1966 by A.W. Burks. The motivation for this approach was to propose a formal framework to model the dynamics of complex systems by means of repeated local interactions between simple components. In this context, von Neumann wanted to investigate what kind of logical organization of an automaton is sufficiently powerful to produce the self-organization principles found in nature. For this purpose he proposed a CA model with twenty-nine states and a five neighborhood, which has universal computation capabilities—it is powerful enough to calculate any computable task equivalent to a Turing machine.

An important instance of CA is the "game of life," which was introduced by mathematician John H. Conway in 1970. The game of life is a CA that consists of a two-dimensional grid of square cells with a nine neighborhood where each cell (automaton) has just the two states "alive" and "dead." Cells die if they have less than two or more than three live neighbors and become alive if they have exactly three live neighbors. It has been shown that Conway's very simple CA resembles a universal computer. The game of life is capable of producing complex organizational patterns, which, depending on the initial states of the cells, can be static, periodically changing, or moving. Interestingly, the size versus the frequency of state transitions in the game of life follows a power law relationship, which is a typical phenomenon found among a great variety of complex systems, which are in a state between stability and chaos called *self-organized criticality*. So far no other instance of cellular automata has been found that expresses the same property.

Cellular automata have been mainly investigated in artificial life and complexity science, but have also gained importance in other fields. In biology, CAs serve as simple frameworks for modeling the spatial effects of the interactions between neighbored individuals. In particular, CAs have been used to model space in game theory for various research issues, including the evolution of co-operation.

See also COMPLEXITY; EVOLUTIONARY ALGORITHMS; SELF-ORGANIZATION

Bibliography

Gardner, Martin. "Mathematical Games: The Fantastic Combinations of John Conway's New Solitaire Game 'Life'." *Scientific American* 223, no. 4 (1970):120–123.

von Neumann, John. *The Theory of Self-Reproducing Automata,* edited and completed by Arthur W. Burks. Urbana: University of Illinois Press, 1966.

THIEMO KRINK

AUTOPOIESIS

The modern concept of autopoiesis emerged within biological discourse, was picked up in sociology, and is increasingly present in debates within the philosophy of science. With ontological as well as epistemological implications, it touches religious understandings of God's action in the world and images of the original as well as ongoing creation. It promises to bridge natural and cultural processes.

While the problem itself was already described in the late eighteenth century by the German philosopher Immanuel Kant (1724–1804), the term *autopoiesis* was coined in the 1970s by the Chilean theoretical biologists Humberto Maturana and Francisco J. Varela in order to denote the operative closure of living systems and their ability to produce themselves. Any cell that, by means of molecular processes, reproduces its own building blocks on which it at the same time depends, operates on an autopoietical basis. These molecular elements are part of a complex network of components, which is on the one side constantly reproduced and maintained, and on the other side simultaneously the very basis of this operation.

As a result of this autonomy and operative closure, autopoietic systems lack any immediate contact with their environment even though they are energetically open systems and are forced to produce "order from noise" within this environment. In this regard, the theory of autopoietic systems replaces older ideas of a causal input and output across the border of systems, as well as stimulus/response models.

In reacting to their own inner states, autopoietic systems are self-determined. They are not independent of their environment, but if they respond to it they do it in a nondeterminate way. The environment can only stimulate system-specific processes and states. In epistemological contexts this opens up the possibility of developing an empirical theory of knowledge, which relativizes widespread ontological presuppositions since "reality" is the product of inner-systemic processes of the observer. On the other hand, autopoietic theories also suggest an ontology of multiple autonomous *and* interdependent levels of reality.

While Varela wants to restrict the concept of autopoiesis to cell systems, immune systems, and nerve systems, Maturana has extended it to human societies and epistemological issues, thereby providing support for radical constructivism. The German sociologist Niklas Luhmann (1927–1998) introduced the concept into the social sciences in order to characterize the self-referential operative closure of social systems and psychic systems. Social systems consist of communication, and psychic systems of thoughts. Neither can reach into their environment, but are open to it because of their self-referential closure.

The concept of autopoiesis has been criticized by some Christian theologians because it challenges not only the idea of a teleology immanent to nature but also the notion of total passivity and dependency in creation theology. It seems to replace the very idea of a *creatio ex nihilo*.

However, the concept was constructively used by Niels H. Gregersen in order to overcome the breach between God's activity and the self-productivity of God's own creatures. By distinguishing self-constitution in the sense of a theological ultimate beginning (creation *de novo*) from constituted autopoiesis as ongoing self-creative creativity based on self-constitution, Gregersen describes God as being creative by supporting and stimulating autopoietic processes. Autopoiesis can illuminate the theological notion of God's continuous creation, of providence in nature, and particularly of God's blessing. Within this context of creation the notion of autopoiesis resonates with God's self-giving nature and with the Christian notion of God's internal trinitarian self-realization.

See also CONSTRUCTIVISM; CREATIO CONTINUA; CREATIO EX NIHILO; DIVINE ACTION; PROVIDENCE; SELF-ORGANIZATION

Bibliography

Bosshard, Stefan N. *Erschafft die Welt sich selbst? Die Selbstorganisation in Natur und Mensch aus naturwissenschaftlicher, philosophischer und theologischer Sicht,* 2nd edition. Freiburg, Germany: Herder, 1987.

Gregersen, Niels Henrik. "The Idea of Creation and the Theory of Autopoietic Processes." *Zygon* 33 (1998): 333–367.

Kant, Immanuel. *Critique of Judgement* (1790), trans. Werner Pluhar. Indianapolis, Ind.: Hackett, 1987.

Luhmann, Niklas. "The Autopoiesis of Social Systems." In *Essays on Self-Reference.* New York: Columbia University Press, 1990.

Maturana, Humberto R., and Varela, Francisco J. *The Tree of Knowledge: The Biological Roots of Human Understanding,* rev. edition. Boston and London: Shambhala, 1992.

GÜNTER THOMAS

AVERROËS

The Aristotleanism of Ibn Rushd (Averroës), combined with his thorough training in various aspects of Islamic scientific and philosophical traditions, contributed to the evolution of his discourse on the relationship between science and religion. He lived at a moment in time particularly suited to synthesizing a broad understanding of philosophy and the philosophical sciences in which religion had a central position. Ibn Rushd's dialectical treatment of the role of religion and philosophy in human affairs and his theory of knowledge remain relevant to the contemporary science and religion discourse.

Life and writings

Averroës, whose real name was Abu'l Walid Muhammad ibn Ahmad ibn Muhammad ibn Rushd, was an Arab philosopher known as "The Commentator" to the medieval West because of his commentaries on Aristotle. Ibn Rushd was born in Córdoba, Spain, in 1126 C.E. to an eminent family of jurists. His grandfather had been a *Qadi* (judge) and *Imam* (Muslim leader of the congregational prayers) of the mosque of Córdoba. Ibn Rushd's early education was in the traditional pattern of Islamic education. He studied Arabic, the Qur'an, traditions of the Prophet and, later, natural sciences.

In 1153, Ibn Rushd traveled to Marrakash in Morocco where he helped the Almohad ruler 'Abd al-Mu'min to establish colleges. In 1169 or slightly earlier, Ibn Rushd was introduced to the learned prince Abu Yaqub Yusuf by the philosopher Ibn Tufayl. When Abu Yaqub succeeded 'Abd al-Mu'-min, Ibn Rushd found great favor with him throughout his rule (1163–1184). Ibn Rushd was made the Qadi of Seville in 1169. Two years later, he returned to his favorite Córdoba as Qadi. He traveled to various parts of the country, including longer sojourns in Seville, from where he dates several of his works between 1169 and 1179. In 1182, while in Marakash, Ibn Rushd succeeded Ibn Tufayl as the chief physician to Abu Yaqub Yusuf. Ibn Rushd remained in favor during the reign of Abu Yaqub's successor, Yaqub al-Mansur, except for a short period when his rivals were able to convince the ruler that his philosophical works were against the teachings of Islam. But al-Mansur called him back to his court as soon as he moved to Marrakash, where Ibn Rushd died in1198. He was buried in Marrakash outside the gate of Taghzut but later his body was taken to Córdoba where the young mystic Ibn 'Arabi was present at his funeral.

Ibn Rushd's commentaries on Aristotle can be divided into short (*jawami'*), middle (*talkhis*) and great (*tafsir*); the first two types were written between 1169 and 1178. His greatest medical work, the *Colliget* (*al-Kulliyyat*, Book of generalities), also belongs to this period. He wrote most of his original works between 1174 to 1180. These include *Kitab al-'aql* (Treatises on the intellect), *De substantia orbis* (Nature of heavens), *Fasl al-maqal* (The Decisive chapter), *Kashf al-manahij al-adillah* (Discovery of the methods of proof), and *Tahfut al-Tahafut* (Incoherence of the incoherence).

Philosophy

Ibn Rushd's philosophy was strongly influenced by his training in the principles of jurisprudence (*Usul*) on the one hand and by Aristotle and certain Muslim philosophers (*falasifa*), especially al-Farabi, Ibn Bajja and Ibn Tufayl, on the other hand. He criticized Ibn Sina's (Avicenna) philosophy but respected his medical works (indeed, he wrote a commentary on Ibn Sina's medical poem, *al-Urjuza fi'l tibb* [Recompense for medicine]). Ibn Rushd's relationship with Ibn Tufayl was one of deep respect for the elder philosopher who was also his mentor. But while Ibn Tufayl was mystically inclined, Ibn Rushd was not. The two philosophers

recognized the convergence of philosophy and revelation but whereas Ibn Tufayl leads Absal, the second main character of his celebrated narrative *Hayy ibn Yaqzan* (The Living son of the awake), to a mystic vision of knowledge, Ibn Rushd remains strictly within the philosophical realm.

In his *Fasl al-makal wa-takrib ma bayn al-sharia' wa'l hikma min al-ittisal* (Authoritative treatise and exposition of the convergence of religious law and philosophy), written before 1179, Ibn Rushd formulated a conception of philosophy that was in accordance with the Qur'anic teachings. For him, philosophy was a rational view of creation that leads to the knowledge of the creator. Thus formulated, philosophy becomes a valid path for discovery of truth, which is also to be found in revealed texts. Because different individuals have different levels of comprehension, God speaks to humans through three kinds of discourses: dialectical (*al-aqawil al-jadaliyya);* rhetorical (*al-aqawil al-khitabiyya)* and demonstrative syllogism (*al-aqawil al-burhanniyah*). This validation of philosophy led Ibn Rushd to formulate his theory of knowledge, in which the findings of rational research are collaborated with the revealed text through a reinterpretation of the text in accordance with the established rules of the Arabic language. This interpretation (*Ta'wil),* Ibn Rushd points out, is in accordance with the Qur'an because the Qur'an itself distinguishes between those verses that have fixed and clear meanings (*ayat al-muhkamat)* and those that are open to several interpretations (*ayat al-mutashabihat).*

Ibn Rushd cherished the honor given to scholars by the Qur'an and used this to demonstrate that scholars have the right to interpret those verses that lend themselves to rational speculation, but such interpretation, he held, should remain in the scholarly circles; it should not be passed on to the common folk who do not have the capacity to understand it. He criticized Muslim philosopher al-Ghazali for not following this rule. This criticism is present in many works of Ibn Rushd, in various forms and degrees, but it is in his master piece, *Tahafut al-Tahafut* (The Incoherence of the incoherence), that he forcefully attacks not only al-Ghazali but also all those neo-Platonic philosophers who had distorted Aristotle's teachings, including Ibn Sina and his followers.

Tahafut al-Tahafut deals with some of the basic problems of philosophy and it reconstructs

Ibn Rushd's conclusive ideas about time, eternity, creation, divine action, causality, and other fundamental issues. Using al-Ghazali's *Tahafut al-Falasifa* (Incoherence of the Philosophers) as the lynchpin for his attack, Ibn Rushd attempts to prove the eternity of the world. Ibn Rushd rejects the emanationist doctrine that the "One" can give birth only to one. He also criticizes Ibn Sina's notion of "Necessary Being" on the grounds that it is not possible to separate essence and existence; the distinction is made only in thought. Ibn Rushd's God is conceived as the One who is part of the universe. Unlike Ibn Sina for whom God is transcendent and is situated beyond the moving intelligences, divinity is the cause of the physical order for Ibn Rushd. Thus Ibn Rushd conceives God in purely Qur'anic terms, but through Aristotelian method. He refuses to separate divinity from its attributes. It is only human thinking that distinguishes between the two according to what people consider to be one or another of the infinite divine perfections.

Influence

Ibn Rushd's influence on the Western scholars is well known. In canto four of the *Inferno,* Dante called him *"che'l gran comento"* (the great commentator) and gave him the place of honor along with Euclid, Ptolemy, Hippocrates, Avicenna, and Galen. In Europe, the University of Padua became the main center of Averroism, though the Universities of Paris and Bologna were not far behind. But it is his masterly and clear exposition of Aristotelian thought that earned Ibn Rushd the title of "The Commentator," not his original ideas. His originality was, in fact, belittled by nineteenth-century French philosopher Ernest Renan and those who followed him. However, a more correct appreciation of Ibn Rushd is slowly emerging.

See also ARISTOTLE; AVICENNA; ISLAM; ISLAM, CONTEMPORARY ISSUES IN SCIENCE AND RELIGION; ISLAM, HISTORY OF SCIENCE AND RELIGION

Bibliography

Brockelmann, Carl. *Geschichte der arabischen Litteratur,* Vol.1. Leiden, Netherlands: E. J. Brill, 1943.

Bello, Iysa, A. *The Medieval Islamic Controversy Between Philosophy and Orthodoxy: Ijma' and Ta'wil in the Conflict Between Al-Ghazali and Ibn Rushd.* Leiden, Netherlands: E. J. Brill, 1989.

El-Ehwany, Ahmed Fouad. "Ibn Rushd." In *History of Muslim Philosophy* (1963), ed. M. M. Sharif. Karachi, Pakistan: Royal Book, 1983.

Hourani, George. *The Life and Thought of Ibn Rushd.* Cairo, Egypt: American University Press, 1947.

Ibn Rushd. *Tahafut al-Tahafut,* trans. Simon van den Bergh. London: Luza, 1954.

Ibn Rushd. *Metaphysics,* trans. Charles Genequand. Leiden, Netherlands: E. J. Brill, 1986.

Wahba, Mourad, and Abousenna, Mona, eds. *Averroës and the Enlightenment.* Amherst, N.Y.: Prometheus, 1996.

MUZAFFAR IQBAL

AVICENNA

In spite of the enormous difference between the science of his day and contemporary science, Ibn Sina (Avicenna) remains an essential link in the science and religion discourse. This is so because Ibn Sina addressed some of the most fundamental questions regarding the relationship between science and religion: How did the cosmos come into existence?; What is the role of God in the unfolding of human and cosmic destinies?; How does God interact with created beings? These and many other questions critical to contemporary discussions occupy a central position in Ibn Sina's philosophy, if not his science.

Life and writings

Abu'l'Ali al-Husayn Ibn 'Abd Allah Ibn Sina, whose name was Latinized as Avicenna during the Middle Ages, is known in the Muslim world as Ibn Sina. He was one of the most important representatives of the encyclopedic tradition of learning that was the hallmark of Islamic scholarship. Honorifically called *al-Shaykh al-Ra'is* (the Grand Shaykh), Ibn Sina was born in 980 C.E. in Afshana, his mother's home town near present-day Bukhara, Uzbekistan, during the reign of Amir Nuh ibn Mansur al-Samani.

We know about his life and works from two authoritative sources: an autobiography that covers the first thirty years of his life and a detailed life-sketch left behind by his disciple and friend al-Juzjani. Ibn Sina's father was a high official of the Samanid administration. His native language was Persian and he was first educated at home and then sent to learn jurisprudence from Isma'il al-Zahid. He studied Ptolemy's *Almagest,* Euclid's *Elements,* and logic with the famous mathematician Abu 'Abdallah al-Natili. By the time of his sixteenth birthday, Ibn Sina had mastered physics, medicine, metaphysics, and he was well-known as a physician. During the next two years, he was able to master Aristotle's metaphysics with the help of al-Farabi's commentary.

The first important turning point in the life of Ibn Sina came in the year 997 when, as a physician, he successfully treated the ruler of Bukhara, Nuh ibn Mansur; this opened the doors of one of the best libraries of its time to the young Ibn Sina. He spent the next several months in the palace library and saturated his mind with the best of medieval learning to such an extent that many years later he remarked to his disciple Juzjani, "I now know the same amount as then but more maturely and deeply; otherwise the truth of learning and knowledge is the same."

The earliest of Ibn Sina's surviving works date from 1001 when he was twenty-one; these include the twenty-volume *Kitab al-hasil wa'l-mahsul* (Book of sum and substance) dealing with all sciences, *Kitab al-majmu'* (Book of compilation) on mathematics, and *Kitab al-birr wa'l- ithm* (Book of virtue and sin) on ethics.

The second important turning point in Ibn Sina's life can be traced back to the year 1002 when his father died amidst political turmoil and war, and Ibn Sina left Bukhara for Jurjaniyah, then the capital of the Khwarazmian dynasty, where he found patronage in the court of the ruler, Abu'l Hasan Ahmad ibn Muhammad al-Suhaili. It was for al-Suhaili that Ibn Sina wrote two treatises on mathematics and astronomy, *Kitab al-tadarik li anwa' al-khata fi'l tadbir* (Book of remedy for mistaken planetary positions) and *Qiyam al-ard fi wasat al-sama'* (The Establishment of earth in the middle of the sky). But Ibn Sina had to flee again because of political turmoil. He set out for Jurjan because of the reputation of its ruler as a lover of learning but when Ibn Sina arrived in the kingdom of Qabus in 1012, he discovered that the ruler had died. After ten years of moving from place to place, Ibn Sina finally settled in Ispahan in present day Iran, where he composed his masterpieces during a fifteen-year period of calm and peace. When Masud of Ghaza attacked Ispahan, this

peace came to end, and Ibn Sina returned to Hamadan where he died of colic during the month of Ramadan in the year 1037.

Ibn Sina's surviving works include more than two hundred and fifty books, treatises, and letters on philosophy, cosmology, medicine, and religion. The most important among these are the voluminous *Kitab al-Shifa'* (Book of healing), *Kitaba al-Najat* (Book of salvation), *Danishnama-yi 'ala'I* (Divine wisdom), *'Uyun al-Hikmah, al-Isharat wa'l tanbihat* (Remarks and admonitions), and the famous *al-Qanun fi'l-tibb* (The Canon of medicine).

Philosophy

Ibn Sina's philosophy is based on an ontological foundation in which God, the Necessary Being *(wajib al-wujud),* is the only being that is pure goodness, the source of all existence. Everything else derives its being *(mahiyya)* and its existence *(wujud)* from the Necessary Being and hence is contingent upon God. The contingent beings *(mumkin al-wujud)* are then divided into two kinds: (1) Those that are necessary in the sense that they cannot "not be"; they are contingent by themselves but receive from the First Cause the quality of being necessary. These beings are the simple substances *(mujarradat).* And (2) those beings that are only contingent, the composed bodies of the sublunary world that come into being and pass away. Ibn Sina's importance is based on the fact that he attempted to integrate Greek philosophy and Islam in an original synthesis that places God at the center of a philosophy that is essentially based on self-evident truths. According to Ibn Sina, the idea of "being" is so rooted in the human mind that it could be perceived outside of the sensible, though the first certitude apprehended by the human mind is the one that comes by means of sense perception.

In a prefiguration of the Cartesian *Cogito ergo sum* (I think, therefore I am), Ibn Sina based his philosophy on intuition *(hads)* and on the notion that the human soul is independent of body, and hence capable of apprehending itself directly. According to Ibn Sina, the Necessary Being produces a single Intelligence (because from the One can only come one). This Intelligence possesses a duality of being and knowledge; it introduces multiplicity into the world; from it can derive another Intelligence, a celestial soul, and a celestial body.

Then, according to Ptolemy's system, this creative emanation descends from sphere to sphere as far as a tenth pure Intelligence, which governs our terrestrial world; this terrestrial world is unlike the other worlds because it is made of corruptible matter. This multiplicity surpasses human knowledge but is perfectly possessed and dominated by the active Intelligence, the tenth Intelligence. Ibn Sina demonstrated this in a highly original poetic narration, *Hayy ibn Yakzan* (The living, the son of the Awakened).

Among Ibn Sina's medical works, *Canon of Medicine,* is the ordered summation of all the medical knowledge up to his time. Divided into five books, this major work of Islamic medical tradition was used as the basic textbook for teaching medicine for seven centuries both in the East as well as in the West. Translated by Gerard of Cremona between 1150 and 1187, the *Canon* formed the basis of teaching at all European universities. It appears in the oldest known syllabus given to the School of Medicine at Montpellier, a bull of Pope Clement V dating from 1309, and in all subsequent ones until 1557. The Arabic text was edited at Rome in 1593; in all, eighty-seven translations, some incomplete, exist in various European languages.

Influence

Ibn Sina's influence on the subsequent development of intellectual thought is vast. In the Muslim world, his philosophy was instrumental in the emergence of *Ishraqi* (Illuminist) school of Suhrawardi. Ibn 'Arabi combined it with the Gnostic doctrines and Mulla Sadra integrated it into the intellectual perspectives of Shi'ism. In the West, medieval philosopher Thomas Aquinas embodied some of Ibn Sina's proofs in the Catholic theology and although the Renaissance brought a violent reaction against him, Ibn Sina holds a secure place in the history of Western philosophy through his influence on major Christian philosophers.

See also ARISTOTLE; AVERROËS; ISLAM; ISLAM, CONTEMPORARY ISSUES IN SCIENCE AND RELIGION; ISLAM, HISTORY OF SCIENCE AND RELIGION; THOMAS AQUINAS

Bibliography

Gohlman, William E. *The Life of Ibn Sina: A Critical Edition and Annotated Translation.* Albany: State University of New York Press, 1974.

Gutas, Dimitri. *Avicenna and the Aristotelian Tradition: Introduction to Reading Avicenna's Philosophical Works.* Leiden. Netherlands: E. J. Brill, 1988.

Hamarneh, Sami. "Abu 'Ali al-Hussain bin 'Abdallah bin Sina (Avicenna) (980–1037)." In *The Genius of Arab Civilization: Source of Renaissance,* ed. John R. Hayes. London: Eurabia, 1983.

Corbin, Henry. *Avicenna and the Visionary Recital,* trans. Willard Trask. New York: Pantheon, 1960.

Nasr, Seyyed Hossein. *An Introduction to Islamic Cosmological Doctrines.* Albany: State University of New York Press, 1993.

Marmura, Michael E., ed. *Islamic Theology and Philosophy: Studies in Honor of George F. Hourani.* Albany: State University Press of New York, 1984.

Wickens, G. M., ed. *Avicenna, Scientist and Philosopher: A Millenary Symposium.* London: Luzac, 1952.

MUZAFFAR IQBAL

AXIOLOGY

An axiology is a theory about the nature of values and value judgments. Distinctions are usually made among *aesthetic values* (concerning the beauty of an object or action), *moral values* (concerning whether something is good or right), and *scientific* or *intellectual values* (concerning the coherence and adequacy of a theory). Nondualistic theories (Buddhism, Confucianism, process philosophy) deny these distinctions. Those who think value judgments are objective argue that the value of anything is measured by how well it imitates normative universals or conforms to the will of God. Empiricists, including most modern scientists, reject such objective universals. They treat values as subjective responses or judgments, as creations of personal preference or cultural tradition.

See also AESTHETICS; BEAUTY; VALUE

GEORGE ALLAN

B

BAHÁ'Í

The Bahá'í faith, a new and growing world religion, holds the unity and harmony of science and religion as one of its core principles. Science and religion, according to the Bahá'í teachings, are both equally necessary for humanity to progress. Science is the discoverer of the material and the spiritual reality of things, and it is the foundation of material and spiritual development. Religion develops both the individual and society, fostering the love, fellowship, and will that is necessary for humanity to advance. Science and religion counterbalance each other: Religion without science leads to superstition, whereas science without religion leads to materialism.

Historical origins

The Bahá'í faith originated in nineteenth-century Iran at a time when the country was struggling with economic and political instability, conflict between the religious and secular segments of society, and Russian and British expansionist policies. Iran was in decline under the Qajar dynasty when the Bábí millenarian movement was founded in 1844 by the Báb (Siyyid 'Alí Muhammad, 1819–1850). The rapid rise of the Bábí movement and its prophecy of the coming of a world redeemer led to violent suppression, with its leaders either killed or sent into exile, as was the case for Bahá'u'lláh (Mírzá Husayn 'Alí, 1817–1892).

Bahá'u'lláh nursed the decimated Iranian Bábí community back to health from nearby Baghdad but was further exiled to Constantinople (modern Istanbul), to Adrianople (modern Edirne), and finally to Acre (modern Akko in Palestine). When he announced that he was the redeemer prophesied by the Báb, most of the Bábí community became Bahá'ís, followers of Bahá'u'lláh.

Bahá'u'lláh's teachings were laid out in numerous books, epistles, and letters to a growing community. The central theme was unity: the unity of religion; the oneness of God; the unity of humanity; the equality of women and men; the need for a united world civilization, and the unity of science and religion. Religion promoted amity and concord as its chief aim, and this required the unfettered search after truth and the elimination of prejudice and superstition characteristic of science.

By the early twentieth century, the Bahá'í faith had spread around the world. 'Abdu'l-Bahá (1844–1921)—Bahá'u'lláh's eldest son and successor—traveled and spoke widely throughout Europe and North America, emphasizing that religion must be progressive. The great progress in technical and material spheres wrought by science necessitated similar progress in religion. "When religion, shorn of its superstitions, traditions, and unintelligent dogmas, shows its conformity with science," he told his audiences, "then will there be a great unifying, cleansing force in the world which will sweep before it all wars, disagreements, discords and struggles" (1969, p. 146). Shoghi Effendi (1897–1957) succeeded 'Abdu'l-Bahá. After his death, leadership passed to the Universal House of Justice seated in Haifa, Israel.

Bahá'í teachings about science and religion

The teachings of the Bahá'í faith are "founded upon the unity of science and religion and upon investigation of truth." Science and religion are like the two wings of one bird: "A bird needs two wings for flight, one alone would be useless. Any religion that contradicts science or that is opposed to it, is only ignorance—for ignorance is the opposite of knowledge. Religion which consists only of rites and ceremonies of prejudice is not the truth" ('Abdu'l-Bahá, 1969 p. 129).

The Bahá'í writings describe science as "the discoverer of realities," the means by which humanity explores and understands both material and spiritual phenomena:

> The virtues of humanity are many, but science is the most noble of them all. . . . It is a bestowal of God; it is not material; it is divine. Science is an effulgence of the Sun of Reality, the power of investigating and discovering the verities of the universe, the means by which man finds a pathway to God. Through intellectual and intelligent inquiry science is the discoverer of all things. ('Abdu'l-Bahá, 1982 p. 49)

The purpose of religion is to "safeguard the interests and promote the unity of the human race, and to foster the spirit of love and fellowship amongst men" (Bahá'u'lláh, 1978, p. 168). Human nature is fundamentally spiritual, and the "spiritual impulses set in motion by such transcendent figures as Krishna, Moses, Buddha, Zoroaster, Jesus, and Muhammad have been the chief influence in the civilizing of human character" (Bahá'í International Community). Religion and spiritual commitment are necessary if the fruits of science are to be used for the advancement of humanity: "In every sphere of human activity and at every level, the insights and skills that represent scientific accomplishment must look to the force of spiritual commitment and moral principle to ensure their appropriate application" (Bahá'í International Community).

Religious truth must be understood in the light of science and reason if it is not to become superstition and a source of discord. Religious doctrines that disagree with science are likely to disagree with doctrines of other religions, creating and sustaining religious conflict. However, this does not mean the current scientific point of view is necessarily fully correct, nor does it mean that truth is limited to only what science can explain.

Similarly, science alone is inadequate. Doctrines inspired by science—most notably, the view that only material things are real—have had pernicious and corrosive effects when imposed on the people of the world. These doctrines need to be counteracted by the truths of religion. 'Abdu'l-Bahá in *Paris Talks* emphasized that "with the wing of science alone he would also make no progress, but fall into the despairing slough of materialism" ('Abdu'l-Bahá 1969, p. 143). Furthermore, the commitment and the will that derives from religion is required if the results of science are to be applied to the benefit of the people of the world.

Evolution and the emergence of humanity. The Bahá'í writings address in depth the issue of evolution and the emergence of humanity—a major source of conflict between science and contemporary religion. Humanity is described as emerging by a gradual progression that starts at a simple material stage and advances degree by degree to the human stage. In each stage, according to 'Abdu'l-Bahá, humanity develops capacity for advancement to the next stage: "While in the kingdom of the mineral he was attaining the capacity for promotion into the degree of the vegetable. In the kingdom of the vegetable he underwent preparation for the world of the animal, and from thence he has come onward to the human degree, or kingdom" ('Abdu'l-Bahá 1982, p. 225). Evolutionary processes—indeed, all natural processes—are the expression of God's will and the mechanism for the unfolding of God's creation:

> Nature in its essence is the embodiment of My Name, the Maker, the Creator. Its manifestations are diversified by varying causes, and in this diversity there are signs for men of discernment. Nature is God's Will and is its expression in and through the contingent world (Bahá'u'lláh, p. 142).

Humanity, therefore, was created by God and potentially existed even before being actualized as a "composition of the atoms of the elements."

Humans and animals and are distinct and different kinds of beings, according to the Bahá'í view. It is incorrect to say that humans are descended from animals, even though physically that is the case. This is because humans have a rational and spiritual side in addition to the physical reality they share with animals: "The reality of man is his thought, not his material body. The thought force and the animal force are partners. Although man is part of the animal creation, he possesses a power of thought superior to all other created beings" ('Abdu'l-Bahá 1969, p. 17). The Bahá'í point of view therefore diverges from understandings of evolution that see no distinction between humans and animals. It reconciles two perspectives—natural evolution and divine creation—that many have deemed irremediably in conflict.

Types of knowledge. 'Abdu'l-Bahá describes human knowledge as being of two kinds. One kind "is the knowledge of things perceptible to the senses." The other kind "is intellectual—that is to say, it is a reality of the intellect; it has no outward form and no place and is not perceptible to the senses" ('Abdu'l-Bahá 1981, p. 83). The knowledge that people have of the laws of the universe is such an intellectual reality, as is the knowledge of God. 'Abdu'l-Bahá further describes four criteria for knowledge: sense perception (empiricism), reason (rationality), tradition, and inspiration. By itself, each criterion is inadequate: The senses can be fooled, reasonable thinkers differ, understanding of tradition is reasoned and gives differing interpretations, and the heart's promptings are not reliable. Only when evidence from all criteria is in agreement can a proof be trusted as reliable.

The Bahá'í model of how reliable knowledge is obtained gives a perspective for viewing the roles of science and religion in society. Purely empirical approaches or rational approaches to knowledge, even when combined as they are in science, are inadequate to meet social needs. Approaches based solely on tradition—prophetic or otherwise—or intuition and feeling are likewise inadequate. Rather, contributions from all the approaches are needed. Neither science nor religion separately provides the broad foundations by which society can progress. Both are needed.

Conclusion

The task facing humanity, according to the Universal House of Justice, the global Bahá'í administrative body, "is to create a global civilization which embodies both the spiritual and material dimensions of existence." Carrying out this task requires "a progressive interaction between the truths and principles of religion and the discoveries and insights of scientific inquiry." Science provides the understanding and technical capabilities that allow humanity to overcome the limitations of nature, making the goal of a peaceful and just world civilization an achievable one. Religion provides the moral, ethical, and spiritual strength, the discipline, and the commitment that are necessary if the goal is to become a reality.

See also EMERGENCE

Bibliography

'Abdu'l-Bahá. *Paris Talks: Addresses Given by 'Abdu'l-Bahá in Paris in 1911–1912,* 11th edition. London: Bahá'í Publishing Trust, 1969.

'Abdu'l-Bahá. *Selections from the Writings of 'Abdu'l-Bahá.* Haifa, Israel: Bahá'í World Centre, 1978.

'Abdu'l-Bahá. *Some Answered Questions,* 3rd edition. Wilmette, Ill.: Bahá'í Publishing Trust, 1981.

'Abdu'l-Bahá. *The Promulgation of Universal Peace: Talks Delivered by 'Abdu'l-Bahá During His Visit to the United States and Canada in 1912,* 2nd edition. Wilmette, Ill.: Bahá'í Publishing Trust, 1982.

Bahá'u'lláh. *Tablets of Bahá'u'lláh revealed after the Kitáb-i-Aqdas.* Haifa, Israel: Bahá'í World Centre, 1978.

Bahá'í International Community. *The Prosperity of Humankind: A Statement Prepared by the Bahá'í International Community Office of Public Information.* Haifa, Israel: Bahá'í International Community, 1995.

Universal House of Justice. *Letters of the Universal House of Justice.* Haifa, Israel: Bahá'í World Centre, 1992.

STEPHEN R. FRIBERG

BEAUTY

Beauty, according to the ancient Greek philosopher Plato (c. 427–347 B.C.E.), is the most accessible of the Forms. Forms are transcendent sources of the essential qualities of things, the qualities that make things what they are. The proper relation among these qualities, their harmony, is what makes a thing beautiful. We are naturally drawn to beautiful things, wanting to possess them and to perpetuate their beauty in creations of our own. Our love of beauty leads us to seek it in increasingly more enduring forms of enjoyment and creation: from particular physical objects to friends and children, to public institutions and societal laws, to scientific theories and philosophical systems, and finally to Beauty itself. Thus Beauty is the harmonizing structure that give things their integrity, we desire it above all else, and in its presence we are able to create things of enduring worth. It is both the measure of our good and the enkindling agent for its accomplishment. Western notions of beauty since Plato are but a series of footnotes to these linked notions.

Objective interpretations

Aristotle emphasizes the notion of structure: The beauty of a thing lies in its formal and final causes, in the imposition of appropriate ordering principles of symmetry and unity upon indeterminate matter. He argues that for a work of art, such as a tragedy, to be excellent it must adhere to proper unities of time, place, and narrative sequence. Plotinus (205–270 C.E.) emphasizes the notion of beauty's lure, the ascent by its means to the timeless. Beauty is not merely symmetry and unity; it is a power irradiating them, for which we yearn and through which we can transcend that about us which is perishing. The early Christian theologian Augustine of Hippo (354–430 C.E.) identifies this power as God, through the beauty of whose Word our restless selves find salvation's rest.

Hence in Christianity, as in most religions, the actions and objects associated with worship are as beautifully crafted as possible, their beauty having the power to draw believers into the presence of the holy. Islam excludes the use of images, however, as did early radical Protestantism, finding them distractions rather than inducements. Contrast, for example, the severe elegance of Islam's Dome of the Rock mosque, or a clear-windowed New England Puritan church with the sculptured figures on the facade of the Roman Catholic cathedral at Chartres, or the ballet of icons and censors at a Russian Orthodox Eucharist.

Thomas Aquinas uses the beauty people see in the world around them, their sense of how things fit together, as a proof for the existence of God. Because they act together so as to attain the best result, they must be directed by a purposive being, as the arrow is directed by the archer. The ultimate source of such purposiveness is God. In the eighteenth century, William Paley (1743–1805) revived Aquinas's "argument from design," adapting it to the natural order described by Newtonian science. The well-ordered mechanistic intricacy of the world results from laws that cannot be fortuitous: the precision of a watch entails a watchmaker; the precision of the universe entails a God. People were no longer brought into God's presence through beauty, but from the beauty of nature at least it could be inferred that there must be a God who had created it.

The tendency since the rise of modern science, however, is to claim that nonsensible principles such as Beauty, although still timeless and necessary, are no longer understood as supernatural: they are the laws of nature. The Enlightenment *philosophe* Denis Diderot (1713–1784), for instance, defines beauty as the relations things possess by virtue of which we are able to understand nature in its genuine objectivity. Classicism in the arts is the claim that the timeless laws manifest in nature imply that there are rules derivable from those laws that apply to each artistic genre and that only if those rules are respected will the artist's work be beautiful. Similarly, scientists often argue that a machine works beautifully if it has been well designed, if its parts operate so that it fulfills its function smoothly and efficiently. The laws governing what works beautifully are themselves beautiful, and therefore laws that lack beauty are not likely to be adequate descriptions of what works. In this sense, a criterion of simplicity is often included in the conditions by which to assess a scientific hypothesis. For many purposes, Ptolemy's (90–168 C.E.) astronomy may be descriptively and predictively accurate, but its array of circles and epicycles are unnecessarily complicated and mathematically awkward compared to Johannes Kepler's (1571–1630) elegant ellipses. As William of Ockham (c. 1280–c. 1349) insisted, one should not multiply theoretical entities beyond necessity. Truth and Beauty, it would seem, have much in common after all.

Many thinkers, however, including most non-Western theorists, reject the notion that beauty is a universal objective reality. They argue that it is different in each of its instances. Beauty is the unique character of a thing, the way in which its specific elements are specifically related. The creation or the study of beautiful things is not a science but an art: conducting a tea ceremony, achieving inner peace through meditation or in action, freeing a statue from the marble block, telling an edifying story. For G. E. Moore (1873–1958), beauty is undefinable precisely because it is particular; it can only be directly experienced, like seeing the color red. Contemporary philosopher Mary Mothersill argues that a judgment of beauty is a logically singular judgment, based on radically contextual properties.

Subjective interpretations

Although there have always been those who claim that beauty is only in the eye of the beholder, modern science and the Cartesian separation of mind and body combined to reserve objectivity for physical bodies and their publicly-verifiable quantitative features. Beauty was therefore relegated to the realm of private mental things, to ideas and the sentiments. The Scottish philosopher David Hume (1711–1776) says that beauty is a matter of taste, a disinterested pleasure we take in certain of our sensations. The twentieth-century American poet and philosopher George Santayana (1863–1952) says beauty is pleasure objified: pleasure experienced as the quality of a thing, our subjective responses projected onto their source.

The extreme version of subjectivism is found in the claim by C. K. Ogden and I. A. Richards, made in the 1950s, that aesthetic judgments have no truth functional significance: They are neither true nor false but rather emotive ejaculations akin to saying "wow." Marxist and Postmodernist forms of relativism make this subjectivism a function of race, ethnicity, religion (ideology), economic class, political power, or gender, critiquing objectivity claims as attempts to hide their self-serving character.

People often agree about what is beautiful, however, so even if beauty is a subjective feeling it can be argued that it has an objective cause. In the eighteenth century, the philosopher Francis Hutcheson (1694–1746), for instance, argued that on the basis of our sense perceptions we discern by a sixth sense a uniformity pervading their variety and call our pleasure in this beauty. Immanuel Kant (1724–1804) calls this sixth sense our common sense. As with all our other experiences, the experience of beauty involves both intuition and understanding, both sensations and concepts. But whereas for scientific and practical purposes the concepts are imposed on the sensations, ordering them meaningfully, when we experience something as beautiful we allow the free play of imagination to associate our perceptions with notions of

meaning yet without their being imposed. We take what we experience as fraught with meaning but not any specifiable meaning. We take delight in this experience and so appreciate the world as involving more than what we can know about it or achieve by our actions upon it. Because these judgments involve conceptual and intuitive faculties that are the same for all human beings, they can be valid for others as well as ourselves: We have a common sense of beauty and hence our disputes about it can be rationally resolved.

Back to Plato

So Kant opens a way other than through politics, or religion, or scientific or philosophical theorizing for getting at the deeper realities underlying the world as it appears to us—through aesthetic appreciation and through the creation of works of art. Thus in the nineteenth century, Alexander Baumgarten (1714–1762) claimed that beauty is the sensory recognition of a transcendent unifying perfection. In the twentieth century, Martin Heidegger (1889–1976) argued that the beauty of a work of art, by disclosing the workly character of things, unconceals the creative source of the world's beings, their Being. We are back once more with Plato: There is a nonsensuous Reality disclosed by sensuous beauty, toward which we are drawn because of Beauty's power to break us free from the constraints of scientific understanding and our practical endeavors, to open us to the Good they obscure.

See also AESTHETICS; KANT, IMMANUEL; ORDER; PLATO; VALUE

Bibliography

Heidegger, Martin. "The Origin of the Work of Art." In *Philosophies of Art and Beauty,* eds. Albert Hofstadter and Richard Kuhns. New York: Modern Library, 1964.

Kant, Immanuel. *The Critique of Judgment* (1790), trans. J. H. Bernard. New York: Haefner, 1951.

Mothersill, Mary. *Beauty Restored.* Oxford: Clarendon Press, 1984.

Ogden, C.K. and Richards, I. A. *The Meaning of Meaning: The Influence of Language upon Thought and of the Science of Symbolism.* New York: Harcourt, Brace, 1959.

Plato. *Symposium,* trans. Alexander Nehamas and Paul Woodruff. In *Plato: Complete Works,* ed. John M. Cooper. Indianapolis, Ind.: Hackett, 1997.

Plotinus. *The Enneads,* trans. Stephen MacKenna. London: Faber and Faber, 1969.

Santayana, George. *The Sense of Beauty: Being the Outlines of Aesthetic Theory* (1896). Cambridge, Mass.: MIT Press, 1988.

Watts, Alan. *The Spirit of Zen: A Way of Life, Work, and Art in the Far East.* New York: Grove Press, 1960.

GEORGE ALLAN

BEHAVIORAL GENETICS

Behaviors distinguish human beings from other creatures and from each other. Genetic perspectives could help account for both the universals of human behavior (those shared by all) and the particulars (the individual differences). Behaviors are among the most complex attributes to study, but developments in behavioral genetics and the human genome project are producing new insights in this important area of study.

Behavioral genetics is a field that uses genetic methods to answer three questions about the nature and origin of individual differences in behavior: Is there good evidence for genetic influence on behavioral differences? How strong is this effect? Through what mediating steps do the genes influence the behavior? The manner in which such issues are addressed may have significant implications for one's conceptions of human nature, ethical responsibility, and freedom.

To answer these questions, behavioral geneticists use a variety of methods to study cognitive abilities, personality traits, psychiatric disorders, and other conditions. For example, results from family, twin, and adoption studies are carefully compared in order to analyze the differential effects of genetic background and rearing circumstances on the risk of specific behaviors in the offspring. Since the mid-1990s, the insights and methods developed in the human genome project have begun to shed light on the molecular pathways involved in brain development and function. This knowledge in turn may lead to better methods of intervention or treatment that are adapted to an individual's genetic makeup.

Such a strategy differs from that used in two other approaches. Behaviorism arose as a protest against introspective psychology and emphasized observable behavior in response to environmental stimuli, thus implying that behavior is shaped entirely by environmental forces. Sociobiology, on the other hand, emphasizes the role of an evolved, species-typical, nature for the behavior of a given organism.

Behavioral geneticists accept the view that behavior is influenced by both nature and nurture, but recent studies have shown that these components are not as independent as they were once thought to be. Some genes influence the way individuals select and shape experiences, while other genes can affect an individual's susceptibility to these experiences. Careful research designs are needed to sort out such gene/environment interactions and correlations.

Contrary to reports of a "novelty-seeking gene" or a "schizophrenia gene," researchers do not expect to find a single gene that explains a specific behavior (except in rare cases). Instead, multiple genes are associated with aspects of brain functioning that mediate one's preferences and capacities; these in turn influence one's likelihood of showing that behavior. In such situations any specific gene is likely have only a small effect.

Genetic research methodology may be inherently reductionistic, but this need not lead to explanatory reductionism. Genes never act in isolation, and their effects must always be interpreted in context. Individual genes can be turned on or off in response to signals from their environment, with the result that gene expression can even be modified indirectly by social interaction.

Clearly any evidence that DNA defines human beings and shapes their decision-making would appear to be incompatible with traditional understandings of human freedom and moral responsibility. The findings from behavioral genetics, however, indicate that genetic influences should be understood more as predispositions or limiting factors. An individual's genome may set boundaries on various traits and potential, but it does not determine how one will organize his or her life within those parameters.

In summary, genes are necessary for human existence and give people the ability to express those qualities that are distinctively human. Genes are not sufficient to account for all differences in behavior, however, since interactions with environment and individual experience are involved throughout life. An adequate view of human nature should be informed by an understanding of the effects of genes at many levels. Future research is likely to provide further evidence of the contributions of genes to psychological, social, moral, and religious behaviors.

See also BEHAVIORISM; SOCIOBIOLOGY

Bibliography

Anderson, V. Elving. "A Genetic View of Human Nature." In *Whatever Happened to the Soul? Scientific and Theological Portraits of Human Nature,* Warren S. Brown, Nancey Murphy, and H. Newton Malony, eds. Minneapolis, Minn.: Fortress Press, 1998.

Chapman, Audrey R. *Unprecedented Choices: Religious Ethics at the Frontiers of Genetic Science.* Minneapolis, Minn.: Fortress Press, 1999.

Cole-Turner, Ronald. *The New Genesis: Theology and the Genetic Revolution.* Louisville, Ky.: Westminster and John Knox Press, 1993.

Peters, Ted, ed. *Genetics: Issues of Social Justice.* Cleveland, Ohio: Pilgrim Press, 1998.

Plomin, Robert; DeFries, John C.; McClearn, Gerald E.; and McGuffin, P., eds. *Behavioral Genetics,* 4th edition. New York: W. H. Freeman, 2000.

V. ELVING ANDERSON
AUDREY R. CHAPMAN

BEHAVIORISM

Behaviorism as a positivistic anti-metaphysical science presupposes a highly mechanistic one-dimensional view of the human person and therefore is often seen as an attack on transcendence, the human soul, and human freedom. The British-American psychologist William McDougall (1871-1938) introduced behaviorism in *Psychology: The Study of Behavior* (1912) and independently the American psychologist John B. Watson (1878–1958) in his article "Psychology as a Behaviorist Views It" (1913). Watson began his essay stating: "Psychology as the behaviorist views it is a purely objective experimental branch of natural science. Its theoretical goal is the prediction and control of behavior" (p. 158). McDougall later distanced himself from Watson's mechanistic approach.

The predecessors of behaviorism

Among the predecessors of behaviorism were the British empiricist philosophers, including David Hume (1711–1776), who contended that sense impressions produce all ideas. American philosopher John Dewey (1859–1952), with whom Watson studied at the University of Chicago, introduced functionalism, which was concerned with the use of consciousness and behavior. Biologist Jacques Loeb (1859–1924), one of Watson's professors at Chicago, explained animal behavior in purely physical-chemical terms. Russian reflexology merged the mind with the brain, which was then explained in terms of reflexes; physiologist Ivan Pavlov (1849–1936) introduced experiential analysis of reflexes and their conditioning, and neurologist Vladimir Bekhterev (1857–1927) influenced Watson's interpretation of emotional behavior.

By drawing on neighboring branches of the sciences, behaviorists attempted to turn psychology into a hard science. In 1879, philosopher and psychologist Wilhelm Wundt (1832–1920) established an institute of experimental psychology in Leipzig, Germany. But Watson chided Wundt and his students that despite having made psychology into a science without soul, despite replacing the term *soul* with *consciousness,* they still maintained a dualistic concept of the human being. Since both soul and human consciousness elude the purely objective experimental method, they cannot be quantified and therefore do not exist for Watson. His methodological behaviorism, disallowing for the duality of mind and matter, was a materialistic monism or even a scarcely disguised atheism.

Methodological behaviorism

Between 1912 and the mid-1900s, methodological behaviorism dominated psychology in the United States and also had a wide international impact. Most important for the wider populous was the theory of learning, which was explained wholly or largely on facts and methods of conditioning.

From approximately 1930 to 1950 psychological research moved from the classic behaviorism of Watson to a neo-behaviorism. Psychologist Jacob Robert Kantor (1888–1984), schooled at the University of Chicago, believed that behavior was dependent upon the interaction of an organism with its environment. His "Organismic Psychology," later renamed "Interbehavioral Psychology," was promoted as an antidote to the notion that parts of the organism ad a causal responsibility for the rest of the organism's action.

Radical behaviorism

In his 1938 book *The Behavior of Organisms: An Experimental Analysis,* psychologist B. F. Skinner (1904–1990) introduced radical behaviorism. Skinner insisted that behavior should be studied as a function of external variables apart from any reference to mental or physiological states or processes. For him psychology was an experimental natural science. Fundamental to his approach was the analysis of behavior in light of stimuli. In 1948, he wrote *Walden Two,* a utopian novel where a social environment free of governments, religions, and capitalistic enterprises produced a "good life." In this work, Skinner advocated what some called behavioral engineering. In his book *Beyond Freedom and Dignity* (1971) Skinner asserted that the abolition of the concept of autonomous humanity is overdue. Rather, Skinner believed that human beings are controlled by their environment. The question is whether this control should be left to accidents, to tyrants, or to people themselves. Therefore Skinner opted for designing an existence aided by psychology which enables a happy life, defined by his wholehearted endorsement of the capitalistic system and his critical view of government and religion.

In 1932, psychologist Edward C. Tolman (1886–1959) published *Purposive Behavior in Animals and Man* in which he incorporated motifs and perceptions into psychological consideration. Purpose to him had not a theological, but a teleological meaning. Although Tolman was as skeptical about religion as the behaviorists who preceded him, he introduced a more holistic approach to behaviorism. Nevertheless he developed mechanistic rules to account for observed behavior.

Psychologist Clark L. Hull (1884–1952) distinguished between scientific empiricism and scientific theory in his 1943 book *Principles of Behavior: An Introduction to Behavior Theory.* While Hull did not deny the existence of a mind or a consciousness, he did not insist on its basic, logical, priority. Yet the mind was not a means for solving problems; to the contrary, it itself was a problem. This means that Hull was open to the insights of neurophysiology.

Behaviorism since the 1950s

At least since the 1950s, increasing skepticism arose about the claims of behaviorism, and a new humility emerged. Behaviorism never abandoned its scientific rigor, but rather became more multifaceted. While some continued to pursue the discernment of behavior using the language and the terms of physical science, others pursued a more teleological track by alternatively trying to understand why behavior is created and how behavior is created.

Even a new realism emerged with regard to human nature and its potential. Behavioral scientists such as zoologist Konrad Lorenz (1903–1989) no longer explained away evil, but understood aggressive behavior as an inherent part of life. In its excessive varieties, however, aggression signaled a breakdown of cultural ethos. Ethologists such as Irenaeus Eibl-Eibesfeldt (b. 1928) have shown that humans follow some inborn norms according to which they interact with the environment, such as fear of strangers and smiling during pleasant experiences. Finally, sociobiologists such as Edward O. Wilson (b. 1929) suggest that a species neither responds just to stimuli, as classical behaviorism maintained, nor is it only instinctively fixed. Rather, a species uses whatever is advantageous to its evolution.

Behaviorism has helped the experimental method become a constituent part of psychological research. Psychology has moved from philosophy and physiology to an independent enterprise in its own right by utilizing the tools and methods of physics, chemistry, computer science, and statistics. However, it is evident that although certain principles are demonstrated in the laboratory, there is no guarantee that they are significant outside it. The reductive nature of the laboratory is quite different from the complexity of the natural environment. We can never infer from laboratory experiments that we have identified all or even the most critical influences in nature.

In its history behaviorism has not rejected rigorous experimental and observational emphasis, but has become more discerning and tentative in its claims. It has realized that a human being is a complicated biological being whose socialization has greater influence in its development than is the case with other biological beings. Therefore a strictly mechanistic one-dimensional view has been found wanting. This multifaceted approach to human behavior opens the possibility for a renewed dialogue with the humanities, including theology, on such issues as human freedom and responsibility and even on transcendence.

See also AGGRESSION; HUME, DAVID; PSYCHOLOGY; PSYCHOLOGY OF RELIGION

Bibliography

Hull, Clark L. *Principles of Behavior: An Introduction to Behavior Theory*. New York: Appleton-Century-Crofts, 1943.

McDougall, William. *Psychology: the Study of Behavior* (1913). New York: Oxford University Press, 1959.

O'Donohue, William, and Kitchener, Richard, eds. *Handbook of Behaviorism*. New York: Academic Press, 1999.

Rachlin, Howard. *Introduction to Modern Behaviorism*, 2nd edition. San Francisco: W. H. Freeman, 1976.

Schwartz, Barry, and Lacey, Hugh. *Behaviorism, Science, and Human Nature*. New York: Norton, 1982.

Skinner, B. F. *The Behavior of Organisms: An Experimental Analysis*. New York: Appleton-Century-Crofts, 1938.

Skinner, B. F. *Walden Two*. New York: Macmillan, 1948.

Skinner, B. F. *Beyond Freedom and Dignity*. New York: Bantam, 1971.

Todd, James T., and Morris, Edward K., eds. *Modern Perspectives on John B. Watson and Classical Behaviorism*. Westport, Conn.: Greenwood Press, 1994.

Todd, James T., and Morris, Edward K., eds. *Modern Perspectives on B.F. Skinner and Contemporary Behaviorism*. Westport, Conn.: Greenwood Press, 1995.

Tolman, Edward C. *Purposive Behavior in Animals and Man*. New York: Appleton-Century-Crofts, 1932.

Uttal, William R. *The War Between Mentalism and Behaviorism: On the Accessibility of Mental Processes*. Mahwah, N.J.: Lawrence Erlbaum Associates, 2000.

Wann, T.W., ed. *Behaviorism and Phenomenology: Contrasting Bases for Modern Psychology*. Chicago: University of Chicago Press, 1964.

Watson, John B. "Psychology as a Behaviorist Views It." *Psychological Review* 20 (1913): 158–177.

Watson, John B. *Behaviorism*, Rev. edition. Chicago: University of Chicago Press, 1966.

HANS SCHWARZ

BIBLICAL COSMOLOGY

Cosmogony is the study of the creation of the universe. The Bible begins with God creating the heaven and the Earth, then the sun, moon, and stars, followed by every living creature that moves, and finally human beings, in God's own image (Gen. 1:1, 16, 21, 26). *Cosmology* examines the structure and evolution of the universe. The biblical worldview makes no provision for evolution; its universe is static, except for God's miracles. Regarding structure, God is said to have stretched out the firmament (heaven) like a tent (Ps. 103:2), rather than a sphere or the infinite expanse of later scientific beliefs. God's intervention on behalf of the army of Joshua, when God commanded the sun to stand still (Josh. 10:12–14), implies that the sun revolves around the Earth, rather than Earth rotating. Inevitably, aspects of biblical cosmology written long ago now conflict with changing scientific belief.

See also COSMOLOGY, RELIGIOUS AND PHILOSOPHICAL ASPECTS; GENESIS

NORRISS HETHERINGTON

BIBLICAL INTERPRETATION

See SCRIPTURAL INTERPRETATION

BIG BANG THEORY

The Big Bang Theory is based on the observation that all the stars and galaxies of the universe are in motion and not stationary. The American astronomer Edwin Hubble (1889–1953) discovered in 1929 that the light of all visible stars was redshifted. Hence the movement of the myriad of galaxies is not random but everything is moving further away. If all galaxies are now racing away from one another then at one point all matter must have been clustered together in an infinitely dense space and its present motion might best be explained by an original explosion of matter. Hence the term *Big Bang*. The 1965 discovery by Arno Penzias (b. 1933) and Robert Wilson (b. 1936) of the background radiation produced by the intense heat of this "explosion" served to further confirm the theory. The Big Bang Theory brought to an end the idea of a static universe and made respectable again discussions of the beginning and possible creation of the universe.

See also BIG CRUNCH THEORY; COSMOLOGY, PHYSICAL
ASPECTS; CREATION; INFLATIONARY UNIVERSE THEORY

MARK WORTHING

BIG CRUNCH THEORY

The Big Crunch Theory is made possible by Big Bang cosmology, which states that all matter in the universe is now racing away from all other matter. If there is enough matter in the universe to create a gravitational force sufficient to bring this movement to a halt and to reverse its direction, then at some point in the remote future all matter in the universe will converge into an infinitely dense point in space, resembling a massive black hole. The end of the universe would then resemble its beginning—a singularity at which the laws of physics as we know them no longer apply. Such a universe is called a *closed universe*.

See also BIG BANG THEORY; CLOSED UNIVERSE;
COSMOLOGY, PHYSICAL ASPECTS; SINGULARITY

MARK WORTHING

BIOCULTURAL EVOLUTION

See EVOLUTION, BIOCULTURAL

BIOLOGICAL DIVERSITY

Biological diversity, or biodiversity, is a generic term for the variety of life on Earth. Such variety is described in Genesis as the "swarms" of creatures Earth brings forth (Gen. 1:20-25). One basic measure of biodiversity is species, though other indicators run a spectrum from genetic alleles (variants) through ecosystems and landscapes. Estimates of the total number of existing species vary from three to ten million (and as much as thirty million),

with about 1.5 million described. The unknowns are mostly small invertebrates and microorganisms. Contemporary species inherit their diversity from forms that have gone extinct; diversity overall has increased over evolutionary history. Estimates of the number of species that humans place in jeopardy run from fifteen percent to twenty-five percent of the total. Scientists and religious persons may differ about evolutionary origins but seldom differ about the urgency of conserving biodiversity.

See also ECOLOGY; EVOLUTION

Bibliography

Levin, Simon Asher, ed. *Encyclopedia of Biodiversity*. San Diego, Calif.: Academic Press, 2001.

Rolston, Holmes, III. "Creation: God and Endangered Species." In *Biodiversity and Landscapes,* eds. Ke Chung Kim and Robert D. Weaver. New York: Cambridge University Press, 1994.

HOLMES ROLSTON, III

BIOLOGY

Biology is defined as the science of living organisms. The diversity of activities contained within the field of biology is immense, and includes research into the origins, functions, and interrelationships of organisms, as well as the technological application of biological knowledge.

The idea that living forms gradually emerged through a process of evolution from much simpler forms in a branch-like system is no longer a contested issue in biology. Research into the fossil record, or palaeontology, and other subdisciplines of biology, such as comparative anatomy, biogeography, embryology, and genetics, have helped to trace patterns of common descent, including those between humans and primates. Charles Darwin's (1809–1882) theory of natural selection forms the basis of evolutionary theory, though other processes such as genetic drift and molecular drive have been proposed in addition. The relative pace of natural selection continues to be the subject of ongoing debate. The dynamics of genetic change in a population include mutation rates, migration of individuals from one population to another, genetic drift, and natural selection. The anatomical and behavioral differences within and among known hominid species can be traced. Other extinct species of humans have been discovered, though the consensus seems to be that *Homo sapiens* has a single original ancestor, who probably lived in Africa.

Ecology has enabled scientists to study more closely the way living organisms relate to each other. While early ecologists believed that ecosystems were stable and in equilibrium, this thesis has gradually given way to a more dynamic view, where contingency is predominant. Ecology includes not just the relationship between local communities of living things, but also extends to wider global and planetary systems. Some ecologists emphasize the idea of self-regulation within living systems, or autopoiesis, as well as the idea of emergence, understood in terms of properties that cannot simply be explained by upward causation from molecular mechanisms. Biosemiotics applies concepts from semiotics to elaborate the specific emergence of meaning, intentionality, and a psychic world. The latter can be compared to sociobiology, which tries to explain particular aspects of animal and human behavior by envisaging a shared biological and genetic origin.

The use of biological research to address specific human needs through biotechnology was given a radical boost following the discovery of the structure of deoxyribonucleic acid (DNA) in the 1950s. The ability to move genes from one species to the next has opened up the possibility of even more radical human intervention in the evolutionary process. The most controversial changes are those that manipulate the human species. Nonetheless, changes in the nonhuman world also raise questions that are of concern to environmentalists. The general increase in technological and industrial activity has put considerable strain on the planet, which many biologists consider to be near its carrying capacity in terms of its ability to support the human population. Loss of species through, for example, habitat destruction, climate change, or direct exploitation has promoted a growing concern for an environmental ethic among secular and religious communities. Such questions move biology outside the realm of pure science into the realms of the politics and the economics of poverty, posterity, and social justice.

See also BIOSEMIOTICS; EVOLUTION; LIFE, ORIGINS OF; LIFE, RELIGIOUS AND SPIRITUAL ASPECTS; LIFE SCIENCES; SOCIOBIOLOGY

CELIA DEANE-DRUMMOND

BIOSEMIOTICS

Biosemiotics is a growing field that studies the production, action, and interpretation of signs (such as sounds, objects, smells, movements, but also signs on molecular scales normally not perceived by an organism) in the physical and biologic realm in an attempt to integrate the findings of biology and semiotics (the study of signs and symbols). One goal of biosemiotics is to form a new view of life and meaning as immanent features of the natural world.

Early pioneers of biosemiotics include Charles S. Peirce (1839–1914), Charles Morris (1901-1979), Jakob von Uexküll (1864-1944), Heini Hediger (1908-1992), Giorgio Prodi (1928-1987), Thomas A. Sebeok (1920-2001), and Thure von Uexküll (b.1908). Contemporary scholars include the biologists Jesper Hoffmeyer (b.1942), Kalevi Kull (b.1952), Alexei Sharov (b. 1954), and semioticians Floyd Merrell (b.1937), John Deely (b. 1942), Winfried Nöth (b. 1944), and Lucia Santaella (b.1944).

One of the central characteristics of living systems is the highly organized nature of their physical and chemical processes. These processes are based, in part, on the informational and molecular properties of what came to be known in the 1960s as the *genetic code*. Some distinguished biologists, such as Ernst Mayr, have viewed these properties as processes that distinguish life from anything else in the physical world, except, perhaps, computers. However, although the informational teleology (i.e., god-directedness based on the stored informational code) of a computer program is not an original form of teleology because the program is designed by humans to achieve specific goals, the teleology and informational characteristics of organisms are intrinsic because they evolved naturally through evolutionary processes. Traditional biology has regarded such processes as purely physical, adopting a restricted notion of the physical as having to do with only "efficient causation."

Biosemiotics attempts to use semiotic concepts to answer questions about the biologic and evolutionary emergence of meaning, intentionality, and a psychic world. Such questions are difficult to answer within a purely mechanist and physicalist framework. Biosemiotics sees the evolution of life and the evolution of semiotic systems as two aspects of the same process. The scientific approach to the origin and evolution of life has given us highly valuable accounts of the external aspects of the process, but has overlooked the inner qualitative aspects of sign action, leading to a reduced picture of causality.

Complex self-organized living systems are governed by formal and final causality. Such systems are *formal* in the sense of their *downward causation* from a whole structure (such as the organism) to its individual molecules, constraining their action but also endowing them with functional meanings in relation to the whole metabolism. Systems are *final* in the sense of their tendency to take habits and to generate future interpretants of the present sign actions. In this sense, biosemiotics draws upon the insights of fields like systems theory, theoretical biology, and the physics of complex self-organized systems.

Particular scientific fields like molecular biology, cognitive ethology, cognitive science, robotics, and neurobiology deal with information processes at various levels and thus spontaneously contribute to knowledge about *biosemiosis* (sign action in living systems). However, biosemiotics is not yet a specific disciplinary research program, but a general perspective on life that attempts to integrate such findings, and to build a new foundation for biology. It may help to resolve some forms of Cartesian dualism that are still haunting philosophers and scientists. By describing the continuity between matter and mind, biosemiotics may also help people understand higher forms of mind and the variety of religious experiences, although real interaction between biosemiotics and theology has yet to come.

See also BIOLOGY; CAUSATION; EMERGENCE; SEMIOTICS

Bibliography

Hoffmeyer, Jesper. *Signs of Meaning in the Universe,* trans. Barbara J. Haveland. Bloomington: Indiana University Press, 1996.

Kull, Kalevi, ed. *Jakob von Uexküll: A Paradigm for Biology and Semiotics.* Special issue of *Semiotica* 134, no. 1/4 (2001).

Sebeok, Thomas A., and Umiker-Sebeok, Jean, eds. *Biosemiotics. The Semiotic Web 1991.* Berlin and New York: Mouton de Gruyter, 1992.

Sebeok, Thomas A., Hoffmeyer, Jesper, and Emmeche, Claus, eds. *Biosemiotica.* Special issue of *Semiotica* 127, no. 1/4 (1999).

CLAUS EMMECHE

BIOTECHNOLOGY

Biotechnology is a set of techniques by which human beings modify living things or use them as tools. In its modern form, biotechnology uses the techniques of molecular biology to understand and manipulate the basic building blocks of living things. The earliest biotechnology, however, was the selective breeding of plants and animals to improve their food value. This was followed in time by the use of yeast to make bread, wine, and beer. These early forms of biotechnology began about ten thousand years ago and lie at the basis of human cultural evolution from small bands of hunter-gatherers to large, settled communities, cities, and nations, giving rise, in turn, to writing and other technologies. It is doubtful that, at the outset, the first biotechnologists understood the effects of their actions, and so the reason for their persistence in pursuing, for example, selective breeding over the hundreds of generations necessary to show much advantage in food value, remains something of a mystery.

The world's historic religions emerged within the context of agriculture and primitive biotechnology, and as one might expect they are at home in that context, for instance through their affirmation of agricultural festivals. In addition, Christianity took the view that nature itself has a history, according to which, nature originally was a perfectly ordered garden, but as a result of human refusal to live within limits, nature was cursed or disordered by its creator. The curse makes nature at once historic, disordered, both friendly and hostile to human life, and open to improvement through human work. These effects fall especially on human agriculture and childbirth, both of which are focal areas of biotechnology.

By the time of Charles Darwin (1809–1882), plant and animal breeders were deliberate and highly successful in applying techniques of selective breeding to achieve specific, intended results. Darwin's theory of evolution is built in part on his observation of the ability of animal breeders to modify species. The work of human breeders helped Darwin see that species are variable, dynamic, and subject to change. Inspired by the success of intentional selective breeding, Darwin proposed his theory of natural selection, by which nature unintentionally acts something like a human breeder. Nature, however, uses environmental selection, which favors certain individuals over others in breeding. The theory of natural selection, of course, led to a profound shift in human consciousness about the fluidity of life, which in turn fueled modern biotechnology and its view that life may be improved. While Christianity struggled with other implications of Darwinism, it did not object to the prospect that human beings can modify nature, perhaps even human nature.

The emergence of modern biotechnology

In the twentieth century, as biologists refined Darwin's proposal and explored its relationship to genetics, plant breeders such as Luther Burbank (1849–1926) and Norman Borlaug (1914–) took selective breeding to new levels of success, significantly increasing the quality and quantity of basic food crops. But it was the late twentieth-century breakthroughs in molecular biology and genetic engineering that established the technological basis for modern biotechnology. The discovery that units of hereditary information, or genes, reside in cells in a long molecule called deoxyribonucleic acid (or DNA) led to an understanding of the structure of DNA and the technology to manipulate it. Biotechnology is no longer limited to the genes found in nature or to those that could be moved within a species by breeding. Bioengineers can move genes from one species to another, from bacteria to human beings, and they can modify them within organisms.

The discovery in 1953 of the structure of DNA by Francis Crick (b. 1916) and James Watson (b. 1928) is but one key step in the story of molecular biology. Within two decades, this discovery opened the pathway to the knowledge of the so-called genetic alphabet or code of chemical bases that carry genetic information, an understanding of the relationship between that code and the proteins that result from it, and the ability to modify these structures and processes (genetic engineering). The decade of the 1980s saw the first *transgenic* mammals, which are mammals engineered to carry a gene from other species and to transmit it to their offspring, as well as important advances in the ability to multiply copies of DNA (polymerase chain reaction or PCR). The Human Genome Project, an international effort begun around 1990 to detail the entire DNA information contained in human cells, sparked the development of *bioinfomatics,* the use of powerful computers to acquire, store, share, and sort genetic information. As a result, not only is a standard human DNA sequence fully known (published in February 2001), but it is now possible to determine the detailed code in any DNA strand quickly and cheaply, a development likely to have wide applications in medicine and beyond.

Biotechnology is also dependent upon embryology and reproductive technology, a set of techniques by which animal reproduction is assisted or modified. These techniques were developed largely for agricultural purposes and include artificial insemination, in vitro fertilization, and other ways of manipulating embryos or the gametes that produce them. In 1978, the first in vitro human being was born, and new techniques are being added to what reproductive clinics can do to help women achieve pregnancy. These developments have been opposed by many Orthodox Christian and Roman Catholic theologians, by the Vatican, and by some Protestants, notably Paul Ramsey. Other faith traditions have generally accepted these technologies. In addition, some feminist scholars have criticized reproductive medicine as meeting the desires of men at the expense of women and their health.

Reproductive medicine, however it may be assessed on its own merits, does raise new concerns when it is joined with other forms of biotechnology, such as genetic testing and genetic engineering. In the 1990s, in vitro fertilization was joined with genetic testing, allowing physicians to work with couples at risk for a genetic disease by offering them the option of conceiving multiple embryos, screening them for disease before implantation, and implanting only those that were not likely to develop the disease. This technique, known as *preimplantation diagnosis,* is accepted as helpful by many Muslim, Jewish, and Protestant theologians, but is rejected by Orthodox Christians and in official Catholic statements. The ground for this objection is that the human embryo must be shown the respect due human life, all the more so because it is weak and vulnerable. It is permissible to treat the embryo as a patient, but not to harm it or discard it in order to treat infertility or to benefit another. The usual counterargument is to reject the view that the embryo should be respected as a human life or a person.

The significance of stem cells and cloning

Developments in cloning and in the science and technology of stem cells offer additional tools for biotechnology. In popular understanding, cloning is usually seen as a technique of reproduction, and of course it does have that potential. The birth of Dolly, the cloned sheep, announced in 1997, was a surprising achievement that suggests that any mammal, including human beings, can be created from a cell taken from a previously existing individual. Many who accept reproductive technology generally, including such techniques as in vitro fertilization, found themselves opposing human reproductive cloning, but they are not sure how to distinguish between the two in religiously or morally compelling ways. With few exceptions, however, religious institutions and leaders from all faith traditions have opposed human reproductive cloning, if only because the issues of safety seem insurmountable for the foreseeable future. At the same time, almost no one has addressed the religious or moral implications of the use of reproductive cloning for mammals other than human beings, although it has been suggested that it would not be wise or appropriate to use the technique to produce large herds of livestock for food because of the risk of a pathogen destroying the entire herd.

The technique used to create Dolly—the transfer of the nuclear DNA from an adult cell to an egg, thereby creating an embryo and starting it through its own developmental process—can serve purposes other than reproduction, and it is these other uses that are especially interesting to biotechnology. Of particular interest is the joining of the nuclear transfer technique with the use of embryonic stem cells to treat human disease. In 1998, researchers announced success in deriving human embryonic stem cells from donated embryos. These cells show promise for treating many diseases. Once derived, they seem to be capable of being cultured indefinitely, dividing and doubling in number about every thirty hours. As of 2002, researchers have some confidence that these cells can be implanted in the human body at the site of disease or injury, where they can proliferate and develop further, and thereby take up the function of cells that were destroyed or impaired.

Stem cells, of course, can be derived from sources other than the embryo, and research is underway to discover the promise of stem cells derived from alternative sources. There are two advantages in using these other sources. First, no embryos are destroyed in deriving these cells. For anyone who sets a high standard of protection for the human embryo, the destruction of the embryo calls into question the morality of any use of embryonic stem cells. Second, the use of stem cells from sources other than an embryo may mean that in time, medical researchers will learn how to derive healing cells from the patient's own body. The advantage here is that these cells, when implanted, will not be rejected by the patient's immune system. Embryonic stem cells, which may have advantages in terms of their developmental plasticity, are decidedly problematic because of the immune response.

One way to eliminate the immune response is to use nuclear transfer to create an embryo for the patient, harvesting stem cells from that embryo (thereby destroying it) and implanting these cells in the patient. Because they bear the patient's DNA, they should not be rejected. This approach is medically complicated, however, and involves the morally problematic step of creating an embryo to be destroyed for the benefit of another.

Nonhuman applications

As a result of the developments in the underlying science and technologies, biotechnology is able to modify any form of life in ways that seem to be limited only by the imagination or the market. Biotechnology has produced genetically modified microorganisms for purposes ranging from toxic waste clean-up to the production of medicine. For example, by inserting a human gene into a bacterium that is grown in bulk, biotechnology is able to create a living factory of organisms that have been engineered to make a specific human protein. Such technologies may also be used to enhance the virulence of organisms, to create weapons for bioterrorism, or to look for means of defense against such weapons. Aside from obvious concerns about weapons development, religious institutions and scholars have not objected to these uses of biotechnology, although some Protestant groups question the need for patents, especially when sought for specific genes.

Plants, perhaps the first organisms modified by the earliest biotechnology, remain the subject of intense efforts. Around the year 2000, major advances were made in plant genome research, leading to the possibility that the full gene system of some plant species can be studied in detail, and the ways in which plants respond to their environment may be understood as never before. Some attention is given to plants for pharmaceutical purposes, but the primary interest of biotechnology in plants is to improve their value and efficiency as sources of food. For instance, attempts have been made to increase the protein value of plants like rice. The dependence of farm plants on fertilizer and pesticides may also be reduced using biotechnology to engineer plants that, for instance, are resistant to certain insects.

In the 1990s, the expanding use of genetically modified plants in agriculture was met with growing concerns about their effects on health and on the environment. Adding proteins to plants by altering their genes might cause health problems for at least some who consume the plants, perhaps through rare allergic reactions. Genes that produce proteins harmful to some insects may cause harm to other organisms, and they might even jump from the modified farm plant to wild plants growing nearby. Furthermore, some believe that consumers have a right to avoid food that is altered by modern biotechnology, and so strict segregation and labeling must be required. Deeply held values about food and, to some extent, its religious significance underlie many of these concerns. In Europe and the United Kingdom, where public opposition to genetically modified food has been strong, some churches have objected to excessive reliance upon biotechnology in food production and have supported the right of consumers to choose, while at the same time recognizing that biotechnology can increase the amount and the value of food available to the world's neediest people.

Animals are also modified by biotechnology, and this raises additional concerns for animal welfare. Usually the purpose of the modification is related to human health. Biotechnologists may, for example, create animals that produce pharmaceuticals that are expressed, for instance, in milk, or they may create animal research models that mimic human disease. These modifications usually involve a change in the animal germline—that is, they are transmissible to future generations and they affect every cell in the body. Such animals may be patented, at least in some countries. All this raises concern about what some see as the commodification of life, the creation of unnecessary suffering for the animals, and a reductionistic attitude toward nature that sees animals as nothing but raw materials that may be reshaped according to human interest.

Human applications

It is the human applications of biotechnology, however, that elicit the most thorough and intense religious responses. As of 2002, genetic technologies are used to screen for a wide range of genetic conditions, but treatments for these diseases are slow to develop. Screening and testing of pregnancies, newborns, and adults have become widespread in medicine, and the resulting knowledge is used to plan for and sometimes prevent the development of disease, or to terminate a pregnancy in order to prevent the birth of an infant with foreseeable health problems. Some religious bodies, especially Roman Catholic and Orthodox Christian, vigorously criticize this use of genetic testing. One particular use of prenatal testing—to identify the sex of the unborn and to abort females—is thought to be widespread in cultures that put a high priority on having sons, even though it is universally criticized. It is believed that the uses of testing will grow, while the technologies to treat disease will lag behind.

Attempts at treatment lie along two general pathways: pharmaceuticals and gene therapy. Biotechnology offers new insight into the fundamental processes of disease, either by the creation of animal models or by insight into the functions of human cells. With this understanding, researchers are able to design pharmaceutical products with precise knowledge of their molecular and cellular effects, with greater awareness of which patients will benefit, and with fewer side effects. This is leading to a revolution in pharmaceutical products and is proving to be effective in treating a range of diseases, including cancer, but at rapidly increasing costs and amidst growing concerns about access to these benefits, especially in the poorest nations.

Gene therapy, begun in human beings in 1990, tries to treat disease by modifying the genes that affect its development. Originally the idea was to treat the classic genetic diseases, such as Tay Sachs or cystic fibrosis, and it is expected that in time this technique will offer some help in treating these diseases. But gene therapy will probably find far wider use in treating other diseases not usually seen as genetic because researchers have learned how genes play a role in the body's response to every disease. Modifying this response may be a pathway to novel therapies, by which the body treats itself from the molecular level. For instance, it has been shown that modified genes can trigger the regeneration of blood vessels around the heart. In time these approaches will probably be joined with stem cell techniques and with other cell technologies, giving medicine a range of new methods for modifying the body in order to regenerate cells and tissues.

Religious opinion has generally supported gene therapy, seeing it as essentially an extension of traditional therapies. At the same time, both religious scholars and bioethicists have begun to debate the prospect that these technologies will be used not just to treat disease but to modify traits, such as athletic or mental ability, that have nothing to do with disease, perhaps to enhance these traits for competitive reasons. Many accept the idea of therapy but reject enhancement, believing that there is a significant difference between the two goals. Many scholars, however, are skeptical about whether an unambiguous distinction can be drawn, much less enforced, between therapy and enhancement. Starting down the pathway of gene therapy may mean that human genetic enhancement is likely to follow. This prospect raises religious concerns that people who can afford to do so will acquire genetic advantages that will lead to further privilege, or that people will use these technologies to accommodate rather than challenge social prejudices.

It is also expected that these techniques will be joined with reproductive technologies, opening the prospect that future generations of humans can be modified. The prospect of such germline modification is greeted with fear and opposition by many, usually for reasons that suggest religious themes.

In Europe, germline modification is generally rejected as a violation of the human rights of future generations, specifically the right to be born with a genome unaffected by technology. In the United States, the opposition is less adamant but deeply apprehensive about issues of safety and about the long-term societal impact of what are popularly called "designer babies." Religious bodies have supported these concerns and have called either for total opposition or careful deliberation.

How far biotechnology can go is limited by the complexities of life processes, in particular in the subtleties of interaction between DNA and the environment. Biotechnology itself helps researchers discover these subtleties, and as much as biotechnology depends upon the sciences of biology and genetics, it must be noted that the influence between technology and science is reciprocal. The Human Genome Project, for instance, opened important new questions about human evolution and about how DNA results in proteins. Knowledge of the genomes of various species reveals that the relationship between human beings and distant species, such as single-celled or relatively simple organisms, turns out to be surprisingly close, suggesting that evolution conserves genes as species diverge.

Perhaps even more surprising is the way in which the Project has challenged the standard view in modern genetics of the tight relationship between each gene and its protein, the so-called dogma of one gene, one protein. It turns out that human beings have about one hundred thousand proteins but only about thirty-three thousand genes, and that genes are more elusive and dynamic than once thought. It appears that DNA sequences from various chromosomes assemble to become the functional gene, the complete template necessary to specify the protein, and that these various sequences can assemble in more than one way, leading to more than one protein. Such dynamic complexity allows some thirty-three thousand DNA coding sequences to function as the templates for one hundred thousand proteins. But this complexity, in view of the limited understanding of the processes that define it, means that the ability to modify DNA sequences may have limited success and unpredictable consequences, which should lower confidence in genetic engineering, especially when applied to human beings.

Biotechnology is further limited by financial factors. Most biotechnology is pursued within a commercial context, and the prospect of near-term financial return must be present to support research. Biotechnology depends upon access to capital and upon legal protection for intellectual property, such as the controversial policy of granting patent protection on DNA sequences or genes and on genetically modified organisms, including mammals. This financial dependence is itself a matter of controversy, giving rise to the fear that life itself is becoming a mere commodity or that the only values are those of the market.

A look ahead

There is no reason, however, to think that biotechnology has reached the limits of its powers. On the contrary, biotechnology is growing not just in the scope of its applications but in the range and power of its techniques. Biotechnology's access to the whole genomes of human beings and other species means that the dynamic action and interaction of the entire set of genes can be monitored. In one sense, the completion of full genomes ushers in what some have called post-genomic biotechnology, characterized by a new vantage point of a systematic overview of the cell and the organism. This is proving valuable, for instance, in opening new understandings of cancer as a series of mutation events within a set of cells in the body. Attention is turning, however, from the study of genes to the study of proteins, which are more numerous than genes but also more dynamic, coming quickly into and out of existence in the trillions of cells of the human body according to precise temporal and spatial signals. Most human proteins are created only in a small percentage of cells, during a limited period of human development, and only in precisely regulated quantities. Studying this full set of proteins, in all its functional dynamism, is a daunting task requiring technologies that do not exist at the beginning of the twenty-first century. The systematic study of proteins, called *proteomics,* may in fact become a new international project for biology, leading in time to a profound expansion of the powers of biotechnology.

In time, researchers will develop powerful new methods for modifying DNA, probably with far higher precision and effectiveness than current techniques allow, and perhaps with the ability to transfer large amounts of DNA into living cells and organisms. Computer power, which is essential to undertakings like the Human Genome Project and to their application, continues to grow, along with developments such as the so-called gene chip, using DNA as an integrated part of the computing device. Advances in engineering at the very small scale, known as *nanotechnology* (from *nanometer,* a billionth of a meter), suggest that molecular scale devices may someday be used to modify biological functions at the molecular level. For instance, nanotechnology devices in quantity may be inserted into the human body to enter cells, where they might modify DNA or other molecules. In another area of research, scientists are exploring the possibility that DNA itself may be used as a computer or a data storage device. DNA is capable of storing information more efficiently than current storage media, and it may be possible to exploit this capacity.

It is impossible to predict when new techniques will be developed or what powers they will bring. It is clear, however, that new techniques will be found and that they will converge in their effectiveness to modify life. Precisely designed pharmaceutical products will be available to treat nearly every disease, often by interrupting them at the molecular level and doing so in ways that match the specific needs of the patient. Stem cells, whether derived from embryos or from patients themselves, will probably be used to regenerate nearly any tissue or cell in the body, perhaps even portions of organs, including the brain. The genes in patients' bodies will be modified, either to correct a genetic anomaly that underlies a disease or to trigger a special response in specific cells to treat a disease or injury. It is more difficult to foresee the full extent of the long-term consequences of biotechnology on nonhuman species, on the ecosystem, on colonies of life beyond Earth, and on the human species itself; estimates vary in the extreme. Some suggest that through these means, human beings will engineer their own biological enhancements, perhaps becoming two or more species.

The prospect of these transformations has evoked various religious responses, and scholars from many traditions have been divided in their assessments. Those who support and endorse biotechnology stress religious duties to heal the sick and feed the hungry. Most hold the view that nature is to be improved, perhaps within limits, and that human beings are authorized to modify the processes of life. Some suggest that creation is not static but progressive, and that human beings are co-creators with God in the achievement of its full promise.

Others believe biotechnology will pervert nature and undermine human existence and its moral basis. They argue, for instance, that genetic modifications of offspring will damage the relationship between parents and children by reducing children to objects, products of technology, and limit their freedom to grow into persons in relationship with others. Some warn that saying yes to biotechnology now will make it impossible to say no in the future. Still others suggest that the point is not to try to stop biotechnology but to learn to live humanely with its powers, and as much as possible to steer it away from selfish or excessive uses and toward compassionate and just ends.

See also CLONING; DARWIN, CHARLES; DNA; EVOLUTION; EUGENICS; GENE PATENTING; GENE THERAPY; GENETICALLY MODIFIED ORGANISMS; GENETIC ENGINEERING; GENETICS; GENETIC TESTING; HUMAN GENOME PROJECT; IN VITRO FERTILIZATION; REPRODUCTIVE TECHNOLOGY; STEM CELL RESEARCH

Bibliography

American Association for the Advancement of Science. "Human Inheritable Genetic Modifications: Assessing Scientific, Ethical, Religious, and Policy Issues." Washington, D.C.: AAAS, 2000.

Bruce, Donald, and Bruce, Ann, eds. *Engineering Genesis: The Ethics of Genetic Engineering in Non-Human Species.* London: Earthscan Publications, 1998.

Chapman, Audrey R. *Unprecedented Choices: Religious Ethics at the Frontiers of Genetic Science.* Minneapolis, Minn.: Fortress Press, 1999.

Cole-Turner, Ronald. *The New Genesis: Theology and the Genetic Revolution.* Louisville, Ky.: Westminster and John Knox Press, 1993.

Cole-Turner, Ronald. *Beyond Cloning: Religion and the Remaking of Humanity.* Harrisburg, Pa.: Trinity Press International, 2001.

Dorff, Elliot N. *Matters of Life and Death: A Jewish Approach to Modern Medical Ethics.* Philadelphia, Pa.: Jewish Publication Society, 1998.

Dorff, Elliot N. "Jewish Views on Technology in Health Care." In *Claiming Power Over Life: Religion and Biotechnology Policy,* ed. Mark J. Hanson. Washington, D.C.: Georgetown University Press, 2001.

Evans, John H. *Playing God? Human Genetic Engineering and the Rationalization of Public Bioethical Debate.* Chicago: University of Chicago Press, 2002.

Genome Sequencing Consortium. "Initial Sequencing and Analysis of the Human Genome." *Nature* 409 (2001): 860–921.

Kilner, John F.; Pentz, Rebecca D.; and Young, Frank E., eds. *Genetic Ethics: Do the Ends Justify the Genes?* Grand Rapids, Mich.: Eerdmans, 1997.

National Council of Churches, Panel on Bioethical Concerns. *Genetic Engineering: Social and Ethical Consequences.* New York: Pilgrim Press, 1984.

Peacocke, Arthur R. *God and the New Biology.* San Francisco: Harper, 1986.

Peters, Ted. *Playing God? Genetic Determinism and Human Freedom.* New York: Routledge, 1997.

Peters, Ted, ed. *Genetics: Issues of Social Justice.* Cleveland, Ohio: Pilgrim Press, 1998.

Peterson, James C. *Genetic Turning Points: The Ethics of Human Genetic Intervention.* Grand Rapids, Mich.: Eerdmans, 2001.

Rahner, Karl. "The Problem of Genetic Manipulation." In *Theological Investigations,* Vol. 9, trans. G. Harrison. New York: Seabury, 1966.

Rahner, Karl. "The Experiment with Man: Theological Observations on Man's Self-Manipulation." In *Theological Investigations,* Vol. 9, trans. G. Harrison. New York: Seabury, 1966.

Ramsey, Paul. *Fabricated Man: The Ethics of Genetic Control.* New Haven, Conn.: Yale University Press, 1970.

Shinn, Roger Lincoln. *The New Genetics: Challenges for Science, Faith and Politics.* London and Wakefield, R.I.: Moyer Bell, 1996.

Venter, J. Craig, et. al. "The Sequence of the Human Genome." *Science* 291 (2001): 1304–1351.

Willer, Roger A., ed. *Genetic Testing and Screening: Critical Engagement at the Intersection of Faith and Science.* Minneapolis, Minn.: Kirk House, 1998.

World Council of Churches, Church and Society. *Manipulating Life: Ethical Issues in Genetic Engineering.* Geneva: World Council of Churches, 1982.

World Council of Churches, Church and Society. *Biotechnology: Its Challenges to the Churches and the World.* Geneva: World Council of Churches, 1989.

RONALD COLE-TURNER

BLACK HOLE

Modern astronomy has produced a theory about the life of stars in which the fate of a star crucially depends on how massive it is. Lighter stars might end as red dwarfs, and heavier stars as enormously dense but tiny neutron stars. The heaviest stars collapse in upon themselves, creating black holes. Black holes are called *black* because the gravitational force associated with them is so strong that no light can escape. The infinite gravitational attraction at the edge of an event horizon such as a black hole not only warps space but also warps time for the hypothetical observer near the black hole.

See also ASTROPHYSICS; COSMOLOGY, PHYSICAL ASPECTS; GRAVITATION; SINGULARITY

MARK WORTHING

BOHR, NIELS

For the first half of the twentieth century, as both physicist and natural philosopher, Niels Bohr was at the epicenter of the quantum revolution that gave physicists their understanding of the atomic structure of matter. Bohr's Institute for Theoretical Physics (now the Niels Bohr Institute) in Copenhagen, Denmark, was the central headquarters of this revolution, and Bohr was its most senior and respected spokesperson. His influence made this city of his birth the namesake for the position defended by supporters of the revolution: the so-called Copenhagen Interpretation, which became the dominant or orthodox understanding of quantum theory, even while remaining controversial and beset with numerous conceptual difficulties. Although the quantum revolution transformed theoretical physics utterly, making a return to the worldview of classical physics out of the question, Bohr's viewpoint never received unanimous acceptance; several of Bohr's peers, most notably Albert Einstein and Erwin Schrödinger, remained critical and designed various paradoxes to confront the party of Copenhagen. From 1927 onwards, Bohr and Einstein debated these issues, but the precise implications of their differing views remain a matter of intense discussion among historians and philosophers of science.

Early life and work

Born in 1885, Niels Bohr, and his younger brother Harald, a famed mathematician, came to maturity in Danish academic circles. Their father, a professor of physiology at the University of Copenhagen, was a close friend of the philosopher-psychologist Harald Høffding (1843–1931). The Bohr brothers were auditors and later participants in the intellectual discussions held in the Bohr home with Høffding and their father's other academic friends. Høffding, an eclectic thinker with a broadly Kantian outlook sympathetic to his friend William James's pragmatism, became Bohr's only formal teacher of philosophy.

After receiving his doctorate in physics from the University of Copenhagen in 1911, Bohr found his way to Manchester, England, where Ernest Rutherford had recently discovered a massive positively charged nucleus at the center of the atomic system. The young physicists surrounding Rutherford were eager to develop a theoretical model of a stable atomic system accounting for the then known evidence of atomic behavior. Starting from the assumption that no classical mechanical model would possibly yield a stable system, Bohr quickly sensed that the secret to atomic stability lay in the quantization of action already postulated in 1900 by the German physicist Max Planck (1853–1947) as a heuristic move toward a formula for black-body radiation consistent with observation.

Bohr's 1913 presentation of his atomic model astonished physicists by deriving the observed frequencies of the spectrum of the simplest atomic system, hydrogen. Bohr assumed two nonclassical postulates. The first proposed that atomic systems exist in a series of discrete "stationary states" in which, contrary to classical electrodynamics, they neither emit nor absorb radiation. The second postulate stipulated that when atomic systems interact with electromagnetic radiation, the energy emitted or absorbed is determined by the difference between the energy of the stationary states in which the system existed before and after the interaction and is a function of the frequency of the radiation. While Bohr used classical mechanical models of electrons orbiting a nucleus to derive the energy of the stationary states, those same classical pictures imply a radically unstable system, a conclusion explicitly denied by Bohr's first postulate. Moreover, in classical physics, the energy exchanged with radiation should be a function of the orbital characteristics of the electron in each stationary state, rather than the *difference* between two states. If one imagined the electron in a spatiotemporal trajectory "jumping" from one quantized stationary state to another, the electron would seemingly have to know to which orbit it was going the moment it departed its original orbit. Thus Bohr's 1913 model already gave the interaction between matter and radiation a *wholeness,* implying that the theoretical representation of such interactions in terms of visualizable, mechanical pictures could not be a realistic picture of microphysical processes.

Complementarity

From 1913 to 1925 Bohr pondered how the classical descriptive concepts were to be used in describing microphenomena while his model became the basis of much new research leading towards building up more complex atomic systems. Although it had many successes, ultimately this "old" quantum theory could not derive the intensities of spectral lines. In 1925 the German physicist Werner Heisenberg (1901–1976) formulated a *matrix mechanics* dispensing altogether with spatiotemporal models of atomic systems by replacing single numbered kinematic and dynamic parameters of position and momentum with matrices. A few months later Erwin Schrödinger (1887–1961) produced *wave mechanics,* generally held to be mathematically equivalent to Heisenberg's theory, though in a more tractable form. After intense discussions with Bohr and Schrödinger, Heisenberg derived the indeterminacy relations in the spring of 1927; that summer Bohr formulated his new "viewpoint" for understanding this quantum description, and named it *complementarity.*

Bohr's viewpoint of complementarity, originally presented in 1927 in Como, Italy, remains obscure and controversial, although he repeated the basic argument in many essays. Bohr argues that the use of concepts rests on presuppositions which, upon extending experience into new domains, may be discovered to be of restricted applicability, thus forcing a "rational generalization of classical physics which would permit the harmonious incorporation of the quantum of action"

(1987 [1963], p. 2). The quantization of action introduces a feature of "wholeness inherent in atomic processes, going far beyond the ancient idea of the limited divisibility of matter" (1987, p. 2). Thus a visualizable space-time picture of such interactions is merely a conceptual abstraction used for interpreting phenomena as interactions between microphysical particles and macroscopic observing systems that must be classically described. Measurements are interactions, but this indivisibility of interactions implies that the experimental arrangements required for determining both *kinematic* (space and time) and *dynamic* (momentum and energy) parameters defining a system's state are physically exclusive, although both are required for a complete definition of the system's state. Heisenberg's indeterminacy relations express formally the physical fact that the indivisibility of interaction prohibits defining the state of the system in terms in which both kinematic and dynamic properties have precise values. Classical deterministic predictions were possible because both properties could be predicated of systems only by neglecting the interaction involved in the measurement, but quantum predictions of observables are statistical because the interaction in which a kinematic parameter is well defined excludes the interaction in which a dynamic parameter can be defined.

Classical determinism requiring predication of a mechanical state with simultaneous arbitrarily precise values of kinematic and dynamic parameters now appears as an idealization attainable only in interactions that are enormous compared to the scale of the quantum of action. The paradoxical fact that, for defining the state of both matter and radiation, the system needs to be characterized using both wave and particle "pictures" has misled some interpreters to misread complementarity as a relation between *wave* and *particle* concepts. Classically both kinematic and dynamic measurements can be made in a single experimental arrangement because the effect of the interaction with the measuring system can be left out of the account. Therefore precise values of both position and momentum can be "combined into a consistent picture of the object under investigation" representing its objects as either particles (if matter) or as waves (if radiation). However, because of the wholeness of quantum interactions, Bohr concludes "evidence obtained by different experimental arrangements exhibits a novel kind of complementary relationship . . . which appears contradictory when combination into a single picture is attempted" (1987 [1963], p. 4). Representing the object as a "wave" or a "particle" proves contradictory because defining the state of a material system requires defining the particle's momentum, but in the quantum case to define the particle's momentum one must give it a wavelength, a property defined only by representing it as a wave. To define the state of radiation one must attribute to waves the property of momentum, which requires picturing the object as a particle. Thus *wave-particle dualism* arises from the complementary relation between the phenomena by which measurements of kinematic and dynamic parameters are empirically determined. Bohr held no other conceptual scheme avoiding this complementarity would be possible because to avoid "ambiguity" one must describe the measuring instruments in classical terms. This unambiguity is the foundation for the objectivity of the quantum description; thus Bohr abandons grounding objectivity in an ontological predication of properties of individuals.

Influence beyond physics

Bohr ventured beyond atomic physics to suggest that in other cases where the "analysis and synthesis" of experience encountered indivisible interactions analogous to quantum interactions, one must expect to employ complementary descriptions. In biology the wholeness of the organism-environment interaction necessary for displaying the phenomena of life, excludes the sort of isolation necessary for unambiguously defining the organism's state as a mechanical system, thereby leading to the necessity for a complementary combination of functional descriptions with mechanistic ones. Psychological descriptions of conscious experiences require the well known distinction between *empirical ego* (the object) and the *transcendental ego* (the subject) leading to the complementarity between deterministic description and that employing the notion of free will. In the human sciences Bohr called attention to the complementary relationship between descriptions of experience by persons within a culture or religious tradition and those of observers from another culture standing outside the cultural tradition being described, leading him to speak of different cultures and religious traditions as "complementary."

Bohr has often been presumed to be a positivist holding an antirealist or instrumentalist interpretation of atomic physics; however, his viewpoint arises from a *physical* discovery expressed in the quantization of action rather than an epistemological analysis along positivistic lines. He agrees that quantum physics bars a realistic visualizing of microphysical interactions, but it is clear that he regards atomic systems as independently real entities in nature, not as theoretical constructions. He seeks a radical revision of the conception of physical reality rather than its elimination from atomic physics. Although Bohr emphasized the epistemological lesson following from the indivisibility of observational interactions at the atomic level, he left unexplored the ontological implications of combining complementary descriptions of the same object appearing in different phenomena, thus inviting widely divergent philosophical interpretations of complementarity that continue to be debated.

See also COMPLEMENTARITY; COPENHAGEN
    INTERPRETATION; DETERMINISM; EINSTEIN, ALBERT;
    PHYSICS, QUANTUM; WAVE-PARTICLE DUALITY

Bibliography:

Beller, Mara. *Quantum Dialogue: The Making of a Revolution.* Chicago: University of Chicago Press, 1999.

Bohr, Niels. *Atomic Theory and the Description of Nature.* New York: Macmillan, 1934; Reprinted as *The Philosophical Writings of Niels Bohr: Volume 1.* Woodbridge, Conn.: Ox Bow Press, 1987.

Bohr, Niels. *Atomic Physics and Human Knowledge.* New York: Wiley, 1957; Reprinted as *The Philosophical Writings of Niels Bohr: Volume 2, Essays 1932–1957 on Atomic Physics and Human Knowledge.* Woodbridge, Conn.: Ox Bow Press, 1987.

Bohr, Niels. *Essays 1958–1962 on Atomic Physics and Human Knowledge.* New York: Wiley, 1963; Reprinted as *The Philosophical Writings of Niels Bohr: Volume 3.* Woodbridge, Conn.: Ox Bow Press, 1987.

Bohr, Niels. *The Philosophical Writings of Niels Bohr: Volume 4, Causality and Complementarity—Supplementary Papers,* eds. Jan Faye and Henry J. Folse. Woodbridge, Conn.: Ox Bow Press, 1998.

Faye, Jan. *Niels Bohr: His Heritage and Legacy. An Anti-Realist View of Quantum Mechanics.* Dordrecht, Netherlands: Kluwer Academic, 1991.

Faye, Jan, and Folse, Henry J., eds. *Niels Bohr and Contemporary Philosophy*. Dordrecht, Netherlands: Kluwer Academic, 1994.

Folse, Henry J. *The Philosophy of Niels Bohr: The Framework of Complementarity*. Amsterdam: North Holland Physics, 1985.

Honner, John. *The Description of Nature: Niels Bohr and the Philosophy of Quantum Physics*. Oxford: Clarendon Press, 1987.

Hooker, C. A. "The Nature of Quantum Mechanical Reality: Einstein vs Bohr." In *The Pittsburgh Studies in the Philosophy of Science*, Vol. 5, ed. R. G. Colodny. Pittsburgh, Pa.: University of Pittsburgh Press, 1972.

Murdoch, Dugald. *Niels Bohr's Philosophy of Physics*. Cambridge, UK: Cambridge University Press, 1987.

Pais, Abraham. *Niels Bohr's Times: in Physics, Philosophy, and Polity*. Oxford: Clarendon Press, 1991.

Petruccioli, Sandro. *Atoms, Metaphors, and Paradoxes: Niels Bohr and the Construction of a New Physics*. Cambridge, UK: Cambridge University Press, 1992.

HENRY J. FOLSE, JR.

BOTTOM-UP CAUSATION

See UPWARD CAUSATION

BOUNDARY CONDITIONS

Physical laws are characterized by their mathematical form, the values of universal constants, and the contingencies to which the laws apply—known as boundary conditions. For instance, Newton's Law of Universal Gravitation is an inverse square law (its mathematical form), employs the gravitational constant (a universal constant), and applies to certain boundary conditions (like the positions and momentums of the planets at a given time). Boundary conditions, because of their inherent contingency, hamper the physicist's search for a theory of everything. In addition, when the mathematical form of physical laws is nonlinear, as in chaotic systems, slight changes in boundary conditions can lead to enormous changes downstream.

See also COMPLEXITY; CHAOS THEORY

WILLIAM A. DEMBSKI

BUDDHISM

Originating with the life of the historical Buddha, Siddhartha Gautama, born in present-day Nepal in the sixth century B.C.E., varieties of Buddhism have developed and spread across the globe for the past 2,500 years. Though Buddhism by no means presents a uniform face in all cultures and time periods, Buddhist traditions do reveal certain common experiential contours, doctrinal themes, and ritual practices. Speaking experientially, Buddhism emphasizes disciplined introspection through a combination of meditative, recitative, and gestural sequences. Doctrinally, Buddhist teachings call attention to four primary themes: suffering, liberation, emptiness, and interdependence. And in terms of ritual practice, Buddhists engage in a combination of devotional offerings, initiatory rites, and other ceremonies to mark important spiritual and life-cycle transitions.

Buddhist history reflects three primary "vehicles" of Buddhist thought and practice: *Nikāya* (Individual Tradition, of which *Theravāda* Buddhism represents one strand); *Mahāyāna* (Great Vehicle); and *Vajrayāna* (Diamond Vehicle, also known as Tantric Buddhism). However, from a contemporary perspective, it remains difficult to know the extent to which these traditions operated autonomously from one another. It seems likely that a great degree of overlap existed between Buddhist traditions, as, for example, when a practitioner espousing Mahāyāna precepts also may have engaged in Tantric practices. Adherents of all three traditions exist throughout the world, though one traditionally associates Nikāya (primarily Theravāda) Buddhism with Southeast Asia; Mahāyāna Buddhism with historical India, China, and parts of Southeast Asia; and Vajrayāna Buddhism with historical India, Tibet, Japan, and, since the late nineteenth century, the West.

Buddhism concerns itself with science in, for example, its Tantric Vehicle. Tantric Buddhist texts occupy themselves with questions of cosmology, astronomy, embryology, and physiology, and they concisely weave religion and science together into a seamless fabric. An eleventh-century Sanskrit Buddhist Tantric text, the *Śrīlaghu Kāla-cakratantra* (or *Śrī Kālacakra* [Auspicious short Kālacakra Tantra]), constitutes a primary example of a religious text oriented toward meditative practice that also serves as the repository for highly developed scientific observations of the time. Divided into five chapters, the *Śrī Kālacakra* and its corresponding twelve-thousand-verse *Vimalaprabhā-tīkā* commentary contain five chapters in both Sanskrit and Tibetan redactions: (1) cosmology, the realm-space section; (2) physiology, the inner-self section; (3) initiation, the empowerment section; (4) generation stage, the practice section; and (5) completion stage, the gnosis section.

More specifically, the first chapter of the *Śrī Kālacakra,* sometimes referred to as *Outer Kāla-cakra,* presents a cosmological alternative to traditional Buddhist cosmology as articulated in the fourth century in Vasubandhu's *Abhidharmakośa* (Treasury of manifest knowledge) and its *Auto-commentary,* the *Abhidharmakośabhāsya.* The second chapter, sometimes referred to as *Inner Kālacakra,* outlines the physiology of the "subtle body" (Sanskrit, *śuksmadeha*), including its structure and function. This chapter also addresses the time cycle of breaths taken by a person during a day. According to this system, the vital-wind processes, which Tantric practitioners seek to control, situate the temporal divisions of the universe in the body. The third to fifth chapters of the *Śrī Kālacakra,* sometimes referred to as *Alternative Kālacakra,* include an explanation of the qualifications necessary for both guru and disciple and also describe the activities that precede empowerment, which include examining the initiation site, accumulating ritual materials, taking control of the site, creating a protective circle, and constructing the *Kālacakra* mandala. This third chapter also describes disciples' progress through the mandala, the guru's conferral of empowerment, and the concluding rituals that follow the empowerment ceremony. The fourth and fifth chapters of the *Śrī Kālacakra* focus on the practice of *Kālacakra's* six-limbed yoga. These practices include both *generation stage* and *completion stage* yogas.

See also BUDDHISM, CONTEMPORARY ISSUES IN SCIENCE AND RELIGION; BUDDHISM, HISTORY OF SCIENCE AND RELIGION

Bibliography

Dwivedi, Vrajavallabh, and Bahulkar, S. S., eds. *Vimala-prabhātīā of Kalki Śrī Pundarīka on Śrī Laghukāla-cakratantrarāja by Śrī Mañjuśrīyaśas,* Vol. 2. Sarnath, Varanasi, India: Central Institute of Higher Tibetan Studies, 1994.

Sopa, Geshe Lhundub. "The Kalachakra Tantra Initiation." In *The Wheel of Time: The Kalachakra in Context,* by Geshe Lhundub Sopa, Roger Jackson, and John Newman. Madison, Wis.: Deer Park Books, 1985.

Zahler, Leah. "Meditation and Cosmology: The Physical Basis of the Concentrations and Formless Absorptions According to dGe-lugs Tibetan Presentations." *Journal of the International Association of Buddhist Studies* 13, no.1 (1990): 53–78.

JENSINE ANDRESEN

BUDDHISM, CONTEMPORARY ISSUES IN SCIENCE AND RELIGION

Buddhist reflections on science are based on insights, doctrines, and practices that have evolved from the teachings and life of Siddhartha Gautama (c. 563–486 B.C.E.), the founder of Buddhism. The assumption that reality is in constant flux, together with the principle of *pratītyasamutpāda* (dependent co-arising or interdependence), the primacy of mind, and a holistic appreciation of health and the world, are a few of the ideas from which Buddhists have understood and critiqued science, its methods, and its conclusions. *Pratītyasamutpāda* articulates the Buddha's Weltanschauung and is the basis for his teachings. The subsequent development of Buddhist thought and practice explores different facets of this insight.

Pratītyasamutpāda and science

A compound of *pratitya* (meaning "based on" or "dependent on") and *samutpada* (meaning "to spring up together"), *pratītyasamutpāda* affirms the temporal efficacy between a cause and its result. This efficacy underlies the belief in karmic retribution and reward. The principle also recognizes the importance of conditions or indirect causes in generating a result; and explains the origin, persistence, disintegration, and disappearance of existents. *Pratītyasamutpāda* further asserts the formal and spatial reciprocity of all existents. This reciprocity pertains not just to physical entities but also mind (or cognition) and apprehended object. Mind and object are both the cause and the result of the other's existence.

Most Buddhists are open to the discoveries and theories of science, and they seek common ground between the findings of modern science and Buddhist doctrines and beliefs. Thus, though Darwinism met great resistance in the West, the Japanese, for example, deeply ingrained in the Buddhist acceptance of transience, found no difficulty with the concept that humans evolved from lesser forms of life. Transcience is an indisputable thesis for Buddhists. Buddhists examine in great detail the process of change, its phases and their duration, and its practical consequences.

The flowering of Buddhism in the West coincided with the interest in science that emerged from the post-Darwinian need to ground religious belief in new scientific understanding of reality. Moreover, Buddhists understand that objects and individuals are comprised of an ever-changing composite of elements of reality called *dharmas.* Originally dharma referred to social norms and responsibilities. Buddhists broadened its usage to mean the Good, Truth, Teaching, and Law. Dharma (meaning, literally, "thing") is peculiar to Buddhism and in early Buddhism designated the enduring building blocks of transient phenomena. This was an assertion that later, Mahāyān thinkers, came to dismiss. Dharma also refers to mind and its cognitive functions. Although distinct and irreducible, dharmas relate to other dharmas in time and space. The consideration of the momentary spatial and temporal intersection of dharmas prompted Chinese Buddists to further expand the meaning of dharma to include the notion of "event."

The Buddha left a legacy of "benevolent skepticism" of the unproven, an appreciation for relative values, and an empirico-rational problem solving method. As such, Buddhist "truths" are to be discarded if and when they are no longer beneficial. However, investigations into mind and the natural world are not ends in themselves, but are pursued for the purpose of relieving suffering, and many Asian Buddhists are troubled by certain advances of the biological sciences, such as cloning

and organ transplant, that challenge traditional views of life, death, and family lineage.

Beliefs and doctrine

Siddhartha Gautama began his spiritual journey with the question of human suffering. After six years of spiritual exercises Gautama realized the Dharma, the truth of *pratītyasamutpāda,* and became the Buddha, which means "Enlightened One." Buddha awakened to the reality that all things, beings, and events, are mutually dependent and irrevocably interrelated. *Pratītyasamutpāda* can be understood as a further development of the law of karma. Karma, literally "action" by living beings, explains the creation, persistence, and disintegration of the universe (*loka-dhātu*). Later, the *Avatamsaka sūtra* and other Mahāyāna Buddhist documents, which emerged in the first and second century, claimed that the universe is a creation and projection of mind. Existentially, karma accounts for an individual's present life situation, which was determined by the moral quality that his or her actions generated in the past. Similarly, deeds performed in one's present life determine one's station in the next.

Mahayana Buddhists accepted the early Buddhist understanding of the temporal efficacy of karma, but proceeded to expand *pratītyasamutpāda* to describe the formal and spatial relationship between and among dharmas. The relationship of a single dharma with the world, as well as with every other dharma, is outlined by the doctrine of *fajie yuanqi* (universal *pratītyasamutpāda*). In a mutually dependent world, each dharma assists in the creation and support of the world and every other dharma. At the same time, each dharma is supported by all other dharmas.

Fazang (643–712), the third patriarch of the Chinese Huayen school, detailed the temporal and spatial relationships among all dharmas with the "Ten Subtle Principles of the Unimpeded Fusion of *Pratītyasamutpāda,*" which is discussed in his *Huayen tanxuanji,* a commentary on the *Huayenching* (*Avatamsaka sūtra*). The Ten Principles describe the relationship between each dharma and every other dharma. Similarly, an individual is never conceptualized in isolation, but as part of a dynamic and ever-evolving society of other persons and the universe. Morally, *pratītya-samutpāda* engenders the virtues of responsibility and gratitude. More concretely, this vision of inter-dependence is true for the human person. Health is understood to be a balance among all the bodily functions and an integration of body and mind. The health of the individual is intimately linked with the health of society and the environment. While Buddhists are primarily interested in karma and *pratītyasamutpāda* as a principle of moral and spiritual causality, these notions are also used to explain the formation of and interactions in the physical and cognitive worlds.

Though Theravada and Mahayana Buddhists differ in their understanding of *pratītyasamutpāda*, they agree that change is the nature of reality, that suffering is endemic to the human condition, and that the realization of *Nirvana* results in the transcendence of change and suffering. Both traditions accept *anātman* (selflessness), a notion that the Buddha reasoned reflected the reality of the constantly changing relationships among the five *skandhas* (aggregates)—i.e., form, sensation, perception, mental formations, and consciousness—that constitute the psychological self. The *skandhas* are not substantial or eternally existing forms. The Buddha never denied there was an ontological self.

Theravada, the representative tradition of present-day South and Southeast Asia, and Sarvastivada, a once influential non-Mahayana school, further refined these five *skandhas* into seventy-five dharmas, or ontological elements of reality. Yogacara, a Mahayana tradition, lists a hundred dharmas. Systematic summarizations of these dharmas and their causal relationships are articulated by the fifth-century Theravadin master Buddhghosa in the *Visuddhimagga*, and by Vasubandhu (c. 400–480), a Sarvastivada apologist, in the *Abhidharmakośaśāstra*. In contrast, Mahayana, which represents the tradition of present day North and East Asia, proposed a more radical view, namely that dharmas themselves are devoid of essential essence. This view is proclaimed in the *Prajñaparamita-sutra* (*Heart Sutra*): Form is emptiness and emptiness is form.

Attitudes toward science

Assessment of the scientific method.
Buddhists do not reject the efficacy and benefits of science; they nonetheless critique the scientific method and the validity of the knowledge that is derived from science. Appealing to the *Abhidharmakośaśāstra's*

classification of four conditions, Izumi Yoshiharu faults the narrowness of observation employed by the scientific method to explain the appearance of an event. The *Abhidharmakośaśāstra*, which enumerates, in addition to the four conditions, six causes and five results, states in sum that the occurrence of an event is facilitated by dominant causes and contributory conditions. A dominant cause directly contributes to the fruition of a karmic event. For example, an acorn would be the dominant or direct cause of an oak tree because only an acorn can become an oak tree. Contributory conditions include sunlight and soil conditions, as well as adequate rainfall to nurture and sustain the acorn as it transforms from a sprout to a sapling and into a mature tree. Both causes and conditions are necessary for an event or being to appear. In addition, the *Abhidharmakośaśāstra* cites the necessity of passively efficacious karmic causes and conditions that do not prevent or hinder the occurrence of a result. For example, the violets in a garden have no direct relationship to the phases of the moon, but in so far as their blossoms do not prevent its rotation, they are considered causal conditions. The *Visuddhimagga*, which lists twelve kinds of karma into three categories, details a similar understanding.

Buddhists also question the validity of objective observation, which presumes an unchanging observer and phenomenon, since reality—things and beings—are in constant flux. Not only does an observer continually change, but different observers will observe the same phenomena differently. Further, Buddhists have determined through their meditative exercises that perception determines the way objects and events seem to exist. Taking their cue from such documents as the *Avatamsaka sūtra* and *Prajñāsāmadhi sūtra*, Buddhist thinkers such as Maitreya (c. 270–350), Asanga (c. 310–390), Vasubandu, and others from the Yogācāra tradition argued that the reality one perceives and knows is a transformation of one's mind. When a person sees a red rose, what the mind perceives are neural signals that have been converted from light waves that strike the retina of the eyes. Subsequently, the mind interprets and cognizes these signals. Buddhists do not deny the reality of the physical world. Additionally, one's moods and temperament, as well as one's physical and environmental conditions, influence how one sees the world. Perception varies from moment to moment and differs from person to person.

This mutuality between the observer and observed preoccupied early Buddhist and Yogācāra thinkers who explored in great detail the mutuality of mind and its object of perception. In the twentieth century, the German physicist Werner Heisenberg arrived at a similar conclusion in quantum physics. The Heisenberg Uncertainty Principle claims that on the subatomic level, one cannot know simultaneously with precision the velocity and position of an entity. The observer changes the very nature of the "reality" that is being measured.

The Buddhist doctrine of *pratītysamutpāda* also challenges the validity of scientific principles or any other paradigm as the arbitrator of truth. Science and its method survey only a limited spectrum of reality experienced by human beings. *Pratītysamutpāda*, which recognizes the importance of every dharma, validates multiple centers and shifting paradigms. The tenth of Fazang's Ten Principles, the principle of complete accommodation of principal and secondary dharmas, (*zhuban yuanming jude men*) describes the rationale for shifting paradigms. In an interdependent world, all dharmas are mutually supportive and mutually dependent. When a dharma is singled out, it becomes the principal dharma, and the remaining dharmas are relegated to a secondary status. Every dharma has the potential of alternately assuming the principal or secondary role. On a given occasion, a dharma may be the principal; on another, a second dharma may assume the principal role.

This idea of the shifting perspectives of an event is illustrated by Japanese director Akira Kurosawa's film *Rashomon* (1950). The "truth" is relative to a particular storyteller: the murdered samurai who speaks through a medium, his violated wife, the bandit, and the woodcutter who witnessed the event. Each retelling emphasizes the storyteller's version, while relegating other perspectives to a secondary role. To be truly objective, one must see an event from all possible vantage points. Shifting vantage points offer alternative perspectives of reality. One never fully discovers the nature of reality, which may remain forever ambiguous. Scientific paradigms, as Thomas Kuhn argued in his 1962 book *The Structure of Scientific Revolutions,* are forever shifting and riddled with unexamined prejudices and presumptions. Science, which is a visual rendering technique

perfected during the European Renaissance, sees a view from a single-fixed point, and, as such, it is hardly objective. As early as the third century B.C.E., Nāgājuna (c. 150–250 B.C.E., one of the primary thinker of Mahāyāna Buddhism and founder of the Madhyamaka school, had already established that all conceptual categories of understanding distort reality.

Environmental science. Buddhism shares a holistic paradigm of nature with the environmental sciences. The doctrine of *pratiitysamutpāda* sees the world as a single whole in which sentient life and the world that supports it are irrevocably intertwined. Buddhist "teachings emphasize the importance of coexisting with nature, rather than conquering it. . . . The very core of Buddhism evolves around compassion, encouraging a better respect for and tolerance of every human being and living thing sharing the planet" (Kabilsingh, p, 8). Mary Evelyn Tucker and Duncan Williams's *Buddhism and Ecology: The Interconnection of Dharma and Deeds,* a collection of papers presented at the 1996 proceedings of Earth Charter, set forth the Buddhist vision of ethical principles concerning the environment for the twenty-first century.

Organ transplant. Buddhist reflections of biotechnological advances such as gene therapy, cloning, and organ transplants, which have pushed the traditional boundaries of life, death, and personal identity, are grounded on the meaning of sentience and life. Buddhist medical theory is based on presuppositions of transience, the composite nature of persons, and a holistic understanding of the individual. Buddhists understand human life to be a fortuitous event that involves the coming together of innumerable causes and conditions. Death is the dissolution of the temporary coalescing of mind and body. Life is identified with sentience, which includes feelings and in its broadest sense encompasses animals, plants, and inanimate objects.

Like *Āyurveda,* the classic system of Indian medicine, on which it is based, Buddhist medicine assumes that the living body consists of a substratum of three humoral fluids—phlegm, bile, and wind—that circulate throughout interconnected channels of the body to ensure vital life functions. Health constitutes the proper balance and circulation of these humors. Buddhists learned long ago that a healthy body is required before one can discipline the mind for spiritual exercises. Buddhists have identified life with cardiopulmonary activity. Consequently, the absence of brain activity, the criterion used for organ transplants, does not necessarily signify the death of the person. Many Buddhists are of the opinion that as long as the body is warm, there is life, and they have resisted the harvesting of organs. Additionally, some think that a body, though cold, may feel pain when incisions are made to remove its organs.

Another pervasive attitude against organ transplants is the belief that life is impermanent and death is inevitable. Such efforts to extend life disrupt an individual's karmic life span. Moreover, organ transplants are possible only at the expense of another person's life, a violation of the precept to abstain from taking and profiting from another life. Consequently, some Buddhists advocate the development and use of artificial organs. However, those who favor transplants argue that the gift of life is the greatest gift an individual can give.

While Buddhist doctrine offers ample support for the reluctance of organ transplants among East Asian Buddhists, the Confucian notion of filial piety, which has been incorporated into their ritual and socio-cultural practices, is also influential. The opening lines of the Confucian text *Hsiao Ching* (Classic on filiality) states, "Filial piety is the basis of virtue and the source of our teachings. We receive our body, our hair, and skin from our parents, and we dare not destroy them." Chinese funerary practices insist that a person should be buried with every part of his or her body. Such reasoning sees the donation of one's organs to be an unfilial act. Receiving the heart of another person raises questions of family identity. The Japanese reluctance against organ transplants and organ donation is rooted in a pre-Buddhist notion of personhood, which holds that physical death marks the beginning of the spiritual life of a person. The spirit can mature or proceed to ancestorhood only if the body is interred with all of it parts.

Cloning. As of 2002, Buddhist reflections on cloning and genetic engineering have been few and mostly cautionary. Citing the sanctity of life, some Buddhists are concerned over the unforeseen consequences that biotechnology will have on human life and the environment. Others find repugnant the idea of cloning a human being to produce organs for use in transplantation.

However, invoking the Buddhist assumption that reality is in constant flux, the birth of Dolly, the first successfully cloned sheep, as well as the prospect of a human clone, are part of evolving reality. The birth of Dolly also raises issues of the continuity of family lineage. Genetic manipulation brings into question the relationship between prior generations, their progeny, and future generations.

Cognitive sciences. Buddhists have expended great energy in investigating and speculating on the nature of mind and cognitive functions. Psycho-spiritual phenomena experienced during meditative practice are the basis for the speculations and systemization of mind, mental functions, and the world. Further, the belief in successive rebirths means that mind is not an emergent property of life, but is one of the conditions for it. Thus the Buddhist would say, "I am, therefore I think." Invoking the theory of karma and the idea of successive lives, the energy of consciousness from a previous being is a necessary condition for the arising and development of life in the womb.

For the Yogācārins, mind and object (psychic impressions of the objective world) arise together. Since the mid 1970s, there has been a heightened interest in Buddhism and the neurosciences by academics in the West. The Dalai Lama and a number of neurologists, biologists, psychiatrists, physicists, and philosophers have organized "Mind and Life" meetings centering on the nature of mind. One result of these discussions was the publication of *The Embodied Mind* (1991) by Francisco J. Varela, Evan Thompson, and Eleanor Rosch. They explore the structure of the subjective experience through cybernetics, brain science, psychology, and artificial intelligence using Tibetan Abhidharma categories of mind and mental functions. James H. Austin's *Zen and the Brain* (1998) weaves brain research with his Zen experiences.

Conclusion

Buddhism's interest in science is essentially therapeutic—to relieve human suffering and to care for the earth. Though Buddhists are open to the discoveries of change, Asian Buddhists were almost universally wary of improper use of new knowledge, and thus have been preoccupied with the ethical issues generated by organ transplant and cloning. In contrast, Western scholars and Western converts to Buddhism tended to explore the implications of Buddhist ideas. Finally, different systems of knowledge are built on differing assumptions of reality, which in turn lead to different notions of reality and categories of understanding. For the Buddhist, Western science and its assumptions are just one of many ways of understanding reality. Most Buddhists, while acknowledging the scientific and technological domination of the West, continue to find correspondence and derive legitimacy for their vision of reality. Perhaps, as Izumi suggests, a science based on the complex notions of causality of the *Abhidharmakośaśāstra* might lead to alternative methods of observation, experimentation, and theories of reality (Izumi 1999, p. 63). An alternative science and methodology, for example, can perhaps be extrapolated from currently practiced Tibetan Buddhist medicine, which still preserves much of its original paradigm.

See also BIOTECHNOLOGY; CLONING; CYBERNETICS; DARWIN, CHARLES; ECOLOGY; EXPERIENCE, RELIGIOUS: COGNITIVE AND NEUROPHYSIOLOGICAL ASPECTS; GENE THERAPY; HEISENBERG'S UNCERTAINTY PRINCIPLE; KARMA; NEUROSCIENCES; PARADIGMS; QUANTUM FIELD THEORY

Bibliography

Austin, James A. *Zen and the Brain: Toward an Understanding of Meditation and Consciousness.* Cambridge, Mass.: MIT Press, 1998.

Azariah, Jayapaul; Azariah, Hilda; and Macer, Darryl R. J. *Bioethics in India: Proceedings of the International Bioethics Workshop in Madras: Bioethical Management of Biogeoresources.* Tsukuba Science City, Japan: Eubios Ethics Institute, 1998.

Buddhaghosa. *The Path of Purification* (*Visuddhimagga*), trans. Bhikkhu Ñanamoli. Colombo, Ceylon: R. Semage, 1956.

Capra, Fritjof. *The Tao of Physics: An Exploration of the Parallels Between Modern Physics and Eastern Mysticism.* Boulder, Colo.: Shambhala, 1975.

Dhammavihari, Bhikkhu. "Euthanasia: A Study in Relation to Original Theravāda Buddhist Thinking." Paper presented at the Y2000 Global Conference on Buddhism: In Face of the Third Millennium, Singapore, June 3–5, 2000.

Dow, Tsung-I. "Modern Science and the Rediscovery of Buddhism." In *Buddhism and the Emerging World Civilization: Essays in Honor of Nolan Pliney Jacobson,* eds. Ramakrishna Puligandla and David Lee Miller. Carbondale: Southern Illinois Press, 1996.

Epstein, Ron. "Genetic Engineering: A Buddhist Assessment." *Religion East and West,* no. 1 (2000): 39–47.

Hanh, Thich Nhat. *Interbeing: Commentaries on the Tiep Hien Precepts.* Berkeley, Calif.: Parallax Press, 1987.

Izumi, Yoshiharu. *Kagakusha no toku Bukkyō to sono tetsugaku* (A scientist's reflections of Buddhism and its philosophy). Tokyo: Gakkai shuppan senta, 1992.

Izumi, Yoshiharu. *Kagakusha ga tou: mirai wa aru ka: kagaku to bukkyō no kachi* (a scientist asks: is there a future? Values of science and Buddhism). Kyoto, Japan: Jinbun shoin, 1999.

Jayasuriay, W. F. *The Psychology and Philosophy of Buddhism.* Colombo, Ceylon: Young Men's Buddhist Association Press, 1963.

Kabilsingh, Chatsumarn. "How Buddhism can help protect nature." In *Tree of Life: Buddhism and the Protection of Nature,* ed. Shann Davies. Geneva, Switzerland: Buddhism Perception of Nature Project, 1987.

Kuhn, Thomas S. *The Structure of Scientific Revolutions,* 3rd edition. Chicago: University of Chicago Press, 1996.

Macer, Darryl R. J. *Bioethics is Love of Life: An Alternative Textbook.* Tsukuba Science City, Japan: Eubios Ethics Institute, 1998.

Meyer, Fernard. "Theory and Practice of Tibetan Medicine." In *Oriental Medicine: An Illustrated Guide to the Asian Arts of Healing,* eds. Jan Van Alphen and Anthony Aris. Boston: Shambhala, 1996.

Morioka, Masahiro. "Reconsidering Brain Death: A Lesson from Japan's Fifteen Years of Experience." *Hastings Center Report* 31, no. 4 (2001): 42–46.

Nakasone, Ronald Y. "The Opportunity of Cloning." In *Ethical Issues in Human Cloning: Cross Disciplinary Perspectives,* ed. Michael C. Branningan. New York: Seven Bridges Press, 2001.

Nakasone, Ronald Y. "Buddhist Views on Biotechnology". In *Encyclopedia of Ethical, Legal, and Policy Issues in Biotechnology,* eds. Thomas H. Murray and Maxwell J. Mehlmans. New York: Wiley, 2000.

Nakasone, Ronald Y. "An Unlikely Donor." In *Ethics and World Religions: Cross-Cultural Case Studies,* eds. Regina Wentzel Wolfe and Christine E. Gudorf. Maryknoll, N.Y.: Orbis Books, 1999.

Nakasone, Ronald Y. "Probing the Limits of Buddhist Thought: The Case of Theresa Ann Campo." In *Bukkyō shisō bunkashi ronso: Watanabe Takao kyōu kanreki kinen ronshu.* Kyoto, Japan: Nagata, 1997.

Ratanakul, Pinit. "Buddhism and Science: Allies or Enemies." Paper presented at the Mahidol University-Graduate Theological Union Buddhist Christian Dialogue Conference, Berkeley, Calif., April 6–7, 2001.

Richard, Matthieu, and Trinh Xuan Thuan. *The Quantum and the Lotus: A Journey to the Frontiers Where Science and Buddhism Meet.* New York: Crown, 2001.

Sadakata, Akira. *Buddhist Cosmology: Philosophy and Origins,* trans. Gaynor Sekimori. Tokyo: Kōsei, 1997.

"Shoji o tou-iryogenba o mejutte" (reflections on life and death—in the context of medical care). *Honganji shinpō,* no. 2725 (2001): 2

Sono Ayako. "Meditations on Organ Transplants from Brain-Dead Donors." *Japan Echo* 26, no. 4 (1999): 31–32.

Takefuji, Yoshikazu. "Bukkyōto no bai." (from the Buddhist devotee). In *Shūkyō to shizen kagaku* (religion and the natural sciences), Vol. 4, ed. Iwanami Koza. Tokyo: Iwanami shoten, 1992.

Tucker, Mary Evelyn, and Williams, Duncan R., eds. *Buddhism and Ecology: The Interconnection of Dharma and Deeds.* Cambridge, Mass.: Harvard University Center for the Study of World Religions, 1997.

Varela, Francisco J.; Thompson, Evan; and Rosch, Eleanor. *The Embodied Mind: Cognitive Science and Human Experience.* Cambridge, Mass.: MIT Press, 1991.

Verhoeven, Martin. "Buddhism and Science: Probing the Boundaries of Faith and Reason." *Religion East and West,* no. 1 (2001): 77–97.

Watanabe, Masao. *The Japanese and Western Science,* trans. Otto Theodor Benfey. Philadelphia: University of Pennsylvania Press, 1976.

Yōrō, Takeshi. "The Fuss over Brain Death and the Japanese Psyche." *Japan Echo* 26, no. 4 (1999): 28–32.

Other Resources

Rashomon. Directed by Akira Kurosawa. Daiei Motion Picture Co. Ltd. and Daiei Studio, 1950.

RONALD Y. NAKASONE

BUDDHISM, HISTORY OF SCIENCE AND RELIGION

The fundamental Buddhist ideas of interdependence and impermanence are based on a rational apprehension of the world that can be likened to the modern scientific method. Because of this basic shared approach, Buddhism and science doe not come into serious conflict. The primary concern of Buddhism is to relieve human spiritual suffering and not to clarify the laws of nature. Thus Buddhists have freely adopted the practical scientific technologies of each epoch and place. For Buddhists, scientific technology is neither good nor evil. However, Buddhism recognizes that a self-centered application of technology can harm the integrity of other life forms, and hard to these can in turn harm human beings. Buddhism emphasizes the holistic relationship of life and the harmonious coexistence of all beings and all things.

Essence of Buddhism

Buddhism was founded in northernwestern India by Gautama Buddha (463–383 B.C.E.), who realized the truth of *Pratītya-samutpāda* (interdependent co-arising). For Buddhists, *interdependence* means that all living beings are born through the intersection of causes and conditions, and all lives are supported by the existence of others. The term conveys two meanings. First, interdependence is a fundamental principle of universe. Though the world is full of distinctions, each being exists and evolves in harmony with the vast network of interdependence that sustains all life. The world is an interconnected, interdynamic, cooperative whole, not a collection of separate, oppositional parts. Buddhists understand that no being is unconditional, permanently fixed, or immutable. Nothing exists by itself. Second, interdependence is not a mechanical law of nature but is the reality of compassionate relationships. Awakening to interdependence cultivates a sense of consideration towards all beings. All beings are worthy of respect due to their mutuality. Each being is an irreplaceable existence of the universe. Buddhism teaches one how to see all sentient beings as fellow living beings and cultivate the empathic mind of oneness with others. In the *Sutta-nipata,* one of the oldest Buddhist scriptures, the Buddha discusses his view toward life as follows:

> Whatever living beings there be: feeble or strong, tall, stout or medium, short, small or large, without exception; seen or unseen, those dwelling far or near, those who are born or those who are to be born, may all beings be happy. Just as a mother would protect her only child at the risk of

her own life, even so, let him cultivate a boundless heart towards all beings. Just as a mother would protect her only child at the risk of her own life, even so, let him cultivate a boundless heart towards all beings. (*The Sutta-nipata,* p. 16)

The Buddha, according to this passage, everywhere and at all times respected all beings equally, without discrimination, and wished them happiness. Therefore, human beings should be aware of the truth of coexisting with other life forms through mutual support and should cultivate compassion toward other beings. The ultimate goal of Buddhist is to save both the self and others.

The relationship between Buddhism and science

Historically, Buddhists have placed highest value on a supermundane wisdom that is beyond secular attachments and have encouraged compassionate acts toward all living beings. For Buddhists, there was no need to take part in practices such as sacrificial rituals, divination, or astrology, which have been popular in the societies of the various countries Buddhism has entered. The natural sciences also never became a significant part of Buddhist practice, although Buddhists were eager to introduce into their practices the knowledge of medicine and pharmacology, as well as more practical scientific technologies from paper and ink making to metallurgy, sculpture, and architecture. Such practical knowledge provided them with advanced skills in building temples, carving and casting statues, and printing scriptures, all of which helped in spreading the teaching of Buddhism. It is well known that the concepts of zero and fractions were first discovered in India. The discovery of zero is considered to be related to the Buddhist concept of impermanence or *anatman* (no-self).

Science focuses on the external world and seeks to analyze objectively the phenomena of the universe, including human beings, to clarify the principle behind each phenomenon and to apply its discoveries to society to bring comfort to human lives. On the other hand, Buddhist teaching focuses mainly on the inner self as it faces the reality of suffering. The Buddhist path aims at pinpointing and eradicating causes of suffering for the sake of the accomplishment of the totality of the individual human being and that being's peace of mind.

Therefore, Buddhism, which focuses on the individual, did not develop a standpoint of observing the universe and natural phenomena objectively, and Buddhism did not attempt to formulate a mechanical model of the universe.

Buddhist cosmology is based on the concept that nature and human beings are not mutually opposing, but are harmoniously interdependent. Therefore, nature, or the external world, has never been considered as merely material existence within the cosmology of Buddhism. One of the most representative descriptions of the Buddhist cosmology appears in the *Abhidhaemakosabhasya* composed during the fifth century C.E. by Vasuvandhu, which states that at the foundation of the universe a vast ring of wind floats within empty space. The thickness of the ring is 1,600,000 *yojana* (one *yojana* is approximately seven miles) and its circumference is 1059 *yojanas*. Above the ring of wind there is a ring of water, and on the top of the water ring is a ring of metal. There is a layer of water, an ocean, above the metal ring. At the center of the ocean is a mountain named Sumeru. The height of the mountain is eighty thousand *yojanas*. Mount Sumeru is surrounded by nine mountain ranges and eight oceans, and the sun and moon circle around it. This is the world of the six realms of transmigration known as *samsara*.

The world of the six realms of transmigration consists of hell (*naraka*), the realm of hungry ghosts (*preta*), the realm of beasts (*tiryand*: the realm in which beasts kill each other), the realm of human beings (*manusa*: although humans are in the state of suffering, they have self awareness of their state of impermanence and ignorance and are capable of seeking the true living), the realm of titans (*asura*: deities of anger and fighting), and the realm of heavenly beings (*devas*). These six realms are all the world of suffering.

Until modern Western scientific theories describing the shape of the Earth and the structure of the solar system were introduced into Buddhist nations like India, China, and Japan, the majority of Buddhists believed that this cosmology truly represented the structure of the universe. However, Buddhist cosmology was not created as a chart of the Earth discovered through geographic survey or astronomical observation. Rather, Buddhist cosmology was a vision created spiritually by Indian Buddhist monks, both Theravada and Mahayana, who contemplated upon the towering Himalayan mountains in the north of the subcontinent. The purpose of this cosmological vision is to reveal the reality of this world, which is filled with defilements and sufferings as living beings transmigrate through the six realms of existence.

Buddhists meditate upon the concept of transmigration of the six realms of existence in order to awaken to truths of impermanence and vanity and to achieve the state of enlightenment, which is beyond the realms of ignorance. Even today, this spiritual cosmology of Buddhism remains respected within Buddhist communities throughout Southeast and East Asia.

India. The *Ayurveda,* a traditional Indian book on medicine that was adopted by Buddhism, discusses surgery, pediatrics, toxicology, and divine pharmacology. It even includes a skeletal chart of the human body. The Buddha is often referred to in Buddhist documents as the "Great and Good Physician" and "Great Doctor King." The Buddha's teaching is regarded as a kind of medicine that relieves human suffering and brings spiritual liberation. In the *Anguttara-nikaya,* the Buddha declared, "Caring for the ill is no different from caring for me." One who cares for a dying person, through that act of caring, reciprocally learns about the impermanence and preciousness of life. From the time of early Buddhism, and through the history of the religion in China and Japan, there have continually been movements to provide care compassionately to the sick.

During the third century B.C.E., King Asoka of the Mauryan Empire, after reflecting on the cruelty and evil of war, converted to the teaching of the Buddha, which taught compassion and peace. Based on Buddhism's egalitarian view of the original nature of all human beings, the king protected all religious traditions equally. He built hospitals for humans and animals, grew medicinal herbs, planted trees on the streets, and dug wells and ponds for the well-being of the people.

In the beginning of the second century C.E., during the reign of King Kaniska of the Kusana Empire, the royal physician Caraka, an ethicist and a Buddhist, compiled a great book on medicine. According to the book *Caraka-Samhita: The Collected Medical Treatments of Charaka,* human beings must strive to seek three goals: to respect all

lives, to obtain fulfilled lives, and to attain the happiness of enlightenment. In India, the practice of medicine was not an independent area of science, but was treated as an integrated part of Buddhism, philosophy, and ethics.

China and South East Asia. Numerous Mahayana and Theravada Buddhist scriptures dealing with the cure of general illnesses, eye maladies, and dental problems appear from about the late fourth century C.E., when advances in medicine and pharmacology were made. In Tibet, China, and South East Asia, the study of medicine and pharmacology was based on traditional Indian *ayurvedic* medicine. Additionally, in China Buddhists incorporated existing traditional medical practices including acupuncture, moxibustion (moxa-herb combustion treatment), and medicinal herbs to cure illnesses.

During the Tang dynasty, Chinese Buddhism reached its maturity in part through cultural exchanges with regions to the west. During the early eighth century, the monk Yixing (683–727), famous as an astronomer and mathematician in the capital city Changan, created the Tayan calendar at the request of the emperor Xuanzong in 727. An accurate calendar was essential because it was believed that the movements of the stars and planets had a great influence on the prosperity of the empire. The Tayan calendar was based on the existing Chinese calendar system but enhanced its accuracy through the use of astronomical observations. It remained the basis for calendar making for many centuries thereafter. The Tayan calendar was introduced to Japan in the seventh century and was used as the official calendar for almost one hundred years between the eighth and ninth centuries.

Korea and Japan. Many Buddhist monks from the Korean peninsula traveled to India and China to seek the true Buddhism. Others went to Japan to propagate and establish the foundations of Buddhism in this neighboring country. These monks greatly contributed to the creation of Japanese culture. For example, Huici, a Korean monk from Koguryo, went to Japan in 595 C.E. and was appointed the tutor of Prince Shotoku. In 602, the monk Guanle from Pekche introduced the studies of astronomy, geography, calendar making, and mathematics. In 610, Tanzheng, a Korean monk from Koguryo introduced the Chinese technologies and arts of painting, paper making, and ink production. These technologies were also transmitted to nations to the west as Chinese and Korean monks traveled to propagate Buddhism.

In Japan, Prince Shotoku, who studied the Buddhism and politics of the Chinese Sui Dynasty, is credited with introducing new Chinese architectural technology and encouraging the arts of paper and ink making during the seventh century. He built Buddhist temples for the sake of world peace and social equality. In the eighth century the Empress Komyo, influenced by the compassionate spirit of the Tang Dynasty, built the Hiden-in, a "house of compassion" with social welfare facilities providing shelters for the poor, sick, and orphaned, and the Seyaku-in, a "house of medicine" with its own medicinal herb garden and pharmacy offering free care and medicine for the poor. The world's oldest printed materials were Buddhist scriptures found in Korea and Japan. These include *Hyakumantou-darani,* Buddhist scriptures enshrined in three-story wooden *stupas,* which were made to pay tribute to the war dead in 764.

In Japan, physician-monks appear as early as the seventh century. Although these monks bore the title *zenji* (meditation master), they were not advanced *zazen* practitioners but medical care givers for emperors and aristocrats. The work of physician-monks included the techniques of acupuncture and moxibustion, the creation of medicinal compounds, surgery, internal medicine, pediatrics, ophthalmology, and obstetrics. They did not use the practices of esoteric Buddhism, such as mystical prayers and divination, for curing sickness.

From the seventh to twelfth centuries, monks from China, such as Ganjin, and Japanese monks who had studied in China, such as Saicho and Kukai, continued to introduce medical practices, including new medications and breathing exercises. Records indicate that monks in the Nara area—like Kiogan of Todaiji, Kikogan of Toshodaiji, and Hoshintan of Saidaiji—produced and marketed medicine to support the temple economy. During the thirteenth century, the Tendai School on Mount Hiei established a department of medicine within the monastic complex. From the sixteenth century, Jodo Shinshu temples in particular encouraged the production of medicine by popular medical practitioners and donated medicine for the sick.

During the 1920s, the work-oriented Morita therapy was developed within Japanese psychiatric medicine. Based on the teachings of Zen Buddhism, especially the concept of nonattachment, Morita therapy teaches that the more one tries to eliminate suffering, the more suffering becomes fixed in one's consciousness. Morita therapy involves giving up the attachment to suffering by living with suffering while doing physical work, nurturing the mind, and searching for a new and meaningful way to live. Morita therapy clearly contrasts with modern medical practices, which objectify illness as an enemy to be forcefully conquered.

In the 1980s the modern *vihara* movement in Japan, Korea, and Taiwan was created through the teamwork of specialists in Buddhism, medical care, and social welfare. The word *vihara* has several meanings: a temple (*shoja*) or a monastery (*soin*), peace of body and mind, a place for practicing asceticism, and a place for rest or a hospital. Learning from the spirit of hospice care developed by Christians, the *vihara* movement created a network of caregivers and facilities to provide humane and whole-hearted support for patients and their families. The aspiration of *vihara* is that patients and families are not left alone while they are under medical attention. The *vihara* movement, in accordance with the thought of the Japanese Buddhist cleric Shinran (1173–1262), does not aim to control people's minds to make them peaceful at the end of their lives. Nor does it judge people by the manner in which they die. The *vihara* movement accepts each person's death as a unique individual death. People shed tears in memory of the loved one after they are separated from them. The *vihara* movement is also important for the surviving family to learn from the memories of the deceased as guidance for their lives.

Historically, pharmacological research and the production of traditional medicines developed in areas in which the practice of Buddhism was strong. Buddhists did not believe that prayer cured sickness, nor did they give themselves up easily to illness as their unavoidable fate. Instead, Buddhists understood illness to result from causes and conditions, and they directly sought its eradication through the development of medications and treatments.

Tibet. In Tibetan Buddhism, natural science, medicine, and pharmacology are incorporated within Buddhist practice. Tibetan medicine is highly holistic. It emphasizes the integrated mind and body and their harmony with the entire universe. *Gyu shi* (four medical texts) written in the eighth century is one of the world's oldest documents on psychiatry.

At a Tibetan Buddhist hospital housed in a four-story modern building in downtown Lhasa, doctors who have also studied modern western medicine treat patients according to traditional Tibetan Buddhist medical practice. They consult charts of human anatomy showing the paths of respiratory tracts, arteries, and chi; charts of pressure points in the human body; and charts of plants and animals used for food. Buddhist doctors in Lhasa also use charts explaining how to diagnose illness by analyzing urine and blood, and they refer to *tanka* paintings of astronomical charts. This combination of charts represents the fundamental Tibetan Buddhist concept of the interrelatedness of the human body and the universe. This hospital is also attempting to compile a scientific analysis of the psychology of Buddhist enlightenment through modern psychology.

Buddhist encounters with modern Western science

When modern western science was first introduced to countries with large Buddhist populations, no major conflicts arose. Buddhists accepted western scientific technologies without much resistance. For example, in Japan during the nineteenth century, there emerged an idea of Japanese spirit and Western knowledge (*wakon yosai*), which entailed the introduction of Western knowledge and technology with respect to traditional Japanese spirituality.

Asian society through the twentieth century has never experienced a drastic transformation of worldview to parallel the European scientific revolution or the Renaissance. One explanation for this is that Asian religions do not posit a singular god that governs over human beings. In the West, however, distinctions of self and others, human beings and nature, and human beings and God are clear. Galileo Galilei's (1564–1642) mathematical vision of the universe and René Descartes's (1596–1650) dualistic distinction of matter and spirit became the foundation for the eventual emergence of advanced scientific technologies such as electronics and genetic engineering. Observing a phenomenon objectively to discover the principles of the

phenomenon is the starting point of modern science. For Buddhists, however, there exists no absolute being, and Buddhists need to nurture a sense of harmony and oneness with all things and beings. Humanity and nature are both precious existences, and the universe is composed of mutual supports for each existence. Therefore, modern scientific thinking, which analyzes nature and the universe as material, did not emerge.

Another reason that the modern scientific worldview was readily accepted in Buddhist nations is that Buddhism and science are both founded on the idea that everything in the universe has a cause. The Buddhist truth of interdependent co-arising is the concept that all phenomena are produced by the interrelatedness of things. Modern science also tries to clarify the cause of phenomena by the interrelatedness of matter. Because both Buddhism and science share this kind of rational thinking, Buddhists could easily accept modern science.

However, in Buddhism, understanding phenomena objectively by dividing self from others is considered to be an insufficient partial knowledge that will not bring a holistic understanding of the world. For example, there is a Buddhist analogy of "four visions of one water." For human beings, water is for drinking; for fish, water is a dwelling; for hungry ghosts (*preta*), water looks like a pool of pus; and for heavenly beings (*deva*), water is a beautiful jewel like lapis lazuli. This analogy demonstrates how all beings understand the water in different ways according to their own standpoints. For Buddhists, the existence of beings is not permanently static. Scientific knowledge discovered that a molecular of water consists of oxygen and hydrogen atoms. But this scientific view, while a type of knowledge, by no means captures the true quality of water. In the desert, water is as sweet as honey; for a person washed away by a flood, water is a threat. Buddhism teaches that there can be no understanding of the true quality of existence through attachment to a single viewpoint. Buddhism respects the unity of self and others by going beyond attachment to oneself and one's own perspective.

The Buddhist way of understanding phenomena is perhaps best described by the concept of the four wisdoms of the *Yogacara* school of Mahayana Buddhism. First, the wisdom of the perfect mirror is the wisdom of understanding all phenomena as they are, as if reflected in a clear mirror. Second, the wisdom of equality is the wisdom of understanding the fundamental nature shared by everything that exists. Third, the wisdom of wondrous observation is the wisdom of understanding all existences by their differences through the observation of the characteristics of each existence. Fourth, the wisdom of accomplishing what is to be done is the wisdom of qualitatively transforming the five human senses (touch, sound, sight, smell, taste) so as to act for the benefit and to perfect the existences of all living beings.

Buddhism and science in the twenty-first century

The relationship between science and Buddhism is not contradictory, for each can mutually understand the knowledge and wisdom of the other and bring benefits to humans and the Earth. But Buddhism teaches that people must avoid an extreme dependency on scientific technology because the application of technology has both beneficial and dangerous aspects. In this sense, Buddhists believe that it is necessary to bring a certain degree of regulation into the progress of science.

In order to nurture a productive relationship between Buddhism and science, three important attitudes should be maintained. First, there must be a transformation of viewpoint from self-centered interests to a universal vision. Second, people must respect the values of modern science, yet avoid reducing all existences to material or mathematical formulae. Third, people must stop simply discussing problems and start acting to protect living beings and the environment.

In 1989, the 14th Dalai Lama of Tibet discussed his idea of the relationship between Buddhism and science when he accepted the Nobel Peace Prize. The problems people face today, such as violent conflicts, destruction of nature, poverty, hunger, and so on, are human-created problems that can be resolved through human effort, understanding, and a sense of brotherhood and sisterhood. The Dalai Lama stated that people need to cultivate a universal responsibility for one another and the planet. Buddhists and the spiritual leaders of many other religions support the Dalai Lama's vision. Buddhists believe that people should not negate science simply by pointing out the harms created by modern science. Rather, scientists and religious leaders need to make more efforts to cooperate and depend on each other to bring happiness to Earth and humans.

See also BUDHISM; CHINESE RELIGIONS AND SCIENCE; TRANSMIGRATION

Bibliography

Clifford, Terry. *Tibetan Buddhist Medicine And Psychiatry: The Diamond Healing.* York Beach, Maine: Marine, Samuel Weiser, 1984.

Evelyn, Mary Tucker, and Williams, Duncan Ryuken, eds. *Buddhism and Ecology: The Interconnection of Dharma and Deeds.* Boston: Harvard University Press, 1998.

Hayashima, Kyosho; Takasaki, Jikido; and Maeda, Sengaku, eds. *Bukkyo Indo Shiso Jiten.* Tokyo: Shunjusha, 1987.

Hayward, Jeremy W., and Varela, Francisco J., eds. *Gentle Bridges: Conversations with the Dalai Lama on the Science of Mind.* Boston and London: Shambhala, 2001.

Matsunaga, Yukei. *Bukyo to Kagaku.* Tokyo: Iwanami Shoten, 1997.

Nakamura, Hajime. *Bukkyo-go Dai Jiten.* Tokyo: Tokyoshoseki, 1975.

Nakasone, Ronald Y. *Ethics of Enlightenment.* Freemont, Calif.: Dharma Cloud Publishers, 1990.

Piburn, Sidney, ed. *The Dalai Lama: A Policy of Kindness.* New York: Snow Lion Publications, 1990.

The Sutta-Nipata, trans. H. Saddhatissa. London: Curzon Press, 1985.

Watson, Gay; Batchelor, Stephen; and Claxton, Guy, eds. *The Psychology of Awakening: Buddhism, Science, and Our Day-To-Day Lives.* York Beach, Maine: Samuel Weiser, 2001.

NAOKI NABESHIMA

BUTTERFLY EFFECT

Butterfly Effect is a term coined by the American metereologist Edward Lorenz (b. 1917) to describe a special effect in chaos theory. Because of the iterative character of chaos theory, the slightest change in the initial conditions of a chaotic system can accumulate in the long run into an enormous effect. Because of this sensitivity to initial conditions, the state of a chaotic system is practically unpredictable in the long run, even though such systems are deterministic. Lorenz came up with a fanciful image to illustrate this effect: The flapping of a butterfly's wing in the Amazon can result in a tornado in China. Thus, the sensitivity of chaotic systems to initial conditions came to be called the Butterfly Effect.

See also CHAOS THEORY; UNPREDICTABILITY

WOLFGANG ACHTNER

CALVINISM

The term *Calvinism* was originally a polemical label meant to denigrate those deemed to be followers of the French reformer John Calvin (1509–1564). Those who in fact were most influenced by Calvin chose not to be named after a person—Calvin or anyone else—and instead most commonly referred to themselves as members of the "Church reformed according to the Word of God" or simply as "those of the cause."

If Calvinism cannot be traced exclusively to one person, it also cannot be reduced to the presence of two or three fixed teachings. If one is to judge from the Westminster Confession and Catechisms (1646–1647), the Heidelberg Catechism (1563), and the Second Helvetic Confession (1566), the most prominent components of Calvinism include the centrality of the person and work of the Mediator; the work of the Holy Spirit in the right interpretation of the normative Scriptures of the Old and New Testaments; the emphasis on the Church as the body of the elect and their assurance of salvation; justification and sanctification by grace alone through faith and the positive use of the law in guiding believers; the importance of the ordinary means of grace; and the need to translate the sovereignty of God into transforming political, educational, and economic structures. In polemical debate Calvinists were often divided over the implications of any given doctrine of predestination, especially concerning the question of free will and whether atonement is universal or limited.

See also CHRISTIANITY, REFORMED, ISSUES IN SCIENCE AND RELIGION

Bibliography

Graham, W. Fred, ed. *Later Calvinism: International Perspectives.* Kirksville, Mo.: Sixteenth Century Journal, 1994.

McNeill, John Thomas. *The History and Character of Calvinism.* New York: Oxford University Press, 1962.

Prestwich, Menna, ed. *International Calvinism: 1541–1715.* Oxford: Clarendon, 1985.

E. DAVID WILLIS

CARTESIANISM

Cartesianism is the name given to the philosophical movement initiated by French mathematician and philosopher René Descartes (1596–1650) on the basis of two key innovations. The first is Descartes's claim that material events, including most biological phenomena, can and must be explained without appeal to teleological principles or occult qualities, through laws of motion acting mechanically on microcorpuscular bodies having no properties beyond spatial extension and shape. Descartes's second claim, his *dualism,* is that the distinctive human properties of selective intentionality and free volition, dramatically manifest in the creative freedom of language, mark human beings off from other animals as innately possessed of an immaterial soul or mind that is ontologically independent of matter, characterized by infinite moral freedom, susceptible of a distinct happiness, and capable of continued existence after the body's demise.

In Descartes's day, the first claim was by far the most controversial: how can living, breathing beings, plants and bees and horses, emerge from purely mechanical laws acting invariably on inert matter? As a program for physics, Descartes's elegant reductionism was fatally undermined when Isaac Newton in 1687 successfully accounted for universal gravitation by adding without metaphysical justification the notion of force. However, Cartesian mechanistic parameters continued fruitfully to guide biology and experimental physiology, shaping the speculative outlook of such diverse scientists as Julien de la Mettrie (1709–1751) and Claude Bernard (1813–1878). Today, Cartesianism survives in the methodological premise, also adopted by Newtonians, that a large part of sensible phenomena derives from causes acting invariably, without intention or free volition.

See also DESCARTES, RENÉ; DUALISM; MATERIALISM; NATURALISM; PHYSICALISM, REDUCTIVE AND NONREDUCTIVE; REDUCTIONISM

Bibliography

Gerber, Daniel. *Descartes' Metaphysical Physics*. Chicago: University of Chicago Press, 1992.

Marion, Jean-Luc. *On Descartes' Metaphysical Prism: The Constitution and the Limits of Onto-Theo-Logy in Cartesian Thought*, trans. Jeffrey L. Kosky. Chicago: University of Chicago Press, 1999.

Nadler, Stephen. *Causation in Early Modern Philosophy: Cartesianism, Occasionalism, and Preestablished Harmony*. University Park: Pennsylvania State University Press, 1993.

ANNE A. DAVENPORT

CATASTROPHISM

Catastrophism is a doctrine originally proposed by French zoologist Georges Cuvier (1769–1832) in 1810 to explain large geological and biological changes in the earth's history. The discovery of extinct animal and plant species under a coarse superficial deposit (diluvium) lead English geologist William Buckland (1784–1856) and others to suggest that this was caused by the biblical flood, which was then followed by the divine recreation of the animal and plant species living today (creationism). Scottish geologist Charles Lyell (1797–1875) rejected catastrophism and suggested that the same geological forces apparent today had always been at work on the earth, gradually changing the earth's surface and its biological species (gradualism). Today diluvium is attributed to glacial drift.

See also CREATIONISM; GRADUALISM

ARN O. GYLDENHOLM

CATHOLICISM

See CHRISTIANITY, ROMAN CATHOLIC, ISSUES IN SCIENCE AND RELIGION

CAUSALITY, PRIMARY AND SECONDARY

In the history of Christian thought, the philosopher Thomas Aquinas (c. 1225–1274) refers to God as the "Primary Cause" of the being of everything; Aquinas refers to creatures as "secondary causes" whose activity reaches particular aspects and depends on divine action. These concepts are related to core Christian ideas of God and creatures. God's being does not depend on anything outside God, is self-sufficient, and is the fountain of the being of all that exists. Creatures have their own consistency but require the divine founding action that makes possible their existence and activity.

The Primary Cause is unique. It is not the first of a series of causes belonging to the same level. God's action is different from created action. God does not substitute creatures (except in miracles). God not only respects the activity of the creatures, God is its main guarantee, as created agency corresponds to God's plans.

These ideas have often been appropriated by religion to speak of God's complementary action in the world of creatures. God creates in order to communicate being and perfection, and creatures fulfill God's plans when they deploy their capacities and reach their perfection.

Empirical science studies the nature and activity of secondary causes. Metaphysics and theology study divine action and the spiritual dimensions of the human being. These two perspectives should be different and complementary, but are not necessary opposed.

Difficulties in harmonizing evolution and God's action often resulted from disregarding the distinction between first order and second order causality. Cosmic and biological evolution can be considered as the deployment of the potentialities that God has placed within created beings. Natural finality and God's plans also correspond to two related but different levels.

The modern scientific worldview shows that natural beings possess an inner dynamism that produces new results that have ever increasing degrees of complexity. In natural processes the concept of information plays a central role. Natural information exists coded in dynamic structures, and its deployment produces new structures. Natural activity shows a high degree of creativity which, in conjunction with the subtlety of natural processes and their results, could be seen as coherent with the existence of a divine plan. The new paradigm of self-organization was metaphorically anticipated by Aquinas who wrote in his *Commentary on Aristotle's Physics*: "Nature is nothing but the plan of some art, namely a divine one, put into things themselves, by which those things move towards a concrete end: as if the man who builds up a ship could give to the pieces of wood that they could move by themselves to produce the form of the ship" (p. 124).

This worldview does not lead to metaphysical or theological consequences by itself. Reflection upon it, however, paves the way for an understanding of natural agency as supported by a founding divine action that does not oppose nature but rather provides it with its ultimate grounding. The world can be represented as an unfinished symphony where human beings have a role to play.

See also CAUSATION; DIVINE ACTION; THOMAS AQUINAS

Bibliography

Artigas, Mariano. *The Mind of the Universe: Understanding Science and Religion.* Philadelphia and London: Templeton Foundation Press, 2001.

Gilson, Étienne. *Being and Some Philosophers.* Toronto, Ont.: Pontifical Institute of Mediaeval Studies, 1952.

Thomas Aquinas. *Commentary on Aristotle's Physics,* trans. Richard J. Blackwell, Richard J. Speth, W. Edmund Thirkel. New Haven, Conn.: Yale University Press, 1963. Reprint Notre Dame, Ind.: Dumb Ox Books, 1999.

MARIANO ARTIGAS

CAUSATION

The notion of cause is one of the most common yet thorniest concepts in the history of philosophy. This should come as no surprise. Questions of causation tie up with such divisive issues as determinism and moral responsibility, as well as with the principle of the causal closure of the physical universe and the possibility of divine action. Furthermore, causation is intimately intertwined with the notion of change. Together these two notions stood at the cradle of such momentous intellectual traditions as Western philosophy in Asia Minor, the Vedic hymns and the Upanishads in Central and South Asia, and early Buddhism along the borders of the ancient Ganges. They constituted the first and fundamental challenge to systematic thought, inspiring a variety of solutions still resonating in intellectual debates.

People use causal idiom in everyday life with great ease, yet upon closer scrutiny this family of notions seems to defy analysis and justification. The famous comment of Augustine of Hippo (354–430) regarding the question of time applies with equal force to the analogous question concerning causation: When nobody asks us, we know what it means; when queried, we don't.

Quite generally, a *cause* produces something called the *effect*; and the effect can be explained in terms of the cause. Usually the effect is taken to be a change in something already existing. Yet in traditional theology it has also been assumed that causes may give rise to new substances out of nothing. Thus in the Judeo-Christian tradition God is seen as the creator of the universe, which God created out of nothing. Similarly, theories of self-causation and creation by God were two of the major causal theories in the Vedic tradition. By contrast, early Buddhism rejected these two views, arguing that the idea of self-causation would imply the prior existence of the effect, while the idea of external causation would imply the production of a nonexistent effect out of nothing. Similarly, Thomas Aquinas (c. 1225–1274) rejected the theological notion of self-causation as philosophically untenable. God cannot possibly be regarded as *causa sui,* he argued, since either God existed to cause God, in which case God did not need to cause God; or else God did not yet exist, in which case God could not be anything to be able to cause God.

Aristotle's theory of causation

Aristotle (384–322 B.C.E.), too, regarded causes as producing changes in preexisting substances only. To be sure, when a moth emerges from a caterpillar the change is so striking that a new word is naturally used for the causal product. And yet the moth emerged from the pre-existing caterpillar. By contrast, when a leaf turns red, it is still called a leaf, because the change is less striking. Aristotle called the former type of change *generation,* as opposed to the merely qualitative change—or, in his terminology, motion (*kinesis*)—taking place in the latter kind of case. Yet the distinction is plainly a relative one, opposing rather than licensing the idea of new substances being producible out of nothing by a cause. Indeed, the conception of creation *ex nihilo* is foreign to the whole tradition of ancient Greek thought.

Commenting on Plato (428–347 B.C.E.) as well as on his pre-Socratic predecessors, Aristotle famously distinguished four types of causes or explanatory principles (the Greek word *aitia* is ambiguous between these two rather different meanings). A statue of Zeus, for example, is wrought by a sculptor (its efficient cause or *causa efficiens,* also known as the *causa quod*) out of marble (the material cause or *causa materialis*), which thereby takes on the shape the artist has in mind (the formal cause or *causa formalis*) in order that it may serve as an object of worship (the final cause or *causa finalis,* also known as the *causa ut*). Plato's forms, or formal causes (*causa exemplaris*), had been transcendent ideas in the mind of the Demiurge. By contrast, in Aristotle's theory of natural change the four causes together have an immanent teleological character. The form being developed is an integral part of the thing itself. Thus, the formal cause for an acorn developing

into an oak tree is the seed's intrinsic character disposing it to become an oak tree rather than, say, a maple tree.

Naturally Aristotle's largely teleological theory of causation authorized the abundant use of final causes in explanations of natural phenomena. Thus his theory of motion espoused the principle that objects strive toward their *locus naturalis,* while medieval hydraulics—just to give another example—promulgated the principle that nature abhors a vacuum (*Natura abhorret vacuum*).

Mechanicism and the demise of the teleological theory of causation

While medieval scholastic thought was still dominated by Aristotle's theory of causation, seventeenth-century science opposed its teleological underpinnings. Natural order and change, it claimed, could be produced by "blind" efficient causation alone, without the need of final or formal causes intervening in the process. Having created the matter of the universe together with the laws of mechanics, God could have left the world to its own in any disordered fashion, claims René Descartes (1596–1650) in *Le Monde,* and yet in due course the universe would have taken on its current natural order of celestial motions and "terrestrial" physics mechanically, driven blindly by efficient causes alone and without "striving" to achieve any final perfections or divine purposes.

This conception of the causal "machinery" of the universe being limited to efficient causation presented a stimulating and exceedingly fruitful research program to modern science. In due course its validity was proclaimed to extend not just to mechanics proper, but also to physiology and chemistry, to biology (in the Darwinian program), to ethology, and even to the realm of human action in twentieth-century sociobiology and of human thought in late-twentieth-century cognitive science. And yet, from the very start, the program spawned riddles and grave philosophical difficulties. Chief among these was the difficulty involved in the widely held view that linked (efficient) causation to necessity. David Hume (1711–1776) notoriously pointed out that causal pairs are related neither by logical nor by empirical necessity. It is both logically and empirically possible for an effect to fail to follow a given cause. In fact Hume's influential argument had a theological background.

French theological tradition, including notably Descartes and Nicolas Malebranche (1638–1715), had always been keen to stress the point that God's freedom is unfettered by any restrictions whatsoever. Hence given any cause, God is always free not to permit the effect to follow. Thus, causes alone, unaccompanied by the will of God, are never sufficient conditions for their effects. Nor, given God's omnipotence, can they be allowed to be necessary conditions for their effects. For God is free to bring about the effect by any other mediating cause or even by simply willing it.

Having failed to find an empirical basis for the idea of necessary connection in the case of *singular* causation, Hume turned his attention (without making a clear distinction) to the case of causation as it exists between *classes* of (similar) events. Analyzing this latter notion Hume advanced a regularity theory of causation. Eschewing powers and necessary connections, Hume thought causation could be adequately dealt with in terms of the "constant conjunction" of similar causes with similar effects. In addition, conditions of temporal priority and spatiotemporal contiguity were also required. This analysis, in Hume's view, had the distinct merit of being entirely empirical. Yet subsequent generations of (logical) empiricists have found, to their exasperation, that the empiricist ideals are not that easily fulfilled.

One difficulty is that of distinguishing between accidental and genuinely causal regularities. As the Scottish philosopher Thomas Reid (1710–1796) famously remarked in his *Essays on the Active Powers of the Human Mind* (1788), day is invariably followed by night and night by day and yet neither is the cause of the other. One tempting way to find a distinctive mark is to say that statements of causal regularities, unlike those that express merely accidental generalizations, are supported by corresponding counterfactuals. Thus, it is presumably true that a given piece of metal would have expanded had it been heated. By contrast, even if all the marbles in a given bag happen to be red, that fact alone doesn't add credence to the counterfactual that had the green marble in my hand been a marble in that bag, it would have been red. Yet, reliance on counterfactuals would involve a high price for empiricists to pay. For the truth conditions of counterfactuals are notoriously beyond the reach of empirical verification.

Another difficulty was raised by Bertrand Russell (1872–1970), who noted that in order for events to be causally connected they must be similar not just in arbitrary respects, but in *relevant* respects. For example, two matches may differ only in color or, alternatively, only in one being wet while the other is dry. Yet for the question of whether striking them will cause them to ignite only the latter dissimilarity counts while the former is entirely irrelevant. But how is one going to specify this notion of relevance? One is tempted to rely on an undefined notion of *causal* relevance. But that would critically trivialize Hume's analysis because it would utilize the notion of causation in the very attempt to analyze it.

Oriental theories of causation

For Hume, then, the idea of causation, insofar as it is mistakenly bound up with such unfounded notions as power or necessary connection, does not represent anything objective. The implied idea of necessity does not arise from anything in the external world. Rather it results from a mental response to the constant conjunction of causes and their effects. By comparison, in Indian philosophy the objectivity of causation has been subject to considerable shifts of opinion. The first to deny the principle of causation was the idealist school of the Upanishads. Insisting that reality and soul (*atman*) were permanent and eternal, they denied change and therefore causation. Like Hume, but for different "Parmenidean" reasons, these thinkers considered change and causation mental constructs, or purely subjective phenomena. Conversely, the consequent denial of *atman* or self among early Buddhist materialists led to fruitful speculation regarding causality and change. However, in their extreme aversion to the idealist metaphysics of the Upanishads, these materialists went on to deny all mental phenomena. This annihilationism is opposed to the earlier belief of Upanishad philosophers in eternalism. However, according to the "middle path" preached by the Buddha, both positions are errors stemming from two opposite extremes with regard to causation, which early Buddhism set out to steer clear of: on the one hand the belief in self-causation, resulting in a belief in eternalism; on the other the belief in external causation, fostering a belief in annihilationism. While early Buddhism, like Hume, rejected the belief in a mental substance or "self," it did not share his conclusion that "were all my perceptions remov'd by death […] I shou'd be entirely annihilated … " (Hume, p. 252). The reason for this is precisely that unlike Hume early Buddhism insisted on the objective validity of causal processes, which it referred to as constituting the "middle" between the two extremes of eternalism and annihilationism. Consequently it regarded such causal processes sufficient for sustaining the continuity of a thing without positing a "self" or a "substance."

The importance of causality as an objective category in early Buddhism is brought out clearly by the fact that of the four noble truths discovered by the Buddha, the second and the third refer to the theory of causation. In the early Pali Nikayas and Chinese Agamas causation is not a category of relations among ideas but represents an objective ontological feature of the external world. Yet there has been much debate concerning the notion of *avitathata,* the second characteristic of the causal nexus in Buddhist philosophy. The Buddhist philosopher Buddhaghosa (late fourth and early fifth centuries C.E.) rendered this concept as "necessity," while others have championed a rather deflationary Humean interpretation of mere regularity and constant conjunction. From a more balanced perspective, what seems to be at stake in such discussions is to free causation from strict determinism. Thus a fourth characteristic of causation, *idappaccayata* or conditionality, is supposed to place causality midway between fatalism (*niyativada*), or unconditional necessity, and accidentalism (*yadrc-chavada*), or unconditional arbitrariness. Clearly, the underlying concern here is the problem of moral responsibility, which Buddhist thinkers are anxious to uphold.

Volitional causation

Taking their clue from Hume that causality is not a physical connection inasmuch as one never observes any hidden power in any given cause, philosophers of an empiricist bent have insisted ever since on analyses of causality in terms of necessary and sufficient conditions for the applicability of the term. Thus, they focused on the logical and linguistic aspects of the notion of causality to the neglect of trying to find a physical connection between cause and effect. An example is John L. Mackie's (1917–) sophisticated regularity account

in *The Cement of the Universe* (1974).Yet the contrary opinion has not been without its adherents. Even before Hume, John Locke (1632–1704), while discussing causality, appealed to the model of human volition. When one raises one's arm, he argued, one is directly aware of the power of one's volition to bring about the action.

This *purposive* perspective on causation has independent merits. For one thing it can make perfectly good sense of singular causation. For another, it avoids the vexing problem of so-called causal asymmetry. The fact that one ordinarily refuses to allow effects to precede their causes—Hume's condition of the temporal priority of causes—may on this view simply be seen as a natural consequence of the familiar experience that whatever actions one initiates cannot bring about the past. In fact, this volitional model of causation has been more influential than is generally acknowledged even among protagonists of the scientific revolution. Thus Isaac Newton (1642–1727) toyed with, and George Berkeley (1685–1753) championed, a theological construal of gravitation. Instead of invoking gravitational action-at-a-distance, a notion that Newton himself had deemed embarrassing enough to keep his theory locked up in a drawer for almost twenty years, it was, according to this view, God's own intervention that caused the sun ever so slightly to drift toward such large but immensely distant planets such as Jupiter, in accordance with mathematical patterns and laws that Newton had the genius to unravel. Needless to say, such animistic astronomy fails to carry conviction at the present time. But it is good to realize, if only for expository purposes, that Berkeley's animistic world is not a world without causation. Rather it is a world where all causation is volitional. When this world is stripped of volitional causation, what remains is a "Hume world," a world truly without causation. If philosophers have found such a world equally unconvincing, they could then ask the critical question: What crucial ingredient is the Hume world lacking that our world supposedly possesses?

Recent debates: realist vs. pragmatist views on causation

Apparently there are at least two ways to go from there: One can follow either the realist or the Kantian-pragmatist way out. The opposition in question is neatly exemplified by two contemporary schools of thought on causation, one represented by Wesley Salmon (1925–2001), the other highlighted by the philosophy of Philip Kitcher (1947–). Salmon has argued that there does exist, after all, an empirically verifiable physical connection between cause and effect. It is to be found in the notion of a causal process, rather than in that of a causal interaction, which Hume mistakenly took as his paradigm. Furthermore, thanks to the theory of relativity that sets an upper limit to the transmission of causal signals, we can now empirically distinguish between genuinely causal processes (e.g., light rays traveling at straight lines from a rotating beacon to the surrounding wall of, say, the Colosseum) and mere pseudoprocesses (e.g., a spot of light "traveling" along the inner wall of the Colosseum as a result of a central beacon rotating at very high speed). While pseudoprocesses may travel at arbitrarily high velocities, they cannot transmit information as only causal processes can. Similarly, the actions of a cowboy on a cinema screen are pseudoprocesses. When, in excessive excitement, you shoot him, it has no lasting effect on the cowboy, but only on the screen. Thus, in Salmon's view, the capacity to transmit information (or rather, conserved energy) constitutes empirical proof that the relevant process is genuinely causal in nature rather than a mere pseudoprocess.

According to this realist view, therefore, causation is a robust physical ingredient within our world itself, *entailing* necessary and sufficient conditions (or causal laws, probabilistic or otherwise), rather than *being entailed* by these. Causation is essentially a "local" affair, depending on the intrinsic features of two causally related events. By contrast, causal laws and necessary and sufficient conditions are "global" features, depending on the world as a whole. Consequently, on this realist view, causality may be entirely compatible with indeterminism, while theories couched in terms of necessary and sufficient conditions run into grave difficulties when confronted with the pervasiveness of indeterminacy in the subatomic realm.

Yet Salmon's theory has not been without its detractors. Thus, having confronted the theory with ingenious counter examples, Kitcher has argued that Salmon's theory, just like the empiricist theories before him, ultimately comes to rest on the truth of empirically unverifiable counterfactuals. By contrast, Kitcher's own theory places causality squarely within a Kantian-Peircian perspective. Immanuel Kant (1724–1804), while conceding to Hume that causality may be unobservable in the physical world, contradicted Hume's conclusion that therefore causality is not a real feature of the world *as we know it*. Indeed, causality may not be a feature positively discoverable in what Kant called the *noumenal* world, that is, the world as it exists in itself, without regard to the structural limitations of human knowledge. But then again, nothing is so discoverable or attributable. And yet causality is a property objectively ascribable to the *phenomenal* world, that is, the world as structured by the conceptual and perceptual features inherent in human cognitive capacities. As a result of the necessarily synthetic activities of human reason, one cannot *conceive* of the empirical world except in terms of causes and effects. The causal relation is therefore as firmly and objectively established as are space and time, which constitute the a priori forms of *perception* of the empirical world. These are all verifiable attributes of the physical world, which is part of the phenomenal world, the only kind of world humans are capable of knowing in principle.

Thus, the fundamental notion of causation receives a distinctly epistemological underpinning in Kantian philosophy. This is what ties Kitcher's philosophy of causation in part to the Kantian tradition. Thus, Kitcher has stated that the *because* of causation derives from the *because* of explanation. Rather than being an independent metaphysical notion, what may and may not be recognized as truly causal relations depends in the final analysis on epistemological constraints. In Kitcher's view the ultimate aim of science is to generate theories of the universe as unified and simple (or all-encompassing) as possible. Which theories are finally recognized—in the ideal end of inquiry, to borrow the famous words of the pragmatist Charles Sanders Peirce (1839–1914)—as optimally unified and robust thus determine what causes are recognized as genuinely operative and effective in the only world humans can possibly come to understand. Thus, in Kitcher's view, the metaphysical significance of causation ultimately derives from its key role in the best possible theory of the universe we will be able to generate. In a sense, therefore, causation, rather than being a metaphysically realist notion, is better seen as an unadulterated epistemological notion, dependent not on what we stumble upon in observation of singular cases of causation, as realists like Salmon would have it, but rather on the excellency of the theories that best account for the physical features of the world as a whole.

See also DOWNWARD CAUSATION; UPWARD CAUSATION

Bibliography

Hume, David. *A Treatise of Human Nature,* ed. L. A. Selby-Bigge. Oxford: Clarendon Press, 1888.

Mackie, John L. *The Cement of the Universe: A Study of Causation.* Oxford: Clarendon Press, 1974.

Reid, Thomas. *Essays on the Active Powers of the Human Mind* (1788). Cambridge, Mass.: MIT Press, 1969.

THEO C. MEYERING

CHANCE

In both science and religion there is a lively debate about the role of chance in the universe. In science, this debate usual takes the form of a discussion deciding between determinism (all events follow of necessity from prior initial conditions) and physical indeterminism (some events, at least, are not so determined). In religion, the dispute is between those who accept total predestination (the view that God unilaterally ordains everything that happens) and theological indeterminism (God leaves some things to chance or to determination by finite agents). Most religious views deny any role for pure chance, but many allow some role for chance even in a providentially-governed universe. Debate is often clouded by a failure to define what "chance" is.

Different senses of chance

In its most radical sense, chance is the occurrence of an event without any cause or reason. Thus the universe may be said to come into existence for no reason and without any antecedent cause—by chance. In this sense, absolutely anything might happen at any time, and there is no point in seeking reasons for what happens. If everything happened by chance, in this sense, science would be impossible.

Another, more common, sense of chance is involved in gambling or lotteries. When a gambler throws a die, the side that lands uppermost is a matter of chance. It is not that there are no causes for the position of the die, but that the causes are far too difficult, complex, or tedious to be detected. The roll of the die could be determined in every particular by applying the laws of mechanics, but it would still be considered a matter of chance because the system is set up so that no human can predict the outcome. In this case, chance primarily refers to unpredictability; whether something is chance or not depends on the knowledge available to the observer.

Another sense is that in which something happens "by chance" because it is not intended by any agent. A person may meet a long-lost friend by chance if neither the person nor the friend nor God had intended the meeting to happen, or tried to bring it about. Genetic mutations are said to be random, to occur by chance, in this sense. They have causes, but they are not intended to happen as they do.

This sense can be extended to events that are not parts of any directional process or propensity. Thus, many geneticists would say that genetic mutations do not tend in any particular direction (they do not, for example, always occur so as to maximize the chances of survival for some organism). This view is contentious, for some argue that there are propensities in organic mutation; the process does tend to realize consciousness eventually, and this tendency is inbuilt in the system from the beginning. If this were true, particular mutations could happen by chance (they would not each be determined to increase the chances of consciousness coming into being), but the process as a whole (the whole set of mutations in their environmental context) might have a propensity to terminate in consciousness.

This introduces yet another sense of chance, for which particular events have a specific probability of occurring, but are not sufficiently determined. An event is sufficiently determined when, given its initial conditions and the laws of nature, it could not happen in any other way. An event is not sufficiently determined when, from the very same initial conditions and laws, there are a number of possible effects that could result. In other words, the same cause in the same situation can have different effects. Some physicists have denied this possibility, but the Copenhagen Interpretation of quantum mechanics asserts precisely that particular subatomic events have a highly specific probability of occurring in a specific way, but they may not do so. When large numbers of quantum events occur, however, this probability will turn into a predictable certainty—thus the equations of quantum mechanics are deterministic, though they refer to events that are to some extent indeterminate. Such processes are called "stochastic"; there is a high probability that specific types of events will occur, but particular events may be unpredictable and not sufficiently determined.

Implications for freedom

There are thus two main components of the idea of chance—lack of predictability and lack of sufficient causality. For some philosophers, human freedom requires chance, since humans could not be held responsible for their actions if they were sufficiently caused (if they were determined by some cause, whether natural or divine) to act as they do. According to this view, chance is a necessary condition of responsible freedom. A free act is distinguished from a purely arbitrary (non-caused) act by being intentional, initiated for a purpose.

A believer in God may say that the creation of the universe is the primary instance of a free act. Creation is not caused by any prior initial state or by some general laws, but it is brought about for a reason. God has some value or values in mind, and realizes them by creating the universe. A free act is thus a form of causality for the sake of realizing some envisaged value. This causality distinguishes such an act sharply from pure chance, even though the act may appear unpredictable and undetermined from the point of view of physical laws and prior physical or mental states.

Some theologians have proposed that quantum mechanics shows the fundamental laws of the universe to be stochastic, or statistical, rather than deterministic. This, they claim, would permit both human free acts to occur, and would also allow God to act freely within the statistical probabilities of the physical system without "breaking" any laws of nature. For others, it is much too restrictive to confine God's free actions to scrabbling around in the sub-atomic basement. In any case, quantum indeterminacies cancel out because of the large numbers of probabilistic events involved in supra-atomic events, which means that the overall statistical distribution is virtually uncertain.

The existence of dynamic systems far from equilibrium allows quantum fluctuations to be amplified to produce macrocosmic effects. Thus in the right circumstances (in the brain, for example) quantum indeterminacies could produce huge observable indeterminacies in nature. Or it could be held that, quantum considerations apart, laws of nature are in themselves probabilistic, operating on an "other things being equal" basis, and they do not exclude free, or teleological causality, at all.

Religious views cannot easily live with any supposition of pure chance, in the radical sense. Most classical theistic views are deterministic (all is determined by God), seeing freedom as compatible with determinism. But in the twentieth century there has been an increase in the number of people holding nondeterministic views, for which chance (as probabilistic indeterminism) allows free creative activity both of creatures and of God, and a mutual responsiveness of creaturely and divine acts that may be held to be close to a biblical perspective.

See also COMPLEXITY; CONTINGENCY; CONVERGENCE

Bibliography

Bartholomew, David J. *God of Chance*. London: S.C.M. Press, 1990.

Murphy, Nancey. "Divine Action in the Natural Order." In *Chaos and Complexity: Scientific Perspectives on Divine Action,* eds. Robert John Russell, Nancey Murphy, and Arthur Peacocke. Vatican City State: Vatican Observatory, 1995.

Plantinga, Alvin. *God, Freedom, and Evil*. London: Allen, Unwin, 1974.

Polkinghorne, John. "Chaos Theory and Divine Action." In *Religion and Science,* eds. Mark Richardson and Wesley Wildman. New York: Routledge, 1996.

Russell, Robert J., Murphy, Nancey; and Peacocke, Arthur, eds. *Perspectives on Divine Action,* Notre Dame, Ind.: University of Notre Dame Press, 1997.

Saunders, Nicholas T. "Does God Cheat at Dice? Divine Action and Quantum Possibilities." *Zygon: Journal of Religion and Science* 35, no. 3 (2000): 517–544.

Swinburne, Richard. *Responsibility and Atonement*. New York: Oxford University Press, 1989.

Ward, Keith. *God, Chance, and Necessity*. Oxford: Oneworld, 1996.

Ward, Keith. *God, Faith, and the New Millenium*. Oxford: Oneworld, 1998.

KEITH WARD

CHAOS, QUANTUM

Quantum Chaos connects quantum and chaos physics, giving rise to two fundamentally different versions of indeterminism. Quantum mechanics holds that classical particle trajectories become indeterminate when studied under conditions that bring forth the wave nature of matter. Within classical physics, trajectories follow deterministic laws but are nevertheless unpredictable if the motion is chaotic. Quantum indeterminism and classical chaos conspire to create effects that become observable at the transition between microscopic (atomic) and macroscopic scales. For example, a characteristic phenomenon of quantum chaos is that quantum wave effects help suppress the instability of chaotic motion.

See also CHAOS THEORY; PHYSICS, QUANTUM; UNPREDICTABILITY

WOLFGANG ACHTNER
JENS NOECKEL

CHAOS, RELIGIOUS AND PHILOSOPHICAL ASPECTS

The word *chaos* appears in a variety of scholarly disciplines. This entry will address its use in the Greek philosophical tradition and a number of religious traditions. Chaos will also be explored in its use in scientific cosmology.

Religious and philosophical traditions

It is characteristic of ancient Greek thought to see the world (*cosmos*) as coming into existence through the imposition of order on preexisting *chaos*. The first known usage of the term *chaos* is in the *Theogony* of Hesiod (late eight century B.C.E.); Hesiod probably took up the idea from earlier mythological accounts of the beginning of the universe. For Hesiod, chaos refers to the preexisting undifferentiated state of things. It manifests itself in the gap between heaven and Earth that occurs as the world emerges. This chaotic gap is transformed by the appearance of Eros, a fertilizing force that brings heaven and Earth back into a creative embrace. The word cosmos was used by philosophers from Pythagoras (569–475 B.C.E.) to Archimedes (287–212 B.C.E.) to describe the order that is manifest in the natural world. Both Plato (in *Timaeus*) and Aristotle (in *Physics*) interpreted chaos in terms of the pre-philosophical concept of space. Zeno of Citium (333–264 B.C.E.) associated chaos with water. The Stoics understood chaos as referring to the watery state that occurs periodically when the universe is destroyed by fire.

There are a number of different symbols for chaos among the peoples of the Earth. Two are widespread: the waters of the deep and the cosmic egg or embryo-like form that is the matrix for all things. But chaos is also envisioned as a dragon, as a hybrid human-animal, as a dangerous female mother associated with the waters or the Earth, and as a cosmic giant figure. It appears in popular culture in the figures of the demon, the witch, the trickster, and sometimes the shaman.

Religious traditions from different parts of the world express the defeat of chaos in their myths and rituals of combat. This pattern found expression in the ancient Near East. The Babylonian epic poem *Enuma Elish,* which dates in part back to the second millenium B.C.E., is good example. It tells of a great battle in which a sky god, Marduk, wins a victory over Tiamat, a female chaos figure associated with the primeval waters. Marduk slays Tiamat and divides her body to form the world, using her skin to keep out and confine the waters in the heavens and in the underground. The story establishes the legitimacy of the temple and rule of Babylon. Tiamat has been interpreted as referring to an older impotent order of society and divine beings that is replaced by the new.

In the Canaanite myths of Ugarit, Baal engages in warfare with the adversary Mot, with another adversary called the Sea, and with Leviathan or Shalyat of the seven heads. This kind of combat also appears in the Hebrew Bible, in Isaiah 27:1, where Leviathan is mentioned; in Psalm 74:13–15; 89:10–11; in Isaiah 51:9; and in Job 9:13; 26:12; 38:8–11. In these texts the monster is often constrained rather than destroyed. God is understood as continually creating and defending the universe against disintegration and chaos.

The Bible begins with an account of creation that seems to go back to priestly sources of the sixth century B.C.E. According to the Bible the "the earth was a formless void and darkness covered the face of the deep, while a wind from God swept over the face of the waters" (Gen. 1:2). "Formless void" translates the Hebrew words *tohu wabohu*. The word *tohu* appears in the Bible twenty times, with the meaning of formless, shapeless, and uninhabitable. The word *wabohu* appears three times, with a similar meaning. Two chaotic elements characterize the formless void, the primordial waters and darkness. God vanquishes darkness on the first day of creation with the creation of light. Darkness is not completely destroyed, but is limited to the night, as part of good creation (Gen. 1:5). The chaotic waters that cover the whole Earth (Pss. 104:6) are brought under divine control on the second and third days. God positions a gigantic concave plate or dome to separate the waters above from the Earth below (Gen. 1:7) and then sets boundaries to the seas so that dry land can appear (Gen. 1:9). The explicit idea of creation *ex nihilo* does not appear in Jewish thought until the second century B.C.E. (2 Macc. 7:28).

In the stories and rituals of the indigenous peoples of Australia, Africa, and North and South America, there are times when participants experience a liminal state that can be understood as a return to the creative boundaries between chaos and order. Alongside the religious traditions that emphasize the defeat of chaos, there are those that challenge dualistic polarities and encourage an acceptance of chaos or elements associated with it, such as negativity, unknowing, and darkness. In ancient China, early Daoist texts (as opposed to the later Daoism) support mystical union with *hun-tun* (chaos) and identify hun-tun with the ultimate principle of Dao. Alongside the mainstream Vedic traditions of India there are forms of mysticism, both Upanishadic and Buddhist, that encourage union with "emptiness." Christian theology includes the tradition of apophatic theology, which finds expression in the works of Gregory of Nyssa (c. 335–c.395 C.E.) and Pseudo-Dionysius (c. fifth century C.E.), in the English medieval text *The Cloud of Unknowing*, in the John of the Cross's (1542–1591) symbol of the Dark Night, and in the

twentieth century in Karl Rahner's (1904–1984) theology of God as Incomprehensible Mystery.

In Jewish thought, a theology that can embrace negativity finds expression in various streams of thought, including those concerning God's *Shekinah* and sixteenth-century mystic Isaac Luria's concept of the divine withdrawal that makes space for creation (the *zimsum*). In philosophy since the Holocaust, there has been an attempt to embrace the chaotic strangeness and alterity of reality, particularly in the postmodern rejection of all "totalizing" attempts at comprehension and order and in philosopher Emmanuel Levinas's (1906–1995) insistence on the radical and irreducible otherness of one's neighbor.

Scientific cosmology

In the scientific cosmology that emerged during the twentieth century, ancient ideas of the emergence of cosmos from chaos were replaced by the idea of a universe that has expanded and evolved over the course of twelve billion to fifteen billion years from a tiny, dense, and hot state. The Big Bang theory of cosmology had its origins in models of the universe based on Albert Einstein's theory of General Relativity. According to these theories, space-time itself emerges and stretches in the process of cosmic expansion. Over the last century a number of lines of evidence have supported Big Bang cosmology, particularly the discoveries of the red shifting of galaxies, the abundance of helium and deuterium in the universe, and background microwave radiation. According to standard Big Bang cosmology the universe is expanding and also decreasing in temperature and density, and this points back to a beginning of the universe of unthinkable smallness, density, and heat—to an original singularity. A singularity is a point at which the density and the curvature of space-time are infinite, a point at which the laws of physics no longer hold.

In 1948, physicists Fred Hoyle, Thomas Gold, and Hermann Bondi put forward an alternative to Big Bang cosmology with their *steady-state* idea of the universe. In this theory new matter and new galaxies are continuously brought into being, in a stable universe that has an infinite past. Although the steady-state theory was undermined by the discovery of background microwave radiation, some of its philosophical aims were incorporated into a

Big Bang framework in what physicist Charles Misner called *chaotic cosmology*. Chaotic cosmology seeks to avoid attributing the order of the universe to initial conditions. It is committed to explaining the present nature of the universe without requiring knowledge of its initial state. It seeks to show that no matter how chaotic the state of the universe at the beginning of its expansion, there are processes that can smooth out irregularities and produce the isotropic and uniform universe that people can observe. But no known process could account for this smoothing out process until the rise of inflationary theories in the 1980s.

In the meantime cosmologists had begun to speculate about the beginning of the universe in terms of quantum theory. Quantum field theories differ from their classical predecessors in the way they understand a vacuum. Within quantum theory, a vacuum is not understood simply as nothing at all, but as a sea of continuously appearing and disappearing pairs of oppositely charged particles. These processes are unobservable at the individual level and are called *virtual,* but are measurable at the collective level. The quantum vacuum is an infinite sea of virtual processes. Quantum theory allows for the spontaneous appearance of energy in the quantum vacuum for a very short time, as long as it is unobservable. Quantum cosmology involves a theory of the emergence of the universe from a fluctuation of the quantum vacuum. It thus, once again, suggests that an ordered universe appears from a chaotic initial state.

Chaos was to reenter the language of cosmology in the form of the theory of *chaotic inflation.* In order to solve some of the problems associated with the Big Bang, physicist Alan Guth in 1980 proposed that within a fraction of the first second the universe went through a period of extremely rapid expansion or inflation. Soon after, in 1983, physicist Andrei Linde put forward his theory of chaotic inflation, which dispenses with the idea of most initial conditions including the initial heat. The universe begins from chaos in the form of the seething ocean of different forms of scalar fields. The observable universe began from one such field, as one part of a process that may involve an unlimited ensemble of universes. In many recent models of the expanding universe, particularly those based on a period of rapid inflation, the observable universe would be a small domain within a much bigger universe, perhaps an infinite and eternal one.

In all of these theories, inflation provides the ordering principle, and chaos reappears in the initial conditions of the universe. As astronomer John Barrow has said: "Inflation does not explain the uniformity of the Visible Universe by eradicating primordial chaos, but by sweeping its effects out of sight beyond the boundary of the visible part of the Universe" (p. 239). It is worth keeping in mind that at this stage there is much more evidence for Big Bang cosmology in general than there is for the various forms of chaotic cosmology. In a recent evaluation of the major theories of cosmology, physicist P. James E. Peebles concludes that while there is compelling evidence that the universe has evolved from a hotter and denser state, the theory of inflation is "elegant, but lacks direct evidence and requires huge extrapolation of the laws of physics" (p. 45).

Conclusion

For many communities, chaos represents the strangeness and otherness of reality. As such it may be unwise to understand chaos and cosmos as simply opposed to one another. It is not simply that an ordered cosmos emerges from and replaces chaos. In many cultural systems chaos may be defeated but nevertheless reappears. It can be seen as an ever-returning dimension of human existence in the world. Even in the midst of ordered lives, human beings continually experience the chaotic, in the wildness of the wind in a storm, in the untamable violence of the sea, and in the dark and lonely hours of the night. It can be a threat and a challenge. But it can also have the character of the mysterious and uncontrollable ground or source from which all things spring. It can represent the possibility of creativity and of the new.

See also BIG BANG THEORY; CHAOS THEORY; CREATIO EX NIHILO; DISORDER; INFLATIONARY UNIVERSE THEORY

Bibliography

Barrow, John B. *The Universe that Discovered Itself.* Oxford: Oxford University Press, 2000.

Clifford, Richard J. "Creation in the Hebrew Bible." In *Physics, Philosophy, and Theology,* eds. Robert J. Russell, William Stoeger, and George Coyne. Vatican City State: Vatican Observatory, 1988.

Eliade, Mircea. *Myth and Reality.* New York: Allen & Unwin, 1964.

Giradot, Norman J. "Chaos." In *Encyclopedia of Religion,* ed. Mircea Eliade. New York: Macmillan, 1987.

Kuntz, Paul G., ed. *The Concept of Order*. Seattle: University of Washington Press, 1968.

Linde, Andrei D. *Inflation and Quantum Cosmology*. Boston: Academic Press, 1990.

Peebles, P. James E. "Making Sense of Modern Cosmology." *Scientific American* 284 (2001): 44-45.

DENIS EDWARDS

CHAOS THEORY

Chaos Theory (CT) is a mathematical theory about nonlinear dynamical systems that exhibit exquisite sensitivity to initial conditions, eventual unpredictability, and other intriguing features despite the inevitably deterministic character of mathematical equations. CT has been used to model processes in diverse fields, including physics (quantum chaos, nonequilibrium thermodynamics), chemistry, ecology, economics, physiology, meteorology, zoology, and the neurosciences.

Basic research in mathematics and physics during the twentieth century produced CT. Felix Hausdorff (1869–1942) made essential contributions in mathematics when he created spaces with fractional dimensions. When Benoit Mandelbrot (1924–) applied these spaces to geometry, he discovered new objects that he called *fractals*. These ideas were combined with the study of recursive and iterative mathematical formulas. The simplest formula of this kind, which was explored in great detail by Mitchell Feigenbaum (1944–), is the logistic equation $x_{n+1} = ax_n (1 - x_n)$, where a is a *tuning* constant for the system. The system evolves recursively for $n = 0, 1, 2, 3, \ldots$.

In 1963, meteorologist Edward Lorenz (1917–) used differential equations with chaotic properties to model a physical system, the first time this had been done. In physics Henri Poincaré (1854–1912) used features of CT to demonstrate the stability of the solar system, a result that Isaac Newton (1642–1727) and many other scientists had not been able to achieve because of the potentially chaotic behavior of systems containing three or more bodies. Ilya Prigogine (1917–), who did research in thermodynamics, examined nonlinear systems that are far from equilibrium and showed that such a system could generate novel structural features.

All these developments were independent of each other, but they merged in the new concept of CT in the 1970s. The term *chaos theory* was coined by mathematician and physicist James Yorke around 1972 and was introduced to the scientific literature in 1975 by the mathematician and biologist Robert May. Robert Devaney gave the first mathematical-technical definition of chaos in 1989, although this definition does not cover all features of interest to mathematicians who study chaos. In this technical sense, CT is not to be understood as being opposed to order, and it should not be confused with the metaphorical and colloquial use of the word *chaos*. Rather it describes how order breaks down and reemerges on many levels of complexity within dynamic systems.

Features of chaos theory

There are four essential aspects of CT. First, because of its recursive and iterative character, a chaotic system is exquisitely sensitive to its initial conditions, which means that the slightest variations in the parameters of a system may result in tremendous differences in the system's development. This feature is known as the Butterfly Effect.

Second, within the various modes of a chaotic dynamical system, there are certain levels of stability, especially when movements or changes come to an end. These levels of stability form the mathematical concept of an attractor. The eventual point of rest of a pendulum's movement is an attractor for the mathematical model of the nonchaotic pendulum system. Similarly, in classical thermodynamics the state of maximum entropy can be regarded as an attractor within nonchaotic mathematical models of fluids. Such nonchaotic attractors can be represented geometrically by a single point or a toroid. An attractor is distinguished from a *strange* attractor, the latter being used only in CT. The strange attractor is a fractal, of which the best known are the Hénon, Rössler, and Lorenz attractors. Dynamical systems in chaotic modes stabilize on strange attractors.

Third, the essential difference between the development of a nonchaotic system and the development of a chaotic system has to do with determinism and predictability. Although determinism and predictability are mutually entailing in nonchaotic systems, determinism does not entail predictability in chaotic systems. Chaotic systems possess a certain degree of predictability, measured by the so-called Lyapunov exponent, but all chaotic systems are unpredictable in the long run. Because of this astonishing mixture of determinism and nonpredictability, CT is also called the theory of deterministic chaos.

Finally, in contrast to a nonchaotic deterministic system, a chaotic deterministic system is not reversible due to progressive information loss as the system evolves. Thus, it is not possible to trace a system backwards to its initial conditions. If this mathematical form of CT is applied in physics to open systems that are far from equilibrium, additional features are revealed:

(1) Autopoietic systems, which are self-generating, can be described by CT.

(2) In order for a system to evolve in a chaotic manner, it is necessary constantly to supply it with energy, and the input of energy prevents it from entering a state of stationary equilibrium.

(3) Due to this constant input of energy, chaotic systems can evolve new features, such as those used in certain chemical clocks.

(4) Because chaotic systems are not static, they can adapt to new environmental conditions.

(5) The application of CT to evolving systems that are far from equilibrium requires a refinement of the concept of entropy.

Theological implications

The fact that determinism does not entail predictability in chaos theory means that knowledge of the future of a complex physical system that can be modeled with a chaotic dynamical mathematical system is severely limited in practice. This limitation of knowledge of the future may seem undesirable, but it turns out to be useful when CT is used as a conceptual tool for studying evolutionary and autopoietic systems. If philosophical reasoning is used to relate natural science to theology, then this new distinction between determinism and predictability has to be respected. There are three predominant options when relating CT to theology.

Ontology. The distinction between the mathematical theory of CT and its physical application raises the question of how to relate divine action to CT. If one interprets the eventual unpredictability of CT as an epistemological clue to an underlying

openness in nature, as does John Polkinghorne, one can speculate whether the world is open to divine influences by the concept of "divine information input without energy transfer." On the other hand, if eventual unpredictability is judged to be merely an epistemic limitation with no ontological implications, then CT is not immediately useful for interpreting the natural-law-conforming action of an intentional divine being, though Robert John Russell and others have invoked it to explain how divine action at the quantum level might be amplified to macroscopic dimensions.

Autopoiesis. If CT is linked to the theory of autopoietic systems, the independence of creatures is emphasized rather than their dependence on God. This interpretation is adopted in some contemporary kenotic theologies and it tends to challenge traditional theological teachings such as providence and omnipotence. Generally, CT leads to the conclusion that it is more plausible to think of God as a cooperative partner in a panentheistic way, rather than as an almighty ruler, if God is to be thought of as a being at all, which is itself theologically controversial.

Unpredictability. The eventual unpredictability that is intrinsic to CT offers the possibility of reinterpreting the concept of divine providence. Rather than conceiving of God's knowledge as a deterministic prescience, one can interpret that knowledge as a knowledge of different options within an open future that is vulnerable to the possibilities of failure and error. In light of CT, one could also argue that in God predictability and determinism are again fused. This third interpretation does justice to human freedom. The use of CT in neuroscience invites attempts to relate CT's distinction between predictability and determinism to neurological interpretations of human free will. However, the deeper problem is whether mental phenomena, such as the will, can be reduced to neural activity, and here CT seems to offer no new insights.

See also CHAOS, RELIGIOUS AND PHILOSOPHICAL ASPECTS

Bibliography

Crain, Steven D. "Divine Action and Indeterminism: On Models of Divine Agency that Exploit the New Physics (Chaos)." Ph.D. diss., University of Notre Dame, 1993.

Devaney, Robert L. *An Introduction to Chaotic Dynamical Systems*. Redwood City, Calif.: Addison-Wesley, 1989.

Dinter, Astrid. *Vom Glauben eines Physikers: John Polking-hornes Beitrag zum Dialog zwischen Theologie und Naturwissenschaften.* Mainz, Germany: Matthias Grünewald Verlag, 1999.

Gregersen, Niels Henrik. "Providence in an Indeterministic World." *CTNS Bulletin* 14 (1994): 16–31.

Kellert, Stephen. *In the Wake of Chaos: Unpredictable Order in Dynamical Systems.* Chicago: University of Chicago Press, 1993.

Polkinghorne, John. *The Faith of a Physicist: Reflections of a Bottom-Up Thinker.* Princeton, N.J.: Princeton University Press, 1994.

Russell, Robert John; Murphy, Nancey; and Peacocke, Arthur R., eds. *Chaos and Complexity. Scientific Perspectives on Divine Action.* Vatican City and Berkeley, Calif.: Vatican Observatory Publications and Center for Theology and Natural Sciences, 1995.

Singe, Georg. *Gott im Chaos: Ein Beitrag zur Rezeption der Chaostheorie in Theologie und deren Praktisch-theologische Konsequenz.* Frankfurt am Main, Germany: Peter Lang Verlag, 2000.

Smedes, Taede. "Chaos: Where Science and Religion Meet? A Critical Evaluation of the Use of Chaos Theory in Theology." In *Studies in Science and Theology,* Vol. 8, eds. Niels Henrik Gregersen, Ulf Görman, and Hubert Meisinger. Aarhus, Denmark: University of Aarhus, 2001.

Smith, Peter. *Explaining Chaos.* Cambridge, UK: Cambridge University Press, 1998.

WOLFGANG ACHTNER
TAEDE A. SMEDES

CHEMISTRY

When, in the 1830s, eight authors published Bridgewater Treatises on the goodness and wisdom of God, the series included volumes on astronomy and physics, geology, psychology, human physiology, animal and vegetable physiology, zoology, and the human hand. But chemistry was stuffed into a rag-bag of a book by William Prout (1785–1850) that also covered meteorology and the function of digestion. Yet this was a time when lectures on chemistry attracted large and enthusiastic audiences, and chemistry was perceived as a fundamental science. When most science was popularized in a context of natural theology, why was chemistry seen as problematic?

In the early twenty-first century, *chemicals* are perceived as alarming additives, the chemical industry as a source of pollution, and fertilizers, pesticides, and explosives as dangerous to the planet and its populations. Still, people depend upon plastics, synthetic fibers, pharmaceutical drugs, and paints. Chemistry is everybody's service science, ubiquitous, but highly suspect, which points to the reason for its neglect by natural theologians. Astronomers contemplate the starry heavens; chemists understand the world in order to change it.

Chemical theology in history

The alchemist was an optimist, seeing potential gold where others saw dross. Alchemists often identified the perfecting of base metal into gold with the simultaneous spiritual perfecting of the alchemical practitioner. George Herbert's well-known poem *The Elixir* (1633) is indeed used as a hymn. God's creation of the cosmos from chaos was compared to an alchemical project. In the laboratory, the natural improvement of base metals could be accelerated. But in the second half of the seventeenth century Robert Boyle, one of the fathers of modern chemistry, although deeply interested and involved in alchemy, delighted especially in the mechanical or corpuscular philosophy as a basis for natural theology—comparing God to a clockmaker rather than to an alchemist. He and the other founders of the Royal Society favored the plain words of artisans rather than witty metaphysical conceits or coded messages for initiates. The oblique, resonant, and metaphorical language of alchemy gave way, especially in the 1780s in the hands of chemist Antoine Lavoisier, to sober prose approximating as far as possible to algebra. For Boyle, who was deeply devout, mechanical explanations were particularly satisfying and intelligible. He bequeathed money for lectures demonstrating the existence and wisdom of God. For succeeding generations this meant *astrotheology,* joyfully dwelling upon Isaac Newton's work, and *physico-theology,* showing how humans and other creatures were like beautifully designed little clocks living in an enormous clock.

Whereas astronomy was a science of meditative observation and calculation (with spin-offs into calendars and navigation), chemistry was active and practical. The busy chemist's task was to improve the world by isolating metals, distilling medicines, or making ceramics and dyes. Adam and Eve had been expelled from paradise and sentenced to hard labor: Chemists might be able to do something about that. As the macho English chemist Humphry Davy declared in the early nineteenth century, the chemist is godlike because he exerts a "creative energy" that "entitles him to the distinction of being made in the image of God and animated by a spark of the divine mind" (p. 361). Instead of simply commending this best of all possible worlds and its designer, therefore, chemists seek to understand it in order to change it for the better, using God-given intelligence and manual skills.

Chemistry is essentially an experimental science, concerned with the secondary qualities of color, taste, and smell, and demanding trained fingers, hands, and noses; it cannot be done on paper in an armchair in a study or library. When interrogating nature through experiments, the chemist for Davy is not a passive scholar, but a master, active with his own instruments, exerting the "godlike faculties, by which reason ultimately approaches … to inspiration." In the words of a poet, Davy's lectures disclosed "Nature's coyest secrets." Davy was a friend of Samuel Taylor Coleridge and other Romantic poets, and went from interrogation to worship of nature, as we see in his poems and last writings. Such pantheism was not unusual among scientists of the nineteenth century, who found religious experience in communing with nature both in the laboratory and on mountain tops.

The enthusiastic Samuel Parkes, a Unitarian and a chemical manufacturer, borrowing from church teaching called his elementary and successful book of 1806 *The Chemical Catechism*. Not only did he hope that parents would ensure that their children learned chemistry for its utility, he also sought to defend the youthful mind against "immorality, irreligion, and scepticism." The text (questions and answers) was amplified with footnotes, where chemical detail, poetry, and occasional encomia upon the creator were to be found. The "goodness of the ALMIGHTY" was particularly displayed in the various uses to which different substances may be put, though sometimes the "design of Nature" in assigning properties to things was not yet apparent. The book is pervaded with natural theology, rather than being an exposition of it. In a later popular work *The Chemistry of Common Life* (1855), widely known in translation as well as in English, the Presbyterian James Johnston concluded surprisingly that earthly life was insignificant in the vast general system of the universe. Humans were here solely because God, in a separate act of will, had formed beings to admire God's work. Johnston sought thus to indicate the insufficiency of natural theology without revelation, which told more of God's purposes and character than could ever be inferred from chemical discoveries.

Authors of Bridgewater Treatises were meant to confine themselves to natural theology, and Prout's was thus a straightforward exposition of the design argument, given a particular turn because of his idiosyncratic atomic theory. But chemistry was making rapid progress, and in 1844 George Fownes published his book *Chemistry as Exemplifying the Wisdom and Benevolence of God*, which was awarded the Actonian Prize associated with the Royal Institution, where Davy and Michael Faraday held forth. Fownes began from the position that recent studies (especially with microscopes, enormously improved at this time) had shown how exquisitely animals were adapted to their environment. Then he declared that recent discoveries in chemistry, especially in its organic branch, made it easier to use science to infer design. He urged people to look for God's activity in the commonplace and the everyday world, seeing God's hand in the simple laws of chemical combination, the ubiquity of protein, and the equilibria among reversible reactions that made animal and plant chemistry possible. Natural theology was for Fownes the highest aim of science. His book is also a good account of the current state of chemistry, being transformed at that time through the work especially of Justus Liebig, in whose wake German universities were training large numbers of professional research chemists to work in industry and academia.

Both Prout and Fownes came under friendly fire from George Wilson in his *Religio Chemici* (published posthumously in 1862) for their Panglossian emphasis upon unmixed and unbounded benevolence. Wilson, the first Professor of Technology in Edinburgh University in Scotland, was dogged by bereavements and illness, but supported by staunch religious faith. He believed that while chemical evidence, especially from the earth's atmosphere and the carbon and water cycles, demonstrated design, the demonstration of benevolence was another story. Introducing a gendered perspective, he noted that men read the Bridgewater Treatises and such books chiefly to learn science; women, more perceptive, did not because they were not impressed by such banal optimism. The problem of evil was real, and the dark side must be faced. If human bodies are constantly being renewed, why then do they wear out? Why are there poisons? Wilson noted the formidable weapons of destruction possessed by carnivores—"God has been very kind to the shark"—and the reality and enduring character of pain, animal and human. Evil exists alongside good, and cannot in the manner of the Manicheans be separated from it. Chemistry can show that God *has* love, but not that God *is* love. For Wilson the problem of evil is real and cannot be solved in this world, except in the light of revealed religion and true conversion. Astrotheology might be immune from such criticisms, but physico-theology along with reasoning from chemistry is undoubtedly undermined. Most of those writing natural theology had been, like William Paley, healthier and wealthier than the average person, and Wilson brought in a draft of fresh air.

The twentieth century onwards

Natural theology had made popular chemical books and lectures interesting and indeed momentous. By 1900, however, there were many students (more than in any other science) with examinations to pass and professional qualifications to gain, and their textbooks had become much drier and more factual, presenting chemical theory but not a worldview. Also, natural theology was in retreat for most of the twentieth century, under assault not only from scientific naturalists but also from theologians. And whereas chemistry had seemed a fundamental science to Davy and his contemporaries, in the early twentieth century it appeared that chemistry was being reduced to physics with the work of Ernest Rutherford and Niels Bohr. No doubt experiment was still necessary because the mathematical equations, based upon quantum theory, were too difficult to solve in detail, but genuine chemical explanation would in principle be in terms of physics, or so it seemed to physicists, who enjoyed enormous prestige. Philosophy of science, therefore, was for much of that century focused

upon physics; chemistry seemed necessary, but not exciting. In addition, much nineteenth-century research had been done by individuals. In the twentieth century, the teams and groups that now undertook scientific research needed to include a chemist or two whatever their field, but the glamorous science was physics. Then came the elucidation of the DNA structure, making molecular biology and genetics major areas of interest; here, as in pharmacy, chemistry was essential, but still not the center of interest for the lay person following what was going on. In the United States, Creationism focused the attention of natural theologians upon Charles Darwin's theory of evolution by natural selection, which by the second half of the century incorporated genetics. Only perhaps in the context of ecotheology has chemistry again impinged seriously on religious thinking.

Nevertheless, chemistry was not really reduced to physics any more than architecture has been; builders must take into account the law of gravity, and chemists building molecules cannot defy the laws of physics. Working within such constraints is the basis of art in both fields. Roald Hoffmann emphasizes the creativity that lies behind structural chemistry, designing substances never made before. He also draws attention to the visual and verbal language of chemistry and the role of illustration in the science. Lavoisier's project of abolishing richness has not been achieved, and chemistry can be fun. Hoffmann has also been involved with Shira Schmidt in reflection on Jewish traditions in the light of chemistry, seeing argument as central to both and exploring dichotomies between natural and artificial, symmetry and asymmetry, purity and impurity. This is not the traditional enterprise of natural theology, as in Fownes's book, but much less formal. For the believer, satisfying parallels and analogies reveal themselves in a coherent pattern, and metaphors are refreshed.

A collective study of *Science in Theistic Contexts* (2001) unsurprisingly contains no discussion of chemistry. In their Gifford Lectures, however, published as *Reconstructing Nature* (1998), John Brooke and Geoffrey Cantor investigate the engagement (a useful word with multiple meanings) of science with religion in a historical perspective. They devote a chapter to chemistry, with particular discussion of the theological problems that can arise from the idea that the chemist is perfecting creation. They see process as a feature of chemistry that might bear upon religion. Most people accept that a world with nylon and aluminum is better than one without, and expect more progress in applied chemistry, but people remain uneasy about nineteenth-century chemist Eleanor Ormerod's enthusiastic espousal of chemical pest-control, with its aim of exterminating noxious insects. Brooke and Cantor also look at materialism and reductionism, in which chemistry has been involved—the melancholy may be bracingly told "it's just your chemistry," and may or may not find that consoling.

What emerges is that chemistry has never been nearly as tempting for the natural theologian, wishing to put design beyond reasonable doubt, as astronomy or natural history. While the world of stinks and bangs is fun, atoms and molecules lack sublimity or accessibility. Chemistry is not only the experimental science par excellence, it is also useful in seeking to improve the world and the quality of life. That, and the idea of process, is something that should resonate with anyone pursuing natural theology, especially in an intellectual climate where the argument from design runs up against a deep prevailing skepticism. In such a broader and more sensitive natural theology, there should also be room for the metaphors and analogies from chemistry that can make it aesthetically, rather than logically, compelling.

See also ALCHEMY; DESIGN; DESIGN ARGUMENT; ECOLOGY; ECOTHEOLOGY; NATURAL THEOLOGY

Bibliography

Boyle, Robert. *The Vulgar Notion of Nature* (1686), ed. M. Hunter. Cambridge, UK: Cambridge University Press, 1996.

Brock, William H. *From Protyle to Proton: William Prout and the Nature of Matter, 1785–1985*. Bristol, UK: Adam Hilger, 1985.

Brooke, John H., and Cantor, Geoffrey. *Reconstructing Nature: the Engagement of Science and Religion*. Edinburgh, UK: T&T Clark, 1998.

Brooke, John H.; Osler, Margaret J.; and Van der Meer, Jitse M., eds. *Science in Theistic Contexts: Cognitive Dimensions*. Chicago: University of Chicago Press, 2001.

Davy, Humphry. *Collected Works*, Vol. 9. London: Smith Elder, 1839–1840.

Fownes, George. *Chemistry, as Exemplifying the Wisdom and Beneficence of God*. London: John Churchill, 1844.

Hoffmann, Roald, and Schmidt, Shira Leibowitz. *Old Wine, New Flasks: Reflections on Science and Jewish Tradition*. New York: W. H. Freeman, 1997.

Hoffmann, Roald, and Torrence, Vivian. *Chemistry Imagined: Reflections on Science*. Washington, D.C.: Smithsonian, 1993.

Johnston, James F.W. *The Chemistry of Common Life*. Edinburgh, Scotland: Blackwood, 1855.

Knight, David M. *Ideas in Chemistry: A History of the Science,* 2nd edition. London: Athlone Press, 1995.

Knight, David M. "Higher Pantheism." *Zygon* 35 (2000): 603–612.

Knight, David M., and Kragh, Helge eds. *The Making of the Chemist: The Social History of Chemistry in Europe 1789–1914*. Cambridge, UK: Cambridge University Press, 1998.

Lundgren, Anders, and Bensaude-Vincent, Bernadette, eds. *Communicating Chemistry: Textbooks and their Audiences 1789–1939*. Canton, Mass.: Science History Publications, 2000.

Nye, Mary Jo. *Before Big Science: The Pursuit of Modern Chemistry and Physics 1800–1940*. New York: Twayne, 1996.

Parkes, Samuel. *The Chemical Catechism, with Notes, Illustrations and Experiments,* 3rd edition. London: Lackington Allen, 1808.

Prout, William. *Chemistry, Meteorology, and the Function of Digestion, Considered With Reference to Natural Theology*. London: William Pickering, 1834.

Topham, Jonathan R. "Beyond the 'Common Context': The Production and Reading of the Bridgewater Treatises." *Isis* 89 (1998): 233–262.

Wilson, George. *Religio Chemici: Essays*. London: Macmillan, 1862.

DAVID M. KNIGHT

CHINESE RELIGIONS AND SCIENCE

The three main *Jiao* (systems of teachings and beliefs) in Chinese tradition are Confucianism, Daoism, and Buddhism, which are called the "three religions." However, Chinese scholars generally consider Confucianism, the School of Daoism (*Dao Jia*), and the School of Buddhism (*Fu Jia*) to be philosophies, whereas Daojiao (*Jiao* of Daoism) and Fujiao (*Jiao* of Buddhism) are considered to be religions. In the West, all are regarded as either religions or philosophies or both.

In regard to Chinese science, traditional Chinese scientific discoveries should not be measured by the standards of modern Western science. By doing so, one risks missing many of the real merits in non-Western cultures. One example is that the holistic view and the harmony of the *yin-yang* (shade and sunshine) concept of the human body and soul in Chinese medicine does not correlate directly with the standard Western (Greek) dichotomy of body and soul, although many have tried to make this correlation.

The main themes of traditional Confucianism are to cultivate the person, to regulate the family, to effectively govern the state, and to exemplify virtue throughout the world. The purpose of science and technology is to help a person be a good politician and sage. Moral teachings are considered far more important than scientific findings. Confucianism does not oppose scientific and technological knowledge; the attitude of Confucianism toward science is to leave it alone.

Daoism as a religion can be traced back to ancient China, especially to the philosophers Lao-tzu (c. 604–490 B.C.E.) and Chuang-tzu (c. 399–295 B.C.E.), although Daoist teachings were later radically reinterpreted. Later Daoism is called *Daojiao* (Daoist religion) rather than *Daojia* (School of Daoism), the name for classical Daoism. The Daoist religion sought to lead its adepts into such a harmonious relationship with the world that they would escape the horrors of disease and the tragedy of death. It was not life after death that they sought, but life without death, which they tried to achieve through the use of drugs, meditation, exercise, appropriate sexual activity, and purity of life. These approaches to immortality led to the development of traditional Chinese sciences, which include Chinese medicine, pharmacology, chemistry, and health care techniques. Traditional Chinese science also includes efforts to exploit the outside world in order to find a place for immortals to live. Such efforts constitute the earliest Chinese geographical work.

Buddhism was introduced to China around the first century B.C.E. In order for assimilation to take place, Buddhism had to undergo a process of contextualization in China. Chinese Buddhists declared that Buddhism is different from Daoism. In *The Emptiness of the Unreal,* the Buddhist philosopher Seng Chao (384–414) pointed out that Daoism teaches belief in *wu* (nothingness), which is a metaphysical reality. Buddhists, however, believe in *sunya* (emptiness), which is the negation of any kind of independent reality. Seng Chao also taught that all existences are conditioned by necessary causes and sufficient causes; there are no eternal realities in themselves. He quotes from the teaching of Buddha to assert "no life and no death, no continuousness and no discontinuousness. No universal and no particular, no come and no go … this is the first truth of Buddha." The basic teaching of Buddhism is to release human beings from suffering, which comes from desire. Buddhists strive to leave this world by entering the realm of *nibbana* or *nirvana,* where all the activities of the mind stop. From this point of view, Buddhism contributes little to science in Chinese culture.

See also CHINESE RELIGIONS, CONFUCIANISM AND SCIENCE IN CHINA; CHINESE RELIGIONS, DAOISM AND SCIENCE IN CHINA; CHINESE RELIGIONS, HISTORY OF SCIENCE AND RELIGION IN CHINA

Bibliography

Chan, Wing-tsit. *A Source Book in Chinese Philosophy.* Princeton, N.J.: Princeton University Press, 1963.

Ching, Julia. *Chinese Religions.* New York: Orbis, 1993.

Ropp, Paul S., ed. *Heritage of China: Contemporary Perspectives on Chinese Civilization.* Berkeley: University of California Press, 1990.

Thompson, Laurence G. *The Chinese Way in Religion.* Belmont, Calif.: Wadsworth, 1973.

Ying Siu-leung. *A Study on the Thought of Traditional Chinese Science.* Nanchang, China: Kiangsi People's Publisher, 2001.

HING KAU YEUNG

CHINESE RELIGIONS, CHINESE BUDDHISM AND SCIENCE

See BUDDHISM; BUDDHISM, CONTEMPORARY ISSUES IN SCIENCE AND RELIGION; BUDDHISM, HISTORY OF SCIENCE AND RELIGION

CHINESE RELIGIONS, CONFUCIANISM AND SCIENCE IN CHINA

The term of *Confucianism* is ambiguous. It refers to the ideology developed by a man named Confucius (522–479 B.C.E.), but Chinese scholars prefer to use the term *Rujia,* which means the school or teachings of the scholars. *Ru* was originally used to refer to dispossessed aristocrats of antiquity who were no longer warriors, but lived according to their knowledge of rituals, history, music, arithmetic, and archery. The term eventually became a designation of honor. The "school of *ru*" eventually came to encompass the ethical wisdom of the past that Confucius transmitted to later ages, as well as the entire development of the tradition after his time. In this sense, it constitutes the "religion" of the Chinese because it provides a system of beliefs and values that calls for faith and acceptance from adherents. It also qualifies as a religion in that it provides a way of life for adherents to follow, rather than a body of knowledge for them to master. In this regard, Confucianism is more comparable to Western religions than it is to Western philosophies. However, Confucianism is not a religion in the Western sense because it has no transcendental God, no eschatology or teaching beyond this life, and no organizational structure. It is only a teaching, and it teaches people how to live a noble life in a particular social context.

The teaching of Confucianism

The main teaching of Confucius is *jen,* which literally means "two persons." *Jen* is concerned with human relationships and with the virtue of the superior or noble person. *Jen* is associated with loyalty (*zhong*), referring basically to loyalty to one's own heart and conscience, rather than to a narrower political loyalty. *Jen* also refers to affection and love. The great Confucian thinker Mencius (371–289 B.C.E.) said, "The human being of *jen* loves others." However, *jen* should be guided by *yi* (righteousness), and a superior person must know how to love others and when not to love others. The Confucian interpretation of *jen* as universal love differs from that of Mo-tzu (fifth century B.C.E.), who advocated a love for all without distinction. The followers of Confucius emphasize the need of discernment, of making distinctions, and they reserve for parents and kin a special love. Familial relations provide a model for social behavior by which people should respect their own elders, as well as other's elders, and be kind to their own children and juniors, as well as those of others. This is the reason for the strong sense of solidarity not only in the Chinese family, but also in Confucian social organizations among overseas Chinese communities.

Ritual is an important part of Confucius's teachings as well, and Confucianism is also known as the ritual religion (*li-jiao*). Confucian teachings have helped keep alive an older cult of veneration for ancestors and the worship of heaven. This was a formal cult practiced by China's imperial rulers, who regarded themselves as the keepers of "Heaven's Mandate" of government, and were considered to be "High Priests," mediators between the human order and the divine order.

Before the twentieth century, the calendar of official sacrifices was determined by the Board of Astronomy according to established divinatory procedures and was published well in advance by the Ministry of Rites (*li-Pu*). During the last dynasty (Q'ing, 1644–1912), the Ministry of Rites performed the same functions as they did during the Han dynasty (206 B.C.E.–220 C.E.). The Ministry's most important responsibilities were educational, but it also kept records of all ceremonies the emperor attended, of the descendants of Confucius, and of Buddhist, Daoist, medical, and astronomical officials. All cases of filial piety, righteousness, and loyalty were reported to the emperor for rewards.

Neo-Confucianism

Neo-Confucianism develops the meaning of *jen* through the School of Mind. Wang Yang-ming (1472–1529) understood that the *hsin* (mind and heart) was the root of *jen,* according to which *hsin*-in-itself is the highest good. It exists beyond good and evil to distinguish what is good and evil. This is the substance of morality. Yang-ming called it *liang-chih* (inborn capacity to know the good) and *liang-neng,* which enables one to act according to one's originally good nature. When the mind is in good condition, for example, no human desire occupies it and the mind is clear and intelligent. If one has a clear and intelligent mind, one knows how to apply moral principle to daily life. It does not matter if one is versed in technical knowledge or knows how to complete a task. As Yang-ming puts it, if a person knows what filial piety is, that person will know how to treat his parents well.

Yang-ming does not distinguish between moral knowledge and cognitive knowledge, with the result that in Confucianism, moral knowledge suppresses cognitive knowledge. Contemporary neo-Confucianists understand this, and have revised Yang-ming's theory by stressing cognitive knowledge so as to open the door to modern science and democracy.

Confucianism and science

Traditional Confucianism valued science mainly for its practical applications. Astronomy and mathematics, for example, were valuable for divination and agricultural purposes. Both of them were also needed in making calendars, which were important for the agricultural economy. In addition, Chinese medicine was an early scientific tradition with many practical applications related to the surival of human beings.

Astronomers were active during the East Chou period (722–222 B.C.E.) in China. Almost all Chinese astronomers were also astrologers. They believed that the stars and celestial bodies affected the governmental bureaucracy, but seldom affected individuals or the population in general. The *Shiji* (Records of the historian), written by Sima Qian in 90 B.C.E. during the Han dynasty, includes a systematic chapter on astronomy. The chapter reviews the stars and constellations of the five "Palaces" (circumpolar, east, south, west, and north) and includes an elaborate discussion about planetary movements, including retrogradations, followed by the astrological association of the lunar mansions with specific terrestrial regions, and the interpretation of unusual appearances of the sun and moon, comets and meteors, clouds and vapors, earthquakes, and various harvest signs. The author also warns the emperor to pay attention to astronomy because it can help him learn how to govern the empire.

The most important early writing on mathematics is *Jiuzhang suanshu* (Nine chapters on the mathematical arts), written in 260 C.E. by Liu Hui. This work provides the first Chinese geometrical proofs in connection with finding the areas of a trapezium (a quadrilateral formed by two isosceles triangles) and other figures. The first chapter of *Jiuzhang suanshu* is a "Land Survey" that gives the correct rules for finding the areas of rectangles, trapeziums, triangles, circles, and arcs of circles and annuli. The second chapter, "Millet and Rice," deals with percentages and proportions, and reflects the management and production of various types of grains in Han China. The sixth chapter, "Impartial Taxation," deals with problems of pursuit and alligation, especially in connection with the time required for people to carry their grain contributions from their native towns to the capital.

Nearly one thousand Chinese mathematical treatises from the second century C.E. onward survive. The great majority have to do with the kinds of practical matters that government officials, their clerks, and landowners would encounter, such as surveying land and calculating exchange rates and taxes payable in money and commodities. The predominantly practical orientation of Chinese mathematics makes it neither inferior nor superior to the Western tradition. Its lack of development at the abstract geometric level was balanced by its strength in numerical problem solving.

Another important function of mathematics in premodern China was divination (*shu*) and astrology (*suan*), both of which included numerology. Some divination techniques also identify regularities underlying the flux of natural phenomena.

In general, Confucianism is mainly concerned with ethics, morality, and political theory rather than science and technology. Although Confucianism essentially functioned as the state religion, it was conspicuously un-religious. Confucian scholars who lived during the long period (approx. two thousand years) of unity of Chinese society always set the social agenda concerning how to "cultivate their persons, regulate their families, govern well their states and finally exemplify illustrious virtue throughout the world" (c. fifth to first century, *Great Learning*). The purpose of science and technology in a Confucian society is to help a person to be a good politician and sage. Thus, moral teachings are more important than natural scientific findings, and scientific discourse in Chinese culture tends to be full of speculations and metaphors, rather than accurate factual information.

Confucian tradition has not been concerned with scientific theory, so traditional Chinese sciences have focused on practical applications in medicine, agriculture, arithmetic, and astronomy. Traditional Chinese sciences have also stressed the political and moral implications of science and technology. Nonetheless, Chinese scientists are credited with some important inventions, including paper, the compass, the art of printing, and the production of gunpowder. Although the compass was invented in China around 2700 B.C.E., there was no further scientific theory of the compass. The Chinese people used compasses mostly for determining *Feng Shui* (wind and water), a folk superstition by which people set up a comfortable living environment. Although it can not be denied that technical investigations were fruitful in Chinese history and resulted in many inventions, scientific theorization remained on the level of factual description and empirical interpretation. For example, traditional Chinese medicine involves a great deal of speculation that is not supported by clinical experimentation; it remains on the level of abstract thinking and intuitive observation. Arithmetic was also mainly used for practical calculation that did not require abstract thinking, so no mathematical theory or formal logical system was developed.

Under the ideology of Confucianism, science and technology had to deal with daily issues of human society, and Confucian scholars made little effort to engage in scientific and technological research. Science and technology were generally regarded as merely a means for human beings, with no ultimate value in helping someone become a sage. This may be one of the main drawbacks of the Confucian value system and worldview: It has served as a drag on Chinese scientific and technological development.

See also CHINESE RELIGIONS AND SCIENCE; CHINESE RELIGIONS, HISTORY OF SCIENCE AND RELIGION IN CHINA; MATHEMATICS

Bibliography

Chan, Wing-tsit. *A Source Book in Chinese Philosophy*. Princeton, N.J.: Princeton University Press, 1963.

Ching, Julia. *Chinese Religions*. New York: Orbis, 1993.

de Bary, William Theodore. *Sources of Chinese Tradition*. New York: Columbia University Press, 1960.

Great Learning. c. Fifth to First century B.C.E.

Ho, Peng Hoke. *Li, Qi, and Shu: An Introduction to Science and Civilization in China*. Hong Kong: Hong Kong University Press, 1985.

Needham, Joseph. *Science and Civilisation in China*. Cambridge, UK: Cambridge University Press, 1956.

Ropp, Paul S., ed. *Heritage of China: Contemporary Perspectives on Chinese Civilization*. Berkeley: University of California Press, 1990.

Ying Siu-leung. *A Study on the Thought of Traditional Chinese Science*. Nanchang, China: Kiangsi People's Publisher, 2001.

HING KAU YEUNG

CHINESE RELIGIONS, DAOISM AND SCIENCE IN CHINA

As the native religion of China, Daoism (also spelled Taoism), together with Confucianism and Buddhism, comprises the main body of traditional Chinese culture. Daoists, in pursuit of the ideal of becoming immortals by practicing *Dao*, made great efforts to transcend conventional wisdom about life and knowledge and so helped both to define ancient science in China and to advance it through a great number of inventions.

Relationship between Daoism and science

For a long time, many Western translators, writers, and scholars misunderstood Daoist thought, largely overlooking its scientific and protoscientific aspects. Moreover, different understandings of what constitutes science have rendered the issue more confusing. While some scholars denied any link between Daoism and science, many studies have confirmed an important relationship between them.

Daoist thought is basic to Chinese science and technology. Daoism provided a philosophical foundation for the development of science; its love for nature, its conception of change, its unique mastery of the relationship between human beings and nature, and its pursuit of freedom are based on the exploration of nature. Daoist admiration for ancient scientific inventors, and their absorption of science and technology in history, show that Daoism tried to reach its religious ideal by means of science. In addition, Daoism's cultural structure is favorable for science. The unique Daoist ideal of material immortality is invaluable in stimulating the observation and exploration of nature and life, and the development of techniques of alchemy, medicine, and related fields.

Daoists regard Dao as the origin of all things, including human beings, and they believe that people can return to Dao and thus attain immortality. Because immortality can be acquired through learning, one's life rests with oneself rather than heaven. Daoist scriptures include such sayings as "Probe into the mystery of heaven and earth and understand the root of creation" (*The Taoist Canon,* Vol. 18, p. 671). In fact, such explorations serve the goal of achieving oneness with the Dao, which leads to becoming an omniscient and almighty immortal, a True Human of True Knowledge.

Unrealistic as immortality is, many Daoist ideas, techniques, and practices for longevity are reasonable and scientific. They constituted the most important part of Daoist spiritual heritage in the Middle Ages. Thus, Joseph Needham argues in *Science and Civilization in China* (1956) that Daoism "developed many of the most important features of the scientific attitude, and is therefore of cardinal importance for the history of science in China" (vol. 2, p.161). Similarly, Welch Holmes writes in *Taoism: The Parting of the Way* (1957) that "the Daoist movement has sometimes been called the Chinese counterpart of Western science … To a large extent the Daoists practiced experimental science" (p.134).

Daoist contributions to science

Hua Tuo, a famous Daoist doctor in the third century C.E., was the first to use a type of anesthesia called *ma fei san.* He also formulated the gymnastic techniques called *wu qin xi* (imitation of five-animal playing) for nourishing vitality of life. A text of Daoist prescription *Zhou Hou Bai Yi Fang* (Collection of prescriptions for hundred-and-one diseases fourth century C.E.), written by Ge Hong and enlarged by Tao Hongjing, contains the first known record of the disease of smallpox. It also records therapeutic techniques for dealing with a variety of acute medical conditions, including artificial respiration, bleeding stoppage, abdominocentesis, catheterization, clyster, intestinal anastomosis, *débridement* (sore cleaning), drainage, fracture treatment with superficial fixture, and disjointed articulation restituting. Remarkably, this work recorded an anti-malaria treatment using southernwood (*Artemisia annua* L.). In the 1970s, scientists extracted artemisinin from southernwood, which is a significant discovery in the history of antimalaria

treatments from medicines of the quinoline category. Sun Simiao, a great Daoist doctor, summed up in the seventh century C.E. the prevention of struma by using animal thyroid and the prevention of nyctalopia by using animal livers. And the treatment of restituting mandible disjointing that Sun Simiao put forward is still in use in modern medicine. *Jin Si Xuan Xuan* (The incredible mysteries in the golden box), a Daoist text of parasitology written sometime between the fourteenth and seventeenth centuries C.E., enumerated a "Catalogue of Nine Parasite Species" with illustrations of various kinds of parasites, as well as figures depicting their life cycles.

In seeking elixirs from the bodies of human beings themselves, Daoists made great strides in the field of biochemistry. Both Joseph Needham and Lu Gwei-Djen hold that the medicine named *qiushi,* which was made by medieval Daoists, is a relatively pure preparation of urinary steroid hormones. A similar medicine was made in the West by a German biochemist in the early twentieth century.

Daoists also acquired solid knowledge of certain chemical reaction processes. They accurately described the reversible reactions between mercury and thiosugar. *Long Hu Huan Dan Jue* (The oral formula for cyclically transformed elixir of dragon and tiger), written by Jin Ling Zi, an expert in alchemy in the Tang Dynasty (618–907), recorded precise methods of making arsenic-copper alloy and of extracting pure copper, methods developed by Daoists over many generations. Instead of conforming to an older Daoist tradition of keeping key links secret or of using obscure terminology, this text clearly and definitely states strict rules of operation that are similar to those of modern chemistry.

As the basic components of gunpowder in ancient China were niter, sulfur, and carbonaceous substances, all frequently used in Daoist alchemical experiments, the invention of gunpowder can be traced back to Daoist writings in the Han Dynasty (206 B.C.E.–220 C.E.). The formula included in *Bao Pu Zi Nei Pian* (The inner chapters of the Philosopher Master-Who-Embraces-Simplicity), written by Ge Hong in the fourth century C.E., already covered the basic composition of gunpowder. In the middle of the ninth century C.E., the Daoist scripture *Zhen Yuan Miao Dao Yao Lue* (Classified essentials of the mysterious Tao of the true origin of things) clearly recorded the precise composition of gunpowder. Obviously, the time of its invention was much earlier.

Many Daoists were also metallurgists. The hydrometallurgical technique of smelting copper from cupric sulfate liquor was first used in China in Daoist alchemic practices. It can be traced back to *Huai Nan Zi* (The book of Master Huainan), a Daoist text written in the early years of the first century C.E., it formally appeared in Daoist texts of the Tang Dynasty, and it became the prevailing technique of copper production during the Song Dynasty (960–1279). It was no later than the Song Dynasty that Daoists had identified the element arsenic and extracted pure samples of it. Around the year 550 C.E., a Daoist practitioner invented a technique of steel production called *guan gang fa,* by which pig iron and wrought iron were heated together to a certain temperature for higher quality steel. With its moderate carbon content, this kind of steel was ideal for making high-quality tools. This technique was widely used and refined in China during the succeeding one thousand years.

With seven kinds of materials, Daoist alchemists created the earliest fireproof sealing material called *six-one mud.* They made glass and preserved valuable technical data in their writings. They wrote works on casting techniques such as *Shen Xian Lian Dan Dian Zhu San Yuan Bao Zhao Fa* (Spot casting methods of bronze mirror of the three origins of things by the immortals), in which they recorded in detail the techniques of quality control in casting. Ever since *Huai Nan Zi* in the Han Dynasty, Daoists used mercury-tin alloy and later added lead amalgam to create an ideal media for bronze mirror polishing.

A technique involving the suspending of magnetized needles was used by Daoists to test the quality of lodestone, which was a major healing object in alchemy. Eventually, this technique led to the invention of the magnetic needle compass. In addition, modern scientists found that *Wu Yue Zhen Xing Tu* (Maps of the true topography of the five sacred mountains), drawn in the third or fourth centuries C.E. and treasured by Daoists over the last eighteen centuries, contains the earliest type of contour map. The maps roughly reflect the local terrain and routes of the mountains.

Precise clock devices are of great importance in Daoist practices. Throughout Chinese history, many Daoists participated in the invention and improvement of the water clock. The famous *cheng lou,* a scale-controlled water clock invented by a Daoist named Li Lan, was widely used in the 400 years between the fifth and eighth centuries C.E., and served as an important component of various types of compounded clock devices in China. It was also used in the medieval Islamic world; studies show that Muslims probably learned about such clocks from the Chinese. Daoists of the Quanzhen Sect even invented portable water clock devices. A scripture called *Quanzhen Zuo Bo Jie Fa* (Quanzhen Sect easy preparation for sitting quiet in meditation), written between the tenth and fourteenth centuries C.E., recorded the technical details of making, debugging, and controlling the clocks.

Zhang Zhihe, a Daoist who lived during the Tang Dynasty, expounded the phenomenon of duration of vision, as it was called in modern optics. Later, another Daoist, Tan Qiao, who lived during the Five Dynasties (907–960), discussed the phenomenon of reflection of plane mirrors. Zhao Youqin, a Daoist of the Quanzhen sect who wrote the famous scientific work *Ge Xiang Xin Shu* (New Book on the Investigation of Astronomical Phenomena) in the Yuan Dynasty (1260–1368), conducted a series of large-scale experiments on geometric optical problems, such as rectilinear propagation of light, hole imaging, and intensity of illumination. He came to correct conclusions in these fields two centuries earlier than Galileo Galilei (1564–1642). His rough conclusion that "illumination intensifies as the intensity of light source enhances, but decreases as the image distance increases" appeared four hundred years earlier than Lambert's formula of qualitative illumination published in 1760, according to which "illumination is in reverse proportion to distance squared." In the early years of the nineteenth century, there were still Daoist believers in Guangzhou who studied with an open mind both the traditional Daoist theory of sphere-heavens and modern European astronomy.

In order to avoid losses in their alchemical experiments and for many other religious purposes, Daoists conducted weather observation and forecast. Their scripture *Yu Yang Qi Hou Qin Ji* (The near forcasting of the weather of rain or fine) analyzed scientifically the causes of wind and rain and recorded in terse but vivid verses their observations, which conform with modern meteorological science. They even provided various types of "cloud pictures" in the text.

Daoists not only explored but also wanted to navigate the heavens. The "flying vehicle made of jujube heart timber," recorded by Ge Hong in his *Bao Pu Zi Nei Pian* and regarded as the earliest design for a propeller aircraft, reveals the Daoist knowledge of the aerodynamic principles of flight. Modern scientists have recreated the vehicle according to Ge Hong's records and testified it to be technically reasonable. Ge Hong added that when rising to a height of forty *li* (about 12.44 miles) into the heavens, one can reach the outer space of *taiqing* (super clarity), where the air is powerful enough to support flying objects, helping them to fly naturally by inertia instead of motive forces. This is close to the law of First Cosmic Velocity in the modern science of astronautics. In the fourth century C.E., a hermit Daoist named Wang Jia wrote *Shi Yi Ji* (Record of gleaning), in which he claimed that once there had been a huge space aircraft named *Cha* ridden by the immortals. This aircraft used the sea as its base for launching and landing, and it continually navigated around the four seas, making a circuit every twelve years.

With the invention of gunpowder and the subsequent emergence of applied techniques for the control of its explosive power, the idea arose of using it as a rocket propellant. In the fifteenth century, an official of the Ming Dynasty named Wan Hoo conducted and died in the first attempt at manned rocket flight in human history—propelled by forty-seven gunpowder rockets. A Daoist biographical text formally printed in 1909 includes a description of a Daoist beauty who launched her aircraft into the heavens from a silo by means of a propellant compounded from cyprinoid fat.

Daoists were responsible for rich scientific achievements in many other fields, including cosmology, uranography, calendar making, geography, geology, mineralogy, botany, zoology, pharmaceutics, architecture, porcelain production, dye making, wine making, zymurgy, cerebral science, acoustics, wushu, sex hygiene, strategics, and psychology. Because the impetus for scientific exploration comes for Daoists from their religious belief in immortality, their science was inevitably bound by the ideas, purposes, and the historical development of Daoism. Therefore, it was impossible for

science to gain an independent and deep development within the Daoist framework. Yet the remarkable achievements of Chinese science were also enabled and inspired by the Daoist interpretation of reality.

See also DAO

Bibliography

Dao Zang (The Taoist canon). Beijing: Wenwu Press, 1988.

Holmes, Welch. *Taoism: The Parting of the Way,* Rev. edition. Boston: Beacon Press, 1957.

Hua, Tong-xu. *Zhong Guo Lou Ke* (*Water Clock in China*). Hefei, China: Anhui Science and Technology Press, 1991.

Jiang, Sheng, and Tong, Waihop, eds. *Zhong Guo Dao Jiao Ke Xue Ji Shu Shi: Han Wei Liang Jin Juan* (A history of science and technology in Taoism), Vol. 1. Beijing: Science Press, 2002.

Jin, Zheng-yao. *Taoism and Science,* trans. Joe Smith. New York: Macmillan, 1991.

Needham, Joseph. *Science and Civilization in China,* Vol. 2: *History of Scientific Thought.* Cambridge, UK: Cambridge University Press, 1956.

Needham, Joseph. *Gunpowder as the Fourth Power, East and West.* Hong Kong: Hong Kong University Press, 1985.

Sivin, Nathan. *Medicine, Philosophy, and Religion in Ancient China: Researches and Reflections.* Aldershot, UK, and Brookfield, Vt.: Variorum, 1995.

Sleewyk, Andre Wegener. "The Celestial River: A Reconstruction." *Technology and Culture* 19 (3) (1978): 423–449.

Volkov, Alexei. "Science and Daoism: An Introduction." *Taiwanese Journal for Philosophy and History of Science* 5, no. 1 (1996): 1–58.

Yoshinobu, Sakade. *ChuKoKu ShiSou KenKYu: Iyaku You-Jou, KaGaKu ShiSou ben* (A study of Chinese thought: Essays on traditional medicine, pharmacy, nourishing vitality, and science). Osaka, Japan: Kansai University Press, 1999.

Zhao, Kuanghua, and Zhou, Jiahua. *A History of Science and Technology in China,* Vol.: Chemistry. Beijing: Science Press, 1999.

Zhen-dou, Wang. "The Recreating of Flying Vehicle Recorded in 'The Inner Chapters of the Philosopher Master-Who-Embraces-Simplicity' by Ge Hong." *Magazine of Chinese Museum of History* 6 (1984).

Zhu, Ya-ping. *Dao Jia Wen Hua Yu Ke Xue* (Taoism culture and science). Hefei, China: University of Science and Technology of China Press, 1995.

Zim, Herbert S. *Rockets and Jets.* New York: Harcourt, 1945.

JIANG SHENG

CHINESE RELIGIONS, HISTORY OF SCIENCE AND RELIGION IN CHINA

The terms *religion* and *science,* which were introduced to China in the seventeenth century by Jesuit missionaries, are controversial in a Chinese context. *Religion* in Chinese is *jiao* (systems of teachings and beliefs); in this sense, Chinese religions include Confucianism, Daoism, Buddhism, and the religions of antiquity. Whether Confucianism has a religious dimension is debatable, but Daoism certainly qualifies as a religion. Since Buddhism came from India, its religious character is quite different from those of Confucianism and Daoism. As for the term *science,* the very notion of a "Chinese science" is problematic. The modern concept of science cannot be used to measure ancient Chinese ideas, theories, studies, or inventions because doing so would misrepresent the merits of traditional science in Chinese culture. It cannot be denied that there were great inventions in ancient Chinese history, including gunpowder, the compass, paper making, and the art of printing. However, these inventions did not lead to modern scientific discoveries, and thus there is a gap between traditional Chinese science and modern Chinese science. In fact, modern Chinese science has been a recent development in response to the Western world.

Religion and science in ancient China

During the Shang dynasty (1766–1122 B.C.E.), ancient Chinese people believed that their ancestors, upon death, would continue to exist in heaven, the home of the divine ruler or lord on high (*Shang-ti*), and from heaven they could influence human affairs. According to oracle bones that were discovered at the end of the nineteenth century in Anyang in northern China, Shang-ti watches over human society and regulates the workings of the universe. In view of the close relationship between religious worship and family clans, it is possible that Shang-ti was the chief god of the ruling family clan. Thus, the ascendancy of Shang-ti in religion closely parallels the political ascendancy of the family clan that practiced the cult of Shang-ti. Beneath him are a number of lesser deities of the sun, moon, stars, wind, rain, and particular mountains and rivers.

The oracle bones, which were made from tortoise shells or the shoulder blades of oxen, bore inscriptions written by the Yin or Shang people for purposes of divination. Yin people believed that dead animals had the power to contact divine figures, including the ancestors of humans, in the spiritual world. Divination rituals were performed by three groups of functionaries: persons who posed the questions; persons in charge of the ritual itself, which included cracking the oracle bones with heated bronze rods or thorns; and persons who interpreted the resulting patterns of the cracks. In the case of royal divination, official recorders or archivists also took part. After the fall of the Shang dynasty, people who lived during the early years of the Chou dynasty (1122–1249 B.C.E.) continued to practice divination using shells and bones, then the practice died out.

Divination presupposes a belief in spirits and their power to protect the living. Ancient Chinese people believed that the cosmos consists of three levels: heaven above, the dwelling place of the dead below, and the Earth in between them. When people die, the "upper soul" (the psyche) rises up to heaven while the "lower soul" (the physical body and emotions) descends to the underworld. Ancestors of the royal family were considered to be the most powerful among the dead on account of their special relationship with the gods. It was believed that they dwell in high heaven in the company of the gods, where they continue to have power over the living, either to protect and bless them or to punish and curse them.

From the inscriptions on oracle bones, scholars know not only the divination activities but also the scientific activities of Yin people. Oracle bones record eclipses and novae, as well as names of stars and constellations. They show that Yin people used a lunar calendar with twelve *yues* (moons or lunar months) in one lunar year. Each lunar month consisted of twenty-nine or thirty days, and every two or three years one extra month, known as the intercalary month, was added to keep the lunar year in step with the corresponding solar year. Numerals found on oracle bones also indicate that Yin people used a decimal system.

In the Warring States period (480–381 B.C.E.), the disciples of Mo Zi (479–381 B.C.E.) made great contributions to natural science, especially in the areas of statics, hydrostatics, dynamics, and optics. Mohist physicists understood that light travels in straight lines. By using fixed light sources, screens with pinhole apertures, and possibly the camera obscura, they were able to study the formation of inverted images and the idea of the focal point.

Confucianism

Confucianism is the English word for *Ru-jia* (School of Scholars), which was founded by the philosopher and teacher Confucius (551–479 B.C.E.). The name *Confucius* is the Latinized form of *Kong Fu-tzu,* a respectful way of addressing the master. *Kong* was his family name. Confucius lived in a time when the empire was fragmenting into numerous feudal states. It was a time of change, disorder, and degeneration of the traditional moral and political order. Confucius can truly be said to have molded Chinese civilization to a great extent. The central concept of his teaching is *jen,* a word that literally means the relationship of two persons, and Confucius's teachings focus on human interpersonal relationships. It is a humanistic approach to philosophical thinking. *Jen* is associated with loyalty (*zhong*), that is, loyalty to one's own heart and conscience. *Jen* is also related to reciprocity (*shu*), that is, respect of and consideration for others. Confucius did not care to talk about spiritual beings or even about life after death. Instead, he believed that human beings "can make the Way (Dao) great," and not that "the Way can make man great" (*Analects* 15:28). Although his teachings concentrate on human beings, Confucius's primary concern is good society based on good government and harmonious human relations. To this end he advocated a good government ruled by virtue and moral example rather than by punishment or force. His criterion for goodness is righteousness as opposed to profit. It is the ideal of a sage or a superior person to apply this inner morality to the outside world. Such an approach is called *nei-sheng wai-huang,* or sagacity within and kingliness without. The opposite of a sage is an inferior man.

The Confucian sage does not withdraw from the business of the world. In his inner sagacity, he accomplishes spiritual cultivation; in his outward kingliness, he functions in society. It is not necessary for the sage to be the actual head of the government in his society. From the standpoint of practical politics, a Confucian sage usually had little chance of becoming the head of the state in Chinese history before the twentieth century. The saying "sagacity within and kingliness without" means only that he who has the noblest spirit should, theoretically, be king. A student of Confucius once asked him: "If a ruler extensively confers benefit on the people and can bring salvation to all, what do you think of him? Would you call him a man of humanity?" Confucius replied: "Why only a man of humanity? He is without doubt a sage. Even Yao and Shun [legendary emperors before the Shang dynasty] fall short of it. A man of humanity, wishing to establish his own character, also establishes the character of others, and wishing to be prominent himself, also helps others to be prominent. To be able to judge others by what is near to ourselves may be called the method realizing humanity" (*Analects* 6:28).

Confucianism emphasizes not just social behavior. It confers definite importance on rituals, including religious rituals, and has even been called a "ritual religion" (*li-jiao*). The Chinese word for *ritual* is related to the word *worship* or *sacrificial vessel* with definite religious overtones. The Confucian emphasis on political responsibility explains why during much of Chinese history Confucianism served the function of a civil religion. From the Han dynasty (206 B.C.E.–220 C.E.) on, an elaborate state cult was developed. It has been, rightly or wrong, attributed to Confucian teachings, which include expressions of very ancient beliefs in a supreme deity.

Daoism

Daoism as religion can be traced back to ancient China, especially to Lao-tzu (c. 604–490 B.C.E.) and Chuang-tzu (c. 369–286 B.C.E.). However, the Daoists reinterpreted the teachings of their religion radically in later centuries. In the third century C.E., the first legendary emperor of ancient China, Huang-di (the Yellow Emperor), was worshiped together with Lao-tzu as Huang-Lao in a cult that involved pursuing immortality and changing base metals into gold. From that time on, the Daoist religion identified with the quest for immortality, including physical immortality, through the search for elixirs in alchemy and through yogalike exercises. Elixirs frequently contained toxic compounds derived from mercury, lead, sulfur, arsenic, and so on, certain to cause poisoning. If metallic poisoning might bring death, there was also the hope that such death was temporary, as a necessary phase in the quest for eternal life. Although mercuric and lead compounds can be fatal when swallowed, they are also known to have preservative powers. It may be that Daoists believed the power of faith would protect their physical bodies from corruption, so that their souls would remain with their bodies and eventually attain immortality together.

The strong idea of elixir alchemy for eternal life contributed to traditional Chinese medicine, while yogalike exercises contributed to health care. Yoga techniques are based on the theory of interaction between body and spirit and the possibility of controlling one's mental state by manipulating one's body.

Daoism, according to some scholars, is *the* folk religion of Chinese people. Unlike Confucianism, Daoism seeks to guide its believers beyond this transitory life to a happy eternity. Daoists believe in an original state of bliss, which is followed by the present human condition, the fallen state. Daoists also rely on supernatural powers for help and protection.

Daoists believe in a supreme emperor deity called Yu-huang-da-di, who governs over a heavenly universe of deities and immortals, many of them famous historical figures. The Daoist religion offers its doctrines of the cosmos and the cosmic process and harmony, tracing all back to the great ultimate (*tai chi*) and to the interactions of the two great modes of *yin* and *yang*. Yin, the great feminine mode, denotes all figures, things, and processes of negativity, passivity, staticity, and concealment. Yang, the great masculine mode, denotes all figures, things, and processes of positivity, activity, dynamism, and manifestation. Yin and yang are the basic principles for classification and explanation in traditional Chinese daily life, science and technology, medicine, and philosophy. With such unique categories, a truly traditional "Chinese science" is very different in character from a Westernized scientific enterprise in modern China.

Daoists do not conceive of eternal life in terms of spiritual immortality alone. They anticipate the survival of the whole person, including the body. The means by which Daoism pursues immortality, which should enable immortality to be realized in this life on Earth, are empirical and congenial to the geographical environment, to health care, and to elixir alchemy. Thus, the influence of Daoism on the development of traditional "Chinese science" is substantial.

Mohism

In Chinese, a follower of Confucianism is called a *ru*. The *ru* and the *hsieh* (knights errant) originated as specialists attached to the houses of the aristocrats and were themselves members of the upper classes. In later times the *ru* continued to come mainly from the upper or middle classes, but the *hsieh* were more frequently recruited from the lower classes. In ancient times, such social amenities as rituals and music were exclusively for aristocrats; for the common person, therefore, rituals and music were luxuries that had no practical utility. It was from this vantage point that Mo Zi and the Mohists, who came from the *hsieh* class, criticized the traditional institutions, including Confucius and Confucianism.

Unlike Confucius, Mo Zi believed in a personal God and the existence of spirits, and he submitted himself to the will of God. He saw his mission as rescuing the people from suffering, and he proclaims the all-embracing love. He and his followers explored science and technology so they would have the skills they needed to put their ideas into practice.

The school of Mohism introduced epistemology, as well as formal, abstract, and geometrical notions such as a dimensionless geometrical point in space and time. According to Mohist epistemology, the knowing faculty must be confronted with an object of knowledge. The human mind interprets the impressions of external objects, which are brought to it by the senses. The *Mo Jing* (Book of Mohism) provides various logical classifications of knowledge. For example, names are classified into three kinds: general, classifying, and private. The knowledge of correspondence is that which knows which name corresponds to which actuality. Such knowledge is required for the statement of a proposition like "This is a table." When one has this kind of knowledge, one knows that "names and actualities pair with each other" (*Mo Jing*, Ch. 42).

Mohists also touch on atomic theory in their discussion of the strengths of materials, but they never articulate it clearly or develop its consequences. The *Mo Jing* also contains some remarkable statements about the study of motion. Though ancient Chinese scientists accomplished little in theoretical dynamics, they did consider forces in some detail, and they appear to have come remarkably close to the principle of inertia as stated by Isaac Newton (1642–1727). Mohists also investigated the relativity of motion, motion along inclined planes or slopes, and particular problems of moving spheres. Unfortunately, Mohism disappeared during the first century B.C.E., and its important scientific findings were only rediscovered in the twentieth century.

Cosmology

During the first century B.C.E., an impressive cosmology arose in China. "Before heaven and earth had taken form all was vague and amorphous. Therefore it was called the Great Beginning. The Great Beginning produced emptiness, and emptiness produced the universe. The universe produced material-force, which had limits. That which was clear and light drifted up to become heaven, while that which was heavy and turbid solidified to become earth" (*Huai-nan Tzu* 3:1a). This cosmology is different from that of Buddhism, for Buddhists maintain that the origin of the universe comes from the blind consciousness that is no reality. Daoism, however, maintains that the origin of the universe lies with the great ultimate (tai chi), which is also called *wu* (literally, nothingness or nonbeing). The tai chi emblem, which consists of a circle with an s-shaped curve dividing it into two complementing black and white regions, represents respectively the yin and yang as two great modal forces of the cosmos in mutual interpenetration. Each region being punctured in the middle by a dot of the opposite region, further underscoring this dialectical interpenetration. It is meant to be an empirical sign of the origin of the universe.

The cosmology of Confucianism is explained by the *Tai-chi-t'u-shuo* (An explanation of the diagram of the Great Ultimate) by Chou Tun-i, a scholar who lived during the Sung (Song) dynasty (960–1297 C.E.) and a pioneer of neo-Confucianism. Although Chou Tun-i may have obtained his diagram from a Daoist priest, it is unlike any diagram of the Daoists. For Chou Tun-i, the great ultimate is an abstract principle that is the ultimate metaphysical reality. In his explanation, the myriad things are created through the evolutionary process of creation from the great ultimate through the dialectical interaction of the passive cosmic force, yin, and the active cosmic force, yang. Chou Tun-i faithfully followed the *Book of Changes* or *I-ching* rather than Daoism. He assimilated the Daoist concept of nonbeing with Confucian thought, but in so doing he discarded the fantasy and mysticism of Daoism. This diagram of Chou Tun-i has been described as a cosmology of creation without a creator.

In his diagram he said that the ultimate of nonbeing is also the great ultimate (tai chi). The great ultimate generates yang through movement. When its activity reaches its limit, movement turns into tranquility. The great ultimate generates yin through tranquility. When tranquility reaches its limit, activity begins again. So movement and tranquility alternate and become the cause of each other, giving rise to the distinction of yin and yang, and the two modes are thus established. By the transformation of yang and its union with yin, the five agents, elements, or phases of metal, wood, water, fire, and Earth arise. When the material forces of these five agents are distributed in harmonious order, the four seasons run their course. The creating order is called Dao (the Way), which governs not only the Earth but also human life and society. Following the Dao should be the purpose of all one's activities, including governmental, societal, familial, and personal ones. Thus, Dao as the most fundamental principle or cosmological law is objective and natural.

Other sciences in Chinese history

Astronomy. There was no distinction between astronomy and astrology in traditional China. The oracle bone inscriptions include records of eclipses, novae, and names of stars and some constellations, and star catalogs were produced during the Warring States period. The earliest extant Chinese documents on astronomy are two silk scrolls discovered in 1973 in the Mawangdui tombs in Changsha in the Hunan province. One of them, the *Wuxingzhan* (Astrology of the five planets), which was written between 246 and 177 B.C.E, contains records of Jupiter, Saturn, and Venus, the accuracy of which suggests the use of an armillary sphere for measurement. An important role of Chinese astronomy was calendar calculation. Every emperor regarded calendar making as one of his duties associated with the mandate that he received from heaven. The calendar, issued in the emperor's name, became part of the ritual paraphernalia that demonstrated his dynastic right to rule. Astrological observations could easily be manipulated and thus could be dangerous in the hands of someone trying to undermine the current dynasty. It was therefore a principle of state policy that the proper place to conduct astronomical studies was the imperial court. During certain periods it was illegal to do it elsewhere. Thus, an ancient scientific pursuit such as astronomy was deeply embedded in the social matrix of ancient China, although Chinese astronomy could not be pursued as an independent activity like its modern western counterpart.

Medicine. Classical Chinese medicine has often been represented as an empirical science that is based on the clinically sound use of effective natural drugs and other remedies. Scientific theories served primarily as mnemonic devices or as mystification to confuse the untrained. Some scholars portray classical Chinese medicine as a corpus of theory-based adaptations of the yin-yang and five-agents concepts. As such, the body was understood as a multilevel interconnected system, and illnesses were treated holistically. The most famous medical texts were compiled before the Qin period (before 211 B.C.E.) and completed during the Han dynasty. Among extant texts, the most important are *Huangdi Neijing* (Yellow Emperor's inner canon) and *Shennong Bencao Jing* (Divine husbandry's classic of herbology), which laid the foundation for clinical science with definite treatment and diagnostic principles. Chinese pharmacology also reveals outstanding achievements during this period. Shennong's *Classic of Herbology* presents many effective remedies. It also provides the theoretical basis of drug use, as well as the collection, preservation, and mixing of herbs, and their methods of administration.

From the second century C.E. onward, medical disciplines were professionalized. Clinical medicine developed greatly from the third to the tenth centuries. The *Zouhou Beiji Fang* (Handbook of prescription for emergency) in the fourth century includes information on smallpox and a treatment for hydrophobia that used the brain tissue of a mad dog. The academic standard of Chinese medicine was further upgraded during the Ming and Qing dynasties (1368–1911 C.E.). A new medical school was established to study acute infections, and researchers there successfully tackled many infectious diseases, including B-encephalitis, acute viral hepatitis, and other viral diseases.

Chinese medicine never produced a detailed and accurate picture of anatomy and physiology. The philosophical concept of yin-yang was the basic theory for interpreting complex relationships between the upper and lower emotions, the inner basis and the outer manifestations of the body's activities and functions. Moreover, classical Chinese medicine was not concerned with microorganisms or details of the body's organs and tissues. The strength of classical Chinese medical discourse lies rather in its sophisticated analysis of how bodily functions are related on many levels, from the vital processes of the body to the emotions, to the natural and social environment of the patient. In this sense, traditional Chinese medicine stresses a holistic view of health rather than analytical research on the physical body.

See also CHINESE RELIGIONS AND SCIENCE; CHINESE RELIGIONS, CONFUCIANISM AND SCIENCE IN CHINA; CHINESE RELIGIONS, DAOISM AND SCIENCE IN CHINA

Bibliography

Chan, Wing-tsit. *A Source Book in Chinese Philosophy.* Princeton, N.J.: Princeton University Press, 1963.

Chen, Bangzian. *A History of Chinese Medicine.* Beijing: Commercial Press, 1957.

Ching, Julia. *Chinese Religions.* New York: Orbis, 1993.

Ho, Peng Hoke. *Li, Qi and Shu: An Introduction to Science and Civilization in China.* Hong Kong: Hong Kong University Press, 1985. Reprint edition, Mineola, N.Y.: Dover, 2000.

Needham, Joseph. *Science and Civilisation in China,* Vol. 2: *History of Scientific Thought.* Cambridge, UK: Cambridge University Press, 1956.

Ropp, Paul S., ed. *Heritage of China: Contemporary Perspectives on Chinese Civilization.* Berkeley: University of California Press, 1990.

Yeung, Hing kau. "The Meaning of Theological Knowledge in the Western Dualism and the Chinese Cosmology." *Jian Dao* 5 (1996): 51–64.

Ying, Siu-leung. *Zhongguo Chuantong Kexue Sixiang Yanjiu (A Study on the Thought of Traditional Chinese Science).* Nanchang, China: JiangXi People's Publisher, 2001.

HING KAU YEUNG

CHRISTIANITY

Christians were first called "Christians," according to Acts 11: 26, at Antioch in 40 to 44 C.E. A Christian is one who accepts Jesus of Nazareth as Messiah (or in Greek, the Christ), the Anointed One of God—the one who shows and makes present in history God's nature and purpose for creation.

Normally Christians believe in one creator God, threefold in being (Father, Son, and Spirit). The Son is the Logos or Wisdom of God, the archetype of all creation, who was incarnate in Jesus, reconciling an estranged creation to the divine being through Jesus' death and resurrection. The Spirit, the creative energy of God, is known in the fellowship of the Church, which mediates the presence of the risen Christ to the world. Christians believe that human beings have turned away from the love of God to selfish desire (are "in sin"), but God wills that all should turn back to God, and in Christ calls them and empowers them to return. At the end of history, Christ will be disclosed in glory, and all who have not finally rejected God will receive the gift of eternal life in the presence of God. The "gospel," or good news, is that God forgives sin and offers eternal life to all through Christ.

Christianity has expanded from a small Jewish messianic sect to become the largest religion in the world, with an estimated two billion adherents. It has taken many forms, and there are well over a thousand Christian denominations. Some denominations think of themselves as "Biblical Christians," meaning that they take the Bible as the basis of faith, and often interpret the historical records, including accounts of miracles and of the coming end of the world, as literally as possible. Such groups sometimes find themselves in conflict with the claims of science, most obviously over the age of the universe, the origin of human life, and the probable end of the world.

The mainstream denominations—especially Roman Catholic, Reformed, Lutheran and Anglican—are not committed to biblical literalism. It has become standard to interpret the Genesis accounts and teachings about the end of the world as myths, the purpose of which is to teach the dependence of all things on God, and the final destiny of the universe as lying in union with (or final separation from) God. More radical movements seek to reconstruct Christian faith in terms of personal commitment to agapistic love (to the kingdom of God, seen as a moral community), or of apprehension of the Transcendent, as it is disclosed in Jesus. Nevertheless, belief in God as creator is usually affirmed, and Jesus is seen as a unique instance of God's action in the world, from whose life, death, and resurrection the church originates, as the way of reconciling the world to God. The experimental sciences have flourished in this intellectual environment, since it affirms the rational intelligibility of the universe, as created by a wise God, and gives humans the responsibility for having "dominion" over, or care for, the creation.

See also CHRISTIANITY, ANGLICAN, ISSUES IN SCIENCE AND RELIGION; CHRISTIANITY, EVANGELICAL, ISSUES IN SCIENCE AND RELIGION; CHRISTIANITY, LUTHERAN, ISSUES IN SCIENCE AND RELIGION; CHRISTIANITY, ORTHODOX, ISSUES IN SCIENCE AND RELIGION; CHRISTIANITY, PENTECOSTALISM, ISUSES IN SCIENCE AND RELIGION; CHRISTIANITY, RADICAL REFORMED, ISSUES IN SCIENCE AND RELIGION; CHRISTIANITY, REFORMED, ISSUES IN SCIENCE AND RELIGION; CHRISTIANITY, ROMAN CATHOLIC, ISSUES IN SCIENCE AND RELIGION; SCIENCE AND RELIGION, HISTORY OF FIELD

Bibliography

McManners, John, ed. *The Oxford Illustrated History of Christianity*. Oxford: Oxford University Press, 1990.

Ward, Keith. *Christianity: A Short Introduction*. Oxford: Oneworld Press, 2000.

KEITH WARD

CHRISTIANITY, ANGLICAN, ISSUES IN SCIENCE AND RELIGION

The initial impulse given to Anglican thought in the sixteenth century was a confident belief in God as creator of the world, which, though fallen, was intelligible to human understanding. From biblical, patristic, and medieval sources, Anglican liturgy gave expression to the praise of God, notably in the daily use of the book of Psalms, and of canticles such as the *Benedicite* and *Te Deum*. Although initially the reformed Church of England understood itself as a form of Protestantism, the vision of balancing God's work in creation and in human history was somewhat distinctive, giving its thought a somewhat less anthropocentric character.

Views of nature

This positive perspective on nature comes to expression in the classic theology of Richard Hooker (1554–1600). Within a generally hierarchical and Aristotelian view of nature, Hooker insists on God's work as artist, guide, and providential director within nature. Its constancy and dependability are the source of human knowledge of its laws. Natural objects are moved by God as instruments of his being. The same theme is also evident in the poetry of George Herbert (1593–1633), who assigns to humanity the role of being secretary to the praise offered by the whole of creation. A very powerful and individual voice is that of the Anglican poet Thomas Traherne (1636–1674), who takes a mystical delight in the beauty of the created order.

Interaction with the sciences

Certain specific conditions made England a particularly hospitable place for the burgeoning of natural theology after the condemnation of Galileo Galilei (1564–1642) in 1616 and 1633. The founding of the Royal Society of London for the Improvement of Natural Knowledge (known as the Royal Society) in 1660 benefited both from the comparatively loose structure of authority in the Church of England and from a certain degree of toleration of diversity of opinion. In fact, Thomas Sprat (1635–1713), the first writer of the history of the Royal Society, wrote, "The Church of England therefore may justly be styl'd the Mother of this sort of Knowledge; and so the care of its nourishment and prosperity peculiarly lyes upon it" (quoted in Peacocke, p. 5).

Isaac Newton (1643–1727) was an Anglican reared in the scholasticism of Cambridge, but open to the new influences from mechanical philosophy. In his *Opticks* (1706) Newton assigned to God the duties of preventing the stars from collapsing together and of reforming the mechanism of the world to prevent it from subversion by irregularities. The rationalism of this scheme was complemented by his approach to Scripture, which he denied taught the doctrine of the Trinity. But it is clear that Newton was by intention a pious believer and theological thinker as well as a brilliant scientist.

The same atmosphere of toleration supported the scientific work of non-Anglican Protestants, notable among whom was the naturalist and theologian, John Ray (1627–1705). A fellow of the Royal Society, Ray's exceptional work of taxonomy was carried outside the Anglican universities, and his late work, *The Wisdom of God Manifested in the Works of the Creation* (1691), advanced the argument from design influential throughout the coming century.

Although mechanistic philosophy was strongly attacked by many Anglican theological writers (and poets) of the eighteenth century, the teleological argument for the existence of God remained popular, receiving influential expression in the work of the philosopher William Paley (1743–1805), an Anglican priest, and author of a standard textbook, *Natural History* (1802). This book was studied by Charles Darwin (1809–1882) as a student, and its arguments are still worthy of consideration.

An attempt to find a version of the mechanical philosophy compatible with theism was a feature of the Cambridge scientist, ethicist, and theologian, William Whewell (1794–1866). An ordained Anglican as well as a founding member and early president of the British Association for the Advancement of Science and a Fellow of the Royal Society, Whewell stressed the inductive and historical character of science. At the same time he held that God's creation of the world guaranteed the simplicity and comprehensibility of the laws governing nature.

Darwin's own discoveries and writings provided, and still provide, an enormous stimulus to Anglican, as well as to all English-language theology. The dominant idealism of late nineteenth-century English universities had little difficulty in adapting to the implications of Darwinian thought, and Darwin himself was buried, without controversy, in Westminster Abbey.

The dialogue since Darwin

After Darwin and the opening of Oxford and Cambridge to non-Anglicans, it became more difficult to identify a specifically Anglican strand in the generally vibrant relations of science and theology. After the second world war, however, a further burgeoning took place in Anglican responses to scientific developments. In 1942 an Anglican theologian, Charles E. Raven (1885–1964), produced a major biographical study of John Ray, following it later with a two-volume history of religion and science (*Natural Religion and Christian Theology*, 1953).

From the 1970s two authors, both Anglican priests, biologist Arthur Peacocke (1924–) and physicist John Polkinghorne (1930–) have made major contributions. For Peacocke the theological interpretation of how God is related to the world must be rethought in the direction of panentheism, God suffering in and with the world processes. For Polkinghorne, God is active within the world, though in a self-limited, kenotic way.

Attempts to popularize the discoveries of science have led to a continuing public interest and debate, especially on the ethical problems of gene technology. Notable contributions have been made by an Anglican bishop and geneticist, John Habgood (1927–), Archbishop of York from 1983 to 1995.

See also DARWIN, CHARLES; NATURAL THEOLOGY; NEWTON, ISAAC; PANENTHEISM

Bibliography

Habgood, John. *Religion and Science*. London: Hodder and Stoughton, 1972.

Newton, Isaac. *Opticks: or, A Treatise of the Reflections, Refractions, Inflections and Colours of Light* (1706). 4th edition. London: Bell and Sons, 1931.

Paley, William. *Natural History: or, Evidences of the Existence and Attributes of the Deity, Collected from the Appearances of Nature* (1802). Cambridge, UK: Chadwyck-Healey, 1998.

Peacocke, Arthur R. *Creation and the World of Science: The Brampton Lectures, 1978*. Oxford: Clarendon Press, 1979.

Polkinghorne, John C. *Belief in God in an Age of Science*. New Haven, Conn.: Yale University Press, 1998.

Polkinghorne, John C. *Science and Theology: An Introduction*. London: SPCK/Fortress, 1998.

Raven, Charles E. *Natural Religion and Christian Theology: The Gifford Lectures, 1951*. First Series: Science and Religion. Cambridge, UK: Cambridge University Press, 1953.

Ray, John. *The Wisdom of God Manifest in the Works of Creation*. (1691). London and New York: Olms, 1974.

Whewell, William. *The Philosophy of the Inductive Sciences, Founded Upon Their History*, New edition, 2 vols. London: J. W. Parker, 1847.

STEPHEN SYKES

CHRISTIANITY, EVANGELICAL, ISSUES IN SCIENCE AND RELIGION

The term *evangelical* (from the Greek word for gospel) has several meanings; for the purpose of this entry, it will refer to an English-speaking Protestant development that emphasizes personal religion (focused on Christ), Biblical authority and preaching, missions, and evangelism. The origins of this particular type of evangelical Christianity stretch back to eighteenth-century revivals in England and America, with such leading figures as John and Charles Wesley, Jonathan Edwards, and George Whitefield. Early evangelical leaders and scholars accepted a harmony between natural science and religious faith, typical of the age of British natural theology. Edwards saw the glory of God revealed in a spider's web, while Wesley could find the wisdom of God revealed in creation as understood by the natural science of his day. For the most part, evangelical scientists and theologians sought a harmony between science and Scripture.

Views of nature

Evangelicals understand the natural world in terms of Biblical theism and the doctrine of creation. God is the author of nature and of the contingent order of the natural world. Nature was created good, and exists for the purpose of glorifying God. Sin, however, has distorted and warped nature, especially human nature. God will eventually redeem nature and all things through Christ. Thus the natural world serves as a stage for the great drama of salvation: sin and corruption, salvation and redemption. Because it is subject to a higher, spiritual order, evangelicals believe that the stability of natural law may be altered for a higher purpose, without undermining the reliability of natural science. They defend both the value of natural science and the stability of natural law, along with the reality of miracles in the context of God's plan for nature and history.

Interaction with the sciences

With a few exceptions, the general picture of harmony between faith and science did not change in any marked degree after the publication of Charles Darwin's *Origin of Species* in 1859. Given the vitriolic rejection of Darwinism by populist evangelicals in the early twentieth century, this may seem unlikely; but the fact is that most evangelical scholars and natural scientists before World War I accepted some form of evolution, even if some were attracted to non-Darwinian variations, such as that of Jean Baptiste Lamarck. They rejected "Darwinism" when that term was identified with atheism or naturalism (e.g., the Princeton theologian Charles Hodge). Prominent evangelical theologians and scientists of the late nineteenth century, such as James Orr, B. B. Warfield, and A. H. Strong (theologians), or James D. Dana, David Brewster, and Asa Gray (scientists), could all advocate a combination of biological evolution and Biblical religion. There were, of course, critics of evolution among evangelicals in this period, but that was not the dominant mood. The scientific and religious critics of Darwin in the nineteenth century came from a great variety of religious perspectives, and cannot be typified as predominantly evangelical.

After the first World War, the cultural mood changed in the West, and among evangelicals. The horrors of war stimulated a more world-denying, counter-cultural popular religion. Pre-millennial eschatology became popular in the new movement, soon called "fundamentalism." This eschatology expected the imminent return of Jesus and the decline of worldly culture until his return. In this populist movement, evolution was associated with progress, with liberalism, and even with biblical criticism. Because the Book of Revelation was read in a literal way, so was Genesis. Evolution and Darwin were rejected in favor of biblical literalism and tribulation preaching in which the "tribulation" is the period of woes and sufferings predicted in Revelation. The main spokespersons for this populist pre-millennial movement were not scholars and scientists but preachers and pamphleteers. This is the reason the famous Scopes trial in Dayton, Tennessee, took place in 1925 after the rise of fundamentalism, and not earlier. The anti-evolutionary forces in Dayton were lead by the populist politician William Jennings Bryan, not by scholars. It is no accident that the first major "creation scientists" was an Adventist (George McCready Price) because of the close association of populist pre-millennial eschatology and anti-evolutionary rhetoric in American church history. The rise of this kind of fundamentalism also marked the end of the harmony between natural science and biblical religion as a predominant mood within evangelicalism.

The so-called creation science movement was an attempt to give this anti-evolutionary point of view some scientific respectability. Henry Morris was particularly influential, but few serious biologists joined this association. Despite the work of the Institute for Creation Research in Santee, California, and other loose associations of creationists, creation science has remained a populist movement with little scientific respectability. It thrives predominantly within pre-millennial movements, rather than among associations of scientists and scholars. Like earlier fundamentalists, they are often accused of relying upon popular politics, rather than scientific literature, to oppose evolution.

The dialogue since World War II

After the Second World War, some conservative scholars and church leaders saw a need to engage with culture, including science. Carl Henry, Bernard Ramm, and E. J. Carnell, along with English evangelicals like John Stott, were among the theologians who advocated a rejection of fundamentalism and a return to social engagement and scholarly achievements. In his influential book *A Christian View of Science and Scripture* (1954), Ramm reasserted the older evangelical harmony between science, including evolution, and the Bible. Associations of evangelicals who were also scientists, such as the American Scientific Affiliation (ASA) and the Victoria Institute in England, help promote this reengagement. In 1959, members of the ASA, a group previously noted for its anti-evolutionary stance, published Russell Mixter's *Evolution and Christian Thought Today*, a controversial work cautiously in favor of scientific evolution.

Given this complex history, evangelical scholars and scientists remain conflicted with respect to evolution. Unlike their fundamentalist ancestors, evangelicals embrace natural science and scholarship in general. The majority of evangelical scholars would advocate a Christian approach to the sciences that unites faith and reason, rather than the anti-intellectual rhetoric of the fundamentalist movement. But with respect to evolution, some evangelicals remain dubious. In particular, the Intelligent Design movement (popular among evangelicals) includes scientists, philosophers, and theologians who argue that life on Earth is the result of intelligent design. They seek to reject Darwinism, as they understand it, while still accepting natural science as a whole. On the other hand, many evangelical systematic theologians like Thomas F. Torrance are willing to accept biological evolution, while still holding that the universe is created, sustained, and ordered by God.

See also CREATIONISM; DARWIN, CHARLES; DESIGN; INTELLIGENT DESIGN; SCIENCE AND RELIGION, MODELS AND RELATIONS

Bibliography

Carlson, Richard F., ed. *Science and Christianity: Four Views*. Downers Grove, Ill.: InterVarsity Press, 2000.

Behe, Michael; Dembski, William; and Meyer, Stephen. *Science and Evidence for Design in the Universe*. San Francisco: Ignatius Press, 2000.

Lewis, C. S. *Miracles*. New York: Macmillan, 1947.

Livingstone, David N. *Darwin's Forgotten Defenders: The Encounter Between Evangelical Theology and Evolutionary Thought*. Grand Rapids, Mich.: Eerdmans, 1987.

Livingstone, David; Hart; D. G.; and Noll, Mark, eds. *Evangelicals and Science in Historical Perspective*. New York: Oxford University Press, 1999.

Mixter, Russell Lowell, ed. *Evolution and Christian Thought Today*. Grand Rapids, Mich.: Eerdmans, 1959.

Numbers, Ronald. *The Creationists*. New York: Knopf, 1992.

Ramm, Bernard. *A Christian View of Science and Scripture*. Grand Rapids, Mich.: Eerdmans, 1954.

Sandeen, Ernest R. *The Roots of Fundamentalism: British and American Millenarianism, 1800-1930*. Chicago: University of Chicago Press, 1970.

Torrance, Thomas F. *Divine and Contingent Order*. Oxford: Oxford University Press, 1981.

ALAN G. PADGETT

CHRISTIANITY, HISTORY OF SCIENCE AND RELIGION

The fundamental question facing the Christian scholar in any discipline can be seen as a specific form of a general query that was posed within two centuries of Christ's death by the Carthaginian father Tertullian (c. 155–230): "What indeed has Athens to do with Jerusalem? What concord is there between the Academy and the Church?"

Before the Renaissance

As the phrasing implies, Tertullian's attitude toward Greek philosophy was generally negative, though he acknowledged a legitimate role for reason within the bounds of religion. Other patristic authors looked more favorably on pagan philosophy and literature, especially Origen (c. 185–254), who required his students to read nearly every work available to them at the time and found some truth in most of them. The moderate position of Augustine of Hippo (354–430), who considered reason a divine gift resting on the foundation of faith, was by far the most influential on later Christian thinking. Although he cautioned Christians not to devote too much energy to the study of nature, which cannot lead to salvation, Augustine recognized Greek scientists as reliable authorities on natural matters and cautioned Christians against making nonsensical claims about nature, based on some presumed meaning of scripture, for this would only cause people to laugh at the ignorance of Christians. He also urged believers to study nature, "the great book . . . of created things."

Most patristic writers recognized two valid sources of knowledge—scripture and reason, including most conclusions of reason about nature—but assigned a different status to each. Prior to the Renaissance, philosophy (including what is today called science) was considered a "handmaiden to theology," while theology was "queen of the sciences," where "science" meant knowledge in general and not simply knowledge of nature. This terminology was introduced by the Hellenistic Jewish scholar Philo of Alexandria (30 B.C.E.–50 C.E.) and later was used by Christian writers such as Clement of Alexandria (c. 150–215), Augustine, and Bonaventure (1221–1274). On this view, the proper role of scientific knowledge was to help illuminate biblical references to nature, not to stand on its own as an independent domain of inquiry. This is clearly seen in the numerous commentaries on the six days of creation from this period, such as the *Homilies on the Hexameron* by Basil, Bishop of Caesarea (c. 330–379), in which Aristotelian cosmology and physics were used to help interpret references to the heavens in the first chapter of Genesis.

For nearly twelve hundred years the handmaiden model escaped serious challenge, mainly because copies of most Greek scientific and medical texts were unavailable in northern and western Europe, and what little knowledge Christian scholars did have of such texts was usually obtained indirectly, from handbooks and encyclopedias rather than from the original sources. Consequently, Christian scholars were not confronted with the full force of Aristotle's sophisticated naturalism. On the other hand, they did have Plato's *Timaeus,* a dialogue about creation in which a god imposes mathematical form on undifferentiated matter. Although the differences between Plato's story and Genesis are significant, there are enough similarities that Plato was readily seen as a pagan prophet of Christianity. Plato's rejection of purely natural and unintelligent causes in forming the world, coupled with his belief in the immortality of the soul and the superiority of mind over matter, made him highly attractive to Christian writers. The relative ease with which Platonic elements could be incorporated into a Christian world view—and vice versa, depending on who was doing the philosophizing—gave considerable support to the handmaiden model.

The situation changed dramatically with the reintroduction into northern and western Europe of a large body of Greek scientific and medical works. This process began around 1000 C.E. and led within two centuries to the appearance of universities dominated by Aristotelian natural philosophy, strongly flavored by the ideas of Islamic scholars who had worked with translations of Greek texts for hundreds of years. The influence of Ibn Rushd (known in the West as Averroës, 1126–1198), an extreme rationalist who elevated Aristotle over traditional Islamic teaching, was especially important in this connection. Christian scholars were now faced with a powerful, systematic body of natural knowledge, comprehensive in scope and secular in spirit, and they responded in various ways.

At the University of Paris, the leading theological faculty in Christendom, led by the conservative Bonaventure, grew alarmed at certain teachings promulgated by some masters on the faculty of arts, especially Siger of Brabant, a radical Aristotelian who considered philosophy to be an autonomous discipline, perhaps even superior to theology. Several times in the thirteenth century, Aristotle's books were banned at Paris, culminating in 1277 when the bishop of Paris, Étienne Tempier, condemned 219 specific propositions as heretical. These included several ideas associated with Thomas Aquinas (c. 1225–1274), a moderate Dominican who had taught theology at Paris and had carefully integrated Aristotle with Christian theology. Ironically, Aquinas was canonized in 1323 and his ideas later became the basis for one of the leading Christian systems of thought, Thomism. A further irony is that the condemnation inspired the important Parisian natural philosophers John Buridan (c. 1295–1358) and Nicole Oresme (c. 1320–1382) to consider what a non-Aristotelian science of motion might be like, including the possibility of a rotating Earth. Although their ideas probably did not lead directly to the scientific revolution (as Pierre Duhem and some others have claimed), they do show that theology can stimulate significant scientific insights.

Renaissance to mid-nineteenth century

In the later middle ages and continuing into the Renaissance, partly in reaction to the hold Aristotelianism had gained on the universities, Platonism enjoyed a revival. Many Renaissance thinkers followed Plato by emphasizing mathematics as the key to understanding nature, but differed fundamentally from Plato in their belief that the physical world perfectly embodies God's geometrical design; Plato had taught that physical objects are only imperfect "shadows" of the perfect forms. The difference was a consequence of the Christian doctrine of creation: An omnipotent God would carry out the plan of creation to perfection. For Christian neo-Platonists like Nicolas Copernicus (1473–1543), Galileo Galilei (1564–1642), and Johannes Kepler (1571–1630), God was eternally thinking geometric thoughts. By the right use of geometry, one might literally read the mind of God and discover the deepest secrets of creation. Inspired partly by his neo-Platonist beliefs and strongly encouraged by church authorities to publish his ideas, the quiet and conservative Copernicus advanced a radical new theory of the universe that placed the Earth in motion about a stationary sun. Kepler found this theory attractive for several reasons, including his belief that the three parts of the Copernican universe symbolized the Trinity—the central sun with its emanating light representing God the Father, the starry sphere God the Son, and the intermediate space God the Holy Spirit.

There was no convincing proof for the new astronomy, however, and many scientists and theologians alike saw the hypothesis of the Earth's motion as a challenge to those biblical passages (about a dozen in all) that seemed to speak either of the motion of the sun through the sky, as if it were a real motion rather than an apparent one, or else of the stability of the Earth. In defense of the new astronomy, Kepler (a German Protestant) and Galileo (an Italian Catholic) both employed the Augustinian principle of accommodation to justify the figurative interpretation of biblical references to the motion of the sun. The Bible, they argued, speaks in a human way about ordinary matters in a way that can be understood by the common person, using ordinary speech to convey loftier theological truths. Thus, the literal sense of texts making reference to nature should not be mistaken for accurate scientific statements, but the wise interpreter could show how the book of scripture did not really contradict the book of nature. Citing rules established by the Council of Trent in response to Protestant reformers, Catholic authorities found this unacceptable and ordered Galileo not to teach the new astronomy. Galileo, who often treated opponents arrogantly, ignored this warning and published a vigorous attack on traditional astronomy in which he thoughtlessly insulted his friend, Pope Urban VIII, and Galileo was sentenced to house arrest by the Inquisition in 1633.

Those Christian thinkers who agreed with Kepler and Galileo—and by 1700 a large number did—were implicitly raising the status of science from that of an obedient handmaiden to something like an equal partner in the search for truth—a conception that had been explicitly endorsed just a few years earlier by the English statesman and essayist, Francis Bacon (1561–1626), who was ironically not a Copernican himself. Bacon held that nature served as a "key" to the scriptures, not only by "opening our understanding to conceive the true sense of the scriptures," but mainly by "opening our belief, in drawing us into a due meditation of the omnipotency of God, which is chiefly signed and engraven upon his works." At the same time, however, he cautioned against "unwisely confounding these learnings together."

Because it offered relative autonomy for science while enhancing the authority of theology, the Baconian attitude was widely adopted by Protestants in England and America through the middle of the nineteenth century, and Roman Catholics were increasingly attracted to a similar attitude, partly seen in Galileo but ultimately derived from Aquinas. English natural philosopher Robert Boyle (1627–1691) epitomized this approach, promoting what he called the "mechanical philosophy"—the explanation of natural phenomena in terms of matter and motion—over Aristotelian and Galenic views, for its advantages not only to science (it provided clear, experimentally useful explanations) but also to religion: By denying any immanent intelligence to "Nature," which functioned idolatrously as a "semi-deity," the mechanical philosophy more clearly distinguished the creator from the creation, thus focusing worship where it properly belonged. Boyle further believed that Christian character was highly relevant to the scientific enterprise, such that he considered himself a "priest of nature" whose discoveries only enhanced his appreciation for the wisdom, goodness, and power of God. Like many of his contemporaries, including Isaac Newton (1642–1727), Boyle aggressively pursued an extensive program of natural theology while generally avoiding the use of the Bible as a scientific text.

More than a century later, however, Christian thinkers were much less reluctant to cite scripture on scientific matters, no doubt because the age and origin of the Earth had become topics of serious scientific discussion. Many natural historians and theologians saw in the books of nature and scripture essentially the same story, going beyond the general assumption of harmony to endorse a strong concordism, arguing for close parallels between Genesis and geology and sometimes inventing elaborate hermeneutical schemes to achieve harmonization.

Since the mid-nineteenth century

With the acceptance of Darwinian evolution, however, concordism fell out of favor, though some conservative Protestants still embrace it, and no single approach to theology and science has generated a wide enough following to function as its replacement. The first American Darwinian, botanist Asa Gray (1810–1888), thought that his acceptance of evolution had no bearing on his belief in the miracles of Christ and the doctrines affirmed by the Nicene Creed, thus holding a compatibilist or complementarian view of theology and science. At the same time, Gray tried to rebuild natural theology along evolutionary lines—a combination that has never been common, although a number of orthodox and neo-orthodox thinkers in the following century held some type of complementarian position.

From the 1870s to the 1920s, many Protestant scientists and theologians and some Roman Catholics believed that higher biblical criticism, as well as natural science, mandated the formulation of a new theology stressing divine immanence, God's everyday working in and through the processes of nature. Some liberals took this further, including several modernists from the 1920s who denied miracles and special revelation and essentially identified God with the laws of nature, thus completely rejecting divine transcendence. Liberals saw morality as the essence of religion; asserting the fundamental goodness and perfectibility of humanity, many also believed that the science of eugenics would help them establish the kingdom of God on Earth. Both world wars had a devastating impact on such an optimistic view, leading Karl Barth (1886–1968) and other neo-orthodox theologians to reassert sin, revelation, and divine transcendence. Because he understood God as wholly other, and also because he deplored the ways in which the German churches had capitulated to the state, Barth denied that one can learn about God apart from revelation, thereby completely rejecting natural theology.

Around the same time, the English logician Alfred North Whitehead (1861–1947) argued that the very possibility of modern science depended upon the unconsciously held belief, derived from medieval theology, that the created order must be intelligible, thus finding an inextricable link between theology and science. He also developed a highly sophisticated process metaphysics that has profoundly influenced some important modern theologians, philosophers, and scientists. Motivated partly by a desire to embrace evolution and even more by a desire to mitigate God's responsibility for suffering, process theologians believe that God has only limited power to influence natural and human

events, rather than the omnipotence needed to create the world *ex nihilo*. The world and God are seen as coeval entities evolving together, and many contemporary process thinkers follow Charles Hartshorne (1897–2000) in affirming panentheism rather than traditional theism. Ironically, perhaps the greatest challenge to process theology comes from the modern science it seeks to embrace, but from the evolution of the cosmos rather than the evolution of life. Since the mid-1960s, astronomers have discovered a wealth of evidence favoring the Big Bang theory of cosmology, evidence suggesting not only that the universe had a "beginning" but also that the laws of nature were exquisitely tuned for the presence of living things. Many think that a universe with these features seems more consistent with *creatio ex nihilo* than its denial.

At the dawn of the twenty-first century, a good number of leading Christian scientists and theologians, including some who combine that role, such as Ian Barbour (1923–), Arthur Peacocke (1924–), and John Polkinghorne (1930–), are engaged in a growing international conversation about issues of interest to both communities, and the range of opinion reflects disagreements about the nature of God, the nature of humanity, and the nature of nature.

See also CHRISTIANITY, ANGLICAN, ISSUES IN SCIENCE AND RELIGION; CHRISTIANITY, EVANGELICAL, ISSUES IN SCIENCE AND RELIGION; CHRISTIANITY, LUTHERAN, ISSUES IN SCIENCE AND RELIGION; CHRISTIANITY, ORTHODOX, ISSUES IN SCIENCE AND RELIGION; CHRISTIANITY, PENTECOSTALISM, ISSUES IN SCIENCE AND RELIGION; CHRISTIANITY, RADICAL REFORMED, ISSUES IN SCIENCE AND RELIGION; CHRISTIANITY, REFORMED, ISSUES IN SCIENCE AND RELIGION; CHRISTIANITY, ROMAN CATHOLIC, ISSUES IN SCIENCE AND RELIGION; SCIENCE AND RELIGION, HISTORY OF FIELD

Bibliography

Bacon, Francis. *The Twoo Bookes of Francis Bacon: Of the Proficience and Advancement of Learning, Divine and Humane.* London: Henrie Tomes, 1605.

Barbour, Ian. *Religion in an Age of Science: The Gifford Lectures, 1989–1991*, Vol. 1. San Francisco: Harper-Collins, 1990.

Boyle, Robert. *A Free Enquiry into the Vulgarly Received Notion of Nature* (1686), ed. Edward B. Davis and Michael Hunter. Cambridge, UK: Cambridge University Press, 1996.

Brooke, John H. *Science and Religion: Some Historical Perspectives.* Cambridge, UK: Cambridge University Press, 1991.

Collingwood, R. G. *An Essay on Metaphysics.* Oxford: Oxford University Press, 1940.

Davis, Edward B. "The Word and the Works: Concordism and American Evangelicals." In *Perspectives on an Evolving Creation,* ed. Keith Miller. Grand Rapids, Mich.: Eerdmans, 2002.

Duhem, Pierre. *Le système du monde: Histoire des doctrines cosmologiques de Platon à Copernic,* 10 vols. Paris: Hermann, 1913–1959.

Frye, Roland Mushat. "The Two Books of God." In *Is God a Creationist?,* ed. Roland Mushat Frye. New York: Scribner, 1983.

Galilei, Galileo. *Letter to the Grand Duchess Christina.* In *Discoveries and Opinions of Galileo,* trans. Stillman Drake. Garden City. N.Y.: Doubleday, 1957.

Gray, Asa. *Natural Science and Religion: Two Lectures Delivered to the Theological School of Yale College.* New York: Scribner, 1880.

Hartshorne, Charles. *The Divine Reality: A Social Conception of God.* New Haven, Conn.: Yale University Press, 1948.

Lindberg, David C., and Numbers, Ronald L., eds. *God and Nature: Historical Essays on the Encounter between Christianity and Science.* Berkeley: University of California Press, 1986.

Oakley, Francis. *Omnipotence, Covenant, and Order: An Excursion in the History of Ideas from Abelard to Leibniz.* Ithaca, N.Y.: Cornell University Press, 1984.

Peacocke, Arthur. *Theology for a Scientific Age: Being and Becoming–Natural, Divine, and Human,* rev. edition. Minneapolis, Minn.: Fortress Press, 1993.

Polkinghorne, John. *Belief in God in an Age of Science.* New Haven, Conn.: Yale University Press, 1998.

Westfall, Richard S. *Science and Religion in Seventeenth-Century England.* New Haven, Conn.: Yale University Press, 1958.

EDWARD B. DAVIS

CHRISTIANITY, LUTHERAN, ISSUES IN SCIENCE AND RELIGION

When Martin Luther (1483–1546) in 1517 publicly attacked the notion of merit and grace in scholastic theology, denounced the church practices of penance and indulgence, and soon after opposed the authority of the Pope, he inadvertently triggered a long-term schism between Catholics and Protestants within the Western church. All reformation movements of the sixteenth century are indebted to Luther's notion of unconditional grace, but the movements developed differently. Already in 1524 Luther fiercely opposed the Radical Reformed movement of Thomas Müntzer (1490–1525) and others, and from 1526 to 1528 Luther took issue with the interpretation of the Eucharist among the Swiss reformers. Consequently, relatively few countries in Northern Europe (notably Germany and the Nordic countries) defined themselves as "Lutheran," whereas the Swiss, Dutch, and English reformations were eventually more influenced by John Calvin (1509–1564) than by Luther. In the nineteenth century, new Lutheran emigration churches were formed in the United States, Brazil, and Argentina. During the twentieth century major indigenous Lutheran churches emerged in Africa, especially in Tanzania, Madagascar, and Namibia, and in Asia, especially in India and Indonesia.

Views of nature

In his early career, Luther's view of nature was framed by the contrast between divine grace and human nature. In the *Heidelberg Disputation* (1518) Luther renounced natural theology as a "theology of glory" that vainly sought to identify God in the niceties of life. Not nature, but the cross of Christ is the gateway to God. The target of this critique, however, was not nature but self-centered trust in the capacities of human reasoning in grasping God. Luther regarded life as a divine gift, and according to *Small Catechism* (1529) the human body and soul as well as nature and society are created and preserved by God "out of pure fatherly, and divine goodness and mercy, without any merit or worthiness of mine at all." Luther was not so much interested in "pure nature" as in the manner in which nature and culture interweave in ordinary life: "Our house, home, field, garden and everything is full of the Bible, because God through his wonderful work knocks on our eyes, touches our senses and shines right into our hearts." Thus, even if Luther rejected the pursuit of natural theology, he articulated a rich theology of nature from the existential perspective of faith.

Luther's positive view of nature came to the fore in his controversy with Huldreich Zwingli

(1484–1531) on the Eucharist. Luther insisted on a literal understanding of the words of Jesus Christ: "This is my body." God is not only present in creation as Spirit, but through Christ God is ubiquitous in the midst of the material world, in the natural elements of bread and wine. The Medieval distinction between the natural and the supernatural thus became obsolete, and Luther criticized the Roman Catholic doctrine of *transubstantiation* accordingly. Natural bread and wine are not changed (substantiated) into the supernatural body and blood of Christ. Rather, Christ is present "in, with, and under" natural bread and wine. In later Lutheranism, this idea of *consubstantialization* was developed into a more general principle of *finitum capax infiniti* (the finite is capable of embodying the infinite). In this vein, seventeenth-century Lutheran Orthodoxy developed a theological materialism in contrast to the more spiritual ontologies of Zwingli and Calvin. In the twentieth century, these ideas also influenced the sacramental realism of Anglican theologians such as William Temple (1881–1944) and Arthur R. Peacocke (1924–).

Interaction with the sciences

Luther did not himself show any interest in natural science; he preferred to stay within the Biblical worldview. But Luther's close collaborator Philip Melanchthon (1497–1560), who was in charge of the university reform in Wittenberg, strongly supported natural philosophy, as the sciences were called at that time. In his textbook *The Elements of Natural Philosophy* (1549) Melanchthon taught that the entire physical cosmos manifests God's providential order. Melanchthon also wrote a highly influential textbook *On the Soul* (1552) in which he emphasized the compelling force of the human affects on human reasoning, but also recommended the value of anatomical studies, including Andreas Vesalius's *Fabric of the Human Body* (1543). This textbook of Melanchthon was used by the Calvinist Otto Casmannus, who in 1594 coined the term *anthropologia* for the general field to be further subdivided into *psychologia* and *somatologia*. In Melanchthon's many university orations he emphasized the value of the sciences from astronomy and astrology to medicine and psychology, both for the practical needs of society and for the theological contemplation of divine order in nature. Thereby Melanchthon placed natural philosophy

in the context of a natural theology of Stoic flavor (Frank, 1999).

The impact of Lutheranism on science, however, is difficult to evaluate. Some argue that distrust in the a priori human reasoning led Melanchthon to a stronger empirical orientation (Kusukawa, 1995); others emphasize the traditional Aristotelian character of Melanchthon's philosophy of nature (Methuen, 1998). Some see the Lutheran emphasis on the Bible as disconnecting the Lutherans from any scientific interest (White, 1896, vol. 1); other interpreters see the careful literal reading of the Bible as a motivation for a likewise careful and unbiased study of the book of nature (Harrison, 1998). The case of astronomy may show the complexities. Nicolaus Copernicus's (1473–1543) *On the Revolutions of the Heavenly Spheres* was published in Tübingen in 1543 by the Lutheran theologian Andreas Osiander (1496–1552). In his preface Osiander declares Copernicus's work a fruitful hypothesis, though hardly literally true. Melanchthon was initially hostile to Copernicus, but later claimed "to love and admire Copernicus more." Even though Melanchthon could still not believe the theory to be literally true, he integrated the data and figures of Copernicus into the second edition of his 1562 book *Elements* (Barker, 2000). The Lutheran Copernican Johannes Kepler (1571–1630) came out of this astronomic school, and in 1616, when Copernicus's work was listed on the Papal Index of prohibited books, Copernicus appeared alongside the names of Luther, Erasmus, and Calvin.

Rather than seeking a global theory of a distinctive Lutheran involvement with science, it may be wiser to take one's departure in the observation that the Lutheran tradition in general takes a high view of nature, but a low view of disengaged reasoning. Whereas the Reformed and Anglican traditions highlight rationality (and played a major role in the emergence of classic physics), there are some affinities between Lutheranism and Romanticism. Both Georg Wilhelm Friedrich Hegel (1770–1831) and Friedrich Wilhelm Joseph von Schelling (1775–1854) were self-conscious Lutherans. Much later, Paul Tillich (1886–1965) explained how his own mystic and aesthetic attitude towards nature was nourished, via Schelling, by the Lutheran principle that the finite *is* capable of the infinite.

In this perspective it may be more than a coincidence that some of the most counterintuitive theories of modern science were produced by scientists working in a Lutheran milieu. In 1820 the Danish physicist Hans Christian Ørsted (1777–1851) discovered electro-magnetic force. In line with Schelling, Ørsted believed that the spiritual forces of attraction and repulsion are more basic than material particles, and their laws were claimed to reign in nature as well as in society. The quantum theory of the 1920s involved even more counterintuitive notions, and the embrace of paradoxical statements in the Copenhagen Interpretation by Niels Bohr (1885–1962) and Werner Heisenberg (1901–1976) was probably facilitated by a philosophical climate in which paradoxes could be better guides to truth than more pedestrian appeals to order and rationality. Bohr's indebtedness to Søren Kierkegaard (1813–1855) is an interesting case of a disguised presence of a religious tradition in the heuristics of science as well as in its subsequent interpretation.

There exists no official Lutheran view of the natural sciences, or worldviews. The general distrust in the project of natural theology (despite Melanchthon's legacy) is based on the prior conviction that the preaching of theology does not rely on particular philosophical or scientific foundations. Since the nineteenth century, Luther's doctrine of the two regiments (the spiritual and the secular) also led to a widespread assumption of an autonomy or *Eigengesetzlichkeit* (Max Weber) of the sciences. Rudolf Bultmann's (1813–1855) famous program of demythologization may count as one such example of separation. However, the conviction that natural processes are the "masks of God" present in creation has continued to prompt Lutherans to enter the science-religion dialogue. Since the 1980s significant initiatives have been taken by the German Evangelical Academies (Hans May, 1990), by the Evangelical-Lutheran Church of America (Mangum, 1989) and by the Lutheran World Federation (Mortensen, 1995). But in general the dialogue is left to individual scholars working in nondenominational settings.

See also CHRISTIANITY, HISTORY OF SCIENCE AND RELIGION; NATURAL THEOLOGY

Bibliography

Barker, Peter. "The Role of Religion in the Lutheran Response to Copernicus." In *Rethinking the Scientific Revolution,* ed. Margaret J. Osler. Cambridge, UK: Cambridge University Press, 2000.

Frank, Günther. *Die theologische Philosophie Philipp Melanchthons (1497–1560).* Leipzig, Germany: Benno Verlag, 1995.

Harrison, Peter. *The Bible, Protestantism, and the Rise of Natural Science.* Cambridge, UK: Cambridge University Press, 1998.

Kusukawa, Sachiko. *The Transformation of Natural Philosophy: The Case of Philip Melanchthon.* Cambridge, UK: Cambridge University Press, 1995.

Luther, Martin. *Luther's Works,* 55 vols., eds. Jaroslav Pelikan and Helmut T. Lehman. St. Louis, Mo. and Concordia; Philadelphia: Fortress, 1955–1976.

Mangum, John M. *The New Faith-Science Debate: Probing Cosmology, Technology, and Theology.* Minneapolis, Minn.: Fortress Press; Geneva, Switzerland: World Council of Churches, 1989.

May, Hans; Striegnitz, Meinfried; and Hefner, Philip, eds. *Menschliche Natur und moralische Paradoxa aus der Sicht von Biologie, Sozialwissenschaften und Theologie.* Evangelische Akademie Loccum: Rehburg-Loccum, 1990.

Melanchthon, Philip. *Orations on Philosophy and Education,* ed. Sachiko Kusukawa. Cambridge, UK: Cambridge University Press, 1999.

Methuen, Charlotte. *Kepler's Tübingen: Stimulus to a Theological Mathematics.* Aldershot, UK: Ashgate, 1998.

Methuen, Charlotte. "Order of Nature and Natural Order in the Theology of the Reformers" eds. Niels Henrich Gregersen, Ulf Görmon and Hubert Meisinger. *Studies in Science and Theology* 8 (2002): 57–76.

Metzge, Erwin. *Sakrament und Metaphysik. Eine Lutherstudie über das Verhältnis des christlichen Denkends zum leiblich-materiellen.* Stuttgart, Germany: Kreuz Verlag, 1948.

Mortensen, Viggo, ed. *Concern for Creation: Voices on the Theology of Creation.* Uppsala, Sweden: Svenska Kyrkans Forskningsråd, 1995.

Sparn, Walter. *Wiederkehr der metaphysik. Die ontologische Frage in der lutherischen Theologie des frühen 17. Jahrhunderts.* Stuttgart, Germany: Calwer Verlag, 1976.

Tillich, Paul. "Autobiographical Reflections." In *The Theology of Paul Tillich,* eds. Charles W. Kegley and Robert W. Bretall. New York: Macmillan, 1952.

White, Andrew Dickson. *A History of the Warfare of Science with Theology in Christendom,* Vols. 1 and 2. New York: Appleton, 1896.

NIELS HENRIK GREGERSEN

CHRISTIANITY, ORTHODOX, ISSUES IN SCIENCE AND RELIGION

Historically, Orthodox Christianity dates back to the ancient Church, which was established by the apostles, powerful bishops, and seven Ecumenical Councils (from Nicea in 325 to Constantinople in 727). Orthodox Christianity considers itself as the "right" belief and "right glory," whose Church guards and teaches the true belief about God and represents the Church of Christ on Earth.

The divisions and fragmentation of the initially united Church led to the split of the Orthodox Church with Western Christianity, which is conventionally dated 1054 C.E. The Orthodox Church itself is divided into what can be called Oriental churches (mainly in Iraq and Iran), five non-Chalcedonian churches (in Armenia, Ethiopia, Egypt, and India; sometimes called *monophysite*), and the Eastern Orthodox churches proper.

In modern usage the term *Eastern Orthodoxy* is usually applied to those Christians who are in communion with the Ecumenical Patriarchate of Constantinople, which historically became restricted to the Greek-speaking world and later to other Slavic countries in Eastern Europe. There is no centralized organization in the Orthodox Church (unlike Roman Catholicism); it is a family of self-governing territorial bodies that are called Patriarchates. There are four Ancient Patriarchates and nine other autocephalous churches (the biggest one is the Russian Orthodox Church). All churches are in sacramental communion with each other. The territorial arrangement of the churches does not coincide with the formal boundaries of the states.

View of nature

Orthodox theology has a positive attitude towards the natural world as a good creation of a good God. Nature is never worshiped; it is God-creator who is worshiped through creation. The Fathers of the Church loved nature, but were never captured by the imagery of nature, which could prevent them from having a spiritual life in God. Thus nature was never considered an end in itself; its meaning and purpose can only be revealed in the perspective of Christ who, through the incarnation, recapitulated nature. The Fathers saw nature in the perspective of the hierarchy of the orders of creation, which proceeds from the natural law established by God. This "platonic" approach to nature could not provide any methodology of its investigation. The attitude to nature was speculative; it was interpreted in terms of laws that govern nature, but not their particular outcomes, which are displayed in a variety of phenomena. Nature, however, was never excluded from the general view of communion with God, so that the theology of the Greek Fathers was cosmic in its essence. Maximus the Confessor (c. 580-662) articulated that it is through communion with the Logos (Word) of God in Scriptures, through contemplation of the underlying principles of creation in nature, and in sacramental communion with Christ in Church that the fullness of communion can be achieved. Nature itself as the medium through which and by which communion with God can be established is seen as sacrament. Human being as microcosm and mediator participates in the cosmic Eucharist, which aims to renew and redeem the material world. Science then is treated as a tool to articulate the world in terms of its relationship with God.

Interaction with the sciences

In the first centuries of Christianity, the attitude to the sciences was established in the context of its encounter with classical Hellenistic culture. Since Clement of Alexandria (c. 150–215), philosophy and the sciences were considered human activities cooperating in ultimate truth, as useful tools in order to defend faith and make it demonstrable, and important for Christian education. The Greek Fathers asserted that scientific knowledge is incomplete in itself and must be supported by wider views of reality, which are accessible through faith. Knowledge and the sciences thus have their foundation in faith. Carried out through the centuries this attitude to science did not change, excluding any open conflicts between science and theology, with one exception—the seventy years of "scientific atheism" in Soviet Russia.

There is a perception among leading modern Orthodox theologians that science cannot be excluded from the theological vision of God and creation. The task of Orthodox theology is to reconcile the cosmic vision of the Fathers with the vision that grows out of the results of natural science.

The split between science and religion can be overcome on the grounds of their reinstatement to communion with God. Scientific work can be interpreted as "para-eucharistic" work (John Zizioulas). Scientific progress must be taken into account only in the context of the progress of human spirit and the deepening of human experience of the reality of the divine, which cannot be reduced to a physical or chemical level (Dumitru Staniloae). New conceptual tools for mediation between religion and science must be developed. The most important and urgent problems in the science-religion dialogue are not cosmological (e.g., creation of the universe) or philosophical (e.g., the meaning of evolution), but ecological and bioethical.

The Orthodox Church understands the modern ecological crisis either in terms of the misuse of science or utopian reliance on the power of progress. The Church consequently treats the crisis as essentially anthropological and spiritual. The message of the Church is to be cautious with scientific discoveries and technologies because they are handled by spiritually disorientated human beings, who have lost their roots in the divine. The loss of vision of the unity of the whole creation and human priestly responsibility for nature leads to abuse and degradation of the natural world, which threatens the very existence of humankind. It is in the context of love for nature, inner vigilance and chastity towards nature, and self-restraint in the consumption of natural resources that scientific activity can acquire some "eucharistic" features and nature can become reinstated to its sacramental status.

The Orthodox Church is deeply concerned with the possible moral and social implications of the fast advance of biology and medical science in terms of control and regulation of human life. For Orthodox Christians, life is the gift of God, who creates and preserves human personality. When biology and medicine interfere with human existence on the natural level, and threaten human integrity and personality, Orthodox theology opposes this on moral and social grounds. For example, the official position of the Church, expressed by the Council of Bishops of the Russian Church in 2001, with respect to cloning human beings is strongly negative on social grounds (the "printing" of people with specified parameters can appear

welcome to adherents of totalitarian ideologies), as well as personal grounds (a clone can feel like an independent person, but it is only a "copy" of someone who lives or lived before). However, the cloning of isolated cells and tissues does not threaten the personality and can be helpful in medical practice. Genetic engineering is admissible with the consent of the patient in the case of some hereditary diseases, but the genetic therapy of germ cells is considered dangerous because it involves a change of the genome in the line of generations, which can lead to mutations and can destabilize the balance between the human community and the environment.

See also CLONING; ECOLOGY; GENETIC ENGINEERING; MEDICAL ETHICS

Bibliography

Breck, John. *The Sacred Gift of Life: Orthodox Christianity and Bioethics.* Crestwood, N.Y.: St. Vladimir's Seminary Press, 1998.

Cavarnos, Constantine. *Biological Evolutionism.* Etna, Calif.: Center for Traditionalist Orthodox Studies, 1994.

Gregorios, Paulos Mar. *The Human Presence: Ecological Spirituality and the Age of the Spirit.* New York: Amity House, 1987.

Nesteruk, Alexei V. "Patristic Theology and the Natural Sciences." *SOUROZH: A Journal of Orthodox Life and Thought* 84 (2001): 14–35 (part 1); 85 (2001): 22–38 (part 2).

Sherrard, Philip. *The Rape of Man and Nature: An Enquiry into the Origins and Consequences of Modern Science.* Suffolk, UK: Golgonooza Press, 1991.

Staniloae Dumitru. *Theology and the Church.* Crestwood, N.Y.: St. Valdimir's Seminary Press, 1980.

Vucanovich, V. *Science and Faith: Order in the Universe and Cosmic Evolution Motivate Belief in God.* Minneapolis, Minn.: Light and Life Press, 1995.

Ware, Timothy. *The Orthodox Church.* London: Penguin, 1997.

Ware, Kallistos. *Through the Creation to the Creator.* London: Friends of the Centre, 1997.

Zizioulas, John. *Being as Communion: Studies in Personhood and the Church.* Crestwood, N.Y.: St. Vladimir's Seminary Press, 1997.

ALEXEI NESTERUK

CHRISTIANITY, PENTECOSTALISM, ISSUES IN SCIENCE AND RELIGION

Describing overall Pentecostal attitudes and relationships to science is difficult given the diversity of the movement. What historians call *classical Pentecostalism* (denominational groups whose origins are traced back to the Azusa Street revival in Los Angeles from 1906 to 1908) does not adequately encompass the substantially diverse noninstitutional forms of the movement featured since its beginnings, including the development of its educational structure, much less its neo-Pentecostal aspects emergent since the charismatic renewal of mainline churches during the 1950s. Further, the predominance of oral over written modes of communication, especially among non-Western Pentecostal movements, means that specific documentary evidence regarding Pentecostal attitudes of laypersons to science is relatively meager.

Because of their otherworldly orientation, Pentecostals have been either relatively silent about or dismissive of the sciences. Administrators of Pentecostal institutions have had degrees in the humanities or in education, not in the natural sciences. Pentecostalism, being a missionary religion, felt little need for scientific involvement until the last half of the twentieth century. Some Pentecostals rejected scientific learning, based upon their limited perception of what science actually was, along with some aspects of society and culture as a whole. Yet other facets of the movement, including the emerging Pentecostal educational establishment, provide substantial evidence of growth in scientific studies and applications.

Creation and evolution

Otherworldly aspirations combined with a biblicist mindset and worldview, together with the expectation of the imminent return of Christ, fostered an anti-intellectualism among the vast majority of the first generation Pentecostals. Rather than pursuing a secular education or moving up the social ladder, most early Pentecostals were motivated ideologically primarily by evangelistic concerns, and secondarily by apologetic ones. Pentecostal Bible institutes were focused first and foremost on the development of pastors, missionaries, and church workers, and only minimally, if at all, on scientific education as a liberal art.

Science, insofar as it was understood by these Pentecostals, was an enemy of the faith, primarily because of the popularized claims of evolutionary biologists and paleontologists and their apparent presupposition of the nonexistence of God. At this point in Pentecostal development, these popular claims appeared indistinguishable from the methodology and interests of other branches of science, which were totally unknown territory. Since no Pentecostal expertise was available to sort out the details of experimental evidence and interpretation, the sciences did not seem safe. As with many Christians of their time, Pentecostals rejected the Darwinian theory of evolution as being antithetical to a literal reading of the biblical creation narratives. The widespread influence of the *Scofield Reference Bible* (1909) among early Pentecostals led many to adopt the *gap theory* of temporally ambiguous intervals between the Genesis narrator's "days." Unbeknownst to the Pentecostals, and probably to the writers of the *Scofield Bible*, this interpretation, or one of equating the "days" with temporally ambiguous periods, was equivalent to the mainstream of contemporary European Old Testament and Torah scholarship before, during, and after the introduction, in 1859, of Charles Darwin's speculative thesis with *The Origin of Species*.

Beginning in the 1930s and 1940s, a handful of second and third generation Pentecostals were drawn, out of curiosity and thoughtfulness, to study the sciences at universities, primarily biology, studies not encouraged by the elder generation. It began to dawn that medical missions created the need for biological sciences. At the same time, by distancing themselves from fundamentalism and affiliating with the emergent evangelical movement in the 1940s, Pentecostals purchased some social space for members of the movement interested in the sciences.

By the 1950s and 1960s, the initial avoid-and-reject mentality toward evolutionary biology remained among Pentecostal leaders but existed in tension with the discriminating worldview prevalent among the emerging group of college educated adherents. However, the acquisition of academic history by leaders in education, theology, or various humanities did not always erase an anti-intellectual and suspicious posture toward the sciences. Yet, Bible college and Bible institute educators and administrators sensed the need for providing an alternative "Pentecostal" program of study for Pentecostals desiring a college education. This led to the development of departments in the humanities and the sciences, and the offering of degrees in most of the liberal arts.

The scientific liberal arts, however, proved expensive to offer and did not command the enrollment and tuition dollars of other subjects. The quest for regional accreditation was a strong motivating force, but outside scrutiny and pressure did not overcome the traditional resistance to scientific competence. Faculty were sought with at least graduate, if not terminal, degrees in the humanities, mathematics, and the natural sciences, but the approach was, understandably, geared toward the primary realization that academic history had accreditational benefits. The established tradition in the world's universities and participating governments was that academic history, particularly in the natural sciences, is preparatory to the goal of academic production but this remained a totally unknown domain to Pentecostals. The established link between academic history and scholarly research and production, and between academic history, academic production, and teaching, would take at least another half century or more to be understood and become financially feasible at Pentecostal institutions. As Pentecostalism enters its second century, these scientific traditions are fairly well established at some of the leading Pentecostal institutions like Oral Roberts University (ORU) in Tulsa, Oklahoma, and Lee University in Cleveland, Tennessee.

Meanwhile, Pentecostal attitudes toward creation and macroevolution have continued to develop. The appearance of *Dake's Annotated Reference Bible* (1963) provided further "scientific evidence" for the gap or day-age interpretation already popular among many Pentecostals. The emergence of young earth creationism in fundamentalist and conservative evangelical circles caused alarm among Pentecostal science departments, and the Society for Pentecostal Studies was warned early on by the head of the science department at Lee university, Dr. Myrtle Fleming, to "distinguish between fact and theory, original works (experimental evidence), and philosopher's thinking" (Numbers p. 307). Pentecostal administrators have considered young earth creationism an embarrassment, with some institu-

tions refusing to hire faculty in any discipline, scientific or otherwise, who adhere to this ideology. Many prominent Pentecostal evangelists and leaders have also opposed the Darwinian theory of evolution, while others have adopted literary understandings of the creation narratives that are harmonious with science. For many Pentecostal theologians and scientists the so-called theistic evolution (macroevolution with divine guidance) also appears incompatible both with biblical interpretation and with the experimental findings of modern science.

Yet, increasingly, Pentecostals educated in the sciences are suspicious about dogmatic approaches to superimposing macroevolution upon the physical evidence. There is emerging interest in paleontology, paleoastronomy, paleobiology, and paleogeology. Old style reactionary or rhetorical polemic from evolutionary biologists against the abrupt appearance of species, especially in light of the Cambrian explosion of life forms and, for example, the recent extraction of DNA from a hominid fossil, carries less weight among Pentecostal scientists and educators. As more and more Pentecostals are receiving graduate education and achieving doctoral degrees in the sciences, there is a sense in which the older creation-evolution debates are no longer an issue. New experimental results can now be assessed in an atmosphere where the hidden presupposition of the nonexistence of God is out in the open. The ongoing study of microevolutionary mechanisms, while rejecting ideologically motivated macroevolutionary changes per se until scientific evidence strongly suggests otherwise, is a responsible position taken by the majority of Pentecostal scientists. The ideology of carte blanche macroevolution not only contradicts much scientific evidence outright, but is imbued with unnecessarily confining naturalistic, atheistic, and Darwinian presuppositions that are no longer fashionable to many in the scientific community. Further, while contemporary Pentecostalism may host a few anomalous advocates of young earth creationism, it has made little headway among Pentecostals. Pentecostal, Orthodox, and Jewish interpretation is overwhelmingly in favor of understanding the "days" of the Genesis creation narrative as deliberately ambiguous and temporally indefinite periods. This is consistent with both cosmological observations and with the sudden appearance of diverse species in the extant fossil record as continually investigated by a number of scientific disciplines.

Pentecostalism and medical technology

Another window into the relationship between Pentecostalism and the sciences is provided by Pentecostal attitudes toward the use of medicine and the emerging medical establishment. The biblicism of early Pentecostalism led many to embrace the belief of divine healing insofar as this was explicitly connected with the New Testament practice of speaking in tongues (inspired speech in unlearned language, both human and divine, as conceptually interpreted in the book of Acts, and, differently, in the first epistle of Paul to the Corinthians). In part, given their lack of medical knowledge and the inaccessibility and unaffordability of medicinal supplies, early Pentecostals looked to God for their healing. As such, early Pentecostal attitudes toward medical practitioners and their arts resonated well with faith healer John Alexander Dowie's (1847–1907) widely circulated pamphlet, which identified the most dreaded disease as the "*bacillis lunaticus medicus*" (ridiculous bacteria of medicine). The result was that many sectarian Pentecostal groups, especially in the rural Appalachian part of America, rejected medicine and relied solely on the healing power of God, sometimes resulting in the loss of life.

Yet such early Pentecostal polemics were rampant against not only the emergent class of medical doctors, who often made mistakes and appeared unreliable to some, but also against the spiritual healing technologies of the Christian Science movement. Ironically, whereas North American Pentecostals were wary of combining faith and spiritual healing, throughout Asia, sub-Saharan Africa, and Latin America, Pentecostals have combined the belief in divine healing with shamanistic practices in order to address physical, emotional, and psychological ailments.

However, Pentecostals have always negotiated the tension between a robust belief in faith healing, which repudiated medical technology entirely, and the belief that faith healing and the use of medicine were indeed compatible. As Grant Wacker points out in *Heaven Below* (2001), medical doctors were found attending early Pentecostal revival services and even participating as members in Pentecostal communities of faith. Over the generations, both the upward social mobility of many Pentecostals and their medical missionary emphases led to an increasing acceptance of the use of medicine. In the 1970s, the establishment of a medical graduate program at ORU, a vanguard institution for neo-Pentecostal and charismatic higher education, followed soon after by their City of Faith Medical and Research Center, signaled the full engagement of the medical sciences among Pentecostals. Yet the ORU motto of educating "the whole man in spirit, mind and body" reflected at the same time the Pentecostal concern for holistic health care strategies. Unsurprisingly, then, polls conducted in the mid 1990s among Pentecostal ministers in Britain revealed that 93.7 percent believe that "modern medicine is a God-given blessing" (Kay, p. 121). It is fair to assume that this percentage is reflective at least of Western Pentecostal attitudes toward the medical sciences.

Arguably, given the emergence of the Pentecostal movement at the turn of the twentieth century, early Pentecostalism can be understood, at least in part, as a reaction to the scientific and technological rationality of that time. Glossolalia (speaking in tongues) is symbolic of the resistance of the masses against the hegemonic discourse of Enlightenment rationalism, as well as of a prayerful desire to be filled with the Holy Spirit. The belief in divine healing could be seen by sociologists as a protest against the failures of medical technology to heal the ills associated with the modernization and urbanization of the nineteenth century, as well as an appropriation of New Testament thought regarding spiritual gifts. As such, Pentecostal spirituality signifies an eruption in the Western world of the nonrational elements of human feeling, expression, and experience that opposes not the rational scientific methodology of science and engineering disciplines but the overextended popular claims of biological science.

In the meantime, however, the limits of scientific rationality have been recognized and acknowledged by the scientific community. For many, the impersonal is no longer preferred to the personal in the new "Era of the Glimpse of God" that began in 1965 with the paradigm-shifting discovery of the cosmic microwave background, followed by its spectacular finely tuned variations in 1992. This new era may have reopened the door for the dialogue that is taking place between humanities scholars in the inexact sciences who are studying Pentecostalism and between the many Pentecostals who are studying and practicing the various sciences. At the beginning of the second century of the Pentecostal "reformation," with over a million churches throughout the world, one of the classical Pentecostal institutions, the Church of God Theological Seminary in Cleveland, Tennessee, now offers a Master of Divinity and Doctor of Ministry course in Theology and Science.

See also CREATIONISM; SPIRITUALITY; SPIRITUALITY AND FAITH HEALING

Bibliography

Assemblies of God, General Council of. "The Doctrine of Creation" (August 15–17, 1977). Springfield, Mo.: Author, 1977. Available at http://www.agncn.org/documents/creation.pdf.

Elbert, Paul. "Biblical Creation and Science: A Review Article." *Journal of the Evangelical Theological Society* 39 (1996): 285–289.

Hummel, Charles E. *The Galileo Connection: Resolving Conflicts between Science and the Bible.* Downers Grove, Ill.: InterVarsity Press, 1986.

Kay, William K. "Approaches to Healing in British Pentecostalism." *Journal of Pentecostal Theology* 14 (1999): 113–125.

Krings, Matthias; Stone, Anne; Schmitz, Ralf W.; et al. "Neanderthal DNA Sequences and the Origin of Modern Humans." *Cell* 90 (1997): 19–30.

McHargue, Lawrence T. "The Christian and Natural Science." In *Elements of a Christian Worldview,* ed. Michael D. Palmer. Springfield, Mo.: Logion Press, 1998.

Munyon, Timothy. "The Creation of the Universe and Humankind." In *Systematic Theology,* rev. edition, ed. Stanley M. Horton. Springfield, Mo.: Logion Press, 1995.

Numbers, Ronald. *The Creationists: The Evolution of Scientific Creationism.* Berkeley: University of California Press, 1993.

Thurman, L. Duane. *How to Think about Evolution and Other Bible-Science Controversies.* Downers Grove, Ill.: InterVarsity Press, 1978.

Wacker, Grant. "The Pentecostal Tradition." In *Caring and Curing: Health and Medicine in the Western Religious Tradition,* ed. Ronald L. Numbers and Darrel W. Amundsen. New York: Macmillan, 1986.

Wacker, Grant. *Heaven Below: Early Pentecostals and American Culture.* Cambridge, Mass.: Harvard University Press, 2001.

Walker, Paul L. *Understanding the Bible and Science.* Cleveland, Tenn.: Pathway Press, 1976.

AMOS YONG
PAUL ELBERT

CHRISTIANITY, RADICAL REFORMED, ISSUES IN SCIENCE AND RELIGION

The Radical Reformation began in Switzerland and southern German in the 1520s, when participants in the mainline Reformation objected to state control over churches. The Schleitheim Confession of 1527 was an attempt by Radical Reformers to distinguish their movement from other Protestants. The Radical Reform movement supported baptism for believers, separation from the world, selection of pastors from within the congregation, and the refusal to swear oaths. These elements were designed to nullify the effects of Constantinianism, the identification of the church first with empire and then with nation state.

The Radicals objected to the use of coercion and violence in the name of God. In this sense, they believed God's action in the human world to be noncoercive. Accordingly, they rejected violence and adopted the *ban* (exclusion from the shared life of the community in accordance with Matthew 18) as the most severe form of punishment. The Radicals continue to believe that Christianity has more to do with changing the world than interpreting its meaning, and therefore they have rarely engaged with scientific developments. Nevertheless, it can be argued that understanding God's action in the natural and social world as noncoercive has important consequences for interactions with the natural and social sciences.

When Isaac Newton's (1642–1727) Laws were accepted as a complete account of all the movements of matter in the universe, it became difficult to conceive of God's action in the world. Modern liberal and conservative views differed over characterizations of divine action. Liberal theologians generally rejected the concept of special divine acts because it seemed self-contradictory for God to break natural laws. Conservative theologians, on

---

the other hand, generally accepted that God could and did miraculously break into the natural causal order. By contrast, Radical Reformed theologians claimed that while God does act in the world, God does so noncoercively. With developments in quantum physics, it has become easier, though still not unproblematic, to make sense of this claim. For example, it would not be inconsistent, or coercive, for God to manipulate quantum events since it is widely agreed that there is no self-determination at this level for God to overrule.

Whereas conflict with the natural sciences has not been an issue for Radical Reformed theologians, there are inherent tensions between Radical Reformed thought and modern social science because of the movement's attempt to embody the Sermon on the Mount. From the early modern period, the dominant assumption in social science has been that coercion, and ultimately violence, is necessary to maintain order in society. However, according to the Radical Reformed view the church itself provides empirical evidence that a society based on noncoercive reconciliation is possible. The church can be understood as an experiment whose existence demonstrates that violence is not a necessary part of social relations. From this perspective, a new vision can emerge for society and social science. One concrete example is Jesus' rejection of retribution as a model for justice in the Sermon on the Mount. In its place, the sermon provides for an understanding of justice that focuses on reconciliation and restoration.

See also CHRISTIANITY, ANGLICAN, ISSUES IN SCIENCE AND RELIGION; CHRISTIANITY, EVANGELICAL, ISSUES IN SCIENCE AND RELIGION; CHRISTIANITY, LUTHERAN, ISSUES IN SCIENCE AND RELIGION; CHRISTIANITY, ORTHODOX, ISSUES IN SCIENCE AND RELIGION; CHRISTIANITY, PENTECOSTALISM, ISSUES IN SCIENCE AND RELIGION; CHRISTIANITY, REFORMED, ISSUES IN SCIENCE AND RELIGION; CHRISTIANITY, ROMAN CATHOLIC, ISSUES IN SCIENCE AND RELIGION; SCIENCE AND RELIGION, HISTORY OF FIELD

Bibliography

Murphy, Nancey, and Ellis, George F. R. *On the Moral Nature of the Universe: Theology, Cosmology, and Ethics.* Minneapolis, Minn.: Fortress Press, 1996.

Murphy, Nancey. *Reconciling Theology and Science: A Radical Reformation Perspective.* Kitchener, Ont.: Pandora Press; Scottdale, Pa.: Herald Press, 1997.

Yoder, John Howard. *The Original Revolution: Essays on Christian Pacifism.* Scottdale, Pa.: Herald Press, 1971.

Zehr, Howard. *Changing Lenses: A New Focus for Crime and Justice.* Scottdale, Pa.: Herald Press, 1995.

CHRISTIAN EARLY
NANCEY MURPHY

CHRISTIANITY, REFORMED, ISSUES IN SCIENCE AND RELIGION

The term *Reformed theology,* though sometimes used synonymously with *Calvinism,* refers more broadly to doctrines traceable to a group of sixteenth-century reformers that included Guillaume Farel (1489–1565), John Calvin (1509–1564), Huldrych Zwingli (1484–1531), Heynrich Bullinger (1504–1575), John Knox (1505–1572), and, arguably, Johannes Bucer (1491–1551) and Peter Vermigli (1500–1562). Nonetheless, it was Calvin in the various editions of his *Institutes of the Christian Religion* (1536–1560) who more than anyone set the main trajectories of Reformed theology.

Early reformed senses of nature

Calvin likens Scripture to spectacles by which one can read the benevolent purpose of creation, which includes both the delight and the utility of nature. There is no suggestion that Calvin thought Scripture was a substitute for physical inquiry regarding matters of what are today called the natural sciences. At the same time, there is no evidence that he closely followed the latest scientific discoveries; his relative indifference to the work of Nicolaus Copernicus (1473–1543) is itself, in retrospect, a glaring omission. The necessities of international diplomacy for the Reformed movement, its political theory and practice, demanded more of his attention than did the astronomy of the time. Calvin still worked within a framework that resisted the notion that the Earth moved. He never reached the point of Thomas Digges (d. 1595), who argued that such a movement within a huge expanse of extremely distant stars redounded to God's glory. Digges belongs to that significant group of people active in the transition from a modified Aristotelian natural philosophy to a Newtonian physics. Gisbert Voetius (1589–1676), who sought to hone his particular version of Aristotelianism and who argued for proscribing the writings of René Descartes (1596–1650), was a kind of throwback. That exception, however, is far outweighed by the works of one of the great forerunners of modern science, Francis Bacon (1561–1626), and of Isaac Newton (1642–1727).

The senses in which the word *nature* and its several translations are used by Reformed theologians are even more numerous than those inherited from classical antiquity and the early church. The best way, drawing on Ronald Hepburn in "Philosophical Ideas of Nature" (1967), of getting at this usage is to note the analogies the Reformed theologians chose to deal with the perennial questions about fundamental reality comprising the world and its structure. Those questions are regarded as perennial largely because of the opulence of analogies used by different streams of classical philosophy: geometrical and mathematical analogies in the case of Anaximander and Pythagoras, archetypal and intellective analogies in the case of Plato, organic and motional in the case of Aristotle, cosmic and cyclical in the case of the Stoic philosophers. In these discussions, the terminology was richly varied, especially when translated from one language to another. The word *natura* sometimes translated *physis* ("nature"), sometimes *ousia* ("being"); sometimes *substantia* ("substance") translated them both. When used in Christian doctrine, a workable agreement about several major terms was achieved by the time of the Council of Chalcedon (451), whereby in the West *persona* ("person") translated *hypostasis* ("way of being"), *substantia* translated the unique *ousia* of the Trinity, and *naturae* translated the two *physeis* united in the incarnation. Even so, the so-called monophysite controversy (over whether the one person Jesus Christ had only one nature) showed that this usage was not universally accepted. Each of the main terms had its own history during the course of medieval philosophy.

Nature and grace in reformed orthodoxy

Following one medieval tradition, Reformed theologians sometimes used the term *nature* in contrast to *grace*, sometimes as a synonym for the whole of creation including human life, and sometimes as a synonym for the whole of creation excepting human life. What seems best to characterize their view of nature is that they could draw on any of a number of analogies, so long as the analogies served a view of the universe as that which is created by God out of nothing and is providentially sustained for an ultimately good end. Or, to put it another way, benevolent teleology governed their cosmology in such a way that critical inquiry into the basic structure of reality was encouraged. In their history of interpretation, they read 2 Corinthians 4:6 as making the connection between the human nature united to the eternal word in the incarnation and nature as the whole cosmos brought into being by God's efficacious word: "It is God who said 'Let light shine out of darkness,' that has shone into our hearts to enlighten them with the knowledge of God's glory, the glory on the face of Christ." According to Johann Heinrich Heidegger (1633–1698), the reason God created was to share his love with another. In this way God can be called *natura naturans* (nature which brings about nature), the uncaused cause who created *ex nihilo* (out of nothing) the *natura naturata* (nature thus brought about), including the secondary causes through which God's providentially sustaining word works. The intricacy, order, and beauty of the universe thus benevolently created and sustained (as "creation continued") provided motivation for the study of nature in which the Reformed theologians were convinced that the hand of God could be discerned; that is, the wondrous correlation between the microcosm and the macrocosm helped provide the kind of validation in which physical experimentation, done with a variety of analogical worldviews, would flourish.

This use of the primary-secondary causes scheme, largely developed to claim simultaneously God's all inclusive providence and a measure of creaturely initiative, came to be radically challenged. However, depending on who was using the scheme, it could function to encourage physical investigation. Heidegger, in his 1696 treatment of divine concurrence, pushed this idea to provide an intriguing argument for physical inquiry. To discover order in events necessarily predictable according to natural laws is, of course, commendable; " ... but God's providence is manifested particularly in things contingent" (Heppe p. 248) God alone, says Heidegger, already understands these "uncertain and casual" events which are the subjects of investigation. The distinction between explicable ("natural or necessary") events and events that are not yet explicable ("casual and fortuitous") was proving, with more physical experimentation, to be merely formal. Rather than detracting from providence, the discoveries of greater complexity and diversity were thought especially to bear witness to divine teleological benevolence. For example, according to Reformed theologians like Heidegger, God's glory is more manifest by creation developing over a period of time (creation continued after the singular creation out of nothing) than by a supposedly instantaneous completion. This argument resurfaced later against those who, unnerved by the discoveries of evolutionary biology and geology, insisted on a literal interpretation of the creation accounts in Genesis.

Reformed responses to nineteenth-century science

There was a considerable range of mutual influence between Reformed thinkers and the rise of modern geology, paleontology, and evolutionary zoology, and two contrasting reactions developed. The first was the reaction of two figures at Yale: James Dwight Dana (1813–1895), professor of geology, and Theodore Dwight Woolsey (1801–1889), the Yale president. Both stood in the broader Calvinist tradition tempered by the Reawakening at the hands of Jonathan Edwards (1703–1758) a century earlier. Dana found no fundamental incompatibility between the evidences for Christian doctrine and evidences for evolution, though he disagreed with Darwin's theory of single-line evolution and corresponded with Darwin about it. Dana expressed these ideas on March 29, 1890, in a lecture entitled "The Genesis of the Heavens and the Earth." Woolsey warned against the threat of positivism and secularization, rather than specifically against the work either of Charles Darwin (1809–1882) or Herbert Spencer (1820–1903).

By contrast, the second reaction was represented by the theologian Charles Hodge (1797–1878) of Princeton, whose particular belief in Biblical inerrancy, including the Genesis accounts of creation, led him finally to oppose Darwinism as he understood it. He expressed his ideas in *What is Darwinism?* (1874) However, Hodge's apologetic counterargument, carried on with an irenic intent not always evident in his followers,

was made with what he thought to be the tools of a more valid scientific method. That is, while he opposed Darwin's findings, Hodge himself believed that scientific argument was not opposed to the brand of Calvinism that he represented and that was heavily shaped by the earlier work of Francis Turretin (1623–1687).

Reformed theology and post-Newtonian physics

With the displacement of Newtonian physics came a new era in which the attention shifted from debates over evolution and Genesis to the implications of post-Newtonian physics for Reformed theology and of Reformed theology for honing questions of scientific method. One major development is represented by the recovery of the seriousness with which theology is to be taken as a science. Such an approach does not mean, as it did with nineteenth-century apologetic theology, an attempt to legitimate theology by arguing its similarity to natural science; rather, it means considering theology as a science in the sense that it has its own procedures congruent with the subject matter being studied. Although the tradition of defining theology as a science had never died out, now there was a recovery of the boundaries and the mutual respect necessary to fruitful dialogue. In this, and in many other aspects of theology and culture, Karl Barth (1886–1968) was a leader, though his influence in shaping the content of the dialogue between Reformed theology and the natural sciences was indirect. It was left to others, especially the Scottish theologian Thomas Torrance (1913–) whose study of James Clerk Maxwell (1831–1879), Albert Einstein (1879–1955), and Michael Polanyi (1891–1976) led him to explore analogies between scientific knowledge and theological knowledge and between theories of relativity and dynamic redefinitions of being. Torrance called attention to Athanasius (c. 296–373) and the Cappadocians (Basil the Great, c. 330–379; Gregory Nazianzus, 329–389; and Gregory Nyssa, c. 330–c. 395) whose relational understanding of God's triune nature has provided material for discussions between theologians and contemporary physicists. Representative of the discussion is Torrance's *Transformation and Convergence in the Frame of Knowledge* (1984). James Loder and James Neidhardt pursued this line further, as did Harold Nebelsick from the perspective of a historian of science.

See also CHRISTIANITY; CREATIO CONTINUA; CREATIO EX NIHILO

Bibliography

Gabriel, Ralph H. *Religion and Learning at Yale: The Church of Christ in the College and University, 1757–1957.* New Haven, Conn.: Yale University Press, 1958.

Gregersen, Niels H., and van Huyssteen, J. Wentzel, eds. *Rethinking Theology and Science: Six Models for the Current Dialogue.* Grand Rapids, Mich.: Eerdmans, 1998.

Hepburn, Ronald W. "Philosophical Ideas of Nature." In *Encyclopedia of Philosophy,* Vol. 5, ed. Paul Edwards. New York: Macmillan, 1967.

Heppe, Heinrich. *Die Dogmatik der Evangelisch-reformierte Kirche* (1861), ed. Ernst Bizer. Neukirchen Kreis Moers: Buchhandlung des Erziehungsvereins, 1935. English edition: *Reformed Dogmatics, Set Out and Illustrated from the Sources,* trans. G. T. Thompson. Grand Rapids, Mich.: Baker House, 1950.

Loder, James E., and Niedhardt, W. James. *The Knight's Move: The Relational Logic of the Spirit in Theology and Science.* Colorado Springs, Colo.: Helmers and Howard, 1992.

Nebelsick, Harold P. *The Renaissance, the Reformation, and the Rise of Science.* Edinburgh, UK: T&T Clark, 1992.

Rudolph, Enno. "Wissenschaft." In *Evangelisches Kirchenlexikon,* 3rd edition, Vol. 4. Göttingen, Germany: Vandenhoeck and Ruprecht, 1996.

Torrance, Thomas F. *Transformation and Convergence in the Frame of Knowledge: Explorations in the Interrelations of Scientific and Theological Enterprise.* Grand Rapids, Mich.: Eerdmans, 1984.

Torrance, Thomas F. *The Christian Frame of Mind: Reason, Order, and Openness in Theology and Natural Science.* Colorado Springs, Colo.: Helmers and Howard, 1989.

E. DAVID WILLIS

CHRISTIANITY, ROMAN CATHOLIC, ISSUES IN SCIENCE AND RELIGION

The most distinctive features of Roman Catholicism that influence the religion-science dialogue are its hierarchical and authoritative structure and its emphasis upon the rational foundations for religious belief. Many of the divisions that have occurred within Christianity in the course of history have their origins in one or both of these characteristics of Roman Catholicism. The history of the interaction within Roman Catholicism between science and religion has been dominated by its hierarchical structure. On the other hand the insistence on reason as fundamental to the relationship of human beings to the universe and, therefore, to the creator of the universe has played an important role in the birth of modern science and provides a platform for the dialogue between the belief system of Roman Catholicism and other disciplines, especially science.

Views of nature

The Catholic belief system includes the fundamental affirmation that nature has a rational structure which human intelligence is capable of probing and, in fact, is driven to probe. The basis for this affirmation lies principally in the Johannine tradition of the *Logos.* John the Evangelist confronted early Christian belief with the world of Greek philosophy. In addition, early Christian reflection upon lived, historical events, especially those recorded in John's Gospel, sees in such events the insertion of God's plan, thought, and word into the universe. Thus John's use of the word Logos, inherited from the Greeks: "The Word (Logos) of God became flesh." This revelation, which the Judeo-Christian tradition believes is spoken by God through his chosen spokespersons, has enormous consequences for one's judgment upon scientific knowledge of the universe. The Judeo-Christian experience affirms emphatically the enfleshment of the divine and, since God is the source of the meaning of all things, that meaning too becomes incarnate.

Some see in this religious belief the foundations of modern science. A rigorous attempt to observe the universe in a systematic way and to analyze those observations by rational processes, principally using mathematics, will be rewarded with understanding because the rational structure is there in the universe to be discovered by human ingenuity. Since God has come among human beings in his Son, humans can discover the meaning of the universe, or at least it is worth the struggle to do so, by living intelligently in the universe.

Religious experience thus provides the inspiration for scientific investigation.

To varying degrees this "Logos theology" is at the roots of all Christianity. What in it is peculiar to Roman Catholicism? In addition to the strong affirmation of this "transcendence become incarnate" by the robust system of sacraments in Roman Catholicism (shared, perhaps, also by Anglicanism), there is in Catholicism a long tradition of analogical knowledge. This reached its peak in medieval Scholasticism, and, although it has taken on many forms, is still very prominent in Catholic thought. It seeks to come to a knowledge of God, the creator, through knowledge of creation. In creation, perfections are always mixed with imperfections. If, at least in thought, the two can be separated, the perfect can then be applied to God. This analogical knowledge is also referred to as the *via negativa* because, even as one applies knowledge of the perfect to God, one must deny that God can be limited to this knowledge. So, the philosopher Thomas Aquinas (c. 1225–1274) could rightly say upon the completion of his *Summa Theologica* that "it was all straw."

Analogy refers to a relationship of similitudes, or of things that are similar. For instance, God is perfect love, and that can be compared with other kinds of love that one witnesses, such as the love of a mother for her child, or the long-standing love of a husband and wife for one another in a stable marriage. But then one sees imperfections in human love, and one must deny that these are present in God's love. That is the use of analogy. The implication is that God wishes to tell humans about himself/herself in creation. It follows, therefore, that a scientist, one who is also a religious believer, must find in science one way to seek to know God. Roman Catholicism in its view of nature is profoundly convinced of this.

It is important to note the logical sequence here. It is not that one comes to believe in God by proving God's existence through anything resembling a scientific process. God is not found as the conclusion of a rational process like that. One believes in God because God gave himself/herself to one. Faith is a personal relationship of love with God and God initiated gratuitously that relationship. No one merited it. No one reasoned to it. Faith is "arational." It does not contradict reason, but it transcends it. Once one has entered into that relationship, one can seek to deepen it through a

scientific knowledge of God's creation. This is a very characteristic stance of Catholic intellectuals.

History of the interaction between science and religion

Because of the dominant hierarchical and authoritative structure of the Catholic Church the history of the interaction between science and religion will necessarily focus upon that structure. This is not to deny that influential Catholic thinkers, such as the paleontologist Pierre Teilhard de Chardin (1881–1955), the astronomer and cosmologist George Lemaître (1894–1966), and others, have not had an impact, but they are not typical of Catholicism in regard to the interaction with science.

Four case histories indicate that the relationship between religion and science in Roman Catholicism has, in the course of three centuries, passed from one of conflict to one of compatible openness and dialogue. The four periods of history are: (1) the rise of modern atheism in the seventeenth and eighteenth centuries; (2) anticlericalism in Europe in the nineteenth century; (3) the awakening within the Church to modern science in the first six decades of the twentieth century; and (4) the Church's view at the beginning of the twenty-first century. The approach of science to religion in each of these periods can be characterized respectively as: (1) temptress, (2) antagonist, (3) enlightened teacher, (4) partner in dialogue.

In his detailed study of the origins of modern atheism, Michael Buckley concludes that it was, paradoxically, precisely the attempt in the seventeenth and eighteenth centuries to establish a rational basis for religious belief through arguments derived from philosophy and the natural sciences that led to the corruption of religious belief. Religion yielded to the temptation to root its own existence in the rational certitudes characteristic of the natural sciences. This rationalist tendency found its apex in the enlistment of the new science, characterized by such figures as Isaac Newton (1642–1727) and René Descartes (1596–1650), to provide the foundation for religion. Isaac Newton marks the real beginning of modern science. Although the Galileo case, as it is called, provides the classic example of confrontation between science and religion, it is really in the misappropriation of modern science by Isaac Newton and others to mistakenly establish the foundations for religious belief that the roots of a much more deep-seated confrontation can be found. From these roots, in fact, sprung the divorce between science and religion in the form of modern atheism. Thus, science served as a temptress to religion. The certainties born of the scientific method gave birth to the desire for identical certainties as a foundation for religious belief. That desire was radically misplaced and led to a lengthy period of misunderstanding between religion and science.

Certain episodes during the nineteenth century reveal aspects of the second movement—anticlericalism. Its influence on the development of the relationship between science and religion in Catholicism are described by Sabino Maffeo in the second edition of his history of the Vatican Observatory. In fact, the founding of the Observatory in 1891 by Pope Leo XIII is set clearly in that climate of anticlericalism, and one of the principle motives that Leo XIII cites for the foundation of the Observatory is to combat such anticlericalism. However, after having shown clearly the prevailing mistrust of many scientists for the Church, he terminates the document in which he established the Observatory by stating:

> . . . in taking up this work we have put before ourselves the plan ... that everyone might see that the Church and its Pastors are not opposed to true and solid science, whether human or divine, but that they embrace it, encourage it, and promote it with the fullest possible dedication (quoted in Maffeo, p. 315 ff.)

Although the historical circumstances did not provide a healthy climate for a dialogue between religion and science, the founding of the Vatican Observatory, even if couched in triumphalistic terms, proved to be a positive contribution to the dialogue, both at the time of its foundation and in its subsequent history.

When one speaks of the awakening of the Church to science during the first six decades of the twentieth century, one is really speaking of the personage of Pope Pius XII. The Pope had an excellent college-level knowledge of astronomy and he frequently discussed astronomy with researchers. However, he was not immune to the rationalist tendency and his understanding of the then most recent scientific results concerning the origins of the universe led him to a somewhat concordant approach to seeing in these scientific results a rational support for the scriptural, and derived doctrinal, interpretation of creation. It was only, in fact, through the most delicate but firm interventions of Georges Lemaître, the father of the theory of the primeval atom that foreshadowed the theory of the Big Bang, that the Pope was dissuaded from following a course that would have surely ended in disaster for the relationship between the Church and scientists.

The specific problem arose from the tendency of Pope Pius XII to identify the beginning state of the Big Bang cosmologies, a state of very high density, pressure, and temperature, which was, at that time, thought to have occurred about one to ten billion years ago, with God's act of creation. Lemaître, in particular, had considerable difficulty with this view. Although he was a respected cosmologist, he was also a Catholic priest, and, since solid scientific evidence for his theory was lacking at that time, he was subject to the accusation that his theory was really born of a spirit of concordism with the religious concept of creation. In fact, it was only with the discovery in 1965 of cosmic background radiation that persuasive scientific evidence for the Big Bang became available. Lemaître insisted that the primeval atom and Big Bang hypotheses should be judged solely as physical theories and that theological considerations should be kept completely separate.

Galileo and Darwin

There are two episodes in the history of the interaction between Catholicism and science that merit special attention. The cases of Galileo Galilei (1564–1642) and Charles Darwin (1809–1882) have, at least in the popular mind, become myths that are thought to exemplify the interaction.

In view of Galileo's increasing promotion of Copernicanism the Congregation of the Holy Office of the Catholic Church in 1616 issued a decree that declared that the Copernican theory that the sun moved was absurd in philosophy and heretical, and the theory that the Earth was not immovable was absurd in philosophy and suspect of heresy. These carefully honed distinctions between philosophy and religious belief reveal the exaggerated rationalism of Catholicism at that time. *Philosophy*, of course, referred to the philosophy of nature, what people today call *physics*. *Heretical* meant that the philosophy contradicted Scripture. The physics was that of Aristotle; Scripture was limited to the literal meaning and to the understanding of the Church Fathers. On both accounts the decree was, by hindsight, grossly in error. This is touted as a conflict between science and religion, but of all things it was clearly not that. Science was never a partner in the discussions. Galileo's telescopic observations, which convincingly supported Copernicanism even though they were not proofs, were never subjected to discussion. Furthermore, religion in the name of Scripture was not a principal protagonist. A philosophical conviction that Aristotle was correct led to an insistence on a literal interpretation of Scripture. Uncritical and untested convictions about the nature of the universe dominated the scene on the part of the Church. In 1633 Galileo was condemned to house arrest for life because he had disobeyed, by his publication of the *Dialogue*, a private edict given to him in 1616, as a consequence of the above decree, not to support Copernicanism. A final judgment upon this case must be that the Church erred gravely at that time in not allowing an internationally renowned scientist to pursue his research. It did so because its authoritarian structure embraced a renunciation of reason. Aristotelian natural philosophy was the standard, not because it was reasonable but because it was imbedded in all Catholic theological thinking of that epoch. A fracture had occurred between reason and authority, two basics of the Catholic way.

The case of Darwin is different; in confronting Darwinian evolution, it was Catholic doctrine that was at stake. There are two fundamental doctrinal assertions that appeared to be under attack: The human being is a special creature, in whose origins God directly intervenes; and the supernatural cannot be reduced to the natural.

Since the time of Darwin, as biological, chemical and physical evolution became ever more acceptable scientifically, the Catholic Church has struggled to understand its doctrinal heritage in light of the new science. On October 22, 1996, a message of John Paul II on evolution was received by the members of the Pontifical Academy of Sciences on the occasion of a meeting sponsored by the Academy on *The Origin and Evolution of Life.* This message is in continuity with the posture of openness characteristic of modern Catholicism. Whereas the encyclical of Pope Pius XII in 1950,

Humani Generis, considered the doctrine of evolution a serious hypothesis, worthy of investigation and in-depth study equal to that of the opposing hypothesis, John Paul II states in his message:

> Today almost half a century after the publication of the encyclical [*Humani Generis*], new knowledge has led to the recognition that the theory of evolution is no longer a mere hypothesis.

The Pope wished to recognize the great strides being made in the scientific knowledge of life and the implications that may result for a religious view of the human person. For him, however, some theories of evolution are incompatible with revealed, religious truth. These include materialism, reductionism, and spiritualism. But at this point the message embraces a true spirit of dialogue when it struggles with the opposing theories of evolutionism and creationism as to the origins of the human person. And this is obviously the crux of the message.

The dialogue progresses in the following way: (1) The Church holds certain revealed truths concerning the human person; (2) Science has discovered certain facts about the origins of the human person; (3) Any theory based upon those facts that contradicts revealed truths cannot be correct. Note the antecedent and primary role given to revealed truths in this dialogue; yet note the struggle to remain open to a correct theory based upon the scientific facts. The dialogue proceeds between these two poles. In the traditional manner of papal statements, the main content of the teaching of previous popes on the matter at hand is reevaluated. And so the teaching of Pius XII in *Humani Generis* that, if the human body takes its origins from preexistent living matter, the spiritual soul is immediately created by God. Is the dialogue therefore resolved by embracing evolutionism as to the body and creationism as to the soul? It must be noted that the word *soul* does not reappear in the remainder of the dialogue. Rather the message moves to speak of "spirit" and "the spiritual."

If the revealed, religious truth about the human being is considered, then there is an ontological leap or an ontological discontinuity in the evolutionary chain at the emergence of the human being. Is this not irreconcilable, wonders the Pope, with the continuity in the evolutionary chain seen by science? An attempt to resolve this critical issue is given by John Paul II's statement in his 1996 message that:

The moment of transition to the spiritual cannot be the object of this kind of [scientific] observation, which nevertheless can discover at the experimental level a series of very valuable signs indicating what is specific to the human being.

The suggestion is being made, it appears, that the ontological discontinuity may be explained by an epistemological discontinuity. Is this adequate or must the dialogue continue? Is a creationist theory required to explain the origins of the spiritual dimension of the human being? Are we forced by revealed, religious truth to accept a dualistic view of the origins of the human person, evolutionist with respect to the material dimension, creationist with respect to the spiritual dimension? In the last paragraphs concerning the God of life, the message gives strong indications that the dialogue is still open with respect to these critical questions.

The dialogue at the beginning of the twenty-first century

Although there are many others, the sources for deriving the most recent view from Roman Catholicism concerning the relationship of science and faith are essentially three messages of John Paul II, two of them given in 1979 and 1986 to the Pontifical Academy of Sciences, and the third in 1988 to the Vatican Observatory. The public has emphasized the statements made by the Pope concerning the Copernican-Ptolemaic controversy of the seventeenth century. In his statements concerning Galileo the Pope essentially does two things: He admits that there was wrong on the part of the Church and apologizes for it, and he calls for a serene, studious, new investigation of the history of that time. However, there are matters that are much more forward-looking and of much more significance than a reinvestigation of the Galileo case.

Especially in the 1988 message, given on the occasion of the tricentennial of Newton's *Principia Mathematica*, John Paul II clearly states that science cannot be used in a simplistic way as a rational basis for religious belief, nor can it be judged to be by its nature atheistic or opposed to belief in God.

... Christianity possesses the source of its justification within itself and does not expect science to constitute its primary apologetic. Science must bear witness to its own worth. While each can and should support the other as distinct dimensions of a common human culture, neither ought to assume that it forms a necessary premise for the other. (quoted in Russell et al., p. M9).

The newest element in this view from Rome is the expressed uncertainty as to where the dialogue between science and faith will lead. Whereas the awakening of the Church to modern science during the papacy of Pius XII resulted in a too facile an appropriation of scientific results to bolster religious beliefs, Pope John II expresses the extreme caution of the Church in defining its partnership in the dialogue: " ... Exactly what form that (the dialogue) will take must be left to the future" (quoted in Russell et al., p. M7).

See also DARWIN, CHARLES; GALILEO GALILEI; SCIENCE AND RELIGION, MODELS AND RELATIONS; TEILHARD DE CHARDIN, PIERRE

Bibliography

Buckley, Michael J. *At the Origins of Modern Atheism*, New Haven, Conn.: Yale University Press, 1987.

Hesse, Mary B. *Models and Analogies in Science*. Notre Dame, Ind.: University of Notre Dame Press, 1966.

John Paul II. "Message to the Pontifical Academy of the Sciences," October 23, 1996. Published in the original French in *L'Osservatore Romano*, 23 October 1996. English translation available in *Origins* (Washington, D.C.: Catholic News Service) 26, no. 22 (14 November 1996).

Lemaître, George. "The Primeval Atom Hypothesis and the Problem of Clusters of Galaxies." In *La Structure et L'Evolution de l'Universe*. Bruxelles, Belgium: XI Conseil de Physique Solay, 1958.

Maffeo, Sabino. *The Vatican Observatory: In the Service of Nine Popes,* trans. George V. Coyne. Vatican City: Vatican Observatory Publications, 2001.

Pedersen, Olaf. *The Book of Nature*. Vatican City: Vatican Observatory Publications, 1992.

Pius XII. *Humani Generis: Encyclical letter concerning some false opinions which threaten to undermine the foundations of Catholic doctrine,* August 12, 1950. In *Acta Apostolicae Sedis*, Vol. 44. Vatican City: Tipografia Poliglotta Vaticana, 1950.

Pontifical Academy. *Discourses of the Popes from Pius XI to John Paul II to the Pontifical Academy of Sciences.* Vatican City: Pontificia Accademia Scientiarum, Scripta Varia 66, 1986.

Russell, Robert John; Stoeger, William R.; and Coyne, George V., eds. *Physics, Philosophy, and Theology: A Common Quest for Understanding.* Notre Dame, Ind.: University of Notre Dame Press, 1988.

Teilhard De Chardin, Pierre. *The Phenomenon of Man,* trans. Bernard Wall. New York: Harper, 1959.

Turek, J. *Georges Lemaître and the Pontifical Academy of Sciences.* Vatican City: Vatican Observatory Publications, 1989.

Wallace, William A. *The Modeling of Nature: Philosophy of Science and Philosophy of Nature in Synthesis.* Washington, D.C.: Catholic University of America Press, 1996.

GEORGE COYNE

CHRISTOLOGY

In the Septuagint, the Hebrew word *Messiah* is translated *Christos,* the anointed one. Since the Christian community believed that Jesus of Nazareth was the anointed one, *Christology* is then the teaching about Jesus of Nazareth as the Christ. Prior to Jesus, there were various Jewish hopes of a new age, often involving intermediary or redeemer figures. The Christian community focused these hopes in Jesus of Nazareth, and consequently proclaimed him as the Christ. In the second century, Ignatius could then talk about "our God, Jesus Christ" (Eph. 18:2; Rom. 3:3) implying a unity between God and Christ. Christians believe that the reason for this elevated status of Christ comes through his resurrection because, as Paul claims, "if Christ has not been raised, then our proclamation has been in vain and our faith has been in vain" (1 Cor. 15:14).

For Christians, Jesus' resurrection indicated a duality of the risen one. Jesus "was descended from David according to the flesh," but he was also "declared to be Son of God with power according to the spirit of holiness by resurrection from the dead" (Rom. 1:3–4). Through his resurrection Jesus became the Son of God who stands beside his Father and participates in the power the Father delegated to him. According to Christians Jesus became the Lord of all and the resurrection became the foundation of Christology.

The Christian belief that Jesus is the Christ entails a connection between Christology and the origin, structure, and destiny of the physical world. In the opening sentences of John's Gospel, a rephrasing of the Genesis priestly creation account occurs. "In the beginning was the Word [*Logos*], and the Word was with God, and the Word was God. He was in the beginning with God. All things came into being through him and without him, not one thing came into being" (John 1:1–3; cf.Gen. 1:1). John asserted that Jesus' coming as the redeemer provides an exact parallel to the creation. Moreover, the Logos, similar to the Jewish personification of wisdom, is the mediator of this new creation, as the Logos was the mediator of creation at the beginning of time. In Jesus, "the Word became flesh and lived among us" (John 1:14). This emphasis on Christ as the first-born of all creation and its mediator is expressed again in Colossians 1:15–17, which states that Christ is not only prior to all creation, but also that all earthly and cosmic powers were created through and for him.

Christ is also presented as the goal of creation and as being present in creation. Underlying this claim, affirmed as early as Justin Martyr (c. 100–165), is the identification of the Logos with reason. So taught the Stoa (initially a Greek school of philosophy), the implications of which were that creation was understood as both reasonable and governed by God as manifested in Jesus Christ. It also allowed Christians to accept whatever they found reasonable in non-Christian insights, such as in Greek philosophy.

Paul Tillich (1886–1965) picked up this correspondence of the universal and incarnate Logos in the twentieth century. Delineating the respective tasks of theology and philosophy, however, Tillich states that theologians do not use the universal Logos as their source of knowledge. Rather, the Logos became flesh, manifesting itself in a particular historical event. The medium through which theologians receive the Logos is not reason but the church, its traditions and its present reality.

Although Paul did not develop general cosmic or metaphysical speculations (1 Cor. 8:6), he did concentrate on the meaning of Christ's lordship. Since Adam was "a type of the one who was to come," the righteousness of Jesus "leads to justification and life for all people" (Rom. 5:18), and therefore nothing "in all creation" can separate human beings from "the love of God in Christ Jesus our Lord" (Rom. 8:12–39). For Paul, God exalted Jesus that at his name "every knee shall bow, in heaven and on earth, and under the earth" (Phil. 2:9–11). In and through and for Jesus all things were created, and "by the blood of the cross" all things can be reconciled to Jesus (Col. 1:15–20). This means that personal salvation and the salvation of the whole world are tied together.

With reference to Colossians 1:15–20, at the Third Plenary Assembly of the Ecumenical Council of Churches at New Delhi, India, in 1961 the Lutheran theologian Joseph Sittler (1904–1987) referred to the cosmic Christ, claiming that "a doctrine of redemption is meaningful only when it swings within the larger orbit of a doctrine of creation. For God's creation of earth cannot be redeemed in any intelligible sense of the word apart from a doctrine of the cosmos which is his home, his definite place, the theatre of his selfhood under God, in corporation with his neighbor, and in caring-relationship with nature, his sister" (Sittler, p. 179). Since nature and humanity are threatened by annihilation, it is not plausible, according to Sittler, to proclaim Christ as the light of the world without incorporating the natural world into that proclamation.

The Jesuit paleontologist Pierre Teilhard de Chardin (1881–1955) picked up the concept of a cosmic Christ, claiming in his essay "Note on the Universal Christ" that "the universal Christ of the New Testament is the organic center of the entire universe" (p. 14). If Christ is universal, Teilhard concludes, then redemption and the fall must extend to the entire universe. Therefore the whole of evolutionary activity is centered in a process of communion with God.

Finally, process theology picked up the notion of a cosmic Christ. In *Christ in a Pluralistic Age* (1975), John B. Cobb, Jr. (1925–) claimed: In the Christian tradition "the Logos is the cosmic principle of order, the ground of meaning, and the source of purpose, and is identified with the incarnate form of the transcendent reality, the Christ" (p. 71). From this he concludes: "Christ is the incarnate Logos. As such Christ is present in all things" (p. 142). Since the Logos is the order, "Apart from Christ there is no hope for a better future" (p. 186).

See also TEILHARD DE CHARDIN, PIERRE

Bibliography

Cobb, John B., Jr. *Christ in a Pluralistic Age*. Philadelphia: Westminster, 1975.

Lyons, J.A. *The Cosmic Christ in Origen and Teilhard de Chardin: A Comparative Study*. Oxford: Oxford University Press, 1982.

Schwarz, Hans. *Christology*. Grand Rapids, Mich.: Eerdmans, 1998.

Sittler, Joseph. "Called to Unity." *The Ecumenical Review* 14 (1962):177–187.

Teilhard de Chardin, Pierre. "Note on the Universal Christ." In *Science and Christ,* trans. René Hague. New York: Harper, 1965.

Teilhard de Chardin, Pierre. *The Heart of the Matter,* trans. René Hague. New York: Harcourt, 1978.

Tillich, Paul. *Systematic Theology,* Vol. 1. Chicago: University of Chicago Press, 1951.

HANS SCHWARZ

CLOCKWORK UNIVERSE

Clockwork universe refers to the concept of the universe as a system that behaves in a manner as patterned and dependable as a mechanical clock. Like a clock, the universe could be thought of as something both designed and constructed—something both conceptualized by a divine artificer and made by a divine craftsman. Like a clock, the universe, once set in motion by its creator, could be visualized as something able to operate without corrections or interference from outside. The regular motions exhibited by the sun, moon, stars, and planets provided the basis for elaborate medieval clocks that could mimic the patterned motion of these celestial objects.

See also DEISM; DETERMINISM; DIVINE ACTION; DOUBLE AGENCY; NEWTON, ISAAC; PHYSICS, CLASSICAL; PROVIDENCE; SPECIAL DIVINE ACTION

HOWARD J. VAN TILL

CLONING

Cloning burst upon the scene in February, 1997, with the announcement of the birth of Dolly, the cloned sheep. She was created when researchers took the DNA nucleus from a cell of an adult sheep and fused it with an egg from another sheep. Shortly after Dolly was born, mice, cattle, goats, pigs, and cats were also cloned.

For biologists, however, the word *cloning* refers not to producing new animals but rather to copying DNA, including short segments such as genes or parts of genes. This ability to copy DNA is a basic technique of genetic engineering used in almost every form of research and biotechnology. In Dolly, copying was taken to the ultimate scale, the copying of the entire nucleus or the entire genome of the sheep. The transfer of the nucleus is usually called *somatic cell nuclear transfer* (SCNT), and this is what most people have in mind when they speak of cloning.

Dolly's birth immediately raised the question of human cloning. In principle, a human baby could be made using SCNT. The technical obstacles are, however, greater than most people recognize. Experts in the field doubt that human reproductive cloning can be safely pursued, at least for several decades. In Dolly's case, it took 277 attempts to create one live and apparently healthy sheep, a risk level that is clearly unacceptable for human reproduction. More important, the state of Dolly's health is not fully known. One fear associated with cloning is that the clone, having nuclear DNA that may be many years old, will age prematurely, at least in some respects. Mammalian procreation is a profoundly complicated process, as yet little understood, with subtlety of communication between sperm, egg, and chromosomes, which allows DNA from adults to turn back its clock and become, all over again, the DNA of a newly fertilized egg, an embryo, a fetus, and so forth through a complex developmental process. Using cloning to produce a healthy human baby who will become a healthy adult is decidedly beyond the ability of science as of 2002. Expert panels of scientists all strongly condemn the use of SCNT to produce a human baby.

Therapeutic cloning

Cloning, however, may have other human applications beside reproduction, and many scientists endorse these. Usually such applications are referred to as *therapeutic cloning*, but it should be noted that much research must occur before any therapy can be achieved. Especially interesting is the possibility of combining nonreproductive cloning with embryonic stem cell technologies. Human embryonic stem cells, first isolated in 1998, appear promising as a source of cells that can be used to help the human body regenerate itself. Based on research performed in mice and rats, scientists are optimistic that stem cells may someday be implanted in human beings to regenerate cells or tissues, perhaps anywhere in the body, possibly to treat many conditions, ranging from diseases such as Parkinson's to tissue damage from heart attack.

Embryonic stem cells are derived from embryos, which are destroyed in the process. Some scientists are hopeful that they will be able to find stem cells in the patient's own body that they can isolate and culture, then return to the body as regenerative therapy. Others think that stem cells from embryos are the most promising for therapy. But if implanted in a patient, embryonic stem cells would probably be rejected by the patient's immune system. One way to avoid such rejection, some believe, is to use SCNT. An embryo would be created for the patient using the patient's own DNA. After a few days, the embryo would be destroyed. The stem cells taken from the embryo would be cultured and put into the patient's body, where they might take up the function of damaged cells and be integrated into the body without immune response.

Religious concerns about cloning

While many believe the potential benefits justify research in therapeutic cloning, some object on religious grounds. Many Roman Catholic and Orthodox Christians reject this whole line of research because it uses embryos as instruments of healing for another's benefit rather than respecting them as human lives in their own right. Others believe that if nonreproductive cloning is permitted, even to treat desperately ill patients, then it will become impossible to prevent reproductive cloning, and so they want to hold the line against all human uses of SCNT. A few Protestant and Jewish groups and scholars have given limited approval to nonreproductive cloning.

Outside the United States, most countries with research in this area reject reproductive cloning but permit cloning for research and therapy. In the United States, federal funding is not available as of 2002 for any research involving human embryos. Privately funded research, however, faces no legal limits, even for reproductive cloning. In 2001, one

U.S. corporate laboratory, Advanced Cell Technology, published its work, largely unsuccessful, to create human cloned embryos in order to extract stem cells. Some religious leaders object to this situation in which privately funded research is left unregulated.

When it comes to reproductive cloning, religious voices are nearly all agreed in their opposition, although they may give different reasons. Aside from a few isolated individuals, no one has offered a religious argument in support of reproductive cloning. All religious voices agree with the majority of scientists in their objection to cloning based on the medical risk that it might pose for the cloned person, who, even if born healthy, may experience developmental problems, including neurological difficulties, later in life. Until it is known that these risks are not significantly higher for the clone than for someone otherwise conceived, most scientists and ethicists agree that researchers have no right to attempt cloning.

Some religious scholars and organizations oppose cloning as incompatible with social justice. As an exotic form of medicine that benefits the rich, cloning should be opposed in favor of more basic health care and universal access to it.

Others oppose reproductive cloning because it goes against the nature of sexual reproduction, which has profound benefits for a species. Human beings are sexual beings, it is argued, and the necessity of sex for procreation is grounded in hundreds of millions of years of evolution and should not be lightly cast aside by technological innovation. Transcending the biological advantage of sexual procreation, some argue, are the moral and spiritual advantages of the unity of male and female in love, from which a new life emerges from the openness of being, far more than from the designs of will.

Some believe that cloning would confuse and probably subvert relationships between parents and their cloned children. If one person in a couple were the source of the clone's DNA, at a genetic level that parent would be a twin of the clone, not a parent. Whether biological confusion would amount to psychological or moral disorder is of course debatable, but any test might result in tragic consequences. Furthermore, cloning creates a child with nuclear DNA that, in some way at least, is already known. This nuclear DNA begins a new life, not with the usual uncertainties of sexual recombination but through the controls of technology. Many have said that the power to create a clone gives parents far too much power to define their children's genetic identity. Unlike standard reproductive medicine, even if combined in the future with technologies of genetic modification, cloning allows parents to specify that their child will have exactly the nuclear DNA found in the clone's original. This is assuredly not to say that parents may thereby select or control their child's personality or abilities, because persons are more than genes. But some fear that by its nature cloning moves too far in the direction of control and away from the unpredictability of ordinary procreation, so far in fact that a normal parent-child relationship cannot emerge in its proper course. To move in that direction at all is to risk subverting the virtues of parenting, such as unqualified acceptance.

Finally, some have held that cloning will place an unacceptable burden on the cloned child to fulfill the expectations that motivated their cloning in the first place. The fact that the parents may have some prior knowledge of how the clone's nuclear DNA was lived by the clone's original will lead the clone to think that the parents want a child with just these traits. One can imagine that clones will believe they are accepted and loved because they fulfill expectations and not because of their own unique and surprising identity.

In time, reproductive cloning may be widely accepted, much as in vitro fertilization has become accepted. But within religious communities, opposition to cloning is so strong that it is hard to imagine that religious people will ever accept it as a morally appropriate means of human procreation. Nevertheless, despite the strength of the objections, many recognize that human reproductive cloning will occur in time, and when it does the religious concern will shift from preventing cloning to affirming the full human dignity of the clone.

See also ANIMAL RIGHTS; BIOTECHNOLOGY; DNA; GENETIC ENGINEERING; REPRODUCTIVE TECHNOLOGY; STEM CELL RESEARCH

Bibliography

Brannigan, Michael C., ed. *Ethical Issues in Human Cloning: Cross-disciplinary Perspectives.* New York: Seven Bridges Press, 2001.

Bruce, Donald, and Bruce, Ann, eds. *Engineering Genesis: The Ethics of Genetic Engineering in Non-Human Species*. London: Earthscan, 1998.

Cole-Turner, Ronald, ed. *Human Cloning: Religious Responses*. Louisville, Ky.: Westminster John Knox Press, 1997.

Cole-Turner, Ronald, ed. *Beyond Cloning: Religion and the Remaking of Humanity*. Harrisburg, Pa.: Trinity Press International, 2001.

Hanson, Mark J., ed. *Claiming Power over Life: Religion and Biotechnology Policy*. Washington, D.C.: Georgetown University Press, 2001.

Kass, Leon R., and Wilson, James Q. *The Ethics of Human Cloning*. Washington, D.C.: AEI Press, 1998.

McGee, Glenn, ed. *The Human Cloning Debate*. Berkeley, Calif.: Berkeley Hills Books, 2000.

Nussbaum, M. C., and Sunstein, C. R., eds. *Clones and Clones: Facts and Fantasies About Human Cloning*. New York: Norton, 1998.

Pence, Gregory E. *Who's Afraid of Human Cloning?* Lanham, Md.: Rowman and Littlefield, 1998.

Pence, Gregory E., ed. *Flesh of My Flesh: The Ethics of Cloning Humans*. Lanham, Md.: Rowman and Littlefield, 1998.

Ruse, Michael, and Sheppard, Aryne, eds. *Cloning: Responsible Science or Technomadness?* Amherst, N.Y.: Prometheus, 2001.

RONALD COLE-TURNER

CLOSED UNIVERSE

Within standard Big Bang cosmology essentially only three futures are available for the physical universe. The universe is either *open,* which means it will continue to expand at an ever increasing rate; or it is *flat,* which means it will only expand at a rate just sufficient to avoid collapse; or it is *closed,* which means the universe will expand to a maximum size and then collapse in upon itself. The total mass-density of the universe determines which scenario will be realized. At a critical mass-density, the universe is flat. If the mass-density is higher than the critical level, the universe is closed. Certain astronomical measurements suggest that the universe is very nearly flat, and yet estimates of mass-density are far below the critical level. This has led scientists to suspect that there is a great deal of matter as yet undetected. Whether there is enough of this unseen *dark matter* to cause the recollapse of the universe is a still unresolved question.

See also BIG BANG THEORY; BIG CRUNCH THEORY; COSMOLOGY, PHYSICAL ASPECTS

MARK WORTHING

COGNITIVE DEVELOPMENT

See EXPERIENCE, RELIGIOUS: COGNITIVE AND NEUROPHYSIOLOGICAL ASPECTS; NEUROSCIENCES; PSYCHOLOGY

COGNITIVE FLUIDITY

The term *cognitive fluidity* refers to the capacity of the modern human mind to combine different ways of thinking with stores of knowledge to arrive at original thoughts, which are often highly creative and rely on metaphor and analogy. As such, cognitive fluidity is a key element of the human imagination. The term has been principally used to contrast the mind of modern humans, especially those after 50,000 B.P. (before present), with those of archaic humans such as Neanderthals and *Homo erectus*. The latter appear to have had a mentality that was domain-specific in nature—a series of largely isolated cognitive domains for thinking about the social, material, and natural worlds. With the advent of modern humans the barriers between these domains appear to have been largely removed and hence cognition became more fluid.

See also EXPERIENCE, RELIGIOUS: COGNITIVE AND NEUROPHYSIOLOGICAL ASPECTS; EVOLUTION, HUMAN

Bibliography

Mithen, Steven. *The Prehistory of the Mind: The Cognitive Origins of Art, Religion and Science*. London: Thames & Hudson, 1996.

STEVEN MITHEN

COHERENTISM

Coherentism represents one of the most popular alternatives to foundationalism as a theory of belief justification. The easiest way to introduce the difference between them is to note their response to the problem of epistemic regress. Proponents of both sides agree that some beliefs are inferentially derived from or justified by their relation to other beliefs, which in turn are justified in relation to still other beliefs, and so on. A looming skepticism about the possibility of having *any* justified beliefs threatens if this regress cannot be stopped. The foundationalist halts the regress by identifying foundational (basic) beliefs that are justified not in relation to other beliefs, but by some other criterion, such as self-evidence, incorrigibility, or being evident to the senses. All other beliefs are founded upon these basic beliefs. The coherentist rejects this solution, arguing that the justification of every belief is dependent on its inferential relation to other beliefs and ultimately on its place in the whole web of a person's belief system. Foundationalists use the images of a linear chain or a pyramid to depict the structure of belief justification, while coherentists prefer the images of a web of belief or a raft with interlocking planks of divergent size and color.

It is important to understand the scope of any particular proposal for coherentism. If a comprehensive metaphysical theory of truth is the goal, coherentism may be linked to a radical idealist embracing of antirealism. Such a pure coherentism asserts that a belief is true if, and only if, it is a member of a consistent set of beliefs. In this extreme form, coherentism is open to several objections. For example, it appears to involve a viciously circular argument, in which beliefs mutually justify each other. It also allows for the possibility that two internally consistent sets of beliefs could both be true even if they contain contradictory beliefs between them. Finally, the radical coherentist position can lead to one despairing of ever justifying *any* belief, for how can one evaluate the inner logical consistency of *every* belief and its complex relation to the *whole* web of beliefs?

For these and other reasons, most contemporary coherence theories focus not on the metaphysical issue of truth but on the epistemological concern with knowledge and justification. Moderate forms of coherentism do not deny that sense experience plays a role in the formation of beliefs; they deny that this role is foundational. Beliefs must be justified in the context of the whole. For example, Nicholas Rescher's version of coherentism fits into his broader call for a "pragmatic idealism" that accounts for the role of experience and practice in the formation and justification of beliefs. Niels Henrik Gregersen has shown how a "contextual coherence" theory may provide a common framework of rationality for theology, science, and other modes of human inquiry. Those participants in the religion-science dialogue who prefer some form of critical realism over naïve realism or antirealism typically affirm coherence as a criterion of truth, but not as the definition of truth.

See also CRITICAL REALISM; EPISTEMOLOGY; EXPLANATION; FOUNDATIONALISM; REALISM; TRUTH, THEORIES OF

Bibliography

Gregersen, Niels Henrik. "A Contextual Coherence Theory for the Science-Theology Dialogue." In *Rethinking Theology and Science: Six Models for the Current Dialogue,* eds. Niels Henrik Gregersen and J. Wentzel van Huyssteen. Grand Rapids, Mich.: Eerdmans, 1998.

Haack, Susan. *Evidence and Inquiry: Towards Reconstruction in Epistemology.* Oxford: Blackwell, 1993.

Pappas, George, and Swain, Marshall, eds. *Essays on Knowledge and Justification.* Ithaca, N.Y.: Cornell University Press, 1978.

Rescher, Nicholas. *A System of Pragmatic Idealism,* Vol. 1. Princeton, N. J.: Princeton University Press, 1992.

F. LERON SHULTS

COMMON ANCESTOR

See EVOLUTION, BIOLOGICAL; EVOLUTION, HUMAN

COMPETITION

An important component of the neo-Darwinian theory of evolution, competition describes the theory that there is a struggle among organisms both of the same species (intraspecific) and between species (interspecific) for food, space, reproduction, and other requirements for existence. Through natural selection organisms develop adaptations to overcome or resist their own destruction in competition with the counter-adaptations developed by other organisms. These adaptations include physiological, chemical, and psychological traits. For example, organisms may evolve to become larger, more poisonous, or more aggressive. Such adaptations are not developed on the short timescale of individual lifetime but on the long evolutionary timescale of the species.

See also ADAPTATION; AGGRESSION; EVOLUTION; NEO-DARWINISM

ARN O. GYLDENHOLM

COMPLEMENTARITY

In his 1948/1949 Gifford lectures the Danish physicist Niels Bohr (1885–1962) suggested that theologians make more use of the Complementarity Principle. Articles in *Zygon: Journal of Religion and Science* from 1966 and elsewhere advocate and also oppose such use in regard to both theology and the relation of science and religion (Reich, 1994).

Bohr had introduced complementarity in 1927: "The very nature of the quantum theory thus forces us to regard the space-time co-ordination and the claim of causality, the union of which characterizes the classical theories, as complementary but exclusive features of the description" (Bohr, p. 115). Thus, complementarity here means to keep distinct what has traditionally been merged. In contrast, the complementarity of the particle-like and the wave-like behavior of light brings together "contradictory" models that traditionally are regarded as excluding each other.

A definition of *complementarity* that is applicable to both physics and theology reads as follows: Complementarity refers to the possibility that the same entity/phenomenon manifests itself in distinct, categorically different ways. All the differing manifestations need to be described and explained, and be part of an overarching theory of the entity/phenomenon, but not all occur in the

same spatial, temporal, or situational context, respectively. Unfortunately, the meaning of the terms *complementarity* and *complementary* changes in everyday use (e.g., we are not opposed to or competing with each other but are complementary), as well as in communication theory (in contrast to symmetrical communication between same-level partners, complementary communication takes place between a superior and an inferior position), and in psychotherapy (in a complementary relation between client and psychotherapist the client's wishes regarding mutual love or hate and dominance or subjection are met; in an anti-complementary position none are met).

Given such a difficulty, why nevertheless search for complementarity in regard to science and religion? Because it opens up a logical possibility not covered by the traditional relationships (conflict, independence, dialogue, and integration) as defined by classical logic (Reich, 1996). That logic is binary: If the choice is between *A* and *B*, and *A* is correct, then *B* must necessarily be wrong. Genuine complementarity involves a trivalent logic, articulated by Hugo Bedau and Paul Oppenheimer in 1961 (compatible, incompatible, and noncompatible), which allows for a context-dependence of the respective explanatory powers. For instance, whereas both science and religion can contribute to the understanding and the significance of the origin and the evolution of the universe, science contributes more to an explanation of what actually happened, and religion to what it means for human living.

Complementarity as defined above involves ontology, epistemology, logic, and methodology. *Ontologically,* a meta-relation (entanglement as described in quantum physics by Werner Heisenberg's principle of indeterminacy) is posited between the class of contents/meanings pertaining to science and the class of contents/meanings pertaining to religion. For example, a person to whom God entrusts a mission (religion) also receives the capacity (science) to carry it through. The *epistemology* calls for ascertaining that the statements concerning science and religion are co-extensional, that is, they refer to the same entity/phenomenon. The logic has already been indicated. And finally, the *methodological* issue implies that science and religion/theology each use their own methods. From such a perspective one is led to conclude that complementarity cannot be looked tor in science and religion *tout court,* but (if at all) in selected issues (Reich, 2002).

See also PHYSICS, QUANTUM; SCIENCE AND RELIGION, MODELS AND RELATIONS

Bibliography

Bedau, Hugo, and Oppenheim, Paul. "Complementarity in Quantum Mechanics." *Synthese* 13 (1961): 201–232.

Bohr, Niels. *Collected Works,* ed. E. Rüdinger. Vol. 6: *The Foundation of Quantum Physics I (1926–1932),* ed. J. Kalckar. Amsterdam: North Holland Publishing Company, 1985.

Reich, K. Helmut. "The Relation between Science and Theology: A Response to Critics of Complementarity." In: *Studies in Science and Theology,* eds. George V. Coyne and Karl Schmitz-Moormann. Vol. 2: *Origins, Time, and Complexity.* Geneva, Switzerland: Labor et Fides, 1994.

Reich, K. Helmut "A Logic-Based Typology of Science and Theology." *Journal of Interdisciplinary Studies* 8, nos. 1–2 (1996): 149–167.

Reich, K. Helmut. *Developing the Horizons of the Mind. Relational and Contextual Reasoning and the Resolution of Cognitive Conflict.* Cambridge, UK: Cambridge University Press, 2002.

K. HELMUT REICH

COMPLEXITY

Whereas cosmology explores the boundaries of the very large, and quantum theory the nature of the very small, complexity theory aims to understand the emergence and development of orders at every level, including the medium size world. To the riddles of the macroscopic and the microscopic are added the puzzles of complex pattern formation in semistable dynamical systems known from everyday life.

Semistable systems are usually nonlinear, so small inputs may trigger dramatic changes. Examples are volcanos and tornados, embryologic and ecological evolution, traffic systems, and stock markets. These are not new areas of research, but the computerization of science since the 1970s has made possible new formalistic approaches to the study of dynamical systems. The question is hereby not so much "What are the constituents of nature (quarks, protons, electrons, etc.)?" but rather "How does nature work?"

Complexity theory, however, is not the name of a single theory comparable to, say, Albert Einstein's Theory of Relativity. There hardly exists one overarching "law of complexity" waiting to be discovered. Rather, complexity research is an umbrella term for a wide variety of studies on pattern formation, some more general, some arising under specific organizational conditions. The field builds on thermodynamics, information theory, cybernetics, evolutionary biology, economics, systems theory, and other disciplines. Since complexity research consistently crosses the boundaries between the inorganic and the organic, the natural and the cultural, it is likely to influence the science-religion dialogue significantly.

Algorithmic complexity

There is no consensus on a general definition of complexity. The complex is usually defined in contrast to the simple, but the distinction between simple and complex is a relative one. What is simple in one frame of reference may be complex in another. Walking downstairs, for example, is simple from the perspective of a healthy person, but physiologically it is highly complex. On the other hand, chaos theory shows that complex phenomena can be described by simple nonlinear equations.

An exact measure of *algorithmic complexity* has been available since the 1960s. In the Kolmogorov-Chaitin model, the complexity of a digital code consisting of 0s and 1s is measured by the length of the computer program needed to describe it. Even a long series of digits (e.g., 01010101010101010101 . . .) can be compressed into a compact description: "write 01 x times." By contrast, a complex code is a series without a discernable pattern; in the worst case, the series would simply need to be repeated by the computer program (e.g., 1001110010011000011 . . .). Such systems are by definition random. However, one can never know with certainty whether a series that one sees as random could be further compressed. This is an information-theoretical version of Gödel's incompleteness theorem discovered by Gregory Chaitin.

Similarly, C. H. Bennett suggested a measure for a structure's degree of complexity by referring to its *logical depth,* defined as the time needed (measured by the number of computational steps) for the shortest possible program to generate that structure. Both Chaitin and Bennett presuppose Claude Shannon's mathematical concept of information: The more disordered a message is, the higher is its informational content. While Chaitin's basic definition has the advantage of being extremely economic, Bennett's definition is capable of measuring the discrete operational steps involved in problem solutions. However, none of these formal definitions of complexity can distinguish organized complexity from pure randomness. The main interest of complexity studies, though, is to understand the self-organized complexity that arises in the creative zones between pure order and pure randomness.

Real-world complexity

To catch the idea of organized complexity, it may be useful to distinguish between descriptive, causal, and ontological aspects of complexity of natural and social systems. Systems that require different sorts of analyses have been called *descriptively complex* (Wimsatt, 1976). Fruit flies, for example, require a variety of descriptions, such as physical descriptions of their thermal conductivity, biochemical descriptions of their constitution, morphological descriptions of their anatomical organs, functional descriptions, and so on. This idea of descriptive complexity lends support to an explanatory pluralism, which emphasizes the need for different types of explanation at different levels.

Systems, however, can also be *pathway complex* while simple in structure if their causal effects are highly sensitive to environmental conditions. A hormone is a natural-kind entity with an easily specifiable molecular composition, but since the effects of the hormone depend on a variety of bodily constellations (which cannot be finitely determined), the causal trajectory of the hormone is complex. Systems theory and organicist proposals in biology have focused on this aspect of complexity.

The most difficult thing to define is *ontological complexity*. An element-based definition of complexity defines complexity by its large number of *variegated elements* (Bak, 1997, p. 5). This definition centers on the fact that many large-scale systems (mountains, geological plates, etc.) do not allow for an analytical approach of their microphysical states. A relation-based definition of complexity will rather focus on the *multiple couplings*

of a system in relation to its environments (Luhmann, 1995, p. 23–28). The human brain with its high number of flexible neurons exemplifies that more possibilities of couplings exist than can be actualized in a life history. Since the capacity for complex interactions with the environment is usually increased by operational subsystems, organizational features can be added to the definition of complexity. An organization-based definition of complexity thus emphasizes the *hierarchical structure* of interacting levels. Analogously, a performance-based definition focuses on the *capacity for self-organizing activity*. Systems are thus ontologically complex if they (1) consist of many variegated elements (in terms of sizes and types), (2) have a high capacity for relating to themselves and their environments, (3) are highly organized in subsystems, multilevel structures, and internal programs, and (4) can perform self-organized activities by flexible couplings to the environment. On this scheme it is possible to evaluate different aspects of complexity. A volcano will be more complex than an amoeba on (1) elements and perhaps on (2) relations, but far less complex on the score of (3) hierarchical order and (4) self-organizing activity.

On this scheme, the complex can also be distinguished from the merely complicated (Cilliers, 1998). Even "primitive" natural entities such as genes may be ontologically more complex than sophisticated artificial systems such as airplanes. A Boeing 747 jet consists of highly specified elements, related to one another in predescribed ways, and there exists a clear recipe for how to assemble the elements into a unified system, which again has a predesigned purpose: being able to take off, fly, and land safely. The Boeing is a highly complicated machine but not terribly complex. In this sense, the complex is more than the simple but also more than the complicated.

Noncomputational complexity

Complexity studies fall into two main families of research, one more conceptual (organicism, emergentism, and systems theory) and another more formalistic (information theory, cybernetics, and computational complexity). Both types of research continue to interact in understanding complex phenomena. While a conceptual preunderstanding of complex phenomena guides the construction of computational models, these will afterwards have to be tested on real-world situations.

Complexity studies did not start with computers. The idea that the whole is more than the sum of the parts goes back to Plato's notion of divine providence (*Laws* 903 B-C), and in *Critique of Judgment* (1790) Immanuel Kant describes a naturalized version of the same idea of self-adjustment: "parts bind themselves mutually into the unity of a whole in such a way that they are mutually cause and effect of one another"(B 292).

Embryologists from Karl Ernst von Baer and Hans Spemann up to C. H. Waddington embraced *organicism* as the middle course between vitalism and reductionism. In organicism a materialist ontology ("there exists nothing but matter") was combined with the observation that new properties are causally effective within higher-order wholes. Molecules are not semipermeable, but cell membranes are, and without this capacity organisms cannot survive. In the 1920s writers such as C. Lloyd Morgan, C. D. Broad, and Samuel Alexander developed organicism from an empirical research program into a metaphysical program of *emergent evolutionism*. The point here was that in the course of evolution higher-order levels are formed in which new properties emerge. Whereas the solidity of a table is a mere "resultant" of solid state physics, the evolution of life is ripe with "emergent" properties (for example, metabolism) that require new forms of description and eventually will have real causal feedback effects on the physical system (the atmosphere) that nourished life in the first place.

After World War II the *general systems theory* combined organicistic intuitions with cybernetics. Ludwig von Bertalanffy replaced the traditional whole/part difference by the difference between systems and environments. Systems are constitutionally open for environmental inputs and are bound to develop beyond equilibrium under selective pressures. Thereby systems theory established itself as a theory combining thermodynamics and evolutionary theory. Systems are structures of dynamic relations, not frozen objects.

In the 1960s Heinz von Foerster and others introduced the theory of self-referential systems according to which all systems relate to their environments by relating to their own internal codes or programs. Brains don't respond to cats in the world, but only to the internal firings of its neurons within the brain. "Click, click is the vocabulary of neural language" (von Foerster). In this perspective, closure is the precondition of openness, not its preclusion. In this vein, biologists Francisco J. Varela and Humberto Maturana developed a constructionist research program of *autopoietic* (self-productive) systems. The sociologist Niklas Luhmann has further emphasized how systems proceed by self-differentiation and can no longer be analyzed by reference to global physical features of the world-as-a-whole. In this perspective, each system needs to reduce, by its own internal operations, the complexities produced by other systems. Different systems (for example, biological, social, psychic) operate with different codes (energy, communication, consciousness), and even though they coevolve they cannot communicate with one another on neutral ground. The fleeting experience of consciousness, for example, remains coupled to physiological processes and to social communication, yet has its own irreducible life.

Computational complexity

Computational complexity presupposes the idea of algorithmic compression and embodies the spirit of cybernetics. The dictum of Norbert Wiener that "Cybernetics is nothing if it is not mathematical" (1990, p. 88) could also be said of computational complexity.

The field of cybernetics was developed after World War II by John von Neumann, Ross Ashby, Norbert Wiener, and others. Central to cybernetics is the concept of *automata,* defined as machines open for information input but leading to an output modified by an internal program. In cybernetic learning machines, the output functions are reintroduced into the input function, so that the internal program can be tested via trial and error processes. However, the measure for success or failure is still fixed by preset criteria.

The cybernetic automata were the direct precursors of *cellular automata,* used in the artificial life models designed by John Conway and Chris Langton in the 1970s. Cellular automata use individual based modeling: "Organisms" are placed in cubic cells in a two-dimensional grid, and their "actions" (die or divide) are specified by the number of living cells in their immediate neighborhood. In this way, the positive feedback of breeding can be modeled as well as the negative feedback of competition. The result is self-reproducing loops generated by very simple rules.

With the establishment of the Santa Fe Institute in New Mexico in 1984 a multidisciplinary center for computational complexity was formed. Physicist Murray Gell-Mann, computer scientist John Holland, and others introduced the idea of *complex adaptive systems*. As opposed to simple adaptation (as in a thermostat), there are no preset goals for complex adaptive systems. Like cellular automata, complex adaptive systems are individually modeled systems, but complex adaptive systems also involve "cognition." Complex adaptive systems are able to identify perceived regularities and to compress regular inputs into various schemata. Unlike cybernetic learning machines, there may be several different schemata competing simultaneously, thus simulating cognitive selection processes. In this manner self-adaptation coevolves with adaptation beyond a preset design. Whereas Gell-Mann uses complex adaptive systems as a general concept, Holland uses the term only about interacting individual agents. Complex adaptive systems agents thus proceed by a limited set of interaction rules, governed by simple stimulus-response mechanisms such as (1) tags (e.g., if something big, then flee; if something small, then approach), (2) internal models (or schemata), and (3) rules for connecting building blocks to one another (e.g., eyes and mouth to facial recognition). The result of these local mechanisms, however, is the emergence of global properties such as nonlinearity, flow, diversity, and recognition.

Insofar as complex patterns are generated by simple mechanisms, computational complexity can be seen as a reductionist research paradigm; in contradistinction to physical reductionism, however, the reduction is to interaction rules, not to physical entities. But insofar as higher-level systems can be shown to exert a "downwards" feedback influence on lower-level interaction-rules, computational complexity may also count as an antireductionist research program. The issues of reductionism versus antireductionism, bottom-up versus top-down causality, are still debated within the computational complexity community. But anyway, it is information and not physics that matters.

Computational complexity and real-world complexity

The spirit of computational complexity is not to collect empirical evidence and "reflect" reality, but to "generate" reality and explore virtual worlds of possibility. Computational complexity is nonetheless empirically motivated and aims to understand real-world complexity by computer modeling. The aspiration is to uncover deep mathematical structures common to virtual worlds and real-world dynamical systems.

The mathematical chaos theory is an example of a computer-generated science that has succeeded in explaining many dynamical patterns in nature. Yet the relation between chaos theory and computational complexity is disputed. While chaotic systems (in the technical sense) are extremely sensitive to the initial conditions, complex systems are more robust (that is, they can start from different conditions and still end up in almost the same states). Accordingly, chaos theory can predict the immediate next states but not long-term developments, whereas complex systems can reliably describe long-term prospects but cannot predict the immediate following steps. Moreover, chaos systems do not display the kind of evolutionary ascent and learning characteristic of complex adaptive systems, but oscillate or bifurcate endlessly. It therefore seems fair to say that chaos theory is only a small pane in the much larger window of complexity studies. Chaos, in the colloquial sense of disorder, is everywhere in complex systems (and so are fractals and strange attractors), but the equations of chaos in the technical sense (the specific Lyapunov-exponent, etc.) cannot explain self-organized complexity.

There are also connections between thermodynamics and complexity theory. Beginning in the 1960s, the chemist Ilya Prigogine studied the so-called dissipative structures that arise spontaneously in systems dissipated by energy. While classical thermodynamics described isolated systems where nonhomogeneities tend to even out over time, Prigogine studied nonequilibrium processes of "order out of chaos" (*chaos* in the nontechnical sense). Famous examples are the convection patterns of Bénards cells formed spontaneously under heating or the beautiful chemical clocks of the Belousov-Zhabotinski reaction. While Ludwig Boltzmann's law of entropy from 1865 still holds for the universe as a whole, the formation of local orders is produced by nonequilibrium thermodynamics. The averaging laws of statistical mechanics are not contradicted, but they simply do not explain the specific trajectories that develop beyond thermodynamical equilibrium.

In the wake of Prigogine, a new search for the thermodynamical basis of evolution began (Wicken, 1987). The bifurcation diagrams of Prigogine showed amazing similarities to evolutionary trees. Reaching back to the seminal work of D'Arcy Wentworth Thompson in *On Growth and Form* (1916), many began to think that the interplay of selection and mutation is not self-sufficient for explaining the evolutionary tendency towards complexification. Evolution may be driven by gene selection *and* prebiotic laws of physical economy.

Since the 1970s, theoretical biologist Stuart Kauffmann has constructed computational models of self-organizing principles at many levels. Motivated by the almost ubiquitous tendency of chemical systems to produce autocatalytic systems, Kauffman theorizes that life may have emerged quite suddenly through phase transitions where chemical reactions function as catalysts for one another far below the threshold of the RNA-DNA cyclus. Kauffman uses a similar model for simulating the empirical findings of Francois Jacob and Jacques Monod, who showed that genes switch on and off depending on the network in which they are situated. In the simplest model of Boolean networks, each "gene" is coupled randomly to two other genes with only two possible states, on or off (states that are determined by the states of the two other genes). Running this small system with only three genes and two activities recurrently (and later with much larger networks), Kauffman was able to show that the number of state cycles (attractors) increase with the number of genes. Moreover, their relation is constant so that the number of state cycles is roughly the square root of the number of genes, and Kauffman points out in *The Origins of Order* (1993) that in real-world species one finds roughly the same relation between the number of genes and the number of cell types in a given species. Thus, agents in coupled systems seem to tune themselves to the optimal number of couplings with other agents. In addition, when investigating fitness landscapes of interacting species at the ecological level, Kauffman finds the principle of "order for free." Evolutionary innovations tend to happen "at the edge of chaos," between the strategy of evolutionarily stable orders and the strategy of the constant evolutionary arms race. In *Investigations* (2000), Kauffman pursues a search for laws by which the biosphere is coconstructed by "autonomous agents" who are able run up against the stream of entropy. Kauffman hereby acknowledges the impossibility of prestating finitely what will come to be within the vast configuration space of the biosphere.

The theory of *self-organized criticality* formulated by Per Bak and his colleagues starts in empirically confirmed regularities (such as the Gutenberg-Richter law of earthquakes). Many systems show slow variation over long periods, rare catastrophic activities over short time, and some critical phases in between. The building up of sand piles shows these phase transitions, but so do earthquakes, extinction rates, and light from quasars. Bak's point is that self-organized criticality systems are self-organizing, since they (1) are robust and do not depend on specific initial conditions, (2) emerge spontaneously over time (with no external designer), and (3) are governed by the same mathematical principles in stationary, critical, and catastrophic states. Bak has made both real-world experiments and simplified computer-models of self-organized criticality systems, but he believes that self-organized criticality is only a first approximation of stronger explanations of nature's tendency to build up balances between order and disorder.

Relevance for the science-religion discussion.
While organicist programs of noncomputational complexity have played a major role in the science-religion dialogue since the seminal works of Ian Barbour, Arthur Peacocke, and others, the relevance of computational complexity for theology largely remains to be explored. The following issues are therefore to be taken more as pointers than as conclusions:

(1) The sciences of complexity study pattern formations in the midst of the world rather than in a hidden world beyond imagination. The features of organized complexity resonate with the experiences of being-part-of-a-whole, experiences that since Friedrich Schleiermacher's *On Religion* (1799) have been taken to be essential to religious intuition.

(2) While presupposing a robust naturalism, complexity theory suggests that "information" is as seminal to nature as are the substance and energy aspects of matter. Complexity theory may thus give further impetus

to the dematerialization of the scientific idea of matter in the wake of relativity theory.

(3) By focusing on relations and interactions rather than on particular objects, complexity theory supports a shift in worldview from a mechanical clockwork view of the world to an emergentist view of the world as an interconnected network, where flows of information take precedence over localized entities. Complexity theory also offers a road for understanding the evolution of coevolution. By balancing the principle of individual selection by principles of self-organization, the focus on individual genes is supplemented by the importance of interconnected living organisms, a view closer to ethical and religious sentiments than the inherited view of the omnipotence of selection.

(4) Even though natural evils (from earthquakes to selection) remain a challenge to religions that presuppose a loving almighty God, the costs of evolutionary creativity are now being placed in a wider framework of evolution. If the same underlying dynamics of self-organized criticality produce both stability, criticality, and catastrophes, and the constructive aspects of nature cannot exist without the destructive aspects, a theodicy of natural evils may be facilitated.

(5) The idea of complex adaptive systems gives biological learning and human culture (including science, ethics, and religion) a pivotal role in the understanding of what nature is, and what makes human and animal life grow and flourish. In addition, since complexity theory consistently crosses the boundaries between physics, biology, and the cultural sciences, theologians and human scientists may be prompted to rethink human culture (including religion) in terms of the creative interactions between the inorganic, the organic, and the cultural.

(6) From an external scientific perspective, computational complexity may be used to explain a variety of religious phenomena that arise at the critical interface between adaptation and self-adaptation, such as the interaction between religious groups, individual conversion experiences, and so on. The first computer models in this area have already been completed.

(7) From an internal religious perspective, complexity theory offers religious thought a new set of thought models and metaphors, which (when adopted) can stimulate the heuristics of theology when complex phenomena are redescribed from the perspective of religious symbolics. Self-organization, coupled networks, and adaptation by self-adaption are candidates for such religious self-interpretation. The principles of complexity are in particular consonant with the idea that a divine Logos is creatively at work in the pattern formations of nature and drives nature towards further complexification.

(8) The computational complexity idea of self-organization is a challenge to the Enlightenment idea of a divine designer of all natural processes. Self-organization is also a challenge to the creationist Intelligent Design movement, which gives priority to the idea of "original creation" and tends to perceive novelties as perversions of pre-established designs. However, self-organizational processes never happen from scratch, but always presuppose a framework of laws and natural tendencies that could well be said to be "designed" by God. While a design of specific evolutionary outcomes is obsolete in light of self-organized complexity, the coordination of laws leading towards self-organization and coevolution may be explained by a divine metadesign.

(9) Since emergence takes place in the merging of coupled systems, theology may escape the alternative between an interventionist God, who acts by breaking natural laws, and a God who only sustains the laws of nature uniformly over time. In higher-organized systems, new informational pathways are continuously tried out in adventurelike processes. If the local interaction rules and the overall probability patterns are constantly changed over time, the actual pathways of large-scale coupled systems are not reducible to the general laws of physics. Special divine interaction with the evolving world can thus no longer be said to "break laws" in an interventionist manner, since there are no fixed laws to break in coupled systems.

(10) The seminal idea of self-organization may help overcome the idea that God and nature are contraries, so that God is powerless, if nature is powerful, and vice versa. A more adequate view may be to understand God as the creator who continuously hands over creativity to nature so that natural processes are the signs of a divine self-divestment into the very heart of nature's creativity. On this view, God is at work "in, with, and under" natural and social processes, and self-organization takes place within a world already created and continuously gifted by God.

See also AUTOMATA, CELLULAR; AUTOPOIESIS; CHAOS THEORY; CYBERNETICS; EMERGENCE; INFORMATION THEORY; INTELLIGENT DESIGN; SYSTEMS THEORY; THERMODYNAMICS, SECOND LAW OF

Bibliography

Ball, Philip. *The Self-Made Tapestry: Pattern Formation in Nature.* Oxford: Oxford University Press, 1999.

Bak, Per. *How Nature Works: The Science of Self-Organized Criticality.* Oxford: Oxford University Press, 1997.

Bennett, C. H. "Logical Depth and Physical Complexity." *The Universal Turing Machine. A Half-Century Survey,* ed. Rolf Herken. Oxford: Oxford University Press, 1987.

Chaitin, Gregory. *Algorithmic Information Theory.* Cambridge: Cambridge University Press, 1975.

Cilliers, Paul. *Complexity and Postmodernism: Understanding Complex Systems.* London: Routledge, 1998.

Clayton, Philip. *God and Contemporary Science.* Grand Rapids, Mich.: Eerdmans, 1997.

Cowan, George A.; Pines, David; and Meltzer, David, eds. *Complexity: Metaphors, Models, and Reality.* Cambridge, Mass.: Perseus Books, 1994.

Emmeche, Claus. *The Garden in the Machine: The Emerging Science of Artificial Life.* Princeton, N.J.: Princeton University Press, 1994.

Gell-Mann, Murray. *The Quark and the Jaguar: Adventures in the Simple and the Complex.* New York: W. H. Freeman, 1994.

Gilbert, Scott F., and Sarkar, Sahotra. "Embracing Complexity: Organicism for the 21st Century." *Developmental Dynamics* 219 (2000): 1–9.

Gregersen, Niels Henrik. "The Idea of Creation and the Theory of Autopoetic Processes." *Zygon* 33, no. 3 (1998): 333–367.

Gregersen, Niels Henrik, ed. *From Complexity to Life: On the Emergence of Life and Meaning.* New York: Oxford University Press, 2002.

Holland, John. *Hidden Order: How Adaptation Builds Complexity.* Reading, Mass.: Addison-Wesley, 1995.

Holland, John. *Emergence: From Chaos to Order.* Oxford: Oxford University Press, 1998.

Kauffman, Stuart. *The Origins of Order: Self-Organization and Selection in Evolution.* New York: Oxford University Press, 1993.

Kauffman, Stuart. *At Home in the Universe: The Search for Laws of Self-Organization and Complexity.* New York: Oxford University Press, 1995.

Kauffman, Stuart. *Investigations.* New York: Oxford University Press, 2000.

Luhmann, Niklas. *Social Systems,* trans. John Bednarz Jr. with Dirk Baecker. Stanford, Calif.: Stanford University Press, 1995.

Maturana, Humberto R., and Varela, Fransisco. *The Tree of Knowledge: The Biological Roots of Human Understanding,* rev. edition. Boston: Shambala, 1992.

Peacocke, Arthur. *Theology for a Scientific Age: Being and Becoming—Natural, Divine and Human,* enlarged edition. London: SCM Press, 1993.

Rasch, William, and Wolfe, Cary, eds. *Observing Complexity: Systems Theory and Postmodernity.* Minneapolis, Minn.: University of Minnesota Press, 2000.

Russell, Robert John; Murphy, Nancey; and Peacocke, Arthur A., eds. *Chaos and Complexity: Scientific Perpectives on Divine Action.* Berkeley, Calif.: Center for Theology and the Natural Sciences; Notre Dame, Ind.: Notre Dame University Press, 1995.

Russell, Robert John; Murphy, Nancey; Meyering, Theo; and Arbib, Michael A., eds. *Neuroscience and the Human Person: Scientific Perpectives on Divine Action.* Berkeley, Calif: Center for Theology and the Natural Sciences; Notre Dame, Ind.: Notre Dame University Press, 1999.

Schmidt, Siegfried J., ed. *Der Diskurs des radikalen Konstruktivismus.* Frankfurt am Main, Germany: Suhrkamp, 1988.

Solé, Richard, and Goodwin, Brian. *Signs of Life: How Complexity Pervades Biology.* New York: Basic Books, 2000.

Stengers, Isabelle. *La vie et l'artifice: Visage de l'émergence.* Paris: La Découverte, 1997.

Thompson, D'Arcy Wentworth. *On Growth and Form* (1916). New York: Dover, 1992.

Waldrop, M. Mitchell. *Complexity: The Emerging Science at the Edge of Order and Chaos.* New York: Simon and Schuster, 1992.

Wicken, J. S. *Evolution, Information, and Thermodynamics: Extending the Darwinian Paradigm.* New York: Oxford University Press, 1987.

Wiener, Norbert *God and Golem Inc.: A Comment on Certain Points Where Cybernetics Impinges on Religion.* 1964. Reprint, Cambridge, Mass: MIT Press, 1990.

Wimsatt, William C. "Complexity and Organization." In *Topics in the Philosophy of Biology,* eds. Marjorie Grene and Everett Mendelsohn. Dordrecht, Netherlands: Kluwer, 1986.

NIELS HENRIK GREGERSEN

COMPUTER

See INFORMATION TECHNOLOGY

CONFLICT

See MODELS; SCIENCE AND RELIGION, MODELS AND RELATIONS; SCIENCE AND RELIGION, METHODOLOGIES

CONFUCIANISM

See CHINESE RELIGIONS, CONFUCIANISM AND SCIENCE IN CHINA

CONSCIOUSNESS STUDIES

Consciousness studies is a new, rapidly evolving, highly interdisciplinary field that includes psychology, philosophy, physics, sociology, religion, dynamic systems, mathematics, computer science, neuroscience, art, biology, cognitive science, anthropology, and linguistics. In the early 1990s, most scientists considered consciousness taboo, but by the early 2000s many considered it the most important unsolved problem in science. Consciousness is also a key issue in the ongoing dialogue between science and religion. The dominant view of consciousness in the hard sciences is materialist and reductionist. This view has had important successes, but it also faces important unresolved problems. For example, biologist Francis Crick to wrote of his audience, "You're nothing but a pack of neurons" in parody of Lewis Carroll. But most people, including those in consciousness studies, and even in neuroscience, think there is much more to human life than can be seen at the level of neurons.

Notions of consciousness are important in many religions. The term *God consciousness* figures in the Protestant theology of Friedrich Schleiermacher and his followers, and *Christ consciousness* is used in some Christian and New Age religions, sometimes in a dubious way. *Cosmic consciousness* is important in Hinduism, especially Vedanta, and *pure consciousness* is important in the Buddhist school called *Dzogchen* in Tibetan and *Maha Ati* or *Mahasandhi* in Sanskrit. Consciousness is also a common theme in the Tantric traditions. Reports of meditation experience are taken more seriously in consciousness studies than in the hard sciences, where researchers often dismiss such data as mere subjective experience. On the other hand, due to close connections with various religions, some writers on consciousness have hidden (or not so hidden) agendas, so that caution is called for when approaching some literature on consciousness studies.

In general, the hard sciences tend to reduce consciousness to the material, while religions are more concerned with mental or spiritual aspects. This reflects the heritage of mind-body separation associated with the seventeenth-century French philosopher René Descartes. Although there is no single dominant view of consciousness, nor even any generally accepted definition, consciousness studies has made significant progress.

Shape of the field

At of the turn of the twenty-first century, consciousness studies has a professional society, the Association for the Scientific Study of Consciousness (ASSC); one highly interdisciplinary journal, the *Journal of Consciousness Studies (JCS)*; and three journals devoted mainly to scientific and philosophical studies, *Consciousness and Cognition, Consciousness and Emotion,* and *Psyche,* the latter being an electronic journal. *JCS* sponsors a popular online discussion group. Many other journals, such as *Behavioral and Brain Sciences* and *Mind,* publish articles on consciousness. The University of Arizona in Tucson hosts a research center on consciousness studies and has organized an important biannual conference series since 1994. *Consciousness and Cognition* and *Psyche* are official journals of ASSC, which also organizes a biannual conference. Well known universities offering courses on consciousness include New York University in New York City, Bryn Mawr College in Pennsylvania, Vanderbilt University in Nashville, the University of Colorado in Boulder, the University of Virginia in Charlottesville, and the University of Arizona in Tuscon. Advanced degrees in consciousness studies are offered by the University of Skoevde in Sweden, Greenwich University in Australia, and Birla Institute of Technology and Science in India, among others. John F. Kennedy University in Orinda, California, has a Department of Consciousness Studies, and Brunel University in London offers an MSc degree in Cognition and Consciousness. In addition, there are many specialized conferences, and the emergence of the specialized journal *Consciousness and Emotion* in 2000 is a sign that the field is maturing.

Issues, paradigms, and results

It is difficult to single out any small set of key issues, not only because of the rapid growth of the field, but also because each of its many paradigms defines different sets of issues as central, secondary, marginal, and meaningless. Nonetheless, the following are some issues, paradigms, and results that seem most important in the literature.

The most obvious issue is how to study consciousness. Despite the fact that the advocates of various approaches are in constant, sometimes acrimonious, dialogue, no approach has been completely discredited, except perhaps that of mediums, spiritualists, and the like. This is why the editorial policy of *JCS* calls for a wide diversity of views, and aims to promote dialogue among them, and why the Tucson conference follows a similarly liberal policy. As the distinguished philosopher John Searle famously noted: At our present state of the investigation of consciousness, we don't know how it works, and we need to try all kinds of different ideas. Nevertheless, journals and conferences devoted to specific aspects of consciousness studies can be valuable.

Mind and body relation. The relation between mind and body is another major issue. Are mind and body the same kind of thing, or are they different? Or perhaps the same thing but differently perceived? Monism says there is just one kind of thing, and material monism (also called physicalism) says that all things are material, while mental monism (also called idealism) says that all things are mental. The dualism associated with Descartes says that both material and mental things exist. There are many variants of these and many other positions. Philosophical interpretations of consciousness wedded to reductionist scientific approaches like neuroscience and experimental psychology tend to be material monist. The philosopher David Chalmers is a kind of dualist, who argues that in addition to matter, information is a second fundamental world constituent. The philosopher Paul Churchland is an "eliminative materialist" monist, who argues that there is really no such thing as consciousness. Searle is an "emergent materialist" monist, who argues that consciousness is a distinct level of phenomena, emerging out of lower level brain activity, which only exists when it is experienced.

It is difficult to find adherents of either dualism or mental monism among eminent scientists. The most prominent acception is the Nobel Prize winning physiologist John Eccles, who advocated a form of interaction dualism similar to that of Descartes. Bishop George Berkeley (1685–1753) was the last major Western philosopher to advocate mental monism. On the other hand, dualism is the most common position in Christianity, as is mental monism in South and East Asian religions. For example, the Buddhist school of Yogacara posits a form of mental monism and is considered foundational for Buddhist Tantra. Traditions in Hinduism and Taoism can also be considered mental monist.

In "Conversations with Zombies," Todd Moddy investigates an amusing development in the debate among these positions: The possibility (or impossibility) of "philosophical zombies," creatures having exactly the same physical structure as ordinary humans, but without consciousness. Metaphysical debates about basic world substances seem to contribute little to the understanding of consciousness. Reconceptualizing the two main views as the scientific and phenomenological methods, instead of reifying them as world substances, leads to more fruitful projects such as the refinement of these views and their combination in productive syntheses.

Cognitivism. A once dominant approach in decline well before the end of the twentieth century is that of early cognitive science and artificial intelligence, often called cognitivism. This paradigm's model of the mind identifies cognition with computation, and the brain as the hardware on which it runs. The lineage of cognitivism traces back to pioneering work of Norbert Wiener on cybernetics, and to the Macy Conferences, organized since 1947 by anthropologists Margaret Mead, Gregory Bateson, and others, introducing systems theory to a key cross-disciplinary group. But cognitivists often ignore these antecedents and instead cite linguist Noam Chomsky's scalding review of psychologist B. F. Skinner's 1957 book *Verbal Behavior.* Skinner advocated behaviorism, a psychological theory that tried to ignore internal mental states. Chomsky argued that such states are needed to process even simple syntax. Another seminal cognitivist work, *Plans and the Structure of Behavior* (1960) by George Miller, Eugene Galanter, and Karl Pribram, proposed that human plans have the same structure as a certain simple kind of computer program. This tradition generally relies on formal logical representations of knowledge about the world. The cognitivist paradigm flourished beginning in the 1960s, partly fueled by large military funding for artificial intelligence.

Cognitivism has been much criticized. A famous early attack was Searle's Chinese room argument, which challenged the idea that a program running on a machine could be conscious. Another serious challenge came from James Gibson's work on affordances, showing that many cognitive tasks are greatly simplified by relying on information already in the world, instead of complex internal representations. Work in cognitive linguistics, as represented by George Lakoff and Mark Johnson's *Metaphors We Live By* (1980), showed that many basic metaphors rely on innate sensory-motor schemas. The sociologist Lucy Suchman showed that human plans as actually used can have structure and execution very different from that postulated by Miller, Galanter, and Pribram.

Biologist Francisco Varela, philosopher Evan Thompson, and psychologist Eleanor Rosch (all Buddhists) used empirical evidence in *The Embodied Mind* (1991) to argue that cognition is necessarily embodied, rather than disembodied like a computer. They also drew on Buddhist philosophy to show how cognition is possible without a "self." This book is a brilliant synthesis of cognitive science and religion. Rodney Brooks of the Massachusetts Institute of Technology has built robots which demonstrate that logical representation of knowledge is not necessary for the embodied action of locomotion. The anthropologist Edwin Hutchins argued that real world cognition is often distributed over individuals, rather than localized in a single individual, one example being navigation on large ships. There is also a growing body of work, such as that by Jaak Panskeep, showing that cognition is not entirely rational and disembodied because emotion plays a central role. All these developments are deeply inconsistent with cognitivism, though the significance of the work done before 1900 was not then generally appreciated.

Phenomenology. Phenomenology is an area of philosophy with important implications for consciousness. Phenomenology seeks to ground everything in the actual experience of human beings; in other words it takes a "first person" experiential perspective, rather than "third person" scientific perspective. Important exponents include Edmund Husserl, Martin Heidegger, and Maurice Merleau-Ponty. Heidegger considered implications of embodiment, including finitude and temporality, noting that humans are historical beings, bounded in time, space, and ability. Many of these themes also appear in the anti-cognitivist movement. Another such theme, with origins in Heidegger and especially Merleau-Ponty, but developed by Hubert Dreyfus, is the phenomenological critique of representation, which draws on human experience with routine activities to argue that representations are not necessary for embodied action. The work of Merleau-Ponty predates Gibson and Brooks, but is non-empirical, while Dreyfus makes compelling use of work by Walter Freeman connecting brain dynamics with chaos theory.

Neuroscience. The decline of cognitivism has inspired a return to naturalism, the study of cognition as it actually occurs in living human beings and, in particular, a shift towards neuroscience and evolutionary biology. Neuro-reductionism is perhaps the dominant position at the beginning of the twenty-first century. Certainly one can find neural correlates of consciousness or patterns of neural activity that correlate with various conscious experiences, such as visual perception. But it remains unclear whether such correlates can ever explain the nature of consciousness. A narrower version of this challenge is to explicate *qualia,* which are the qualitative aspects of consciousness, such as "how it feels" when one is angry or when one sees the blue of the sky. David Chalmers has introduced an influential distinction between the "easy" and the "hard" problems of consciousness studies:

> The easy problems are those of finding neural mechanisms and explaining cognitive functions: the ability to discriminate and categorize environmental stimuli, the capacity to verbally report mental states, the difference between waking and sleeping. The hard problem is that of *experience*: why does all this processing give rise to an experienced inner life at all? While progress is being made on the easy problems, the hard problem remains perplexing. (p. 200)

One approach to bridging this gap is to postulate that consciousness is some form of emergent activity of the brain. A familiar example of an emergent property is the liquidity of water, which arises from a sufficiently large collection of water molecules at an appropriate temperature.

Another problem facing neuroscience is the *binding problem,* which is to determine how the brain integrates sensory input from different times and/or different modalities to create a coherent seeming whole. Few doubt that this problem is solvable within the neuro-reductionist paradigm, though the complete answer will likely be complex. Neuro-reductionism has been especially successful in studying perception and this success has inspired interesting speculations on consciousness. In *Art and the Brain* (2000), Joseph Goguen demonstrates the intriguing possibility that such research can help people understand art. Critics have complained, however, that the cultural aspects of art get short changed by neuro-reductionist analyses.

Another problem is to determine the modularity and plasticity of the brain and the mind. Studies have found brain locations associated with many mental functions, but other functions have been shown to be non-local. Recent work has demonstrated physical brain change associated with learning, even relatively late in life. There is strong support for the modularity of many unconscious perceptual processes, and for the non-modularity of many higher level conscious processes. Whether there is a *language module,* as claimed by Noam Chomsky, remains contentious. A growing consensus is against his anti-evolutionary view of the origin of language, in which he claims that "there is no substance to the view that human language is simply a more complex instance of something to be found elsewhere is the animal world" (1972, p. 70).

On the interface between neurophysiology and computer science is the issue of modeling neurons, networks of neurons, and ultimately, brains. In 1943 Warren McCullough and Walter Pitts introduced the first such model, in which neurons were either "on" or "off," firing or not firing. These neurons are similar to the logic gates of computers, but are far simpler than real neurons. Some key ideas introduced by psychologist Donald Hebb include the following: connections between neurons become tighter the more they are used; neurons act in groups called *cell assemblies*; and cell assemblies are the basis of short term memory, but not long term memory. Although these only a rough approximation to the complex functioning of real neurons (involving numerous chemical reactions), they inspired a new generation of models having important engineering applications, such as character recognition. But because of its approximate character, many researchers prefer to call their work *parallel distributed processing* or *connectionism,* rather than neural net modeling.

Meanwhile, experimental neuroscience has uncovered even more complexities, some of which may have profound implications for consciousness. Benjamin Libet found that voluntary acts are preceded by a readiness potential (a gradual negative shift in electrical potential, as recorded at the scalp) about 550 milliseconds before the action occurs, and about 200 milliseconds before subjects recorded a conscious intent to act. This research has generated some controversy, including arguments that it implies that consciousness is constructed well after the fact, and even that consciousness may be unimportant. Mirror neurons are another significant discovery. The Italian neurophysiologist Giacomma Rizolatti found that certain cells in monkey frontal lobes respond to specific actions, not only in the subject, but also when the subject observes another monkey perform that same action. It has been suggested that this phenomenon may help explain many puzzles, such as how people learn by imitation, or how they can put themselves in the place of another in order to outsmart them should be added to this list the capacity for compassion, the ability to empathize with others. Blind sight is another intriguing phenomenon, in which, for example, a subject reports inability to see an object, but can still guess its location with reasonable accuracy (Weiskrantz). This dissociation between perception and awareness raises questions about the relation between conscious and unconscious processes.

Quantum mechanics. Physicists have not been shy to speculate about the relevance of quantum mechanics to consciousness. This is unsurprising, since the two have long been linked by the "Copenhagen interpretation" of Niels Bohr (and as augmented by John von Neumann), which says that, when an experiment is performed, the consciousness of an observer is needed to "collapse" the state probability distribution associated to the wave function down to a single state. This was always controversial, but it remains respectable despite difficulties with quantum coherence. Physicist Roger Penrose, instead of explaining quantum mechanics with consciousness, seeks to explain consciousness with quantum mechanics. The results seem stimulating but disappointing because his major conclusion is that some as yet nonexistent physics (quantum gravity) is needed. Penrose also argues against cognitivism, though he relies on a Platonist philosophy of mathematics, in which abstract mathematical objects are as real as chairs, trees, and people. David Bohm is another physicist who has written about consciousness, particularly in relation to the non-sectarian spiritual teachings of Jiddu Krishnamurthy, which helped inspire novel versions of quantum mechanics having philosophical interpretations that involve information and consciousness.

God and consciousness. Attempts to prove the objective existence of God have a long and important history. Although every such attempt has failed, the dialectic of refutation and refinement has been surprisingly productive, especially in certain areas of formal logic. This is relevant to consciousness studies because if the traditional Christian God exists in a separate realm of spirit, intervening in the material world, then dualism is true, the mind-body problem is solved, and the hard problem of consciousness takes on a very different, more theological, character. Using modern tools from information theory, William Dembski has attempted a sophisticated revival of an ancient proof that an intelligent designer is needed to account for the regularities of the universe. Dembski's work has been greeted with skepticism, and even hostility, by the scientific community, in part because his an anti-Darwinism has been embraced by fundamentalist Christians, who advocate teaching creation science in the schools, and in part because of technical difficulties in his argument.

A very different God is discussed by Anthony Freeman, motivated by the idea of treating conscious states as emergent properties of brain states. Freeman views both God and the soul as emergent from individuals and communities, claiming that this view is neutral between dualism and reductive materialist monism. He draws on work of Schleiermacher, Searle, and recent advocates of a more social approach to biology, such as Raphael Nuñez. A simpler approach than that of Dembski or Freeman may be to avoid ontological questions by placing the existence of God in the category of first person experience, rather than third person fact; one often sees this in contemporary expositions of the Buddhist tantra.

Emerging trends

Biologists are applying sociobiology and evolution to consciousness, though most results are rather speculative—e.g., work about the possible co-evolution of language and consciousness. Some less speculative work is being done in ethics, as illustrated in a brilliant series of essays edited by Leonard Katz and published in 2000 in JCS.

There have been proposals to merge phenomenology and science (such as the neurophenomenology of Francisco Varela), and even proposals to reformulate science based on phenomenology. More such proposals can be expected, in part because experience provides phenomena that demand explanation, including the following aspects of consciousness: it is ineffable, open, fluid, non-local, temporally thick, and involves qualia and a sense of self. Can it be mere coincidence that similar properties are often attributed to God? Reports from experienced meditators suggest additional phenomena, such as certain states of consciousness in which there are no thoughts. Moreover, the emphasis on time in phenomenology resonates well with many issues and results in neuroscience.

Another approach, sometimes called *second person,* is to relate consciousness to society rather than to individuals. One example is the cultural-historical approach, in the tradition of philosophers Giambattista Vico, Wilhelm Dilthey (who built on Schleiermacher), and John Stuart Mill, and of the Russian activity theory of Lev Vygotsky, Alexander Luria, and others. The second person approach is also related to distributed cognition and to the actor-network theory of Bruno Latour and others. The area of sociology called ethnomethodology also seems promising. The hope of second person approaches is to transcend the problematic relationship between mind and body; debates here often parallel those in consciousness studies and emerging syntheses like the cultural psychology of Michael Cole could likely illuminate several issues in consciousness.

Moving away from the social sciences, PET and fMRI techniques will certainly continue to yield provocative results about brain function. Also, dynamical systems and chaos theories seem promising. Perhaps semiotics can also make a contribution. Ideas from ecology, feminism, and literature should also play a role. Definitely, there will be more fermentation, discussion, and progress.

See also ARTIFICIAL INTELLIGENCE; BEHAVIORISM; COPENHAGEN INTERPRETATION; EMERGENCE; EXPERIENCE, RELIGIOUS: COGNITIVE AND NEUROPHYSIOLOGICAL ASPECTS; EXPERIENCE, RELIGIOUS: PHILOSOPHICAL ASPECTS; MIND-BODY THEORIES; MIND-BRAIN INTERACTION; MONISM; NEUROSCIENCES; PHYSICALISM, REDUCTIVE AND NONREDUCTIVE; PHYSICS, QUANTUM

Bibliography

Brooks, Rodney. "Intelligence without representation." *Artificial Intelligence* 47 (1991): 139–159.

Chalmers, David. *The Conscious Mind: In Search of a Fundamental Theory.* Oxford: Oxford University Press, 1996.

Chomsky, Noam. "A Review of B.F. Skinner's *Verbal Behavior.*" *Language* 35, no. 1 (1959): 26–58.

Chomsky, Noam. *Language and Mind,* enlarged edition. New York: Harcourt, 1972.

Chomsky, Noam. Interview with Bridgette Stemmer. *Brain and Language* 68, no. 3 (1999): 393–401.

Churchland, Paul. *A Neurocomputational Perspective: The Nature of Mind and the Structure of Science.* Cambridge, Mass.: MIT Press, 1989.

Cole, Michael. *Cultural Psychology: A Once and Future Discipline.* Cambridge, Mass.: Harvard University Press, 1996.

Crick, Francis. *The Astonishing Hypothesis: The Scientific Search for the Soul.* New York: Scribner, 1994.

Dembski, William. *Intelligent Design: The Bridge Between Science and Theology.* Downers Grove, Ill.: Intervarsity Press, 1999.

Freeman, Anthony. "God as an Emergent Property." *Journal of Consciousness Studies* 8 (9/10) (2001): 147–159.

Freeman, Walter. "The Physiology of Perception." *Scientific American* 264 (1991): 78–85.

Gibson, James. *An Ecological Approach to Visual Perception.* Boston: Houghton Mifflin, 1979.

Goguen, Joseph, ed. *Art and the Brain.* Thorventon, UK: Imprint Academic, 2000. Also available in a special issue of *Journal of Consciousness Studies* 6, nos. 6/7 (1999).

Hebb, Donald. *The Organization of Behavior: A Neuropsychological Theory.* New York: Wiley, 1949.

Hutchins, Edwin. *Cognition in the Wild.* Cambridge, Mass.: MIT Press, 1995.

Katz, Leonard, ed. *Evolutionary Origins of Morality: Cross-Disciplinary Perspectives.* Thorverton, UK: Imprint Academic, 2000. Also available in *Journal of Consciousness Studies* 7 (Metaphors We Live By). Chicago: University of Chicago Press, 1980.

Libet, Benjamin. "Unconscious Cerebral Initiative and the Role of Conscious Will in Voluntary Action." *Behavioral and Brain Sciences* 8 (1985): 529–566.

Miller, George; Galanter, Eugene; and Pribram, Karl. *Plans and the Structure of Behavior.* New York: Holt, 1960.

Moody, Todd C. "Conversations With Zombies." *Journal of Consciousness Studies* 1 (2) (1994): 196–200.

Panskepp, Jaak. *Affective Neuroscience: The Foundations of Human and Animal Emotions.* Oxford: Oxford University Press, 1998.

Penrose, Roger. *The Emperor's New Mind.* Oxford: Vintage, 1990.

Schleiermacher, Friedrich. *The Christian Faith* (1822). Edinburgh, Scotland: T&T Clark, 1989.

Searle, John. "Minds, Brains, and Programs." *Behavioral and Brain Sciences* 3 (1980): 417–457.

Searle, John. *The Mystery of Consciousness.* New York: Granta, 1997.

Suchman, Lucy. *Plans and Situated Actions: The Problem of Human-Machine Communication.* Cambridge, UK: Cambridge University Press, 1987.

Symposium on "Conversation With Zombies." *Journal of Consciousness Studies* 2 (4) (1995).

Varela, Francisco. "Neurophenomenology: A Methodological Remedy for the Hard Problem." *Journal of Consciousness Studies* 3 (4) (1996): 330–349.

Varela, Francisco; Thompson, Evan; and Rosch, Eleanor. *The Embodied Mind: Cognitive Science and Human Experience.* Cambridge, Mass.: MIT Press, 1991.

Weiskrantz, Lawrence. *Consciousness Lost and Found: A Neuropsychological Exploration.* Oxford: Oxford University Press, 1997.

JOSEPH A. GOGUEN

CONSONANCE

See MODELS; SCIENCE AND RELIGION, METHODOLOGIES; SCIENCE AND RELIGION, MODELS AND RELATIONS

CONSTRUCTIVISM

The term *constructivism* denotes a heterogeneous set of theoretical approaches currently stemming from areas so diverse as biology, neurophysiology, philosophy, sociology, cybernetics, cognitive psychology, rhetoric, and literary studies. In all their variety they share the basic idea that knowledge cannot be based on some kind of correspondence to or representation of actual reality but only on the active cognitive constructions or cognitive operations of an observer. Any possible "objects" of experience and knowledge are embedded in cognitive and social processes.

Historically speaking the roots of constructivism begin in ancient skeptical philosophy, pass through the enlightenment philosophy of Immanuel Kant (1724–1804), the philosophy of language, and eventually to pragmatism. The most recent versions are *radical constructivism* and *operational constructivism,* where the term *construction* refers (1) to the construction of reality, (2) the construction of knowledge, and (3) the construction of tools and skills for human cognition.

Important impulses for radical constructivism were provided by Heinz von Foerster (1911–) due to his insights into the epistemological implications of the unspecified coding of external stimuli in the brain. The world as human beings know it, by means of their sense organs, is the product of internal mental activity. In this respect modern versions of constructivism draw on the concept of autopoiesis as it was introduced by the theoretical biologist Humberto Maturana (1928–) into epistemological discourse. According to the principle of autopoiesis every cognitive system operates on the basis of operative closure, that is to say, without direct input from its environment. Any stimulus from the environment can only stimulate the system to recursively produce its own elements and react to its own inner states. Hence any kind of knowledge or insight is an internal construction. However, this neither leads to relativism nor to the denial of an external reality. Constructivism should not be conflated with strong forms of idealism or antirealism. Yet any correspondence or mirror-theory of knowledge and truth is rejected because nothing corresponds to the internal categories, structures, and elements. Instead, categories of "compatibility," "fitting," or "viability" are of ultimate importance for constructivism since the external reality discriminates among the human constructions in favor of acceptable and fitting knowledge, assumptions, and cognitive skills. In addition, the self-referential and recursive operations inside the cognitive system produce stable states that tend to be taken as "givens" and can furthermore be socially stabilized in a broader culture.

In Niklas Luhmann's (1927–1998) operative constructivism, any production of explicit knowledge is "second-order-observation" since it is not data but other observations that are observed. This second order observation can see the distinction between the analyzed observation and its contingent and constructed character, yet without simultaneously being able to see the contingency of its own observation. What is observed are contingent constructions, but the "own" observation is—due to the blind spot within every observation—assumed to be "realistic." In modern society, where every social subsystem observes "the world" in its own way, this hybrid combination of constructivism and realism leads to a polycontextual ontology.

Due to the strong and widely held realistic assumptions within science and theology, constructivism so far has not attracted very much attention in the dialogue between religion and science. Constructivism does however argue for a nonfoundationalist view of knowledge that opens up new avenues for this dialogue. Moreover, based on the idea of autopoiesis in cognitive systems and its pragmatic orientation, constructivism vividly rejects any notion of reductionism between various cognitive approaches that seek to cope with "reality." Instead it emphasizes the limitedness and fragmentary nature of all human knowing. In addition, constructivism highlights the intimate bond between knowledge and ethics. Unexplored is the contribution of more socially oriented forms of constructivism in answering the question of the way in which, for example, the Christian faith exercises a subtle yet crucial influence on the nonreligious constructions of the wider culture. However, in order to fully embrace constructivism as religious epistemology, theology would have to accept the objectionable claim of God being a human construction for coping with life. And yet constructivism reflects at least one aspect of a central religious insight: Religious knowledge cannot secure its own stability, adequacy, and truth unless God makes Godself present in human understanding and knowing—a process often called revelation.

See also AUTOPOIESIS; CONTEXTUALISM; DUALISM; FUNCTIONALISM; NONFOUNDATIONALISM; PRAGMATISM

Bibliography

Foerster, Heinz von. *Observing Systems,* 2nd edition. Seaside, Calif.: Intersystems, 1984.

Glasersfeld, Ernst von. *Radical Constructivism. A Way of Knowing and Learning*. Washington, D.C.: Falmer Press, 1995.

Luhmann, Niklas. "The Cognitive Program of Constructivism and a Reality that Remains Unknown." In *Self organization: Portrait of a Scientific Revolution,* eds. Wolfgang Krohn and Günter Küppers. Dordrecht, Netherlands: Kluwer, 1990.

Luhmann, Niklas. *Die Wissenschaft der Gesellschaft*. Frankfurt, Germany: Suhrkamp, 1990.

Maturana, Humberto R., and Varela, Francisco J. *Autopoiesis and Cognition: The Realization of the Living*. Dordrecht, Netherlands: Reidel, 1980.

Maturana, Humberto R., and Varela, Francisco J. *The Tree of Knowledge: The Biological Roots of Human Understanding,* rev. edition. Boston and London: Shambhala, 1992.

GÜNTER THOMAS

CONTEXTUALISM

Contextualism comes in stronger and weaker versions. What these versions all have in common is the idea that the context, the situation, or the particularities are taken to be of outmost importance. Contextualism is a reaction against the strong emphasis on universality and common human reason characteristic of the Enlightenment tradition and modernity. The catchwords are "*Whose* truth, rationality, science, religion, ethics, or gender?" For instance, there are titles of book that read *Whose Justice? Which Rationality?* (by Alasdair MacIntyre) and *Whose Science? Whose Knowledge?* (by Sandra Harding). The idea is that it makes a crucial difference for the issues discussed whether one succeeds or fails to take the "whose" aspect or the contextual aspect into account.

Exactly what it is that could or should be contextualized in this way (whether it is, for example, theology, rationality, justice, or gender) varies from contextualist to contextualist. What also differs is the degree or depth of this contextualization. For instance, is the argument that one cannot determine what it is rational to believe without specifying who the agent is, including his or her particular historical and social context? Or is it that the standards of rationality (and not merely the particular application of them) or even truth is context-determined? If the latter, but not the former, is it the case then that rationality or truth would vary from one context (that is, culture, religion, gender, etc.) to another?

In the science-religion dialogue there are those who maintain that one cannot sensibly talk about science and religion in some abstract, universal, ahistorical, or gender-unrelated way. Instead one must be specific about, for instance, which religion (or what religious tradition within that religion), which science (or part of science), which historical period, which cultural setting, and the like, one is dealing with. For instance, John Brooke and Geoffrey Cantor argue that neither religion nor science is reducible to some timeless essence, but must be understood in their historical particularities. Science and religion are inextricable from the times in which they arise. But there are also those who make different and perhaps more radical contextual claims. D. Z. Phillips, Peter Winch, and others who have followed the Austrian-born philosopher Ludwig Wittgenstein (1889–1951) maintain that there are no practice-transcending standards of rationality, that is, science and religion do not have any standard of rationality or criteria of intelligibility in common. Therefore, it makes no sense to compare or relate them. Science and religion are two autonomous practices with totally different languages, functions, and standards of rationality.

Contextualism in many of its forms is a healthy reaction against the tendency in Western tradition to talk about, for example, "man," "human nature," "science," "religion," "reason," and "rationality" as if these are universal categories unsullied by the particularities of history, culture, traditions, gender, and the like. It is an open question, however, whether the strong emphasis of many contextualists on the local, the contextual, or the particular is just as questionable—if it is in fact to go from one ditch of the road to the other.

See also CONSTRUCTIVISM; NONFOUNDATIONALISM; PRAGMATISM

Bibliography

Brooke, John and Geoffrey Cantor. *Reconstructing Nature: The Engagement of Science and Religion.* New York and Oxford: Oxford University Press, 1998.

Harding, Sandra. *Whose Science? Whose Knowledge? Thinking from Women's Lives.* Ithaca, N.Y.: Cornell University Press, 1991.

MacIntyre, Alasdair. *Whose Justice? Which Rationality?* Notre Dame, Ind.: University of Notre Dame Press, 1988.

Phillips, D. Z. *Religion without Explanation.* Oxford: Blackwell, 1976.

Stenmark, Mikael. *Rationality in Science, Religion, and Everyday Life: A Critical Evaluation of Four Models of Rationality.* Notre Dame, Ind.: University of Notre Dame Press, 1995.

Winch, Peter. *The Idea of a Social Science and Its Relation to Philosophy* (1958). 2nd edition. London: Routledge, 1990.

MIKAEL STENMARK

CONTINGENCY

A proposition is *necessary* when there is no possible case in which it is false ("a vixen is a female fox"). A proposition is *contingent* when it is true in some cases and false in others ("it is raining now"). By extension, a state of affairs is contingent if it could have been other than it is. A state of affairs is necessary if there is no possible alternative to it. Most philosophers think that all physical states are contingent. Some physicists argue that the universe has to exist, whereas some theologians argue that God has to exist, but creates a contingent universe.

See also CHANCE

KEITH WARD

CONVERGENCE

When an octopus and a human being gaze at one another through the aquarium glass, they both do so through a camera-like eye. A human is a vertebrate and the occupant of the tank is a cephalopod mollusc. Their common ancestor lived more than one-half billion years ago, and since it did not have a camera-like eye the fact that humans can exchange gazes with octopuses can only mean that such an eye evolved independently. This is a classic example of convergent evolution—i.e., the emergence of a similar biological feature, not by descent from a common ancestor but from organisms that are effectively unrelated. Yet biologists also know that this eye-type has evolved independently at least four other times. For eyes to work the lens must be transparent. This property is conferred by employing particular proteins called *crystallins*. Their small molecular size enables a close packing in the watery medium of the lens, thus providing the necessary transparency. Yet the origins of human (and mammalian) and cephalopod crystallins are different. So here is an example of biochemical convergence. In both cases the crystallin is recruited from a protein originally involved with stress control; in mammals it came from a small heat-shock protein, but in cephalopods it derives from a detoxification protein. Both octopus and human end up seeing in much the same way, even though their respective ancestors could not.

Problems with the theory of convergent evolution

In the literature, such examples of convergence often provoke exclamations of "remarkable," "astonishing," and even "uncanny." It is almost as if there was a latent fear of the teleological principle being smuggled back into evolutionary biology. But are the eyes of humans and octopuses really convergent? After all, both employ the protein rhodopsin, which allows a chemical process whereby light is converted into an electrical signal that humans understand as vision. But this does not undermine the principle of convergence; it merely demonstrates that pre-existing structures will be recruited when necessary in a way analogous to the lens crystallins.

There is, however, a more serious obstacle in accepting convergence. This is in the form of the developmental gene known as *Paired-Box* (or *Pax*) *6*. This gene now has an almost iconic status: *Pax-6* "makes" eyes in most, and perhaps all, groups of animals. Does this not undermine the principle of convergence? Hardly. In the developing embryo, the activity of *Pax-6* is much more widespread. Originally it probably evolved in connection with the emerging needs for sensory systems in general: not only vision but also olfaction. *Pax-6* is necessary but not sufficient; it is little more than a genetic switch. In human and octopus, it will ensure camera-eyes, but in flies and lobsters it "makes" compound eyes.

As already noted, camera-like eyes have evolved separately at least six times, while compound eyes—most familiar in insects—have evolved independently at least three times. These examples, involving vision, are surely more significant than the other familiar instances of convergence, such as the streamlining of aquatic vertebrates or warm-bloodedness in birds and mammals. This is because such sensory assimilation implies nervous activity and a brain, with the further link to cognition and sentience.

There are also striking instances of convergence in both hearing and olfaction. Even when a nose stops being used for olfaction, as in the star-nosed mole, its tactile sense is actually strongly convergent on the neurology of vision. Even senses that are decidedly alien to humans, such as echolocation (in bats and dolphins) and the generation of electric fields in fish, show splendid examples of convergence.

Scientific and theological implications

Few textbooks on evolutionary biology neglect to mention convergence, but curiously its wider implications are seldom addressed. These concern (1) its ubiquity, which implies (2) the reality of natural selection and thereby adaptation, and (3) the inevitability of evolutionary trends. Moreover, if the natural world is seen as part of God's great order, then convergence may also have theological implications. In brief, how different can this world—or any world—really be? Put another way, if intelligent life exists elsewhere in the universe, will it be humanoid or, in Robert Bieri's phrase, the equivalent of a thinking pancake?

Convergence is, therefore, central to understanding organic evolution. First, it confirms its reality. The eyes of octopus and human are similar, but they are not identical. The structure of the lens and the position of the retina, for example, are different. Convergence does not guarantee the identical, only the emergence of particular biological properties. Second, the ubiquity of convergence implies the prevalence of selective pressure: how else could biological systems come so closely to resemble each other? So too with adaptation; it is a biological reality and not some incidental by-product of effectively random processes. Third, the reality of convergence has the implicit assumption that starting points will be disparate, but there will be defined and repeatable evolutionary trajectories in evolution. Trends are real, and if the end-point is not perfect, is it emphatically better than what came before.

Yet all this is strongly at odds with a widespread perception that contingent happenstance is the determining reality in evolution. Thus, to paraphrase American paleontologist Stephen Jay Gould's metaphor of the tape of life, if the history of the world were to be re-run, the end result would utterly different. Historians might meditate on the untimely demise of Hitler or the death at an advanced age of Alexander the Great, but the consensus amongst biologists is that even a nudge in one direction half a billion years ago would preclude entirely the emergence of humans. As individuals this must be true, given that all humans were conceived by their parents against the odds. Yet biologically this view is deeply credulous. It is no accident that those who suppose the emergence of humans to be the product of individual and contingent history, also believe that humans are not only free (as indeed they are) but may mold their morality to a scheme of their choosing.

The realities of biological evolution and the inevitability of convergence suggest, however, a new view of life. Creation presupposes a history and an end-point, but this does not constrain choice and acceptance (or the opposite). The universe is so arranged that sooner or later, somewhere or other, certain properties, biological and ultimately spiritual, will emerge. The quip by British geneticist and physiologist J.B.S. Haldane remarking upon the creator's inordinate fondness for beetles is thereby turned on its head. Creation is indeed rich, but the modalities of convergence suggest that ultimately it is otiose to speak of accidents. Seeded in the act of creation was the inevitability of sentience endowed with free will.

See also ADAPTATION; CHANCE; DESIGN; EVOLUTION; EVOLUTION, BIOLOGICAL; SELECTION, LEVELS OF

Bibliography

Bieri, Robert. "Humanoids on Other Planets?" *American Scientist* 52 (1964): 452–458.

Catania, Kenneth C. "A Nose That Looks Like a Hand and Acts Like an Eye: The Unusual Mechanosensory System of the Star-Nosed Mole." *Journal of Comparative Physiology A* 185 (1999): 367–372.

Conway Morris, Simon. *The Crucible of Creation: The Burgess Shale and the Rise of Animals.* Oxford: Oxford University Press, 1998.

Marino, Lori. "What Can Dolphins Tell Us About Primate Evolution?" *Evolutionary Anthropology* 5, no. 3 (1996): 81–85.

Moore, Janet, and Willmer, Patricia. "Convergent Evolution in Invertebrates." *Biological Reviews* 72 (1997): 1–60.

Mueller, Ulrich G.; Rehner, Stephen A.; and Schultz, Ted R. "The Evolution of Agriculture in Ants." *Science* 281 (1998): 2034–2038.

Strausfeld, Nicholas J., and Hildebrand, John G. "Olfactory Systems: Common Design, Uncommon Origins." *Current Opinion in Neurobiology* 1 9 (1999): 634–639.

Wistow, Graeme. "Lens Crystallins: Gene Recruitment and Evolutionary Dynamism." *Trends in Biochemical Sciences* 18 (1993): 301–306.

SIMON CONWAY MORRIS

COPENHAGEN INTERPRETATION

The Copenhagen Interpretation, developed primarily by Danish physicist Niels Bohr (1885–1962) and other researchers in Copenhagen in the first third of the twentieth century, is the standard interpretation of quantum mechanics. It ascribes physical reality only to observed reality. Quantum mechanics can predict only the probability that measurements will have particular outcomes. No observation has ever been found to conflict with the experimental predictions of this theory. However, there is much debate about the correctness of this interpretation of the measurement process, and there are several rival interpretations of quantum mechanics, notably the Many Worlds Interpretation proposed in 1957 by physicists Hugh Everett and John Wheeler. A major problem of the Copenhagen Interpretation is the lack of a precise definition of what constitutes a "measurement" or an "observation." It is also problematic if a theory of quantum cosmology is to be developed because the Copenhagen Interpretation requires an "observer" for the universe.

See also EPR PARADOX; MANY-WORLDS HYPOTHESIS; PARADOX; PHYSICS, QUANTUM; SELF-REFERENCE

Bibliography

Deutsch, David. *The Fabric of Reality.* London: Penguin, 1997.

Herbert, Nick. *Quantum Reality: Beyond the New Physics.* London: Rider, 1985.

Rae, Alistair I. M. *Quantum Physics: Illusion or Reality?* Cambridge, UK: Cambridge University Press, 1986.

JOHN D. BARROW

COSMOLOGICAL ARGUMENT

Cosmological arguments aim to establish the causal or explanatory dependence of the world on a wholly independent being, usually identified with God. These arguments typically proceed from the claim that familiar things are dependent in various ways upon other things—that is, for their origin, movement, and continued existence. The crux of traditional cosmological arguments is the contention that not every being can be dependent in the relevant way; that is, any chain of dependence must ultimately be grounded in a being that admits of no such dependence.

History of cosmological argument

The history of cosmological arguments goes back at least to Aristotle, though his understanding of the Prime Mover bears little resemblance to theism. After Aristotle, the history divides naturally into two categories: (1) In the Middle Ages, philosophers in all three major theistic traditions defended cosmological arguments. Prominent among them were Ibn Sina (Avicenna), St. Thomas Aquinas, and Moses Maimonides, all thinkers within the Aristotelian metaphysical framework; and (2) By the early modern period, the principles of Aristotelian metaphysics that had supported cosmological arguments were no longer in vogue. But it proved natural to formulate a cosmological argument in fresh terms, as Samuel Clarke did in 1705. Clarke insisted that whatever comes to be is dependent on other things to provide an account or reason for its existence, and he argued that an account is incomplete if it is not ultimately grounded in some independent thing. Clarke's contemporary, Gottfried Leibniz, also defended a cosmological argument, while both David Hume and Immanuel Kant provided famous criticisms. Variations on deductive cosmological arguments (like that of Clarke) are the most important in the literature, and are still discussed today.

Deductive cosmological argument

It is incontrovertible that some things and events are explanatorily dependent on other things in the way described above. But a central question in debates over cosmological arguments of the deductive sort concerns the possibility of an infinite series of things or events, each providing an adequate explanation for the existence (or motion) of the next. Setting Aristotelian principles aside, there is no obvious way to rule out such a series based on contemporary physical theory or metaphysical accounts of causation. But many cosmological arguments reject the possibility of such a series on the grounds that an explanation is incomplete if that which explains (the *explanans*)

requires explanation itself. This implies that a complete explanation for any thing or event must ultimately be grounded in something that has no explanatory dependence. Finally, it is often claimed that only a necessary being (a being that could not have failed to exist) requires no explanation for its existence. And God is considered the most natural example of a necessary being with causal powers.

Two responses to this argument are common. First, the critic can reject the notion of complete explanation just sketched. Since every individual thing in an infinite series of dependent beings is explained by the thing immediately prior to it, the existence of that individual remains intelligible despite the lack of an independent being in the series. Second, the critic can claim that the infinite series itself provides a complete explanation for the existence of whatever follows it. But the series itself is not dependent on anything else for an explanation.

In order to rule out both of these responses, some theists have propounded a very strong principle: not just the familiar facts of experience, but *every contingent state of affairs* must have an explanation outside of itself (the Principle of Sufficient Reason). If this principle were true, not only would every individual in an infinite series of causes require explanation, but the existence of the series itself would require explanation. (A contingent state of affairs is one that might not have been the case.) However, the principle seems overly strong and quite difficult to motivate. In fact, even a theist has good grounds for rejecting it. After all, traditional theism maintains that God created freely and could have chosen otherwise; so God's deciding to create the world is a contingent occurrence. And since it is contingent, it cannot be completely explained (i.e. deduced) from any necessary truths about God. In response, the theist could weaken the original principle somewhat, allowing that only free acts of persons are suitable contingent grounds for explanation. But if exceptions to the rule are allowed, why not allow the unexplained existence of an infinite series, or of a first contingent physical event like the Big Bang?

It is important to clarify that even a successful deductive cosmological argument would not establish the truth of theism. First, such an argument would not entail the conclusion that there is a *single* independent and necessary being, since there could be a number of them. Second, even if there were only one such being, a cosmological argument would provide no guarantee that the being is personal, all-powerful, or good. (Perhaps it is an impersonal force or a great demon.) But these limitations do not mean that cosmological arguments are useless for justifying theism. For a great many competing theories would be ruled out by a successful deductive cosmological argument.

Evidential cosmological argument

An importantly different kind of argument is presented by Richard Swinburne's *The Existence of God* (1979). Swinburne rejects cosmological arguments aiming at deductive proof. Rather than insisting that some principle of reason rules out the possibility that the physical universe could simply exist unexplained, he compares the creation hypothesis with its rivals by using criteria such as simplicity and explanatory power. In this respect, the existence of God is treated as an explanatory postulate akin to the existence of electrons. Swinburne builds a cumulative case based on several types of facts that he believes are best explained by theism. Among these facts is the mere existence of a complex and contingent physical universe. Nevertheless, because there is no established standard for comparing the merits of ultimate explanations, the evidential cosmological argument is widely considered inconclusive at best. Swinburne's conclusions receive a sophisticated critique in J. L. Mackie's *The Miracle of Theism* (1982).

See also ARISTOTLE; AVICENNA; CAUSATION; COSMOLOGY; MAIMONIDES; ONTOLOGICAL ARGUMENT; TELEOLOGICAL ARGUMENT; THEISM; THOMAS AQUINAS

Bibliography

Brown, Patterson. "Infinite Causal Regression" (1966). In *Readings in the Philosophy of Religion: An Analytic Approach,* ed. Baruch A. Brody. Englewood Cliffs, N.J.: Prentice-Hall, 1992.

Hume, David. *Dialogues Concerning Natural Religion* (1779), ed. H. Aiken. New York: Macmillan, 1948.

Mackie, J. L. *The Miracle of Theism: Arguments For and Against the Existence of God.* Oxford: Oxford University Press, 1982.

Rowe, William L. *The Cosmological Argument.* Princeton, N.J.: Princeton University Press, 1975.

Swinburne, Richard. *The Existence of God* (1979). Oxford: Clarendon, 1991.

DAVID MANLEY

COSMOLOGY

Many, perhaps all, early cosmologies or descriptions of the structure of the world were anthropocentric (focused on the role and fate of human beings) and they envisioned a universe subject to whims of gods. As such, cosmology and religion were closely intertwined.

From the ancient Greeks through the Middle Ages, over some two millennia, the geocentric cosmology or worldview of Aristotle (384–322 B.C.E.) dominated much of the Western intellectual world. Circular and unalterable heavens rotated around the Earth, which was motionless in the center of the one and only world. Created during roughly the same period and in the same regions of the world, Aristotelian philosophy and Biblical accounts of cosmology and cosmogony are, not surprisingly, congruent in some respects. Aristotle's teleological explanations assumed that the world was fulfilling a purpose formed by a superhuman mind; Christian philosophy also is inherently meaningful and purposive.

During the Middle Ages, Aristotelian cosmology was subordinated to religious concerns. In the sixteenth century Nicolaus Copernicus (1473–1543) displaced the Earth, though not the solar system, from the center of the universe, and increasingly from the center of God's attention as well. In the seventeenth century Galileo Galilei (1564–1642) destroyed Aristotelian cosmology. The subsequent mechanical cosmology of Isaac Newton (1642–1727), though initially requiring God's intervention to keep the planets circling the sun, eventually replaced God completely with the universal law of gravity.

Early in the twentieth century, the American astronomer Harlow Shapley (1885–1972) showed that the solar system is not at the center of our galaxy, but off to the side, and that our galaxy is many times larger than previously contemplated. A few years later, Edwin Hubble (1889–1953) showed that our galaxy is but one of many island universes, and that the acentric universe is expanding. Each new cosmological discovery displaced humankind farther from the center of the universe and seemed to render humans less significant in an increasingly immense universe.

A contemporary resurgence of dialogue between scientific cosmology and religious thought late in the twentieth century involved yet another version of the traditional design argument for God. The Anthropic Principle noted that values of the fundamental constants of nature (the speed of light, Planck's constant, etc.) and the fundamental physical laws are "fine-tuned" to precisely what is needed for the evolution of life. As with earlier cosmologically based arguments for the existence of God, the Anthropic Principle has proven highly vulnerable to theory-change in science. The inflationary Big Bang cosmological model now explains much fine-tuning without recourse to God.

The history of the relationship between cosmology and religion, particularly in Western thought, has been enlivened by changes in cosmological understanding and beliefs. As the Earth has been increasingly displaced from the center of the universe and observed phenomena have been increasingly brought under the rule of natural physical laws, humankind's relationship with and understanding of God has required revisions.

See also ANTHROPIC PRINCIPLE; BIBLICAL COSMOLOGY; BIG BANG THEORY; BIG CRUNCH THEORY; FEMINIST COSMOLOGY; GALILEO GALILEI; GEOCENTRISM

Bibliograpy

Danielson, Dennis Richard. *The Book of the Cosmos: Imagining the Universe from Heraclitus to Hawking*. Cambridge, Mass.: Perseus, 2000.

Gribbin, John. *Companion to the Cosmos*. London: Weidenfeld & Nicolson, 1996.

Hetherington, Norriss S. *Encyclopedia of Cosmology: Historical, Philosophical, and Scientific Foundations of Modern Cosmology*. New York and London: Garland, 1993.

North, John. *The Norton History of Astronomy and Cosmology*. New York and London: Norton, 1995.

NORRISS HETHERINGTON

COSMOLOGY, PHYSICAL ASPECTS

The scientific understanding of the origin, nature, and possible future of the universe dramatically changed during the twentieth century. This burst of scientific discovery triggered a complex series of responses among religious thinkers, particularly after about 1960, which marks the beginning of the contemporary resurgence of dialogue between science and religion. The recent interaction between scientific cosmology and religious thought is one of the richest and most instructive examples of contemporary science-religion dialogue.

Theologians have related physical cosmology most often to the doctrine of creation. In its Christian form, creation theology typically includes two components: *creatio ex nihilo* (creation out of nothing) and *creatio continua* (continuous creation). Judaism and Islam explicate similar ideas, but the formal distinction is an invention of Christian theology to express different features of the God-world relation. *Creatio ex nihilo* stresses the dependence or contingency of all that exists on God as its transcendent source while *creatio continua* stresses God's continuing and immanent action in the universe. Together, these ideas portray God both as the ultimate source of nature's causal efficacy, faithfully maintaining its regularities, which we describe in terms of the laws of nature, and as creating in time by acting in, with, under, and through the laws of nature, bringing forth the order, beauty, and complexity of the physical world and the rich diversity found in the biological evolution of life.

Creation *ex nihilo* has been explored extensively in relation to two particular features of Big Bang cosmology: $t = 0$, which represents the beginning of time and thus the age of the universe, and the Anthropic Principle, which points to the remarkable conditions that the fundamental constants and the laws of nature must meet if the evolution of life in the universe is to be possible. These will be discussed in turn, each followed by theological discussions of its significance for *creatio ex nihilo*. The *creatio continua* form has been discussed in terms of the temporal, developmental, and historical character of the universe; it will not be treated here. Finally, inflationary and quantum cosmologies will be discussed in advance of a survey of theological responses.

Big Bang cosmology

During the decade following the 1905 publication of his Special Theory of Relativity, Albert Einstein worked on a relativistic theory of gravity. His basic insight was to reconceptualize gravity as the curvature of space-time instead of as a (Newtonian) force in Euclidean space. According to Einstein, masses move along geodesics, curves describing the shortest possible path in space-time. Their motion, in turn, alters the curvature of space-time, thus giving the field equations of the General Theory of Relativity their complicated nonlinear form.

Shortly after the discovery of the General Theory of Relativity, solutions to Einstein's equations were developed for two distinct classes of problems: (1) point masses, which when applied to the solar system led to several key tests of the theory and their eventual confirmation (including the deflection of starlight by the sun and the precession in the perihelion of the orbit of Mercury); and (2) dust, which when eventually applied to the distribution of galaxies and galactic clusters described the universe as expanding in time. Beginning in the 1920s, telescopic observations by Edwin Hubble showed that galaxies were indeed receding from us and at a velocity proportional to their distance. In essence, the expansion of the universe had been discovered.

There are in fact three standard types of expansion possible. In the so-called closed model, the universe has the shape of a three-dimensional sphere of finite size. It expands up to a maximum size, approximately one hundred to five hundred billion years from now, then contracts, eventually collapsing to vanishing size with infinite temperatures and densities. The so-called open model has two variations, one in which the universe is flat, and one in which it is saddle-shaped. In both versions of the open model, the universe is infinite in size. In both cases the universe will expand forever and cool towards absolute zero. The future of these three models is often used to characterize them as "freeze" (open) or "fry" (closed).

All three models came to be called Big Bang models because they describe the universe as having a finite past life of twelve to fifteen billion years and as beginning in a singularity, an event of infinite temperature, infinite density, and zero volume in which the laws of physics as we know them break down. Since the age of the universe t is calculated as starting here, it is convenient to label the singularity "$t = 0$"; technically this event is referred to as an *essential singularity*. In the 1960s, Stephen Hawking, Roger Penrose, and Robert Geroch proved key theorems demonstrating that the existence of an essential singularity such as $t = 0$, given Einstein's General Theory of Relativity, was unavoidable.

The relevance of $t = 0$ to creation *ex nihilo*

To what extent is $t = 0$ relevant to the doctrine of creation *ex nihilo*? Responses have ranged widely from direct relevance to complete irrelevance.

Direct relevance.   For some scholars, the scientific discovery of an absolute beginning of all things (including time) provides empirical confirmation, perhaps even proof, of divine creation. This was the position taken by Pope Pius XII in 1951 in an address to the Pontifical Academy of Sciences. In 1978 Robert Jastrow, then head of NASA's Goddard Institute for Space Studies, spoke metaphorically about scientists who, after climbing the arduous mountain of cosmology, came to the summit only to find theologians there already. The idea that $t = 0$ provides strong, even convincing, support for belief in God is frequently advanced by conservative and evangelical Christians such as Hugh Ross. Early in the debate, Lutheran theologian Ted Peters advanced a more nuanced argument elucidating the theological importance of a beginning to the universe in terms of "consonance" between theology and Big Bang cosmology. A sophisticated argument for the temporal finitude of the universe based on $t = 0$, as well as on an argument that rejects the possibility that the universe is also actually infinite in size, has been developed by philosopher William Craig, partially through an explicit debate with atheist Quentin Smith. More recently, philosopher Phil Clayton has suggested that contemporary cosmology affords a clear case of divine activity.

$t = 0$ also has served indirectly to inspire the construction of an alternative, and quite successful, cosmology. In the 1940s, Fred Hoyle, an outspoken atheist, together with colleagues Hermann Bondi and Thomas Gold, constructed a cosmology that would have no temporal beginning or end. Their "steady state cosmology" depicted the universe as eternally old and expanding exponentially forever. For two decades, the Big Bang and the steady state models seemed equally viable given the empirical evidence then available. By the mid-1960s, however, the Big Bang model was vindicated, at least in most scientists' minds, by the discovery of the microwave background radiation, the successful prediction of the cosmological abundances of hydrogen and helium, and other effects. What is important here, however, is Hoyle's motivation in developing the steady state cosmology. One reason, although probably only secondary, was his concern that Big Bang cosmology seemed, at least in the public mind, to support Christianity. Of course, the scientific community must test strictly any cosmological proposal—steady state or Big Bang—regardless of its possible ideological origins. As philosophers put it, the "context of discovery" should not influence the "context of justification." Nevertheless, the story of Hoyle demonstrates that very fruitful ideas can come from "extra scientific" disciplines, such as philosophy and theology, and lead even if indirectly to scientific theories with testable consequences.

Complete irrelevance. Several of the most important scholars in the theology and science interaction see *creatio ex nihilo* as an entirely philosophical argument regarding contingency for which specific empirical evidence is irrelevant. This includes scientists such as Arthur Peacocke, John Polkinghorne, Bill Stoeger, and Ian Barbour (in his early writings) as well as Thomistic scholars such as Steven Baldner and William Carroll.

Indirect relevance. There are a variety of positions that one can take between the two extremes of direct relevancy and complete irrelevancy. Those who find various forms of indirect relevance include scientists such as Ian Barbour (in later work), George Ellis, Walter Hearne, and Howard Van Till; and philosophers and religious scholars such as Ernan McMullin, Nancey Murphy, Ted Peters (in later work), Mark Worthing, and Robert John Russell. Russell's way of articulating indirect relevance is to point out that $t = 0$ is relevant to the aspect of contingency within the idea of creation to various degrees depending on the sort of contingency considered. For example, three basic types of contingency can be distinguished: global contingency, local contingency, and nomological contingency. The first of these, global contingency, includes both the existence of the universe as such (global ontological contingency) and contingent theoretical or empirical aspects of the universe as a whole (global existential contingency). The particular sort of contingency associated with $t = 0$ would come under the latter—it is a form of past temporal finitude, which is a form of finitude and thus a species of global existential contingency—but not the former. Thus, the universe's existence and its beginning relate to different strands of global contingency. It is important to note, however, that the infinite size and infinite future of the two open models of the universe argue against contingency in the very same respect. In other words, if $t = 0$ is "consonant" with creation theology in respect of "global existential contingency" then these infinities are "dissonant" with creation and other theological doctrines, such as the eschatological views of Western religions, in exactly the same respect.

The Anthropic Principle

The term Anthropic Principle was coined by physicist Brandon Carter in 1974 to bring together various apparent coincidences about the universe that had received scattered attention throughout the twentieth century. Although formulated in a variety of ways, in its strongest form the Anthropic Principle poses the following question: How are we to explain the fact that the values of the fundamental constants of nature (e.g., the speed of light, Planck's constant, etc.) and the form of the fundamental physical laws are "fine-tuned" to precisely what is needed if the evolution of life is to be possible? Estimates have been made suggesting that if the values of the natural constants differed from their actual values by one part in a million, it would have been impossible for life to have evolved in the universe.

To some, then, the universe seems "fine-tuned" for life, suggesting a cosmological version of the traditional design argument for God. Opponents have deployed a variety of "many-worlds" arguments to suggest that there are many universes besides our own, each with different values of the natural constants, perhaps even different physical laws. In that scenario, by definition, life would evolve in the particular universe that satisfies the conditions for life but not in others, which explains cosmic fine-tuning without having to invoke a designer to explain the anthropic coincidences. What are the relative scientific, philosophical, and theological merits of these opposing positions?

As early as 1979, Peacocke gave the Anthropic Principle an indirect but important role within his discussion of the doctrine of creation, using metaphors of God as elaborating a fugue and as a bell-ringer sounding the changes. George Ellis has explored what he calls the "Christian Anthropic Principle," combining design perspectives with a theology of divine omnipotence and transcendence, drawing from William Temple. Nancey Murphy, however, treats Ellis's thesis as an argument for God. She reconstructs Ellis's paper to show that theology can be seen as a science and that cosmological fine-tuning can serve as an "auxiliary hypothesis" in such a theological program. Richard Swinburne and John Polkinghorne have also drawn on the Anthropic Principle in constructive ways.

The endorsements are not universal, however. Theologian Mark Worthing cautions that the "designer" of the universe need not be the creator God of theism: both a divine demiurge, including the universe itself, as Richard Dawkins suggests, or an emerging divinity, as John Barrow and Frank Tipler propose, take into account the empirical evidence of fine-tuning. According to Barbour, the theological virtues of construing the Anthropic Principle as a modern design argument are minimal.

Philosopher John Leslie's overall evaluation is that the two opposed sides are equally strong as arguments but also equally incorrect because a fully adequate conception of God is neutral to cosmological details—Leslie articulates God in terms of a neo-Platonic aesthetic/ethical principle. Most variations on the Platonic idea of God as the form of the Good and the neo-Platonic idea of God as Ground of Being are neutral to cosmological details, and their defenders are inclined to regard design arguments based on the Anthropic Principle and the many-worlds opponents as premature. Historian of science Ernan McMullin points out that the Anthropic Principle is highly vulnerable to theory-change in science. A quantum cosmology needs to gain widespread acceptance before the force of the Anthropic Principle can be assessed properly.

The Anthropic Principle can, however, play a fruitful role if incorporated within ongoing constructive theology, illuminating its inner meaning and suggesting connections between theological topics we might not otherwise have recognized. For example, the Anthropic Principle underscores the key role that Planck's constant plays in the particular overall structure of the universe, a role that a theology of creation *ex nihilo* would need to take seriously. The same constant may be a critical factor in compatibilist discussions of free will and thus for theological anthropology: For us to act freely, nature at the physical level must, arguably, be indeterministic. It also functions pivotally in some approaches to noninterventionist divine action, particularly in the context of theistic evolution.

Inflationary and quantum cosmologies

Since the 1970s, scientists have pursued "inflationary Big Bang" and beyond that "quantum cosmologies." The motivation for this has been both to solve a variety of technical problems in the standard Big Bang model and to blend cosmology with quantum physics, which studies atomic and subatomic physical systems. The term *quantum cosmology* sounds oxymoronic, but the Big Bang entails that the very early universe was extremely small and thus subject as a whole to quantum physics. Physicists were also seeking to produce a theoretical unification of gravity and the other physical forces (the electroweak and strong nuclear forces), a unity that is thought to be physically evident only at extraordinarily high energies such as those present in the early stages of the Big Bang.

With the introduction of the "inflationary Big Bang" scenario by Alan Guth and colleagues in the 1970s and further developments in this direction in the 1980s, the technical problems were basically solved. According to inflation, the extremely early universe (roughly from $t = 0$ until the Planck time, which is 10^{-43} seconds) expands extremely rapidly, then quickly settles down to the expansion rates of the standard Big Bang model. During inflation, countless cosmic domains may arise, separating the overall universe into huge portions of space-time in which the natural constants and even the specific laws of physics might vary. The effect of inflation on the problem of $t = 0$ is fascinating, however, because the Hawking-Penrose theorems mentioned above do not apply during the inflationary epoch. In these cosmologies we may never know whether or not an essential singularity was part of the universe's history.

Many physicists have proposed methods to unify quantum physics and gravity, subsequently applying the results to create quantum cosmologies: Hawking and Jim Hartle, Andrei Linde, Chris Isham, Guth, Hawking and Alan Turek, and others. All of these proposals are still highly speculative, but there are some indications of what different quantum cosmologies might look like, including models with or without an initial singularity (eternal inflation), with open or closed domains embedded in an open or a closed megauniverse, and so on. In most quantum cosmologies, our universe is just one part of an eternally expanding, infinitely complex megauniverse. Quantum cosmology is a highly speculative field chiefly because the underlying theories of quantum gravity are notoriously hard to test empirically, and they lift the philosophical issues already associated with quantum mechanics to a much more complex level since the domain of application is now the entire universe.

$t = 0$ revisited in inflationary and quantum cosmologies. Given the speculative status of quantum cosmology, some scholars have kept the theological conversation focused on the standard Big Bang model. Others, though, have asked what effects quantum cosmology might have on their theology of creation.

One argument is to invoke, once again, the argument for God from the sheer existence of the universe. Thus, even without an initial singularity, even the endless number of universes suggested by inflation and most quantum cosmologies is contingent in some sense and so invites a creator God as their necessary complement and creative source. A related point is that the prior universe or ensemble of universes out of which our universe arose includes quantum fields governed by the laws of physics (both of which are needed to give what passes in quantum cosmologies for a scientific account of the quantum creation of the universe). But the Christian view of *creatio ex nihilo* relies on the meaning of "nothingness" out of which God created all that is as the absolute lack of anything. Hawking, for example, seems to argue in part in this way in *A Brief History of Time* (1988). At times in the book Hawking seems to agree that without a $t = 0$ there is nothing left for God to do, but not at the end, for he also writes: "even if there is only one possible unified theory, it is just a set of rules and equations. What is it that breathes fire into the equations and makes a universe for them to describe? The usual approach of science … cannot answer the question of why there should be a universe for the model to describe" (p. 190).

It is also possible to see, in the debates over approaches to quantum cosmology, the striking presence of extrascientific factors. A fascinating example occurs in comparing proposals by Penrose and Hawking and Hartle. In Penrose's view, our universe arises as an arbitrary quantum fluctuation in a homogeneous background superspace filled with quantum fields. But why should any point in superspace be singled out as creating a universe like ours? As Isham puts it, the problem was preempted by the response of Augustine of Hippo

(354–430) to the question of what God was doing before God made the universe. Augustine's answer was that God did not create the universe in time, since the decision as to which point in time to create it would be arbitrary and would imply that God's will is mutable. Instead Augustine claimed that God created time along with the creation of the universe. But as Isham points out, the same reasoning leads us to reject Penrose's approach: It is thoroughly arbitrary to pick a creation point in superspace. The Hawking-Hartle model, on the other hand, circumvents the need for such a point, making it more attractive to many scientists. This is a striking example of the potentially positive role philosophy and theology can play in stimulating new insights and directions of inquiry within the natural sciences.

In short, then, inflation and quantum cosmologies can point to the grandeur and mystery of God's creativity and undercut our anthropocentrism by stressing a creation far beyond anything we could ever observe, one in which God relishes and delights in its sheer diversity. Moreover, none of the scientific cosmologies explains why the "universe" exists as such, leading us once again to the possibility of recognizing God as the creative ground of being.

Anthropic principle revisited in inflationary and quantum cosmologies. In the inflationary Big Bang scenario, the "universe" (or megauniverse) includes an infinity of domains, each a "universe" unto itself, with its own values of the fundamental constants, perhaps even differing laws of nature. In Linde's quantum cosmology, the universe eternally inflates into an infinity of bubble universes, themselves inflating into others endlessly. These scenarios suggest a far more ontologically stark "many-worlds" character than those of standard Big Bang cosmology, though they are far less defensible empirically. At least in theory they seem to explain fine-tuning by means of a kind of "cosmic Darwinism," rendering the design argument irrelevant.

Those defending an application of the Anthropic Principle to a design argument tend to stress the technical and philosophical problems with inflation and quantum cosmologies. They also tend to appeal to Ockham's Razor against many-worlds or multiverse theories and in support of the Big Bang, and they invoke God as the simplest explanation of fine-tuning. Critics of an application of the Anthropic Principle to a design argument tend to view standard Big Bang cosmology as outdated while appealing to philosophical criticisms to the effect that judgments of design are unreliable because they are necessarily limited by human imaginations.

Conclusion

Perhaps the most important result to emerge from the shifts in cosmology over the late twentieth century is the emergence of the hot Big Bang as a "permanent" description of *our* universe from the Planck time some twelve to fifteen billion years ago until the present. Gone is the time when the Big Bang theory enjoyed a serious challenger in the form of Hoyle's steady state model, with its picture of a single, ever-expanding universe whose fundamental features were time-independent. Instead the domain of debate has shifted to the pre-Planck era and what might lie endlessly "before" the Big Bang in quantum superspace. We have witnessed what Joel Primack and Nancy Abrams call an "encompassing" revolution as distinguished from the kind of Kuhnian "replacing revolution" one usually thinks of when scientific paradigms change. In such an encompassing revolution, the new paradigm contains the old one as a limit case; that is, quantum cosmology encompasses Big Bang cosmology as a special case when quantum effects can be ignored. To paraphrase a point made by Charles Misner, we can have confidence in relying on the Big Bang scenario because we know just where it fails: prior to the Planck time. In this sense the Big Bang is here to stay.

See also ANTHROPIC PRINCIPLE; BIG BANG THEORY; COSMOLOGY; COSMOLOGY, RELIGIOUS AND PHILOSOPHICAL ASPECTS; CREATIO CONTINUA; CREATIO EX NIHILO; INFLATIONARY UNIVERSE THEORY; MANY-WORLDS HYPOTHESIS; QUANTUM COSMOLOGIES; STEADY STATE THEORY; T = 0

Bibliography

Nontechnical introductions to physical cosmology

Goldsmith, Donald. *Einstein's Greatest Blunder? The Cosmological Constant and Other Fudge Factors in the Physics of the Universe.* Cambridge, Mass.: Harvard University Press, 1995.

Hawking, Stephen W. *A Brief History of Time: From the Big Bang to Black Holes* (1988). New York: Bantam, 1998.

Trefil, James S. *The Moment of Creation: Big Bang Physics from Before the First Millisecond to the Present Universe.* New York: Macmillan, 1983.

Trefil, James S., and Hazen, Robert M. *The Sciences: An Integrated Approach,* 2nd updated edition. New York: Wiley, 2000.

Technical introductions to physical cosmology

Barrow, John D., and Tipler, Frank J. *The Anthropic Cosmological Principle.* Oxford: Clarendon Press, 1986.

Misner, Charles W.; Thorne, Kip S.; and Wheeler, John Archibald. *Gravitation.* San Francisco: Freeman, 1973.

North, J. D. *The Measure of the Universe: A History of Modern Cosmology* (1965). New York: Dover, 1990.

Weinberg, Steven. *Gravitation and Cosmology: Principles and Applications of the General Theory of Relativity.* New York: Wiley, 1972.

Cosmology and creation—books

Barbour, Ian G. *Religion in an Age of Science, Gifford Lectures; 1989–1990.* San Francisco: Harper, 1990.

Clayton, Philip. *God and Contemporary Science.* Grand Rapids, Mich.: Eerdmans, 1997.

Craig, William Lane, and Smith, Quentin. *Theism, Atheism, and Big Bang Cosmology.* New York: Oxford University Press, 1993.

Drees, Willem B. *Beyond the Big Bang: Quantum Cosmologies and God.* La Salle, Ill.: Open Court, 1990.

Kragh, Helge. *Cosmology and Controversy: The Historical Development of Two Theories of the Universe.* Princeton, N.J.: Princeton University Press, 1996.

Leslie, John. *Universes.* London: Routledge, 1989.

Leslie, John, ed. *Physical Cosmology and Philosophy.* New York: Macmillan, 1990.

Murphy, Nancey, and Ellis, George F. *On the Moral Nature of the Universe: Theology, Cosmology, and Ethics.* Minneapolis, Minn.: Fortress Press, 1996.

Peacocke, Arthur. *Creation and the World of Science: The Bampton Lectures, 1979.* Oxford: Clarendon Press, 1979.

Peacocke, Arthur. *Theology for a Scientific Age: Being and Becoming—Natural, Divine, and Human.* Minneapolis, Minn.: Fortress Press, 1993.

Peters, Ted, ed. *Cosmos as Creation: Theology and Science in Consonance.* Nashville, Tenn.: Abingdon Press, 1989.

Peters, Ted, ed. *Science and Theology: The New Consonance.* Boulder, Colo.: Westview Press, 1998.

Polkinghorne, John C. *The Faith of a Physicist: Reflections of a Bottom-up Thinker.* Minneapolis, Minn.: Fortress Press, 1994.

Richardson, W. Mark, and Wildman, Wesley J., eds. *Religion and Science: History, Method, Dialogue.* New York: Routledge, 1996.

Russell, Robert John; Stoeger, William R.; and Coyne, George V., eds. *Physics, Philosophy, and Theology: A Common Quest for Understanding.* Vatican City State: Vatican Observatory Publications, 1988.

Russell, Robert John; Murphy, Nancey C.; and Isham, Chris J., eds. *Quantum Cosmology and the Laws of Nature: Scientific Perspectives on Divine Action.* Vatican City State: Vatican Observatory Publications; Berkeley, Calif.: Center for Theology and the Natural Sciences, 1993.

Southgate, Christopher, et al., eds. *God, Humanity, and the Cosmos: A Textbook in Science and Religion.* Harrisburg, Pa.: Trinity Press International, 1999.

Worthing, Mark W. *God, Creation, and Contemporary Physics.* Minneapolis, Minn.: Fortress Press, 1996.

Cosmology and creation—articles

McMullin, Ernan. "How Should Cosmology Relate to Theology?" In *The Sciences and Theology in the Twentieth Century,* ed. Arthur R. Peacocke. Notre Dame, Ind.: University of Notre Dame Press, 1981.

Russell, Robert John. "Cosmology, Creation, and Contingency." In *Cosmos as Creation: Theology and Science in Consonance,* ed. Ted Peters. Nashville, Tenn.: Abingdon Press, 1989.

Russell, Robert John. "Finite Creation Without a Beginning: The Doctrine of Creation in Relation to Big Bang and Quantum Cosmologies." In *Quantum Cosmology and the Laws of Nature: Scientific Perspectives on Divine Action,* eds. Robert John Russell, Nancey C. Murphy, and Chris J. Isham. Vatican City State: Vatican Observatory Publications; Berkeley, Calif.: Center for Theology and the Natural Sciences, 1993.

ROBERT JOHN RUSSELL

COSMOLOGY, RELIGIOUS AND PHILOSOPHICAL ASPECTS

Presumption of inevitable battle often dominates discussions of interactions between cosmology and religion, and dictates the history produced. The image of war, though modified since Andrew Dickson White's 1897 *History of the Warfare of Science with Theology in Christendom,* persists.

As he watched workers chip away at the ice barrier across the River Neva binding together the piers and the old fortress of the czars, White, the American ambassador to Russia, likened the ice to outworn creeds and noxious dogmas attaching the modern world to medieval conceptions of Christianity. He hoped that both barriers might be swept away by floods, the former by water and the latter by increased knowledge and new thought. White had experienced dogmatic opposition in the course of steering through the New York state legislature the enabling legislation in 1868 for Cornell University in Ithaca, which he subsequently guided and served as its first president. Clergymen had warned against the atheism of the proposed university with its emphasis on science, but White refused to stretch or cut science to fit "revealed religion." The controversy bore in upon White a sense of antagonism, subsequently reflected in his book. "In all of modern history," White wrote, "interference with science in the supposed interest of religion ... has resulted in the direst evils both to religion and to science" (p. viii).

Early interaction between cosmology and religion

The ancient Greek philosopher Anaxagoras (500–428 B.C.E.) was seemingly an early victim of the conflict between cosmology and religion. Greek cosmology moved away from astrological superstition, magical powers, and myth toward a more rational spirit and a picture of a universe with unchanging ways ascertainable by human reason but beyond the control of human action. Anaxagoras' new theory of universal order collided with popular faith—the belief that gods ruled the celestial phenomena—and he was expelled from Athens. Impiety, however, may have been an incidental charge; the indictment also included an accusation of corresponding with agents of Persia. The rise of a new scientific attitude and mode of thought may have accelerated the downfall of traditional religious and political beliefs, and helped shape their replacements.

An earlier religious belief of the Babylonians—that the movements of celestial bodies functioned as a sort of message board with which the gods foretold human affairs—had promoted observations and mathematical analysis. Many ancient religions associated planets with gods and found religious significance in configurations of celestial arrangements. Egyptian temples were aligned with specific stars and Stonehenge in southwestern England faced sunrise at summer solstice.

Religion motivated Greek as well as Babylonian cosmological studies. Plato's fourth-century B.C.E. conception of cosmic order was permeated with ethical overtones and moral significance, and during the second century C.E. Ptolemy cultivated cosmology particularly with respect to divine and heavenly things. He wrote "I know that I am mortal and the creature of a day; but when I search out the massed wheeling circles of the stars, my feet no longer touch the Earth, but, side by side with Zeus himself, I take my fill of ambrosia, the food of the gods" (p. 55).

Similarly for Christians, "The Heavens declare the glory of God" (Ps. 19:1). During the early Middle Ages, cosmology was regarded as a handmaiden, subservient to theology, pursued not for its own sake but for its usefulness in the interpretation of Holy Scripture. Both Augustine of Hippo (354–430) and Thomas Aquinas (c. 1225–1274) insisted that the truth of scripture is inviolable. Given possible alternative interpretations of scripture, however, they warned against rigid adherence to any one of them. A hasty choice could prove detrimental to faith, were science later to prove that choice untenable. Study and contemplation of the cosmos, the perfect expression of divine creativity and providence, were for some a way to know God.

Scientific knowledge was not precious enough to prevent the Roman emperor Justinian (483–565), a Christian, from closing the Academy at Athens in 529 C.E. and forbidding pagans to teach. Leading philosophers left Athens for Persia, though some returned after a few years and the Academy may have continued in some form. Further impeding cosmological inquiry was a growing inability to recruit competitively against the church as a profession for bright young minds. Cosmological study had received little patronage in ancient societies, with the exception of the Museum at Alexandria, and its precarious position was not altered significantly under early Christianity.

Greek science almost disappeared from Western Europe between 500 and 1100 C.E., before it was recovered through translations of the works of Aristotle and Plato, and in Arabic treatises and commentaries on Aristotle. Cosmological studies flourished within Muslim culture and civilization, sometimes under rulers interested in astrology. A few Islamic traditionalists criticized these practices for leading to the establishment of schools for heretics and the teaching of magic. The Istanbul observatory, built in 1577, was torn down shortly after its completion. In the wake of the famous comet of 1577 there had followed in quick order plague, defeats of Turkish armies, and deaths of several important persons. These misfortunes were attributed to the attempt, manifested in construction of the observatory, to pry into the secrets of nature.

After transmission from Islam to the West, Aristotelian cosmology fused with Christian theology into Scholasticism. In this form, Aristotle's cosmology permeated thought in Western Europe between roughly 1200 and 1500, especially in universities. The Aristotelian position that necessary cosmological principles can be known conjured the specter of truths necessary to cosmology but contradictory to dogmas of the Christian faith. For example, the Aristotelian assertion that the world had no beginning and no end, and thus was indestructible, seemingly conflicted with the possibility of a Day of Judgment. In 1270 the bishop of Paris condemned several propositions derived from the teachings of Aristotle, including the eternity of the world and the necessary control of terrestrial events by celestial bodies. In 1277 Pope John XXI directed the bishop of Paris to investigate intellectual controversies at the university. Within three weeks the bishop condemned 219 propositions. Excommunication was the penalty for holding even one of the damned errors.

Though intended to contain and control scientific inquiry, the condemnation may have helped free cosmology from Aristotelian prejudices and modes of argument. The Scientific Revolution may owe something to the condemnation of 1277, even if cosmologists waited until the seventeenth century to repudiate Aristotelian cosmology.

The condemnation of 1277 with its emphasis on God's absolute power undisputedly led to the nominalist thesis. The Aristotelian position that the necessary principles of cosmology and physics can be established was rejected. Cosmology now was understood to be a working hypothesis in agreement with observed phenomena. The truth of any particular hypothesis could not be insisted upon, because God could have made the world in a different manner but with the same observational consequences. Cosmologists might come to conclusions, but they could not insist that their conclusions limited God's power to have created the world in another way. Tentative, but not necessary, cosmological theories posed no challenge to religious authority.

While conceding the divine omnipotence of Christian doctrine and acceding to religious authority, the nominalist, instrumentalist, positivist thesis also freed science from religious authority. It was a convenient stance in a time when religious matters were taken seriously and heretical cosmological thoughts could place their adherents in serious trouble with powerful ecclesiastical authorities. In the new intellectual climate, imaginative and ingenious discussions flourished.

Hypothetical cosmologies, however, were not the stuff of revolution. It was not until the goal of "saving the appearances," as the nominalist endeavor has been called, was replaced with a quest to discover physical reality, that Aristotelian cosmology was destroyed and replaced with a new worldview. Confidence that the essential structure and operation of the cosmos is knowable seems to have been a prerequisite to the work of Nicolaus Copernicus (1473–1543), Galileo Galilei (1564–1642), Johannes Kepler (1571–1630), and Isaac Newton (1642–1727). Some of their necessary cosmological principles would conflict with dogmas of the Christian faith.

To account for the apparent daily motion of the heavens, Copernicus placed the sun in the center of the universe and the Earth in revolution around the sun and rotating on its axis. An unauthorized foreword to Copernicus's 1543 *De revolutionibus orbium caelestium* (*On the Revolutions of Heavenly Spheres*) presented the heliocentric theory as a convenient mathematical fiction. Copernicus, however, believed that he was describing the real motions of the world.

Copernicus anticipated criticism, acknowledging in the preface to *De revolutionibus* "that to ascribe movement to the Earth must indeed seem an absurd performance on my part to those who know

that many centuries have consented to the establishment of the contrary judgment, namely that the Earth is placed immovably as the central point in the middle of the Universe" (p. 137). Copernicus, however, did not anticipate criticism from the Catholic Church, in whose service he had long labored as a canon and advised the papacy on calendar reform. Indeed, Copernicus dedicated his book to Pope Paul III, in hope that "my labors contribute somewhat even to the Commonwealth of the Church, of which your Holiness is now Prince. For not long since the question of correcting the ecclesiastical calendar was debated" (p. 143).

Citation of scripture against the new cosmology was not long in coming. Even before Copernicus' book was published, the reformer Martin Luther (1483–1546) warned that "this fool wishes to reverse the entire science of astronomy; but sacred Scripture tells us that Joshua commanded the Sun to stand still, and not the Earth" (Josh. 10:13). Literal adherence to the Bible was the foundation of Protestant revolt against Catholic religious hegemony. Prior to the Counter-Reformation, the Catholic Church was more liberal in its interpretation, and more accepting of Copernican cosmology. It was taught in some Catholic universities and used for the new calendar promulgated by Pope Gregory XIII in 1582.

Galileo and the Church

Revolutions in science, as in politics, often go beyond the limited changes that the people who start a revolution have in mind. In Copernican cosmology, the rotation of the Earth caused the stars' observed motion. Hence, the notion of the starry sphere that carried the stars around was obsolete, and soon human imagination distributed the stars throughout a perhaps infinite space. Also, the Earth was no longer unique; now it was merely one of several similar objects in the solar system. And humankind was but one of possibly many intelligent inhabitants of the universe. Soon questions arose: If the Earth were a celestial planet, how did it differ from the divine heavens? Had each planet been visited by an Adam and an Eve? Faith in an anthropocentric universe lay shattered, leaving humankind's relationship with God uncertain. John Donne's 1611 poem *The Anatomy of the World,* with its opening line the "new Philosophy calls all in doubt," and later "all Relation: Prince, Subject, Father Son, are things forgot," refers to Christian morality as well as the physical locations of the sun and the Earth.

That the Earth was no longer unique was most dramatically emphasized by Galileo. His telescopic observations of the moon's surface emphatically demanded the revolutionary conclusion that the moon was not a smooth sphere, as Aristotelians had maintained, but was uneven and rough, like the Earth. Another similarity, between Jupiter and the Earth, was furnished by Galileo's discovery of four satellites of Jupiter, similar to the Earth's single satellite.

Galileo's arguments in support of the new Copernican cosmology culminated in a clash with Catholic authorities so dramatic that it forms the foundation of the most widely held stereotype regarding the general relationship between science and religion. The conflict, however, was far from inevitable. Initially, the primary opposition to Galileo came from Aristotelian philosophers in Italian universities. At around the same time, a church official remarked that the Bible tells how to go to heaven, not how the heavens go. Wisely, the Church was not eager to enter a scientific dispute. As Augustine had suggested earlier, no cosmological doctrine should ever be made an article of faith, lest some better informed heretic exploit misguided adherence to a scientific doctrine to impugn the credibility of proper articles of faith.

Galileo's Aristotelian philosophical opponents were eager, however, to enlist the Church on their side in their battle against Galileo, and a few individual priests were induced to charge that the motion of the Earth was contrary to the Bible. Galileo, in turn, sought to win the Church to his side, and to silence potential objections to Copernican cosmology based on scripture. In an open letter of 1615, Galileo appealed to the authority of Augustine in support of the thesis that no contradiction can exist between the Bible and science when the Bible is interpreted correctly. But Galileo was out of step with the times. The Counter-Reformation, following the Council of Trent, which had met from 1545 to 1563, now demanded tight control over Church doctrine, the better to counter Protestants. Galileo also cited Augustine's warning not to make cosmological doctrine an article of faith. This was especially good advice when new scientific facts from telescopic observations were still coming in.

In 1616 Pope Paul V submitted the questions of the motion of the Earth and the stability of the sun to the official qualifiers of disputed propositions. It is not clear why he chose to act. Galileo expected the qualifiers to read the Bible metaphorically, but they read it literally and found both the motion of the Earth and the stability of the sun false and absurd in philosophy. They did not rule on the truth of Copernican cosmology in terms of its agreement with nature. The qualifiers found the motion of the Earth at least erroneous in the Catholic faith and the stability of the sun formally heretical. Here they exceeded their authority, because only the pope or a Church Council could decree a formal heresy, and Pope Paul ignored this finding. Galileo was instructed no longer to hold or defend the forbidden propositions: the motion of the Earth and the stability of the sun. The Congregation of the Index issued an edict forbidding reconciliation of Copernicanism with the Bible and assertion of literal truth for the forbidden propositions. One passage about scriptural interpretation and passages calling the Earth a star, implying that it moved like a planet, were ordered removed from Copernicus' *De revolutionibus*. Catholics could still discuss Copernican cosmology hypothetically, and little damage was done to the science.

Had Galileo at his meeting with Church officials resisted the instruction not to hold or defend the forbidden Copernican propositions, the Commissary General of the Inquisition was prepared to order him, in the presence of a notary and witnesses, not to hold, defend, or teach the propositions in any way, on pain of imprisonment. Galileo did not resist, but the Commissary General may have read his order anyway. It appears in the minutes of the meeting, unsigned and unwitnessed. Galileo may have been advised to ignore the unauthorized intervention. Subsequent rumors that Galileo had been compelled to abjure caused him to ask for and receive an affidavit stating that he was under no restriction other than the edict applying to all Catholics.

In 1623, a new pope was chosen. Urban VIII was an intellectual, admired his friend Galileo, granted him six audiences in 1624, and encouraged him to write a book on Copernican cosmology. The book, Urban hoped, would demonstrate that the Church did not interfere with the pursuit of cosmology, only with unauthorized interpretations of the Bible. The *Dialogue* on world systems was published in 1632, with Church approval. Urban, however, became angry when he found his own thoughts attributed to the Aristotelian representative in the *Dialogue,* who lost every argument. Also, the timing was unfortunate for Galileo, his book appearing in a climate of heightened suspicion, even paranoia. A Spanish cardinal had recently criticized Urban for his interference in a political struggle, and Urban had responded with a purge of pro-Spanish members of his administration, including the secretary who, coincidentally, had secured permission for printing the *Dialogue.*

Galileo was called to Rome and charged with contravening the (unsigned and unauthorized) 1616 order of the Commissary General of the Inquisition not to hold, defend, or teach the Copernican propositions in any way. Galileo produced his affidavit, signed and dated, but nonetheless was found guilty. He was compelled to abjure, curse, and detest his errors and heresies. Henceforth even hypothetical discussion of Copernican cosmology was heresy for Catholics.

The Galileo fiasco has long been a major embarrassment for the Catholic Church, and in 1978 Pope John Paul II acknowledged that Galileo's theology was sounder than that of the judges who condemned him. Galileo's battle with religious authority is the major historical source for the stereotype of an ineluctable conflict between science and religion, but the stereotype is a vast oversimplification, as most stereotypes are. This clash between cosmology and religion was avoidable.

The Mechanical universe

Copernican cosmology, though revolutionary in important respects, clung to Aristotelian circular motion, whose cause generally was attributed to God. Kepler, using Tycho Brahe's (1546–1601) observations, showed that planetary orbits are elliptical. Kepler also found several mathematical relationships, such as the proportionality of the cubes of the mean planetary distances to the squares of the periodic times. Initially he attributed planetary motion to moving souls, but within a few years was searching for a physical principle. Kepler's cosmology was strongly Christian. He was convinced that the creator had used mathematical archetypes to design the universe, and this religious belief drove his cosmological research and shaped his results, which were "a sacred sermon, a veritable hymn to God the Creator," showing "how great are His wisdom, power, and goodness."

An explanation of how the planets continue to retrace the same paths forever around the sun became a central problem of seventeenth- and eighteenth-century cosmology. Newton showed mathematically that Kepler's elliptical orbits as well as several mathematical relationships, including the proportionality of distances and times, were consequences of a universal inverse-square law of gravity. For Newton, the medium conveying action must be immaterial. The omnipresence of God, an immaterial ether, pervaded the Newtonian cosmos, offering no resistance to bodies, but moving them.

Theological implications of Newton's cosmology were criticized in 1715 in a letter to Caroline, Princess of Wales, from the philosopher and mathematician Gottfried Leibniz (1646–1716). Leibniz was a rival of Newton in the invention of the calculus, each accusing the other of plagiarism. Newton's friend Samuel Clarke answered in a letter to Caroline, which she forwarded to Leibniz. In the course of the debate Leibniz wrote five letters and Clarke five replies, which were published in 1717. Newton thought that his discoveries provided new evidence of the existence and providence of God. Irregularities in planetary motions caused by the disturbing influence of other planets would increase until the system wanted reformation. Leibniz charged that Newtonian views were contributing to a decline of natural religion in England. The implication that God occasionally intervened in the universe, much as a watchmaker has to wind up and mend his work, derogated from God's perfection. Clarke admitted that God had to intervene in the universe, but only because intervention was part of God's plan.

Eighteenth-century belief in the orderliness of the universe made determination of that order an important theological, philosophical, and scientific endeavor. William Whiston (1667–1752), Newton's successor at Cambridge University in 1703, argued that the system of the stars, the work of the creator, had a beautiful proportion, even if frail humans were ignorant of the order. In 1750 the English astronomer Thomas Wright (1711–1786) proposed a model for the Milky Way (a luminous band of light circling the heavens). Inspired by an incorrect summary of Wright's book, Immanuel Kant (1724–1804) explained the Milky Way as a disk-shaped system viewed from the Earth, which was located in the plane of the disk. Thoroughly imbued with a belief in the order and beauty of God's work, Kant went on to suggest that nebulous patches of light in the Heavens are composed of stars and are other Milky Ways, or island universes. In the absence of large telescopes and revealing observations of distant stars, philosophical and theological speculations dominated cosmology. This situation began to change after the English astronomer William Herschel (1738–1822) proposed a cosmological model rooted in observations. From the 1780s onward, the heavens, penetrated by Herschel's large telescopes, increasingly were understood as an expanded firmament of three dimensions.

The universe was also thought of as a clock, which Newtonians had argued required God's occasional reformation. But in 1786 the last major problem in celestial mechanics was solved when Pierre-Simon Laplace (1749–1827) demonstrated that the gravitational interactions of Jupiter and Saturn were self-correcting, not in need of divine intervention. Laplace also proposed a plausible mechanism for the formation of the solar system, which Newton had cited as reason for belief in divine providence, given the small likelihood that random chance could have been responsible. Reflecting the atheistic approach to nature of the French Enlightenment, Laplace attempted to replace the hypothesis of God's rule with a purely physical theory that could also explain the observed order of the universe. He was successful, at least in his own mind. According to legend, when Napoleon asked Laplace whether he had left any place for the creator, Laplace replied that he had no need of such a hypothesis.

Changing status of cosmology and religion

Cosmology and Christianity, formerly joined in Western thought, were now estranged. Furthermore, science, flush with triumphant reductions of all known phenomena of the system of the world to the universal law of gravity, was replacing religion as the source to which people turned to for inspiration, direction, and criteria of truth. The divorce of God from the physical universe may well have been inevitable with the rise of modern cosmology, however convinced were its founding fathers that they were exploring and demonstrating God's wonders.

Christian conceptions increasingly were relegated to aspects of cosmology not yet susceptible to scientific observation and analysis. They continue to play a powerful role in debates over the question of intelligent life elsewhere in the universe, in which extraterrestrials are potential evidence of God's omnipotence and benevolence. The idea of intelligent life elsewhere in the universe also challenges the conception of God as redeemer. Actual contact with extraterrestrials could well prove devastating; anthropological studies of primitive societies confident of their place in the universe find them disintegrating upon contact with an advanced society pursuing different values and ways of life.

Once theology was king of the disciplines, autonomous, the supreme principle by which all else was understood, its fundamental postulates and principles derived from divine revelation, interpreted and formulated within the tradition, and producing knowledge of ultimate value. Cosmology was a handmaiden, neither controlling fundamental knowledge nor ways of getting at it, its truths holding a lower logical status and value. The relationship between cosmology and religion is now largely reversed; both religion and politics now direct appeals for legitimacy to science.

An example is found in Georges Lemaître (1894–1966), an early proponent of an expanding universe. Lemaître was a Belgian astrophysicist and a Catholic priest, and from 1960 until his death he was president of the Pontifical Academy of Sciences. He offered a second chance for the Catholic Church to embrace and be embraced by a second Galileo. Also, in 1952, Pope Pius XII argued that modern Big Bang cosmology affirmed the notion of a transcendental creator. At the same time, Fred Hoyle (1915–2001), a leading creator and proponent of the rival steady state cosmology, was using it to further his anti-religious polemic, arguing that there was no room in his theory for a creator.

In politics, also, cosmology is appealed to for validation. Another early proponent of an expanding universe, the Russian mathematician Alexander Friedmann (1888–1925), was hailed as an example of great Soviet science, no matter that difficult conditions in revolutionary Russia in the early 1920s and Friedmann's early death from typhoid fever severely limited his scientific output. During Stalin's rule, Soviet cosmologists were expected to serve the party by providing a cosmology congruent with official party ideology.

After serving for many centuries as handmaiden to religion, science, including cosmology, now commands supreme status among intellectual disciplines. When appeals for validation and legitimacy are made, now it is more often to cosmology than to religion. Once intertwined, cosmology and religion have become estranged. Relative to cosmic time and space, human concerns approach insignificance. Much of modern cosmology has become "naturalized," shorn of its former human connections, particularly religion.

See also ARISTOTLE; AUGUSTINE; COSMOLOGY, PHYSICAL ASPECTS; EXTRATERRESTRIAL LIFE; GALILEO GALILEI, KANT, IMMANUEL; NEWTON, ISAAC; PLATO; THOMAS AQUINAS

Bibliography

Alexander, H. G. *The Leibniz-Clarke Correspondence, Together with Extracts from Newton's* Principia *and* Opticks. Manchester, UK: Manchester University Press, 1956.

Copernicus. *On the Revolution of Heavenly Spheres.* In Thomas S. Kuhn, *The Copernican Revolution: Planetary Astronomy in the Development of Western Thought.* Cambridge, Mass.: Harvard University Press, 1957.

Crowe, Michael J. *The Extraterrestrial Life Debate 1750–1900: The Idea of a Plurality of Worlds from Kant to Lowell.* Cambridge: Cambridge University Press, 1986.

Drake, Stillman, trans. and ed. *Discoveries and Opinions of Galileo.* New York: Doubleday, 1957.

Gilkey, Landon, "The Structure of Academic Revolution." In *The Nature of Scientific Discovery,* ed. Owen Gingerich. Washington, D.C.: Smithsonian Institution Press, 1975.

Grant, Edward. "The Condemnation of 1277, God's Absolute Power, and Physical Thought in the Late Middle Ages." *Viator* 10 (1979): 211–244.

Hetherington, Norriss S. *Cosmology: Historical, Literary, Philosophical, Religious, and Scientific Perspectives.* New York: Garland, 1993.

Kragh, Helge. *Cosmology and Controversy: The Historical Development of Two Theories of the Universe.* Princeton, N.J.: Princeton University Press, 1996.

Lindberg, David C., and Numbers, Ronald L. *God and Nature: Historical Essays on the Encounter between Christianity and Science.* Berkeley: University of California Press, 1986.

Odum, Herbert H. "The Estrangement of Celestial Mechanics and Religion." *Journal of the History of Ideas* 27 (1966): 533–548.

Olson, Richard. "Science, Scientism and Anti-Science in Hellenic Athens: A New Whig Interpretation." *History of Science* 14 (1978): 179–199.

Ptolemy. "Epigram to the Almagest." In Owen Gingerich, *The Eye of Heaven: Ptolemy, Copernicus, Kepler.* New York: American Institute of Physics, 1993.

White, Andrew D. *A History of the Warfare of Science with Theology in Christendom* (1897). New York: George Braziller, 1995.

NORRISS HETHERINGTON

CREATED CO-CREATOR

A dynamic theological anthropology with the concept of the created co-creator in its core is elaborated by theologian Philip Hefner: Humans are created by God to be co-creators in the creation that God has purposefully brought into being. The word *created* thus relates to being created by God as part of the evolutionary reality (a view sometimes criticised for demeaning humans understood as *imago dei*). The word *co-creator* reflects the freedom of humans to participate in fulfilling God's purposes (a view sometimes criticised for super-elevating humans to the same level as God). The paradigm of the created co-creator is Jesus Christ who reveals that the essential reality of humans has never been outside God.

See also EVOLUTION, BIOLOGICAL; EVOLUTION, HUMAN

Bibliography

Hefner, Philip. *The Human Factor: Evolution, Culture, and Religion.* Minneapolis, Minn.: Fortress Press, 1993.

Klein, Ralph W. ed. *Philip Hefner: Created Co-Creator. Currents in Theology and Mission* 28, no. 3–4 (2001).

HUBERT MEISINGER

CREATIO CONTINUA

The term *creatio continua* refers to God's continuing creative activity throughout the history of the universe. In a sense, most theologians accept *creatio continua,* since creation is the dependence of the whole of space-time on God. But more traditional views hold that because God is timeless and immutable, there is only one divine creative act, which originates the whole of space-time from first to last. Those who speak of *creatio continua* think of creation taking place in many successive acts, partly in response to events in time. Thus, at any particular time God's creation has not been completed, and the future is partly open, in some theological views, even for God.

See also CREATIO EX NIHILO

KEITH WARD

CREATIO EX NIHILO

Creatio ex nihilo (Latin for "creation from nothing") refers to the view that the universe, the whole of space-time, is created by a free act of God out of nothing, and not either out of some preexisting material or out of the divine substance itself. This view was widely, though not universally, accepted in the early Christian Church, and was formally defined as dogma by the fourth Lateran Council in 1215. *Creatio ex nihilo* is now almost universally accepted by Jews, Christians, and Muslims. Indian theism generally holds that the universe is substantially one with God, though it is usually still thought of as a free and unconstrained act of God.

See also CREATIO CONTINUA

KEITH WARD

CREATION

Creation refers to the idea that the whole universe is brought into being and sustained by a personal agent, God, who is beyond the universe. Since creation is an intentional act, God is usually said to envisage what will be created, and to intend that it will come into existence. Knowledge and will are thus attributes of a creator God.

Creation in various religions

Many religions have the concept of a creator God. In the late nineteenth century, the anthropologists Edward Tylor and James Frazer thought that the idea of God was in effect an early scientific hypothesis to explain why things happen as they do. They thought the hypothesis was false or superfluous, an instance of primitive science. Contemporaries, like Max Müller or the theologian Friedrich Schleiermacher, pointed to a more affective or experiential source of the idea of a creator in something like an intuition or apprehension of the infinite, or in a sense of *absolute dependence* (Schleiermacher's later term). It would not then be a scientific theory, but a primal sense of an unchanging, self-existent reality beyond the changes of the natural world.

Primal religious traditions usually contain some idea of a creator god, but often one who is remote and not particularly concerned with human affairs, delegating that to lesser gods. In the Chinese or East Asian religious stream, as represented in Daoism and Confucianism, the idea of creation is not denied, but it is not especially important. What is important is the Way of Heaven, the balance and harmony of nature itself, as reflecting in human life and society the order that obtains in the universe. The ultimate source of being, perhaps the Dao (or Way), is not seen as a personal agency. For that reason, these religious views do not have a doctrine of creation. They stress the interrelatedness and sacredness of nature, and they connect the best way of human life with insight into the natural order the universe should have. Chinese and East Asian religions tend to say, however, that questions of how the universe began or what a God might be like are both insoluble and spiritually irrelevant.

Buddhism shares with the East Asian traditions a lack of interest in, or even a rejection of, a doctrine of creation. For many Buddhists, the suffering involved in the natural world is too great to permit any thought of a good creator, and again the idea is seen as too theoretical to be of any practical use. The Buddhist way is one of disciplining the mind to overcome attachment, so that one might realize that state of wisdom, compassion, and bliss that is *nirvana*. In *Mahayana* Buddhism, there develops the idea of *bodhisattvas,* compassionate beings who help suffering beings, and who may even generate from themselves worlds in which sentient beings exist. This can come near to a doctrine of creation, but the emphasis is on a plurality of liberated beings, who may be of great compassion, knowledge, and power, but who are not creators of all reality.

In general, these religious traditions find the existence of suffering too great a problem to allow for a good creator. They find belief in a creator spiritually superfluous; their spiritual quest is for compassionate mindfulness and wisdom, and devotion to a personal god is seen as a lesser vehicle or lower path. They also find such belief too theoretical, regarding it as unprofitable speculation.

Most orthodox Indian traditions, however, have developed the idea of one supreme spiritual reality—Brahman—from which everything in the universe derives its existence. This reality can be described as *sat-cit-ananda,* or being, consciousness, and bliss. Sometimes, as in Ramanuja, the twelfth-century Indian philosopher, the one supreme reality is characterized as a supreme person. Sometimes, as in Sankara (perhaps the best-known Indian philosopher of the eighth century C.E.) it is said to be beyond personhood, though it appears as a person, and to be one undifferentiated reality of which all finite things are illusory appearances. It is a common doctrine that "all is Brahman," so that the Lord is the material cause of the universe, which is the Lord's appearance or (in Ramanuja) his "body." For Hindus in these traditions, all the gods are aspects or diverse forms of the one all-inclusive Brahman. The universe comes into being in order to work out the *karma,* the accumulated merit or demerit, of finite souls. Each universe has a finite, though vastly long, life. Then it dies, and after a period when all the potentialities of being exist in unevolved form in Brahman, they are realized again in a new universe, perhaps a repetition of the one before it. Universes come into being and pass away without beginning or end, and only Brahman remains unchanging, the one source of all.

This is a doctrine of creation, since every universe comes into being as the result of an act of knowledge, will, and desire of the Supreme Lord, who says, in the holy scriptures, the Upanishads, "May I become many" (Chandogya Upanishad, VI, ii, 3). It is usually held that each universe is necessarily what it is, and that everything in each universe is part of, or one with, Brahman. For that reason, some might prefer to call this a doctrine of *emanation,* or necessary self-manifestation of the supreme Lord. However, it is an act of will, not a sort of unconscious seepage of being. And in that self-manifestation, there are infinite souls working out their own karma, so that there is an "otherness" between each finite soul and the Supreme, even though they are ontologically one. It may be that the most obvious difference from the Abrahamic traditions—where creation is said to be a free act of the creator, and where creatures are ontologically quite distinct from the creator —is largely verbal. For in the Abrahamic faiths, freedom and necessity are often said to be compatible, so that even though the act of creation is "free," it is nonetheless an unforced yet necessary expression of the divine nature. Moreover, no creature can exist without the upholding presence of God, from which creatures can never be separated, even in hell. This doctrine of divine omnipresence is not far removed from the Indian doctrine that all things are, in a sophisticated sense, "one" with Brahman. There are divergences of doctrine, to be sure, but the conceptual differences are neither absolute nor unchangeable.

Hindu traditions deal with the problem of suffering by attributing it to the free actions of finite souls, in the sequence of rebirths, without beginning or end, which each soul experiences until it achieves release or liberation into a realm beyond suffering. So creation by a good God is ontologically necessary. God, whose essential nature is perfect intelligence and bliss, is not to blame. Moreover, Hindu traditions permit creaturely freedom and promise final bliss for all souls that choose it. And God enters into nature in many forms to help suffering beings, so that God can truly be called good.

Hindus would say that God is not spiritually superfluous, since the perfect state of intelligence and bliss is realized in one supreme being, and to know the supreme being is the greatest happiness for finite souls. Nor is God a speculative concept, since the doctrine of creation is not primarily a doctrine about the beginning of the universe (there have always been universes). It is a doctrine about the present union of all finite beings with and their dependence on the one Supreme Lord, conscious realization of which is the supreme spiritual goal.

Abrahamic faiths

In the Abrahamic faiths, mainly Judaism, Islam and Christianity, there is a shared doctrine that the universe is the creation of one supreme and perfect

God. This is usually said to be a free, nonnecessitated act of bringing into being things other than God. In Christianity, creation is through the Logos, the eternal Son, who is construed as the archetype of all creation and the uncreated image of the divine Wisdom. So the universe is seen to be contingent—it did not have to be as it is—and yet supremely rational. Some have argued that such a belief made modern science possible because it encouraged the view that nature can be understood by reason, that it is ordered and unitary, having one rational creator, yet because it is contingent, observation is necessary to discern its laws. Moreover, since nature is not divine, but it is a created object, humans can investigate it without offending the spirits. It may even be held that such investigation, at first encouraged but also impeded by the excessive authority given by the Church to Aristotle in the thirteenth to sixteenth centuries, really began to flourish only when, after 1500, that Church authority was challenged by the Reformation. So the scene was set for the rise of the natural sciences in a European culture in which reliance on close observation, insistence on critical freedom, and belief in the rational structure of nature all coalesced in one dynamic matrix.

The word *creation* has usually been used to refer to the origin of the universe, but theologically it has always been clear that it more properly refers to the relationship of every time and place to God. In this sense, when and how the universe originated is not of primary importance. Some theologians and scientists have held that if the universe can be shown to have a beginning in time, this would raise the probability that it was created. For many years it was argued that if the universe had no beginning in time, the universe would not be created, since it would necessarily always be there. Medieval philosopher and theologian Thomas Aquinas argued in Summa Theologica (1a; qq. 46, art. 2) that this view is a misunderstanding. If creation means that nothing can exist unless it is part of a world-system that God wills, it does not matter whether that system has existed forever or if it had a beginning. What the believer needs to know is not that God was needed to start the universe, but that the universe, whatever its age or size, could not exist at any moment without a self-existent creator. The doctrine of creation depends on the truth of the assertion that the material universe is not self-existent, and that it can reasonably be seen as the effect of a free act of a conscious being that is of supreme value—God.

Creation and science

All the great religious traditions formulated their views of the universe long before the rise of modern science, and they incorporate theoretical beliefs that need to be reconstructed if the findings of science are to be fully accepted. East Asian traditions in practice embody many quasi-magical practices—*Feng Shui* and astrology, for example—that would be regarded by most scientists as superstitious, and based on misunderstanding of or simple errors about how the laws of nature work. In the Indian traditions, the ideas of rebirth and of the soul as distinct from matter create tensions with evolutionary biology, neurophysiology, and genetics in particular. The Abrahamic faiths have traditionally believed in six-day creation, in a primal paradisal state without suffering or death, and in a very short history for the universe, with earth at its center, all of which is rendered obsolete by evolutionary cosmology, with its fifteen billion year history for the universe, and belief in the principle of natural selection as at least a major driving force of biological evolution.

If religious belief in creation is not primarily a speculative hypothesis, but an existential apprehension of dependence on a transcendent reality, these traditional beliefs can be revised without much difficulty. They can simply be said to express spiritual insights into the limited terms of their understanding of the universe. Their creation stories can be seen as myths, as primarily symbolic attempts to depict the human situation of alienation from a supreme transcendent reality, and the way to overcome that alienation.

It will remain important, and it is part of the drive to understanding that motivates science, to have some view, however provisional, of how the universe relates to the transcendent spiritual goal of religion. The scientific investigation of nature is important to religion because it reveals the sort of universe there is, and therefore by implication the way in which the universe could be related to a transcendent reality. If this is an evolutionary universe, in which consciousness and freedom evolve from a simple primal singularity as emergent properties of matter itself, and if this happens through the interplay of mathematically ordered laws and processes of random variation and natural selection, a number of questions need to be asked before a doctrine of creation could seem plausible. One will need to ask whether the system is well-designed, whether it shows signs of rational order or of creative freedom, whether it can be seen as purposive or directional, and whether it could be willed by a being who can be termed good.

Since humans will in all likelihood continue to give different answers to these questions, the "religious transcendent" will not always be interpreted in terms of a creator god. Many in the renouncing traditions will continue to focus on an "impersonal" state of wisdom, compassion, and bliss which has no causal role in the universe, but which can be attained by humans. In the Western Christian tradition, the element of design has been so strongly emphasized that sometimes the universe has been seen as a quasi-machine, with the creator as a cosmic clockmaker. However, some contemporary theologians, like Arthur Peacocke, have preferred to picture God as an artist, expressing the divine being in creation. Process theologians have adopted an even more organic view of the relation between the universe and its creator. In this respect they have drawn nearer to the dominant Indian traditions, which speak of the creation as "one" with the creator—meaning that the universe realizes elements of the divine nature that are in some way essential to its being what it is.

Often a contrast is drawn between Indian cyclic view of time and Semitic linear views. It is true that the Indian tradition speaks of vast repetitive cycles of creation, and the Semitic tradition speaks of this universe as having a definite beginning, end, and purpose. But it needs to be remembered that even the early Christian theologian Augustine acknowledged in Book 11 of *City of God* that God could create many universes, and for Indian thinkers each universe can be said to have the purpose of expressing the creative play of Brahman, of working out the destiny of souls, and of making liberation possible. Both these traditions agree that, however finite or infinite time may be, however repetitive or creatively new, it is wholly dependent on the intentional act of a being of supreme value that is supra-temporal. That is the heart of the idea of creation. It is widely shared between Semitic and Indian religious traditions. And while some revision of the original creation myths of these traditions is required by science, the new understanding of the cosmos that science brings may well be felt not to challenge a basic belief in creation, but to increase a sense of the wisdom, power, and infinity of the creator.

See also CREATIO CONTINUA; CREATIO EX NIHILO; DESIGN; GENESIS; LIFE, ORIGINS OF

Bibliography

Frazer, James. *The Golden Bough* (1922), Abridged edition. London: Penguin, 1996.

Harvey, Peter. *An Introduction to Buddhism: Teachings, History and Practices*. Cambridge, UK, and New York: Cambridge University Press, 1990.

Lott, Eric. *Vedantic Approaches to God*. New York: Harper, 1980.

Müller, F. Max. *Introduction to the Science of Religion* (1873). Varanasi, India: Bharata Manisha, 1972.

Paley, William. *Natural Theology* (1802). New York: Harper & Brothers, 1847.

Peacocke, Arthur. *Creation and the World of Science*. New York: Oxford University Press, 1979.

Polkinghorne, John. *Science and Creation: The Search for Understanding*. Boston: New Science Library, 1989.

Richardson, W. Mark, and Wildman, Wesley J., eds. *Religion and Science: History, Method, and Dialogue*. New York: Routledge, 1996.

Schleiermacher, Friedrich. *The Christian Faith*. (1830-1831), trans. Hugh R. Mackintosh and James S. Stewart (1928). Edinburgh, UK: T&T Clark, 1989.

Tylor, Edward B. *Primitive Culture* (1929). Gloucester, Mass.: Peter Smith, 1970.

Ward, Keith. *Religion and Creation*. London: Oxford University Press, 1996.

Yao, Xinzhong. *An Introduction to Confucianism*. New York: Cambridge University Press, 2000.

KEITH WARD

CREATIONISM

The meaning of the term *creationism* has varied greatly over time. In the history of Christian theology it once designated the idea that God creates a new soul for each person born, in contrast to *traducianism,* which envisions the soul as propagating in a manner similar to the way bodies propagate.

In contemporary culture, however, the term has taken on a number of substantially different meanings that need to be distinguished. For the purposes of this entry, the term *theological creationism* designates the basic belief, held by members of many religious communities, that the universe is not self-existent but is a creation; that is, the universe has being only because a self-existent creator-God gives it being. The existence of a creation is held to be dependent on the effective will of a creator not only to give it being at a beginning but also to sustain it in being from moment to moment.

But the term *creationism* usually entails more than this basic belief that the universe is a creation. The term now ordinarily designates the conviction that the creator-God of which the Bible speaks has both (1) brought the basic material of "the heavens and the earth" into being from nothing at the beginning of time, and (2) conferred specific forms on that basic material in the course of time through occasional episodes of divine intervention. Because of its strong emphasis on the need for several episodes of form-conferring supernatural action, this perspective will here be called *episodic creationism* to distinguish it from *theological creationism* as defined above. Episodic creationism has historically been called *special creationism* because of its idea that each basic kind of creature was specially created (given a specific form) to function in its environment.

Within the category of episodic creationism, however, there are numerous and vastly differing concepts of the particular manner and timetable of the creator's form-conferring interventions. Following are the basic tenets of the most common versions of these creationist portraits of God's creative action.

Young-earth episodic creationism

Young-earth episodic creationism is committed to the belief that the universe was brought into being recently (usually taken to be six thousand to ten thousand years ago) and that God's form-conferring interventions (or "acts of creation") were performed during a week of six twenty-four-hour days immediately following the beginning. The primary basis for this perspective is the belief that this portrait of the creation's formational history is the clear teaching of the Bible and that all faithful believers of biblical faiths must accept it.

Bible inerrancy. Understanding the creationists' beliefs concerning the nature and authority of the Bible is essential for understanding all forms of episodic creationism. The Bible (made up of the Hebrew Scriptures plus the New Testament writings of the early Christian era) is generally taken to be not only a trustworthy guide for faith and practice, but also an inerrant source of information on any topic that it addresses. How does the Bible come to have this remarkable character? The Bible has this quality because, inerrantists believe, the Bible is the inspired Word of God. The Bible is believed to be the product, not of human knowledge or of human experience alone, but of divine revelation of information and divine guidance in the writing of the text. As God's revelation and as the product of divine inspiration, what the Bible says can be trusted to be true and unblemished by error of any sort.

This concept of the Bible, combined with an interpretive approach that favors "the plain reading of the text," has led many to insist upon a literal interpretation of biblical narratives unless there is strong reason (derived from the Bible itself) to read it in a more figurative or artistic sense. The application of this belief to the first three chapters of Genesis has led a large proportion of the Christian community (at least in the past century) to treat the creation narratives of Genesis 1–3 as literature that is more like a documentary photograph than an artistic portrait. Consequently, Genesis 1–3 is taken to be a chronicle of God's acts of creation—a concise account of what happened and when during the first week of time. Young-earth episodic creationists read Genesis 1 as a divine revelation that God not only brought the universe into being at the beginning of time but also performed a series of form-conferring interventions over the next six days. Similarly, Genesis 6–9 is taken to be a chronicle of a catastrophic global flood event that occurred within human history, perhaps four thousand to five thousand years ago.

Creation science. Furthermore, if the Bible is the inspired Word of God, it must be true. And if it is true, then it must be open to empirical confirmation. Empirical confirmation of the recentness and episodic character of divine acts of creation is the task of a science-styled enterprise known as *creation science.* Creation science stands in the tradition of *flood geology,* which presumes that the major structural features of the earth's surface were formed as a consequence of the great flood of Noah. In both cases, selected empirical evidence is reinterpreted in such a way as to reach the conclusions that: (1) the age of the universe is not fourteen or fifteen billion years—as conventional science has concluded—but more like six thousand years; (2) new forms of life could not have evolved in the manner that most biologists believe, but must have been specially created by supernatural means; and (3) the Noachian flood can account for all of the major geological structures that characterize the surface of the earth.

There are several societies and institutions that actively promote young-earth episodic creationism, flood geology, and creation science. The Creation Research Society (CRS), for example, was founded in 1963. Its members must subscribe to a statement of belief that affirms, in the order listed:

(1) that the Bible, as the inspired Word of God, is historically and scientifically true;

(2) that all basic types of life forms were made by direct creative acts of God in six days;

(3) that the Noachian flood was a worldwide historical event: and

(4) that salvation through Jesus is necessary because of Adam and Eve's fall into sin.

The CRS has published its technical journal, the *Creation Research Society Quarterly,* since 1964 and now supports a variety of "creation-related research" projects at its Van Andel Creation Research Center in north central Arizona.

Creation science is taught in many conservative Christian schools and colleges. Graduate degrees in creation science can be earned at the Institute for Creation Research (ICR) in Santee, California. The ICR maintains an extensive resource center for books, pamphlets, research monographs, textbooks, and videos prepared for a variety of age and educational levels. Its educational outreach programs include *Back to Genesis* regional seminars, *Good Science* workshops at a variety of grade levels, creation science camps, *Case for Creation* community seminars, and creation/evolution debates in which biochemist Duane Gish defends young-earth creationism against various representatives for evolution. Programs of this sort are presented not only throughout the United States but in countries around the world.

The ICR supports research expeditions to locate the remnants of Noah's Ark on Mount Ararat in Turkey and to study catastrophic phenomena at Mount St. Helens in Washington. It sponsors both research trips and public tours in the Grand Canyon—research trips "looking for evidence to support a young-age creation interpretation of the formation and history of the Canyon," and Grand Canyon outreach tours that are "devoted to reaching pastors, teachers, professionals, and business leaders with the creation message" and designed to give its participants "an opportunity to see evidences for the Genesis Flood firsthand."

Other forms of creationism

Creationism has many variants. Three of the most prominent interpretations are old-earth episodic, progressive, and Intelligent Design creationism.

Old-earth episodic creationism. The tenets of old-earth episodic creationism are very similar to those of young-earth creationism with the exception of the timetable. The Bible is taken to be the inspired and scientifically inerrant Word of God. The formational capabilities of the created world are presumed to be inadequate to sustain biotic evolution, so that a succession of episodes of form-conferring supernatural intervention remains an essential feature of the creation's formational history, and the Noachian flood was a historical event within human history. However, the "days" of the Genesis 1 creation narrative could have been extended periods of time so that the scientifically-derived timetable for the universe's formational history may be accepted without fear of contradicting the Scriptures.

Progressive creationism. Like old-earth episodic creationism, progressive creationism is open to the contributions of science on such matters as the timetable of the creation's formational history. It also gives recognition to the idea, rooted in the Augustinian tradition, that the creation was provided by God with the formational capabilities needed to actualize the structures and life forms that God intended to appear in the course of time. Progressive creationism envisions God giving being at the beginning to the raw materials of the universe and generously providing them with formational powers. Then, in a progressive manner, the Spirit of God is thought to have stimulated and enabled these causal powers to actualize a vast array of preordained physical structures (like dry land and seas) and life forms (like plants, cattle, fish, and birds). The formational history of the creation is envisioned as a progressive and cooperative venture in which both divine and creaturely action contribute to the outcome.

Intelligent Design creationism. The Intelligent Design movement is a recent entry into this arena of creationist perspectives on the character and role of divine action in effecting the assembly of new creaturely forms—especially new life forms—in the course of time. Proponents of Intelligent Design argue that there is empirical evidence that the universe's system of natural capabilities for forming things is inadequate for assembling certain information-rich biological structures. And if the system of natural capabilities is inadequate, as Intelligent Design proponents argue, then these biological structures must have been assembled by the action of some non-natural agent, usually taken to be divine. Exactly how and when this divine action might have occurred is not specified. Little or no appeal is made to the biblical text to support the theological implications of this concept.

See also CREATION; CREATION SCIENCE; DESIGN; DESIGN ARGUMENT; DIVINE ACTION; GOD; INTELLIGENT DESIGN; SCOPES TRIAL; SCRIPTURAL INTERPRETATION

Bibliography

Behe, Michael J. *Darwin's Black Box: The Biochemical Challenge to Evolution.* New York: Free Press, 1996.

Dembski, William A. *Intelligent Design: The Bridge Between Science and Theology.* Downers Grove, Ill.: InterVarsity Press, 1999.

Gilkey, Langdon. *Maker of Heaven and Earth: A Study of the Christian Doctrine of Creation.* Garden City, N.Y.: Doubleday, 1959.

Johnson, Phillip E. *Defeating Darwinism by Opening Minds.* Downers Grove, Ill.: InterVarsity Press, 1997.

Morris, Henry M. *The Modern Creation Trilogy.* Green Forest, Ark.: Master Books, 1996.

Numbers, Ronald. *The Creationists: The Evolution of Scientific Creationism.* New York: Knopf, 1992.

Ramm, Bernard. *The Christian View of Science and Scripture.* Grand Rapids, Mich.: Eerdmanns, 1956.

Ross, Hugh. *Creation and Time: A Biblical and Scientific Perspective on the Creation-date Controversy.* Colorado Springs, Colo.: NavPress, 1994.

Young, Davis A. *Christianity and the Age of the Earth.* Grand Rapids, Mich.: Eerdmanns, 1982.

Young, Davis A. *The Biblical Flood: A Case Study of the Church's Response to Extrabiblical Evidence.* Grand Rapids, Mich.: Eerdmanns, 1995.

HOWARD J. VAN TILL

CREATION SCIENCE

Creation science is a science-styled activity dedicated to the goal of providing observational, experimental, and theoretical support for the basic tenets of young-earth episodic creationism. These tenets are: (1) that the world was brought into being recently (a few thousand years ago); and (2) that the basic types of physical structures (like the sun, moon, and stars) and the basic kinds of living creatures were formed by episodes of supernatural intervention during the first week after the beginning. On the basis of its interpretation of selected empirical data, creation science argues that the universe cannot be as old as the natural sciences have concluded, and that the full array of life forms could not possibly be the outcome of uninterrupted evolutionary development.

See also CREATIONISM; DESIGN; DESIGN ARGUMENT; INTELLIGENT DESIGN; SCOPES TRIAL

HOWARD J. VAN TILL

CRITICAL REALISM

Critical realism is a philosophical view of knowledge. On the one hand it holds that it is possible to acquire knowledge about the external world as it really is, independently of the human mind or subjectivity. That is why it is called *realism*. On the other hand it rejects the view of *naïve realism* that the external world is as it is perceived. Recognizing that perception is a function of, and thus fundamentally marked by, the human mind, it holds that one can only acquire knowledge of the external world by critical reflection on perception and its world. That is why it is called *critical*.

History

Critical realism arose in German philosophy in the late nineteenth and early twentieth centuries as a reaction to idealistic and phenomenalist types of philosophy. German critical realists took account of Immanuel Kant's (1724–1804) view of the subjectivity of knowledge but denied that this precludes access to "things-in-itself." In American philosophy, critical realism designates a movement initiated by Roy Wood Sellars (1880–1973) in 1916. It purported to integrate insights of both idealism and new realism, which was a naïve realist reaction to idealism. Through the work of Wilfrid Sellars (1912–1989), Roy Wood Sellars's son, critical realism influenced scientific realism, which arose in the 1950s in opposition to positivistic phenomenalism. Scientific realism basically claims that mature scientific theories are approximately true (in the sense of corresponding to the external world) and that their postulated central entities really exist.

The term *critical realism* was introduced into the dialogue between science and theology in 1966 by Ian Barbour. Barbour used the term to cover both scientific realism and a theological realism that takes seriously the cognitive claims of religion, that is, religion's claims to convey knowledge of a mind-independent divine reality. Subsequently Barbour pointed to the cognitive role of metaphors, models, and paradigms in scientific as well as religious language. His ideas were later assimilated and elaborated by Arthur Peacocke, John Polkinghorne, J. Wentzel van Huyssteen, and others. Actually, critical realism has been the dominant epistemology in the dialogue between science and theology for several decades. However, since the 1990s the transfer of critical realism from science to theology has increasingly been disputed, mainly on the ground that it does not, or does not sufficiently, do justice to the specific nature of theology.

Analysis

On closer inspection, critical realism as a view of scientific and theological knowledge comprises three theses:

(1) *Metaphysical realism,* which holds that there exists a mind-independent reality. In scientific realism this reality is the material world; in theological realism this reality is the material world and also, primarily, God.

(2) *Semantic realism,* which holds that science and theology contain propositions, that is statements capable of being true or false in the sense of correspondence to the reality to which they refer. In scientific realism the focus is on propositions about unobservable entities; in theological realism the focus is on propositions about God.

(3) *Epistemic realism,* which holds that it is possible to put forward propositions that are approximately true, that some propositions actually are approximately true, and that belief in their approximate truth can be justified. In scientific realism this applies primarily to theories and theoretical propositions about unobservable entities; in theology it applies to propositions and theories about God.

The first thesis distinguishes critical realism from idealism and positivism, but also from Hilary Putnam's (b. 1926) "internal realism," which defines reality as a function of human conceptualization of the world. The second thesis distinguishes scientific realism from an instrumentalism that regards statements about unobservable entities as useful fictions without propositional content. Similarly, it distinguishes theological critical realism from the Wittgenstein-inspired view of religious language as mere expression or recommendation of a way of life. The third thesis distinguishes critical realism from a skepticism that affirms the first and second theses but denies that it is possible to acquire justified approximate knowledge of a mind-independent reality. On the other hand, the qualification "approximate" entails a dissociation from the naïve realist claim that reality is as it is perceived.

Discussion

The main arguments in favour of scientific realism are:

(1) The fact that observation and experiments again and again compel scientists to change their prior ideas points to a substantive external input into science.

(2) The predictive success of mature theories can only (or at least best) be explained by the view that the processes, structures, and entities postulated by those theories approximate reality.

(3) The effectiveness of science-based technology can only (best) be explained by the view that mature scientific theories match nature to a substantive degree.

The main arguments against scientific realism are:

(1) Scientific theories are underdetermined by the empirical data; that is, the same data permit different theories that explain them. Therefore, empirical success is not a sufficient reason to assume that a theory is true.

(2) The history of science abounds with once empirically succesful theories that are now abandoned (e.g., a whole cluster of nineteenth-century theories assuming the existence of ether as a central entity). Therefore, empirical success is not a sufficient reason to assume that a theory is true.

(3) Scientific realism claims that those theories that offer the best explanation of the data are (approximately) true. This claim is thought to be supported by the argument that realism is the best explanation of the predictive success of science. However, this argument is viciously circular because it employs the kind of reasoning the validity of which it has to vindicate.

The main arguments in favour of transferring critical realism from science to theology are:

(1) Like science, theology makes cognitive claims.

(2) Science seeks to explain sense-experience with reference to the natural world, just as theology seeks, or should seek, to explain religious experience with reference to a divine reality.

(3) Both science and theology employ metaphors and models as approximative descriptions of an external reality.

The main arguments against transferring critical realism from science to theology are:

(1) Religious language has an expressive or recommending function, rather than a cognitive one. Therefore, theology should not be concerned with an external divine reality.

(2) Theology concerns itself with God, who is wholly different from the natural world, which is the subject matter of science.

(3) Theology cannot refer to a similar predictive success as science. Therefore, theology lacks a counterpart of the principal reason for a realistic view of science.

In evaluating a critical realist view of science and theology it may be useful to realize that the discussion of scientific realism has focused on scientific theories, especially on unobservable theoretical entities. One should not forget, however, that science is more than theories. It comprises also a wealth of observation statements and statements of primary relations, such as the statement that the specific gravity of lead is approximately 11.4. Although such statements are not theory-free, they will often have a realist plausibility that will even be acknowledged by most instrumentalists. As a consequence, a realist understanding of large parts of science seems to be a plausible option. However, scientific realism can hardly be a global view of science. Realistic plausibility has in principle to be established for each proposition and theory in particular. It would seem that this specification lessens the force of those arguments against scientific realism that aim at a global view.

As for the plausibility of transferring critical realism from science to theology, it should be realized that there are great differences between theology and science. As a reflection on religion, theology is primarily concerned with the question of the meaning of life, which implies that theology, unlike science, has an existential dimension. This does not, however, alter the fact that theological statements, insofar as they are propositions about God, make cognitive claims. Hence, critical realism is at least a logically possible view of theological propositions. But since God is not accessible to sense experience and experimental control, critical realism can hardly have the same rational plausibility for theology as for science. It would seem that a critical realist view of theology, or rather of particular theological propositions about God, is only a viable option within the context of faith.

See also COHERENTISM; EPISTEMOLOGY; KANT, IMMANUEL; REALISM

Bibliography

Barbour, Ian G. *Issues in Science and Religion* (1966). New York: Harper and Row, 1971.

Barbour, Ian G. *Myths, Models, and Paradigms: A Comparative Study in Science and Religion.* New York: Harper and Row, 1974.

Leplin, Jarrett, ed. *Scientific Realism.* Berkeley: University of California Press, 1984.

McMullin, Ernan. "Enlarging the Known World." In *Physics and Our View of the World,* ed. Jan Hilgevoord. Cambridge, UK: Cambridge University Press, 1994.

Peacocke, Arthur. *Intimations of Reality: Critical Realism in Science and Religion.* Notre Dame, Ind.: University of Notre Dame Press, 1984.

Polkinghorne, John. *One World: The Interaction of Science and Theology.* London: SPCK, 1986.

Psillos, Stathis. *Scientific Realism: How Science Tracks the Truth.* London: Routledge, 1999.

van Huyssteen, J. Wentzel. *Theology and the Justification of Faith: Constructing Theories in Systematic Theology.* Grand Rapids, Mich.: Eerdmans, 1989.

van Kooten Niekerk, Kees. "A Critical Realist Perspective on the Dialogue Between Theology and Science." In *Rethinking Theology and Science: Six Models for the Current Dialogue,* eds. Niels Henrik Gregersen and J. Wentzel van Huyssteen. Grand Rapids, Mich.: Eerdmans, 1998.

KEES VAN KOOTEN NIEKERK

CULTURE, ORIGINS OF

The dawn of culture may be the single most important development in human evolution. Sometimes people find their dependence on culture frustrating, but overall it is far more an enabler than a limitation. The human ability to think would be grossly constrained without language, however often people find themselves at a loss for words. Humans would not be human without culture to mediate their relationships with the environment, with other humans, with spirits and deities, and with abstract or imagined worlds like mathematics and the future.

Despite many suggestions, the definition E. B. Tylor used when introducing the term *culture* to anthropology is still popular: "that complex whole which includes knowledge, belief, art, morals, custom and any other capabilities and habits acquired by man as a member of society" (p. 1). Lee Cronk and others have preferred not to include behavior, seeing culture as socially transmitted information

or, as Clifford Geertz, puts it, patterns for behavior, not patterns of behavior.

Most traditional peoples have explanations of cultural origins, myths about the first fire or the gift of corn. Intensifying this quest for knowledge of cultural origins with new information about cultures all over the world, Enlightenment philosophers tried to imagine an original "state of nature." The seventeenth-century philosopher Thomas Hobbes envisioned perpetual war, concluding that individuals would gladly give up unbounded liberty for the protection of government. The eighteenth-century philosopher Jean-Jacques Rousseau's vision was a celebration of freedom, equality, and the unfettered, uncorrupted individual. But whatever life can or should be it is clear that for humans the "natural" state is within society, enveloped by culture.

What is known about the prehistory of cultural origins is easily outlined. The following scenario is primarily derived from Richard Klein, with insights from Merlin Donald on the interrelation of culture and cognition. The data suggest brief periods of rapid transition, which is one reason many paleoanthropologists prefer the Eldredge-Gould punctuated-equilibrium model of evolution to neo-Darwinism.

The appearance of flaked stone tools 2.5 million years ago, the earliest known evidence for culture, coincides with the appearance of the first people with brains proportionally larger than apes. This is Donald's *mimetic stage* of cognitive development, representing emergence of the ability to mime, to imitate, and to re-enact events. The appearance of the first people with fully human body proportions about 1.7 million years ago was probably coincident with invention of the hand axe and the first hominid movement out of Africa.

A rapid increase in brain size about six hundred thousand years ago correlates with developments in lithic technology and the appearance of archaic *Homo sapiens.* This development corresponds to Donald's *mythic stage,* in which the increased pace of technological innovation is evidence of true human language. The timing of language, however, remains deeply contentious.

The "creative explosion" or "Big-Bang" of human cultural development occurred about forty-five to fifty thousand years ago with the appearance of the fully human creative use and manipulation of culture. This development corresponds to

Donald's *theoretic* or *modern culture* stage, which was marked by the ability to enhance what is possible with the brain alone through externalization of memory.

When did human culture first appear?

One could legitimately place culture's origins at any of these stages. One could even place the origin of culture earlier, since stone tools may not be the first products of culturally based behavior; this would place the origins of culture well before the appearance of the human species. As recently as the 1970s it was a virtual truism that only humans had culture. But by 1973 Jane Goodall had recorded thirteen forms of tool use and eight social activities distinguishing the chimpanzees of Gombe in Tanzania from those at other study sites. Goodall proposed a cultural origin for these variations, and recent work has amply reinforced that view. Andrew Whiten and Christophe Boesch argue that chimpanzees display not only individual cultural traits but sets of distinctive behaviors that can be thought of as, for example, "Gombe culture" or "Teï culture."

Nonhuman culture or proto-culture is widespread among primates. Indeed, John Bonner provides many examples of animals, including birds, that are capable of behavioral transfer of information. But human culture is cumulative and makes use of symbolism. Human culture is also uniquely creative, flexible, diverse, and capable of both rapid change and remarkable stasis, even in changing environments. The "creative explosion" or "Big Bang" of human development likely represents the move from proto-culture to a truly human symbolic and cumulative culture. Human culture has become a newly emergent property of life that no longer needs to wait generations for genetic changes but can rapidly effect behavioral changes.

Sources, causes, and correlates of culture

What follows is a sampling of major contemporary theories of cultural origins, beginning with models of cultural evolution. Though not strictly theories of origins, they are essential for understanding how culture works and how cultural diversity came about.

For sociobiologists, natural selection is central, controlling even the details of human thought. Cultural origins and contemporary diversity are based on genetic differences in human populations. A recent variant, evolutionary psychology, accepts the criticism that genetic change cannot even remotely keep pace with cultural change, but retains the view that what people believe and do is based on genetic adaptations. Thus, how contemporary humans think is constrained by genes selected for the ways of life of earlier humans. Contemporary humans are basically hunter-gatherers ripped from the savanna, with mind ill suited and ill at ease with city life—a modern "expulsion from the garden" myth that attributes deep human dilemmas to gene-environment mismatch. With great clarity Holmes Rolston presents many important reasons why strong versions of these theories do not succeed. Early humans lived under varying conditions, not a single environment of adaptedness, and behaviors are not directly programmed by genes. Further, ideas can be transmitted to unrelated, even unknown, individuals.

Some scholars prefer to understand culture as radically separate from biology. This is the traditional anthropological perspective; Alfred Kroeber's influential "superorganic" notion views culture almost as having a life of its own, molding each individual far more than individuals mold culture. Memetics proposes a new kind of replicator, the *meme* an element of culture passed on by non-genetic means. Culture is a meme's way of replicating itself; beliefs and opinions are survival tricks memes use for self-perpetuation. Strict forms of these theories, however, would only work if cultures were composed of genuinely distinguishable units. In addition, the transmission processes (analogies with disease organisms abound) presume an unreasonable passivity in human communication.

Recognizing that human lives are influenced both by genes and by culturally transmitted ideas, *gene-culture co-evolution* or *dual inheritance* models ask how these influences relate. Importantly, it can be acknowledged that beliefs and behaviors are selected and transmitted by various means; it is only the overall mix that must be adaptive. William Durham demonstrates in, for example, his lactose tolerance case study that culture can be a causal force in human genetic evolution.

Sexual selection. Geoffrey Miller believes much of human culture (e.g., the arts, ritual, ideology) makes more sense as courtship display than as survival adaptation. Mate choice selects for indicators of fitness, which can explain interesting features of humanity. For example, because courtship displays need only indicate fitness, belief systems could develop that "work" even though they do not accurately depict the world.

Causal events, triggers, and mechanisms.

Another approach is to isolate one or a few variables as causes for the development of culture. Distinguishing human labor from animal behavior, the nineteenth-century social scientist Friedrich Engels proposed production as the primary factor, while Randall White and others suggest a trend toward increased group size. Social groups comprised of more people required more complicated social organization than do small, family-size groups, creating demands on communication. Michael Pfieffer has proposed an environmental change as the causal event. Rick Potts argues that the human innovation was to develop flexible cognitive abilities to face regular climate changes. Richard Klein argues that a single genetic mutation completed the modern brain, triggering the human capacity for culture. There is growing reason to believe genes are only indirectly connected to phenotype, yet there is also evidence that one change can make a dramatic difference. Michael Tomasello believes that a new form of social cognition, the ability to see other humans as intentional beings, triggered cognitive-cultural co-evolution.

Cooperation, altruism, and love.
Elliott Sober and David Sloan Wilson argue in *Unto Others* (1998) that self-giving behaviors may benefit a group enough to compensate evolutionarily for any harm caused to individuals within the group. And Adrienne Zihlman points to the great importance of mother-infant interaction in the development of primate sociality. This emotional closeness and communication prepares individuals for culturally based cooperation and self-giving better than if society is, as alternative interpretations suggest, an endless power struggle. For Catherine Key and Leslie Aiello as well, cooperation defines humanity.

Blood relations.
The developing human brain came with great costs especially to females whose reproductive strategy would have emphasized helping offspring reach maturity. The primate male strategy would have been to fertilize as many females as possible. Culture began, Chris Knight argues, when females obtained male energetic investment by confusing the males about the

female's fertility state, thus tricking the males into sticking around. Menstruation is an obvious clue to pending fertility, and males, with only one thing on their minds, would turn away from nursing females to more fertile females just when most needed. Solution? Females could paint themselves red and all would appear equally fertile.

Relevance to science-religion dialogue

Whatever else one may conclude, Knight's proposal suggests that human agency and purpose are part of what needs to be explained. From this brief survey of theories of cultural origins, it is clear that human thought is probably not genetically determined in detail. And because cultural origins and transmission are quasi-independent of genetics, one can ask of an idea not just whether it spreads genes but how well it describes the world. Humans regularly create new ideas and pass them on non-genetically. One implication is that, to the extent values and virtues are culturally based, they do not need to be explained by natural selection on genes.

It would still be valuable to know whether altruism and true other-regarding love can arise by natural selection. John Polkinghorne and his colleagues have argued that love may be a deep feature of the universe itself, not just of human cultural beliefs. The study of human cultural origins may have something to contribute to this debate.

Understanding human cultural origins is also important for the science-religion dialogue because it raises important issues for understanding each of these elements of culture. For example, to the extent that human culture and behavior are only loosely tied to our genetic variation and to our evolutionary history, the religious and scientific quests could do more to put us in touch with a reality outside of our individual subjective selves than some existing models of human nature allow. As another example, religion and ethics are very likely human universals, originating early in human cultural evolution. If love is a significant feature of reality and to the extent that human culture evolved out of cooperation and self-giving as Zilman suggests, religion and ethics could be more central to and indicative of human culture than we usually allow. Their origins could, in turn, be important in cultural origins. Could it be that the origins of the human religious, spiritual and ethical sense was an essential piece in the puzzle of the origins of human culture and so of humanity itself?

See also ALTRUISM; ANTHROPOLOGY; ART, ORIGINS OF; EVOLUTIONARY PSYCHOLOGY; EVOLUTION, BIOCULTURAL; MEMES; PALEOANTHROPOLOGY; PUNCTUATED EQUILIBRIUM; SOCIOBIOLOGY

Bibliography

Aunger, Robert, ed. *Darwinizing Culture: The Status of Memetics as a Science*. Oxford: Oxford University Press, 2000.

Bonner, John Tyler. *The Evolution of Culture in Animals*. Princeton, N.J.: Princeton University Press, 1980.

Chimpanzee Cultures. Available from: http://chimp.st-and. ac.uk/cultures.

Cronk, Lee. *That Complex Whole: Culture and the Evolution of Human Behavior*. Boulder. Colo.: Westview, 1999.

de Waal, Frans B. M., ed. *Tree of Origin: What Primate Behavior Can Tell Us About Human Social Evolution*. Cambridge, Mass.: Harvard University Press, 2001.

Donald, Merlin. *Origins of the Modern Mind: Three Stages in the Evolution of Culture and Cognition*. Cambridge, Mass.: Harvard University Press, 1991.

Dunbar, Robin; Knight, Chris; Power, Camilla, eds. *The Evolution of Culture: An Interdisciplinary View*. New Brunswick, N.J.: Rutgers University Press, 1999.

Durham, William H. *Coevolution: Genes, Culture, and Human Diversity*. Stanford, Calif.: Stanford University Press, 1991.

Klein, Richard G., and Edgar, Blake. *The Dawn of Human Culture: A Bold New Theory on What Sparked the "Big Bang" of Human Consciousness*. New York: Wiley, 2002.

Knight, Chris. *Blood Relations: Menstruation and the Origins of Culture*. New Haven, Conn.: Yale University Press, 1991.

Polkinghorne, John, ed. *The Work of Love: Creation as Kenosis*. Grand Rapids, Mich.: Eerdmans, 2001.

Potts, Rick. *Humanity's Destiny: The Consequences of Ecological Instability*. New York: William Morrow, 1996.

Rolston, Holmes, III. *Genes, Genesis, and God: Values and Their Origins in Natural and Human History*. Cambridge, UK: Cambridge University Press, 1999.

Sober, Elliott, and Wilson, David Sloan. *Unto Others: The Evolution and Psychology of Unselfish Behavior*. Cambridge, Mass.: Harvard University Press, 1998.

Tattersall, Ian. *The Monkey in the Mirror: Essays on the Science of What Makes Us Human*. New York: Harcourt, 2002.

Tomasello, Michael. *The Cultural Origins of Human Cognition*. Cambridge, Mass.: Harvard University Press, 1999.

Tylor, E.B. *Primitive Culture: Researches into the Development of Mythology and Philosophy*. London, UK: J. Murray, 1871.

Wild Chimpanzee Foundation. Available from: http://www.wildchimps.org.

PAUL K. WASON

CYBERNETICS

The term *cybernetics* is derived from the Greek word *kybernetes* (steersman). The term was introduced in 1948 by the mathematician Norbert Wiener (1894–1964) to describe how systems of information and control function in animals and machines (steersmanship). Cybernetics is inherently interdisciplinary; it is related to systems theory, chaos theory, and complexity theory, as well as artificial intelligence, neural networks, and adaptive systems. Cybernetics was formulated by thinkers such as Wiener, Ludwig von Bertalanffy (1901–1972), W. Ross Ashby (1903-1972), and Heinz von Foerster (1911–). It developed as a consequence of multidisciplinary conversations among thinkers from a variety of disciplines, including economics, psychiatry, life sciences, sociology, anthropology, engineering, chemistry, philosophy, and mathematics. Cybernetics contributed greatly to the development of information theory, artificial intelligence, artificial life, and it foresaw much of the work in robotics and autonomous agents (hence the term *cyborg* for robot).

After control engineering and computer science became independent disciplines, some cyberneticists felt that more attention needed to be paid to a system's autonomy, self-organization, and cognition, and the role of the observer in modeling the system. This approach became known as *second-order cybernetics* in the early 1970s. Second-order cybernetics emphasizes the system as an agent in its own right and investigates how observers construct models of the systems with which they interact. At times, second-order cybernetics has resulted in the formulation of philosophical approaches that, according to some critics, are in danger of losing touch with concrete phenomena.

Cybernetics moves beyond Newtonian linear physics to describe and control complex systems of mutual causalities and nonlinear time sequences involving feedback loops. It seeks to develop general theories of communication within complex artificial and natural systems. Applications of cybernetic research are widespread and can be found in computer science, politics, education, ecology, psychology, management, and other disciplines. Cybernetics has not become established as an autonomous discipline because of the difficulty of maintaining coherence among some of its more specialized forms and spin-offs. There are thus few research or academic departments devoted to it.

Because of the diffuse interdisciplinarity of cybernetics, theological, religious, and philosophical concerns and engagements are multiple. Some conversations concern the social and economic impact of computer networks, such as the internet, on culture and nature. Others concern the development of artificial life and artificial intelligence and its impact on how human intelligence and life is understood. Other theological and philosophical concerns of cybernetics include the shape of divine activity in the world, the "constructed" nature of knowledge and of ethical values, the boundaries between bodies and machines and the implications for creation, the promises of salvific technology, and a tendency to strive for a metanarrative or grand unifying theory.

See also ARTIFICIAL INTELLIGENCE; ARTIFICIAL LIFE; CHAOS THEORY; COMPLEXITY; CYBORG; PROCESS THOUGHT; SYSTEMS THEORY

Bibliography

Ashby, W. Ross. *An Introduction to Cybernetics* (1956). London: Chapman and Hall, 1999.

Hayles, N. Katherine. *How We Became Post-Human: Virtual Bodies in Cybernetics, Literature, and Informatics.* Chicago: University of Chicago Press, 1999.

Heylighen, Francis, and Joslyn, Cliff. "Cybernetics and Second-Order Cybernetics." In: *Encyclopedia of Physical Science and Technology,* 3rd edition, ed. R. A. Meyers. New York: Academic Press, 2001.

Heylighen, Francis; Cliff, Joslyn; and Turchin, V., eds.: *Principia Cybernetica Web.* Brussels, Belgium: Principia Cybernetica. Available from: http://pespmc1.vub.ac.be.

MARION GRAU

CYBORG

Cyborgs are human beings who have technical parts attached to their bodies on a semipermanent or permanent basis to enhance their capabilities. The term *cyborg* was first used in science fiction literature and refers to a convergence of human and robotic life forms; it can also be used to describe someone enmeshed in the World Wide Web. In Artificial Intelligence, the term is used to define people who wear ubiquitous computer parts (chips, storage, processors, etc.) hidden in clothes, as well as people with special glasses that enable them to be constantly online. Often the term raises fears as cyborgs challenge the boundaries of the human-machine interaction and thus our human uniqueness.

See also ARTIFICIAL INTELLIGENCE; ARTIFICIAL LIFE; CYBERNETICS; TECHNOLOGY

ANNE FOERST

CYCLICAL UNIVERSE

Within closed universe models there exists the possibility that a final Big Crunch may not be the end of the universe. It has been speculated that perhaps some mechanism exists at such infinite density that would trigger another Big Bang. Hence the Big Crunch really becomes the "Big Bounce," with the universe recycling itself for infinity. Also known as an oscillating or reprocessing universe, this idea has ancient parallels, both in the Hindu Vedas and in ancient Greece, and was even taken up by the early Christian theologian Origen (185–254 C.E.). The mechanism of a cyclical universe is considered beyond the reach of human understanding, however, because the laws of physics break down at the space-time singularity of the rebound. For this reason, and perhaps also due to a certain philosophical prejudice against the notion of a cyclical universe, the idea has never been popular in modern scientific cosmology.

See also BIG BANG THEORY; BIG CRUNCH THEORY; COSMOLOGY, PHYSICAL ASPECTS; COSMOLOGY, RELIGIOUS AND PHILOSOPHICAL ASPECTS; SINGULARITY

MARK WORTHING

DAO

The root meaning of the Chinese word *Dao* is "path" or "way." It is more commonly known in English by the older transliteration *Tao* and is one of the few Chinese words that have been adopted into the English language. This is largely due to the broad appeal of an ancient Chinese text (c. fourth century B.C.E.) known as the *Daode jing* (or *Tao-te-ching*), which, it is said, is the most widely translated book in the world after the Bible.

During the period in Chinese history known as the Warring States (481–220 B.C.E.) the Zhou dynasty empire had disintegrated into several smaller states governed by rival feudal lords. This chaotic state of affairs led intellectuals to ask "Where is the Dao?" By this they meant: What path should leaders follow to bring harmony and stability to the country? Confucians said that the way lay in restoring ancient moral and ritual codes. Legalists said that the way lay in imposing by force a single language and legal system upon the country. Daoists, whose names are not known, compiled the *Daode jing,* a collection of terse aphorisms, which states that the way that humans should follow is precisely the same "Way" that governs the operation of nature. This Way is "self-so" or "spontaneous," that is, it is naturally self-generating and cannot be artificially engineered by human intelligence or culture. To give a modern analogy, in nature acorns marvelously grow into oak trees and the various species live in an overall state of organic harmony. Nobody tells acorns or the various species what to do, yet somehow they develop

their innate potential (*de*) and entirely of their own accord follow a path (*dao*) that leads to a state of maximal perfection and harmony. The Dao may thus be understood as the wellspring of natural creativity that brings everything in the world into an organic, harmonious existence. In this respect there are many broad parallels with the process philosophy of Alfred North Whitehead (1861–1947).

In his investigations into science and civilization in China, the British biochemist Joseph Needham (1900–1995) concluded that Daoists had a natural affinity with what is now called "science," since to investigate the Way, Daoists had to pay close attention to the operation of things in nature. The difference is that science holds nature to be in principle explainable, whereas Daoists generally understand the Dao to be fundamentally mysterious and beyond human understanding.

This wondrous aspect of the Dao led to a mystical reverence for nature's marvelous capacity for self-transformation: Who could possibly have imagined that an acorn would grow into an oak tree? Some Daoists, such as Ge Hong (283–343 C.E.), became alchemists and aimed to capture for themselves the extraordinary power for change that is pregnant within nature, and to reverse it to create an elixir of immortality. Other Daoists revered this mystical aspect of the Dao in the form of gods and spirits who have power over human life and death. Still others cultivated this Dao within themselves through meditation and *Qi*-energy practices. All aimed through their various methods to attain the Way for themselves.

JAMES MILLER

DAOISM

See CHINESE RELIGIONS, DAOISM AND SCIENCE IN CHINA

DARWIN, CHARLES

Author of the *Origin of Species* (1859) and the *Descent of Man* (1871), Charles Darwin (1809–1882) famously challenged the popular belief that every species had been separately and immediately created by divine fiat. His theory of evolution by natural selection was based on what he considered an empirical fact: the presence of variation among members of every species. Darwin's powerful argument was that, in competition for limited resources, those variants having characteristics that favored them in their struggle would tend to be preserved and produce more offspring than those less advantaged. Over many generations the gradual accumulation of advantageous variations would lead to the emergence of a new species markedly different from its progenitor. Applied to humankind the argument was particularly contentious for the continuity it affirmed between animals and humans, and because the idea of species transformation was often associated with political radicalism and materialism. Darwin himself recalled that admitting the mutability of species had been like confessing to murder.

Providing a naturalistic account of species production and then of human evolution, Darwin risked offending the piety of those, including his own wife Emma Wedgwood, who wished to give the moral sense a transcendental significance. If humans had evolved from humbler species could humans be said to be made in the image of God? Was it possible to speak of an immortal soul? What remained of the argument for design, which in Christian natural theology had often presupposed the perfect adaptation of organic structures to the needs of the organism that possessed them?

Darwin was not the atheist vilified in ultra-conservative religious literature, but he did become increasingly agnostic. Attacked in the name of religious orthodoxy, he found it "ludicrous" that he had once intended to become a clergyman. This was a reference to his Cambridge education, which had followed an abortive preparation in Edinburgh for a medical career. At Cambridge, the young Darwin encountered divines such as John Henslow and Adam Sedgwick who combined scientific enthusiasm with reverence for nature as a work of creation. In Edinburgh he had moved in free-thinking circles and had been introduced to the evolutionary theory of the French naturalist Jean-Baptiste Lamarck. Darwin also knew that his grandfather Erasmus Darwin had proposed organic transformation, but Charles Darwin was not yet a convert to such ideas. On leaving Cambridge his destiny would be to find ways of explaining the appearance of design in such intricate mechanisms as the human eye without recourse to the divine "Contriver" celebrated by the theologian and philosopher William Paley in his *Natural Theology* (1802).

Darwin's research

This destiny was shaped by a five-year voyage on which Darwin embarked in December 1831 as companion to Robert Fitzroy, captain of HMS *Beagle*. The ship was sailing for South America, enabling Darwin to enlarge his horizons as a naturalist and geologist. Having been captivated by the travelogues of Alexander von Humboldt he soon luxuriated in the rain forests of Brazil. As Adrian Desmond and James Moore have observed, their sublimity afforded a surrogate religious experience: "twiners entwining twiners, beautiful lepidoptera, silence, hosanna" (p. 122). Thoughts of a Christian ministry gradually receded as Darwin was enchanted by the study of nature, delighted by the discovery of fossil bones, staggered by the number of species that had become extinct. He was intrigued by resemblances between lost and living forms, by tantalizing patterns in the distribution of flora and fauna, and by disruptive natural forces. Entering the city of Concepción in Chile he found the cathedral shattered by an earthquake. At the Southern tip of South America natives of the Tierra del Fuego were struggling to survive in one of the most inhospitable regions on Earth. The world was perhaps not the "happy world" of

Paley's English garden. Even before reading economist Thomas Malthus's *Essay on Population* in September 1838, Darwin had been "well prepared" to appreciate the struggle for existence that Malthus's arithmetic on reproductive fecundity convinced him was inexorable.

Of his visit to the Galapagos Islands it is often said that Darwin recognized that each island had its own distinctive species, eventually concluding that the different finches, for example, had diverged from a mainland ancestor, molded by nature to occupy different niches. But there was no such "Eureka" moment. Darwin had muddled his finch specimens from various islands and it was not until March 1837, following his return to England, that the ornithologist John Gould broke the exciting news that three forms of mockingbird, from different islands, were genuinely different species. Gould identified fourteen species of finch from Darwin's specimens. The enthralling question was why so many similar species lived in such proximity, but Darwin was unable to prove that the geographical isolation of each island had been responsible for the proliferation.

Darwin's earliest speculations on evolutionary change preceded his reading of Malthus. They show him playing with the idea that nature employs bisexual reproduction as a way of introducing variation into each new generation, so permitting continuing adaptation to changing conditions of existence. Darwin flirted with, but quickly rejected, the possibility of sudden mutation as a source of evolutionary change. As with the naturalist Alfred Russel Wallace later, it was when reading Malthus that the penny finally dropped and a theory of natural selection took shape.

The metaphor of "natural selection" allowed Darwin to exploit a simple analogy. Domestic animals and birds showed a degree of plasticity as breeders chose which specimens to mate when selecting for characteristics they wished to accentuate. Darwin crossed social barriers in fraternizing with pigeon fanciers and he emphasized the diversity of form ultimately derived from the common rock pigeon. Even a trained ornithologist, he argued, would be tempted to think that the pouter, runt, and fantail were not merely different varieties but different species. If, through human "selection," such effects could be produced, might not nature achieve much more in the millions of years

at its disposal? For insight into the age of the Earth and for an emphasis on the incompleteness of the fossil record, which would help him to explain the absence of transitional forms in the fossil record, Darwin was indebted to the geologist Charles Lyell.

Darwin's view of religion

Did the metaphor of "selection" imply a divine selector in the management of the evolutionary process? Some of Darwin's contemporaries believed so. Darwin's own emphasis, however, was on the interplay of unconscious forces. Without denying a creator on whom the existence of everything ultimately depended, Darwin rejected the kind of deity who might be micromanaging the process. Rejecting the argument for design as formulated by Paley, Darwin's extension of natural law to explain how new species had arisen did not preclude a transcendent legislator. In his first transmutation notebook, he wrote of a "Creator who creates through laws," one who had "impressed" certain laws on nature, as a consequence of which beautiful organic forms had evolved. Darwin resembled earlier deists, admitting the existence of a creator but doubting there had been divine revelation or intervention

In certain respects his science corroded a residual faith. The more people know of the fixed laws of nature, he wrote in his *Autobiography*, "the more incredible do miracles become" (p. 86). As his wife recognized, the questioning mentality demanded of a scientist could induce skepticism. Debating the question whether evolution was under divine control, Darwin stressed the elements of randomness in the process. His conclusion was that the variations on which natural selection worked appeared without a prospective use in mind. The presence of so much pain and suffering also affected Darwin deeply. This was difficult to square with belief in a beneficent deity, but was consistent with his hypothesis of natural selection and with what in the first full sketch of his theory (1842) he called the "concealed war of nature."

To ascribe Darwin's agnosticism to his science would, however, be simplistic. During the *Beagle* voyage he was already asking himself whether an intuitive sense of God was universal among humankind, concluding it was absent among Fuegians and native Australians. Some Christian teaching he found morally repugnant. Aware of high moral standards among the freethinkers he met in the circle of the English writer and social reformer Harriet Martineau, he declared in his *Autobiography* that the idea of eternal damnation for those outside the fold was a "damnable doctrine" (p. 87). Although opinions differ as to when he finally renounced Christianity, the death early in 1851 of his young daughter Annie produced a crisis in which belief in a beneficent God became unsustainable. His agnosticism was to be peculiar since he retained the conviction that the universe as a whole could not be the result of chance. But so nuanced was his thinking that he came to mistrust his own conviction. If the human mind was itself the product of evolution, what guarantee was there that it could be trusted when engaging such metaphysical issues?

Religious responses to Darwin's science

Religious responses to Darwin's science have varied enormously. From 1859 until the 1930s, when a powerful new synthesis of genetics and Darwinian theory appeared, the controversial status of natural selection left plenty of scope for supplementary or alternative mechanisms for evolution in which divine control was affirmed. Strictly speaking, as the biologist Thomas Henry Huxley insisted, Darwinism had no implications for the central tenets of theism. Huxley even conceded that it was still possible to assert design in an original cosmic state from which all had developed through natural processes. Modern atheists and materialists, by contrast, frequently stress the apparently directionless aspects of biological evolution, weaving them into a completely secular and naturalistic world view.

Within the Christian churches the theory of evolution, not surprisingly, continues to be a divisive issue compounding the problems posed by historical criticism of the Bible. In some religious communities it has become the symbol of secular and liberalizing values and is still vehemently resisted. Yet religious writers have also appropriated Darwin's theory for constructive purposes, as did one of Darwin's early converts, Charles Kingsley, who concluded that a deity who could make all things make themselves exhibited greater wisdom than one who simply made things. Might a unified process of evolution testify more eloquently to a single creator than piecemeal creation? Darwin's

American correspondent Asa Gray, a botanist, even suggested the theory might assist the theologians with their greatest difficulty—the problem of suffering. If competition and struggle were the prerequisites of a creative process, without them there could not have been the evolutionary development that had culminated in human intelligence and responsiveness. Darwin himself had toyed with the idea that a deity who had created the *possibility* for humans to evolve might be considered less directly responsible for the uglier facets of nature that had also been possible in such a world. Sophisticated theologians have invoked the Darwinian theory to illuminate what they see as God's self-limitation rather than coercive agency. Others have seen in evolution evidence of divine immanence and participation in the world. It was the view of nineteenth-century Oxford theologian Aubrey Moore that, under the guise of a foe, Darwin had done the work of a friend, destroying infantile images of a conjuring god who was inactive except when intervening.

See also CREATIONISM; CREATION SCIENCE; DEISM; DESIGN; DESIGN ARGUMENT; DIVINE ACTION; EVOLUTION; EVOLUTION, BIOCULTURAL; EVOLUTION, BIOLOGICAL; EVOLUTION, HUMAN; EVOLUTION, THEOLOGY OF; GENETICS; IMMANENCE; INTELLIGENT DESIGN; REVELATION; SCOPES TRIAL

Bibliography

Bowler, Peter. *Reconciling Science and Religion: The Debate in Early-twentieth-century Britain*. Chicago: University of Chicago Press, 2001.

Browne, Janet. *Charles Darwin: Voyaging*. London: Pimlico. 1995.

Burkhardt, Frederick, ed. *The Correspondence of Charles Darwin*. Cambridge, UK: Cambridge University Press, 1985.

Darwin, Charles. *The Autobiography of Charles Darwin* (1876), ed. Nora Barlow. London: Collins, 1958.

Darwin, Charles. *The Descent of Man* (1871). Amherst, N.Y.: Prometheus, 1997.

Darwin, Charles. *On the Origin of Species by Means of Natural Selection* (1859). New York: Bantam, 1999.

Dawkins, Richard. *The Blind Watchmaker*. London and New York: Penguin, 1986.

Dawkins, Richard. *Climbing Mount Improbable*. London and New York: Penguin, 1996.

Desmond, Adrian, and Moore, James. *Darwin*. London: Michael Joseph, 1991.

Durant, John, ed. *Darwinism and Divinity: Essays on Evolution and Religious Belief*. Oxford: Blackwell, 1985.

Haught, John. *God After Darwin: A Theology of Evolution*. Boulder, Colo.: Westview Press, 2000.

Hodge, Jonathan, and Radick, Gregory, eds. *The Cambridge Companion to Darwin*. Cambridge, UK: Cambridge University Press, 2002.

Kohn, David, ed. *The Darwinian Heritage*. Princeton, N.J.: Princeton University Press, 1985.

Kohn, David. "Darwin's Ambiguity: The Secularization of Biological Meaning." *British Journal for the History of Science* 22 (1989): 215–239.

Larson, Edward. *Evolution's Workshop: God and Science on the Galapagos Islands*. London and New York: Penguin, 2001.

Livingstone, David. *Darwin's Forgotten Defenders: The Encounter Between Evangelical Theology and Evolutionary Thought*. Grand Rapids, Mich.: Eerdmans, 1987.

Moore, James. *The Post Darwinian Controversies: A Study of the Protestant Struggle to Come to Terms with Darwin in Great Britain and America, 1870–1900*. Cambridge, UK: Cambridge University Press, 1979.

Numbers, Ronald. *The Creationists*. New York: Knopf, 1992.

Roberts, Jon. *Darwinism and the Divine in America: Protestant Intellectuals and Organic Evolution 1859–1900*. Madison: University of Wisconsin Press, 1988.

Ruse, Michael. *Can a Darwinian be a Christian? The Relationship Between Science and Religion*. Cambridge, UK: Cambridge University Press, 2001.

Ward, Keith. *God, Chance, and Necessity*. Oxford: One World, 1996.

JOHN HEDLEY BROOKE

DARWINISM

See DARWIN, CHARLES; EVOLUTION, BIOLOGICAL; EVOLUTION, HUMAN; NEO-DARWINISM

DARWINISM, NEO

See NEO-DARWINISM

DARWINISM, NEURAL

See NEURAL DARWINISM

DARWINISM, SOCIAL

See EVOLUTION, BIOCULTURAL; SOCIOBIOLOGY

DEATH

Within the popular Western Judeo-Christian tradition, death has usually been understood to be a consequence of original sin. This has, of course, not been a scientifically informed belief. And where theology has been in conversation with science on this point, or when theology is indirectly informed by a growing ecological consciousness, natural death in and of itself is increasingly seen as a natural piece of the creation that God called good.

Western religious perspectives

The growing perspective that death according to natural processes is not necessarily a consequence of sin would cohere with the early Christian tradition, as well as with Eastern Orthodox theology. The second-century Christian theologian Irenaeus, for example, emphasized how the first parents, as described in one of the Genesis accounts, were driven out of paradise so that they would not eat of the tree of life after they had sinned. Their being secured from that temptation by expulsion into a hard life was thus a gift—for who would want to live eternally estranged from God?—and presupposes that they were mortal beings. Indeed, death was already part of the natural order designed by God. Eastern Orthodoxy reiterates this anthropology with its emphasis on the incarnation as more a leading of humanity into the next aspect of

God's creative work than of rescue from sin and evil; the need for Christ to redeem the creation from the new exigency of sin was, as it were, added to the original agenda of leading the creation into the new age.

Western theology is beginning to adapt this perspective. Christian theologians like Karl Rahner (1904–1984) and Karl Barth (1886–1968) at the beginning of the twentieth century already recognized this impulse, and such thought is more advanced in this ecumenical age. Death is not so readily understood as an "evil." It is, rather, a "problem" in Christianity because sin became attached to it. Sin constitutes alienation from God, and thus the experience of death most often is attended by fear, loneliness, and loss. Though biblical scholars still debate the meaning of the apostle Paul's assertions that the wages of sin are death (Rom. 5:12) and that the travails of the creation are attributable to human sin, more and more exegetes are less willing to claim biblical warrant for the dominant Augustinian idea that physical death, along with physical suffering and corruptibility, are consequences of the Fall. Further, an ever more scientifically informed consciousness, one that ever more understands how consciousness itself has evolved from simple matter, is also less inclined to fix material processes, including natural physical death, in dualistic terms of good and evil. Concurrently, such consciousness may recognize that its own knowledge of finitude—and so, an intuited transcendence—is precisely the "problem" that is occasioned by fear of death.

Other religious perspectives are less ambivalent in asserting a spiritual origin to death, and will ascribe death more to God's direct agency than to natural processes. Islamic thought, like some Christian perspectives, links natural death more specifically to the will of God. The Qur'an teaches of death that God determines the span of a person's life: "He creates man and also causes him to die" (Qur'an, XLV:26). How this might cohere with Western religious notions of divine agency, design of creative processes, and so forth, are a ripe field for exploration as the science-theology dialogue begins more to engage Islamic scholars.

Eastern religious perspectives

Hindu tradition, with all its variety, is distinguished by the doctrine of the transmigration of the soul, that is, the passing at death of the soul from one body or being to another. Life and death are aspects of an eternal cycle, as over and against the linear understanding of time embedded in Western science and theology. This process of *samsara* refers to journeying or passing through a series of incarnational experiences. One's karma accompanies one through these stages, and can be roughly defined as the moral law of cause and effect. Some popular reflection attempts to correlate karmic doctrine with Newtonian physics. The thoughts and actions of the past determine the present state of being, and in turn present choices influence future states. This karmic process characterizes the ever-changing flow of everyday experience, as well as the successive rounds of deaths and rebirths. Each moment conditions the next, and karma impacts the reincarnational flow of being.

An interesting new trajectory might yet be explored with respect to the linking of the spirituality of Hindu self-abnegation and new science. According to Hinduism, underlying the apparent separateness of individual beings is a unitary reality. Just as the ocean is composed of innumerable drops of water, so undifferentiated being manifests itself in human experience as apparently separate selves. The goal of life—lives—is, in the end, to realize the eternal self, or Atman, which by nature defies description. This assuredly difficult task (of the realization of something beyond description) aspires to deliverance from a potentially endless cycle of birth, death, and rebirth. To achieve deliverance, one must act with pure insouciance and detachment, with no attentiveness to cause or effect or reward; "one must act without desire or purpose, independently of the results of the action (Kramer, p. 33)." Thereby the detached self dies to self and into Krishna, becoming a "True Self." The goal of Hindu religion, in other words, is to transcend or leave karma and its cause and effect activity behind, which is perhaps not unlike new science's movement away from Newtonian physics.

The general understanding of death in Buddhism in all its varieties (Zen, Tantric, etc.) is not greatly different from Hindu thought. Generally (there are notable variations in Buddhist thinking) Buddhism understands death as a transition toward either phenomenal rebirth or release from the phenomenal realm into pure *nibbana* (nirvana). Practicing a life that would ensure the latter, or at least ensure a return to a desirable station after rebirth, requires total moderation of self-will and desire. Death itself involves grieved losses; thus, a certain kind of pastoral care obtains at Buddhist funerals. Even so, death is a phenomenon to be transcended, and so a reality that is not as real or as significant as the transcendent. A Buddhist, in other words, might well question the relevance of an entry about death. Likewise with other Asian religions. Confucianism, the philosophy of Lao Tze, and Daoism, for example, significantly moderate the Buddhist perspective of death, and locate the meaning of life more in practiced simplicity and propitious behavior than in preparing for a hereafter. There are ritually correct ways to conduct life and death, and so human consciousness is at its best simply when it is attentive to the fullness of the present.

Death and ultimate destiny

Finally, the question of whether death is an *end* is, to be sure, energetically discussed. This, of course, is where religious faiths diverge from final entropy as the last word. Christians believe in a resurrection of the dead—though not necessarily in physicalist terms—which is subject to a coming judgment by God and the possibility of eternal joy (heaven) or despair (hell). Within Judaism, only the most mystical and apocalyptic fundamentalists share any similar concept. In the main, Judaism understands the legacy of a person's life as the moral example left to the next generations. Biophysically there is nothing more. Islamic thought, on another hand, is more detailed with respect to an afterlife and the Qur'an vividly describes the spiritual cum physical states of bliss or torment that await after death. Some of the above, though certainly not all, could cohere with contemporary scientific perspectives. Natural science understands death as the final expenditure of energy, as dissipation into stasis. Yet, that which has decomposed may well be fodder for the recycling of life. Stars turn to dust, stardust has come to mind in human being, human being may become again stuff for stars, and untold other phenomena. Nevertheless, death as a modus unto new, organized, and sentient life is not a theme that natural science readily explores or articulates.

See also ESCHATOLOGY; FALL; ETERNITY; KARMA; LIFE AFTER DEATH; TRANSMIGRATION

Bibliography

Hefner, Philip. *The Human Factor: Evolution, Culture, and Religion*. Minneapolis, Minn.: Fortress Press, 1999.

Kramer, Kenneth, *The Sacred Art of Dying: How World Religions Understand Death*. New York: Paulist Press, 1988.

Pannenberg, Wolfhart. *Anthropology in Theological Perspective,* trans. Matthew J. O'Connell. Philadelphia: Westminster, 1985.

Reynolds, Frank E. "Death as Threat, Death as Achievement." In *Death and Afterlife: Perspectives of World Religions,* ed. Hiroshi Obayashi. New York: Greenwood Press, 1992.

Reynolds, Frank E., and Waugh, Earle H., eds. *Religious Encounters with Death: Insights from the History and Anthropology of Religions*. University Park: Pennsylvania State University Press, 1977.

DUANE H. LARSON

DEEP ECOLOGY

The term *deep ecology* was coined by Norwegian philosopher Arne Naess (b. 1912) in 1973 to contrast two different approaches to environmental concerns. Whereas *shallow ecology* merely seeks to avoid excessive pollution and resource depletion, deep ecology advocates the need for fundamental shifts in perception, values, and lifestyles. Its basic premises are the intrinsic value of nature, the critique of industrial materialism and technology, and the application of ecological principles to human moral evaluations and actions. The word *deep* refers to the level at which human purposes and values are questioned. The goal of deep ecology is to clarify value priorities when establishing policies and practices.

Naess, influenced by Dutch philosopher Baruch de Spinoza and Indian political and spiritual leader Mohandas Gandhi, advocates a philosophy of ecological harmony and equilibrium (*ecosophy*) through four levels of questioning: (1) ultimate premises based on a person's worldview, for example, a particular religion or philosophy; (2) eight "Platform Principles" as common core principles independent of worldview; (3) general consequences derived from the platform; and (4) concrete decisions chosen by individuals and groups. Deep ecology challenges religions to respond to the concerns of environmental philosophy and so encourages the interconnection between religious and philosophical worldviews, scientific and empathetic studies of nature, and public policy and ethics. Deep ecology has been criticized for insufficient attention to gender issues, biocentric egalitarianism, and not adequately addressing economical and political injustices.

See also ECOFEMINISM; ECOLOGY; ECOLOGY, ETHICS OF; ECOLOGY, RELIGIOUS AND PHILOSOPHICAL ASPECTS; ECOLOGY, SCIENCE OF; GAIA HYPOTHESIS

Bibliography

Devall, Bill, and Sessions, George. *Deep Ecology: Living as if Nature Mattered.* Salt Lake City, Utah: Gibbs Smith, 1985.

Naess, Arne. "The Shallow and the Deep: Long-range Ecology Movements." *Inquiry* 16 (1973): 95–100.

Naess, Arne. *Ecology, Community and Lifestyle,* trans. and ed. David Rothenberg. Cambridge, UK: Cambridge University Press, 1989.

Reed, Peter, and Rothenberg, David. *Wisdom in the Open Air: The Norwegian Roots of Deep Ecology.* Minneapolis, Minn.: University of Minnesota Press, 1993.

Rothenberg, David. *Is It Painful to Think? Conversations with Arne Naess.* Minneapolis, Minn.: University of Minnesota Press, 1993.

Sessions, George, ed. *Deep Ecology for the Twenty-First Century.* Boston and London: Shambala, 1995.

ROALD E. KRISTIANSEN

DEISM

Deism is the belief in a creator God who does not have any subsequent influence upon the world. Deism became influential in the West beginning in the seventeenth century, when it was seen that modern physics is compatible with an initial act of supernatural creation but appears to leave no room for subsequent interventions by God into the natural order. Although deism stands in marked contrast to traditional Jewish, Christian, and Muslim accounts of God's providential activity in the world, it is often advanced as an answer to the problem of evil: If God is unable to act in the

world, God cannot be responsible for the suffering that arises within it.

See also CLOCKWORK UNIVERSE; EVIL AND SUFFERING; GOD; MONOTHEISM; NATURAL THEOLOGY; PANENTHEISM; PANTHEISM; THEISM

PHILIP CLAYTON

DESCARTES, RENÉ

René Descartes's philosophical importance for the advent of the modern scientific age is matched only by the difficulty of fully evaluating what his doctrines imply for religion. Born in Poitou, France, in 1596, Descartes lived most of his adult life in Holland, incurring the opposition, but also gaining the support, of Catholics and Protestants alike. He died in 1650 in Stockholm, where Queen Christina of Sweden had invited him to reside and instruct her in philosophy.

In his lifetime, he published works in both French and Latin, aimed at two slightly different audiences: *Discourse on the Method of Rightly Conducting Reason and Reaching the Truth in the Sciences* (French, 1637), *Meditations on First Philosophy* (Latin, 1641), *Principles of Philosophy* (Latin, 1644), and *Passions of the Soul* (French, 1649). Descartes also left unfinished works, notably *Rules for the Direction of the Mind* (Latin), *The Search for Truth* (Latin), *The Universe or Treatise on Light* (French), and *Treatise on Man* (French), as well as a voluminous correspondence in both French and Latin.

Method and faith

As a boy, Descartes attended the Jesuit College of La Flèche. Recalling his education in *Discourse on the Method*, Descartes denounces bookish learning and the vain pretense of scholastic philosophy, but favorably cites his love of poetry, his delight in mathematics, and his reverence for "our" theology. He emphasizes being firmly taught that revealed truths are above human intelligence. Stating moreover that the truths of faith have "always been first" in his beliefs, he explicitly says that these truths must be "set apart" from human opinions and must not be subjected to his method of universal doubt.

Descartes consistently maintains this position throughout his work, from the early and unpublished *Rules for the Direction of the Mind* to the mature *Principles of Philosophy,* where article seventy-six gives divine authority unambiguous precedence over human reason. Youthful diaries dating from his years of wandering and soldiering (1618–1620) reveal a feverish, unconventional, religious imagination, coupled with devout impulses.

A critical aspect of Descartes's mature philosophy for issues of science and religion is that his theory of mind (*res cogitans*) explicitly privileges free will over cognition. During an extended stay in Paris from 1620 to 1627, Descartes had frequent exchanges with leading religious figures: Marin Mersenne (1588–1648), who was also educated at La Flèche; Guillaume Gibieuf, a priest of the Oratory busy writing a book on freedom of the will; and Cardinal Pierre de Bérulle, who encouraged Descartes to pursue his reform of philosophy as a duty and vocation. In *Rules for the Direction of the Mind,* composed in the immediate wake of these meetings, Descartes affirms that revealed truths are held with even greater certainly than natural truths since "faith rests, not on an act of intelligence, but an act of will." He also distinguishes between cognition as such and the faculty of "affirming and denying" in an attempt to explain error, but the second faculty is not yet clearly identified with the free will, as it will be in the *Meditations* (1641) and in article thirty-two of the *Principles of Philosophy* (1644).

In 1628, Descartes moved to Holland in search of solitude. A letter to Mersenne dated April 15, 1630, reveals the extent to which physics and metaphysics were indivisibly combined in this search. Descartes explains that he would not have discovered the foundations of physics if he had not started with the rational discovery of self and God, which is indeed everyone's "first duty." God, Descartes maintains further, is "the first and most eternal" truth from which "all other truths proceed." Most dramatically, Descartes affirms that eternal truths are created: God has freely decreed that two and two make four, so that mathematical truths "depend on God's will no less than creatures." By 1630, while solving problems of mechanics and conducting dissections in his home, Descartes thus conceptualized divine freedom, the new physics, human self-knowledge, and dependence on God as intricately connected.

Cartesian naturalism

When Descartes learned of Galileo's condemnation in 1633, he cancelled plans to publish the cosmological *Universe or Treatise on Light* designed to unveil his new philosophy, citing at a later date "those whose authority has hardly less power over my action than my own reason over my thoughts." Instead, he published the *Discourse on the Method* anonymously in Leiden in 1637, along with "samples" of what his new method could achieve in geometry, optics and meteorology. Presenting his proof of self and God as pivotal to his own intellectual awakening, Descartes launches a framework in which physical phenomena, including biological phenomena, can be investigated experimentally according to materialist principles, while special mental events exhibiting voluntary features and characteristic of human beings are set apart and assigned to a distinct immaterial principle. In the *Discourse,* Descartes proceeds naturalistically in so far as he cites the empirical evidence of languages to conclude that the human "rational soul" is "in no way drawn from the potentiality of matter" and is therefore "not liable" to die with the body.

Cogito and freedom

Objections from all sides greeted Descartes's radical move to explain biological phenomena by means of inert microcorpuscular processes, as well as Descartes's bold noetic proof of self ("I think, therefore I am") and God. In 1639, desirous to clarify his views and to answer his critics, Descartes began writing his masterpiece, *Meditations on First Philosophy,* published in Paris in 1641. Composed in Latin, the text of the *Meditations* is followed by objections and answers, and is dedicated to Paris theologians. This time, the reader is led through a six-day journey of introspection and analysis designed to purge the mind of naïve empiricism, secure new grounds of noetic truth by rooting the human soul in God, and promote scientific investigation of the material universe (*res extensa*) as a way to cultivate personal happiness while working for the common good. From the demonic ordeal of the first day to the orderly reintegration of soul and body on the last, Descartes's core concern is to champion the inalienable gift of freedom that marks human beings as created in God's image. God, Descartes explains, has "left it in my power not to err" since he is always free to suspend judgment when evidence is insufficient. No evil demon, however powerful, can compel him to affirm as true what is merely doubtful. Human freedom thus manifests the will's inherent predilection for what is good and true, even in the absence of any known good or truth. Moreover, clarification in *Meditation* VI that the senses are meant for immediate survival and must therefore not usurp the function of reason in proposing to our freedom truths to be affirmed allows the same responsible exercise of judgment afforded by geometry to extend to the physical and experimental sciences.

The moral value of the scientific project thus lies primarily in the special opportunity it provides for deliberately searching out and affirming the truths that God has freely decreed. Significantly, in the *Principles of Philosophy,* charmingly dedicated to his favorite pupil Elizabeth of Bohemia, the principle of human freedom (article six) precedes the principle of cognitive certainty or *cogito* (article seven): The freedom to abstain from error is even more fundamental than the first cognitive certainty *I think; I am.* And as article thirty-seven goes on to explain, a human being's principle perfection lies in having a free will, and people act worthily whenever they deliberately choose what is true.

Further development of Descartes's views relating to proper use of the free will, truth, and human happiness, is found in Descartes's numerous letters to Elizabeth, and in the treatise on *The Passions of the Soul,* published in 1649. Descartes distinguishes between autonomous acts of will that terminate in bodily actions and those that terminate "in the soul itself, as for example, when we resolve to love God, or more generally, apply our thought to some immaterial object." Acts of the will that are based on false opinions leave one vulnerable to regret and remorse, while those that are securely based on knowledge of the truth lead instead to happiness and inner serenity. Descartes's letter to Queen Christina dated November 20, 1647, may serve to summarize Descartes's integration of religion and science since he declares that the highest good, for each and every human being, consists in "a firm will to do what is good and in the serenity to which this leads."

Influence

Although what is crudely described as *Cartesian dualism* has been mostly rejected by later philosophy, the problem of human freedom raised by Descartes and explained by him on the basis of a distinct, substantial, and immaterial spiritual principle (*res cogitans*), has be no means disappeared. The linguist Noam Chomsky has repeatedly drawn attention to some of the advantages of Cartesian rationalism for the defense of universal human dignity. In France, the philosopher Nicolas Grimaldi continues to emphasize the relevance of Cartesian freedom, while Jean-Luc Marion has in turn used Descartes as a springboard to elaborate new perspective on ethics. Most importantly, Cartesian scholars continue to discover seminal ideas in Descartes regarding the spiritual dimension of science. Daniel Garber, in particular, has shed light on the distinctive metaphysical features of Cartesian physics; Gary Hatfield has called attention to the deeply religious character of Descartes's notion of force; and Matthew Jones has initiated new questions on the spiritual dimension of Descartes's mathematics.

See also CARTESIANISM; FREEDOM; MODERNITY

Bibliography

Chomsky, Noam. *Language and Thought.* Wakefield, R.I.: Moyer Bell, 1993.

Cottingham, John, ed. *Descartes.* Oxford: Oxford University Press, 1998.

Cottingham, John, ed. *The Cambridge Companion to Descartes.* Cambridge, UK: Cambridge University Press, 1992.

Descartes, René. *Oeuvres de Descartes,* eds. Charles Adam and Paul Tannery. Paris: Cerf, 1897–1913.

Garber, Daniel. *Descartes' Metaphysical Physics.* Chicago: University of Chicago Press, 1992.

Gaukroger, Stephen. *Descartes: An Intellectual Biography.* Oxford: Clarendon Press, 1995.

Grimaldi, Nicolas. *Six Etudes sur la Volonté et la Liberté chez Descartes.* Paris: Vrin, 1988.

Hatfield, Gary. "Force (God) in Descartes' Philosophy." *Studies in the History and Philosophy of Science* 10 (1979): 113-140.

Jones, Matthew. "Descartes's Geometry as Spiritual Exercise." *Critical Inquiry* 28 (2000): 40-71.

Marion, Jean-Luc. *Sur la theologie blanche de Descartes.* Paris: Presses Universitaires de France, 1981.

Rorty, Amélie Oksenberg, ed. *Essays on Descartes' Meditations.* Berkeley and Los Angeles: University of California Press, 1986.

Rodis-Lewis, Genevieve. *Descartes.* Paris: Librairie Generale Française, 1984.

ANNE A. DAVENPORT

DESIGN

The apparent evidence of intelligent design in the universe has historically provided a kind of argument for the existence of God. The argument from design has evolved over time and in relation to changing scientific and philosophical perspectives. Interestingly, it has been formulated and reformulated in ways that show responsiveness to the discoveries and challenges it has encountered from science. This history of interaction reflects both the tensions and support at play between science and religion. Whatever tensions lie between science and religion, however, are in many instances eclipsed by tensions within them. Scientists, for example, disagree with one another as to whether there is, in fact, evidence of intelligent design in the universe. Theologians, conversely, differ as to whether and to what extent such evidence should have bearing upon the question of the existence of God.

The argument from design (the teleological argument) should first be distinguished from its close relative, the cosmological argument. In the cosmological argument, existence of the cosmos as a whole, because it is contingent and is not self-explanatory, serves as a kind of argument for the existence of God. God becomes the answer to the question "Why is there something and not nothing?" The cosmological argument for the existence of God is put forward on the ground *that* something exists, whereas the argument from design works from *what* exists. The world evidences order, adaptation, directionality—design, therefore an intelligent designer must have brought it into being.

This argument gets the name *teleological* from the Greek word *telos,* which means "end" or "goal." Teleological order entails the notion that processes or structures are fitted to bring about certain results, and in that sense are "designed." The concept of teleological ordering is not simple causal ordering. To say that the wind is fitted to circulate dust in the air is an example of causal ordering, but to say the eye is fitted for sight is an example of teleological ordering, pertaining to the adjustment of means to ends.

Greek philosophy and the early church

Accounting the history of the argument from design presents something of a challenge because the argument has followed a long and winding road with many interesting turns and occasional dead ends along the way. Historian Norma Emerton gives a fuller accounting of this history in "The Argument from Design in Early Modern Theology" (1989), but this brief treatment can only present an aerial survey of the landscape the argument has traversed. Forms of the argument in Western classical tradition go back at least as far as the early Greeks. The pre-Christian Stoics believed that the order and harmony of the cosmos demanded explanation. In 45 B.C.E. the Roman lawyer Cicero in his book *The Nature of the Gods* presented both pro and con arguments. Speaking for the Stoics, who favored a teleological view, Cicero posed the question, "When we see a mechanism such as a planetary model or a clock, do we doubt that it is the work of a conscious intelligence? So how can we doubt that the world is the work of the divine intelligence?" Cicero also presented the contrary view of the Atomists (Epicureans) that "The world is made by a natural process, without any need of a creator. . . . Atoms come together and are held by mutual attraction" (2.97). No intelligent designer need be postulated. If there were an intelligent designer, the atomist Lucretius argued, the world in some respects is really badly designed.

The early Christian church eagerly took up the idea of nature as a witness to God. In *Against Marcion* (1.18) Tertullian even spoke in terms of a double revelation in "God's two books": the book of nature (God's work) and the Bible (God's Word). Nature's design, as seen in the order and beauty of the heavens, the anatomy and physiology of living creatures, and the suitability of the environment to support life, became and has continued to be for Christian theology a pointer to God.

The Middle Ages: classic formulation

After the fall of the Roman Empire in the fifth century C.E., interest in the natural world dwindled and with it the pursuit of both science and natural theology. It was not until the thirteenth century that long lost classical philosophy and science were rediscovered. With this turn the argument from design reemerged and received its classic formulation.

Aristotelian physics with its emphasis on causality became widely influential. Purely physical processes were frequently explained in terms of "ends." For Aristotle there were four distinguishable types of cause: *final cause* (the maker of an object), *formal cause* (the design or blueprint according to which it is made), *material cause* (the raw material from which it is made) and *efficient cause* (the effort applied in actually making the object). At this time, the debate turned upon whether there is a formal cause (a design) and, having established that, proceeded to make theological claims of a final cause (a designer); if there is a design there must be a designer.

Christian theologian Thomas Aquinas was conversant with the science and philosophy of his day, and Aristotelian physics shaped his theology. The assumptions that an effect cannot be greater than its cause and that something can be *known* of the cause by observing the effect became building blocks of his particular formulation of the argument from design. Aquinas's arguments for the existence of God work *a posteriori* from observed facts of existence (effects) to what must be the case in the way of a *cause* to bring about such an effect. The most famous of his arguments are the "five ways."

Aquinas's "fifth way"(*Summa Theologica,* Part I, Question 2, Article 3) is perhaps the closest to the present concern. It starts from the orderly character of mundane events. Things meet their goals, even things that lack consciousness. Yet nothing that lacks awareness can tend toward a goal without direction from something that has awareness. As an arrow requires an archer to reach its goal, so also universal order points to the existence of an intelligent *orderer* of all things. For Thomas all causes acting in the physical universe are instrumental and have to be "used," as it were, by a primary agent. To assume that all this causation is self-explanatory is like expecting that a bed will be constructed if only one puts the tools and materials together "without a carpenter to use them." Aquinas then images God on the model of an artisan (in the mode of final cause).

Also relevant is the first of the "five ways." In thirteenth-century physics and astronomy, the four basic elements were thought to be under the dynamic influence of the stars, and lower celestial bodies were considered to be moved about by those at greater distance from the Earth. Everything that moved did so because it was moved by something else. God was the *Unmoved Mover* behind all the motion.

The section in the *Summa Theologica* where the "five ways" are presented is a response to the question, "Is there a God?" It begins with the objections that there must not be a God because there is evil in the world and because natural effects can be explained by natural causes. Interesting, these same objections still play an important part in contemporary discussions.

The scientific revolution: challenges and new forms

When Isaac Newton began working out the physical laws of nature during the late seventeenth century, he demolished one form of Aquinas's argument from design when he explained the motion of bodies according to fundamental mechanical physical laws. There was no longer need to appeal to direct divine intervention to move things around in space. However, in another sense, Newton only reformulated the argument, for he assumed God was the architect of the physical laws he had discovered. Science could explain matter and motion without recourse to supernatural forces, but these mechanical secondary forces were simply the working out of structural conditions given by God at the creation.

As many new discoveries were made during the scientific revolution, there came to be greater ambivalence about the place of natural theology. Some theologians were concerned that natural theology might usurp revelation. Conversely, some scientists were concerned that appeal to final causes might usurp attention to physical causes. Science needed to preserve its integrity and avoid becoming a "quarry" that was mined for theological arguments. Nevertheless most theologians, philosophers, and scientists (people like Francis Bacon, Robert Boyle, René Descartes, and Newton) assumed the legitimacy of natural theology.

Eighteenth and nineteenth centuries: new form and challenges

In the eighteenth century philosopher William Paley in *Natural Theology: Or, Evidences of the Existence and Attributes of the Deity, Collected from the Appearances of Nature* (1802) reformulated the argument from design by attending to specific instances of design. He took the eye as a case in point and the ways in which the parts of the eye cooperate to produce sight. To explain this adaptation of means to ends, he claimed, one needs to postulate an intelligent designer, much as one would if one found a watch while crossing a heath; rather than assume the watch had come together by chance, one would assume an intelligent designer put it together.

David Hume in *Dialogues Concerning Natural Religion* (1779) attacked Paley's position for privileging the model of human design of artifacts. This approach, he claimed, skews the argument. Why not use another model, for instance the model of biological generation, which does not require intentional design? One could as easily say the universe is like an organism, therefore there must be a cosmic womb.

Paley had his defenders, those who preferred his analogy to Hume's. They observed that in biological generation creatures reproduce themselves rather than producing new and various things. When one asks why a rabbit has organs that are so well adapted to meet its needs, one is not helped by the answer that this is because it springs from other rabbits that were similarly adapted. Hume countered that if the best answer to such a problem is that there is an intelligent designer, then one still has to give an account for why the designer has a mind that is so well-fitted for designing. If the design comes from the designer, where does the designer come from? With either option, one ends up with an infinite regress.

Immanuel Kant in his *Critique of Practical Reason* (1788) also put forward objections to the argument from design. He thought that science and religion should be completely separate, and natural theology was for him a contradiction in terms. Nevertheless, he said in the conclusion to the *Critique,* "Two things fill my mind with wonder and awe . . . the starry sky above and the moral law within" (p. 166). Still, it was the latter—the moral law within—and not the former that he took to be the clearer pointer to God and God's goodness.

With the publication of Charles Darwin's *Origin of the Species* in 1859, the argument from design met a truly formidable challenge to its credibility. In the theory of evolution there came to the fore a genuine alternative explanation for apparent design in organisms. One was not left with mere chance on the one hand, or intelligent design on the other. Organic structures come to be what they are by development from simpler forms through purely natural processes of mutation and natural selection over an extended period of time.

No intelligent designer is needed to design the eye for sight.

Twentieth century: new forms and new challenges

One might think that Darwin had dealt arguments from design the decisive blow, but the argument arose with new vitality in the twentieth century. The shape was, however, no longer examination of the particular instances of design but the general principles behind apparent design. In a manner parallel to what happened with Newton's discovery of physical laws, with Darwin's discovery of principles of natural selection the theological interest shifted from particular divine interventions to the wider divine design. What makes mutation and natural selection work in the way that it does? How did material existence come to be self-organizing in the way that it is?

This approach began taking shape in the 1920s with the work of Frederick R. Tennant in *Philosophical Theology* (1928–1930). He presents a fresh discussion of the teleological argument pointing to six kinds of adaptation that seem to evidence design and, when taken together, to point toward a theistic interpretation:

(1) The intelligibility of the world.

(2) The adaptation of living organisms to their environment.

(3) The ways in which inorganic life is conducive to the emergence and maintenance of life.

(4) The way in which the natural environment nurtures moral development in human beings through coping with hardships.

(5) The overall progressiveness of the evolutionary process.

(6) The aesthetic value of nature.

Here, in rudimentary form, are the elements of what became the argument from design in the contemporary discussion—the intelligibility of the universe and its suitability for life. Interestingly, these newly emerging forms of the argument arise from science, while some of the direct challenges to grounding intelligent design thinking in observations of the natural world come from of theology.

Theologian Karl Barth, for example, exemplifies a twentieth-century theological disillusionment with natural theology—the idea that there is a point of contact whereby one may easily perceive who God is by studying the natural world. Barth's context, Germany during the rise of the Third Reich, shaped his theological critique. The risk of natural theology is that what one discovers will not be God, but one's own reflection, which one then names as God. It is too easy to find God in one's race, culture, and interests. Barth observed the failure of Protestant liberalism to issue a prophetic challenge. He insisted on the prophetic distance of revelation over against the "culture Christianity" of his day. So the early Barth said no (*Nein!*) to natural theology and cautioned that God is "wholly other."

A second theological challenge to intelligent design thinking arose in twentieth-century experience with the problem of evil. This is not a new challenge, but one to which any form of the argument from design (in any age) has to give a thoughtful response. But during the twentieth century, the challenge of the problem of evil was sharpened in new ways. The optimism of the Enlightenment and the nineteenth century was severely chastened. With two world wars, the Holocaust, and ethnic cleansing, evil has proven too pervasive and too heinous to be dismissed as a brief passage on the way to God's good ends, the necessary dark shades in God's beautiful painting.

Theological responses to this challenge have been mixed. In response to the problem of evil, for example, some maintain design, by which they mean a kind of divine blueprint is working itself out inexorably and in all its detail. If one could but see world processes from God's perspective, all evil would be only *apparently* evil, a matter of one's limited perspective or a necessary means to some greater good. Other theologians, especially process theologians, are willing to rethink the meaning of design in the face of evil. If absolutely everything that happens comes about by God's design, then what does one make of all the blind alleys, waste, suffering, and evil that have attended this process so carefully designed and closely controlled by God?

Design in the early twenty-first century

In the early twenty-first century, the discussion of design is being engaged with renewed vigor. Discussion centers on the somewhat negative evaluations emerging from chaos theory and evolutionary biology, and around more positive evaluations based upon the intelligibility of the universe and the suitability of the universe for the emergence of life. In these discussions, there are differences of viewpoint within the fields of theology and science that are every bit as great as some of the differences between these fields. It is not uniformly the case that theology affirms design while science denies it; the discussions are much more nuanced than that.

The reintroduction of the role of chance and contingency in the way the world works has, for many, challenged notions of design. Ian Stewart in *Does God Play Dice? The Mathematics of Chaos* (1989) has noted that with the advent of quantum mechanics the clockwork universe of Newton's day has become a cosmic lottery. "The very distinction . . . between the randomness of chance and the determinism of law, is called into question. Perhaps God can play dice, and create a universe of complete law and order, in the same breath." As one learns more about chaos theory, the question becomes "not so much *whether* God plays dice but *how* God plays dice" (p. 1–2).

Biologist Jacques Monod in *Chance and Necessity* (1972) expressed the conclusion of some: "The ancient convenant is in pieces: Man at last knows that he is alone in the unfeeling immensity of the universe, out of which he has emerged only by chance. Neither his destiny nor his duty have been written down" (p. 167).

Theologians who wish to uphold design are responding variously to chaos theory and the observations of science that much of what occurs in the universe is random activity, pure chance. A great deal depends upon their differing understandings of what one must mean by God's "design" as presented above. Those who mean "a detailed preexisting blueprint in the mind of God" hold a view that is antithetical to chance. These theologians tend to argue that what appears to be random is only apparently so. They point out that even Albert Einstein held the position that what appears to be a random occurrence would prove not to be random if only the causal activity behind it could be seen.

Other theologians do not understand design in such a constraining mode. They would allow that it might be part of the "design" that some things happen by necessity, others by chance, and others in open interplay of relative freedom. The design might include contingency as well as regularity, chaos as well as order, novelty as well as continuity. Design might simply mean setting the systemic conditions that make life and consciousness possible, and then allowing it all to unfold. This view has the capacity to incorporate elements of chance as well as necessity into "design." This shift has profound implications for the way in which God and God's relation to the world are viewed. As John Polkinghorne expressed it, this view is "consistent with the will of a patient and subtle Creator, content to achieve his purposes through the unfolding of process and accepting thereby a measure of the vulnerability and precariousness which always characterize the gift of freedom by love" (1987, p. 69).

Process theology takes this general approach but allows for a more interactive role for God. God's purposes are expressed not only in setting the unchanging structural conditions and then letting things be, but also in the novel possibilities introduced. Divine creativity works within order and chaos, persuading toward good ends. It works with and does not coerce the self-creating activity of creatures.

Evolutionary biology, generally speaking, excludes appeal to the notion of intelligent design in organisms. The explanation of life in all its diversity, according to neo-Darwinist Francisco Ayala, lies in the blind, unguided, and mechanical process of natural selection. There are teleological processes internal to organisms; the heart, for example, has the purpose of pumping blood. However, these are not to be accounted for by divine design but through the process of natural selection and the development over time of features that prove reproductively successful. This process needs no external teleology directing it from outside. If there is anything like a "goal" or "end" to which things tend, it is reproductive efficiency.

To these assumptions, most contemporary theologians (except for creationists who reject evolutionary theory altogether) would accede. The question may still be posed as to why all things are oriented toward reproductive success. Can one infer, for example, that ultimate reality is in some sense fecund and biophilic? Why does natural selection work in the way that it does? How did material existence come to be self-organizing in the way that it is? Moreover, the mode of operation of evolution is a source of wonder that seems to point

beyond itself. Differentiation, self-organization, and interrelation seem to characterize the evolutionary process. As Paul Davies points out, life forms have emerged from primeval chaos in a sequence of self-organizing processes that have progressively enriched and complexified the evolving universe in a more or less unidirectional manner. All this diversity, as John Haught has noted, comes from the informational sequencing of only four DNA acid bases. It is a remarkable state of affairs.

Nature seems to operate with a kind of "optimization principle" whereby the universe evolves to create maximum richness and diversity. Davies observes "that this rich and complex variety emerges from the featureless inferno of the Big Bang, and does so as a consequence of laws of stunning simplicity and generality, indicates some sort of matching of means to ends that has a distinct teleological flavor to it" (1994, p. 46).

As Paul Davies observed, "Human beings have always been struck by the complex harmony and intricate organization of the physical world. The movement of the heavenly bodies across the sky, the rhythms of the seasons, the pattern of a snowflake, at the myriads of living creatures so well adapted to their environment—all these things seem too well arranged to be a mindless accident. It was only natural that our ancestors attributed the elaborate order of the universe to the purposeful workings of a deity" (1994, p. 44). However, with the increased understanding that science has brought, one no longer needs explicit theological explanations for these phenomena. The questions that remain concern why the universe is lawful, coherent, and unified in this way. Why is it intelligible? Scientists themselves normally take for granted that people live in a rational, ordered cosmos subject to precise laws that can be uncovered by human reasoning. Yet why this is so remains a "tantalizing mystery" (Davies 1992, p. 20). Ian Barbour quotes Einstein as saying, "the only thing that is incomprehensible about the world is that it is comprehensible" (1990, p. 141).

Not all scientists agree here, however. Theoretical physicist Steven Weinberg at the end of his book, *The First Three Minutes* (1977), makes the statement, "the more the universe seems comprehensible, the more it also seems pointless" (p. 149). Analysis of cosmos does not, for him, yield clear and evident purpose. Advocates of the anthropic principle, John Barrow and Frank Tipler (also theoretical physicists), make a different interpretation. The very laws that Weinberg takes to be indifferent to human beings seem to them to suggest the presence of an intelligence that "wanted" human beings to evolve.

Biological systems do have some very particular requirements and these requirements are in fact met by nature. There are cosmic coincidences of striking proportions. For example, if the expansion rate of the universe after the Big Bang were greater by an infinitesimally small proportion, stars and planets would not have formed. If it were any smaller, the universe would have collapsed upon itself. Similarly, the inverse square laws that apply to gravitational, electric, and magnetic forces are essential to the stability of the atoms and solar systems. Even a small change in the force-distance relation would jeopardize life as we know it. There are countless other instances of what Barbour has called "remarkable coincidences" (p. 136)

The odds against this special set of physical conditions and natural laws that make our lives possible are astronomical. The theoretical physicist Stephen Hawking has said, "The odds against a universe like ours emerging out of something like the Big Bang are enormous. I think there are clearly religious implications" (p. 121).

Detractors will say that one could only observe a universe that is consistent with one's existence (the weak form of the anthropic principle). Moreover, there is a possibility that there are an infinite number of universes. It is also possible that other, vastly different, forms of life have emerged elsewhere under different initial conditions and physical laws, although, as of 2002, none are known and this remains an open question.

If it is the case that the existence of life requires finely tuned conditions and these do in fact exist, then the suggestion of intelligent design does not seem an extravagant metaphysical claim. It is not more extravagant than the claim for infinite random universes. Some would apply the criterion of Ockham's Razor and argue that the hypothesis that there exists an intelligent designer serves as a simpler and therefore better explanation (applying Ockham's Razor criterion).

Theological responses to the argument from design emerging from some scientific accounts of the intelligibility of the universe and its suitability for life are mixed. From this scientific picture of the universe, many theologians are willing to make the interpretive leap to the existence of an intelligent designer—a creator with an investment in life, and even, apparently, intelligent life. If one does see design, it is hard not to make the leap to thoughts of an intelligent designer. While one may imagine a designer without a design, a design without a designer would be a surprising thing indeed.

Nevertheless, many theologians do not want to invest too much import in the argument from design. This is, in part, because the evidence is ambiguous. Scientists do not all agree, for example, that evolution manifests the directionality that is often appealed to as evidence of design. Paleontologist Stephen Jay Gould holds that while early evolution might be said to *complexify* (there was no other direction to go), as things steadied out life randomly got simpler as often as it got more complex. Complex life forms are actually disadvantageous; they are easy prey to mass extinctions that periodically plague the planet.

Even if the weight of scientific opinion were clearly in the side of design in the universe, the leap to an intelligent designer is still a large interpretive leap, and not one that all impartial observers would make. And even if this be granted as a reasonable inference from the evidence, a "designer" is not yet "God" in the sense of the creator of all things visible and invisible, infinite in goodness, wisdom, and power.

Theologically speaking, the argument from design is somewhat limited in its efficacy. At best, it is a pointer toward God; it cannot offer a convincing proof for God's existence. For the believer, evidence of design in the universe seems a kind of confirmation that there is reason to believe that it is not *unreasonable* to believe. Whether one believes or does not believe is a question of interpretation, as some would have it, "a leap of faith." One that is inevitably "underdetermined by the data."

The current state of the discussion between theologians and scientists is one of active engagement and mutual illumination. There are exciting new directions and many diverse perspectives represented. Old assumptions that theologians will uniformly support arguments from design while scientists will uniformly oppose them, simply do not hold. Scientists, for example, disagree with one another as to whether there is in fact evidence of intelligent design in the universe. Theologians, conversely, differ as to whether and to what extent such evidence would have bearing upon the question of the existence of God. The questions remain open and interesting.

See also ANTHROPIC PRINCIPLE; ARISTOTLE; CHAOS THEORY; CONTINGENCY; COSMOLOGICAL ARGUMENT; CREATION; CREATIONISM; CREATION SCIENCE; DESCARTES, RENÉ; DESIGN ARGUMENT; DIVINE ACTION; EINSTEIN, ALBERT; EMERGENCE; EVIL AND SUFFERING; EVOLUTION; EVOLUTION, BIOLOGICAL; GOD; INTELLIGENT DESIGN; MUTATION; NATURAL THEOLOGY; NEWTON, ISAAC; PROCESS THOUGHT; REVELATION; SUPERNATURALISM; TELEOLOGICAL ARGUMENT; THOMAS AQUINAS; TWO BOOKS

Bibliography

Alston, William P. "Teleological Argument for the Existence of God." In *Encyclopedia of Philosophy*, ed. Paul Edwards. New York: Macmillan, 1967.

Ayala, Francisco. "Darwin and the Teleology of Nature." In *Science and Religion in Search of Cosmic Purpose*, ed. John Haught. Washington D.C.: Georgetown University Press, 2000.

Barbour, Ian. *Religion in an Age of Science*. San Francisco: HarperCollins, 1990.

Bourke, Vernon J. "St. Thomas Aquinas." In *Encyclopedia of Philosophy*, ed. Paul Edwards. New York: Macmillan, 1967.

Davies, Paul. *The Mind of God: The Scientific Basis for a Rational World*. New York: Simon and Schuster, 1992.

Davies, Paul. "The Unreasonable Effectiveness of Science." In *Evidence of Purpose: Scientists Discover the Creator*, ed. John Marks Templeton. New York: Continuum, 1994.

Emerton, Norma. "The Argument from Design in Early Modern Theology." *Science and Christian Belief* 1, no. 2 (1989): 129–147.

Genet, Russell Merle. "Is Evolution Evolving: Evolutionary Direction and Humanity's Place In It." *Science and Spirit* 9, no. 1 (1998): 2–3, 20–21.

Haught, John, ed. *Science and Religion in Search of Cosmic Purpose*. Washington, D.C. Georgetown University Press, 2000.

Hawking, Stephen. *Stephen Hawking's Universe*. New York: William Morrow, 1985.

Kant, Immanuel. *Critique of Practical Reason*, trans. Lewis White Beck. Indianapolis, Ind.: Bobbs Merrill, 1956.

Monod, Jacques. *Chance and Necessity: An Essay on the Natural Philosophy of Modern Biology,* trans. Austryn Wainhouse. London: Collins, 1972.

Murphy, Nancey, and Ellis, George, eds. *On the Moral Nature of the Universe: Theology, Cosmology, and Ethics*. Minneapolis, Minn.: Fortress, 1996.

Paley, William. *Natural Theology: Or, Evidences of the Existence and Attributes of the Deity, Collected from the Appearances of Nature* (1802). Indianapolis, Ind.: Bobbs-Merrill, 1964.

Polkinghorne, John. *One World: The Interaction of Science and Theology*. Princeton, N.J.: Princeton University Press, 1987.

Polkinghorne, John. "A Potent Universe." In *Evidence of Purpose: Scientists Discover the Creator,* ed. John Marks Templeton. New York: Continuum, 1994.

Stewart, Ian. *Does God Play Dice? The Mathematics of Chaos*. Oxford: Basil Blackwell, 1989.

Templeton, John Marks, ed. *Evidence of Purpose: Scientists Discover the Creator*. New York: Continuum, 1994.

Tennant, Frederick R. *Philosophical Theology*. Cambridge, UK: Cambridge University Press, 1928–1930.

Weinberg, Steven. *The First Three Minutes: A Modern View of the Origin of the Universe*. New York: Basic Books, 1977.

Wilcox, David. "How Blind is the Watchmaker?" In *Evidence of Purpose: Scientists Discover the Creator,* ed. John Marks Templeton. New York: Continuum, 1994.

ANNA CASE-WINTERS

DESIGN ARGUMENT

The argument from design argues from the order, adaptation, and directionality evident in the cosmos that an intelligent designer (whom theologians call God) must have brought it into being. In religion and science discussions this argument has held a prominent place historically and is continually reformulated in response to discoveries and challenges from science. There is an ongoing discussion among scientists as to whether the cosmos in fact manifests sufficient order, adaptation, and directionality to indicate design. Discussion continues among theologians as well concerning the effectiveness and limitations of an argument from design for establishing the existence of God.

ANNA CASE-WINTERS

DETERMINISM

The concept of determinism conveys the idea that everything that happens could not have happened in a different way than it actually did. Or alternatively, everything that happens, happens by necessity. However, as simple as this may sound, the concept of determinism is one of the most difficult and controversial concepts in Western philosophy.

Philosophers often distinguish different kinds of determinism. First, there is *scientific determinism,* which was inspired by classical physics. One interpretation entails that everything in the universe is governed by universal laws. *Universal* in this context means that the laws are the same everywhere in the universe and at all times, and that they apply to all events and objects. A second interpretation of scientific determinism holds that every event has a sufficient cause. These two interpretations of scientific determinism combined can yield an argument for *Laplacian determinism*: If every event has a sufficient cause, and if every event is governed by universal laws, then one could in principle predict exactly the subsequent evolution of the universe if one had knowledge of all the initial conditions of all objects in the universe combined with knowledge of all the laws of nature.

Note first that this interpretation denies the existence of chance or probabilistic laws. Since the second half of the twentieth century, however, more and more scientists argue that not all natural laws are deterministic, but that some of these laws may be inherently statistical in nature. This line of argument could constitute an argument for indeterminism, and is explored further by Karl Popper (1902–1994). Note furthermore that, though Laplacian determinism is an ontological view, it is mostly formulated in epistemic terms, relating to knowledge and predictive capabilities. Hence, as John Earman argues, one must keep in mind that scientific determinism is first of all a claim about how the world is constituted. As such one must distinguish this ontological claim from the epistemological claim to predictability, even though both often go together. That determinism does not always entail predictability is testified by chaotic systems, which display deterministic though unpredictable behavior.

If scientific determinism is taken seriously, it can result in a worldview that affirms the concept of *metaphysical determinism.* Metaphysical determinism conveys the idea that if everything in the universe is governed by universal laws, and if every event has a sufficient cause, then there is only one history possible. One can clarify this idea by using possible-world semantics. If a possible world starts off with exactly the same initial conditions as the actual world and with exactly the same universal laws, its evolution would look the same in every detail. As such, metaphysical determinism entails scientific determinism, but not necessarily vice versa, even though scientific determinism could be used to defend metaphysical determinism.

Both metaphysical and scientific determinism are threatened by the indeterminism of quantum mechanics, when interpreted as an ontological feature of the world. If at the quantum level there is genuine indeterminism, then, it might be argued, not everything has a sufficient cause, so that the histories of two possible worlds with exactly the same initial conditions, but with quantum indeterminism, might develop in completely different ways. However, scientists like David Bohm (1917–1992) have tried to restore determinism at the quantum level by invoking hidden variables, though this proposal is not uncontroversial. Furthermore, it must be kept in mind that quantum theory might not be the final theory, but might in the future be replaced by an alternative theory that forces its philosophical interpretation to affirm either determinism or indeterminism.

A third kind of determinism, closely related to scientific determinism, is *mathematical determinism.* Mathematical determinism is the "logical" complement of scientific determinism, and has become increasingly important in chaos theory. In mathematical determinism the initial conditions are numerical inputs, and a mathematical function takes the place of the universal law. Mathematical determinism now entails that, given an arbitrary value of the initial conditions, calculating the mathematical function will yield one and only one outcome. In other words, given an arbitrary value of the initial conditions and a mathematical function, there is only one outcome possible. In the case of mathematical chaotic systems, problems arise with specifying the initial value. Because knowledge of the initial conditions is limited, the outcome of a chaotic evolution cannot be predicted, yet as a mathematical system it is deterministic, which means that the outcome of the calculation, given the initial conditions, could not be other than it actually is.

A fourth kind of determinism is *logical determinism*. Logical determinism is about propositions, and entails that any proposition about the past, present, or future of the world is either true or false. As such, logical determinism is grounded in Aristotle's law of the excluded middle, which holds that a proposition cannot be both true and false at the same time. Developments in so-called "fuzzy logic" have challenged this kind of determinism.

Theological determinism constitutes a fifth kind of determinism. There are two types of theological determinism, both compatible with scientific and metaphysical determinism. In the first, God determines everything that happens, either in one all-determining single act at the initial creation of the universe or through continuous divine interactions with the world. Either way, the consequence is that everything that happens becomes God's action, and determinism is closely linked to divine action and God's omnipotence. According to the second type of theological determinism, God has perfect knowledge of everything in the universe because God is omniscient. And, as some say, because God is outside of time, God has the capacity of knowing past, present, and future in one instance. This means that God knows what will happen in the future. And because God's omniscience is perfect, what God knows about the future will inevitably happen, which means, consequently, that the future is already fixed.

All forms of determinism (except perhaps mathematical determinism) challenge the idea of free will. Or rather, they render the experience of free will an illusion. Theological determinism moreover raises big problems for the idea that God is perfectly good. For, if everything is God's action, the evil and suffering that happens is also due to God's actions. Or, alternatively, if God already knows what evil will happen, why does God not prevent it from happening? Some theologians have argued for divine self-limitation (*kenosis*) of God's omniscience and omnipotence to warrant human freedom.

See also CAUSALITY, PRIMARY AND SECONDARY; CHANCE; CHAOS THEORY; CLOCKWORK UNIVERSE; CONTINGENCY; DIVINE ACTION; FREEDOM; HEISENBERG'S UNCERTAINTY PRINCIPLE; INDETERMINISM; KENOSIS; OMNIPOTENCE; OPEN UNIVERSE; PHYSICS, CLASSICAL; PHYSICS, QUANTUM

Bibliography

Berofsky, Bernard. *Determinism.* Princeton, N.J.: Princeton University Press 1971.

Earman, John. *A Primer on Determinism.* Dordrecht, Netherlands: D. Reidel, 1986.

Laplace, Pierre Simon Marquis de. *A Philosophical Essay on Probabilities,* trans. from the 6th edition by Frederick Wilson Truscott and Frederick Lincoln Emory. New York: Dover, 1952.

Polkinghorne, John, ed. *The Work of Love: Creation as Kenosis.* Grand Rapids, Mich.: Eerdmans; London: SPCK, 2001.

Popper, Karl. *The Open Universe: An Argument for Indeterminism.* London: Routledge 1982.

Weatherford, Roy. *The Implications of Determinism.* London and New York: Routledge 1991.

TAEDE A. SMEDES

DEUS EX MACHINA

See GOD OF THE GAPS; SKYHOOKS

DHARMA

Dharma literally means "what holds together" and thus is the basic Hindu concept for all order, whether individual, social, or cosmic, as established by the Veda. For moral or social behavior it is codified in the teachings of the Laws of Manu. For traditional views of scientific knowledge, arising from the Veda, it is knowledge of the cosmic order of the universe. According to Mimamsa philosophy, dharma is what is enjoined in the Veda. It is religious duty which, when performed, brings merit to the individual and fosters the inherent order of the universe. Its neglect brings personal demerit and cosmic chaos.

See also BUDDHISM; HINDUISM

HAROLD G. COWARD

DIALOGUE

See MODELS; SCIENCE AND RELIGION, METHODOLOGIES; SCIENCE AND RELIGION, MODELS AND RELATIONS

DIRECTIONALITY

See CONVERGENCE; TEILHARD DE CHARDIN, PIERRE

DISORDER

Disorder can be described as the absence of structure and differentiation. Its religious and scientific connotations have been negative in many cultures, identifying God as the source of creational order. In thermodynamics, the entropy of a closed system is a measure of its disorder, which can only increase in due course of time. Chaotic systems show disorder, insofar it is impossible to indefinitely predict the behavior of their elements. Still, an overall structural order can emerge from inherent disorder, which may indicate that systemic order is transcended disorder and that a certain amount of disorder is necessary for emergent and adaptive structural processes.

See also CHAOS THEORY; EMERGENCE; ENTROPY

DIRK EVERS

DISSIPATIVE STRUCTURES

Dissipative structures are nonequilibrium thermodynamic systems that generate order spontaneously by exchanging energy with their external environments. Dissipative structures include physical processes (e.g., whirlpools), chemical reactions

(e.g., Bénard cell convection), and biological systems (e.g., cells). Chemist and physicist Ilya Prigogine (b. 1917), whose research on dissipative structures has been seminal, found that these structures, when far from equilibrium, can transform small-scale irregularities into large-scale patterns. The most intriguing application of Prigogine's ideas is to the origin of life and biology generally. It is an open question whether the complexity and specificity inherent in biological systems can be reduced to the thermodynamics of dissipative structures.

See also COMPLEXITY; ENTROPY

WILLIAM A. DEMBSKI

DISSONANCE

See MODELS; SCIENCE AND RELIGION, METHODOLOGIES; SCIENCE AND RELIGION, MODELS AND RELATIONS

DIVINE ACTION

One fundamental theme in the theistic religious traditions has been that God acts purposefully to call the world into being and to guide its history. Judaism, Christianity, and Islam all include in their sacred scriptures substantial (and overlapping) collections of stories about divine action. These stories present a drama of magnificent scope, setting human events in the wider context of cosmic history and portraying God's relationship with humans as an ongoing dialogue characterized by repeated divine initiatives, inconstant human responses, painful reversals, and renewed opportunities. The God of the biblical narratives establishes a covenant with Abraham, liberates the Hebrew people from slavery and gives them the law, makes Israel an independent kingdom, raises up prophets who call the nation to justice, and judges and sustains the people in their tragedies of political defeat and exile. Christians take up these stories and interpret them in terms of their conviction that God has acted in a stunning new way in Jesus of Nazareth, and Muslims later proclaim that the history of divine action receives its definitive articulation in the text of Qur'an given by Allah to the Prophet Mohammed. Each of these religions of the book places stories of divine action at the center of its understanding of God; God is known, in part, as the One Who Acts in these ways, and divergences in the stories told by these traditions contribute crucially to differences in their conceptions of the character and purposes of God. The canonical narratives, therefore, do not remain simply a record of past understandings of God's activity; rather they set the context within which communities of faith interpret their contemporary experience as part of an ongoing history of divine action in the world.

Modern challenges

In addition to playing this central role in the theistic traditions, the idea that God acts in the world raises a host of difficult questions. The transition from sacred stories to theological claims about divine action involves subtle interpretive judgments. The biblical texts, for example, do not speak with a single voice, but rather depict God in strikingly diverse ways; in order to construe them as contributing to a relatively unified narrative of God's acts, decisions must be made about which elements are central and which are peripheral, and these theological choices can generate a wide range of different readings. Further, modern techniques of critical scholarship have contributed greatly to understanding the literary forms, functions, and history of these texts. One effect of this scholarship has been to show how complicated it is to move from scriptural stories to conclusions about historical events. A theologian who appeals to biblical and liturgical talk about God's mighty acts in history must think through what this language means once it is granted that the stories are not straightforward reports of surprising things that happened long ago. If, for example, one acknowledges the legendary and symbolic character of significant aspects of the exodus story, and if one doubts that each of the miraculous divine interventions occurred just as it is related in the text, then what should one say about what God did to liberate the Hebrew people from slavery in Egypt? This is a question that Langdon Gilkey (1919–) pressed with great effectiveness against the biblical theology movement, represented by theologians

like G. Ernest Wright (1909–1974) and Reginald H. Fuller (1915–), who insisted that God is known through mighty acts in history but who were unwilling to take at face value the biblical stories of those acts.

The natural sciences raise additional powerful questions for traditional claims about divine action. In a prescientific view of the world, one compelling way to make sense of events is to ascribe them to the action of person-like but super-human powers. With the rise of the sciences, these supernatural agencies and teleological (i.e., purposive) explanations tend to be displaced in favor of appeal to efficient causes that are themselves a part of nature. As the various sciences developed, the web of explanations they offer has expanded and become increasingly integrated in interlocking structures of natural law. At the same time, the sciences have progressively eliminated from their theories the remaining elements of explicit theological explanation that reflect the close historic association of science and religion. A paradigm here, perhaps, is the transition from Isaac Newton (1642–1727) to Pierre-Simon Laplace (1749–1827). Newton's calculations indicated that there would be accumulating errors in the orbits of the planets. This, he suggested, is corrected by God, who intervenes periodically to set the solar system aright. A hundred years later, Laplace demonstrated that these variations in orbital speed are part of a mathematically predictable cycle, and it is said that when he was asked about the role of God in his physics, he triumphantly replied that he had "no need of that hypothesis." The sciences, it appears, can get along perfectly well without appealing to God as a element in their account of the world. Theologians have had to grapple, therefore, with questions about the relation between the traditional affirmation that God acts in the world and scientific accounts of that world as an intelligible natural order. How do God's purposes engage a world whose history develops within a finely woven skein of natural law?

Creation as God's fundamental act

At the heart of virtually any theological account of divine action will be some understanding of God's fundamental activity as creator. Creation has been construed in various ways in the history of the theistic religions, but one particularly prominent view has understood creation as a free and intentional divine act that calls the world into being and continuously sustains its existence. There are four elements in this account. First, creation is a free divine act in the sense that it does not follow necessarily from the divine nature; God could exist without the world in undiminished fullness of being. God chooses to create not because God must have the creature, but because it is good for the creature to be. The act of creation, therefore, is an expression of generosity and love. Second, creation is an intentional action insofar as God brings the world into existence knowingly and purposefully. These first two claims distinguish classical accounts of creation from emanationist accounts, such as that of the neo-platonic philosopher Plotinus (205–270 C.E), according to which the perfection of being in God necessarily overflows into a progression of diminishing forms of existence. Third, perhaps the most striking feature of this theological view is that God's creative act accounts for the very being of the creature. There is no pre-existing unformed "stuff" that constrains and shapes God's creative choice. God creates from nothing (*ex nihilo*), that is, apart from God's creative act, nothing at all would exist other than God. Finally, the world that God creates has no power to continue to exist on its own. Finite things depend at every moment on a divine creative action that continuously sustains, or conserves, their existence. Creation, therefore, is not a one-time event completed at some moment long ago but rather is an ongoing active relationship of God to the whole finite world throughout its history. This stands in contrast to the view associated with eighteenth century deism, which responded to the rise of Newtonian mechanics by arguing that the creator establishes the structure of the world and then leaves it to exist and to operate on its own.

This way of thinking about God's action at the foundation of the world will pervasively shape one's interpretation of traditional talk about God's action within its history. On this account of creation, every event in the world depends upon the action of God; it will be true to say that God acts in all things. Theologians have not wanted to conclude from this, however, that God is the only effective cause or agent, or that created causes merely appear to bring about effects in the world while God alone directly produces all change. Views of this sort came to be called *occasionalism,*

because they regard created causes merely as occasions for the action of God in bringing about the effect. In rejecting this view, Thomas Aquinas (c. 1225–1274) affirmed that God gives created things active and passive causal powers of their own, that is, the capacity to affect other things and to be affected by them. God is always the primary cause who directly sustains the existence of every creature, but God also chooses to act indirectly through the operation of created, or secondary, causes. This provides a further sense in which events in the world may be understood as God's acts, namely, that God acts by means of the order of nature to produce effects in the world. This mode of divine action is analogous to indirect human action in which various means are used to achieve one's ends. Aquinas notes that when the artisan uses a hammer and chisel to shape stone, the effect is produced both by the tools and by the human agent who wields them, though the two causes operate on different levels. Similarly, God acts by means of the entire network of causal relations that constitutes the created world. God's engagement with finite causes goes much deeper, of course, than the involvement of human agents with the tools they use. For God directly sustains the very existence of the finite cause (traditionally called *divine conservation*) and, on some accounts, empowers it to act as it does (traditionally called *divine concurrence*). Hence, by establishing the lawful structures of nature and setting the boundary conditions under which they operate, God indirectly produces the vast range of effects that together make up the history of the universe. Indeed, if the universe were a causally closed, deterministic system, then everything that happens would be an indirect act of God. On the other hand, if the universe includes moments of indeterministic openness within its structure (e.g., either as chance or as self-determining freedom), then God will set the direction of cosmic history but not necessarily specify all of its details.

The classical conception of creation that underlies this account of divine action is by no means the only view found in the theistic traditions. Process, or neo-classical, theologies reflect a contemporary alternative approach that has different implications for divine action in the world. These theologians make use in various ways of the thought of Alfred North Whitehead (1861–1947) and Charles Hartshorne (1897–2000). Within

Whitehead's metaphysical scheme, every entity, from the simplest elements of the physical world to God, is a creative synthesis of relations to others. God is not the absolute source of the world's existence, rather God and the world together constitute the basic structure of reality, which is a process of creative becoming. God plays a central role, however, in the world's unfolding history, for God makes a crucial contribution to the direction of each entity's development and God embraces that individual's achievement within the ongoing divine experience. On this view, God acts in every event to lure and persuade, and though God's power is limited, the reach of God's influence is not. Charles Hartshorne explores similar ideas about the inherently social nature and persuasive power of God, but develops them through the analogy of divine embodiment in the world. God and world form an organic unity of many distinct sub-centers of activity; God shares the experience of all the parts and acts through them with an immediacy analogous to (but even more profound than) that with which humans act through their bodies. Once again, God's powers of action are limited by the given structure of the divine life as a social organism and by the partial independence and self-creativity of the constituents that are united in this structure. One of the strengths of this approach, however, is that it provides a vivid expression of God's universal responsiveness and preeminent influence in shaping the destiny of the cosmos.

Particular divine action

The theistic traditions have affirmed not only that God shapes the overall direction of cosmic history through the act of creation, but also that God acts in particular events to advance the divine purposes for the world. The mighty acts of God related in the biblical stories provide paradigmatic examples of this form of divine action. Modern theologians have struggled to know what to say about particular divine action. There are at least three senses in which specific events might be singled out as acts of God in a special way. First, an event may be distinguished from others by virtue of its disclosive, or revelatory, importance. Particular events may become the occasion through which individuals and communities recognize with special clarity the presence and purposes of God. It need not be the case that God acts in these events in a way that is different from God's universal action in every event. What marks them out as special is not a distinctive mode of divine action within them but rather their power to reveal and exemplify the direction of God's work in history. If, for example, the escape of the Hebrew people across the shallows of the Red Sea involved only the ordinary processes of nature coupled with free human decisions, this event may reveal for this community God's liberating purposes. Second, an event may be distinguished from others by virtue of its causal role in advancing God's purposes in the world. Once again, the event need not be brought about by God in any distinctive way; one can suppose that God acts in this special event in just the way God acts everywhere, namely (on the classical account) as the creator and sustainer of a system of natural causes and free human agents. Yet this event may in fact mark a turning point in the progress of God's purposes in history. The escape of Hebrew people, according to this view, not only discloses God's intentions to humankind, it also advances God's intentions in a particularly significant way. Third, an event may be distinguished from others because God acts directly in it to turn events in a direction they would not otherwise have gone. What makes the event special is that God acts, on this occasion, to alter the course of the world's history. On this view, God not only acts indirectly through created causes and agents, God also acts directly in the world to bring about particular states of affairs. An event of this sort may or may not evoke a recognition of God's working, and it may or may not represent an especially significant turning point in the course of events, but even if it remains hidden in the minutia of history, it constitutes a particular divine action in the world.

Many modern theologians have sought to avoid this third, and strongest, claim about divine action and have interpreted traditional talk about God's acts in history exclusively in terms of the first two. This treats particular divine action as a subset of God's universal activity as creator; it incorporates the idea of divine providence entirely into the doctrine of creation. At the founding of modern Protestant theology, for example, Friedrich Schleiermacher (1768–1834) contended that God bears the same relation to every event, though some events play a special role in awakening in human beings a deepened experience of their absolute dependence upon God as the source of all things. This approach has important implications for a number of central topics in Christian theology (e.g., in giving an account of the person and work of Christ), and is a matter of controversy. There are powerful considerations that push in this direction, however, not the least of which are those derived from the impact of the natural sciences.

It has become commonplace for modern theologians to argue that a scientifically informed understanding of the world presents fatal objections to the assertion that God acts in history to affect the course of events. Rudolph Bultmann (1884–1976), for example, contended that one cannot embrace a scientific world view and also affirm that God acts within objective history. The lawful structures described by the sciences leave, in Bultmann's phrase, "no room for God's working," and any divine action will necessarily be a miraculous intervention that disrupts the natural order. Similar claims have been made by a succession of contemporary theologians. Bultmann's solution was to insist that God's action should be understood as an engagement with the human self that leaves the natural order untouched. This strategy can succeed, of course, only if one thinks that selves can be affected without altering their physical conditions, and if this idea is rejected, then it is far from clear that God can interact with embodied persons without affecting the natural world.

There are at least two considerations at work in these scientifically based worries about particular divine action. Both have to do with miracles, understood in the rather artificial but familiar modern sense of divine actions that contravene the structures of nature. The first concerns the epistemic status of claims about miracles. Although it is sometimes said that science has shown that miracles cannot occur, there is little prospect of vindicating this general claim. It is more plausible to note that scientifically literate people find their expectations about the world to have been shaped in ways that raise significant evidential barriers to accepting claims about miracles. David Hume (1711–1776) gave early and elegant expression to an argument that it will always be more reasonable to conclude that testimony about miracles is mistaken or fraudulent than to believe that a well-evidenced law of nature has been abrogated. There are also distinctively theological objections to giving miracles a pervasive role in one's account of divine action. Nonetheless, while there are good reasons for caution about claims regarding miracles, it important

to note that, at least on a classical account of creation, there is no theological ground for denying that the creator of the universe is free to act in ways that exceed the causal powers of creatures.

The second issue concerns the claim that any divine action that affects the course of events will necessarily constitute a miraculous intervention in the lawful structures of nature. This conclusion may appear inevitable if one thinks of the natural order as a deterministic system; it appears that in a closed structure of sufficient finite causes, God can act either by determining the design of the structure in the initial act of creation or by miraculously intervening within it. In the modern discussion of divine action it has often been assumed that universal causal determinism has been endorsed by the natural sciences, either as result of its investigations or as a presupposition of its methods. There are good reasons not to embrace this conclusion, however. Determinism has neither been established nor refuted by the sciences to date; rather, it represents a metaphysical view that extrapolates beyond the findings of the sciences and that need not be assumed in scientific research.

A number of theologians have sought ways to conceive of particular divine actions that do not involve any disruption of the structures of nature. Arthur Peacocke (1924–) notes that the world described by the natural sciences is structured as a complex, nested hierarchy of causal systems; for example, biochemical processes operate within a cell located within an organ that functions within an organism. The higher levels of organization constrain the operation of their parts without abrogating the causal laws proper to those parts. Peacocke couples this picture of the natural order with a panentheistic conception of God according to which the world is encompassed within God, and God constitutes the ultimate whole that unites all finite systems. This opens the way to proposing whole-part as the model for God's action; God affects the world as a higher level system affects is parts, channeling their operation in particular ways without violating the lawful structures that govern them. Note that this account would allow for nonmiraculous particular divine influences upon the course of events whether or not the world constitutes a closed system of sufficient (i.e., deterministic) causes. The crucial task facing such a position is to vindicate the claim that God can affect the operations of finite causal systems without this divine influence registering as a discontinuity in the causal series.

Another strategy in developing an account of particular divine action explores the theological possibilities that arise if the universe is not in fact thoroughly deterministic in its structure. If the order of nature does not constitute a lock step of deterministic law but rather includes elements of under-determination, whether as mere chance or as self-determining freedom, then perhaps God can act in the world without in any way disrupting its inherent structures. The world that God created might, that is, incorporate both lawful regularities and openness to novel developments that are not entirely prescribed by the past.

John Polkinghorne (1930–) has proposed that the science of chaotic systems, which are highly sensitive to initial conditions and functionally unpredictable, provides a window on what may be a more supple and flexible network of relations in nature. Although these systems are described in deterministic equations, Polkinghorne notes that the laws of nature formulated by the sciences are a simplification and abstraction from the actual complexities of nature. This suggests that God might act by affecting the conditioning context within which these malleable systems operate. Other thinkers have explored the possibilities created by indeterministic interpretations of quantum mechanics. William Pollard (1911–) was the first to develop a proposal of this kind, but the idea has been explored and refined by a number of others. On what is arguably the dominant (though by no means the only) interpretation of quantum mechanics, there are transitions in quantum systems (namely, from a probabilistically described superposition of states to a determinate value for a measured variable) that have necessary but not sufficient conditions in preceding states. If the effects of these chance transitions are sometimes amplified by the larger systems in which they occur, then they can make a difference in the macroscopic course of events. Robert John Russell (1946–) has argued that this amplification can be found in a number of natural structures, notably in genetics. The structures of nature, in this case, would be open and flexible in such a way that God could, without disrupting the probabilistic regularity of those structures, act through them to bring about particular effects in the world. It might be objected that this represents a return to the

God-of-the-Gaps, that is, the hasty appeal to divine action at points of scientific ignorance. In this case, however, the relevant gaps occur in nature, not simply in human knowledge of nature. If the Copenhagen Interpretation of quantum theory is correct, then the deepest structures in nature are indeterministically open, and that is a fact about the world that theological reflection will need to take into account. Of course, the viability of particular theological proposals of this sort will depend in part on developments in the relevant sciences. Given the multiple options in interpreting quantum theory and the persistence of unresolved fundamental questions within the theory itself, any theological use of this science must remain a tentative exploration of intriguing possibilities.

Conclusion

The affirmation that God acts in the world has played a central role in the theistic religious traditions, and there are a number of ways in which this idea can be understood. God acts as the creator who calls all finite things into being and sustains their existence at every moment. In this way God acts directly with every causal operation or intentional action of creatures. By virtue of endowing created things with causal powers of their own, God can be also understood to act indirectly by means of the order of nature. Theists have typically affirmed that particular events can be identified as special acts of God, at least in the sense that they play a distinctive epistemic or causal role, and perhaps also in the sense that they reflect a direct divine action that affects the course of events or the lives of individuals. The latter form of special divine action raises difficult questions of theological interpretation, and it presents one of the points at which the dialogue between religion and science has been most fascinating and fruitful.

See also CLOCKWORK UNIVERSE; COPENHAGEN INTERPRETATION; CREATIO EX NIHILO; DEISM; DETERMINISM; DOUBLE AGENCY; GOD OF THE GAPS; MIRACLE; PANENTHEISM; PROCESS THOUGHT; PROVIDENCE; SPECIAL DIVINE ACTION; SPECIAL PROVIDENCE; THEISM; WHITEHEAD, ALFRED NORTH

Bibliography

Aquinas, Thomas. *Summa Theologiae* (1266–1273), Ia, QQ. 22–23, 103–05, ed. Timothy McDermott. London: Blackfriars, 1964.

Barth, Karl. *Church Dogmatics* (1935), Vol. 3, Part 3: *Doctrine of Creation, the Creator, His Creature,* eds. G. W. Bromiley and T. F. Torrence. Edinburgh, UK: T&T Clark, 1977.

Bultmann, Rudolph. *Jesus Christ and Mythology.* New York: Scribner, 1958.

Burrell, David. *Aquinas: God and Action.* Notre Dame, Ind.: University of Notre Dame Press, 1979.

Calvin, John. *Institutes of the Christian Religion* (1535–1559), Vols. 1 and 2, ed. John T. McNeill. Louisville, Ky.: Westminster John Knox Press, 1960.

Gilkey, Langdon. "Cosmology, Ontology, and the Travail of Biblical Language." *Journal of Religion* 41 (1961): 194–205.

Gilkey, Landgon. *Reaping the Whirlwind: A Christian Interpretation of History.* New York: Seabury Press, 1981.

Hartshorne, Charles. *Man's Vision of God and the Logic of Theism.* Hamden, Conn.: Archon Books, 1964.

Hume, David. "On Miracles" In *An Enquiry Concerning Human Understanding* (1748), Section 10. The Clarendon Edition of the Works of David Hume, ed. Thomas L. Beauchamp. New York: Oxford University Press, 2001.

Kaufman, Gordon. *God the Problem.* Cambridge, Mass.: Harvard University Press, 1972.

Morris, Thomas V., ed. *Divine and Human Action: Essays in the Metaphysics of Theism.* Ithaca, N.Y.: Cornell University Press, 1988.

Peacocke, Arthur. *Theology for a Scientific Age: Being and Becoming, Natural and Divine.* Oxford: Basil Blackwell, 1990.

Polkinghorne, John. *Science and Providence: God's Interaction with the World.* London: SPCK Press, 1989.

Pollard, William. *Chance and Providence: God's Action in a World Governed by Scientific Law.* New York: Scribners, 1958.

Russell, Robert John; Murphy, Nancey; Isham, C.J., eds. *Quantum Cosmology and the Laws of Nature: Scientific Perspectives on Divine Action,* rev. edition. Vatican City State: Vatican Observatory Publications, 1996.

Russell, Robert John; Murphy, Nancey; Peacocke, Arthur, eds. *Chaos and Complexity: Scientific Perspectives on Divine Action.* Vatican City State: Vatican Observatory Publications, 1995.

Russell, Robert John; Stoeger, William; Ayala, Francisco J., eds. *Evolutionary and Molecular Biology: Scientific Perspectives on Divine Action.* Vatican City State: Vatican Observatory Publications, 1998.

Russell, Robert John; Murphy, Nancey; Meyering, Theo C.; Arbib, Michael A., eds. *Neuroscience and the Person: Scientific Perspectives on Divine Action.* Vatican City State: Vatican Observatory Publications, 1999.

Russell, Robert John; Clayton, Philip; Wegter-McNelly, Kirk; Polkinghorne, John, eds. *Quantum Mechanics: Scientific Perspectives on Divine Action.* Vatican City State: Vatican Observatory Publications, 2001.

Schleiermacher, Friedrich. *The Christian Faith* (1830–1831), Vols. 1 and 2, trans. H. R. Mackintosh. Edinburgh, UK: T&T Clark, 2001.

Tanner, Kathryn. *God and Creation in Christian Theology: Tyranny or Empowerment.* London: Basil Blackwell, 1988.

Tracy, Thomas F., ed. *The God Who Acts: Philosophical and Theological Explorations.* University Park: Pennsylvania State University Press, 1995.

Ward, Keith. *Divine Action.* London: Collins, 1990.

Whitehead, Alfred North. *Process and Reality: An Essay in Cosmology.* New York: Macmillan, 1929.

Wiles, Maurice. *God's Action in the World: The Bampton Lectures for 1986.* London: SCM, 1986.

Wright, G. Ernest, and Fuller, Reginald H. *The Book of the Acts of God.* Garden City, N.Y.: Doubleday, 1957.

THOMAS F. TRACY

DNA

DNA (*deoxyribonucleic acid*) carries design information between generations, and thus accounts for inherited biological traits (*phenotypes*). At conception, a father's sperm injects a set of DNA molecules into a mother's egg, which already contains a nearly matching set. Those molecules contain the designs for all the material components their child needs for growth, development, and daily living.

Structure of DNA

The designs are called *genes*. Some genes play a role in regulating other genes, and some design *ribonucleic acid,* a close relative of DNA. But mostly, the designs in DNA are for the class of chemicals called proteins. The human body contains tens of thousands of kinds of proteins, which do all the body's work. Interactions among those proteins, and interactions between them and environmental factors account for the processes and structures of the body. Those processes and structures are manifested as inherited traits. DNA is comprised of chains of chemical subunits called *nucleotides,* each of which contains one nitrogenous base: *adenine* (*A*), *thymine* (*T*), *cytosine* (*C*), or *guanine* (*G*). The design instructions in DNA are spelled out as particular sequences of these four bases. This is analogous to conveying instructions in printed books by particular arrangements of the twenty-six letters of the alphabet. In the case of genes, however, there are only four letters in the alphabet. Hundreds of nucleotides are linked in a DNA chain in a sequence that spells out instructions for a single gene.

There are two complementary chains in the structure of DNA. Each nucleotide in DNA has a sugar component joined to a phosphate group at one point on the sugar, and to a nitrogen-containing base attached at another point. The chains in DNA have the phosphate of one nucleotide linked to the sugar of the next nucleotide to form a strand of alternating sugars and phosphates with dangling nitrogenous bases. DNA contains two such chains, twisted around each other to form a double-stranded helix with the bases on the inside. Every *A* on one chain forms weak bonds with a *T* on the other strand, and every *C* on a strand bonds weakly to a *G* on the opposite chain. The two strands, held together weakly by the pairing of *A* with *T*, and *G* with *C*, are thus complementary, and the sequence in one can be deduced from the other's sequence.

Design information is transmitted as new DNA to new cells during development and growth. The complementarity of the two DNA strands allows their information to be copied. Each old strand is used as a template in synthesizing a new complementary one. Intricate cellular machinery makes new copies of the DNA when a fertilized egg divides into two progeny cells. When each of the progeny divides again, the new progeny all receive complete copies of the parental DNA. As the fertilized egg grows to become successively an embryo, a fetus, a child, and finally an adult, cells go through many rounds of division with replication of the DNA in each round. Finally, adult humans have trillions of cells, each one (except sperm and ovum) containing complete copies of the DNA initially contributed by the parents.

On rare occasions mutations (changes) are made in nucleotides by chemicals, radiation, or errors in copying DNA. In a nucleotide chain, one nucleotide may be substituted for another, or one or more nucleotides might be inserted or deleted. Sometimes the change in DNA structure has little or no effect on the function of the gene's product, but it frequently harms the function to some degree, or very rarely enhances it. Harmful mutations cause gene-based diseases, but enhancing mutations allow organisms to evolve new or more effective functions. Like normal phenotypes, disease phenotypes usually require the products of multiple genes, so most defective genes predispose an organism to disease rather than directly causing it. The accumulation of mutations within the human species accounts for such phenotypic differences as eye color, stature, or skin pigmentation. The number of mutations among human genes is so large that no two persons, except for identical twins, have exactly the same nucleotide sequence in the three billion bases of their DNA.

Control of gene expression

DNA information is expressed as proteins and their feedback networks. The information resident in nucleotide sequences is used not only for replicating DNA, but also for synthesizing proteins. Proteins are chains of a few hundred subunits called *amino acids,* of which there are twenty kinds. The amino acids in a protein are arranged in a specific sequence by cellular machinery that translates the genetic information coded in DNA. The sequence of nucleotides, read three at a time, corresponds to the sequence of amino acids in a protein. The amino acids differ among themselves in chemical character so that every kind of protein differs in chemical character from others. For the work of the human body many thousands of proteins are needed, each having a highly specific function like catalyzing a chemical reaction or transporting oxygen. Observable phenotypes are the result of protein action, usually the coordinated action of many proteins. The functions of many proteins are integrated into large networks, and these webs of chemical processes act as feedback control systems allowing organisms to shift the balance of their activities to adapt to changes in the demand for the system's output. Often the networks possess alternate pathways for achieving a desired output.

Differentiation into specialized cells requires the control of gene expression. The development of a human being starts with a single-celled, fertilized egg. As the egg divides into two cells, and as successive rounds of cell division occur, every progeny cell receives a complete copy of parental DNA. In the first few divisions, the cells produced are identical in all observable characteristics, but as cell division continues, cells are produced that differ in phenotype even though all the cells continue to have identical DNA. In this differentiation, particular genes are controlled by blocking their expression, not by changing nucleotide sequence. Regulatory molecules block particular sites in DNA preventing translation of the corresponding genes into their products. Specific blocking thus generates different patterns of gene expression. Changing patterns of gene expression produce distinct populations of cells, diverging in phenotype as differentiation progresses. Eventually, differentiation in humans produces more than two hundred cell types, organized into different tissues and organs. In any one cell type the majority of its approximately 35,000 genes is repressed, leaving a small subset of expressed genes that differs from the subsets expressed in other cell types. Phenotypic differences between progeny in a given cell generation depend on the location of the cells in different microenvironments. During differentiation cells adapt to a succession of environmental changes produced by changes in their neighboring cells and extracellular fluids. Each successive adaptation is superimposed on its predecessor so that each terminally differentiated cell manifests the entire history of its lineage and not merely its immediate state. Since differentiation is irreversible in animals, (except in special cases), history as well as DNA designs a person, even in the material sense.

Feedback networks and regulation of genes allow individual organisms to adapt to changing conditions throughout life. When environment increases the need for the product of a network of chemical reactions, the overall process will be accelerated, and when need decreases the process will be inhibited. Obviously, adaptation to environment is induced by contact with physical and chemical forces, but adaptation can be evoked even without physical contact, as in the adaptation of the brain through learning, and emotional reaction. Many of these adaptive responses affect patterns of gene expression, and therefore environment, as well as history, joins with DNA in designing persons.

At the level of populations, long-term adaptation to environment occurs more by changes in gene structure than by changes in the expression of genes. The mechanism for this adaptation is the natural selection that underlies evolution. For example, skin pigmentation may be an adaptation that protects against exposure to the sun, and the genes that design the pigment systems would be naturally selected in successive generations that are exposed to much sunlight. Similarly, sickle-cell hemoglobin seems to have evolved in Africa because it offers resistance to malaria that is prevalent there.

Long-term adaptation through natural selection is most obvious in the case of physical and chemical aspects of human beings. Less obvious is the adaptation of behaviors through natural selection of genes, a possibility actively studied under the title "sociobiology." Although the mechanisms producing material phenotypes may seem more obvious than those producing social behaviors, a mechanism giving rise to a certain behavior may be thoroughly materialistic, although far more complex. Behavior modification by psychoactive drugs reveals a material mechanism for behavior. A mechanism can be pictured, for example, in the courting and mating behaviors that are correlated with the release of hormones from the brain, when an animal or human senses that a potential mate is near. Those released hormones induce particular chemical reactions at many sites throughout the body, giving rise to an appropriate pattern of bodily actions. Moreover, feedback responses between the mates guide further behavioral interactions between them. The hormonal system that links brain functions to bodily functions is, of course, designed by genes, and the mechanism just sketched is clearly materialistic. The frequent association of natural selection with notions of "survival of the fittest," makes altruism an especially challenging kind of behavior to study in testing the validity of sociobiology theory, and much of the research of sociobiologists is focused on the evolution of a gene for altruism.

Genes affect behavior, but as is the case with most human phenotypes, genes act in combinations and their expression is modulated by the histories and environments of individuals, as already described. Through the invariability of individual histories and environments, natural selection must be able to recognize the difference between organisms that possess a particular behavioral gene, and those that do not possess it. In order for a behavioral gene to evolve through natural selection it must be powerful enough in determining the behavior, to avoid substantial compromise by variable non-genetic factors. Sociobiology, then, tends to favor a strongly deterministic and materialistic view of behavior.

Human nature and genetic determinism

Choosing is part of human nature, but its degree of autonomy is debated. All agree that choice is constrained by genes, history, and environment, but does any degree of freedom remain? Science describes material brain mechanisms as chains of causes and effects, but every cause is an effect having a prior cause. Since the initial cause is not recognized by science, some say thought initiation is due to chance. Others look for initiation outside the material realm of science by distinguishing between mind and brain, or even spirit and brain.

Some degree of genetic determinism is necessary in describing human nature. All the possible scenarios of a person's life must conform to the designs in DNA, and thus genes set rigid, though spacious boundaries on what a person can be and do. But genes are insufficient for explaining what actually happens. What actually happens within the boundaries set by genes, depends on factors that control genes, including environment, history, and mental state. The question arises whether spiritual forces can be added to the list of controlling factors. Material determinism argues that a complete physicochemical description of the history and state of a person would explain everything without including a spiritual component. Some, however, argue that human spirituality is a capacity that emerged as gene-based human biology evolved, and that its activity cannot be fully comprehended at the molecular level. Still others add spirit as a control factor in human nature in accepting a dualism where body and spirit are distinct, though coexistent, in a person. The disparity in these views of human nature has theological consequences.

A view of human nature according to material determinism fits atheism and deism. It provides no locus for personal interaction with God, although deists might suppose that God influences humans through environment. Belief in human spirituality, either as an emerged capacity or as a distinct part of human nature does provide such a locus. Scientific understanding of gene-based human biology does not perceive a spiritual component in human nature, but it might not be expected that a physico-chemico-molecular description of humans would be capable of such discernment in the first place.

See also GENE PATENTING; GENETIC DEFECT; GENETIC DETERMINISM; GENETICS; HUMAN GENOME PROJECT; MUTATION; NATURE VERSUS NURTURE

Bibliography

Avise, John C. "Evolving Genomic Metaphors: A New Look at the Language of DNA." *Science* 294 (2001): 86-87.

Barbour, Ian. *Religion in an Age of Science.* New York: Harper Collins, 1990.

Dawkins, Richard. *The Selfish Gene.* Oxford: Oxford University Press, 1989.

Dennis, Carina; Gallagher, Richard; and Campbell, Philip, eds. "The Human Genome." *Nature* 409 (2001): 813-958.

Edelman, Gerald M. *Bright Air, Brilliant Fire: On the Matter of the Mind.* New York: Basic Books, 1992.

Goldsmith, Timothy H. *The Biological Roots of Human Nature: Forging Links Between Evolution and Behavior.* New York: Oxford University Press, 1991.

Hefner, Philip. "Determinism, Freedom, and Moral Failure." In *Genetics: Issues of Social Justice,* ed. Ted Peters. Cleveland, Ohio: Pilgrim Press, 1998.

Kitcher, Philip. *The Lives to Come: The Genetic Revolution and Human Possibilities.* New York: Simon and Schuster, 1996.

Kotulak, Ronald. *Inside the Brain: Revolutionary Discoveries of How the Mind Works.* Kansas City, Mo.: Andrews McMeel, 1996.

Peters, Ted. "Genes, Theology, and Social Ethics." In *Genetics: Issues of Social Justice,* ed. Ted Peters. Cleveland, Ohio: Pilgrim Press, 1998.

Raven, Peter H., and Johnson, George B. *Biology,* 6th edition. New York: McGraw Hill, 2002.

Stevens, Raymond C.; Shigeyuki, Yokoyama; and Wilson, Ian A. "Global Efforts in Structural Genomics." *Science* 294 (2001): 89-92.

On the philosophical front, materialists often have difficulty capturing the evident existence of consciousness or felt experiences. Human thinking, sensing, and feeling appear to be different in kind from brain processes and other bodily activity. At a minimum, there is a profound causal relation between the two (one's thinking is contingent on neurological events), and yet a causal relation is not the same thing as identity. The mental and physical may be causally interdependent without being identical. Since 1980, a range of philosophers who are materialists either in their convictions or inclinations (e.g., Thomas Nagel, Colin McGinn, Jaegwon Kim, and John Pollock), have insisted that there are serious problems with identifying consciousness with physical states and processes.

A shift in contemporary science has also bolstered the case for dualism. So long as a strictly deterministic physical science dominated the view of nature, it appeared that something nonphysical (states of consciousness or the soul) would have no causal role in explaining events in the world. This would render a dualist account of action absurd. But quantum mechanics has advanced an indeterminist view of the cosmos, and it is more difficult to rule out dualism.

From a religious point of view, dualism is in play with most but not all traditions that acknowledge an afterlife. Some religions believe in a resurrection of the dead in which a person survives death by their material body being either reconstituted or re-created. But even these religions often preserve some immaterial locus or referent to secure a person's identity; in between physical death and resurrection a person might still be thought of as present to God. Virtually all religions that include a belief in reincarnation allow that there is some immaterial aspect to a person's or a soul's identity. If persons are identical with their bodies, then what happens to persons and bodies are the very same; dualism allows persons and souls to share a different fate from their bodies.

Dualism also receives some support from cultures that routinely adopt different methods for studying and talking about persons as opposed to studying and talking about their bodies. Consider a modest example in English: It can make sense to say that someone is in class but that his or her mind is far away.

History of the concept

Historically, the ancient Greek philosopher Plato (428–347 B.C.E.) was a key advocate of a form of dualism. Dualism is integral to his case for the immortality of the soul, as expressed in the *Phaedrus, Phaedo,* and *Republic.* Plato posited not just a postmortem existence but life before material embodiment (prenatal existence). Plato thought of a person's material embodiment as good but also as something that impedes the soul's longing for the good, the true, and the beautiful. Compared with the beauty and glory of disembodied life, material existence can be like a prison. The early Christian leader Augustine of Hippo (354–430 C.E.) developed a Platonic form of Christianity, rejecting some of Plato's beliefs (Augustine rejected pre-natal existence, as well as Plato's view of the divine as a finite reality) but preserving his dualism and the centrality of the good.

Some Platonic Christians in the medieval period speculated that God creates a host of various forms of intelligence in either embodied or disembodied form. This formed part of the principle of plentitude in medieval thought. The philosopher Thomas Aquinas (1225–1274) preserved much of the Platonic, Augustinian tradition but he more firmly insisted that human beings are comprised of matter and form. He still allowed that a person's soul persists after death, so Aquinas's reservations about radical dualism were limited.

Modern philosophy in Europe focussed on three philosophies of human nature. Dualism was championed by René Descartes (1596–1650); Cartesian dualism was advanced based on the conceivability of the self without the body. Thomas Hobbes (1588–1679) was very much on the other side. According to Hobbes, only matter exists and the very notion of there being something immaterial was nonsense. Hobbes insisted that even God is a material reality. A third position was championed by George Berkeley (1685–1753) who held that matter was not a fundamental, mind-independent reality. The cosmos is made up of minds and their sensory experiences. Berkeley's thesis that only minds and their states and activities exist is called *idealism.* In the eighteenth century it was possible to see dualism as a mediating, moderate choice between the extremes of materialism and idealism.

Many contemporary Christian theologians see dualism as part of an undesirable body-hatred;

dualism is accused of foisting on people an excessively fragmented view of embodiment. Moreover, dualism is thought to reflect a vain attempt by humans to distinguish themselves from the rest of creation. These objections all seem answerable. There is no necessity for dualists to see embodiment in negative terms. And while a person's psychological and physical life can be fragmented, there is no need for dualism to regard human embodiment as always laden with bifurcation. Dualists may see the embodied person as a functional unity. As for the question of human pride, Descartes famously denied nonhuman animals were like humans in possessing (or being) minds. Descartes read nature in mechanical terms while he tried to secure an exception for human life. But most contemporary dualists see the emergence of consciousness as something involving nonhuman animal life; people share with some nonhumans in having experiences and possessing psychological abilities. Dualists tend to see the emergence of consciousness as something that prevails throughout the animal world and not something limited exclusively to human beings.

See also AUGUSTINE; EMBODIMENT; MATERIALISM; MIND-BODY THEORIES; MIND-BRAIN INTERACTION; MONISM; PLATO; THOMAS AQUINAS

Bibliography

Cooper, John. *Body, Soul and Life Everlasting: Biblical Anthropology and the Monism-Dualism Debate.* Grand Rapids, Mich.: Eerdmans, 1989.

Foster, John. *The Immaterial Self: A Defence of the Cartesian Dualist Conception of the Mind.* London: Routledge, 1991.

Hart, W. D. *The Engines of the Soul.* Cambridge, UK: Cambridge University Press, 1988.

Hasker, William. *The Emergent Self.* Ithaca, N.Y.: Cornell University Press, 2000.

Lovejoy, Arthur O. *The Great Chain of Being: A Study of the History of an Idea* (1936). Cambridge, Mass.: Harvard University Press, 1970.

Nagel, Thomas. "What is It Like to Be a Bat?" *Philosophical Review* 83 (1974): 435–450.

Smythies, John R., and Beloff, John, eds. *The Case for Dualism.* Charlottesville: University of Virginia Press, 1989.

Swinburne, Richard. *The Evolution of the Soul.* Oxford: Oxford University Press, 1986.

Taliaferro, Charles. *Consciousness and the Mind of God.* Cambridge, UK: Cambridge University Press, 1994.

CHARLES TALIAFERRO

E

ECOFEMINISM

The term *ecofeminism* was first used by French radical feminist Françoise d'Eaubonne (b. 1920) in 1974 to synthesize two movements previously thought of as separate: ecology and feminism. D'Eaubonne saw clear interconnections between the domination of women and that of nature, and she hoped, by making these interconnections explicit, to rescue the planet from the destructive effects of "the male system" and restore it for the benefit of humanity's future.

Ecofeminism offers a range of theoretical positions in which the prefix *eco* signifies the whole household of life. These positions include stringent critiques of reductionist ecological science because of its destructive effects on the whole. Ecofeminism is defined, however, by politically and socially multivalent feminist analyses that seek a positive understanding of the dialectic between nature and humanity in order to move beyond masculine domination of both women and nature.

The relationship between nature and human culture remains problematic for ecofeminists because the feminization of nature has contributed conceptually to downgrading women's cultural role and status. Ecofeminists reject a male elite model of human culture that inferiorizes and excludes groups of people, as well as nature. Within industrially developed societies, ecofeminists debate the issue of gender difference within cultures in dialogue with movements such as deep ecology, antimilitarism, animal liberation, antiracism, and environmental justice. Globally, ecofeminists consistently critique the environmental effects of gendered science and resource management, together with economic development models that have a disproportionate and often disastrous impact on women.

Ecofeminism also offers a potentially transformative philosophy of the self and of society. Influenced by process thought and Gaia science, every entity is seen as internally related to all aspects of its environment, with that relationship as part of what the entity is in itself. This awareness of ecological interdependence calls for an essentially nonviolent ethic of care within societies. It includes care for the fundamental elements of life in recognition of their limits, as well as attention to their present and future ecological and social costs.

Worldwide, ecofeminism focuses on relationships between global economic policies and global ecological crises, arguing that addressing the first in the form of a radical transformation of capitalist production, from an overwhelmingly competitive system to a cooperative one, benefits the global environment. Therefore ecofeminists unite with social justice organizations in order to reach out and care for those statistically most at risk from, but powerless to avert, environmental degradation: the poor, women, children, and indigenous peoples.

Ecofeminism encourages, indeed, requires a reshaping of the image of God from a hierarchical God above and beyond Earth to one continuously involved with, while not confined by, the evolutionary history of life on Earth. Therefore, ecofeminism fosters a sense of our belonging within, rather than being in control of, the community of life. The insights of process theology, feminist theology, non-traditional spiritualities, and the spiritualities of indigenous communities with a strong matriarchal tradition are used to highlight ecological interdependence and the value of biodiversity in all its forms. Many of these insights demonstrate a diversity of response to what is called sacred or divine.

See also ANIMAL RIGHTS; DEEP ECOLOGY; ECOLOGY; ECOLOGY, ETHICS OF; ECOLOGY, RELIGIOUS AND PHILOSOPHICAL ASPECTS; ECOLOGY, SCIENCE OF; ECOTHEOLOGY; FEMINISMS AND SCIENCE; FEMINIST COSMOLOGY; FEMINIST THEOLOGY; GAIA HYPOTHESIS; WOMANIST THEOLOGY

Bibliography

d'Eaubonne, Françoise. "The Time for Ecofeminism," trans. Ruth Hottell. In *Ecology: Key Concepts in Critical Theory,* eds. Carolyn Merchant and Roger S. Gottlieb. Atlantic Highlands, N.J.: Humanities Press International, 1994.

Merchant, Carolyn. *Earthcare: Women and the Environment.* London and New York: Routledge, 1996.

Mies, Maria, and Shiva, Vandana. *Ecofeminism.* London and Atlantic Highlands, N.J.: Zed Books, 1993.

Plumwood, Val. *Feminism and the Mastery of Nature.* London and New York: Routledge, 1993.

Primavesi, Anne. *Sacred Gaia: Holistic Theology and Earth System Science.* London and New York: Routledge, 2000.

Sturgeon, Noël. *Ecofeminist Natures: Race, Gender, Feminist Theory, and Political Action.* London and New York: Routledge, 1997.

Warren, Karen, ed. *Ecological Feminism.* London and New York: Routledge, 1994.

ANNE PRIMAVESI

ECOLOGY

The term *ecology* is, etymologically, the logic of living creatures in their homes, a word suggestively related to *ecumenical,* with common roots in the Greek *oikos,* the inhabited world. Named in 1866 by German biologist Ernst Haeckel (1834–1919), ecology is a biological science like molecular biology or evolutionary theory, though often thought to be less mature. Ecosystems are complicated; experiments are difficult on these open systems,

often large, that resist analysis. Ecology has nevertheless been thrust into the public arena, with the advent of the ecological crisis. Ecology has also become increasingly global, and still more complex, as when planetary carbon dioxide cycles affect climate change.

Ethics, policy, theology, and ecology

Ecology mixes with ethics, an ecological (or environmental) ethics urging that humans ought to find a lifestyle more respectful of, or harmonious with, nature. Ethics, which seeks a satisfactory fit for humans in their communities, has traditionally dwelt on justice, fairness, love, rights, or peace, settling disputes of right and wrong that arise among humans. Ethics now also concerns the troubled planet, its fauna, flora, species, and ecosystems.

American forester Aldo Leopold urged a new commandment in "The Land Ethic," a chapter in his 1968 book *A Sand County Almanac*: "A thing is right when it tends to preserve the integrity, stability, and beauty of the biotic community. It is wrong when it tends otherwise" (pp. 224–225). Since the United Nations Conference on Environment and Development, held in 1992 in Rio de Janeiro, Brazil, the focus of environmental policy, often referred to as ecosystem management, has been a sustainable economy based on a sustainable biosphere.

Theologians have argued that religion needs to pay more attention to ecology, and perhaps also vice versa. Partly this is in response to allegations that Christians view humans as having God-given dominion over nature; they dominate nature and are responsible for the ecological crisis. An ecological theology may hope to find norms directly in ecological science, but often an ecological perspective rather freely borrows and adapts various goods thought to be found in ecology into human social affairs, such as wholeness, interrelatedness, balance, harmony, efficiency, embodiment, dynamism, naturalness, and sustainability.

Leading concepts in ecological science

Leading concepts in ecology involve ecosystems, succession of communities rejuvenated by disturbances, energy flow, niches and habitats, food chains and webs, carrying capacity, populations and survival rates, diversity, and stability. A main claim is that every organism is what it is where it is because its place is essential to its being; the "skin-out" environment is as vital as the "skin-in" metabolisms. Early ecologists favored ideas such as homeostasis and equilibrium. Contemporary ecologists emphasize a greater role for contingency or even chaos. Others emphasize self-organizing systems (*autopoiesis*), also an ancient idea: "The earth produces of itself [Greek: automatically]" (Luke 4:28). Some find that natural selection on the edge of chaos offers the greatest possibility for self-organization and survival in changing environments, often also passing over to self-transformation.

The stability of ecosystems is dynamic, not a frozen sameness, and may differ with particular systems and depend on the level of analysis. There are perennial processes—wind, rain, soil, photosynthesis, competition, predation, symbiosis, trophic pyramids or food chains, and networks. Ecosystems may wander or be stable within bounds. When unusual disturbances come, ecosystems can be displaced beyond recovery of their former patterns. Then they settle into new equilibria. Ecosystems are always on historical trajectory, a dynamism of chaos and order entwined.

Michael E. Soulé and Gary Lease have demonstrated in their 1995 book, *Reinventing Nature? Responses to Postmodern Deconstruction,* that ecology as a science has not proven immune from postmodernist and deconstructionist claims that science in all its forms—astrophysics to ecology—is a cultural construct of the Enlightenment West. Science is pragmatic and enables scientific cultures to get what they want out of nature; science is not descriptive of what nature is really like, apart from humans and their biases and preferences. According to this view, humans should make no pretensions to know what nature is like without them, but can choose what it is like to interact with nature, living harmoniously with it, which will result in a higher quality life. This fits well with a bioregional perspective. Environmental ethics is as much applied geography as it is pure ecology.

Some interpreters, such as Mark Sagoff, conclude that human environmental policy cannot be drawn from nature. Ecology, a piecemeal science in their estimation, can, at best, offer generalizations of regional or local scope, and supply various tools (such as eutrophication of lakes, keystone species, nutrient recycling, niches, succession) for

whatever the particular circumstances at hand. Humans ought to step in with our management objectives and reshape the ecosystems we inhabit consonant with our cultural goals.

Other interpreters, such as David Pimentel, Laura Westra, and Reed Noss, argue that human life does and ought to include nature and culture entwined, humans as part of, rather than apart from, their ecosystems. Ecosystems are dependable life support systems. There is a kind of order that arises spontaneously and systematically when many self-actualizing units interactively pursue their own programs, each doing its own thing and forced into informed co-action with other units.

In culture, the logic of language or the integrated connections of the market are examples of such co-action. We legitimately respect cultural heritages, such as Judaism or Christianity, or democracy or science, none of which are centrally controlled processes, all of which mix elements of integrity and dependability with dynamic change, even surprise and unpredictability. We might wish for "integrity, stability, and beauty" in democracy or science, without denying the elements of pluralism, dynamism, contingency, and historical development.

Ecosystems, though likewise complex, open, and decentralized, are orderly and predictable enough to make ecological science possible—and also to make possible an ethics respecting these dynamic, creative, vital processes. The fauna and flora originally in place, independently of humans, will with high probability be species naturally selected for their adaptive fits, as evolutionary and ecological theory both teach. Misfits go extinct and unstable ecosystems collapse and are replaced by more stable or resilient ones (perhaps rejuvenated by chaos or upset by catastrophe).

This ecosystemic nature, once flourishing independently and for millennia continuing along with humans, has in the last one hundred years come under increasing jeopardy—variously described as a threat to ecosystem health, integrity, or quality.

Ecosystem management

Since the 1990s, emphasis has been ecosystem management. This approach appeals alike to scientists, who see the need for understanding ecosystems objectively and for applied technologies, and also to humanists, who find that humans are cultural animals who rebuild their environments and who desire benefits for people. The combined ecosystem/management policy promises to operate at system-wide levels, presumably to manage for indefinite sustainability, alike of ecosystems and their outputs. Such management connects with the idea of nature as "natural resources" at the same time that it has a "respect nature" dimension. Christian ethicists note that the secular word "manage" is a stand-in for the earlier theological word "steward." Adam was placed in the garden "to till and keep it" (Gen. 2:15).

Pristine natural systems no longer exist anywhere on Earth (the insecticide DDT has been found in penguins in Antarctica). Perhaps 95 percent of a landscape will be rebuilt for culture, considering lands plowed and grazed, forests managed, rivers dammed, and so on. Still, only about 25 percent of the land, in most nations, is under permanent agriculture; a large percentage is more or less rural, still with some processes of wild nature taking place. The twenty-first century promises an escalation of development that threatens both the sustainability of landscapes supporting culture as well as their intrinsic integrity.

Scientists and ethicists alike have traditionally divided their disciplines into realms of the "is" and the "ought." No study of nature can tell humans what ought to happen. This neat division has been challenged by ecologists and their philosophical and theological interpreters. The analysis here first distinguishes between interhuman ethics and environmental ethics. The claim that nature ought sometimes to be taken as norm within environmental ethics is not to be confused with a different claim, that nature teaches us how we ought to behave toward each other. Nature as moral tutor has always been, and remains, doubtful ethics. Compassion and charity, justice and honesty, are not virtues found in wild nature. There is no way to derive any of the familiar moral maxims from nature: "One ought to keep promises." "Do to others as you would have them do to you." "Do not cause needless suffering." No natural decalogue endorses the Ten Commandments.

But, continuing the analysis, there may be goods (values) in nature with which humans ought to conform. Animals, plants, and species, integrated into ecosystems, may embody values that,

though nonmoral, count morally when moral agents encounter these. To grant that morality emerges in human beings out of nonmoral nature does not settle the question whether we, who are moral, should sometimes orient our conduct in accord with value there. Theologians will add that God bade Earth bring forth its swarming kinds and found this genesis very good. Palestine was a promised land; Earth is a promising planet, but only if its ecologies globally form a biosphere.

Environmental science can inform environmental ethics in subtle ways. Scientists describe the "order," "dynamic stability," and "diversity" in these biotic "communities." They describe "interdependence," or speak of "health" or "integrity," perhaps of their "resilience" or "efficiency." Scientists describe the "adapted fit" that organisms have in their niches. They describe an ecosystem as "flourishing," as "self-organizing." Strictly interpreted, these are only descriptive terms; and yet often they are already quasi-evaluative terms, perhaps not always so but often enough that by the time the descriptions of ecosystems are in, some values are already there. In this sense, ecology is rather like medical science, with therapeutic purpose, seeking such flourishing health.

Ecology in classical religions

Is there ecological wisdom in the classical religions? Religion and science have to be carefully delineated, each in its own domain. One makes a mistake to ask about technical ecology in the Bible (such as the Lotka-Volterra equations, dealing with population size and carrying capacity). But ecology is a science at native range. Residents on landscapes live immersed in their local ecology. At the pragmatic ranges of the sower who sows, waits for the seed to grow, and reaps the harvest, the Hebrews knew their landscape. Abraham and Lot, and later Jacob and Esau, dispersed their flocks and herds because "the land could not support both of them dwelling together" (Gen. 13:2-13; 36:6-8). There were too many sheep and goats eating the sparse grasses and shrubs of their semi-arid landscape, and these nomads recognized this. They were exceeding the carrying capacity, ecologists now say.

Here academic ecologists can learn a great deal from people indigenous to a landscape for centuries. Such ecological wisdom might be as readily found with the Arunta in Australia, or with the Navajos in the American Southwest on their landscapes. This would be indigenous wisdom rather than divine revelation. Such wisdom is often supported more by mythology than by science. Such wisdom is also frequently mixed with error and misunderstanding.

Christian (and other) ethicists can with considerable plausibility make the claim that neither conservation, nor a sustainable biosphere, nor sustainable development, nor any other harmony between humans and nature can be gained until persons learn to use the earth both justly and charitably. Those twin concepts are not found either in wild nature or in any science that studies nature. They must be grounded in some ethical authority, and this has classically been religious.

One needs human ecology, humane ecology, and this requires insight more into human nature than into wild nature. True, humans cannot know the right way to act if they are ignorant of the causal outcomes in the natural systems they modify—for example, the carrying capacity of the Bethel-Ai rangeland in the hill country of Judaea. But there must be more. The Hebrews were convinced that they were given a blessing with a mandate. The land flows with milk and honey (assuming good land husbandry) if and only if there is obedience to Torah. Abraham said to Lot, "Let there be no strife between me and you, and between your herdsmen and my herdsmen" (Gen. 13:8), and they partitioned the common good equitably among themselves. The Hebrews also include the fauna within their covenant. "Behold I establish my covenant with you and your descendants after you, and with every living creature that is with you, the birds, the cattle, and every beast of the earth with you" (Gen. 9:5). In modern terms, the covenant was both ecumenical and ecological.

See also ANIMAL RIGHTS; AUTOPOIESIS; CHAOS THEORY; DEEP ECOLOGY; ECOFEMINISM; ECOLOGY, ETHICS OF; ECOLOGY, RELIGIOUS AND PHILOSOPHICAL ASPECTS; ECOLOGY, SCIENCE OF; ECOTHEOLOGY; FEMINISM AND SCIENCE; FEMINIST COSMOLOGY; FEMINIST THEOLOGY; GAIA HYPOTHESIS; WOMANIST THEOLOGY

Bibliography

Golley, Frank. *A Primer for Ecological Literacy*. New Haven, Conn.: Yale University Press, 1998.

Gumbine, R. Edward. "What is Ecosystem Management?" *Conservation Biology* 8 (1994): 27-38.

Leopold, Aldo. "The Land Ethic." In *A Sand County Almanac*. New York: Oxford University Press, 1968.

Northcott, Michael S. *The Environment and Christian Ethics*. Cambridge, UK: Cambridge University Press, 1996.

Pimentel, David; Westra, Laura; and Noss, Reed F., eds. *Ecological Integrity: Integrating Environment, Conservation, and Health*. Washington, D.C.: Island Press, 2000.

Rolston, Holmes, III. "The Bible and Ecology." *Interpretation: Journal of Bible and Theology* 50 (1996): 16–26.

Sagoff, Mark. "Ethics, Ecology, and the Environment: Integrating Science and Law." *Tennessee Law Review* 56 (1988): 77-229.

Soulé, Michael E., and Lease, Gary, eds. *Reinventing Nature? Responses to Postmodern Deconstruction*. Washington, D.C.: Island Press, 1995.

HOLMES ROLSTON, III

ECOLOGY, ETHICS OF

Ecological (or environmental) ethics is the study of what humans, individually and corporately, ought to value, ought to be, and ought to do in relationships with all other beings and elements in the biosphere. As in normative ethics generally, ecological ethics involves evaluating, justifying (or not), and prescribing values, norms, and standards of character and conduct in view of the ecological conditions that contribute to the well-being of humans and other life forms. This discipline is diverse in types, methods, values, problems, foundational perspectives, and other elements of ethics. Ecological ethics comes in both philosophical and religious versions; the problems and values are often the same, though the methods and ultimate rationales are often different.

The topical agenda of ecological ethics is molded by contemporary environmental problems. The primary concerns are climate change, multiple forms of pollution, human population growth, scarcities of some renewable and nonrenewable resources, human-induced losses in biodiversity, the interactive dynamics of ecological degradation and economic patterns of consumption and distribution, and, increasingly relevant, the environmental effects of genetic manipulations.

Models and value systems

Much ethical thought about the environment has been an expansion of the concern in traditional ethics to cover the adverse effects of environmental conditions on human interests. Classical moral values and norms remain basically unchanged. Only humans count for direct moral consideration. Other life forms are strictly instrumental values—means—for human needs and wants, such as scientific, aesthetic, and various economic purposes. The basic moral assumption has been: Humans ought to take care of the environment so that the environment can take care of humans.

In reaction to this anthropocentric model, the clear majority of contemporary ecological ethicists interpret their discipline as a reformation of moral values and duties. The bounds and rules of relationships are reshaped by a new consciousness of three fundamental facts about planetary existence: the biological, coevolutionary kinship of all life forms; the systemic interdependence of all beings and elements; and the biophysical limits of all planetary goods. Ethics itself must change to fit the reality that humans are not only social animals, as recognized in classical ethics, but also ecological animals.

Consequently, a prominent feature—some, indeed, would say a defining feature—of ecological ethics is the extension of moral standing beyond the human community. The questions are perplexing: Who or what has moral claims on humans for consideration of their interests? Are animals, plants, and other biological classes included? What about individuals, species, and ecosystems as the holistic interactions among organisms and elements? Where is the line to be drawn, if at all? What are the justifications or reasons for recognizing moral status?

Some ethicists limit this extension to organisms that satisfy certain criteria, such as sentience in the case of animal rights advocates. Critics claim, however, that this limitation leaves the vast majority of the biota with the instrumental status of "things."

Most ecological ethicists now argue that all organisms have some moral claims on humans, because they are intrinsic values, goods, or ends for themselves. Many contend that species also have moral claims as genetic lifelines that carry these values. Only a few argue for equal value among species; most allow for graded valuations in accord with significant and relevant differences. An increasing number also claim that ecosystems are values for themselves that warrant direct moral consideration.

At this point, the field is split between so-called biocentric and ecocentric value systems—or, more accurately, individualistic and holistic perspectives on moral duties. The debate is sometimes confused and polemical. Biocentrists focus on protecting or promoting the welfare of individual lives, often mammals, but sometimes other species, in a given context. Ecocentrists stress systemic values, arguing that our primary or only responsibility is to the integrity of ecosystems.

These positions, however, need not be mutually exclusive. For a fully adequate ecological ethics, some in the field propose, we need a basis for respecting both life forms (individuals, populations, and species) and collective connections—that is, diverse and whole ecosystems in a healthy ecosphere, which alone provide the essential conditions for the good of all individuals and species. The individualistic and holistic poles may not be contraries but rather complementary sides of a comprehensive ecological ethics.

Sustainability

Sustainability has been a prominent norm in ecological ethics—largely because of the perception that present patterns of using the planet as source and sink are unsustainable. Sustainability is living within the bounds of the regenerative, assimilative, and carrying capacities of the planet indefinitely, in fairness to future generations. It seeks a just distribution of goods between present and future generations, without sacrificing one for the other. Human beings have obligations to future generations because what they are and do will have profound effects on them for good and ill. Since they do not yet exist but can reasonably be expected to do so, future generations can be said to have anticipatory rights, and every present generation has anticipatory obligations to them.

Sustainability is often interpreted as an anthropocentric norm, but that limitation is not at all inherent in the idea. Ecological ethicists usually interpret sustainability as responsibilities to future generations of both humankind and other kinds. This inclusive vision may significantly change the prevailing principles and practices of sustainability.

Reflecting practitioners' commitments to sustainability, social equity, and ecological integrity, two issues have been prominent on the agenda of ecological ethics: high levels of human population and consumption. From an ecological perspective, these are intertwined problems. Population and consumption are two interactive sides of a species' impact on its environmental base, whether by too many humans contending over a depleted base or by an economic elite using that base disproportionately. The basic moral questions are: What are the responsibilities of humans, individually and collectively, to the rest of humanity, other species, and future generations? What then are the material and demographic conditions that humans must respect to fulfill these responsibilities? Ecological ethicists frequently urge moral limits on both economic consumption and sexual reproduction for the sake of the social and ecological common good.

Conclusion

From the perspective of ecological ethicists, their discipline is not another branch or subdiscipline of ethics, such as medical or business ethics. It is rather the expansion of every branch of ethics, the wider context for every ethical focus. Business ethics, for example, must now think not only socially and economically, but also ecologically—considering moral responsibilities to other life forms and their habitats, present and future, in economic planning. Henceforth, all ethics must be done in the context of ecological ethics—or else they will be distorted and constricted ethics.

The intention of ecological ethicists, with rare exceptions, is not to substitute biotic values for anthropic ones, but rather to weave these two sets together coherently for the enhancement of both—in short, to integrate the quests for social justice and ecological integrity, for the present and future.

See also ANIMAL RIGHTS; DEEP ECOLOGY; ECOFEMINISM; ECOLOGY; ECOLOGY, RELIGIOUS AND PHILOSOPHICAL ASPECTS; ECOLOGY, SCIENCE OF; ECOTHEOLOGY; GAIA HYPOTHESIS; FEMINISMS AND SCIENCE; FEMINIST COSMOLOGY; FEMINIST THEOLOGY; WOMANIST THEOLOGY

Bibliography

Des Jardins, Joseph R. *Environmental Ethics: An Introduction to Environmental Philosophy,* 3rd edition. Belmont, Calif.: Wadsworth, 2001.

Johnson, Lawrence. *A Morally Deep World: An Essay on Moral Significance and Environmental Ethics.* New York: Cambridge University Press, 1991.

Nash, James A. *Loving Nature: Ecological Integrity and Christian Responsibility.* Nashville, Tenn.: Abingdon Press, 1991.

Rasmussen, Larry. *Earth Community, Earth Ethics.* Maryknoll, N.Y.: Orbis Books, 1996.

Rolston, Holmes, III. *Environmental Ethics: Duties to and Values in the Natural World.* Philadelphia: Temple University Press, 1988.

Taylor, Paul W. *Respect for Nature: A Theory of Environmental Ethics.* Princeton, N.J.: Princeton University Press, 1986.

Westra, Laura. *An Environmental Proposal for Ethics: the Principle of Integrity.* Lanham, Md.: Rowman and Littlefield, 1994.

JAMES A. NASH

ECOLOGY, RELIGIOUS AND PHILOSOPHICAL ASPECTS

The word *ecology* has two meanings. It refers to a discipline within biology that studies ecosystems, and it refers to the ecosystems that biologists study. These ecosystems can include the local biotic communities with which, for example, indigenous peoples and farmers often have special bonds. But the concept of ecosystem can also apply to the whole of the Earth and the whole of the cosmos.

To call these larger wholes "ecosystems" is not to suggest that they are static or stable. Indeed, even local biotic communities are not static. Contemporary ecologists say that such communities are evolving and naturally subject to dramatic and sometimes chaotic changes, as is the larger whole, which scientists call the universe.

Religious people have different names for this larger and more inclusive whole. Jews, Christians, and Muslims often speak of the integrated whole as "the creation" and its ongoing development as "continuing creation." They say that creation includes the heavens as well as the Earth, that it has invisible as well as visible dimensions, and that humans are a part of, not apart from, this larger whole. Some Jews, Christians, and Muslims believe that the future of this whole is already determined by God, quite apart from decisions made in the present. Others believe that the future, at least of the Earth, is not yet determined and depends on present decisions. Religion, like science, has its determinists and nondeterminists.

For many religious people, it is the smaller ecosystems—the bioregions and their many forms of life on planet Earth—that are of greatest immediate concern. Environmental crises have prompted their concerns. They have been forced to ask: In what ways does my religion encourage or discourage healthy ways of (1) behaving toward, (2) thinking about, and (3) apprehending landscapes, life-support systems, and other forms of life?

On this matter Buddhist environmentalism is especially instructive. It does not speak of the universe as creation; rather it presents the universe as a beginningless and endless series of cosmic epochs. But Buddhist environmentalism points out that a healthy religious approach to nature includes all three forms of response just named: (1) moral conduct toward other living beings, (2) intellectual understanding of the interconnectedness of all things, and (3) mindful awareness of other living beings, on their own terms and for their own sakes, without projection. It emphasizes that mindful awareness can be nurtured, not simply by reading books about ecology, but by meditation and direct exposure to the palpable presences of the Earth.

Can science help religion?

As religious people face environmental crises, they can simultaneously ask: How might insights and information from the ecological sciences, and from other forms of science as well, help my religion to become more responsible and sensitive than it might otherwise be? The response is twofold.

On the one hand, most religious people realize that science provides relevant information that can help people make wise decisions in terms of land use, population, and pollution control. Additionally, some appreciate ways in which science can help humans better understand human continuities with other forms of life, both genetically and evolutionarily; better understand the interconnected nature of the whole of reality, as is affirmed in many Buddhist, Daoist, and Confucian points of view; and better understand that the Earth and cosmos are creative, containing potentialities for creative adaptation and renewal, even when things seem hopeless. Finally, some ecologically minded and religiously interested writers, Thomas Berry and Ursula Goodenough, for example, propose that science offers a common epic—the epic of evolution—that can itself inspire a sense of purpose and adventure, leading people to realize that "the great work" of our time is to help create mutually enhancing bonds between humans and the rest of the Earth.

On the other hand, many ecologically minded religious people simultaneously reject certain forms of materialism and reductionism that are characteristic of some but not all science. Particularly problematic are those (1) that reduce galactic and biological evolution to an amoral and purposeless process devoid of intrinsic worth or any capacity for divine guidance; (2) that insist that scientific ways of knowing—and those alone—provide wisdom concerning nature; and (3) that reduce living wholes—animals who are subjects of their own lives, for example—to mechanical wholes devoid of subjectivity and creativity. These rejections suggest that religious approaches to ecology, particularly at the level of worldview, will often differ from scientific approaches, even as they learn from science.

Ecotheologies and ecophilosophies

As religious people face the environmental crises, they are led to develop what are often called *ecotheologies* or *ecophilosophies*. Typically these theologies and philosophies explore the histories of religious traditions for usable insights and practices, criticize those aspects of the past that seem problematic rather than helpful, and develop new ideas that build upon, but also move beyond, inherited ways of acting, thinking, and feeling.

The development of these perspectives has been underway for several decades, but it has been catalyzed and brought into focus by work done at the Center for the Study of World Religions at Harvard University in Cambridge, Massachusetts, in collaboration with the Center for Respect of Life and Environment in Washington, D.C., and Bucknell University in Lewisburg, Pennsylvania. From May 1996 until July 1998, the Center for the Study of World Religions hosted a series of ten conferences, each involving scholars from the world's religions, all of which "explored particular intellectual and symbolic resources of a specific religious tradition regarding views of nature, ritual practices, and ethical constructs in relation to nature" (Tucker). The scholarly anthologies produced by these conferences offer a multivolume anthology on world religions and ecology.

Equally important is the work being done by creative scholars from the thousands of small scale, indigenous societies in the world, including Native American, African, Aboriginal, and South Asian. The religions of these peoples are indistinguishable from their cultures and there is much variation among them. Still, it is generally recognized, by scholars of classical religions and by representatives of indigenous traditions themselves, that the life-ways of indigenous peoples emphasize reciprocal relations between human beings and their local bioregions in ways that are more typically absent from classical traditions. The Harvard series included a conference on iIndigenous traditions, highlighting ways in which, even as these peoples offer no technological fixes for modern problems, they nevertheless offer examples of "a loving experience of place" from which many can learn.

Also important to religion and ecology is the work of philosophers around the world, some affiliated with religions and some not, who have simultaneously explored and criticized the past, and simultaneously developed new perspectives emphasizing human embeddedness in the larger web of life. Deep ecology and ecofeminist philosophies are prime examples. While some versions of these perspectives are philosophical rather than religious if the word *religion* implies allegiance to a classical religious tradition, all are religious in the sense that they are interested in helping guide humans toward sensitive ways of perceiving and responding to nature.

All of these ecotheologies and ecophilosophies have their distinctive features. Ecotheologies emerging out of the Abrahamic traditions often emphasize:

(1) that human beings are a part of, not apart from, a larger evolving whole;

(2) that they are kin to fellow creatures on Earth;

(3) that the whole of creation, including Earth, is embraced by a surrounding presence, namely God, who cares about the whole of creation and each living being within it;

(4) that God calls humans to embody alternatives to the more greed-driven lifestyles of consumer society;

(5) that God calls humans to be good stewards of the Earth and compassionate participants in the ongoing development of creation.

This compassionate participation involves commitment to four values advocated by "The Earth Charter": respect and care for the community of life; ecological integrity; social and economic justice; and nonviolence, democracy, and peace.

Among the Abrahamic ecotheologies that stress these five ways of thinking, process theology is especially important for people interested in the dialogue between religion and ecology; although it is environmentalist in orientation, it draws deeply from quantum theory, ecological biology, and evolutionary biology. It is an especially science-based form of contemporary ecotheology. It is also important because it wrestles with the reality of suffering in creation, proposing that the God who calls humans toward environmental responsibility is a counter-entropic and influential lure within creation, who is nevertheless not all-powerful in the classical sense of having unilateral power. From the perspective of process theology, the very God who calls toward compassion is a God who shares in the suffering of all creation and who is impoverished by a reduction in the Earth's biological diversity. The Earth and the whole of the universe is God's body.

Ecophilosophies emerging out of the various East Asian and South Asian traditions do not emphasize the role of God, but rather ground their commitments to a sustainable future in a deep sense of interconnectedness that is likewise consonant with many dimensions of science. To this emphasis on interconnectedness, they also add the importance of mindfulness in the present moment and the importance of having a nongrasping approach to life that allows other living beings simply "to be" without "being exploited." Here nonattachment does not mean nonappreciation, but rather nongrasping, precisely so that other living beings and the rest of nature can be appreciated on its own terms, without being a mere "commodity" for the consumer-driven mindset. With this emphasis they add to the critique of consumerism likewise offered by Abrahamic ecotheologians.

The deep ecology perspective and ecofeminist orientations add distinctive but complementary emphases to the Abrahamic and Asian perspectives just noted. Not unlike Buddhism, deep ecology emphasizes the notion of an ecological self whose inner horizons transcend the illusion of a skin-encapsulated ego and live from a deeper sense of kinship with the whole. Ecofeminism adds that the very illusion of a skin-encapsulated ego is often grounded in patriarchal habits of thought and feeling.

In short, the environmental crisis stimulates a great deal of work within religions and among those interested in religiously based alternatives to consumerist habits of thought and feeling. Some but not all of this work is enriched by insights from the sciences, even as some but not all is also critical of certain dimensions of science, especially its reductionistic and more determinist strands. The dialogue between religion and science involves a dialogue with the Earth, with which both religion and science are jointly and sometimes collaboratively engaged.

See also ANIMAL RIGHTS; BUDDHISM; CHINESE RELIGIONS, CONFUCIANISM AND SCIENCE IN CHINA; CHINESE RELIGIONS, DAOISM AND SCIENCE IN CHINA; DEEP ECOLOGY; ECOFEMINISM; ECOLOGY; ECOLOGY, ETHICS OF; ECOLOGY, SCIENCE OF; ECOTHEOLOGY; GAIA HYPOTHESIS; FEMINISMS AND SCIENCE; FEMINIST COSMOLOGY; FEMINIST THEOLOGY; PROCESS THOUGHT; WOMANIST THEOLOGY

Bibliography

The Earth Charter Initiative. "The Earth Charter." Available from http://www.earthcharter.org.

Tucker, Mary Evelyn. "Culminating Conferences on Ecology." Center for the Study of World Religions. Available from http://www.hds.harvard.edu/cswr/publications/5-2eco.htm.

JAY MCDANIEL

ECOLOGY, SCIENCE OF

Ecology is the study of the relationships of organisms with other organisms and with their physical environment. Ecology also includes study of the structure and functions of natural systems. The word *ecology* was first used in 1866 by the German biologist Ernst Haeckel (1834–1919), who based it on the Greek words *oikos,* meaning "household," and *logos,* meaning "study." Though modern ecology is less than a hundred years old as a science, it has quickly diversified into a number of subdisciplines, each with different concepts and research methods. Some subdisciplines can be described by organism (plant ecology, animal ecology) or by habitat (terrestrial ecology, marine ecology). Other forms of ecology reflect applied use of the science, as in restoration ecology or agroecology. In this entry, ecology will be described in terms of the scale and orientation of the scientists working on ecological questions. Common to all ecological perspectives are the role of evolution and historical change, the impacts of human activities on organisms and environments, and the use of models to represent complex interactions.

Approaches to ecology

There are six predominant approaches to ecology.

Some of the earliest work has been done by *community ecologists* who study patterns and processes in groups of species, asking questions about species diversity and complexity. A community can be defined in several ways: as the residents of a localized place, the historical presence of species in an area, a collection of co-existing populations, or as the collective interactions of species members moving through a place. Community ecology focuses on species relationships and abundance in specific places such as a desert wash, a peat bog, or a sandy beach. Typical research examines patterns of change over time such as plant succession after a fire. Scientists also study species distribution according to soil and climate conditions, and strategies used to cope with these conditions. Analytical methods include gradient analysis, diversity mapping, and computer modeling.

Population ecologists examine how and why the size of populations changes over time and place. They consider environmental factors such as temperature and rainfall as well as biological interactions such as predation. Growth rate, density, rate of reproduction, and mortality are key to understanding population flux. Population models show such things as changes in age classes over time or variability in predator-prey cycles. Factors of population regulation are important in managing game harvests and agricultural pests, as well as protecting endangered species. Population ecologists rely on field data, experimental studies, and computer modeling to chart population dynamics.

Behavioral ecologists focus on adaptive behaviors in animals that have been successful in survival and reproduction. Unlike community and population ecology, which address broad groups of organisms, behavioral ecology looks at the individual and how its behaviors have evolved to serve the individual's fitness. Life history strategies reflect the tradeoffs animals make between survival and reproduction. Drawing on field observations as well as experimental tests, behavioral ecologists use cost-benefit models and game theory to propose explanations for animal behaviors. How an animal forages for food, chooses a mate, or raises its young reveal something about the ecological contexts in which the species has evolved.

Physiological ecologists look at the biochemical constraints that define whether an organism survives or not. Variation in environmental factors such as habitat temperature, nutrient availability, and light level can be optimal or stressful, depending on an individual's tolerance. Below freezing, sensitive plant cells can burst; starved for oxygen, fish in a polluted lake can die. Thermoregulation and other mechanisms of homeostasis help stabilize organisms in response to changing abiotic conditions. To describe the dimensions of a species's ecological niche, physiological ecologists measure metabolic chemistry, energy use, and rates of growth. Radiotelemetry instruments are used to collect data on heart rate, body temperature, and environmental conditions from such animals as deep-diving whales or far-ranging wolves. In the related field of ecotoxicology, scientists track the impacts of human-made chemicals such as DDT and dioxin.

Ecosystem ecology along with landscape ecology, is one of the most recent subdisciplines to emerge in the science of ecology. The goal of ecosystem ecology is to understand the movement of energy and matter as they circulate through organisms and the environment. Studies of nutrient cycling in an ecosystem ask questions about flow patterns, seasonal variation, and biological productivity. As human activities accelerate the degradation of ecosystem functions, increasing attention has been focused on ecosystem resilience and sustainability. Many ecosystem level questions originate in the field, with information integrated into sophisticated models using statistical analyses and flow diagrams. Both restoration of damaged ecosystems and clean-up of toxic contaminants draw on the knowledge base of ecosystem ecology.

Landscape ecology examines even broader scale patterns of environmental change. Landscape-level studies focus on mosaics of habitat patches to understand causes and consequences of long-term historical change. Clearcutting or forest fires, for example, set up ecological dynamics that can change the shape of the landscape in many ways. Likewise, changes in climate or the Earth's surface through mountain-building or erosion affect species composition and habitat distribution. Aerial photographs are used to collect broad-scale information which is then stored in computerized geographic information systems (GIS). Landscape ecologists engage land management issues of patch viability and habitat connectivity, using complex maps and models to compare the impacts of different land-use policies.

Conclusion

Ecological theories have changed significantly over the last century as ecologists ask different questions and use different tools to gather and process information. From traditional natural history observation to complex modern computer modeling, ecology has made enormous advances. Ideas of nature have likewise changed and influenced the development and application of ecological theories. Earlier views of climax communities as the inevitable outcome of competition have been replaced with more dynamic views of nature. The role of human agents in ecosystem change has become more widely included in ecological analysis. While much early research was oriented to management and production goals, modern ecologists are motivated by the desire to protect and restore biological diversity and ecosystem health. As human population and consumption continue to impact the environment, the science of ecology will have a critical role to play in leading the way toward a sustainable future.

See also ANIMAL RIGHTS; DEEP ECOLOGY; ECOFEMINISM; ECOLOGY, ETHICS OF; ECOLOGY, RELIGIOUS AND PHILOSOPHICAL ASPECTS; ECOTHEOLOGY; GAIA HYPOTHESIS; FEMINISMS AND SCIENCE; FEMINIST COSMOLOGY; FEMINIST THEOLOGY; WOMANIST THEOLOGY

Bibliography

Dodson, Stanley I.; Allen, Timothy F.H.; Carpenter, Stephen R.; et al. *Ecology.* New York: Oxford University Press, 1998.

Forman, Richard T. T., and Godron, Michael. *Landscape Ecology.* New York: Wiley, 1986.

Jordan, William R, III; Gilpin, Michael E.; and Aber, John D. *Restoration Ecology.* Cambridge, UK: Cambridge University Press, 1987.

Meffe, Gary K., and Carroll, C. Ronald, eds. *Principles of Conservation Ecology,* 2nd edition. Sunderland, Mass.: Sinauer Associates, 1997.

Miller, G. Tyler, Jr. *Living in the Environment.* Belmont, Calif.: Wadsworth, 1990.

Noss, Reed F., and Cooperrider, Allen Y. *Saving Nature's Legacy.* Washington D.C.: Island, 1994.

Smith, Robert L., and Smith, Thomas M. *Elements of Ecology,* 4th edition. Menlo Park, Calif.: Addison-Wesley, 1998.

Soule, Michael, ed. *Conservation Biology.* Sunderland, Mass.: Sinauer Associates, 1986.

STEPHANIE KAZA

ECONOMICS

The field of economics encompasses the study of how natural resources are drawn from nature and processed by human activity to become value-added products for consumption or commodities for exchange; the study of how complex services are developed by coordinating human activities so that particular services can be rationally provided, bought, or sold; and the study of how the resulting resources are allocated, and how the costs and benefits of these processes are calculated.

Highly specialized subdisciplines of this vast field developed after the Industrial Revolution, the rise to social dominance of the modern business corporation, the sharp debates between capitalist and socialist theories during the nineteenth and twentieth centuries, and the increased globalization of the contemporary world. *Econometrics* seeks to measure actual processes and their consequences in a delimited institutional range—a family, firm, nation, industry, or segment of the population such as a race or a class. *Regression analysis* seeks to develop models that can interpret the relative effects of a variable or a set of variables. Other subdisciplines focus on policy-making and are intended to bring desired social results. *Macroeconomics,* for example, focuses on tax or other governmental policies that aim to enhance development or public services, reduce poverty or inequality, or control behaviors that damage the common welfare (crime, environmental damage, drug abuse, child pornography, health or safety, etc.). *Microeconomics* seeks to enhance the efficiency, productivity, profitability, and viability of companies that operate in various markets. *Labor economics,* which often engages in advocacy, studies both political and business policies from the standpoint of their effects on employees and workers' unions. Despite their differences in focus, experts in all economic subdisciplines agree that without a sound economic infrastructure, societies falter and people suffer.

History

Economic activity has always been a part of human existence. Hunting, gathering, and cooking have taken place since humans first appeared. Production by craftsworkers to supply goods for trade and for merchants has been present in all of recorded history. Early theories of economic life date back to discussions about farmers and peddlers in the *Arthashastra,* an Indian treatise on governance from about the third century B.C.E. The concept of *shangye* (commercial occupation) in early Confucian texts sought to spell out the relationships of economic actors to political and social life. Economic theories also turn up in ancient Greek writings. Plato (c. 428–347 B.C.E.) saw the foundation of *The Republic* as rooted in economic life (Book 2), and in *Politics* Aristotle (384–322 B.C.E.) developed the idea of the "management of the household" (*oikonomia*) and applied it to the *polis.*

Moreover, economic issues were taken up by religious prophets and moral philosophers in all known cultures, and in the West the blend of biblical themes and Greek philosophy has decisively shaped the social and ethical perceptions of economic life and policy. That is so despite the fact that economics in its modern mode has sought to differentiate itself from these social, ethical, and spiritual philosophies. Indeed, it has become a truly autonomous science on the model of the natural sciences since, at least, the French physiocrats and the English post-mercantilist economists from Adam Smith (1723–1790) through the utilitarians to John Maynard Keynes (1883–1946) and the German socialists and the Austrian libertarians. It is these modern Western sets of perspectives and debates that have most shaped what is today understood as the discipline of economics.

Economics as a discipline, for all its achievements, is not identical to economic life. The heirs of Adam Smith, and those of Karl Marx (1818–1883) or Friedrich Hayek (1899–1992), have developed refined theories that describe how the "rational choices" of persons, families, classes, governments, businesses, or market mechanisms (such as a stock exchange, employment and wage rates, or a futures market) typically manifest themselves, although economists know that they are working with abstract models. The great advantage of such models is that they can be developed and applied in many concrete circumstances by ruling out idiosyncratic and extrinsic contingencies that may also influence decisions or policies but are not directly economic factors. The best economic theories not only have a mathematical and philosophical mark of elegance, they also have a high degree of reliability when applied to specific questions and adjusted to specific contexts.

These models work best in an environment that shares a common society, a common culture, and, since they deeply influence the perceptions and expectations of persons and communities, something of a common set of religious convictions. That is because the "conditionalities" of behavior, what strict economic theory considers to be idiosyncratic or extrinsic contingency, are different where divergent cultural, social, or religious convictions shape morality in distinctive ways. It is true that no one wants to be cheated and that stealing or exploitation is recognized as wrong in every culture, even if it occurs. And it is true that people seek the well-being of the persons or groups that are most important to them in all sorts of social,

cultural, or religious conditions. But it is also the case that a polygamous tribal person, for example, or a Hindu caste member, a dedicated leader of an Islamic brotherhood, or a Buddhist nun will have different senses of what constitutes the well-being of persons and groups. It is, thus, not at all surprising that the banking systems in different parts of the world are operationally different, that corporations are formed in distinctive ways and led with diverse understandings of the proper role of leadership, and that workers variously evaluate their obligations to firm, family, nation, political ideology, and faith.

Basic disputes and issues

The attempts to account for these contextual differences are among the key subjects of cultural studies, the sociology of religion, and comparative religious ethics to the extent that these fields bear on economic matters; the issues are paralleled by political, legal, and aesthetic studies. In the West, John Locke (1632–1704) and Thomas Hobbes (1588–1679) can be considered exemplars of a primal disagreement about how economic life works in society. For Locke, persons have a right to their *"proprium,"* that property that they appropriate from nature by honest labor and that is necessary both for their individual existence and for the support of their family. On these bases, people form a civil society with others and construct a political society for the protection of their own and others' well-being. They are aided in this effort by the fact that all persons can, in some measure, recognize the "self-evident truths" of a universal moral law, guaranteed both by reason and by Christian scripture. If the political society does not work, or violates the moral law, the people have a right to alter it to restore their economic and social well-being.

For Hobbes, perpetual conflict over scarce resources could not be resolved by either reason or religion, and thus a sovereign had to impose a collective order by force. Politics must control economics, and no rebellion was allowed. The obvious and brutal conflicts of interests, ideologies, and religions demanded state power so that economic well-being could be obtained beyond the natural state of war. In this paradigmatic dispute, one finds not only the question of the relationship of the bee to the hive in economic life, but the issue of the relative priority of civil society to political society as determinants of economic existence.

A second set of disputes can be seen in the controversies of those who follow Georg Wilhelm Friedrich Hegel (1770–1831) and those who follow his disputatious disciple, Marx. Hegel held that spiritual or mental (*geistliche*) realities fundamentally shape material realities in a decisive dialectic. Marx, famously turning Hegel on his head, argued that it was not "superstructural" factors that shaped "substructural" factors, but rather the material realities of life that determined human consciousness. Any correlation between religious orientation and economic life was an effect of economic forces that evoked the religious sighs of the people, while those who had control of the means of production perpetuated these dreams to control the workers.

These theories combine in mixed ways. A version of the materialist view can be found among various contemporary disciples of Charles Darwin (1809–1882). Some of them, including the Nobel Prize winning economist Gary Becker (1930–), hold to an "evolutionary psychology" in which individuals make "rational choices" about not only business matters but also about whom to marry and whether to have children on the basis of their calculation of material interests. A collectivist view of economic behavior is set forth by Edward O. Wilson (1929–) in his sociobiological theories; this view sees religion as an illusory cultural by-product of collective material and instinctual dynamics.

More influential in the understanding of the relationship of religion and economic life is the work of Max Weber (1864–1920). His five volumes on the *Sociology of Religion* and his three volumes on *Economy and Society,* written early in the twentieth century, argued that different religions have distinct effects on economic (and political) life and on various classes and occupational groups in society. Weber saw not only that the late medieval Roman Catholic faith had an economically positive influence in the emerging free cities of northern Europe in the very early stages of modernity, but that the Protestant ethic gave impetus to the formation of what is now known as the break with traditional, feudal economies and the development of modern capitalist industries. Weber's arguments were doubted during the harsh realities of the Great Depression (which saw greater use of Marxist theory and the rise of Fascism), and were often ignored after World War II when Keynes's economic theories came to ascendancy, but Weber's work regained attention after the collapse of the Soviet Union in the early 1990s and the resurgence of religion all over the world. Today, few economists think that Weber's treatments of India and China were fully adequate, and questions about aspects of his views of Catholicism, Protestantism, and Islam are manifold. Yet, it is widely held that the questions he raised and the methods of investigation he developed are among the most definitive for the ongoing discussions between religion and economic life.

In a postmodern age, the predicted certainties of inevitable secularization that seemed beyond dispute, of a purely scientific view of reality that could provide firm foundations for progressive public policy, clear-minded corporate decision-making and personal rational choices without illusion, and the end of both ideology and religious myth seem positively silly. Indeed, it turns out that a deep convergence of inter-contextual reasonability and moral conviction, not equally available in all religions, are critical for the economic well-being of persons and peoples. The body of contemporary literature that points in this direction is found in a host of Weber-influenced studies that document the interactions of religion and economic life, and point out that the basic assumptions behind contemporary secular economic theory are, in fact, echoes of religious convictions that are well, but not fully, masked.

See also CULTURE, ORIGINS OF; MATERIALISM; MORALITY

Bibliography

Berger, Peter. *The Capitalist Revolution: Fifty Propositions about Prosperity, Equality, and Liberty.* New York: Basic Books, 1986.

Harrison, Lawrence E., and Huntington, Samuel P., eds. *Culture Matters: How Values Shape Human Progress.* New York: Basic Books, 2000.

Küng, Hans. *A Global Ethic for Global Politics and Economics.* New York: Oxford University Press, 1999.

Landis, David S. *The Wealth and Poverty of Nations: Why Some are So Rich and Some So Poor.* New York: Norton, 1997.

Nelson, Robert H. *Economics as Religion: From Samuelson to Chicago and Beyond.* University Park: Pennsylvania State University Press, 2001.

Sen, Amartya. *Development as Freedom.* New York: Anchor, 1999.

Stackhouse, Max L.; McCann, Dennis P.; Roels, Shirley J., eds. *On Moral Business: Classical and Contemporary Resources for Ethics in Economic Life.* Grand Rapids, Mich: Eerdmans, 1995.

Stackhouse, Max L., with Peter Paris, eds. *God and Globalization,* Vol. 1: *Religion and the Powers of the Common Life.* Harrisburg, Pa.: Trinity Press International, 2000

Stackhouse, Max L, with Don S. Browning, eds. *God and Globalization,* Vol. 2: *The Spirit and the Modern Authorities.* Harrisburg, Pa.: Trinity Press International, 2001

Stackhouse, Max L., with Diane B. Obenchain, eds. *God and Globalization,* Vol. 3: *Christ and the Dominions of Civilization.* Harrisburg, Pa.: Trinity Press International, 2002.

Weber, Max. *Economy and Society: An Outline of Interpretive Sociology,* trans. Ephraim Fischoff and others, eds. Guenther Roth and Claus Wittich. Berkeley: University of California Press, 1978.

Weber, Max. *Sociology of Religion,* trans. Ephraim Fischoff. Boston: Beacon Press, 1993.

MAX L. STACKHOUSE

ECOTHEOLOGY

The term *ecotheology* came into prominence in the late twentieth century, mainly in Christian circles, in association with the emergent scientific field of ecology. Ecotheology describes theological discourse that highlights the whole "household" of God's creation, especially the world of nature, as an interrelated system (*eco* is from the Greek word for household, *oikos*). Ecotheology arose in response to the widespread acknowledgment that an environmental crisis of immense proportions was threatening the future of human life on the earth. Ecotheology also arose in response to what has been called "the ecological complaint" against Christianity.

The ecological complaint

Some scholars and critics maintain that the Christian faith helped set the stage for the global environmental crisis by instructing generations of believers that God transcends nature, that humans likewise transcend nature, and that nature therefore has meaning in the Christian schema only as an instrument for God's purposes with humans.

The signature Christian teaching in this respect was the theology of human dominion over nature (also called *stewardship*), a theology that encouraged manipulation, even exploitation, of nature for the sake of human purposes. According to these scholars and critics, Christianity is unavoidably anthropocentric, no longer relevant to the ecological world, and even, in a sense, spiritually dangerous.

The historical truth, however, is more complex, as a review of Christian theology since 1500 will show. While the emergence of ecotheology is relatively recent, its historic roots in the Christian theology of nature are deep. Christians have held a variety of views about nature, all of them rooted in widely divergent socioeconomic and cultural situations. A nuanced understanding of Christian attitudes to nature must address those differing contexts as well as the explicit theological teachings themselves.

A critical case is the Christian understanding of human dominion over nature. The meanings of this teaching varied substantially from one period to another. From about 1500 to 1750, human dominion was understood in terms of survival in the midst of a threatening world. Much economic life in those times was carried on at a subsistence level, highly dependent on the precarious cycles of small-scale agriculture. Except for the most wealthy, the vast majority of the people had to struggle, with minimal aid from technology and with pervasive dependence on farm animals, such as oxen, in order to hack out agricultural spaces from the primeval forests, where threatening predators, such as wolves, roamed freely, and where a sustainable level of agricultural productivity was highly uncertain. Moreover, although many people lived in the same buildings with their farm animals, which were part of their domestic world, their attitudes toward wild animals tended to be negative, especially within the ranks of the wealthy, who sometimes fostered a hunting culture predicated on delight in killing.

In this socioeconomic context, the biblical idea of human dominion over the earth would have been read and enacted in terms of a life-and-death struggle with the vicissitudes of nature. After the mid eighteenth century, towns and cities emerged in significant numbers in Europe, and human dominion over nature was no longer interpreted in the context of an agricultural struggle for survival, but more in terms of an increasingly crowded urbanized world that was predicated on the exploitation of nature, a world that sometimes prompted a romantic nostalgia for the remembered beauties and purities of life in the country. Human dominion over nature came to be viewed by some believers as a problem, rather than as a self-evident mandate in the quest for survival.

By the beginning of the twentieth century, trends of massive urbanization and industrialization, constantly expanding applications of earth-shaking technologies, especially in mining and agriculture, and concomitant pollution of the land, sea, and air in virtually every region of the planet had increased to the breaking point. Issues of human survival on the earth began to emerge, heightened by a growing awareness of the related problems of global poverty, exhaustion of nonrenewable natural resources, and enormous population growth. This global crisis, in turn, posed unprecedented questions to Christian communities around the world. The Christian teaching of human dominion over the earth came under attack, both by believers and by critics hostile to the Christian tradition, because it seemed to symbolize much that was wrong with the way humans had chosen to live on the earth. By the end of the twentieth century, the theme of human dominion over nature had become, in the eyes of many, a scandal. On the other hand, the same theme continued to be affirmed by a few leading Christian theologians and by numerous prominent Christian public policy-makers, who wrote and acted as if the world needed nothing more than business-as-usual.

Such were the major socioeconomic contexts to which Christian theologians responded, consciously or unconsciously. Significantly, these trends were made possible by the burgeoning natural sciences, above all by the mechanistic science championed by Isaac Newton at the turn of the eighteenth century and by the evolutionary science advocated by Charles Darwin during the nineteenth century. Theology was buffeted by these cultural forces, too, especially by Darwinism, which sent tidal waves of anti-religious sentiment coursing through the intellectual world of the times. On the other hand, many theologians thought of their work not as responding to questions raised by socioeconomic or cultural trends, but as a creative exposition of the whole body of

traditional Christian teachings, according to the tradition's own norms.

The world of nature and Protestantism

Self-conscious theological reflection about the world of nature was most prominently launched by the two major Protestant reformers of the sixteenth century—Martin Luther and John Calvin—who gave voice to a rich theology of nature. "In every part of the world, in heaven and on earth," Calvin wrote in his *Institutes,* God "has written and as it were engraven the glory of his power, goodness, wisdom and eternity . . . For the little singing birds sang of God, the animals acclaimed him, the elements feared and the mountains resounded with him, the river and springs threw glances toward him, the grasses and the flowers smiled." Calvin even suggested that when humans contemplate the wonders of God in nature "we should not merely run them over cursorily, and, so to speak, with the fleeting glance, but we should ponder them at length, turn them over in our mind seriously and faithfully, and recollect them repeatedly."

Luther had a similar view of the glories of God in the whole creation and of creation's marvels. "If you truly understood a grain of wheat," he once wrote, "you would die of wonder." In his commentary on Genesis, Luther imagined Adam and Eve before the fall enjoying a common table with the animals. In the same spirit, both reformers thought theocentrically about human interactions with nature: God and his righteousness will set very real limits for the reaches of human pride and arrogance. The created world belonged first and foremost to the Creator and humans were mandated by God to exercise dominion over the earth. But that dominion was understood to be a restoration of Adam's and Eve's lives as caretakers or gardeners, not as a license for exploitation.

Further, both Calvin and Luther affirmed the immediacy of God in nature. For them, God was not detached from the world, far above in some spiritualized heaven. On the contrary, as Luther often said, God is "in, with, and under" the whole created world. This view of nature as divinely given and divinely charged came to its completion in their the reformers' teachings about "last things" (eschatology). Both theologians strongly emphasized the traditional Christian teaching about the resurrection of the body. Both also projected a view of the end of the world as a cosmic consummation, the coming of the "new heavens and new earth" announced in biblical traditions. Nature itself would be "saved" and consummated at the very end.

Fatefully, however, the issues that preoccupied Luther and Calvin had to do not with God and nature, but with God and human salvation. Their theologies, accordingly, took on an anthropocentric character. "Justification by grace through faith alone" was the theological teaching that most occupied their attention. Furthermore, Calvin accented the responsibility of Christians to change the world for the better, teaching that the world was the arena for righteous work and faith-driven social transformation.

The theological heirs of Luther and Calvin, especially in the nineteenth century and thereafter, took the reformers' measured anthropocentrism as a given, but tended to leave behind the reformers' rich teaching about God and the natural world. As a result, Christian theology became more exclusively anthropocentric. There were many reasons for this marked shift of emphasis, not the least of them being the rise of Newtonian mechanistic science and Darwinian evolutionary science, and the need by these post-Reformation theologians to root religious faith in the intangible human spirit or human subjectivity, so as to leave the objective world of nature to natural scientists, and also to protect faith from the attacks of some scientists and scientifically informed philosophers. This anthropocentric dynamic also made it easy for both theologians and Christian lay people to be swept along by the dynamics of industrial society, which were predicated on the exploitations of the earth for the sake of human progress.

Accordingly, many theologians in the first half of the twentieth century, like Emil Brunner and Karl Barth, self-consciously refused to project theologies of nature. Their theologies focused on God and humankind alone. When they did talk about nature, it was typically in highly anthropocentric terms. Both Brunner and Barth affirmed, for example, that the purpose for which God created the world was to have a redemptive history with humankind. Brunner called nature merely "the scenery" for the divine-human drama.

Catholic theologians had to deal with the same socioeconomic and cultural trends, but the officially sanctioned teachings of the Catholic Church tended to be mainly reactive to the expanding claims of the natural sciences, until well into the twentieth century. Traditional Catholic teachings about God's creation of the world and human dominion over the earth were simply affirmed against the advances in science represented by Newton and Darwin. Thus the work of twentieth-century Catholic paleontologist and theologian Pierre Teilhard de Chardin, who claimed evolution as a theological theme, were banned by the Papacy until the middle of the twentieth century.

The ecological turn

It was not until the second half of the twentieth century that Christian theology began to take an ecological turn. Teilhard himself had led the way by incorporating evolutionary thought into the corpus of his theology, although Teilhard's theology remained anthropocentric in many ways. The mid-century Protestant thinker Paul Tillich was also a prophetic voice, eschewing the anthropocentrism of theologians like Brunner and Barth, radically criticizing the destructive power of modern "technical reason," and richly reaffirming and reinterpreting Luther's theology of nature in terms of Tillich's own doctrine of God as "the Ground of Being." The era of ecotheology fully emerged, however, only in the 1960s. It was first announced publicly by the pioneering Protestant ecotheologian Joseph Sittler. Drawing on Paul's Letter to the Colossians, Sittler called for a new theology of grace that included rather than excluded nature. Sittler was the first to give the term *ecology* public prominence as a theological construct and also took the lead in establishing conversations with ecologists like Aldo Leopold and reconsidering Christian poets of ecological consciousness such as Gerard Manly Hopkins.

Perhaps the single most important advocate of ecotheology toward the end of the twentieth century was the ecumenically oriented Protestant theologian Jürgen Moltmann. Drawing on the theologies of the reformers, the fruits of twentieth century studies of biblical eschatology, and immanentalist insights from the traditions of Jewish mysticism, Moltmann projected a theology of hope for the whole cosmos, giving a holistic, ecological shape to Christian teaching, including an impressive response to issues of global poverty, so much a part of the emergent global environmental crisis. The Protestant theologian John Cobb also made substantial contributions to Christian thought about nature, especially by his explorations of the resources offered to ecotheology by process thought, associated with the work of the twentieth century philosopher Alfred North Whitehead.

Ecotheological ethics emerged, too, as a theological field in its own right through the labors of scholars like the Protestant theologian James Nash, who argued that "loving nature" must be an essential theme for Christian theology. Catholic thinkers, such as Thomas Berry and Denis Edwards, made significant contributions to ecotheology drawing respectively on the findings of twentieth-century scientific cosmology and on the wisdom theology of the Bible. In addition, a number of Christian ecofeminists, most prominent among them Rosemary Radford Ruether and Sallie McFague, offered a range of fresh theological methodologies and insights, often reading between the lines of traditional texts to discern how the experience of women and the theological appreciation of nature had been suppressed by normative patriarchal theologians. In addition, the testimony of Eastern Orthodox theology, voiced by thinkers such as Paulos Gregorios, was heard in ecumenical circles emerging from centuries of affirmation of nature by many Orthodox communities. Toward the end of the twentieth century, a growing number of biblical scholars moved away from the anthropocentric assumptions of the previous generation to new and often highly suggestive understandings of the biblical theology of creation.

Vision of ecotheology

All these thinkers presented visions of nature much more consonant with the theologies of Luther and Calvin—although often departing from the reformers' thought in significant ways—than with later anthropocentric trajectories of Christian thought. Viewed as a theological movement, these late twentieth-century ecotheologians can be said to have shared a single vision, rooted in early modern theologies of nature. Characteristically, they championed:

(1) the idea of divine immanence in the whole cosmos;

(2) a relational, ecological rather than a hierarchical understanding of God, humans, and the created world;

(3) a radically reinterpreted view of human dominion over nature in terms of partnership with nature; and

(4) a commitment to justice for all creatures, not just humans, highlighting the needs of the impoverished masses and endangered species around the globe.

Their theological labors, along with the work of numerous other theologians, reflected theological concerns that emerged from the grass roots in churches around the world. These concerns came to public expression in the second half of the twentieth century in the form of a number of prophetic teachings promulgated by denominational and ecumenical bodies in order to address the global environment crisis. By the year 2002, Christian ecotheology had emerged as a theological movement that had begun to speak with a new and powerful voice on behalf of the whole creation "groaning in travail" (Rom. 8:22).

See also ANIMAL RIGHTS; ANTHROPOCENTRISM; DEEP ECOLOGY; ECOFEMINISM; ECOLOGY; ECOLOGY, ETHICS OF; ECOLOGY, RELIGIOUS AND PHILOSOPHICAL ASPECTS; ECOLOGY, SCIENCE OF; GAIA HYPOTHESIS; FEMINISMS AND SCIENCE; FEMINIST COSMOLOGY; FEMINIST THEOLOGY; PROCESS THOUGHT; WHITEHEAD, ALFRED NORTH; WOMANIST THEOLOGY

Bibliography

Bakken, Peter W.; Engel, Johan Gibb; and Engel, J. Ronald. *Ecology, Justice, and Christian Faith: A Critical Guide to the Literature*. Westport, Conn.: Greenwood, 1995.

Berry, Thomas. *The Dream of the Earth*. San Francisco: Sierra Club, 1988.

Birch, Charles, and Cobb, John B., Jr. *The Liberation of Life: From the Cell to the Community*. Cambridge, UK: Cambridge University Press, 1981.

Bouma-Prediger, Steven. *For the Beauty of the Earth: A Christian Vision for Creation Care*. Grand Rapids, Mich.: Erdmans, 2001.

Bouma-Prediger, Steven. *The Greening of Theology: The Ecological Models of Rosemary Radford Ruether, Joseph Sittler, and Juergen Moltmann*. Atlanta, Ga.: Scholars Press, 1995.

Calvin, John. *Institutes of the Christian Religion* (1559). Philadelphia: Westminster Press, 1960.

Cobb, John B., Jr. *Is It Too Late? A Theology of Ecology,* rev. edition. Denten, Tex.: Environmental Ethics Books, 1995.

Edwards, Denis. *Jesus and the Wisdom of God.* Maryknoll, N.Y.: Orbis, 1995.

Fowler, Robert Booth. *The Greening of Protestant Thought.* London and Chapel Hill: University of North Carolina Press, 1995.

Fox, Matthew. *The Coming of the Cosmic Christ: The Healing of Mother Earth and the Birth of a Global Renaissance.* New York: Harper, 1988.

French, William. "Subject-Centered and Creation-Centered Paradigms in Recent Catholic Thought." *Journal of Religion* 70 (1990): 48–72.

Gregorios, Paulos Mar. *The Human Presence: An Orthodox View of Nature.* Geneva, Switzerland: World Council of Churches, 1978.

Haught, John. *The Promise of Nature: Ecology and Cosmic Purpose.* New York: Paulist Press, 1993.

Hessel, Dieter, and Rasmussen, Larry, eds. *Earth Habitat: Eco-injustice and the Church's Response.* Minneapolis, Minn.: Fortress Press, 2001.

Hessel, Dieter T., and Ruether, Rosemary Radford, eds. *Christianity and Ecology: Seeking the Well-Being of Earth and Humans.* Cambridge, Mass.: Harvard University Press, 2000.

Hiebert, Theodore. "Reimaging Nature: Shifts in Biblical Interpretations." *Interpretation* 50 (1996): 36–46.

Linzey, Andrew. *Animal Theology.* Urbana: University of Illinois Press, 1995.

McFague, Sallie. *The Body of God: An Ecological Theology.* Minneapolis, Minn.: Fortress Press, 1993.

Moltmann, Jürgen. *God in Creation: A New Theology of Creation and the Spirit of God,* trans. Margaret Kohl. San Francisco: Harper, 1985.

Nash, James A. *Loving Nature: Ecological Integrity and Christian Responsibility.* Nashville, Tenn.: Abingdon Press, 1991.

Nash, Roderick Frazier. *The Rights of Nature: A History of Environmental Ethics.* Madison: University of Wisconsin Press, 1989.

Rasmussen, Larry L. *Earth Community, Earth Ethics.* New York: Orbis, 1996.

Rossing, Barbara R. "River of Life in God's New Jerusalem: An Eschatological Vision for Earth's Future." In *Christianity and Ecology: Seeking the Well-Being of Earth and Humans,* eds. Dieter T. Hessel and Rosemary Ruether. Cambridge, Mass.: Harvard University Press, 2000.

Ruether, Rosemary Radford. *Gaia and God: An Ecofeminist Theology of Earth Healing.* San Francisco: Harper, 1992.

Santmire, H. Paul. *Nature Reborn: The Ecological and Cosmic Promise of Christian Theology.* Minneapolis, Minn.: Fortress Press, 2000.

Santmire, H. Paul. *The Travail of Nature: The Ambiguous Ecological Promise of Christian Theology.* Philadelphia: Fortress Press, 1985.

Simkins, Ronald A. *Creator and Creation: Nature in the Worldview of Ancient Israel.* Peabody, Mass.: Hendrickson, 1994.

Sittler, Joseph. *Evocations of Grace: The Writings of Joseph Sittler on Ecology, Theology, and Ethics,* eds. Steven Bouma-Prediger and Peter Bakken. Grand Rapids, Mich.: Eerdmans, 2000.

Teilhard de Chardin, Pierre. *The Hymn of the Universe,* trans. Simon Bartholomew. New York: Harper, 1965

Thomas, Keith. *Man and the Natural World: A History of the Modern Sensibility.* New York: Pantheon, 1983.

Tillich, Paul. "Nature and Sacrament." In *The Protestant Era,* trans. James Luther Adams. Chicago: University of Chicago Press, 1957.

White, Lynn, Jr. "The Historical Roots of Our Ecological Crisis." *Science* 155 (1967): 1203–1207.

H. PAUL SANTMIRE

EINSTEIN, ALBERT

Albert Einstein is generally regarded as the greatest theoretical physicist of the twentieth century, if not of all time. Modern physics bears his mark more than any other physicist. His Special Theory of Relativity changed our conceptions of space, time, motion, and matter, and his General Theory of Relativity was the first new theory of gravitation since Isaac Newton's. Yet his work went beyond the boundaries of physics as he engaged himself in the educational, cultural, and philosophical concerns of his generation. Less known is Einstein's interest and personal engagement in religious matters. In specific, he strongly opposed the proposition that science and religion are irreconcilable.

Early life and influences

Albert Einstein, whose ancestors had lived in southern Germany for many generations, was born on March 14, 1879, in Ulm, Germany. The fact that his parents, Hermann Einstein and Pauline Einstein, née Koch, did not call him Abraham after his deceased grandfather, as Jewish tradition required, and that his sister, his only sibling, born 1881, was called Maria, shows that his parents did not observe religious rites although they never renounced their Jewish heritage. In 1889, the Einstein family moved to Munich, where Albert at the age of six was sent to a Catholic elementary school. At home a distant relative introduced him to the principles of Judaism and evoked in him such a fervent religious sentiment, that he observed Jewish religious prescriptions and even chided his parents for eating pork. At age ten he entered the interdenominational Luitpold Gymnasium, where he excelled in mathematics and Latin.

Ironically, his religious enthusiasm ended abruptly as the result of the only religious custom his parents observed, the hosting of a poor Jewish student for a weekly meal. This beneficiary was Max Talmud, a medical student older than Albert by ten years. He gave Albert books on science and philosophy, amongst them Ludwig Büchner's (1824–1899) materialistic *Force and Matter* (1874). Albert was particularly impressed by Büchner's survey of theriomorphic and therianthropic religions, in which animals or their combinations with humans were apotheosized. As Einstein, in his autobiographical notes, wrote, "through the reading of these books I reached the conclusion that much in the stories of the Bible could not be true. The consequence was a fanatic freethinking . . . suspension against every kind of authority . . . an attitude which has never again left me, even though later on, because of a better insight into the causal connections, it lost much of its original poignancy" (Schlipp p. 5).

In 1894, Albert's parents, for commercial reasons, moved to Italy. Left alone and hating the authoritarian discipline at the Gymnasium, Albert joined his parents before finishing school. At the Swiss cantonal school in Aarau he obtained the diploma that enabled him to enroll in the Swiss Federal Polytechnic School (ETH) in Zurich, where he studied physics and mathematics and graduated in 1900. Unable to find a regular academic position, he supported himself by tutoring and part-time school teaching until June 1902, when he obtained the appointment of technical expert third class at the patent office in Berne. A year later he married Mileva Maric, a Greek Orthodox Serbian, with whom he had fallen in love when they were classmates at the ETH. Little is known about their daughter Lieserl, who was born in 1902 before their marriage during Mileva's visit to her parents. Albert seems never to have seen her. Their first son, Hans Albert, was born in 1904, and their second son, Eduard, in 1910.

Theories and career

Einstein liked the job at the patent office because it was interesting and also left him time to pursue his own work in theoretical physics. He already had a number of important publications, mostly on thermodynamics, to his credit. But the year 1905 became his *annus mirabilis*. In March he completed his paper on the light-quantum hypothesis, in May his paper on Brownian motion, and in June his celebrated essay on the special theory of relativity, which was followed in September by his derivation of the famous mass-energy relation $E = mc^2$, the most famous equation in science.

In 1908 Einstein became Lecturer at the University of Berne, in 1911 full professor in Prague, and a year later he became a professor at the ETH. In April 1914, less than four months before the outbreak of the First World War, he moved to Berlin with his wife and two sons to serve as university professor without teaching obligations and as director of the Kaiser Wilhelm Institute of Physics.

Mileva disliked Berlin and returned with the children to Zurich. In February 1919 Albert and Mileva got divorced. Six months later Einstein married his cousin, the divorced Elsa Löwenthal, mother of two daughters, Ilse and Margot. Einstein detested the military enthusiasm that swept Germany after the declaration of war and courageously refused to sign the manisfesto, in which German intellectuals declared their solidarity with German militarism.

Einstein continued his work on the general theory of relativity, which he had begun in 1907. In November 1915, he derived the exact value of the perihelion precession of the planet Mercury, which for over sixty years had been an unresolved problem, and he predicted how much a ray of light, emitted by a star and grazing the sun, should be deflected by the gravitation of the sun. In 1917 he applied general relativity to the study of the structure of the universe as a whole, raising thereby the status of cosmology, which theretofore had been a jumble of speculations, to that of a respectable scientific discipline. His prediction of the gravitational deflection of light was confirmed in 1919 by two British eclipse expeditions to West Africa and Brazil. When their results were announced in London, Einstein's theory was hailed by the President of the Royal Society as "perhaps the greatest achievement in the history of human thought." From that day on Einstein gained unprecedented international fame. In 1922, he was awarded the Nobel Prize for physics. But when the Nazi terror began in Germany, he, as a Jew and pacifist, and his theory, became the target of brute attacks. At Adolf Hitler's rise to power early in 1933, Einstein was in Belgium and, instead of returning to Germany, accepted a professorship at the Institute for Advanced Study in Princeton, New Jersey, where he remained until his death on April 18, 1955.

Later life and influence

During the twenty-two years in Princeton he resumed his work on quantum theory. Although he was one of its founding fathers, he rejected its generally accepted probabilistic interpretation because, influenced by the philosopher Baruch Spinoza (1632–1677), whom he had read in his youth, he was utterly convinced of the causal dependence of all phenomena. Nor did he accept the prevailing view that the concept of a physical phenomenon includes irrevocably the specifics of the experimental conditions of its observation. For him "physics is an attempt conceptually to grasp reality as it is thought independently of its being observed" (Schlipp, p. 81). His famous 1935 paper, written in collaboration with physicists Nathan Rosen and Boris Podolsky challenged the completeness of orthodox quantum mechanics and had far-reaching consequences debated still today. But most of his time, until the day of his death, he devoted to the last great project of his life, the search for a unified field theory, which however remained unfinished.

Apart from his scientific work Einstein, using his prestige, engaged himself in promoting the causes of social justice, civil liberty, tolerance, and equity of all citizens before the law. He believed in the ideal of international peace and in the feasibility of establishing a world government, led by the superpowers, to which all nations should commit all their military resources. Although having signed in August 1939 the famous letter to President Franklin Delano Roosevelt proposing the development of an atomic bomb, he later admitted that, had he known that the Germans would not succeed in producing an atomic bomb, he "would not have lifted a finger."

Having been, during his later years in Berlin, a victim of anti-Semitic propaganda, and being aware of the cruel persecutions of Jews by the Nazis, Einstein most actively supported Zionism, which he regarded as a moral, not a political, movement to restore his people's dignity necessary to survive in a hostile world. When once, in this context, he declared: "I am glad to belong to the Jewish people, although I do not regard it as 'chosen'" (Schlipp, p. 81) he obviously referred to his disbelief in the Bible, which he retained from his adolescence. And when he said, as quoted above, that he later recanted his juvenile freethinking "because of a better insight into causal connections," he referred to his realization that science, by revealing a divine harmony in the universe expressed by the laws of nature, imbued him with a feeling of awe and humility that made him believe in a "God who reveals himself in the harmony of all that exists." He defined the relation between science and religion in a much-quoted phrase: "Science without religion is lame, religion without science is blind." But retaining his early uncompromising rejection of anthropomorphisms, he stated that, following Spinoza, he cannot conceive of a God who rewards or punishes his creatures or has a will of the kind humans experience. In his Princeton years, Einstein wrote numerous articles and addresses on what he called his "cosmic religion" and protested strongly against the identification of his belief in an impersonal God with atheism. The philosophy of religion and the quest for religious truth had occupied his mind in those years so much that it has been said "one might suspect he was disguised as a theologian," as the Swiss playwright Friedrich Dürrenmatt once said.

On December 31, 1999, the well-known weekly newsmagazine *Time* proclaimed Albert Einstein "Person of the Century" on the grounds that he was not only the century's greatest scientist, who altered forever our views on matter, time, space, and motion, but also a humanitarian, who fought for the causes of justice and peace, and "had faith in the beauty of God's handiwork."

See also GRAND UNIFIED THEORY; GRAVITATION; PHYSICS, QUANTUM; RELATIVITY, GENERAL THEORY OF; RELATIVITY, SPECIAL THEORY OF; SPACE AND TIME

Bibliography

Einstein, Albert. *The World as I See It.* New York: Covici-Friede, 1934.

Einstein, Albert. *Ideas and Opinions.* New York: Crown, 1949.

Einstein, Albert. *Out of My Later Years.* New York: Philosophical Library, 1950.

Fölsing, Albrecht. *Albert Einstein: A Biography,* trans. Ewald Osers. New York: Viking, 1997.

Holton, Gerald, and Elkana, Yehuda, eds. *Albert Einstein: Historical and Cultural Perspectives.* Princeton, N.J.: Princeton University Press, 1982.

Jammer, Max. *Einstein and Religion.* Princeton, N.J.: Princeton University Press, 1999.

Pais, Abraham. *Subtle is the Lord—The Science and Life of Albert Einstein.* Oxford and New York: Oxford University Press, 1982.

Schilpp, Paul Arthur, ed. *Albert Einstein: Philosopher-Scientist.* New York: Tudor, 1949.

MAX JAMMER

EMBODIMENT

What concept of *embodiment*—of the bodily becoming of life itself and of any life-form—emerges in the interstices of religion and science? All religions minister to the vulnerabilities and passions of the body, lending meaning to mortality through practices of ritual, discipline, and narrative. Such interpretive practices nestle the human body into its cosmic environment of fellow creatures, even as they distinguish it in its humanity. The biblical creation narratives, for example, stress the goodness of all species in their interdependence. Christianity offered a dramatic symbolization of God-becoming-flesh, heightening the importance of the body, whose resurrection as part of the "Body of Christ" defined salvation itself. Presumably this radicalization of embodiment, against the background of the

unqualified goodness of nature itself, helps to explain why it is on Christian soil that natural science in its full modern sense arose. Yet paradoxically the same Christian paradigm effected some of humanity's most dualistic discourses, inhibiting full-bodied appreciation of the material world and perhaps explaining why the rise of science took the form of a polarizing struggle. It may also conversely shed light upon why Christianity has failed to inhibit the more devastating effects of scientific technology upon the planetary ecology.

This paradox, pulsing with ambivalence toward the body, lies at the heart of Western history. As the early Christian movement first struggled to translate its gospel into the terms of Greco-Roman culture (for which science and philosophy were inseparable), there was no greater stumbling block than "the body." The body, in its ceaseless metamorphosis from birth to death, signified for classical thought the realm of change. By the same logic, God would be incapable of change. Thus it is the source of truth, of the unchanging ideas—or forms—that organize the changing world of nature (*physis*). The categorical distinction between the eternal "One" and the mortal "Many" accounts for the compatibility between philosophical Hellenism and the Jewish monotheism of the Christians. But the Greek dichotomy between changeless "Being" and the changing world of bodies, between Aristotle's (384–322 B.C.E.) unmoved "Mover" and the moving world, did not fit the Christian proclamation of an incarnation of the divine. The orthodox Christian solution finally made it fit: In the form of the "two natures" of Christ, the divine Word inhabited the human body, but remained in itself free of change, feeling, or flesh. The paradox was institutionalized.

It took nearly a thousand years for Christianity to develop genuine interest in the mortal human body. A seemingly subtle shift in the classical sources effected a dramatic change: Appropriated from Muslim scholars during the crusades, Aristotle's texts—and a different, scientific reading of Aristotle—came to the fore of Christian thought. Unlike Plato (428–347 B.C.E.) , true knowledge, according to Aristotle, can only arise out of sense experience. Such embodied experience requires the illumination of reason and then, in its Christian reception, the completion by faith. Although the fundamental Greek ontological binary of unchanging reason and bodily phenomena remained intact, the epistemology changed radically. In the new Western universities of the thirteenth century, that shift gave rise to a certain autonomy of the discipline of "philosophy" (which included what is meant today by the sciences) from theology. The Dominican Albertus Magnus (c. 1193–1280) and his pupil Thomas Aquinas (c. 1225–1274) developed systematically the implications of this new interest in the integrity of the embodied senses and the world of bodies. Aquinas read the human rational soul as the form, or actualization, of its own body. The body is the potentiality, enmeshed in a prima matter or pure potentiality comprised of contiguous bodies of varying densities.

The Platonic dualism however soon reconquered theology on the whole. When in the Renaissance a more favorable attitude toward the body became again apparent, it took a Platonic form, propelled largely by the idealized body-forms of art. Within the milieu of a Renaissance neo-Platonic mysticism, driven by a powerful mathematics in which the multiple infinities of the embodied universe were articulated, Cardinal Nicholas da Cusa (d. 1464) and his martyred disciple Giordano Bruno (1548–1600) initiated a fresh, proto-scientific theological discourse, in which God and world fold in and out of each other. The Protestant Reformation, by contrast, reacted against the paganism of these new arts, as well as against the sensuality of the sacramental system. It was, to twist the above paradox further, the extreme form of Platonic dualism of René Descartes (1596–1650), boiled down to "mental substance" and "extended substance," that provided the initial framework for modern science. The mechanistic rather than the mystical approach to the spirit/world, mind/body relation prevailed in science and theology, even as the gap widened between the disciplines. The body as a machine, as a closed system to which spirit, mind, and God, if they exist, were posited as external agents, dominated the western imagination until the twentieth century.

The dynamic unfolding of the organism through chance in evolution, the relativity of the physical universe, and the indeterminacy of the quanta begin to reopen the system. The mathematician and cosmologist Alfred North Whitehead (1861–1947) first conceptualized the philosophical and theological potentialities of this shake-up of the old modern reductionisms. His conversion of

something like the Aristotelian passive prime matter into the activity of a primal "Creativity," from which God and world unfurl freely and in immanent relation, has had tremendous influence on the formation of the field of religion and science. Process theology can thus present God as embodied—not as a sum of bodies à la pantheism, but as the spirit of the universe, partly and differently incarnate in all creatures. This panentheism thus redistributes the incarnation throughout reality: All actualization is embodiment, including the divine self-actualization in the world; the unique incarnation of God in the symbolism of the Christ no longer represents an exception that proves the rule of spirit/body dualism. Feminist and ecological theologies have been evolving in close proximity to this sense of inclusive embodiment, emphasizing the implications for social and environmental justice of a new profoundly spiritual attention to interdependent, vulnerable human bodies, within their systemic contexts of socio-material interchange.

New developments in genetics, for example, offer stunning contributions to the human sense of embodiment. The recipe that links heredity to the metabolism of human life is "a code, an abstract message that can be embodied in a chemical, physical or even immaterial form" (Ridley, p. 15). The secret of this code lies in its ability to replicate itself in the form of proteins: and so to produce bodies from an ancient alphabet of infinitesimal filaments. "In the beginning was the word," avers a science writer with no specific interest in religion. "The word proselytized the sea with its message, copying itself unceasingly and forever. The word discovered how to rearrange chemicals so as to capture little eddies in the stream of entropy and make them live. The word transformed the land surface of the planet from a dusty hell to a verdant paradise. The word eventually blossomed and became sufficiently ingenious to build a porridgy contraption called a human brain that could discover and be aware of the word itself" (Ridley, p. 11). This gospel of genetics may be put to reductionist or commercial use. But it articulates awe in the face of the alphabetic code of the four bases (A, C, G, and T) that in its four million year simplicity writes the recipes for the endless complexity emerging with startling order out of the chaotic potential of the world. Nowhere has the interconnectivity and common source of all living creatures been more clearly demonstrated as in this emergent genetics, outside of religious narratives of genesis.

As science begins to outgrow its modern model of bodies as closed systems, as increasingly bodies are inscribed in cosmological and ecological contexts of such irreducible complexity as to solicit awe rather than certainty, religion may find the resources for healing the split between its words of spirit and its bodies of shared flesh.

See also ARISTOTLE; CHRISTOLOGY; DESCARTES, RENÉ; ECOTHEOLOGY; FEMINIST THEOLOGY; GENETICS; GOD; HUMAN NATURE, PHYSICAL ASPECTS; HUMAN NATURE, RELIGIOUS AND PHILOSOPHICAL ASPECTS; INCARNATION; ISLAM; PANENTHEISM; PHYSICS, QUANTUM; PLATO; SOUL; THOMAS AQUINAS; WHITEHEAD, ALFRED NORTH

Bibliography

Ashley, Benedict. *Theologies of the Body: Humanist and Christian*. Braintree, Mass.: National Catholic Bioethics Center, 1985.

McFague, Sallie. *The Body of God: An Ecological Theology*. Minneapolis, Minn.: Fortress Press, 1993.

Prigogine, Ilya, and Stengers, Isabelle. *Order Out of Chaos*. New York: Bantam, 1984.

Ridley, Matt. *Genome: The Autobiography of a Species in 23 Chapters*. New York: Harper Collins, 1999.

Whitehead, Alfred North. *Science and the Modern World*. New York: Free Press, 1967.

CATHERINE KELLER

EMERGENCE

The term *emergence* refers to the appearance of a new property in an evolving system or entity. As the system changes over time, a new property that was not present before comes to be associated with it, often through an increase in complexity. Emergent phenomena are not fully reducible (in a causal, explanatory, or ontological sense) to the lower-level phenomena from which they arise. Emergence thus represents the hypothesis that the whole story (in science, and perhaps in religion) can only be told by multiple causal stories at multiple levels.

In the religion-science discussion, uses of the term *emergence* fall roughly into three broad categories: (1) *Scientific emergence* concentrates on individual instances and patterns of emergence in the natural world. Many emergent phenomena can be categorized and analyzed in a purely scientific manner without needing to raise broader questions about their philosophical or theological significance. (2) *Philosophical emergence theories* look for broader patterns or similarities between emergent phenomena and attempt to formulate general criteria for classifying a phenomenon as emergent. (3) *Metaphysical* or *theological emergence theories* presuppose that the natural world is hierarchically structured and that it is a fundamental feature of reality that new emergent levels are produced in the course of cosmic history. At the metaphysical level, emergence theories attempt to describe and account for the broad pattern of emergence over time. In theological theories, the ladder of emergence is associated with the nature and action of God. Both presuppose the fundamental nature of change or development and emphasize creativity or novelty as a basic feature of ultimate reality.

Critics of emergence complain that it is either trivial, untestable, or false. *Trivial* because it seems obvious that, as systems increase in complexity, they will express new properties not manifest at earlier stages. Thus the critic might complain that emergence just restates the concept of complexity—and in a less clear, more obscure fashion. *Untestable* because how could one ever test whether there is a broad pattern of emergence in natural history? And *false* if emergentists are claiming that mysterious new things emerge in cosmic history that cannot be understood at all in terms of more basic levels. After all, critics complain, the success that physics has enjoyed is simply success at explaining "new things" in terms of more fundamental laws.

Some classical theists have criticized emergence theories by responding that the basic nature of the world was set by the last day of creation. Humanity may move toward or away from God, but human nature as such does not change—and certainly God does not change or emerge over time, as both Augustine of Hippo (354–430) and Thomas Aquinas (c. 1225–1274) maintained. Process thinkers have argued that emergence is not as metaphysically satisfactory as, for example, Alfred North Whitehead's (1861–1947) thought, since in place of the unified framework of actual occasions (panexperientialism), emergence offers only a confusing variety of fundamental entities arising within natural history.

Instances of emergence in the natural world

The first cases of emergence arise already in quantum mechanics. (Indeed, one could speculate that spontaneous symmetry breaking constitutes the earliest instance of emergence.) In the fractional quantum Hall effect, electrons act together in strong magnetic fields to form new types of "particles." Likewise, atomic structures and the properties of bulk matter are the emergent and relatively stable results of increasing complexity in physical systems.

Thermodynamics is inherently concerned with emergence, since it relates exchanges of heat to macroscopic phenomena such as temperature, pressure, and volume. Ilya Prigogine studied the thermodynamics of irreversible processes, developing laws for the emergence of order (anentropy) in specified systems ("order through fluctuations"). To take an example from fluid turbulence, heating a fluid from below results in the Bénard phenomenon, in which the convecting fluid spontaneously forms complex hexagonal "cells." Using similar physical principles, meteorologists study emergent patterns in the weather, which demonstrate very sensitive dependence on small changes in initial conditions (e.g., Edward Lorenz's Butterfly Effect). In such systems "matter displays its potential to be self-organizing and thereby to bring into existence new forms . . . under the constraints and with the potentialities afforded by their being incorporated into systems the properties of which, as a whole, now have to be taken into account" (Peacocke, 1986, p. 53).

The emergence of life depends on emergent properties in chemistry, such as the folding properties of proteins, which in turn are products of their underlying physical structure. Likewise, auto-catalytic (self-catalyzed) processes in chemistry play a key role in increasing complexity to the level required for life. Such processes allow for the role of feedback mechanisms, which can foster an iterative, self-correcting process that leads to the formation of new structures.

Eventually, ordered dissipative structures emerged. Life requires only that they have the potential to replicate and to incorporate environment-induced changes into their physical structure. At this point biological evolution begins, in which differential survival rates depend on reproductive success in a given environment. Emergence connotes both the unbroken chain of development backward through time and the continual emergence of new forms: bio-molecules, cells (including neurons), organelles, organs, and "autonomous agents," which Stuart Kauffman defines as systems that are able to reproduce and also able to carry out at least one thermodynamic work cycle.

Emergence may involve the evolution of new structures according to as many as six metrics:

(1) evolution temporally or spatially;

(2) evolution in the progression from simple to complex;

(3) evolution in levels of inner organization, feedback loops, and self-catalyzing autopoiesis (Niels Gregersen);

(4) evolution in increasing levels of information-processing;

(5) evolution in the development of "subjectivity" (e.g., perception, awareness, self-awareness, self-consciousness, spiritual intuition);

(6) evolution in the ladder of emergence of new properties (e.g., physiological, psychological, sociological; or physical, biological, psychological, spiritual).

Philosophical analysis and implications

Understood as a philosophical position, emergence theory is derived from the details of cosmic evolution as revealed through the various natural and social sciences. Philosophical emergence generally includes some combination of the following eight theses:

(1) *Emergentist monism*: There is one natural world composed of matter and energy (Peacocke and Clayton in Russell, 2000).

(2) *Hierarchy*: This world is hierarchically structured; more complex units are formed out of more simple parts, and they in turn become the "parts" out of which yet more complex entities are formed.

(3) *Temporal ontology*: This process of hierarchical structuring takes place over time; cosmic evolution moves from the simple to the

more complex, and new structures and entities emerge in the process.

(4) *Emergentist pluralism*: The manner of the emergence of one level from another, the qualities of the emergent level, the degree to which the "lower" controls the "higher," and many other features vary depending on which instance of emergence is being studied (e.g., the biophysicist Harold Morowitz has identified at least twenty-eight different levels). Emergence should thus be viewed as a family resemblance term.

(5) *Logical features*: The various instances of emergence in natural history do tend to share certain features. For any two levels, L_1 and L_2, where L_2 emerges from L_1, (a) L_1 is prior in natural history; (b) L_2 depends on L_1, such that if the states in L_1 did not exist, the qualities in L_2 would not exist; (c) L_2 is the result of a sufficient degree of complexity in L_1; (d) one might be able to predict the emergence of some new or emergent qualities on the basis of what one knew about L_1. But one would not be able to predict the precise nature of these qualities, the rules that govern their interaction (or their phenomenological patterns), or the sorts of emergent levels that they may in due course give rise to; (e) L_2 is not reducible to L_1 in any of the standard senses of "reduction" in the philosophy of science literature (causal, explanatory, metaphysical, or ontological reduction).

(6) *Downward causation*: In some cases, phenomena at L_2 exercise a causal effect on L_1, which is not reducible to an L_1 causal history. This causal nonreducibility is not just epistemic, in the sense that humans cannot tell the L_1 causal story but an omnipotent being could. It is ontological: The world is such that it produces systems whose emergent properties exercise their own distinct causal forces among each other and on (at least) the next lower level in the hierarchy.

(7) *Against dualism*: Although the emergence of consciousness in the brain is significant to humans, it is not the defining moment of emergence. Emergence theory refers to the process of emergence as a whole, not merely to a single instance of emergence.

(8) *Against dual aspect monism*: Traditionally, as in Baruch Spinoza (1632–1677), dual aspect monism implies that there is no causal interaction between mental and physical properties, whereas emergence theories maintain that there is a dependence of the mental upon the physical and two-way causal influence between them.

Metaphysical or theological emergence

Emergentist theologies take several different forms, some focusing on emergence within the world, and some on emergence and the nature of God. Regarding the former, three forms are possible, here listed in order of increasing strength of divine involvement.

(1) The process of emergence might represent a basic feature of the natural world. Fundamental laws and constants and the nature of matter and energy are such that increasingly complex entities and states of affairs are formed, and more complex systems naturally give rise to new emergent properties. The emphasis is on the lawlike nature of the process: Once such basic features are set, emergence will occur naturally. It may have no broader significance outside itself.

(2) The same view of emergence being presupposed, a teleological dimension might be added. God established these features with the intention that the world would produce ever more complex entities and properties, such as complex biochemical molecules, living organisms, and the brains of the higher primates, as well as culture, art, philosophy, and perhaps religious understanding. In all cases, the pattern of complexification, once the preconditions are given, requires no divine intervention to be carried out.

(3) God might be more directly involved in bringing about emergent levels of reality. This might involve a general "lure," a constant introduction of creativity into the natural process, as argued by Whitehead and most process thinkers; it might involve the claim that in nature emergent levels (life, experience, self-consciousness) would not have occurred except for the role of God; or, the theist may assert, the entire process reflects God's providential role in history,

working the divine will in to mold reality to God's image, for example, bringing about humankind in the image of God (*imago Dei*) through God's constant creative or redemptive activity.

It is important to note that one can advocate an emergence theory of the natural world without maintaining any emergence within God. Thus one might hold an Augustinian view of God, such that God is completely immutable and dwells in a timeless eternal realm, yet through an act or series of acts preordained before creation God brings about its emergent history (its levels of emergence). On this view, emergence is divinely caused and entails a temporal process in the world, but it does not entail any change in God (Ernan McMullin).

Various forms of dipolar theism allow emergence within God, without asserting that "God comes into being" along with the process of emergence of the cosmos. So, for example, the essential or "antecedent" nature of God might be eternal and unchanging through the cosmic process, whereas the "consequent" nature of God—the side of God that interacts with and responds to the world—grows, develops, and even changes over the course of cosmic history. There is emergence within God at least in the sense that the divine experience becomes richer, containing experiences and responses that were not there *ab initio,* even though the essential nature of God remains constant.

Finally, the strongest forms of "emergentist theism" maintain that God comes to be along with the process of history. The world and the divine are inextricably wed: Where there is no world, there is no God. The world and God then come into being together, and perhaps the process will culminate in a deification of the world through this identity or association.

See also AUTOPOIESIS; COMPLEXITY; SUPERVENIENCE

Bibliography

Holland, John. *Emergence: From Chaos to Order.* Reading, Mass.: Addison-Wesley, 1998.

Kauffman, Stuart. *Investigations.* New York: Oxford University Press, 2000.

Peacocke, Arthur. *God and the New Biology.* London: Dent; San Francisco: Harper, 1986.

Peacocke, Arthur. *Theology for a Scientific Age: Being and Becoming—Natural, Divine, and Human.* Minneapolis, Minn.: Fortress, 1993.

Prigogine, Ilya. *From Being to Becoming: Time and Complexity in the Physical Sciences.* San Francisco: W. H. Freeman, 1980.

Russell, Robert John; Murphy, Nancey; and Meyering, Theo C., eds. *Neuroscience and the Person: Scientific Perspectives on Divine Action.* Vatican City State: Vatican Observatory; Berkeley, Calif.: Center for Theology and the Natural Sciences, 1999.

PHILIP CLAYTON

EMERGENCE OF CONSCIOUSNESS

See COGNITIVE FLUIDITY; COMPLEXITY; EMERGENCE

EMERGENCE OF LIFE

See EMERGENCE; LIFE, ORIGINS OF

EMPIRICISM

The term *empiricism* describes a philosophical position emphasizing that all concepts and knowledge are derived from and justified by experience. Empiricists disagree on the nature of experience, including whether it is individual or social and whether sense experience is to be emphasized. Empiricism often is associated with other positions, including nominalism, naturalism, materialism, atheism, secularism, humanism, behaviorism, and emotivism.

Empiricism usually contrasts with views that truths can be derived from tradition, Scripture, revelation, intuition, or reason. Empiricists often have a special attitude toward mathematics, acknowledging its role in understanding the world yet denying that it gives direct truths about the world apart from experience. In the last third of the twentieth century, Anglo-American discussion has tended to contrast empiricism with holism or coherentism.

Classic empiricism

Despite earlier roots, empiricism really began with the seventeenth- and eighteenth-century British philosophers John Locke (1632–1704), George Berkeley (1685–1753), and David Hume (1711–1776). Locke rejected the existence of innate ideas, including truths of religion and morals and held that the mind is a "blank slate" at birth. All of one's ideas are derived, either directly or indirectly, from either sensation (the source of one's knowledge of external objects) or reflection (the source of one's knowledge of one's mental processes). Berkeley, holding that perception requires a perceiver, developed a theory that required individual minds and God as perceivers of the world. Hume pushed empiricism in a skeptical direction, questioning beliefs in causation, self, and God.

Early in the twentieth century, the Vienna circle of logical positivists made a major impact on philosophy in England and the United States. They used empiricism as a criterion for meaning, holding that the only meaningful propositions are either tautologies (including mathematical statements), which tell nothing about the world, or else statements that are empirically verifiable. Logical positivism ran into two problems: It was difficult to state the principle of verification precisely, and it had a self-contradiction at its heart because the criterion of meaning is neither a tautology nor empirically verifiable. Thus the criterion of meaning seems to be meaningless. The later holism of American philosopher W. V. O. Quine (1908–2000) also challenged the positivist distinction between tautologies and empirical statements, pointing out that meanings may vary so much between contexts that the dichotomy is hard to maintain.

American empiricism

In the United States, William James (1842–1910) and John Dewey (1859–1952) developed an empiricism (called *radical empiricism* by James) that challenged some of the assumptions of British empiricism, especially the commitment to the existence of separate sensations. James held instead that people experience complexes of sensations in a matrix of relations. Thus they are not left with a choice between Hume's world of separate pieces and the non-empirical containers of these pieces (mind, God) of idealism. Values, the worth of things, can be perceived. Thus values are not subjective and arbitrary additions to empirical facts as

held by most empiricists (and by modern culture generally). Dewey's subject-object transactionalism avoids the subject-object dichotomy. This more "generous empiricism" has influenced such thinkers as Henry Nelson Wieman, Bernard Meland, William Dean, Nancy Frankenberry, and Jerome A. Stone. Later Quine held that since empirical propositions are embedded in a network of commonsense or scientific theories, no statement can be verified in isolation. Confirmation or disconfirmation always affects a range of theories.

That vast conglomeration of ideas typically labeled *postmodern* has also impacted empiricism. A common theme of postmodernism is that there is no theory-free observation, that theories are not completely determined by data, and consequently that science is merely one of the many stories that people can tell each other. A major task confronting people who value science is how to honor the insights of postmodernism, including the tentativeness of verification and the hegemonic motive of the Enlightenment grand narrative of progress toward rationality, while at the same time articulating the ways in which scientific procedures have a relative and tentative yet significant value. A number of thinkers work towards this, including Richard Bernstein, Frederick Ferré, Susan Haack, J. Wentzel van Huyssteen, Lynn Hankinson Nelson, and Robert Neville.

It has been asked whether human gender influences empirical procedures, either through biological or cultural factors. Sandra Harding, Helen Longino, Evelyn Fox Keller, Lynn Hankinson Nelson, and others have been pursuing this question from differing perspectives.

Cross-cultural perspectives

To turn to a cross-cultural analysis, it should be observed that in developing their various technologies all cultures seem to have pursued empirical methods, sometimes in combination with non-empirical approaches. However, only the Western philosophical tradition seems to have developed the exclusiveness of empiricism as a theoretical option. In South Asia the Carvakas, Nyaya-Vaisesikas, and early Buddhists might be classified as empiricists. In China, Korea, and Japan the principle of "the investigation of things" occasionally took an empiricist direction, although not with the exclusiveness of European empiricism. "The investigation of things" usually included an investigation of the worth of things. One might speak of the empiricism of Mozi, Xunzi, Wang Fuzhi, Yan Yuan, Dai Zhen, and others of the "Investigations Based on Evidence" movement, and of the Korean Yi Yulgok.

Empiricism in the science-religion dialogue

As for science-religion issues, the topic of empiricism relates to virtually every question. For example, ideas on God, the soul, heaven, or reincarnation will be greatly influenced by a person's stance toward empiricism. That stance will also affect a person's ideas on the questions of the worth of tradition, revelation, scripture, or reason in religion and ethics. Related questions are whether the divine or the sacred as a quality of natural processes can be appreciated or responded to, as some "religious naturalists" hold, and whether such awareness is a complement to or an extension of a more strict empirical method. Another approach is to ask whether religious ideas can be vetoed by empirical procedures, whether they must be strictly based on or may be more loosely informed by them, or whether science and religion are such distinct orientations that neither can interfere with the other. Writers such as Douglas Clyde Macintosh and Henry Nelson Wieman have attempted to treat theology as an empirical study. The success of this depends on how one conceives God and also empirical method.

See also COHERENTISM; POSITIVISM, LOGICAL

Bibliography

Ayer, Alfred Jules. *Language, Truth, and Logic.* New York: Dover, 1952.

Ferré, Frederick. *Knowing and Value: Toward a Constructive Postmodern Epistemology.* Albany: State University of New York Press, 1998.

Frankenberry, Nancy. *Religion and Radical Empiricism.* Albany: State University of New York Press, 1987.

Locke, John. *An Essay concerning Human Understanding* (1690), ed. P. H. Nidditch. Oxford: Clarendon Press, 1975.

Nelson, Lynn Hankinson. *Who Knows: From Quine to a Feminist Empiricism.* Philadelphia: Temple University Press, 1990.

Quine, W. V. O. "Two Dogmas of Empiricism." In *From a Logical Point of View.* New York: Harper, 1963.

Stone, Jerome A. *The Minimalist Vision of Transcendence: A Naturalist Philosophy of Religion.* Albany: State University of New York Press, 1992.

van Huyssteen, J. Wentzel. *The Shaping of Rationality: Toward Interdisciplinarity in Theology and Science.* Grand Rapids, Mich.: Eerdmans, 1999.

JEROME A. STONE

END OF THE WORLD, PHYSICAL

See COSMOLOGY, PHYSICAL ASPECTS; ESCHATOLOGY

END OF THE WORLD, RELIGIOUS AND PHILOSOPHICAL ASPECTS OF

Beliefs in the "end of the world" (loosely speaking, *eschatology*), generally from a massive cataclysm, appear in many cultures, especially those with creation myths. Those who believe this "end of the world" is imminent, that is, *apocalyptic* believers, have produced a vast literature focused on the destructive nature of the "end" of the physical creation. By creating this "sense of an ending" these catastrophic scenarios knit up a culture's cosmogony in a great cycle of time during which creation "lives out" its allotted span. Because the physical world of time and space (Latin *saeculum,* which in French, *siècle,* means both "century" and "secular") are so concrete, the temptation to measure the length of the world's existence and hence to "date" its end has existed in all cultures. Nowhere, however, did this concern become more intense than in Western European culture, birthplace of modern notions of time and modern techniques of time measurement.

End-time calculations and great cycles

These "great cycles" generally take some combination of two forms: the circular and the linear. In circular cosmogonies, the most widespread variant, creation goes through cycles from origins to annihilation and then to a new beginning, repeating indefinitely. These cycles tend to be extremely long, measured in chronological units ranging from the

Roman and Greek *millennia* (one thousand years), to the Babylonian *sar* (3,600 years), to Hindu *kalpas* (8.64 billion years). From such cycles, people looked upon the yearly cycle as a microcosm and celebrated the completion and new beginning of a cycle as a "myth of eternal return." Greek philosophical thought leaned heavily toward cyclical cosmologies in which everything repeated, or even replicated exactly, the details of the previous cycle *ad infinitum.*

In the less common linear cases, the current cycle receives a teleological significance, rendering it unique among ages, or even making it the only created age. Thus the "end of the world" becomes an ultimate moment in a divine scheme. In monotheism, with its typically moral focus, the "end" brings a *Last Judgment* in which the good receive their reward and the evil their punishment. This radical shift from circular to linear time sometimes involved equally significant shifts from viewing the passage of time as a declining process to a progressive one, looking *forward* to a golden age. Characteristically, adepts of these linear, moral schemata tended to shorten the time separating the present from the "end of the age," thus intensifying the imminence of judgment.

In both linear and cyclical cases, the future end of the world had more than merely conceptual significance to various degrees, depending on what trends these schemata attributed to the cycle, and where they placed the present in the larger process. The most prominent approach viewed the cycle as one of monotonic declension from a golden age to the current (worst) age. Often these schemes placed the present time toward the middle of the final age. In the most extreme case, Hindu scriptures (e.g., *Surya Siddhanta*) place the beginning of the last and most debased cycle, the *kaliyuga*, in 3102 B.C.E., placing the present in the early millennia of that *yuga*, and the cataclysmic "end" some 420 *millennia* away. The final conflagration in these scenarios often appears as both a destructive and a purging flame that wipes out impurities and reunites creation with eternity. Greek and Roman ideas of these cycles appear in most philosophical schools (Pythagorean, Platonic, Stoic), although the associated cycles are measured in chronological units taken from Babylonian astronomical calculations, but significantly reduced. Drawing on the second-century B.C.E. Babylonian astronomer

Berossos's 12,960,000-year cycle, the Roman statesman and author Cicero (106–43 B.C.E.) dated the *magnus et verus annus* (the great and true year) to 12,954 years.

With more careful astronomical observation, calculators in antiquity increasingly tried to measure more precisely both the yearly cycle (that inelegant 365.242199 days) and the greater cosmic cycle from creation to end of the world, thus wedding cosmologies of religious importance to measurement and calculation of time. In both the case of the (liturgical) year and the (apocalyptic) cycle of the age, this attention to time played a major role in religious passions attached to the celebration and innovation of collective rituals, and from there in cultural identity formation and the widespread emergence of new religious movements that proliferated throughout late antiquity. This close connection between temporal measurement and religious beliefs and behaviors also participated in a crucial shift from cyclical to linear models and from distant to closer (more apocalyptic) end-times. These developments have a particular vigor in the Hellenistic intersection between the "scientific" spirit of Greco-Roman culture and the apocalyptic spirit of Jewish and Christian culture.

Whereas Chinese chronographers affixed a length of 23,639,040 years to a great (astronomical) cycle, and the Hindus attributed 4.32 million years to a single *mahayuga*, Near Eastern and Mediterranean cultures measured in the more restrained *millennia* and counted ages within a cycle by sevens (planets) or twelves (zodiacal signs). Among the many variants, the six- or seven-thousand year cycle proved most popular and found adepts in Mithraic, Mazdean, Jewish, and Christian circles. The marriage of astronomical cycles from Zoroastrian sources in Babylon to the linear eschatology of the exiles from the tribe of Judah (sixth century B.C.E.) produced the most vigorous strain of calculations of the approaching end. During the last quarter of the first millennium B.C.E., Jewish writers produced a rich and innovative literature of apocalyptic visions anticipating an imminent cataclysmic transformation of the world.

Theodicy and the Last Judgment in monotheistic eschatologies

For Jews and later for Christians and Muslims, end-time beliefs offered an answer to the monotheistic problem of God's justice (theodicy). These personal and morally charged visions looked *forward* to an imminent apocalyptic "Day of Judgment" that would separate out those evil people who will go to destruction and those good who will receive cosmic rewards. This intensified focus on justice and reward shifted some of the great-cycle thinking from that of the world's end to its continuation, here become a messianic age of peace and prosperity (millennialism). In any case, these eschatological beliefs, driven by a moral and social urgency, preferred shorter timelines. By the later Hellenistic age, Jewish and, still more avidly, Christian circles focused on a world cycle of a millennial week of seven thousand years. In this reading, which dramatically reversed the more pessimistic visions of the creation cycle, the current age was made up of six 1,000-year "days" of toil and travail, and looked forward to the advent, in the year-6,000 *annus mundi* (The year of the world [the year since creation]), of a sabbatical millennium, or thousand-year period of messianic peace where swords turn into plowshares and spears into pruning hooks.

Calculations of the imminent apocalyptic advent of a messianic age, based on prophetic signs, astronomical calculations, chronologies (especially based on Daniel) proliferated around the turn of the common era. Despite the invariable failure of such calculations, believers (in Islam they are known as the *exact men*) continued to engage in them, posing serious problems for those who tried to control the unpredictable explosions of strange behavior that accompany apocalyptic beliefs that "the end is at hand." One rabbi, reflecting on the catastrophes brought on by those who prematurely announce the end, cursed those who calculate the end (*Sanhedrin,* 97b), and Augustine of Hippo (354–430) commanded these types to "quiet their busy fingers," that is, stop counting (*The City of God,* 18.54.2).

The desire to "date the end" became especially vigorous in Christianity, which, from an early age (c. 100 C.E.) openly associated the apocalyptic moment with the chronological date of 6,000 *annus mundi.* Early-third-century chronographers produced the first widely accepted Christian era, *annus mundi,* calculating the years since creation based on figures in the Septuagint (the Greek translation of the Hebrew Bible, at significant chronological variance with the Masoretic Hebrew text). These chronographers located the incarnation at 5,500 *annus mundi,* their present at 5,700, and the advent of the sabbatical millennium for 6,000 (500 C.E.), some three centuries off. This open and explicit textual commitment to a date, even though at the time it might have seemed far away (though not to Hindus), wedded both *computus* (Easter dating) and chronology to apocalyptic expectations and encouraged a peculiar Christian obsession with dating that intensified at the approach of various end-time dates (500 C.E.; 801 C.E.—the second "year-6,000" *annus mundi;* 1000/1033 C.E.; 1260 C.E.; 1500/1533 C.E.; etc.). A "fever of computation," as one modern historian has termed it, appears repeatedly in the scriptoria of medieval Europe (500–1500) and marks one of the most striking aspects of Renaissance science and historiography.

End-time beliefs and scientific thinking

Western notions of the end of the world have paradoxically provided fuel for scientific developments, irresistibly urging people to "date" the end as accurately and imminently as possible on the one hand, and invariably producing failure on the other. For example, motivated by his concerns about the approach of the next "year-6,000" *annus mundi* (801 C.E.), the English historian and theologian Bede (c. 673–735) worked intensively on problems in chronology and, among other things, solved the problem of the Easter cycle: 532 years (*de temporum ratione,* On the reckoning of times), a feat that had escaped the computists of antiquity.

The obsession with measuring the end never abated, not even with the advent of a supposedly more rational age. Repeatedly chronographers (including Isaac Newton) computed the end, and repeatedly they were wrong. Each failure, however, produced a sharper, more extensive knowledge of chronology and the calculations of time, making time measurement one of the distinguishing obsessions of the West. Thus, precision time measurements, one of the hallmarks of all scientific and historical work, may well be the unintended consequence of failed apocalyptic calculations, which left in their wake a religious disappointment and refined the tools for time measurement now available for other uses, a process that evolutionary scientists call *exaptation.*

At another level, the constant failure of cataclysmic eschatological scenarios gave increased credibility to more millennial notions of a redeemed and transformed physical world. The Western fascination with "progress" and the "new" draws much of its inspiration from a notion that the future held not decay and destruction but renewal and rejoicing. This fairly unusual cultural optimism, where one sought to transform the world rather than date its end, whose most striking early expressions are primarily (though not exclusively) biblical, played a central role in the emergence of modern science, especially in the earliest centuries of the printing press.

Similarly, the failure of apocalyptic expectations may have contributed to a de-enchantment or a demystification of the ways in which Westerners have "read" the universe. No religious belief is more subject to "objective" disconfirmation than eschatological calculations, especially the specific, apocalyptic ones. These beliefs tend to excite a state of exegetical arousal, in which all observed phenomena become part of a coherent and urgent pattern of meaning. With the collapse of expectations, a cognitive dissonance ensues, which generates a wide range of behavior, some of it increasingly grounded in a focus on neutral "observation." After the immense disappointment of the Joachite year 1260, the Franciscan monk Salimbene (c. 1221–1288) wrote in his *Chronicle*: "I have sworn to believe only what I see with my eyes." The difference between Danish astronomer Tycho Brahe's interpretation of the nova of 1572 as a sign of the imminent *Parousia* (the Second Coming of Christ), and his assistant Johannes Kepler's more clinical treatment of the 1604 nova, illustrates the kind of de-eschatologizing shifts that such failures of expectation might inspire. Furthermore, this renunciation of eschatological schemata, forced by repeated and quite precise failures, may have contributed over time to the emergence of non-teleological notions (such as inertia and evolution), that have proved so fruitful in scientific inquiry.

Beliefs in the "end of the world" also played a villain's role in the persecution of scientific thinking in the medieval period. One of the major conflicts for philosophers who sought to reason about the nature of the universe concerned whether the cosmos, the physical universe, was created (and hence had an end) or eternal. Drawing on Aristotelian works, some philosophers—most notably the Arab philosopher Averroës (Ibn Rushd, 1126–1198) and the Flemish philosopher Siger of Brabant (d. 1284)—argued that the physical world was eternal. This contradicted the eschatological claims that, with their lurid threats of coming punishment for evil deeds, played a critical role in the moral education of Christian and Muslim societies. This built-in friction between rational (scientific) and revealed (theological) approaches to the physical universe provoked the repression of philosophical inquiry in the Arabo-Islamic world (and perhaps also in rabbinic Judaism). In Latin Christendom, however, despite determined efforts in inquisitorial circles to eliminate such teachings (most famously in Paris in the 1260s to 1270s, with the attacks on Siger of Brabant and the "Latin Averroists"), these dissident forms of thinking persisted and developed.

Ironically, after having hindered scientific thought for centuries, the medieval framework has, in some sense, returned to modern scientific cosmology, including both a creation (Big Bang) and some sort of cosmic destruction (either of the Earth when the sun goes nova, or of the entire universe). Of course the periods of time involved are immense—the universe is about ten to twenty billion years old, or, in Hindu cosmology, about three to five *kalpas* (4.32 billion years). Even the period left to our solar system (five billion years) makes any imminent framework for apocalyptic beliefs impossible, thus driving a scientific wedge between the monotheistic pair: the end of the world and the Last Judgment.

The ironies of modern technology of destruction

Unfortunately, what becomes conceptually inconceivable (the natural end of the world any time soon) has reappeared in a new form of unnatural ends, especially the threat of nuclear weapons and other technological agents of mass destruction. This ironic and extremely dangerous relationship of technological development to end-time beliefs is best understood within the context of millennialism, but expectations of the end of the world also play a significant role. Briefly in Western Europe, where these beliefs have been especially widespread, each disappointed expectation of God's intervention in human history seems to have inspired believers to take on more and more of the task of bringing about the apocalypse (from passive to active apocalypticism), repeatedly driving technological innovation well beyond the limits of what necessity demanded. Already in the later thirteenth century, Roger Bacon (c. 1220–1292), a younger contemporary of Salimbene and a fellow Franciscan, argued that science would provide an apocalyptic defense against the Antichrist, allowing the Church to spot the Antichrist's deceptive miracles, which he will perform using scientific techniques.

In particular, the awesome power of the atomic bomb inspired end-time imagery from one of its inventors, the American physicist Robert Oppenheimer (1904–1967). As he watched the first test bomb explode, he thought of a line from the Bhagavad Gita: "Now I am become death, the shatterer of worlds." Moreover, the arming of these weapons in the United States occurred in Amarillo, Texas, where a community of "pre-millennial dispensationalists" (passive cataclysmic apocalyptic) believed that in so doing they advanced divine plans for the time of the "tribulation." At the turn of the third millennium in a period of rapid and penetrating globalization, more active cataclysmic apocalyptic groups like the Japanese Aum Shinrikyo and the Muslim Al Quaeda have tried to make the use of these weapons of mass destruction a focus of their "redemptive" violence—destroying the world to save it. At the approach of 2000, astronomical warnings and popular films (e.g., Michael Bay's *Armageddon* and Mimi Leder's *Deep Impact*) depicted the Earth threatened by an extinction-level catastrophe, with the destructive power of modern science then arrayed in defense of human beings. Thus, while many Western Europeans may have awaited the end of the world in *anno Domini* 1,000 only to be disappointed, after the year 2000, when most intellectuals no longer believe in a God who intervenes in history, humans live, perhaps permanently, in the shadow of their own ability to destroy themselves, their own humanly wrought end of the world.

See also ESCHATOLOGY; MILLENNIALISM

Bibliography

Burgess, Ebenezer, trans. *Surya Siddhanta: A Text-Book of Hindu Astronomy*. New Haven, Conn.: American Oriental Society, 1858. Reprint, Kila, Mont.: Kessinger, 1998.

Carroll, Robert P. *When Prophecy Failed: Cognitive Dissonance in the Prophetic Traditions of the Old Testament*. New York: Seabury Press, 1979.

Cohn, Norman. *Cosmos, Chaos, and the World to Come: The Ancient Roots of Apocalyptic Faith*. New Haven, Conn.: Yale University Press, 1993.

Cumont, F. "La fin du monde selon les mages occidentaux." *Revue de l'histoire des religions* 103 (1931): 29–96.

Eliade, Mircea. *The Myth of the Eternal Return*. New York: Pantheon, 1965.

Festinger, Leon. *When Prophecy Fails: A Social and Psychological Study of a Modern Group that Predicted the Destruction of the World*. New York: Harper, 1956.

Landes, Richard. "Owls, Roosters, Bata, and Apocalyptic Time: A Historical Method for Reading a Refractory Documentation." *Union Seminary Quarterly Review* 49 (1996): 165–185.

Lifton, Robert Jay. *Destroying the World to Save it: Aum Shinrikyo, Apocalyptic Violence, and the New Global Terrorism*. New York: Metropolitan, 1999.

Schwartz, Hillel. *Century's End: A Cultural History of the Fin-de-siècle from the 990s to the 1990s*. New York: Doubleday, 1990.

Thompson, Damian. *The End of Time: Faith and Fear in the Shadow of the Millennium*. London: Vintage, 1999.

Whitrow, G. J. *Time in History: The Evolution of our General Awareness of Time and Temporal Perspective*. Oxford: Oxford University Press, 1988.

RICHARD LANDES

ENTROPY

Entropy is a thermodynamic quantity whose value depends on the physical state or condition of a system. It is useful in physics as a means of expressing the Second Law of Thermodynamics. That is, while the law may be stated in terms of it being impossible to extract heat from a reservoir and convert it totally to usable work, in terms of entropy the law states that any changes occurring in a system that is thermally isolated from its surroundings are such that its entropy never decreases.

This behavior corresponds to the fact that entropy is a measure of the disorder of a system. On average all of nature proceeds to a greater state of disorder. Examples of irreversible progression to disorder are pervasive in the world and in everyday experience. Bread crumbs will never gather back into the loaf. Helium atoms that escape from a balloon never return. A drop of ink placed in a glass of water will uniformly color the entire glass and never assemble into its original shape.

Entropy as a measure of disorder can be shown to depend on the probability that the particles of a system are in a given state of order. The tendency for entropy to increase occurs because the number of possible states of disorder that a system can assume is greater than the number of more ordered states, making a state of disorder more probable. For example, the entropy of the ordered state of the water molecules in ice crystal is less than it is when the crystal is melted to liquid water. The entropy difference involved corresponds to the transfer of heat to the crystal in order to melt it.

It may appear that there are exceptions to the general rule of ultimate progression to disorder; the growth of crystals, plants, animals, and humans are all remarkable examples of order or organization. However, these are open systems that exchange matter and energy with their surroundings for their growth and sustenance. If a composite of the system plus its environment is considered, then it can always be shown that its entropy will never decrease, as long as the composite system is isolated.

Entropy is defined in physics as the ratio of the heat absorbed by a system to its absolute temperature (i.e., temperature based on the Kelvin scale). When a certain amount of heat passes to a system from one at a higher temperature, the entropy of the two systems combined increases. This is an irreversible process characterizing the general tendency of matter to seek temperature equilibrium, a state of maximum entropy or disorder.

This progressive tendency of nature toward disorder has been considered by many scholars as one of the primal natural processes that serve as a gauge for the irreversible nature of time. Accordingly, a considerable number have identified the relentless increase of entropy with what they term the *thermodynamic arrow of time*. In addition, the degradation associated with the increase of entropy has been discussed by some scholars of science and religion as a meaningful metaphor for evil.

See also DISORDER; THERMODYNAMICS, SECOND LAW OF

Bibliography

Feynman, Richard P. *The Feynman Lectures on Physics,* Vol. 1. Reading, Mass.: Addison-Wesley, 1963.

Coveney, Peter, and Highfield, Roger. *The Arrow of Time: A Voyage Through Science to Solve Time's Greatest Mystery*. New York: Ballantine, 1990.

Russell, John Robert. "Entropy and Evil." *Zygon: Journal of Science and Religion* 19 (1984): 449–468.

Sears, Francis W. *Thermodynamics*. Reading, Mass.: Addison-Wesley, 1953.

Zemansky, Mark W., and Dittman, Richard H. *Heat and Thermodynamics,* 6th edition. New York: McGraw-Hill, 1979.

LAWRENCE W. FAGG

ENVIRONMENTALISM

See ECOLOGY; ECOLOGY, ETHICS OF; ECOLOGY, RELIGIOUS AND PHILOSOPHICAL ASPECTS; ECOLOGY, SCIENCE OF

EPISTEMOLOGY

The need for an entry on epistemology—the theory of knowledge—illustrates the important mediating role of philosophy in key aspects of the science-religion interface. More specifically, the problems occasioned for religious traditions by the rise of science have extended beyond particular disputes to a more pervasive sense that science stands as the measure of all valid knowledge. The result has been a significant questioning as to whether religious traditions can still be viewed as routes to truth. For those seeking to maintain that these traditions can be so viewed, and that the sciences might even profit by appropriating some of the practices of wisdom enshrined therein, epistemological analysis is inescapable.

A number of interrelated issues apply: What is knowledge? What can one know? Does knowledge require certainty, and how can one know?

What is knowledge?

Taking these in order, the standard philosophical definition of knowledge is that of justified true belief. The need for justification and the related concern for its mode of operation links to the fourth issue listed. The need for true beliefs raises the question as to what truth is in regard to propositions. There are three standard approaches: the *correspondence,* the *coherence,* and the *pragmatic.*

The instinct behind correspondence views of truth—whether in scientific or religious contexts—is that true propositions bring something of reality to conceptual articulation. Despite the lasting importance of this instinct, questions exist about the adequacy of the metaphor of correspondence. How in the scientific context, for example, can concepts be thought to correspond to an intrinsically unconceptualized material reality? Does this not inevitably trade off the assumption that real knowledge, although unavailable to humans, is of an intuitive, unconceptualized form? And does that not in turn inevitably serve to denigrate the only forms of knowing of which humans are capable?

Implicit in the above statement of the instinct behind so-called correspondence approaches is the recognition that no one proposition can be fully adequate to the complexity of even one aspect of reality. For their part, coherentist approaches maintain that the best guide to truth consists in the maximally coherent configuration of all relevant statements pertaining to a given aspect of reality. Further, to the extent that all aspects of reality are viewed as being interrelated, coherentist approaches tend towards the aspiration for the maximally coherent configuration of all possible information pertaining to all aspects of reality. In scientific terms this might equate with the heuristically useful, although unattainable, hope for a perfected science and in Judeo-Christian terms with the hope for the eschatological gathering, fulfilling, and true configuring of all things in God.

Integrating the diversity of pragmatist views is the conviction that standard truth talk requires expanding to reflect the fact that human engagement with reality extends beyond the concern to know reality aright to include also the concern to live within it well: Truth is a matter of practical action as well as of conceptual articulation. This resonates with the emphasis within religious traditions upon the need to integrate attentiveness, discernment, and wise practice. While the sciences are justifiably viewed as the clearest example of the human capacity for knowing the world, the scientific community may have something to receive here in the form of a more explicit attentiveness to the specific practical objectives and potential applications of any proposed research project.

What can one know?

The question "What can one know?" has traditionally been answered in two different, but perhaps ultimately complementary, ways: the realist and the idealist. The strong realist maintains that knowledge must involve a real knowing of the world as it really is. The idealist maintains that human knowledge can only ever be a knowing of reality as mediated by human concepts. The bind for both science and religion has been to be caught between a strongly realist-correspondentialist definition of truth and the recognition that all truth claims are inextricably shaped by human concepts. Much philosophy of science has sought to counter the charge that science is simply a useful construct that does not actually convey knowledge. Likewise, much philosophical theology sets itself against the charge that religion is simply a human mythic creation or emotive projection.

A potential way beyond the realist-idealist impasse lies in the dual recognition that while all human engagement with reality is mediated by concepts, such concepts themselves reflect a long process of interaction with the world and, for the religious domain, with the reality of God in such a fashion as renders them at least partially adequate to the reality of things.

Knowledge and fallibility

The move to any such critical-realist position clearly requires one to relinquish an absolute connection between certainty and knowledge. As noted earlier, however, principles already exist that encourage one to view both scientific and religious knowledge in its full and final sense more as an aspiration than a present reality, and this without devaluing the partial knowledge already available. Recognizing the fallibility of scientific knowledge should keep science open to revision. So also, recognizing the inexhaustible richness of God should keep religious understanding open to there always being more.

Two different constructional metaphors have been offered in response to the question of how one can justify one's beliefs: that of a building resting on sure foundations and that of an interconnected web, the strength of which derives from mutual support between members. In spite of their dominance throughout much of the eighteenth, nineteenth, and even twentieth centuries, foundationalist models of justification have tended to recede, along with the strongly correspondential definition of truth with which they are associated, as the inextricable role of language and concept in all human engagement with reality has emerged more broadly into view.

Quite apart from the unrealizable character of foundationalist aspirations, alternative systemic, coherence-based approaches to justification have been claimed to fit the actual practices of scientific and religious reasoning better. It can be claimed that any danger of promoting a move towards closed systems wherein coherence is won at the cost of insularity and ossification can be offset by a recognition of the permanent fallibility of present understanding and a consequent continual drive towards ever more extensive coherence.

While pragmatist views are generally seen as having a limited contribution to make to the justification of propositions, some accord them a greater role in choosing between methods of ascertaining truth. Perhaps their real value is in reminding us of the various factors that may influence someone in finding one system, rather than another, truth-bearing. While that is particularly appropriate in the religious context, it may also be more appropriate in the scientific context than many scientists care to admit.

See also CRITICAL REALISM; FOUNDATIONALISM; IDEALISM; NONFOUNDATIONALISM; POSTFOUNDATIONALISM; PRAGMATISM; TRUTH, THEORIES OF

Bibliography

Banner, Michael C. *The Justification of Science and the Rationality of Religious Belief.* Oxford: Clarendon, 1990.

Clayton, Philip. *Explanation from Physics to Theology: An Essay in Rationality and Religion.* New Haven, Conn.: Yale University Press, 1989.

Deane-Drummond, Celia E. *Creation Through Wisdom: Theology and the New Biology.* Edinburgh: T&T Clark, 2000.

Murphy, Nancey. *Theology in the Age of Scientific Reasoning.* Ithaca, N.Y.: Cornell University Press, 1990.

Murphy, Nancey, and Ellis, George F. R. *On the Moral Nature of the Universe: Theology, Cosmology, and Ethics.* Minneapolis, Minn.: Fortress, 1996.

Murray, Paul D. "Truth and Reason in Science and Theology: Points of Tension, Correlation and Compatibility." In *God, Humanity and the Cosmos: A Textbook in Science and Religion,* ed. Christopher Southgate. Harrisburg, Pa.: Trinity Press International, 1999.

Rescher, Nicholas. *A System of Pragmatic Idealism, Volume I: Human Knowledge in Idealistic Perspective.* Princeton, N.J.: Princeton University Press, 1992.

Soskice, Janet Martin. *Metaphor and Religious Language.* Oxford: Clarendon, 1985.

van Huyssteen, J. Wentzel. *The Shaping of Rationality: Toward Interdisciplinarity in Theology and Science.* Grand Rapids, Mich.: Eerdmans, 1999.

PAUL D. MURRAY

EPR PARADOX

EPR paradox is a seeming paradox conceived as a thought experiment by Albert Einstein (1879–1955), Boris Podolsky, and Nathan Rosen in 1935 as a challenge to the Copenhagen Interpretation of quantum mechanics. The title of the published paper was "Can Quantum-Mechanical Description of Physical Reality be Considered Complete?" Einstein did not believe that objects only had properties when they were observed. He tried to conceive of a situation in which the observation of one thing would lead to a situation in which it was one hundred percent certain that another state would be completely certain irrespective of whether it had been observed.

Atomic states can be created so that their total spin is zero. If the state is allowed to decay into two spinning particles that move off rapidly in opposite direction close to the speed of light then the particles must have spin of +1 and −1 respectively, so that they add to zero, as required by the conservation of spin. According to the Copenhagen Interpretation of quantum mechanics the spin of either of the two particles does not exist until it is measured. Before any spin is measured any one of the two decay particles has a fifty percent chance of having spin +1 or spin −1. But EPR argued that if you measure one particle and find its spin to be +1 then you know that the other must be −1 without a measurement taking place. Einstein argued that this undermined Niels Bohr's (1885–1962) interpretation of quantum measurement. The word *paradox* became associated with this set up because it appears mysterious how the second particle to have its spin measured can "know" what the outcome of the measurement of the spin of the first particle turned out to be. However, Bohr showed that this was not in fact the case. The two particles are entangled by quantum reality in such a way that there is no violation of the Copenhagen Interpretation of quantum reality. The measurement of the spin of the first particle brings into being the spin of the second particle. More recently, experiments of this sort have been performed by Alain Aspect and colleagues in 1982 in ways that allow the predictions of quantum mechanics to be tested to see if there is any conflict with observation. So far, the predictions of quantum mechanics agree with all observations to high precision.

See also COPENHAGEN INTERPRETATION; EINSTEIN, ALBERT; PARADOX; PHYSICS, QUANTUM

Bibliography

Aspect, Alain; Dalibard, Jean; and Roger, Gnard. "Experimental Test of Bell's Inequalities Using Time Varying Analyzers." *Physical Review Letters* 49 (1982): 1804.

D'Espagnet, Bernard. *In Search of Reality.* New York: Springer-Verlag, 1983.

Herbert, Nick. *Quantum Reality: Beyond the New Physics.* London: Rider, 1985.

Einstein, Albert; Podolsky, Boris; Rosen, Nathan. "Can Quantum-mechanical Description of the Universe be Considered Complete?" *Physical Review* 47 (1935): 777-780.

JOHN D. BARROW

ESCHATOLOGY

Eschatology, from the Greek word *eschaton* (the last), is the theological study of the last things, the final state of each individual, of the community of all individuals, and of reality itself. Thus, traditionally eschatology has dealt with the themes of death, judgment, heaven, hell, purgatory, the resurrection of the dead, the end of the world, and "the new heavens and the new Earth." Generally, eschatology deals with the ultimate destiny of individuals and creation, and what it is legitimate to hope for. For Christians, that destiny is envisioned as the resurrection of each individual with Christ and the transformation and unification of all things with him in God forever. In theological reflection since late 1960s, there has been a shift in stress to the present realities, which through God's active presence in the risen Christ and in the Spirit are considered the seeds or partial realizations of this ultimate destiny (realized eschatology). Full flowering and completion will only be achieved after death and the "final consummation" of the universe.

It is at this point that the natural sciences have a contribution to make. Biology, paleontology, geology, and astronomy help one appreciate the transience and fragility of all that exists, even though nature is continually bringing new things and new life out of dissolution and death. No individual entity or species continues forever. Cosmology assures that the observable universe itself will eventually become sterile and evanesce as it expands forever, undergoing heat death. The natural sciences are, of themselves, unable to discern anything beyond physical dissolution and biological death. However, because theologically there must be a continuity between present reality and its final transformation at the *eschaton,* certain key characteristics of reality, such as relationality and pattern, will undoubtedly be the enhanced basis for its eschatological completion.

See also DEATH; ETERNITY; LIFE AFTER DEATH

Bibliography

Polkinghorne, John, and Welker, Michael, eds. *The End of the World and the Ends of God: Science and Theology on Eschatology.* Harrisburg, Pa.: Trinity Press International, 2000.

WILLIAM R. STOEGER

ETERNAL LIFE

See ESCHATOLOGY; ETERNITY; LIFE AFTER DEATH

ETERNITY

The concept of *eternity* qualifies both discussion about God and about human destiny, although in different but analogous way. Most believers would profess that God is eternal and many of them believe that eternal life is the prospect of human life in the wider context of the divine life. However, believers, theologians, and philosophers disagree about the meaning of these professions. With the declaration "God is eternal" religious believers express their faith that God encompasses all time for them as creatures because divine life has all the time it needs without beginning or end. God is present at any time in the course of history; divine existence is everlasting, so it endures without any possible limitation. This notion of eternity is found in biblical literature.

The word *eternal,* meaning "everlasting," can be used in a strong and weak sense. In the strong sense it refers only to God with the entire divine reality, which always has existed and will exist without end. In the weak sense *eternal* might be used to describe creatures that enjoy eternal life that has a temporal beginning but will have no end. Human beings have their creaturely constraints (birth and death), and it is God's grace when they (or their soul) receive eternal life beyond death, which is life in relation to the eternal God. Apart from these meanings, *eternity* is sometimes used in a nontemporal way: To live *sub specie aeternitatis* means to lead one's life according to eternal ultimate normativity.

Theologians and philosophers often disagree about how to interpret *eternal.* Many of them understand "God is eternal" as affirming "God is wholly timeless." So they imagine the divine being as outside time, without a temporal location (a moment of existence), and without duration (a period of subsistence). There is an anthropological argument *pro* timelessnes, presupposing a realistic theory of time (time flows and exits independent from events) that runs as follows: Human life is limited both by the borderline cases of birth and death (moments) and by the periods of its past, which are no longer available, and of its future to which it has no access. As temporally living beings, humans are imprisoned in time, continually losing parts of their lives (present events). Such an "imprisonment" in any temporal series is considered to be a denial of the perfectness of the divine being. Therefore, the Roman philosopher Boethius (c. 480–524) equated God's perfect eternal life with timelessness: "eternity is the instantaneously whole and perfect possession of illimitable life."

So far, the argument entails that God knows everything simultaneously because the past, present, and future of God's life are instantaneously grasped in all its relations to creation. Therefore, the past, present, and future are all present to God in one divine point of view. Boethius illustrates God's point of view outside of time with the image of a person standing on a mountaintop who sees what happens along the road in the valley. That person sees, as it were, simultaneously the past, the present, and the future of people walking along the road. The mountain metaphor, however, makes unequivocally clear that this all-encompassing simultaneity spatializes the concept of time: God observes all temporal relations between events as if they were spatial relations between objects in a landscape. If the omniscient God knows all the events of past, present, and future simultaneously, God is simultaneous both with these individual events in order to observe them, and with the sum total of these events because God must be outside of time to observe the temporal series as a unity. Because divine knowledge is true by definition, God's observation of the temporal order is how it "really" is; all events are simultaneous, synchronized. In other words, the notion of a causal chain as a temporal structure is useless because causes and effects are simultaneous, which makes the temporal order arbitrary and causal circularity a serious option. This appears to be equivalent to the assertion that time has no temporal metric and merely a spatial topology. Given this reconstruction, time is merely illusion or appearance (in line with an idealistic theory of time). And therefore, the temporal "imprisonment" human beings might experience is illusory as well. Without coping with such issues, a timeless view of God's eternity is incoherent.

For classical theists, however, eternity conceived as sempiternality (of never-ending duration) raises several theological problems. Divine essence cannot be identical with existence because a temporal God continually loses part of being as past and is not fully actual because of the divine future. Moreover, a temporal God cannot be simple because the divine existence is composed of past, present, and future, each with its own logic. Lastly, to reach the present for a sempiternal God takes an infinite amount of time, subdividable in a finite and an infinite part *ad infinitum.* These interpretations of essence and simplicity, however, are disputed, whereas the third issue misses the existential point that there is no moment in history in which God is absent. The use of temporal language has the advantage that it can make sense of the notion of divine action and involvement in history.

Contemporary theologians like Wolfhart Pannenberg (1928–) and Jürgen Moltmann (1926–) argue that God's future already exists (in a tenseless sense) from which God acts in the present, a movement opposite to the arrow of time. So God's eternity is an entering in time in which everything is shaped by and from God's future, which is declared to have ontological priority over past and present. However, God's action from God's future implies that all past, present, and creaturily future are simultaneous with God's future. Thus, in God's view, the complete history of created reality appears to be a timeless block universe, whereas from the perspective of creatures history is experienced as temporally ordered. Pannenberg interprets the divine eternity as simultaneity, the perfect possession of the fullness of life, which is claimed to be the opposite of timelessness. Both the whole of creaturely history and this divine life is present to God in such a way that God's eternity embraces the totality of time.

See also LIFE AFTER DEATH; TIME: RELIGIOUS AND PHILOSOPHICAL ASPECTS

Bibliography

Craig, William Lane. "Omniscience, Tensed Facts, and Divine Eternity." *Faith and Philosophy* 17 (2000): 225–241.

Helm, Paul. *Eternal God: A Study of God Without Time.* Oxford: Oxford University Press, 1990.

Leftow, Brian. *Time and Eternity.* Ithaca N.Y.: Cornell University Press, 1991.

Moltman, Jürgen. *The Coming of God: Christian Eschatology.* London: SCM Press, 1996.

Padgett, Alan. *God, Eternity, and the Nature of Time.* New York: St. Martin's Press, 1992.

Pannenburg, Wolfgang. *Systematic Theology,* Vol. 3. Grand Rapids, Mich.: Eerdman's, 1998.

Pike, Nelson. *God and Timelessness.* London: Routledge and Kegan Paul, 1970.

Stump, Eleonora, and Kretzmann, Norman. "Eternity." *The Journal of Philosophy* 78 (1981): 429–458.

Stump, Eleonora, and Kretzmann, Norman. "Eternity, Awareness, and Action." *Faith and Philosophy* 9 (1992): 463–482.

Swinburne, Richard. "God and Time." In *Reasoned Faith: Essays in Philosophical Theology in Honor of Norman Kretzmann,* ed. Eleonora Stump. Ithaca N.Y.: Cornell University Press, 1993.

LUCO J. VAN DEN BROM

ETHICS

See ALTRUISIM; MEDICAL ETHICS; MORALITY; TECHNOLOGY AND ETHICS; VALUE

ETHNICITY

This entry probes the intersections of religion and science from a cultural perspective. Culture and ethnicity are crucial to the ongoing dialogue about meaning, nature, and the role of humankind in the cosmos, Historically, it was assumed that dominant cultures provided the only reliable scientific methodologies and theological interpretations. This preoccupation with rationality, objectivity, and neutrality relegated the wisdom of indigenous people to myth and mystery. Yet scientific findings are more congruent with ancient wisdom than modernist deductions. Ancient intuitions hint at a universe that is expansive rather than exclusive, connected rather than isolated.

Both religion and science offer intriguing insights about the universe, culture, and human nature. Both disciplines, however, have been complicit in the oppression of racial/ethnic people. Historically, religion was used as a catalyst for domination, wars, atrocities, and abuses of humankind are still perpetrated in the name of God. In North America, Christian slave masters hoped that Christian conversion would encourage slave to accept their fate. The promise of freedom in heaven relieved owners of the need to redress immediate and grievous breaches of human rights. During the civil rights movement, it was the unified efforts of local clergymen who urged Martin Luther King Jr. to slow his initiatives for justice.

Theological discourses also rely upon problematic dyads of light and dark to signify good and evil. This is done even though biblical texts refer to a God who is identified with light but who also dwells in darkness. People live in a world that is seduced by light, intrigued by its properties, and theologically persuaded that evil is synonymous with darkness. This paradigm allows people with dark skin to be deemed pariahs and strangers within the world community.

Despite cultural assumptions to the contrary, most scholars agree that race is not a biological or physical category, yet racial perceptions persist. Race always develops within a matrix of superiority and inferiority. Distinctions based on color, physical traits, or ethnicity mask issues of power, fear of difference, and social control. Those who envision an egalitarian society in the twenty-first century will be challenged to use all of the resources at hand to deconstruct mythologies about race.

Seekers of justice usually rely on the discourses of religion to describe their visions of freedom and reconciliation, but reject the metaphors of science when they try to delineate the contours of the beloved community. Even though both science and religion incorporate issues of power, hierarchy, and the assignment of inferiority, ethnic communities have a historical mistrust of scientific contributions to issues of race.

In scientific circles, eugenics attempted to tie social constructions of inferiority to physical attributes. In the eighteenth century, Swedish botanist Carolus Linnaeus (1707–1708) created "scientific" racial classifications and descriptive characteristics. In the nineteenth century, Louis Agassiz (1807–1873), a Swiss-born Harvard professor, argued that human beings do not share a common ancestry (monogenism); instead, he argued that God created the races as separate and distinct human categories (polygenism). On the medical front, the Tuskegee Syphilis experiments conducted at the Tuskegee Institute in Alabama from 1932 to 1972 allowed syphilis to advance untreated in African-American male subjects despite the eventual availability of penicillin. Nazi experiments on Jewish prisoners are also ignominious moments in history.

The sciences also influence social institutions, laws, and theological perspectives. As physicist Nick Herbert notes, Isaac Newton's description of the world "as a giant clock" was translated in cultural contexts into "atomicity, objectivity, and determinism" (p. xi). A rigid and mechanistic view of the universe influenced political and social initiatives that oppressed those deemed to be at the bottom of the hierarchy. The case can be made that both science and religion can reflect the best and the worst in human culture.

Despite these problems, the quest for justice is not just a social and spiritual construct; it also reflects the view of the universe and the human task within the cosmos. Accordingly, liberation initiatives require the resources of both science and religion. The questions change when science and religion inform discussions of race and ethnicity. What does race mean in a scientific context, when darkness is no longer an indicator of inferiority, but instead becomes a cosmological metaphor for the power and predominance attributed to dark matter? Biology teaches that social separations based on difference are false. People are connected through a common human ancestry and genome. Cosmology teaches that separation is not the way of the universe. Instead connections that defy rational processes abound. By means of the Uncertainty and Complementarity Principles, physics demonstrates that observations and attempts to know other humans connect people at the most fundamental levels.

Conflicts based on race, ethnicity, gender, class, or sexuality are power struggles that attempt to define social acceptability through force or appropriation of the public narrative. The addition of religious and scientific concepts and discourses offer a rhetorical corrective to social and legal theories about life in diverse and multicultural spaces.

See also ANTHROPOLOGY; EUGENICS; LIBERATION THEOLOGY; WOMANIST THEOLOGY

Bibliography

Herbert, Nick. *Quantum Reality: Beyond the New Physics.* New York: Anchor/Doubleday, 1985.

Montagu, Ashley. *Man's Most Dangerous Myth: The Fallacy of Race,* 6th edition. Walnut Creek, Calif.: AltaMira Press, 1997.

Rothman, Barbara Katz. *The Book of Life: A Personal and Ethical Guide to Race, Normality and the Implications of the Human Genome Project.* Boston: Beacon Press, 2001.

BARBARA A. HOLMES

EUGENICS

Eugenics is a science that aims to purify the gene pool, especially of humans, by controlling reproduction to assure the birth of offspring with desired traits. The roots of eugenics go back to ancient Greece, where Plato's *Republic* lauds procreation by the best parents. The term *eugenics,* derived from the Greek word *eugenes* (good in birth), was first used in 1883 by the British scientist Francis Galton. Advocates of eugenics sought to counter Charles Darwin's theory of natural evolution with human-controlled outcomes. American biologist Charles Benedict Davenport (1866–1944), founded the Eugenics Records Office at Cold Spring Harbor, New York, in 1910. Davenport's work there led some of the first research in human eugenics during the early 1900s.

Environmental eugenicists emphasized prenatal care and a clean environment to ensure "positive" eugenics. Negative eugenics reached its apex during the Nazi regime (1933–1945) in Germany, which sterilized and murdered the "racially unfit." By the late twentieth century, eugenics and the Holocaust were linked. Yet earlier, some states and the U.S. government mandated sterilization for persons with severe genetic disabilities, and immigration laws in 1924 sought to reduce the number of immigrants from areas considered less desirable, such as eastern and southern Europe. In the 1950s, and most dramatically since the 1980s, human genetics replaced eugenics as the accepted approach to planned reproduction. Genetic counseling and sophisticated screening for genetic or chromosomal diseases or disorders inform parents about reproductive options. Will labeling fetuses "defective" or "less desirable" reintroduce selection by abortion, voluntary sterilization, or birth control? Some feminists and liberal religious groups embrace freedom of reproductive choices, while persons with disabilities, Roman Catholics, and conservative Protestants fear that it will lead to a disregard of human life from conception forward.

With the completion in the year 2000 of the sequencing of the human genome, determining genetic anomalies or, some say, even the genetic roots of destructive social behavior will trigger the wide dissemination of genetic information. Confidentiality becomes crucial. Some fear that human hubris, like that exhibited by the mythic figures Prometheus or Pandora, will engineer the engineer as well as the engine along an unknown track. Eugenics merged with genetic engineering produces scientific triumphs, moral challenges, and fears about things like human germline alteration and dissemination of pathogenic bacteria. There are dangers in policies of noninterference (as plagues and epidemics testify) as well as in genetic enhancement in which the definition and social policies establishing the "fit" are externally, rather than individually, determined. The slippery slope argument suggests that once certain traits are screened (e.g., color blindness or skin color) they will be eliminated or altered. The challenge is to determine the difference between therapeutic and eugenic measures.

At heart, one's definition of moral dilemmas surrounding eugenics is affected by one's view of knowledge as neutral or value-laden. If "improving" the human condition is a laudable end that genetic engineering can achieve, then this knowledge is good. Some believe that obligations to future generations and exorbitant health care costs provide a moral mandate to screen and treat curable diseases. Is consideration of supremely compromised fetuses, profoundly disabled persons, or comatose elderly from the perspective of financial and social burdens a sign of a highly moral society or an irresponsible one? Hermann Muller, for one, argues that the gene pool is at risk without positive eugenics, while Gregory Pence argues in *Classic Works in Medical Ethics* that even with sperm and eggs from genetically "superior" fathers and mothers, predicting "perfect" children is uncertain at best.

See also ABORTION; BIOTECHNOLOGY; DARWIN, CHARLES; ETHNICITY; GENE PATENTING; GENETIC ENGINEERING; GENETICS; GENETIC TESTING; HUMAN GENOME PROJECT; PLATO; PLAYING GOD; REPRODUCTIVE TECHNOLOGY; SOCIOBIOLOGY

Bibliography

"Genetics and Faith." *The Park Ridge Center Bulletin* 13 Jan/Feb (2000).

Kass, Leon R. "The New Biology: What Price Relieving Man's Estate?" *Science* 174 (1971): 779–787.

Muller, Hermann J. "Genetic Progress by Voluntarily Conducted Germinal Choice." In *Man and His Future,* ed. Gordon Wolstenholme. Boston: Little, Brown, 1963.

National Institutes of Health. *Draft National Institutes of Health Guidelines for Research Involving Human Pluripotent Stem Cells.* Bethesda, Md.: NIH, 1999.

Pence, Gregory E., ed. *Classic Works in Medical Ethics: Core Philosophical Readings.* Boston: McGraw Hill, 1998.

Reich, Warren Thomas, ed. *Encyclopedia of Bioethics,* rev. edition. New York: Macmillan, 1995.

ABIGAIL RIAN EVANS

EVANGELICAL THEOLOGY

See CHRISTIANITY, EVANGELICAL, ISSUES IN SCIENCE AND RELIGION

EVIL

See EVIL AND SUFFERING; THEODICY

EVIL AND SUFFERING

Evil is whatever frustrates or opposes goodness, and goodness is what is, or ought to be, desired by conscious rational agents. Suffering is thus one sort of evil, since no conscious rational agent would desire to suffer, just for its own sake. Other sorts of evil lie in the frustration of the aims and goals of rational agents (one might also include the aims of God, and some would include the aims and goals of any beings whatsoever, insofar as they could reasonably be said to have aims or goals), or in factors that restrict the normal activities and dispositions of rational or sentient agents.

Buddhism

The faith that most obviously takes the fact of evil as one of its basic starting points is Buddhism, whose first noble truth is that "all is suffering" (*dukkha*). This is not merely the view that there is much frustration and suffering in life. It is the view that material existence essentially involves suffering, so that no enduring happiness can be found in such existence. Not only is there the obvious suffering to be experienced in birth, disease, and

death. There is the fact that pleasure is short-lived, misfortune is always possible, and the transitory nature of time itself means that the past is lost forever, the present cannot be held fast, and the future is always tinged with anxiety. The one who sees deeply into the nature of things will therefore see that only in the acceptance of total transience can any stability be found. All things are empty of enduring substantial existence, and there is not even an enduring substantial soul or self that remains the same throughout all change. All things are in perpetual flow, interdependent and perpetually perishing. *Dukkha* is the first noble truth of the Buddhist way, which sees suffering and evil as the basic human problem, which may, with some difficulty, be overcome.

Buddhists are not usually concerned with answering the question of how suffering arises. It is just there, a fact of existence. However, the cause of suffering is said to be the sort of desire that consists in attachment to finite things—wishing to possess them, or bemoaning the lack of them. So it might be said that suffering is intrinsic to a world in which attachment and desire are possible. In addition, specific sufferings are caused by *karma,* by the accumulated attachments of many past existences. So it might be held that souls "fall" into this world of the senses, of transience and time, because of desire, and they have to work out the consequences of their desires over many lives until they achieve liberation from the wheel of rebirth—*samsara*—and, all desire exhausted, never again experience rebirth.

Karma **and moral causality**

Insofar as rebirth is essential to Buddhist belief, there needs to be a spiritual or mental part of human nature that is capable of rebirth. There needs to be a form of moral causality in nature, which ensures that actions have appropriate consequences in future lives. And there needs to be some form of correlation between practices of morality and meditation and the achievement of those higher mental states of mindfulness, compassion, and bliss, in which the practitioner approaches liberation, or *nirvana.*

To devise precise and measurable tests of these claims is, however, extremely difficult, if not impossible. Neurophysiology may lead to the establishment of links between brain and mental functions, but it is highly disputable whether it can establish either that mental functions are nothing but brain functions, or that they can have separate existence. At present, evidence suggests a high degree of correlation, in a rather general sense, between brain states and mental states. But attempts to show, for example, that there can be "out of the body" experiences, are viewed skeptically by most scientists. While claims that complete physical accounts of mental activity are possible are viewed equally sceptically by most philosophers.

Similarly, attempts to establish or disprove rebirth are unsatisfactorily vague or uncontrolled. The alleged evidence for memories of past lives is highly contested, and the theoretical difficulty of aligning souls that have highly developed propensities and desires with appropriate genetic materials may suggest that a completely new individual is created with each random combination of genetic material at fertilization, but it is hardly conclusive.

Most physicists would probably think of laws of nature as operating in an impersonal, universal, and morally neutral way, thus throwing doubt on the existence of any general principles of a morally ordered causality, which could ensure that all persons get the just deserts that their past lives have accumulated. Scientific views have developed in contexts in which rebirth has not been a major issue, and the belief is at present beyond the competence of the physical sciences to determine. It may even be held that the study of discarnate mental states is beyond the competence of science altogether. Buddhist appeals to laws of karmic consequences, and to the causal connectedness of desire and suffering, to explain the existence of evil and suffering, must be regarded as coherent and possible, even though they are in some tension with the world-view, if not with the particular established findings, of the natural sciences.

There are far less metaphysically committed forms of Buddhism that might regard belief in rebirth itself as an irrelevant question. They may not seek theoretical explanation at all, but remain concerned only with the practical question of how to overcome suffering and attain mindfulness and equanimity. In that case, Buddhism would be almost entirely a matter of moral commitment and mental discipline aiming at enlightenment. Evil and suffering would be purely practical problems, and would not be subject to scientific evaluation, except possibly for psychological tests to determine whether Buddhist techniques of meditation produce the desired results.

Hindu traditions

Belief in karma and rebirth is common to most Indian religions, and so in general an explanation of the occurrence of suffering is given in terms of the consequences of wrong acts or attachments in past lives. However, most Indian traditions are theistic, with devotion to one or more gods as central to their practice. Sometimes the gods are regarded as caught up in the cycle of *samsara* just like human beings. They have finite existences, which are much happier and longer-lasting than those of humans. But they will come to an end, and even the gods may fall down through the chain of beings into greater suffering, if they do not attain final liberation.

Those Indian traditions that are fully monotheistic (such as the two major traditions of Saivism, worship of Siva, and Vaisnavism, worship of Vishnu) usually identify the highest god with Brahman, the absolute reality, and assert that in some sense all things are one with, parts of, or expressions of Brahman. Since Brahman, appearing as the Supreme Lord, Isvara, is perfect in wisdom, intelligence, and bliss, and is the cause of the universe, there is a "problem of evil" in those traditions. The problem is how a perfect being can originate, or even be identical with, a universe so full of evil and suffering.

This is not usually felt to be a severe problem, however, since Brahman, though perfect in intelligence and bliss, contains the potentialities of all finite things in its own infinite reality, and those potentialities necessarily manifest themselves in the origination of an infinite number of worlds. The combination of a necessary manifestation of all possible realities, and a karmic law by which all finite souls receive the consequences of their own choices through a huge succession of embodied lives, effectively draws the sting out of the problem of evil. The imperfect manifests by necessity from the perfect, which remains changeless and unaffected by all imperfection. And in the realm of the imperfect, it is the acts and desires of finite souls themselves that cause both their suffering and happiness. The Supreme Lord is not responsible, and can in no way be blamed, as though he had chosen to inflict suffering on helpless and innocent creatures.

Very traditional or literalist readings of the Hindu scriptures may lead to tensions with evolutionary biology, since they depict a degeneration from an earlier golden age, when the gods were more intimately known, to the present. There may also be difficulties with belief in rebirth, since the number of human souls now in existence exceeds that of past history, and according to most scientific accounts there were millions of years when no souls existed at all. However, Hindus say that rebirth can take place in many different worlds or planes of existence. This cosmos is only one of an infinite number of worlds in which souls might be reborn in various forms. Moreover, Hinduism is not committed to literalism any more than Christianity is. In general the Hindu view is that evil and suffering arise from ignorance (*avidya*) of the truly spiritual nature of reality, and the mistaken belief that souls are essentially material. This view entails no particular account of the past history of this cosmos, since souls may have existed in other planes of being. To the extent that the natural sciences allow for such a belief in the ultimate primacy of spirit, and for belief in rebirth, and to the extent that Hindus interpret the classical myths as legendary, the Hindu account of evil and suffering as due to karmic fruits of action raises no particular problems for the relation of religious and scientific beliefs.

Semitic religions

The Semitic religious faiths (Judaism, Christianity, Islam, and their offshoots) have a different account of the human soul. They do not think, as most Indian religious traditions do, that souls exist without beginning or end, and are reborn in countless forms. They believe that human persons are formed of dust—they are material, and begin to exist with, or some short time after, the conception of a genetically unique individual. This means that the theory of karma is not available to the Semitic faiths to explain evil and suffering. Furthermore, since Semitic religions interpret creation as the freely chosen act of an omnipotent God, there is a serious problem about why there is evil and suffering in the world at all.

It could be held, and often Jews and Muslims do hold, that the creator is beyond assessment in moral terms. The divine nature is inaccessible to human understanding, and it is impious to question God or to judge whatever reasons for creating God might have. That, however, clearly raises the question of whether God can be called good. According to such a view, there are three main senses in which an omnipotent and incomprehensible creator could be called good. First, God can be good because God is the supremely desirable object of rational choice. God is desirable above all things. The divine being is unsurpassed in beauty, wisdom, knowledge, and power, and is supremely good in the sense that a beautiful picture might be called good.

Second, God is merciful and compassionate, showing mercy to thousands of those who love him, and God can forgive sins and help and support whomsoever he wills. God is also rigorously just, and will visit the sins of the fathers on the third and fourth generation of their descendents. The divine will is simply unquestionable. But God will be merciful to those who sincerely seek to obey his will.

Third, God offers incomparable rewards to the just. At the day of resurrection, he will condemn the unjust (perhaps not for ever), but grant to the just unending life in paradise, a share in the world to come, which will make all the suffering of this life as nothing by comparison.

Theodicy and science

Such a view does not seek to offer any reason why evil and suffering exist, rooting them in the unfathomable will of God. For many people it is difficult, however, to think of God as truly just when so many innocent beings suffer so much. And to some, appeal to rewards after death cannot compensate for immense suffering in life, when an omnipotent God could presumably have abolished such suffering. So attempts have often been made to justify the ways of God to men, with varying degrees of success.

At this point the natural sciences, perhaps surprisingly, offer a certain amount of help. It would be almost impossible to understand the universe if events in it did not occur in accordance with general and predictable laws. So a condition of scientific understanding, and of the growth of the ability to adapt and control our environment, is the existence of general laws of nature, which will be both mathematically precise and virtually universal in scope.

Such laws are "nested" in an extremely complex way, so that the elementary and highly unstable forces of the subatomic world form stable atoms and molecules at a higher level. These in turn form the solid bodies and organic unities that are found at the level of human perception. And they make possible the formation of central nervous systems and brains, which are the conditions of consciousness and eventually of rational agency. Thus the natural world seems to be a developing system of levels of emergence, whereby on the basis of a few elementary laws and particles complex communities of rational agents can come into being. These agents are not alien intrusions into the material world. They are its highest emergent forms, and manifest the amazing capacity of matter to come to understand and shape itself.

The development of quantum mechanics strongly suggests that there is a deep interconnectedness in nature, whereby each part is connected with every other, and it is not possible simply to remove even a few electrons, and leave the rest of the universe unchanged. In other words, one cannot just change a few parts of the universe for the better, and otherwise leave everything as it is. Either you have the system as an interconnected whole, or you have something completely different. To put it bluntly, as a rational agent, a human soul, who is an integral part of this material universe, either you exist in this universe, with all its faults, or you, as the precise and unique individual you are, do not exist at all.

At the level of biological existence, as it is presently understood, humans have come to exist largely by the operation of the principles of random mutation and natural selection. It is as if living things shuffle through the possibilities of existence, creatively seeking new forms of adaptive life. Consciousness and creativity are perhaps, as biochemist and theologian Arthur Peacocke (b. 1924) suggested, inherent potentialities or *propensities* of matter, which will be realized in time through the shuffling and adaptive processes of natural selection. Human nature is essentially the product of these processes, and the lust and aggression of humans, as well as their interdependence and altruism, has been built up through the adaptive process over many generations of evolution. Being parts and products of this natural process, humans cannot be basically different from what they are, creatures that are partly competitive and violent, and partly cooperative and loving.

If the universe disclosed by the sciences is roughly like this, its basic nature will include the operation of general laws of nature, the emergence according to such laws of consciousness and agency, the existence of humans as an integral part of a general system that cannot be different from what it is, and the gradual evolution of humans through processes of mutation and competition. Evil and suffering will be ineliminable from such an evolutionary world-system. Destruction and violence are built into the system from the decay of nuclear particles to the explosion of supernovae and the elimination of life-threatening organic competitors.

The moral of the story is that God cannot create human beings without creating a universe like this, with all its evil and suffering, of which such beings are an integral part. In this sense the natural sciences offer a sort of theodicy, the giving of reasons why a good Creator might create a universe with suffering in it. It might be wrong to think that God can create absolutely anything we can imagine—human beings in a universe without suffering, for example. There could be beings in a universe without suffering, but they would not be human. They would not be us. So if human existence is worthwhile, maybe the suffering in this universe has to exist.

For some contemporary scientists, like Steven Weinberg, human existence is not worth-while enough to justify so much suffering. Or maybe evolution is seen as too random or accidental to be purposive. To these scientists, chance and necessity are enough and rule out any idea of a good God who chooses to create the universe. But this may not be a strictly scientific judgment. A good God could create this universe, if the suffering in it is a necessary condition or consequence of an overwhelmingly great good—and such a good might be the creation of rational agents who could enjoy eternal fellowship with one another and with God.

This conclusion would be strengthened if the creation of a universe like this was somehow necessary to God, as flowing from the changeless divine nature. At this point most theists insist that the act of creation must be free, not compelled, and must be intended, not accepted reluctantly by God. But when speaking of the divine nature, the distinction between freedom and necessity may not apply—some theologians suggest that God is necessarily what God freely chooses to be. As long as God is not compelled by some external or undesired force, the act of creation may be both free and necessary—as the being of God itself may be. As Thomas Aquinas (c. 1224–1275) put it in his *Summa Theologiae*, God's willing is identical with God's essence, which is necessarily what it is. Yes, as Aquinas notes, this is compatible with God's freely creating the universe.

Thus evil and suffering may be in some way necessary to the creation of humans. In traditional terms, evil and suffering are privations of goodness, not positively intended states. This is a viewpoint to which scientific investigation of nature makes a positive contribution.

Other explanations in theistic traditions

In the Abrahamic traditions, and especially in the Christian tradition, there has always existed another explanation for suffering—it may be the result of the maleficent or egoistic actions of rational beings. Satan is an angelic being whose evil is perhaps the cause of natural evils like earthquakes, and he successfully tempted Adam and Eve to disobey God. From a primal Paradisal state, Adam and Eve were ejected into the harsh world of an already *fallen* nature. In the Western Christian view, all their descendents were born in *original sin,* guilty before God even at birth because of the sin of their ancestors. Suffering and death entered the world mainly as a result of Adam's sin, and are now punishments for moral evil.

This literalist interpretation of Genesis (not accepted in this form either by Jews or by Eastern Orthodox Christians) is obviously at odds with any evolutionary account, for which suffering and death were intrinsic parts of the biological world long before humans even existed, and for which there is no paradisal world at the beginning of human history. Most Christian theologians now regard the Genesis accounts as legendary, and reinterpret the fall in terms of a general human condition of moral weakness and ignorance of God, which was caused or intensified by the moral and spiritual failures of the first humans.

Some theologians, like Paul Tillich, regard the fall as a necessary part of human evolution, which requires an *epistemic distance* between humans and God to enable moral autonomy to exist. Others think of the primal human estrangement from God as originally due to voluntary moral failure, though now all humans are born into an estranged society, and so not onto an equal moral playing-field. In contrast to Jews and Muslims, most Christians insist that reconciliation with God cannot be achieved by good works, but requires divine grace, or some act of divine self-sacrificial love, which was manifest supremely in the life and death of Jesus.

It is generally held in all Abrahamic traditions that much evil and suffering is caused by the free immoral acts of past and present human beings. Such an account can easily be held together with a commitment to the necessary possibility of such evil, and its actual existence to some degree. Human moral evil would be seen as intensifying the amount and degree of actual evil and suffering.

Evolutionary biology requires some revision of traditional views, especially of original sin. However, it offers a helpful account of how moral failure follows naturally, if not inevitably, from the dispositions to lust and aggression that are part of the human biological inheritance and have been necessary conditions of human dominance in the processes of natural selection. On a literalist biblical account, it is hard to see why the first humans should have sinned against God at all, except by a sheer irrational act. But in an evolutionary context, sin becomes the natural expression of biologically inbred tendencies. Such expression becomes "sin" only when expressed in opposition to divine commands to love and reconciliation. One still cannot explain why humans sin—that is a free and therefore inexplicable choice. But one can give good reasons why they might sin—it is an inherent possibility of their nature, and offers temptations of sensual desire that might well, though they should not, counteract the impulse to love God, which also, according to this hypothesis, lies present, though perhaps only implicitly, in their biologically evolved nature.

A third explanation for evil and suffering in theistic traditions is that they are not the natural consequences of egoistic acts, but punishments inflicted by God for moral evil. This explanation has played a part in much religious thought, and biblical narratives often connect natural and human disasters with lack of obedience to God's law, while happiness and long life are seen as rewards for obedience. The scientific perception of laws of nature that are not morally ordered, of the chance elements involved in natural selection, and of the biological basis and the possibility of medical treatment for most diseases has largely led to the collapse of such views. In the Bible it was also perceived that God causes rain to fall on the just and on the unjust, and that the innocent suffer. Any easy equation of immorality and suffering is undermined by the Book of Job. While it is not absurd to posit a general tendency toward altruistic acts to produce happiness, and toward egoistic acts to produce suffering, the attribution of diseases to demonic influence, and of natural disasters to direct decisions of God to punish sin, has largely disappeared from informed theological debate.

Conclusion

Perhaps the greatest influence of modern science on these matters has been the supercession of belief in the direct causal acts of good and bad spirits by belief in the general operation of impersonal laws of nature. God's action in the world is largely seen in the setting up of a general system in which good is effectively selected and evil becomes finally self-destructive, rather than in continual divine interventions in nature. Particular divine actions (miracles) need not be denied, but they will be, almost by definition, very occasional transcendences of the usual processes of nature for a spiritual purpose, not the normal causes of happenings in the universe.

All these traditions accept that evil and suffering are either necessary or the result of freely chosen acts, and that in either case one should seek either to abolish evil and suffering or to overcome them by altruistic action, non-attachment to selfish desires, and perhaps by devotion to God. Science does require a reconstruction of traditional ways of formulating these positions, but it is reasonable to see the scientific view of nature as helpful in developing a deeper religious understanding of the place of suffering in the world, and offering more effective practical ways of overcoming it.

See also SIN; THEODICY

Bibliography

Bowker, John. *Problems of Suffering in Religions of the World*. Cambridge, UK: Cambridge University Press, 1970.

Davies, Brian. *The Thought of Thomas Aquinas*. New York: Oxford University Press, 1992.

Fiddes, Paul, S. *The Creative Suffering of God*. New York: Oxford University Press, 1988.

Griffin, David Ray. *God, Power and Evil: A Process Theology*. Philadelphia: Westminster Press, 1976.

Hardy, Friedhelm, *The Religions of Asia*. London: Routledge, 1988.

Helm, Paul. *The Providence of God*. London: InterVarsity Press, 1993.

Hick, John. *Evil and the God of Love*. San Francisco: Harper, 1978.

Peacocke, Arthur. *Theology for a Scientific Age*. London: SCM Press, 1990.

Plantinga, Alvin, *God, Freedom and Evil*. Grand Rapids, Mich.: Eerdmans, 1977.

Surin, Kenneth. *Theology and the Problem of Evil*. Oxford and New York: Blackwell, 1976.

Swinburne, Richard. *The Existence of God*. New York: Oxford University Press, 1979.

Tennant, F.R. *The Origin and Propagation of Sin: Being the Hulsean Lectures Delivered Before the University of Cambridge in 1901-2*. Cambridge, UK: Cambridge University Press, 1902.

Tillich, Paul. *Systematic Theology*. Chicago: University of Chicago Press, 1957.

Vanstone, W. H. *Love's Endeavour, Love's Expense*. London: Darton, Longman, and Todd, 1977.

Ward, Keith. *Religion and Human Nature*. Oxford: Oxford University Press, 1998.

Weinberg, Steven. *Dreams of a Final Theory*. London: Vintage, 1993.

KEITH WARD

EVOLUTION

There is a common belief that evolution and religion, Darwinian evolution and Christianity especially, are world pictures that are forever opposed. This is a belief today endorsed and promulgated both by extreme evangelical Christians (who support some version of Biblical literalism) and ardent ultra-Dawinians (who hold that their theory necessarily falls into an atheistic mode of thinking). Traditionally, however, this opposition has not been universally accepted. Many people find that there is much in common between the two systems and, thus, great opportunities for sympathetic dialogue. Much of the difficulty and debate arises from ignorance about the various positions involved. This is especially true of evolution. In discussing the idea of selection, it is convenient to make a three-fold distinction between the *fact* of evolution, the *path* of evolution, and the *theory* or *mechanism* of evolution.

The fact of evolution

The fact of evolution is simply the idea that all organisms, living and dead, came into being by a long developmental process, governed by natural laws, from organisms of a different, probably much simpler, kind. The fact of evolution includes the belief that the original organisms themselves developed by natural processes from inorganic materials. If one wanted to extend from the biological to the cosmological, one would see the fact of evolution as including all developmental change from the time of the Big Bang.

Claims for the fact of evolution were first mooted in the seventeenth century with the extension of Newtonian ideas from the mere running of the universe to its supposed development through natural laws. It was later argued—by, among others, Immanuel Kant—that this happened in a regular fashion as suns and planets were formed from gaseous nebulae. Biological evolutionary ideas began to appear towards the end of the eighteenth century. A prominent exponent in England was the physician and naturalist Erasmus Darwin, grandfather of Charles Darwin; in France a little later the chief advocate of the idea was the biologist Jean Baptiste de Lamarck.

The evidence offered for evolution (then more generally called *transmutation*) tended to be anecdotal. A major reason why few endorsed the idea with enthusiasm was that it was seen to be a reflection of the ideology of progress—upward change in the human social world, and upward change in the history of life, from "monad" to "man." Critics, like the father of comparative anatomy, the French biologist Georges Cuvier, found the idea religiously offensive less because it clashed with literal interpretations of the Bible than because of its underlying philosophy of progress. Such a world picture, in which humans can make the difference unaided, was at odds with the Christian notion of providence, where all depends on God's grace. Although by the mid nineteenth century religious worries were still much in evidence,

Charles Darwin met this challenge head on in the *Origin of Species* (1859), the groundbreaking work in which he introduced his theory. Darwin was not the first to argue for the fact of evolution, but by marshaling so much evidence from paleontology, embryology, geographical distributions, and more, he made the fact of evolution empirically plausible and no longer reliant on an underlying social philosophy for acceptance.

The path of evolution

The path of evolution, or *phylogeny,* is simply the history of the past as given in the fossil record and as can be discerned indirectly from anatomical and embryological causes and, increasingly, molecular evidence. Thanks to various sophisticated methods of dating, researchers can say that the universe itself is (since the Big Bang) about fifteen billion years old, that the Earth is about 4.5 billion years old, and that life first appeared on the planet about 3.75 billion years ago. Complex life began with the Cambrian explosion about six hundred million years ago; the Age of Mammals began about sixty-five million years ago (although the first mammals go back two hundred million years); the first known ancestors of humans are about four million years old (upright but with ape-sized brains); and, depending on how one measures things, the modern human species *Homo sapiens* is between five hundred thousand and a million years old.

Traditionally, life is pictured as a tree with contemporary organisms at the ends of the upper branches. However, Lamarck and some other early evolutionists thought that life developed upwards in separate but parallel lines, with variations laid over these. Alternatively, some researcher believe that viruses may carry genes from one line to other, very different, lines, so perhaps a better picture is that of a net. Paradoxically, the main outlines of the history of life were worked out in the first part of the nineteenth century, primarily by those who did not subscribe to evolution, and only later was the process of life given an evolutionary interpretation.

The theory or mechanism of evolution

The theory or mechanism of evolution has garnered many hypotheses. Notorious before Darwin was Lamarck's idea of the inheritance of acquired characteristics, which had not originated with him; Erasmus Darwin had accepted it, as did Charles Darwin much later. In the *Origin of Species,* Darwin described the mechanism that is generally accepted as the chief force for change: *natural selection.* More organisms are born than can survive and reproduce, leading to a struggle for survival and, more importantly, reproduction. Given naturally occurring variation, and the fact that those that survive will tend on average to be different from those that do not, there will be a *differential reproduction,* natural selection. In time this leads to full-blown evolution, and evolution of a particular kind, for selection produces organisms with *adaptations.* The eye and the hand come naturally as a result of Darwin's causal process.

Conclusion

In the years subsequent to the publication of Darwin's *Origin,* there have been a multitude of putative alternatives to Darwinian selection, including *orthogenesis* (a life force driving things), *mutationism* (major one-step changes), *genetic drift* (randomness), and *molecular drive* (DNA has its own built-in ways of change); none has established itself as a full and genuine rival to natural selection. This is not to say that all controversy is therefore quelled. Apart from the question of whether selection can be applied profitably to such issues as the origin of life, there are also questions about the form that life's history will take given selection as the main mechanism of change. Will it be smooth and gradual (*phyletic gradualism*), as supposed by Darwin and his followers, or will it be jerky and abrupt (*punctuated equilibria*), as supposed by some leading paleontologists, notably Stephen Jay Gould? Controversy about these issues, however, should not be taken as controversy about other matters. The fact of evolution is firmly established, the main outlines of the path of evolution have been worked out and details are being filled in (for example, that birds are descended from dinosaurs), and selection is taken to be the major mechanism of change even though there are debates about its applicability and its precise results and consequences.

Evolution as fact, path, and theory is a thriving part of the biological sciences, and it is also seen to have extensions and implications for thinking about many other parts of human experience. Social scientists are increasingly turning to evolutionary ideas to flesh out their understanding of human nature and society; philosophers have (after many hesitations) begun to see how evolution, selection even, can profitably deepen their understandings of epistemology (theory of knowledge) and ethics (theory of morality); novelists and poets use evolutionary themes to illuminate aspects of human understanding and motivation; linguists turn to Darwinism for help in grasping the developments of languages; and so it is in many other subjects and disciplines. Although there is still much opposition to evolutionary ideas on various religious fronts, there is realization by theologians and historians that the old story of the warfare between science and religion was much overblown, and many see evolution as an aid to faith and understanding rather than a hindrance.

See also DARWIN, CHARLES; EVOLUTIONARY EPISTEMOLOGY; EVOLUTIONARY ETHICS; LAMARCKISM; SELECTION, LEVELS OF; SOCIOBIOLOGY

Bibliography

Bowler, Peter. *Evolution: The History of an Idea.* Berkeley: University of California Press, 1984.

Depew, Daniel J., and Weber, Bruce H. *Darwinism Evolving.* Cambridge, Mass.: MIT Press, 1994.

Desmond, Adrian, and Moore, James. *Darwin: The Life of a Tormented Evolutionist.* New York: Warner, 1992.

Richards, Robert J. *The Meaning of Evolution: The Morphological Construction and Ideological Reconstruction of Darwin's Theory.* Chicago: University of Chicago Press, 1992.

Ruse, Michael. *Monad to Man: The Concept of Progress in Evolutionary Biology.* Cambridge, Mass.: Harvard University Press, 1996.

Ruse, Michael. *The Darwinian Revolution: Science Red in Tooth and Claw,* 2nd edition. Chicago: University of Chicago Press, 1999.

Ruse, Michael. *Can a Darwinian be a Christian? The Relationship Between Science and Religion.* Cambridge, UK: Cambridge University Press, 2001.

Ruse, Michael. *Darwin and Design: Science, Philosophy, and Religion.* Cambridge, Mass.: Harvard University Press, 2003.

MICHAEL RUSE

EVOLUTIONARY ALGORITHMS

Evolutionary algorithm is a term that describes the use of evolutionary models and methods in the design of computer programs, robots, and artificial life. Incorporating evolutionary strategies into computer programs was first proposed by Lawrence Fogel in the early 1960s. This work was significantly advanced by the invention of genetic algorithms by John Holland in 1975. Widespread interest in evolutionary computing, however, did not develop until the late 1980s and early 1990s, with the first conference on evolutionary computing being held in 1992 in La Jolla, California. Evolutionary computing methods are now used in a wide range of civilian and military applications, and the techniques of evolutionary computing are seen by some to be the future of both computer programming generally and artificial intelligence specifically.

Traditional computer programs rely on a sequence of precise instructions (algorithms) that commands a computer or robot to perform specific actions. Evolutionary computing mimics biological evolution by developing a program that considers a set of possible solutions for a given problem, evaluates the solutions according to fitness criteria, mutates the solutions according to set rules, and then repeats the sequence until a sufficiently optimal solution is found. Programs that utilize genetic algorithms attempt to more closely mimic neo-Darwinian evolution by providing each solution with a chromosome. Solutions then "mate" with one another, creating a new generation of solutions. The most fit solutions are selected out, and are allowed to mate and mutate further, until an optimal solution is found.

Much of the interest in evolutionary algorithms is due to their success in solving problems that are computationally difficult or impossible by traditional means. The most famous of these is the "traveling salesman problem," which attempts to find the shortest path between any two destinations. While the individual task may sound trivial, it represents a class of problems that are mathematically quite important. The techniques of evolutionary computing have also been used in the development of artificial life, creating virtual organisms that feed, reproduce, and compete within a computer-generated environment. In 2000, Hod Lipson and Jordan Pollack applied evolutionary computing to robotics, developing a program that creates mobile robots through a process of mutation and selection.

These and similar successes have led some to conclude that evolutionary algorithms provide basic insights into evolutionary theory, confirming basic neo-Darwinian principles of natural selection. Richard Dawkins's distribution of his biomorphs program along with his book *The Blind Watchmaker* (1986) is an early instance of this sort of claim in a popular science work. Critics of evolution, such as William Dembski, however, have argued that evolutionary computing does not provide evidence for neo-Darwinism because the algorithms must first be designed by a human being.

Evolutionary algorithms are also held to provide insight into the nature of intelligence itself. Thinkers as diverse as Daniel Dennett, Karl Popper, and Michael Ruse have argued for a similarity between evolution by natural selection and basic cognitive tasks, and evolutionary computing began, in part, to solve issues related to the development of artificial intelligence.

See also AUTOMATA, CELLULAR; COMPLEXITY

Bibliography

Dawkins, Richard. *The Blind Watchmaker: Why the Evidence of Evolution Reveals a Universe without Design.* New York: Norton, 1986.

Dembski, William. *No Free Lunch: Why Specified Complexity Cannot Be Purchased Without Intelligence.* Lanham, Md.: Rowman & Littlefield, 2001.

Fogel, Lawrence. *Intelligence Through Simulated Evolution: Forty Years of Evolutionary Programming.* Somerset, N.J.: Wiley, 1999.

Holland, John. *Adaptation in Natural and Artificial Systems: An Introductory Analysis with Applications to Biology, Control, and Artificial Intelligence* (1975). Cambridge, Mass.: MIT Press, 1992.

GREGORY R. PETERSON

EVOLUTIONARY COMPUTING

See EVOLUTIONARY ALGORITHMS

EVOLUTIONARY EPISTEMOLOGY

Evolutionary epistemology widens the scope of traditional epistemology by inclusion of considerations of the evolutionary origins of human cognitive capacity. The roots of evolutionary epistemology extend back to Charles Darwin's idea of natural selection, set forth in 1859, and to subsequent vivid discussions of the evolutionary origin of human rational capacity put forth by Darwin's followers. Contemporary evolutionary epistemology is based on the work of three seminal thinkers: Karl Popper, Konrad Lorenz, and Jean Piaget. Evolutionary epistemology is an interdisciplinary and constructive theory that aims to unite philosophical views on human knowledge with theories of both human origin and life in general.

Program

Evolutionary epistemology suggests that human cognitive capacity is the result of evolutionary development and can be understood only with the help of evolutionary theories that describe the development of this capacity. In fact, evolution itself is understood as a cognition-gaining process: Thus, Gerhard Vollmer suggests that "knowledge is an adequate reconstruction of the outside structures in the subject, and cognition is the process leading to knowledge" (p. 70). Consequently, knowledge can be seen as a tiered phenomenon: On each level, only those responses "fitting" their environment are retained for the future. On the *genetic level* of knowledge, basic information about the environment is captured in the physical construction of the body by natural selection of those characteristics fitting the environment. A second level is *preconscious cognition,* which includes reflex-based responses to sudden environmental changes. The third level is that of *rational knowledge,* in which a person's reaction to the environment is guided by rational judgment.

Lorenz used these principles of evolutionary epistemology to critique the Kantian concept of *a priori*: If cognition is a capacity acquired through the evolutionary process, it is, to any given individual, *ontogenetically a priori.* However, the origins of human cognitive capacity and knowledge as products of evolutionary processes reach back to nonhuman ancestors, and in that sense should be viewed as *phylogenetically a posteriori.* Thus, human cognitive functions are shaped by the environment that is known. Furthermore, human knowledge, including its a priori component, is provisional: It is neither infallible nor arbitrary. Its success lies in examining the long-term "fit" between the world and physical/mental appropriations to the world, as found in neural and mental structures of the knowing subject. Therefore, evolutionary epistemology subscribes to *hypothetical realism,* a special type of realism which claims that human knowledge of the external world is a well-founded and reliable hypothesis about external reality. While it is possible to see the parallel between biological evolution and conceptual evolution (the later being the evolution of ideas) as literal, the real strength of evolutionary epistemology is in applying it analogously to all processes involved in the acquisition of knowledge.

Such an extension was established by Karl Popper. His philosophy transforms the principle of elimination of "unfit hypotheses" about reality (occurring on the planet since biological evolution began) to an abstract level of scientific hypotheses. The resulting system claims to provide the basis for the objectivity of knowledge: While social circumstances influence the expressions of beliefs, the beliefs themselves are not caused by these circumstances alone but have an objective component.

These principles of selective retention of fitting structures, both physical and mental, lead to a very high efficiency in the entire cognition-gaining process: Only successful variations are retained, thereby becoming a basis for future selective processes. Cases where blind chance seemingly operates in evolutionary processes are in the system of *nested hierarchies,* preselected by past successes. These principles are applicable to all levels and forms of knowledge-gaining processes, but at the same time do not allow for the reduction of culture to biology. What is emphasized is the parallel to knowledge-gaining processes in biological and cultural evolution.

Consequently, evolutionary epistemology is capable of examining the formal structure of any kind of human knowledge, including areas traditionally barred from scientific study, such as religions. Donald T. Campbell suggests that, from a scientific point of view, human sociocultural inheritance is as reliable as biological inheritance.

Impact on science and religion

Campbell's proposal was theologically appropriated by Ralph Wendell Burhoe, who attempted to employ the ideas of evolutionary epistemology to relate scientific and religious thought. For Burhoe there is, in principle, no difference between the discernment of the validity of religious beliefs and the discernment of the validity of scientific claims: Knowledge in both areas is acquired through methods described by evolutionary epistemology. Therefore, natural sciences should no longer claim methodological and epistemic superiority over religion. Burhoe, however, went even further, stating that "religious belief systems characteristically involve man's relation or adaptation to some ultimate realities" (p. 30). Implicitly, such a claim points to the reality of God: If one presupposes that selection processes take place through confrontation with reality, and result in the acquisition of information about selecting reality, then "adaptation to ultimate reality" can be translated into "acquisition of knowledge about an independently existing God."

Theologically, evolutionary epistemology represents an important new methodological tool. While it does not fall into the trap of natural theology by attempting to argue about God on the basis of knowledge of the world, it advocates that the acquisition of religious knowledge follows the same principles as the acquisition of knowledge of the material world. Since the reliability of cognitive claims is based on the methods used to derive them, religious claims are no longer epistemically inferior to any other kind of knowledge.

Critiques

Critics of evolutionary epistemology argue that survival and reproduction are the only ends of evolutionary development, and that selected knowledge is not true information about reality but merely a situationally successful resolution of a given situation. The success of such a solution is understood by these critics without relating it to reality. While it is correct that knowledge-gaining processes described by evolutionary epistemology do not lead to true knowledge but rather to truly reliable hypotheses, this charge is based on the faulty presupposition that long-term solutions based on evolutionary selection could result from false assessments of external reality.

Other critics lament that evolutionary principles are inherently egoistic and, consequently, that the realm of ethics and religion can not be described by evolutionary epistemology. This criticism is, again, based on the faulty presupposition that evolution's primary value is mere survival. Evolutionary epistemology, however, redefines evolution as a knowledge-gaining process that makes the outcome of the evolutionary process dependent upon what has been retained and what is learned.

Recently, the findings of evolutionary epistemology have been confirmed by new trends in several disciplines. The most promising discipline is evolutionary psychology, along with new studies in human development and paleontology. While the slowly emerging picture of human cognitive ability seems to be inviting theology as a dialogue partner, advances made during the last two decades of the twentieth century suggest that theology will benefit greatly from including evolutionary epistemology among its methodological tools.

See also EPISTEMOLOGY; EVOLUTIONARY ETHICS; EVOLUTIONARY PSYCHOLOGY; HYPOTHETICAL REALISM

Bibliography

Burhoe, Ralph Wendell. "Natural Selection and God." *Zygon* 7 (1972): 30–63.

Campbell, Donald T. "On the Conflicts Between Biological and Social Evolution and Between Psychology and Moral Tradition." *Zygon* 11, no. 3 (1976): 167–208.

Elman, Jeffrey L.; Bates, Elisabeth A.; Johnson, Mark H.; Karmiloff-Smith, Annete; Parisi, Domenico; and Plunkett, Kim. *Rethinking Innateness: A Connectionist Perspective on Development.* Cambridge, Mass.: Bradford Books, 1996.

Lorenz, Konrad. "Kant's Doctrine of the A Priori in the Light of Contemporary Biology." In *Learning, Development, and Culture,* ed. Henry Plotkin. Chichester, UK: Wiley, 1982.

Mithen, Steven J. *The Prehistory of the Mind: The Cognitive Origins of Art, Religion, and Science.* London: Thames and Hudson, 1996.

Piaget, Jean. *Biology and Knowledge.* Edinburgh, UK: Edinburgh University Press, 1971.

Popper, Karl Raimund. *Objective Knowledge: An Evolutionary Approach.* Oxford: Clarendon Press, 1972.

Vollmer, Gerhard. "Mesocosm and Objective Knowledge: On Problems Solved by Evolutionary Epistemology." In *Concepts and Approaches in Evolutionary Epistemology: Towards an Evolutionary Theory of Knowledge,* ed. Franz M. Wuketits. Dordrecht, Netherlands: D. Reidel, 1984.

TOMAS HANCIL

EVOLUTIONARY ETHICS

The term *evolutionary ethics* refers to three different fields of inquiry that share a concern for the relationship between ethics and evolutionary theory. First is the question of how the human capacity for ethics could have arisen through natural selection—the evolution of ethics. Second is the issue of how the process of evolution appears to exacerbate the problem of natural evil and theodicy—the ethics of evolution. Third is the question of what implications Darwinian theory has for ethical understanding and whether it is possible to derive an ethical system from evolutionary biology—ethics from evolution.

Evolution of ethics

Charles Darwin (1809–1882) speculated on, but did not resolve, the question of how ostensibly sacrificial social cooperation, and especially human morality, could be established by natural selection, which entails the preferential transmission of biological characteristics that confer reproductive advantage to their possessor. In the 1970s, breakthroughs in the application of Darwinian theory to animal social behavior by the emerging discipline of sociobiology shed light on this problem through the notion of reciprocal altruism, suggesting that organisms sacrifice for others in proportion to the likelihood of a compensatory return. Some species, such as social insects, achieve high cooperation in large group sizes, at the cost of rigid and therefore predictable behaviors. Other species, such as nonhuman primates, can achieve high cooperation with significant behavioral flexibility, within the constraints of small group sizes where relational history can be monitored. Human morality is widely viewed as facilitating the unique capacity for significant cooperation in the context of both high behavioral flexibility and large group sizes. Morality not only

urges us, but in a sense enables us, to be kind to strangers.

Far from settling the biological origin of ethics however, these notions have stimulated vigorous debate. One controversy is over whether ethical behavior can be understood as invariably benefiting the actor's or others' reproduction; that is, is morality an individual or group level adaptation? Extending the influential ideas of George Williams and Richard Dawkins, in his seminal work, *The Biology of Moral Systems* (1987), Richard Alexander maintains that moral acts, even those not directly paid back, benefit the individual by indirect reciprocity or reputational enhancement. We are as morally good as it takes to enhance our social standing, and conscience is a reputation alarm that goes off when we are cheating in a way likely to get caught. Conversely, David Wilson and Christopher Boehm argue that human evolution has established the capacity for moral acts that entail uncompensated personal sacrifice and benefit the group relative to competing groups.

Another debate waged both within and outside evolutionary biology involves the question of whether morality is adequately explainable by natural selection at all. One view considers morality not as an evolutionary adaptation but as a byproduct of other biologically adaptive capacities, such as intelligence and the capacity for group cooperation. Another position, coevolutionary or hierarchy theory, views moral systems and other higher cognitive functions as influenced by nongenetic evolutionary processes that are not constrained by natural selection. Proponents reject genetic reductionism and affirm both genuine moral freedom and radical outgroup sacrifice. Scientific and theological critics maintain it is dualistic, even Gnostic, in viewing beneficence as a nonmaterial imposition on an innately selfish human biology. These disputes mirror longstanding theological differences over embodiment and the work of grace.

Ethics of evolution

In his 1893 Romanes lectures, Thomas Henry Huxley (1825–1895) reflected on the relationship between natural evil and evolutionary ethics. While natural evil is considered by many religious and wisdom traditions, evolutionary theory has been viewed as intensifying the quandary in three ways. First, it extends the temporal and biological scope of suffering and death. They become primal features rather than post-hoc additions to creation; moreover, death ravages not only individuals but also entire species, previously considered fixed in divine providence. Second, the role of natural evil changes from an ancillary intrusion upon God's mode of creation to the central driving force of the process itself. The very engines of creation seem to be the competition and selective carnage of natural selection. Third, not just the process but the products of natural selection raise ethical questions: In many representations, the Darwinian picture of the world is colored by dominant hues of self-interest and an utter absence of natural beneficence. A century after Huxley, George Williams argued that evolutionary theory and sociobiology paint an even bleaker picture.

Some theodicies respond to this view of the world by affirming eschatological extrapolations of evolutionary progress. Others criticize the picture itself. Darwin maintained death was most often swift, and selection favored pleasure over pain in behavioral motivation. Moreover, natural selection is actually not driven by selective mortality, but by differential fecundity. Finally, symbiotic cooperation may be as important in evolution as competitive displacement. Whether the most apt metaphor for evolution is "nature is red in tooth and claw" or "exuberant in youth and bough" is an object of ongoing debate, and the controversy itself has significant theological implications.

Ethics from evolution

The relationship of evolution to ethical theory is debated along two main lines. First is the metaethical question of whether a naturalistic origin of ethics makes divine command theory, or any form of moral realism, untenable. Michael Ruse argues that evolution entails moral relativism because what seems right is merely what happens to work in conferring reproductive success. Conversely, Nancy Murphy and some process thinkers argue that the universe operates in such a way that what works actually tends toward the right and good.

Another controversy involves the normative ethical question of whether evolution can inform moral understanding. Advocates of this view, such as Ruse and natural law proponent Larry Arnhart, argue evolution can contribute, first, by elucidating

what is biologically impossible in light of natural selection and therefore errant to command. Ruse thus claims the New Testament's radical love command is biologically perverse. Second, if we understand the evolutionary function of human behavioral traits, we can discern what is most likely to facilitate or subvert fulfillment, and therefore inform ethical judgments. Critics argue that limiting our ethical vision to what conforms with prevailing views of the natural dismisses the work of grace in redeeming, or moral imagination in reforming, nature. Especially since the evolutionarily natural may not be so good, we are cautioned to avoid the naturalistic fallacy of attempting to infer a moral *ought* from a brute *is*. Furthermore, evolution-based ethics cannot adjudicate between conflicting impulses: If the function of all behavior is reproductive advantage, then slavery is not ethically preferable to benevolence, assuming both sustainably maximize fitness. Huxley's *Evolution and Ethics* (1894) made these criticisms of Herbert Spencer's (1820–1903) evolutionary ethics, and the debates continue to this day.

See also ECOLOGY, ETHICS OF; EVOLUTION,
    BIOCULTURAL; EVOLUTIONARY EPISTEMOLOGY;
    NATURE; NATURE VERSUS NURTURE; SOCIOBIOLOGY

Bibliography

Alexander, Richard D. *The Biology of Moral Systems.* New York: De Gruyter, 1987.

Arnhart, Larry. *Darwinian Natural Right: The Biological Ethics of Human Nature.* Albany: State University of New York Press, 1998.

Boehm, Christopher. "How, When, and Why Did the Unique Aspects of Human Morality Arise?" In *Evolutionary Origins of Morality: Cross-Disciplinary Perspectives,* ed. Leonard D. Katz. Bowling Green, Ind.: Imprint Academic, 2000.

Dawkins, Richard. *The Selfish Gene* (1976), rev. edition. Oxford: Oxford University Press, 1989.

Huxley, Thomas H. *Evolution and Ethics and Other Essays.* New York: Appleton, 1894.

Murphy, Nancy, and Ellis, George. *On the Moral Nature of the Universe: Theology, Cosmology, and Ethics.* Minneapolis, Minn.: Fortress Press, 1996.

Nitecki, Matthew H., and Nitecki, Doris V. *Evolutionary Ethics.* Albany: State University of New York Press, 1993.

Ruse, Michael. "Evolutionary Theory and Christian Ethics: Are They in Harmony?" *Zygon* 29, no. 1 (1994): 5–24.

Sober, Elliott, and Wilson, David Sloan. *Unto Others: The Evolution and Psychology of Unselfish Behavior*. London and Cambridge, Mass.: Harvard University Press, 1998.

Williams, George C. "Huxley's Evolution and Ethics in Sociobiological Perspective." *Zygon* 23, no. 4 (1988): 383–407.

JEFFREY P. SCHLOSS

EVOLUTIONARY PSYCHOLOGY

Evolutionary psychology assumes that operating beneath the surface of historical and cultural variability, the human mind is a system of functionally specialized, developmentally constructed neural information processors that were naturally selected because they solved particular adaptive problems faced during the evolution of the hunter-gatherer ancestors of human beings. Evolutionary psychology assumes a computational theory of mind rooted in the information processing revolution of the 1960s. It also draws on insights from the sociobiology of the 1970s, which describes how "selfish" genes, in benefiting their own replication and that of copies amongst kin (William D. Hamilton's "inclusive fitness"), direct the generation of organic structures, including those that may incidentally benefit the organism. With the natural selection of species-wide characteristics, evolutionary psychology considers sexual selection, including the effects of parental investment, and has made empirical contributions to understanding the proximal mechanisms behind mate choice, cheater detection, and language acquisition.

Evolutionary psychology avoids a collapse to genetic determinism through its attention to development and environment, including social interaction and coevolutionary systems. Nevertheless, any computational theory of mind may ultimately be inadequate, and there are questions about the empirical robustness of its findings.

See also EVOLUTIONARY EPISTEMOLOGY; EVOLUTIONARY ETHICS; SELFISH GENE; SOCIOBIOLOGY

Bibliography

Hamilton, William D. "The Genetic Evolution of Social Behavior." *Journal of Theoretical Biology* 7 (1964): 17–18.

Pinker, Steven. *How the Mind Works*. New York: Norton, 1997.

Wright, Robert. *The Moral Animal: The New Science of Evolutionary Psychology*. New York: Pantheon, 1994.

JOHN A. TESKE

EVOLUTION, BIOCULTURAL

From its beginnings in the eighteenth century, evolution—the idea that organisms are descended through a gradual development, ruled by natural law, from original, simple, primitive forms—was intermingled with thoughts of culture. In fact, it is difficult to distinguish the two, since early evolutionists tended to start with a theory about culture, generalize to the biological world, then use biology to support beliefs about culture. In particular, especially as represented in the writings of the English physician and naturalist Erasmus Darwin (1731–1802, the grandfather of Charles) and the French biologist Jean Baptiste de Lamarck (1744–1829), one encounters ideas about social and cultural progress. Darwin, Lamarck, and others promoted the belief that knowledge and society can be improved through unaided human effort; such ideas were read into the animal and plant realm (monad to man, to use the popular phrase), then read back into the human realm to support ideas of social and cultural progress.

Three problem areas

The study of biocultural evolution presents three problematic issues. First, there is the fact of evolution and its causes as applied to the organic world generally. The big question concerning evolution is the "mechanism," and the major debate is over the adequacy and extent of the causal process proposed by Charles Darwin (1809–1882) in his *Origin of Species* in 1859. Does one accept, and to what extent does one accept, the mechanism of natural selection, according to which more organisms are born than can survive and reproduce, producing a struggle that results in a differential reproduction of the fittest, which leads to change in the direction of adaptation? Should the mechanism of selection be limited or replaced? The consensus among practicing biologists is that selection is extremely significant, and, although there is disagreement, most would say that selection is by far the most important mechanism.

A second problem concerns the application of evolutionary theory to humans. Few scientists today would dispute that human beings evolved, but again there is debate about the extent to which selection is significant, with nearly all agreeing that it has had some significant role. The hand and the eye, for example, are adaptations produced by selection. How much and how far selection has affected and shaped human behavior and thought, however, is still a matter of (sometimes bitter) debate. Some researchers, particularly those called human sociobiologists or evolutionary psychologists, grant selection a major role in determining human behavior and thought. Others, in particular cultural anthropologists and those with ideologies opposed to certain aspects of biology (a group that often includes feminists, Marxists, and postmodernists), tend to downplay the importance of biology in shaping behavior. Most concede to biology some role, but even here there is dispute. For example, male and female (human) physical differences are obviously a function of biology; whether male and female psychological and social differences are a function of biology is less clear.

A third problem is the question of cultural evolution or change. There is, of course, continuity in science or religion. Albert Einstein (1879–1955) did not just appear, he arose out of a physics tradition that dates back at least to Isaac Newton (1642–1727). Christianity did not just appear but goes back to Judaism, with introgressions of a greater or lesser extent from Greek philosophy. The question is whether one can develop a theory of such change, and if so what kind of theory. In particular, do biological theories help one to understand cultural change? Moreover, does natural selection offer a causal insight into the way and reasons that culture changes? From Newton to Einstein, from Moses to Paul, are the processes that rule such changes the same process that ruled the evolution of the reptile to the bird, or the monkey to the human being?

Assuming acceptance of the first point (evolution in general) and of the second point (evolution of humans), then the third point (cultural evolution) becomes the critical question. If one accepts the possibility of cultural evolution of some kind—and it is hard not to, at least in a general sense—then does one start with the second point (evolution of humans) and work to the third point (cultural evolution)? Or does one jump straight to the third point (cultural evolution)? In other words, is cultural evolution autonomous in some sense, sitting at the summit of the biological sciences (as many cultural anthropologists would argue), or does cultural evolution arise as a consequence of human biological evolution? And returning to the issue of causes, what role does selection play in this process, and how does it affect one's answer?

Nineteenth-century discussions

It is fair to say that Erasmus Darwin and Lamarck were evolutionists, and they applied evolutionary theory to humans, although neither was aware of natural selection, though in Erasmus Darwin's writings there are hints of sexual selection, the competition for mates. Darwin and Lamarck were not, however, sufficiently sophisticated in their thinking to address cultural evolution; it is probably best to say that they thought of cultural evolution as autonomous, but fueled by the same processes as biological evolution, chiefly the inheritance of acquired characteristics. Although such a view is now known as *Lamarckism,* it also appeared in writings by Erasmus Darwin. People often note that the Lamarckian evolutionary mechanism of the inheritance of acquired characteristics seems cultural. They are right. It was taken from culture, so it is not surprising that it can be read back to culture. Much the same can be said of later pre-Darwinian evolutionists. However, by the mid-1850s, cultural evolution was definitely being seen as autonomous, although biology and culture were considered ultimately part of the same process, in which things moved in Lamarckian fashion from simple to complex, from homogeneous to heterogeneous. As the philosopher Herbert Spencer (1820–1903) remarked:

Now we propose in the first place to show, that this law of organic progress is the law of all progress. Whether it be in the development of the Earth, in the development of Life upon its surface, in the development of Society, of Government, of Manufactures, of Commerce, of Language, Literature, Science, Art, this same evolution of the simple into the complex, through successive differentiations, hold throughout. From the earliest traceable cosmical changes down to the latest results of civilization, we shall find that the transformation of the homogeneous into the heterogeneous, is that in which Progress essentially consists. (Spencer 1857)

Spencer was not much interested in selection, even though the idea occurred to him independently of Darwin. Others took a similar approach to Spencer but included selection in their theories. Thomas Henry Huxley (1825–1895) was probably the first to argue that there is a struggle for existence among ideas, and the fittest win. Einstein triumphed over Newton because Einstein's ideas are in some way better than Newton's. For Huxley, who invented the term *agnostic*, Darwin beat out Christianity because Darwin's ideas were better than Christianity.

What about Darwin himself? He certainly wrote about humans and was interested in culture. At times he sounds as if he believed culture to be reasonably autonomous, but one senses that he was not convinced of this. In the *Descent of Man* (1871) he is more inclined to start with human evolution and then work outward and backward to culture. Morality, for example, has biological value because it helps keep the tribe together. Thus, there is evolution toward a moral sense, which then feeds back to biology because creatures that are more moral are also more biologically successful. Similarly, social practices, particularly social sexual practices, start with biology, get encoded into culture, and then feed back into biology. Even capitalism can be conceived in Darwinian terms as something that aids evolution and hence is cherished and adaptive.

In general, it seems fair to say that for the century after Darwin, the biology to culture approach did not thrive. Thanks to the popularity of Spencer and his followers, as well as to the rise of the social sciences and to the difficulty of understanding the biology of behavior and thought, cultural evolution was considered to be a process in its own right. The philosopher William James (1842–1910), for instance, takes a Darwinian approach in his *Principles of Psychology* (1890), although in the more philosophical *Pragmatism* (1907), he treats culture as more autonomous. And although Spencer is no longer highly regarded as a thinker,

and although few would subscribe to Spencer's beliefs about the nature and course of evolution, many still treat culture as Spencer did, as autonomous but with causes that are analogous to biology. In fact, many follow in the steps of Huxley in seeing selection as key to understanding cultural, particularly scientific, change.

Twentieth-century discussion

Such an approach is often called *evolutionary epistemology*. Its best-known proponent was the philosopher Karl Popper (1902–1994), who combined an evolutionary approach with his own criterion for distinguishing science from nonscience: *falsifiabilty*. One starts with a problem, say a discovery that seems not to fit with existing theory. One then proposes an idea or hypothesis intended to solve the problem, or more likely, one proposes a number of ideas or hypotheses. One then subjects the ideas to rigorous testing, choosing the idea that survives or solves the problem best. All the others must be rejected, including ideas or hypotheses one may have held earlier. In effect, a change has occurred through a process analogous to natural selection. One then continues until another problem arises.

Those sympathetic to Popper's approach include Stephen Toulmin and David Hull, the latter having applied the approach to the eclipse of traditional evolutionary methods of biological classification with the new *cladistic* approach. This is a method of classification that uses only shared characteristics as the method of classification, aiming to represent lines of descent and nothing else. Richard Dawkins's theory about units of belief called *memes,* which are analogous to genes, also fits here. Dawkins believes that memes invade brains (rather like viruses) and then multiply and succeed in a Darwinian fashion, inasmuch as they have good cultural adaptations. Religion, in particular, is something that Dawkins thinks has no objective truth but nevertheless succeeds because it has good adaptations. It exploits people's need to belong and their need for comforting answers about life after death and other matters.

Thomas Kuhn (1922–1996), who is usually regarded as representing an approach to the understanding of science diametrically opposed to that of Popper, also liked to think of his "paradigm" theory of science as evolutionary. A paradigm is proposed, and another is rejected, in Darwinian fashion. Popper was a realist, committed to the idea of an independent, real world, unlike Kuhn, for whom reality, inasmuch as it exists, is a function of human perception. The important question of progress remains. Is science progressive? Does it progress toward an understanding of the real world, or is it simply going nowhere and just subject to fashion? Popper certainly thought of his epistemology as progressive. Kuhn, who was more ambiguous, saw progress in a Darwinian sense, in which certain ideas are better than rivals, rather than in an absolute sense, in which some ideas are better on some independent scale. Dawkins would probably take an even more relativistic approach than Kuhn.

With the rise of human sociobiology (or evolutionary psychology) there is an increasing interest in the Darwinian approach to culture. This interest results, in part, from dissatisfaction with the alternative approach. But if culture is Darwinian, then how can one explain the fact that biological mutations are random (in the sense of undirected), whereas cultural mutations are apparently nonrandom? The sociobiologist Edward O. Wilson, working with physicist Charles Lumsden, argues that culture is founded on various rules of thought, which he calls *epigenetic rules,* or which might be called "innate dispositions." As the philosopher W. V. O. Quine (1908–2000) argued, mathematical rules or the laws of logic may be ingrained in human biology because protohumans who thought logically were more likely to survive than those who did not. So culture, which can then elaborate in ways unknown to biology, nevertheless has its base in biology. It is not so much that Einstein's ideas beat out Newton's in a struggle for existence, but that both theories are based on rules that are rooted in biology. The success of one over the other is simply an observation, and not really biological at all.

A number of scholars, including Wilson and Michael Ruse, have applied this approach to morality, arguing that supreme imperatives, like the Christian love commandment, are held because those human ancestors who took them seriously were more successful than those who did not. Such an approach does not preclude cultural developments alongside those of biology. For example, whether it is ever obligatory to tell lies—as to a child dying of cancer—is not something determined by natural selection, although the tendency to be kind to such children certainly is.

What of religion in all of this? Wilson certainly thinks that religion is promoted by biology inasmuch as it reinforces morality and promotes group harmony and cohesion. Like Dawkins, however, he is something of a nonrealist on these matters and thinks that religious beliefs are not objectively true. Indeed, he would replace Christianity with a better myth (his word), namely Darwinian materialism. Others who take this approach, including the ethologist Konrad Lorenz (1903–1989), incline to a more realist approach. Whether or not they themselves accept religious beliefs as true, they would allow the possibility that they could be found true.

There are, in fact, scholars who apply biology to an understanding of religion. They do not treat religion as culturally autonomous but as a system of beliefs that can feed back into biology and vice versa. In other words, they would probably not regard such beliefs as innate but as one of a cluster of characteristics that have biological, and not just cultural, adaptive advantage, and hence serve as an aid to the possessors. Religious beliefs maintain a kind of halfway position between the two extremes described above (culture as autonomous and culture as an epiphenomenon of biology). Primatologist Vernon Reynolds and R. Tanner, a student of religion, have argued that different religions speak to different biologically adaptive needs. Using standard biological theory, which distinguishes between adaptations that are needed when resources are not stable or predictable and adaptations that are needed when resources are stable and predictable, they argue that religions reflect these conditions. Their theory predicts that organisms will tend to have numerous offspring that require minimal parental care during periods of instability or unpredictability, and few offspring requiring much care during periods of stability. Reynolds and Tanner argue that in a place like Great Britain, which has stable resources, one finds (expectedly) a religion like Anglicanism that stresses restraint and care, whereas in a place like Ireland, where resources fluctuate, one finds Catholicism with its exhortation to have many children. Other practices discussed by Reynolds and Tanner include food rules and prohibitions (as in Judaism), attitudes toward women, and much more.

Even though it is now nearly 150 years since the *Origin of Species* appeared (and two hundred since the start of evolutionary thinking), it is probably too early to say that a generally acceptable biocultural theory has been formulated. There are, however, many stimulating, if controversial, ideas, which promise to cast light on culture, including science and religion, and the relationship between them.

See also CULTURE, ORIGINS OF; EVOLUTION, BIOLOGICAL; EVOLUTIONARY EPISTEMOLOGY; EVOLUTIONARY ETHICS; EVOLUTIONARY PSYCHOLOGY; HUMAN NATURE, PHYSICAL ASPECTS; SOCIOBIOLOGY

Bibliography

Hull, David. *Science as a Process: An Evolutionary Account of the Social and Conceptual Development of Science.* Chicago: University of Chicago Press, 1988.

Lumsden, Charles J., and Wilson, Edward O. *Genes, Mind, and Culture: The Coevolutionary Process.* Cambridge, Mass.: Harvard University Press, 1981.

Popper, Karl R. *Unended Quest: An Intellectual Autobiography.* LaSalle, Ill.: Open Court, 1976.

Reynolds, Vernon, and Tanner, R. *The Biology of Religion.* London: Longman, 1983.

Ruse, Michael. *Taking Darwin Seriously: A Naturalistic Approach to Philosophy,* 2nd edition. Buffalo, N.Y.: Prometheus, 1983.

Spencer, Herbert. "Progress: Its Law and Cause." *Westminster Review* 67 (1857): 244–267.

Toulmin, Stephen. *Human Understanding.* Oxford: Clarendon, 1972.

MICHAEL RUSE

EVOLUTION, BIOLOGICAL

Biological evolution encompasses three issues: (1) the fact of evolution; that is, that organisms are related by common descent with modification; (2) evolutionary history; that is, when lineages split from one another and the changes that occur in each lineage; and (3) the mechanisms or processes by which evolutionary change occurs.

The fact of evolution is the most fundamental issue and the one established with utmost certainty. During the nineteenth century, Charles Darwin (1809–1882) gathered much evidence in its support, but the evidence has accumulated continuously ever since, derived from all biological disciplines. The evolutionary origin of organisms is today a scientific conclusion established with the kind of certainty attributable to such scientific concepts as the roundness of the Earth, the motions of the planets, and the molecular composition of matter. This degree of certainty beyond reasonable doubt is what is implied when biologists say that evolution is a *fact*; the evolutionary origin of organisms is accepted by virtually every biologist.

The theory of evolution seeks to ascertain the evolutionary relationships between particular organisms and the events of evolutionary history (the second issue above). Many conclusions of evolutionary history are well established; for example, that the chimpanzee and gorilla are more closely related to humans than is any of those three species to the baboon or other monkeys. Other matters are less certain and still others—such as precisely when life originated on earth or when multicellular animals, plants, and fungi first appeared—remain largely unresolved. This entry will not review the history of evolution, but rather focus on the processes of evolutionary change (the third issue above), after a brief review of the evidence for the fact of evolution.

The evidence for common descent with modification

Evidence that organisms are related by common descent with modification has been obtained by paleontology, comparative anatomy, biogeography, embryology, biochemistry, molecular genetics, and other biological disciplines. The idea first emerged from observations of systematic changes in the succession of fossil remains found in a sequence of layered rocks. Such layers have a cumulative thickness of tens of kilometers that represent at least 3.5 billion years of geological time. The general sequence of fossils from bottom upward in layered rocks had been recognized before Darwin proposed that the succession of biological forms strongly implied evolution. The farther back into the past one looked, the less the fossils resembled recent forms, the more the various lineages merged, and the broader the implications of a common ancestry.

Although gaps in the paleontological record remain, many have been filled by the researches of paleontologists since Darwin's time. Millions of fossil organisms found in well-dated rock sequences represent a succession of forms through time and manifest many evolutionary transitions.

Microbial life of the simplest type (i.e., procaryotes, which are cells whose nuclear matter is not bound by a nuclear membrane) was already in existence more than three billion years ago. The oldest evidence of more complex organisms (i.e., eukaryotic cells with a true nucleus) has been discovered in flinty rocks approximately 1.4 billion years old. More advanced forms like algae, fungi, higher plants, and animals have been found only in younger geological strata. The following list presents the order in which increasingly complex forms of life appeared:

Life form	Millions of years since first known appearance (approximate)
Microbial (procaryotic cells)	3,500
Complex (eukaryotic cells)	1,400
Multicellular animals	670
Shell-bearing animals	540
Vertebrates (simple fishes)	490
Amphibians	350
Reptiles	310
Mammals	200
Nonhuman primates	60
Earliest apes	25
Australopithecine ancestors	5
Homo sapiens (modern humans)	0.15 (150,000 years)

SOURCE: Steering Committee on Science and Creationism, National Academy of Sciences. *Science and Creationism: A View from the National Academy of Sciences*, Second Edition. National Academy Press: Washington, DC, 1999.

Forms of life by year of origin.

The sequence of observed forms and the fact that all (except the procaryotes) are constructed from the same basic cellular type strongly imply that all these major categories of life (including plants, algae, and fungi) have a common ancestry in the first eukaryotic cell. Moreover, there have been so many discoveries of intermediate forms between fish and amphibians, between amphibians and reptiles, between reptiles and mammals that it is often difficult to identify categorically along the line when the transition occurs from one to another particular genus or from one to another particular species. Nearly all fossils can be regarded as intermediates in some sense; they are life forms that come between ancestral forms that preceded them and those that followed.

Inferences about common descent derived from paleontology have been reinforced by comparative anatomy. The skeletons of humans, dogs, whales, and bats are strikingly similar, despite the different ways of life led by these animals and the diversity of environments in which they have flourished. The correspondence, bone by bone, can be observed in every part of the body, including the limbs: Yet a person writes, a dog runs, a whale swims, and a bat flies with structures built of the same bones. Such structures, called *homologous*, are best explained by common descent. Comparative anatomists investigate such homologies, not only in bone structure but also in other parts of the body as well, working out relationships from degrees of similarity.

The mammalian ear and jaw offer an example in which paleontology and comparative anatomy combine to show common ancestry through transitional stages. The lower jaws of mammals contain only one bone, whereas those of reptiles have several. The other bones in the reptile jaw are homologous with bones now found in the mammalian ear. What function could these bones have had during intermediate stages? Paleontologists have discovered intermediate forms of mammal-like reptiles (*Therapsida*) with a double jaw joint—one composed of the bones that persist in mammalian jaws, the other consisting of bones that eventually became the hammer and anvil of the mammalian ear. Similar examples are numerous.

Biogeography also has contributed evidence for common descent. The diversity of life is stupendous. Approximately 250,000 species of living plants, 100,000 species of fungi, and 1.5 million species of animals and microorganisms have been described and named, and the census is far from complete. Some species, such as human beings and our companion the dog, can live under a wide range of environmental conditions. Others are amazingly specialized. One species of the fungus *Laboulbenia* grows exclusively on the rear portion of the covering wings of a single species of beetle (*Aphaenops cronei*) found only in some caves of southern France. The larvae of the fly *Drosophila carcinophila* can develop only in specialized grooves beneath the flaps of the third pair of oral appendages of the land crab *Gecarcinus ruricola*, which is found only on certain Caribbean islands.

How can one make intelligible the colossal diversity of living beings and the existence of such extraordinary, seemingly whimsical creatures as *Laboulbenia*, *Drosophila carcinophila*, and others? Why are island groups like the Galápagos inhabited by forms similar to those on the nearest mainland but belonging to different species? Why is the indigenous life so different on different continents? The explanation is that biological diversity results from an evolutionary process whereby the descendants of local or migrant predecessors became adapted to diverse environments. For example, approximately two thousand species of flies belonging to the genus *Drosophila* are now found throughout the world. About one-quarter of them live only in Hawaii. More than a thousand species of snails and other land mollusks are also only found in Hawaii. The explanation for the occurrence of such great diversity among closely similar forms is that the differences resulted from adaptive colonization of isolated environments by animals with a common ancestry. The Hawaiian Islands are far from, and were never attached to, any mainland or other islands, and thus they have had few colonizers. No mammals other than one bat species lived on the Hawaiian Islands when the first human settlers arrived; very many other kinds of plants and animals were also absent. The explanation is that these kinds of organisms never reached the islands because of their great geographic isolation, while those that reached there multiplied in kind, because of the absence of related organisms that would compete for resources.

Embryology, the study of biological development from the time of conception, is another source of independent evidence for common descent. Barnacles, for instance, are sedentary crustaceans with little apparent similarity to such other crustaceans as lobsters, shrimps, or copepods. Yet barnacles pass through a free-swimming larval stage, in which they look unmistakably like other crustacean larvae. The similarity of larval stages supports the conclusion that all crustaceans have homologous parts and a common ancestry. Human and other mammalian embryos pass through a stage during which they have unmistakable but useless grooves similar to gill slits found in fishes—evidence that they and the other vertebrates shared remote ancestors that respired with the aid of gills.

The substantiation of common descent that emerges from all the foregoing lines of evidence is being validated and reinforced by the discoveries of modern biochemistry and molecular biology, a biological discipline that has emerged in the mid twentieth century. This new discipline has unveiled the nature of hereditary material and the workings of organisms at the level of enzymes and other molecules. Molecular biology provides very detailed and convincing evidence for biological evolution.

The genetic basis of evolution

The central argument of Darwin's theory of evolution starts from the existence of hereditary variation. Experience with animal and plant breeding demonstrates that variations can be developed that are "useful to man." So, reasoned Darwin, variations must occur in nature that are favorable or useful in some way to the organism itself in the struggle for existence. Favorable variations are ones that increase chances for survival and procreation. Those advantageous variations are preserved and multiplied from generation to generation at the expense of less advantageous ones. This is the process known as *natural selection*. The outcome of the process is an organism that is well adapted to its environment, and evolution occurs as a consequence.

Biological evolution is the process of change and diversification of organisms over time, and it affects all aspects of their lives—morphology, physiology, behavior, and ecology. Underlying these changes are changes in the hereditary material (DNA). Hence, in genetic terms, evolution consists of changes in the organism's hereditary makeup. Natural selection, then, can be defined as the differential reproduction of alternative hereditary variants, determined by the fact that some variants increase the likelihood that the organisms having them will survive and reproduce more successfully than will organisms carrying alternative variants. Selection may be due to differences in survival, in fertility, in rate of development, in mating success, or in any other aspect of the life cycle. All these differences can be incorporated under the term *differential reproduction* because all result in natural selection to the extent that they affect the number of progeny an organism leaves.

Evolution can be seen as a two-step process. First, hereditary variation takes place; second, selection occurs of those genetic variants that are passed on most effectively to the following generations. Hereditary variation also entails two mechanisms: the spontaneous mutation of one variant to another, and the sexual process that recombines those variants to form a multitude of variations.

The information encoded in the nucleotide sequence of DNA is, as a rule, faithfully reproduced during replication, so that each replication results in two DNA molecules that are identical to each other and to the parent molecule. But occasionally "mistakes," or *mutations,* occur in the DNA molecule during replication, so that daughter molecules differ from the parent molecules in at least one of the letters in the DNA sequence. Mutations can be classified into two categories: gene, or point, mutations, which affect one or only a few letters (nucleotides) within a gene; and chromosomal mutations, which either change the number of chromosomes or change the number or arrangement of genes on a chromosome. Chromosomes are the elongated structures that store the DNA of each cell.

Newly arisen mutations are more likely to be harmful than beneficial to their carriers, because mutations are random events with respect to adaptation; that is, their occurrence is independent of any possible consequences. Harmful mutations are eliminated or kept in check by natural selection. Occasionally, however, a new mutation may increase the organism's adaptation. The probability of such an event's happening is greater when organisms colonize a new territory or when environmental changes confront a population with new challenges. In these cases there is greater opportunity for new mutations to be better adaptive. The consequences of mutations depend on the environment. Increased melanin pigmentation may be advantageous to inhabitants of tropical Africa, where dark skin protects them from the Sun's ultraviolet radiation; but it is not beneficial in Scandinavia, where the intensity of sunlight is low and light skin facilitates the synthesis of vitamin D.

Mutation rates are low, but new mutants appear continuously in nature because there are many individuals in every species and many genes in every individual. More important is the storage of variation, arisen by past mutations. Thus, it is not surprising to see that when new environmental challenges arise, species are able to adapt to them. More than two hundred insect species, for example, have developed resistance to the pesticide DDT in different parts of the world where spraying has been intense. Although the insects had never before encountered this synthetic compound, they adapted to it rapidly by means of mutations that allowed them to survive in its presence. Similarly, many species of moths and butterflies in industrialized regions have shown an increase in the frequency of individuals with dark wings in response to environmental pollution, an adaptation known as industrial melanism. The examples can be multiplied at will.

Dynamics of genetic change

The genetic variation present in natural populations of organisms is sorted out in new ways in each generation by the process of sexual reproduction. But heredity by itself does not change gene frequencies. This principle is formally stated by the Hardy-Weinberg law, an algebraic equation that describes the genetic equilibrium in a population.

The Hardy-Weinberg law plays in evolutionary studies a role similar to that of Isaac Newton's First Law of Motion in mechanics. Newton's First Law says that a body not acted upon by a net external force remains at rest or maintains a constant velocity. In fact, there are always external forces acting upon physical objects (gravity, for example), but the first law provides the starting point for the application of other laws. Similarly, organisms are subject to mutation, selection, and other processes that change gene frequencies, and the effects of these processes are calculated by using the Hardy-Weinberg law as the starting point. There are four processes of gene frequency change: mutation, migration, drift, and natural selection.

Mutations change gene frequencies very slowly, since mutation rates are low. *Migration,* or *gene flow,* takes place when individuals migrate from one population to another and interbreed with its members. The genetic make-up of populations changes locally whenever different populations intermingle. In general, the greater the difference in gene frequencies between the resident and the migrant individuals, and the larger the number of migrants, the greater effect the migrants have in changing the genetic constitution of the resident population.

Moreover, gene frequencies can change from one generation to another by a process of pure chance known as *genetic drift.* This occurs because populations are finite in numbers, and thus the frequency of a gene may change in the following generation by accidents of sampling, just as it is possible to get more or less than fifty "heads" in one hundred throws of a coin simply by chance. The magnitude of the gene frequency changes due to genetic drift is inversely related to the size of the population; the larger the number of reproducing individuals, the smaller the effects of genetic drift. The effects of genetic drift from one generation to the next are quite small in most natural populations, which generally consist of thousands of reproducing individuals. The effects over many generations are more important. Genetic drift can have important evolutionary consequences when a new population becomes established by only a few individuals, as in the colonization of islands and lakes. This is one reason why species in neighboring islands, such as those in the Hawaiian archipelago, are often more heterogeneous than species in comparable continental areas adjacent to one another.

Natural selection

Darwin proposed that natural selection promotes the adaptation of organisms to their environments because the organisms carrying useful variants leave more descendants than those lacking them. The modern concept of natural selection is defined in mathematical terms as a statistical bias favoring some genetic variants over their alternates. The measure to quantify natural selection is called *fitness*.

If mutation, migration, and drift were the only processes of evolutionary change, the organization of living things would gradually disintegrate because they are random processes with respect to adaptation. Those three processes change gene frequencies without regard for the consequences that such changes may have in the welfare of the organisms. The effects of such processes alone would be analogous to those of a mechanic who changed parts in a motorcar engine at random, with no regard for the role of the parts in the engine. Natural selection keeps the disorganizing effects of mutation and other processes in check because it multiplies beneficial mutations and eliminates harmful ones. Natural selection accounts not only for the preservation and improvement of the organization of living beings but also for their diversity. In different localities or in different circumstances, natural selection favors different traits, precisely those that make the organisms well adapted to the particular circumstances.

The origin of species

In everyday experience we identify different kinds of organisms by their appearance. Everyone knows that people belong to the human species and are different from cats and dogs, which in turn are different from each other. There are differences among people, as well as among cats and dogs; but individuals of the same species are considerably more similar among themselves than they are to individuals of other species. But there is more to it than that; a bulldog, a terrier, and a golden retriever are very different in appearance, but they are all dogs because they can interbreed. People can also interbreed with one another, and so can cats, but people cannot interbreed with dogs or cats, nor can these breed with each other. Although species are usually identified by appearance, there is something basic, of great biological significance, behind similarity of appearance; namely, that individuals of a species are able to interbreed with one another but not with members of other species. This is expressed in the following definition: *Species* are groups of interbreeding natural populations that are reproductively isolated from other such groups.

The ability to interbreed is of great evolutionary importance, because it determines that species are independent evolutionary units. Genetic changes originate in single individuals; they can spread by natural selection to all members of the species but not to individuals of other species. Thus, individuals of a species share a common gene pool that is not shared by individuals of other species, because they are reproductively isolated.

Adaptive radiation is a form of speciation that occurs when colonizers reach geographically remote areas, such as islands, where they find an opportunity to diverge as they become adapted to the new environment. Sometimes a multiplicity of new environments becomes available to the colonizers, giving rise to several different lineages and species. This process of rapid divergence of multiple species from a single ancestral lineage is called adaptive radiation.

Examples of speciation by adaptive radiation in archipelagos removed from the mainland have already been mentioned. The Galápagos Islands are about six hundred miles off the west coast of South America. When Darwin arrived there in 1835, he discovered many species not found anywhere else in the world—for example, fourteen species of finch (known as Darwin's finches). These passerine birds have adapted to a diversity of habitats and diets, some feeding mostly on plants, others exclusively on insects. The various shapes of their bills are clearly adapted to probing, grasping, biting, or crushing—the diverse ways in which these different Galápagos species obtain their food. The explanation for such diversity (which is not found in finches from the continental mainland) is that the ancestor of Galápagos finches arrived in the islands before other kinds of birds and encountered an abundance of unoccupied ecological opportunities. The finches underwent adaptive radiation, evolving a variety of species with ways of life capable of exploiting niches that in continental faunas are exploited by different kinds of birds. Some striking examples of adaptive radiation that occur in the Hawaiian Islands were mentioned earlier.

Rapid modes of speciation are known by a variety of names, such as *quantum, rapid,* and *saltational* speciation, all suggesting the short time involved. An important form of quantum speciation is *polyploidy,* which occurs by the multiplication of entire sets of chromosomes. A typical (diploid) organism carries in the nucleus of each cell two sets of chromosomes, one inherited from each parent; a polyploid organism has several sets of chromosomes. Many cultivated plants are polyploid: bananas have three sets of chromosomes, potatoes have four, bread wheat has six, some strawberries have eight. All major groups of plants have natural polyploid species, but they are most common among flowering plants (angiosperms) of which about forty-seven percent are polyploids.

In animals, polyploidy is relatively rare because it disrupts the balance between chromosomes involved in the determination of sex. But polyploid species are found in hermaphroditic animals (individuals having both male and female organs), which include snails and earthworms, as well as in forms with parthenogenetic females (which produce viable progeny without fertilization), such as some beetles, sow bugs, goldfish, and salamanders.

Gradual and punctuational evolution

Morphological evolution is by and large a gradual process, as shown by the fossil record. Major evolutionary changes are usually due to a building up over the ages of relatively small changes. But the fossil record is discontinuous. Fossil strata are separated by sharp boundaries; accumulation of fossils within a geologic deposit (stratum) is fairly constant over time, but the transition from one stratum to another may involve gaps of tens of thousands of years. Different species, characterized by small but discontinuous morphological changes, typically appear at the boundaries between strata, whereas the fossils within a stratum exhibit little morphological variation. That is not to say that the transition from one stratum to another always involves sudden changes in morphology; on the contrary, fossil forms often persist virtually unchanged through several geologic strata, each representing millions of years.

According to some paleontologists the frequent discontinuities of the fossil record are not artifacts created by gaps in the record, but rather reflect the true nature of morphological evolution, which happens in sudden bursts associated with the formation of new species. This proposition is known as the *punctuated equilibrium* model of morphological evolution. The question whether morphological evolution in the fossil record is predominantly punctuational or gradual is a subject of active investigation and debate. The argument is not about whether only one or the other pattern ever occurs; it is about their relative frequency. Some paleontologists argue that morphological evolution is in most cases gradual and only rarely jerky, whereas others think the opposite is true. Much of the problem is that gradualness or jerkiness is in the eye of the beholder.

DNA and protein evolution

The advances of molecular biology have made possible the comparative study of proteins and the nucleic acid DNA, which is the repository of hereditary (evolutionary and developmental) information. Nucleic acids and proteins are linear molecules made up of sequences of units—nucleotides in the case of nucleic acids, amino acids in the case of proteins—which retain considerable amounts of evolutionary information. Comparing macromolecules from two different species establishes the number of their units that are different. Because evolution usually occurs by changing one unit at a time, the number of differences is an indication of the recency of common ancestry.

Changes in evolutionary rates may create difficulties, but macromolecular studies have two notable advantages over comparative anatomy and other classical disciplines. One is that the information is more readily quantifiable. The number of units that are different is precisely established when the sequence of units is known for a given macromolecule in different organisms. The other advantage is that comparisons can be made even between very different sorts of organisms. There is very little that comparative anatomy can say when organisms as diverse as yeasts, pine trees, and human beings are compared; but there are homologous DNA and protein molecules that can be compared in all three.

Informational macromolecules provide information not only about the topology of evolutionary history, but also about the amount of genetic change that has occurred in any given branch. Studies of molecular evolution rates have led to the proposition that macromolecules evolve at fairly constant rates and, thus, that they can be used as evolutionary clocks, in order to determine the time when the various branching events occurred. The molecular evolutionary clock is not a metronomic clock, like a watch or other timepiece that measures time exactly, but a stochastic clock like radioactive decay. In a stochastic clock, the probability of a certain amount of change is constant, although some variation occurs in the actual amount of change. Over fairly long periods of time, a stochastic clock is quite accurate. The enormous potential of the molecular evolutionary clock lies in the fact that each gene or protein is a separate clock. Each clock "ticks" at a different rate—the rate of evolution characteristic of a particular gene or protein—but each of the thousands of genes or proteins provides an independent measure of the same evolutionary events.

Evolutionists have found that the amount of variation observed in the evolution of DNA and proteins is greater than is expected from a stochastic clock; in other words, the clock is inaccurate. The discrepancies in evolutionary rates along different lineages are not excessively large, however. It turns out that it is possible to time phylogenetic events with accuracy, but more genes or proteins must be examined than would be required if the clock were stochastically accurate. The average rates obtained for several DNA sequences or proteins taken together provide a fairly precise clock, particularly when many species are investigated.

See also ADAPTATION; DARWIN, CHARLES; ECOLOGY; FITNESS; GENETICS; LIFE, ORIGINS OF; LIFE SCIENCES; MUTATION; SELECTION, LEVELS OF; SOCIOBIOLOGY

Bibliography

Ayala, Francisco J., and Valentine, James W. *Evolving: The Theory and Processes of Organic Evolution.* Benjamin/Cummings: Menlo Park, Calif.: 1979.

Ayala, Francisco J., and Fitch, Walter M., eds. *Genetics and The Origin of Species: From Darwin to Molecular Biology 60 Years After Dobzhansky.* Washington, D.C.: National Academy Press, 1997.

Ayala, Francisco J.; Fitch, Walter M.; and Clegg, Michael T., eds. *Variation and Evolution in Plants and Microorganisms: Toward A New Synthesis 50 Years After Stebbins.* Washington, D.C.: National Academy Press, 2000.

Dawkins, Richard. *Climbing Mount Improbable.* New York and London: Norton, 1996.

Eldredge, Niles. *Reinventing Darwin: The Great Debate at the High Table of Evolutionary Theory.* New York: Wiley, 1995.

Fitch, Walter M., and Ayala, Francisco. J., eds. *Tempo and Mode in Evolution.* Washington, D.C.: National Academy Press, 1995.

Fortey, Richard. *Life: A Natural History of the First Four Billion Years of Life on Earth.* New York: Knopf, 1998.

Futuyma, Douglas J. *Evolutionary Biology,* 3rd edition. Sunderland, Mass.: Sinauer, 1998.

Hartl, Daniel L., and Clark, Andrew G. *Principles of Population Genetics,* 2nd edition. Sunderland, Mass.: Sinauer, 1989.

Howells, W. W. *Getting Here: The Story of Human Evolution.* Washington, D.C.: Compass Press, 1997.

Johanson, Donald C.; Johanson, Lenora; and Edgar, Blake. *Ancestors: In Search of Human Origins.* New York: Villard, 1994.

Levin, Harold L. *The Earth Through Time,* 5th edition. Philadelphia: Saunders College, 1996.

Lewin, Roger. *Patterns in Evolution: The New Molecular View.* New York: Scientific American, 1996.

Mayr, Ernst. *Populations, Species, and Evolution: An Abridgment of Animal Species and Evolution.* Cambridge, Mass.: Harvard University Press, 1970.

Mayr, Ernst. *One Long Argument: Charles Darwin and the Genesis of Modern Evolutionary Thought.* Cambridge, Mass.: Harvard University Press. 1991.

Moore, John A. *Science as a Way of Knowing: The Foundations of Modern Biology.* Cambridge, Mass.: Harvard University Press, 1993.

Porter, Duncan M., and Graham, Peter W. *The Portable Darwin.* New York: Penguin, 1993.

Strickberger, Monroe W. *Evolution,* 3rd edition. Sudbury, Mass.: Jones and Bartlett, 2000.

Weiner, Jonathan. *The Beak of the Finch: A Story of Evolution in Our Time.* New York: Knopf, 1994.

Zimmer, Carl. *At the Water's Edge: Macroevolution and the Transformation of Life.* New York: Free Press, 1999.

FRANCISCO J. AYALA

EVOLUTION, HUMAN

Human evolution is a field of science that falls within the larger area of physical anthropology. Human evolutionary studies are broadly synonymous with paleoanthropology, although paleoanthropology is a slightly wider concept that covers the host of fields contributing to the understanding of the human biological past in all its varied aspects. The central concern of human evolution involves sorting anatomical and behavioral differences within and among hominid species in order to delineate their ranges of variation through geological time and across geographical space. *Hominid* is often used as a colloquial term to indicate membership of fossil forms in the family *Hominidae,* the taxonomic group that includes anatomically and behaviorally modern humans and their precursors of the last six million years. The term *human* is a more subjective notion, whose limits can be debated. Some writers use it to include all members of the hominid family, while others restrict it to the genus *Homo* or to the species *Homo sapiens.*

In pre-evolutionary times, the Swedish naturalist Carolus Linnaeus (1707–1778), in his first edition of the *Systema Naturae* (1735), classified all organic organisms into a natural order using a hierarchical system with binominal nomenclature. He included humans (under the genus *Homo* and the species *sapiens,* derived from the Latin words for "man the wise"), along with lemurs, monkeys, and apes, in the order Primates. Intriguingly, in place of supplying physical characteristics to define this new species, Linnaeus avoided controversy by simply writing *nosce te ipsum* ("know thyself"). More than two and a half centuries later, physical anthropologists are still unable to agree on what constitutes modern humanity.

In terms of the morphological definition of modern humans, only a small number of unique anatomical characteristics stand out: (1) *Homo sapiens* is the only surviving member of the family *Hominidae,* a group anatomically committed to terrestrial bipedalism; (2) Members of this species have (not uniquely) relatively large brains—averaging 1,350 milliliters—with the most complex neocortex of all primates; (3) their chin-bearing faces are small compared to their neurocrania; and (4) they have a brow region structured into two parts. Behaviorally, modern humans are identified by the unique presence of: (1) a spoken language; (2) the cognitive faculties to generate mental symbols, as expressed in art; (3) the ability to think, reason, and plan; and (4) a bizarre inability to sustain prolonged bouts of boredom. Are anatomically modern humans and behaviorally modern humans the same thing? Not entirely. Anatomically and behaviorally modern humans appear in the archaeological and fossil records at different times.

Approximately one hundred thousand years ago, or perhaps somewhat earlier, anatomically modern humans appear in the fossil records of the Middle East and Africa; they are similar both cranially and postcranially to modern humans today, yet these earliest forms left no archaeological evidence to lead us to believe they had incorporated a modern behavioral repertoire. At seventy to fifty thousand years ago, we detect no change in the morphology of early anatomically modern humans, but there is dramatic evidence of a change in behavior. Splendid murals painted on the walls and ceilings of caves, musical instruments, and elaborate notations, together with a complex technology of stone and bone, are known from western Europe beginning about thirty thousand years ago. But these dramatic expressions were rather late, compared to the suggestions of similar symbolic behaviors known from as long ago as seventy thousand years, and maybe even more, in Africa. Similarly, modern humans had arrived in Australia by sixty thousand years ago, and an effectively modern level of cognition must have been present in these people to have allowed them to cross at least fifty miles of open ocean to get there. Obviously, a cognitive gulf was breached at some time after about seventy thousand years ago (perhaps earlier). This arose first of all in Africa, and spread thence to other parts of the world. Once *Homo sapiens* was in this behavioral mode, the speed of technological and other behavioral innovation (formerly episodic and rare) increased out of all proportion to what had gone before. At what point religious awareness was acquired is not known, but it was probably part of an overall biological potential for modern cognition that was achieved as a single "package." The huge range of behaviors made possible by this potential was only gradually discovered—and indeed, *Homo sapiens* is still enlarging its behavioral range today.

The human species and religious doctrine

By nature humans are inquisitive beings with an unquenchable thirst to understand and explain the meaning of life, especially their own. Since the days of the ancient Greek philosopher Aristotle (384–322 B.C.E.), the organic world had been looked upon as stable and unchanging, ascending steadily from the simplest forms to the most complex. Under the doctrine of the "Great Chain of Being," humans were perceived as godly creations and were positioned just below the angels on the top branch of a nicely ordered tree of life. All flora and fauna were designed for the purposes in nature that they were perceived to fulfill. The humanistic ideas of the Renaissance period centered all philosophy on human values and exalted human autonomy and superiority to the rest of nature. By the late seventeenth century, René Descartes's (1596–1650) philosophical idea that animals were complex machines with no higher sense of purpose had been expanded by French and German philosophers to create new foundations for a human social order. Morality was no longer considered to descend from an absolute truth enshrined in Christian beliefs, nor was the notion of accountability in the afterlife. The study of human nature became the key to understanding moral order in decent, complex societies. At a later period some struggled to integrate humans and nature with materialistic philosophy, but this view lost support during the turmoil of the French Revolution.

From Cuvier to Darwin

It would not be until the eighteenth century that the study of human origins became an approachable,

but still controversial, topic within the budding science of natural history. Doubts raised by some natural historians questioned the interpretations of biblical literalists as to how humans came to exist on Earth, especially as increasing fossil discoveries in recognizably ancient sediments came to reveal that Earth's fauna did indeed appear to have a biological past. It was evident to naturalists that the Earth bore scars of an ancient history that contained puzzling geological phenomena, such as fossil fish on the tops of mountains, that were inexplicable within the boundaries even of the rudimentary scientific understanding that then existed.

It was impossible, then, to avoid the question as to where humans fitted into the picture. In 1830, the French naturalist Georges Cuvier's (1769–1832) treatise on fossil fauna and flora that was discovered in ancient geologic strata reported no evidence of human fossils coeval with these ancient genera. Since the geologic deposits involved varied greatly from one layer to the next, with bony evidence of once living creatures present in places where they had either gone extinct or now existed only on other continents, Cuvier reasoned that divinely instigated catastrophes and re-creations were responsible for the many extinction and replacement events he perceived. He argued that human fossils could be found if one were to look under the deepest of oceans, as suggested by the Old Testament's story of the great flood. Other naturalists, like Etienne Geoffroy Saint-Hilaire (1772–1844) and Jean Baptiste de Lamarck (1744–1829), provided strict evolutionary reasons for the drastic changes observed in the fossil record. Lamarck, for example, postulated that anatomical and behavioral changes acquired in a creature's lifetime might be passed on to its descendants. However, the Lamarckian paradigm of evolution would shift when two important events took place: (1) the 1858 announcement of Charles Darwin's (1809–1882) and Alfred Russel Wallace's (1823–1913) mechanism of natural selection to explain how species gradually change over time; and (2) the 1856 discovery (and the 1864 naming) of an extinct human species.

Charles Darwin, who rejected the basic tenets of the inheritance of acquired characteristics, enormously popularized a different evolutionary explanation for life on Earth with his the *On the Origin of Species,* published in 1859. Darwin proposed that biological organisms gradually evolve over time by adapting to their environments. Those individuals who are optimally suited to their environments end up producing more descendants than those who are not. If the features that make them better "adapted" are passed along by biological inheritance to their offspring, those features will become more common in the population, whose aspect will thus change over time. Keenly aware of the controversy it would generate, the retiring Darwin minimized any reference to humans in his publication, and did not broach the problem of human origins until many years later. Darwin's theory of "descent with modification" generated a great deal of controversy within religious and scientific communities. The highly public and politico-religious uproar that resulted centered on the distasteful suggestion that humans and apes share a common ancestor, especially in view of the long held belief that other animals are unable to think and are effectively nothing more than soulless automatons. Coming to Darwin's defense, Thomas Henry Huxley (1825–1895) fervently defended the tenets of Darwinian evolution, most publicly in his debate with Bishop Samuel Wilberforce (1805–1873) in 1860. In his influential 1863 publication of a series of public lectures titled *Evidence as to Man's Place in Nature,* Huxley argued that humans should be seen as biological organisms, and subject to the same natural laws that all other organic entities obey.

Interpreting the hominid fossils

The second epochal event for human evolutionary studies was the 1856 discovery of a fossil human at the Feldhofer Grotto in the Neander Valley, Germany. Most authorities of the day dismissed this find as the remains of a "barbarous" type of *Homo sapiens.* However, in 1864 the anatomist William King named the new form *Homo neanderthalensis,* thereby implying that there had been at least one ancient human extinction and speciation event. With further discoveries of the remains of extinct fossil humans, evolutionary concepts were more palatably applied to modern humans. The British geologist Charles Lyell (1797–1875), once a firm believer in God's role, abandoned many of his theological notions and accepted Darwin's theory of descent with modification after examining the remains of the Feldhofer Neanderthal.

At the turn of the twentieth century, the rediscovery of Mendelian genetics provided a basis for Darwin's evolutionary mechanism. Nonetheless, some paleontologists continued the attempt to integrate Christian beliefs with the idea of evolution. One such was the French Jesuit Pierre Teilhard de Chardin (1881–1955). While in Jesuit training in England, Teilhard also trained in paleontology and archaeology, and became embroiled in the Piltdown controversy that was just erupting. In 1912, he was invited to the Piltdown site in Sussex, which had yielded fossil bones including those of a human, and flint tools. Upon arrival he found a tooth. Reconstruction of the fragmentary hominid pieces seemingly offered the perfect transitional candidate from apes to humans—perhaps too perfect.

In 1912, "Piltdown Man" was introduced to the world as *Eoanthropus dawsoni.* At that time, the large brain was considered to be the hallmark of humanity; and for forty years British anatomists would disregard many significant fossil human discoveries because of their prized and large-brained Piltdown fossil. Teilhard later continued his paleontological research at the "Peking Man" site of Zhoukoudian in China. The Chinese fossils helped Teilhard to reconcile his now expansive knowledge of the human fossil record with his Christian beliefs. In *The Phenomenon of Man* (1938–1940), Teilhard proposed a theory of human evolution in which humans were evolving towards a final spiritual unity, also known as *Finalism.* This notion elicited the disapproval of his Jesuit superiors.

Early in the 1950s, Piltdown was exposed as a hoax—the doctored remains of a human and orangutan—and Teilhard has even been fingered as the hoaxer, though he remains only one of the more unlikely suspects of many. By the late 1950s the human fossil record had greatly expanded, as had the plethora of names used to describe it. A tidying-up was in order, and this was gradually achieved under a gradualist and progressivist model of human evolution.

In the 1970s and 1980s, new systematic methods began to transform the understanding of the constantly expanding human fossil record. Further, molecular studies were providing new perspectives. In particular, the "molecular clock" shortened the ape-human divergence to as little as five to six million years ago (from maybe twelve to fourteen). From around 1970 researchers uncovered bipedal but otherwise rather apelike hominids from sites in eastern Africa. These joined the *Australopithecus* fossils already known from southern Africa in the 2.5 to 1.5 million years ago range, and dated mostly from about 3.5 to 2.0 million years ago. Interpreted using an underlying gradualist model, these archaically-proportioned fossil hominids mostly reflected the search for an "earliest ancestor."

The situation at the beginning of the twenty-first century

Over the following few decades, hundreds of fossil human discoveries offered fuel for systematic debates. The "single species hypothesis," which stated that the human ecological niche was so wide that only one species of hominid could have existed at any one time, was rapidly invalidated by new finds, but still lingers in models of human origins that find deep roots in time for contemporary geographical groups of humankind. Evolutionary theory, as well as the rather sparse fossil record, imply in contrast that the species *Homo sapiens* must have had a single origin at one time and in one place, probably Africa. All of the human diversity familiar today has apparently appeared within the past 150 thousand years or so.

Despite minor differences of opinion, it is clear that the diversifying pattern of human evolution is similar to that of other mammalian taxa. Hominid phylogeny is a story of evolutionary experimentation, with multiple speciations and extinctions. The hominid family comprises at least five genera and eighteen known species (see Fig. 1, p. 302), some of which shared territories in both time and space. At present, all geographical varieties of modern humans occupy the single surviving twig of what appears once to have been a densely branching bush.

See also ANTHROPOLOGY; EVOLUTION; EVOLUTION, BIOCULTURAL; EVOLUTION, BIOLOGICAL; EVOLUTION, THEOLOGY OF; PALEOANTHROPOLOGY; PALEONTOLOGY; SOCIOBIOLOGY; TEILHARD DE CHARDIN, PIERRE

Bibliography

Bowler, Peter J. *Evolution: The History of an Idea*. Berkeley: University of California Press, 1984.

Darwin, Charles. *The Origin of Species* (1859). New York: Bantam Classic, 1999.

Eldredge, Niles. *The Triumph of Evolution and the Failure of Creationism*. New York: W. H. Freeman, 2000.

Huxley, Thomas Henry. *The Major Prose of Thomas Henry Huxley*, ed. Alan P. Barr. Athens: University of Georgia Press, 1997.

Johanson, Donald, and Blake, Edgar. *From Lucy to Language*. New York: Simon and Schuster, 1996.

Schwartz, Jeffrey and Tattersall, Ian. *Extinct Humans*. Boulder, Colo.: Westview Press, 2000.

Tattersall, Ian. *The Fossil Trail: How We Know What We Think We Know About Human Evolution*. New York: Oxford University Press, 1995.

Tattersall, Ian. *Becoming Human: Evolution and Human Uniqueness*. New York: Harcourt, 1998.

Tattersall, Ian. *The Monkey in the Mirror: Essays on the Science of What Makes Us Human*. New York: Harcourt, 2001.

Teilhard de Chardin, Pierre. *The Phenomenon of Man*. New York: Harper, 1976.

Wolpoff, Milford. *Paleoanthropology*, 2nd edition. Boston: McGraw-Hill, 1999.

KENNETH MOWBRAY
IAN TATTERSALL

EVOLUTION, THEOLOGY OF

The term *theology of evolution* connotes the systematic study of the religious implications of biological evolution. Any intellectually plausible theology today must face the challenges arising from the notion of life's common descent and Charles Darwin's (1809–1882) theory of natural selection.

The dominant religious and theological traditions, where they have not been utterly hostile to it, have generally ignored evolutionary science. Consequently, when philosophers such as Daniel Dennett (b. 1942) refer to Darwinian evolution as "dangerous," partly because it seemingly destroys in principle any rational basis for religious life and thought, theologians must respond to such a provocation. However, the theological encounter with Darwinian science is not limited simply to an apologetic reaction to those scientists and philosophers who interpret evolution in terms of materialist philosophy. From the days of Darwin himself some theologians (for example, the Anglican Charles Kingsley) have eagerly embraced evolutionary biology as a great gift, one that allows theology to express its understanding of God in fresh

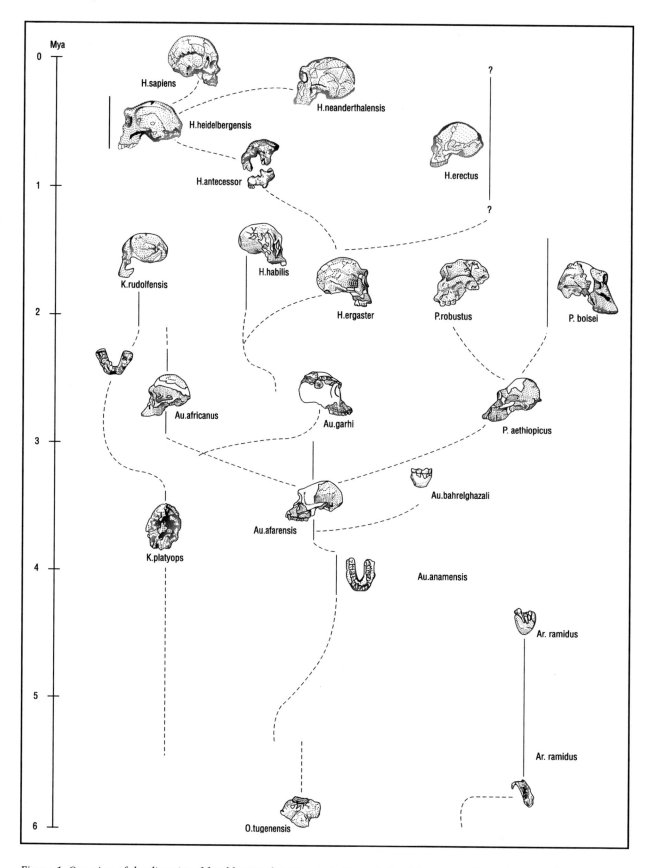

Figure 1. One view of the diversity of fossil hominid species and of the relationships among them. Courtesy of Ian Tattersall.

and fertile ways. In the same spirit a theology of evolution continues the quest to understand religious views of deity in light of new scientific information about the story of life on earth.

That theology can enthusiastically appropriate evolution, however, may initially seem incompatible with the apparent randomness, waste, vast temporal duration, and blind natural selection associated with Darwin's theory of "descent with modification." According to the Darwinian theory, since organisms produce more offspring than are able to survive, some of these simply by chance will be better *adapted* than others to their habitats. The better-adapted organisms will on average produce more offspring than other members of the species, and so nature will *select* their descendants for survival. Over a long period of time this process of natural selection can account for all of the diversity in life, as well as for the intricate *design* in organisms.

The synthesis of Darwinian ideas with the more recent understanding of genetics, which explains variations in terms of mutations of genes, is generally known as *neo-Darwinism*. In the present entry, the term evolution will refer to the ideas of Darwin as well as those of neo-Darwinism.

The theory that all living forms descend with modification from a single source by way of the *mechanism* of natural selection has proven difficult for many religious people and theologians to embrace, especially when natural selection is presented, as it is by many scientists, as the adequate explanation of life's design and diversity. Evolutionists hold that the relative differences that render one organism more adaptive (reproductively fit) than others are apparently random or undirected. For theology this raises the question of whether life in particular, and the universe in general, might not be utterly devoid of any providential guidance. The competitive struggle for survival between the strong and the weak, in which the best adapted are selected and the ill-adapted perish, suggests that we live in an indifferent, impersonal universe. The entire process of evolution is accompanied by what seems to be an enormous amount of suffering, waste, and an unnecessary enormity of time, thus making us wonder what sense we could possibly make of the notion of an intelligent, compassionate God who truly cares for life, humans, and the universe.

All of the world's dominant religious traditions originated long before we had any inkling of the fascinating but shocking Darwinian account of life's story on earth. It would seem, therefore, that all of these religions, if they are to remain intellectually persuasive to their scientifically educated devotees, must now respond to evolutionary biology in ways other than simply ignoring or repudiating the neo-Darwinian convictions shared by the vast majority of contemporary scientists. So, even though the present entry focuses primarily on the implications of evolution for Western theology, much of what is said here may be applicable also to the religious thought of other traditions as they begin to look closely at the story of life on Earth.

Theological responses to Darwin

Theological responses to the Darwinian challenge fall naturally into three classes: opposition, separatism, and engagement. Here the first two will be given only brief treatment, since the third alone seems to encounter the science of evolution with the spirit of gratitude and enthusiasm that can lead to a constructive theology of evolution.

The first response is to insist that Darwinian evolution is incompatible with any religious or theological vision of the universe. The so-called creationists and scientific creationists can be located here. Interpreting the biblical creation accounts literally, creationists claim that Darwin's theory offers a whole new creation story, one that contradicts the biblical accounts. The idea of evolution seems to conflict with the accounts in Genesis of human origins and of the Fall. If there were no historical Adam and Eve and no "original sin" then, the creationists ask, what need would there be for a savior? Scientific creationists go even farther, claiming that the Scriptures give us a better scientific understanding of life's origin than do contemporary biologists.

Other representatives of this opposition response include contemporary proponents of *Intelligent Design Theory* such as Phillip Johnson, William Dembski, and Michael Behe. Representatives of this movement are not necessarily biblical literalists, but they view Darwinism as incompatible with every form of theism. Evolutionary science, at least in their view, is inseparable from philosophical naturalism or scientific materialism, a vision of reality that explicitly rules out the existence of God. Johnson, for example, repeatedly asserts that Darwinian biology is inherently atheistic and that secularists are now using evolutionary ideas as a weapon in a culture war whose objective is to topple traditional religious cultures and concomitant ethical values. Theologians from the second and third group (discussed below) likewise observe that at least some prominent Darwinians present evolutionary science in the guise of materialist ideology. However, they vehemently reject the assumption that evolutionary biology is inherently materialistic or atheistic.

The second of the three responses is the *separatist* one. Separatists are those who prefer in general to keep theology and science as far apart from each other as possible. They claim that unnecessary confusion on issues in science and religion occurs if we fail to distinguish scientific ideas from religious beliefs. In their view, theology deals with a completely different set of questions from those that scientists are asking. Theology is concerned with questions about God, human destiny, or ultimate meaning, whereas evolutionary science inquires about physical, efficient, material, or mechanical—that is, proximate—causes of events in nature. These two sets of questions, the religious and the scientific, are so distinct that, logically speaking, they cannot contradict each other. Consequently, since evolutionary theory is part of science, it cannot in principle be placed in a competitive relationship with theology. Many followers of the neo-orthodox theology of Karl Barth (1886–1968) as well as existentialist theologians fall in this separatist camp.

A good number of theologians, philosophers and scientists are comfortable with this separatist position. But others question whether this is the most courageous and fruitful approach that theology can take when it comes to evolution. A third position, *engagement,* goes further than separatism. It endorses the latter's concern to avoid conflating or confusing science and religion, but it advocates a more positive theology of evolution. Engagement theologians are aware that in the real world science inevitably affects our theological understanding. Evolutionary biology, therefore, will in some way influence our ideas of God. One can hardly expect to have precisely the same thoughts about ultimate reality after Darwin as people did before. Evolution, this third approach suggests, can even enrich our theological conceptions of God. Darwin's great idea, instead of being theologically

dangerous (as the opposition camp holds) or simply innocuous (as the separatists maintain), may turn out to be a great stimulus to constructive theology. Recent examples include the contemporary work of Denis Edwards, John F. Haught, and Holmes Rolston III.

A theology of evolution does not seek refuge in pre-Darwinian design arguments, a quest that is destined to bring theology into unnecessary tension with science. Scientists, after all, seek to provide purely natural explanations of design, including the ordered complexity of living organisms; so the attribution of organic design directly to special divine intervention will be taken as an inappropriate intrusion of theology into an inquiry that lies in the domain of potential scientific illumination. Moreover, focus on design may cause us to ignore the randomness and disorder that accompany the emergence and evolution of life.

An understanding of God as self-emptying love, on the other hand, may provide the foundations for an evolutionary theology that neither interferes with scientific exploration nor edits out the messiness in Darwinian portraits of life. While it is obliged to reject what it takes to be the deadening materialist ideology within which neo-Darwinians often package their popular renditions of evolution, a theology of evolution based on a kenotic understanding of God as humble, self-giving love seems, at least to an increasing number of theologians, to be consonant with, and illuminative of, the astounding discoveries of evolutionary science itself. (The Greek word *kenosis* literally means "emptying").

Prospects for a theology of evolution

Theology, therefore, may begin its reflections on the life process by asking not whether evolution is compatible with the idea of an intelligent designer, but whether the sense of God as it is operative in actual religious awareness can, without in any way interfering with scientific work, plausibly contextualize the findings of evolutionary science. A theology rooted in actual religious experience is obliged to understand the natural world, including its evolutionary character, in terms of a specifically religious notion of God. And so, if the ultimately real is thought of by religious believers as endlessly self-emptying compassion, then theology must strive to understand Darwinian evolution as somehow consonant with such an understanding.

Evolutionary scientists, of course, will immediately want to know how any theology could plausibly reconcile trust in divine providence, the belief that God provides or cares for the world, with the fact of randomness or contingency in life's evolution. A theology of evolution would not try to brush this question aside with the reply that the idea of the "accidental" is simply a cover-up for human ignorance. Accident or chance is no illusion, but a very real aspect of nature. Moreover, an element of indeterminacy is just what theology should expect if the universe is grounded in a God whose essence, as Christians and others believe, is self-giving love. For if God really loves the world as something truly distinct from the divine being itself, then the cosmos must always have possessed some degree of autonomy, even during the long span of prehuman evolution. As even medieval philosopher and theologian Thomas Aquinas observed in *Summa Contra Gentiles*, there has to be room for contingency and chance in any universe that is distinct from God.

Not only indeterminacy, however, but also the remorseless regularity of the laws of nature, including natural selection, seems providential. If nature is not to dissolve into chaos at each instant of its becoming there must be a high degree of consistency to the cosmic process. In this respect, the impersonal rigidity of natural selection would not be regarded as any more theologically problematic than the laws of physics.

Furthermore, if nature is truly distinct from God, as most theists maintain, a theology of evolution would not be surprised that nature is given considerable amplitude for wandering about experimentally, as evolutionary biology has shown to be the case with life on earth. If God's creative and providential activity includes a liberating posture of letting the world be something distinct from God, rather than of manipulatively controlling it, theology can hardly be surprised that the world's creation does not take place in a single, once-and-for-all magical moment, but instead takes many billions of years. The reason theologians give for this temporal extravagance is that God cannot give the divine self, in grace and unrestricted love, to a universe that is not first allowed to be itself, that is, something truly "other" than God. We may wonder,

then whether a universe created instantaneously in complete finished perfection would possess the requisite "otherness" to be loved by its creator.

Of course, to scientists skeptical of theology the prodigality of evolution's multi-millennial journey seems impossible to reconcile with a religious trust in divine intelligence and providence. Surely, if God were intelligent and all-powerful, creation would never have taken so long or ambled so awkwardly over thirteen or so billions of years. Here the scientific skeptics would be joined by creationists and intelligent design defenders in a common objection: a truly competent creator would not have gone about the business of creating a universe in so bumbling a fashion as Darwin's science has pictured it.

However, a theology of evolution would argue that a God of love wills the independence of the universe, and that all of the evolutionary indeterminacy in the journey of life is consistent with the idea of a God who longs for a universe of emergent freedom. A theology of evolution would even claim that any universe embraced by divine love must inevitably have the opportunity to try out many different ways of existing. Evolution's randomness and deep temporal duration, therefore, are not necessarily signs of a universe devoid of providence, but are features that could be seen as essential to the genuine emergence of what is truly other than God.

A theology of evolution portrays providence, therefore, as rejoicing in the evolving autonomy of a self-creating universe. It claims that only a narrowly coercive deity would have collapsed what is in fact a long and dramatic story of creation into the dreary confines of a single originating instant. Instead of freezing nature into a state of finished perfection, a God of love would generously endow the universe with ample scope to become a self-coherent world rather than letting it be a passive, puppet-like appendage of deity. A divine providence that assumes the character of self-humbling love would risk allowing the cosmos to exist and unfold in relative liberty. And so the story of life would take on an evolutionary character not in spite of but because of God's care for the cosmos. For this reason, attempts to cover up the messiness of evolution by portraits of nature as consisting essentially of order or design devised by an intelligent designer would be taken as theologically impoverishing.

A theology of evolution, therefore, revels in Darwin's ragged vision of life rather than trying to trim off its uneven edges. It maintains that evolution may help theology realize more clearly than ever that God is more interested in promoting freedom and arousing adventure in the world than in preserving the status quo or legislating impeccable design. Biblical faith has always been aware of God's concern for human liberation. Now evolutionary science allows theology to connect its ideas of a liberating deity more expansively to the larger story of life's ageless emancipation from triviality.

What then about the problems of original sin, evil, and the fact of suffering in evolution? The idea of original sin after Darwin cannot refer literally to events in a historically factual Eden. One interpretation then is that original sin means that each person is born into a world already vitiated by humanity's habitual turning away in despair from the imperatives of life and the evolutionary adventure of self-transcendence. Furthermore, as Jesuit geologist and paleontologist Teilhard de Chardin (1881–1955) often noted, as long as the universe remains unfinished it will have a dark side to it. Original sin and evil in general cannot be understood apart from the fact that the universe has not yet been perfected. In this context, one meaning of *sin* would be our deliberate resistance to the world's ongoing evolution. An unfinished universe allows for hope, and an evolutionary theology would claim that the world's inhabitants are given the opportunity to participate in the momentous work of continuing creation. Not to do so would, in an evolutionary context, be disobedience to the will of God.

Finally, an evolutionary theology would also extend the picture of God's empathy far beyond the human sphere so as to have it embrace and redeem all the struggle and pain in the entire emergent universe. It sees God as responsively enfolding the whole of creation and not just human history.

See also EVIL AND SUFFERING; EVOLUTIONARY EPISTEMOLOGY; EVOLUTIONARY ETHICS; HUMAN NATURE, RELIGIOUS AND PHILOSOPHICAL ASPECTS; KENOSIS; SIN; THEODICY

Bibliography

Darwin, Charles. *The Origin of Species* (1859). New York: Bantam Classic, 1999.

Dembski, William. *The Design Inference: Eliminating Chance Through Small Probabilities.* New York: Cambridge University Press, 1998.

Dennett, Daniel C. *Darwin's Dangerous Idea: Evolution and the Meanings of Life.* New York: Touchstone, 1995.

Edwards, Denis Edwards. *The God of Evolution: A Trinitarian Theology.* Mahwah, N.J.: Paulist Press, 1999.

Haught, John F. *God After Darwin.* Boulder, Colo.: Westview Press, 2000.

Korsmeyer, Jerry D. *Evolution and Eden: Balancing Original Sin and Contemporary Science.* Mahwah, N.J.: Paulist Press, 1998.

Rolston, Holmes, III. *Genes, Genesis, and God: Values and Origins in Natural and Human History.* New York: Cambridge University Press, 1999.

Schmitz-Moormann, Karl. *Theology of Creation in an Evolutionary World,* in collaboration with James F. Salmon. Cleveland, Ohio: Pilgrim Press, 1997.

Teilhard de Chardin, Pierre. *Christianity and Evolution,* trans. Rene Hague. New York: Harcourt, 1969.

JOHN F. HAUGHT

EXAPTATION

See GOULD, STEPHEN J.; ADAPTATION

EXOBIOLOGY

Exobiology, also known as *astrobiology* and *bioastronomy,* is the study of the potential for life beyond Earth and the active search for it. Nobel geneticist Joshua Lederberg coined the term *exobiology* in 1960, and the field grew significantly with space exploration, especially the Viking landers on Mars. Exobiology draws largely from four disciplines: planetary science, planetary systems science, origins of life studies, and the Search for Extraterrestrial Intelligence (SETI). The field has been invigorated by claims of fossil life in an ancient Mars rock, the discovery of a possible ocean on the Jovian moon Europa, extrasolar planets around sun-like stars, life in extreme environments on Earth, and complex organic molecules in interstellar molecular clouds. Life itself, however, has not yet been found beyond Earth.

See also EXTRATERRESTRIAL LIFE

STEVEN J. DICK

EXPERIENCE, RELIGIOUS: COGNITIVE AND NEUROPHYSIOLOGICAL ASPECTS

In a neurocognitive approach to the study of religious and spiritual experiences, it is important to consider two major avenues towards attaining such experiences: (1) group ritual, and (2) individual contemplation or meditation. A phenomenological analysis reveals that the two practices are similar in kind, if not intensity, along two dimensions: (1) intermittent emotional discharges involving the subjective sensations of awe, peace, tranquility, or ecstasy; and (2) varying degrees of unitary experience correlating with the emotional discharges. These unitary experiences consist of a decreased awareness of the boundaries between the self and the external world, sometimes leading to a feeling of oneness with other perceived individuals, thereby generating a sense of community.

The experiences of group ritual and individual meditation overlap to a certain degree, such that each may play a role in the other. In fact, it may be that human ceremonial ritual provides the "average" person access to mystical experience ("average" in distinction to those who regularly practice intense contemplation, such as highly religious monks). This by no means implies that the mystic or contemplative is impervious to the effects of ceremonial ritual. Precisely because of the intense unitary experiences arising from meditation, mystics are likely to be more affected by ceremonial ritual than the average person. Because of the essentially communal aspect of ritual, it tends to have immeasurably greater social significance than individual meditation or contemplation. However, meditation and contemplation, almost always solitary experiences, typically produce unitary states that are more intense and more extended than the relatively brief flashes generated by group ritual.

Human ceremonial ritual is a morally potent technology. Depending on the myths and beliefs in which it is imbedded and which it expresses, therefore, ritual can either promote or undermine both the structural aspects of a society and overall aggressive behavior. In *The Ritual Process* (1969) Victor Turner uses the term *communitas* to refer to the powerful unitary social experience that usually arises out of ceremonial ritual. If a myth achieves its incarnation in a ritual that defines the unitary experience as applying only to the tribe, then the result is *communitas tribus*. It is certainly true that aggression within the tribe can be minimized or eliminated by the unifying experience generated by the ritual. However, this may only serve to emphasize the special cohesiveness of the tribe in relation to other tribes. The result may be an increase in intertribal aggression, even though intra-tribal aggression is diminished. The myth and its embodying ritual may, of course, apply to all members of a religion, a nation state, an ideology, all of humanity, or all of reality. As one increases the scope of what is included in the interpretation of the experience, the amount of overall aggressive behavior decreases. If indeed a ceremonial ritual gave flesh to a myth of the unity of all being, then one would presumably experience a brief sense of *communitas omnium*. Such a myth-ritual experience approaches meditative states, such as the "cosmic consciousness" described in 1961 by Richard Bucke, or even the "Absolute Unitary Being" described in Eugene d'Aquili and Andrew Newberg's *Mystical Mind* (1999). However, such grand scope is normally unusual for group ritual.

A neurocognitive perspective on spiritual experiences

It appears that there are a variety of spiritual experiences that may seem to be different, but actually have a similar neurocognitive origin, and therefore, lie along a continuum. This continuum might be thought of from a unitary experiential perspective. On one end of the spectrum are experiences such as those attained through participating in a church liturgy or watching a sunset. These experiences carry with them a mild sense of being connected with something greater than the self. On the other end of the spectrum are the types of experiences usually described as mystical or transcendent. This unitary element of spiritual experience should not be thought of as limiting the specific aspects and experiences associated with them. It simply appears to be the case that unitary feelings are a crucial part of spiritual experiences. Most scholars have focused on the more intense experiences because of ease of study and analysis—the most intense experiences provide the most robust responses, which can be qualitatively and perhaps even quantitatively measured. For example, in "Language and Mystical Awareness" (1978), Frederick Streng described the most intense types of spiritual experiences as relating to a variety of phenomena, including occult experience, trance, a vague sense of unaccountable uneasiness, sudden extraordinary visions and words of divine beings, or aesthetic sensitivity. In *The Religious Experience of Mankind* (1969), Ninian Smart distinguished mysticism from an experience of "dynamic external presence." Smart argued that certain sects of Hinduism, Buddhism, and Daoism differ markedly from prophetic religions, such as Judaism and Islam, and from religions related to the prophetic-like Christianity, in that the religious experience most characteristic of the former is "mystical," whereas that most characteristic of the latter is "numinous."

Similar to Smart's distinction between mystical and numinous experiences is the distinction Walter T. Stace makes in *Mysticism and Philosophy* (1960) between what he calls "extrovertive" and "introvertive" mystical experiences. According to Stace, extrovertive mystical experiences are characterized by: (1) a "Unifying Vision" that all things are one; (2) a concrete apprehension of the "One" as an inner subjectivity, or life, in all things; (3) a sense of objectivity or reality; (4) a sense of blessedness and peace; (5) a feeling of the holy, sacred, or divine; (6) paradoxicality; and (7) that which is alleged by mystics to be ineffable. Introvertive mystical experiences are characterized by: (1) "Unitary Consciousness," or the "One," the "Void," or pure consciousness; (2) a sense of nonspatiality or nontemporality; (3) a sense of objectivity or reality; (4) a sense of blessedness and peace; (5) a feeling of the holy, sacred, or divine; (6) paradoxicality; and (7) that which is alleged by mystics to be ineffable. Stace then concludes that characteristics 3 through 7 are identical in the two lists and are therefore universal common characteristics of mystical experiences in all cultures, ages, religions, and civilizations of the world. Characteristics 1 and 2 ground the distinction between extrovertive and introvertive mystical experiences in his typology. There is a clear similarity between Stace's extrovertive

mystical experience and Smart's numinous experience, and between Stace's introvertive mystical experiences and Smart's mystical experience.

A neurocognitive analysis of mysticism and other spiritual experiences might clarify some of the issues regarding mystical and spiritual experiences by allowing for a better typology of such experiences based on the underlying brain structures and their related cognitive functions. In terms of the effects of ceremonial ritual, rhythmicity in the environment (visual, auditory, or tactile) drives either the *sympathetic* nervous system, which is the basis of the fight or flight response and general levels of arousal, or the *parasympathetic* nervous system, which is the basis for relaxing the body and rejuvenating energy stores. Together, the sympathetic and parasympathetic systems comprise the *autonomic* nervous system, which regulates many body functions, including heart rate, respiratory rate, blood pressure, and digestion. During spiritual experiences, there tends to be an intense activation of one of these systems, giving rise to either a profound sense of alertness and awareness (sympathetic) or oceanic blissfulness (parasympathetic). It has also been shown that both the sympathetic and the parasympathetic mechanism might be involved in spiritual experiences since such experiences contain both arousal and quiescent-like cognitive elements.

For the most part, this neurophysiological activity occurs as the result of the rhythmic driving of ceremonial ritual. This rhythmic driving may also begin to affect neural information flows throughout the brain. The brain's posterior superior parietal lobe (PSPL) may be particularly relevant in this regard because the inhibition of sensory information may prevent this area from performing its usual function of helping to establish a sense of self and distinguishing discrete objects in the environment. The result of this inhibition of sensory input could result in a sense of wholeness becoming progressively more dominant over the sense of the multiplicity of baseline reality. The inhibition of sensory input could also result in a progressive loss of the sense of self. Ceremonial ritual may be described as generating these spiritual experiences from the "bottom-up," since it is through rhythmic sounds and behaviors that rituals eventually drive the sympathetic and parasympathetic systems and, ultimately, the higher order processing centers in the brain. In addition, the particular system initially activated depends upon the type of ritual. Rituals themselves might therefore be divided into the "slow" and the "fast." Slow rituals involve, for example, peaceful music and soft chanting to generate a sense of quiescence via the parasympathetic system. Fast rituals might include, for example, frenzied dancing to generate a sense of heightened arousal via the sympathetic system.

Individual practices like prayer or meditation may also access a similar neuronal mechanism, but from the "top-down." In such a practice, a person begins by focusing the mind as dictated by the particular practice, thereby affecting higher-level processing areas of the brain and ultimately the autonomic nervous system. For example, a meditation practice in which the person focuses on a visualized object of spiritual significance might begin with activation of the brain's prefrontal cortex (PFC), which is normally active during attention-focusing tasks. The continuous fixation on the image by the areas of the brain responsible for high order visual processing begins to stimulate the limbic system, which is primarily involved in emotional processing and memory. Several scholars have implicated this area as critical for religious experience because of its ability to label experiences as profound or real and also because certain pathological conditions, such as seizures in the limbic areas, have been particularly associated with extreme religious experiences. The limbic system is connected to a structure called the hypothalamus, making it possible to communicate the activity occurring in the brain to the rest of the body. The hypothalamus is a key regulator of the autonomic nervous system, and therefore such activity in the brain ultimately activates the arousal (sympathetic) and quiescent (parasympathetic) arms of the autonomic nervous system. Part of the result of meditation and other spiritually oriented practices is also to block sensory input into the PSPL, resulting in a loss of the sense of self and a loss of awareness of discrete objects. Thus, a comparison of ceremonial ritual and individual practices like meditation suggests that the end result can be the same for both. It is, of course, difficult to attain the same degree of spiritual experience through ritual as through meditation, because the former requires the maintenance of the rhythmic activity necessary for the continued driving of neurocognitive systems. However, ceremonial ritual still can result in powerful unitary experiences.

The cognitive state in which there is a unity of all things, including the self, the world, and objects in the world, is described in the mystical literature of all the world's great religions. When a person is in that state all sense of discrete being is lost and the difference between self and other is obliterated. There is no sense of the passage of time, and all that remains is a timeless undifferentiated consciousness. When such a state is suffused with positive affect there is a tendency to describe the experience, after the fact, as personal. Such experiences may be described as a perfect union with God, as in the *unio mystica* of the Christian tradition, or else the perfect manifestation of God in the Hindu tradition. When such experiences are accompanied by neutral affect they tend to be described, after the fact, as impersonal. These states are described in concepts such as the "abyss" of Jacob Boeme, the "void" or "*nirvana*" of Buddhism, or the "absolute" of a number of philosophical and mystical traditions. There is no question that whether the experience is interpreted personally as God or impersonally as the "absolute" it nevertheless possesses a quality of transcendent wholeness without any temporal or spatial division.

Techniques for studying spiritual experiences

Clearly, one of the most important aspects of a study of spiritual experiences is to find careful, rigorous methods for empirically testing hypotheses. One such example of empirical evidence for the neurocognitive basis of the spiritual experiences described above comes from a number of studies that have measured neurophysiological activity during states in which there is activation of the holistic operator. Meditative states comprise perhaps the most fertile testing ground because of the predictable, reproducible, and well-described nature of such experiences. Studies of meditation have evolved over the years to utilize the most advanced technologies for studying neurophysiology.

Originally, studies analyzed the relationship between meditative states and electrical changes in the brain as measured by electroencephalography (EEG). Proficient meditation practitioners have been shown to demonstrate significant changes in the electrical activity in the brain, particularly in the frontal lobes. Furthermore, the EEG patterns of meditative practice indicate that it represents a unique state of consciousness different from normal waking and sleep. Unfortunately, EEG is limited in its ability to distinguish particular regions of the brain that may have increased or decreased activity.

For this reason, more recent studies of meditation have used brain imaging techniques, such as single photon emission computed tomography (SPECT), positron emission tomography (PET), and functional magnetic resonance imaging (fMRI). Since about 1990, neuroimaging techniques have been used to explore cerebral function during various behavioral, motor, and cognitive tasks. These studies have helped to determine which parts of the brain are responsible for a variety of neurocognitive processes. These imaging techniques have also allowed for the uncovering of complex neural networks and cognitive modules that have become a basis for cognitive neuroscience research. Activation studies using these functional neuroimaging techniques have helped researchers determine the areas in the brain that are involved in the production and understanding of language, visual processing, and pain reception and sensation. In a typical activation study, the subject is asked to perform such tasks as reading and problem solving while being scanned, and the activation state during the task is then compared to some control state (usually resting). Since most spiritual practices and their concomitant experience might be considered from the perspective of an activation paradigm, functional brain imaging techniques may be extremely useful in detecting neurophysiological changes associated with those states. Researchers can also use PET and SPECT to explore a wide variety of neurotransmitter systems within the brain. Neurotransmitter analogues have been developed for almost every neurotransmitter system, including the dopamine, benzodiazepine, opiate, and cholinergic receptor systems.

There are limitations in each technique for the study of meditation. It is important to ensure that the technique is sensitive enough to measure the changes. Also, each of these techniques may interfere with the normal environment in which spiritual practices take place. Early data of meditative practices has generally shown increases in brain activity in the region comprising the PFC, consistent with focusing attention during meditation. Studies have also observed decreases of activity in

the area of the PSPL, possibly consistent with inhibition of sensory input into this area. However, more studies, with improved methods will be necessary to elucidate the neurocognitive aspects of meditation and spiritual experiences. That the underlying neurophysiology of extreme meditative states can be considered at all allows for the conceptualization of many other spiritual experiences that lie along the spiritual continuum.

In all, these studies can provide a starting point to develop a more detailed neurocognitive model of religious and spiritual experience. This kind of analysis can also be utilized as the hypothesis for future investigations of such experiences.

See also CONSCIOUSNESS STUDIES; EXPERIENCE, RELIGIOUS: PHILOSOPHICAL ASPECTS; MIND-BODY THEORIES; MIND-BRAIN INTERACTION; NEUROSCIENCES

Bibliography

Bucke, Richard M. *Cosmic Consciousness: A Study in the Evolution of the Human Mind* (1901). Secaucus, N.J.: Citadel, 1961.

d'Aquili, Eugene G., and Newberg, Andrew B. "Religious and Mystical States: A Neuropsychological Substrate." *Zygon* 28 (1993): 177–200.

d'Aquili, Eugene G., and Newberg, Andrew B. *The Mystical Mind: Probing the Biology of Religious Experience.* Minneapolis, Minn.: Fortress, 1999.

Durkheim, Emile. *The Elementary Forms of the Religious Life: A Study in Religious Sociology* (1915), trans. Joseph Ward Swain. New York: Macmillan, 1926.

Eliade, Mircea. *The Sacred and the Profane: The Nature of Religion,* trans. Willard R. Trask. New York: Harcourt, 1959.

Gellhorn, E. and Kiely, W.F. "Mystical States of Consciousness: Neurophysiological and Clinical Aspects." *Journal of Nervous and Mental Diseases* 154 (1972): 399-405.

Joseph, Rhawn. *Neuropsychology, Neuropsychiatry, and Behavioral Neurology.* New York: Plenum, 1996.

Newberg, Andrew B.; Alavi, Abass; Baime, Michael; Mozley, P. David; and d'Aquili, Eugene. "The Measurement of Regional Cerebral Blood Flow During the Complex Cognitive Task of Meditation: A Preliminary SPECT Study." *Psychiatry Research: Neuroimaging* 106 (2001): 113–122.

Otto, Rudolph. *The Idea of the Holy: An Inquiry into the Non-rational Factor in the Idea of the Divine and its*

Relation to the Rational (1923), trans. John W. Harvey. New York: Oxford University Press, 1970.

Peng, C.K., Mietus J.E., Liu Y., et al. "Exaggerated Heart Rate Oscillations During Two Meditation Techniques." *International Journal of Cardiology* 70 (1999): 101-107.

Smart, Ninian. *Reasons and Faiths: An Investigation of Religious Discourse, Christian and Non-Christian.* London: Routledge and Kegan Paul, 1958.

Smart, Ninian. *The Religious Experience of Mankind.* London: Macmillan, 1969.

Stace, Walter T. *Mysticism and Philosophy.* London: Macmillan, 1960.

Streng, Frederick. "Language and Mystical Awareness." In *Mysticism and Philosophical Analysis,* ed. Steven Katz. New York: Oxford University Press, 1978.

Turner, Victor. *The Ritual Process: Structure and Anti-Structure.* Ithaca, N.Y.: Cornell University Press, 1969.

ANDREW B. NEWBERG

EXPERIENCE, RELIGIOUS: PHILOSOPHICAL ASPECTS

Although Protestants had previously used the phrase *religious experience* as a rough synonym for spiritual biography, William James (1842–1910) first employed *religious experience* to denote a generic category, applicable to all religions and susceptible to scientific analysis. James's *The Varieties of Religious Experience* (1902) gave the new category a broad extension. He described his topic as "personal religion in the inward sense," contrasted with institutional religion and theology (p. 42). From a psychological standpoint James aimed to provide a "descriptive survey of the religious propensities" (p. 22), including religious feelings and emotions, religious impulses, religious motivations, and nonritualized religious actions. James's methodological decision to focus on the extreme expressions of personal religion exhibited by "religious geniuses" (p. 24) has contributed to a tendency to narrow the category of religious experience to include primarily extraordinary, paranormal experiences and mystical states of consciousness.

With his "descriptive survey of the religious propensities," James hoped to contribute to a "Science of Religions" as he conceived it. His Science of Religions would distill the beliefs of various religions until they harmonized with each other, and then formulate hypotheses that reconciled this universal content with the rest of science. James identified as common to religions the consciousness of something "more" that is continuous with the higher part of oneself. To render this generalized religious content palatable to science, he invoked the subconscious. He hypothesized that "whatever it may be on its farther side, the 'more' with which in religious experience we feel ourselves connected is on its hither side the subconscious continuation of our conscious life" (p. 386). James believed that a Science of Religions would commend itself to believer and scientist alike, and could prove as credible as the natural sciences. Though others too have hoped to reconcile science and religious experience, few have entertained so sanguine an expectation.

An early theory

Despite the fact that James adopted the term *religious experience* at the turn of the twentieth century, the scientific interest in what James and later thinkers would call *religious experience* dates to the eighteenth century. David Hume's (1711–1776) essay "Of Superstition and Enthusiasm" (1741) represents one of the earliest psychological explanations of religious experience. It attempts, moreover, a sociology of religious experience. With the notable exception of Emile Durkheim's (1858–1917) *The Elementary Forms of Religious Life* (1912), most later theories focus exclusively on either the psychology of religious experience or the sociology of religious experience—its social determinants and social uses. Hume wanted to establish general principles with which to explain human nature (moral philosophy) in the same way that Newton had established general principles with which to explain physical nature (natural philosophy). Hume drew on his science of human nature to explain religion. Superstition and enthusiasm, he argued, represent different implicit explanations of anomalous emotional states. A superstitious person, ignorant of the physiological cause of objectless fear, attributes it to the existence of invisible malevolent beings who require appeasement through rites and mortifications. An enthusiast, by contrast, ignorant of the physiological cause of unwarranted hope or pride, attributes it to divine inspiration and experiences transports, raptures, and ecstasies. In both cases the subject resorts to imaginary causes to satisfy an explanatory interest.

Hume believed that the proportions of superstition and enthusiasm in a religion had important social consequences. He argued that superstition requires priests to interpose on behalf of the cowed fearful, whereas enthusiasm will not abide priests because the enthusiast believes his sacred commerce with God obviates institutions and their representatives. Enthusiastic religions begin tumultuously, even violently, but quickly moderate because their weak institutional structure cannot sustain the fervor. Nevertheless, enthusiasm's spirit of self-reliance and autonomy bolsters civil liberty. Superstition, by contrast, gains ground gradually by taming its adherents and ends in tyranny. Despite the fact that Hume emphasizes only the influence an individual's emotions have on his religion and overlooks the extent to which the doctrines of a religion inform the quality of the individual's emotions, his account is superior to many later theories for at least one major reason. Hume stresses the cognitive nature of religious experience, that explanatory commitments are constitutive of religious experience. The subject's own tacit or implicit commitments about the proper explanation of the experience are what makes the experience the experience it is. Many later theorists, including James, elide this feature of religious experience.

Polemics and apologetics

Hume's theory had a polemical tenor. He labeled both superstition and enthusiasm "species of false religion" (p. 73), and the essay has a political subtext. Hume is instructive in this regard. The study of religious experience, like the study of religion itself, had its origin in polemics and apologetics. This history explains the contours of the concept. Religious experience was forged in response to the modern challenge to religion. Since the Enlightenment, rational inquiry had impugned the traditional sources of religious knowledge. Baruch Spinoza (1632–1677) and the subsequent development of higher textual criticism undermined scriptural authority. The creation of modern probability theory

eroded the once intrinsic connection between doctrinal authority and credibility. Hume and Immanuel Kant (1724–1804) effectively thwarted the aspiration for natural theology, while Hume, furthermore, produced what he called a "check" against the credibility of miracle claims. By way of rejoinder, apologists turned to spiritual or mystical experience as a ground for religious commitment. They argued that religious experience is cognitively immediate (i.e., not influenced by, or a product of, prior beliefs) and, therefore, unassailable by rational and historical inquiry into the defensibility of religious beliefs. If religious experience were, in part, a product of prior religious beliefs, one could not use religious experience as an independent ground for religious commitment. Armed with this understanding of religious experience, the increasing exposure to the vast diversity of religions presented not a challenge, but a defense in numbers. Despite incompatible beliefs and practices, all religions at bottom stem from the same or similar experiences, feelings, or sentiments.

Friedrich Schleiermacher (1768–1834) inaugurated this apologetic conception of religious experience. In *On Religion: Speeches to its Cultured Despisers* (1799) he explained that religion consists in piety, a distinct moment of consciousness that he construed as "a sense or taste for the Infinite." In his later systematic theology, *The Christian Faith* (1830) he described piety as the "feeling of absolute dependence" that accompanies all self-consciousness. In both works he sharply distinguished piety from belief and insisted on the immediacy of piety. Ultimately, he heralded an "eternal covenant" between science and religion, whereby religion allows to science all that is of interest to it (1981, pp. 64–65). The immediate, noncognitive nature of piety, he claimed, eliminated the possibility of a conflict. The tendency to treat religious experience as immediate and to consider it the source of religion became widespread after Schleiermacher. Despite James's refusal to distinguish sharply between feelings and beliefs in his more psychological and philosophical works, he too displays this tendency in *The Varieties of Religious Experience* when he claims that personal religious feelings are immediate, primordial, and ultimately productive of beliefs.

Naturalistic explanations of religious experience, such as Hume's, had their effect on the concept of religious experience as well. Ann Taves, in her book *Fits, Trances, and Visions* (1999) has shown how American religious groups, especially among the elite, tended to construct their notions of genuine religious experience by contrasting it with experiences that could be explained naturalistically. Furthermore, they often adopted the naturalistic explanations for experiences they wished to discourage. In the eighteenth century, for instance, Jonathan Edwards (1703–1758), the Calvinist divine, distinguished in his mature writings between genuine religious affections and enthusiasm, the latter involving "imaginary ideas . . . strongly impressed upon the mind" (Taves, p. 39). In the nineteenth century, religious explanations of religious experience continued to compete with naturalistic explanations, now phrased in terms of mesmerism. Seventh Day Adventists and Christian Scientists explained false religion by invoking mesmerism, while mainline denominations tended likewise to dismiss the experiences of Adventists and Christian Scientists as products of mesmerism. Some religious movements, such as Spiritualism, embraced mesmerism as a natural and sufficient means for attaining access to the spirit world and, therefore, attempted a form of religious naturalism. Taves's work demonstrates that thought about religious experience has implicitly been thought about naturalistic explanation as well.

The polemical and apologetic history informing the concept of religious experience has shaped its connotation. The concept suggests ethereal experiences like those that have come to be called mystical because these states seem more resistant to naturalistic explanation, more plausibly immediate, and more promising as a ground for religious commitment than somatic automatisms or visionary experience. The latter seem pathological and best explained naturalistically. James's ultimately unsuccessful labors to neutralize "the bugaboo of morbid origin" in the very first chapter of *The Varieties of Religious Experience,* before even defining his topic, reflects this concern to hedge religious experience from pathology (p. 35). The insistence in many mystical texts on ineffability—that the experience cannot be described—has lead many to consider mystical states of consciousness the paradigmatic religious experiences. Ineffability is taken to signal immediacy. The modern interest in religious experience has frequently led to interpretive mistakes. Some religious thinkers engaged in negative theology, such as Pseudo-Dionysius, who assert the ineffability of its conclusions, have been mistakenly read as describing altered states of consciousness.

Contextualists and perennialists

The alleged immediacy of mystical states continues to be a point of controversy in the study of religious experience. So-called contextualists or constructivists follow in Hume's footsteps. They argue for the cognitive nature of religious experience. In *Religious Experience* (1985) Wayne Proudfoot argued on logical grounds that the subject's implicit explanation of their experience in religious terms makes their experience a religious experience. The commitments the subject harbors about the causes of their experience and the terms appropriate to describe it are constitutive of the experience. They determine its intentionality, or what the experience is of. For this reason subjects who adopt commitments derived from different religious traditions have different experiences. Proudfoot argues, moreover, that one should not understand the ineffability reported in mysticism as an unanalyzable, descriptive characteristic of experience indicating its immediacy but rather as a feature of the theological concepts and commitments informing the intentionality of the experience.

So-called perennialists follow in Schleiermacher's footsteps. They argue for the immediacy of certain forms of religious experience. Robert Forman has argued largely on phenomenological grounds for the existence of states of wakeful, nonintentional consciousness. He calls episodes of this state of contentless consciousness *Pure Consciousness Events* (PCEs). They are nonintentional because they are not experiences of anything. Forman sees evidence of PCEs in a number of meditative traditions around the world. Because PCEs have no content, he claims, they cannot be culturally specific. Mystics of any tradition achieving PCEs have the qualitatively identical ineffable experience. Contextualists reply that the textual evidence adduced by perennialists does not support the assertion of a cross-cultural uniformity of experience. They also argue that phenomenological descriptions of what feels like contentless consciousness do not necessarily mean that the experiences are immediate (i.e., unconditioned by prior beliefs). Regardless, one should note that even if Forman has indeed identified a form of contentless, immediate consciousness, that fact has no intrinsic religious significance. Religious significance could only come ex post facto from interpretation. Because PCEs have no intrinsic religious import, they cannot by themselves serve the apologetic motivations that inspire the search for immediate experience.

Neuroscience

Advances in neurobiology have fostered the hope that a better understanding of the brain can explain religious experience. For some scholars brain function (or malfunction) provides models for accounts of extraordinary religious states. Michael Persinger, for instance, observes the similarities between the psychological effects produced by temporal lobe epilepsy and what he calls "God Experiences." On this basis and with no intention of stigmatizing religion, he infers that transient electrical microseizures in the temporal lobe of the brain explain "God Experiences." Eugene d'Aquili and Andrew Newberg offer a different neurological explanation of religious experience. They provide a complex model whereby ritual and meditation, by different routes, lead to the activation of the autonomic nervous system. This stimulation, in conjunction with the subsequent activation of some and isolation of other higher brain areas, creates various forms of religious experience, including contentless mystical states of Absolute Unitary Being (AUB). Like Schleiermacher and James, they view religious experience as the source of theology and institutions. They maintain that these circuits of neurophysiological stimulation, which affect areas of the brain responsible for causal and holistic cognition, produce religious concepts and even mystical traditions. D'Aquili and Newberg's theory is generally considered highly speculative. It also slights the cognitive dimension of religious experience. The physiological underpinning or component of experience does not suffice to make an experience a religious experience. The subject's implicit commitment to a religious explanation of the experience makes an experience a religious experience. To this extent a social or cultural explanation of religious experience is necessary. Neurology by itself is insufficient.

See also CONSCIOUSNESS STUDIES; EXPERIENCE, RELIGIOUS: COGNITIVE AND NEUROPHYSIOLOGICAL ASPECTS; HUME, DAVID; MIND-BODY THEORIES; MIND-BRAIN INTERACTION; MYSTICISM; NEUROSCIENCES; PSYCHOLOGY OF RELIGION; SOCIOLOGY

Bibliography

Bagger, Matthew. *Religious Experience, Justification, and History*. Cambridge: Cambridge University Press, 1999.

D'Aquili, Eugene, and Newberg, Andrew. *The Mystical Mind: Probing the Biology of Religious Experience*. Minneapolis, Minn.: Fortress Press, 1999.

Durkheim, Emile. *The Elementary Forms of Religious Life* (1912), trans. Karen Fields. New York: Free Press, 1995.

Forman, Robert, ed. *The Problem of Pure Consciousness: Mysticism and Philosophy*. New York: Oxford University Press, 1990.

Forman, Robert, ed. *The Innate Capacity: Mysticism, Psychology, and Philosophy*. New York: Oxford University Press, 1998.

Hume, David. "Of Superstition and Enthusiasm" (1741). In *Essays: Moral, Political, and Literary*. Indianapolis, Ind.: Liberty Fund, 1985.

James, William. *The Varieties of Religious Experience* (1902). New York: Mentor Books, 1958.

Katz, Steven, ed. *Mysticism and Philosophical Analysis*. New York: Oxford University Press, 1978.

Katz, Steven, ed. *Mysticism and Religious Traditions*. New York: Oxford University Press, 1983.

Lewis, I. M. *Ecstatic Religion: A Study of Spirit Possession and Shamanism*, 2nd edition. London: Routledge, 1988.

Persinger, Michael. *Neuropsychological Bases of God Beliefs*. New York: Praeger, 1987.

Proudfoot, Wayne. *Religious Experience*. Berkeley: University of California Press, 1985.

Schleiermacher, Friedrich. *The Christian Faith* (1830), trans. H. R. Mackintosh and J. S. Stewart. Edinburgh, UK: T&T Clark, 1928.

Schleiermacher, Friedrich. *On the Glaubenslehre: Two Letters to Dr. Lucke (1829)*, trans. James Duke and Francis Fiorenza. Chico, Calif.: Scholars Press, 1981.

Schleiermacher, Friedrich. *On Religion: Speeches to its Cultured Despisers* (1799), trans. Richard Crouter. Cambridge, UK: Cambridge University Press, 1996.

Taves, Ann. *Fits, Trances, and Visions: Experiencing Religion and Explaining Experience from Wesley to James*. Princeton, N.J.: Princeton University Press, 1999.

MATTHEW C. BAGGER

EXPLANATION

When one wants to understand something, one asks for an explanation. In principle, everything can be the object of explanation. Some explanations, such as in classification and interpretation, explain *what* something is: What is a whale? It is a mammal; Could you explain the movie *Dr. Strangelove* to me? It is about the Cold War. Some explanations explain *how* something works or how something is possible: How does the door open? Press the button; How is it possible that some children survive the most cruel experiences? There are adults who love them and care about them. Finally, some explanations explain *why* something happens: Why did the aircraft crash? Because one of its motors came loose. In all three cases, the explanation is supposed to yield knowledge. Concerning the why-questions, however, not all are requests for an explanation and, thus, not every answer to a why-question yields knowledge. Some why-questions express the wish to find consolation (Why have you abandoned me?) or the wish to get rid of prejudices (Why should men and women not get the same salary for the same job?). In the science and religion discussion it is intensely debated whether religious answers to such a question as "Why is the universe so special and finely tuned for life?" are explanations, yielding knowledge, or whether they have other functions in the believer's life.

The covering law model

Quite often explanations of why something is the case are related to causation. Other explanations are functional or teleological, as they are also called. The white fur of the polar bear is explained by its camouflage function. A common view is that those explanations actually are causal explanations referring to past causes in evolution that led to the natural selection of the biological trait in question. Causal and functional or teleological explanations are seen as two different variants of the so-called covering law model.

According to the covering law model, an explanation of an event consists in subsuming it under a causal law: All metals expand when heated; this rod is metallic and it was heated; therefore, it expanded. There are four conditions for such a scientific explanation:

(1) The *explanandum* (The rod has expanded.) has to follow logically from the *explanans* (All metals expand when heated; this rod is metallic and it was heated.). Only if the explanandum can be deduced from the initial circumstances and the applied causal laws, the explanandum is really explained and justifies the prediction of a similar event, even if it has not been observed yet.

(2) The applied causal laws (All metals expand when heated.) have to be laws proper and not only all-statements. It is not an explanation to say: "All apples in this basket are red; this apple is from the basket; therefore, the apple is red."

(3) The explanans needs to have empirical content; it should be possible, at least in principle, to confirm or falsify the explanans through experience. Without this condition explanations like God's wrath as the cause of historical catastrophes could not be excluded from science.

(4) The explanans has to be true. If it were false, the implication between the explanans and any explanandum would be true for logical reasons and the explanandum would not be explained.

Although the covering law model cannot be applied everywhere in its strict form, it is supposed to represent an ideal that at least all explanations in the natural sciences that are answers to why-questions ought to strive to attain. It satisfies one feature that one would expect of such explanations, namely, that it explain why a certain event occurred and not another. By subsuming an event under causal laws, it is shown that the event had to occur. The price to be paid for this is determinism, excluding the possibility of exceptions. One way of coping with this difficulty is to allow deterministic as well as nondeterministic explanations. Thus, the explanation of a patient's death from lung cancer may take the form of a statistical explanation referring to the frequency of dying from lung cancer and smoking heavily. According to this variant of the covering law model, the explanandum is not deduced from the explanans. It is supposed to follow with an inductive probability. The reference is not to exceptionless laws but to statistical regularities concerning events and to tendencies concerning human actions.

Rational reconstruction

Another model of explanation that is supposed to be an alternative to the covering law model in, for instance, historical research consists in explaining an event as the result of human action by rational reconstruction. First, an event is shown to be an intentional act that the agent in question has undertaken in accordance with beliefs that seemed reasonable in the situation at issue. Second, the critical examination of the agent's beliefs, whether true or reasonable, contributes to explain why the action resulted in precisely that event. So, in some historical cases, the fact that the belief in the enemy's strength was false may explain why the army was defeated in a certain battle.

Explanation in the science-religion dialogue

One frequently discussed question in theology and in philosophy of religion concerns the relationship between scientific and religious explanations: whether they are on the same categorical level or belong to completely different domains. The difference between scientific and religious explanations is sometimes identified by pointing out that science causes questions that go beyond its own power to answer, for instance, the question "Why is the universe so special and finely tuned for life?" Since this question is not a question formed within science, it cannot be answered scientifically. Instead, the question is a metaphysical why-question, wherefore it can be answered, for instance, theistically by saying "because the universe is created by God who wills that it be so." Since it is not always clear to what extent cosmological theories about the beginning of the universe are metaphysically laden, it is also not clear to what extent the theistic answer competes with scientific explanations or with the metaphysical aspects of some of these theories.

See also CAUSALITY, PRIMARY AND SECONDARY; CAUSATION

Bibliography

Clayton, Philip D. *Explanations from Physics to Theology: An Essay in Rationality and Religion.* New Haven, Conn.: Yale University Press, 1989.

Collingwood, Robin George. *The Idea of History,* rev. edition. Oxford: Clarendon Press, 1993.

Dray, William H. *Laws and Explanation in History.* Oxford: Oxford University Press, 1957.

Gregersen, Niels Henrik, and van Huyssteen, J. Wentzel, eds. *Rethinking Theology and Science: Six Models for the Current Dialogue.* Grand Rapids, Mich.: Eerdmans, 1998.

Hempel, Carl G. *Aspects of Scientific Explanation and Other Essays in the Philosophy of Science.* New York: Free Press, 1965.

Polkinghorne, John Charlton. *Quarks, Chaos, and Christianity: Questions to Science and Religion.* London: Triangle, 1994.

van Fraassen, Bas C. *The Scientific Image.* Oxford: Clarendon Press, 1980.

von Wright, Georg Henrik. *Explanation and Understanding.* London: Routledge and Kegan Paul, 1971.

EBERHARD HERRMANN

EXTINCTION

See EVOLUTION

EXTRATERRESTRIAL LIFE

The concept of extraterrestrial life, embodied in the discipline known as exobiology, astrobiology, or bioastronomy, is one of the oldest in the history of science. Although the search for life beyond Earth has always been intrinsically difficult, and intermingled with philosophy and theology, it has usually been a reflection of the science of its times.

The idea of an infinite number of worlds was part of the ancient Greek atomist system, but was opposed by the physical principles of the philosopher Aristotle. Beginning in the sixteenth century, Copernican theory made the Earth a planet, and the other planets potential Earths. In the seventeenth and eighteenth centuries, Cartesian cosmology extended the idea to other planetary systems, as did Newtonian cosmology, at first in conjunction with natural theology and later with the nebular hypothesis. Only in the twentieth century, and especially with the space age, has empiricism become a major component of the search for extraterrestrial life. It has done so under the banner of cosmic evolution, the idea that the universe has evolved from the Big

Bang to planets, stars, galaxies, life, and intelligence. Although at the limits of science, the question of the abundance of life in the universe has been passionately pursued because it bears so strongly on humanity's place in the universe. As such, "the biological universe," as it has been called, has generated considerable and ever increasing theological and philosophical discussion.

Research on extraterrestrial life

Research on extraterrestrial life is pursued in at least four areas: planetary science, planetary systems science, origins of life studies, and the Search for Extraterrestrial Intelligence (SETI). Not surprisingly, the planet Mars was the focus for much of the twentieth century, beginning with the canals of Mars controversy and culminating with the Viking missions in 1976. The latter demonstrated to the satisfaction of most scientists that no organic molecules were present on the surface of Mars at the Viking lander sites, samples of which were analyzed down to parts per billion. Surprisingly, the problem of life on Mars was again highlighted in 1996 when scientists at NASA announced possible fossils in an ancient Mars rock found in the Antarctic. This conclusion caused an uproar and is still hotly debated. Meanwhile, the discovery of a possible liquid ocean under the ice of the Jovian moon Europa raised the unexpected possibility of life in the solar system beyond the ecosphere usually considered hospitable for life.

Although Earth-like conditions have not been found elsewhere in the solar system, extrasolar planets provide potential abodes of life. After a long and fruitless search during most of the twentieth century, in 1995 the first planet was found around the solar-type star 51 Pegasi. In the following six years, with increasingly refined technology, more than eighty planets were found around sun-like stars within a few hundred light years of Earth. More are being discovered monthly. The evidence is indirect, and the planets discovered through 2001 are gas giants like Jupiter, many in highly eccentric orbits or very close to their parent stars. The search continues for Earth-size planets, and the technology is advancing to the point where their detection may be possible within the next decade.

Because there is no guarantee that life will arise even on Earth-like planets, an understanding of the mechanisms of the origin of life is essential. Unfortunately, these mechanisms are not well understood, even on Earth. Nevertheless, the discovery of life in extreme environments—inside rocks, several kilometers below the surface of the Earth, and deep in the ocean—indicates that extraterrestrial life might develop under conditions considerably broader than thought possible. In particular, the exploration of deep-sea hydrothermal vents and their associated life, including tube worms several meters in length, has provided insights into the limits of life, and even the possible origin of life on Earth. Delivery of organic materials, and even life, from beyond the Earth remains an alternative possibility for the origin of life.

SETI programs seek artificial signals emanating from planets around sun-like stars, using a variety of assumptions about signal frequency and targets. For forty years, beginning with Frank Drake's Project Ozma in 1960, SETI relied mainly on radio telescope technology. During the 1990s, the search began expanding to include optical techniques, even as dedicated facilities were being built and increasingly complex software constructed for signal detection. While there have been some false alarms, no unambiguous signals from extraterrestrial intelligence have been detected. In fact, aside from the controversial Mars rock, no form of extraterrestrial life has yet been discovered.

Implications for religion and humanity

The human implications of the existence of extraterrestrial life have almost always been discussed in terms of extraterrestrial intelligence. For centuries religious implications have been a center of attention, especially in the Christian context, beginning with medieval commentaries on Aristotle and increasing significantly in the wake of heliocentrism. In the post-Newtonian era, scriptural objections were largely met by demonstrations of the benefits of extraterrestrials to natural theology, in which a universe full of life was seen as a demonstration of God's omnipotence and the magnificence of divine creation. During the nineteenth century, in the absence of techniques to resolve the scientific question of life on other worlds, the religious implications were explored in considerable detail. Three options were considered and adopted: religion and extraterrestrial life could be reconciled, certain religious doctrines could be rejected, or the idea of inhabited worlds could be rejected. No consensus has been reached on these options. Nor is there consensus on the effect of the discovery of extra-terrestrials on Christian thought, particularly the doctrines of redemption, incarnation, and salvation. A few religions, including Mormonism, have incorporated the concept of life on other worlds into their religious doctrine. The implications for non-Western religions have only begun to be explored, but in general it seems that the effect on non-Adamist religions would be less than on those that teach salvation through a single God-head.

In a broader sense, the biological universe may be seen as a worldview analogous to the Copernican and Darwinian worldviews. It is possible that the implications for humanity will be similarly widespread, and may follow the general outlines of the reception of past world views, for which there is a rich literature in the history of science. Science fiction, both literature and film, has also addressed the human implications. In particular the work of Olaf Stapledon, Arthur C. Clarke, Stanislaw Lem, Carl Sagan, and Maria Dorrit Russell, have treated the theme of alien life in a thoughtful manner.

Finally, extraterrestrial intelligence may relegate all human knowledge to the status of a specific instance of a more general knowledge possessed, and perhaps shared, by civilizations scattered throughout the universe. On the other hand, in the absence of extraterrestrial intelligence, human destiny may be to spread throughout the galaxy on some variation of the model adopted in Isaac Asimov's *Foundation* series of novels, as opposed to the complex interactions with extraterrestrials found in Clarke's work. Either way, the implications are sobering.

See also EXOBIOLOGY; SCIENCE FICTION

Bibliography

Crowe, Michael J. *The Extraterrestrial Life Debate, 1750–1900: The Idea of a Plurality of Worlds from Kant to Lowell.* Cambridge, UK: Cambridge University Press, 1986.

Dick, Steven J. *Plurality of Worlds: The Origins of the Extraterrestrial Life Debate from Democritus to Kant.* Cambridge, UK: Cambridge University Press, 1982.

Dick, Steven J. *The Biological Universe: The Twentieth Century Extraterrestrial Life Debate and the Limits of Science.* Cambridge, UK: Cambridge University Press, 1996.

Dick, Steven J. *Life on Other Worlds: The Twentieth Century Extraterrestrial Life Debate.* Cambridge, UK: Cambridge University Press, 1998.

Dick, Steven J., ed. *Many Worlds: The New Universe, Extraterrestrial Life, and the Theological Implications.* Philadelphia: Templeton Foundation Press, 2000.

Goldsmith, Donald, and Owen, Tobias. *The Search for Life in the Universe,* 3rd edition. Mill Valley, Calif.: University Science Books, 2001.

Harrison, Albert. *After Contact: The Human Response to Extraterrestrial Life.* New York and London: Plenum, 1997.

Tough, Allen, ed. *When SETI Succeeds: The Impact of High-Information Contact.* Bellevue, Wash.: Foundation for the Future, 2000.

Ward, Peter, and Brownlee, Donald. *Rare Earth: Why Complex Life is Uncommon in the Universe.* New York: Springer-Verlag, 2000.

STEVEN J. DICK

FAITH

Faith as the heart of religious adherence is chiefly a Christian concept and a matter of Christian self description that has been used in the West to describe not only Christianity but other religions as well. In many other religions there are strong analogies to the Christian concept of faith, but they are still by and large analogies. Thus, this entry will deal with the Christian concept of faith and only analogously with other religions.

Definition

Faith would appear to be one of the chief problems in the relations between science and religion. Not only do Christians believe certain things that appear to conflict with scientific accounts of the world, and that are in principle inaccessible to scientific method, it is a theological virtue and necessity to believe them. To believe certain things about God (*credere Deo*) is to believe them because one believes God (*credere Deum*) (i.e., because one believes what God says and reveals because God is God); and one is willing to do that because one believes or trusts in God (*credere in Deo*). This is according to the definition of Augustine of Hippo (354–430), reiterated by Thomas Aquinas (c. 1225–1274). According to them, it is this sort of faith, never mere belief, that defines a Christian. As Augustine observed, the devil believes the same things as the saint but cannot, of course, be considered to have faith because the devil does not trust in God. The reformers Martin Luther (1483–1546) and John Calvin (1509–1564) did not use this same formula; both, however, insisted that Christian faith always involved an inner element of trust and assurance. Never was it mere belief of facts or propositions.

Explanation or virtue?

This way of stating the problem, by stressing the inner aspect of faith, has not always been emphasized in debates over faith since the Enlightenment. Beginning with John Locke (1632–1704), who certainly had the ground prepared for him by others, and continuing through David Hume (1711–1776), philosophical and even theological concern with the concept of faith has largely been, with a few exceptions such as Søren Kierkegaard (1813–1855) and John Henry Newman (1801–1890), over what is believed. Such a perspective assumes that religious beliefs are formed in much the same way as scientific beliefs or that religious beliefs answer to the same sort of inquiries as scientific beliefs. In this case, religion is assumed from the outset to be an explanation for, say, how the world came to be; as such it competes directly with scientific accounts. It can then be assessed on the same methodological bases as scientific accounts. Locke, for example, thought Christian beliefs were credible because, he argued, one could (1) demonstrate that God exists and (2) have reason to believe what God had revealed whenever the propositions proposed for belief were attended by miracles, which served as evidence of their divine origin. Once one had such good reasons for belief, one could give one's will to propositions about God. Hume did not dispute this approach; he simply argued that one cannot demonstrate the existence of God and that miracles, though possible in principle, were never actually believable because they were, by definition, violations of what is normal. Thus, he argued, one should always be skeptical about miracles and reports about miracles.

Although Christians, on the Augustinian understanding, certainly confessed numerous objective beliefs about God, it was the inner virtue of trust that was paramount; trust was always prior to belief, and always linked to it. For Locke and Hume and the philosophical tradition after them, however, the relation between outer confession and inner trust is reversed: One ought not to give one's assent to God until the evidence dictates it. Even then, faith should be proportioned to the degree of certitude possessed by the evidence. Whether faith that is formed by certain or even highly probable chains of reason is actually faith is, of course, disputable, for there is no special personal virtue in committing oneself this way. Neither is there anything to be discovered by faith since the assent depends entirely on external evidence, accessible in principle to anyone who does not have faith.

On this account, then, faith and science would be comparable. Both are seen as explanations, and both depend on comparable sorts of evidence, giving answers to the same sort of inquiries. For example, religion and God might be considered explanations upon inquiry by early human ancestors into "how we got here." If primitive people were concerned by human and cosmic contingency and felt the need to explain it, so too are modern people, but they have much higher standards, such as the ones that Locke and Hume proposed. Or so the argument goes.

However, neither Jews nor early Christians actually seemed much given to this sort of speculation about cosmic origins. Rather, they conceived of their relations with God in much more personal categories. Since their relations with God were personlike, they required personal sorts of concepts for discussing matters about God, and such concepts require certain personal virtues, such as openness, loyalty, truthfulness, and love. These factors are central in the Augustinian definition of faith, where what is believed is important, but what is more important is the inner, personal nature of faith. In Christianity this inner aspect of

faith was never meant to be static; faith was considered to develop and transform the believer through the exercise of the personal virtues. According to the biblical witness, this is a transformation whereby a person in faith is "in Christ" and Christ is in the believer. Faith is thus theologically never a set of beliefs *simpliciter* about God and Jesus Christ; it is the very means by which God dwells in the lives of the faithful. It is important to recognize that much of what is believed about God, as in the analogous case of believing things about other human beings, can only be discerned by those whose developing life in faith equips them with the proper sensibilities. These sensibilities rarely include the epistemic distance and methodological indifference that scientific inquiry requires. These sensibilities require the thinker to put his or her own thoughts into question.

A holistic approach to faith

To approach faith in this way can cause one to reconceive many (but not all) of the problems commonly thought to exist between science and religion. If the heart of faith is a personal openness and an ongoing moral and spiritual transformation of the thinker, then there is a certain shift in the weight given to faith's "what is believed" when one considers the relations between science and religion. To be sure, the objective beliefs of faith are never irrelevant to faith; nevertheless, if the thinker who holds them is in the process of transformation, surely what is believed is continually subject to ongoing interpretation. Any literalism that suggests that a human thinker enjoys a God's-eye view is not tenable. Furthermore, insofar as faith stretches itself to see the world as God created it and seeks to reproduce itself through the rational teaching of others, it is not innately unscientific, unmethodical, dogmatic, or credulous. It can invite method, freedom of opinion, and critical judgement. Barring therefore any definitive reductionism by science, discussion between faith and what science proposes may always be open ended.

In addition, many of the personal habits and dispositions required for faith may contribute to the personal habits and dispositions needed by scientists who want to do cooperative research with intellectual integrity. Insofar as faith requires deep self-reflection on the moral stance of the thinker and on the purposes of human knowledge gained by research, and insofar as it causes the scientific questioner to put him or herself into question, it may even cause one to look at how science contributes or does not contribute to overall human flourishing, including aesthetic, moral, and spiritual flourishing, since science is a function of beings for whom these things are vital.

If, however, approaching faith in this Augustinian way lessens the need for direct confrontation with science over one's specific beliefs about the world, it also raises what may be a deeper problem, namely, the difference in the way faith and scientific method think and imagine. Newman suggested that if faith's appeal to the human mind should ever be overcome, it will not be because faith has been out-reasoned, but because the human mind has lost the ability to imagine itself approaching the world by any method other than the scientific, and because it must always provide explanations of the sort provided by science, for which a distanced and impersonal approach is required. This would result, in the poet T. S. Eliot's phrase, in a "dissociation of sensibility" whereby faith's native imaginative means and sensibilities for dealing with the world and human life are replaced with other incommensurate sensibilities, thus effectively overcoming faith.

See also ATHEISM; CHRISTIANITY; SPIRITUALITY

Bibliography

Allen, Diogenes. *Christian Faith in a Postmodern World: The Full Wealth of Conviction.* Louisville, Ky.: Westminster/John Knox Press, 1989.

Aquinas, Thomas. *On Faith*: *Summa Theologiae*, 2–2, QQ. 1–16, trans. and ed. Mark Jordan. Notre Dame, Ind.: University of Notre Dame Press, 1990.

Aubert, Roger. *Le Problème de l'Acte de Foi*, 3rd edition. Louvain, Belgium: Publications Universitaires de Louvain, 1950.

Augustine. *Homilies on the Gospel of John.* In Vol. 7: *The Nicene and Post-Nicene Fathers* (First series; 1886–1889), ed. Philip Schaff. Reprint, Grand Rapids, Mich.: Eerdmans, 1974.

Buckley, Michael J. *At the Origins of Modern Atheism.* New Haven, Conn.: Yale University Press, 1987.

Dulles, Avery. *The Assurance of Things Hoped For: A Theology of Christian Faith.* New York: Oxford University Press, 1994.

Kierkegaard, Søren. *Philosophical Fragments*; *Johannes Climacus* (1844), trans. and eds. Howard V. Hong and Edna H. Hong. Princeton, N.J.: Princeton University Press, 1985.

Kierkegaard, Søren. *Concluding Unscientific Postscript to Philosophical Fragments* (1846), trans. and eds. Howard V. Hong and Edna. H. Hong. Princeton. N.J.: Princeton University Press, 1992.

Louth, Andrew. *Discerning the Mystery: An Essay on the Nature of Theology.* Oxford: Oxford University Press, 1983.

Newman, John Henry. *An Essay in Aid of a Grammar of Assent* (1870). Westminster, Md.: Christian Classics, 1973.

Smith, Wilfred Cantwell. *Belief and History.* Charlottesville: University Press of Virginia, 1977.

Springsted, Eric O. *The Act of Faith: Christian Faith and the Moral Self.* Grand Rapids. Mich.: Eerdmans, 2002.

Wolterstorff, Nicholas. *John Locke and the Ethics of Belief.* Cambridge, UK: Cambridge University Press. 1996.

ERIC O. SPRINGSTED

FAITH HEALING

See SPIRITUALITY; SPIRITUALITY AND FAITH HEALING

FALL

According to the theology of the early Christian church fathers, Adam not only possessed complete human harmony, he also possessed an encompassing knowledge of nature such that God brought all the animals to him so that he could name them (Gen. 2: 19–20). Adam and Eve lost not only these gifts as a result of the fall, but suffering and death became part of their lives and were passed on to their offspring. Eastern theologians, therefore, spoke of death by heredity, while Augustine of Hippo and other early Western theologians spoke of original sin that is passed on by heredity from one generation to the next. According to this view, only the Bible, as God's revelation, offers true knowledge.

During the Middle Ages, the influences of the theologies of creation and Christology, as well as the reception of Aristotelian and other ancient Greek writings, brought about a new understanding of the regularity and independence of the laws of nature. Scholars began to see nature as a second book of God's revelation, in addition to the Bible. Consequently, the idea appeared that humans had to study the book of nature to regain partly the knowledge that Adam had lost in the fall. This idea was important in English physico-theology during the sixteenth and seventeenth centuries, which strongly influenced the emerging natural sciences.

Criticism against the doctrine of original sin emerged with Enlightenment philosophy, which, contrary to the natural sciences and their conception of deterministic laws, emphasized human freedom and deemed the conception of passing on sin by heredity a confusion of categories in which sin was an aspect of history, and heredity an aspect of nature. Enlightenment philosophy interpreted the fall as a necessary step in human development from a dreaming, childlike consciousness toward the full adult consciousness that befitted humanity. For nineteenth-century philosopher Søren Kierkegaard, angst, which distinguishes humans as ecstatic beings from animals, is the actual occasion for sin. Kierkegaard rejects, however, any attempt to scientifically construe a cause for sin because this would create only myths.

The theory of evolution challenged the traditional doctrine of original sin from still another angle. How could primordial humans, who hardly differed in their abilities from animals, have had a comprehensive knowledge of nature, and how could they have determined the whole of human history that was to come? Evolutionary theory also weakens arguments against the doctrine of original sin that stem from Enlightenment philosophy. Evolutionary theory, in effect, transcends the juxtaposition of nature and history that the Enlightenment had assumed because it can show how behavior is, in fact, passed on through heredity, and contingent (historical) events can become structural elements of a living organism.

The doctrine of the fall, on the one hand, intends to emphasize that evil, which has been the cause of great suffering in the course of history, is rooted deep within humanity, and therefore is not easily overcome. It rejects all simplified, quick, and utopian solutions to the problem of evil. On the other hand, the doctrine precludes human nature from being identified with evil, and thus leaves the way open for potential, however laborious, progress. It addresses a depth in the human person

that can only be addressed in a language of its own, such as myth.

Furthermore, evolutionary theory explains how events and developments that are experienced as negative or evil by single creatures (e.g., suffering, being killed, being fed on) are conducive to the development of life in general. In this way, evolutionary theory provides a new context for theological reinterpretations of the traditional doctrine of the fall. These reinterpretations are developed within the framework of either classical theology (Raymund Schwager), process theology (Jerry Korsmeyer), or as part of a common theory of religions (Eugen Drewermann and Philip Hefner).

See also AUGUSTINE; EVIL AND SUFFERING; EVOLUTION; HUMAN NATURE, RELIGIOUS AND PHILOSOPHICAL ASPECTS; NATURAL THEOLOGY; TWO BOOKS

Bibliography

Drewermann, Eugen. *Strukturen des Bösen.* Paderborn, Germany: Schöningh, 1977–1978.

Hefner, Philip. "Biological Perspective of Fall." *Zygon* 28 (1993): 77–101.

Kierkegaard, Søren. *The Concept of Anxiety* (1844), trans. and ed. Reidar Thomte. Princeton, N.J.: Princeton University Press, 1980.

Korsmeyer, Jerry. *Evolution and Eden: Balancing Original Sin and Contemporary Science.* New York: Paulist Press, 1998.

Ricoeur, Paul. *The Symbolism of Evil,* trans. Emerson Buchanan. Boston: Beacon Press, 1969.

Schwager, Raymund. *Erbsünde und Heilsdrama.* Münster, Germany: Lit Verlag, 1994.

RAYMUND SCHWAGER

FALLIBILISM

Fallibilism is the view that human knowledge lacks a secure and an infallible foundation. Fallibilism is associated in particular with American scientist and philosopher Charles S. Peirce (1839–1914) and Austrian-born philosopher Karl Popper (1902–1994). In its most comprehensive form the fallibilist maintains that people cannot know anything with certainty. In its more restricted forms uncertainty is attributed to a particular domain of beliefs, such as empirical or religious beliefs. What separates fallibilists from others is the confidence each gives to epistemological success in general or within a particular domain. Participants within the science/religion discussion quite frequently affirm fallibilism. Its merit seems to be that it opens up possibilities for a dialogue on more even terms than foundationalism does.

See also FALSIFIABILITY; POSTFOUNDATIONALISM

Bibliography

Peirce, Charles S. *Collected Papers,* eds. Charles Hartshorne, Paul Weiss, and Arthur W. Burks. Cambridge, Mass.: Belknap Press, 1931–1958.

Popper, Karl. *Conjectures and Refutations: The Growth of Scientific Knowledge.* London: Routledge and Kegan Paul, 1963.

Van Huyssteen, J. Wentzel. *The Shaping of Rationality: Toward Interdisciplinarity in Theology and Science.* Grand Rapids, Mich.: Eerdmans, 1999.

MIKAEL STENMARK

FALSIFIABILITY

In opposition to the verification criterion of the logical positivists, Austrian-born philosopher Karl Popper (1902–1994) defended the idea of falsifiability. According to Popper's falsification criterion scientists should develop theories that can be falsified by observation. They should then try to falsify them, and those that survive testing should then be tentatively accepted and regarded as corroborated, that is, as closer to the truth than theories that have been falsified. The criterion was intended to demarcate science from pseudo-science. In the mid-twentieth century these ideas and their consequences for religious beliefs were at the center of the science/religion debate, but because of doubts about whether science itself could satisfy Popper's requirements, issues of falsifiability have had a less prominent place in the debate since the 1980s.

See also FALLIBILISM; POSITIVISM, LOGICAL

Bibliography

Mitchell, Basil, ed. *The Philosophy of Religion.* Oxford: Oxford University Press. 1971.

Popper, Karl. *The Logic of Scientific Discovery* (1934). London: Hutchinson, 1968.

Stenmark, Mikael. *Rationality in Science, Religion and Everyday Life: A Critical Evaluation of Four Models of Rationality.* Notre Dame, Ind.: University of Notre Dame Press, 1995.

MIKAEL STENMARK

FEMINISMS AND SCIENCE

At their most basic level, feminist perspectives on science begin with the observation that women have been excluded from the practice of science. This exclusion has sometimes been overt. For example, women have often been barred from getting the education required to become scientists. Overall, feminists have demonstrated that, for women, it is difficult to get in, difficult to stay in, and difficult to advance to positions with the power to control the direction of scientific study. Exclusion has also been more covert, as demonstrated by the lack of women's perspectives within science.

Feminists argue that a number of problems are related to this exclusion, including depletion of natural resources, tainted food sources, pollution, and impending viral disaster. They argue for a number of different causes and solutions for this exclusion of women—some compatible, some conflicting—which makes it more proper to speak of "feminisms" and science, rather than feminism. Despite these differences—or, perhaps, because of them—feminist perspectives remain a rich resource for understanding science and for rethinking the relationship between science and religion.

Margaret Wertheim, for example, in her book *Pythagoras' Trousers: God, Physics, and the Gender Wars* (1995) argues that there is a connection between the exclusion of women in physics and the exclusion of women from positions of authority in Western religion. From the mystic Pythagoras, to the revival of physics in medieval monasteries, to Albert Einstein's observation that "in this materialistic age of ours, the serious scientific workers are the only truly profoundly religious people," physics has been permeated with a religious sensibility. Wertheim explores how women have been excluded both from the right to interpret Scripture and from the right to interpret God's other revelation, nature.

Feminists have examined the diverse ways that women have been excluded from science and how male perspectives and bias have influenced the selection of problems to examine and decisions about how to organize and interpret data. What these arguments have in common is that the problem is seen as external: The results may be biased, but that bias is unrelated to the basic methods and assumptions of science. In fact, bias occurs because exclusion of women leads to a distortion of proper scientific method. These eternal explanations lead to external solutions: Remove the barriers for women in science; get them in and get them into positions where they can influence the direction, programs, and interests of science. Wertheim, for example, argues that women should be involved in physics in order to influence the direction of the research and to create a new culture of physics.

From this perspective, there is no such thing as "women's science," except to the extent that women may choose different problems to address or, perhaps, organize data differently. Including more women will bring about a better science, truer to its ideals and goals, but it will not bring about a different science.

Internalist arguments

Some feminists see this as a partial solution. Post-Kuhnian philosophies of science suggest that scientific concepts, theories, methodologies, and truths are not objective, but instead bear the marks of their collective and individual creators. The social location of the scientist not only influences the direction of science, it can influence the shape of science itself and even the truths it discovers. Feminists focused on gender as one of the aspects of culture that shape science.

All cultures sort human beings by sex, but there are variations in the roles, duties, characteristics, and so on that define those divisions. These variations are what is meant by *gender*. Feminists have argued that in the West, science is constructed around gendered assumptions, with "male" categories privileged over "female." It is not just the centrality of "rational man" that is problematic, but that what counts as rational or objective is that which has been given a masculine meaning.

Women have demonstrated this connection between gender and science in a number of ways. One of the most influential works in this regard is Carolyn Merchant's, *Death of Nature: Women, Ecology, and the Scientific Revolution* (1976). Merchant argues that prior to the sixteenth century, nature was seen as female: a mother, a lover, and so on. Further, nature was seen as a living, dynamic entity with a body and a soul. This conception carried with it an ethic towards nature that was marked by moderation. If one abused or exploited nature, one faced the consequences.

In the 150 years from Nicolaus Copernicus to Isaac Newton, this view completely changed. Nature became a machine, made up of discrete, interchangeable parts. Because nature was no longer alive, with no spirit and no animation, it could be exploited at will. This change had a religious dimension. Merchant, Rosemary Reuther, Evelyn Fox Keller, and others have argued that the scientific revolution was a child of the Reformation in that the removal of the divine presence from within nature contributed to the transformation from nature as mother to nature as machine. There was a further connection in that the Fall of Genesis was seen as both a fall from innocence and a fall from dominion. Innocence could be regained through religion, dominion through science (*techne*).

This change was, of course, gradual, but it was not always subtle, especially in its use of gendered language. Women and nature were connected: Women threatened man's innocence; nature threatened his dominion. And, just as God intended that man should dominate and control woman, God intended that man should dominate and control nature. In the early seventeenth century, Francis Bacon encouraged scientific endeavor by declaring that nature, like a woman, locked her secrets away in her womb. But, like a women, she wanted to be penetrated and her secrets taken. The male scientist should extract the truth by force, and thereby command nature and compel her to serve him.

These insights have been influential in the development of ecofeminist thought, as well as feminist philosophies of science. They suggest that the problems with science are not external; rather, its epistemological assumptions and methodologies are themselves biased. The problem is not bad science, the problem is science itself. Unlike internal approaches that seek to get women into labs, these feminists insist that it is necessary to transform science, to promote a different science based on a feminist epistemology.

Feminist epistemologies and feminist science

Feminists have offered several alternatives to existing "masculinist science." Feminist empiricists, such as Helen Longino, have sought to integrate feminist concerns with existing empiricist assumptions, arguing that the social identity of the observer is not irrelevant to the practice of science. Instead, values are imbedded in science, and scientists should therefore be intentional about which values they bring to their work. Feminist empiricists have been criticized for retaining certain aspects of empiricism: the primacy of reason, the centrality of the (experiencing) individual, and the separation between public and private in science. Further, feminist empiricists do not challenge the assumption that there is but one science and one nature waiting to be discovered by it.

As an alternative, feminists such as Sandra Harding have argued in favor of *standpoint theory*. This arises out of German philosopher Georg Wilhelm Friedrich Hegel's (1770–1831) dialectic between master and slave, and the observation that the standpoint of the slave offers a more complete, less distorted view of the world. The master thinks that the slave responds only to the master's commands. The slave knows that the slave also dreams, intentionally thwarts the master's plans, reads in secret, and even plots rebellion. In other words, the master only knows one reality, but the slave knows there are more. Feminist standpoint theorists suggest that starting from—or at least including—women's perspectives on and experiences of the world can give science a more comprehensive and reliable view of the world.

A third position, *feminist postmodernism*, begins with the observation that there is no single standpoint. Donna Haraway, for example, links women's experiences with the experiences of other "others," such as African Americans. Just as contemporary science blurs boundaries between human and animal, organism and machine, physical and nonphysical, this approach blurs boundaries between standpoints and embraces the partiality of a feminist point of view—indeed any view—and the possibilities that partiality opens up.

Despite their differences, these positions converge on the point that there is something essentially wrong with the way that science is done, and they argue for a "feminist science." This does not mean that feminist epistemologies should be equated with relativism; few if any feminist philosophers of science would take an antirational or anti-objective stance. Most would argue that feminism is a way to increase the objectivity of science, although it is an objectivity that is not grounded in the detached observer.

Feminist rationality is a responsive rationality, what Hilary Rose refers to as "thinking from caring" and what Evelyn Fox Keller sees as knowledge arising from a relationship between knower and known. This knowledge does not require, and in fact rejects, distance between the observer and the observed. Nature is not a "thing," separate or separable from a speaking and knowing "we." What people know about nature they know because they interact with and are embedded in it. People know the world, because they are a part of the world and because they are in a relationship with it.

In addition, feminists argue that it is not subjectivity—the context and desires of the observer—that leads to bad science, but the illusion of objectivity. Values do not distort science; it is only coercive values—racism, classism, sexism—that threaten objectivity. Participatory values decrease rather than increase distortions, so objectivity is enhanced when people are intentional about their subjective preferences and can choose those that are most effective. Feminists have gone so far as to suggest that these participatory values are the preconditions of objectivity.

Multicultural and global feminisms

An additional feminist approach is emerging in the recent writings of Sandra Harding, where she explores the intersection of post-Kuhnian, feminist, and postcolonial science and technology studies. Just as feminists argue that feminist science involves more than bringing women into laboratories, multicultural approaches require more than just tacking on issues of women of color. The frameworks set by Western women can themselves block concerns from other perspectives, and alternative frameworks give way to different institutional contexts and different concepts. For example, Western science thinks in terms of nature, which is distinct from the human being, while in developing countries the focus is on the environment, which is something with which human beings interact.

The issue is not whether knowledge is universal, or whether the law of gravity is the same everywhere. The question is whether there is one best way to represent the world. Women's science is problematic to the extent that, like men's science, it retains the view that there is *a* science.

Each culture is a tool box containing different resources for understanding nature. Because different cultures are exposed to different parts of nature, they develop distinctive resources. In addition, each culture has distinctive metaphors, models, and languages that enable them to see their particular parts of the world in diverse ways. These resources generate both systematic knowledge and systematic ignorance about nature.

If people settle on one "science," these diverse ways of organizing and producing systematic knowledge will be lost, reducing knowledge of the world. Diverse perspectives not only allow people to see more, they enable people to see better, promoting a more rigorous objectivity by revealing aspects of nature that may be difficult or even impossible to detect from within the dominant culture and perspective. In the same way that the world needs biodiversity to continue to renew itself, so too does knowledge of the world need different sciences to maintain its creativity.

What is needed is what Sandra Harding calls a *borderlands epistemology* that values the distinctive understandings of nature that different cultures generate. The goal is not to integrate them into an ideal knowledge system, because that would necessarily sacrifice the advantages of the differing conceptual schemes that different cultures have developed. Instead of a single science, scientists would learn when to use one science and when to use another, what to value in modern sciences and what to value in other knowledge systems. What they would learn is which approaches provide the best set of maps for each particular journey.

See also ECOFEMINISM; ETHNICITY; FEMINIST
 COSMOLOGY; FEMINIST THEOLOGY; LIBERATION
 THEOLOGY; WOMANIST THEOLOGY

Bibliography

Harding, Sandra. *The Science Question in Feminism.* Ithaca, N.Y.: Cornell University Press, 1986.

Harding, Sandra. *Is Science Multicultural?: Postcolonialisms, Feminisms, and Epistemologies.* Bloomington: Indiana University Press, 1998.

Keller, Evelyn Fox. *Reflections on Gender and Science.* New Haven, Conn.: Yale University Press, 1985.

Keller, Evelyn Fox. *Secrets of Life, Secrets of Death: Essays on Language, Gender, and Science.* New York: Routledge, 1992.

Longino, Helen. *Science as Social Knowledge: Values and Objectivity in Scientific Inquiry.* Princeton, N.J.: Princeton University Press, 1990.

Merchant, Carolyn. *Death of Nature: Women, Ecology, and the Scientific Revolution.* San Francisco: Harper, 1976.

Rose, Hilary. *Love, Power and Knowledge: Towards a Feminist Transformation of the Sciences.* Bloomington: Indiana University Press, 1994.

Rossiter, Margaret. *Women Scientists in America: Struggles and Strategies to 1940.* Baltimore, Md.: Johns Hopkins University Press, 1982.

Tuana, Nancy. *Feminism and Science.* Bloomington: Indiana University Press, 1989.

Tuana, Nancy. *The Less Noble Sex: Scientific, Religious, and Philosophical Conceptions of Woman's Nature.* Bloomington: Indiana University Press, 1993.

Schiebinger, Londa. *Nature's Body: Gender in the Making of Modern Science.* Boston: Beacon Press, 1993.

Wertheim, Margaret. *Pythagoras' Trousers: God, Physics, and the Gender Wars.* New York: Random House, 1995.

LISA L. STENMARK

FEMINIST COSMOLOGY

Feminist cosmology is both a critical and constructive model of the cosmos. Feminists criticize the mechanistic, dualistic, patriarchal model of the cosmos informed by Enlightenment philosophy and modern science. This dominant model creates hierarchical dualisms: human over nature, mind over body, male over female, subject over object. The subjugation of nature is linked to the subjugation of women. Feminist cosmologies restructure these pairs, like nature and humans, as intimately and interdependently related to each other in a web of moral responsibility. Ecofeminists lead the charge in developing a cosmology that not only reconstructs a new world view, but also calls for radical change in the way that humans live with the natural world.

See also COSMOLOGY, RELIGIOUS AND PHILOSOPHICAL ASPECTS; ECOFEMINISM; FEMINISMS AND SCIENCE; FEMINIST THEOLOGY; WOMANIST THEOLOGY

Bibliography

Howell, Nancy R. *A Feminist Cosmology: Ecology, Solidarity, and Metaphysics.* Amherst, N.Y.: Prometheus, 2000.

ANN PEDERSON

FEMINIST THEOLOGY

Feminist theology emerged from the notion that Christian theology and the institutional embodiment of Christianity not only excluded women's voices and experiences, but also developed practices that are sexist, patriarchal, and androcentric. Contemporary feminist theology finds its historical roots with those who question authors of sacred texts and those who challenge theologians who defined what it meant to be a human being from the perspective of patriarchal, male experience. For centuries, male experience was the standard by which the worth and contribution of women was judged. In the 1960s, contemporary feminist theologians began to challenge and protest these fundamental doctrines and practices of institutional Christianity.

Feminist theology is not limited to the Christian tradition. Jewish and Islamic feminist theologians also examine the patriarchal assumptions that support the subordination and oppression of women. Judith Plaskow, for example, calls for a retrieval and redefinition of the past in order for women to reform Torah; Jewish women must rewrite texts, author new liturgies, and disclose voices from the past. Islamic feminist theologians, such as Riffat Hassan, speak not only about patriarchy, but also about mixing modernization and Westernization with Islam. These are two examples of the growing diversity of feminist voices in theology. While feminist theologians come from diverse cultural and religious traditions, they share similar hopes and common interests.

Methodologies and types

Feminist theologians employ similar methodological strategies that result in substantive, constructive changes within Christian theology and practice. Three important steps must follow. First, feminist theologians reflect critically on the patriarchal and androcentric nature of the churches' practices and theological doctrines. This critical step challenges the values and theological paradigms that support patriarchy. For example, Sallie McFague (b. 1933), a European-American ecofeminist theologian, challenges the patriarchal model of God and the world as one that sanctions and supports an understanding of divine power and human power that dominates and excludes women. Second, feminist theologians return to the tradition to delve deeper and discover voices that have been previously ignored and discarded. These acts of retrieval expand and deepen the liberatory voices already within the tradition. Third, many feminist theologians begin the process of reconstructing theological doctrines with new paradigms. McFague utilizes the metaphor of the body of God to reconstruct the relationship between God and the world. This paradigmatic shift emphasizes mutual and reciprocal relationships between God and the world instead of hierarchical and dominating ones.

Generally, three types of feminist theology have developed in their relationship to Christianity. First, some feminist theologians seek modest changes in the traditions from within Christianity. For the most part, these theologians are less critical of the structure of Christianity. Other feminist theologians, while still working from within a Christian framework, seek not only to critique the theology, but also to reimagine and reconstruct new models of thinking about and practicing Christianity. Radical transformation of both doctrines and the institutional practices of Christianity is sought. Another category of revolutionary feminist theologians find the nature of Christianity so thoroughly patriarchal, that their only way to remain committed to feminist concerns is to leave Christianity. These voices can be described as post-Christian.

The first phase of feminist theology concentrated primarily on issues related to gender. Later, the development of feminist theology from a white, privileged standpoint began to embrace and connect with other women's voices and experiences. In fact, the category of women's experience, while embraced early on in feminist theology, has become problematic since it so often only seemed to describe the experience of one voice: that of privileged, white women. Feminist theologians were primarily white, privileged women working within the confines of the academy. As feminist theologians linked their projects to other liberation movements, the challenge was to examine their own bias of class and race. Feminist theologians began to question the category of "women's experience." There is no monolithic experience, no single way of being women. Feminist theology consequently linked the voices and experiences of those excluded because of race, class, sexual orientation, disability, age, and gender. Consequently, feminist theologians are now a worldwide company of voices, having expanded from American white feminists to Asian feminists, Womanists, Mujerista theologians, and many others. Feminist theology continues to expand upon and celebrate the variety of voices and experiences. Tensions and dissonances that reside in these differences are opportunities for creative new theological explorations.

Links with science and ethics

Feminist theology is also linked to other feminist projects in fields like science and bioethics. For example, in religion and science, feminists are critical of the patriarchal systems in which both disciplines are embedded. Science, like religion, is a socially-situated institution that has excluded women from its theory and practice. Contemporary feminist philosophers of science are linked to feminist theologians in their common critique of the Enlightenment ways of knowing the world (epistemologies) and their institutional embodiment, which support patriarchal and androcentric viewpoints. Feminists are critical of the convergence of modern science with the modern or Enlightenment worldview because it excludes women as valuable knowers and participants in the scientific process. Feminist philosophers of science criticize the Enlightenment epistemology that sees those "in the know" as impartial, detached, impersonal, value-free, and dispassionate.

Similarly, feminist philosophers of science have different ways of critiquing science. Sandra Harding examines three different kinds of feminist scientists. First, feminist empiricists uncover sexist and androcentric biases in the sciences. The addition of more women in the institution of science might be enough of a corrective. Feminist empiricists, like the reformist feminist theologians, don't directly link science to politics. Both groups are less critical of the institutions themselves. Second, feminist standpoint theorists claim that knowledge grounded in the perspectives and experiences of women's lives is actually a more comprehensive, objective way of knowing. They criticize the dominant standpoint of patriarchal science. Much like the revisionist theologians, they insist that research and data collection must begin with voices that have been systematically excluded. Finally, feminist postmodernists reject the foundationalism of modern epistemologies and sciences, calling for a new science. This position is similar to the post-Christian feminist theologians who reject Christianity itself and call for new ways of expressing spirituality. Both feminist theology and feminist philosophers of science require narratives of those who have been marginalized. They both require beginning the research, data collecting, and questions from the perspectives of the voices of "the other."

In both religion and science, feminists insist that epistemology and ethics are inextricably linked together: People are accountable for what they do with what they know. Substance and praxis follow together. Feminist research develops postmodern epistemologies that value multidimensional perspectives to expand and widen the definition of reason, begins research with the excluded voices, and constructs the subject/object relationship on the same epistemological plane. Feminist research becomes a model for research and living: Multiple voices are used for research, and conversational praxis is the methodological means of including voices of those formerly excluded. In the field of religion and science, the research program of Anne Foerst in artificial intelligence and theology constructs an embodied theology and epistemology that redefines what it means to be human. The theology of Nancy Howell explores how the subjugation of women and nature is interconnected. Her ecofeminist theology offers new ways of constructing models of God and the world. These are two examples of the constructive feminist engagement between religion and science.

See also ECOFEMINISM; ECOLOGY, ETHICS OF;
    ECOTHEOLOGY; EPISTEMOLOGY; FEMINISMS AND
    SCIENCE; FEMINIST COSMOLOGY; LIBERATION

THEOLOGY; POSTFOUNDATIONALISM; POSTMODERNISM; WOMANIST THEOLOGY

Bibliography

Foerst, Anne. "Cog: A Humanoid Robot, and the Question of the Image of God." *Zygon* 33 (1998): 91-111.

Harding, Sandra. *Whose Science? Whose Knowledge? Thinking from Women's Lives.* Ithaca, N.Y.: Cornell University Press, 1991.

Hassan, Riffat. "Challenging the Stereotypes of Fundamentalism: An Islamic Feminist Perspective." *The Muslim World* 91, nos. 1/2 (2001): 55-69.

Howell, Nancy R. *A Feminist Cosmology: Ecology, Solidarity, and Metaphysics.* Amherst, N.Y.: Humanity Books/Prometheus Books, 2000.

Johnson, Elizabeth. *Women, Earth and Creator Spirit.* New York: Paulist Press, 1993.

LaCugna, Catherine, ed. *Freeing Theology: The Essentials of Theology in Feminist Perspective.* San Francisco: Harper, 1993.

McFague, Sallie. *Metaphorical Theology.* Minneapolis, Minn.: Fortress Press, 1997.

Pederson, Ann. *Where in the World Is God? Variations on a Theme.* St. Louis, Mo.: Chalice Press, 1998.

Plaskow, Judith. *Standing Against Sinai: Judaism from a Feminist Perspective.* San Francisco: Harper, 1991.

ANN PEDERSON

FIELD

The term *field* designates a variety of different, closely related concepts in mathematics and physics that have been carried over into everyday language to designate a context or region of influence. In geometry a field is a function that is defined (i.e., has values) at every point of a manifold (smooth continuous surface). Similarly, in physics a field (e.g., an electric, magnetic, or gravitational field) is a function describing a physical quantity (e.g., electric, magnetic, or gravitational influence or forces) at all points of a region of space and time. Sometimes the region that is under the influence of an electric, magnetic, gravitational, or other source or agent is also referred to as a field. A similar and almost equivalent definition of a field in physics, especially in contemporary physics, is as a continuous dynamical system, or a dynamical system with infinite degrees of freedom. Fields are essential to the description of physical phenomena, particularly of the interaction between particles or other physical entities, and to the quantitative and qualitative modeling of forces, especially those that act at a distance without any medium.

See also FIELD THEORIES; GRAVITATION; PHYSICS, QUANTUM

WILLIAM R. STOEGER

FIELD THEORIES

Most of classical and quantum physical phenomena are fundamentally described and explained in terms of fields, such as the electromagnetic and gravitational fields. These physical entities are not localized objects or particles, they generally vary in time, and they are defined at every point in space. They represent the influence, or force, an object or particle would experience at each point in space, at the time indicated. These fields are represented mathematically by functions of space and time. Field theories are the systematic theoretical mathematical-physical descriptions and elaborations of these fields, including their generation, detection, behavior, and relationships with one another and with other physical entities, such as particles. Generally, field theories are expressed in terms of partial differential equations that describe the relation of the fields to the entities that cause, or source, the fields.

There are also energy and momentum conservation equations that further constrain the fields, as well as the closely related equations of motion, which describe how particles or objects move at every point under the influence of the fields. All of these equations are generally derivable from a very special function, called a *Lagrangian,* which gives the kinetic energy minus the potential energy of the entire system. The behavior of the system described by the field equations and the equations of motion is always given by an *extremum* (maximum or minimum) of the Lagrangian action.

In physics there are four basic interactions, or forces: electromagnetism, the strong nuclear interaction, the weak nuclear interaction, and gravity.

All of these are represented by fields, and their description, generation, behavior, and associated phenomena are treated and explained by field theories. As just indicated, these fields are generated by sources. For example, an electric field has charge as its source, and a magnetic field has a magnetized object or a current as its source. A gravitational field is generated by anything that has mass-energy. As also mentioned, these fields can be time-varying and they can propagate. Time-varying, propagating fields are often referred to as *waves,* or *radiation.* Thus, we have electromagnetic radiation—light, X-rays, radio-waves—which are really time varying electromagnetic fields. Similarly, a gravity wave or gravitational radiation is a time-varying gravitational field, or the time-varying, propagating changes of curvature through space. Fields also have particles associated with them, both those that function as sources and those that are quanta of their waves (photons for electromagnetic waves and gravitons for gravitational waves). These *bosons* (integer-spin particles) are the force carriers of their respective fields between other particles, or distributions of particles, usually those that constitute matter (half-integer spin particles, like quarks, protons, neutrons, and electrons—the *fermions*).

Finally, at the highest energies, these four fundamental interaction fields probably undergo unification. That is, they become indistinguishable from one another at very high energies. At a relatively low energy, equivalent to a temperature of 10^{15} K (kelvin), the electromagnetic and the weak nuclear interaction become indistinguishable—the electroweak interaction.

Electroweak unification has been securely demonstrated and described; this theoretical achievement is due to Stephen Weinberg and Abdus Salam. At a much higher energy (equivalent to 10^{27} K) the electroweak interaction and strong interaction unify in the Grand Unified Theory (GUT) interaction, and this in turn probably unifies with gravity at an energy equivalent to 10^{32} K, above which is the realm of quantum gravity and quantum cosmology. As of 2002, there was no theory adequately describing these last two levels of unification, nor were there experiments and observations unequivocally requiring them. However, there has been very promising theoretical and experimental progress made on both fronts. If and

when total unification of all four fundamental interactions is attained this will complete the unification program that began with James Clerk Maxwell's brilliant unification of the electric and magnetic fields in 1864.

The early history of field theory

The concept of a field first appeared in hydrodynamics in the treatment of continuous media, such as fluids. Many mathematical physicists of the seventeenth and eighteenth centuries treated fluids or continuous bodies by dividing them up into small volumes or elements, but it was John Bernoulli who in 1732 first wrote down the equations of motion for these elements, considering them as point particles. Using this approach, Leonard Euler fashioned hydrodynamics into a field theory by modeling the motion of a fluid by giving its velocity at each point in the fluid, and using partial differential equations of these velocity components as functions of time and of the spatial coordinates. In doing this, the molecular structure of the fluid was neglected and it was treated as a continuum, with key parameters being determined at every point. This enabled researchers to describe the transmission of effects through the fluids. Somewhat later the more challenging problem of the propagation of displacements in solids, where elastic forces are prominently involved, was tackled. This was adequately solved by George Stokes in 1845.

Thus, field theory first emerged to describe the behavior of a continuous medium. There was at that time a different set of important physical phenomena (gravity, and electric and magnetic attraction and repulsion), which seemed to involve action at a distance. In these cases, such as in Isaac Newton's theory of gravity, it was assumed that there was no medium transmitting these interactions and that their effects occurred instantaneously. During the nineteenth century, due to the work of Joseph-Louis Lagrange, Pierre-Simon Laplace, and Siméon-Denis Poisson, the action at a distance in these cases began to be considered somewhat like a field, but without the presence of a fluid or a medium. In the case of gravity, for instance, the force of attraction at any location outside of a massive body can be designated in terms of what a point test mass would experience at each of those coordinate positions. This can be expressed in terms of the gravitational potential V at each position, which satisfies the well known second-order differential equations of Laplace (empty space) or Poisson (nonempty space). Thus, both the gravitational force and the gravitational potential are fields. As such, they are no longer properties of discernable matter, but of empty space itself.

Despite its representation by a potential field, gravity continued to be considered an action at a distance throughout the nineteenth century because the gravitational potential could not be associated with any discernable medium. The propagation of gravitational effects was not affected by any material changes in the intervening space; it appeared instantaneous, no mechanical model for the action of a medium could be conceived, nor could any energy be located between the gravitationally interacting bodies. It was only in the early twentieth century, with the advent of Albert Einstein's General Relativity (his theory of gravity), that gravitation became recognized as a field theory in the strict physical sense. Electromagnetism, in contrast, began to be considered as a genuine field-theory in the nineteenth century, precisely because it clearly fulfilled these same criteria.

Classical field theory

It was Michael Faraday who in the mid-nineteenth century first showed that action at a distance provides an inadequate description of electric and magnetic phenomena. His studies convinced him that electrical and magnetic influences propagated through a medium and not at a distance. The basic idea is that of a "continuous action" of forces filling space, not of a continuous mechanical action. Faraday's diagrams of lines of force originating in and returning to conductors and magnets stimulated Baron Kelvin (William Thomson) and Maxwell to formulate electromagnetic behavior in terms of fields. In comparing gravitational forces with electromagnetic forces, however, Faraday was unable to extend to gravity his arguments for propagation through a medium. Thus, Newtonian gravity continued to be considered by most, from a physical point of view, to be an "action at a distance" theory.

Faraday's key insights concerning electromagnetism were confirmed by Kelvin, who in the 1840s was able to show that the same mathematical formulae could be used to describe fluid and heat flow, electrical and magnetic behavior, and elastic

behavior. Kelvin thus established the important analogies among all five classes of phenomena, as well as that representing electric and magnetic phenomena by lines of force was consistent with their inverse-square falloff. Both Kelvin and Maxwell were careful not to draw conclusions about the reality of physical media from these detailed mathematical analogies. However, once Maxwell had formulated his highly successful electromagnetic field equations, which really provide a detailed quantitative unified description of electrical and magnetic phenomena, he and other physicists began to interpret these fields as a form of matter, so much so that matter in the usual sense gradually came to be looked upon in terms of fields, rather than vice versa. This was especially true once it was clear from Maxwell's theory that propagation of electromagnetic fields is not instantaneous and that electromagnetic energy, which can be transformed into other forms of energy, is contained in the fields themselves. Maxwell also succeeded in associating momentum with the electromagnetic field, and the physicist John Henry Poynting later developed the concept of energy-flux, and showed that this applied in a concrete way to electromagnetic fields and electromagnetic radiation. These developments have all contributed to supporting the conception of electromagnetic fields as a genuine form of matter, and they presaged the discoveries in Special Relativity that mass and energy are equivalent, and later in relativistic quantum theory that all forms of matter are fundamentally interacting fields. Maxwell's theory was the first fully successful and complete field theory, and remains the best example of a classical field theory.

The influence of Special and General Relativity

Along with Maxell's electromagnetic theory, Special and General Relativity strongly reinforced the usefulness and strength of the field-theory perspective, and even the realistic physical interpretations given to fields. The formulation and confirmation of Special Relativity have been especially influential in effecting this. Besides the discovery of mass-energy equivalence, mentioned above, perhaps the most influential event was the 1887 experiment by Albert Michelson and Edward Morley, the most compelling interpretation of which held that "the ether" does not exist and that therefore the velocity of light is constant with respect to any inertial frame (any coordinate system moving at a constant velocity). Thus, there is no absolute standard of rest. Moreover, there is no medium needed for electromagnetic fields to propagate. The fields themselves are fundamental and are, in a sense, their own media. Furthermore, since nothing propagates instantaneously, there are no perfectly rigid bodies or incompressible fluids, as envisioned in Newtonian mechanics. These are idealizations that, strictly speaking, are never realized. What is most impressive is that Maxwell's electromagnetic field theory turns out to be completely consistent with Special Relativity and can be explicitly formulated as such (in Lorentz-invariant fashion) in a natural and straightforward way. This confirms the insights that fields are a basic form of matter and that they are integral and indivisible.

Newton's theory of gravity was not generally looked upon as a field theory in the same way electromagnetism was, but rather as an "action at a distance" theory. Einstein changed that. In formulating his theory of gravitation, he fundamentally conceived space and time as fields that obey field equations, connecting space and time with the mass-energy distribution that they "contain." These space and time fields are the components of the metric tensor that makes space-time measurements possible. They are like, and in fact replace, the gravitational potential of Newton, but they are not defined in a pre-existing background space-time. They *are* the space-time. And this space-time is, in general, not flat but curved, depending on the density and pressure of the mass-energy on the space-time manifold, including all nongravitational (e.g., electromagnetic) fields. As a result, light rays (electromagnetic radiation) and freely moving particles follow the geodesics in curved space-time. Gravity is no longer conceived as a force, strictly speaking, but rather as the curvature of space-time. And light is affected by this curvature, unlike in Newtonian gravitational theory. This is consistent also from the point of view that light possesses energy, which is equivalent to mass, according to Special Relativity. Through observations of the bending and the red-shifting of light rays in gravitational fields, as well as through other observations (including the evidence for the existence of black holes), General Relativity has been impressively confirmed. General Relativity also predicts the existence of gravitational radiation—the propagation, at the speed of light, of variations in the curvature of space-time. This has been indirectly detected. And there is a massive effort to detect these gravity waves directly.

Quantum mechanics and quantum field theory

One of the great accomplishments of twentieth-century physics was the development and experimental confirmation of quantum theory. This began with failures of classical physics to account for the stability of atoms, the photoelectric effect, the explanation of the Planck blackbody spectrum, wave-particle duality, and the intrinsic uncertainties in certain types of measurements. Essentially, it became clear that physical reality, at its most fundamental level, could not be modeled in a continuous way, but only in terms of discrete quanta of energy, angular momentum, spin, and so on. Furthermore, any measurement of a system automatically affects that system in some way, with the Uncertainty Principle always applying. In any quantum measurement, the outcome is never precisely predictable. The theory gives probabilities that any one of a set of possible outcomes will result from a given measurement. All of these issues have been more or less satisfactorily incorporated into quantum mechanics by Erwin Schrödinger, Werner Heisenberg, and others. Paul Dirac properly formulated quantum mechanics within the framework of Special Relativity, yielding relativistic quantum mechanics. As such, in both these formulations, quantum mechanics is not a field theory, but rather a quantum theory of discrete bodies and individual particles in their interactions with one another.

Relativistic quantum mechanics, however, is plagued by a serious problem: it allows for negative-energy states, which would seem to predict an infinite series of decays. It turns out that this problem can be solved only by moving from consideration of single particles to indefinitely many particles. This automatically leads us to consider quantum fields as fundamental, with the particles being localized realizations (modes or quanta) associated with these fields. The result is the development of the extraordinarily successful quantum field theory. The fundamental structure of physical reality has come to be understood in terms of the interaction of these quantum fields, some of which are bosonic, or force-carrying, and some which are fermionic, or particle-constituting.

As mentioned at the beginning, there is strong evidence that at higher and higher energies or temperatures the four fundamental field interactions (electromagnetism, the strong and weak nuclear interactions, and gravity) unify step by step, and become indistinguishable. There are still many unknown details and challenges in constructing a completely adequate unified field theory and in explaining some of the features that physical reality manifests, particularly with respect to the quantum connections between gravity and space-time, as well as gravity and the other three interactions. But quantum field theory as it is understood in the early twenty-first century provides an impressive and reliable, though provisional and incomplete, description and guide to how reality at its most fundamental levels is constituted and behaves.

Relevance to the religion-science dialogue

The principal relevance of field theory to the religion-science dialogue is that it gives a reliable, well tested, and nearly comprehensive account of how reality is put together at its most fundamental levels. It also ultimately sheds light, through its applications in cosmology, on how the universe evolved from an extremely hot, homogeneous, simple, and undifferentiated quantum-dominated state to its present cool, lumpy, complex, and highly differentiated state. This strongly constrains theology in speaking about how creation occurred and about how God acts in creating and in sustaining what has been created. The relationships, processes, interactions, and regularities described by field theory—the laws of nature and physics—must be acknowledged to play a key role as channels of God's creative ordering power in reality. The concept of dynamic interacting fields, along with the auxiliary concepts and phenomena connected with them, can also provide analogies that can be employed in constructive theological programs.

See also FIELD; GRAND UNIFIED THEORY; GRAVITATION; PHYSICS, QUANTUM; RELATIVITY, GENERAL THEORY OF; RELATIVITY, SPECIAL THEORY OF

Bibliography

Auyang, Sunny Y. *How Is Quantum Field Theory Possible?* Oxford: Oxford University Press, 1995.

Berkson, William. *Fields of Force: The Development of a World View from Faraday to Einstein.* New York: Wiley, 1974.

Hesse, Mary B. *Forces and Fields: The Concept of Action at a Distance in the History of Physics.* London: Thomas Nelson and Sons, 1961.

Landau. L. D., and Lifshits, E. M. *Classical Theory of Fields.* Oxford and New York: Pergamon, 1971.

Lorrain, Paul, and Corson, Dale R. *Electromagnetism: Principles and Applications.* San Francisco: W. H. Freeman, 1978.

Peskin, Michael E., and Schroeder, Daniel V. *An Introduction to Quantum Field Theory.* Reading, Mass.: Addison-Wesley, 1995.

Raymond, Pierre. *Field Theory: A Modern Primer,* 2nd edition. Reading, Mass.: Addison-Wesley, 1990.

Ryder, Lewis H. *Quantum Field Theory,* 2nd edition. Cambridge, UK: Cambridge University Press, 1996.

Sachs, Mendel. *The Field Concept in Contemporary Science.* Springfield, Ill.: Thomas, 1973.

Sen, D. K. *Field and/or Particle.* London and New York: Academic Press, 1968.

Williams, L. Pearce. *The Origins of Field Theory.* New York: Random House, 1966.

WILLIAM R. STOEGER

FITNESS

Fitness is a measure of the relative performance or adaptedness of an organism represented by its genotype in a given environment. The term *fitness* is sometimes also used to describe other biological units, such as the gene or the population. Classically *fitness* is used to describe differences in survival (viability selection as described by Charles Darwin (1809–1882) with the phrase "survival of the fittest"), mating success (sexual selection), and reproductive output (fecundity selection) between individuals characterized by their genotypes and measured as their relative contribution to the next generation in terms of the number of offspring a genotype succeeds in producing and rearing to sexual maturity. A genotype that leaves more offspring will thus have a higher fitness.

In the field of classical population genetics theory, evolutionary changes are exemplified by the change in gene frequency at a single gene locus with two alleles, *A1* and *A2*, in a diploid organism. The modes of selection depend on the fitness of the heterozygote *A1A2* compared to that of the homozygotes *A1A1* and *A2A2*. If one homozygote (e.g., *A1A1*) has the highest fitness, directional selection will favor that genotype and eventually lead to fixation of allele *A1*. A famous example of directional selection is the industrial melanism of the peppered moth (*Biston bitularia*) in England, where the black or melanic morph increased in frequency after the industrial revolution, then decreased in the 1950s when "smokeless zones" were established and tree trunks became lighter, thus giving the black morph a disadvantage due to increased risk of predation by birds.

If the heterozygote has the highest fitness, stabilizing selection or heterozygote advantage will usually maintain both alleles in the population (an example is variation at the beta–globin gene in humans, where heterozygotes have an advantage in regions with malaria, while one type of homozygotes gets sickle cell disease), while heterozygote disadvantage will lead to disruptive selection favoring both homozygotes. This simple theory was developed for one locus in infinite populations and for constant fitness coefficients by, among others, R. A. Fisher (1890–1962) and J. S. B. Haldane (1892–1964) in the 1920s and 1930s. The theory was later modified and expanded to include multiple loci and variable environments, as well as population substructure and finite populations.

The shifting balance theory of Sewall Wright (1889–1988) describes the fitness landscape of more complex multilocus genotypes, where the fitness of certain genotypes has local peak values, while simple changes in genotype will lead to a fitness decrease. Shifts from one peak to another in that landscape require more complex changes with intermittent genotypes of reduced fitness. In small populations random genetic drift may counteract the selective forces that are driven by fitness differences and push populations from one peak to another.

Darwin considered fitness to be a property of the individual; later biologists sometimes use the term to refer to lower levels of organization, such as, for example, a property of the gene (the idea of the selfish gene is based on this unit) or of higher levels, such as, for example, the population. So-called group selection is based on higher units, and the concept of inclusive fitness includes contributions of related individuals who share genes. This concept of fitness has been used to explain the evolution of altruistic behaviors, such as warning calls in birds, which may bring the altruistic individual to higher risk but may benefit its genes by improving the chance of survival of relatives.

See also ADAPTATION; ALTRUISM; EVOLUTION; SELECTION, LEVELS OF; SELFISH GENE; SOCIOBIOLOGY

Bibliography

Darwin, Charles. *On the Origin of Species by Means of Natural Selection or the Preservation of Favored Races in the Struggle for Life.* London: Murray, 1859.

Haldane, J. B. S. *The Causes of Evolution.* Green, New York: Longmans, 1932.

Fisher, R. A. *The Genetical Theory of Natural Selection.* Oxford, UK: Clarendon Press, 1930.

Wright, Sewall. "Evolution in Mendelian Populations." *Genetics* 16 (1931): 97–159.

VOLKER LOESCHCKE

FORCES OF NATURE

The term "forces of nature" refers to the capabilities of the natural world that enable its various members to act on and interact with one another. Nature—the whole system of galaxies, stars, planets, and living things, along with the atoms and molecules of which they are composed—is interactive. Each of its parts interacts with its environment—both near and distant—and responds to the various forces acting on it. In current physics, these forces number four: the strong and weak nuclear forces, the electromagnetic force, and the gravitational force. In discussions relating science and religion, there is considerable interest in comparing or contrasting action by the forces of nature with divine action on the natural world.

See also DIVINE ACTION; GRAVITATION; LAWS OF NATURE; PHYSICS, PARTICLE

HOWARD J. VAN TILL

FOUNDATIONALISM

The term *foundationalism* usually refers to theories about the structure of belief formation or belief justification. Beliefs may be formed or justified in one of two ways: non-inferentially (immediately) or inferentially (mediately). The division between "basic" and "nonbasic" beliefs is asymmetrical; nonbasic beliefs are formed or justified by appealing to basic beliefs, which are foundational. For *classical* foundationalists, a basic belief must be self-evident or incorrigible. *Modest* foundationalists argue that meeting other criteria, such as "evident to the senses," may also qualify a belief as basic; further, basic beliefs can be defeasible. Foundationalists in the science-religion dialogue often focus on defending the propriety of basic beliefs and inferences from them.

See also NONFOUNDATIONALISM;
  POSTFOUNDATIONALISM

F. LERON SHULTS

FREEDOM

Freedom as understood in the modern West is self-determination by an autonomous being with a rational mind. Precursors to this understanding of freedom begin with Plato in ancient Greece, who shifted the locus of freedom from the political distinction between citizen and slave to the internal will that exercises influence on external events. Aristotle saw in the human will the capacity to harmonize itself with the will of God and the pursuit of the transcendent good and the good life.

Conceptions in Various Religious Traditions

In Hinduism and sister traditions such as Buddhism the doctrine of *karma* places the human person in a causal nexus of moral determinism where past life behavior determines present life status. Liberation (*moksha*) consists of being freed from the wheel of reincarnation, freed for eternity from the effects of karma. A variant of the dispute between grace and merit appears in Hinduism over the role of free human action in salvation. The cat school (*Tenkalai*) argues that God's irresistible grace saves the adept like a mother cat carries her young by the nape of the neck; whereas the monkey school (*Vatakalai*) argues that human free will is required in a way that a baby monkey is required to cling to its mother.

Islam teaches that God (Allah) is in control of the outcome of human acts, whether those acts are free or not. Human beings are free to choose between good and evil; the Qur'an teaches that God will judge mortals on the Last Day according to good and bad deeds. Some Muslims find comfort in predestination as a doctrine that affirms divine control over the course of events. "God leads astray whom he pleases and guides whom he pleases" (Surah 74:34). Human moral responsibility is not obviated by strong reliance upon divine control.

Freedom according to Christian theology belongs preeminently to God, who is absolutely free. God is the one, original, and authentic person through whose creative self-expression all other persons come into existence and are sustained. Human freedom derives from divine freedom, expressed as divine grace. God liberates Hebrew slaves from their Egyptian taskmasters and liberates faithful believers from the threat of sin, death, and the power of the devil. Christian advocates of predestination hold that human salvation is the result of free divine action, a gracious action that bestows eternal life as a gift rather than as a reward required by a legal structure of merit.

Commitment to belief in a single all-powerful God, which Christians share with Jews and Muslims, has led to three theological struggles over the nature of freedom that provide background to the contemporary conversation with science. The first is the predestination controversy. Once it is accepted that human salvation is a gift of divine grace and not the product of human moral achievement, then the question arises: Why do some persons exhibit strong faith in God and others do not? Predestination answers this question by contending that God has eternally decreed that some individuals would be infallibly guided to saving faith and, thereby, to eternal salvation. Those who do not have faith either were not included in the eternal decree; or, according to the double predestination school, they were actually predestined to damnation. The import of predestination is to make salvation solely a product of divine action, not a matter of human freedom. Humans remain free on a daily basis to make routine choices, but their salvation is a matter of divine decree alone.

The second theological struggle focuses on divine power, on God's omnipotence. Once it is accepted that God is all-powerful, metaphysical questions arise regarding the application of omnipotence to causal efficacy. Is God the cause of all things? Of every event? Should we eliminate causal efficacy, contingency, and human action as factors in the created world? If so, is God responsible for evil and suffering? This tempts some to affirm a thoroughgoing predestination, a complete determinism; and to do so not as a corollary to grace but as an implication of omnipotence. The unspoken assumption is that of a fixed pie image of power in the universe: if God gets more power then human beings get less. The fixed pie assumption has led two contemporary theological schools to compromise divine omnipotence. Process theologians in the tradition of Alfred North Whitehead (1861–1947) deny divine omnipotence and proportionately increase the power that local human free decision-making has on the future. Similarly, certain classical theists adopt the Kabbalistic notion of *zimsum,* a primordial self-withdrawal on God's part to permit contingency in nature and freedom in human life. In this case, the self-restriction on God's part is voluntary; whereas for the process theologians it is metaphysically necessary. For both these schools of thought, power is finite and competitive; so to have room for human freedom some proportion of power must be denied to God.

The third struggle in theological conceptuality is to clarify how power begets power, and how freedom begets freedom. Rejected here is the assumption of a fixed pie of power. Rather, theologians influenced by Karl Barth (1886–1968) and liberation theologians posit that God is the absolutely free one and that divine freedom is contagious; when God exerts divine power, it liberates the creation. The creation of the universe from nothing, *creatio ex nihilo,* took an act of divine power; and God's continuing work of creation, *creatio continua,* is similarly an exertion of divine action in the world. Yet this is fully compatible with natural causation, contingency in events, and willful human action. The prayerful cry of petitionary prayer is for God to exert divine power to liberate us from natural disaster, disease, political oppression, or our personal bad habits.

The historical struggles over divine power and human freedom set the stage in Western history for the contemporary debate regarding the relationship of determinism to free will. Rather than see God as the opponent to human freedom, modern Westerners see the causal ubiquity of natural law playing this opposing role. The word 'determinism' refers to lack of contingency in natural events, lack of noncaused events; it is a philosophy deriving from scientific reductionism.

Contemporary definitions of freedom

In the contemporary discussion of freedom versus determinism raised by reductionism among natural scientists, four definitions of freedom are of interest to theologians. First, *political freedom* or liberty is understood as independence from external coercion by government power. Liberation movements pursue freedom to escape economic and cultural coercion as well as political restriction. Philosophies of political liberty usually presuppose belief in natural freedom applied to the individual. Second, *natural freedom* or freedom of the will is the ability of a rational mind to choose between alternatives and make decisions that lead to actions. The locus of natural freedom is the choosing self. This is the Enlightenment view of freedom as self-expression, self-determination, and self-pursuit of happiness. Choosing between good and bad things and acting voluntarily are attributes of an individual's free will. Third, *moral freedom* refers to what the disciples of Aristotle dubbed 'virtue,' the freedom gained when conforming one's life to a higher truth or higher good that transcends the choosing self. For Augustine of Hippo (354–430 C.E.) and Martin Luther (1483–1546) the human self, to be truly free, must be freed from being curved in upon itself; such freedom can come only from a bestowal of God's liberating grace. The Christian variant of moral freedom expresses itself in selfless love of neighbor. Fourth, *future freedom* is the release of human creativity through designing, engineering, organizing, and building in such a way as to influence future events. Freedom here consists of transcending the confines of past precedents and constraints.

Determinism in modern science

Determinism is a philosophical idea that may or may not be attached to a scientific understanding of natural law. The essence of the deterministic view is that natural law is exhaustive and total in its causal application. Once initial conditions are established, every event that follows is bound to happen as it does and in no other possible way. Nothing in nature is contingent; so no room exists for natural freedom or future freedom. Hard determinists hold that no human act of will is free, even if it appears so. Free will is a delusion. Soft determinists hold a version of compatibilism; they believe that human actions are physically caused, but room remains for exercise of free will.

The mechanistic model of the natural world bequeathed to modern science by Newtonian physics presents a closed causal nexus, an exhaustive nexus of events without contingency. If the laws of nature never go on holiday, then what follows is eighteenth-century philosopher David Hume's (1711–1776) repudiation of miracles as events that deviate from unbreakable laws. What also follows is the eclipse of freedom, both divine and human. What appears to be freedom in human experience must be reducible to lawful physical activity, and the appearance of freedom as something supraphysical or spiritual must be a delusion.

In the early twentieth century Newtonian mechanism in physics was replaced by quantum mechanics; determinism was replaced by indeterminism. The activity of the individual electron is contingent, unpredictable; it can be predicted only in statistical quanta. Some contemporary theologians such as Robert John Russell argue that indeterminism at the fundamental physical level is a necessary condition for human free will to appear at the psychological level. Some physicists repudiate indeterminism by posing the theory of many worlds, according to which every potential physical state becomes actual in one or another universe. This would in principle apply to every human state as well, eliminating natural freedom.

Near the end of the twentieth century, Newtonian mechanism reappeared in genetics and neuroscience. Genetic determinism—the widespread belief that human essence is found in DNA and that DNA is determinative of both traits and behavior—has indirect implications for freedom understood as political liberty. The cultural response to the Human Genome Project (initiated in 1990) in conjunction with controversies over gene patenting, cloning, and stem cells lead many to fear an alliance between big science and big money; it is the populist fear that a powerful invisible elite will make decisions regarding human evolutionary future that will release forces beyond the average person's control.

Neuroscience and cognitive theory prompt some philosophers to reduce psychological and cognitive processes to neuronal activity in the human brain. This has led to an alliance between genes and brains that seems to challenge natural freedom with ferocity. If DNA through neural activity turns out to govern behavior, then the genes would turn out to govern human choices. What appears to be a self who makes decisions would be reducible to a complex interaction of genes with environment. Genes might even be found responsible for predispositions to choose between what is moral and what is immoral. Crime and virtue would then be predetermined. No self would need to be transcended by moral freedom, because no self would exist in the first place.

Some opponents of genetic determinism argue for a two-part determinism, genes plus environment. Other opponents defending the Enlightenment doctrine of freedom as self-determination hold to a three-part determinism: genes, environment, and self. In the latter case, the self is an emergent entity not reducible to either genes or environment.

Future freedom is enhanced by the Promethean dimension of genetic determinism, according to which molecular biologists are gaining the knowledge and technology to alter the human germline in such a way as to influence directly the future of human evolution. This future freedom elicits anxiety on the part of many people, because it raises specters of Frankenstein the mad scientist who lets evil loose on society. Those fearing Promethean pride on the part of scientists try to curtail research by saying, "thou shalt not play God." This warning appeals to something allegedly essential or sacred in nature prior to technological intervention; so the commandment against playing God is an attempt to avoid violating nature by legislating against future freedom.

Freedom in theology and science

The commandment against playing God in secular society shares the assumption made by some theologians that there is a fixed pie of power in the universe, that God's power competes with human power. These theologians believe that if God's power is restricted then human power is increased, thereby making human freedom possible. Those who forbid playing God in genetics or other scientific endeavors follow the opposite logic, namely, if human power is restricted then God is freer to act through natural processes.

The advantage for theologians in adopting either the process model or the *zimsum* model is that they can hold to a doctrine of divine creation while allotting to Big Bang cosmology and biological evolution principles such as deep time, contingency, self-organization, and development. The absence of divine power opens an arena within which a dialectic of regularity and chance governs natural occurrences. This is theologically significant because it solves the theodicy problem: suffering and evil on the part of sentient creatures is now the responsibility of self-organization through natural selection. God is exempt from responsibility for what goes wrong. Science and technology fill the hole vacated by God. God's absence makes natural freedom and future freedom possible.

The difficulty faced by theologians who cling to divine omnipotence is that nature's victims, such as the predator's prey or extinct species, must be judged to be part of God's plan. By allowing such waste and suffering, God risks being thought of as cruel. The theological advantage to omnipotence is that God is viewed as the very power by which development is energized and guided, leading the human race through scientific and medical discoveries toward taking control of its own health and wellbeing. God is viewed as the healer, the redeemer. Science and technology become liberating vocations, expanding the horizon of human freedom while imposing increased environmental responsibilities. God's presence makes natural freedom and future freedom possible.

Finally, reductionism raises the question of the status of the human self. Biologist Francis Crick (b. 1916) would eliminate any ontological status to the self or the soul, on the grounds that it is reducible to gene expression and neural firing patterns in our brain. Many who oppose a strict biological determinism substitute a two-part determinism, genes plus environment. In this case 'environment' can refer to the cytoplasm within the cell or to the food our parents place on our plate. Two-part determinism is just as eliminative of the human self or soul as is raw genetic determinism.

What most defenders of natural freedom actually advocate is three-part determinism: genes, environment, and self. The self functions as a determinant. The self can be thought of materialistically as an emergent property within evolutionary development; or it can be thought of metaphysically as a divinely imparted soul. It need not have any material substrate other than genes and environment; but its deliberations, decisions, and actions are observable and can be empirically confirmed.

See also DETERMINISM; FREE WILL DEFENSE

Bibliography

Adler, Mortimer J. *Six Great Ideas.* New York: Macmillan, 1981.

Barth, Karl. *Church Dogmatics.* New York: Scribner's, 1936-1962.

Cobb, John B., and Griffin, David Ray. *Process Theology: An Introductory Exposition.* Louisville, Ky.: Westminster/John Knox, 1976.

Crick, Francis. *The Astonishing Hypothesis: The Scientific Search for the Soul.* New York: Scribners, 1994.

Hartshorne, Charles. *The Divine Relativity.* New Haven, Conn.: Yale University Press, 1948.

Luther, Martin, "Freedom of A Christian." In *Luther's Works,* Vols. 31-55: Minneapolis, Minn.: Fortress, 1955-1986.

Marcoulesco, Ileana, "Free Will and Determinism." In *The Encyclopedia of Religion,* ed. Mircea Eliade: New York: Macmillan, 1987.

Moltmann, Jürgen. *The Coming God.* Minneapolis, Minn.: Fortress Press, 1996.

Peacocke, Arthur. *Theology for a Scientific Age.* Minneapolis, Minn.: Fortress Press, 1993.

Peters, Ted. *Playing God? Genetic Determinism and Human Freedom.* London and New York: Routledge, 1997.

Russell, Robert John; Murphy, Nancy; Meyering, Theo C.; and Arbib, Michael A., eds. *Neuroscience and the Person: Scientific Perspectives on Divine Action.* Vatican City State: Vatican Observatory; and Berkeley, Calif.: Center for Theology and the Natural Sciences, 1999.

Searle, John R. *The Mystery of Consciousness.* New York: New York Review of Books, 1997.

Taylor, Charles. *Sources of the Self.* Cambridge, Mass.: Harvard University Press, 1989.

TED PETERS

FREE PROCESS DEFENSE

Process theology's solution to the problem of evil derives from its conception of divine power. God cannot be held culpable for failing to prevent the occurrence of genuine evil because God cannot override, veto, or withdraw the freedom that creatures possess when committing evil. God's power entails the persuasion, never coercion, of free creatures. Conceiving of divine power in this way allows process theists to affirm divine love unequivocally. It also allows them to acknowledge the commonsense notion that some events occur that make the world a worse place than it might have been.

The free process defense originates from the philosophies of Alfred North Whitehead (1861–1947) and Charles Hartshorne (1897–2000). David Ray Griffin (1939–) has further developed and explained this defense. Scientist-theologians such as John Polkinghorne (1930–) and Arthur Peacocke (1924–) have been attracted to the process answer to the problem of evil, and each uses variations of it in his own work. In their view, God has chosen to let the world develop itself in a continual interplay with chance and the necessities embodied in the divinely installed laws of nature, in order for nature to explore its own potentialities. Thus understood, the free process defense is an extension of the free will defense.

See also EVIL AND SUFFERING; FREEDOM; FREE WILL DEFENSE; PROCESS THOUGHT; THEODICY; WHITEHEAD, ALFRED NORTH

Bibliography

Griffin, David Ray. *God, Power, and Evil: A Process Theodicy*. Philadelphia: Westminster, 1976.

Griffin, David Ray. *Evil Revisited: Responses and Reconsiderations*. Albany: State University of New York Press, 1991.

Inbody, Tyron L. *The Transforming God: An Interpretation of Suffering and Evil*. Louisville, Ky.: Westminster John Knox, 1997.

THOMAS JAY OORD

FREE WILL

See DETERMINISM; FREEDOM; FREE WILL DEFENSE

FREE WILL DEFENSE

The occurrence of evil, despite the existence of a perfectly loving and perfectly powerful God, poses a theoretical and existential problem. The Scottish philosopher David Hume (1711–1776) put the problem in the form of questions: "Is [God] willing to prevent evil, but not able? Then he is impotent. Is he able, but not willing? Then he is malevolent. Is he both able and willing? Whence then is evil?"

The free will defense solves the problem of evil by claiming that creatures have power to exert freely some control over their circumstances. Creatures can use freedom for good or evil; evil results from improper creaturely use of freedom. The free will defense solution to the problem of evil provides a basis for claiming that creatures, not God, are culpable for the genuine evil that occurs.

Accidental free will theism. Two general forms of the free will defense exist: *accidental free will theism* and *essential free will theism*. Accidental free will theism purports that although God essentially possesses all power as omnipotent, God voluntarily gives up power and becomes self-limited so that creatures might act freely. While creatures possess power for freedom on loan from God, this omnipotent God retains the capacity to veto (i.e., withdraw or override) this divinely given power. Accidental free will theists claim that God voluntary became self-limited at the creation of the universe as God bestowed the universe with the birthright of freedom. God grants freedom voluntarily in each present moment as the direct and constant source of power for all creatures. While God always uses divine power lovingly, creatures sometimes use God-derived power in evil ways.

Many forms of accidental free will theism have been proposed. Alvin Plantinga (1932–) advocates one form, in which he argues that although it is possible for an omnipotent God to create a world in which creatures are not free, a loving God would not create such a world. Instead, a loving God would create a world in which creatures have the opportunity to make genuinely free decisions among various morally conditioned options. Such a world is the best of all possible worlds that God could have created.

John Polkinghorne (1930–) and Arthur Peacocke (1924–) also advocate a form of accidental free will theism. The form they embrace, correlated to the Greek word *kenosis,* entails that God is self-emptied of some power in order for creatures to possess power for freedom. This self-limitation occurs because God lovingly desires others with which to relate and create. Some forms of accidental free will theism suppose that God's loving nature drives the divine desire for others to express freedom, even when the expression of creaturely freedom occasionally results in pain and suffering.

Critics of accidental free will theism argue that if God is omnipotent in every possible world, the best possible world that God would create would be one in which people invariably choose rightly. Other critics acknowledge that it may be logically possible that a perfectly loving and all-powerful God exists despite the occurrence of genuine evil, but the amount of evil makes the existence of such a God evidentially implausible. Perhaps the most severe criticism of accidental free will theism is that it does not explain why God does not prevent genuine evils. A God who is voluntarily self-limited ought to become un-self-limited occasionally, in the name of love, to veto the freedom expressed by perpetrators of genuine evil.

Essential free will theism. Essential free will theism, also known as the *free process defense,* views divine omnipotence as meaning that God is the most powerful being in existence, rather than possessing all power in the universe. This form of the free will defense speculates that all individuals necessarily posses some power that cannot be completely overridden, withdrawn, or vetoed by anyone, including God. Advocates of this position claim that culpability for genuine evil rests upon the shoulders of creatures that use their own power wrongly.

Process theist David Ray Griffin (1939–) posits a form of essential free will theism that entails that God is metaphysically unable to determine creaturely decisions unilaterally. Creatures possess self-determinative power that cannot be withdrawn or overridden by God, and the fact that individuals possess power for freedom is an eternal metaphysical law. God cannot circumvent these metaphysical laws of freedom, partly because God did not create them. God is not indictable for failing to prevent genuinely evil events from occurring because these metaphysical laws prevent God from removing power and freedom away from creatures who misuse freedom. Griffin's free will defense solves the problem of evil by denying that God is able to prevent genuinely evil occurrences resulting from free creaturely decisions.

The recurring criticism of Griffin's hypothesis ultimately derives from the claim that God did not create the metaphysical laws that govern actual existence. Most theists have assumed that part of what it means for God to be the creator is that God created the metaphysical laws that govern what it means for all things to exist. Griffin's process free will defense also envisions God as always relating to and creating from some realm of nondivine entities. This hypothesis undermines the classic Church doctrine of God's capacity voluntarily to create the world out of absolute nothingness (*creatio ex nihilo*).

Dialogue with science. Both the accidental and essential forms of the free will defense posit a theodicy that reinterprets the concept of divine omnipotence in light of creaturely freedom. Culpability of genuine evils is removed from a perfectly loving God and is placed upon creatures that have the ability to exert freely a degree of control over their circumstances. This reinterpretation of divine power and creaturely responsibility is profoundly important for the science and religion dialogue, partly because many atheists have chosen not to believe in the existence of God due to the problem of evil. If convinced by the free will defense that God can be considered perfectly loving despite the occurrence of evil, a platform may be secured for discussing other dialogue issues.

See also EVIL AND SUFFERING; FREEDOM; FREE PROCESS DEFENSE; KENOSIS; THEODICY

Bibliography

Davis, Stephen T., ed. *Encountering Evil: Live Options in Theodicy: A New Edition.* Louisville, Ky.: Westminster John Knox, 2001.

Griffin, David Ray. *God, Power, and Evil: A Process Theodicy.* Philadelphia: Westminster, 1976.

Griffin, David Ray. *Religion and Scientific Naturalism: Overcoming the Conflicts.* Albany: State University of New York Press, 1999.

Haught, John. *God After Darwin: A Theology of Evolution.* Boulder, Colo.: Westview Press, 2000.

Inbody, Tyron. *The Transforming God: An Interpretation of Suffering and Evil*. Louisville, Ky.: Westminster John Knox, 1997.

Moltmann, Jürgen. *The Crucified God: The Cross of Christ as the Foundation and Criticism of Christian Theology*. Minneapolis, Minn.: Fortress Press, 1993.

Peacocke, Arthur. *Theology for a Scientific Age: Being and Becoming—Natural, Divine, and Human*. Minneapolis, Minn.: Fortress Press, 1993.

Plantinga, Alvin. *God, Freedom and Evil*. Grand Rapids, Mich.: Eerdmans, 1983.

Polkinghorne, John. *The Faith of a Physicist*. Princeton, N.J.: Princeton University Press, 1994.

Polkinghorne, John. *Belief in God in an Age of Science*. New Haven, Conn.: Yale University Press, 1998.

Polkinghorne, John., ed. *The Work of Love: Creation as Kenosis*. Grand Rapids, Mich.: Eerdmans, 2001.

THOMAS JAY OORD
MATTHEW HENRY

FREUD, SIGMUND

Sigmund Freud, well known as the founder of psychoanalysis, was born in 1856 in Freiberg, Moravia. He moved with his family to Vienna, Austria, at the age of four. Freud received a thorough scientific training in his early years and went on to a distinguished career in scientific research, establishing himself as a leading neuropathologist. He made important contributions to the study of the *neuron* (nerve cell) and wrote influential treatises on aphasia and cerebral palsy. In his later career, Freud labored to establish psychoanalysis as a form of natural science. As a late representative of Enlightenment thinking, Freud joined the issue of the relation between science and religion most directly in his long drawn out debate with Oskar Pfister (1873–1956), a Swiss Lutheran pastor and his devoted friend of many years.

Debate with Pfister

The debate came to a head in Freud's writing of *The Future of an Illusion* (1927). Pfister took up the challenge and responded in a lengthy article, "The Illusion of the Future" (1928). The interchange was, in fact, the high point of a dialogue contained in letters exchanged over more than thirty years. The two men differed radically in their assessment of and attitudes toward religious experience and belief. Freud viewed religious beliefs as forms of illusion (if not delusion) and religious experience and practice as universal forms of obsessional neurosis. Freud continually presented himself to Pfister as an unbeliever, a "godless Jew" (1928, p. 170).

The analytic insistence on the resolution of transference, rather than the dependence (as he saw it) of religion on transference in the sense of emptional attachment and dependence, was central in Freud's assessment of religion. In 1928, Freud wrote to Pfister:

> The rift, not in analytic, but in scientific thinking which one comes on when the subject of God and Christ is touched on I accept as one of the logically untenable but psychologically only too intelligible irrationalities of life. . . . In contrast to utterances as psychologically profound as "Thy sins are forgiven thee; arise and walk," . . . if the sick man had asked: "How knowest thou that my sins are forgiven?" the answer could only have been: "I, the Son of God, forgive thee." In other words, a call for unlimited transference. And now, just suppose I said to a patient: "I, Professor Sigmund Freud, forgive thee thy sins." What a fool I should make of myself. To the former case, the principle applies that analysis is not satisfied with success produced by suggestion, but investigates the origin of and justification for the transference. (Meng and Freud, pp. 125–126)

Yet, Freud clearly envied the power of religion: "As for the possibility of sublimation to religion, therapeutically I can only envy you. But the beauty of religion certainly does not belong to psychoanalysis. It is natural that at this point in therapy our ways should part, and so it can remain" (Meng and Freud, p. 63).

Freud's argument in *The Future of an Illusion* was fairly straightforward. In opposition to nature, civilization exacts a heavy price in the form of instinctual renunciation. In addition to prohibitions and privations, imposed externally or internally by the superego, culture proposes certain ideals as its highest achievements. The satisfaction associated with such ideals is basically narcissistic. In this unending struggle between civilization and the forces of nature, religion serves to defend civilization against nature. Thus, "Man's self-regard, seriously menaced, calls for consolation; life and the universe must be robbed of their terrors; moreover his curiosity, moved, it is true, by the strongest practical interest, demands an answer" (1927, p. 16). In their hopelessness, mankind turn the forces of nature into gods with whom they can associate on relatively human terms. But this transformation follows the prototype of the original infantile state of helplessness in relation to one's parents. The gods thus are transformed fathers, who could be both feared and looked to as sources of protection against unknown dangers.

Religious ideas, therefore, are in essence illusions. They are enunciated as dogmatic teachings rather than as the product of experience or of argument and proof. As Freud proclaimed: "They are illusions, fulfillments of the oldest, strongest, and most urgent wishes of mankind. The secret of their strength lies in the strength of those wishes. As we already know, the terrifying impression of helplessness in childhood aroused the need for protection—for protection through love—which was provided by the father; and the recognition that this helplessness lasts throughout life made it necessary to cling to the existence of a father, but this time a more powerful one" (1927, p. 30). Religion, like obsessional neurosis in childhood, becomes a universal obsessional neurosis of humanity, arising out of the Oedipus complex, specifically out of the relationship to the father.

Science and religion

Freud's polemic against religion was cast in the form of a radical opposition between natural science and religion. Religion had failed in making the majority of people happy or, for that matter, in bringing them to a more moral condition of life. Rather it achieved little more than keeping them submissive to religious beliefs and practices. Freud attributed the decline of religion to the rise of natural science. He observed:

> We have heard the admission that religion no longer has the same influence on people that it used to. . . . And this is not because its promises have grown less, but because people find them less credible. Let

us admit that the reason—though perhaps not the only reason—for this change is the increase of the scientific spirit in the higher strata of human society. Criticism has whittled away the evidential value of religious documents, natural science has shown up the errors in them, and comparative research has been struck by the fatal resemblance between the religious ideas which we revere and the mental products of primitive peoples and times. (1927, p. 38)

Anticipating the grim vision later enunciated in *Civilization and Its Discontents* (1930), Freud painted a dire picture of the weakening of the influence of religion on the mass of people. He argued that incestuous and murderous passions would surge to the surface without the suppressive force of religious convictions—"If the sole reason why you must not kill your neighbor is because God has forbidden it and will severely punish you for it in this or the next life—then, when you learn that there is no God and that you need not fear His punishment, you will certainly kill your neighbor without hesitation, and you can only be prevented from doing so by mundane force" (1927, p. 39).

Freud's answer, of course, is to replace religion with science. Since religion has proven so deceitful, misguided, untrustworthy, and oppressive, humankind is obviously better off without it. Moreover, people can do without illusions, and the sooner they abandon their dependence on such infantile illusions, the better off they will be. Moreover, those who abandon such illusions are not without resources or assistance. Their scientific knowledge, which is increasing every day, gives them power to deal with and control their environment, to face the demands of harsh reality more effectively. And, Freud says, "as for the great necessities of Fate, against which there is no help, they will learn to endure them with resignation." (1927, p. 50)

Freud's reply to this imagined argument seems to lack conviction. Certainly, he says, no one has to tell him about the difficulty of avoiding illusions, and perhaps his own hopes, rooted in scientific methodology, are illusory too. But at least his illusions are not, like religious ones, incapable of correction. To that extent, they are not delusions, as religious convictions would be. Finally, he holds out some optimism that people can overcome and free themselves from their neurotic entanglements in virtue of better scientific knowledge, specifically psychoanalysis.

Freud stakes his modest claim for the superiority of the human intellect to religious beliefs:

We may insist as often as we like that man's intellect is powerless in comparison with his instinctual life, and we may be right in this. Nevertheless, there is something peculiar about this weakness. The voice of the intellect is a soft one, but it does not rest until it has gained a hearing. Finally, after a countless succession of rebuffs, it succeeds. . . . It will presumably set itself the same aims as those whose realization you expect from your God (of course within human limits—so far as external reality, "Ananke," allows it), namely the love of man and the decrease of suffering. (1927, p. 53)

In "The Illusion of the Future," Pfister summarized the Freudian viewpoint in one trenchant sentence: "The God, Logos, hurls the God of religion from the throne and reigns in the realm of necessity, about whose meaning we, in the meantime, do not know the least." (p. 172)

See also PSYCHOLOGY; PSYCHOLOGY OF RELIGION

Bibliography

Freud, Sigmund. *The Future of an Illusion* (1927). In *Standard Edition of the Complete Psychological Works of Sigmund Freud,* trans. and ed. James Strachey, Vol. 21. London: Hogarth Press, 1961.

Freud, Sigmund. "A Religious Experience" (1928). In *Standard Edition of the Complete Psychological Works of Sigmund Freud,* trans. and ed. James Strachey, Vol. 21. London: Hogarth Press, 1961.

Freud, Sigmund. *Civilization and Its Discontents* (1930). In *Standard Edition of the Complete Psychological Works of Sigmund Freud,* trans. and ed. James Strachey, Vol. 21. London: Hogarth Press, 1961.

Gay, Peter. *Freud: A Life for Our Time.* New York: Norton, 1988.

Irwin, J. E. G. "Pfister and Freud: The Rediscovery of a Dialogue." *Journal of Religion and Health* 12 (1973): 315–327.

Meissner, W.W. *Psychoanalysis and Religious Experience.* New Haven, Conn.: Yale University Press, 1984.

Meng, Heinrich, and Freud, Ernst L., eds. *Psychoanalysis and Faith: The Letters of Sigmund Freud and Oskar Pfister,* trans. Eric Mosbacher. New York: Basic Books, 1963.

Pfister, Oskar. "Die Illusion einer Zukunft" ("The Illusion of the Future"). *Imago* 14 (1928): 149–184; Available in English in *International Journal of Psychoanalysis* 74 (1993): 557–579.

WILLIAM. W. MEISSNER, S.J.

FUNCTIONALISM

Functionalism is a schema of explanation: All parts of a system fulfil a necessary, latent function for the system as a whole, its stable equilibrium (principle of homeostasis), or its survival. Functionalism, thus, is a descendant of earlier teleological or finalistic conceptions. It can be applied to nearly all complex systems, but functional explanations are not a unitary phenomenon across disciplines.

Functionalism in sociology

Stimulated by Auguste Comte (1798–1857), Herbert Spencer (1820–1903), and especially Emile Durkheim (1858–1917), and encouraged through the anthropologists Bronislaw Malinowski (1884–1942) and A. R. Radcliffe-Brown (1881–1955), functionalism became important in sociology. Specific structural-functional macro-theories, such as that proposed by Talcott Parsons, describe religious institutions, norms, and symbols with respect to their output on integration, legitimization, compensation, and socialization for the society as a whole, its equilibrium, or its survival. The function of religion is destined for its power of integration (e.g., Durkheim), its role to institutionalize cultural-social norms (Parsons), or its ability to cope with experiences of contingency and reducing complexity (Nikklas Luhman).

This functional conception of religion has been criticized with respect to the epistemological and cognitive status of religious notions, regardless of the contribution of religion to the survival of human cultures. In addition, though the notion of stable equilibrium in functional analysis enables one to define what is dysfunctional and allows the search for functional equivalents, it needs to be defined in its temporal context and can hardly cover social change; in other words, it was accused of being conservative. However, functionalists can easily dismiss this criticism: Contributing to an optimum is adaptive, not legitimate. Some functional theories do not even have a static or equilibrium bias (Luhmann). Modern (neo)functionalism (which takes cybernetic concepts into account), theories about the evolution of religion proposed by Robert Bellah (which mediate the structural-functional model and historic-genetic model of social evolution), and autopoietic systems theories like that of Luhmann all try to avoid this and other criticism mentioned below.

Functionalism in biology

The form of a functional explanation in biology is the same as in sociology: It explains the presence of a trait as solution to a hypothetical design problem to assure that the needs of the individual or group are satisfied. Functional explanations for the needs of the genes are especially popular in sociobiology. Intentions are not involved.

Controversies in sociology and biology roughly concern (1) evidence, (2) explanation, and (3) the selection question. First, opponents like Richard Lewontin argue that stories are being told in sociobiology that have little statistical evidence, are incomplete, and are not empirically testable. Functionalism is accused of "adaptive failure": Adaptiveness does not assure presence of a trait, and it does not give criteria for normality and empirical measures for survival. In the same vein, functionalism is accused of eliminating the truth-question: The issue is not whether the propositions are true or whether there is evidence for believing them to be true, but how holding beliefs is functional. Second, the issue of different levels of explanation is controversial: Is the gene level sufficient for sociobiological explanations? Or do also the individual or the group level have to be considered? Also, the relation of functional explanations to mere functional descriptions and to chemical, causal explanations is controversial. Third, functional explanations in biology do better than those in sociology, it is argued, because they offer an answer to the selection question, natural selection, whereas mechanisms for cultural selection have not been satisfactorily developed. Nevertheless, as Wolfgang Stegmüller posits, functional analysis can be logically correct, empirically substantial, and highly valuable as a heuristic research program. Despite

these controversies, (neo)functionalism dominated mainstream sociological and anthropological theories for most of the twentieth century. Functionalist approaches are also prominent in biology.

Functionalism in philosophy of mind

In contemporary philosophy of mind, functionalism is one of the most important theories. Developed in the 1960s by Hilary Putnam and Jerry Fodor, a wide range of different versions has been developed since. The basic thesis is: Mental states are functional states caused by external sensory inputs, causing external behavioral outputs, and causally related to other functional states. One function may be realized in different ways in different cases (multiple realizability). One can roughly distinguish between *common-sense or analytic functionalism,* which deals with meanings of mental vocabulary; *scientific, empirical, or psycho-functionalism,* in which neurobiology lays down the characteristics of functional roles of mental states; and *machine- or computer-functionalism,* where the relation of mind to brain is thought to be equivalent to the relation of software to hardware, usually excluding intentionality and teleology. This computer functionalism, supported by fruitful research on artificial intelligence, has been investigated by Putnam, as well as others, as a worthwhile reaction to a materialistic or physicalistic view of mind because it does not attribute mental states only to humans or living organisms with a similar central nervous system. Like functionalism in general, it hardly gives sufficient justice to qualitative phenomena.

Functionalism in science and religion

Functional approaches are also highly relevant to the science and religion dialogue, mainly in interpretations of ideas about nature and God. An approach that historians of science and religion like John H. Brooke have found useful is to ask what function theology plays within the sciences and vice versa. Religious belief can function as a presupposition of, or sanction for, science. Religious belief could even provide a motivation for science if one happened to believe that the more one uncovered of the intricacies of nature the greater the evidence of divine intelligence. Robert John Russell has even suggested that scientific research programs such as Big Bang Theory and Steady State

Theory have been motivated by religious respectively atheistic worldviews. Religion may also have reinforced aesthetic criteria, such as ideas of simplicity, elegance, and harmony in theory selection. The aim of a functional analysis is to uncover the uses to which natural theology was put, even in the fields of politics.

Ralph Wendell Burhoe's scientific theology is a functional approach to religion. Based upon writings of the sociologist Donald T. Campbell, Burhoe argues for a positively selected role for religion in the survival of cultures: Only religions can enable the shift from selfishness to altruistic behavior. He even argues for a continuing role for religion or a functional equivalent in the development and survival of human culture, proposing his scientific theology, which incorporates the scientific worldview. Critical reactions to this approach show that a functional approach to religion within a scientific framework has to be complemented by a functional approach to science within a religious or theological framework. This has been done by Philip Hefner from the point of view of a distinct theological anthropology. The integration of both concepts could have an even more liberating effect on the science and religion dialogue.

See also ARTIFICIAL INTELLIGENCE; MIND-BODY THEORIES; MIND-BRAIN INTERACTION; NEUROSCIENCES; TELEOLOGY

Bibliography

Abrahamson, Mark. *Functionalism*. Englewood Cliffs, N.J.: Prentice-Hall, 1978.

Alexander, Jeffrey C. *Neofunctionalism and After*. Malden, Mass., and Oxford, UK: Blackwell, 1998.

Block, Ned. "Art. Functionalism (2)." In *A Companion to the Philosophy of Mind,* ed. Samuel Guttenplan. Cambridge, Mass., and Oxford, UK: Blackwell, 1994.

Braddon-Mitchell, David, and Jackson, Frank. *Philosophy of Mind and Cognition*. Oxford, UK, and Cambridge, Mass.: Blackwell, 1996.

Brooke, John, and Cantor, Geoffrey. *Reconstructing Nature: The Engagement of Science and Religion*. Edinburgh, UK: T&T Clark, 1998.

Burhoe, Ralph Wendell. *Toward a Scientific Theology*. Belfast, Northern Ireland: Christian Journals Limited, 1981.

Hefner, Philip. *The Human Factor: Evolution, Culture, and Religion*. Minneapolis, Minn.: Fortress Press, 1993.

Kincaid, Harold. "Functionalism Defended." In *Philosophical Foundations of the Social Sciences: Analyzing Controversies in Social Research*. Cambridge, UK: Cambridge University Press, 1996.

Lycan, William G. "Art: Functionalism (1)." In *A Companion to the Philosophy of Mind,* ed. Samuel Guttenplan. Cambridge, Mass., and Oxford, UK: Blackwell, 1994.

Meisinger, Hubert. "Christian Love and Biological Altruism." *Zygon* 35 (2000) 745–782.

Putnam, Hilary. *Representation and Reality*. Boston: MIT Press, 1988.

Root, Michael. *Philosophy of Social Science: The Methods, Ideals, and Politics of Social Inquiry*. Oxford, UK, and Cambridge, Mass.: Blackwell, 1993.

Richardson, W. Mark, and Russell, Robert John. *Science and the Spiritual Quest: New Essays by Leading Scientists*. London and New York: Routledge, 2002.

Sober, Elliott, and Wilson, David Sloan. *Unto Others: The Evolution and Psychology of Unselfish Behavior*. Cambridge, Mass.: Harvard University Press, 1998.

Stegmüller, Wolfgang. *Probleme und Resultate der Wissenschaftstheorie und Analytischen Philosophie*. Vol. 1: *Erklärung, Begründung, Kausalität,* 2nd edition. New York, Heidelberg, and Berlin: Springer, 1993.

Turner, Jonathan H., and Maryanski, Alexandra. *Functionalism*. Menlo Park, Calif.: Benjamin Cummings, 1979.

HUBERT MEISINGER

FUNDAMENTALISM

Two sets of complex ways by which contemporary people look at reality coexist and often clash. The code word most frequently used for one set of views is *fundamentalism*. The other is referred to as *science,* as in "the scientific worldview." Science has developed over many centuries and has taken different forms since at least ancient Egypt, Greece, and Rome. At its heart are notions such as these: Scientists must be able to observe cause and effect, and they must be able to replicate experiments to test their validity. Such notions have to do with methods and serve mainly practical purposes.

It happens, however, that many scientists and science theorists become so engrossed in the method and its many positive results that they see it as an all-purpose explanation of the world. Anything that cannot be subjected to the cause-and-effect approach is suspect. Almost inevitably, habits of attention to science become preoccupying. More than a few devotees of the scientific worldview come to regard it as exclusive. Any alternatives that challenge it have to be refuted or repudiated.

The term *fundamentalism* was first applied to Protestants in the United States in the 1920s, but it now represents a set of phenomena that can be observed in most cultures where religion has influence and especially in cultures where religion dominates. Fundamentalism is almost always associated with religion, but some scholars also see it as an outlook on life that can characterize the nonreligious as well. In fact, some theological scholars claim that those who are devoted without question to the scientific worldview sometimes approach it as uncritically as most scientists see religious fundamentalists defending their worldviews.

If the word *fundamentalism* was coined in the twentieth century, it must have been needed to describe a new reality. By common consent, the word points to phenomena different from what is suggested by the related words *conservatism, traditionalism,* or *orthodoxy.* The difference lies chiefly in the fact that fundamentalism is reactive. Its defenders "fight back" against what they feel might undercut or assault what they believe. Such fundamentalism is especially present in the "religions of the book": Christianity, Islam, and, to a lesser extent, Judaism. Fundamentalism is present in other forms in Buddhism and Hinduism, but the lines between religion and science are drawn differently in these traditions.

Religions of the book also speak of cause and effect. In their case, the cause is philosophy's "First Cause," which translates into "God." The means of producing effect is the revelation of God through prophets, events, and a sacred book. It is difficult for devotees of the book to subject it to experiment. How does one "replicate" the creation of the world or the presence of prophets who profess to speak about realities that are not testable in the laboratory? How does one "repeat" events that belong to faith, such as the resurrection of a God-Man or a journey into the heavens by a prophet Muhammad on his horse?

Ordinarily people can live with the two worldviews, which do not always have to be seen as competing. Religion can address some aspects of life and science can address others. But fundamentalists have great difficulty picturing how the two worldviews can coexist in the same mind and the same culture. To fundamentalists, one worldview must be right and the other wrong. One is of God and the other is anti-God, perhaps of Satan.

Fundamentalists react or fight back against threats to their communities, traditions, and ways of life. Usually the term for what they attack is *modernization* and all that goes with it. Fundamentalism took shape in countering the assaults of what modernity brings. Not to fight back is to play into the hands of God's enemy and to see the possible destruction of all that one believes.

Technology provides the most profound impact of modernization among citizens around the globe and in all the religions. Technology might include mass communication, rapid means of travel, highly developed weaponry, and the like. With it may come social arrangements that disrupt community. In the modern world, guided by technology, people migrate and spread alien ideas in traditional cultures. While many adapt, fundamentalists say their adherents dare not.

Paradoxically, however, most fundamentalists are very comfortable with technology. Jewish fundamentalists in Gush Emunim in Israel have highly proficient weapons and systems of communication. The modern revolutionary Islamic movements, from that of the Ayatollah Khomeini in Iran in the 1970s to the al-Qaeda terrorists in Wahhabi Islam at the beginning of the twenty-first century, have exploited technologies from tape recordings to the Internet. In the United States, Christian fundamentalist broadcasters are much more effective in the use of technical media than are their nonfundamentalist competitors.

What has happened? Is there, in fact, compatibility between two worldviews that were opposed root and branch? As one studies Islamic and Christian fundamentalisms, it becomes clear that the leaders are able to separate the practical instruments of technology from the scientific theories and experiments that made them possible.

This does not mean that all fundamentalists oppose all science. Many are, in fact, experts in hard sciences. The largely fundamentalist American movement called *creation science* includes people with Doctor of Philosophy degrees, often in the hard sciences where "facts" are determinative. They might accept but one miracle: That their book is the utterance of God. From there on, they will draw "facts" from the sacred book and approach those facts the way they would approach species in biology.

Islamic and other non-Western fundamentalists aim their reactionary efforts against the West, which is the source of so much science and the philosophy of science. The West is seen as the intrusive agent that has exported science and made the non-West dependent upon its hated alternative. And the science that comes from the West tends to arrive with trappings, which may include scientists and technicians who ignore or have disdain for religion. In a world that is gradually being dominated by technology, whether in medicine, opinion formation, or weaponry, the fundamentalist rejection of science is seen as dangerous among moderate coreligionists or people of secular mentality.

Cultures dominated by fundamentalism may eventually be able to overcome suspicion and retrieve from their heritage the variety of approaches that helped them lead in science, as was the case with medieval Islam. Until then, it will remain necessary for regimes dominated by fundamentalists to borrow some coveted features of scientific development, such as modern medicine. Whether such regimes can remain players on the global scene and serve their constituents without developing their own scientific research traditions is a fateful question both for fundamentalist-ruled nations and those who experience the dangerous expressions of their reaction.

See also CHRISTIANITY, EVANGELICAL, ISSUES IN SCIENCE AND RELIGION; CREATIONISM; CREATION SCIENCE

Bibliography

Antoun, Richard T. *Understanding Fundamentalism: Christian, Islamic, and Jewish Movements.* Walnut Creek, Calif.: Altamira, 2001.

Bassam Tibi. "The Worldview of Sunni Arab Fundamentalists: Attitudes toward Modern Science and Technology." In *Fundamentalisms and Society: Reclaiming the Sciences, the Family, and Education,* ed. Martin E. Marty and R. Scott Appleby. Chicago: University of Chicago Press, 1993.

Farhang Rajaee. "Islam and Modernity: The Reconstruction of an Alternativbe Shi'ite Islamic Worldview in Iran." In *Fundamentalisms and Society: Reclaiming the Sciences, the Family, and Education,* ed. Martin E. Marty and R. Scott Appleby. Chicago: University of Chicago Press, 1993.

James Moore. "The Creationist Cosmos of Protestant Fundamentalism." In *Fundamentalisms and Society: Reclaiming the Sciences, the Family, and Education,* ed. Martin E. Marty and R. Scott Appleby. Chicago: University of Chicago Press, 1993.

Lindberg, David C., and Numbers, Ronald L., eds. *God and Nature: Historical Essays on the Encounter between Christianity and Science.* Berkeley: University of California Press, 1986.

Mendelsohn, Everett. "Religious Fundamentalism and the Sciences." In *Fundamentalisms and Society: Reclaiming the Sciences, the Family, and Education,* ed. Martin E. Marty and R. Scott Appleby. Chicago: University of Chicago Press, 1993.

Moore, James. *The Post-Darwinian Controversies: A Study of the Protestant Struggle to Come to Terms with Darwin in Great Britain and America, 1870-1900.* Cambridge, UK: Cambridge University Press, 1991.

MARTIN E. MARTY

GAIA HYPOTHESIS

Gaia is the name of the Greek goddess of the Earth. The Gaia hypothesis is that the Earth is more worthy of the respect and reverence once shown to Gaia than modern people have supposed. According to this hypothesis, the Earth is a self-regulating system, of which humans are an unruly part. In particular, the organisms on the Earth's surface play a major role in determining the composition of the atmosphere to ensure that it is favorable to life. Some proponents judge from the scientific evidence that the Earth has its own intelligence and depict it in almost personal, quasi-divine, terms. This provides religious support for concern about particular features of the global ecosystem.

See also ANIMAL RIGHTS; BIOLOGICAL DIVERSITY; DEEP ECOLOGY; ECOFEMINISM; ECOLOGY; ECOLOGY, ETHICS OF; ECOLOGY, RELIGIOUS AND PHILOSOPHICAL ASPECTS; ECOLOGY, SCIENCE OF; ECOTHEOLOGY; SACRAMENTAL UNIVERSE

Bibliography

Lovelock, James E. *Gaia: A New Look at Life on Earth*. Oxford: Oxford University Press, 1979.

JOHN COBB

GALILEO GALILEI

The condemantion of Galileo by the Roman Catholic Church in 1633 is one of the most dramatic incidents in the long history of the relations between science and religion. Galileo claimed in his *Dialogue on the Two Chief World Systems,* published the year before, that the sun-centered system of Copernicus was not only a convenient mathematical device for calculating the position of the planets but that it was the physical truth. This appeared to many Christians to run counter to statements in the Bible where the sun is described as mobile and the earth as stationary.

The clash between scientific truth and biblical revelation could have been avoided if Galileo, who had no decisive proof that the earth moves, had been more cautious and if theologians, who tended to be dogmatic, had not assumed that the Bible was to be interpreted literally whenever it mentioned natural events.

Early life

Galileo Galilei was an Italian astronomer, physicist, and natural philosopher. He was born in Pisa on February 15, 1564, and died in Arcetri on January 8, 1642. Galileo studied at the University of Pisa where he became Professor of Mathematics in 1589. Three years later he moved to the University of Padua where he taught elementary astronomy, mathematics, and physics. Medical students made up the majority of his audience, and he also lectured on fortification and military engineering to young noblemen.

Copernicanism

The first indication of Galileo's commitment to the Polish astronomer Nicolaus Copernicus (1473–1543) appeared in a letter that Galileo wrote to his former colleague at Pisa, Jacopo Mazzoni, in 1597. In August of that year he received a copy of Johannes Kepler's *Mysterium Cosmographicum,* in which the heliocentric theory of the solar system was vindicated on mathematical and symbolic grounds. After reading the preface, Galileo wrote to Kepler (1571–1630) to voice his approval of the view that the earth is in motion, but also to express his fear of making his position known to the public at large.

Around 1602, Galileo began making experiments with falling bodies in conjunction with his study of the motion of pendulums. He first expressed the law of freely falling bodies, namely the fact that speed increases as the time squared, in 1604, but claimed to have derived it from the assumption that speed is proportional to distance (whereas, as he later realised, speed is proportional to the square root of the distance). In the autumn of 1604, the appearance of a supernova gave him the opportunity to argue that heavenly matter is not unchangeable.

In July 1609, after hearing that a Dutchman had invented a device to make distant objects appear nearer, Galileo built one himself and gave a demonstration of his telescope from the top of the Campanile of San Marco in Venice. The practical value for sighting ships at a distance impressed the Venetian authorities who confirmed Galileo's appointment for life and raised his salary from 520 to 1,000 florins, an unprecedented sum for a professor of mathematics. Galileo never quite mastered the optics of his combination of a plano-convex objective and a plano-concave eyepiece (an opera glass), but he succeeded in producing a twenty-power telescope, which he turned to the sky in 1610. What he saw is reported in the *Sidereus Nuncius* (The Starry messenger), which appeared in March 1610. The work was to revolutionize astronomy. The moon was revealed as covered with mountains, new stars appeared as out of nowhere, the Milky Way dissolved into a multitude of starlets and, more spectacular still, four satellites were found orbiting around Jupiter. This was particularly important since, if Jupiter was revolving around a central body with four attendant planets, it could no longer be objected that the earth could not carry the moon around the sun. Jupiter's satellites were not a decisive argument for Copernicanism, but they removed a major obstacle to having it seriously entertained by astronomers.

The Grand Duke of Tuscany, Ferdinand, died in January 1609 and was succeeded by his son, Cosimo II. Galileo had wanted to return to Florence for some time and he realised that his newly-won fame might assist him in effecting a change of residence. He christened the satellites of Jupiter Medicean stars in honour of Cosimo and, in July 1610, he was appointed Mathematician and Philosopher of the Grand Duke of Tuscany. Soon thereafter he discovered that Venus has phases like the moon, and that sunspots move across the surface of the sun.

Theological objections

In December 1613, theological objections were raised at a dinner at the court of the Grand Duke in Pisa. Galileo was absent but his disciple Benedetto Castelli defended his views when questioned by Christina of Lorraine, the Grand Duchess of Tuscany and the mother of the Grand Duke. Galileo felt that the matter was important enough to write a long letter to Castelli, dated December 21, 1613, in which he argued that the heliocentric system was not at variance with the Christian faith. On the fourth Sunday of Advent 1614, a Dominican friar, Tommaso Caccini, inveighed against the Copernican system from the pulpit of the church of Santa Maria Novella in Florence. Another Dominican, Nicolo Lorini, denounced Galileo to the Inquisition. Galileo then wrote a long letter to Christina of Lorraine, where he developed the view that God speaks through the book of nature as well as through the book of Scripture, and that the Bible teaches people how to go to heaven, not how the heavens go. In 1615, Cardinal Robert Bellarmine wrote a letter stating that in the absence of a conclusive proof for the motion of the earth, Galileo and astronomers should content themselves with speaking hypothetically. The Cardinal added that should such a proof become available then the passages in the Bible that seem to say that the earth is at rest would have to be reinterpreted. In 1616, Copernicus's *On the Revolutions of the Heavenly Spheres* was placed on the list of proscribed books and Galileo was privately, but nonetheless officially, warned not to teach orally or in writing that the earth revolves around the sun.

The debate on the comets and Galileo's trial

In 1618 great excitement was generated over the appearance, in rapid succession, of three comets. Galileo thought that they were merely optical phenomena caused by refraction in the atmosphere and he wrote a *Discourse on the Comets* to criticise the account of Father Orazio Grassi (1583–1654), a professor of mathematics at the Collegio Romano, who claimed the comets were real bodies beyond the moon. Grassi published a rejoinder, to which Galileo replied. The result was bitter enmity between himself and the Jesuits.

What changed Galileo's Copernican fortune was the election of Cardinal Maffeo Barberini to the Roman Pontificate in 1623. The following spring Galileo journeyed to Rome, and the new Pope, Urban VIII (1623–1644), granted him no less than six audiences. Galileo returned to Florence feeling that he could now write about the motion of the earth. In January 1630 his long awaited *Dialogue on the Two Chief World Systems* was ready for publication and the manuscript was sent to Rome where a friend, Giovanni Ciampoli, played a vital role in securing permission to print the book. Ciampoli exceeded his powers and was largely responsible for Galileo's subsequent trouble.

The *Dialogue* had gone to press in Florence in June 1631. The publisher had decided to print a thousand copies, a large edition for the time, and the work was not completed until February 1632. Copies did not reach Rome until the end of March or early April. Pope Urban VIII created a commission to investigate the licensing of the *Dialogue*. In the file on Galileo at the Holy Office the commission found an unsigned memorandum of 1616 stating that he had been enjoined not to teach that the earth moves. The commission concluded that Galileo had disobeyed a formal order of the Holy Office, and Galileo was summoned to Rome, arriving, after much delay, on February 13, 1633. Despite his vigorous denial, Galileo was judged to have contravened the orders of the Church. On the morning of June 22, 1633, he was taken to a hall in the convent of Santa Maria Sopra Minerva in Rome and was made to kneel while the sentence condemning him to imprisonment was read out aloud. Still kneeling, Galileo formally adjured his error. He was allowed to leave for Siena and later, in 1634, to return to Florence, where he was confined to his house in Arcetri.

Later years and modern assessment

Galileo sought comfort in work, and within two years he completed the *Discourse on Two New Sciences,* the book on which his lasting fame as a scientist rests. In this work Galileo studied the structure of matter and the strength of materials, and explained motion in the light of the times-squared law of falling bodies and the independent composition of velocities. Together these laws enabled him to give an accurate description of the parabolic path of projectiles. When he cast about for a publisher, he came up against a new problem: the Church had issued a general prohibition against printing or reprinting any of his books. Galileo's manuscript was sent to the Protestant Louis Elzevier in Holland, where it appeared in 1638. Galileo became blind in that year, and he remained under house arrest until his death on January 8, 1642, five weeks before his seventy-eighth birthday.

In contemporary times, the Roman Catholic Church has recognized that the trial of Galileo rested on a misunderstanding of the moral authority of the Church. This was clearly expressed by Pope John Paul II in 1983 at a commemoration of the 350th anniversary of the publication of the *Dialogue on the Two Chief World Systems.* The Pope declared that divine revelation does not involve any particular scientific theory of the universe, and that the Holy Spirit does not guarantee our human explanations of the physical constitution of reality. Galileo had made exactly that point in his letter to Christina of Lorraine.

See also ASTRONOMY; CHRISTIANITY, ROMAN CATHOLIC, ISSUES IN SCIENCE AND RELIGION; COSMOLOGY; GRAVITATION; MATHEMATICS; SCIENCE AND RELIGION, MODELS AND RELATIONS

Bibliography

Blackwell, Richard J. *Galileo, Bellarmine, and the Bible.* Notre Dame, Ind.: Notre Dame University Press, 1991.

Fantoli, Annibale. *Galileo: For Copernicanism and for the Church,* 2nd edition. Rome: Vatican Observatory Publications, 1996.

Finocchiaro, Maurice A. *The Galileo Affair: A Documentary History.* Berkeley: University of California Press, 1989.

Galileo Galilei. *Le Opere di Galileo Galilie,* ed. Antonio Favaro. Florence: G. Barbèrea, 1890-1909.

Koyré, Alexandre. *Galileo Studies.* Atlantic Highlands, N.J.: Humanities Press, 1978.

Machamer, Peter. *The Cambridge Companion to Galileo.* Cambridge, UK: Cambridge University Press, 1998.

Redondi, Pietro. *Galileo Heretic.* Princeton, N.J.: Princeton University Press, 1987.

Sharratt, Michael. *Galileo: Decisive Innovator.* Cambridge, UK: Cambridge University Press, 1996.

Shea, William R. *Galileo's Intellectual Revolution.* New York: Science History Publications, 1972.

Shea, William R. "Galileo and the Church." In *God and Nature: Historical Essays on the Encounter Between Christianity and Science,* eds. David C. Lindberg and Ron L. Numbers. Berkeley: University of California Press, 1986.

WILLIAM R. SHEA

GAY GENE

See HUMAN GENOME PROJECT

GENE-CULTURE COEVOLUTION

See BEHAVIORAL GENETICS; CREATION; DESIGN; EVOLUTION, BIOCULTURAL; EVOLUTION, HUMAN; GENETIC DETERMINISM; GENETICS; NATURE VERSUS NURTURE; SOCIOBIOLOGY

GENE PATENTING

Patents give the patent-holder the right to exclude others from making, using, or selling an invention for a limited period of time (generally fifteen to twenty years). They do not confer on patent holders the right to do anything they wish with the invention. Countries regulate patents differently: Many grant patents to the *first to file,* while the United States grants patents to the *first to invent.* Patent rights are extended internationally through trade negotiations and political treaties. In the biotechnology arena, patents protect large financial interests.

Patent law in the United States

U.S. patent law requires that the invention (process or product) be: (1) novel—not already in the public domain; (2) non-obvious—not an obvious extension of prior art; (3) useful; and (4) fully disclosed. Interpretations of each criterion are contested.

Prior to 1930, products of nature could not be patented in the United States. The Plant Patent Act of 1930 permitted plant breeders to patent new plants. Until 1980, however, nonplant living matter was not patentable. Two legal cases changed the picture. By determining that a strain of bacteria constituted a patentable invention *(Diamond v. Chakrabarty),* the U.S. Supreme Court set the stage for patenting organisms as human inventions. (However, at least one critic, Mark Sagoff, argues that Chakrabarty's work did not involve a unique process and should not have been considered a human invention.) Within a few years, the Patent and Trademark Office was granting patents on bio-engineered mice and other living organisms.

The second crucial case was *Moore v. Regents* in 1990. Tissue excised from John Moore during medical treatment was used to develop a commercially valuable line of cells on which a patent was granted to the researcher. Moore sued. The California Supreme Court determined that Moore did not have a proprietary right to his excised tissue or to the cell line developed from it. This decision opened the door for additional efforts to derive patentable tissues from "excess" body parts.

Once patents were granted for living organisms and tissues derived from body parts, it was not long before the Patent and Trademark Office began to permit patents on genes and DNA fragments. Efforts to map and sequence the human genome then sparked a "gold rush" on patents for human genes. By the end of 2000, Human Genome Sciences, Inc., a pharmaceutical company, was reported to hold over one hundred patents on human genes, with applications pending for more than 7,500 additional patents.

Objections to gene patenting

The patenting of genes, organisms, and tissues derived from the human body has not gone undisputed. In 1995, representatives of some eighty religious organizations signed a *Joint Appeal Against Human and Animal Patenting.* For many religious representatives, permitting patents on life forms is arrogating to humans what rightly belongs only to God: "We believe that humans and animals are creations of God, not [of] humans, and as such should not be patented as human inventions."

Indeed, for some, the very framing of the issue as a question of patenting is problematic, since the language of patent rights already determines what questions can be raised. Those who believe that God alone is the author and inventor of living beings would prefer to speak in terms of God's dominion and human duties of stewardship rather than in the language of human rights and patents to human "inventions." Thus, public discourse may already privilege some perspectives and disadvantage others; the very framing of the issues eliminates some ways of seeing the question.

Another argument against gene patenting rests on the notion that the human genome is part of our common human heritage. As such, the genome should be seen as public property and no single person, organization, or group should have the right to exclude others from access to public property. Native Americans, in spite of their diversity of religious and ethical views, generally oppose gene patenting, seeing it as a new form of *biopiracy* in which colonizers steal from natives anything of value. Serious issues of international justice are raised by such concerns.

In the popular mind, gene patenting is linked with practices such as buying and selling of human body parts. Hence, gene patenting evokes prohibitions against ownership of human beings. If parts of a body can be owned, then there is no reason that all the parts could not be owned, resulting in the ownership of persons. Prohibitions against buying and selling body parts or owning persons exist worldwide. In the West in particular, early Christian belief in a literal resurrection of the body continues today, as Paul Rabinow states, in an "enduring cultural understanding that the 'person' is inextricably tied to the sheer materiality of the body or its parts . . . ." (p. 185). To patent human genes is thus perceived as patenting persons, which is repugnant to many. One critic argues that current patent law in the United States would permit patenting processes for germline genetic intervention, thus leading to rights over a genetically altered human being. The shared presumption that people cannot be owned thus generates some resistance to patenting of human genes.

Even those who do not utilize explicitly religious arguments often wish to set bodies and body parts aside as something that cannot be owned or patented. The European Union Directive of 1998 states that the human body "and the simple discovery of one of its elements, including the sequence of a gene, cannot constitute patentable inventions." Similarly, lawyer and bioethicist George Annas has argued strongly against any "ownership" of human body parts.

Arguments for gene patenting

Proponents of gene patenting counter that patents are not granted on humans or their bodies, but only on genes or gene fragments. More importantly, what is patented is in the laboratory, not in the living person; holding a patent on a gene does not grant ownership of the gene inside someone's body. For example, Article 5(2) of the European Union Directive does permit patenting of gene sequences that are "isolated from" the body or produced by a technical process, provided their industrial application is disclosed. Here, the Directive balances the conviction that life forms per se should not be patentable with the reality that in the contemporary international market access to patents may be crucial for scientists and investors.

Two major arguments are proffered for gene patenting. First, such patents are part of the *intellectual property rights* tradition in which people have rights over things they have invented. Article 27 of the Universal Declaration of Human Rights specifically provides that every person has a right to "protection of the moral and material interests resulting from any scientific . . . production of which he is the author." The notion that there is a *right* of ownership deriving from authorship has deep roots. Seventeenth-century philosopher John Locke held that each person had a "property" in his own person and therefore in the work of his hands; by "mixing his labor" with objects (within certain constraints), a person gained a property right in those objects. This labor theory of property forms the basis for a deeply held conviction that patents are justified because they embody a right to the work of one's hands or one's mind.

However, under contemporary conditions, the one who discovered a gene may not hold the patent. More often, the patent holder is an employing institution or corporation that sponsors the research. Hence, the notion that there is a right to the work of one's hands or mind applies only ambiguously to the modern circumstances of gene patenting.

The second and more prominent argument for patenting genes and DNA fragments is a utilitarian one: patents, as William Haseltine writes, "ensure the rapid and open dissemination of new knowledge, encourage innovation, and promote commerce" (p. 59). Since patents are granted only where there is full disclosure of the invention, patents promote open dissemination of knowledge. Since they exclude others from using the invention, they provide time for commercial developments and thus encourage innovation. These are typical arguments made in the biotechnology industry.

Whether the patenting system has these good effects is difficult to ascertain. Both the Council for Responsible Genetics and the Human Genome Organization (HUGO), representing the coordinated mapping and sequencing efforts of many scientists worldwide, assert that patents work against the tradition of shared knowledge among researchers. The current climate of collaboration between universities and private industry raises particular concerns that patenting may not encourage open sharing of information but rather discourage it in the interests of developing commercial applications. Patent holders often permit free access to information for those doing basic research but restrict access for those doing applied research with commercial potential. In light of these and other considerations, some urge a moratorium on any further gene patenting. Others argue that even if patenting does contribute to the free flow of information, stimulate innovation, and promote commerce, these good effects must be balanced by principles of international justice and the common good, which might require some limitations on gene patenting.

See also BIOTECHNOLOGY; CREATION; DNA; GENETICS; HUMAN GENOME PROJECT

Bibliography

Andrews, Lori B., and Nelkin, Dorothy. *Body Bazaar: The Market for Human Tissue in the Biotechnology Age.* New York: Crown, 2001.

Annas, George J. "Outrageous Fortune: Selling Other People's Cells." *Hastings Center Report* 20, no. 6 (1990): 36–39.

Chapman, Audrey R. "A Human Rights Perspective on Intellectual Property, Scientific Progress, and Access to the Benefits of Science." In *Intellectual Property and Human Rights,* World Intellectual Property Organization, Publication # 762 (E). Geneva, Switzerland: WIPO, 1999a.

Chapman, Audrey R., ed. *Perspectives on Genetic Patenting: Religion, Science, and Industry in Dialogue.* Washington, D.C.: American Association for the Advancement of Science, 1999b.

Chapman, Audrey R. *Unprecedented Choices: Religious Ethics at the Frontiers of Genetic Science.* Minneapolis, Minn.: Fortress, 1999c.

Gold, E. Richard. *Body Parts: Property Rights and the Ownership of Human Biological Materials.* Washington, D.C.: Georgetown University Press, 1996.

Haseltine, Willliam. "The Case for Gene Patents." *Technology Review* 5 (2000): 59.

Hensley, Scott. "Celera's Human Genetic Code Will be Available on Web Site," *Wall Street Journal.* 8 February 2001.

Howard, Ken. "The Bioinformatics Gold Rush." *Scientific American* 283, no. 1 (2000): 58–63.

Kondo, LeRoy L. "Major Considerations in Meeting Requirements for Patents in Biotechnology." *Biotechnology Law Report* 17, no. 6 (1998): 794.

Locke, John. "Second Treatise on Civil Government" (1690). In *Social Contract: Essays by Locke, Hume, and Rousseau,* ed. Ernest Barker. New York: Oxford University Press, 1962.

Mattei, Ugo. *Basic Principles of Property Law: A Comparative Legal and Economic Introduction.* Westport, Conn.: Greenwood, 2000.

Rabinow, Paul. "Severing the Ties: Fragmentation and Dignity in Late Modernity." *Knowledge and Society: The Anthropology of Science and Technology* 9 (1992): 169–187.

Regalado, Antonio. "The Great Gene Grab." *Technology Review* 5 (2000): 50.

Sherry, Stephen F. "The Incentive of Patents." In *Genetic Ethics: Do the Ends Justify the Genes?* eds. John F. Kilner, Rebecca D. Pentz, and Frank E. Young. Grand Rapids, Mich.: Eerdmans, 1997.

Shulman, Seth. "Toward Sharing the Genome." *Technology Review* 5 (2000): 60.

Wright, Karen. "The Body Bazaar: The Market in Human Organs is Growing." In *Bioethics, Justice and Health Care,* eds. Wanda Teays and Laura Purdy. Belmont, Calif.: Wadsworth, 2001. First published in *Discover* 19 (1998): 115–120.

Court Cases

Diamond v. Chakrabarty (447 U.S. 303, 1980).

Moore v. Regents (793P.2d 479. Cal 1990 cert.den.111 S.Ct.1388, 1991).

Internet Resources

Sagoff, Mark. "Patented Genes: An Ethical Appraisal." *Issues in Science and Technology Online.* National Academy of Sciences, Spring 1998. Available from http://stills.nap.edu/issues.

Who Owns Life? The American Journal of Bioethics Online. Produced by the University of Pennsylvania Center for Bioethics and the MIT Press. Available from http://ajobonline.com.

KAREN LEBACQZ

GENERAL THEORY OF RELATIVITY

See RELATIVITY, GENERAL THEORY OF

GENESIS

The importance of the Old Testament book of Genesis in the history of science stems largely from the fact that the narrative begins with an account of creation. A wide variety of theological cosmologies were based on differing interpretations of these few verses. Most of these views hinged on two major issues of interpretation: the nature of the "beginning" and the primordial materials described in Genesis 1:1–2; and the six "days" described in Genesis 1:4–2:3.

Interpretations of Genesis 1: 1–2 varied with the version of the Bible that was used. The Hebrew version begins with a relative clause: "In the beginning when God created the heavens and the earth, the earth was a formless void . . . ." (New Revised Standard Version), much like the parallel Hebrew construction in Genesis 2:4. So the Hebrew version of Genesis began with the primordial materials of formless earth, water, and darkness (Genesis 1:2). Various interpretations of this "beginning" were possible. Some rabbis accepted the inference that God began with a pre-existent chaos

and then created an ordered cosmos (Genesis Rabbah 1:5). Others brought in texts like Proverbs 8:22–24 to demonstrate that God had created the water and the darkness and that the "beginning" of Genesis 1:1 was God's own wisdom as encoded in the Torah (Jubilees 2:2–3; Genesis Rabbah 1:1, 9). Still others argued that God must have created worlds before this one (Genesis Rabbah 3:7; 9:2).

Most Diaspora Jews and early Christians, however, used the Greek translation of the Old Testament, known as the *Septuagint.* This text begins with the absolute statement: "In the beginning God created the heavens and the earth," which implied an absolute beginning for this universe. It also implied that the unformed earth and water were included in the initial act of creation. This reading was followed by pioneering theologians like Basil of Caesarea (c. 329–379) and Augustine of Hippo (354–430) and became the standard interpretation for Christians.

The meaning of the six days of Genesis 1 was also debated. Some exegetes thought there was a temporal sequence of days without specifying their exact length (Jubilees 2:2; Genesis Rabbah 1:3). For those who accepted the idea of an absolute beginning, this implied that God created the cosmos in two stages: God made the building materials (unformed earth, water, etc.) at the beginning of the first day; then God illuminated and formed those materials as described in the narrative (Wisdom of Solomon 11:17; 4 Ezra 6:38–40; Justin Martyr).

Others exegetes saw inconsistencies in the idea of a temporal sequence of days. For example, the first "day" that is described is assigned a cardinal number ("one day" rather than "first day," Genesis 1:5) in both the Hebrew and Greek versions (Genesis Rabbah 2:3; 3:9; Basil); the sun, moon, and stars appear in the narrative three days after the first evening and morning. Some Rabbis saw a nontemporal parallelism between the first three and the second three days (Genesis Rabbah 12:5). Others suggested that the ten utterances ("God said") of the narrative were patterned after the Ten Commandments or the construction of the Tabernacle (Pirqei Avot 5:1; Midrash Tanhuma). Other scholars argued that divine creation required no effort (Genesis Rabbah 12:10) and that it all might have taken place in a single instant (Philo; Midrash Tanhuma). This idea of a simultaneous creation of all things was followed by early Christian theologians like Origen (c. 185–254), Athanasius (c. 293–373), Basil, and Augustine.

See also COSMOLOGY, RELIGIOUS AND PHILOSOPHICAL ASPECTS; CREATIO EX NIHILO; LIFE, ORIGINS OF

Bibliography

Fretheim, Terence E. "Genesis." In *The New Interpreter's Bible,* Vol. 1. Nashville, Tenn.: Abingdon Press, 1994.

Greene-McCreight, Kathryn E. *Ad Litteram: How Augustine, Calvin, and Barth Read the "Plain Sense" of Genesis 1–3.* New York: Peter Lang, 1999.

Levenson, Jon D. *Creation and the Persistence of Evil.* San Francisco: Harper, 1988.

Neusner, Jacob, trans. *Genesis Rabbah: The Judaic Commentary to the Book of Genesis,* Vol. 1. Atlanta, Ga.: Scholars Press, 1985.

CHRISTOPHER B. KAISER

GENE THERAPY

Gene therapy refers to the repairing or replacing of malfunctioning genes that cause a deleterious illness or condition. There are two forms of gene therapy: *somatic* and *germline.*

Somatic and germline therapies

Somatic therapies are used to replace or repair malfunctioning genes that are expressed in such conditions as cystic fibrosis or sickle cell disease. Since these therapies attempt to remedy the causes rather than alleviate the effects of disease, they presumably will provide more effective and beneficial medical treatments. Although initial attempts to develop somatic gene therapies proved largely unsuccessful, experimental treatments since the mid 1990s of severe combined immunodeficiency disease (SCID) and sickle cell disease have renewed public optimism regarding its potential efficacy.

Like somatic therapies, germline therapies attempt to repair or replace malfunctioning genes. The principal difference is that the corrected gene, rather than the deleterious one, is passed-on to subsequent generations. Consequently, the potential benefits or effects of germline therapies could be much more widespread than those of somatic therapies. As of 2002, no experimental procedures employing human germline techniques had been undertaken.

Ethical and moral objections

In principle, somatic gene therapy has raised few ethical objections. Because these therapies treat the underlying causes of disease at the molecular level rather than concentrating on affected organs or compromised biological processes, somatic therapies have been largely perceived as more sophisticated and potentially more effective extensions of established medical procedures. So long as these therapies are safe, there is nothing inherently wrong in deploying them. The issue of safety, however, came to the forefront with the death in 1999 of a patient undergoing an experimental genetic treatment for ornithine transcarbamylase (OTC) deficiency, an incident that prompted calls for greater public oversight or regulation.

The prospect of germline therapy has proven much more controversial. The primary objection is that humans should not attempt to construct the genetic inheritance of future generations. This objection usually takes one of two forms. First, since so little is known about the complex relationship between genes and larger environmental factors, it would be imprudent to introduce genetic alterations that would be inherited by future generations. Although the goal would be to eliminate a severely debilitating disease or condition, there might be unintended or unforeseen consequences that would adversely affect subsequent generations. Individuals carrying a recessive deleterious gene, for example, might in the future incur certain survival advantages in response to changing environmental factors. Since the effects of germline therapy are so much more widespread than those of somatic therapies, large populations could be potentially devastated. The seemingly harmless or even beneficial intervention into the human germline could wreak havoc down the road.

The second form of this objection invokes a more sweeping moral imperative. Humans do not have a right to shape the genetic endowment of their descendants, and correspondingly, individuals have the right to be born with unaltered genomes. People must simply resist the temptation to play God in shaping the destiny of humans, both as individuals and as a species.

The principal defense against this objection, in both its forms, is that it does not sufficiently take into account the nature of evolutionary change, thereby imposing unwarranted responsibilities regarding the possible fate of future generations. Other than identical twins, there are no unique genomes that parents do not have a right to alter or that offspring have a right to inherit in an unaltered form. Human reproduction entails the creation of a unique genome, derived from the genes of parents but also including mutations. It is difficult to imagine what an unaltered genome might be in the future in evolutionary terms. If individuals have a right to inherit an unaltered genome, then presumably cloning should become the preferred method of human reproduction. In addition, many argue that the prudential claim that current ignorance should prohibit germline interventions is unwarranted. Every action entails unforeseen consequences, and it is not known whether failing to intervene will prove better or worse than intervening. It cannot be known in advance whether the consequences of germline therapies will be any more or less devastating than those of natural selection upon future generations.

Some religious and moral concerns have also been raised, not so much with the prospect of genetic therapy per se, but with the fear that their introduction might exacerbate some already troubling trends. For instance, it is argued that the growing knowledge of human genetics is not being used, at least initially, to develop more effective therapies, but to prevent the birth of offspring with debilitating or undesirable genetic traits. Some fear that parents will turn increasingly to embryonic testing and screening techniques, such as preimplantation genetic diagnosis, to prevent the implantation of embryos carrying certain genetic abnormalities, leading in turn to the destruction of embryos deemed to be undesirable.

The issue is further compounded because the same techniques being developed as therapies may also be applied to select, and perhaps someday enhance, certain genetic characteristics of offspring. The bar of parental expectation would then be raised dramatically regarding what constitutes a desirable or even healthy child. The prospect of so-called designer babies will exert social pressure on parents not only to prevent the birth of offspring with severely debilitating conditions, but to select or enhance their genetic endowment in the hope of giving their children the best possible start in life. Although the development of genetic therapy is motivated by a humane impulse, its advent could fuel parental anxieties and prejudicial attitudes toward individuals with physical and mental disabilities, thereby unwittingly supporting a new, implicit, and insidious form of eugenics.

Proponents of genetic therapy counter that these worries are both unfounded and inflammatory. Legal protections against discrimination can be enacted as needed. Moreover, the best way prevent the destruction of so-called undesirable embryos is to develop effective genetic therapies as quickly as possible. More importantly, the distinction between genetic therapy and genetic selection and enhancement is spurious. Any therapy is also an enhancement, because the restoration of health is presumably an improvement over illness. In addition, many non-genetic medical procedures are enhancing, rather than therapeutic, in character, and genetic therapies will make them more effective. Genetically enhancing an individual's immune system, for example, is merely a more effective form of inoculation. Despite the moral and religious objections, the development of effective gene therapies may alleviate the suffering of many people.

See also BIOTECHNOLOGY; DNA; ETHNICITY; EUGENICS; EVOLUTION; GENE THERAPY; GENETIC ENGINEERING; GENETIC TESTING; GENETICALLY MODIFIED ORGANISMS; GENETICS; HUMAN GENOME PROJECT; MUTATION; NATURE VERSUS NURTURE; PLAYING GOD; REPRODUCTIVE TECHNOLOGY

Bibliography

Chapman, Audrey R. *Unprecedented Choices: Religious Ethics at the Frontiers of Genetic Science.* Minneapolis, Minn.: Fortress Press, 1999.

Engelhardt, H. Tristram, Jr. *The Foundations of Bioethics.* New York and Oxford: Oxford University Press, 1996.

Fletcher, Joseph. *The Ethics of Genetic Control: Ending Reproductive Roulette.* Garden City, N.Y.: Anchor Books, 1974.

Parens, Eric, ed. *Enhancing Human Traits: Ethical and Social Implications.* Washington D.C.: Georgetown University Press, 1998.

Peterson, James C. *Genetic Turning Points: The Ethics of Human Genetic Intervention*. Grand Rapids, Mich.: Eerdmans, 2000.

Ramsey, Paul. *Fabricated Man: The Ethics of Genetic Control*. London and New Haven, Conn.: Yale University Press. 1970.

Walters, LeRoy, and Palmer, Julie Page. *The Ethics of Human Gene Therapy*. New York: Oxford University Press, 1997.

BRENT WATERS

GENETICALLY MODIFIED ORGANISMS

Humans have tried to influence the development of organisms for centuries by selectively breeding plants and animals. Advances in genetics make it possible to engineer organisms at the cellular level to improve everything from the productivity of crops to the viability of animal organs and tissues for transplantation to humans. There are basically two ways to genetically alter an organism: A *transgenic* animal has been modified by the introduction of a new gene, whereas a *knock out* is an animal in which a given gene is no longer expressed. Religious and ethical concerns include respect for the well being of future generations of the organisms and possible effects on the environment.

See also BIOTECHNOLOGY; DNA; GENE THERAPY; GENETIC DETERMINISM; GENETIC ENGINEERING; GENETICS; XENOTRANSPLANTATION

Bibliography

Applegate, John S. "The Prometheus Principle: Using the Precautionary Principle to Harmonize the Regulation of Genetically Modified Organisms" *Indiana Journal of Global Legal Studies* 9, no. 1 (2001): 207–264. Available from http://ijgls.indiana.edu/

Pontifical Academy for Life. "Prospects for Xenotransplantation: Scientific Aspects and Ethical Consideration." September 26, 2001. Available from http://www.vatican.va/roman_curia/pontifical_academies/acdlife/

Wolfenbarger, L. L., and Phifer, P. R. "The Ecological Risks and Benefits of Genetically Engineered Plants." *Science* 2088 (2000): 290.

DONNA M. MCKENZIE

GENETIC DEFECT

A genetic defect occurs when a gene fails to express a certain function or produce a particular protein. Such a defect may cause or be a contributing factor to a debilitating disease or illness. The defect occurs when DNA is miscopied, resulting in what geneticists call a *mutation*. It should be noted that virtually every human being carries a small number of mutations, but they usually are not expressed in a deleterious manner.

Mutations can be passed from parents to offspring. If only one parent carries a mutated gene it will usually be overridden by a second copy of the gene. If both parents carry the mutated genes, offspring are at risk of being affected. For example, if one parent carries the recessive gene for cystic fibrosis but the other parent does not, there is no risk that offspring will be afflicted with the disease. If both parents carry the recessive gene, however, there is a one-in-four chance that they will give birth to a child with cystic fibrosis. In addition, mutations can occur through exposure to certain levels of radiation or chemicals.

The term *genetic defect* is falling into disfavor because of its pejorative connotation. To identify a gene as "defective" implies that this determination is made in comparison to a natural, normative standard. Consequently, it suggests that individuals affected by defective genes are themselves defective or inferior human beings. A genetic "defect," however, denotes a statistical abnormality within a given population. The degree to which such an abnormality is judged to be defective is as much a social as it is a medical determination. Short stature, for example, is a "defect" only in a culture that places a high value on being tall.

A principal religious concern is to insure that individuals expressing certain genetic traits that are perceived to be undesirable are not stigmatized or subjected to unwarranted discrimination. A similar concern holds for parents of children with genetically related illnesses (particularly illnesses that could be prevented through embryonic or fetal testing), or communities in which there are high incidents of certain conditions such as sickle-cell anemia or Tay Sach's disease. Moreover, there is also some apprehension that recent advances in embryonic and fetal testing will promote a new and more subtle round of eugenics in which parents will select against offspring with genetic traits judged to be defective or undesirable. These religious concerns are derived from a conviction that the value or worth of an individual is not derived from the presence or absence of genetic characteristics, thereby implying a natural hierarchy among human beings.

The idea of a genetic defect also raises vexing theological questions. For instance, since mutations can be passed from parents to offspring, does this imply that nature is flawed and is itself in need of redemption? But if this is the case, what would a redeemed or perfected nature be like? Or, to the contrary, is the possibility of deleterious mutations the necessary price that must be paid in order to spur evolutionary development within the human species? But if this is true, what is one to make of a God who seemingly requires the suffering of individuals in order to promote the flourishing of the species?

See also GENETIC TESTING; GENETICS; MUTATION

Bibliography

Cole-Turner, Ronald, and Waters, Brent. *Pastoral Genetics: Theology and Care at the Beginning of Life.* Cleveland, Ohio: Pilgrim Press, 1996.

Kilner, John F.; Pentz, Rebecca D.; and Young, Frank E., eds. *Genetic Ethics: Do the Ends Justify the Genes?* Grand Rapids, Mich.: Eerdmans, 1997.

Song, Robert. *Human Genetics: Fabricating the Future.* Cleveland, Ohio: Pilgrim Press, 2002.

Peacocke, Arthur. *God and the New Biology.* San Francisco: Harper, 1986.

BRENT WATERS

GENETIC DETERMINISM

With rising public attention given to the Human Genome Project in the early 1990s, there grew an increased belief in genetic determinism. Scholars referred to this widespread belief variously as *geneticism,* the *strong genetic principle, genetic essentialism, genetic fatalism,* and the *gene myth.* Generic determinism was fed minimally by molecular biology but maximally by behavioral genetics and sociobiology. In the classic war between nature and nurture, genetic determinists sided with nature.

The gene myth can be dissected into three sub-tenets: puppet determinism, promethean determinism, and the commandment against playing God. The first is seemingly fatalistic; DNA defines human beings, and the genes, like a puppeteer, pull the strings that make people dance. The second, promethean determinism, assigns to scientists the task of understanding just how the genes work plus that of developing appropriate technologies based upon this understanding, giving humans control over what nature bequeaths. The third sub-tenet voices an ethical maxim: Thou shalt not play God. This sub-tenet derives from the Frankenstein fear of the mad scientist who, in trying to take control of the mysterious forces of life, oversteps the invisible boundary intended by nature to contain human pride and lets loose uncontrollable destructive forces.

See also BEHAVIORAL GENETICS; DETERMINISM; DNA; FREEDOM; GENETICS; HUMAN GENOME PROJECT; NATURE VERSUS NURTURE; SOCIOBIOLOGY

Bibliography

Hubbard, Ruth, and Wald, Elijah. *Exploding the Gene Myth.* Boston: Beacon, 1993.

Peters, Ted. *Playing God? Genetic Determinism and Human Freedom.* London and New York: Routledge, 1997.

TED PETERS

GENETIC ENGINEERING

The term *genetic engineering* refers to technologies that modify genes. Unlike selective breeding, which merely chooses traits that are already found in nature, genetic engineering acts directly on the genetic material itself in order to alter an organism's traits. Genetic engineering is the cornerstone of modern biotechnology, and through it human beings have the power to modify the molecular basis of all forms of life.

A brief history

The concept of genetic engineering emerged in the 1960s and was first realized in the 1970s. Its development depended upon a century of advances in science, beginning in the 1860s with Gregor

Mendel's discovery of the existence of factors that govern inheritance. In the 1940s, it was learned that these factors, now called *genes,* are composed of a complex molecule, deoxyribonucleic acid or DNA. In 1953, Francis Crick and James Watson described the structure of DNA as the famous double helix along which are found pairs of chemicals. Soon it was learned that the sequence of these chemicals, known as bases, carries information that instructs the cell how to make proteins that are essential to the structure and function of the cell.

By the 1960s, it was becoming clear that scientists would soon learn how to manipulate this chemical information and thereby engineer genes. In the ensuing decades, various techniques for manipulating DNA have been developed, beginning in the early 1970s with the discovery of the use of *restriction enzymes,* which exist in nature and which cut and join strands of DNA at precise locations. This allows scientists to cut and splice DNA. A later discovery called *polymerase chain reaction* (PCR) made it possible for researchers to produce huge quantities of specific DNA sequences. Further advances in the use of computers to decode, store, and manipulate DNA means that researchers can discover and modify DNA on a broad scale and with considerable precision.

Methods

Genetic engineering uses various methods in pursuit of many goals. One method is to transfer a gene from one organism to another. For instance a human gene may be transferred to a microorganism in order to develop a new strain of microorganism that will produce a human protein, such as insulin, for pharmaceutical purposes. Much of the insulin used by diabetics comes from this process. It is possible in fact to transfer many genes into an organism by packaging them together as a kind of artificial chromosome, sometimes called a *gene cassette.* Plants, too, are genetically engineered to produce pharmaceutical products, to enhance their protein value as foods, to allow them to grow with less reliance on pesticides or fertilizers, to resist freezing or spoiling, to enhance flavor, or perhaps to grow in seawater. Another method is to incapacitate a particular gene by deliberately causing it to mutate and shut itself down. For instance if scientists know that an impaired human gene is linked to a disease such as cancer, they will find the corresponding gene in laboratory rats, shut it

down, and create a strain of rats with this gene knocked out, and therefore with a high likelihood for cancer, in order to have animals on which to test possible therapies.

In human beings, scientists have attempted to modify or replace genes in some of the cells of patients' bodies in order to treat diseases with genetic basis. This strategy, called *gene therapy,* began in 1990 with mixed success. In time it will likely become widely used to treat a variety of diseases. Still another method is to modify a tiny portion of the gene—one or two bases of DNA—by constructing a special small molecule that can trigger what is called a *mismatch repair.* Ordinarily the body corrects for the mutations that occur naturally inside the body all the time, and scientists are learning how to exploit the body's own repair mechanisms to correct mutations that may have been inherited. These strategies used so far on human beings differ sharply from what scientists are attempting to do with other animals. In human beings, researchers are attempting to change the genes only in selected cells that are affected by the disease. In animals, however, the modifications affect every cell and are passed on to future generations. That strategy, often called *germline modification,* has been proposed for use on human beings but remains controversial from the standpoint of safety.

Religious concerns

From the time genetic engineering was first considered in the 1960s, religious scholars and institutions have commented on its value and limits. Often scientists themselves, not to mention science journalists, report on developments in genetics in religious terms, speaking of DNA as the mystery of life or the human genome as the holy grail of biology. Not surprisingly, the general public sometimes responded to these developments with religious fervor, sometimes in favor of them, but often opposed to developments that people saw as, for instance, *playing God.*

One concern of special importance to many religious scholars and leaders has been the use of the system of patenting, by which governments give exclusive rights for a time to inventors, to protect developments in genetics. Particularly troubling has been the granting of patents to gene sequence information. Many have argued that knowledge of genes is discovery, not invention, and should not be eligible for patent protection. Many have also argued that granting biological patents amounts to patenting life, therefore making life a mere commodity. Other religious scholars recognize that patenting, while not perfect, is essential to the financial development of the full potential of genetic engineering, and that opposition to patenting is tantamount to opposing the benefits of research.

Beyond these general concerns, many religious scholars and organizations have considered developments in genetic engineering on a case-by-case basis. For instance, many religious organizations have responded to the use of genetic engineering to modify food by recognizing its potential for increasing the quality and quantity of food, but with cautions having to do with the viability of small farms, global inequities, the power of corporations in view of intellectual property rights, and the right of consumers to know what they are eating. Similarly, religious scholars have raised concerns, but generally have not objected categorically, to genetic engineering of animals. Of special concern is the prospect of herds of genetically identical livestock becoming vulnerable to disease, or to the use of genetic engineering to create strains of animals whose sole purpose is to suffer a disease for the benefit of medical research.

Quite understandably, human applications evoke the most intense religious responses. Religious responses to the use of genetic engineering for pharmaceutical purposes have been positive, with concerns limited to patenting, to the high costs of medicines, and to the need for socially just patterns of distribution. Furthermore, almost without exception, human gene therapy has met with approval not just by the public, but by religious institutions and scholars, who assess it morally as an extension of traditional medicine. Issues of safety remain, and many are concerned that the technique, when shown to be beneficial, will not be justly distributed.

The greatest concern, however, is that the technique will not be limited in its application to therapy but will be used for enhancement of human health and possibly of traits that are unrelated to health. Those who voice this concern point not just to cosmetic surgery and to performance enhancing drugs in sports but to the use of mood-altering pharmaceutical products, such as the drugs known as selective serotonin reuptake inhibitors (SSRIs). Evidence exists that people request these drugs not to treat anxiety or depression but to improve their mood and thus their performance in life. If that is true, some argue, how much more will people request gene modification that enhances their state of being and their performance. As of 2002, it is not at all clear which human traits will become susceptible to enhancement by genetic engineering. Height, most definitely, will be modifiable, but perhaps mental and emotional traits may be modifiable too. The concern here is the lack clarity about the distinction between therapy and enhancement, and thus the lack any publicly credible way to prevent those with economic or political means from acquiring new ways to improve themselves to the competitive disadvantage of others.

Sometime in the twenty-first century, many believe, humans will learn how to modify the genes of their offspring. Such germline modification, as it is usually called, is already done in other mammals, although not reliably. Many technical obstacles lie ahead, but learning to do this in human beings has a strong attraction, for some, in the promise that a family might be freed of a genetic disease that has afflicted it for generations. Other techniques, such as testing an embryo for disease before it is implanted, will probably achieve the same result at less cost and risk. If so, it may turn out that the real advantage of germline modification is not to eliminate disease but to improve the next generation, perhaps by enhancing resistance to disease or by producing other traits. The prospect of children born with such enhancement, often referred to as designer babies, is widely opposed by the general public, secular scholars, and religious leaders, even though most analysts concede that it probably cannot be prevented.

Religious objections to germline modification are that the resulting children will enter the world as objects, engineered according to the will of their designers and not as persons who emerge from the love of their parents. The intrusion of technology perverts the relationship between parent and child, difficult under any circumstance, but all the more so if parents can use technology to express their desires for the kind of child they want to have. Others believe that designed children will face impossible expectations in achieving that for which they are designed, and that they will likely resist their makers' intentions.

See also BIOTECHNOLOGY; CLONING; DNA; EUGENICS; GENE PATENTING; GENE THERAPY; GENETICALLY MODIFIED ORGANISMS; GENETICS; HUMAN GENOME PROJECT; PLAYING GOD; STEM CELL RESEARCH

Bibliography

Bruce, Donald, and Bruce, Ann, eds. *Engineering Genesis: The Ethics of Genetic Engineering in Non-Human Species.* London: Earthscan, 1998.

Chapman, Audrey R. *Perspectives on Genetic Patenting: Religion, Science, and Industry in Dialogue.* Washington, D.C.: American Association for the Advancement of Science, 1999.

Chapman, Audrey R. *Unprecedented Choices: Religious Ethics at the Frontiers of Genetic Science.* Minneapolis, Minn.: Fortress Press, 1999.

Chapman, Audrey R., and Frankel, Mark S. *Human Inheritable Genetic Modifications: Assessing Scientific, Ethical, Religious, and Policy Issues.* Washington, D.C.: American Association for the Advancement of Science, 2000. Available at http://www.aaas.org/spp/dspp/sfrl/germline/report.pdf.

Cole-Turner, Ronald. *The New Genesis: Theology and the Genetic Revolution.* Louisville, Ky.: Westminster John Knox Press, 1993.

Cole-Turner, Ronald. *Beyond Cloning: Religion and the Remaking of Humanity.* Harrisburg, Pa.: Trinity Press International, 2001.

Evans, John H. *Playing God? Human Genetic Engineering and the Rationalization of Public Bioethical Debate.* Chicago: University of Chicago Press, 2002.

Hanson, Mark J., ed. *Claiming Power over Life: Religion and Biotechnology Policy.* Washington, D.C.: Georgetown University Press, 2001.

Fletcher, Joseph. *The Ethics of Genetic Control: Ending Reproductive Roulette.* Garden City, N.Y.: Doubleday, 1974.

Kilner, John F.; Pentz, Rebecca D.; and Young, Frank E., eds. *Genetic Ethics: Do the Ends Justify the Genes?* Grand Rapids, Mich.: Eerdmans, 1997.

Mackler, Aaron, ed. *Life and Death Responsibilities in Jewish Biomedical Ethics.* New York: Louis Finkelstein Institute and Jewish Theological Seminary of America, 2000.

National Council of Churches, Panel on Bioethical Concerns. *Genetic Engineering: Social and Ethical Consequences.* New York: Pilgrim Press, 1984.

Peters, Ted. *Playing God: Genetic Determinism and Human Freedom.* New York: Routledge, 1997.

Peters, Ted, ed. *Genetics: Issues of Social Justice.* Cleveland, Ohio: Pilgrim Press, 1998.

Peterson, James C. *Genetic Turning Points: The Ethics of Human Genetic Intervention.* Grand Rapids, Mich.: Eerdmans, 2001.

Rahner, Karl. "The Problem of Genetic Manipulation." In *Theological Investigations,* Vol. 9, trans. G. Harrison. New York: Seabury, 1966.

Rahner, Karl. "The Experiment with Man: Theological Observations on Man's Self-Manipulation." In *Theological Investigations,* Vol. 9, trans. G. Harrison. New York: Seabury, 1966.

Ramsey, Paul. *Fabricated Man: The Ethics of Genetic Control.* New Haven, Conn.: Yale University Press, 1970.

Shinn, Roger Lincoln. *The New Genetics: Challenges for Science, Faith and Politics.* Wakefield, R.I., and London: Moyer Bell, 1996.

Willer, Roger A., ed. *Genetic Testing and Screening: Critical Engagement at the Intersection of Faith and Science.* Minneapolis, Minn.: Kirk House, 1998.

World Council of Churches, Church and Society. *Manipulating Life: Ethical Issues in Genetic Engineering.* Geneva: World Council of Churches, 1982.

World Council of Churches, Church and Society. *Biotechnology: Its Challenges to the Churches and the World.* Geneva: World Council of Churches, 1989.

RONALD COLE-TURNER

GENETIC FUTURISM

See GENETICS

GENETICS

Genetics is the field of scientific research that studies gene activity in plants, animals, and humans. Genes are segments of DNA (deoxyribonucleic acid) found in each living cell; each of these DNA segments codes for a protein, thereby yielding a phenotypic effect. All life on Earth shares the chemical make-up of DNA, even though each species differs in the number and function of genes. Scientists estimate that human DNA contains between thirty-one and thirty-six thousand genes arrayed over two pairs of twenty-three chromosomes. The forty-six human chromosomes are strands of DNA, with each of the twenty-three strand pairs arranged as a double helix. The DNA strands are composed of four base chemicals: adenine (*A*), guanine (*G*), cytosine (*C*), and thymine (*T*). These four bases are typically identified by their single letter abbreviations (*A,G,C,T*) and constitute an alphabet, so to speak, that carries genetic information from DNA to tissue formation and bodily activity.

Modern genetics began in the nineteenth century with the research of an obscure Austrian monk, Gregor Mendel (1822–1884), who discovered patterns of inheritance in pea plants. Mendelian laws of inheritance still stand as the foundation for contemporary genetics. The twentieth century added the chemical work of molecular biology, including the post World War II discovery of the double helix structure of DNA by James Watson (b. 1928) and Francis Crick (b. 1916). At the turn of the twenty-first century, the Human Genome Project had sequenced the three billion base pairs and nearly identified all the genes in the human genome. The complete genomes of a handful of plants and animals had also been identified.

In addition to molecular biology, which directly studies the chemical processes of genes, two other branches of genetics have become significant for religious reflection: behavioral genetics and sociobiology. Behavioral genetics employs statistical studies of phenotypical characteristics and social preferences to discern heritability probabilities. Central to such studies are monozygotic and heterozygotic twins raised apart. The assumption in such studies is that twins raised apart are excellent subjects because they provide opportunity to distinguish between genetic and environmental influences.

Sociobiology appeared in 1975 with publications by Harvard entomologist Edward O. Wilson (b. 1929). Wilson, having studied how ant societies are socially held together by chemical signals, purported by analogy that human breeding patterns, gender dominance, and caste systems are similarly explainable. Zoologist Richard Dawkins (b. 1941) shortly thereafter coined the term "selfish gene," which reinforced the central thesis of sociobiology.

In Darwinian fashion the human organism does not live for itself; rather, its function in nature is to reproduce the genes for which it is the temporary carrier. In short, genetic forces drive evolution, including human evolution, and human social history, including religious history, can be explained by reference to genetic drives.

Theological issues raised by genetics

The apparent growth in knowledge regarding human nature cultivated by genetic research leads some religious thinkers to review their inherited anthropologies. Most theologians see the field of genetics as a challenge requiring response; a few see new genetic knowledge as a complement to long standing religious insight. Distinctively theological issues are few and are frequently embedded within the more plentiful and visible issues of ethics and public policy. Theological issues will be taken up immediately; ethical issues surrounding cloning and stem cell research will follow.

The first theological concern is *genetic reductionism*. Reductionism poses a theological threat everywhere in modern science. The form it takes in genetics is the vague cultural belief that "it's all in the genes." In the laboratory, methodological reductionism is necessary to foster research into gene function, but a threat comes with ontological reductionism and surmises that all of what constitutes human nature is reducible to the genes. During the early years of the Human Genome Project, DNA was described by some scientists as the "code of codes" or the "blueprint of humanity." Such biological reductionism seems to leave no room for independent influence on the part of spirit or culture, the dimensions wherein most religious traditions work.

A second and related concern is *genetic determinism*. If "it's all in the genes" and the DNA is the blueprint of who human beings are, then genes move into the position of determiners of human nature and human value. In the historical struggle between nature and nurture in the minds of intellectuals trying to explain human complexity, the new breed of genetic determinists stake their claim on nature. Relatively few molecular biologists advocate strong genetic determinism, whereas behavioral geneticists and sociobiologists reinforce it. Molecular biologists and philosophers who oppose an exclusive genetic determinism frequently appeal to two part determinism: genes plus environment. Some theologians locate human freedom in three part determinism: genes, environment, and the human self or person. In the latter case, the human self is emergent; the self is not reducible to either biological or environmental influences. Divine action in the human reality here is said to be holistic—that is, present to all three dimensions of biology, environment, and person.

A third and related concern is *neo-Darwinian evolution*. Nineteenth century Darwinism employed natural selection as the mechanism for explaining evolutionary change over time. Twentieth century neo-Darwinists such as Fransisco Ayala or Stephen Jay Gould add genetic mutation to the theory, adding detail to the manner in which natural selection works. Sociobiology extrapolates on neo-Darwinism by attempting to explain all of human culture including religious belief in terms of biological determinism. Sociobiologists (sometimes called evolutionary psychologists) contend that human culture is on a leash, a short leash, held by a genetic agenda. That agenda is the self-replication of genes using the human species as its vehicle. Human culture is structured so as to encourage reproduction and, hence, the perpetuation of genes. Human religion and human morality, whether theologians know it or not, is reducible to the agenda of selfish genes.

Those theologians who are attempting to incorporate sociobiology into their religious vision feel they must justify human transcendence of biology and the emergence of soul or spirit. Philip Hefner's theological anthropology, for example, argues that through evolutionary processes the genes have determined that we humans would be free. Some Christology's contend that Jesus marks a significant advance in evolutionary history, because with the Nazarene a precedent-setting life is led that transcends the selfish genetic agenda, and the possibility is opened for self-sacrificial loving. In contrast, some Muslim scholars find they must simply reject neo-Darwinian evolutionary theory because it makes no room for human spirit and because it fails to cohere with the anthropology of the Qur'an.

In summary, the theological community is accepting of the methodological reductionism within molecular biology that functions to yield advance in scientific research. However, theologians resist philosophical extrapolations that tend toward ontological reductionism or genetic determinism. Reductionism and determinism are insufficient, say theologians, to explain spiritual reality or ethical transcendence. Theologians defend human freedom and moral transcendence whether it complements the science or requires abandoning the science.

Genetic engineering

Genetic engineering consists of selecting, inserting, or removing individual genes in order to manipulate the genome of an organism. In agriculture and animal husbandry selective breeding to obtain preferred strains has been practiced for millennia. Modern genetic engineering adds chemical and mechanical methods for more sophisticated results.

In agriculture the genomes of plants are altered by genetic engineering to confer resistance to blight or resistance to herbicides in order to eliminate weeds while preserving the crops. Tomato genomes, for example, can be modified so as to stall final ripening during transport to market and then ripen just prior to going on sale. Such techniques dramatically increase the percentage of produce that becomes marketable. In Europe and other parts of the world popular movements against *genetically modified foods* (GMFs) have arisen. Fearing unknown possible health effects, opponents of GMFs lobby for accurate labeling so that the market can freely choose whether to consume them or not.

The engineering of farm animal genomes has two purposes. One is to obtain preferred strains of livestock, especially beef cattle. The other is to produce foods or pharmaceuticals for human consumption. An example of the latter case is the insertion of a human gene into a sheep genome to produce in the animal's milk a certain protein usable for treatment of a human disease. This use of animals for human betterment is itself controversial, with opponents arguing that turning animals into a means for human ends violates animal dignity.

To date, the genetic engineering of human genomes in the reproduction process has been limited to gene selection; it has not included gene insertion or removal. When in vitro multiple fertilized ova are examined, only those with the preferred genome may be implanted in the mother's uterus. This process is typically employed to eliminate known deleterious genes such as that for cystic fibrosis. In somatic therapy on living persons, however, more than selection is being tried. Genes that produce healthy blood have been inserted into bone marrow cells. Attempts are being made to send "knock out" genes into cancer tumors to turn off tumor growth by turning off telomerase activity.

An implicit theological issue that arises more often in the wider cultural debate than within specific religious communities is *naturalism*. Naturalism is the belief that nature apart from intervention by human technology is the source of value. Genetic engineering is a form of technology that alters the natural world people have inherited from evolutionary history. The promethean question arises implicitly: Is the natural world the source of human value, or, on the basis of humanly superimposed purposes, do people have the right to manipulate nature to meet these purposes? Much of the energy driving opposition to GMFs derives from naturalism. A similar naturalism is implicit in theological arguments, which presume that God's will is manifest in the genetic lottery resulting from sexual intercourse rather than through deliberate selection in vitro of the genetic code of future children.

The promethean question also arises with genetic futurism. As the present generation manipulates plant, animal, and human genomes, will this place humans in the position of guiding our evolutionary future? Does the human race possess the wisdom to choose a wholesome future or, like Prometheus of ancient Greek tragedy, will humans overstep their finite bounds and create an irreparable tragedy? Conservative theologians along with naturalist advocacy groups wish to put the brakes on genetic engineering and let nature take its course; whereas other religious leaders foresee immense benefits for health and wellbeing to be gained through genetic technology and contend that the human race must steward scientific advance.

Cloning

The two most virulent ethical controversies over genetic research have been cloning and stem cells. The two are linked. The first successful experiment in reproductive animal cloning was accomplished at the Roslin Institute in Edinburgh, Scotland, where embryologist Ian Wilmut cloned the world famous sheep, Dolly. The details were published in the February 27, 1997, issue of *Nature*. Wilmut's Roslin team removed cells from the udder of a pregnant Finn Dorset ewe, placed them in a culture, and starved them of serum nutrients for a week until the cells became quiescent—that is, they arrested the normal cycle of cell division, inviting a state akin to hibernation. Second, they took an unfertilized egg, or oocyte, from a Scottish Blackface ewe and removed the nucleus. When removing the nucleus with the DNA, they left the remaining cytoplasm intact. Third, the scientists placed the quiescent cell next to the oocyte; then they introduced pulses of electric current. The gentle electric shock caused the cells to fuse, and the oocyte cytoplasm accepted the quiescent DNA. A second electric pulse initiated normal cell division. Fourth, after six days of cell division, the merged embryo was implanted into the uterus of another Blackface ewe and brought through pregnancy to birth on July 5, 1996. The newborn babe was named Dolly. The procedure was called *somatic cell nuclear transfer* (NT).

An important scientific question was answered with this experiment: Is cell differentiation reversible? The answer seems to be yes. Embryonic cells are predifferentiated. Adult cells are normally differentiated in order to perform the particular tasks of particular parts of the body. For example, genes for hair are turned on in the hair while genes for toenails are turned off in hair but on where the toenails belong. In theory, cloning could be accomplished by employing embryonic cells in their predifferentiated state. The accomplishment here was to make an adult differentiated cell function as an undifferentiated embryonic cell.

The procedure was not clean and easy. The successful cloning of Dolly was accompanied by numerous misfires. Out of 277 tries, the Roslin scientists were able to make only twenty-nine embryos survive beyond six days. At fourteen days 62 percent of the fetuses in ewe wombs were lost, a significantly greater proportion than the estimate of 6 percent after natural mating. Eight ewes gave birth to five lambs, with all but one dying shortly thereafter. Dolly was the only one to survive. Triumph is accompanied by loss. Noting this, many scientists including Wilmut himself have opposed the prospect of human cloning because of the safety argument—that is, until the process is perfected, too many human embryos would be destroyed as misfires.

Ethical issues raised by cloning

Ethical issues arising from cloning technology can be divided into two areas, human reproductive cloning and human therapeutic cloning. Therapeutic cloning will be taken up later in the discussion of stem cells. The public discussion over reproductive cloning seems to focus on human reproduction, not animals. Cloned cattle and sheep do not elicit the religious opposition connected to human births.

The overriding ethical issue is this: Should human beings be cloned? Back in 1971 James Watson predicted this debate. Watson, along with Francis Crick, won the 1962 Nobel Prize for medicine or physiology for the discovery of the double helix structure of DNA. Writing on cloning for the May 1971 issue of the *Atlantic,* Watson predicted that the first reaction of most people to the arrival of these asexually produced children would be one of despair. He then went on to suggest that people with strong religious backgrounds would want to de-emphasize all those forms of research that would circumvent the normal sexual reproductive process. The Watson prophecy seems to have found its fulfillment.

In a February 22, 1997, press release, Donald Bruce, Director of the Society, Religion and Technology Project of the Church of Scotland, said that cloning human beings would be ethically unacceptable as a matter of principle. According to Christian belief, he said, cloning would be a violation of the uniqueness of human life, which God has given to each of us and to no one else. The argument that each individual person has a unique identity that would be violated by cloning has been repeated in religious and secular circles with a high degree of frequency.

The structure of this argument applies three assumptions to the issue of cloning. The first assumption is that in order for a human person to have an individual identity he or she must have a unique genome. The second assumption is that God has ordained that each person have a genome that differs from every other person. The third assumption is that through this genetic technology human beings could accidentally produce two persons with the same identity and, thereby, violate

the divine creator's intention. On the basis of these scientific and theological assumptions, the ethical conclusion drawn here is this: no cloning.

Those holding the alternative position reject these assumptions. Scientifically speaking, even though two individuals might end up with identical genotypes, they would not end up with identical phenotypes. DNA does not always express itself in lock step fashion. There are variations in expression and spontaneous mutations. In addition, environmental factors such as food and exercise and health care influence gene activity. If the DNA donor and clone are reared a generation apart in time let alone in separate locations, similarities will be noticeable, but differences will abound.

The existence of monozygotic twins is instructive. Like clones, identical twins are born with identical genomes. Despite what they share in common, they grow up as separate and distinct individuals. Each has his or her own interior consciousness, sense of self, thought processes, and ethical responsibility. Even if studies in behavioral genetics eventually show strong DNA influence on predispositions to certain forms of behavior, they remain two separate individuals with separate lives to lead. A clone would in effect be a delayed twin; due to the delay, a clone would probably experience even more independence than two born at the same time.

During the debate, the question arose: Would two clones share a single soul? No theological position to date has held that two twins share a single soul. Each has his or her own soul, his or her own connection to God. This by analogy would seem to apply to clones as well. The human soul, theologically speaking, is not formed from DNA as the phenotype is formed from the genotype. The soul is not a metaphysical appendage to the physical. In sum, the theological argument against cloning based on an alleged violation of a God-given identity appeared early in the debate but eventually dissipated under critical review.

The United States National Bioethics Advisory Commission (NBAC) studied cloning—a study that included interviews with leaders in Judaism, Islam, Hinduism, Buddhism, Evangelical Protestantism, Liberal Protestantism, and Roman Catholicism—and issued a report on June 6, 1997, with the following conclusion: At this time it is morally unacceptable for anyone in the public or private sector, whether in a research or clinical setting, to attempt to create a child using somatic cell nuclear transfer cloning. The principle argument against cloning was the safety argument, as enunciated above by Ian Wilmut. The report went on to ask the U.S. Congress to pass legislation setting a three to five year moratorium on the use of federal funding in support of human cloning, and it asked non-federally funded private sectors to comply voluntarily with this moratorium. The NBAC further recommended that religious groups carry on an ongoing discussion of the ethics of cloning. Even though legislation did not follow, religious groups have carried on the recommended discussion.

In addition to the safety and the identity arguments, a third has been raised against human reproductive cloning: the commodification argument. Cloning—as a form of designer baby making—might lead to the commodification or commercialization of children; this would constitute an assault on a child's dignity. Dignity in this case is not based upon genetic individuality but upon treatment as an end rather than a means. Designer babies serve the ends of the designers, the parents, not the ends of the child. Cloning along with other genetic technologies, critics fear, may play into the hands of economic forces that will tend to commodify newborn children. Commodification, not genetic uniqueness, would deny the sacred character of human individual life.

Stem cells

The cloning controversy deals primarily with human reproduction. The stem cell controversy moves into therapeutic cloning and related matters. The therapeutic promise is dramatic. Specifically, rejuvenation through transplantation of tissue grown in a laboratory from stem cells would be of enormous value for *cardiomyocytes* to renew heart muscle to prevent congestive heart failure; replacement of *hematopoietic stem cells* for producing healthy blood in bone marrow to resist infection by the HIV virus and to treat AIDS and possibly sickle cell anemia; cultivating *endothelial cells* to reline blood vessels as treatment for atherosclerosis, angina, and stroke due to arterial insufficiency; rejuvenating *islet cells* in the pancreas to produce natural insulin to fight diabetes; renewal of *neurons* in the brain to treat Parkinson's disease and victims of stroke; *fibroblast* and *keratinocyte cells* to heal skin in the treatment of burns; and

chondrocytes or cartilage cells to treat osteoarthritis or rheumatoid arthritis. All this promise arises from human embryonic stem cells (hES cells), which are self-renewing—virtually immortal—and have the capacity to develop into any or all tissue types in the human body.

Two momentous laboratory discoveries are relevant. First is the isolation of human embryonic stem cells (hES cells) in August 1998 by James Thomson, an associate veterinarian in the University of Wisconsin's Regional Primate Research Center. Thomson began with fertilized ova—spare embryos from in vitro fertilization (IVF) not placed in a uterus—and cultured them to the blastocyst stage, about four to six days. At this point he removed the outer shell of the blastocyst, separated out the individual cells, and placed them on a feeder tray. The cells divided. They reproduced themselves. Because these cells are as yet undifferentiated—that is, they are pluripotent and able to make any part of a human body—they are the cells from which other cells stem. Because they replicate themselves indefinitely, Thomson in effect created an immortal line of embryonic stem cells.

Second, John Gearhart, a professor of gynecology and obstetrics at Johns Hopkins University School of Medicine, drew human embryonic germ cells (hEG cells) from fetal gonadal tissue in September 1998. These cells, when taken from an aborted fetus, resemble in nearly all respects the pluripotent stem cells described above.

It is not yet clear whether or not hES cells are identical to hEG. Both are pluripotent and equivalent in function. Yet, it may be discovered that different alleles appear in different hES, because hES cells could be imprinted by either the male or female source. The blastocyst stage of embryogenesis is a stage that avoids the gender imprint. What is not yet known is whether original gender imprint will matter. For the foreseeable future the two types of stem cells will be treated the same, yet controversy rages over Thomson's destruction of the blastocyst to obtain hES cells.

One goal of the research agenda is to learn just what turns genes on and off. Once scientists have gained the knowledge of triggering gene expression, they can apply it to pluripotent stem cells and direct the growth of selected bodily tissue. Particular organs could be grown in culture. Heart tissue or entire organs such as the pancreas or liver could be grown in the laboratory. These would be healthy rejuvenating organs ready for transplantation.

In order to transplant the laboratory grown organs, however, medical scientists need to override our immune system in order to avoid organ rejection. Two scenarios lie before us. One would be to create a *universal donor* cell that would be compatible with any organ recipient. The task here would be to disrupt or alter the genes within the cell responsible for the proteins on the cell's outer surface that label them as foreign to the recipient's immune system. This approach would be difficult. It would involve disrupting genes within the same DNA in which researchers are trying to express certain other genes. Exposing such cells to harsh conditions with rounds of different drugs may damage more than just the targeted surface proteins.

A preferable second scenario would be to make cells that are genetically compatible (histocompatible) with the organ recipient—that is, to make cells with an identical genotype. If the organ genotype matches that of the recipient, no immune system rejection will take place.

This is the connection to cloning, or somatic cell nuclear transfer. One hypothetical scenario is to begin with an enucleated human oocyte, an egg with the DNA nucleus removed. Via somatic nuclear transplantation—cloning—one could insert the DNA nucleus of the future transplant recipient. By turning on selected genes, selected tissue could be grown *ex vivo,* outside the body, and then through surgery placed within the recipient. Because the implanted heart or liver tissue has the same genetic code as the recipient, no rejection would occur. This is in part the Dolly scenario, although it differs in that it grows only organ tissue and not an entire fetus.

Another variant or second scenario distinguishes itself sharply from Dolly, namely, one that eliminates the use of a fresh oocyte. Instead of an oocyte, the recipient's DNA nucleus would be placed in a non-egg cell, in the stem cell itself. The goal here would be to accomplish laboratory organ growth in a stem cell that is not an egg. To accomplish this, further research on cytoplasm's role in gene expression is required, as well as development of the nuclear transfer technology for insertion into the tiny stem cell.

Ethical issues raised by stem cells

On August 9, 2001, U.S. President George W. Bush announced that his government would support research on existing lines of stem cells, but would refrain from supporting the destruction of embryos to create new cell lines. The president thought he was settling an ethical dispute. Public policy, science, and ethics are inextricable.

Formulating the central ethical question raised by stem cell research is difficult because each of the two sides is oriented toward a different question. The *embryo protection* position begins with the question: How can we protect the dignity of the embryo? The *beneficence* or healing opportunity position begins with the question: How can scientific research lead to advances in human health and well-being? Each position is internally coherent, yet they are locked in controversy.

Those holding the embryo protection position lift their voices in defense of the apparently helpless embryo threatened with death at the hands of the laboratory executioner. The use of blastocysts and aborted fetuses leads opponents to criticize the scientific community for devaluing human life. They argue that the devaluation of humans at the very commencement of life encourages a policy of sacrificing the vulnerable, and this could ultimately put other humans at risk, such as those with disabilities and the aged, through a new eugenics of euthanasia. Pope John Paul II (1978–), in an elocution at Castel Gandolpho in August 2001, likened the destruction of blastocysts to obtain hES cells with infanticide. In effect, the embryo protection position sees the stem cell debate in terms of the abortion debate.

The major premise of this position is that each human embryo is the tiniest of human beings. The unspoken second premise is that, because an embryonic stem cell is a tiny human being, it has dignity. And, having dignity, the embryo providing the stem cell deserves protection from scientists who would use the name of medical research to destroy it. The nonmalificence or "do no harm" medical maxim applies here, and this maxim is violated in embryonic stem cell research.

In contrast, the healing opportunity position notes that the principle of beneficence goes beyond that of nonmalificence. Beyond avoiding harm, appeal to beneficence requires the active pursuit of human health and wellbeing. The central focus here is the good promised by stem cell research. Beneficence is a form of *agape,* selfless love. Decisive in the thinking of Christian supporters of medical research is Jesus' own ministry of healing, which set an example for his disciples. In many cities Christian groups have named their hospitals "Good Samaritan" after the key figure in one of Jesus' parables who administered healing to an abandoned victim of violence. From this perspective, secular medical research contributes to God's healing work on earth.

Embryo protectors accuse beneficence supporters of crass utilitarianism, of sacrificing innocent human beings in vitro for future hospital patients. Stem cell supporters repudiate the charge of utilitarianism, some even conceding the possibility of dignity applied to the early embryo. Relevant here is the observation that hES cells are derived from surplus embryos, from fertilized ova discarded in clinics. Such surplus embryos are slated for destruction in any case, either due to freezer burn or overt disposal. The beneficence position does not necessarily endorse the actual creation of new embryos for sacrifice to laboratory research; rather, it is satisfied with drawing some life-giving potential from an entity otherwise marked for disposal. Rather than deny dignity to the early embryo, beneficence advocates believe they can affirm embryo dignity yet still sustain justification for proceeding with health yielding research on stem cells.

The deliberate creation of fresh embryos for destruction in the laboratory would require an additional premise to attain ethical justification. The additional premise could be supplied by the developmentalists. Ethicists holding the developmentalist position frequently apply the fourteen-day rule. This is based on the observation that until an embryo attaches itself to the uterine wall and gastrulation occurs, a single individual fetus is not yet formed. Twining can still occur up until the appearance of the primitive streak that will become the backbone, thereby defining a single individual rather than multiple fetuses. By denying individuality to the embryo prior to the fourteenth day, some ethicists justify research at prior stages of development. Stem cells are harvested between the fourth and sixth days.

The Vatican has steadfastly rejected the fourteen-day rule. *Donum Vitae* in 1987 and subsequent papal elocutions have reiterated the classic doctrine of creationism and applied it to the so-called moment of conception. When the sperm fertilizes the egg during sexual intercourse, says Pope John Paul II, a third factor is present. God imparts a freshly created soul to the zygote. The presence of this eternal soul establishes personhood and dignity to the embryo. This makes it morally inviolable and, hence, protectable.

Genetics, culture, and religion

With the field of genetics the unavoidable interpenetration of science, culture, and religion becomes visible. Laboratory researchers cannot separate their daily work from wider cultural interpretations, and the wider culture in this case has elected to interpret genes deterministically. Theologians, who represent the intellectual segment of religious traditions, find themselves simultaneously listening to the bench scientists and the wider cultural cacophony, trying to respond to both. The pressure is increased by the demand from the political sector to establish public policy regarding what is permissible in basic research and resulting medical technology. Society cannot do without either the scientists or the theologians.

See also BEHAVIORAL GENETICS; BIOTECHNOLOGY; CLONING; DNA; EUGENICS; FREEDOM; GENE THERAPY; GENETICALLY MODIFIED ORGANISMS; GENETIC DEFECT; GENETIC DETERMINISM; GENETIC ENGINEERING; GENETIC TESTING; HUMAN GENOME PROJECT; MEMES; MUTATION; NATURALISM; NATURE VERSUS NURTURE; SELFISH GENE; SOCIOBIOLOGY; STEM CELL RESEARCH

Bibliography

Bruce, Donald, and Bruce, Anne, eds. *Engineering Genesis: The Ethics of Genetic Engineering.* London: Earthscan, 1998.

Chapman, Audrey R. *Unprecedented Choices: Religious Ethics at the Frontiers of Genetic Science.* Minneapolis, Minn.: Fortress, 1999.

Cole-Turner, Ronald, ed. *Human Cloning: Religious Responses.* Louisville, Ky.: Westminster/John Knox, 1997.

Congregation for the Doctrine of the Faith. *Donum Vitae: Instruction on Respect for Human Life in its Origin and on the Dignity of Procreation: Replies to Certain Questions of the Day* (February 22, 1987). Washington, D.C.: United States Catholic Conference, 1987.

Crick, Francis. *Of Molecules and Men.* Seattle: University of Washington Press, 1966.

Evangelical Lutheran Church in America. *Human Cloning: Papers from a Church Consultation.* Chicago: ELCA, 2000.

Genome Sequencing Consortium. "Initial Sequencing and Analysis of the Human Genome." *Nature* 409 (2001): 860-921.

Hefner, Philip. *The Human Factor.* Minneapolis, Minn.: Fortress Press, 1993.

Holland, Suzanne; Lebacqz, Karen; and Zoloth, Laurie. *The Human Embryonic Stem Cell Debate.* Cambridge, Mass.: MIT Press, 2002.

John Paul II. Encyclical Letter *Evangelium Vitae* (March 25, 1995). Vatican City: Vatican, 1995.

Kass, Leon, and Wilson, James Q. *The Ethics of Human Cloning.* Washington, D.C.: AEI Press, 1998.

Lebacqz, Karen; Mendiolla, Michael M.; Peters, Ted; Young, Ernlé W. D.; and Zoloth-Dorfman, Laurie. "Research in Human Embryonic Stem Cells: Ethical Considerations." *Hastings Center Report* 29, no. 2 (1999): 31-36.

National Bioethics Advisory Commission. *Cloning Human Beings.* Springfield, Va.: National Technical Information Service, 1997.

National Institutes of Health. *Stem Cells: Scientific Progress and Future Research Directions.* Bethesda, Md.: NIH, 2001.

Peters, Ted. *Playing God? Genetic Determinism and Human Freedom.* New York: Routledge, 2002.

Pedersen, Roger A. "Embryonic Stem Cells for Medicine." *Scientific American* 280, no. 4 (1999): 68-75.

Peters, Ted. *For the Love of Children: Genetic Technology and the Future of the Family.* Louisville, Ky.: Westminster John Knox, 1998.

Peters, Ted, ed. *Genetics: Issues of Social Justice.* Cleveland, Ohio: Pilgrim, 1998.

Shamblott, Michael J.; Axelman, Joyce; Wang, Shumping; et al. "Derivation of Pluripotent Stem Cells from Cultured Human Primordial Germ Cells." *Proceedings of the National Academy of the Sciences* 95 (1998): 13726-13731.

Shannon, Thomas A., ed. *Bioethics,* 3rd edition. New York: Paulist Press, 1987.

Shinn, Roger L. *The New Genetics: Challenges for Science, Faith, and Politics.* Wakefield, R.I., and London: Moyer Bell, 1996.

Thomson, James A.; Itskovitz-Eldor, Joseph; Shapiro, Sander S.; et al. "Embryonic Stem Cell Lines Derived from Human Blastocysts." Science 282 (1998): 1145-1147.

Venter, J. Craig, et al. "The Sequence of the Human Genome." *Science* 291 (2001): 1304-1351,

Watson, James. "Moving Toward the Clonal Man: Is This What We Want?" *Atlantic* 227, no. 5 (1971): 50–53.

Wilmut, Ian. "Viable Offspring Derived from Fetal and Adult Mammalian Cells." *Nature* 385 (1997): 810-813.

TED PETERS

GENETIC TESTING

Advances in the science of human genetics since 1980 (particularly the Human Genome Project) have prompted the development of techniques that identify a growing range of deleterious traits or predispositions. As researchers gain greater knowledge about the genetic components of many diseases or disorders, individuals are enabled to take precautionary measures reducing the chances of contracting an illness or mitigating its effects. In addition, genetic testing may be used to prevent the birth of offspring with a severely debilitating illness or disability.

Individuals, for example, may be tested for genetic traits indicating a proclivity for various forms of cancer or heart disease. If these genetic indications are present, individuals can avoid certain lifestyles or diets, take prescribed medications, or undergo invasive surgical techniques (in rare instances), which may help prevent the onset of cancer or heart disease. Moreover, individuals may also be tested for genetic abnormalities that may be passed on to offspring. Individuals may use this knowledge to inform their reproductive decisions. An individual carrying a recessive gene for cystic fibrosis, for instance, may avoid reproducing, limit mate selection to individuals not carrying the same recessive gene, or use a reproductive technology that employs donated gametes.

Genetic testing may also be used to prevent the birth of offspring with a debilitating illness or disability. Using amniocentesis or chorionic villus sampling, for example, a fetus can be tested for a genetically based condition such as Tay-Sachs syndrome. If the test is positive, parents may choose to prepare themselves to care for a terminally ill child or terminate the pregnancy. In addition, preimplantation genetic diagnosis in conjunction with in vitro fertilization may be employed to test a number of embryos, implanting only those that are unaffected by the deleterious gene.

As genetic testing becomes more sophisticated, it offers great promise for advances in diagnostic and preventive techniques. As the understanding of the complex relationship between genes and environmental factors increases, it is hoped that drugs can be developed that will prevent a wide range of late onset diseases. Some envision a day, for example, when individuals with a genetic predisposition for Alzheimer's disease will be able to take prescribed drugs preventing the onset of the disease, or at least mitigating its effects.

Although genetic testing undoubtedly benefits many people, it also raises a number of important ethical, pastoral, and religious issues. There are concerns over privacy. Some worry that genetic testing will be used to discriminate against individuals in employment or insurance coverage. There are concerns over the moral status of the fetus and embryo. Although prenatal testing may prevent the birth of children suffering from severely debilitating illnesses, the techniques also entail destruction of selected fetuses and embryos. More broadly, genetic testing raises intriguing implications for theological anthropology. How will a burgeoning knowledge of human genetics, as well as the ability to manipulate genes, inform religious accounts of what it means to be human?

See also BIOTECHNOLOGY; DNA; GENETIC
  DETERMINISM; GENETICS; HUMAN GENOME
  PROJECT; NATURE VERSUS NURTURE;
  SOCIOBIOLOGY

Bibliography

Chapman, Audrey R. *Unprecedented Choices: Religious Ethics at the Frontiers of Genetic Science.* Minneapolis, Minn.: Fortress Press, 1999.

Cole-Turner, Ronald. *The New Genesis: Theology and the Genetic Revolution.* Louisville, Ky.: Westminster John Knox Press, 1993.

Cole-Turner, Ronald, and Waters, Brent. *Pastoral Genetics: Theology and Care at the Beginning of Life.* Cleveland, Ohio: Pilgrim Press, 1996.

Peterson, James C. *Genetic Turning Points: The Ethics of Human Genetic Intervention.* Grand Rapids, Mich.: Eerdmans, 2001.

BRENT WATERS

GEOCENTRISM

In geocentric worldviews, the earth is the center of the universe. The ancient Greek philosopher Aristotle (384–322 B.C.E.) thought of celestial bodies as beautiful and pure, travelling on the surface of perfect spheres, and of the earth as an imperfect place that had fallen to the center of the universe. In the second century B.C.E., Ptolemy adjusted the geocentric theory with *epicycles* (orbits imposed on the orbits of the planets) and *eccentrics* (orbits that were centered to the side of the universe) so that the theory was better able to predict the orbits of the sun, moon, and stars. The geocentric view of the universe was replaced by the heliocentric (sun-centered) view that was pioneered by Nicolaus Copernicus (1473–1543), adopted and defended by Galileo Galilei (1564–1642), and much refined by Johannes Kepler (1571–1630), who discovered the elliptical nature of planetary orbits.

See also ANTHROPOCENTISM; COSMOLOGY, PHYSICAL
  ASPECTS; GALILEO GALILEI

DENIS EDWARDS

GEOMETRY, MODERN: THEOLOGICAL ASPECTS

The discovery of mathematics in deep Antiquity, together with its essential pair, geometry, was an important factor shaping rationalistic tendencies of the European spirit. From Plato's belief that "God geometrizes" through Einstein's conviction that the goal of science is nothing else but "to discover the mind of God," interaction between geometry and theology continued with change a changing rate and intensity.

Middle Ages through the nineteenth century

During the Middle Ages theology formed the natural environment for the sciences. For instance, the shift in theology from the understanding of God's presence in the world in terms of "his power" to the understanding of his omnipresence in terms of "all places" fostered the gradual emergence of the modern idea of space extending to infinity. This process culminated with the French philosopher and mathematician René Descartes (1596–1650), who identified matter with only one of its attributes, extension: body is nothing but an extended thing. Descartes was doubtless inspired by his monumental discovery of analytic geometry—the first really important discovery in geometry after Euclid and Apollonius. In Descartes's view, science, which should be done "in a geometric manner" (*more geometrico*), is concerned with extended bodies, thus leaving to philosophy the realm of consciousness.

In the seventeenth century a kind of fusion occurred between science and theology (called *physico-theology*) to an extent unheard before. This is clearly seen, for instance, in the writings of Isaac Newton (1642–1727). In creating his concept of absolute space Newton was a direct successor of former disputes on God's omnipresence. Newtonian absolute space, which "in its own nature, without relation to anything external, remains always similar and immovable" (*Principia*; 1687), has three attributes: homogeneity, immobility, and infinity, which qualify it as both the universal arena for physical processes and the "sense organ" of God (*sensorium Dei*). The enormous successes of Newton's physics overshadowed his theology and only the former function of the Newtonian space continued to exercise its influence on subsequent generations of thinkers.

Newton's absolute space as an arena for physical processes constituted an inherent element of the mechanistic worldview, and it came as a shock when it turned out that Euclidean space is not the only possibility. The dispute concerning Euclid's "fifth postulate" lasted from antiquity. The question was whether the fifth postulate has to be accepted as an independent assumption or could be deduced from other postulates. Many proofs of the fifth postulate produced during the centuries invariably turned out to fail. Around 1830, three mathematicians—Nikolai Ivanovich Lobachevsky (1793–1856), Janos Bólyay (1802–1860), and Carl Friedrich Gauss (1777–1855)—demonstrated independently but almost simultaneously that one can obtain a new geometry, a geometry that is absolutely consistent from a logical point of view, based on the negation of Euclid's fifth postulate. This shows that Euclid was right: The fifth postulate is an independent assumption and cannot be derived from other postulates. This long expected

conclusion was overshadowed, however, by the fact that a new non-Euclidean geometry was possible. Soon it became manifest that by playing with axioms an infinite number of geometries could be created. In fact, in the second half of the nineteenth century many new geometric systems were created and extensively explored. The philosophical significance of this mathematical revolution was comparable to that of Copernicus (1473–1543): Humans are not only creatures from the outskirts of the universe, but even the universe, at least conceptually, is not unique; it is a member of an infinite family of geometric universes.

German mathematician Georg Friedrich Bernhard Riemann (1826–1866) in his 1854 inaugural lecture created a broad conceptual setting for modern geometry, which admitted more than three spatial dimensions. He also foresaw its physical applications: The world, with all its physical fields, could be but a system of fluctuating geometries.

Relativity

At the end of the nineteenth century, peoples' imaginations were fed with multidimensional geometric pictures. Some philosophers started speculating on "other dimensions" as living places for spirits, and the popular writer Edwin A. Abbot published a book in 1884 entitled *Flatland,* the principal aim of which was criticism of Victorian England, but which in fact inspired both philosophers and scientists to deal with new geometric spaces.

With the advent of the special and general theories of relativity the concept of space-time entered the imaginary requisites of popular and philosophical literature and became a powerful tool of scientific investigation. From then on, geometry would not only deal with the problem of space but also with at least some aspects of the time problem. Consider only two such problems that have repercussions in theological matters. The first problem concerns the nature of time flow and its relationship to eternity. The theory of relativity favors, but does not require, a picture of space-time as existing in one totality with the idea of the flowing time being only a "projection" of human psychological experience onto the world. Such a picture is consonant with the traditional idea of God's eternity (going back to Augustine of Hippo [354–430 C.E.] and Boethius [c. 480–c. 526 C.E.]) as existence outside time rather than existence in time flowing from minus infinity to plus infinity. The second problem concerns the interpretation of the initial singularity appearing in some solutions of Einstein's equations describing the evolution of cosmological models. The question whether such a singularity (for instance the one corresponding to the Big Bang in the standard cosmological model) could be identified with God's act of creation was once heatedly discussed. The prevailing view at the start of the twenty-first century is that such interpretations should be postponed (if they are methodologically legitimate) until a trustworthy quantum cosmology becomes available

Rapid progress in relativity theory, especially during the second half of the twentieth century, greatly contributed to the development of geometry. New physical problems required the sharpening of known geometric methods and the invention of new ones. In fact, the necessity to consider more and more abstract spaces gradually led to the broadening of the notion of geometry itself. The process of the geometrization of physics has changed both physics and geometry.

Noncommutative geometry

It seems that a long dialogue between science and religion has made people more cautious about drawing theological conclusions from scientific premises, but there is still one lesson the theologian can learn from this process. The degree of generalization of spatial and temporal concepts one meets in geometry and its applications to physics is a good warning against anthropomorphisms in theological language.

One notable achievement in geometry at the end of the twentieth century is the creation and rapid progress in the so-called noncommutative geometry, which has some roots in the mathematical formalism of quantum mechanics. One of its aims is to deal with spaces that are intractable with the help of the usual geometric methods. Noncommutative spaces are, in general, purely global entities; no local concepts have, in general, any meaning. For example, the concept of point, as a typically local concept, has no meaning in many noncommutative spaces. The number of attempts to apply noncommutative geometry to physics, for instance to create a fundamental physical theory, is

constantly increasing. Some such attempts can have a profound philosophical meaning. For example, it is possible to create a model of the fundamental physical level in which there is no space and no time in their usual senses (space consisting of points and time consisting of instants, which are local concepts) and yet, in spite of this, an authentic dynamics (i.e., equations modeling behavior of physical systems under the action of forces) can be defined in them. Even if such models will turn out to be false, they demonstrate, by being logically consistent, that time (in the usual sense as transient succession of events) is not the necessary condition for an authentic activity. This seems to falsify the claim of some theologians that the idea of an active agent existing outside the flow of time is contradictory in itself.

Conclusion

To conclude, it could be said that although in the past there were many direct influences coming from geometry to theology, it seems unlikely that this will happen in the future. However, one could expect an indirect influence. Modern geometric methods and their application to physics and other natural sciences doubtless shape people's sense of rationality, and this feeling for the rational will continue to be a powerful source of theological inspirations.

See also BIG BANG THEORY; EINSTEIN, ALBERT; MATHEMATICS; NEWTON, ISAAC; PHYSICS, QUANTUM; RELATIVITY, GENERAL THEORY OF; SINGULARITY; SPACE AND TIME

Bibliography

Boyer, Carl B. *A History of Mathematics*. New York: Wiley, 1968.

Connes, Alain. *Noncommutative Geometry*. New York: Academic Press, 1994.

Davies, Paul C. W. *The Mind of God: The Scientific Basis for a Rational World*. New York: Simon and Schuster, 1992.

Funkenstein, Amos. *Theology and the Scientific Imagination from the Middle Ages to the Seventeenth Century*. Princeton, N.J.: Princeton University Press, 1986.

Kline, Morris. *Mathematics in Western Culture*. London: Penguin Books. 1977.

Torrance, Thomas F. *Space, Time, and Incarnation.* Oxford: Oxford University Press, 1969.

MICHAEL HELLER

GEOMETRY: PHILOSOPHICAL ASPECTS

The theological and religious importance of geometry needs to be addressed in conjunction with the much wider question of the relationship between those religious aspirations that strive to lay hold upon abstract eternal truths embedded and embodied in God and others that emphasize the importance of contingent, temporal, and ephemeral features of existence. To some extent this antithesis reflects the differences between the ancient Greek philosophers Plato (427–347 B.C.E.) and Aristotle (384–322 B.C.E.) in their attitudes toward the status of mathematical objects.

For Plato, neither geometrical objects such as points, lines, and circles, nor arithmetical objects such as numbers could be conceived as existing in the physical world. Since two shapes could not be the same, nor two objects equal, concepts such as shape and number had to belong to a realm beyond sense and experience, the realm of forms or ideas. Aristotle rejected this notion, preferring to think of geometrical and arithmetic objects as reductive abstractions from experience that give rise to mental generalities. During the Middle Ages, the Christian philosopher Thomas Aquinas was to make much of this in terms of intellective and abstractive knowledge, and in their turn John Duns Scotus (c. 1265–1308) and William of Ockham (c. 1285–1347) were to contribute to the debate by relating the issues to questions of universal and particular knowledge. Even so, the issue of the grounding of geometrical truth did not challenge the self-evident truth of Euclidean geometry; that had to await the advent of non-Euclidean geometries and the philosophical criticisms of John Stuart Mill (1806–1873) during the nineteenth century.

Euclidean geometry

Greek mathematics culminated around 300 B.C.E. in Euclid Alexandria's *Elements,* whose achievement was to treat geometry axiomatically through a rigorous system of deduction. This abstraction reflected the value placed upon eternal ideas by the platonic school, and rid geometry of reliance upon particular instances of such things as circles and lines. Euclid's achievement was to classify rather than discover the theorems he systematized. He was able to see that the entire edifice of geometry could be captured in a deductive system based upon five foundational assumptions or *postulates.* Granted those assumptions, no reference to the physical world was required, and the truths of the theorems he was able to deduce became tautological. Albert Einstein (1879–1955), writing long after the monopoly of Euclidean geometry had been broken, reiterated essentially the same point about the relationship between geometry and experience in his essay of that name where he observed that only one assumption is required in addition to a geometrical system: the further postulate that it is a model for the real world.

Whether the configuration and behavior of the physical world conforms to a deductive geometrical system is nonetheless an open question. If it does, there is a remarkable harmony between an abstract construction of the human mind and the workings of the world—part of what contemporary physicist Stephen Weinberg has called "the unreasonable effectiveness of mathematics," but the effectiveness of geometry may say more about the limitation and consistency of human thought and action than it does about the behavior of the world. As the Italian philosopher Giambattista Vico (1668–1744) put it in the *Nuovo Scienza* (New Science, 1725), the dilemma arises from the fundamental question of the relationship between the "found" and the "made" (*verum et factum*).

Euclidean geometry dominated mathematics for the subsequent two thousand years. Problems posed in antiquity that provided the stimuli for the development of enormous areas of mathematics—construction of a square with area exactly that of a given circle, the doubling of the volume of the altar at Delos, or the trisection of an angle (all to be solved using only straightedge and compasses)—remained unresolved until modern times, when all three were proved to be impossible. The influence of Euclidean geometry permeated education, architecture, science, and literature. The mediaeval *trivium* and *quadrivium* made geometry an essential ingredient of education. The Italian poet Dante Alighieri (1265–1321) designed the structure of Hell, Purgatory, and Heaven around it in his epic poem *The Divine Comedy*. First Ptolemy (c. 85–165 C.E.) and then Nicolaus Copernicus (1483–1543), Johannes Kepler (1571–1630), and Isaac Newton (1642–1727) devised their world systems upon it. Prohibition of images in Islam encouraged the intricate geometrical patterns used to decorate mosques.

Perhaps the most significant change in the study of geometry occurred with René Descartes's (1596–1650) invention of algebraic or *analytic* geometry as described in the *Discourse on Method* (1637) by envisaging geometrical figures superimposed on a grid, thereby making their properties susceptible to algebraic analysis. It is impossible to exaggerate the importance of this change, for it allowed geometry to be integrated into the calculus as discovered by Newton and Gottfried Wilhelm Leibniz (1646–1716), and so into the emerging theories of the physical world. Immanuel Kant (1724–1804) took it as an obvious a priori truth in the *Critique of Pure Reason* in 1781 that the sum of the angles of a triangle is 180 degrees, and Euclid continues to be taught throughout the world as a quintessential example of a deductive system to assess the potential of young mathematicians. Carl Friedrich Gauss (1777–1855), prompted by his study of curvature, was experimenting with alternative geometries, and the nineteenth century saw them proliferate through the work of Nikolai Ivanovitch Lobachevsky (1793–1856), Gauss's pupil Georg Friedrich Bernhard Riemann (1826–1866), and others.

Non-Euclidean geometries

From Euclid's own time there had been persistent attempts to deduce the "fifth postulate"—often cited as "through any point not in a given line one and only one line can be drawn parallel to the given line"—from the other four. These attempts continued until beyond Gauss's time, but he gradually became convinced that they were futile, that the fifth postulate was independent of the others, and therefore that it could be modified to produce non-Euclidean geometries. Lobachevsky was similarly obsessed with proving the fifth postulate, but, unlike Gauss, between 1826 and 1829 he worked on and eventually published his discovery of non-Euclidean geometry, thus dealing a blow to the Kantian system similar, as Carl Boyer puts it, to the impact on Pythagoreanism of the discovery of incommensurables. The "Copernicus of geometry,"

Lobachevsky was the first to generate an entirely consistent and coherent geometry that rejected Euclid's fifth postulate (although Janos Bólyay [1802–1860] also developed one almost simultaneously), but even he was so bemused by its counter-intuitive properties that he called it "imaginary" geometry. Non-Euclidean geometry nonetheless remained an obscure mathematical curiosity until taken up and generalized by Riemann. He realized that geometry need not be based upon quasi-Euclidean postulates at all, but could be regarded as a set of *n-tuples* (co-ordinates) combined according to certain rules. These rules define a *metric* and give rise to different kinds of Riemannian "space" governed by *tensors*. These spaces were to prove fundamental to the revolution in physics brought about by Einstein.

The realization that there were non-Euclidean geometries shook the foundations of mathematics and contributed to the demise of absolute foundationalism in philosophy, even though the discovery of different and mutually exclusive axiomatic geometries gave new momentum to the study of deductive systems based upon "foundations." Whereas for Kant and his predecessors there had seemed to be no element of choice in the determination of the geometry of the world because there was only one geometry, and that Euclid's, after Gauss and Lobachevsky it became necessary to add the postulate that Einstein was to remark on, that a particular geometry should also be chosen as the geometry of "real world." As he was to show in his theory of General Relativity, the "natural" geometry of the universe is not Euclidean at all, but Riemannian.

Implications for theology

In theological terms, the ubiquity and power of geometry have often been regarded as evidence for the work of God, whose mind has come on such a basis to be thought of as a perfect deductive system. But there are serious difficulties with such a view. One concerns the parallelism between deduction and determinism; another concerns the problem of the found and the made.

Deductive systems self-consciously avoid the introduction of any new material whatever; proof involves rendering explicit what is already implicit by applying the rules of deductive logic. A universe governed by physical laws equivalent to such deductive systems would be deterministic; there would quite literally be "no new thing under the sun" (Eccles. 1:9). At best, as occurs when implicit truths are rendered explicit by the articulation and proof of a new theorem in geometry, people would find themselves surprised by the unforeseen; but any freedom, either for God or for human beings, would be illusory, the outworking of an implicit and inevitable necessity.

Since Kant, people have been forced to take seriously the notion that what they regard as the intelligibility of the world is in reality the inner coherence of their modes of thought: in Vico's language, the intelligibility of the made, not the found. Objections to the employment of geometry as a model for the world reiterate this view in the context of doubts about the fine structure of the world and the limits of observation. Such doubts have been reinforced by the development of quantum mechanics and relativity, which suggest that human intuitions about the world are mistaken (although even these suggestions are still to be construed within a conceptual system, and not as grounded in a noumenal world).

Nonetheless, the expansion of elementary geometry into analytic geometry, topology, and linear algebra, preserves the sense of the "unreasonable effectiveness of mathematics," and suggests that, all doubts to the contrary notwithstanding, there may remain some sense in Newton's designation of the universe as the divine *sensorium,* albeit construed as a creation embodying the structure of a divine geometry, and intelligible only to a divine mind.

John Stuart Mill (1806–1873) was one of the first to challenge Kant's view that the a priori truths of geometry are necessary consequences of the possibility conditions of rational thought, in other words, that to be rational people have to think the world, amongst other things, in Euclidean terms. Mill did not know of non-Euclidean geometry, but attributed the apparent inescapability of Euclidean geometry to paucity of imagination, and its domination to the kinds of experiences to which human beings are susceptible. Mill seems to have been vindicated by the predilection of physical theory—in both quantum mechanics and relativity—for non-Euclidean geometries that defy everyday human intuitions.

Towards the end of the nineteenth century fundamental changes in philosophy of mathematics occurred, most notably the articulation of *logicism* by German mathematician and philosopher Gottlob Frege (1848–1925). Frege attempted to reduce arithmetic to logical categories by employing the theory of sets and the non-Euclidean geometries of Riemann that discard the intuitive notions of line and plane familiar from Euclid in favor of abstract *n-tuples* governed by arbitrary rules.

Attempts to reduce mathematics to logic were associated with Frege's attack on *psychologism,* itself a descendant of Kant's view that the nature of intelligible reality is governed not by properties of an objective world but by the rules of thought. Often called a modern platonism, Frege's work struggled to ground mathematics in an inviolable world independent of experience. Unfortunately, by adopting the theory of sets, Frege fell foul of Bertrand Russell's (1872–1970) celebrated paradox that the "set of all sets that are not members of themselves" both is and is not a member of itself, thus demonstrating that there is an apparent antinomy in the theory of sets.

Quite apart from its relevance to ontology and epistemology, and thus to theology, geometry has played a major role in the more everyday development of religion. Closely associated with the educated and priestly classes, with astronomy and astrology, with numerology and mysticism, geometry has repeatedly had an impact on the way people have viewed the order and mystery of the world. The Pythagoreans regarded number as the basis of all knowledge and truth, many religions and cults have seen mystical significance in the properties of geometrical shapes, especially the golden rectangle/ratio and the pentangle, widely employed in magic.

The fundamental religious importance of geometry nevertheless emerges from questions of the relationship between divine creative purpose, the structure and operation of the natural world, and the conceptual capacities of the human mind. If, as Einstein suggested, "the only unintelligible thing about the world is that it is intelligible," there seems to be an intrinsic harmony between all three, and geometry seems able, at least in the limit, to embody the structure of the world as found. If, as others suggest, following Kant, "the only intelligible thing about the world is that it is unintelligible," then geometry is a fabrication designed to render the world intelligible at the expense of misrepresenting its intrinsic structure, and geometry can do no more than embody a structure of the world as made in the image of the human mind.

See also KANT, IMMANUEL; MATHEMATICS; NEWTON, ISAAC; PHYSICS

Bibliography

Boyer, Carl B. *A History of Mathematics*. Princeton, N.J.: Princeton University Press, 1985.

Conway, John H., and Guy, Richard K. *The Book of Numbers*. New York: Springer-Verlag, 1996.

Coxeter, H. S. M. *Introduction to Geometry*. New York: Wiley, 1961.

Gulberg, Jan. *Mathematics: From the Birth of Numbers*. New York: Norton, 1996.

Heath, Thomas L. *The Thirteen Books of Euclid's Elements, Books 1 and 2*. New York: Dover, 1956.

Hofstadter, Douglas R. *Gödel, Escher, Bach: An Eternal Golden Braid*. New York: Basic Books, 1999.

Stewart, Ian. *Flatterland: Like Flatland, Only More So*. London: Macmillan, 2001.

JOHN C. PUDDEFOOT

GERMLINE INTERVENTION

See GENE THERAPY

GLOBAL WARMING

Three important indicators suggest that the Earth's climate is going through a period of global warming: (1) an increase in atmospheric temperatures near the Earth's surface; (2) an increase in the surface temperature of the Earth's oceans; and (3) an increase in sea levels. Since global weather patterns are extraordinarily complex, with different systems influencing one another, the effects of global warming will vary from region to region. For instance, as global warming continues, some regions should have dramatic increases in annual precipitation levels, whereas other regions should have dramatic decreases—even desertification. Within the science

and religion literature, discussions of global warming occur most frequently within ecological ethics. Ethicists draw from the climatology sciences to inform their reflection and analysis.

See also ECOLOGY; ECOLOGY, ETHICS OF; ECOLOGY, RELIGIOUS AND PHILOSOPHICAL ASPECTS; ECOLOGY, SCIENCE OF

RICHARD O. RANDOLPH

GOD

Taken in its subjective sense, the word *God* refers to whatever is the object of one's ultimate concern. Thus one might judge about a person, "Money or power is his god." But one can also ask whether his "god" really is God, whether what he treats as god possesses the properties one would expect in an object of ultimate concern. In this second or more objective sense, then, *God* refers to whatever is truly ultimate: the greatest being, the highest object of belief, the ground of all being. Most often, to believe in God means to believe that the ultimate reality is personal. That is, the divine possesses all the positive features that one associates with "mind" (intellect, will, self-consciousness, and perhaps emotions), but possesses them in an infinitely higher and more perfect form than humans do. For virtually all theists, God is understood as the creator of all things. For most theists, God is also understood as providentially involved in guiding the world subsequent to its creation.

Two major sources have added more specific content to the notion of God. The various religious traditions have developed extensive beliefs about the nature of God, the actions and self-revelation of God in the world, and the sorts of ethical and moral principles that most correspond to the divine nature. In a similar fashion, but not always in lockstep, the philosophical traditions have reached conclusions on what most appropriately count as attributes of God, how (if at all) the divine could be known, and why an infinite God could never be fully comprehended by finite knowers. Theologians have combined features from both of these approaches. They draw on beliefs from one or more of the religions, while analyzing and reformulating these beliefs using conclusions and conceptual tools developed by philosophers over the centuries. The result is a spectrum of positions on whether there are many gods or only one, on what it means to say that God is personal, and on how God is related to the world.

A brief history of God

Before there was belief in one God (monotheism), there was belief in many gods (polytheism). The earliest cultural remnants show humans relating to parts of the natural world (mountains, bodies of water, thunder and lightening, changes in climate) as if they were the product of personal forces. Finding reasons for natural events was perhaps the first step toward science, which gives explanations based on impersonal forces rather than on supernatural agents.

As cultures became more sophisticated, the gods took on personalities distinct from natural objects. Some of this evolution is visible in the Hebrew Bible, an authoritative text for Jewish, Christian, and Muslim views of God. Yahweh, the God of Abraham and his clan, was "a jealous God" (Exod. 20:5) who would allow "no other gods" before him (Deut. 5:7). Gradually the Israelites realized that Yahweh was "a great King above all gods" (Ps. 95:3), indeed so all-encompassing that there could be no other gods: "For I am God, and there is no other" (Isa. 45:22). Hence, the three Western monotheisms came to hold that God's power must be unlimited (omnipotence), as must be God's perception (omnipresence), God's knowledge (omniscience), and God's goodness (omnibenevolence). Yahweh must be the sole creator of all that is. All must stem from God, and God must have created all out of nothing (*creatio ex nihilo*). God became the ultimate ground and explanation of all things, the One who alone is worthy of worship.

In addition to this shared basis, the Western monotheisms also evidence important differences, regarding, for example, whether the divine nature is *trinitarian* (three-in-one) or not. Even if the full variety of specific beliefs about God cannot be treated in this entry, the differences remain vital for many believers. Indeed, many would resist the notion of "generic theism." That is, many would say that they are not believers in God in general but believers in "the God of Abraham, Isaac, and Jacob," or disciples of Allah as he revealed himself to the prophet Mohammed, or believers in the Holy Trinity of "God the Father, His Son Jesus Christ, and the Holy Spirit."

God and contemporary science

Some leading philosophers and scientists (for example, in the twentieth century, Bertrand Russell, Antony Flew, Edward O. Wilson, and Richard Dawkins) hold that belief in God as an explanatory principle is incompatible with science. Clearly, if science entails some form of metaphysical naturalism (physicalism, materialism, or nontheistic emergence), then all forms of theism are excluded; belief in a single act of divine creation would be no better off than the belief that one must sacrifice to the rain god. By contrast, other leading scientists are theists and find no conflict between their religious belief and the practice of science.

Among the latter group one finds stronger and weaker claims. For example, many hold that science and personalist theism are at least compatible and can coexist without contradiction or tension. Perhaps science explains the "how" of the universe, theism its ultimate "why." Perhaps divine actions concern only the "before" and "after," the moment of creation that led to the existence of physical laws and the final act that establishes "a new heaven and a new Earth" (Rev. 21:1). Or perhaps God-language refers to the ground of all existence and all value but can never be used to explain any particular thing or event.

Others make stronger claims: The order in the universe is best understood as an expression of the nature of God. Without God one cannot finally make sense of the lawfulness and mathematical simplicity of the physical world (John Polkinghorne), or of the evolution of intelligent life (theistic evolutionists and Intelligent Design theorists such as William Demski), or of human rationality and morality (Alvin Plantinga). It is argued that the fundamental physical constants are "fine-tuned" so as conjointly to make it possible, or even likely, that intelligent life would emerge, and that a supernatural agent offers the best explanation of this fact. To use Robert John Russell's distinction, they argue either that the universe is consistent with what the believer in God would expect (the theology of nature) or that the fine-tuning of physical constants actually provides evidence that God exists (natural theology).

Those who find science and theism in conflict suggest two different answers. One group responds that belief in God has to be eliminated, or at least radically modified so that it fits into the gaps left by science and makes no claims incompatible with it (the "god of the gaps"). For example, theistic language could be viewed as an expression of a cultural, emotional, or psychological particularity, similar to one's manner of dressing or speaking. If God-talk makes no truth claims, it cannot conflict with scientific results. Another group responds that the results and methods of science should instead be set aside whenever they conflict with theological truths. Religious fundamentalism may employ scientific-sounding language, as in "young Earth creationism"; it may refute science by appeal to scriptural texts; or it may associate God with "truths beyond the reach of reason" seen only through "the eyes of faith."

In summary, the differences in the logic of scientific theories and God-language are generally acknowledged. Proponents differ on whether the differences are tensions and, if so, how serious they are. Should the tensions be minimized, bringing science and religion into the greatest consonance possible, or should they be maximized, making the contrasts as stark as possible?

Issues on God and science

The God-science relationship has continually fascinated reflective persons for its alternating resonances and dissonances.

The problem of divine action. For Jews, Christians, and Muslims, God creates the world, sustains it in existence, and acts providentially to bring about divine purposes. Far from being deists, these traditions espoused miracles (supernatural interventions into history that set aside natural law). Indeed, the miracle of the resurrection lies at the center of Christian faith. But such miracles are by definition inaccessible to scientific study; indeed, they seem to imply the negation of scientific results and methods. Contemporary efforts to minimize the conflict include developing noninterventionist accounts of divine action in the world, reducing God's role to a single all-encompassing act, and offering fully naturalized reworkings of the traditional religions that eschew all miracle claims.

Evidences for and against God. Do human beings inhabit a cosmos that displays the signs of creation by a benevolent, omnipotent deity? Some say no. Vast regions are cold and uninhabitable; does all this exist just for the sake of intelligent animals on one planet? Entropy means the universe will wind down; what sign is there of "a new heaven and a new Earth"? Finally, why would a benevolent God allow such incredible evil, suffering, and wastefulness of life—both in the natural world and at the hands of man?

Others argue that the cosmos does display signs of creation by God. Could a random origin and evolution have produced beings capable of rational thought and moral action? The improbability suggests design. Moreover, they argue, the result is different in kind from physical evolution; consciousness, rationality, and morality are better explained by a "first cause" that itself possesses these features. The universe possesses a mathematical simplicity that evokes a religious (or quasi-religious) response from many scientists, and a beauty that for some is both awe-inspiring and sublime. The argument for God as the best explanation becomes more compelling when supplemented with personal religious experience of the divine or, in Immanuel Kant's phrase, of "the moral law within."

God and specific scientific results. In cosmology, the "singularity" of the Big Bang seemed to offer support for a doctrine of creation. In Jim Hartle and Stephen Hawking's quantum cosmology, however, there would be no $t = 0$ (time equals zero), hence no time at which God could create. Perhaps creation could be understood as the contingency of the world on God, even if there were never a "moment of creation," as Robert John Russell posits.

Neo-Darwinian evolution involves random genetic variation and selective retention by the environment. Denying evolution seems impossible, but theists have argued that the process may be "guided" by God in ways not yet fully visible or understood. Sociobiology and evolutionary psychology also challenge the ontological uniqueness of the human animal and hence challenge claims that humans are created "in the image of God."

The neurosciences can increasingly reconstruct the neural correlates of cognitive functions. Will they someday be able to detect the neurological footprints of God's interactions with individuals?

Might they discriminate between genuine and counterfeit experiences of God? Or will God's interactions with the world always escape human detection and rational analysis?

"God beyond God," experience, and mystery

The history of the interrelations between God and science mirror something of the history of God and philosophy. Like philosophy, science uses its analytic tools to falsify an ever larger number of specific claims about God. Yet neither can verify the divine, and neither can rule out God's existence. The experiences of something transcendent, someone divine, remain; hence room remains for conceiving God in a way that conflicts with neither science nor philosophy (the Transcendent Other, the "God beyond God"). New philosophical theologies, such as panentheism, can reformulate traditional claims about God's relationship with the world in new and more adequate ways. In the end, the question of God remains part of the ultimate mystery that faces humans in their walk between birth and death.

See also CREATIO EX NIHILO; DIVINE ACTION; EMERGENCE; GOD OF THE GAPS; MONOTHEISM; NATURAL THEOLOGY; OMNIPOTENCE; OMNIPRESENCE; OMNISCIENCE; PANENTHEISM; THEISM; THEOLOGY

Bibliography

Armstrong, Karen. *A History of God: The 4000-Year Quest of Judaism, Christianity, and Islam.* London: Heinemann, 1993.

Clayton, Philip. *God and Contemporary Science.* Grand Rapids. Mich.: Eerdmans, 1998.

Clayton, Philip. *The Problem of God in Modern Thought.* Grand Rapids, Mich.: Eerdmans, 2000.

Davies, Paul. *God and the New Physics.* New York: Simon and Schuster, 1983

Moltmann, Jürgen. *God in Creation: A New Theology of Creation and the Spirit of God.* Minneapolis, Minn.: Fortress Press, 1993.

Peacocke, Arthur. *Theology for a Scientific Age: Being and Becoming—Natural, Divine, and Human.* Minneapolis, Minn.: Fortress, 1993.

Polkinghorne, John. *Belief in God in an Age of Science.* New Haven, Conn.: Yale University Press, 1998.

PHILIP CLAYTON

GÖDEL'S INCOMPLETENESS THEOREM

By the early part of the twentieth century, the work of mathematical logicians such as Gottlob Frege, Bertrand Russell, and Alfred North Whitehead had honed the axiomatic method into an almost machine-like technique of producing mathematical theorems from carefully stated first principles (axioms) by means of clear logical rules of inference. In 1931, however, Kurt Gödel (1906–1978), an Austrian logician, uncovered a surprising limitation inherent in any axiomatic system intended to produce theorems expressing the familiar mathematical properties of integer arithmetic.

Gödel developed a method, whose reach was slightly extended by J. Barkley Rosser in 1936, that shows how, given any such (consistent) system of axioms, one can produce a true proposition about integers that the axiomatic system itself cannot produce as a theorem. Gödel's incompleteness result follows: Unless the axioms of arithmetic are inconsistent (self-contradictory), not all arithmetical truths can be deduced in such machine-like fashion from any fixed set of axioms. This result, that here consistency implies "incompleteness," has striking implications not only for mathematical logic, but also for machine-learning (artificial intelligence) and epistemology, although its precise significance is still debated.

Gödel's work was stimulated by a program of the mathematician David Hilbert (1862–1943), whose goals included showing that the consistency of higher mathematics need not be based solely upon faith in the reasonableness of its axioms and methods, but could be established using means no more questionable than those of elementary arithmetic. The link Gödel discovered between consistency and completeness of elementary arithmetic, however, led him to a further result strongly suggesting that this goal, as originally envisioned by Hilbert, is unattainable. Although relatively few nonspecialists have mastered Gödel's proof, many general readers have attained an appreciation of his argument through popular accounts of its connection with familiar paradoxes involving self-reference.

See also ARTIFICIAL INTELLIGENCE; MATHEMATICS; PARADOX, SELF-REFERENCE

Bibliography

Hofstadter, Douglas R. "Analogies and Metaphors to Explain Gödel's Theorem." In *Mathematics: People, Problems, Results,* eds. Douglas M. Campbell and John C. Higgins. Belmont, Calif.: Wadsworth International, 1984.

Nagel, Ernest, and Newman, James R. *Gödel's Proof.* New York: New York University Press, 1958.

W. M. PRIESTLEY

GOD, EXISTENCE OF

Most theists tend to think of God as the Supreme Being. Human knowledge and power are strictly limited, while God is omniscient and omnipotent. But humans are beings and God is a vastly superior being. Hence human beings exist and God exists in exactly the same sense. The tradition of Christian theology, however, also contains conceptions of the differences separating God and creatures that are more radical. According to Thomas Aquinas (c. 1225–1274), for example, there is in human beings a distinction between essence, which is to say what human beings are, and existence. But in God essence and existence are identical; God's essence is to exist. God is Being Itself, not one being among others. Thus humans exist and God exists in different though analogously related senses. And an even more radical separation is found in the mystical theology of Meister Eckhart (1260–1328). He distinguishes between God (*Gott*) and the Godhead (*Gottheit*). The Godhead is an aspect or dimension of divine reality that is above or beyond being. It is neither a being nor Being Itself. Paradoxically, it cannot be said to exist, even though it is the Ultimate Reality. Jean-Luc Marion develops a conception of this sort in his aptly titled *God Without Being* (1991).

Evidential support for claims about the existence of God comes from several sources. They include religious experience, revelation, and theological reflection. According to William P. Alston's *Perceiving God* (1991), claims about how God is interacting with a human subject of religious experience derive prima facie epistemic justification from a kind of nonsensory perception in which it seems to the subject that God is performing actions of various sorts. The God encountered in such experiences is taken to be a being capable of interacting with human beings. In the Hebrew Bible, when Moses asks God to make known the divine name, God says in response to Moses, "I am who I am" (Exod. 3:14). According to some interpretations, it is revealed by means of this response that God is Being Itself. The idea that God is not just a being among beings thus derives epistemic warrant from scriptural revelation. And in *The Courage to Be* (1952), Paul Tillich speaks of the God above the God of theism. He also claims that the divine Ultimate Reality is not a being or even Being Itself, but is instead the Ground of Being. Theological reflection therefore lends credibility to the claim that God is somehow beyond being.

However, one must turn to certain parts of natural theology if one wishes to find a source of evidence for the existence of God that is sensitive to empirical science. According to Immanuel Kant (1724–1804), natural theology's main arguments for God's existence may be classified as ontological, cosmological, or teleological. Anselm of Canterbury (c. 1033–1109) is the author of the first and most famous ontological argument. He attempted to derive the existence of God from the idea of God as a being greater than which cannot be conceived. But since the premises of ontological arguments are supposed to be knowable a priori and so independent of human experience of the world, such arguments do not in any way rely on scientific knowledge of that world.

Cosmological arguments do appeal to premises about the empirical world that is the object of scientific inquiry. Two familiar cosmological arguments are among Aquinas's celebrated five ways of proving the existence of God. One starts from the premise that there are now things undergoing change and things causing change; it concludes that an unchanging first cause of change exists. The other starts from the premise that there are contingent things that might not have existed; it concludes that there is a necessary being on which contingent things depend for their existence. Because the premises of these two arguments invoke only very general features of the world that humans experience, their truth does not depend on the details of the scientific worldview. There are, however, cosmological arguments that are sensitive to such details. In his contribution to *Theism, Atheism, and Big Bang Cosmology* (1993), William Lane Craig argues for God's existence from physical cosmology. According to Big Bang cosmology, the cosmos began to exist twelve to fifteen billion years ago. Reasoning from the principle that anything that begins to exist must be brought into existence by something, Craig concludes that God brought the cosmos into existence. Craig's argument is, of course, quite controversial. In his contribution to *Theism, Atheism, and Big Bang Cosmology,* Quentin Smith contends that Big Bang cosmology provides the basis for a successful argument to atheism.

But science bears most directly on natural theology through teleological or design arguments. The best known design argument is contained in William Paley's *Natural Theology* (1802). Paley argues for an analogy between the order displayed by biological structures, such as the human eye, and the order of mechanical devices, such as watches that are known to be products of design, and he concludes that God designed those biological structures. This sort of analogical design argument was subjected to devastating criticism by David Hume (1711–1776), and Darwinian mechanisms involving variation and natural selection have successfully explained a great deal of biological order. So Paley's design argument has lost its popularity.

More recent design arguments appeal to other sorts of natural order. In *The Existence of God* (1979), Richard Swinburne argues that the temporal order in the cosmos expressed by natural laws together with the fact that nature is composed of only a few elementary building blocks are evidence of design. He concludes that this evidence boosts the probability of God's existence. Others have drawn attention to the fact that various parameters such as certain physical constants and initial conditions of the cosmos at the Big Bang must lie within narrowly restricted limits if life is to evolve. They contend that God fine-tuned those parameters for the purpose of producing either life of some sort or other, or human life in particular. These arguments too have turned out to be controversial.

And in the United States, the Intelligent Design creationism movement aims to overthrow Darwinism. Michael Behe, one of the prominent figures in this movement, argues in *Darwin's Black Box* (1996) that molecular and cell biology have revealed irreducible biological complexity that cannot be explained in terms of Darwinian mechanisms of variation and natural selection. Behe's

view is that such complexity is the product of divine design. Intelligent Design creationism has been vigorously disputed by many scientists and philosophers. A balanced and comprehensive presentation of the views on both sides of this new outbreak of warfare between science and religion may be found in *Intelligent Design Creationism and Its Critics* (2001), a volume edited by Robert T. Pennock. It remains an open question whether any part of scientific knowledge supports or undermines belief in the existence of God.

See also COSMOLOGICAL ARGUMENT; DESIGN; INTELLIGENT DESIGN; ONTOLOGICAL ARGUMENT; TELEOLOGICAL ARGUMENT

Bibliography

Alston, William P. *Perceiving God: The Epistemology of Religious Experience.* Ithaca, N.Y.: Cornell University Press, 1991.

Behe, Michael. *Darwin's Black Box: The Biochemical Challenge to Evolution.* New York: Free Press, 1996.

Craig, William Lane, and Smith, Quentin. *Theism, Atheism, and Big Bang Cosmology.* New York and Oxford: Oxford University Press, 1993.

Marion, Jean-Luc. *God Without Being,* trans. Thomas A. Carlson. Chicago: University of Chicago Press, 1991.

Paley, William. *Natural Theology.* London: Faulder; Philadelphia, Pa.: John Morgan, 1802.

Pennock, Robert T., ed. *Intelligent Design Creationism and Its Critics.* Cambridge, Mass.: MIT Press, 2001.

Swinburne, Richard. *The Existence of God.* Oxford: Clarendon Press, 1979.

Tillich, Paul. *The Courage to Be.* New Haven, Conn.: Yale University Press, 1952.

PHILIP L. QUINN

GOD OF THE GAPS

The phrase *God of the gaps* refers to attempts to use statements about divine intervention in the physical world to fill in the "gaps" in scientific explanation. It is the attempt to introduce God as an explanatory hypothesis on the level of efficient causality to make up for limitations in current scientific understanding. The approach simply does not work because eventually scientific understanding closes the gap, making the appeal to divine explanation irrelevant. The approach is not taken seriously as a way of relating science and religion because it violates several fundamental principles of causal analysis and explanation in both science and theology.

History

The phrase *God of the gaps* is often credited to Charles A. Coulson in his book *Science and Christian Belief* (1955). This is certainly one of the first places where the phrase appears in material directly related to the science and religion discussion, but there are antecedents that appear years or even centuries earlier. In his *Letters and Papers from Prison,* German theologian Dietrich Bonhoeffer in correspondence from May 25, 1944, observes in response to Carl F. von Weizsacker's *The Worldview of Physics* that:

> Weizsacker's book . . . brought home to me how wrong it is to use God as a stop-gap for the incompleteness of our knowledge. For the frontiers of knowledge are inevitably being pushed back further and further, which means that you only think of God as a stop-gap. He also is being pushed back further and further, and is in more or less continuous retreat. We should find God in what we do know, not in what we don't . . . (p. 190–191).

Bonhoeffer clearly saw the danger of placing God on the level of secondary causal explanation. God and the God hypothesis would be edged out, just as the astronomer Marquis de Laplace replied "I had no need of that hypothesis" when Napoleon asked why he did not discuss God in his writings. According to Ian Barbour in *Religion and Science: Historical and Contemporary Issues* (1997):

> The "God of the gaps" was as unnecessary in biology after Darwin as it had been in physics after Laplace. Adaptive changes could be accounted for by random variation and natural selection without involving divine intervention. We have Darwin to thank for finally making it clear that God is neither a secondary cause operating on the same level as natural forces nor a means for filling gaps in the scientific account. (p. 73)

The concept of God intervening from beyond to fill in inadequate knowledge or to resolve human problems actually goes back in Western culture to the ancient Greeks and the understanding of a *deus ex machina* (god of the machine) found in Greek theater. When a plot became too convoluted (or the audience's patience and endurance was wearing thin) an actor wearing the mask of the appropriate Greek deity would literally be lowered onto the stage from above by a crane (the machine) and resolve the plot conflicts, restore order, and serve out justice. In later thought, the phrase *deus ex machina* came to refer to any theological concept that involved God directing human or earthly events by dropping out of the supernatural into the natural. The *ad hoc* character of the concept expresses a form of theological desperation in which divine involvement cannot be understood in a coherent way with other forms of rational explanation.

Analysis

Since the time of Aristotle in Western culture a distinction has been made between primary and secondary causal analysis. Primary causal analysis (formal and final) has to do with the ends or purposes of any physical existent and secondary analysis with the means for its arisal (material and efficient). The great gains in scientific analysis have been accomplished at least in part by focusing on secondary analysis, which is observable, measurable, and repeatable. The power of scientific analysis lies precisely in the intentional limiting of the questions to the physically empirical and verifiable. Science as part of its methodology assumes that there will be material and efficient explanations of physical phenomena, that is, the methodology is inclusive of secondary causal analysis. This focus is at the heart of the scientific revolution of the seventeenth century. Theology and philosophy on the other hand have focused on the origins and ends of physical existence. To introduce God as a part of the secondary causal analysis violates principles of scientific understanding and commits a category mistake in causal analysis.

It must also be said that a constructive relationship between religion and science would involve connecting the two forms of causal analysis. Multiple strategies have been proposed for this with God working either "before" or "behind" the physical systems. The former was approached in

Enlightenment deism, where God arranged every-thing "before" the creation like a divine clock-maker and then left the created order to run on its own. This position, while popular in the eighteenth century, was later seen to deny the understanding of God involved in a continuing creation (*creatio continua*) and to be contradictory to the Abrahamic faith traditions.

Since about 1990 attention has been devoted to formulating theories where God works in and through the physical systems, such as in quantum indeterminacy, without violating known physical or biological laws. This "causal joint" discussion has resulted in a number of new theories of divine action ranging from *top-down* or *whole-part* causation (Arthur Peacocke) to *bottom-up* (Robert John Russell), *Persuasion* (John Cobb, David Griffin), *Information* (John Polkinghorne), or *Self-Limitation* (W. H. Vanstone), to name a few. What unites these diverse approaches is their commitment to respect the various physical and life sciences in their causal analyses and yet provide opportunities for dialogue on boundary questions, the ethical application of scientific technology, and other areas of common concern. Mutual respect between science and religion permits this in a way that a "God of the gaps" approach does not because it violates the integrity of both. For these reasons, among others, both "God of the gaps" and *deus ex machina* are not seen as viable concepts for theological understanding in relating science and religion.

See also ARISTOTLE; CAUSALITY, PRIMARY AND SECONDARY; CAUSATION; CREATIO CONTINUA; CREATIO EX NIHILO; CREATION; DEISM; DIVINE ACTION; GOD; GOD, EXISTENCE OF; SKYHOOKS

Bibliography

Barbour, Ian. *Religion and Science: Historical and Contemporary Issues.* San Francisco: Harper, 1997.

Berg, Christian. "Leaving Behind the God-of-the-Gaps: Toward a Theological Response to Limit Questions." In *Expanding Humanity's Vision of God,* ed. Robert Hermann. Philadelphia: Templeton Foundation Press. 2001.

Bonhoeffer, Dietrich. *Letters and Papers From Prison,* ed. Eberhard Bethge. New York: Macmillan, 1953.

Coulson, Charles A. *Science and Christian Belief.* Chapel Hill: University of North Carolina Press, 1955.

Southgate, Christopher, et al. *God, Humanity, and the Cosmos: A Textbook in Science and Religion.* Harrisburg, Pa.: Trinity Press, 1999.

ERNEST SIMMONS

GOULD, STEPHEN JAY

Stephen Jay Gould was born on September 10, 1941, in New York City. He was educated at Antioch College in Ohio and then trained as a paleontologist, doing his doctoral work at Columbia University in New York. His first academic position was at Harvard University in Cambridge, Massachusetts, where he remained for the rest of his life, later adding to his responsibilities a curatorship in paleontology at the American Museum of Natural History in New York. Gould received many honors, including numerous honorary doctoral degrees, and was a member of the National Academy of Sciences.

Gould's early scientific work focused on land snails in Bermuda, and at first he worked in a fairly conventional Darwinian fashion, seeing natural selection as the main cause of evolutionary change. But soon, he and paleontologist Niles Eldredge began trying to break the paradigm of conventional Darwinism, which sees the fossil record as essentially flowing from one form to another, with all gaps due to inadequacies in the record. Gould and Eldredge forwarded a theory of *punctuated equilibrium,* arguing that the fossil record shows stasis (no appreciable change, for periods of time, in some particular line of organisms), followed by very rapid change. The gaps in the record therefore reflect real gaps in the fossilization process.

Gould held to the theory of punctuated equilibrium throughout his life, although the causal mechanism for the process was often in flux and not entirely clear. For a while, Gould floated the idea of *saltations* (real macromutations that jump from one species to another), but this theory was criticized by population geneticists, causing Gould to look for other non-Darwinian, nonselective mechanisms. Together with molecular evolutionist Richard Lewontin, Gould argued that many aspects of organic nature are nonadaptive and could not have been produced by selection. Lewontin and

Gould argued that many features of plants and animals are like spandrels (the tops of columns in medieval churches); they are simply byproducts of the building process and thus without any great biological significance.

Much of Gould's work was not presented directly to his fellow professionals. He was a master at writing for a general audience, especially in essay form. For thirty years he wrote a monthly column called "This View of Life" in the magazine *Natural History.* In this column, Gould explored hundreds of different topics, not all of them related to biology. The essays were collected in several very successful volumes, beginning with *Ever Since Darwin* (1977). Gould also wrote books on general topics, including the history of brain science in *The Mismeasure of Man* (1981) and the fossils of the Burgess Shale in Canada in *Wonderful Life* (1989). At the scholarly level, Gould published numerous articles on the nature of the fossil record, usually in the journal *Paleobiology,* and the book *Ontogeny and Phylogeny* (1977) on the importance of development. Just before he died, Gould completed *The Structure of Evolutionary Theory* (2002), a comprehensive book covering all of his thoughts about evolution. In this last book, Gould turned to the history of science, as he had often done earlier, not merely to develop his ideas but to demonstrate that he was part of a respectable tradition, while his opponents were not.

Gould was admired by the general public, but many of his fellow evolutionists were less open in their praise, perhaps because of professional jealousy combined with discomfort at Gould's arrogant nature. Some critics felt that Gould's ideas were, scientifically speaking, somewhat shallow: Detailed examination did not always bear them out. By the time of Gould's death, consensus on the Eldredge-Gould claim about the nature of the fossil record was that it probably has merit, although there are many exceptions. The lack of a convincing causal hypothesis for punctuated equilibrium certainly counts against it. However, Gould's early stress on the importance of development for a full understanding of the evolutionary process seems fully borne out as molecular biologists turn their interests to questions of history.

Gould admitted that he always wrote with a concern for the morality beneath the surface of his science. A nonpracticing Jew with a Marxist background (the lasting influence of which was a matter of debate), he felt strongly about all matters of prejudice. In the 1970s, Gould was one of the leaders against sociobiology's attempts to explain human nature in terms of biology. Gould argued that sociobiology was not real science, but simply conservative ideology in fancy dress. For him, culture is essentially a spandrel, with no real biological importance. Undoubtedly the Lewontin-Gould attack on adaptation was motivated in part by this continued critique. Sociobiologists argued strongly that human nature is directly adaptive, such that men and women, for example, are psychologically as well as physically different because of their biology. Gould was determined to counter such views.

Gould also saw claims about biological progress as being part and parcel of the offensive ideology against which he fought, which set humans at the top of the animal hierarchy, with white gentiles at the top of the human chain. Gould saw Darwinism, with its emphasis on the success of the fittest, as badly bound up with claims about progress, and this was another reason to attack adaptationism. Many of Gould's popular works, especially *The Mismeasure of Man* and *Wonderful Life,* were explicit critiques on progressionism. Whether or not Gould was correct, such views brought him into conflict with many of his fellow evolutionists. British science writer Richard Dawkins, an ardent Darwinian and progressionist, took strong offence at Gould's thinking, which Dawkins felt distorted and belittled the opposition. In one of his essays, Gould accused the Jesuit paleontologist Pierre Teilhard de Chardin of being responsible for the Piltdown hoax. Many critics, particularly many Catholics, took umbrage at this accusation, since Gould's evidence was slim. Careful examination of the essay, however, shows that Gould's real intent may have been to read Teilhard out of science. As the twentieth century's most ardent progressionist, Teilhard had to be exposed as a man without moral or scientific authority.

Despite this attack on Teilhard, Gould's attitude toward religion was far more complex than that of a typical atheist. Although a nonbeliever, Gould had a passion for singing oratorio, which was equaled by his passion for baseball. He was, in a sense, a deeply religious man, despite the absence of any formal theology. He knew the Bible, both the Old and New Testaments, very well, and he frequently used biblical stories or allusions to illustrate points in his science writing. As an ardent evolutionist, Gould stood firmly against biblical literalists and creationists, and in 1981 he served as an expert witness for the American Civil Liberties Union in its successful litigation against a creationist law that had been passed in Arkansas. One of his last books, *Rocks of Ages* (1999), deals explicitly with issues of science and religion. Gould takes the position of the neo-orthodox (like Langdon Gilkey), arguing that science and religion are different dimensions for understanding and feeling— he calls them *magisteria*—and hence can not come into conflict if properly understood.

Unfortunately, Gould never really explored the ways in which conflict is avoided, and one is left with the impression that any compromise is going to favor religion. Gould's worldview would not allow miracles, for instance, and hence it would be necessary to interpret the resurrection symbolically or metaphorically. Such an approach may be acceptable to some Christians, but not to all, or indeed to most. In a way, therefore, Gould comes across as a logical positivist who is prepared to allow a role for religion as long as it is confined to sentiment, feeling, and morality, but makes no claims about matters of fact.

Gould died on May 20, 2002, in New York City. It is difficult to make long-term predictions about his lasting influence, although he will surely always be celebrated as a brilliant popular writer. It is less likely that he will be remembered as a significant scientist or as a major player in the debate about science and religion.

See also ADAPTATION; CREATIONISM; DARWIN, CHARLES; EVOLUTION, BIOLOGICAL; POSITIVISM, LOGICAL; SOCIOBIOLOGY; TEILHARD DE CHARDIN, PIERRE

Bibliography

Eldredge, Niles, and Gould, Stephen Jay. "Punctuated Equilibria: An Alternative to Phyletic Gradualism." In *Models in Paleobiology,* ed. Thomas. J. M. Schopf. San Francisco: Freeman Cooper, 1972.

Gould, Stephen Jay. *Ever Since Darwin: Reflections in Natural History.* New York: Norton, 1977.

Gould, Stephen Jay. *Ontogeny and Phylogeny.* Cambridge, Mass.: Belknap, 1977.

Gould, Stephen Jay. "The Piltdown Conspiracy." *Natural History* 89 (1980): 8–28.

Gould, Stephen Jay. *The Mismeasure of Man.* New York: Norton, 1981.

Gould, Stephen Jay. *Wonderful Life: The Burgess Shale and the Nature of History.* New York: Norton, 1989.

Gould, Stephen Jay. *Rocks of Ages: Science and Religion in the Fullness of Life.* New York: Norton, 1999.

Gould, Stephen Jay. *The Structure of Evolutionary Theory.* Cambridge, Mass.: Harvard University Press, 2002.

Ruse, Michael. *The Darwinian Paradigm: Essays on Its History, Philosophy, and Religious Implications.* London: Routledge, 1989.

Ruse, Michael. *Monad to Man: The Concept of Progress in Evolutionary Biology.* Cambridge, Mass.: Harvard University Press, 1996.

Ruse, Michael. *Mystery of Mysteries: Is Evolution a Social Construction?* Cambridge, Mass.: Harvard University Press, 1999.

Ruse, Michael. *Darwin and Design: Science, Philosophy, Religion.* Cambridge, Mass.: Harvard University Press, 2003.

MICHAEL RUSE

GRADUALISM

Gradualism, also called *phyletic gradualism,* is the view that the course of evolution is gradual with small changes accumulating through time. Gradualism is opposed to *punctualism,* where evolutionary change is thought to happen in short episodes of rapid evolution followed by long periods of stasis when little or no evolutionary change occurs. The latter view is based on the interpretation of the fossil record and is common among palaeontologists, whereas the former view builds on a version of population genetics theory. However, most evolutionary biologists hold the view that the two concepts are not necessarily contradictory because gradual changes in genotype may occasionally lead to major changes in phenotype.

See also CATASTROPHISM; EVOLUTION; PUNCTUATED EQUILIBRIUM

VOLKER LOESCHCKE

GRAND UNIFIED THEORY

A Grand Unified Theory (GUT) unifies, or interrelates in a single quantum field interaction, the three fundamental nongravitational forces: electromagnetism, the weak nuclear interaction, and the strong nuclear interaction. These three forces are each characterized by a *coupling constant,* which gives the strength of the interaction by a range over which the force acts (long-range like electromagnetism, or short-range like the two nuclear forces), and by certain characteristic symmetries that are described by mathematical symmetry groups. A successful GUT would show how the three different coupling constants become identical at some very high energy, subsume the symmetries of the three individual interactions in a much larger symmetry group, and explain all of the masses, processes, couplings, decays, ranges, and other behaviors of all particles at lower energies—lower than the GUT unification energy. The current standard model of particle physics, though highly successful in other ways, does not do this. Further, there are strong indications that a more complete and adequate explanation, describing deep connections that have so far evaded our understanding, awaits a successful GUT model.

A GUT would express the fact that at the most fundamental level all nongravitational interactions, and all particles, quarks, electrons, and neutrinos, are intimately interrelated and, in fact, identical above the unification energy. Their difference at low energies is expressed in a GUT by saying that the symmetries characterizing the interactions at very high energies, rendering particles and forces identical or equivalent, are "spontaneously broken" below the unification energy. Such spontaneously broken symmetries are present in the underlying relationships characterizing the system, but are not expressed—are hidden—in a given equilibrium state of the system, such as that realized in the present state of the universe. Construction of a GUT theory is an essential step towards achieving total unification, which would also include gravity. Although promising and detailed progress has been made on a number of fronts, there was no adequate GUT as of 2002.

There are strong indications that all the basic physical interactions are intimately related and that they can be unified. In the mid nineteenth century, the Scottish physicist James Clerk Maxwell began realizing this intuition by unifying electrical and magnetic phenomena in his electromagnetic theory. In the 1970s, Sheldon Glashow, Stephen Weinberg, and Abdus Salam succeeded in developing an adequate electroweak theory, which describes how electromagnetism and the weak nuclear interaction are related, and how they are identical at temperatures above 10^{15} K (kelvin). This electroweak theory was confirmed in 1983 by the discovery of the W and Z massive bosons, which carry the electroweak force and which were predicted by the theory. A completely successful GUT would incorporate the strong nuclear interaction with this electroweak interaction in an analogous way at some higher temperature above 10^{27} K.

Part of the motivation for a GUT is the lack of explanation for many of the parameters and characteristics of the standard model, and of the universe itself. For example, there is no explanation for the baryon-anti-baryon asymmetry, which means that there is more matter in the universe than there is antimatter. There is also some positive experimental support for a GUT, including equality of the magnitude of the charges of the proton and the electron and the non-zero rest-mass of the neutrino. Furthermore, GUT candidates generically predict the decay of protons at some very slow rate, as well as the presence of monopoles and other topological defects, which are localized regions in which the vacuum energy is different from the rest of the universe (false vacuum). Observational limits on these phenomena are being used, and will continue to be used, to identify the most adequate GUT candidates.

From a cosmological point of view, the success of a GUT would mean that at some very early stage in the history of the universe—well before one second after the Big Bang, when the temperature of the universe was greater than 10^{27} K—the physics of the universe was characterized by just two interactions: gravity and the GUT interaction. The universe would have been much too hot for protons, neutrons, and electrons to exist, as they do at lower temperatures. As the universe expanded, it cooled. And, as it cooled below 10^{27} K, the GUT interaction split into the strong nuclear and the electroweak interactions. A short time later—still much less than one second after the Big Bang—when the temperature had plummeted below 10^{15} K, the electroweak interaction split further into the weak nuclear and the electromagnetic interactions. From that point on, the basic physics of the universe was the same as it is today, but devoid of the complex macroscopic and microscopic structures that developed much later.

Implications for theology

There are no direct implications of GUT unification for religion and theology, but there are several important indirect influences. First, GUT unification, when it is finally achieved, will contribute to describing how everything in material reality is intimately interconnected in very basic ways. Those relationships constitute reality as it is and are an essential part of how God's continuing creative action is realized—through these "laws of nature." Second, a GUT characterizes a definite, very early stage in the evolution of the universe. A successful GUT will strengthen the already strong case for the evolution of the presently lumpy, cool, complex, and highly differentiated cosmos from a very hot, simple, homogeneous, and relatively undifferentiated primordial state, which was characterized by a much simpler physics. For the theistic thinker, a GUT represents one of the key ways in which God gradually brought into being the reality of which human beings are a part.

See also FIELD THEORIES

Bibliography

Bailin, David, and Love, Alexander. "Grand Unified Theory." In *Introduction to Gauge Field Theory,* rev. edition. Bristol, UK, and Philadelphia: Institute of Physics, 1993.

Börner, Gerhard. "Grand Unification Schemes." In *The Early Universe: Facts and Fiction,* 3rd edition. Berlin, Heidelberg, and New York: Springer-Verlag, 1993.

Collins, P. D. B.; Martin, A. D.; and Squires, E. J. "Grand Unified Theories." In *Particle Physics and Cosmology.* New York: Wiley, 1989.

Davies, Paul. "The New Physics: A Synthesis." In *The New Physics,* ed. Paul Davies. Cambridge, UK: Cambridge University Press, 1989.

Georgi, Howard. "Grand Unified Theories." In *The New Physics,* ed. Paul Davies. Cambridge, UK: Cambridge University Press, 1989.

Guth, Alan, and Steinshardt, Paul. "The Inflationary Universe." In *The New Physics,* ed. Paul Davies. Cambridge, UK: Cambridge University Press, 1989.

Kaku, Michio. "Gauge Field Theories." In *Quantum Unified Theory: A Modern Introduction.* New York and Oxford: Oxford University Press, 1993.

WILLIAM R. STOEGER

GRAVITATION

Gravitation is a universal attractive force exerted by any two physical bodies on each other, even though they may be separated by a large distance. Gravitation is responsible for making objects fall to the surface of the Earth (gravitational attraction of the object by the Earth), for the nearly circular motions of the planets around the sun (gravitational attraction of the planets by the sun), for the structure of stars and planets (gravitational attraction balanced by pressure forces of constituent particles towards each other), and for the structure of star clusters and galaxies (hundreds of millions of stars would fly apart from each other if not held together by gravity). Gravitation also controls the rate at which the universe expands, and is responsible for the growth of small inhomogeneities in the expanding universe into galaxies and clusters of galaxies.

Gravity is the weakest of the four fundamental forces known to physics, but it dominates on large scales because it is a long-distance force that is locally always attractive (in contrast to the far stronger electromagnetic force, which can both attract and repel, and cancels itself out on large scales). Thus gravitation is a dominant force in every day life, as well as in the motions of stars and planets and in the evolution of the cosmos. Indeed, it is one of the forces that makes our existence possible by enabling the formation and stability of plants like Earth that are hospitable to life. Without gravity (at approximately the strength it has on Earth) evolution of life would be difficult if not impossible. This fact can naturally lead to speculation that the existence and specific nature of gravitation could be part of a grand design allowing self-assembling structures to come into existence and lead to intelligent life. In this way, gravity can have theological significance.

Classical physics

Italian astronomer Galileo Galilei (1564–1642) first recognized in the early seventeenth century that when air resistance can be neglected, objects accelerate at the same rate towards the surface of the earth, irrespective of their physical composition. Thus a feather and a cannon ball will arrive at the same time at the earth's surface if simultaneously released from rest at the same height in a vacuum chamber. This means there is a universal rate of acceleration downwards caused by the earth's gravitational field—approximately 32 feet per second squared—irrespective of the nature of the object considered. Gravitational potential energy can be converted to kinetic energy, with total energy conserved, as for example in a roller coaster or a pole vaulter. This enables gravity to do useful work, as in a clock driven by weights or a water mill, but it also means people must work to go uphill. Gravity can also be a danger to people, who can fall or be hurt by falling objects. Despite this danger, gravity is an essential part of the stability of every day life—it is the reason that objects stay firmly rooted on the ground rather than floating into the air.

In the late seventeenth century, Isaac Newton (1642–1727) showed that the gravitational attraction of objects towards the earth and the motion of the planets around the sun could be described accurately by assuming a universal attractive force between any two bodies, proportional to each of their masses and to the inverse of the square of the distance between them. The attractive nature of gravity results because masses are always positive. On this basis he was able to explain both the universal acceleration towards the surface of the earth observed by Galileo and the laws of motion of planets around the sun that had been observationally established earlier in the century by Johannes Kepler (1571–1630). This was the first major unification of explanation attained in theoretical physics, showing that two phenomena that initially appeared completely unrelated had a unified origin. Newton's account of gravitation also explained why the direction of gravity varies at different places on the surface of the earth (always being directed towards its center), allowing "up" to be different directions at different places on the earth's surface (Australia and England, for example).

In conformity with the rest of theoretical physics, Newton's theory of gravity can be reformulated as a variational principle (Hamilton's principle or Lagrange's equations) based on minimisation of particular combinations of kinetic energy and gravitational potential energy along the trajectory followed by a particle. Gravity by itself is a conservative theory (energy is conserved), so there is no friction associated with the motion of stars and planets in the sky, and their motion is fully reversible; the past and future directions of time are indistinguishable, as far as gravity is concerned. Newton was puzzled as to how the force of gravity, as described by his equations, could succeed in acting at a distance when there was no apparent contact between the bodied concerned. Pierre Laplace (1749-1827), a French physicist and mathematician, essentially resolved this puzzle by introducing the idea of a gravitational force field that fills the empty space between massive bodies and mediates the gravitational force between them. The concept of such fields became one of the major features of classical physics, particularly in the case of electromagnetism. In quantum theory the idea gravitational fields is revised and understood as a force mediated by the interchange of force-carrying particles.

Einstein and after

In the early twentieth century, Albert Einstein (1879–1955) radically reshaped the understanding of gravity through his proposal of the general theory of relativity, based on the idea that space-time is curved, with the space-time curvature determined by the matter in it. This theory predicts the motion of planets round the sun more accurately than Newtonian theory can, and also predicts radically new phenomena, in particular, black holes and gravitational radiation. Insofar as science has been able to test these predictions, they are correct. A problem with the theory is that it predicts that under many conditions (for example, at the start of the universe and at the end of gravitational collapse to form a black hole), space-time singularities will occur. Scientists still do not properly understand this phenomenon, but presumably it means that they will have to take the effect of quantum theory on gravity into account. General Relativity does not do so; it is a purely classical theory.

Quantum gravity theories try to develop a theory of gravity that generalizes Einstein's theory and is also compatible with quantum theory. Even the way to start such a project is unclear. Approaches include twistor theory, lattice theories, noncommutative geometries, loop variable theories, and superstring theories. None has reached a satisfactorily developed state, however, much less been tested and shown to be correct. Indeed, in many ways such theories are likely to be untestable. The most ambitious are the superstring theories, now extended into a metatheory of uncertain nature known as *M-theory,* which promises to provide a unified theory of all fundamental forces and particles. M-theory still has far to go before making good on that promise.

Despite the lack of a definite quantum theory of gravity, various attempts have been made to develop quantum theories of cosmology. These theories also face considerable conceptual and calculational problems. The satisfactory unification of quantum theory and general relativity theory, perhaps in some unified theory of all the fundamental forces, remains one of the most significant outstanding problems of theoretical physics.

The desire to develop a practical antigravity machine remains one of humanity's outstanding wishes. No present theory offers a way to such a machine, but the negative gravitational effect of the vacuum energy will continue to inspire some to hope that one day such a machine might exist.

See also BLACK HOLES; COSMOLOGY, PHYSICAL ASPECTS; FORCES OF NATURE; GALILEO GALILEI; NEWTON, ISAAC; PHYSICS, QUANTUM; QUANTUM THEORY; RELATIVITY, GENERAL THEORY OF; SINGULARITY; STRING THEORY; SUPERSTRINGS

Bibliography

Begelman, Mitchell, and Rees, Martin. *Gravity's Fatal Attraction: Black Holes in the Universe.* New York: W. H. Freeman, 1996.

D'Inverno, Ray. *Introducing Einstein's Relativity.* Oxford: Oxford University Press, 1996.

Ellis, George F. R., and Williams, Ruth M. *Flat and Curved Spacetimes.* Oxford: Oxford University Press, 2000.

Hawking, Stephen W., Ellis, George F. R. *The Large-scale Structure of Spacetime.* Cambridge, UK: Cambridge University Press, 1973.

Misner, Charles W.; Thorne, Kip S.; and Wheeler, John A. *Gravitation.* San Francisco: W. H. Freeman, 1973.

Thorne, Kip S. *Black Holes and Time Warps.* New York: Norton, 1994.

GEORGE F. R. ELLIS

GREENHOUSE EFFECT

In the Earth's atmosphere, there are five important greenhouse gases that occur naturally: carbon dioxide, methane, ozone, halocarbons, and nitrous oxide. In correct proportion, these greenhouse gases provide important protection for the Earth's surface. However, if the greenhouse gases become too concentrated in the Earth's atmosphere, then they create a greenhouse effect that overheats the Earth. Although a few scientists continue to dissent, there is near unanimity among climatologists that current global warming is caused by the dramatic increase in atmospheric carbon dioxide since the advent of the Industrial Revolution and the extraordinary increase in the combustion of fossil fuels. In her essay, "The Greening of Science, Theology, and Ethics," Audrey Chapman has argued that ecological ethicists must understand the science behind concepts such as the greenhouse effect in order to contribute meaningful ethical analysis.

See also ECOLOGY; ECOLOGY, ETHICS OF; ECOLOGY, RELIGIOUS AND PHILOSOPHICAL ASPECTS; ECOLOGY, SCIENCE OF

Bibliography

Chapman, Audrey R. "The Greening of Science, Theology, and Ethics." In *Science And Theology: The New Consonance,* ed. Ted Peters. Boulder, Colo.: Westview Press, 1998.

RICHARD O. RANDOLPH

HEALING

See SPIRITUALITY AND FAITH HEALING; SPIRITUALITY
AND HEALTH

HEISENBERG'S UNCERTAINTY
PRINCIPLE

In 1927 the German physicist Werner Heisenberg
(1901–1976) showed that quantum mechanics
leads to the conclusion that certain pairs of quantities can never be measured simultaneously with
arbitrarily high precision, even with perfect measuring instruments. For example, it is not possible to
measure the position and the momentum of a particle with unlimited precision. If one denotes the
uncertainty in the measurement of its position by
Δx and the uncertainty in its momentum by Δp
then Heisenberg's Uncertainty Principle states that
the axioms of quantum mechanics require that

$$\Delta x \times \Delta p \geq h/4\pi$$

where h is Planck's constant
($h = 6.626\ 068\ 76 \times 10^{-34}\ Js$).

The Uncertainty Principle is often presented as
a manifestation of the fact that the act of measurement inevitably perturbs the state that is being
measured. Thus, the smaller the particle being
observed, the shorter the wavelength of light
needed to observe it, and hence the larger the energy of this light and the larger the perturbation
it administers to the particle in the process of

measurement. This interpretation, while helpful for
visualization, has its limitations. It implies that the
particle being observed does have a precise position and a precise momentum which we are unable to ascertain because of the clumsiness of the
measurement process. However, more correctly,
we should view the Uncertainty Principle as telling
us that the concepts of position and momentum
cannot coexist without some ambiguity. There is
no precise state of momentum and position independent of the act of measurement, as naïve realist philosophers had assumed. In large, everyday
situations this quantum mechanical uncertainty is
insignificant for all practical purposes. In the subatomic world it is routinely confirmed by experiment and plays a fundamental role in the stability
of matter. Note that if we take the limit in which
the quantum aspect of the world is neglected (so
Planck's constant, h, is set to zero), then the
Heisenberg Uncertainty would disappear and we
would expect to be able to measure the position
and momentum of any object with perfect precision using perfect instruments (of course in practice this is never possible).

The Uncertainty Principle has had a major effect upon the philosophy of science and belief in
determinism. It means that it is impossible to determine the present state of the world (or any small
part of it) with perfect precision. Even though we
may be in possession of the mathematical laws that
predict the future from the present with complete
accuracy we would not be able to use them to predict the future. The Uncertainty Principle introduces an irreducible indeterminacy, or graininess,
in the state of the world below a particular level of

observational scrutiny. It is believed that this inevitable level of graininess in the state of matter in the universe during the first moments of its history led to the production of irregularities that eventually evolved into galaxies. Experiments are underway in space to test the detailed predictions about the variations left over in the temperature of the universe that such a theory makes.

Of the other pairs of physical quantities that Heisenberg showed cannot be measured simultaneously with arbitrarily high precision, the most frequently discussed pair is energy and time. Strictly, this pair is not a true indeterminate pair like position and momentum because time is not an observable in the way that energy, position, and momentum are in quantum mechanics. By using a time defined externally to the system being observed (rather than intrinsically by it), it would be possible to beat the requirement that the product of the uncertainty in energy times the uncertainty in time be always greater than Planck's constant divided by 4 π.

The physicist Niels Bohr (1885–1962) called quantities, like position and momentum, whose simultaneous measurement accuracy was limited by an uncertainty principle *complementary pairs*. The limitation on simultaneous knowledge of their values is called *complementarity*. Bohr believed that the principle of complementarity had far wider applicability than as a rigorous deduction in quantum mechanics. This approach has also been adopted in some contemporary religious apologetics, notably by Donald Mackay and Charles Coulson. There has also been an interest in using quantum uncertainty, and the breakdown of rigid determinism that it ensures, to defend the concept of free will and to provide a channel for divine action in the world in the face of unbreakable laws of nature.

The Uncertainty Principle also changes our conception of the vacuum. Quantum uncertainty does not allow us to say that a volume of space is empty or contains nothing. Such a statement has no operational meaning. The quantum vacuum is therefore defined differently, as the lowest energy state available to the system locally. This may not characterize the vacuum uniquely and usually a physical system will have more than one possible vacuum state. Under external changes it may be possible to change from one to another. It is therefore important to distinguish between the nonscientific term "nothing" and the quantum mechanical

conception of "nothing" when discussing creation out of nothing in modern cosmology.

See also CREATIO EX NIHILO; DETERMINISM; DIVINE ACTION; FREEDOM; INDETERMINISM; PARADOX; PHYSICS, QUANTUM; DOWNWARD CAUSATION

Bibliography

Barrow, John D. *The Book of Nothing*. London: Jonathan Cape, 2000.

Heisenberg, Werner. "'Über den Anschaulichen Inhalt der Quantentheoretischen Kinematik und Mechanik." *Zeitschrift für Physik* 43 (1927): 127.

Herbert, Nick. *Quantum Reality: Beyond the New Physics*. London: Rider, 1985.

Jammer, Max. *The Philosophy of Quantum Mechanics: The Interpretations of Quantum Mechanics in Historical Perspective*. New York: Wiley, 1974.

Pais, Abraham. *Inward Bound*. Oxford: Oxford University Press, 1986.

JOHN D. BARROW

HERMENEUTICS IN SCIENCE AND RELIGION

Hermeneutics is the branch of philosophy that deals with theory of interpretation. It can be argued that any discussion of the relationship between science and religion is implicitly or explicitly a matter of interpretation. This can be seen, for instance, in Ian Barbour's (1923–) advocacy of "critical realism" in matters both religious and scientific. Interpretation theory necessarily stands at the intersection of the dialogue between science and religion, though few authors in the field have articulated formal theories of interpretation as part of this exploration.

The etymology of the word *hermeneutics* begins with the ancient Greek god, Hermes, who was a messenger between the gods of Olympus, the gods of the underworld, and the mortal humans. Hermeneutics could literally be translated as the "science of Hermes." Called Mercury in the Roman tradition, Hermes was unique in the ancient pantheon as the singular interpreter between worlds, but one should not forget that he was also something of a trickster. The apparently simple task of interpretation turns out to be remarkably complicated and can make fools of everyone.

Hermeneutics first arises in the disciplines of interpreting sacred texts, historical events, and legal codes, but philosophers increasingly see its application to theories of understanding in the broadest sense. The book, poem, event, or law to be interpreted is referred to generically as the "text." The interpretation of texts is seen as a metaphor for all kinds of nontextual interpretative problems, for instance in social and psychological theories and increasingly also in the biophysical sciences.

Hermeneutics in science

Scientists tend to have a formalist approach to their disciplines, believing that science is a singular methodology leading to objective, realist accounts of phenomena. While this is often pragmatically justified in the narrow domains of particular sciences, philosophical reflection on the practice of science in the last century points to a much more nuanced and complicated view. The positivist view of science advocated by Moritz Schlick (1882-1936), Karl Popper (1902–1994), and others has largely fallen to a more contextual and constructivist understanding of science. Willard V. O. Quine (1908–2000), Arthur Fine (1937–), Hillary Putnam (1926-), and Thomas Kuhn (1922–1996) have argued persuasively that science is not a singular methodology, but a complex of diverse disciplines situated within particular historical and social contexts. The philosophical task now becomes explaining the progressive and efficacious results of scientific investigations and insights in spite of this situatedness.

A few examples will suffice to show how science engages in interpretation. In contemporary cosmology, the problems of quantum entanglement and the apparent "fine-tuning" of perhaps a dozen cosmological parameters leads to the extravagant and often nonempirical speculations of string theory, multiverse theory, and numerous accounts of the significance of quantum weirdness. In the case of multiverse theory, it remains to be seen whether these speculations will ever be more enlightening than debates about how many angels can fit on the head of a pin.

In molecular biology, the genome is increasingly referred to as a text or code, which is then interpreted in particular organisms to varying degrees, sometimes with a great deal of stochastic latitude, for instance as seen in the probabilistic occurrences of many genetically based diseases. Biology turns out to be all nature and all nurture, and the two cannot easily be separated in spite of reductionistic predilections.

Because of the historical nature of evolutionary biology, scholars continue to debate whether evolution has teleological biases or structures. Because researchers can only simulate evolution and cannot subject theories of evolution to laboratory-like replication and verification, they are not likely to ever resolve these questions. These arguments will always take on the status of interpretations in which empirical facts and logical arguments are mustered to support competing views to varying degrees of satisfaction.

Primatologists regularly draw analogies between humans and their primate relatives in order to decode the biological nature of human sexuality, sociability, and aggression. When primatologists compare baboons, gorillas, chimpanzees, or bonobos, let alone apparent cultural differences between groups within one of these species, it would be hard to know what is biologically normative for humans. These primate analogies to humans could be seen as an example of what philosophers denounce as the *naturalistic fallacy,* in which humans justify or deduce an "ought" of culture from an "is" of nature. The human species, however, exhibits a ubiquitous and perennial tendency, if not necessity, to extrapolate and analogize between the "is" and the "ought" as we develop our sense of individual selves and culture identity. The question is not *whether* to commit the naturalistic fallacy, but *how.* Again this is a matter of interpretation.

Hermeneutics in religion

Religions have long dealt with the problem of interpretation. When confronted with an archaic or foreign language in a sacred text, simple translation itself becomes an interpretative task. Sacred texts and traditions are full of other interpretative problems. Even if readers begin with the presupposition that the text is divinely revealed and in some sense perfect, as for instance with the status of the Koran for most Muslims, they must still confront their own finitude as the readers of such revealed texts. Ambiguity and conflict within the Koran necessarily give rise to a body of interpretation and case law that places this foundational religious text within a tradition of jurisprudence. Talmudic interpretations of Torah in Judaism are another explicit example of a hermeneutical process at work in religion.

Augustine of Hippo (354–430) and others in the early and medieval Christian movement argued that the Bible was often allegorical and not to be understood as literal. The parables of Jesus are explicitly metaphorical and thus also in need of interpretation. With the Protestant Reformation, Martin Luther (1483–1546), John Calvin (1509–1564), and others tended to reject allegorical interpretation as mere manipulation of the text for the political purposes of the Catholic hierarchy. A literal and univocal hermeneutics was advanced in which the Bible was open to the self-interpretation of every competent reader, even as it was widely translated in vernacular languages for the first time. Curiously, the Christian reform movement, which advanced this literal and univocal Biblical hermeneutics, quickly splintered into competing Protestant denominations. Radical Protestants argued that Biblical interpretation must be guided by the Holy Spirit, the same Spirit in which the text was written, or it could never be properly understood. As the New Testament itself warns us, even the devil quotes scripture.

Hermeneutics in philosophy

Hermeneutics rose as a formal philosophical discipline in the modern period. While one should be mindful of the rich histories and reflections on hermeneutics in other civilizations and traditions, the context in which modern European philosophers began to articulate formal theories of hermeneutics arises out of the life and death battles of the Reformation.

Friedrich Schleiermacher (1768–1834) and Wilhelm Dilthey (1833–1911) are widely credited with the rise of modern hermeneutics. Schleiermacher, for instance, united problems in biblical interpretation with the interpretation of other genres of literature, history, law, and philosophy. Schleiermacher articulated the problem of a hermeneutical circle in which the reading of a particular passage could only be understood in the context of the whole text and the reading of the whole text could only be understood in light of the interpretation of particular passages. Thus the correct reading of a text also needed to draw on other sources, including an understanding of the author's life and intentions. The goal was to "understand an author better than he understood himself." This also required an understanding of the entire cultural context in which the author's work emerged. At every level, the problem of a part and whole circularity arose for Schleiermacher, but he had a kind of sanguine optimism about the endeavor of achieving an objective reading of a text. One also sees in Schleiermacher's approach an affinity with early psychology and the other human sciences.

Others argue that authors do not actually understand themselves and that it is the job of the interpreter to decode the hidden meanings of the author's text. For instance, the self-understanding of the author or the surface reading of a text are covers for "false consciousness" of economic interests (Karl Marx) or the "unconscious projections" of psychological forces (Sigmund Freud). This critical turn toward a hermeneutics of suspicion, however, soon implicated the "objective" interpreter himself, since all interpreters and interpretations are ideologically biased. The reader is thus drawn into the hermeneutical circle as part of problem. A reader necessarily approaches the reading of a significant text with all kinds of assumptions; prejudices can simply predetermine the interpretation. The challenge of interpretation begins to look like a vicious circle in which readers project any and all prejudices onto the text.

Hans-Georg Gadamer (1900–2002) articulated a theory of interpretation that took the reader's situatedness fully into account. Interpretation was an encounter between the two worlds of the author and the reader. The text became an independent entity with a life of its own. Good interpretation sought for a "fusion of horizons" between the reader, the author, and the life of the text. The task was to reflect critically about the prejudgments brought to the table by the reader, seek a provisional critical distance from these prejudices, and be open to encountering some new understanding through a new reading, which might then inform a new set of assumptions for future readings. The goal was to turn what was understood to be a solipsistic hermeneutical circle into an open-ended and progressive hermeneutical spiral.

Postmodern hermeneutics

The hermeneutics of suspicion and the self-implication of the reader in the hermeneutical dynamic, however, also gave rise to the more extreme formulations of radical deconstruction and postmodern hermeneutics. Michel Foucault (1926-1984), Jacques Derrida (1930–), Richard Rorty (1931–), and others have argued for the impossibility of interpretative truth claims. Because one cannot escape prejudice, delusion, and interested rationalization in every interpretative move, the best one can do is not delude oneself through an endless process of deconstruction (the double meaning is intentional). The challenge of postmodernism is to live in the flux of change without the crutch of artificially willed certainty.

Scientism has come to be seen by many in the humanities as just such an oppressive metanarrative. There has been a major movement to apply social-critical theory to the understanding of scientific knowledge as socially constructed. Historians and social critics enter the scientific discourse like anthropologists in a foreign land. They read the ethnography of the laboratory, the economics of the pharmaceutical research, the history of physics, and the metaphoric symbolism of genetic engineering in order to uncover hidden meanings that are not self-apparent to members of the "tribe." These studies often offer some enlightening insights into how the actual practice of science differs from the philosophy of science or the self-understanding of scientists, but the hermeneutical circle also puts into question the ethnography, economics, psychology, and symbolism of the new cultural critics of science.

Contemporary hermeneutic theory tends toward philosophical and ethical pragmatism. The truth of a theory or interpretation is understood not through some direct correspondence to reality but through the practical consequences of its applications. In this sense, postmodernism can be seen as having deep affinities with some religious and scientific philosophies. The reluctance of physicists to draw metaphysical implications from quantum mechanics can be seen as a kind of pragmatism. Plato (428–347 B.C.E.) offers the notion of a Noble Lie necessary for well-being of the Polis and the individual. Jesus' warning to judge the false prophets on the consequences of their ministry, to be wary of rotten "fruit" in "sheep's clothing," can also be seen as a pragmatist apologetic.

Buddhism includes the notion of *Upaya*, effective teachings that are not necessarily true but that work nonetheless. Even if foundational theories of knowledge are unattainable, one might still find in lived experience some practical guidance.

That science is a socially and historically constructed form of knowledge is in retrospect an obvious truism. That science is merely a socially constructed form of knowledge without reference to a "real" reality is a highly problematic assertion. The problem is compounded by the either/or, subjective/objective, rational/irrational dichotomies upon which the modernist worldview is founded. Here, too, an understanding of postmodernism is helpful to the science and religion interdisciplinary dialogue.

Religion, which has long been attacked and deconstructed as mythic delusion, can now claim some pragmatic parity with the scientific worldview that attacked it within this pragmatist hermeneutic. History, anthropology, psychology, sociology, gender studies, and literary theory have long been conversation partners in serious religious thought and inquiry, but they are now new dialogue partners for the biophysical sciences.

Once perceived as hostile to a committed life of faith, modernist critical theory has turned into a postmodernist helpmate for religion in nurturing deep and intellectually vibrant religious belief. The fact that there are invisible social and psychological processes that corrupt and distort one's understanding of the divine (or nature) and that unconscious processes can be exposed and demystified through critical interpretative theory is an occasion to reaffirm human finitude and humbleness before the divine and the larger nature that contains human "be(ing) longingness." After all, in most faith traditions such humility is prescribed. The Judaic prohibition against idolatry, the *via negativa* of medieval Christianity, the *Neti Neti* of Hinduism, the *Sunyata* of Buddhism, and the Islamic sense of divine transcendence are all rich affirmations of human epistemological finitude before the Ultimate.

Many in the biophysical sciences, however, tend to feel threatened by these social constructionist studies. Most scientists believe that their theories, models, and measurements are in some sense directly related to reality and not simply an elaborate projection of social prejudice and power. The strong social constructionist argument would render the predictive and explanatory power of science as nonsensically coincidental. Airplanes really fly; cell phones really work. Science produces untold efficacious results in daily life. And while belief in antibiotics or acupuncture will improve the effect of the remedy, they will also work independently of belief system. The truths of science, like the truths of religion, must surely lie somewhere between relativistic social constructionism and naive realism, though scholars are struggling to find a new philosophical language to account for this in-between knowing.

Hermeneutics in linguistics

These hermeneutical conundrums are also characterized by a linguistic movement in philosophy of science and philosophy in general. Ludwig Wittgenstein (1889–1951), for instance, came to reject his own earlier positivist theory of language and science. Wittgenstein recognized that all languages, from mathematical formalism to one's mother tongue, are internally self-referential (Kurt Gödel (1906-1978) proved the even mathematical languages are self-referential). Language is understood as a kind of game playing, in which the rules are arbitrary to each particular user-group. One can talk about language games within the boundaries of rational, irrational, and other rational. Within the rules of their respective language games, an Orthodox Jew can be every bit as rational as a particle physicist; indeed, they can be one and the same person. There is, however, no master language or logic of truth, contrary to the hopes of the scientific positivists and religious fundamentalists.

Paul Ricoeur (1913–) carefully considers this new linguistic analysis and argues that far from being merely arbitrary, human language builds upon a deep symbolic structure of the universe itself. It is not just that human language reflects a semiotic/semantic structure internally; the universe itself is constituted through semiotic/semantic processes. Ricoeur advocates metaphoric realism. Words achieve their denotative function only through connotative associations in established usage. Because the function of language is first established in connotation, the result is a theory of metaphors as linguistically primordial. Ricoeur avoids descending into relativistic nonsense by grounding human language in a semiotic and semantically rich universe.

Many religions consider language to be somehow primordial to the material constitution of the universe. In Hinduism, the Upanishads talk of a primal word, *Om*, which functions as the creative source of all nature. The Greeks, including Plato, drew upon Heraclitus' notion of *Logos*, viewing the embodied word as that fire that animated and ruled the world. In Jewish Midrash, the grammatical ambiguity of the first line of Genesis, leads to philosophical speculation about a pre-existent *Torah*, which God uses to speak reality into being. In Medieval Judaism, this rabbinic tradition gave rise to the wild speculations and philosophical subtleties of the Kabbalists. In the Gospel of John, Christians celebrate this Word or Logos in a radical incarnationalist vision of a cosmic Christ by whom and through whom all things are made and from whom everything that was created received life.

So, too, throughout the sciences theoretical and research projects point beyond mere materialism and reductionism to a new kind of ontological entity called "information." Contemporary scientists take matter-energy and space-time as metaphysical foundations, but increasingly need to include some concept of "information" in their metaphysics, even though information is somehow immaterial, ephemeral, and context dependent.

The relativistic tendencies of postmodern hermeneutics and culture at large now present a great challenge at a time in human history that also requires intellectual rigor and committed moral action in the face of theoretical and existential uncertainty. The hermeneutical dynamic may be unavoidable, but it need not be a self-confirming or paralyzing circle of prejudice. While unavoidable, the cultural biases of the interpreter are not necessarily bad, for a tradition is paradoxically the sustaining foundation upon which deconstructive hermeneutics builds new meanings. All deconstructions are parasitic on some functional metanarrative. Nor does interpretation always necessarily confirm the prejudgments of interpretation. The text presents a limited matrix of possible and plausible interpretations. The trick will be not to deny one's hermeneutical finitude through some fundamentalist dogmatism or callous rhetorical will-to-power, but to honor the hermeneutical process and open the solipsistic circle into an evolving spiral. New and different voices in one's social and biophysical ponderings can help provide powerful insights, even as the text or phenomenon have the capacity sometimes to direct one to new insights in spite of oneself.

Human reason, like the universe, is polyglot. But interdisciplinary, cross-cultural, and intra-phenomenological translation projects are possible and necessary. With a combination of interpretative insights of science and religion, like the blind men describing the elephant in the Jainist-Buddhist myth, a "fusion of horizons" and a fuller understanding of science, society, self, and the sacred might be gained. A rigorous and open-ended conversation of tolerance and humility is an ethical and epistemological prescription for both science and religion as we confront the extraordinary challenges of our time and the stunning complexities of the universe and ourselves.

See also SCRIPTURAL INTERPRETATION

Bibliography

Barbour, Ian. *Religion in an Age of Science: The Gifford Lectures 1989–1991:* Vol. 1. San Francisco: Harper, 1990.

Boyd, Richard, et al. *The Philosophy of Science.* Cambridge, Mass.: MIT Press, 1991.

Caputo, John D. *Radical Hermeneutics: Repitition, Deconstruction, and the Hermeneutic Project.* Bloomington: Indianna University Press, 1987.

Dreyfus, Hubert L., and Rabinow, Paul. *Michel Foucault: Beyond Structuralism and Hermeneutics.* Chicago: University of Chicago Press, 1983.

Foucault, Michel. *The Foucault Reader,* ed. Paul Rabinow. New York: Pantheon, 1984.

Gadamer, Hans-Georg. *Philosophical Hermeneutics,* ed. David E. Linge. Berkeley: University of California Press, 1976.

Geertz, Clifford. *The Interpretation of Cultures.* New York: Harper, 1973.

Haraway, Donna. *Simians, Cyborgs, and Women: The Reinvention of Nature.* New York: Routledge, 1991.

Harding, Sandra, ed. *The "Racial" Economy of Science: Toward a Democratic Future.* Bloomington: Indiana University Press, 1993.

Heidegger, Martin. In *Poetry, Language, Thought* (1951), trans. Albert Hofstadter. New York: Harper & Row, 1971.

Heidegger, Martin. *Martin Heidegger: Basic Writings* (1962), ed. David F. Krell. New York: Harper & Row, 1977.

Krieger, David. *The New Universalism: Foundations for a Global Theology.* Maryknoll, N.Y.: Orbis, 1991.

MacIntyre, Alasdir. *After Virtue.* South Bend, Ind.: University of Notre Dame Press, 1984.

MacIntyre, Alasdir. *Three Rival Versions of Moral Enquiry: Encyclopaedia, Genealogy and Tradition.* South Bend, Ind.: University of Notre Dame Press, 1990.

Merchant, Carolyn. *The Death of Nature: Women, Ecology, and the Scientific Revolution.* New York: Harper & Row, 1980.

Rabinow, Paul, and Sullivan, William, eds. *Interpretive Social Science: A Reader.* Berkeley: Univeresity of California Press, 1979.

Ricoeur, Paul. *Interpretation Theory: Discourse and the Surplus of Meaning.* Forth Worth: Texas Christian University Press, 1976.

Ricoeur, Paul. *Hermeneutcis and the Human Science.* New York: Cambridge University Press, 1981.

Ricoeur, Paul. *Lectures on Ideology and Utopia.* New York: Columbia University Press, 1986.

Ricoeur, Paul. *From Text to Action: Essays in Hermeneutics, II* (1986). Evanston, Ill.: Northwestern University Press, 1991.

Rolston, Holmes, III. *Science and Religion: A Critical Survey.* Philadelphia, Pa.: Temple University Press, 1987.

Rolston, Holmes, III. *Environmental Ethics: Duties and Values in the Natural World.* Philadelphia, Pa.: Temple University Press, 1988.

Rolston, Holmes, III. *Philosophy Gone Wild: Environmental Ethics.* Buffalo, N.Y.: Prometheus Books, 1989.

Rorty, Richard. *Philosophy and the Mirror of Nature.* Princeton, N.J.: Princeton University Press, 1979.

Rorty, Richard. *The Consequences of Pragmatism.* Minneapolis, Minn.: University of Minnesota Press, 1982.

WILLIAM J. GRASSIE

HIERARCHY

The word *hierarchy* stems from the Greek word *hierarches,* and early usage referred primarily to ecclesiastical structure and authority. The term is now widely used in a number of fields and generally denotes an inter-level relationship, usually conceived as a vertical layering of levels that implies higher value, power, or centralization at the top, and less of these qualities at the bottom.

History of the concept

The ancient Greek philosopher Plato has had an enormous influence on hierarchical thinking. In works such as the *Republic* and *Phaedo,* Plato argued that the world is divided into a lower, chaotic material reality, and a higher reality of forms that is the genuine source of truth, beauty, and the good. For Plato, this ontological distinction was necessarily related to epistemological and moral ones, for the realm of the forms are the source of true knowledge as well as being the ultimate good that all seek. Human beings were seen as a composite of the two worlds, the irrational world of matter and the rational world of the forms. In Plato's framework, the good person is one who shuns material things and pursues rational inquiry in accordance with one's true, nonmaterial nature.

During the Roman era, Plotinus (205–270) and other neo-Platonists expanded Plato's dualism into what twentieth-century philosopher Arthur Lovejoy (1873–1962) called the great chain of being. According to this view, God is the most real, out of which all other things emanate. Material reality is that which is most distant from the plenitude of God and, in a sense, the least real. As a composite of the different levels of reality, human beings stand at a halfway point, both material and spiritual. Neo-Platonism profoundly influenced the development of Christian theology, particularly through the writings of Augustine of Hippo (354–430), Pseudo-Dionysus (c. fifth century C.E.), and Bonaventure (1217–1274). In a Christian framework, angels naturally fit into a neo-Platonic framework as beings who occupied a higher level of reality. For Augustine in particular, evil could be explained as the absence of good, an irrational move from the most real (God) towards the unreal.

The rise of modern science played a significant role in the demise of hierarchical understandings of the world. Early scientific thinkers were influenced by philosophers such as William of Ockham (c. 1285–c. 1347), who denied Plato's theory of forms and hierarchical ontologies. This and other factors led to an understanding of the physical world that emphasized material causes alone, a tendency that seemed vindicated by the work of Galileo Galilei (1564–1642) and Isaac Newton (1642–1727). Such materialistic views were typically reductionistic in character. Materialist reductionists inverted and then rejected the neo-Platonic hierarchy of being, claiming not only that it is the material world that is most real, it is the only reality. Such materialism not only influenced scientists such as Pierre-Simon Laplace (1749–1827), but also the whole trajectory of nineteenth-century philosophy.

In the twentieth century, the legitimacy of ontological and moral hierarchies was intensely debated within specific fields of philosophy and theology. Debates about ontological hierarchies focused on questions of reductionism and emergence or holism, much of which centered on the status of the mind and human person. Reductionists emphasize that the material constituents of the world are all that there is, and that higher-order realities such as the human mind and culture can ultimately be explained by the laws of physics and chemistry. Reductionists often point to the success of neo-Darwinism and the discovery of DNA as justification for their approach. Likewise, categories of mind and the human person, so reductionists argue, can best be understood in terms of the activities of the brain. In the late twentieth century, reductionism was most associated with the popular writings of Richard Dawkins and Francis Crick in biology and the thought of Daniel Dennett, Paul Churchland, and Patricia Churchland in the philosophy of mind.

Modern opposition to reductionism has early roots in the movement of British emergentism, typified by the work of C. D. Broad. Opponents to reductionism have frequently endorsed the category of emergence, arguing that there are higher-order levels that emerge from, but are not reducible to, the lower levels of reality. Generally speaking, emergentists do not deny the validity of the lower-level sciences, only their sufficiency for explaining higher-order phenomenon. Emergentism came to be particularly important for the defense of biology as a legitimate and separate field of inquiry from physics and chemistry, and has been vigorously supported by such prominent thinkers as biologist Ernst Mayr and philosopher Karl Popper. Emergence has also been complemented by the concept of supervenience, which provides a philosophical framework for understanding the relation of different levels of reality. Philosophers such as Jaegwon Kim have argued, however, that supervenience ultimately leads to causal reduction of higher-level to lower-level physical properties. Within the paradigm of computational complexity theory, a similar suspicion has been raised against emergence by John Holland and others.

Hierarchy in the science-religion dialogue

Science and religion scholars have tended to support emergentist positions and reject reductionist ontologies. Both the physicist and theologian Ian Barbour and the biochemist and theologian Arthur Peacocke have strongly criticized reductionist interpretations of science. Both have noted that while science employs methodological reductionism in its attempt to analyze physical reality, such practice does not entail ontological reductionism. Going a step further, Peacocke has argued that the whole of reality should be understood as a complex hierarchy that begins at the bottom with physics and chemistry, and moves towards increasing levels of complexity, moving towards living organisms, human beings, cultures, and eventually God at the very top. Peacocke's analysis has had tremendous influence, and has been developed in different ways by philosophers Nancey Murphy and Philip Clayton.

Despite this, the value of hierarchical thinking has been much questioned in broader theological circles. Feminist theologians such as Sallie McFague have criticized traditional moral hierarchies because of their tendency to oppress women. Environmental theologians and philosophers have also criticized moral hierarchies as contributors to abuse of animals and destruction of ecosystems. Because traditional moral hierarchies have been justified by reference to ontological hierarchies, these too have come under attack. Serious dialogue between these differing theological perspectives has yet to occur and represents a likely step in the science-religion dialogue.

See also EMERGENCE; HOLISM; ORDER; PLATO; SUPERVENIENCE

Bibliography

Ayala, Francisco, and, Dobzhansky, Theodosius, eds. *Studies in the Philosophy of Biology: Reductionism and Related Problems.* Berkeley: University of California Press, 1974.

Broad, C. D. *The Mind and Its Place in Nature.* New York: Harcourt, 1929.

Kim, Jaegwon. *Supervenience and Mind: Selected Philosophical Essays.* Cambridge, UK: Cambridge University Press, 1993.

Lovejoy, Arthur. *The Great Chain of Being: A Study of the History of an Idea* (1936). Cambridge, Mass.: Harvard University Press, 1970.

McFague, Sallie. *Models of God: Theology for an Ecological, Nuclear Age.* Philadelphia: Fortress Press, 1987.

Peacocke, Arthur. *Theology for a Scientific Age: Being and Becoming—Natural, Divine, and Human,* enlarged edition. Minneapolis, Minn.: Fortress Press, 1993.

GREGORY R. PETERSON

HINDUISM

Unlike the Western religions, Hinduism does not have an easily identifiable beginning. Although records of its early history are not available, Hinduism dates back at least three thousand years in the subcontinent of India. However, within Hinduism there is a great diversity of practice and belief so that it is difficult to identify a distinctive essence. Hinduism contains many traditions that share distinctive characteristics such that they are identifiable as members of the same cultural family. Some traditions share more of these characteristics, making them more strongly Hindu. Over the centuries one such characteristic has been the practice of caste distinctions. Another is seeing Hinduism as a religious way of life that in one way or another reaches back to scriptures, the oldest of which is the Veda.

Historical origins

The term Hindu derives from the Indus River in the northwest part of the Indian subcontinent. Flowing some three thousand kilometers from the Himalayas to the Arabian Sea, the Indus served as a natural boundary for those attempting to enter India through the passes of the Hindu Kush. During the period 1500 to 1000 B.C.E., people known as the Aryans, who may have come through these mountain passes, began to dominant the Indus River area of northwest India. Their view of the world was described in the Veda, spoken and written in the Sanskrit language. In the oldest portion of the Vedas, called the *Rg samhita,* there are references to a river called the *Sindhu,* which may have been the Indus. By association, the word *Sindhu* seems also to have been used to refer to the people who lived in the Indus valley. The later term *Hindu* seems to have derived from *Sindhu.*

From the earliest historical times, military invasions and trade have flowed through the mountain passes of the northwest, such as the Khyber. Those who invaded India from the Mediterranean area (e.g., the Persian Darius I and Alexander of Macedon) used the term Hindu to refer to those who lived on or beyond the Sindhu River boundary. Over the centuries the term Hindu has increasingly been used to refer to those Indians who share some connection with the Veda as a basis for their way of life. Within the Vedic scriptures are found the overarching concepts of caste, karma, and rebirth that knit together the many diverse Hindu groups. Karma is the idea that each action or thought leaves behind a seed or memory trace that predisposes one to a similar action or thought in the future. These karmic traces, stored up in one's unconscious, as it were, originated not only in this life but also from previous lives, and cause one to be reborn in a future life. This cycle of birth, death, and rebirth is held to be beginningless (*anandi*) and is seemingly endless. However, for those wishing to escape from this cycle of rebirth, the Hindu scriptures offer three general paths or disciplines (*Yogas*) by which release may be realized: the paths of knowledge, work, and devotion. In orthodox or Brahmanical Hinduism, the source of these paths, and indeed of all knowledge, including science, is said to be the Vedic scriptures.

Cosmology and the concept of God

In the Hindu view, the whole of the universe is held to have existed beginninglessly as a series of cycles of creation going backward into time infinitely. Although the Hindu scripture is spoken anew at the start of each cycle of creation, what is spoken is identical with the scripture that had been spoken in all previous cycles. The very idea of an absolute point of beginning for either creation or the scripture is not present in Hindu thought. A close parallel to this Hindu notion of the eternal presence of scripture is found in the Western idea of the Logos, especially as expressed in the Gospel of John: "In the beginning was the Word, and the Word was with God, and the Word was God" (1:1). The *rsis* or seers, identified as speakers of particular Vedas, are understood to be channels through which the divine word passes to make itself available to humans at the start of each creation cycle. The same *rsis* are said to speak the same Vedas in each cycle of creation, and the very language in which the Vedas are spoken, Sanskrit, is itself held to be divine.

This view of the Vedas and Sanskrit as being divine had important implications for the traditional Hindu understanding of all forms of knowledge, including science. The *rsi's* initial mystical vision is of Brahman's consciousness, God's omniscient knowledge. This unitary vision is broken down and spoken as the words and sentences of the Veda so that through this revelation people will be enabled to realize release. In addition to this ultimate spiritual goal, the Veda, as the authoritative speaking of divine omniscience, contains in seed form the fundamental knowledge of all the disciplines—the arts, medicine, and science. This is why the Grammarian philosophers of India argue that correct word use (following Sanskrit rules) is essential for science for two reasons. First, it is essential because only when language is spoken and heard correctly will the seeds of scientific ideas inherent in the Veda be able to manifest themselves. Second, correct word use is essential in formulating and communicating scientific knowledge so that it does not become confused but is clearly conveyed.

Such thinking lies behind the traditional Hindu notion that all knowledge, including science, comes from and through the Vedas. It is just this kind of thinking that anchors the claim of the modern Hindu reformer Swami Vivekananda (1863–1902) that science and religion are complementary, cross-validating, and are both based on experience of the same Brahman. Just as science is based on the empirical experience of the outer world (whose essence is Brahman) so also religious knowledge arises from the direct experience of the Vedic word; at base both are experiences of the same ultimate reality.

See also KARMA

Bibliography

Coward, Harold G. and Raja, K. Kunjunni. *The Philosophy of the Grammarians.* Princeton, N.J.: Princeton University Press, 1990.

Coward, Harold. *Scripture in the World Religions: A Short Introduction.* Oxford: Oneworld, 2000.

Klostermaier, Klaus K. *A Survey of Hinduism.* Albany: State University of New York Press, 1994.

Rambachan, Anantanand. *The Limits of Scripture: Vivekananda's Reinterpretation of the Vedas.* Honolulu: University of Hawaii Press, 1994.

HAROLD COWARD

HINDUISM, CONTEMPORARY ISSUES IN SCIENCE AND RELIGION

Modern science was brought to India during the 1800s by the British as a part of the colonization process. The goal of science in the colony was not the advancement of science but rather the exploration of natural resources, flora, and fauna to feed the needs and demands of Britain and its ongoing industrial revolution. In the colonial context of India there was also discrimination against deserving Indian scientists who were relegated to positions below their entitlement and paid half the salary of their British counterparts.

Scientists in modern India can be divided into three categories. First there were transplanted European scientists employed by the British government who served as "gatekeepers" of colonial science. In the second category were British scientific personnel called by the colonial administration to undertake specific tasks. They had no commitment to the advancement of science in India. When these scientists completed their assignments, they returned home taking with them their knowledge and experience. A third category was composed of Indian scientists who became prominent after the 1870s. They were supported by a small group of British settler scientists and Christian missionaries who devoted themselves to the establishment of professional science in India. They numbered a few hundred including such key persons as David Hare, Eugene Lafont, William Carey, Prafulla Chandra Ray, Jagadish Chandra Bose, Chandrasekhara Venkata Raman, Meghnad N. Saha, and Mahendra Lal Sircar. While scientists in the first two categories were part of the colonial enterprise, it was the third group that struggled to transform colonial structures and create an indigenous and autonomous culture of science in India.

Within Hinduism, during the same time period, the Hindu reformer Swami Vivekananda (1863–1902) was revising Hindu thought to accommodate European rationality and science. Among the Bengali intelligentsia of the late nineteenth century it was widely felt that science as a method of obtaining knowledge about humans and nature was the key to human progress. Therefore, all systems of thought, including religion, needed to be validated by reason and science. Following the lead of earlier Brahmo Samaj thinkers such as Keshub Chandra Sen (1838–1884), Vivekananda attempted to show the compatibility of Hindu Advaita philosophy with science. Continued efforts in contemporary Hindu studies to draw analogies between Advaita and science are evidence of Vivekananda's influence. Just as science allows for the discovery of physical laws through the application of the scientific method, so also said Vivekananda, the *rsis* or seers who wrote the Vedas are the discoverers of spiritual laws. Rather than depending for their authority on their status as revelation, the Vedas can be shown to be timeless impersonal laws (like the law of gravity) that one accepts not on the basis of faith but by testing out and proving for oneself in one's own experience (just as the scientist does in verifying, by experiment, the discoveries of others.) Thus, the Advaita teaching on the realization of knowledge of Brahman (*brahmajñāna*) is, according to Vivekananda, a method, like the scientific method, for the discovery of spiritual facts. Although one must begin with reliance on the Veda, one must eventually go beyond such a faith basis and prove the truths of the Vedas in personal experience. For Vivekananda, this method of attaining one's own spiritual knowledge is based on the Yoga of Patanjali (c. 200 B.C.E–200 C.E.), with its focus on the direct experience of truth, and is parallel to the process of attaining and verifying knowledge in science.

Following the lead of Vivekananda, Hindu philosophers and theologians typically see themselves as presenting an approach in which spiritual and scientific knowledge coalesce, and through which they can win back their selfhood. For Hinduism the European scientific and technological tradition cannot be ignored or rejected, but must be absorbed and "worked-through" until the heart of Hinduism is reclaimed. This "working-through" is manifesting itself in contemporary cosmology and applied sciences such as medicine, ecology, and genetic engineering.

Cosmology

Hindu thinkers approach the still unresolved mystery of the universe by looking back to Brahman (the Divine) as somehow associated with the creation or production of the universe. Scientific theory has speculated that the universe may arise from a quantum vacuum state, which is a peculiar mixture of emptiness and activity. Ancient sages, say Hindu thinkers, had similar thoughts. The Sanskrit concept of zero, when applied to Brahman, is identified with both fullness and emptiness. Zero also makes possible advances in mathematics and modern digital technology. The universe is ontologically characterized by the term *Brahman* from the root *brh* "to expand." The *risis* thought of the universe as an "expanding Brahman," which is consistent with contemporary cosmological thinking. The current idea of a Big Bang in which very dense matter explodes into an expanding universe is seen to be prefigured by the Upanishadic notion *bindu*—a dimensionless point that is a unity of both static and dynamic forces, the dynamic expressing itself as the universe of multiplicity while essentially remaining a unity or order (*rta*). Or, as cosmologists put it, about 100 billion stars, including the sun, make up the Milky Way galaxy, a spiral wheel-shaped structure. This galaxy is part of a group of galaxies that form a cluster, while clusters in turn form superclusters of many thousands of galaxies. Cosmologists suggest that this pattern of hierarchical clustering prevails throughout the cosmos with gravitational forces holding the whole thing together. This contemporary theorizing recalls the Upanishadic words of the *rsi* Yajñvalkya to his pupil Aruni: "This world and the next world and all beings and all natural phenomena are strung together by the thread, the Inner Controller, the Immortal, the Brahman." (Brhad-arañyaka Upanishad III:7:3).

The vast collection of Hindu scripture leaves ample room for speculations as to ancient Vedic precursors of the latest thinking in India's strong scientific traditions in mathematics and astronomy, represented by the outstanding twentieth-century mathematician, Srinivasa Ramanujan (1887–1920), and Chandrasekhara Venkata Raman (1888–1970), the 1930 Nobel prize winner in physics. As A. K. Bag shows, contemporary Indian excellence in mathematics and astronomy may be traced back to the Vedic concerns with the correct construction of strangely shaped altars and the correct astronomical time for the conducting of both individual and social events (p.186).

Medicine

British colonization brought to India modern Western medicine, where it met *Ayurveda* or traditional Indian medicine, which traces itself back to the Vedas. Modern medicine, and its assumption of René Descartes's mind-body dualism, has often viewed the body as a mechanical object to be exercised, fed, and kept in order with drugs and the miracles of modern technology. By contrast, traditional Indian medicine sees the person as a sacred entity, a microcosm corresponding to the whole cosmological order. Consequently all Hindu thinking about the person and, to take an example, one's reproductive activity takes place within the larger context of the divine-human cosmos. To study the health of the Hindu bather who goes to the river at daybreak, one must include the mantras chanted, the purifying experience of the body in water, the vegetarian *sattvic* quality of the food eaten, and so on—a gestalt of human-within-nature/culture/religion analysis. The Western mechanistic view of the isolated body was held by British medicine to be the scientific replacement for the sense of the healthy person as a unity of body, mind, and environment as maintained by Hindu medicine. In the attempted superimposition of British ways upon India, the colonization of the body by modern Western medicine was a key strategy, especially when it assumed the right to define health and illness, and a monopoly to treat the latter. This particular colonization did not succeed, however, for many Hindus continue to practice Ayurveda and homeopathy alongside modern biomedicine.

A second colonization of the body is that of the patriarchal social order that has dominated Hindu thought and practice from the seventh century B.C.E. to the present. This colonization of women and their bodies, when combined with modern medical technology, raises serious ethical issues for contemporary Hindus. Since the patriarchal biasing of Hindu culture has led some Hindus to value boys more than girls, clinics have appeared in India and in Western diaspora communities where sonograms and amniocenteses are performed, and female fetuses aborted, even though this practice finds no justification in Hindu texts unless the life of the mother is in danger. Given the Hindu teaching of reincarnation, to engage in abortion is to commit murder.

In the realm of new reproductive technologies, the importance of popular Hindu notions of biological descent entail that artificial insemination with sperm other than that of the husband is not tolerated. But clinics that can help a childless couple conceive by implanting the husband's sperm are welcomed. In vitro fertilization (IVF), however, presents complicated issues for Hinduism. Fertility is important, especially the conception and birth of a son. Thus IVF is attractive to couples having difficulty conceiving and giving birth. Although modern India is using IVF enthusiastically, when considered by Hindu scholars IVF becomes a serious issue since the destruction of any embryo is considered murder—thus all fertilized embryos are to be implanted. Hinduism has religious rituals that must be performed by a son if one's afterlife is to be secured, and the dowry practice makes sons a source of wealth and daughters a drain on family fortunes. Thus, the conflict between the desire for sons (and the possibility of ensuring them through the new technologies) and the proscription against abortion places severe moral strains on some families, especially upon the mothers involved.

Ecology

Hindu texts speak of a close relationship between dharma (righteousness, duty, justice) and the ravaging of the earth. When dharma declines, humans take it out on nature. Modern science and technology, introduced into India during the British colonization and fostered by Jawaharlal Nehru's plans to industrialize India (undertaken after Indian attained independence in 1947), have led to serious pollution of the rivers, land, and air. This has been made worse by the country's population explosion and the desire of India's well-off classes (estimated at 200 to 250 million people) to consume conspicuously. This overpopulation and overconsumption has led to serious environmental degradation and an ecological crisis. The challenge for future science and Hinduism is how to use the resources of both to foster a sustainable future for generations to come. A key Hindu text, the Bhagavad Gita, offers a vision of the universe as the body of God towards which Hindus are to behave with respect. In addition, there are dharma texts in the Ramayana, Mahabharta, and Puranas that call for ecological action. The destruction of forests is condemned and the planting of trees encouraged. Temples such as the Tirumala Tirupati in South India, a famous place of pilgrimage, have established large nursery forests and, in place of the traditional food *prasada* (favor of the deity which

gives one divine grace), have begun to give saplings to pilgrims to take home and plant. Hindu gurus have begun to cite previously obscure texts such as "one tree is equal to ten sons." When political officials visit the temple they are given a tree to plant as a symbol that all trees are worthy of respect as part of God's body.

The Hindu tradition emphasizes bathing in rivers as a way to be morally cleansed and to acquire spiritual merit. Thus rivers, especially the Ganges, are seen as sacred. Rapid industrialization, however, has led to the release of toxic wastes into India's rivers. Overpopulation and the lack of basic sanitary facilities have resulted in the rivers being used as latrines despite the injunctions of dharma texts against such practices. Rivers that are supposed to be a pure part of God's body, and to be able to ritually purify people, stand stagnant due to dams and are polluted with waste—the results of *adharma* or unrighteous behavior. The Hindu view of rivers as nurturing goddesses is under severe challenge due to contemporary environmental degradation, which is linked by some scholars, such as Vasudha Narayanan, with the denigration of women. A comparison can be made between the plight of rivers and the plight of women, both being targets of greed and power. Yet it is women, as in the Chipko (hugging trees) movement, that are leaders in the protection of forests and the stopping of dams. Women are also involved in communicating the tragedy of ecological disasters using traditional religious art forms of song, dance, and story. The challenge for science is to join forces with such ecological movements within Hinduism so as to respond to the current crisis.

Genetic engineering

In hopes of responding to India's overpopulation and the attendant need for increased food production, both government and industry have turned to genetic engineering for help. Science in India has responded quickly with research ranging from genetic studies of the human population to various agricultural and medical applications. Such studies raise ethical questions for Hinduism. Pharmaceutical companies use the traditional genetic knowledge of village and tribal peoples, and then engineer and patent products for which the local people receive no credit and for which they have to pay. Similarly the genetic altering and patenting of seeds takes them out of the hands of ordinary farmers and places them under corporate control. For example, Monsanto in partnership with Mahyco (a seed company in India), has genetically engineered hybrid cotton seed to produce the Bacillus thuringiensis (Bt) enzyme, so that chemical insecticide sprays will no longer be needed for pest control (e.g., bollworms). While this may be beneficial for the preservation of insect diversity, more problematic has been the activity of Monsanto in India in testing the "terminator gene," which allows plants to grow but not produce seed for future crops. This led to protests by farmers' groups, ecofeminist activity by Vandana Siva, and charges of biopiracy against Monsanto. In the face of this protest the Indian government reversed its position and declared that the terminator gene will pose a serious threat to Indian agriculture. The government implemented regulations to cover every phase of genetic engineering from laboratory research to field trials and final release.

Such regulations, however, may not cover the important ethical questions that an application of Hinduism will raise. For example, given that all of nature is God's body, are there moral limits that genetic engineering must respect? Or do the requirements of dharma allow for the patenting and commercial (for profit) ownership of forms of life? And is the crossing of species in genetic engineering acceptable? Hindu answers to these questions may well differ from responses of the Western religions given the strong Hindu view (*karma-samsara*) that there is no radical separation between humans and other forms of life, which from a Jaina perspective extends from humans to animals, plants, air, water, and molecules of matter. Instead, a radical continuity is proposed that has ethical implications for much genetic engineering. Hindu reverencing of plant and animal life offers an important corrective to tendencies in modern science and technology to view the results of genetic engineering strictly from the perspective of the benefits that will accrue to humans. Although medical therapeutic uses of genetic engineering may, at first glance, seem more defensible, they are open to similar ethical examination. Although therapeutic goals seems more clearly good than enhancement goals (e.g., more intelligence, better memory), once one begins to make genetic modifications, one is unsure of the biological and social consequences for the individual and for the collective ecosystem of which the individual is but a part. While the government of India still looks to genetic engineering for help in feeding India's population of 950 million and growing, the Hindu peasant farmer still plants his seed with the prayer, "Let the seed never be exhausted, let it bring forth seed next year." The challenge to science is to help feed the hungry and heal the sick while still respecting the requirements of dharma or righteousness in which the farmer trusts.

See also ECOFEMINISM; ECOLOGY; SPIRITUALITY

Bibliography

Arnold, David. *Colonizing the Body: State Medicine and Epidemic Disease in Nineteenth-Century India*. Oxford: Oxford University Press, 1993.

Bag, A. K. "Mathematical and Astronomical Heritage of India." In *Science, Philosophy and Culture*, ed. D. P. Chattopadhyaya and Ravinder Kumar. Delhi, India: Munshiram Manoharlal, 1996.

Chattopadhyaya, D. P., and Kumar, Ravinder, eds. *Science, Philosophy, and Culture in Historical Perspective*. Delhi, India: Munshiram Manoharlal, 1995.

Grover, Sudarshan. *History of the Development of Mathematics in India*. Delhi, India: Atma Ram, 1993.

Halbfass, William. *India and Europe: An Essay in Understanding*. Albany: State University of New York Press, 1988.

Krishna, V. V. "Reflections on the Changing Status of Academic Science in India." *International Social Science Journal* 53, no. 168 (2001): 231–246.

Narayanan, Vasudha. "'One Tree is Equal to Ten Sons': Some Hindu Responses to the Problems of Ecology, Population, and Consumption." In *Visions of a New Earth*, ed. Harold Coward and Daniel Maguire. Albany: State University of New York Press, 2000.

Radhakrishnan, S. *The Principal Upanisads*. London: Allen and Unwin, 1968.

Rambachan, Anantanand. *The Limits of Scripture: Vivekananda's Reinterpretation of the Vedas*. Honolulu: University of Hawaii Press, 1994.

Saraswati, Baidyanath, and Torres, Yoloti Gonzales. *Cosmology of the Sacred World*. Varanasi, India: N. K. Bhose Memorial Foundation, 1999.

Siva, Vandana. *Biopiracy*. Boston: South End Press, 1997.

HAROLD COWARD

HINDUISM, HISTORY OF SCIENCE AND RELIGION

Hinduism is not the name of a particular religion in the narrow modern sense but it stands for a cultural tradition that developed over thousands of years on the South-Asian subcontinent, now embracing many different religions, such as Vaiṣṇavism, Śaivism, Śāktism, and others. Hinduism comprises, besides rituals and festivities and detailed ethical regulations for individuals and communities, also the arts and sciences. Hinduism never knew the Western antagonism between philosophy and theology, nor does it have a history of warfare between science and religion. It was the highest aim of Hindus to find *satyam,* truth/reality, which could be approached in many ways and appear in many forms.

The well organized, publicly sponsored ancient Indian universities such as those at Taxilā and Nālandā (considered venerable institutions already at the time of Gautama the Buddha [late sixth and early fifth centuries B.C.E.]), with thousands of teachers and tens of thousands of students, taught not only the Veda (revealed scripture) and the *Vedā·gas* (auxiliary disciplines), but also the "eighteen sciences." The basic curriculum included *śabda-vidyā* (linguistics), *Śilpasthāna-vidyā* (arts and crafts), *cikitsa-vidyā* (medicine), *hetu-vidyā* (logic and dialectics), and *adhyātma-vidyā* (spirituality). Religion, while suffusing all life and activity, was not isolated from other subjects or given exclusive attention. The *brahmins,* the custodians of the sacred texts, were also the leading intellectuals who studied and taught secular subjects.

Hindu scriptures and thought

The Hindus called their most ancient and most venerated scripture *Veda* (from the verbal root *vid-,* to know). *Vidyā,* from the same root, designated knowledge acquired in any subject (a medical doctor was called a *Vaidya*), particularly that of the highest reality/truth taught by the Upanishads. The term *śāstra* (from the root *śās-,* to order) became the most general designation for *science* (in the sense of French *science* or Italian *scienza*): authoritative, systematic teaching, ranging from *Dharma-śāstra,* the exposition of traditional law, and *Artha-śāstra,* the teaching of statecraft and administration, to *Śilpa-śāstra,* instruction in art and architecture,

and *Kṛṣi-śāstra,* the theory and practice of agriculture. A learned person carried the title of *Śāstrī,* respected by the community regardless of the subject of his learning. Graduation was a "third birth": members of the three higher castes became *dvijati* (twiceborn) through *upanayana* (initiation), the *śāstrī* degree made them *trijati.*

Traditional Indian thought is characterized by a holistic vision. Instead of breaking experience and reality up into isolated fragments, the Indian thinkers looked at the whole and reconciled tensions and seeming contradictions within overarching categories. Thus the poets of the *Ṛgveda* speak of *viśva-jyoti,* cosmic light as the principle and source of everything, and of *ṛta,* the universal cosmic order connecting and directing all particular phenomena and events. The Upanishads organize the world by relating everything to the *pañca-bhūtas* (five elements: earth, water, light, wind, ether) and identify in Brahman an all-embracing reality-principle. The name of the major deity of later Hinduism is *Viṣṇu,* the "all-pervading," whose body is the universe. Nature (*prakṛti*) was never seen as mere object, but always as productive agent. The Hindu view of life found expression in the four *puruṣārthas*: a person was to acquire wealth (*artha*), enjoy life (*kāma*), practice morality and religion (*dharma*), and seek final emancipation (*mokṣa*) in appropriate balance. Religion was a natural part of the universally accepted order of things. Texts dealing with medicine contain religious regulations, and theological treatises also frequently refer to worldly matters. The study of *Nyāya* (logic and epistemology) was undertaken to achieve *mokṣa* (spiritual emancipation). The notion of *atman* was applied to humans, animals, and plants. Many Indian scientists show an interest in religious issues, and Hindu spiritual leaders frequently appeal to science to illustrate their instructions. They would never relegate science to pure reason and religion to pure faith and treat them as natural enemies, as is often done in the West.

According to the Vedas, only one-fourth of reality is accessible to the senses, which also include *manas,* instrumental reason. Supersensual reality revealed itself to the *ṛṣis,* the composers of the Vedic *sūktas.* The Upanishads know an ascending correlation of subject/consciousness and object/reality: Only the lowest of four stages (*jāgarita*) concerns sense perception of material objects. The three higher levels of reality are intuited through meditative introspection, which culminates in the insight that *ātman* is Brahman: Spirit-self alone is supreme reality.

The central ritual of Vedic culture was the *yajña* (sacrifice of material objects according to fixed rules). *Brahmin* students had to train for many years to learn to perform *yajña*, which involved, besides the priest and the patron, the *devas* (the deities of earth, space, and heaven who were invited to attend). It was offered on altars built with specifically produced bricks arranged in a prescribed geometric pattern, performed at astronomically fixed times. The altar was conceived as symbol of the human body as well as of the universe: One text relates the 360 bricks of an altar to the 360 days of the year and the 360 bones in the human body. The building of altars of different configurations, and more so their change in shape and volume, as required in certain rituals, involved a sophisticated geometry. *Śulva-sūtras* (part of *Kalpa-sūtras*, ritual texts) provided the rules for constructing a variety of shapes of altars and their permutations. They exhibit an algebraic geometry older and more advanced than early Egyptian, Babylonian, or Greek geometry. The exact timing of the performance of the sacrifices was accomplished by people conversant with the movement of the stars. *Jyotiṣa*, one of the six early *Vedā·gas* (auxiliary sciences of the Veda), reveals a good deal of astronomical knowledge.

Study was mandatory for *brahmins*. They had to devote the first part of their lives up to age twenty-four to systematic training under the supervision of a *guru*. Later they had to practice *svādhyāya* (study on their own.) While the study of the Vedas and the *Vedā·gas* was reserved for *brahmins,* the study of the *Upavedas* was open to all higher castes. These comprise *Āyur-veda* ("life-science," medicine), *Dhanur-veda* ("bow-science," martial arts), *Gandharva-veda* ("art-science," music and dancing), and *Stāpathya-veda* ("building science," architecture, sculpture, and painting). The universities, where these subjects were taught, attracted a large body of students from all over Asia. Reports from fourth and sixth century Chinese guest-students praise the physical amenities as well as the high standard of learning. In the eleventh century, after the Muslim invaders had already destroyed much of India's cultural infrastructure, the Muslim scholar-diplomat Al-Biruni spent a decade in India researching and documenting many aspects of traditional Indian science in his *Al-Hind.*

The practical sciences of Hindu India

Research in the history of Indian science is still in an early stage and much work remains to be done. New material is regularly published in the well established *Indian Journal for the History of Science, Vedic Science,* and other periodicals. In the following, elementary information is offered on some specific areas only. The dates for early Indian literature are still a matter of controversy; expert opinions often differ by thousands of years.

Astronomy. Astronomical knowledge of a fairly high order was required for the performance of Vedic *yajñas*. According to Subhash Kak, the structures both of the *Ṛgveda* text and the Vedic altars contain an "astronomical code," embodying precise and fairly accurate information about distances and revolutions of planets and more general astronomical data. The *Ṛgveda* has some astronomical markers that have been used for dating these texts to the fourth millenium B.C.E. From the *Jyotiṣa Vedā·ga* (third century B.C.E.) onwards there is a rich Indian astronomical literature. Indians operated with various cycles of lunar and solar years and calculated cosmic cycles of 10,800 and 432,000 years. Their findings and theories are embodied in numerous *siddhāntas,* of which the most famous is the *Sūrya-siddhānta* (fourth century C.E.). Indian astronomers calculated the duration of one *kalpa* (a cycle of the universe during which all the heavenly bodies return to their original positions) to be 4,320,000,000 years. Several *Purāṇas* contain cosmogonic and cosmological sections utilizing astronomy, describing periodic creations and destructions of the universe, and also suggesting the existence of parallel universes. While the main purpose of the *Purāṇas* is to recommend a specific path of salvation, this is always set into a cosmic context. Many popular *stotras* (hymns, prayers) recited at religious gatherings allude to cosmic events as well. One of the most interesting figures among Indian astronomers is Varāhamihira (fifth to sixth century C.E.), the author of the celebrated *Pañcasiddhāntika amd* of the *Bṛhat-Saṃhitā,* which besides astronomical information teaches astrology and all kinds of occult arts.

Mathematics. Indian mathematics developed out of the requirements for the Vedic *yajña*. The *Yajurveda* knows terms for numbers up to 10^{12} (by comparison the highest number named by the Greeks was 10^4). Later on the Indians coined terms for numbers up to 10^{24} and 10^{53}. Algebra, in spite of its Arabic name, is an Indian invention, and so are the zero and the decimal system, including the "Arabic" numerals. The names of some great Indian mathematicians and some particulars of their accomplishments are known. Thus Āryabhaṭa I (fifth century C.E.), a link in a long chain of unknown earlier master mathematicians, knew the rules for extracting square and cubic roots. He determined the value of π to four decimals and developed an alphabetical system for expressing numbers on the decimal place value model. His *Āryabhaṭīya* was translated into Latin (from an Arabic translation) by a thirteenth century Italian mathematician. Brahmagupta (seventh century C.E.) formulated a thousand years before the great Swiss mathematician Leonhard Euler (1707–1783) a theorem based on indeterminate equations. Bhāskara II (twelfth century) is the author of the *Siddhānta-śiromaṇī*, a widely used text on algebra and geometry. Hindus have continued to show great aptitude for mathematics. Ramanujan (1887–1920), practically untutored, developed the most astounding mathematical theorems.

Medicine. The *Atharva-veda*, considered by some to be the oldest among the four Vedas, contains invocations relating to bodily and mental diseases. Its *Upa-veda*, the *Āyur-veda* (life-science) was cultivated systematically from early on. It was mainly oriented towards preventing diseases and healing through herbal remedies, but it also later developed other medical specialties. Good health was not only considered generally desirable, but also priced as a precondition for reaching spiritual fulfillment. Medicine as a charity was widely recommended and supported by the rulers. Two Indian medical handbooks, the result of centuries of development, became famous in the ancient world far beyond India: the *Caraka-saṃhitā* and the *Suśruta-saṃhitā*. They were later translated and utilized by the invading Muslims. Caraka deals mainly with general medicine and identifies hundreds of medical conditions for which mainly plant pharmaca are prescribed. *Suśruta* focuses on surgery, which by that time was already highly developed, with an array of specific surgical instruments. Indian surgeons were famous in the ancient world; their skills were especially appreciated by the wounded in the frequent wars. Hindus also called upon the divine physician of the gods Dhanvantari, "the one who removes arrows." The theory of *Āyurveda* was based on the *tri-doṣa* theory, which is older than the similar Greek three-humours teaching, used for diagnosis as well as in the treatment of diseases. While the healthy body has a perfect balance of *vata, pitta,* and *kapha,* disease is a disturbance of that harmony, to be cured by re-establishing the right proportion.

Āyur-veda was also applied to animals and plants. There is an ancient *Vṛkṣāyurveda,* a handbook for professional gardeners, and a *Gavāyur-veda* for veterinarians of cattle. Other texts deal with veterinary medicine relating to horses and elephants. Ancient India also had hospitals as well as animal clinics, and *gosalās,* places in which elderly cattle are tended, are still popular in some parts of India. *Āyurveda* was the source of much of ancient Greek and Roman, as well as mediaeval Arabic, medical knowledge. The scientific value of Āyurvedic pharmacology is being recognized by major Western pharmaceutical companies who apply for world-wide patents on medicinal plants discovered and described by the ancient Indian *Vaidyas.*

Architecture. The ancient Indus civilization exhibits a high degree of architectural achievement. The well-laid out cities, the carefully built brick houses, the systems of drainage, and the large water tanks reveal the work of professional town-planners and builders. This tradition was continued and enhanced in later centuries, especially in connection with the building of temples to provide abodes for the deity. No village or town was deemed fit for human habitation if it did not possess a temple. Careful selection and preparation of the ground preceded the building activity proper. The edifice had to be constructed according to an elaborate set of rules that took into account not only structural engineering and quality of materials, but also circumstances of caste and religious affiliation. The Upaveda of *Sthāpatya-vidyā* was expanded into a professional *Vāstu-śāstra* and *Śilpa-śāstra.* Elaborate handbooks like the *Mānasāra* and the *Mayamata* provide detailed artistic and religious canons for the building of temples and the making of images. Temples and images of deities were consecrated only if they conformed to the standards established. The temple (*maṇḍira*) was a visible symbol of the universe, showing the entire range of entities from the highest to the lowest. The image (*mūrti*) was the very body of God, who descended into it for the purpose of receiving worship. Thousands of large and beautiful temples dot the landscape of India, and millions of images adorn *maṇḍiras* and homes.

Linguistics. While India's medical doctors, architects, metallurgists, mathematicians, astronomers, and others were appreciated for their knowledge and skills in their fields, the pride of place in the world of brahminic knowledge always belonged to the study of the Word (*vāk*), which from early on was seen as embued with divine power. The *brahmins* who preserved and investigated the Word occupied the highest social rank. Sanskrit, the refined language of the Veda and of higher learning, was considered a gift of the gods.

The Sanskrit alphabet, in contrast to the chaotic alphabets used in Western languages, is based on a scientific system: All vowels are arranged in an orderly fashion according to acoustic principles. The consonants are organized in five classes (guttural, palatal, cerebral, dental, labial) and, in each of these, five varieties were distinguished (hard, hard-aspirate, soft, soft-aspirate, nasal). This system shows great ingenuity and a keen sense of observation and proved conducive to formulating general grammatical and phonetical laws. It was in place already by one thousand B.C.E. By six hundred B.C.E., Pāṇini, a linguistic genius of the first order, systematised Sanskrit in his *Aṣṭādhyāyī* by deriving all verbs and nouns from about eight hundred roots and formulating four thousand interconnected grammatical rules—an achievement unparalleled in any other language until the twenty-first century. Pāṇini was followed by a long line of commentators, who continued his work: The best known is Patañjali, the author of the *Mahā-bhāṣya*. Traditional Indian scholarship was based on memorizing enormous amounts of literature and transmitting it orally over thousands of years. In the process Indians developed very sophisticated mnemotechnical devices.

Ancient Indian theoretical sciences

Among the *ṣaḍ-darśanas*, the traditional "six orthodox philosophical systems" of Hinduism, *Sāṃkhya* stands out as possibly the oldest and certainly the most interesting in the religion and science context. It offers a general theory of evolution based on the interactive polarity of nature and matter (*prakṛti*), and spirit and soul (*puruṣa*). All reality is subsumed under five times five principles (*tattvas*), originating from one substratum (*pradhāna*), covering all possible physical, biological, and psychological categories. *Sāṃkhya* shows the interconnections between the various components of our world in order to unravel the evolutionary process (which is seen as the cause of all unhappiness and misery) and to return to the changeless bliss of spirit-existence. The twenty-five categories to which *Sāṃkhya* reduces the manifold world became widely accepted in Hindu thought. The *Yoga* system of Patañjali is wholly based on it. The *Purāṇas* also accept it as their philosophical basis, with one amendment: *Prakṛti* and *puruṣa* are overarched by *īśvara*, a personal creator-maintainer-savior God.

Vaiśeṣika, another one of the six orthodox *darśanas*, offers a theory of atomism more ancient than that of the Greek philosopher Democritus, and a detailed analysis of *viśeṣas*, qualities and differences, after which the system is named. The *Vaiśeṣika-sūtra* describes the formation of physical bodies from atoms (*aṇu*) through dyads (*dvyāṇuka*) and triads (*tryāṇuka*) in a strict cause-effect series. The positioning of the atoms determines the qualities of a body. *Vaiśeṣika* also developed the notion of impetus, a concept that appeared in Western science only in the fourteenth century. In *Vaiśeṣika* the relation of science to religion is less clear than in the case of *Sāṃkhya*. However, the other *darśana* with which it has been paired, *Nyāya*, concerned with epistemology and logic, declares that such analysis is necessary for obtaining spiritual liberation.

Spiritual sciences

Among the prescribed subjects of the ancient Indian university curriculum was *adhyātma-vidyā*, the science relating to spirit. As the most important level of reality, *Brahman* was the subject of the highest science, employing personal experience (*anubhāva*), a coherent epistemology (*yukti*), and the exegesis of revealed utterances (*śruti* or *śabda*). The Upanishads mention thirty-two *vidyās*, paths leading to the goal of all science: "One who knows *Brahman* becomes *Brahman*." The ideas of the Upanishads were further developed into the systematics of Vedānta philosophy laid down mainly in commentaries (*bhāsyas*) on the *Brahma-sūtras* ascribed to Bādarāyaṇa (second century B.C.E.). Beginning with Śa·kara (eighth century C.E.), through Rāmānuja (eleventh century) to Madhva (thirteenth century), the greatest minds of India have endeavored to cultivate science that concerns itself with the eternal reality of the spirit. *Yoga* too, in the form in which it was systematized by Patañjali (*Rāja-yoga*) is proceeding scientifically by analyzing the world of experience in terms suitable to spiritual enlightenment and describing experiential steps to be taken to find enlightenment.

India's spiritual fame in the West is of long standing. During the fourth century B.C.E., Alexander the Great, intrigued by the proverbial wisdom of the *brahmins,* sought out the company of what the Greeks called *gymnosophists* on his Indian expedition (eventually replacing his mentor Aristotle by Kálanos, an Indian sage). Six centuries later, the philosopher Plotinus joined the expedition of Emperor Gordian in order to meet the famed Indian sages. No less a modern Western scientist than Austrian physicist Erwin Schrödinger (1887–1961), who won the Nobel prize for physics in 1933, has paid tribute to that "other" science: "The subject of every science is always the spirit and there is only that much true science in every endeavour as it contains spirit" (p. 495).

India and scientific technological progress

Glazed pottery appeared in Mohenjo Daro fifteen hundred years earlier than in Greece. Indian steel was so famous three-thousand years ago that the ancient Persians were eager to obtain swords from India. Indian silk and cotton fabrics were among the most prized imports of ancient Rome. The famous Iron Pillar in Delhi, almost eight meters high and weighing more than six tons, has weathered more than fifteen hundred monsoons without showing a trace of rust. Amazing engineering feats were displayed in the construction of numerous temples of huge dimensions. The capstone of the Bṛhadīśvara temple of Tanjavur, weighing eighty

tons, was moved up to a height of sixty-five meters in the eleventh century. The skills of ancient Indian craftsmen, who created innumerable tools and works of art from ivory, wood, metal, and stone, show a broad based technical culture that had few equals in its time.

Many of the intellectual or practical achievements later ascribed to the Babylonians, the Greeks, or the Arabs had originated in India. India was the envy and the marvel of the ancient world before it fell victim to Muslim invaders, who massively disrupted its cultural, scientific, and religious traditions. The British who succeeded them encountered a weak, backward, fragmented, and demoralized India. Together with machine-made fabric, British India imported Western education and with it a hitherto unknown tension between culture and religion. Modern science and technology were touted as an accomplishment of Christian Europe and seen as the most effective instruments in overcoming superstitious Hinduism. Ram Mohan Roy, an early Hindu reformer, believed in the possibility of harmonizing Hinduism with modern Western science and the teachings of Christ. He founded English-language schools in which modern Western scientific knowledge was taught. Swami Dayanand Saraswati asserted that the ancient Hindus had known the principles of Western science long ago, had anticipated some of the technological marvels like steam-engines and airplanes, and did not need a new religion. He founded a traditional *Gurukula* with Sanskrit medium and only traditional Indian subjects. By the late twenty-first century, there are thousands of Indian scientists with a Hindu background. Most do not see a conflict between their religion and their science, but some do notice a difference in orientation. Some have been led to astounding discoveries through the application of ancient Hindu insights to new fields of enquiry. Thus the biologist Jagdish Chandra Bose (1860–1937) used the Upanishadic idea of the universal *ātman* to conduct groundbreaking research in plant physiology. The traditional Hindu holistic and personalistic orientation could serve as a necessary corrective to mainstream Western science with its Cartesian legacy of an impersonal mechanistic worldview and a purely pragmatic, analytic approach to nature.

See also ASTRONOMY; MEDICINE; SPIRITUALITY

Bibliography

Al Biruni. *Al Biruni's India,* trans. Edward C. Sachau. New Delhi, India: S. Chand, 1964.

Bose, D. M; Sen, S. N.; and Subbarayappa, B.V., eds. *A Concise History of Science in India* (1971). New Delhi, India: Indian National Science Academy, 1984.

Gosling, David. L. *Science and Religion in India.* Madras, India: CSL, 1976.

Heimann, Betty. *Facets of Indian Thought.* London: George Allen and Unwin, 1964.

Iyengar, T. Renga Rajan. *Hinduism and Scientific Quest.* Delhi, India: Motilal Banarsidass, 1997.

Jaggi, O. P. *History of Science, Technology, and Medicine in India,* 15 vols. Delhi, India: Atma Ram, 1973–1986.

Kak, Subhash. *The Astronomical Code of the Rgveda.* New Delhi, India: Munshiram Manoharlal, 2000.

Klostermaier, Klaus K. *Hinduism: A Short History.* Oxford: Oneworld, 2000.

Kramrisch, Stella. *The Hindu Temple* (1946), 2 vols. Delhi, India: Motilal Banarsidass, 1976.

Ravindra, Ravi, ed. *Science and Spirit.* New York: Paragon House, 1991.

Schrödinger, Erwin. *My View of the World.* London: Cambridge University Press, 1964.

Schrödinger, Erwin. "Der Geist der Naturwissenschaft." *Eranos-Jahrbuch* 14. Zurich: Rhein-Verlag, 1947.

Seal, Brajendranath. *The Positive Sciences of the Ancient Hindus* (1915). Delhi, India: Motilal Banarsidass, 1958.

Seidenberg, Abraham. "The Geometry of the Vedic Rituals." In *Agni: The Vedic Ritual of the Fire Altar,* ed. Frits Staal. Berkeley, Calif.: Asian Humanities Press, 1983.

Singhal, Damodar P. "Naturalism and Science in Ancient India." In *India and World Civilization,* 2 vols. East Lansing: Michigan State University Press, 1969.

Staal, Frits. "The Sanskrit of Science." *Journal of Indian Philosophy* 23 (1995): 73–127.

Subbarayappa, B. V. "India's Contribution to the History of Science." *Dilip* 1, no. 2 (1974): 15–33.

KLAUS K . KLOSTERMAIER

HISTORICAL CRITICISM

It would be difficult to argue that there was extensive interrelation between the rise of historical criticism and the emergence of modern science. True, both of these developments raised the most serious questions about the viability of traditional theological notions. In addition, the growing confidence in scientific explanations for events in nature, especially from the Enlightenment on, clearly eroded trust in traditional biblical authority. Yet the languages and the trajectories of criticism and science were mainly independent and parallel, as if taking place on the opposite sides of a high fence. And they raised different kinds of problems for the theological enterprise.

Method

Historical criticism of the Bible, sometimes referred to as *higher criticism* in contrast to the *textual criticism* that sought to determine the most accurate reading (or original texts) of the received biblical documents, sought to apply to the scriptures the same sort of analysis commonly used for other (especially ancient) literary documents—though it should be said that biblical scholars contributed perhaps more than any others to the origin and refinement of this kind of literary analysis. Prescinding from the traditional notions about authorship and "inspiration," historical criticism sought to answer anew questions about the origin and development of the scriptural literature, both by internal analysis and by relating the biblical texts to other records of ancient times. Fresh attention was given to such questions as: What is the relation of the biblical books to each other? How and why were they written? By whom? When? What did the writers intend to say? Were there historical causes that might account for the events recorded in the scriptures?

While such methods had been employed even in ancient times by some opponents of the church and by a small minority of Christian scholars, biblical studies in the church had continued to be largely insulated from literary criticism or defensive in reaction to it. Historical criticism began to be most extensively employed after the Renaissance and Reformation. The multiple levels of medieval interpretation, especially the allegorical or spiritual meanings, which through the Middle Ages had been favorite means of dealing with apparent difficulties and contradictions in the texts, were largely abandoned in favor of the "plain" or literal sense. In connection with their insistence on the authority of scripture rather than tradition, the Reformers, especially Martin Luther and William

Tyndal, had argued (though not consistently) for the "plain meaning."

Evolution of historical criticism

Early landmarks in the rise of historical criticism can be found in Thomas Hobbes's *Leviathan* (1651), with the implication that the Bible was not the word of God but rather contained the record of some men who had been inspired by God, and with doubts about the Mosaic authorship of the Pentateuch. Similarly, Baruch Spinoza, in the *Tractatus Theologico-Politicus* (1670), discussed the literary incoherencies, the historical contradictions, and chronological difficulties in Genesis. Spinoza was followed by the French oratorian Richard Simon (1638–1712), who noted the double accounts of some events in the Pentateuch and suggested a diversity in authorship, as well as the late origin of the present form of the Old Testament (i.e., only after the Exile). Simon is thus sometimes hailed as the true founder of historical criticism.

Application to the Old Testament. The full development of such criticism, however, came in the eighteenth and nineteenth centuries. Because the early application was mainly to the Hebrew scriptures, it was thus less threatening to Christian sensitivities. That criticism did not actually function much in the early adjustments to scientific (especially geological) views of the age of the world—for example, the notion popularized by James Ussher (1581–1656), the Irish Archbishop of Armagh, that creation had occurred in 4004 B.C.E., was easily abandoned by reinterpretation of the "days" of creation in the Genesis story. Yet historical criticism did raise serious questions about the reliability of the Old Testament chronology. And the uniformitarianism of the new geology of James Hutton in the eighteenth century and Charles Lyell (especially Lyell's *Principles of Geology,* 1830–1833) in the nineteenth century gradually replaced the popular catastrophism as a theory for the development of the earth. Equally important was reinterpretation of the nature of the Old Testament writings in general. For example, Johann Gottfried von Herder's *The Spirit of Hebrew Poetry* (1782–1783) and *History of the Education of Humanity* (1774), reflected both the Enlightenment critique of religious authority and the newly emerging Romantic movement. This was both parallel to and in protest against the Enlightenment (and especially Kantian) emphasis on the sole authority of the moral in religion.

Analysis of the sources and development of the Old Testament writings can be said to culminate in the Graf-Wellhausen theory (1876–1877) of the composition of the Hexateuch (the first six books of the Old Testament), which came to dominance by the end of the nineteenth century. To the basic distinction between the names for God in the *J* (Jahvist) and *E* (Elohim) sources were added the *D* (for Deuteronomic) and *P* (for Priestly) sources. Thus the famous *JEDP* documentary hypothesis, with subcategories in each (for some scholars).

It is of special interest that the biblical critical analysis played little or no role in Friedrich Schleiermacher's contention in *Der Christliche Glaube* (The Christian faith, 1821) that the Genesis stories of the creation and fall had no proper place in the Christian doctrines of creation and sin because those doctrines had properly to be derived strictly from the fundamental experience of utter dependence on God. Thus, for example, the controversy over whether creation is eternal or temporal has no bearing on the content of the feeling of utter dependence and is therefore a matter of indifference. On the other hand, it is plain that the scientific view of the world, or Nature, as a system of interconnected causality is crucial, and it is this which must go back to the divine causality as an explanation of the feeling of utter dependence. Thus cosmology is given over to the scientific view of things, yet the integrity of the religious affirmation is preserved, in what Schleiermacher in the second of his famous letters 1829 to his friend Friedrich Luecke called "an eternal covenant between the living Christian faith and a free, independent scientific inquiry, so that faith does not hinder science and science does not exclude faith" (p. 64). This statement has sometimes been hailed as the precursor of a fundamental dichotomy between the interests of theology and those of natural science that frequently appeared in the nineteenth and twentieth centuries.

Application to the New Testament. The application of the historical-critical method to the life of Jesus really began with German philosopher Hermann Samuel Reimarus (1694–1768), some of whose writings were published by Gothold Ephraim Lessing in the *Wolfenbuettel Fragments*

(1777–1778). This became the center of violent controversy with David Friedrich Strauss's *The Life of Jesus, Critically Examined* (1835). For both of these authors, of course, it was clear that certain events could not have happened in the way they were described in the gospels, because those accounts contravene scientific explanation. Strauss lists this as the first of his "negative" criteria for identifying the nonhistorical account; along with either internal inconsistency or contradiction to other accounts, a narrative can be "irreconcilable with the known and universal laws which govern the course of events" (p. 88). In this way, a scientific view is presupposed by historical criticism.

Closely related to this kind of argument was the rejection of the favorite traditional arguments from miracle and prophecy. The latter was partly a product of biblical criticism, with the recognition that the so-called prophecies in the Old Testament were properly to be understood in relation to current events rather than, for example, to the appearance of Jesus. The rejection of the argument from miracle was classically expressed in David Hume's critique in section ten of *An Enquiry Concerning Human Understanding* (1748). The argument here was not strictly a denial of the possibility of miracle, as a violation of the laws of nature, but was a devastating attack on the evidential value of such claims. Assumed here, but only in a general way, is the view of natural science as the primary explanatory category.

The historical-critical trajectory with respect to the New Testament continued particularly through varying analyses of the relations of the synoptic gospels, with the most widely accepted view that Luke and Matthew were dependent on Mark and that John was of much less value as an historical account. A culmination of this process was the judgment by the end of the nineteenth century that it was impossible to write a genuine biography of Jesus, for, as one fairly conservative thinker, Martin Kaehler, put it in 1892, we have "only a vast field strewn with the fragments of various traditions" (p. 49) out of which no sure account of the life of Jesus can come.

The most extreme case of the separation of science and theology was doubtless found in the work of the German liberal Protestant theologian Wilhelm Herrmann (1846–1922). Not only was natural scientific study irrelevant to the interests of religion, though within their limits the methods and results of science were "unassailable." Even metaphysics had to be rejected. So also "historical science," while it could serve the purposes of eliminating "false props" for faith, could have no positive value at all for the certainty or "full assurance" that faith requires.

See also SCRIPTURAL INTERPRETATION

Bibliography

Harrisville, Roy A., and Sundberg,Walter. *The Bible in Modern Culture: Theology and Historical-Critical Method from Spinoza to Kasemann.* Grand Rapids, Mich.: Eerdmans,1995.

Hermann, Wilhelm. *The Communion of the Christian With God* (1892), ed. Robert T. Voelkel. Philadelphia: Fortress Press, 1971.

Hobbes, Thomas. *Leviathan* (1651), ed. C. B. Macpherson. New York: Penguin, 1982.

Hume, David. *An Enquiry Concerning Human Understanding* (1748). *A Critical Edition,* ed. Tom L. Beauchamp. New York: Oxford University Press, 2001.

Kaehler, Martin. *The So-called Historical Jesus and the Historic Biblical Christ,* trans. Carl E. Braaten. Philadelphia: Fortress Press, 1964.

Schleiermacher, Freidrich. *The Christian Faith* (1821), trans. H.R. Mackintosh and J.S. Stewart. Edinburgh, UK: T&T Clark, 1948.

Schleiermacher, Friedrich. *On the Glaubenslehre* (1821-1822), trans. James Duke and Francis Fiorenza. Atlanta, Ga.: Scholars Press, 1981.

Schweitzer, Albert. *The Quest of the Historical Jesus* (1906), trans. William Montgomery. New York: Macmillan, 1961.

Spinoza, Baruch de. *Tractatus Theologico-Politicus* (1670), trans. Samuel Shirley. Leiden, Netherlands, and New York: E. J. Brill, 1991.

Strauss, David Friedrich. *The Life of Jesus Critically Examined,* ed. Peter C. Hodgson and trans. George Eliot. Philadelphia: Fortress Press, 1972.

CLAUDE WELCH

HOLISM

Holism is any attitude toward explanation that places emphasis on the importance of a whole system as against that of its individual parts. *Holism* is thus an epistemological term, reflecting a particular approach to explanation. The term was first used in English by South African statesman and author Jan Christiaan Smuts in 1926. Its roots within Western philosophy, however, go back to the German thinker George Wilhelm Friedrich Hegel (1770–1831), with his insistence that "the truth is the whole."

The concept of holism is important to three areas of the science-religion debate: (1) in the philosophy of science, where it is in particular tension with falsificationism; (2) in considerations of causation, including divine action, where holism is in tension with reductionism; and (3) in ecological thinking, where it is in tension with dualism and anthropocentrism.

Holism in the philosophy of science rests on an insight initially developed by Pierre Duhem (1861–1916), and refined by W. V. O. Quine (1908–2000), to the effect that scientific theories face the bar of experience as a whole, as a complex web of interrelated postulates and hypotheses. When an experimental result conflicts with current theory, proponents of the theory have a wide choice as to which elements to re-evaluate, not only altering the hypothesis being tested, but rejecting the result as an artifact, rejecting the apparatus as inappropriate, questioning the mathematical framework used to draw inferences from the result, or altering other hypotheses to fit the data. This runs counter to Karl Popper's proposal that science unfolds by a process of empirical falsification of discrete hypotheses.

Holism in the debate about causation

In discussions of holism and causation it is necessary to mention an important result in quantum theory, as well as a wider debate as to whether systems in any way cause the behaviour of their parts.

Quantum holism.

It is a remarkable feature of the mathematical framework of quantum mechanics that all the elements of an interacting system must be considered together. The wave function of all the components of a quantum system is collapsed by contact with an act of measurement, which gives rise to a definite behavior in all the particles concerned, be they electrons, photons, or some other particle. Thus, measurement of an electron's spin could simultaneously determine the spin of another electron with which it had once been paired, even if the second particle were on the other side of the universe. However, the EPR Paradox proposed by Albert Einstein and colleagues in the 1930s challenged this view. The experimental vindication of the predicted quantum result by physicist Alain Aspect in 1982 confirmed that reality must be viewed as more interconnected than classical science would have supposed. The Aspect result has given rise to highly speculative proposals, including explanations for telepathy. The precise implications of nonlocal interactions between quantum particles remain unclear.

Whole-part causation.

Can the behavior of individual elements of a system be influenced by the character of the larger system of which they are a part? That the answer to this is "yes" can be demonstrated in quite simple chemical systems, such as the Bénard cell, where coordinated geometric structures form when a liquid is heated in a certain way. A commonsense view of conscious agency might suggest that this sort of causation is also present when a person decides to move his arm. Donald T. Campbell and Roger W. Sperry developed the concept of *top-down causation* to describe instances in which larger wholes constrain the behavior of their components. This remains a contentious area of debate, especially in the study of the mind-brain relationship, where it focuses on the question as to *what* is doing the causing, other than the component neurons of the brain.

However, few thinkers would not concede that complex entities such as the cell, the multicellular organism, and the ecosystem, do have to be described in terms of *emergent properties,* types of explanation not necessary for lower levels of complexity. For example, molecules such as hormones are sent round the human body as "messengers," reflecting the state of the body as a whole. These messages change the state of molecules within the cells they reach. Moreover, the science of chaos emphasises that the behavior of many important types of systems, from the weather to the human heart, is exquisitely sensitive to the boundary conditions of the system. These considerations limit the effectiveness of scientific reductions, efforts to describe complex phenomena in terms of their component parts. The attempt to effect such reductions is essential to scientific methodology, but the experience of science is that explanations in terms of the functioning of larger wholes remain indispensable.

Two words of caution are in order in developing holistic accounts of causation. First, the previous paragraph simply states that description in terms of wholes influencing parts is a necessary explanatory device within scientific epistemology. It does not, however, establish an ontology of efficient causes of the sort to which the physics of forces lays claim. Second, sensitivity to initial conditions shows how important the overall environment is to chaotic systems; even a tropical rainforest is a whole within larger wholes.

John Polkinghorne and Arthur Peacocke have taken a lead in proposing that top-down causation can function as an analogy for the activity of God within the created order. Polkinghorne has focused on the mathematics of chaos as indicative of the flexibility and openness of creation to the input of divine information. In response to criticism that the equations of chaos are fundamentally deterministic, he speculates whether they may only be approximations to a more holistic account of reality. Peacocke's emphasis is, rather, on (1) the hierarchy of emergent properties of the universe and (2) that assertion that interaction between God and human minds is the highest known level of that hierarchy. Peacocke's terminology for the sort of physical causation to which divine action might be analogous has shifted from *whole-part causation,* to *whole-part constraint,* and finally to *whole-part influence.*

The words of caution above show the difficulties of the analogy. There is no model for how wholes can be causally effective, other than through the causal interactions of their components, and there are no wholes in the cosmos that are not themselves wholes-within-environments. Models of divine agency that stress whole-part causation do no more than indicate that two analogies may be somewhat helpful: the analogy of human mind-in-body conscious agency, and the analogy of God as the environment of the world.

Holism in ecological thinking

Discussions of holism in ecology draw on American naturalist Aldo Leopold's *Sand County Almanac* (1949), in which he emphasizes the importance of the overall health of the biotic community. These discussions also draw on the insistence of Norwegian philosopher and ecologist Arne Naess

as to the need for a "deep-ecological" attention to the whole network of relationships in an ecosystem. These emphases marked an ethical shift away from a focus on the interests of humans (anthropocentrism), and towards a sense that humans are no more than one part of the natural world. This sense is thus in tension with any dualistic view of humans that values only the status of their souls.

The understanding of the relation between humans and the nonhuman world is a major interface between scientific exploration of ecosystems and religious and ethical perspectives. The deep-ecological emphasis on the moral status of whole systems serves as a provocative corrective to the assumption that environmental problems can be best resolved by hierarchical, technocratic thinking. However, such holism raises an important question in environmental ethics: Is the whole system—be it the Brazilian rainforest or the total biosphere of the planet—the overriding locus of value, to which other values, such as the aspirations of individual humans, should be sacrificed? At their most radical such views smack of "ecofascism," and are themselves reductive of the complexity of biological systems. An alternative view is that of Holmes Rolston III, who asserts that the system is valuable because it is the protective matrix within which other sorts of value can be exchanged. Duties to a whole ecosystem, as Don Marietta insists, supplement, rather than supplant, duties to humans and other living things.

Holism is an important ingredient in a network of philosophical and physical explanations; it becomes weakened when its adherents neglect the importance of causative and evaluative explanations in terms of the components of systems.

See also BOUNDARY CONDITIONS; CHAOS THEORY; DOWNWARD CAUSATION; ECOLOGY; EPR PARADOX; HIERARCHY; PHYSICS, QUANTUM

Bibliography

Clayton, Philip. *God and Contemporary Science.* Edinburgh, Scottland: Edinburgh University Press, 1997.

Marietta, Don E. *For People and the Planet: Holism and Humanism in Environmental Ethics.* Philadelphia: Temple University Press, 1994.

Polkinghorne, John. *Belief in God in an Age of Science.* New Haven, Conn.: Yale University Press, 1998.

Rolston, Holmes, III. *Conserving Natural Value*. New York: Columbia University Press, 1994.

Russell, Robert John; Murphy, Nancey; Meyering, Theo C.; Arbib, Michael A., eds. *Neuroscience and the Person: Scientific Perspectives on Divine Action*. Vatican City and Berkely, Calif.: Vatican Observatory and Center for Theology and the Natural Sciences, 1999.

Sessions, George, ed. *Deep Ecology for the Twenty-First Century*. Boston, Mass.: Shambhala, 1995.

Smuts, Jan Christiaan. *Holism and Evolution*. New York: Macmillan, 1926.

Southgate, Christopher, ed. *God, Humanity, and the Cosmos: A Textbook in Science and Religion*. Edinburgh, UK, and Harrisburg, Pa.: T&T Clark and Trinity Press International, 1999.

CHRISTOPHER SOUTHGATE

HOLY SPIRIT

The term *Holy Spirit* occurs in only two historically late texts in the Old Testament (Isa. 63:10.11; Ps. 51:13), but much can nonetheless be deduced about the term. God's spirit (*ruah Yahweh*) is the "wind," the breath of life, which proceeds from and will return to Yahweh. It determines life spans (Gen. 6:3; Ps. 104:29–30; Job 33:4) and tames natural forces (Ex. 15:8). Psalm 33:6 ("by the word of the Lord the heavens were made, and all their host by the breath of his mouth"), uses it synonymously with *word* (*dabar*), which Genesis uses to explain how God created the world.

God's spirit is not just a life-giving power. Job 32:8 includes the assertion, "But truly it is the spirit [*ruah*] in a mortal, the breath [*neshamah*] of the Almighty, that makes for understanding." God's spirit leads to wisdom and imparts exceptional qualities. To tackle a threatening famine, for instance, Pharaoh looked for someone "in whom is the spirit of God" (Gen. 41:38). The spirit of God can also endow "ability, intelligence, and knowledge in every kind of craft" (Ex. 31:3). Only the spirit of God leads to right living and fulfillment of the will of God (Ps. 51:10–10).

The New Testament retains the Old Testament notion that the spirit of God can perform unusual deeds and is an eschatological sign (Matt. 12:28). Similar to the creation of the world, God now generates a new creation through the spirit (*pneuma*: Matt 1:18; Luke 1:35). While Matthew and Mark seldom mentioned the Holy Spirit, Luke believed that the presence of the spirit characterizes the time of the church. At Pentecost the Holy Spirit filled the disciples (Acts 2:4), and all who are baptized receive the Holy Spirit. Through the identification of God with the spirit, the latter assumes a cosmological function for John: "God is spirit, and those who worship him must worship in spirit and truth" (John 4:24). The spirit is also the life empowering factor: "It is the spirit that gives life, the flesh is useless. The words that I have spoken to you are spirit and life" (John 6:63). Paul, too, identified Jesus Christ with the spirit and wrote: "Now the Lord is the Spirit, and where the Spirit of the Lord is, there is freedom" (2 Cor. 3:17). Unlike Gnosticism, the spiritual and the physical are not opposites but are unified because of Christ's resurrection (1 Cor. 15:44).

The Church Fathers saw a unity between the *logos* (word) that became flesh, the *pneuma* (spirit), and the *sophia* (wisdom) of God. The Council of Constantinople (381 C.E.) clarified the function of the Holy Spirit. It asserted that Jesus Christ "was incarnate by the Holy Spirit and the Virgin Mary" and referred to the Holy Spirit as "the Lord and life-giver, Who proceeds from the Father, Who is worshiped and glorified together with the Father and the Son, Who has spoke through the prophets" (Leith, p.33). While the spirit is still seen as the life-giver, the main accent is on soteriology, an emphasis that intensified in the Reformation. From that time until the twentieth century, little reflection has been given to the spirit's activity in the world.

Two well-known twentieth-century theologians who have articulated a doctrine of the Holy Spirit in relation to contemporary science are the French Jesuit Pierre Teilhard de Chardin (1881-1955) and Wolfhart Pannenberg (1928–). In *The Divine Milieu* (1960), Teilhard clarified his evolutionary concept of life: "The same beam of light which christian spirituality, rightly and fully understood, directs upon the Cross to humanize it (without veiling it) is reflected on matter so as to spiritualize it" (p. 105). Matter generally drifts toward spirit, and one day "the whole divinizible substance of matter will have passed into the souls of men; all the chosen dynamisms will have been recovered; and then our world will be ready for the Parousia" (p. 110). The goal of the creative process is the spiritualization and divinization of all matter and its reception into the *christosphere*. According to Teilhard, the spirit is not independent of matter but elevates and moves it toward God.

Wolfhart Pannenberg regards the spirit "as the marvelous depth of life out of which all life originates" (1973, p. 106). Pannenberg understands the spirit as active in the self-transcendence of life, and he has used the field theories developed by Michael Faraday (1791–1867) and his successors to understand the spirit's activity in the world. According to Pannenberg, these field theories "claim a priority of the whole over the parts. This is of theological significance because God has to be conceived as the unifying ground of the whole universe if God is to be conceived as creator and redeemer of the world. The field concept could be used in theology to make the effective presence of God in every single phenomenon intelligible" (1988, p. 12).

Pannenberg sees the Stoic doctrine of the divine *pneuma* as a direct predecessor of the field theory that "was conceived as a most subtle matter which penetrates everything and holds the cosmos together by the powerful tension between its different parts, thus accounting for their cohesiveness as well as for the different movements and qualities of things" (1988, p. 13). Just as patristic theology rejected the Stoic notion that *pneuma* is a material element, modern field theorists, such as Albert Einstein in his first paper on special relativity of 1905, rejected ether, a hypothetical substance, as being necessary for the expansion of electromagnetic waves within the field. However, since the 1970s, quantum field theory of the vacuum has once again raised the idea of an ether, as has string theory.

Pannenberg contends that "since the field concept as such corresponds to the old concept of *pneuma* and was derived from it in the history of thought, theologians should also consider it obvious to relate the field concept of modern physics to the Christian doctrine of the dynamic presence of the divine Spirit in all of creation" (1988, p. 13). Field theory becomes Pannenberg's paradigm to show God's activity through the Holy Spirit. Pannenberg knows that there is a difference between how physics and theology perceive the world. Nevertheless he develops the doctrine of the Holy Spirit using field theory, although neither God nor the Holy Spirit can be conceived as a field in any sense

known to physics. Here Pannenberg has been strongly challenged. It remains interesting that modern physics reflects what the Old Testament asserted in speaking of the *ruah* (spirit) of Yahweh.

See also CHRISTIANITY; FIELD THEORIES; PNEUMATOLOGY; SPIRIT

Bibliography

Horn, Friedrich W. "Holy Spirit." In *The Anchor Bible Dictionary,* ed. David Noel Freedman. New York: Doubleday, 1992.

Pannenberg, Wolfhart. *Gegenwart Gottes: Predigten*. Munich: Claudius, 1973.

Pannenberg, Wolfhart. "The Doctrine of Creation and Modern Science." *Zygon* 23 (1988): 3–21.

Pannenberg, Wolfhart. *Systematic Theology,* 3 vols. Grand Rapids, Mich.: Eerdmans, 1991.

Teilhard de Chardin, Pierre. *The Divine Milieu*. New York: Harper Torchbooks, 1960.

Torrance, Thomas F. *The Trinitarian Faith: The Evangelical Theology of the Ancient Catholic Church*. Edinburgh, UK: T&T Clark, 1988.

Worthing, Mark W. *God, Creation, and Contemporary Physics*. Minneapolis, Minn.: Fortress, 1996.

HANS SCHWARZ

HOPE

The word *hope* refers to a concept, emotion, attitude of mind, and object of expectation that is expressed in different ways in different cultures. Its meaning develops in association with other notions, as in the cluster of faith, hope, and love. It may be focused on one central object—hope in God, or much less definite—sometimes people may half-hope for things. Such reflection is a human activity; rabbits do not reflect much on what they will do when they retire.

In order to survey the shape of hope an element of systematization is necessary. This will be invariably selective. Surveys of the Christian doctrine of hope have to try to avoid finding harmony in a tradition where there are significant elements of dissonance. There is a risk of assimilating too easily notions of hope in non-Christian sources with Christian paradigms. Linguistic usage, even in distinctive discourses, is rarely monolithic. Generalizations about the Greek view of hope, or whatever, are liable to be limited in their usefulness, and may easily obscure the balance of overlap and diversity in particular usage.

Reflections on hope

With these reservations, the tradition of theological reflection on hope may be instructive. Reflection upon possible futures, in optimistic anticipation, in trepidation, in trust, in resignation, does not always occur in a religious context. But it is an activity described and assessed as centrally important in major world religions. God is the source and the object of hope, of a positive future for the created order. Prophets are seen as sources of hope. Their return in various forms is anticipated as the expected fulfilment of hope. Transformation of the present world order, of the religious community, and of the self, as a physical or spiritual entity or both, as part of this process, is the content of hope. How this transformation is to be achieved is differently envisaged, from the cave paintings of Neolithic times to modern images of virtual reality. Hope is the antidote to despair, a widespread and damaging aspect of human life. The transformation may be encouraged by appropriately empathic human activity, from human sacrifice to psychotherapy.

The ancient Mediterranean world produced a huge variety of reflection on hope, sacred and secular, from the Greek poet Pindar (c. 520–438 B.C.E.) to Roman statesman and orator Cicero (106–43 B.C.E.) and beyond through the Church Fathers. These variations were accessibly documented by Rudolf Bultmann (1884–1976) in his standard article on hope in Gerhard Kittel's *Theological Dictionary of the New Testament,* which emphasized the different usages, and in Geoffrey Lampe's *A Patristic Greek Lexicon* (1961). Drawing on an early monograph by Hans Georg Gadamer (1900–2002), Bultmann illustrated from Plato the twin aspects of objective hope and subjective expectation in human reflection on existence, reflection that is essential to give people something to live for. Hope is associated with love, for it is drawn towards the good and the beautiful. In a religious context, as in the Mysteries, hope may be sustained by the promise of eternal life. Plato was aware that hope may be dangerous and deceptive. Hence perhaps the turn by the Stoic philosophers to an avoidance of

hope—if one does not hope for too much, one will not suffer disappointment.

Hope in the Hebrew Bible and, following this tradition, in the New Testament is centered upon God and the promise of God for the future of the people of God. In the Psalms a secure hope is based on God; any other basis is a false security. In the New Testament, especially in the Pauline writings, there is patient trust in God, in the expectation of the unfolding of God's future. In 1 Corinthians 13 hope is bound up with faith and love. The resurrection of Jesus Christ becomes the cornerstone of hope. The New Testament is everywhere colored by the overarching hope in eschatological expectation of the coming of the Kingdom. This foundation of hope on the presence of God—past, present, and to come—is taken up in the Fathers and in the theologies of the medieval, Reformation, and modern periods, reshaped according to the cultural imagination of the period (classically in the tradition of the three theological virtues of faith, hope, and love). Augustine of Hippo (354–430 C.E.) reflects the dialectic between hope and memory. For Thomas Aquinas (c. 1225–1274), hope is not simply the fruit of experience but hope in God is a learned habit of will. Not to hope is sinful. Martin Luther (1483–1546) and John Calvin (1509–1564) both interpret the gospel as promise, though this promise is of course firmly based on past and present action by God.

Notions of eschatological hope tended to be replaced in modern Western thought by ideas of progress and evolution. There is a unique amalgam of eschatological hope, apocalyptic imagery, and Enlightenment progress in Karl Marx (1818–1883) whose work was classically taken up by the mid-twentieth century philosopher Ernst Bloch in his massive *The Principle of Hope* (1952–1959). Bloch in turn famously inspired Jürgen Moltmann to write his *Theology of Hope* (1964), which sparked off a rediscovery of the importance of hope and a reorientation towards the future in theology. The turn to eschatology, and the thought of the determination of the present by the future, continues to be developed by Wolfhart Pannenberg and others.

For Luther hope was basically individual hope. Moltmann stressed the social and political dimensions, providing an important stimulus for a theology of liberation or emancipation, and for a new turn to the future as a focus for theology. This continues to be developed as a liberation of the oppressed through the freedom of the gospel, and through black, gay, feminist, and other theologies. A theology of the Holy Spirit understands the future as a future of Christlikeness.

Science and the theology of hope

What does theology of hope have to do with the dialogue between science and religion? Hope has objective as well as subjective dimensions. The future of the physical universe is certainly relevant to one strand of the complex thread of Christian hope. Exploration of divine action in relation to human life, through the natural sciences from cosmology to neuroscience, is seminal to grounds for hope. Hope is more than wishful thinking or blind optimism despite unpleasant facts. It is the hope of love, of corporate participation in the life of God.

A great deal of Christian theology has been devoted to engagement with the past and with the sense of tradition. Doctrines of creation have been especially past-oriented. Faith believes that the future of tradition may be much longer, and much more exciting, than its past. Creation points forward to new creation, to the unfolding of the divine purpose for the cosmos. Here the concept of hope is central. The future is not to be feared, for it is God's future. This is in turn a challenge to be open to new ideas and ready to revise existing paradigms. Hope suggests humility in the face of an unfolding mystery, an openness to surprise, and willingness to accept risk. Hope rests on the past fulfilment of God's promise for humanity and is resolved to look forward with confidence.

See also ESCHATOLOGY; HOLY SPIRIT; LIBERATION; LIBERATION THEOLOGY; PLATO; PROGRESS; THOMAS AQUINAS

Bibliography

Bloch, Ernest. *The Principle of Hope* (1952-1959), trans. Neville Plaice, Stephen Plaice, and Paul Knight. Cambridge, Mass.: MIT Press, 1995.

Bultmann, Rudolf. "Hope." In *Theological Dictionary of the New Testament,* ed. Gerhard Kittel, trans. Geoffrey W. Bromiley. Grand Rapids, Mich.: Eerdmans, 1967.

Kittel, Gerhard, ed. *Theological Dictionary of the New Testament,* trans. Geoffret W. Bromiley. Grand Rapids, Mich.: Eerdmans, 1964–1976 .

Moltmann, Jürgen. *Theology of Hope: On the Ground and the Implications of a Christian Eschatology.* London: SCM Press, 1964.

Newlands, George. *Generosity and the Christian Future.* London: SPCK, 1997.

Watts, Fraser. "Subjective and Objective Hope." In *The End of the World and the Ends of God: Science and Theology on Eschatology,* eds. John Polkinghorne and Michael Welker. Philadelphia, Pa.: Trinity Press International, 2000.

GEORGE NEWLANDS

HUMAN ECOLOGY

Human ecology is the interaction between humans and their environment, particularly the living ecosystems on which human life depends. An *ecosystem* is all the living organisms in a habitat, such as the fish and algae in a pond or the trees and earthworms in a forest, and the physical factors that support and affect them, such as sunlight and precipitation. Humans collect or grow food and fuel resources from Earth's ecosystems and are part of the Earth's food chains, where plants fix energy via photosynthesis, then animal herbivores consume the plants, and animal predators consume the herbivores. In the wake of global industrialization and a great increase in human population size, people are having an ever greater impact on the function and structure of the Earth's ecosystems. Humans are clearing much of the world's forest land, damming many of the world's rivers, and managing a majority of the Earth's most productive soils for agriculture.

Although science and engineering can develop new technologies that damage the environment, scientific research can conversely provide new environmentally friendly technologies for controlling pollution, collecting energy, and improving crop yields. Scientists studying ecosystems guide human interactions with the environment by documenting and monitoring human-initiated disturbances that result from, for example, the harvesting of timber, the catching of fish, or the building of cities, and they test new methods of restoring damaged ecosystems.

The world's religions also encourage human respect and care for ecosystems by providing explanations for natural phenomena and by discouraging destructive human activities and attitudes. The myths of Pacific Northwest Indians, for example, describe the cycle of salmon returning from the sea to spawn in rivers. The First Fish ceremony, held at the beginning of the salmon runs, temporarily halts all salmon harvest, thereby allowing some fish to escape and lay their eggs. Religious rituals or teachings can guide planting times and soil-conserving fallow on farm fields. Some Christian and Jewish farmers follow biblical instructions to provide a Sabbath year for the land to allow the soil to recover from crops. Islamic law provides guidance in managing wells, irrigation, and grazing lands. Religion may also protect the environment by discouraging greed and waste, and by encouraging respect for all creatures. The Jewish law found in the Torah, for example, prohibits wanton destruction of natural features, such as trees. Buddhists carefully replace insects and worms disturbed by plowing agricultural fields.

Religions may also designate ecosystems or species as sacred or provide them with special status, thus reducing over-harvest and conserving ecosystem components, such as predators. Native Hawaiian religion, for example, identifies some large sharks as family deities, thereby prohibiting their capture. Australian aborigines learn to respect plants and animals by adopting them as clan totems. Christian Ethiopian monks allow wildlife to remain undisturbed on their monastic grounds. Many religions identify scared trees or groves that may not be cut, or holy springs or rivers that may not be polluted.

Although they are frequently portrayed as opposites, both science and religion guide human environmental decision-making by identifying the best management alternatives, and encouraging human respect for, care of, and right relationship with the Earth's ecosystems.

See also BIOLOGICAL DIVERSITY; CHRISTIANITY, HISTORY OF SCIENCE AND RELIGION; ECOFEMINISM; ECOLOGY, ETHICS OF; ECOLOGY, RELIGIOUS AND PHILOSOPHICAL ASPECTS; ECOLOGY, SCIENCE OF; ECOTHEOLOGY; ISLAM, CONTEMPORARY ISSUES IN SCIENCE AND RELIGION; JUDAISM, CONTEMPORARY ISSUES IN SCIENCE AND RELIGION

Bibliography

Cooper, David E., and Palmer, Joy A. *Spirit of the Environment: Religion, Value, and Environmental Concern.* London: Routledge, 1998.

Kinsley, David. *Ecology and Religion: Ecological Spirituality in Cross-Cultural Perspective.* Upper Saddle River, N.J.: Prentice Hall, 1995.

SUSAN POWERS BRATTON

HUMAN GENOME PROJECT

The worldwide effort, originally named the *Human Genome Initiative* but later known as the *Human Genome Project* or HGP, began in 1987 and was celebrated as complete in 2001. When begun, HGP was dubbed "big science" comparable to placing human beings on the moon. It was international in scope, involving numerous laboratories and associations of scientists around the world and receiving public funding in the United States of $200 million per year with a scheduled fifteen year timeline. The U.S. Department of Energy (DOE) began funding the project in 1987, followed by the National Institutes of Health (NIH) in 1990.

History and goals

The scientific goal was to map the genes and sequence human DNA. Mapping would eventually reveal the position and spacing of the then predicted one hundred thousand genes in each of the human body's cells; sequencing would determine the order of the four base pairs—the *A* (adenine), *T* (thymine), *G* (guanine), and *C* (cytosine) nucleotides—that compose the DNA molecule. The primary motive was that which drives all basic science, namely, the need to know. The secondary motive was perhaps even more important, namely, to identify the four thousand or so genes that were suspected to be responsible for inherited diseases and prepare the way for treatment through genetic therapy. This would benefit society, HGP architects thought, because a library of DNA knowledge would jump start medical research on many fronts. Many early prophecies found their fulfillment. Some did not.

What was not anticipated was the competition between the private sector and the public sector. J.

Craig Venter (b. 1946) led the private sector effort. While on a grant from NIH, Venter applied for nearly three thousand patents on Expressed Sequence Tags (ESTs). The ESTs located genes but stopped short of identifying gene function. A furor developed when researchers working with government money applied for patents on data that merely reports knowledge of what already exists in nature—knowledge of existing DNA sequences—and this led to the 1992 resignation of James Watson (b. 1928) from the directorship of NIH's National Center for Human Genome Research (NCHGR). Watson, who along with Francis Crick (b. 1916) is famed for his discovery of the double helix structure of DNA, was the first to head the NCHGR

Venter then established The Institute for Genomic Research (TIGR) and began using Applied Biosystems automatic sequencers twenty-four hours per day to speed up nucleotide sequencing and the locating of ESTs. By 1998 Venter had established Celera Genomics with sequencing capacity fifty times greater than TIGR, and by June 17, 2000, he concluded a ninety percent complete account of the human genome. It was published in the February 16, 2001, issue of *Science*.

Francis Collins (b. 1950) took over NCHGR leadership from Watson and found himself driving the public sector effort, racing with Venter toward the mapping finish line. Collins drew twenty laboratories worldwide with hundreds of researchers into the International Human Genome Sequencing Consortium, which he directed from his Washington office. Collins repudiated patenting of raw genomic data and sought to place DNA data into the public domain as rapidly as possible so as to prevent private patenting. His philosophy was that the human genome is the common property of the whole human race. The public project finished almost simultaneously with the private, and the ninety percent complete Collins map appeared one day prior to Venter's on February 15, 2001, in *Nature*.

Human DNA, as it turns out, is largely junk— that is, 98.6 percent does not code for proteins. Half of the junk DNA consists of repeated sequences of various types, most of which are parasitic elements inherited from our distant evolutionary past. Only 1.1 percent to 1.4 percent constitute sequences that code for proteins that function as genes.

Of dramatic interest is the number of genes in the human genome. At the time of the announcement, Collins estimated there are 31,000 protein-encoding genes; he could actually list 22,000. Venter could provide a list of 26,000, to which he added an estimate of 10,000 additional possibilities. For round numbers, the estimate in 2001 stood at 30,000 human genes.

This is philosophically significant, because when the project began in 1987 the anticipated number of genes was 100,000. It was further assumed that human complexity was lodged in the number of genes: the greater the number of genes, the greater the complexity. So, confusion appeared when, nearing the completion of HGP, scientists could find only a third of the anticipated number. Confusion was enhanced when the human genome was compared to a yeast cell with 6,000 genes, a fly with 13,000 genes, a worm with 26,000 genes, and a rice cell with 50,000 genes. On the basis of the previous assumption, a grain of rice should be more complex than Albert Einstein.

With the near completion of HGP, no longer could human uniqueness, complexity, or even distinctiveness be lodged in the number of genes. Collins began to speculate that perhaps what is distinctively human could be found not in the genes themselves but in the multiple proteins and the complexity of protein production. Culturally, DNA began to lose some of its magic, some of its association with human essence.

The theology and ethics of HGP

At the outset, HGP scientists anticipated ethical and public policy concerns; they were acutely aware that their research would have an impact on society and were willing to share responsibility for it. When in 1987 James Watson counseled the U.S. Department of Health and Human Services to appropriate the funds for what would become HGP, he recommended that three percent of the budget be allotted to study the ethical, legal, and social implications of genome research. Watson insisted that society learn to use genetic information only in beneficial ways; if necessary, the government should pass laws at both the federal and state levels to prevent invasions of privacy and discrimination on genetic grounds. Moral controversy broke out repeatedly during the near decade and a half of research.

Religious responses to the advancing frontier of genetic knowledge emerge mainly from people's concern to relieve human suffering and employ science to improve human health and well-being. A statement prepared by the National Council of Churches under the leadership of Union Seminary ethicist Roger L. Shinn affirms that churches in the United States must be involved with genetic research and therapy. "The Christian churches understand themselves as communities dedicated to obeying the will of God through service to others. The churches have a particular concern for those who are hurt or whose faith has been shaken, as demonstrated by the long history of the churches in providing medical care .... Moreover, the churches have a mission to prevent suffering as well as to alleviate it."

In 1990 the Center for Theology and the Natural Sciences (CTNS) at the Graduate Theological Union (GTU) in Berkeley, California, obtained one of the first grants offered by the Ethical, Legal, and Social Issues (ELSI) division of NCHGR. A team of molecular biologists, behavioral geneticists, theologians, and bioethicists monitored the first years of HGP research to articulate theological and ethical implications of the new knowledge. Many religious and ethical issues eventually became public policy concerns. These are adumbrated below.

Genetic discrimination. When Watson recommended the establishment of ELSI, the first public policy concern was what he called *privacy,* here called *genetic discrimination.* An anticipated and feared scenario took the following steps. As researchers identify and locate most if not all genes in the human genome that either condition or, in some cases, cause disease, the foreknowledge of an individual's genetic predisposition to expensive diseases could lead to loss of medical insurance and perhaps loss of employment opportunities. As HGP progressed, the gene for cystic fibrosis was found on chromosome seven, and Huntington's chorea on chromosome four. Alzheimer's disease was sought on chromosome twenty-one, and colon cancer on chromosome two. Disposition to muscular dystrophy, sickle-cell anemia, Tay Sachs disease, certain cancers, and numerous other diseases turned out to have locatable genetic origins. More knowledge is yet to come. When it comes, it may be accompanied by an inexpensive method for testing the genome of each individual to see if he or she has any genes for any diseases. Screening for all genetic diseases may become routine for newborns just as testing for phenylketonuria (PKU) has been since the 1960s. A person's individual genome might become part of a data bank to which each person, as well as health care providers, would have future access. The advantage is clear: Medical care from birth to grave could be carefully planned to delay onset, appropriately treat, and perhaps even prevent or cure genetically-based diseases.

Despite the promise for advances in preventative health care, fear arises due to practices of commercial insurance. Insurance works by sharing risk. When risk is uncertain to all, then all can be asked to contribute equally to the insurance pool. Premiums can be equalized. Once the genetic disorders of individuals become known, however, this could justify higher premiums for those demonstrating greater risk. The greater the risk, the higher the premium. Insurance may even be denied those whose genes predict extended or expensive medical treatment.

Some ethicists are seeking protection from discrimination by invoking the principles of confidentiality and privacy. They argue that genetic testing should be voluntary and that the information contained in one's genome be controlled by the patient. This argument presumes that if information can be controlled, then the rights of the individual for employment, insurance, and medical care can be protected. There are grounds for thinking this approach will succeed. Title VII of the 1964 Civil Rights Act restricts pre-employment questioning about work-related health conditions. Paragraph 102.b.4 of the Act potentially protects coverage for the employee's spouse and children. Legislative proposals during the 1990s and early 2000s seem to favor privacy.

Other ethicists argue that privacy is a misguided cure for this problem. Privacy will fail, say its critics, because insurance carriers will press for legislation fairer to them, and eventually protection by privacy may slip. In addition, computer linkage makes it difficult to prevent the movement of data from hospital to insurance carrier and to anyone else bent on finding out. Most importantly, the privacy argument overlooks the principle that genome information should not finally be restricted. The more society knows, the better the health care planning can be. In the long run, what society needs is information without discrimination. The only way to obtain this is to restructure the employment-insurance-health care relationship. The current structure makes it profitable for employers and insurance carriers to discriminate against individuals with certain genetic configurations—that is, it is in their best financial interest to limit or even deny health care. A restructuring is called for so that it becomes profitable to deliver, not withhold, health care. To accomplish this the whole nation will have to become more egalitarian—that is, to think of the nation itself as a single community willing to care for its own constituents.

The Abortion controversy. Given the divisiveness of the abortion controversy in the United States and certain other countries, fears arise over possible genetic discrimination in the womb or even prior to the womb in the petri dish. Techniques have been developed to examine in vitro fertilized (IVF) eggs as early as the fourth cell division in order to identify so-called defective genes, such as the chromosomal structure of Down syndrome. Prospective parents may soon routinely fertilize a dozen or so eggs in the laboratory, screen for the preferred genetic make up, implant the desired zygote or zygotes, and discard the rest. What will be the status of the discarded embryos? Might they be considered abortions? By what criteria does one define "defective" when considering the future of a human being? Should prospective parents limit themselves to eliminating "defective" children, or should they go on to screen for enhancing genetic traits such as blue eyes or higher intelligence? If so, might this lead to a new form of eugenics, to selective breeding based upon personal preference and prevailing social values? What will become of human dignity in all this?

Relevant here is that the legal precedent set by *Roe v. Wade* (1973) would not serve to legitimate discarding preimplanted embryos. This Supreme Court case legalized the use of abortion to eliminate a fetus from a woman's body as an extension of a woman's right to determine what happens to her body. This would not apply to preimplanted embryos, however, because they are life forms outside the woman's body.

The Roman Catholic tradition has set strong precedents regarding the practice of abortion. The

Second Vatican Council document *Gaudium et spes* (1965) states the position still held today: "… from the moment of its conception life must be guarded with the greatest care, while abortion and infanticide are unspeakable crimes." The challenge to ethicists in the Roman Catholic tradition in the near future will be to examine what transpires at the preimplantation stage of the embryo to determine if the word *abortion* applies. If it does, this may lead to recommending that genetic screening be pushed back one step further, to the gamete stage prior to fertilization. The genetic make up of sperm and ovum separately could be screened, using acceptable gametes and discarding the unacceptable. The Catholic Health Association of the United States pushes back still further by recommending the development of techniques of gonadal cell therapy to make genetic corrections in the reproductive tissues of prospective parents long before conception takes place—that is, gametocyte therapy.

Genetic determinism, human freedom, and the gene myth. Religious thinkers must deal not only with laboratory science but with the cultural interpretations of science, as well as public policy influenced by both. A cultural myth has grown up with media coverage of the Human Genome Project that assumes "it's all in the genes." DNA has emerged as a cultural icon, holding the "blueprint" for humanity or being thought of as the "essence" of what makes a person a person. Even though molecular biologists withdraw from such extreme forms of genetic determinism, a cultural myth has arisen. Some commentators refer to it as the *strong genetic principle*; others call it the *gene myth*.

Genes, sin, crime, and racial discrimination. The belief in determinism promulgated by the gene myth raises the question of moral and legal culpability. Does a genetic disposition to antisocial behavior make a person guilty or innocent before the law? Over the next decade legal systems will have to face a rethinking of the philosophical planks on which concepts such as free will, guilt, innocence, and mitigating factors have been constructed. There is no question that research into the connection between genetic determinism and human behavior will continue and new discoveries will become immediately relevant to the prosecution and defense of those accused of crimes. The focus will be on the concept of free will, because the assumption of the Western philosophy coming down from Augustine that underlies understanding of law is that guilt can only be assigned to a human agent acting freely. The specter on the genetic horizon is that confirmable genetic dispositions to certain forms of behavior will constitute compulsion, and this will place a fork in the legal road: Either the courts declare the person with a genetic disposition to crime to be innocent and set him or her free, or the courts declare him or her so constitutionally impaired as to justify incarceration and isolation from the rest of society. The first fork would jeopardize the welfare of society; the second fork would violate individual rights.

That society needs to be protected from criminal behavior, and that such protection could be had by isolating individuals with certain genetic dispositions, leads to further questions regarding insanity and race. The issue of insanity arises because the genetic defense may rely upon precedents set by the insanity defense. The courts treat insanity with a focus on the insane person's inability to distinguish right from wrong when committing a crime. When a defendant is judged innocent on these grounds, he or she is incarcerated in a mental hospital until the medical evaluators judge that the individual is cured. Once cured, the person may be released. In principle, such a person might never be judged "cured" and may spend more time in isolation than the prison penalty prescribed for the crime, maybe even the rest of his or her life. Should the genetic defense tie itself to the insanity defense, and if one's DNA is thought to last a lifetime, then the trip to the hospital may become the equivalent of a life sentence. In this way the genetic defense may backfire.

With this prospect, we have returned to the specter of genetic discrimination. The current discussion of possible genetic influence on antisocial behavior is riddled with fears of discrimination, especially its racial overtones. Because the percentage of black men among the population of incarcerated prisoners is growing, society could invoke the gene myth to associate genes with criminal predispositions and with race. A stigma against black people could arise, a presumption that they are genetically predisposed to crime. University of California sociologist Troy Duster fears that if we identify crime with genes and then genes with race, we may inadvertently provide a biological support for prejudice and discrimination.

The gay gene. Theological and ethical debate has arisen over the 1993 discovery of a possible genetic disposition to male homosexuality. Dean H. Hamer and his research team at the U.S. National Cancer Institute announced that they discovered evidence that male homosexuality—at least some male homosexuality—is genetic. Constructing family trees in instances where two or more brothers are gay combined with actual laboratory testing of homosexual DNA, Hamer located a region near the end of the long arm of the X chromosome that likely contains a gene influencing sexual orientation. Because men receive an X chromosome from their mother and a Y from their father (women receive two X's, one from each parent), this means that the possible gay gene is inherited maternally. Mothers can pass on the gay gene without themselves or their daughters being homosexual. A parallel study of lesbian genetics is as yet incomplete; and the present study of gay men will certainly require replication and confirmation. Scientists do not yet have indisputable proof.

The ethical implications, should a biological basis for homosexuality be confirmed, could point in more than one direction. The scientific fact does not itself determine the direction of the ethical interpretation of that fact. The central ethical question is this: Does the genetic disposition toward homosexuality make the bearer of that gene innocent or guilty? Two answers are logically possible.

On the one hand, a homosexual man could claim that because he inherited the gay gene and did not choose a gay orientation by his own free will, he is innocent. The biological innocence position could be buttressed by an additional argument that homosexual activity is not itself sinful; it is simply one natural form of sexual expression among others. One could go still further to say that because it is biologically inherited that it is God's will; that a person's homosexual predisposition is God's gift.

On the other hand, one could follow the opposite road and identify the gay gene with a carnal disposition to sin. Society could claim that the body inherited by each person belongs to who they are—people are determined at least in part by what their parents bequeathed them—and that an inherited disposition to homosexual behavior is just like other innate dispositions such as lust or greed, which are shared with the human race generally; all this constitutes the state of original sin into which we are born. Signposts point in both ethical directions.

Beyond the question of guilt or innocence ethicists anticipate another issue, namely, the risk of stigma. Might the presence of the gay gene in an unborn fetus be considered a genetic defect and become grounds for abortion? Would routine genetic testing lead to a wholesale reduction of gay men in a manner parallel to that of children with Down Syndrome? Would this count as class discrimination?

Somatic therapy versus germline enhancement. The debate over two distinctions—somatic versus germline intervention and therapy versus enhancement intervention—involves both secular and religious discussions. The term *somatic therapy* refers to the treatment of a disease in the body cells of a living individual by trying to repair an existing defect. The term *germline therapy* refers to intervention into the gametes, perhaps for the purpose of eliminating a gene such as that for cystic fibrosis so that it would not be passed along to future generations. Both somatic and germline therapies are conservative when compared to genetic enhancement. Enhancement goes beyond mere therapy for existing genes that may be a threat to health by selecting or adding genes to make an individual "superior" in some fashion. Enhancement might involve genetic engineering to increase bodily strength or intelligence or other socially desirable characteristics.

Ethical commentators almost universally agree that somatic therapy is morally desirable, and they look forward to the advances HGP will bring for expanding this important work. Yet they stop short of endorsing genetic selection and manipulation for the purposes of enhancing the quality of biological life for otherwise normal individuals or for the human race as a whole. New knowledge gained from HGP might locate genes that affect the brain's organization and structure so that careful engineering might lead to enhanced ability for abstract thinking or to other forms of physiological and mental improvement.

Religious ethicists argue that somatic therapy should be pursued, but enhancement through germline engineering raises cautions about protecting human dignity. In a 1982 study, the World Council of Churches stated: "Somatic cell therapy may provide a good; however, other issues are raised if it also brings about a change in germline cells. The introduction of genes into the germline is a permanent alteration .... Nonetheless, changes in genes that avoid the occurrence of disease are not necessarily made illicit merely because those changes also alter the genetic inheritance of future generations .... There is no absolute distinction between eliminating defects and improving heredity" (quoted in Peters, ed., 1998, pp. 6–8). The primary caution raised by the WCC here has to do with the lack of knowledge regarding the possible consequences of altering the human germline. The present generation lacks sufficient information regarding the long term consequences of a decision today that might turn out to be irreversible tomorrow. Thus, the WCC does not forbid forever germline therapy or even enhancement; rather, it cautions people to wait and see.

The Catholic Health Association is more positive: "Germline intervention is potentially the only means of treating genetic diseases that do their damage early in embryonic development, for which somatic cell therapy would be ineffective. Although still a long way off, developments in molecular genetics suggest that this is a goal toward which biomedicine could reasonably devote its efforts" (p. 19)

Another reason for caution regarding germline enhancement, especially among the Protestants, is the specter of eugenics. The word *eugenics* connotes the ghastly racial policies of Nazism, and this accounts for much of today's mistrust of genetic science in Germany and elsewhere. No one expects a resurrection of the Nazi nightmare; yet some critics fear a subtle form of eugenics slipping in the cultural back door. The growing power to control the design of living tissue will foster the emergence of the image of the "perfect child," and a new social value of perfection will begin to oppress all those who fall short.

Gene patenting. A controversy exploded in 1991 over gene patenting prompted by the filing for intellectual property rights by J. Craig Venter on nearly three thousand ESTs, expressed sequence tags. Each of these ESTs consisted of three hundred to five hundred base pairs made from cDNAs, copies of DNA sequences produced by polymerase chain reaction. ESTs are gene fragments, not whole genes; hence they mark the location of a gene but cannot identify gene function. Two issues became the focus of controversy. First, should the U.S. Patent and Trademark Office grant patents on genomic data? Even though the patents applied for were on copies of DNA sequences, their only value was to report raw genomic information. It appeared to critics that these applications failed to meet the three patenting criteria: novelty, utility, and nonobviousness. Second, should the U.S. government apply for and receive such patents in competition with the private sector? Venter's first patent applications were filed while he was working on a government grant; later he moved to the private sector and continued filing for intellectual property rights on his discoveries. James Watson followed by Francis Collins at the NIH both opposed patenting raw genomic data.

Cloning. Technically known as "somatic cell nuclear transfer," cloning techniques were developed in 1996 by Ian Wilmut at the Roslin Institute near Edinburgh, Scotland. Wilmut announced the cloning of Dolly the sheep in February 1997. The scientific breakthrough consisted of returning an already differentiated DNA nucleus to its pre-differentiated state and then transferring it to an ennucleated oocyte to make an embryo. The new embryo thus contains the genome of the donor nucleus. In the worldwide controversy that broke out in 1997 and continues in bioethical discussion, the debate seems to bypass the science of nuclear transfer; rather, the focus is on producing multiple human beings with duplicate genomes. Critics of reproductive cloning argue that children produced by cloning would suffer from loss of individuality, identity, and dignity. Roman Catholic critics along with Wilmut himself oppose human reproductive cloning on the grounds of safety—that is, the imperfect technology would lead to the destruction of many early embryos. Defenders of nuclear transfer research distinguish sharply between reproductive cloning, which they oppose, and therapeutic cloning, which is necessary for stem cell research.

Stem cells. The isolation of human embryonic stem cells (hES cells) was accomplished in August 1997 by James Thomson at the University of Wisconsin on funds from the Geron Corporation. The hES cells are removed from the inner mass of the blastocyst, an embryo at four to six days old. When isolated and placed on a feeder tray, hES cells become immortal—that is, they divide indefinitely. In addition, they are pluripotent and able to differentiate into any and every tissue. The research goal is to control gene expression so as to make designated tissue for rejuvenating human organs. Some progress in gene control has been achieved. The next hurdle to jump is histocompatibility, namely, to avoid organ rejection by matching donor and recipient genetic codes. It is likely that experiments with somatic cell nuclear transfer will be required to attain histocompatibility. Ethical objections to stem cell research from Roman Catholics center on destruction of blastocysts for research purposes. Ethical support for stem cell research stresses beneficence; it emphasizes the marvelous advances in human health and well-being that this medical science might offer the human race.

Conclusion: theological commitments to human dignity

Virtually all Roman Catholics and Protestants who take up the challenge of the new genetic knowledge seem to agree on a handful of theological axioms. First, they affirm that God is the creator of the world and, further, that God's creative work is ongoing. God continues to create in and through natural genetic selection and even through human intervention in the natural processes. Second, the human race is created in God's image. In this context, the divine image in humanity is tied to creativity. God creates; so do human beings. With increasing frequency, humans are described by theologians as *co-creators* with God, making their human contribution to the evolutionary process. In order to avoid the arrogance of thinking that humans are equal to the God who created them in the first place, people must add the term *created* to make the phrase *created co-creators*. This emphasizes human dependency on God while pointing to human opportunity and responsibility. Third, these religious documents place a high value on human dignity.

By *dignity* they mean what eighteenth-century German philosopher Immanuel Kant meant, namely, that each human being is treated as an end, not merely as a means to some further end. As church leaders respond responsibly to new developments in HGP, one thing can be confidently forecast: This affirmation of dignity will become decisive for thinking through the ethical implications of genetic engineering. Promoting dignity is a way of drawing an ethical implication from what the theologian can safely say, namely, that God loves each human being regardless of his or her genetic makeup and, therefore, people should love one another according to this model.

See also BEHAVIORAL GENETICS; BIOTECHNOLOGY; CLONING; DNA; EUGENICS; FREEDOM; GENE PATENTING; GENE THERAPY; GENETIC DETERMINISM; GENETIC ENGINEERING; GENETICS; GENETIC TESTING; NATURE VERSUS NURTURE; PLAYING GOD; SIN; SOCIOBIOLOGY; STEM CELL RESEARCH

Bibliography

Catholic Health Association of the United States. *Human Genetics: Ethical Issues in Genetic Testing, Counseling, and Therapy.* St. Louis, Mo.: CHA, 1990.

Chapman, Audrey R. *Unprecedented Choices: Religious Ethics at the Frontiers of Genetic Science.* Minneapolis, Minn.: Fortress, 1999.

Coffey, Maureen P. "The Genetic Defense: Explanation or Excuse?" *William and Mary Law Review* 35, no.353 (1993): 352-396.

Cole, David. "Genetic Predestination?" *Dialog* 33, no. 1 (1994): 20-21.

Cole-Turner, Ronald. *The New Genesis: Theology and the Genetic Revolution.* Louisville, Ky.: Westminster John Knox Press, 1993.

Cole-Turner, Ronald, ed. *Human Cloning: Religious Responses.* Louisville, Ky.: Westminster John Knox Press, 1997.

Cooke-Deegan, Robert. *The Gene Wars: Science, Politics, and the Human Genome.* New York: Norton, 1996.

Davies, Kevin. *Cracking the Genome: Inside the Race to Unlock Human DNA.* New York: Free Press, 2001.

Duster, Troy. *Backdoor to Eugenics.* New York: Routledge, 1990.

Eisenberg, Rebecca S. "Genes, Patents, and Product Development." *Science* 257 (992): 903-908.

Genome Sequencing Consortium. "Initial Sequencing and Analysis of the Human Genome." *Nature* 409 (2001): 860–921.

Halley, Janet E. "Sexual Orientation and the Politics of Biology: A Critique of the Argument from Immutability." *Stanford Law Review* 46, no. 3 (1994): 503-568.

Hamer, Dean H.; Hu, Stella; Magnuson, Victoria L.; et al. "A Linkage Between DNA Markers on the X Chromosome and Male Sexual Orientation." *Science* 261 (1993): 321–327.

Holland, Suzanne; Lebacqz, Karen; and Zoloth, Laurie. *The Human Embryonic Stem Cell Debate.* Cambridge, Mass.: MIT Press, 2001.

Kevles, Daniel J., and Hood, Leroy, eds. *Code of Codes: Scientific and Social Issues in the Human Genome Project.* Cambridge, Mass.: Harvard University Press, 1992.

Lewontin, Richard C.; Rose, Steven; and Kamin, Leon J. *Not In Our Genes: Biology, Ideology, and Human Nature.* New York: Pantheon, 1984.

National Council of Churches. *Human Life and the New Genetics.* New York: Author, 1980.

Nelkin, Dorothy, and Lindee, M. Susan. *The DNA Mystique: The Gene as a Cultural Icon.* New York: W.H. Freeman and Company, 1995.

Paul VI. *Gaudium et Spes.* Pastoral Constitution on the Church in the Modern World (December 7, 1965). In *Vatican Council II: Constitutions, Decrees, Declarations,* ed. Flannery Austin. Northport, N.Y.: Costello: 1996.

Peters, Ted. *Playing God? Genetic Determinism and Human Freedom.* New York: Routledge, 1997.

Peters, Ted. *For the Love of Children: Genetic Technology and the Future of the Family.* Louisville, Ky.: Westminster John Knox, 1998.

Peters, Ted, ed. *Genetics: Issues of Social Justice.* Cleveland, Ohio: Pilgrim, 1998.

Reichenbach, Bruce R., and Anderson, V. Elving. *On Behalf of God: A Christian Ethic for Biology.* Grand Rapids, Mich.: Eerdmans, 1998.

Rifkin, Jeremy. *Algeny.* New York: Viking, 1983.

Shinn, Roger L. *The New Genetics: Challenges for Science, Faith, and Politics.* Wakefield, R.I. and London: Moyer Bell, 1996.

Venter, J. Craig, et al. "The Sequence of the Human Genome," *Science* 291 (2001):1304–1351.

World Council of Churches. *Manipulating Life: Ethical Issues in Genetic Engineering.* Geneva, Switzerland: Author, 1982

TED PETERS

HUMANISM

The term *humanism* over the past several centuries of Western thought has been used to express two different concepts. It is not too much to say that humanism in its original form created the intellectual foundation of the Renaissance. In modern times, humanism has most often come to mean an approach that characterizes all things in a human, rather than theistic, framework and emphasizes human rationality and experience in contrast to classic authority. It is arguable, however, that the adversarial relationship between theism and the human, including scientific knowledge and rationality, that is often imputed to modern humanism is unnecessarily simplistic, ignoring, for example, today's Christian humanists. Moreover, it is possible to detect the evolution of a new, more integrative, humanism as a response to a world whose natural cycles and processes are increasingly dominated by the human.

Humanism in its original sense meant simply the rediscovery and study of classic Greek and Latin language and texts, and the use of them to assess the work of doctrinal Scholastics and secondary commentaries of late Medieval Europe. Humanism during this time was more a cultural attitude and an academic program than a formal conceptual framework or a particular philosophy. Indeed, the first self-conscious humanist, the Italian poet Francis Petrarch (1304–1374), is notable for urging a new curricula based on original classical sources—the *studia humanitatis,* consisting of grammar, rhetoric, poetry, history, and moral philosophy. During this period, the term *humanist* had no ideological content and simply referred to anyone, layperson or Church official, who had a competence in classical Greek, Latin, and to a lesser extent Hebrew, and some familiarity with classical texts.

Early humanism led to the recovery of the direct study of the Bible. Many early medieval Church figures such as Thomas More (1478–1535) and Desiderius Erasmus (1469–1536), and a number of reformers, strongly supported the humanist approach. In general, however, early humanism was stronger in Italy than in the more medieval north of Europe. Thus, Pope Nicholas V (1447–1455) is referred to by Bertrand Russell in *A History of Western Philosophy* (1945) as "the first humanist Pope" (p. 498). Nicholas's apostolic secretary was the epicurean humanist Lorenzo Valla (1407–1457). Reflecting their culture, the vast majority of humanists were practicing Christians, although they tended to react against the medieval Scholastic veneration of authority. Valla, for example, wrote a long treatise somewhat inelegantly titled *Restructuring of All Dialectic with the Foundations of the Whole of Philosophy,* in which he purported to demonstrate the invalidity of Aristotelian logic, a foundation of Scholasticism.

As Western culture evolved, however, humanism inevitably began to challenge medieval worldviews in fundamental ways. Rather than the authority of Aristotle (384–322 B.C.E.), Augustine of Hippo (354–430), and Thomas Aquinas (c. 1225–1274), humanists rediscovered and began to teach classical texts of all types. These not only greatly broadened the knowledge base available to scholars and the educated, but stimulated both increased curiosity about the world in general and a different concept of validity. During the early medieval period, reference to accepted authority was the highest demonstration of truth; humanism over time led to increased reference to the physical world as the ultimate source of validity in argument. The authority of Galen (c. 130–201 C.E.) in medicine or Aristotle in physics was increasingly challenged by data and argument derived not from accepted texts but from observation of the world itself. In doing so, humanism created the foundations for the profound ontological shift from the otherworldliness of medieval faith to scientific knowledge that characterized the Enlightenment and, subsequently, modernity.

The Enlightenment is often characterized as a conflict between faith and reason, but that is misleading. Major Enlightenment figures, including on the nascent rationalist side Francis Bacon (1561–1626) and, later, Isaac Newton (1642–1727), clearly viewed their scientific work as aligned with the Christian faith, even mandated by it. On the literary side, the Romantic project was seen by many of its leading figures as an effort to modernize and humanize Christian theology in light of Enlightenment science, which had come to represent an independent and in some ways equally powerful ontology. Thus, the poet John Keats (1795–1821) saw his goal as creating "a system of Salvation which does not affront our reason and humanity" (quoted in Abrams, p. 33), a goal that can be broadly attributed to the Romantic movement in general.

Attitudes toward modern humanism mirror the distortions of the Enlightenment characterization.

In particular, the attacks by Christian fundamentalists on "secular humanism" in the United States, especially regarding the teaching of evolution, have created an impression that humanism is necessarily opposed to religion. Secular humanism, a tradition flowing from eighteenth-century Enlightenment rationalism and subsequent freethinking movements, is indeed characterized by a Promethean suspicion of theism and religious authority, and a belief that humans are the measure of all things; it is, however, but one branch of the humanist project. Modern humanists fall into many categories, including *literary humanism,* characterized by a devotion to the humanities; *cultural humanism,* the rational, empirical tradition derived from ancient Greece and Rome that forms the basis of modern Western societies; and *philosophic humanism,* systems of thought focused on human needs and realities.

Of particular interest, however, are the schools of humanism that explicitly integrate religious and scientific worldviews. Thus, Christian humanism, the philosophy that posits the self-fulfillment of humans within the framework of Christian principles and beliefs, has evolved from More and Erasmus through elements of the Anglican and German pietist traditions and philosophers such as Immanuel Kant (1724–1804). It is represented by modern theologians such as Jacques Maritain, Hans Küng, Paul Tillich, and James Luther Adams. More explicitly, the Unitarian Universalist tradition includes among its seven Principles three that are obviously humanist; they affirm (1) the "inherent worth and dignity of every person," (2) justice, "equity and compassion in human relations," and (3) a "free and responsible search for truth and meaning." The Unitarian Universalists also identify as among the sources of their tradition humanist "teachings which counsel us to heed the guidance of reason and the results of science, and warn us against idolatries of the mind and spirit."

This integration of faith and rationality will become increasingly important in light of the recognition that, as a result of the Industrial Revolution, population and economic growth, and globalization, the dynamics of most major natural systems are increasingly influenced by human activity. Since this results in a world where teleologies and belief systems are increasingly reified in natural systems through intentional human activity, a rational humanistic understanding, combined with

the religious faith that is central to the human experience—perhaps an "Earth systems" humanism—may well be a future evolutionary path of humanism.

See also ARISTOTLE; AUGUSTINE; CHRISTIANITY; CREATIONISM; EVOLUTION; NEWTON, ISAAC; TELEOLOGY; THOMAS AQUINAS

Bibliography

Abrams, M. H. *Natural Supernaturalism: Tradition and Revolution in Romantic Literature.* New York: Norton, 1971.

Adams, James Luther. *On Being Human Religiously: Selected Essays in Religion and Society.* Boston: Beacon, 1976.

Allen, Michael J. B. "Humanism." In *The Columbia History of Western Philosophy,* ed. Richard H. Popkin. New York: Columbia University Press, 1999.

Allenby, Braden Richard. "Observations on the Philosophic Implications of Earth Systems Engineering and Management." Batten Institute Working Paper. Charlottesville, Va.: Batten Institute at the University of Virginia Darden School of Business, 2002.

Derr, Thomas Sieger. *Environmental Ethics and Christian Humanism.* Nashville, Tenn.: Abingdon, 1996.

Küng, Hans, and, Schmidt, Helmut, eds. *A Global Ethic and Global Responsibilities: Two Declarations.* London: SCM, 1998.

Noble, David F. *The Religion of Technology.* New York: Knopf, 1998.

Russell, Bertrand. *A History of Western Philosophy* (1945). New York: Simon and Schuster, 1972.

Unitarian Universalist Association. "Principles and Purposes." Available from http://www.uua.org/aboutuua/principles.html.

BRAD ALLEBY

HUMAN NATURE, PHYSICAL ASPECTS

A consideration of the physical aspects of human nature leads to viewing human nature as embodied. Embodiment as a concept is fluid, taking its forms from pathways of inquiry that inevitably remake it, however provisionally, according to the task at hand. But surely this is not true of the body. The body as a physical object, a thing, is solid. One points to it, sees its movement, hears the sounds it makes, feels its heart beating, smells its fragrance, and tastes its sharp salinity. Having a body is an undeniable fact of life, a solid place of unity between one human and another, even between human beings and the more than human world. But having a body may do no more to unify than would having a car, wearing clothes, having a mother, speaking English, and dying. Establishing links between the concepts of body and concepts such as human unity requires much more than the simple facts associated with being bodied. Apart from pathways of inquiry, then, the fact of body—its sensory undeniability—seems indeed solid, unmovable, a mountain of inertia.

So the challenge is to give a technical review that transforms some of this inertia into movements along paths of inquiry linking science and religion. Sadly, this requires that much that is wonderful about the body will be left out. Further, some scientific results summarized below (e.g., in relation to physical beauty, human emotion, etc.) may be susceptible to cultural context; most of the studies summarized in this entry relied on Western approaches to science and worked exclusively with subjects within Western cultures.

The major dynamical systems of the body

Human biology partitions the functions of the human body into eleven major dynamical systems: cardiovascular, endocrine, gastrointestinal, hematologic, integumentary, lymphatic, musculoskeletal, nervous, reproductive, respiratory, and urinary (Seeley, Stephens, and Tate, 1995).

The cardiovascular (or circulatory) system includes the structures of the heart, blood vessels, and blood. Its functions include the transport of oxygen and waste gases (e.g., carbon dioxide), nutrients, waste products, and hormones; the regulation of body temperature; the regulation of blood pressure; and a contribution to the immune response.

The endocrine system includes the structures of the pituitary, thyroid, parathyroid, thymus, and adrenal glands, as well as the pancreas, ovaries, and testis. Its major functions are the regulation of the following: metabolism and growth, the absorption of nutrients, fluid balance and ion (i.e., chemicals in the body with a positive or negative charge) concentration, the stress response, and sexual characteristics, reproduction, birth, and lactation.

The gastrointestinal system includes the oral cavity, salivary glands, esophagus, stomach, liver, gallbladder, small intestine, large intestine, and rectum. Its functions include the breakdown of food, the absorption of nutrients, and the elimination of wastes from the body.

The hematologic system includes blood plasma (91.5 percent water by volume), blood cells, red bone marrow, spleen, liver, and kidneys. Blood cells include erythrocytes (i.e., red blood cells) for the transport of oxygen and waste gases; neutrophils for consuming microorganisms and other substances in the blood (i.e., phagocytosis); basophils for the release of histamine in inflammatory responses and heparin to prevent blood clots; eosinophils for the reduction of inflammation and the attack of some worm parasites; lymphocytes for the production of antibodies and other substances to destroy microorganisms and other substances foreign to the body (e.g., transplanted organs); monocytes for the phagocytosis of bacteria, dead cells of the body, cell fragments, and other tissue debris; and platelets for clotting blood. Red bone marrow is the only source of blood formation in adults and occurs mainly in bones along the body's central axis and in the joints of limbs (i.e., epiphyses) that are closest to the center of the body. The spleen holds a reservoir of blood, which is released in emergencies. The kidneys release a chemical, erythropoietin, to stimulate erythrocyte production. Enlarged monocytes in the liver, called *macrophages,* consume old or defective erythrocytes. The liver also produces most of the body's clotting factors.

The integumentary system includes the structures of the skin, hair, nails, and sweat glands. It functions mainly to protect other areas of the body against abrasions and ultraviolet light, to prevent the entry of microorganisms and other harmful substances, to reduce water loss, to regulate body temperature, to produce precursors to vitamin D (increases calcium and phosphate uptake in the intestine), and to provide sensory information about the body and the body's environment.

The lymphatic, or immune, system includes lymph (a clear fluid that is returned to the blood via the lymphatic vessels; three liters per day), lymph vessels, lymph nodes, lymph ducts, the tonsils, spleen, thymus gland, and red bone marrow. The functions of the lymphatic system include removing foreign substances from the blood and lymph, defending the body against elements of disease, maintaining fluid balance in the tissues, and absorbing fat. The two major cell types in the lymphatic system are B cells, which mature to secrete antibodies, and T cells, which recognize foreign molecular patterns on the surface of the body's own cells. Once T cells identify something that is foreign to the body, they either kill the cell or they activate other immune responsive cells in the body (e.g., B cells, macrophages).

The musculoskeletal system includes the bones of the skeleton and all the muscles attached to the skeleton. Its main functions are to provide movement of the body, to maintain body posture, and to produce body heat. This system does not include the muscle of the heart or the smooth muscles that are not typically under voluntary control.

The nervous system includes the brain, the spinal cord, the nerves, and sensory receptors (e.g., photoreceptors in the eye). Its main functions are to provide sensory input for bodily action, to control bodily action (the somatic nervous system), to control physiological processes typically beyond voluntary control (the autonomic nervous system), and to allow for human experience.

The reproductive system in women includes the vagina, uterus, uterine tube, and ovary, and in men the penis, prostate, seminal vesicle, ductus (or vas) deferens, the testis, the epididymis, and scrotum. Its main functions are to assist in the control and performance of sexual behavior.

The respiratory system includes the nose, nasal cavity, pharynx, oral cavity, larynx trachea, bronchi, and lungs. Its major functions are to transport oxygen to the lungs, to exchange waste carbon dioxide for oxygen, and to regulate the acidity of the blood (i.e., blood pH).

The urinary system includes the kidneys, ureter, urinary bladder, and urethra. Its major functions are to remove wastes from the cardiovascular system; to regulate blood pH, ion balance and fluid balance; and to assist in regulating blood pressure.

Paleoanthropology, archaeology, and the body

Humanity's origin narratives within Western science depend largely on the bodily remains of humanity's ancestors. Where were the remains found? What is their three-dimensional character? How old are they? What damage have they sustained? According to Ann Gibbons in "In Search of the First Hominids" (2002), recent unearthings of ancient primate bones have generated controversies in human evolution on questions ranging from whether bipedalism evolved on the savannah to what makes a primate a hominid. Nicknames given to some of these recently uncovered remains, such as Flat-Faced Man and Little Foot, are consistent with the importance of the body in paleoanthropology.

Since the discovery of Lucy, then the earliest known hominid, in Ethiopia in 1973, early hominids have been defined by their bodily resemblance to Lucy. Lucy was small, about the size of a female chimpanzee, had long arms, a relatively small volume inside her skull (i.e., intracranial volume), thick tooth enamel, large molars, smaller canines than earlier paleoanthropological fossils, foot bones that suggested bipedalism, and curved fingers. However, there have also been attempts by scientists to classify hominids by one or a few bodily characteristics: *Ardipithecus ramidus* (Aramis, Ethiopia; 4.4 million years ago) because its canines are more like human canines than those of chimpanzees (the converse is true for its molars); *Ardipithecus ramidus kadabba* (Aramis, Ethiopia; 5.2 to 5.8 million years ago) because the bones of its feet suggest bipedalism; *Orrorin tugenensis* (Tugen Hills, Kenya; 5.7 to 5.9 million years ago) because its thighbone (i.e., femur) looks more like human femurs than do those of Lucy and other Australopithecines, it has even thicker tooth enamel than Ardipithecus, and it has molars more like human molars than those of chimpanzees (the converse is true for its canines).

Controversy is also present in identifying the number and nature of the evolutionary step(s) to *Homo sapiens* from its ancestor, due to the differences in scientific opinions as to which measurements of the body are the deciding ones. Daniel Lieberman has proposed replacing the typically long list of measurements used to classify hominid skulls with two: the roundness of the skull and the degree to which the face and eyes are tucked under the frontal bone (Balter, 2002). Reducing the number of measurements would, in Lieberman's view, reduce the complexity involving theories regarding the evolutionary appearance of *Homo sapiens*. Typically, however, measurements of human skulls (i.e., human craniometry) in paleoanthropology and archaeology involve over sixty different measures (Howells, 1989; White, 2000).

Beauty and the body

Bodily symmetry is generally the most consistent factor to correlate with assessments of physical beauty (Geary, 1998). Women prefer men with high bodily symmetry, a strong chin and cheekbones, and an emotionally expressive mouth. These preferences may have adaptive value in that illnesses during puberty are known to reduce the secretion of male hormones (i.e., androgens) which in turn decreases bone size and density (Thornhill and Gangstad, 1993). Additionally, lower facial symmetry in men correlates with higher baseline metabolism (Manning, Koukourakis, and Brodie, 1997) and higher incidents of depression, anxiety, and minor illnesses (Schakelford and Larsen, 1997). Note, however, that this correlation does not hold for individuals who are assessed as either very attractive or as unattractive (Kalick et al, 1998). Men's assessments of physical beauty in women also correlate with bodily symmetry but rely more on facial features showing youthfulness relative to a man's own age (Kenrick and Keefe, 1992), except during male adolescence (Kenrick et al, 1996). Finally, men think women with a waist-to-hip ratio of around 0.7 are more attractive than women with other ratios, and men find women of average weight with this ratio to be more attractive than heavier or thinner women who have this ratio (Geary, 1998). There is evidence suggesting that women with ratios larger than 0.85 become more ill and have a harder time conceiving children than women with ratios around 0.7 (Singh, 1995).

Smell also plays a role in assessing physical beauty. Evidence associates women's ratings of the bodily fragrances of men with differences between their *major histocompatibility complex* (MHC). Men who differ more in MHC from women raters are assessed as having more pleasant fragrances than men more similar to the women's MHC (Apanius et al, 1997). Having a more variable MHC is associated with greater flexibility in one's immune response, and thus this fragrance preference could reflect the effects of natural selection.

Self determination according to the immune system

The immune system provides for both innate immunity and adaptive immunity. Innate immunity applies to parts of the immune system that do not adapt within an individual organism to a particular immune challenge. Adaptive immunity includes those systems that adapt within an organism to respond in ways specific to each challenge event.

Innate immunity as an organismal function is evolutionarily old since its components are found in both plants and animals. Even single-celled organisms have the capacity to recognize "microbial nonself" (Medzhitov and Janeway, 2002). Genetic changes in the molecular structure of components of innate immunity (i.e., pattern recognition receptors, or PRRs) happen slowly via evolution (Janeway and Medzhitov, 2002). This in turn forces innate immunity to act only against those molecular patterns on nonself bodies (i.e., pathogen-associated molecular patterns, or PAMPs) that do not change rapidly across generations (i.e., antigens that are evolutionarily conserved). PRRs available in the blood or tissue fluid bind to PAMPs, providing a signal for pathogen destruction by cells such as macrophages or neutrophils or by complement. Complement is a group of proteins in blood plasma that undergo transition from inactive to active forms via action by PRRs and participate in the destruction of pathogens, largely by making a hole in the pathogenic cell (i.e., cell lysis). PRRs that are bound to cells are called *Toll-like receptors* (TLRs, because of similarities to immune-related proteins of the *Drosophila* Toll family). PRRs cannot differentiate between microorganisms that are pathogenic to the body and microorganisms that are beneficial to the body (e.g., those in the gustatory system) but are prevented from acting on beneficial microorganisms by physical barriers preventing their access.

Innate immunity also is responsible for what is called the recognition of *missing self* (Medzhitov and Janeway, 2002). The term *missing self* (instead of nonself) was chosen to highlight the observation that some components of innate immunity, instead of responding to molecular patterns of pathogens, respond to lower levels of molecular patterns specifically expressed by a body's own cells. This concept was introduced to account for observations that natural killer (NK) cells mainly kill tumor cells that lack MHC class I proteins. MHC class I proteins are adaptive immunity structures that can combine with parts of the body's own cells and are displayed on the surface of those cells to indicate the presence of a self cell. When cells in the body become cancerous, they display fewer or no MHC class I proteins bound with their own fragments. NK cells have proteins on their surfaces, called *receptors,* that recognize MHC class I proteins bound to self fragments and stop NK cells from killing (Medzhitov and Janeway, 2002). Other examples of innate immunity acting by recognizing a missing self include the activation mechanism of C3, a complement protein; the inhibition of macrophages and neutrophils through receptors on those cells that recognize sialic acid, which is expressed on vertebrate cells but generally not on microorganisms; and the inhibition of macrophages by the protein CD47, largely responsible for distinguishing between functioning and nonfunctioning erythrocytes. Note that these missing self strategies can be fooled if pathogens acquire the DNA that makes the self-specific molecules directly from the body's cells. Then they start looking like self according to the innate immune system. This is known to happen and is called *horizontal gene transfer.*

Adaptive immunity relies strongly on signals from the innate immune system. It is only present in jawed vertebrates, and its molecular components change in a challenge-specific manner. All jawed fish exhibit adaptive immunity, which is lacking in vertebrates without jaws, such as lampreys. Charles A. Janeway names this sudden appearance in the evolutionary record the "immunological 'Big Bang'" (Janeway et al, 2001, p. 602). In a series of experiments culminating in 1998, it was discovered that the genes mediating the genetic recombination underlying adaptive immunity could also mediate the insertion of one DNA fragment into others, a process known as *transposition* (Hiom, Melek, and Gellert, 1998; Agrawal, Eastman, and Schatz, 1998). Scientists infer from this result that adaptive immunity was acquired from a transposable element that inserted itself into the

DNA of an ancestor of jawed vertebrates. Significantly, adaptive immunity, unlike innate immunity, is not hereditary. Genetic modifications that occur in adaptive immunity occur in somatic cells, not in the germline cells (sperm or eggs). This leads immunologists to say that the "memory" of adaptive immunity is limited to the lifespan of the individual, and immunizations must be repeated for each generation. Adaptive immunity is thought to contribute to greater lifespan, though it is the cause of rejection in organ transplantation.

Antibodies, or B-cell receptors, are a key component of molecular pattern recognition in the adaptive immune system. There are on the order of one hundred billion different antibody specificities in the human body (Janeway et al, 2001). The structure of an antibody molecule is modeled as a Y-shape. The stem of the Y is called the *constant region,* and the arms of the Y are called *variable regions.* There are five different classes of antibody: IgA, IgD, IgE, IgG, and IgM. IgG is the most abundant antibody class in humans. Each arm of an antibody's Y structure is composed of a heavy (H) chain and a light (L) chain. Moreover, each H and L chain in each arm of the Y is composed of a constant (C) and a variable (V) region, connected by a hinge.

Antibody diversity is produced in four major ways. The first two are controlled genetic recombination of gene segments forming the gene for the V-regions. Light chain V-region genes include the V gene segment (because it codes for most of the final V protein, 95 to 101 amino acids long) and the J gene segment (because it joins the V-region to the C-region, coding for up to thirteen amino acids). Heavy chain V-region genes include the V, J, and D (or diversity) gene segments. In addition to genetic recombination, diversity arises in different combinations of V and H chains at the protein level through different combinations of protein subunits. Finally, specialized mutations within B cells, occurring only at rearranged V-region DNA, add to the diverse antibody repertoire.

T-cell receptors are diversified much in the same way as B-cell receptors and are structurally similar to antibodies. T cells work in conjunction with the MHC, a gene complex whose proteins combine with small protein fragments inside a cell and take these fragments to the cell surface where they can be accessed by T cells. There are two different classes of MHC: I and II. T cells with CD8 proteins on their surface bind to MHC class I molecules, and those with CD4 proteins bind to MHC class II molecules. Both MHC class I and II molecules bind to protein fragments of the body's own cells if those cells are uninfected or otherwise harmed, though class II MHC molecules are largely responsible for binding to protein fragments from pathogenic microorganisms. CD4 T cells then recognize infection and activate other cells in the immune response. Human immunodeficiency virus (HIV) is particularly toxic to CD4 T cells, resulting in a lower level of these cells, which leads to acquired immunodeficiency syndrome (AIDS).

Emotions and bodies

Emotions are patterns of bodily activity that are often thought to have evolved because they allow an organism to respond to its environment in ways that enable survival and successful reproduction (Rosenberg and Ekman, 1997). In *The Emotional Brain* (1996) Joseph LeDoux says that "Emotions evolved not as conscious feelings, linguistically differentiated or otherwise, but as brain states and bodily responses. The brain states and bodily responses are the fundamental facts of an emotion, and the conscious feelings are the frills that have added icing to the emotional cake" (p. 302). The bodily responses LeDoux refers to include changes in position, posture and movement, facial expression, vocal expression, skin tone, heart rate, blood pressure, breathing rate, and hormone production.

Social affiliation and aversion are correlated with the amount of distance between two bodies, the orientation of one body to another, how much one body leans forward toward another, and the degree of welcome contact between two bodies (Collier, 1985). Two people who disagree but who like each other can show welcome physical contact during arguments (Scheflen and Scheflen, 1972; Collier, 1985). Bodily movement also indicates when someone is startled or suddenly afraid. In these cases, the eye blinks and the bodily movement freezes for a time (e.g., "My spine was frozen in fear."). Observers can infer happiness, sadness, anger, and occasionally pride simply from watching people move (Planalp, 1999).

Perhaps the main route of emotional communication in everyday human interaction is the face. Facial expression includes both the arrangement of the facial anatomy and the direction of eye gaze.

There are sixteen muscles used to control facial expression, excluding those involving gaze direction. Surprise is expressed via the occipitofrontalis on the forehead; frowning is accomplished by the corrugator supercilii and the procerus, both of which work on the eyebrows, and by the depressor anguli oris, the depressor labii inferioris, the risorius, and the mentalis; and smiling (or sneering) is mediated by the levator labii superioris alaeque nasi, the levator labii superioris, the zygomaticus major and minor, and the levator anguli oris. Eyelids, the degree to which the eyes are closed, and the openness of the tear duct (i.e., the lacrimal gland) are controlled by the orbicularis oculi. Nasal dilation is controlled by the nasalis, levator labii superioris alaeque nasi, and depressor septi. The lips are controlled by the orbicularis oris. Gaze direction is mediated by the extraocular muscles, which are comprised of four rectus muscles (superior, medial, inferior, lateral) and two oblique muscles (superior, inferior).

Although there have been numerous studies of human facial expression before and since the time of Duchenne's *The Mechanism of Human Facial Expression* (1862) and Charles Darwin's *The Expression of the Emotions in Man and Animals* (1872), it did not receive great attention in modern psychology until behaviorism waned (Rosenberg, 1997). Facial expressions are assessed using either the *maximally discriminative facial movement coding system* (MAX); the *Facial Action Coding System* (FACS), or *electromyography* (EMG) of facial muscles. Both MAX and FACS rely on visual information about faces, while EMG depends only on electrical outputs of facial expression muscles, measured either at or under the skin. While MAX is framed in terms of what are generally considered universally recognizable features of emotional facial expression, FACS attempts to characterize all "visibly discernible facial movement" (Rosenberg, p. 12). However, FACS does not include gaze direction as a parameter.

Using these methods in combination with emotionally evocative stimuli and subject reports, there is evidence that (1) facial expressions and reports of some emotions cohere (Rosenberg and Ekman, 1997; Ruch, 1997); (2) verbal instruction can lead to the involuntary or voluntary suppression and enhancement of facial expressions relating to lower back pain (Craig, Hyde, and Patrick, 1997); (3) lowering the brows, tightening the areas around the eyes, and raising the lips are consistent signs that a person is in pain (Prkachin, 1997); (4) liars control their facial expressions more successfully than other bodily movements while lying; (5) it is possible to detect smiles while lying if one allows for different types of smile (Ekman, Friesen, and O'Sullivan, 1997); and (6) untrained adults have a difficult time distinguishing between what a baby is tasting (e.g., bitter versus sweet) simply by facial expression (Rosenstein and Oster, 1997).

See also HUMAN NATURE, RELIGIOUS AND PHILOSOPHICAL ASPECTS

Bibliography

Agrawal, A.; Eastman, Q. M.; and Schatz, D. G. "Transposition Mediated by RAG1 and RAG2 and Its Implications for the Evolution of the Immune System." *Nature* 394 (1998): 744–751.

Apanius, V.; Penn, D.; Slev, P. R.; Ruff, L. R.; and Potts, W. K. "The Nature of Selection on the Major Histocompatibility Complex." *Critical Reviews in Immunology* 17 (1997): 179–224.

Balter, Michael. "What Made Humans Modern?" *Science* 295 (2002): 1219–1225.

Collier, Gary. *Emotional Expression.* Hillsdale, N.J.: Lawrence Erlbaum, 1985.

Craig, Kenneth D.; Hyde, Susan A.; and Patrick, Christopher J. "Genuine, Suppressed, and Faked Facial Behavior During Exacerbation of Chronic Low Back Pain." In *What the Face Reveals: Basic and Applied Studies of Spontaneous Expression Using the Facial Action Coding System (FACS),* ed. Paul Ekman and Erika L. Rosenberg. New York: Oxford University Press, 1997.

Darwin, Charles. *The Expression of the Emotions in Man and Animals,* 3rd edition (1872). New York: Oxford University Press, 1998.

Duchenne, G. B. *The Mechanism of Human Facial Expression* (1862), trans. R. A. Cuthbertson. New York: Cambridge University Press, 1990.

Ekman, Paul, and Friesen, W. V. *The Facial Action Coding System (FACS): A Technique for the Measurement of Facial Action.* Palo Alto, Calif.: Consulting Psychologists Press, 1978.

Ekman, Paul, and Rosenberg, Erika L. "Coherence Between Expressive and Experiential Systems in Emotion." In *What the Face Reveals: Basic and Applied Studies of Spontaneous Expression Using the Facial Action Coding System (FACS),* ed. Paul Ekman and Erika L. Rosenberg. New York: Oxford University Press, 1997.

Ekman, Paul; Friesen, Wallace, V.; and O'Sullivan, Maureen. "Smiles While Lying." In *What the Face Reveals: Basic and Applied Studies of Spontaneous Expression Using the Facial Action Coding System (FACS),* ed. Paul Ekman and Erika L. Rosenberg. New York: Oxford University Press, 1997.

Geary, David C. *Male, Female: The Evolution of Human Sex Differences.* Washington, D.C.: American Psychological Association, 1998.

Gibbons, Ann. "In Search of the First Hominids." *Science* 295 (2002): 1214–1219.

Grauer, Anne L., ed. *Bodies of Evidence: Reconstructing History Through Skeletal Analysis.* New York: Wiley, 1995.

Hiom, K.; Melek, M.; and Gellert, M. "DNA Transposition by the RAG1 and RAG2 Proteins: A Possible Source of Oncogeneic Translocations." *Cell* 94 (1998): 463–470.

Howells, W. W. "Skull Shapes and the Map: Craniometric Analyses in the Dispersion of Modern Homo." *Papers of the Peabody Museum of Archaeology and Ethnology* 79 (1989):1–189.

Izard, C. E. *The Maximally Discriminative Facial Movement Coding System (MAX).* Newark, Del.: Instructional Resource Center, University of Delaware, 1979.

Janeway, Charles A., and Medzhitov, Ruslan. "Innate Immune Recognition." *Annual Review of Immunology* 20 (2002):197–216.

Janeway, Charles A.; Travers, Paul; Walport, Mark; and Shlomchik, Mark. *Immunobiology: The Immune System in Health and Disease.* New York: Garland, 2001.

Kalick, S. M.; Zebrowitz, L. S.; Langlois, J. H.; and Johnson, R. M. "Does Human Facial Attractiveness Honestly Advertise Health? Longitudinal Data on an Evolutionary Question." *Psychological Science* 9 (1998): 8–13.

Kenrick, D. T., and Keefe, R. C. "Age Preferences in Mates Reflect Sex Differences in Human Reproductive Strategies." *Behavioral and Brain Sciences* 15 (1992): 75–133.

Kenrick, D. T.; Keefe, R. C.; Gabrielidis, C.; and Cornelius, J. S. "Adolescents' Age Preferences for Dating Partners: Support for an Evolutionary Model of Life-History Strategies." *Child Development* 67 (1996): 1499–1511.

LeDoux, Joseph. *The Emotional Brain: The Mysterious Underpinnings of Emotional Life.* New York: Simon and Schuster, 1996.

Manning, J. T.; Koukourakis, K.; and Brodie, D. A. "Fluctuating Asymmetry, Metabolic Rate and Sexual Selection in Human Males." *Evolution and Human Behavior* 18 (1997): 15–21.

Medzhitov, Ruslan, and Janeway, Charles A. "Decoding the Patterns of Self and Nonself by the Innate Immune System." *Science* 296 (2002): 298–300.

Planalp, Sally. *Communicating Emotion: Social, Moral and Cultural Processes.* Paris: Cambridge University Press, 1999.

Prkachin, Kenneth. "The Consistency of Facial Expressions of Pain: A Comparison Across Modalities." In *What the Face Reveals: Basic and Applied Studies of Spontaneous Expression Using the Facial Action Coding System (FACS),* ed. Paul Ekman and Erika L. Rosenberg. New York: Oxford University Press, 1997.

Rosenberg, Erika L. "The Study of Spontaneous Facial Expressions in Psychology." In *What the Face Reveals: Basic and Applied Studies of Spontaneous Expression Using the Facial Action Coding System (FACS),* ed. Paul Ekman and Erika L. Rosenberg. New York: Oxford University Press, 1997.

Rosenstein, Diana, and Oster, Harriet. "Differential Facial Responses to Four Basic Tastes in Newborns." In *What the Face Reveals: Basic and Applied Studies of Spontaneous Expression Using the Facial Action Coding System (FACS),* ed. Paul Ekman and Erika L. Rosenberg. New York: Oxford University Press, 1997.

Ruch, Willibald. "Will the Real Relationship Between Facial Expression and Affective Experience Please Stand Up: The Case of Exhilaration." In *What the Face Reveals: Basic and Applied Studies of Spontaneous Expression Using the Facial Action Coding System (FACS),* ed. Paul Ekman and Erika L. Rosenberg. New York: Oxford University Press, 1997.

Schakelford, T. K., and Larsen, R. J. "Facial Asymmetry as an Indicator of Psychological, Emotional and Physiological Distress." *Journal of Personality and Social Psychology* 72 (1997): 456–466.

Scheflen, Albert E., and Scheflen, Alice. *Body Language and Social Order: Communication as Behavioral Control.* Englewood Cliffs, N.J.: Prentice-Hall, 1972.

Seeley, Rod R.; Stephens, Trent D.; and Philip Tate. *Essentials of Anatomy and Physiology,* 2nd edition. St. Louis, Mo.: Mosby, 1995.

Singh, D. "Female Health, Attractiveness and Desirability for Relationships: Role of Breast Asymmetry and Waist-to-Hip Ratio." *Ethology and Sociobiology* 16 (1995): 465–481.

Tauber, Alfred I. *The Immune Self: Theory or Metaphor?* New York: Cambridge University Press, 1994.

Thornhill, R., and Gangstad, S. W. "Human Facial Beauty: Averageness, Symmetry, and Parasite Resistance." *Human Nature* 4 (1993): 237–269.

White, Tim D. *Human Osteology,* 2nd edition. San Diego, Calif.: Academic Press, 2000.

MICHAEL L. SPEZIO

HUMAN NATURE, RELIGIOUS AND PHILOSOPHICAL ASPECTS

The suggestion that there is such a thing as human nature implies a specific stance with relation to what a human being is. Do humans have something like a nature? If so, in what does human nature consist? These questions can not be answered from a sole description of specific characteristics, which is one of the main reasons there is a continuous debate over this issue. To say something about what a human being essentially (or in nature) *is,* implies saying something about what humans *ought to be.* Consequently, there is always a kind of normative self-reference in the way the question "What is human nature?" is answered. It is not simply a question of how humans are to understand this or that case, but an articulation of how humans understand, or ought to understand, themselves.

Theories about human nature state something about the place of humans in nature. They also try to define what specifically makes a human being different from other living things. However, as made clear by theologian Wolfhart Pannenberg in *Anthropology in Theological Perspective* (1985), one has to distinguish between the human being as part of nature, and the nature of the human being. These two issues do not necessarily coincide. The former implies a descriptive approach and investigates different empirical and phenomenological aspects that help people better understand their place in nature. The latter is a more normative issue, related to the destiny of humanity in general, as well as to the individual's future and the meaning of the individual life. Its importance is thus also related to interpretation of the place of human beings in history and culture. Taken separately, these approaches offer a basis for the interpretation of human nature from a more naturalistic or humanistic view. Consequently, the sciences usually offer more material relevant to the understanding of the place of humans in nature than for answering questions about human destiny.

A theory about human nature that also takes into consideration an understanding of the human place in nature usually has to account for some or all of the following issues: What specifically makes the human being as a species different from other species? What does it mean to be a person? Do human beings have free will? How does one understand morality, religion, and culture? How are these elements related to language and to human self-consciousness (subjectivity)? Is religion necessarily connected to humanity? Are humans able to act on reasons and principles that cannot be reduced to causes? What is one to think of death? What is the basis for human dignity? Some of these questions can be seen as attempts to differentiate between issues that, in the past, were discussed with reference to the difference between body and soul.

Human nature in non-Western world religions

The variety of ways to understand human nature is expressed also in different world religions. In Hinduism and Buddhism human nature is partly understood from the perspective of the self as part of all that is, and given the task of becoming the nonself. Like other pantheistic religions, both Hinduism and Buddhism affirm that human beings are related to all that is and, simultaneously, how the self is essentially divine. Beyond the empirical human is the human essence, *atman,* which is identical with the ultimate reality, *Brahman.* To overcome individuality and to become part of the encompassing world is the aim of human life. This can be done by transcending the world of the senses. This aim is realized when the self dissolves into the whole after death, but also can be anticipated in different forms of meditational practices.

Whereas Hinduism and Buddhism emphasize how human nature is related to divine nature, the self is generally thought of as distinct from the divine in Semitic religions such as Islam and Judaism. Islam is the religion that most strongly stresses the

distinction between God and the world; humanity is seen as dependent upon God and God's will. As in Judaism, God is the creator of humans. The aim of humanity is to realize this dependence and live accordingly—i.e., in gratitude toward God. In Islam, sin is understood as disobedience (*ma'siya*) and not as rooted in human nature. This is different from the most dominant traditions in Christianity. An original aspect of Islam is that all humans are understood as to be born Muslim. It is the cultural environment that changes their essentially Muslim nature in to something else

The Bible offers no developed theory about human nature. Genesis 1: 26–28 describes human beings as created in the image of God (*imago Dei*); this description has given rise to many different interpretations through the history of doctrine. Whoever is made in the image of God is given the task of representing God as the steward of creation, thereby reminding others of God and taking care of God's creation on God's behalf. Hence, human beings are understood in terms of their relation with God; it is this relation that is thought to make humans unique compared to other species. In Psalm 8, humans are placed between the angels and God, indicating their high rank in the order of creation.

Humans are accordingly responsible to God. Simultaneously, they are themselves part of nature; they are made of earth, and without the life-giving breath of God they return to dust. The Bible depicts human life as dependent on the continuous creative activity of God. Humans are not understood in terms of the Greek dichotomy between soul and body, but human life is viewed from different perspectives, such as flesh, body, heart—all notions that can also take on different spiritual meanings. There is a positive affirmation of human embodiment in the Hebrew Bible, echoed in the New Testament teachings on the resurrection of the body and the human need for bodily health, as well as spiritual salvation. One could suggest that human nature from a Judeo-Christian point of view is to be an embodied image of God. This position is affirmed in Christianity, where Jesus Christ is seen as the true human being, and thus reveals what humans are meant to be.

When entering into dialogue with Greek modes of thought, Christian theologians had to articulate the relationship of humans with God from points of view offered by existing philosophical knowledge. This challenged theology to develop an understanding of what it meant to be created in the image of God. The dominating point of view through the Middle Ages became that human nature is unique in rational faculties, understanding, consciousness, and spirit. This view, as expressed by Augustine of Hippo, draws on Platonism, which emphasized rationality and the eternity of the human soul. It also included the view developed by Aristotle in ancient Greece and by Thomas Aquinas during the Middle Ages that put humans on the same level as the rest of nature, but with rationality as the species-unique skill. The eighth-century theologian Johannes Damascenus expresses the prevalent understanding of human nature in the Middle ages: The human being is the image of God because it has reason and free will and is able to be its own master.

Philosophical patterns for a theory of human nature

Two main philosophical trends have had a major influence on understandings of human nature. From the ancient Greek philosopher Plato onwards, the human being alone is able to understand and grasp rationally the world as it is in itself, beyond every change. This ability derives from the rational faculties, expressed in the ability to think. Thus, human nature is closely linked to the ability to think, and to act with thinking as a guide.

Plato articulated the paradigm for a rationalist understanding of human nature. He assumed a dichotomy between body and soul. The soul is the site of reason, and as such it is understood as eternal and (partly and potentially) independent of the body. The body, on the other hand, is mortal and will die. The central struggle in a person's life is to gain control over the physical by means of the rational. As a consequence, Plato sees the flourishing of human nature in its ability to control life with rational means.

The importance of this paradigm is most clearly seen in the seventeenth century rationalism of the French philosopher and mathematician René Descartes, who maintains a sharp dichotomy of body and soul. Descartes claims that while the external world (*res extensa*) operates by mechanistic principles, this is not the case with humans, who are guided by reason. Animals are without reason

and hence to be understood according to mechanistic causation only. This view separates the human being sharply from the rest of nature, and suggests that what is specifically human cannot be investigated by the same principles that were utilized by the emerging modern natural sciences.

Philosophically, theories of human nature before the Enlightenment are either rationalist or empiricist in outlook. The empiricist outlook puts more stress on human experience as a condition that shapes actual fulfillment in human life. Hence, one's participation in nature is given a larger role when it comes to determining who a person is. This approach also put more emphasis on the continuity of humans with the rest of nature, and, combined with the experimental approach to investigation of nature, it contributed greatly to the development of modern science. As a result, human nature is here regarded as part of nature, and not something unique. This view is consonant with a religious position that sees the human soul as a function of a complex physical organism rather than as an independent substance.

Challenges from evolutionary thinking

A process similar to the one that began when Christian theology met Greek philosophy developed with the rise of biological insights during the nineteenth century. Theology had to articulate views on human nature that were able to respond to, oppose, and integrate the insights offered by the research of Charles Darwin and others. Obsolete theological theories about the constancy of human nature were now challenged; humans could no longer be seen as a species directly created by God outside of the evolutionary process. Some theological traditions, however, were reluctant to enter into a positive reception of what biology could mean for understanding humanity as part of natural history. Some continue to believe that the biblical stories tell the actual prehistory of humans. This view cannot, however, be held without ignoring the massive amounts of data resulting from scientific inquiry into the prehistory of humans and nature.

Following the rapid development during the nineteenth century of more biologically informed views on human nature, the first half of the twentieth century gave rise to other ways of thinking about human nature. In Germany a special discipline developed called *philosophical anthropology.*

Still tying to appropriate the insights of biology, representatives of this movement attempted to show how humans must be seen as a species that participates in a spiritual realm and is able to relate to the world in a way not available to other living creatures. Some theologians, notably Pannenberg, tried to direct this trend toward integration or mediation between scientific and humanistic insights. Here, physiological traits of humanity are seen as conditions for a religious attitude.

The ability of human beings to transcend themselves is interpreted as the basic trait that can relate us to and realize our divine destiny. On the other hand, the estrangement from this destiny (i.e., sin), is understood by Pannenberg to be conditioned by our constitutional self-centeredness. The content of human life, human identity, and human will are developed in tension between selfishness and divinity.

Integrating scientific knowledge with theological anthropology

Attempts to explain moral behavior (and also religion) in the light of biological evolution have stirred much discussion in which human action is judged by moral standards that reflect the extent to which actions contribute to evolutionary advancement or progress. Critics claim that proponents of this position "fail to demonstrate why the promotion of biological evolution by itself should be the standard to measure what is morally good" (Ayala, p. 47).

The interaction between science and theology has generally consisted of two tasks: determining the range of the validity of the claims offered by biology and sociobiology; and integrating these insights into a more coherent pattern of interpretation of humanity that also takes into account other realms that shape human life and development, such as culture, sociality, history, and subjectivity. The second task has led to more modest positions on what theology can say about the place of humans in nature, and there has been no unconstrained reception of the evolutionary approach to morality or religion in theological anthropology. Generally, theological anthropology that is in dialogue with the sciences tends to navigate between biological reductionism and cultural constructivism. Here, the sciences are seen as elucidating the conditions for a religious or moral position, rather than actually explaining them solely on the basis of biology.

The debate over morality in relation to human nature also exhibits a basic challenge concerning the relation between science and theology: Should theology offer interpretations of insights from science, or should theology try to balance, correct, or contradict these in relation to its own definition of humanity? An example of this problem can be found in the discussion of altruism. Some scientists consider acts of altruism to be contrary to the mechanisms promoting human evolution, while others sees altruism as a positive device for evolution. Theological anthropology seems bound to contradict the first view, while it can relate affirmatively to the second, claiming that evolution operates on other, not naturally given, principles in humanity. Here, culture is seen as a process that is reducible to natural selection. Religion takes part in this. "It makes human beings open to a greater reality before which each individual has infinite value and is absolutely equal" (Theissen, p. 49). Again, a basic pattern seems to underlie any discussion of human nature: Is it to be determined from the point of view of nature and the sciences only, and in accordance with the principles given there, or is it necessary to also establish other independent sources as a means for determining human nature?

Recently, the discussion about human nature has taken a new turn as new developments in biology, especially genetics, contribute to what can be called an *essentialist* view of human nature. This implies that what a human being is, or is to become, is determined by his or her genetic dispositions. Thus, there is an identification of human nature with the given genetic conditions. This view puts little emphasis on the social impact on the formation of humans.

An alternative view, *social constructivism,* emphasizes how humans become what they are as a result of specific cultural conditions communicated within a specific social, social-psychological, and cultural context. Here the actual outcome of biological and other functions is seen as shaped by socially determined conditions. This view is often presented as anti-essentialist, and contains a tacit program for emancipation as gender-based or other socially ascribed roles and demarcations are seen as the result of contingent social developments rather than biological conditions. In psychology, this leads to emphasis on how human relations and culture shape a person's "inner world."

Hence, the way human beings relate to and interpret the world is constituted by them as being relational and social. People are more than "containers" of drives and desires that express themselves in the social and cultural world.

From a phenomenological point of view, humans appear as participants in a multitude of realms related to aspects of both nature and culture. Nature and history is deeply interwoven with human life. This multidimensionality also influences the ways humans understand themselves and relate to the world. However, this phenomenon also suggests that to reduce the interpretation of what human nature is to one or a few aspects implies restricting the possibilities for human self-understanding, and thus, in the long run, for human self-fulfillment.

Consequently, one of the issues that theological anthropology must address when integrating elements from scientific understandings of human nature is the possibility for understanding human beings as more than a product of natural evolution. This is partly due to tendencies towards naturalist reductionism, but also in order to safeguard the human ability to transcend the naturally given conditions of life. This self-transcendence is an important element in human personhood, and is closely linked to the affirmation of human freedom.

Conclusion

There is presently no general agreement as to how to relate to and appropriate insights from the natural sciences in the development of philosophical or religious theories of human nature. Such an agreement should not be expected as long as there is no unified opinion about what a human being is. However, it is possible to distinguish three different models for developing the relationship between religious and philosophical theories of human nature and the sciences:

(1) The natural sciences can be seen as the basis for interpreting religious or philosophical doctrines about human nature, with philosophy and theology working in continuation of what the sciences offer.

(2) A more dialectic or mediating approach tries to incorporate different perspectives on the human being within a coherent theoretical (philosophical or theological) framework. Here, informed by natural sciences, one can formulate theological or philosophical insights without giving them alone the task of determining the overall hermeneutic framework for the development of the theory or doctrine.

(3) A non-dialogical approach denies the relevance of natural science for the understanding and development of philosophical and religious theories of human nature. From the point of view of the sciences, this position can be reversed by one who denies the relevance of philosophy or theology for the understanding of humanity, a position that usually implies a very strong empiricism combined with traits of reductionism.

See also EVOLUTION, HUMAN; HUMAN NATURE, PHYSICAL ASPECTS; IMAGO DEI; PSYCHOLOGY; SOCIOBIOLOGY

Bibliography

Ayala, Fransisco J. "Human Nature: One Evolutionist's View." In *Whatever Happened to the Soul? Scientific and Theological Portraits of Human Nature,* eds. Warren S. Brown, Nancey Murphy, and H. Newton Malony. Minneapolis, Minn.: Fortress, 1998.

Darwin, Charles. *The Descent of Man.* London: John Murray, 1874.

Darwin, Charles. *On the Origin of the Species.* Oxford: Oxford University Press, 1996.

Dawkins, Richard. *The Selfish Gene.* Oxford: Oxford University Press, 1989.

Gergen, Kenneth J. *An Invitation to Social Construction.* London: Sage, 1999.

Gregersen, Niels Henrik; Drees, Willem B.; and Görman, Ulf. *The Human Person in Science and Theology.* Edinburgh: T&T Clark, 2000.

Hügli, Anton; Grawe, Christian; Kiefhaber, M.; et al. "Mensch." In *Historisches Wörterbuch der Philosophie* Vol. 5, 1059–1106.

Jones, James W. *Religion and Psychology in Transition: Psychoanalysis, Feminism, and Theology.* New Haven, Conn.: Yale University Press, 1996.

Knapp, Andreas. *Soziobiologie und Moraltheologie. Kritik der ethischen Folgerungen moderner Biologie.* Weinhein, Germany: VCH, Acta Humaniora, 1989.

Pannenberg, Wolfhart. *Anthropology in Theological Perspective.* Philadelphia: Westminister, 1985.

Peacocke, Arthur. *Theology for a Scientific Age: Being and Becoming, Natural, Divine, and Human.* London: SCM, 1993.

Scheler, Max. *Man's Place in Nature*, trans. Hans Meyer-hoff. New York: Noonday Press, 1961.

Stevenson, Leslie. *Seven Theories of Human Nature*. Oxford: Oxford University Press, 1974.

Theissen, Gerd. *Biblical Faith: An Evolutionary Approach*. Philadelphia: Fortress, 1985.

van Huyssteen, J. Wentzel. *Duet or Duel? Theology and Science in a Postmodern World*. London: SCM, 1998.

Wilson, Edward O. *Sociobiology: The New Synthesis*. Cambridge, Mass.: Harvard University Press, 1975.

Wilson. Edward O. *On Human Nature*. Cambridge, Mass.: Harvard University Press, 1978.

JAN-OLAV HENRIKSEN

HUME, DAVID

David Hume (1711–1776) was born in Edinburgh, Scotland, on April 26, 1711. He was educated at home in the Presbyterian parish of Chirnside, near Berwick, and studied at the University of Edinburgh from 1723 until 1726, without taking a degree. Before leaving the university, he had projected his *Treatise of Human Nature,* and between the ages of fifteen and twenty-three he read widely and methodically in philosophy and other branches of learning, making the study of human nature his principal concern and the source from which he would draw all true conclusions in philosophy, morality, and criticism. In 1734 Hume went to France where he lived quietly for three years composing his revolutionary systematic study of human nature, which was published in three volumes in London from 1739 to 1740. The first volume concerns the understanding, the second the passions, and the third morality.

Finding that the work "fell dead-born from the press without reaching such distinction, as even to excite a murmur among the zealots," Hume penned a review of his own work, which he had anonymously published as a pamphlet: *An Abstract of a Book lately Published, Entitled, A Treatise of Human Nature, &c. Wherein The Chief Argument of that Book is farther Illustrated and Explained* (1740). This remarkable pamphlet is still the best brief guide to the central arguments and conclusions of Hume's theoretical philosophy, so it

is unfortunate that a copy of it did not come to light until 1933. Though Hume's *Treatise* was a commercial failure during his lifetime, it is now almost universally regarded as one of the greatest works of systematic philosophy in the English language. However, because he was so disappointed with its reception and was inclined to blame himself for this fact, he recast the first volume into *An Enquiry Concerning Human Understanding* (1748), and the third volume into *An Enquiry Concerning the Principles of Morals* (1758), both of which have become philosophical classics.

The *Treatise* is firmly within the empiricist tradition of John Locke (1632–1704). No ideas are innate: all are derived, either directly or indirectly, from outer or inner experience. Experience is also the arbiter of all belief. Hume may be regarded as advancing a sophisticated Lockean viewpoint that has benefited greatly from the acute criticisms of Locke made by George Berkeley (1685–1753) and others. The universally accepted maxim that "every event has a cause" has no basis in reason. Nor does the ubiquitous assumption that what has happened in the past will happen in the future have any basis in reason. The problem of induction is emphasized and shown to be insoluble by reason alone. The faculty of reason is demoted from its historical hegemony at the same time as the nonrational faculty of imagination is promoted. The imagination, however, does not associate or connect ideas at random. It operates according to principles and associates resembling ideas, or ideas of objects that are contiguous in space and time or that are causally related: "Here is a kind of attraction, which in the mental world will be found to have as extraordinary effects as in the natural, and show itself in as many and as various forms." Reason gives way to instinct, custom, and habit. The three types of association "are the only ties of our thoughts," so "they are really *to us* the cement of the universe." Many items that reason allegedly discerns are reduced to projections or expressions of human nature. In the *Abstract*, Hume unequivocally describes his system as "very sceptical": "Philosophy wou'd render us entirely *Pyrrhonian*, were not nature too strong for it." His considered position is that of a moderate or mitigated scepticism, or one whose otherwise extreme conclusions have been somewhat "corrected" by common sense. This is the Hume who woke Immanuel Kant (1724–1804) from his "dogmatic slumber."

Philosophy of religion

From an early age Hume was preoccupied with religion and science. Before he was twenty, he set down in a notebook "the gradual progress" of his thoughts on theism: "It begun with an anxious search after arguments to confirm the common opinion: Doubts stole in, dissipated, return'd, were again dissipated, return'd again; and it was a perpetual struggle of a restless imagination against inclination, perhaps against reason." It therefore is unsurprising that the *Treatise* as originally written contained several antireligious sections and remarks that Hume prudently removed before publication. In 1737 he told a friend that he was "castrating" his manuscript, or "cutting off its nobler parts" so that it would "give as little offence as possible." He deleted an essay on miracles and probably also one on the immortality of the soul. But notwithstanding these precautions, the very first notice of the work warned readers of its "evil intentions," evident from the book's motto alone: "Seldom are men blessed with times in which they may think what they like, and say what they think".

Hume must have realized that a discerning reader of the *Treatise* would have detected echoes of principles and doctrines prominent in the works of Pierre Bayle (1647–1706), Anthony Collins (1676–1729), Thomas Hobbes (1588–1679), Baruch Spinoza (1632–1677), and other "free thinkers." He therefore should not have been surprised when, in 1745, he applied for a chair in philosophy at the University of Edinburgh, and the local clergy defeated his candidacy by charging him with advocating "universal scepticism" and "downright atheism." They also accused him of "denying the immortality of the soul" and of "sapping the foundations of morality, by denying the natural and essential difference between right and wrong, good and evil, justice and injustice; making the difference only artificial, and to arise from human conventions and compacts." Hume defended himself against these misunderstandings and misrepresentations, but thereafter his writings became increasingly antireligious.

In 1748 Hume published his essay on miracles, in which he argued that there is no reason to believe that any miracle has ever occurred. His argument was attacked by many contemporaries, including William Adams, John Douglas, Richard Price, and George Campbell, whose criticisms are still worth reading. In the same collection Hume devoted an essay to arguing that there is no reason to believe in a particular providence or a future state. This attack on the argument from design was elaborated in Hume's posthumously published *Dialogues Concerning Natural Religion* (1779), which is modelled upon Cicero's *De Natura Deorum*.

The historian Edward Gibbon (1737–1794) regarded the *Dialogues* as "the most profound, the most ingenious, and the best written of Hume's philosophic works." It remains the classic discussion of the argument from design (or argument *a posteriori*), and some regard it as the most important work in the philosophy of religion in English. Had William Paley (1743–1805) carefully studied it, he might never have written *Evidences of Christianity* (1794) or *Natural Theology* (1802). Along the way Samuel Clarke's (1675–1729) *a priori* argument for the existence of God is refuted, and the objections to theism from the existence of evil are forcefully presented.

The *Dialogues* involves three disputants: the orthodox rationalist theologian Demea, the "careless sceptic" Philo, and the scientific theologian Cleanthes, who frequently echoes Bishop Butler's *Analogy of Religion* (1736). Though the argument from design is subjected to sustained criticism, and the attentive reader may be convinced that the canons of scientific reasoning do not issue in theism, at the end Cleanthes seems to emerge as the winner, leading some mistakenly to conclude that Cleanthes speaks for Hume himself. But the *Dialogues* were so "artfully written" that Philo the sceptic only appears to be "silenced." In a private letter Hume said that he objected "to everything we commonly call religion, except the Practice of Morality, and the Assent of the Understanding to the Proposition that God exists." But in the *Dialogues* the concept of God is virtually evacuated of all meaning, so such "assent" amounts to little or nothing. Hume's friend Dr. Hugh Blair, who advised against publishing the *Dialogues* during Hume's lifetime, remarked that they are "exceedingly elegant" and "bring together some of his most exceptional reasonings, but the principles themselves were in all his former works." Most scholars now hold that Philo represents Hume himself. Hume denied that he was an atheist or a deist, so he is perhaps best viewed as a not-so-careless sceptic.

In the *Treatise* Hume argued that morality is not founded on reason, but on passion. Reason alone cannot motivate people to act, and one cannot logically derive statements about what one "ought" to do from statements about what "is" the case. One's sense of justice rests upon self-interest, limited generosity, utility, human conventions, and sympathy or fellow-feeling with the sentiments of others. Jeremy Bentham (1748–1832) said that the scales fell from his eyes when he read this part of Hume's work. Though utility enters into his explanation of the evolution of morality, Hume himself was not a utilitarian. But he was one of the first to insist upon the autonomy of morality, and especially its independence from religious belief. In the *Natural History of Religion* (1757) he inquired into the causes of religion and speculated as to how monotheism had evolved from primitive polytheism, while emphasizing the absurd doctrines and immoral consequences of most world religions. His critics argued that, though his temperament enabled him to be just without being religious, most people require the sanctions of religion in order to be just.

Anonymous writings

Hume counted several of the more liberal Church of Scotland ministers as friends but resented those evangelical ministers who had lobbied against his appointment to a professorship at Edinburgh and Glasgow and who, in the mid-1750s, had unsuccessfully tried to have the Church of Scotland excommunicate him. He carefully cultivated the character of a "virtuous infidel" by encouraging the literary projects of his clerical friends (and potential literary rivals) such as Hugh Blair, Adam Ferguson, and Robert Wallace; and by anonymously publishing favourable reviews of William Robertson's *History of Scotland,* William Wilkie's epic poem the *Epigoniad,* and Robert Henry's *History of Great Britain,* as well as of Adam Smith's *Theory of Moral Sentiments.* The extent of Hume's clandestine literary activity has yet to be determined.

In "My Own Life" (1777), Hume asserted that he was "a man of mild dispositions, of command of temper, of an open, social, and cheerful humour, capable of attachment, but little susceptible of enmity." Adam Smith (1723–1790) testified that his "constant pleasantry was the genuine effusion of good nature and good humour ... without even the slightest tincture of malignity, so frequently the disagreeable source of what is called wit in other men." Nevertheless, under cover of anonymity,

Hume composed several satires against the clergy and corrupt politicians. "The Bellman's Petition" (1751) is directed against an increase in the stipends of ministers of the Church of Scotland. The far more ambitious, lengthy, and scathing *Sister Peg* (1760) is directed against politicians who had defeated his friends' struggle to reestablish a militia in Scotland. An anonymous satire from 1758 is directed against the commonly felt "antipathy to the corn merchant" during times of famine and "affection for the Parson" who at such times inveighed against the supposedly greedy corn merchants. In it Hume argued that these popular sentiments were based upon ignorance, superstition, and bad reasoning; good reasoning should direct one's passions in the opposite direction, so that one should instead feel affection for the useful corn merchants and antipathy for the useless parsons who "cram us with Nonsense, instead of feeding us with Truth." In these works Hume appears to have revenged himself against those who had previously opposed him.

Political history

In the eighteenth and nineteenth centuries Hume was best known as an historian. His multivolume *History of England* is not only a narrative history but is a philosophical study of the English constitution in which he never misses an opportunity to satirize the folly and hypocrisy of self-interested politicians and clergymen. His historical research was informed by his political and economic theories, which were less conservative than many have assumed. Believing that the first duty of a historian is to be accurate and impartial, while the next is the be instructive and entertaining, he succeeded so well in fulfilling these obligations that his history is still read, while those of most of his contemporaries have sunk into oblivion. Though born a Scotsman, Hume always strove to write an elegant and correct English and to surpass the best English stylists. Occasionally some vanity is evident in his writings, which gives them a conversational tone and an engaging character. Hume believed that good writing "consists of sentiments, which are natural, without being obvious." He repeatedly revised his works in order to perfect them. His views in philosophy, politics, economics, theology, history, and criticism were generally original and unobvious and so artfully expressed as to disguise his artfulness.

Hume died on August 25, 1776, and was buried in Calton Hill cemetery, overlooking Edinburgh. At his internment someone was overheard to say: "Ah, he was an atheist." To which another answered: "No matter, he was an honest man."

See also DESIGN ARGUMENT; EMPIRICISM; GOD; HUMAN NATURE, RELIGIOUS AND PHILOSOPHICAL ASPECTS; IMAGINATION; KANT, IMMANUEL; MIRACLE; MONOTHEISM; MORALITY; NATURAL THEOLOGY

Bibliography

Gaskin, J. C. A. *Hume's Philosophy of Religion,* 2nd edition. London: Macmillan, 1988.

Hume, David. *An Abstract of a Treatise of Human Nature, 1740: A Pamphlet Hitherto Unknown,* eds. John Maynard Keynes and Piero Sraffa. Cambridge, UK: Cambridge University Press, 1938.

Hume, David. *Sister Peg: A Pamphlet hitherto unknown,* ed. David R. Raynor. Cambridge, UK: Cambridge University Press, 1982.

Jeffner, Anders. *Butler and Hume on Religion: A Comparative Analysis.* Stockholm, Sweden: Diakonistyrelsens Bokforlag, 1966.

Mackie, John L. *The Miracle of Theism: Arguments For and Against the Existence of God.* Oxford: Clarendon Press, 1982.

Millican, Peter., ed. *Reading Hume on Human Understanding: Essays on the First Enquiry.* Oxford: Clarendon Press, 2002.

Mossner, Ernest C. *The Life of David Hume,* 2nd edition. Oxford: Clarendon Press, 1980.

Norton, David Fate, ed. *The Cambridge Companion to Hume.* Cambridge, UK: Cambridge University Press, 1993.

Penelhum, Terence. *Themes in Hume: The Self, The Will, Religion.* Oxford: Clarendon Press, 2000.

Raynor, David R. "Hume's Abstract of Adam Smith's *Theory of Moral Sentiments.*" *Journal of the History of Philosophy* 22 (1984): 51–79.

Raynor, David R. "Who Invented the Invisible Hand? Hume's Praise of Laissez-faire in a Newly Discovered Manuscript." *Times Literary Supplement* (August 14, 1998): 22.

Stewart, John B. *Opinion and Reform in Hume's Political Philosophy.* Princeton, N.J.: Princeton University Press, 1992.

Stewart, M. A. *The Kirk and the Infidel.* Lancaster, UK: Lancaster University Press, 1995.

DAVID RAYNOR

HYPOTHETICAL REALISM

Realism, generally, is the view according to which knowledge refers to objects that actually exist. Hypothetical realism is a weak form of realism based on the theory of the growth of knowledge put forward by evolutionary epistemology. The basic assumption is that human cognitive capacity has evolved through an interaction with the external world. Therefore even if our knowledge has only a hypothetical character and must be open to improvements, the ontological reality of the known (i.e., external reality) is certain.

See also CRITICAL REALISM; EVOLUTIONARY EPISTEMOLOGY; REALISM

TOMAS HANCIL

IBN RUSHD

See AVERROËS

IBN SINA

See AVICENNA

IDEALISM

Idealism as an ontological or epistemological doctrine holds that reality, or what can count as reality for human beings, is determined by mind. The various ways of specifying the basic role of mind ontologically or epistemologically yield various forms of idealism. As an *ontological* doctrine idealism can hold that reality is basically mental in nature; the physical world is an expression of this mental reality. An argument for the position that what one takes to be material is actually spiritual is that what is actual is process or activity, and mind or spirit is the model of activity. In this sense, *metaphysical idealism* is contrasted with *materialism*. An example is the doctrine of Gottfried Wilhelm Leibniz (1646–1716) that reality consists of active substances, or monads.

As an *epistemological* doctrine, idealism can hold that humans do not have access to a mind-independent reality. However, an epistemological idealism along this line can easily be transformed into an ontological one to the effect that there *is* no mind-independent reality. Idealism in this sense is constrasted with *realism*. The position of George Berkeley (1685–1753) that *esse est percipi* (to be is to be perceived) could be read as an example of an epistemological idealism with radical antirealist claims, which amounts to an ontological *immaterialism*. But Berkeley also argues that sensible things exist independently of human beings in that they exist in the mind of God (*theistic idealism*).

An ontological idealism can hold precisely that there is a reality *beyond* the physical world of sense experience, and this transcendent reality is the basic or true one in that it accords actuality to the relentlessly changing world of sense experience. Humans have access to the ultimate reality beyond the world of sense experience through higher forms of mind, but the true or divine reality transcends the human mind. This form of metaphysical idealism is thus an ontological *realism* (claiming that reality is independent of the human mind). The classic example of a metaphysical idealism as a *transcendent* idealism is the doctrine of the world of ideas in Plato (428–347 B.C.E.).

Epistemological idealism can be reformulated as *transcendental* idealism. The critical philosophy of Immanuel Kant (1724–1804) not only attacks dogmatic metaphysical positions that imply that humans have access to things in themselves beyond the world of sense experience, but also Berkeley's subjective idealism (as Kant takes it to be), which dissolves reality into what humans experience. Instead, according to Kant, space and time, and the categories (e.g., the category of causality) are, as structures of the human mind, also conditions of possibility for the experience of the world. However, this opens the problem that reality is on the one hand "reality-for-us," while on the other hand an ultimate reality beyond this reality is postulated. This problem is dealt with by Johann Gottlieb Fichte (1762–1814), Friedrich Wilhelm Joseph von Schelling (1775–1854), and Georg Wilhelm Friedrich Hegel (1770–1831), whose various positions are collectively labelled *German Idealism.*

Absolute idealism in Hegel seeks to overcome the Kantian split between the world of sense experience and ultimate reality (thing-in-itself) without returning to a dogmatic position. Hegel points out that in having an experience, human understanding of the world and human self-understanding can be changed. This possibility of self-transcendence implied in experience cannot be accounted for if ultimate reality is placed beyond the limits of experience. Hegel's absolute idealism solves the basic task of German Idealism left over by Kant, namely, to account for both freedom inherent in rationality (autonomy) and the embodiment of that freedom. While Fichte emphasizes the activity of the human mind as a productive activity, Schelling sets out to overcome this (as he called it) *subjective idealism* in Fichte by combining a transcendental philosophy and a philosophy of nature. In Hegel's absolute idealism, mind (*Geist*) transcends the divide between freedom and nature by coming to itself through nature and history. Accordingly, Hegel's idealism is not to be captured by the opposition between idealism and materialism, or between realism and antirealism.

As the complex position of Hegel indicates, idealism needs to be reformulated in opposition to its traditional forms. Basically, idealism concerns the problem that human access to reality must tell something about that very reality. From the brief outline above one can extract the insight that in relating to reality human beings are doing something. Thinking is an activity. Humans only relate to reality in interpreting it. This does not imply, however, that reality is what people interpret it to be or that reality is a mental construction. If mind were basic in this sense, people would not be able to discuss the reality of the mind. Instead the crucial argument could be the following: A comprehensive theory of reality must be able to account for the reality of mind and self-consciousness that

it itself presupposes. Following this line of argument, idealism could be reformulated as a response to reductive forms of *naturalism* in that it points to the presupposition that human beings as subjects relate to the world, and only as self-interpreting animals are they able to form theories about the world in which they live. The task is to account for both the embodiment of mind and this presupposition of mind.

The question of idealism is thus not only the basic question of science concerning the reality of interpretations and models of reality. Idealism also concerns religious questions about the place of human beings in the world. Religion need not be interpreted along the lines of an idealism that posits a second world beyond the world of sense-experience. A reformulation of idealism as outlined above can instead draw upon the understanding to be found in religion that human consciousness reflects the problem of the embodiment of consciousness itself.

See also MATERIALISM; NATURALISM; REALISM

Bibliography

Berkeley, George. *A Treatise Concerning the Principles of Human Knowledge* (1710). In *The Principles of Human Knowledge with Other Writings,* ed. G. J. Warnock. London: Fontana Library, 1962.

Hegel, Georg Wilhelm Friedrich. *The Phenomenology of Mind* (1807), trans. J. B. Baillie. London: Allen and Urwin; New York: Humanities Press, 1977. Revised reprint of 1931 edition.

Kant, Immanuel. *Critique of Pure Reason* (1781), trans. Norman Kemp Smith. London: Macmillan, 1978.

ARNE GRØN

IMAGINARY TIME

See COSMOLOGY, PHYSICAL ASPECTS

IMAGINATION

Since Plato, thinkers have recognized human mental capacities for producing images and combining them in ways that do not copy experience.

Philosophers have held many theories about the origin of images. One of the most original is expressed by the seventh-century Chinese Buddhist philosopher Hsuan-tsang in his interpretation of the *Yogacara* writings of the Indian thinker Vasubandhu (c. fifth century C.E.). Hsuan-tsang suggested that the mind has a great storehouse consciousness of images or "seeds" that are "perfumed" into consciousness (as smells incite otherwise hidden memories) by other conscious seeds that have an emotional vector. David Hume, the eighteenth century Scottish Enlightenment philosopher, had a theory of imaginative association modeled on mechanical principles.

Synthesis and construction

Immanuel Kant, Hume's younger contemporary, revolutionized thought about imagination in the first edition of his *Critique of Pure Reason* (1781). He claimed that imagination is a foundational capacity for synthesis in the mind whereby stimuli or impingements from the external world are organized into the basic structures of experience such as a spatiotemporal field and the applicability of concepts to sense data, as explained in Robert Cummings Neville's *Reconstruction of Thinking* (1981). Romantic philosophers such as Thomas Carlyle and Ralph Waldo Emerson developed the view that the structures of imagination are more basic than the surface affirmations of conscious thought and reveal assumptions about reality that are presupposed by other forms of thought. Myths reveal truths more basic than science, for instance. The pragmatic philosopher Charles Sanders Peirce (1839–1914) gave an evolutionary interpretation of imagination such that its deep structures are more likely to be true about basic issues, because corrected over a long evolutionary development, than the reasonings of philosophers. Ray L. Hart in the twentieth century argued that imagination is central to the constitution of human beings before God and is the very form of revelation, inspiring a movement of "theologies of imagination," as analyzed by Fritz Buri in his 1985 article "American Philosophy of Religion."

Imagination has been particularly important in science. For Plato the ideal scientific imagination was mathematical, as Robert Brumbaugh has shown in his *Plato's Mathematical Imagination* (1954) and for Aristotle imagination was the wit to

hit upon the third term connecting two otherwise unrelated topics. Whereas some people in Western philosophy might have thought that science is merely a reading off of the lessons of nature, Kant, in the *Critique of Pure Reason,* argued that post-Copernican science forces nature to answer questions of our own imaginative devising. Peirce, at the beginning of the twentieth century, argued at length that all hypothesis construction in science begins with an imaginative guess at the answer and then proceeds by imagination to articulate the guess in theoretical terms that might be tested. Although certain positivistic trends in mid-twentieth century philosophy of science minimized imagination in the testing of hypotheses by focusing closely on the performance of controlled experiments, a counter-movement associated with Thomas S. Kuhn (1922–1995) has been extremely influential. Kuhn argued that the controlled testing of hypotheses, or "normal science," takes place within larger assumed paradigms of what is at stake in the tests, their assumptions and their interpretations as defined by the instruments involved. "Revolutionary science" is when the paradigms themselves are criticized and changed, and this involves much imagination in stepping outside of linear inference. Imagination plays a large role in contemporary thinking about scientific creativity.

In the last two centuries scholars have used the notion of imagination to describe the set of assumptions, thought patterns, and ways of seeing or sensing peculiar to an age or culture. For instance, the imagination of the Hellenistic world of antiquity, when rabbinic Judaism and Christianity arose, included the view that the cosmos is a stack of many spatial levels of which the Earth occupies one, with perhaps many heavens above and hells below. Each level has its characteristic agents, bodies, movements, and patterns of causation. Aristotle's theory that motion above the orbit of the moon is circular whereas that below is straight-line illustrates one version of the multilevel theory; when his theory or others became unquestioned assumptions they formed part of the age's imagination. Biblical references to angels are to be understood as to beings from certain higher levels crossing the boundaries into the earthly level. God often was imagined to occupy the highest level as a being within a spatiotemporal system that includes earthly life at a different place. God's nature might be very different from that of things on the earthly level, for instance that of a pure, immaterial, infinite spirit, but it is connected with the earthly plane by the geography of the cosmic levels. In Christianity (Phil. 2) God's "Son," who has the form of God when with God in the divine heaven, descends to Earth, taking on a nature proper to the earthly level (indeed that of a slave in earthly terms). When human beings make the reverse journey to God, they must take on natures appropriate to the divine heavenly level, for instance "celestial bodies" (1 Cor. 15).

The challenge of science

The challenge of modern science to the imaginative structures of the religions formed in the ancient world is that science itself shapes contemporary imagination to make it incompatible with them. Because of modern science, people know, and assume deep in their imaginations, that beneath the Earth's surface is a molten core, not hell, and that traveling upward leads to outer space, not one or more heavens with different causal structures. Indeed the imagination shaped by modern science assumes a uniformity of measure throughout the entire cosmos: An inch is always and everywhere an inch, a chemical reaction on Earth is the same as it would be in any part of the cosmos with the same conditions, and mathematics applies equally everywhere.

So, in the modern imagination there is no "proper heavenly place" for God if God is extremely different from earthly beings. Theologians have responded to this in various ways. Process theologians (e.g. Charles Hartshorne [1897–2000]) say that God is not so different and is part of the cosmos. They explain this by saying that the differences between God and humans can be expressed within a set of metaphysical measures that apply to the finite God and ordinary things alike. Other theologians (e.g. Paul Tillich [1886–1965]) deny that God is a being at all because to be a being requires having a place; God rather is the ground or creator of all beings and places. Yet other thinkers (pantheists) say that God is identical with the cosmos and differs from any particular finite thing by being all of the things together. Many thinkers reflecting on the differences between the ancient and the modern scientific imaginations say that belief in God is simply incompatible with science, and hence are atheists. Some religious people are able to divide their imagination into one structure for religious matters and another for engaging the world in other respects, although this makes the integrating intent of religion difficult.

The study of "science and religion" sometimes attempts to reconcile contemporary scientific imagination with the ancient imagination that forms the symbols and rhetoric of traditional religions. One approach, called *demythologizing* and associated with Rudolf Bultmann (1884–1976), is to treat the ancient imagination as metaphorical, searching for "religious meaning" distinct from "scientific meaning." Another is to treat the modern imagination and scientific conceptions as themselves open to the literal kinds of beings and causation depicted as heavenly in the ancient imagination. So it is argued that science still allows for miracles and divine agency without denying scientific causation, as discussed in Mark Richardson and Wesley Wildman's 1996 book *Religion and Science* (especially case study one). The problem for religious imagination is related to but not the same as the problem of reconciling ancient and modern theories: It is a problem of apparently conflicting imaginative presuppositions that affect how people perceive and act.

Contemporary scientific imagination poses a potentially more explosive problem for modern life. Until the mid-twentieth century the modern European scientific imagination could picture atoms interacting within the void, or fields of forces affecting material objects within them. Even quantum mechanics could picture the world as having particles that travel along a path but skipping some sections relative to observation. More recent physical science has moved into a mathematical imagination that is not picturable in terms of customary space-time models. Quarks are not like tiny spinning suns, as people had earlier imagined electrons, photons, and neutrons. Only highly sophisticated mathematicians are able to comprehend the relations that added together in bulk might give rise to picturable images. Popularized expressions of many fundamental ideas in microphysics and astrophysics we know to be just plain false to the sophisticated science. This is exactly like the situation regarding certain kinds of theology whose conceptions of God are not picturable in any way and that need to be understood in purely conceptual terms, like mathematics though perhaps with a different dialectical logic. Popular religious expressions, like popular expressions of certain scientific ideas, must be said to be "just plain false," or at least highly misleading, relative to some sophisticated theology that cannot be understood except by the sophisticated. The elitism common to the mathematical imagination in science and the dialectical imagination in theology is more problematic in the religious realm. Whereas technologists can deliver the results of science to a popular world that cannot picture its theory, religions no long have technological priesthoods to mediate unpicturable truths easily to people whose credulity requires traditional religious language.

See also KANT, IMMANUEL

Bibliography

Brumbaugh, Robert S. *Plato's Mathematical Imagination*. Bloomington: Indiana University Press, 1954.

Brumbaugh, Robert S. *Platonic Studies of Greek Philosophy*. Albany: State University of New York Press, 1989.

Bultmann, Rudolf. *Jesus Christ and Mythology*. New York: Scribners, 1958.

Buri, Fritz. "American Philosophy of Religion from a European Perspective: The Problem of Meaning and Being in the Theologies of Imagination and Process," trans. Harold H. Oliver. *Journal of the American Academy of Religion* 53, no. 4 (1985): 651–673.

Chan, Wing-tsit, trans. and ed. *A Source Book in Chinese Philosophy*. Princeton, N.J.: Princeton University Press, 1963.

Hart, Ray L. *Unfinished Man and the Imagination: Toward an Ontology and a Rhetoric of Revelation*. New York: Herder and Herder, 1968.

Hartshorne, Charles. *The Divine Relativity: A Social Conception of God*. New Haven, Conn.: Yale University Press, 1948.

Kuhn, Thomas S. *The Structure of Scientific Revolutions*. Chicago: University of Chicago Press, 1962.

Neville, Robert Cummings. *Reconstruction of Thinking*. Albany: State University of New York Press, 1981.

Neville, Robert Cummings. *The Truth of Broken Symbols*. Albany: State University of New York Press, 1996.

Richardson, W. Mark, and Wildman, Wesley J., eds. *Religion and Science: History, Method, Dialogue*. New York and London: Routledge, 1996.

Tillich, Paul. *Systematic Theology*, Vol. 1. Chicago: University of Chicago Press, 1951.

Toulmin, Stephen. *Human Understanding: The Collective Use and Evolution of Concepts*. Princeton, N.J.: Princeton University Press, 1972.

ROBERT CUMMINGS NEVILLE

IMAGO DEI

Imago Dei is Latin for "image of God," a theological doctrine common to Jews, Christians, and Muslims that denotes humankind's relation to God on the one hand and all other living creatures on the other. Traditionally, only human beings are in the image of God, and it is by virtue of this image that human beings are moral and spiritual creatures. Because the image of God is ultimately a doctrine of human nature, it has also been inappropriately used historically to justify racism and sexism.

The term *image of God* is originally found in the biblical book of Genesis, where it occurs three times (1: 26–27, 5: 1–3, 9:1–7). The meaning of the term in the original Hebrew context has been much debated, although current scholarship has moved to understanding it as a designation of stewardship or representation of God's sovereignty. This understanding of the image of God seems to be significantly changed in the Christian New Testament, where it is used primarily by the apostle Paul, who speaks of Christ as being in God's image and of human beings becoming in the image of Christ.

In the Christian theological tradition, the image of God has been interpreted in a wide variety of ways. Most ancient and medieval theologians identified the image of God primarily with the human ability to reason, and it was this quality that was seen to distinguish human beings from all other organisms. Irenaeus of Lyon (second century) made a further distinction between the image and likeness of God, as both terms are used in Genesis 1. As a consequence, later theologians argued whether or not human beings are still in the image of God after the Fall, or whether human beings have lost the image and are now merely in God's likeness. On this understanding, the Fall permanently altered human nature for the worse, the image being restored only through the redeeming action of Christ.

In the wake of the Reformation, the image of God came to be reinterpreted along two primary lines. The first, following Martin Luther (1483–1546), interpreted the image of God primarily in terms of human relationality with God, a move followed especially by Karl Barth (1886–1968) and the neo-orthodox movement. The second followed the dominant philosophical interpretations of human nature in the Enlightenment and after. Particularly after Friedrich Schleiermacher (1768–1834), the image of God has often been seen in the human capacity for self-consciousness.

Many modern theologians continue to be influenced by one of these two strands of thought. The chief influence of the sciences has been to emphasize human continuity with nature, either because of humankind's evolutionary heritage or because of humankind's increased knowledge of the animal world. For this and other reasons, theologians such as Langdon Gilkey (1919–) and Gregory Peterson (1966–) have argued that all of nature should be understood as being in the image of God. Nevertheless, interpretation of the image of God continues to be dynamic, and will no doubt be increasingly influenced by both scientific perspectives and inter-religious dialogue.

See also FALL; HUMAN NATURE, RELIGIOUS AND PHILOSOPHICAL ASPECTS; SOUL

Bibliography

Borresen, Kari Elisabeth, ed. *The Image of God: Gender Models in Judaeo-Christian Tradition.* Minneapolis, Minn.: Fortress Press, 1985.

Gilkey, Langdon. *Nature, Reality, and the Sacred: The Nexus of Science and Religion.* Minneapolis, Minn.: Fortress Press, 1993.

Johnson, Gunnlaugur A. *The Image of God: Genesis 1: 26–28 in a Century of Old Testament Research.* Stockholm, Sweden: Almqvist & Wiksell, 1988.

Peterson, Gregory. "The Evolution of Consciousness and the Theology of Nature." *Zygon* 34 (1999): 283–306.

GREGORY R. PETERSON

IMMANENCE

In theological discourse, *immanence* refers to the presence of God in the world. Conventionally, immanence contrasts with the term *transcendence,* which emphasizes God's separateness and superiority to the world. The two terms, however, are not exclusive opposites, and many theologians balance doctrines of God's transcendence with God's immanence. Historically, theologians have tended to emphasize God's transcendence over God's immanence. In the past two centuries, however, this emphasis has shifted, and many theologians now give more weight to God's immanence. Advocates of panentheism such as Arthur Peacocke (1924–) argue that a theology emphasizing God's immanence is most compatible with modern science.

See also GOD; PANENTHEISM; TRANSCENDENCE

Bibliography

Peacocke, Arthur. *Theology for a Scientific Age: Being and Becoming—Natural, Divine, and Human,* enlarged edition. Minneapolis, Minn.: Fortress Press, 1993.

GREGORY R. PETERSON

IMMORTALITY

See LIFE AFTER DEATH

IN VITRO FERTILIZATION

See REPRODUCTIVE TECHNOLOGY

INCARNATION

From the Latin noun *caro,* or *carnis,* meaning "flesh," the term *incarnation* was appropriated by Christianity to designate its belief that in the historical existence of the man Jesus, known to Christians as the Christ, the very being of God has entered fully into human history and the created universe. The incarnation of God implies for believers not only that the person of Christ is the dwelling place of God, his human nature held to be substantially united with the *Logos* (the eternal Word) of God, but that by extension the entire material cosmos is the domicile of God.

In the history of religions, representations of incarnate deities have been a powerful way of communicating a common human intuition that the realm of the sacred is not separate or remote from the empirically given world and that the tangible world is embedded in a mysterious dimension of divine depth. In fact the idea of a divine incarnation is itself a specification of the more generically sacramental character of religions as such. Religions have almost always had a sacramental aspect, by which is meant that their devotees grasp the presence of God or the sacred primordially through the mediation of concrete things, events, or persons that function as revelatory symbols of the divine. The natural world in particular, with its sunlight, flowing water, fertility, life, oceans, mountains, and storms has provided a rich array of symbols by which the sense of a sacred mystery has been communicated to religious awareness. The idea of a divine incarnation in a human being may be understood in the context of the richly sacramental character of religions.

Incarnation in Christian doctrine

A *sacrament* is any property of the visible world through which humans have gathered the impression that the sacred or the divine is expressing itself in an especially intense way. In Christianity, for example, the person of Christ is taken to be the primary symbol or sacrament of God. Theological reflection has even led to the Christian conviction that the fullness of the Godhead has disclosed itself incarnately through the compassion and self-sacrifice of Jesus. Early Christian controversies about how to understand the incarnation led to the teachings of the early Ecumenical Councils (especially First Nicea in 325 and Chalcedon in 451) that Jesus is the incarnate Logos or "Word" of God.

It was an arduous and politically tumultuous process that led to the Christian doctrinal formulations surrounding the incarnation. Denials of Christ's divine nature in the early centuries took the form of Arianism and Nestorianism, both eventually condemned as heretical. And at the other extreme, the humanity of Christ was dissolved into his divinity, in a heresy known as *monophysitism* (literally, "having a single nature"). Christianity has never been completely divested of the tendency to deny that Jesus was fully human, and in recent centuries a decidedly monophysitic leaning has shaped much Christian spirituality. A case can be made that this monophysitic bias has brought needless complications into the dialogue between religion and science.

At the heart of Christian quarrels about the incarnation was the question of how the unchanging, eternal, and almighty God could coherently be said to be fully present in a finite man, one vulnerable enough to be killed by crucifixion. The doctrine of God's incarnation coincides at this point with the shocking idea of a divine *kenosis,* according to which the infinite God empties out the divine substance into the finite world in self-sacrificing love. The God-human paradox of Christ is one that subsequent centuries and contemporary theological discussion have not yet reduced to clarity. Moreover, attempts to clarify the so-called "mystery" of the incarnation have usually led either to the nonacceptance of Christ's divinity or to the suppression of a sense of his humanity. In either case the rejection of a divine incarnation entails a denial of the divine kenosis. The notion of a self-emptying God is one that even Christians have not yet come to terms with, even though it is an idea that can possibly contribute much to the reconciliation of religion and science.

Incarnation in the age of evolutionary science

In this age of evolutionary science, theological reflection on the doctrine of the incarnation has led to speculation that in God's taking on the corporeal reality of Christ the whole universe is, by extension, taken into the divine life. The physical body of Christ is, like every other living organism, the outcome of a cosmic and biological evolution. Hence one may conjecture theologically that the story of the entire universe is inseparable from the existence of the incarnate God. The cosmic story itself, therefore, becomes sacramentally the revelation of God. In light of the idea of God's incarnation in matter the notion of "revelation" can no longer be restricted simply to a brief series of salvific events in the narrow province of terrestrial human history as recorded in the Bible. Rather, the universe as a whole is now seen by many to be the sacramental disclosure of the incarnate God. To some Christian thinkers, especially the Jesuit geologist and paleontologist Pierre Teilhard de Chardin (1881–1955), the epic of evolution is endowed with the deeper meaning that it is from start to finish the process in which God becomes increasingly incarnate in matter, clothing the divine being in the stuff of the universe.

However, as Teilhard de Chardin repeatedly emphasized, "true union differentiates." God's incarnate union with the world is one in which the world becomes even more, not less, distinct from God. Incarnation implies that God foregoes any annihilating relationship to the world. The doctrine of the incarnation, at least as understood by the Council of Chalcedon, implies that God wants to relate to a world that is "other" than God. In order to constitute such a relationship to the universe, however, the presence of God to the world cannot be one in which the divine presence dissolves the world. To seek such an annihilating union of the world in God is an expression of monophysitism, the view that the distinctively human nature of Christ loses itself in the divine nature.

A case could be made that the longing on the part of some anti-Darwinian theists to have a world carefully designed by God, rather than one that evolves more self-creatively and spontaneously, is by implication indicative of a hidden longing for a divine presence that abolishes the world's distinctness from its divine ground. Beneath much current religious anxiety about the implications of Darwinian evolution perhaps there is evidence of a persistent monophysitic hankering for a kind of divine union with the world that melts the world into God.

Any concept of God that theology hopes to reconcile with biological and cosmic evolution, however, would not obliterate the cosmos or human existence in freedom, but would allow for a world that could become increasingly independent. Today a number of Christian theologians see in the doctrine of divine incarnation the basis for such an understanding of the relationship of God to the world.

See also CHRISTOLOGY; EMBODIMENT; KENOSIS; REVELATION; TEILHARD DE CHARDIN, PIERRE

Bibliography

Brown, Raymond E. *Jesus, God, and Man: Modern Biblical Reflections.* Milwaukee, Wis.: Bruce, 1967.

Grillmeier, Aloys. *Christ in Christian Tradition,* trans. John Bowden. Atlanta, Ga.: John Knox Press, 1975.

Pannenberg, Wolfhart. *Jesus, God and Man,* trans. Lewis L. Wilkins and Duane A. Priebe. Philadelphia: Westminster Press, 1977.

Rahner, Karl. *Foundations of Christian Faith,* trans. William V. Dych. New York: Crossroad, 1978.

Teilhard de Chardin, Pierre. *Christianity and Evolution,* trans. Rene Hague. New York: Harcourt, 1969.

JOHN HAUGHT

INCOMPLETENESS

See GÖDEL'S INCOMPLETENESS THEOREM; MATHEMATICS

INDEPENDENCE

See MODELS; SCIENCE AND RELIGION, MODELS AND RELATIONS; SCIENCE AND RELIGION, METHODOLOGIES

INDETERMINISM

In quantum mechanics there is deterministic evolution only of the wave function describing a situation: The present state of the wave function determines its future state uniquely and completely. However, the wave function is not directly observable. It determines the probability that measurements will have particular outcomes. This probabilistic aspect is not a consequence of an incomplete description, loss of information, or imperfect observing equipment. It is intrinsic to the nature of quantum reality. It is a manifestation of the limits of classical concepts, such as position, momentum, and energy that are used to describe nature.

The standard interpretation of quantum mechanics includes indeterminism in principle. Perfect knowledge of the present state of the world cannot be obtained even with perfect measuring instruments. In Isaac Newton's (1642–1727) picture of the world (which does not contain the quantum aspects of reality but which can be obtained from the quantum theory as a limiting case when the sizes of objects are much larger than their quantum wavelengths) there appears to be determinism in principle but not in practice. Newton's laws allow the complete prediction of the future from the present state of the world if it is known with perfect accuracy, as envisaged by astronomer and mathematician Pierre Laplace (1749–1827). However, it is impossible for the present state of the world to be determined with perfect accuracy and scientists know that many configurations of matter have the property that any small uncertainty in their initial state is amplified exponentially rapidly with the passage of time. Thus there is indeterminacy in practice. This feature of the Newtonian world is called *chaos*. There have been many attempts to arrive at a full understanding of the quantum version of this type of chaotic unpredictability, but a complete understanding is still to be arrived at.

See also CHAOS, QUANTUM; PHYSICS, QUANTUM

Bibliography

Barrow, John D. *The Universe that Discovered Itself*. Oxford: Oxford University Press, 2000.

Earman, John. *Primer on Determinism*. Dordrecht, Netherlands: Kluwer, 1978.

JOHN D. BARROW

INFINITY

Infinity in a rigorous sense is a mathematical concept, but the notion of boundless entities, such as the number series and time, have since antiquity touched a deep philosophical and religious chord in the human heart.

Ancient and medieval conceptions

To the ancient Greek religious sect known as the Pythagoreans, the notion of limit was valued as conferring intelligibility and definition, while the infinite (*apeiron*) was associated with void and primordial matter, imperfection and instability. Plato (c. 428–327 B.C.E.) captures this negative sensibility in *Philebus* when he reports that "the men of old" viewed all beings "as consisting in their nature of Limit and Unlimitedness" (16c). Drawing on this background as well as reacting to it, Aristotle (384–322 B.C.E.) adopted the solution of banning anything actually infinite from philosophy. The infinite, he declared, is only "potential," denoting limitless series of successive, finite terms. Time is infinite in this potential sense, without a first beginning or end, but space, which exists all at once, is finite. A similar treatment of infinity is found in Euclidean mathematics, namely in Book 5, definition 4, which allows finite magnitudes as small or as large as desired, but precludes anything actually transfinite.

With the first-century Jewish philosopher Philo and the founder of neoplatonism Plotinus (c. 205–270 C.E.), an actual infinite perfection is attributed in a new positive sense to God to mean that divine perfection transcends every finite case and is immense, eternal, incomprehensible, and unsurpassable. The early Christian leader Augustine of Hippo (354–430 C.E.) in turn stresses in *Confessions* Book 7 that God is infinite according to a special immaterial measure of perfection, invisible to the bodily eye. The eighth-century theologian John Damascene speaks of God in *De Fide Orthodoxa* as "a certain sea of infinite substance" (1, 9). Medieval Jewish mystics such as Isaac the Blind and Azriel of Gerona who were active around the thirteenth century enlist the Hebrew *en-sof* (infinite) to describe the infinite extension of God's thought. Later cabbalists will use the actual infinite as a proper name and refer to "the En-Sof, Blessed be He."

In the mid-thirteenth century, Latin scholastics became concerned with rationalizing divine infinity by framing a coherent philosophical language to discuss various types of infinity and to explore the properties of the actual infinite, such as its noninductive and reflexive character. Two trends are discernible. Thomas Aquinas (c. 1225–1274) built on Aristotle to reach God philosophically as infinite (unrestricted) Being, while his Franciscan counterpart, Bonaventure (1221–1274), drawing more centrally on Augustine, started with a finite degree of ontological perfection and allowed this perfection to be raised to infinity. A new appreciation of the distinction between extension and intensity was thus brought to bear on the infinite, with the notion of intensity serving to mask the paradoxes inherent in the notion of an actual infinite extension. Bonaventure promoted an approach that is introspective rather than cosmological, involving the key premises that the human soul longs for an infinite good (God) and cannot find rest short of reaching it.

Another Franciscan, Peter John Olivi (c. 1248–1298), clarified the difference that exists between a concept taken unrestrictedly (e.g. being) and the determinate infinite case falling under the concept and denoting God (being of infinite intensity). John Duns Scotus (c. 1265–1308), also a Franciscan, formulated on this basis a *univocal* theocentric metaphysics based on adopting the intensive infinite as the "most perfect concept of God naturally available to us in this lifetime." Finally, by stressing the purely semiotic character of the concept and explaining that denoting God by means of the actual infinite does not imply comprehending God, William of Ockham (1288–1348) helped to secularize the discussion and to give the actual infinite a legitimate place in philosophy. The scientists who introduced ideal elements at infinity in geometry in the seventeenth century, namely Johannes Kepler, René Descartes, and Blaise Pascal, were fully familiar with scholastic mainstreaming of the actual infinite.

Modern conception of infinity

In the seventeenth century, Descartes made infinity a keystone of his metaphysics and philosophy of science. The idea of an actually infinite being is innate in the human mind, he argues, and cannot derive from anything finite, not even by extrapolation. Rather, the human ability to conceptualize the limit of an infinite process proves that the concept of the actual infinite is in us prior to the finite. Descartes also insisted that God alone is actually infinite, so that physical space must be described as merely indefinite rather than infinite. Another seventeenth-century scientist to make creative apologetic use of the actual infinite, based on its mathematical properties, was Blaise Pascal (1623–1662). In his famous "wager" argument, he invoked the disproportion of an infinite reward to urge human beings to bet their lives on God, no matter how small the odds. Pascal also invoked mathematical incommensurability to argue that charity infinitely exceeds a life devoted to science, just as a life of science infinitely exceeds a life spent on material pleasure.

The taste for images of absolute transcendence has waned among theologians in recent times, prompting renewed interest in the potential infinite. Process theology, in particular, inspired by mathematician and philosopher Alfred North Whitehead (1861–1947), has explored metaphors connected with the inner unfolding of time and the evolving universe to depict human beings as partners of God's open-ended creativity. Meanwhile, the actual infinite has found rigorous mathematical expression in transfinite set theory, fathered by mathematician Georg Cantor (1845–1918). Cantor not only extended classical number theory by introducing transfinite numbers but proved that there is a hierarchy of transfinite

magnitudes, such that, for instance, the infinite cardinality of the continuum (denoted by c) is larger than the infinite cardinality of the rational numbers (denoted by $aleph$-$zero$). The religious dimension of transfinite ideation by no means evaporated on account of this new rigor: Cantor actively sought to enlist Catholic theologians in support of his mathematical discoveries, citing as a personal inspiration Augustine's speculation about God's perfect knowledge of numbers. Cantor's fellow mathematician David Hilbert has perhaps best summarized the dual religious and scientific appeal of infinity in the 1925 address designed to herald Cantor's discovery: "the infinite has always stirred the emotions of mankind more deeply than any other questions; the infinite has stimulated and fertilized reason as few other ideas have; but also the infinite, more than any other notion, is in need of clarification."

See also THOMAS AQUINAS; ARISTOTLE; PLATO; PROCESS THOUGHT; SPACE AND TIME

Bibliography

Davenport, Anne. *Measure of a Different Greatness: The Intensive Infinite 1250-1650.* Leiden, Netherlands: Brill, 1999.

Field, Judith. *The Invention of Infinity: Mathematics and Art in the Renaissance.* Oxford: Oxford University Press, 1997.

Kretzmann, Norman, ed. *Infinity and Continuity in Antiquity and the Middle Ages.* Ithaca, N.Y.: Cornell University Press, 1982.

Sweeney, Leo. *Divine Infinity in Greek and Medieval Thought.* New York: Peter Lang, 1992.

ANNE A. DAVENPORT

INFLATIONARY UNIVERSE THEORY

The Inflationary Universe Theory proposes a brief period of extremely rapid accelerating expansion in the very early universe, before the radiation dominated era called the *hot big bang*. This acceleration is believed to be driven by a quantum field (in effect, some exotic kind of matter) with a repulsive gravitational effect. This can be achieved if the pressure of the field is extremely large and negative (unlike ordinary matter, which has positive pressure).

A specific example is a *scalar field* associated with a potential energy. Such a field "rolls down" the energy surface defined by the potential, and if it is slow-rolling can act like an effective cosmological constant, driving an exponential expansion with constant acceleration. During this epoch, any matter or radiation density other than that of the scalar field is negligible; one is left with an almost constant energy density of the field, often called a *false vacuum* because it behaves like the highly energetic vacuum of quantum field theory. Every 10^{-37} seconds the size of an inflating patch doubles with its energy density remaining constant, so the total mass in the region increases by a huge factor. Inflation ends through decay of the repulsive material into a mixture of matter and radiation, this decay taking place by quantum processes similar to radioactive decay of ordinary matter. The resulting hot expanding gas provides the starting point for the hot big bang era in the early universe.

This scenario provides explanations for some puzzles in cosmology: why the universe is so large, why it is so uniform, and why it is so nearly flat (scientists can not detect the large-scale spatial curvature effects associated with general relativity). Most importantly, this scenario provides an explanation for the origin of large-scale structure in the universe: Clusters of galaxies arise from seed perturbations generated by quantum fluctuations in the very early universe, amplified vastly in size by the inflationary expansion of the universe and in amplitude by gravitational instability after the decoupling of matter and radiation. A major triumph of the theory is that the subtle variations in the cosmic background radiation it predicted have been observed from satellites and balloons.

One popular version of the theory (*Chaotic Inflation*) proposes that ever more inflationary bubbles are generated and expand to vast size, so that on the largest scales the universe is an eternally reproducing foam-like structure of interleaved inflating and post-inflation regions. It should be noted, however, that this proposition is not observationally testable. Indeed, despite its successes, inflation is not yet a fully developed physical theory; in particular the field (or fields) causing inflation (the *inflaton*) has neither been identified nor shown

actually to exist. Moreover, various theoretical conundrums remain, for example the problem of exactly how inflation ends, how probable it is that inflation will succeed in starting in an extremely inhomogeneous and anisotropic situation, and how successful inflation can be in smoothing out the universe if arbitrary initial conditions are allowed. (A cosmology is anisotrophic if the physical situation appears very different when we observe from different directions in the sky.) Despite these theoretical problems, and the difficulties in testing the physics proposed, inflation is currently the dominant explanatory paradigm for the physics of the early universe. It has generated immense interest because it provides a major link between particle physics and cosmology, allowing cosmological observations to be used for testing theories in particle physics.

See also BIG BANG THEORY; COSMOLOGY, PHYSICAL ASPECTS; PHYSICS, PARTICLE; PHYSICS, QUANTUM

Bibliography

Guth, Alan. *The Inflationary Universe: The Quest for a New Theory of Cosmic Origins.* Reading, Mass.: Addison Wesley, 1997.

Kolb, Edward W., and Turner, Michael S. *The Early Universe.* New York: Wiley, 1990.

Liddle, Andrew R., and Lyth, David H. *Cosmological Inflation and Large-scale Structure.* Cambridge, UK: Cambridge University Press, 2000.

Linde, Andrei D. *Particle Physics and Inflationary Cosmology.* Chur, Switzerland: Harwood Academic, 1990.

Peacocke, J. A. *Cosmological Physics.* Cambridge, UK: Cambridge University Press, 1999.

GEORGE F. R. ELLIS

INFORMATION

The word *information* is used in three principal senses: (1) the mathematical sense from which arises the theory of digital communication or information theory; (2) the linguistic sense in which it is synonymous with the dissemination of meanings understood by members of a culture; and (3) the formative sense in which information denotes the process of giving shape to some medium or substance.

Kinds of information

Counting-information is mathematical information as defined by American mathematician and engineer Claude Shannon (1916–2001) in a paper on communication theory written in 1948. It has nothing directly to do with meaning; rather it relates solely to an arbitrary measure based upon the theory of probability.

Meaning-information is information in the colloquial sense of knowledge. It is completely different from Shannon's concept of information; it is interpretation-, language-, and culture-dependent.

Shaping-information denotes information as a noun describing the action of giving form to something. It is the oldest sense of the word, originating in the Latin verb *informare,* further reflected in current usage in the German *informieren* and the French *informer.* In this sense, one can speak of the "information" of a system when one imposes constraints upon its degrees of freedom, for example by giving content and structure to a spreadsheet.

Construed in these three ways, *information* crosses boundaries between physics, culture, and mind. In its modern, counting-information sense, especially in the realm of information technology, it seems to have taken on a life of its own, as if the process of rendering things digitally had some intrinsic value apart from its use in conveying meaning and enabling people to shape the world. As with any new technology—the telephone, the television, the motor car, the mobile phone—there is a period during which fascination with the technology itself supplants the wisdom that governs its use, but eventually the more important purposes resume their ascendancy, and the technology once again comes to be seen as no more than a tool.

The religious significance of the science of information is best understood in terms of the articulation of meaning and the establishment of a balanced view of the place of information in human life. That process is in full swing as digitization, the Internet, global communication, and the dissolution of historical boundaries reshape how people conceive of themselves and how they decide to live their lives.

If technology is to serve rather than dictate human needs, it is essential that people retain their capacity to think creatively, which is to generate the ideas that give shape to the technology by investing it with significant meanings. Otherwise human needs will increasingly be at the mercy of the agendas of those individuals, corporations, and nation-states that control the technology, and people will be powerless to resist their influence by giving expression to their own objectives. Articulation of worthy religious goals is one contribution that theology can make to the restoration of the balance between creative thought and technological power.

Counting-information

The mathematical concept of counting-information is based upon binary arithmetic, on the ability to distinguish between two states, typically represented as 0 and 1, in an electronic device. One such distinguishable state is called a *binary unit* or *bit.* Combinations of these states allow data to be encoded in strings, such as 01110101010, that can be stored in two-state devices and transmitted down communication channels. Electronic circuits that can distinguish between only two states are relatively easy to devise, although higher-state devices are possible. The process of encoding facts about the world in such binary strings is called *digitization,* although any particular encoding is arbitrary.

A string of n bits can exist in 2^n; different states and so can represent 2^n different symbols. For example, when $n = 3$, the string can be 000, 001, 010, 011, 100, 101, 110, or 111. If a particular encoding treats these strings as binary numbers, they represent 0, 1, 2, . . . , 7; another encoding might treat them as $a, b, . . . , h$. In the early years of computing it was thought that 256 different strings would be sufficient to encode most common letters, numbers, and control codes. The number of bits required to store a given amount of data is therefore usually measured in eight-bit units called *bytes* because of the number of different states of a single byte ($2^8 = 256$). Numbers of bits are counted in powers of 2, so a *kilobyte* is $2^{10} = 1024$ bytes; a *megabyte* is 1024 kilobytes (1024K); and a *gigabyte* is 1024 megabytes. Typical hard disks can now store between 20 and 100 gigabytes.

The states of a binary system are typically called *0* and *1, True* and *False,* or *Yes* and *No.* The system itself is oblivious to these interpretations of the two possible states of a bit, and it is helpful to distinguish between system states and interpretations of those states, for example using the terminology of counting-, meaning- and shaping-information.

The physics of information

The physics of information has given rise to some remarkable results. Shannon showed that there are limits to the rate at which information can be transmitted down a channel with a particular capacity if it is to retain its integrity. Leo Szilard and Leon Brillouin demonstrated that there are fundamental limits to the rate at which information can be processed at given temperatures. Jacob Bekenstein showed that the amount of information that an object can contain—the Bekenstein bound—is directly related to its mass. Some, such as Carl Friedrich von Weizsäcker, have attempted to reconstruct all of physics in information-theoretic terms by conceiving of all physical processes as streams of information. Still others have employed information to look for a fundamental link between entropy and thermodynamics.

The ability to transfer information digitally requires data to be encoded in a binary form; the limitations of such transmission are the subject of information theory as first elaborated by Shannon. However, information is not always easily converted to digital form, especially when it arises from continuous analogue processes, when strict conversion into a discrete coded form is not possible. Neither are the processes that arise from and are useful to human beings easily distilled into the pure digital states required by computers. Some of the most difficult problems faced by those who work in information technology concern the accommodation of computer systems to the untidiness of the data and processes that are typical of human life.

The question of the fundamental nature of information is philosophically and physically deep. It is irrelevant whether one counts to base 2 (as in binary systems) or some other base, but the question of what one is measuring cannot be avoided, and touches some of the hardest questions in physics.

The state of a bit cannot be detected without degrading energy and so increasing the net entropy of the universe. This familiar phrase encapsulates the physical truth that one cannot obtain something for nothing. The Scottish physicist James Clerk Maxwell (1831–1878) once proposed a thought experiment in which a demon capable of

detecting the movement of molecules of gas could open and close a trapdoor to allow fast molecules through and keep slow atoms out, thus increasing the temperature of one side of the partition and infringing the second law of thermodynamics. It is now generally accepted that the flaw in this argument arises from the need to increase the entropy of the universe in order to ascertain the state of the molecule; in other words, reading a certain number of bits of information has a thermodynamic cost.

Encoding and encryption

Although encryption is important in the social and political realms affected by information technology, the fundamentals are mathematical and fall within the realm of information theory. The details of modern encryption involve difficult mathematics, but the essential process is not hard to understand. In a simple code or cipher one typically expects to move from an everyday symbol such as 1 or *a* to a binary string such as 000, to store and manipulate that string in a computer, and then to decode the result by reversing the encoding process. Unfortunately, anyone familiar with the encoding can decode the results, and there are times when one does not wish one's messages to be read—perhaps because they contain private commercial information, perhaps because they contain the plans of criminals or terrorists, perhaps because they contain state secrets. So people would like a way to transmit messages in code. But, if the recipient is to decode them, it seems that the decoding rules must also be transmitted, and they could themselves be intercepted, thus compromising the integrity of the message. What is more, it is far harder to know whether an electronic communication has been intercepted than a physical communication such as a book or letter. Instead people need a way to transmit code that does not require the recipient to be told what the encoding process involves. Fortunately, a way to do this has been devised. It is now embodied in the RSA procedure and is as strong or as weak as the number of bits employed in the encryption. This procedure works as follows. Two very large prime numbers that are intrinsically difficult to guess or find (the private key) are used with another number to generate a pair of numbers (the public key) that everyone knows. This process is essentially irreversible in that there is no tractable way to regenerate the original two prime numbers from the public key. This key is then used by anyone who wishes to send me an encoded message to encrypt it, and I, when I receive it, by using my private key, can decode it. Anyone intercepting the encrypted message, even if in possession of the public key, cannot decrypt the message, because they cannot get back to the private key necessary to do so. The strength of the system lies in the size of the public key: a 40-bit number is deemed very difficult to crack; a 128-bit number is deemed almost impossible with current hardware; a 256-bit number could not be decrypted within the lifetime of the universe.

See also INFORMATION TECHNOLOGY; INFORMATION THEORY

Bibliography

Leff, Harvey S., and Rex, Andrew F. *Maxwell's Demon: Entropy, Information, Computing*. Bristol, UK: Adam Hilger, 1990.

Puddefoot, John C. "Information and Creation." In *The Science and Theology of Information: Proceedings of the Third European Conference on Science and Theology*, ed. Christoff Wassermann, Richard Kirby, and Bernard Rordorff. Geneva, Switzerland: Labor et Fides, 1992.

Puddefoot, John C. "Information Theory, Biology, and Christology." In *Religion and Science: History, Method, Dialogue*, eds. W. Mark Richardson and Wesley J. Wildman. New York and London: Routledge, 1996.

Rényi, Alfréd. *A Diary on Information Theory*. New York: Wiley, 1984.

Shannon, Claude E. "A Mathematical Theory of Communication." *The Bell System Technical Journal* 27 (1948): 379–423, 623–656.

Singh, Simon. *The Code Book: The Science of Secrecy from Ancient Egypt to Quantum Cryptography*. London: Fourth Estate, 1999.

JOHN C. PUDDEFOOT

INFORMATION TECHNOLOGY

Information technology (IT) is a general term used to cover most aspects of computer-related technology. Intimately connected with information and information theory, IT deals with the representation, storage, manipulation, and transmission of information in digital form. The religious significance of information technology must be considered in the light of a general theological view of the nature and purpose of human life. Wherever any medium comes to permeate and shape almost all aspects of social and individual existence, questions can be asked about the direction in which such changes lead, and whether they are favorable or inimical to the purpose of human life as conceived theologically.

At the center of the debate lies the broader question of the way in which human beings represent, model, and shape the world. As computer scientist Joseph Weizenbaum (1923–) once put it, ". . . the computer is a powerful new metaphor for helping us to understand many aspects of the world, but . . . it enslaves the mind that has no other metaphors and few other resources to call on" (p.277).

IT began as a tool that human beings could use as they saw fit. In less than half a century it came to occupy an indispensable place in the world. No single human being altogether controlled that rise, and no single human being understands all its implications. The question is rapidly becoming whether human beings will control information technology or information technology will control human beings. Is the demand that people render the processes of human life in forms that are susceptible to digitization forcing them to alter the way they live their lives without giving them a chance to decide whether those changed lives are the ones they wish to lead? That question forces people to examine, perhaps as they have never examined before, the things they think valuable about human life.

Digitization adds a new dimension to the philosophical issues associated with representation. Their sensory system limits what humans can experience, and their intellectual systems attempt to compensate with imagination for those limitations. By universalizing concepts and generalizing theories from experience of particulars, humans have achieved an understanding of the universe of extraordinary power, but that power is not without its costs and its drawbacks. Universal concepts overwrite the particularities of specific instances, just as Plato believed they should, but they lose sight of detail when number and quantity, statistics and probability, replace specificity. Once the world is digitized, this process takes another step toward unreality: A computer stores data in a medium that is incapable of retaining all the detail and presents people with clear-cut images, data, and their constructs that bear a more remote connection to the "real world" than their usual appropriation in human intellectual systems.

Conceptual clarity, of course, has its power and its uses. By concentrating first on idealized simplified situations, processes that are unimaginably complex in reality can begin to be grasped. Computer-generated models of the workings of a living cell—its DNA-replication and division, its immune-system response to attack by viruses, and so forth—illuminate and clarify. But the reality is far less clear-cut, like the digital signals that are represented as beautifully symmetric square waves.

The more pervasive IT becomes, the more it will tend to influence, shape, and direct human lives. In itself it is no more a force for good or evil than other tools, but the range of its influence makes it unlike most other technological changes. The way colored glass affects everything seen through it affords an analogy: As people come to conceptualize the world more and more in terms borrowed from IT, does a time arise when IT comes to shape their view of the world rather than transmit and interpret the world for them to view? At a very basic level, IT does not answer questions about what people should do with it. It is open and indifferent to that use. But it is easy to overlook the way it constrains what people can see, what they aspire to see, and how they see it.

Uses and impact

Security and surveillance. Information transmitted down wires or by radio waves is inherently more vulnerable to interception than information retained in a vault, and so security measures have been developed to match the increased threat. Chief among these are advanced methods of data encryption using encoding systems that are virtually impossible to break, even by the most advanced computer systems.

The ability to render data safe by encryption also has the potential to prevent those responsible for surveillance from decoding messages between subversives, terrorist groups, criminals, pedophiles, and others deemed socially undesirable. There have therefore been attempts to restrict access to high-performance encryption systems, to forbid the transmission of heavily encrypted signals over the Internet, and to prohibit the export of encryption software likely to enable data to be made impregnable to snooping.

Weaponry and conflict. Many of the pressures that have produced advances in the understanding and command of guidance and control systems have arisen from military applications. Warfare has been transformed by advanced technology. "Smart" bombs that seek specific targets, "jamming" devices that interfere with the ability of an enemy to communicate on the battlefield, software viruses that disrupt control systems, eavesdropping on email and digital telephone calls, and electronically disseminated misinformation are all part of the stuff of modern warfare and state security. But smart bombs are not as smart as people are led to believe, and the technology has proved less reliable than military and political leaders insinuate.

Work and society. Information technology significantly alters the parameters governing the way human beings cooperate to achieve their goals. The manufacture of physical objects requires people to be physically present at the site of their construction, in however widespread a way the components are manufactured. Before electronic mail and data communication through the Internet, office work similarly required people to be collected together in their workplaces. Where added value arises largely from the manipulation of data strings—through programming, database design and construction, composing and editing text, and so forth—this physical juxtaposition is unnecessary. People can relate across digital channels through video conferencing in ways that significantly reduce the need and opportunity for physical meetings.

It is not yet clear what the consequences of this shift in work patterns will be, and they are not unique in human history. Just as the industrial revolution drew populations to the cities and the invention of the telephone and radio communication had a major impact on the relationship between society and work, so decentralized but cooperative data-working will effect further changes in that relationship. The threat of loneliness will increase alongside the opportunities for freer work patterns and wider circles of friends, and many have found their experiences of "virtual communities" deeply unsatisfying and unfulfilling.

Viruses, hacking, and censorship

The destruction of the modern Eden of computer-generated communication by deliberately made viruses is a story of almost biblical proportions. The fact that computers must be accessible to a public domain to receive email or access Internet websites makes them vulnerable to attack from malicious software that attaches itself to email and downloadable packages. Executable files and attachments, once opened, infect the host machine, and commonly export themselves to other machines by spawning copies of themselves in bogus messages sent to all or some of the entries in the local address book. The cost to commerce, worldwide, of damage caused by viruses is already measured in billions of dollars, and the cost of antivirus software that struggles to keep up with ways to immunize systems against attack by viruses that become more sophisticated every day has added to that cost.

Hacking, as the process of gaining unauthorized access to another computer is known, is also a major problem. Just as authors of software viruses regard every new defensive shield as a new challenge, so all the sophisticated mechanisms that are employed to prevent unauthorized access to a computer represent a similar challenge. Hackers' conventions set up competitions where the winners are those who can most successfully penetrate the defenses devised by other competitors, and there have been many instances where commercial, national defense, and other secure systems have been penetrated. Some hackers are motivated by no more than the intellectual challenge; some are malicious; some are politically motivated; some are disgruntled employees; some are just socially disenfranchised and angry.

The location of the physical machine hosting a website is not easy to discover. As a result, it is difficult to police the Internet in order to impose any kind of censorship. But it is not clear whose responsibility or entitlement it is to act either as censor or police force. National governments and international organizations are frequently thwarted in their attempts to track subversive, criminal, or other groups by the lack of boundaries on the Internet.

The most obvious cases where some believe censorship should be imposed are sites posting, advertising, and selling sexual material. Others include terrorist organizations, industrial saboteurs, and all sorts of political activists. But here as everywhere the boundaries between public security and private freedom are hard to define.

On the other hand, the difficulty of policing the Internet affords a means to support and help oppressed minorities in countries where they are persecuted. It enhances freedom of speech and expression. It joins together those who find themselves in minorities. It affords the means for all kinds of propaganda wars to be waged. It allows books and art and music to be made available to the poor and to those who live where some material is prohibited or circumscribed. All of these opportunities can, of course, be used for good and ill, and whether the good outweighs the ill remains to be seen.

Reality and virtual reality

Sciences and religions strive to increase knowledge and awareness of what they take variously to be "reality." They have argued extensively and bitterly about the boundaries of "reality," even though their conceptions of reality have grown and changed through the centuries.

The term *virtual reality* is generally taken to denote that new realm of experience fabricated with the aid of IT from the connections between people throughout the world and the capabilities of software to generate new kinds of communication and even new fictional environments in which they can interact. There is nothing in principle to prevent people living on opposite sides of the globe from donning some sort of virtual-reality headset and sharing the exploration of an entirely unreal virtual habitat.

Virtual habitats are not, of course, new. Every fictional book ever written has created virtual habitats for the human imagination, and so, more recently, have films. It is the interactive capacity of virtual realities that is new and poses sharp questions about what people take to be the nature and purpose of human existence.

Individuals and societies

A person's sense of self has typically been associated with a certain geographical locality, a workplace, and a group of friends largely drawn from his or her own nation. People and their cultures are intimately intertwined, even if every culture consists of a myriad of subcultures with their own mores and customs. Selves are distributed through these cultures, and people know themselves as reflected and invested in them.

Because information technology offers people the opportunity to associate with anyone in the world with access to the Internet in a way that far surpasses in immediacy and intimacy anything possible through the telephone or "snail-mail"—through email, video conferencing, websites, chat rooms, and so forth—it is now possible to withdraw from the community defined by a locality, a geographically defined subculture, or a nation-state, and to find (or lose) oneself in the greater culture that exists through the interactions of persons on the Internet.

It is often suggested that computer technology has made human beings less sociable or neighborly. Now that people can choose like-minded conversational partners from anywhere in the world, they are supposedly less minded to socialize with their neighbors. It is not obvious that this is true. Computer technology is as ambiguous as was the television, the telephone, or the motorcar.

Computer communities do, however, break national boundaries without the need for expensive travel, and it is certainly arguable that greater international fraternization will reduce rather than increase the long-term threat of war. What is not clear is the extent to which having the world as one's neighbor will make one less able to negotiate tolerantly with those physical neighbors who surround one every day, or whether exposure only to those who agree will make one less tolerant of those who do not.

Although it is not true that the Internet has spawned "virtual" communities as an entirely new phenomenon—they have always existed through newsletters, journals, conferences, and the like—it has certainly made their activities more widespread and the frequency of their interactions much greater.

Whatever interest people have, there is almost certainly an Internet community that shares that interest. Through online discussions, websites, mass-circulation email, and so forth, such groups establish both their mutual interest and, usually, considerable interpersonal rapport that spills over into wider aspects of life. Participants will commonly share their joys and sorrows, support one another, and exercise general pastoral care for the group. This phenomenon has led some to suggest that the World Wide Web may facilitate the generation of a new kind of religious community in which mutual care and even worship arise within a virtual world rather than geographically close localities or through meeting eclectically in physical buildings.

Embodiment and realism challenged

Science and religion agree that human beings are embodied: finite, physical existence in a physical world, the fact that life has a beginning and an end. These things occasion no disagreement, even if the nature of the beginning and the end do. Human evolutionary history has been dictated by this physicality, and the need to reproduce, feed, and survive as individuals and species has been deeply influential in making all creatures what they are. Virtual selves challenge this history by providing an intelligible alternative in which people might one day come to exist not as physically embodied selves but as remote functional intellectual agents that would stand evolution on its head by adapting the world to fit human imaginations rather than adapting human bodies to fit the world.

Most people recoil from this suggestion because they do not want to lose their physical embodiment. The pleasures of physical contact, whatever they may be, seem so central to what it is to be human that people want to stop in its tracks any process that would render them less than fully physical and embodied.

This instinctive reaction raises clear questions about what people really and genuinely and deeply value as human beings. Science, in its popularly conceived objectivity, cannot answer those questions because it is indifferent to them. For science, human beings and all living and nonliving things simply are what they are; there is no justifiable scientific view of what anything "ought to be." As soon as one asks how things "ought to be," one is in philosophical or religious or ethical territory; science strikes rock, and its spade is turned.

Philosophy and psychology enable people to see that there is no such thing as a raw perception neither filtered nor colored nor shaped by certain sorts of conceptual apparatuses. The world and what is designated *reality* are complex mixtures of sensory stimulation and intellectual construction. Software and hardware change the way human beings see the world, first as a matter of programming necessity, and later because the image of the world they have has been distorted by the information-theoretic format. One is also tempted to believe that the sheer quantity of information available on the Internet somehow replaces the filtered, processed knowledge imparted through more traditional means of dissemination.

IT models and reality

A theology of creation identifies the physical embodiment of persons as playing a major part in the achievement of the creator's purpose. Physical embodiment entails certain limitations imposed by sensory parameters and necessitates certain kinds of community and cooperation. The nature of the world comes to be construed in accordance with certain kinds of gregarious cooperative endeavor.

IT has the power to change the relationship between human's perceptual and conceptual systems and the world. Digital clarity, arising from the cleansing of data of its inconvenient messiness, encourages one to reconfigure the world; virtual communities encourage one to reconfigure the parameters of friendship and love; software models first imitate and then control financial, political, and military worlds. The beginning of the twenty-first century is an age when the residual images of a predigital worldview remain strong; one can still see that there is a difference. A theology of creation suggests that this analogical unclarity is deliberate and purposive; a digital worldview may prove more incompatible with that creative story than currently supposed. The digital reconfiguration of epistemology may yet prove to be the most profound shift in human cognition in the history of the world, and the changes impression of reality that it will afford will present any theology of creation with a deep new challenge.

See also EMBODIMENT; INFORMATION; INFORMATION THEORY

Bibliography

Hofstadter, Douglas R. *Gödel, Escher, Bach: An Eternal Golden Braid* (1979). London, Penguin, 1996.

Ullman, Ellen. *Close to the Machine: Technophilia and Its Discontents*. San Francisco: City Lights Books, 1997.

Weizenbaum, Joseph. *Computer Power and Human Reason: From Judgment to Calculation* (1976). London: Pelican, 1984.

JOHN C. PUDDEFOOT

INFORMATION THEORY

The version of information theory formulated by mathematician and engineer Claude Shannon (1916–2001) addresses the processes involved in the transmission of digitized data down a communication channel. Once a set of data has been encoded into binary strings, these strings are converted into electronic pulses, each of equal length, typically with 0 represented by zero volts and 1 by + 5 volts. Thus, a string such as 0100110 would be transmitted as seven pulses:

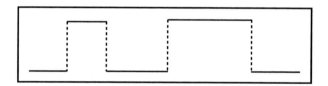

It is clear from the example that the lengths of pulses must be fixed in order to distinguish between 1 and 11. In practice, the diagram represents an idealized state. Electronic pulses are not perfectly discrete, and neither are the lengths of pulses absolutely precise. The electronic circuits that generate these signals are based upon analogue processes that do not operate perfectly, and each pulse will consist of millions of electrons emitted and controlled by transistors and other components that only operate within certain tolerances. As a result, in addition to the information sent intentionally down a channel, it is necessary to cater for the presence of error in the signal; such error is called *noise*.

This example illustrates the dangers inherent in the differences between the way one represents a process in a conceptual system and the underlying physical processes that deliver it. To conceive of computers as if they operate with perfectly clear 0 and 1 circuits is to overlook the elaborate and extensive error-checking necessary to ensure that data are not transmitted incorrectly, which is expensive both in time and cost.

In 1948, Shannon published what came to be the defining paper of communication theory. In this paper he investigated how noise imposes a fundamental limit on the rate at which data can be transmitted down a channel. Early in his paper he wrote:

> The fundamental problem of communication is that of reproducing at one point either exactly or approximately a message selected at another point. Frequently the messages have *meaning*; that is they refer to or are correlated according to some system with certain physical or conceptual entities. These semantic aspects of communication are irrelevant to the engineering problem. (p.379)

The irrelevance of meaning to communication is precisely the point that encoding and the transmission of information are not intrinsically connected. Shannon realized that if one wishes to transmit the binary sequence 0100110 down a channel, it is irrelevant what it means, not least because different encodings can make it mean almost anything. What matters is that what one intends to transmit—as a binary string—should arrive "exactly or approximately" at the other end as that same binary string. The assumption is that the encoding process that produces the binary string and the decoding process that regenerates the original message are known both to the transmitter and the receiver. Communication theory addresses the problems of ensuring that what is received is what was transmitted, to a good approximation.

See also INFORMATION; INFORMATION TECHNOLOGY

Bibliography

Shannon, Claude E. "A Mathematical Theory of Communication." *The Bell System Technical Journal* 27 (1948): 379–423, 623–656.

JOHN C. PUDDEFOOT

INTEGRATION

See also SCIENCE AND RELIGION, MODELS AND RELATIONS; SCIENCE AND RELIGION, METHODOLOGIES

INTELLIGENT DESIGN

Intelligent Design is the concept that some things—especially some life forms or parts of life forms—must have been assembled (at least for the first time) by the direct action of a non-natural agent. Proponents of Intelligent Design argue that there is empirical evidence that the universe's system of natural capabilities for forming things is inadequate for assembling certain information-rich biological structures. And if the system of natural capabilities is inadequate, then these biological structures must have been assembled by the action of some non-natural agent, usually taken to be divine.

See also CREATION; CREATIONISM; CREATION SCIENCE; DESIGN; EVOLUTION; SCOPES TRIAL.

HOWARD J. VAN TILL

INTERNET

See INFORMATION TECHNOLOGY

ISLAM

Six centuries after Jesus Christ, the religion of Islam was born in Arabia. By the beginning of the twenty-first century, Muslims, as its followers have always called themselves, number more than 1.2 billion worldwide.

According to Muslim tradition, in 611 C.E. at the age of forty, Muhammad of Mecca received a revelation from God during a spiritual retreat in a cave on Mount Hira outside the city. God's special envoy who brought the message was the archangel Gabriel. At Gabriel's instruction, the illiterate Muhammad recited five short verses that portrayed the spirit of the new religion. In this first revelation, Muhammad—thus by extension all humans—is called upon to know the unknown in the name of God, whose nature is to create things. Humans are then reminded of how, from their lowly animal origin, they became thinking and knowing creatures thanks to God's generous gifts of instruments of knowledge that are best symbolized by the pen. Knowledge is the supreme symbol of

God's infinite bounty and the key to his treasures. Through sacred knowledge—that is, knowledge through and for the sake of God—humans can attain salvation. In thus emphasizing the saving function of knowledge, Muhammad's maiden revelation as well as many other revelations that were to follow, clearly portrayed the new faith as a way of knowledge. As for Muhammad himself, as told by Gabriel, he had been chosen as the new messenger of God. Fourteen centuries later, Muhammad is widely regarded as one of the world's most influential persons.

Revelations came intermittently to Muhammad over a period of twenty-three years. All of these revelations were systematically compiled into a book known as the Qur'an. According to tradition, the precise arrangement of the Qur'an itself was divinely inspired. This book is central to the religion. It is the most authentic and the most important source of teachings of the religion. The Qur'an is the most influential guide to Muslim life and thought, both individual and collective, spiritual and temporal.

Submission and faith

The word *Islam* means "surrender or submission" to God's will. It also means "peace." In a sense, it is through submission to the divine will that a human attains inner peace. One who submits to the divine will is called *Muslim*. In the Qur'an, the word Muslim refers not only to humans but also to other creatures and the inanimate world. From the Qur'anic point of view, this is not surprising. The divine will manifests itself in the form of laws both in human society and in the world of nature. In Islamic terminology, for example, a bee is a Muslim precisely because it lives and dies obeying the *shavīrah* that God has prescribed for the community of bees, just as a person is a Muslim by virtue of the fact that he or she submits to the revealed "*shavīrah*" ordained for the religious community. In fact, the Qur'an maintains that "every animal species is a community like you," thus implying that God has promulgated a law for each species of being. From its beginning, Islam never made any distinction between what has generally been known in the Western tradition as the "laws of nature" and "the laws of God." In principle, there is harmony between the laws of natural phenomena (*nāmūs al-khilqab*) and the laws of the prophets governing human societies (*nāwamūs al-anbiyā*)

since both kinds of laws come from the same source: God the Law-Giver. In asserting such a view, Islam provides an illustrative example of how it seeks to establish points of convergence in the encounter of religion and science.

Islam is noted for the simplicity of its teachings. By professing the testimony of faith "There is no god but God, and Muhammad is the Messenger of God," one enters into the fold of Islam. The whole teachings of the religion are summarized in the six articles of faith (*arkān al-īmān*) and the five pillars of submission (*arkān al-islām*). Muslims must believe in six fundamental truths: God, angels, revealed books, divine messengers, life in the hereafter, and divine plans and decrees. Necessary beliefs go hand in hand with necessary actions, since a human is both a thinking and a believing creature and a creature who acts and does all kinds of things. There are five fundamental obligatory duties for every Muslim, male and female:

(1) To bear witness that "There is no god but God," and to bear witness that "Muhammad is the Messenger of God";

(2) To perform five daily prayers;

(3) To fast from dawn to dusk during the month of Ramadan;

(4) To pay personal and property tax (*zakāt*, literally meaning purification);

(5) To perform pilgrimage (*ḥajj*) in Mecca once in a lifetime, if possible.

The rest of the teachings of the religion are consequences and further elaborations of these pillars of the faith and devotional practices.

Allah and the Qur'an

God, or *Allāh* in Arabic, is of course the most fundamental reality on which the religion of Islam is based; God created the Muslim soul and shaped the Muslim's thoughts and consciousness. Islam has come to reaffirm the monotheisms of Adam and Abraham. God is absolutely one; the origin and the end of the universe; its creator, sustainer, and ruler. Allah has created the universe for the sake of humans, the best of all creatures. A human being's purpose of existence is in turn to know God. By knowing the universe, humans can know God. This is possible, since God has imprinted numerous signs in the universe. One can also say that

God has imprinted "names" in creation, which are many. Muslim tradition speaks of ninety-nine beautiful names of God, the most mentioned in the Qur'an and the most uttered by the Muslim tongue being *Al-Rahmān* (The Most Compassionate). Muslims adore and celebrate these divine names in numerous ways. Children in kindergartens and Muslim schools called *madrasahs* memorize them by reciting them with melodious voices in a chorus. Artists visualize them with their beautiful Arabic calligraphies. Philosophers exert their intellects to penetrate the deeper meanings of these names through their profound conceptual analysis. Mystics or Sufis contemplate them in their spiritual retreats so that "the heart is empty of everything except God." Such is the profound impact of the divine names as conceived by Islam on the Muslim soul and intellect.

The role of the Qur'an in Muslim life is inseparable from that of Muhammad. He is seen as the perfect embodiment of the Qur'an. A husband and father, a teacher and a businessman, a leader in war and peace, and most of all a spiritual and moral guide, Muhammad is thus the role model for every Muslim of every generation. In Muhammad's own words, his community of believers will not err as long as they are guided by the Qur'an and his way of life.

See also AVERRÖES; AVICENNA; GOD; ISLAM, HISTORY OF SCIENCE AND RELIGION; ISLAM, CONTEMPORARY ISSUES IN SCIENCE AND RELIGION; LIFE AFTER DEATH; SOUL

Bibliography

Azzam, A. Rahman. *The Eternal Message of Muhammad.* Cambridge, UK: Islamic Texts Society, 1993.

Bakar, Osman. *Classification of Knowledge in Islam.* Cambridge, UK: Islamic Texts Society, 1997.

Bakar, Osman. *The History and Philosophy of Islamic Science.* Cambridge, UK: Islamic Texts Society, 1999.

Esposito, John L. *Islam: The Straight Path.* New York: Oxford University Press, 1991.

Gulen, M. Fethullah. *The Essentials of Islamic Faith.* Konak, Turkey: Kaynak, , 1997.

Hamidullah, Muhammad. *Introduction to Islam.* Gary, Ind.: International Islamic Federation of Students Organizations, 1970.

Nasr, Seyyed Hossein. *Ideals and Realities of Islam.* Chicago: Kazi Publications, 1997.

Schuon, Fritjhof. *Understanding Islam.* Bloomington, Ind.: World Wisdom Books, 1994.

OSMAN BAKAR

ISLAM, CONTEMPORARY ISSUES IN SCIENCE AND RELIGION

In the nineteenth century, the Muslim world's encounter with modern science took the form of a double challenge, simultaneously material and intellectual. The Ottoman Empire's defense against the military rise of Western countries, followed by successful colonization, made it necessary to acquire Western technology, and, therefore, the science behind it. The pressure of modern science on Islam has remained very strong. The West appears as the model of progress that the Muslim world has to reach, or at least follow, through the training of technicians and engineers and through the massive transfer of those technologies that are key to development. But more than anything else, the encounter of Islam with modern science stimulated philosophical and doctrinal thinking, provoked in some fashion by an inaugural event, the now famous lecture titled "Islam and Science," which Ernest Renan (1823–1892) delivered at the Sorbonne in 1883. In the lecture, where he expressed his own positivist perspective, Renan criticized the Muslims' utter inability to produce scientific discoveries, as well as their supposed inability to think rationally. Intellectual Muslims of the time, who were in contact with the Western intelligentsia, considered the lecture offensive. Those intellectuals, with precursor Jamal-al-Din al-Afghani (1838–1897), then championed the idea that Islam never experienced a rupture between science and religion, whereas Christianity, and especially Catholicism, had known a long period of conflict with science. They argued that modern science is nothing other than "Muslim science" developed long ago in the classical era of the Umayyad and Abbasid caliphates, and finally transferred to the West in thirteenth-century Spain, thanks to translations that later would make possible both the Renaissance and the Enlightenment.

For the intellectuals who founded the "modernist" movement within Islam, there is nothing wrong, in principle, with science. What remains unacceptable, however, are the distortions imposed upon science by the materialistic and positivist views held by Western philosophers and antireligious scientists. Modern science could not emerge in the Muslim world, even though it was quite advanced at a certain time, because of "superstitions" that were added to the original religion and encouraged quietist fatalism more than action. The result of this awakening of consciousness as to the progressive slipping into torpor (*jumūd*) of Islamic societies is the modernists' call for a renaissance (*nahḍah*) through reform (*Iṣlāḥ*) of Islamic thinking.

Muslim intellectuals who study relationships between science and religion draw their ideas from Islam's epistemology. Indeed, Islamic tradition emphasizes the search for "knowledge" (*'ilm*), a word that recurs more than four hundred times in the Qur'an and in many prophetic traditions in such forms as "the search for knowledge is a religious obligation," or "search for knowledge all the way to China." This knowledge has three aspects: religious knowledge transmitted through revelation, knowledge of the world acquired through investigation and meditation, and knowledge of a spiritual nature granted by God. Different attitudes about the relationship between science and religion proceed from the different emphases placed on those three aspects. The word (*âyât*) describes both God's signs in the cosmos and the verses in the Qur'anic text. Many passages, called "cosmic verses" (*âyât kawniyyah*) by commentators, direct the reader's attention to nature's phenomena, where the reader is to learn to decipher the creator's work. Islam's fundamental perspective is to affirm divine uniqueness (*tawḥīd*), which ensures oneness of knowledge, insofar as all true knowledge leads back to God. Therefore, there could not be disagreement between data resulting from knowledge of the world and data delivered through revelation, nor could there be the "double truth" (*duplex veritas*) condemned in the Western medieval world and falsely attributed to Muslim philosophers.

The fundamental idea of oneness of knowledge appears in the positions of two major players in the history of Muslim thinking, whose works are still very much read today. Abū Hāmid al-Ghazâl (1058–1111), in *The Deliverer from Error* (*al-Munqidh minī aḍ-Ḍalâl*), champions that rational certitude is granted by divine gift. If there is dis-

agreement between the results of *falsafah* (philosophy and science of Hellenic inspiration) and the teachings of religious tradition, it is because philosophers took their investigations outside the domain of validity of their own fields, which led them to enunciate flawed propositions. In the long test-case opinion (*fatwā*)—the format he used in his book, *On the Harmony of Religion and Philosophy* (*Kitāb Faṣl al-Maqāl*)—Abū al-Walīd Muhammad Ibn Rushd (1126–1198) states that the practice of philosophy and of science is a canonical religious obligation. For him, if there is apparent disagreement between philosophy and revelation, then religious texts must be subjected to interpretation (*ta'wil*) or risk impiety by making God say things that are manifestly false. Contemporary Muslim positions on science fall into three main categories that keep to the idea, in one way or another, of the oneness of knowledge.

The majority position considers, in step with of the reformers of the nineteenth and twentieth centuries, that there is nothing essentially bad about science. The West, the current producer of scientific discoveries, may be blamed only for its materialistic vision and its indifference to morals. What this trend identifies as science are essentially the natural sciences, not human sciences permeated with the West's antireligious values. Science is considered as the means to convey "facts" that are, in essence, totally neutral. What the West lacks is the sense of ethics that some Western scientists exhibit personally, but which is not visible enough or at all in Western societies. Some great Muslim scientists, such as Mohammed Abdus Salam (1926–1996), who won the Nobel Prize in physics in 1979, have advocated the development of modern science in the Muslim word. Such defenders of science evoke the glorious hours of the great period of science in Islam, invoke the long list of Muslim scientists whom "history forgot," and strive to build a future that promotes the emancipating role of education.

This trend has enjoyed considerable growth, while being used, in some fashion, for apologetic purposes. In 1976, Maurice Bucaille, a French surgeon, released *The Bible, the Qur'an, and Science*, a study of the scriptures "in light of modern knowledge," and concluded the Qur'an to be authentic because of "the presence in the text of scientific exposés which, examined in our times, are a challenge to human analysis" (p. 255). The original intent was not to tackle the relationships between science and religion in Islam but rather to take part in the debate between contemporary Orientalists and Islamists on the status of the Qur'an and to bring into the debate elements supporting its authenticity. This idea of the "scientific evidence" of the truth of the Qur'an spread through the Muslim world with the many translations of Bucaille's work, and it became amplified to the point of being a major force in contemporary Muslim apologetics, where the traditional theme of "the inimitability of the Qur'an" (*i'jāz al-qur'ān*) is fully reinterpreted from the perspective of "Qur'anic science." Throughout, "Western scientists" identify in the Qur'an the latest discoveries of modern science (cosmology, embryology, geophysics, meteorology, biology), thereby affirming the truth of Islam. The supporters of this position hold a concept of science that gives no thought to its vision of the world, nor to its epistemological or methodological presuppositions. Some go even further, when—calling on the scripture to deliver quantitative scientific information, such as the very precise measure of the speed of light—they claim to be founding an "Islamic science" on entirely new methods. But, as physicist Pervez Hoodbhoy points out in his *Islam and Science* (1991), which takes a stand against such diversion, "specifying a set of moral and theological principles—no matter how elevated—does not permit one to build a new science from scratch" (p.78). There is only one way to make science, and "Islamic science" of the glorious past was nothing but universal science being practiced by scientists belonging to the Arab-Islamic civilization.

View of the presuppositions of modern science

The second trend rejects this idea of universal science and emphasizes the necessity of examining the epistemological and methodological presuppositions of modern science of Western origin. These presuppositions may not be accepted by the Muslim world. This trend has its roots in critics from philosophy and history of science. Karl Popper (1902–1994), Thomas Kuhn (1922–1996), and Paul Feyerabend (1924–1994) contributed, each in his way, to questioning the notion of scientific truth, the nature of experimental methods, and the independence of science's productions with regard to the cultural and social environment in which they appear. In a climate heavily influenced by the

relativism and antirealism of postmodern deconstruction, Muslim critics of Western science reject the idea that there is only one way to pursue science. They strive to define founding principles for an "Islamic science" by planting scientific knowledge and technological activity in the ideas of Islamic tradition and the values of religious law (*sharī'ah*), but with nuances that result from differences of interpretation.

That is how Isma'il Raji Al-Faruqi (1921–1986) elaborated a program of Islamization of knowledge, carried out with the creation in 1981 in Herndon, Virginia, of the *International Institute of Islamic Thought* (IIIT), in response to the experiences and the thinking of Muslims working in North American universities and research institutes. This program is based on the observation of a malaise within the Muslim community (*ummah*), which originates in the importation of a vision of the world totally foreign to the Muslim perspective. For the IIIT, the Islamization of knowledge is all encompassing: It starts with God's word, which can and must apply to all areas of human activity, since God created man as his "representative" or "vice-regent on Earth" (*khalifāt Allāh fī al-ard*). The IIIT's work leads to the conception of a project for the development of a scientific practice at the heart of a religious vision of the world and of society. In fact, the IIIT's undertaking aims more at the social sciences than at the natural sciences, which are considered to be more neutral from the standpoint of methodology.

Other intellectuals, such as Ziauddin Sardar (1951–) and the members of the more or less informal school of thought known as *ijmālī* (self-designated in this fashion in reference to the "synthetic" vision it offers), are also aware of the threat that the West's vision of the world, as it is conveyed by science, represents for Islam. Deeply influenced by Kuhn's analysis of scientific development, they note that Western science and technology are not neutral activities but partake of a cultural project and become a tool for the dissemination of the West's ideological, political, and economic interests. To import modern science and technology into Islam, one needs to rebuild the epistemological foundations of science, keeping in mind the perspective of interconnections between the various domains of human life—a perspective that is peculiar to Islam. Sardar himself has compared the ijmalis' position to al-Ghazālī's.

Assessment of the metaphysical foundations of science

The third trend in Islamic thought is characterized by a deep assessment of the metaphysical foundations that support the vision of the world suggested by Islamic tradition. Seyyed Hossein Nasr (1933–) is its most important proponent. He has been a champion of a return to the notion of "Sacred Science." This trend originates in the criticism of the modern world put forth by French metaphysicist René Guénon (1886–1951), and later by authors in his wake, such as Frithjof Schuon (1907–1994) and Titus Burckhardt (1908–1984), all Muslims of Western origin. Guénon explained how modern Western civilization is an anomaly insofar as it is the only civilization in the world that developed without reference to transcendence. Guénon mentions the universal teaching of humanity's religions and traditions, all of which are nothing but adaptations of the original—essentially metaphysical—tradition. The destiny of human beings is the intellectual knowledge of eternal truths, not the exploration of the quantitative aspects of the cosmos. In this context, Nasr denounces not so much the malaise of the Muslim community, but rather that of Western societies that are obsessed with developing a scientific knowledge anchored in a quantitative approach to reality and in the domination of nature, which results in its pure and simple destruction.

Nasr's position and that of the other defenders of this traditional trend—which some chose to call *perennialist* (in reference to *Sophia perennis,* the "eternal wisdom" of divine origin, which they perpetuate)—inscribes itself not only in the critique of Western epistemology, but in a deep calling into question of the Western idea of a reality reduced to matter alone. The perennialists propose a doctrine of knowledge as a succession of epiphanies, where truth and beauty appear as complementary aspects of the same ultimate reality. They call for a return to a spiritual view of the world and the rehabilitation of a traditional "Islamic science," which would preserve the harmony of the being within creation. In contrast, critics of such a radical position denounce its elitism and emphasize the difficulty of implementing its program in current circumstances.

The various currents within contemporary Muslim thinking are evidence of the intense questioning of the relationship between science and religion. In this context, the Muslim academic world has been operating as a kind of melting pot, where numerous ideas of Islamic or Western origin are elaborated anew in an effort to synthesize them. The fundamental elements remain true to Islamic thinking: the repeated affirmation of God's uniqueness, which unites both creation and humanity; the open nature of the very process of acquisition of knowledge of the world, which, by essence, is unlimited since it originates and ends in the knowledge of God; the narrow interconnection of knowledge and ethics; and, finally, the responsibility of human beings on Earth in their capacity as vice-regents, who must use the world but not abuse it and behave as good gardeners must in their garden. In addition, the metaphysics underlying epistemology and ethics is deeply marked by the dialectic of the visible and of the invisible. Phenomena are the signs of divine action in the cosmos. In fact, God is present in the world, the creation of which God ceaselessly "renews" at every moment (*tajdīd al-khalq*). The articulation of this form of "opportunism" with causality—and modern science's determinism and indeterminism—remains to be elaborated.

Critical thinking on the very elaboration of science as an activity marked by culture is now part of the discourse. In contrast, one must acknowledge that the latest developments in contemporary science—notably those dealing with mathematical undecidability, the uncertainty of quantum physics, the unpredictability of chaos theory, as well as the questioning by biology of evolution, and by neuroscience of conscience—need, no doubt, some further thinking. Indeed, these developments may provide interesting ways to shatter the reductionist and scientist view of the world. They constitute a kind of cornerstone for a metaphysics and epistemology that could give meaning to science as it is done in laboratories and research institutes.

Finally, one has to provide content to the term *Islamic science.* The issue is simultaneously one of ethics (personal and collective), of epistemology, and of the metaphysical *Weltanschauung* it presupposes. When passing from theory to practice, each current of thought must face specific problems resulting not only from its specific position but also from the Muslim world's economic and social difficulties. What remains to be established is the degree to which the most ambitious project—that of Islamic science as Sacred Science—can amount to more than a nostalgic glance at the past and move on to the stage of its actual implementation by a spiritual and intellectual elite. The future of the Islamic civilization's contribution to the development of universal knowledge is tied to the answer that will be given to that question.

See also AVERROËS; AVICENNA; ISLAM; ISLAM, HISTORY OF SCIENCE AND RELIGION

Bibliography

Acikgenc, Alparslan. *Islamic Science: Towards a Definition.* Kuala Lumpur, Malaysia: International Institute of Islamic Thought and Civilization, 1996.

Al-Afghani, Jamal-al-Din. "Refutation of the Materialists." In *An Islamic Response to Imperialism, Political and Religious Writings of Sayyid Jamâl-al-Dîn al-Afghânî,* ed. and trans. Nikki R. Keddie. Berkeley: University of California Press, 1982.

al-Attas, Seyd Muhammed Naquib. *Prelegomena to the Metaphysics of Islam: An Exposition of the Fundamental Elements of the Worldview of Islam.* Kuala Lumpur, Malaysia: International Institute of Islamic Thought and Civilization, 1995.

Al-Faruqi, Isma'il Raji, ed. *Islamization of Knowledge: General Principles and Work Plan.* Washington, D.C.: International Institute of Islamic Thought, 1982.

Al-Ghazālī, Abū Hāmid. *Al-Munqidh min aḍ-Ḍalāl* (Freedom and fulfillment), trans. and ed. R. McCarthy. Boston: Twayne, 1980.

Arkoun Mohammed. "Le Concept de Raison Islamique." In *Pour une Critique de la Raison Islamique.* Paris: Maisonneuve et Larose, 1984.

Bakar, Osman. *Tawhid and Science: Essays on the History and Philosophy of Islamic Science.* Kuala Lumpur, Malaysia: Secretariat for Islamic Philosophy and Science, 1991.

Bucaille, Maurice. *La Bible, le Coran, et la Science: Les Écritures Saintes Examinées à la Lumière des Connaissances Modernes.* Paris: Seghers, 1976. Available in English as *The Bible, the Qur'an, and Science: The Holy Scripture Examined in the Light of Modern Science,* trans. Alastair D. Pannell and the author. Indianapolis, Ind.: American Trust, 1979.

Butt, Nasim. *Science and Muslim Societies.* London: Grey Seal, 1991.

Guénon, René. *Le Règne de la Quantité et les Signes des Temps.* Paris: Gallimard, 1945. Available in English as *The Reign of Quantity and the Signs of the Times,* trans. Lord Northbourne. London and Baltimore, Md.: Penguin, 1953.

Hoodbhoy, Pervez. *Islam and Science: Religious Orthodoxy and the Battle for Rationality.* London: Zed Books, 1991.

Hourani, Albert. *Arabic Thought in the Liberal Age: 1798–1939.* Cambridge, UK: Cambridge University Press, 1983.

Ibn Rushd (Averroës). *On the Harmony of Religion and Philosophy* (*Kitāb Fassl al-Maqāl wa Taqrīr mā bayna ash-Sharī'ah wa al-Hikmah min al-Ittiṣāl*), ed. and trans. George Hourani. London, Luzac, 1976.

Lewis, Bernard. *The Muslim Discovery of Europe.* New York: Norton, 1982.

Modh Nor Wan Daud, Wan. *The Concept of Knowledge is Islam.* London: Mansell, 1989.

Nasr, Seyyed Hossein. *Science and Civilization in Islam,* 2nd edition. Cambridge, UK: Islamic Texts Society, 1987.

Nasr, Seyyed Hossein. *The Need for a Sacred Science.* Albany: State University of New York Press, 1993.

Salam, Mohammed Abdus. *Ideals and Realities: Selected Essays of Abdus Salam,* ed. C. H. Lai. Singapore: World Scientific, 1987.

Sardar, Ziauddin. *Explorations in Islamic Science.* London: Mansell, 1989.

Sardar, Ziauddin. *Islamic Futures: The Shape of Ideas to Come.* London: Mansell, 1985.

Sardar, Ziauddin, ed. *An Early Crescent: The Future of Knowledge and the Environment in Islam.* London: Mansell, 1989.

Stenberg, Leif. *The Islamization of Science: Four Muslim Positions Developing an Islamic Modernity.* Lund, Sweden: Lunds universitet, 1996.

BRUNO GUIDERDONI

ISLAM, HISTORY OF SCIENCE AND RELIGION

An account of science and religion in Islam must examine the attitudes of the faith of Islam towards science, as well as the scientific enterprise in Islamic civilization. The first aspect assumes that the perspective of religious thinkers and religious institutions play a determinative role in science through their coercive power or influential authority. The second aspect tempers and even challenges this assumption, for it investigates actual factors that facilitate or hinder scientific practice during particular historical periods and examines how and why particular social and political contexts promote or inhibit science.

These two aspects illustrate the complexity surrounding the term *Islam*. Primarily, *Islam* denotes a faith with particular beliefs, practices, and institutions within its historical and contemporary diversity of expressions. Beyond faith, *Islam* denotes an empire and then a series of successor states during particular periods in world history over a vast expanse of territory in Asia, Africa, and Europe. Despite inherent differences, these regions shared the bond of participating in Islamic civilization, although many inhabitants, including practitioners of science, were not Muslims. The flow of goods, ideas, fashions, and movements of peoples through these regions and the common strands in their intellectual, political, aesthetic, and social outlooks and the social institutions of their elite classes, broadly speaking, characterize these regions with those particular features that are the hallmarks of Islamic civilization. The account of the relationship of science to the faith of Islam at particular locales and times must acknowledge the unifying role played by this civilization. On the other hand, discourse regarding the relationship between religion and science in contemporary Islam is largely dominated by the notion that science, albeit a universal human endeavor, is nevertheless largely developed and exported from external sources, namely the Western world.

Faith to civilization

The faith of Islam was established in seventh century C.E. by the Prophet Muhammad (570-632 C.E.), who, according to Muslim belief, was the recipient of divine revelations, which are collected in the Qur'an, the Muslim sacred text. Facing hostility and opposition, Muhammad fled his birthplace of Mecca, in present-day Saudi Arabia, to Medina. By the end of his life in 632 C.E., he overcame opposition and united almost the entire Arabian peninsula under the banner of Islam. Muhammad had commanded both religious and political authority, and his death raised the issue of the scope and manner of the subsequent exercise of authority. Not surprisingly, there were, and continue to be, a range of responses. Over the centuries, these responses solidified into religious and political institutions, as well as a multiplicity of attitudes regarding their power and authority. Although

sectarianism played a role in shaping some attitudes, the lack of a centralized religious institution fostered a diversity of attitudes on all subjects, including the relationship of religion to science.

The nascent community established the primarily political institution of the caliphate following the death of Muhammad. Disagreement between supporters of ʿAlī (d. 661 C.E.) and his opponents over succession and the scope of this office was to later crystallize into the Shīʿī and Sunnī branches of Islam. Over the next three decades, under the leadership of companions of Muhammad, the community commenced a campaign of expansion whereby Palestine, Syria, Egypt, and Iran were soon incorporated into the emerging Islamic empire. These "rightly-guided" caliphs were succeeded by the Umayyads (661–750 C.E.), who continued the expansionist policy. The Umayyads faced several rebellions because of their perceived Arabo-centrism. They also resisted the efforts of religious elites to establish normative frameworks for religious study and institutionalization of religious authority. Since this venture was external to, and at times actively opposed by, the Umayyad court, the genesis of a recurrent conflict between religious and political authorities in Islamic polity was born.

By the early eighth century, the Islamic empire reached its greatest expanse, extending from Spain to the Indus and the borders of China, thereby incorporating Hellenistic and Iranian centers of science, philosophy, and learning. Like its predecessors, this vast empire, with its diversity of peoples, languages, faiths, traditions, and administrative and monetary systems, was susceptible to divisive forces. ʿAbd al-Mālik (r. 692–705 C.E.) therefore sought to unify the empire by instituting Arabic coinage and the Arabic language as the administrative language of the empire. Arabic was soon catapulted beyond the language of revelation and then language of governance to the language of literature, humanities, philosophy, science, and indeed all learned discourse. The attitude towards science at the Umayyad court was utilitarian. Evidence suggests that the court sought physicians who were primarily non-Arab and non-Muslim.

In 750 C.E, the Umayyads were overthrown and replaced by the Abbasids everywhere but in Spain. Even though they had capitalized on the anti-Umayyad sentiment of the religious elite, the

Abbasids soon distanced themselves from their former allies. The litterateur Ibn al-Muqaffaʻ (d. 757 C.E.) advised the Abbasid Caliph al-Manṣūr (r. 754–775 C.E.) to bring the religious elite under state supervision and to enforce doctrinal and legal uniformity to replace diverse and opposing views. Even though this advice was ignored, the episode illustrates the continuing fluidity of political and religious institutions.

The Abbasids consciously promoted a new order. This was most evident in their establishment of the city of Baghdad in 762 C.E. in present-day Iraq. Baghdad soon became a thriving commercial center and magnet. Above all, it represented the civilization of Islam with its own distinctive literary and aesthetic preferences, attitudes, institutions, and fashion of refinement. The Arabo-centrism of the early Umayyads was replaced by a bustling engagement of peoples of many faiths and persuasions from all parts of the empire. The splendor and richness of the early Abbasid period, under the reign of the Caliph Hārun al-Rashīd (r. 786-809 C.E.), was later immortalized in the *Thousand and One Nights*. But this prosperity came at a price, as the Caliph was forced to grant fiefs to commanders and strongmen. The fiefs soon became semi-independent principalities, leading to the disintegration of the unified empire by the mid-ninth century. Nevertheless, the vision of a unified Islamic civilization endured for several centuries in a number of successor and competing principalities, thriving in even small provincial centers, as well as still-Umayyad Spain.

The "sciences of the Ancients" and religious sciences of Islamic civilization

In his *Introduction to History*, the fourteenth-century historian Ibn Khaldūn (1332-1382 C.E.) notes that urban civilization is characterized by sciences and crafts: ". . . as long as sedentary civilization is incomplete . . . people are concerned only with the necessities of life. . . . The crafts and sciences are the result of man's ability to think . . . (they) come after the necessities" (p. 2:347). Ibn Khaldūn includes agriculture, architecture, book production, and medicine among crafts of urban civilization. With regards to the sciences: "one [kind] . . . is natural to man . . . guided by his own ability to think, and a traditional kind that he learns from those who invented it" (p. 2:436). The first kind are

the "philosophical sciences"; the second, the "traditional, conventional sciences." Such a distinction was already recognized by Muhammad al-Khwārizmī (d. 997 C.E.) in the tenth century. He divided the sciences into "sciences originating from foreigners such as the Greeks and other nations" and "the sciences of the Islamic religious law and ancillary Arabic sciences." Al-Khwārizmī understood that these attributes denoted origins and were not judgments of intrinsic worth. The religious and Arabic language disciplines were peculiar to Muslims, originating after the advent of Islam; science and philosophy originated in pre-Islamic civilizations and were appropriated into Islamic civilization. Within Islamic civilization, the religious and Arabic language disciplines preceded the appropriation of the "sciences of the Ancients," but the mature development of both was largely coterminous.

The disciplines of philosophical theology (*kalām*) and Islamic law (*fiqh*, *sharīʻa*) are paramount to an account of the relationship between religion and science in Islam. By the late eighth century, Muʻtazilī philosophical theology was immersed in cosmological questions, primarily, creation *ex nihilo* (from nothing), the fundamental constituents of the world, the nature of man, and God's causal role in the world. Notwithstanding a plethora of views in the early period, the late ninth-century consensus held that the world was created *ex nihilo*; its material, temporal, and spatial structure is atomistic; human beings are complex compositions of such atoms (i.e., material beings); and God, who is completely different from created beings, is the primary causal agent, although for the Muʻtazilīs, human beings have a limited causal role (the dissenting Ashʻarī view denied human causal agency). These positions are directly opposed to the Aristotelian bent of the "philosophical" sciences.

Reason played a primary role in the epistemology of the Muʻtazilī philosophical theologians. Reason also played a role in early Islamic legal theory. The primacy of reason was attacked by conservative religious scholars, who instead upheld the primacy of revelation and the inspired example of the Prophet Muhammad's personal practice (*sunna*). These sources, in conjunction with the consensus of the religious elite (*ijmāʻ*) narrowly confined to the two sources of revelation and Muhammad's practice, provided, in their view, the "Islamic" basis for all spheres of human activity.

The conservative movement clashed with the Abbasid Caliph al-Ma'mūn (r. 813–833 C.E.), who, wishing to establish state control over religion, promoted the teachings of the philosophical theologians. Al-Ma'mūn required all judges (who were state appointees) to uphold the doctrine that the Qur'an (technically, God's direct speech) was created. The conservative scholar Aḥmad ibn Hanbal refused to conform and was imprisoned. His continuing refusal resulted in severe beating and home confinement until al-Mutawakkil (r. 847–861 C.E.) revoked this policy.

The early Abbasids were more successful in their policy of encouraging the translation of scientific and philosophical texts into Arabic. This movement began with al-Manṣūr's commission to his physician to translate medical texts into Arabic. By their commitment to a program of appropriating the pre-Islamic scientific and philosophical legacy into Arabic, the early Abbasid view of science went beyond the utilitarian. This perspective is evident in the Abbasid establishment of the institution of a royal library, the House of Wisdom (bayt al-ḥikma), which played a role in scientific activity and perhaps translation. These policies resulted in the translation into Arabic by the middle of the tenth century of almost the entire scientific and philosophical corpus of Classical and Late Antiquity and a handful of Sanskrit and Pahlavi texts. This endeavor relied on Nestorian Christian and other translators and financing by patrons beyond the court. The sons of Mūsā are an interesting example. Their father, a former brigand, was befriended by al-Ma'mūn. Mūsā's orphaned sons were raised at the palace and their education was supervised by the caliph. Subsequently prosperous, they patronized additional translations, apart from being excellent mathematicians in their own right. Translation activity was not haphazard. Manuscripts of texts to be translated were eagerly sought. Moreover, entire areas of the classical tradition, for example Greek drama and tragedy, were bypassed deliberately.

Despite the engagement of the Abbasid court, the translation enterprise was not uncontroversial. The scientist and philosopher al-Kindī (d. ca. 870 C.E.), tutor to al-Mu'taṣim's (r. 833–847 C.E.) son and patron of an early translation of Aristotle's *Metaphysics,* addresses critics in his *On First Philosophy*: "We ought not to be ashamed of appreciating truth and of acquiring it wherever it comes from, even if it comes from races distant and nations different from us." He rejects "those who are in our day acclaimed for speculation, who are strangers to the truth . . . because of their narrow understanding. . . . [They] traffic in religion, though they are devoid of religion" (p. 58–59). The targets of his remarks are undoubtedly philosophical theologians and legal scholars. Despite such controversy, the translation project was a resounding success. It initiated a vigorous scientific and philosophical tradition that extended and flourished beyond Baghdad, persisting in various forms until modern times. During the tenth century, scientists and philosophers were patronized at the courts of the Hamdanids in Syria, the Buyids in Iran and Iraq, the Fatimids in Egypt, and the Ghaznavids in Central Asia, among others.

The movement to appropriate was followed by the naturalization of the "sciences of the Ancients." The extent of naturalization is evident in the education of Ibn Sīnā (980–1037 C.E.), also known as Avicenna. Residing in the eastern city of Bukhara in present-day Uzbekistan, he learned arithmetic from a grocer, then studied with an iterant philosopher, and then, having surpassed his instructor, taught himself the "Ancient" sciences from books that he purchased. An opportunity to examine the private library of the local ruler led to finding rooms of books on all subjects. Ibn Sīnā's account illustrates the widespread engagement with knowledge and the extent of the naturalization of "the sciences of the Ancients," from the practical arithmetic of the grocer, to the iterant philosopher who sought eager students in peripheral locations, to the availability of books in the markets, as well as in private collections. The tenth-century *Epistles of the Sincere Brethren* illustrates another aspect. The epistles represent a sectarian educational program in ethics, politics, mathematics, physics, metaphysics, and the religious sciences, providing an Islamic worldview steeped in a Neoplatonism. Such a perspective was also promoted by the tenth-century Shī'ī Fatimid dynasty in Egypt.

The age of Ibn Sīnā represents the culmination of the naturalization of the "sciences of the Ancients" in Islamic civilization. These sciences were flourishing almost everywhere. Ibn Sīnā was based primarily in Iran. His contemporaries include the astronomer and mathematician al-Bīrūnī (973-1050 C.E.) in Central Asia; the physicist, astronomer, and mathematician Ibn al-Haytham (965-1039 C.E.) and the astronomer Ibn Yunus (d. 1009 C.E.), who were both in Egypt; the physician al-Zahrawī (963-1013 C.E.) in Andalusia; and others. These scientists were at the frontiers of research, yet they were critical of the scientific tradition they had received via the translations and its early proponents. In his encyclopedic work *The Cure*, Ibn Sīnā presents an integral worldview of the "philosophical sciences" encompassing logic, mathematics, physics, and metaphysics. Ibn Sīnā's writings were extremely influential. Many in later generations studied Ibn Sīnā's works, whether as proponents of the "sciences of the Ancients" or as critics.

The fundamental premises of the worldview of the "philosophical sciences" as explicated by Ibn Sīnā are as follows. The world is eternal, produced by cascading emanations of the Divine, who is otherwise removed from, and not directly involved in, creation. The world comprises celestial and terrestrial realms. The celestial realm is constant and unchanging, consisting of emanated spiritual beings—intellects and souls—associated with celestial spheres, which house each of the planets. Planetary motion is voluntary, exhibiting the desire of intellects and souls to imitate the divine. In contrast, the terrestrial realm, consisting of the mineral, plant, and animal kingdoms, is always in flux. Man, possessing intellect, are at the head of the terrestrial chain of being. The celestial realm influences events in the terrestrial realm through emanation. The phenomenon of prophecy, for example, occurs when a particularly receptive human with a powerful imagination is able, through the guidance of a celestial intellect via emanation, to represent pure knowledge in symbolic and cultural garb. Most men are incapable of grasping pure truth and thereby need symbols, rewards, and threats to preserve public order. Revelation is thus replete with symbols, necessitating allegorical interpretation by those with access to pure, theoretical knowledge, namely, the philosophers.

Critique and defense of the "sciences of the Ancients"

Soon after Ibn Sīnā's death, the Shī'ī Buyids were replaced by the Saljuqs, who favored Sunni restoration. By 1055, the Saljuqs controlled Baghdad. They then seized control of the eastern Mediterranean and Mecca and Medina from the Shī'ī Fatimids, and in 1071 they overcame Byzantine resistance in eastern Turkey. Like their Buyid predecessors, the Saljuqs were protectors of the powerless Abbasid caliph. The Saljuq vizier Niẓām al-Mulk (r. 1064–1092 C.E.) established Niẓāmīya *madrasas* (colleges) that, while nominally private, represented official sponsorship of the Shāfi'ī legal school. Already active at the end of the Buyid period, partisans of Ahhmad ibn Hanbal intensified their drive to promote the conservative perspective and caliphal authority. They staged popular uprisings against Mu'tazilī philosophical theology, the mystic al-Hallāj (859-992 C.E.), and even the Hanbalī scholar Ibn Aqīl (1040-1119 C.E.). The movement culminated with the appointment of the Hanbalī Ibn Hubayra (d. 1165 C.E.) to the vizierate by the caliphs al-Muqtafī (r. 1136–1160 C.E.) and al-Mustanjid (r. 1160–1170 C.E.). During the early years of the reign of the later, the property of a judge who had fallen out of favor was seized, and his books on philosophy, including Ibn Sīnā's *The Cure* and the *Epistles of the Sincere Brethren,* were burned.

In a similar environment in 1091, Niẓām al-Mulk appointed the religious thinker al-Ghazālī (1058–1111 C.E.) to teach Shāfi'ī law at the Niẓẓāmīya in Baghdad. Al-Ghazālī spent the first year studying Ibn Sīnā's works and then publishing *The Aims of the Philosophers.* Soon after, he published *The Incoherence of the Philosophers,* with the aim of "[refuting] the ancients, showing the incoherence of their beliefs and the contradiction of their doctrines with regards to metaphysics" (p. 3). The *Incoherence* attacks the cosmology of the "philosophical sciences," in particular, the propositions of the eternity of the world, God's lack of direct involvement in the world evident through God's ignorance of particular events, the determination of particular events in the world by celestial souls, natural causality, and the denial of physical resurrection as described vividly in the Qur'an. Al-Ghazālī's attack, albeit utilizing Ibn Sīnā's philosophical vocabulary, is a defense of the cosmology of the philosophical theologians. The *Incoherence* concludes by charging those who pursued the "philosophical sciences" with unbelief (*kufr*) on the grounds of their denial of creation *ex nihilo,* God's knowledge of particulars, and bodily resurrection.

When al-Ghazālī himself was accused of unbelief, he composed the legal work *The Clear Criterion for Distinguishing between Islam and Unbelief.* He notes that this charge was hurled for sectarian purposes by the Hanbalīs against the Ash'arī philosophical theologians, or the Mu'tazilīs against the Ash'arīs, and so on. Thus, this work is primarily directed against the philosophical theologians and conservative Hanbalīs. Al-Ghazālī asserts interpretive flexibility where the Qur'anic text is susceptible to interpretation, although he proposes strict guidelines. Nevertheless, his attitude of extreme caution in taxing a Muslim with unbelief raises the question of whether he had reevaluated the charge of unbelief against the philosophers in the *Incoherence*.

In his magnum opus, *The Revival of the Religious Sciences,* al-Ghazālī discusses the classification of knowledge from a religious perspective. He divides knowledge into religious and secular, namely, knowledge derived from prophets, and knowledge guided by intellect, observation, or social convention (e.g., arithmetic, medicine, and language). The pursuit of secular sciences beneficial to human activity (e.g., medicine and arithmetic) is praiseworthy even though one need not engage too deeply into them. Geometry and arithmetic are neutral, although some may be led astray by them. Physical sciences, apart from medicine, do not have any utility, and lead people astray. Metaphysics also leads people astray. Thus, most natural sciences and metaphysics are blameworthy. Al-Ghazālī does not evaluate logic, although he describes it as the examination of methods and conditions of proof. He had argued for the Qur'anic basis of logic in many treatises and incorporated logic into his major work on legal theory. Since Aristotelian categorization and analysis were indispensable to logic, al-Ghazālī's action provided a foothold for the "philosophical sciences" at the heart of the religious sciences.

The Andalusian jurist and philosopher Ibn Rushd (1126–1198 C.E.), also known as Averroës, rebutted al-Ghazālī's critique of the "philosophical sciences." Andalusia had undergone a series of social upheavals since the end of Umayyad rule in 1031. After a divisive period of the petty states (1031–1091 C.E.), Andalusia came under the control of the Berber Almoravids (1091–1147 C.E.) and then the Almohads (1147–1269 C.E.), who were invited to defend Spain against the Christian drive to reconquer Spain and oust the Muslims (known as the Christian Reconquista). Under the Umayyad rulers Hishām (r. 788–796 C.E.) and Ḥakam I (r. 796–822 C.E.), Mālikī law became the official Islamic legal school in Andalusia. Andalusian Mālikī law was highly conformist, rejecting any exercise of independent judgment. Mālikī scholars were deeply suspicious of the "philosophical sciences" and theological philosophy, and they even prevented the circulation of al-Ghazālī's works.

When Ibn Rushd was introduced to the Almohad ruler Abū Ya'qūb ibn Yūsuf (r. 1163–1184 C.E.), he hesitated engaging in a discussion regarding the eternity of the world. The ruler then commissioned him to write commentaries on the works of Aristotle, for which Ibn Rushd became known as "the Great Commentator" in medieval Europe. Abū Ya'qūb also appointed Ibn Rushd as judge in Córdoba, Spain. In his *Incoherence of the Incoherence,* Ibn Rushd rebutted each point of al-Ghazālī's critique of the "philosophical sciences." His *Decisive Treatise on the Harmony between Religion and Philosophy* is a legal defense of the "philosophical sciences." Ibn Rushd argues that the Qur'an commands Muslims to recognize their Creator through the study of creation. Since the "philosophical sciences" study creation via demonstration, which is the best manner possible, they permit capable minds to obey the Qur'anic edict. For the masses who cannot grasp demonstrative proof, rhetorical and dialectical knowledge is sufficient. Thus revelation is couched in rhetorical and dialectical language so that the masses can believe, perform religious acts, and maintain public order. Towards the end of his life, Ibn Rushd was briefly imprisoned by the Almohads, who were under external threat from the Reconquista and had to placate Mālikī demands.

Appraisal

It would be a mistake to conclude that the episodes described above illustrate unmitigated religious opposition to science in Islam. The pursuit of science was not explicitly driven by the Qur'anic edict to study creation, despite Ibn Rushd's argument to the contrary. Nevertheless some Muslim scientists, for example al-Bīrūnī, reflect upon the Qur'an in their works. In *The Determination of the Coordinates of Positions for the Correction of Distances between Cities,* al-Bīrūnī quotes the Qur'anic verse, "They consider the creation of the heavens and the earth [and exclaim], Oh our Sustainer, You have not created this in vain" (3:191). He then comments, "This noble verse incorporates all that I have explicated in detail. Only after carrying out its instruction will man arrive at the heart of the sciences and understanding" (p. 3). Al-Bīrūnī illustrates the attitude that prompted the exploration of scientific problems connected to religious practice—the determination of times and direction of prayer, the sighting of the crescent moon, and the determination of the twilight and sunset. As a result, the office of the timekeeper versed in mathematics and astronomy and affiliated with the Friday congregational mosque became an important institution in some regions.

The "philosophical sciences" had always been studied privately and had no place in the curricula of the post-eleventh century, increasingly dominant institution of the *madrasa*. The exceptions of arithmetic and medicine at some *madrasas*. Yet the "philosophical sciences" were deeply rooted in the Islamic world and were incorporated into the religious sciences, as evidenced by Al-Ghazālī's incorporation of logic into Islamic legal theory. In his massive commentary on the Qur'an, Fakhr al-dīn al-Rāzī (1149-1209 C.E.) turns to the "philosophical sciences" to discuss theories of light, planetary motion, and other such matters. This attitude is also evident in the philosophical theologian al-Ijī (d. 1355 C.E.), whose work *The Stations of Philosophical Theology* became the standard textbook in the Sunnī *madrasas* and was the subject of numerous commentaries across the Muslim world. The same can be said of other popular texts. Clearly the interaction of religion and science in premodern Islam was a complex phenomenon and requires due diligence to the specific contexts that supported, or opposed, the scientific enterprise.

See also AVERRÖES; AVICENNA; CREATION; GOD; ISLAM; ISLAM, CONTEMPORARY ISSUES IN SCIENCE AND RELIGION; METAPHYSICS

Bibliography

al-Bīrūnī, Abū al-Rayḥān. *The Determination of the Coordinates of Positions for the Correction of Distances between Cities,* trans. Jamil Ali. Beirut, Lebanon: American University of Beirut, 1967.

al-Ghazālī, Abū Ḥamīd. "The Clear Criterion for Distinguishing Between Islam and Heresy." In *Freedom and Fulfillment: An Annotated Translation of al-Ghazali's Muqidh min al-Dalal and Other Relevant Works of al-Ghazali,* trans. Richard McCarthy. Boston: Twayne, 1980.

al-Ghazālī, Abū Hamīd. *The Book of Knowledge, Being a Translation with Notes of the Kitāb al-'ilm of al-Ghazālī's Iḥyā' 'ulūm al-dīn,* trans. Nabih Amin Faris. Delhi, India: International Islamic Publishers, 1988.

al-Ghazālī, *The Incoherence of Philosophers,* trans. Michael Marmura. Provo, Ut.: Brigham Young University Press. 1997.

al-Kindī, Abū Ya'qūb. *Al-Kindī's Metaphysics,* trans. Alfred L. Ivry. Albany: State University of New York Press, 1974.

Dhanani, Alnoor. "Science and Religion in Islam." In *Science and Religion: A Historical Introduction,* ed. Gary B. Ferngren. Baltimore, Md.: Johns Hopkins University Press, 2002.

Goldziher, Ignaz. "The Attitude of Orthodox Islam Towards the 'Ancient Sciences'." In *Studies in Islam,* trans. M. Schwartz. New York: Oxford University Press, 1981.

Gutas, Dimitri. *Greek Thought; Arabic Culture: The Graeco-Arabic Translation Movement in Baghdad and Early 'Abbāsid Society (2nd–4th/8th–10th Centuries).* London: Routledge, 1998.

Huff, Toby. *The Rise of Early Modern Science: Islam, China, and the West.* Cambridge, UK: Cambridge University Press, 1993.

Ibn Khaldun. *The Muqadimmah: An Introduction to History,* trans. F. Rosenthal. Princeton, N.J.: Princeton University Press, 1958.

Ibn Rushd. *On the Harmony of Religion and Philosophy,* trans. George Hourani. London: Luzac, 1967.

Ibn Rushd. *The Incoherence of the Incoherence,* trans. Simon van den Bergh. London: Luzac, 1978.

Ibn Sina. *The Life of Ibn Sina,* trans. William Gohlman. New York: State University of New York Press, 1974.

King, David. *Astronomy in the Service of Islam.* Aldershot, UK: Variorum, 1993.

Marmura, Michael. "Al-Ghazali's Attitude Towards the Secular Sciences and Logic." In *Essays on Islamic Philosophy and Science,* ed. George F. Hourani. Albany: State University of New York Press, 1975.

Rashed, Roshdi, ed. *Encyclopedia of the History of Arabic Science.* London and New York: Routledge, 1996.

Sabra, A. I. "The Appropriation and Subsequent Naturalization of Greek Science in Medieval Islam: A Preliminary Statement." *History of Science* 25 (1987): 223–243.

Sabra, A. I. "Philosophy and Science in Medieval Islamic Theology: The Evidence of the Fourteenth Century."

Zeitschrift für Geschichte der arabisch-islamischen Wissenschaften 9 (1994): 1–42.

Sabra, A. I. "Situating Arabic Science: Locality versus Essence." *Isis* 87 (1996): 654–670.

Urvoy, Dominique. "The '*Ulamā*' of al-Andalus." In *The Legacy of Muslim Spain,* ed. Salma Khadra Jayyusi. Leiden, Netherlands, and New York: Brill, 1994.

ALNOOR DHANANI